ALL-IN-ONE

BIBLE REFERENCE GUIDE

ZONDERVAN

ALL-IN-ONE

BIBLE REFERENCE GUIDE

KEVIN GREEN, COMPILER

ZONDERVAN®

 **ZONDERVAN®**

Zondervan All-in-One Bible Reference Guide
Copyright © 2008 by The Zondervan Corporation

Requests for information should be addressed to:

Zondervan, *Grand Rapids, Michigan 49530*

ISBN 978-1-60751-560-9

Interior design by Ben Fetterley

Printed in the United States of America

INTRODUCTION

Most people today do not have the money or time to purchase and wade through several reference volumes to find the information they need. Whether you are a Sunday school teacher, pastor, or interested lay-leader who wants to understand the Bible better, the *Zondervan All-in-One Bible Reference Guide* is a one-stop resource that combines the elements of a Concordance, Bible Dictionary, and Topical Bible into a single, easy-to-use volume. Arranged alphabetically, this reference work provides a helpful resource for studying and understanding the world of the Bible. Although the *Zondervan All-In-One Bible Reference Guide* is based on the NIV Bible, its scope of topics, people, places, events, and themes make it a wonderful resource regardless of what version of the Bible you use.

This project seeks to repurpose the content currently found in the *NIV Compact Concordance*, the *NIV Compact Dictionary*, and the *NIV Compact Nave's Topical Bible*.

HOW TO USE THIS RESOURCE

You hold in your hands a unique Bible study resource tool that combines the most common entries found in a Concordance, Topical Bible, and Bible Dictionary all in one volume. The main benefits of combining these three components are saving time in your research, understanding the Bible better in both its details and its "big picture," and seeing things fit together more easily in your study of God's Word.

Each of these components serves a different purpose.

A Concordance is a word index. It is a listing of the words used in the text of a particular translation of the Bible, in this case the *New International Version*. Each word is followed by the Scripture references and a brief excerpt from the verse in which the word occurs. Thus, a concordance may be used to do word studies, locate and trace biblical themes, and find forgotten references to verses.

A Topical Bible — not literally a Bible, but rather a tool for Bible study — references key Scripture verses under numerous topics and provides short descriptions, enabling you to find the exact information you desire about a particular topic or theme, even though the topic itself may not be among the words found in the Scripture text. It is essentially a subject index.

The function of a Bible Dictionary is to make accessible information not found in the Bible itself that enables you to understand better the meaning of the text you are reading. It provides biographical, chronological, geographical, historical, and cultural backgrounds on biblical topics.

Dictionary entries make up the bulk of this reference book. The length of the articles reflects the relative importance of the various topics addressed. For example, entries such as "God," "Moses," and the "Bible" comprise longer articles, while entries on such topics as "Abaddon," "Cana," and "Ecology" comprise shorter articles. Each article includes cross-references to Scripture, thereby supplying a biblical context for the information.

Some topics in this book include all three of these aids while some include only one or two kinds.

All entries are arranged alphabetically and include up to six distinct types of information about the entry topic. In addition to the three mentioned above, there will be a G/K number, a word pronunciation, and a basic Hebrew/Greek root meaning.

G/K (Goodrick-Kohlenberger) numbers refer to the Hebrew or Greek root word(s) used in reference to the topic as found in the *NIV Exhaustive Concordance*. Students of the Bible who wish to dig deeper into word studies relating to a particular topic or word are able to utilize these numbers.

A word pronunciation guide is also provided along with a term's basic Hebrew or Greek root meaning. The root meaning only includes a simple gloss of the term and does not provide the information that can be found in the *NIV Exhaustive Concordance* relating to the G/K numbers.

The sample page below identifies and illustrates these six informational aspects of this Bible reference book.

Goodrick-Kohlenberger (G/K) numbers as found in the *NIV Exhaustive Concordance*

Word pronunciation, Hebrew/Greek root of word, and basic meaning

ABINADAB [44] (a-bĭn′a-dăb, Heb. *’ăvînādhāv, [my] father is generous* or *[my] father is Nadab*).

1. A Levite living in Kiriath Jearim to whose home the ark was brought from the land of the Philistines. About a century later, David removed the ark to Jerusalem (1Sa 7:1 – 2; 2Sa 6:3 – 4; 1Ch 13:7).

2. The second of the eight sons of Jesse. He was in Saul's army when Goliath gave his challenge (1Sa 16:8; 17:13; 1Ch 2:13).

3. Son of Saul (1Sa 31:2), also called Ishvi (1Sa 14:49). He was killed with his father by the Philistines at Mount Gilboa (1Sa 17:13; 31:2; 1Ch 8:33; 9:39; 10:2).

4. Father of one of Solomon's governors who supplied provisions for the king and the royal household. Also called Ben-Abinadab (1Ki 4:11).

ABNER [46, 79] (ăb′nêr, Heb. *’ăvnēr, [my] father is Ner [lamp]*). The son of Ner, who was the brother of Kish, the father of King Saul. Abner and Saul were therefore cousins. During Saul's reign, Abner was the commander in chief of Saul's army (1Sa 14:50). It was Abner who brought David to Saul following the slaying of Goliath (17:55 – 58). He accompanied Saul in his pursuit of David (26:5ff.) and was rebuked by David for his failure to keep better watch over his master (26:13 – 16).

Cousin of Saul and commander of his army (1Sa 14:50; 17:55 – 57; 26); Made Ish-Bosheth king after Saul (2Sa 2:8 – 10); Later defected to David (2Sa 3:6 – 21)

ABOLISH

Da	11:31	and will **a** the daily sacrifice.
Hos	2:18	and sword and battle I will **a** from
Mt	5:17	come to **a** the Law or the Prophets;
	5:17	not come to **a** them but to fulfill

Dictionary entries are numbered if there is more than one meaning for a given topic. Each entry provides biblical references that support the information given for that subject.

Topical references for entry

Concordance references

ABBREVIATIONS

BOOKS OF THE BIBLE

Old Testament

Genesis	Ge
Exodus	Ex
Leviticus	Lev
Numbers	Nu
Deuteronomy	Dt
Joshua	Jos
Judges	Jdg
Ruth	Ru
1 Samuel	1Sa
2 Samuel	2Sa
1 Kings	1Ki
2 Kings	2Ki
1 Chronicles	1Ch
2 Chronicles	2Ch
Ezra	Ezr
Nehemiah	Ne
Esther	Est
Job	Job
Psalm(s)	Ps
Proverbs	Pr
Ecclesiastes	Ecc
Song of Songs	SS
Isaiah	Isa
Jeremiah	Jer
Lamentations	La
Ezekiel	Eze
Daniel	Da
Hosea	Hos
Joel	Joel
Amos	Am
Obadiah	Ob
Jonah	Jnh
Micah	Mic
Nahum	Na
Habakkuk	Hab
Zephaniah	Zep
Haggai	Hag
Zechariah	Zec
Malachi	Mal

New Testament

Matthew	Mt
Mark	Mk
Luke	Lk
John	Jn
Acts	Ac
Romans	Ro
1 Corinthians	1Co
2 Corinthians	2Co
Galatians	Gal
Ephesians	Eph
Philippians	Php
Colossians	Col
1 Thessalonians	1Th
2 Thessalonians	2Th
1 Timothy	1Ti
2 Timothy	2Ti
Titus	Tit
Philemon	Phm
Hebrews	Heb
James	Jas
1 Peter	1Pe
2 Peter	2Pe
1 John	1Jn
2 John	2Jn
3 John	3Jn
Jude	Jude
Revelation	Rev

BIBLE VERSIONS, REFERENCE WORKS, AND OTHER SOURCES

BDB	Brown, Driver, and Briggs, *A Hebrew and English Lexicon of the Old Testament*
G/K	Goodrick/Kohlenberger (Hebrew/Greek numbers)
ICC	*International Critical Commentary*
IDB	*The Interpreter's Dictionary of the Bible*
JB	Jerusalem Bible
KB	Koehler-Baumgartner, *Lexicon in Veteris Testament Libros*
KJV	King James Version
NASB	New American Standard Bible
NEB	New English Bible
NIV	The New International Version
RSV	Revised Standard Version
TR	*Textus Receptus*

AARON [195, 2] (âr′ŭn, Heb. ʾahărôn, meaning uncertain). Aaron was the oldest son of Amram and Jochebed, of the tribe of Levi, and brother of Moses and Miriam (Ex 6:2; Nu 26:59). He was born three years before Moses and before Pharaoh's edict that all male infants should be destroyed (Ex 7:7). His name first appears in God's commission to Moses when Moses protested that he did not have sufficient ability in public speaking to undertake the mission to Pharaoh. In response God declared that Aaron would serve as a spokesman for his brother (Ex 4:10 – 16). So Aaron met Moses at "the mountain of God" (Ex 4:27) after forty years of separation, took him back to the family home in Goshen, introduced him to the elders of the people, and persuaded them to accept him as their leader. Together Moses and Aaron went to Pharaoh's court, where they carried on the negotiations that finally ended the oppression of the Israelites and precipitated the exodus.

Aaron married Elisheba, daughter of Amminadab and sister of Nahshon, a prince of the tribe of Judah (Ex 6:23; 1Ch 2:10). They had four sons: Nadab, Abihu, Eleazar, and Ithamar (Ex 6:23). After Israel left Egypt, Aaron assisted Moses during the wilderness wandering. On the way to Sinai, in the battle with Amalek, Aaron and Hur held up Moses' hands (Ex 17:9 – 13), which held the staff of God. Israel consequently won the battle. With the establishment of the tabernacle, Aaron became high priest in charge of the national worship and the head of the hereditary priesthood.

Later Aaron and Miriam criticized Moses for having married a Cushite woman and challenged his position as Israel's sole mouthpiece (Nu 12:1 – 2). Aaron's own authority as priest did not go unchallenged. It becomes clear that when Korah and his company (Nu 16) challenged Moses' leadership, Aaron's priesthood was also called into question. By the miraculous sign of the flowering and fruit-bearing staff, the Lord identified Aaron as his chosen priest (Nu 17:1 – 9) and accorded him a perpetual priesthood by ordering his staff to be deposited in the sanctuary (Nu 17:10). When Moses went up Mount Sinai to receive the tables of the Law from God, Aaron gave assent to the people's demand for a visible god that they could worship. He melted their personal jewelry in a furnace and made a golden calf similar to the familiar bull god of Egypt.

The people hailed this image as the god who had brought them out of Egypt. Aaron did not protest but built an altar and proclaimed a feast to the Lord on the next day, which the people celebrated with revelry and debauchery (Ex 32:1 – 6). When Moses returned from the mountain and rebuked Aaron for aiding this abuse, Aaron disingenuously replied: "They gave me the gold, and I threw it into the fire, and out came this calf!" (Dt 32:24). Perhaps Aaron meant to restrain the people by a compromise, but he was wholly unsuccessful. Two months later, when the revelation of the pattern for worship was completed, Aaron and his sons were consecrated to the priesthood (Lev 8 – 9).

At the end of the wilderness wandering, Aaron was warned of his impending death. He and Moses went up Mount Hor, where Aaron was stripped of his priestly robes, which were passed in succession to his son Eleazar. Aaron died at age 123 and was buried on the mountain (Nu 20:22 – 29; 33:38; Dt 10:6; 32:50). The people mourned for him thirty days.

Genealogy of (Ex 6:16 – 20; Jos 21:4, 10; 1Ch 6:3 – 15); Priesthood of (Ex 28:1; Nu 17; Heb 5:1 – 4; 7); Priesthood opposed (Nu 16); Garments of (Ex 28; 39); Consecration of (Ex 29); Ordination of (Lev 8); Spokesman for Moses (Ex 4:14 – 16); Built the golden calf (Ex 32; Dt 9:20); Forbidden to enter the Promised Land (Nu 20:1 – 12); Death of (Nu 20:22 – 29; 33:38 – 39)

ABADDON [3] (a-băd′ŭn, Heb. ʾăvaddôn, ruin, perdition, destruction). A Hebrew word for the underworld or the abode of the dead. In the OT it is a synonym of death (hell) and Sheol. Its six OT occurrences (Job 26:6; 28:22; 31:12; Ps 88:11; Pr 15:11; 27:20) have the idea of "ruin." Abaddon is found once in the NT (Rev 9:11) where it refers to the angel who reigns over the infernal regions.

| Rev | 9:11 | whose name in Hebrew is **A** |

ABBA [5] (ăb′a, Heb. *'abbā'*). Aramaic word for "father," which is a customary title of God in prayer. It was transliterated into Greek and then into English and is found three times in the NT (Mk 14:36; Ro 8:15; Gal 4:6). The corresponding Hebrew word is *Ab*. The word *abba* is found in the Babylonian Talmud where it is used as an address of a child to his father and as a type of address to rabbis. It is equivalent to *papa*. This term conveys a sense of warm intimacy and also respect for the father. Because the Jews found it too presumptuous and nearly blasphemous, they would therefore never address God in this manner.

Jesus called God "Father" and gave that same right to his disciples (Mt 6:5 – 15). Paul sees this as symbolic of the Christian's adoption as a child of God and of possession of the Spirit (Mk 14:36; Ro 8:15; Gal 4:6).

Mk	14:36	"**A**, Father," he said,
Rom	8:15	And by him we cry, "**A**, Father."
Gal	4:6	the Spirit who calls out, "**A**, Father."

ABEDNEGO [6284, 10524] (a-bĕd-nē-gō̄ Heb. *'ăvē-dhneghô, servant of Nego*). His Hebrew name was Azariah. He was taken as a captive to Babylon with Daniel, Hananiah, and Mishael, where each was given a Babylonian name (Da 1:6 – 20; 2:17, 49; 3:12 – 30). Azariah was given the Akkadian name Abednego, which was the Babylonian god of wisdom, connected with the planet Mercury. Shadrach, Meshach, and Abednego were chosen to learn the language and the ways of the Chaldeans (Babylonians) so that they could enter the king's service (Da 1:3 – 5, 17 – 20). They were given responsibility over the affairs of the province of Babylon (Da 3:12). These three individuals were eventually thrown into Nebuchadnezzar's furnace because they refused to bow down and worship his golden image, but they were saved by God (Da 3:1, 4 – 6, 8 – 30).

ABEL [64, 2040, 6] (ā′bĕl, Heb. *hevel*). The Hebrew spelling of this word means "breath," "vapor," that which is "insubstantial"; but more likely the name should be linked with an Accadian word meaning "son." He was Adam and Eve's second son who was murdered by his brother Cain (Ge 4). Disaffection between the two brothers arose when Cain brought a vegetable offering to the Lord, and Abel brought a lamb. Perhaps God had previously (at Ge 3:21?) revealed that humans must approach him with a blood sacrifice. God accepted Abel's offering either because it was an animal sacrifice or because of the spirit in which it was offered (Ge 4:4 – 5). Thus Abel became the first example of the way of righteousness through faith.

Second son of Adam (Ge 4:2); Offered proper sacrifice (Ge 4:4; Heb 11:4); Murdered by Cain (Ge 4:8; Mt 23:35; Lk 11:51; 1Jn 3:12)

ABIGAIL [28] (ăb′ĭgāl, Heb. *'ăvi{dec103}hayil, [my] father is rejoicing*).

1. The wife of Nabal and, after his death, of David (1Sa 25:3, 14 – 44; 27:3; 30:5; 2Sa 2:2; 2Sa 3:3), to whom she bore his second son, Kileab (or, 1Ch 3:1, Daniel).

2. A sister or stepsister of David. In 1Ch 2:13 – 17 she apparently belongs to Jesse's family and is, along with Zeruiah, a sister of David. But in 2Sa 17:25 she is mentioned as a daughter of Nahash. The probability is that Nahash was the first husband of Jesse's wife — this would account for the slightly unusual way in which she and Zeruiah are recorded in Chronicles, not as Jesse's daughters but as his sons' sisters. She was married to an Ishmaelite, Jether (2Sa 17:25; 1Ch 2:17), and became the mother of Amasa, Absalom's commander in chief (2Sa 17:2), who was also for a time David's commander in chief (2Sa 17:25; 19:13; 1Ch 2:16 – 17).

ABIJAH [23, 31, 32, 7] (a-bī'ja, Heb. 'ăvîyâh or 'ăvîyāhû, *Jehovah is father; [my] father is Yahweh*).

1. The wife of Judah's grandson Hezron and mother of Ashhur the father of Tekoa (1Ch 2:24).

2. The seventh son of Beker, the son of Benjamin (1Ch 7:8).

3. The second son of the prophet Samuel. Appointed with his brother Joel as a judge by his father, but did not follow in Samuel's ways. They followed after dishonest gains, bribes, and perverted justice. Because of this the Israelites demanded a king to lead them (1Sa 8:1 – 5; 1Ch 6:28).

4. A descendant of Aaron. He was the ancestral head of the eighth of the twenty-four groups into which David had divided the priests (1Ch 24:10). The father of John the Baptist belonged to this group (Lk 1:5).

5. A son of Jeroboam I of Israel (1Ki 14:1 – 18). He died from illness when still a child, in fulfillment of a prediction by the prophet Ahijah, to whom the queen had gone in disguise to inquire regarding the outcome of the child's illness. The death was a judgment for the apostasy of Jeroboam.

6. The second king of Judah, the son and successor of Rehoboam, and the grandson of Solomon (1Ch 3:10). Name is spelled "Abijam" in 1Ki 14 and 15. He made war on Jeroboam in an effort to recover the ten tribes of Israel. In a speech before an important battle in which his army was greatly outnumbered, he appealed to Jeroboam not to oppose the God of Israel, for God had given the kingdom to David and his sons forever. Abijah gained a decisive victory (1Ki 15:1 – 8; 2Ch 11:22; 13). Prosperity tempted him to multiply wives and to follow the evil ways of his father. He reigned three years (2Ch 12:16 – 14:1) and was succeeded by Asa his son (1Ki 15:8; 2Ch 14:1).

7. The daughter of Zechariah and mother of king Hezekiah (2Ch 29:1). "Abi" in 2Ki 18:2 (KJV, NASB, NEB, RSV).

8. A chief of the priests who returned from Babylon with Zerubbabel (Ne 12:4, 17).

9. A priest of Nehemiah's time (Ne 10:7). Probably the same as no. 8.

ABILITY

Ge	47:6	of any among them with special **a**,
Ex	31:3	with skill, **a** and knowledge
	35:31	with skill, **a** and knowledge
	35:34	the **a** to teach others.
	36:1	to whom the LORD has given skill and **a**
	36:2	the LORD had given **a**
Dt	8:18	for it is he who gives you the **a**
Ezr	2:69	According to their **a** they gave to the treasury
Da	5:12	and also the **a** to interpret dreams,
Mt	25:15	each according to his **a**.
Ac	8:19	"Give me also this **a**
	11:29	each according to his **a**,
2Co	1:8	far beyond our **a** to endure,
	8:3	and even beyond their **a**.

ABIMELECH [43] (a-bǐm'ě-lěk, Heb. 'ăvîmelekh, *[my] father is a king* or *[my] father is Molech*).

1. A Philistine king of Gerar, south of Gaza in the foothills of the Judean mountains. It was at his court that Abraham, out of fear, said that Sarah was his sister. Struck by her beauty, Abimelech took her to marry but, when warned by God in a dream, immediately returned her to Abraham (Ge 20:1 – 18). Later, when their servants contended over a well, the two men made a covenant (21:22 – 34).

2. A second king of Gerar, probably the son of the one mentioned in no. 1, at whose court Isaac tried to pass off his wife Rebekah as his sister (Ge 26:1 – 11). Abimelech rebuked Isaac when the falsehood was detected. Later their servants quarreled, and they made a covenant between themselves just as Abraham and the first Abimelech had done.

3. The son of Gideon by a concubine (Jdg 8:31; 9:1 – 57, w 6:32 & 7:1). After the death of his father, aspiring to be king, he murdered seventy sons of his father. Only one son, Jotham, escaped. Abimelech was made king of Shechem. After he had reigned only three years, rebellion broke out against him; in the course of the rebellion he attacked and

destroyed his own city of Shechem. Later he was killed while besieging the nearby Thebez.

4. A Philistine king mentioned in the title of Ps 34, who very likely is the same as Achish, king of Gath (1Sa 21:10 – 22:1), with whom David sought refuge when he fled from Saul. It is possible that Abimelech was a royal title of Philistine kings, not a personal name.

5. A priest in the days of David. A son of Abiathar (2Sa 8:17; 1Ch 18:16). Also called Ahimelech in the LXX and in Chronicles (1Ch 24:6).

ABINADAB [44] (a-bĭn′a-dăb, Heb. *'ăvînādhāv, [my] father is generous* or *[my] father is Nadab*).

1. A Levite living in Kiriath Jearim to whose home the ark was brought from the land of the Philistines. About a century later, David removed the ark to Jerusalem (1Sa 7:1 – 2; 2Sa 6:3 – 4; 1Ch 13:7).

2. The second of the eight sons of Jesse. He was in Saul's army when Goliath gave his challenge (1Sa 16:8; 17:13; 1Ch 2:13).

3. Son of Saul (1Sa 31:2), also called Ishvi (1Sa 14:49). He was killed with his father by the Philistines at Mount Gilboa (1Sa 17:13; 31:2; 1Ch 8:33; 9:39; 10:2).

4. Father of one of Solomon's governors who supplied provisions for the king and the royal household. Also called Ben-Abinadab (1Ki 4:11).

ABLE

Ge	13:6	that they were not **a** to stay together.
Lev	26:37	not be **a** to stand before your enemies.
Nu	14:16	not **a** to bring these people into the land
Jos	24:19	"You are not **a** to serve the LORD.
1Sa	17:33	not **a** to go out against this Philistine
1Ki	3:9	who is **a** to govern this great people
1Ch	29:14	be **a** to give as generously as this?
2Ch	2:6	who is **a** to build a temple for him,
Job	41:10	Who then is **a** to stand against me?
Ps	36:12	not **a** to rise!
Isa	36:20	of these countries has been **a**
Eze	7:19	and gold will not be **a** to save them
Da	2:26	"Are you **a** to tell me what I saw
	3:17	the God we serve is **a** to save us
	4:37	And those who walk in pride he is **a** to humble.
Hos	5:13	But he is not **a** to cure you,
Mt	9:28	"Do you believe that I am **a**
	26:61	'I am **a** to destroy the temple of God
Lk	13:24	will try to enter and will not be **a** to.
	14:30	to build and was not **a** to finish.'
	21:15	none of your adversaries will be **a** to
	21:36	pray that you may be **a** to escape
	21:36	that you may be **a** to stand before
Ac	5:39	you will not be **a** to stop these men;
	15:10	nor our fathers have been **a** to bear?
	22:13	that very moment I was **a** to see him.
Ro	8:39	will be **a** to separate us from the love of God
	11:23	for God is **a** to graft them in again.
	12:2	Then you will be **a** to test
	14:4	for the Lord is **a** to make him stand.
	16:25	Now to him who is **a** to establish you
1Co	12:28	those **a** to help others,
2Co	8:3	they gave as much as they were **a**,
	9:8	And God is **a** to make all grace abound to
Eph	3:4	**a** to understand my insight into the mystery
	3:20	who is **a** to do immeasurably more
	6:13	you may be **a** to stand your ground,
1Ti	3:2	respectable, hospitable, **a** to teach,
2Ti	1:12	is **a** to guard what I have entrusted
	2:24	**a** to teach, not resentful.
	3:7	but never **a** to acknowledge the truth.
	3:15	which are **a** to make you wise
Heb	2:18	he is **a** to help those who are being tempted.
	3:19	we see that they were not **a** to enter,
	5:2	He is **a** to deal gently
	7:25	Therefore he is **a** to save completely
	9:9	not **a** to clear the conscience

Jas	3:2	**a** to keep his whole body in check.
	4:12	the one who is **a** to save and destroy.
2Pe	1:15	always be **a** to remember these
Jude	1:24	To him who is **a** to keep you
Rev	5:5	He is **a** to open the scroll

ABNER [46, 79] (ăb'nêr, Heb. *ăvnēr, [my] father is Ner [lamp]*). The son of Ner, who was the brother of Kish, the father of King Saul. Abner and Saul were therefore cousins. During Saul's reign, Abner was the commander in chief of Saul's army (1Sa 14:50). It was Abner who brought David to Saul following the slaying of Goliath (17:55 – 58). He accompanied Saul in his pursuit of David (26:5ff.) and was rebuked by David for his failure to keep better watch over his master (26:13 – 16).

At Saul's death, Abner espoused the cause of Saul's house and had Ish-Bosheth, Saul's son, made king over Israel (2Sa 2:8). Abner and his men met David's servants in combat by the pool of Gibeon and were overwhelmingly defeated. During the retreat from this battle, Abner was pursued by Asahel, Joab's brother, and in self-defense killed him (2:12 – 32).

Soon after this, Abner and Ish-Bosheth had a quarrel over Saul's concubine. Ish-Bosheth probably saw Abner's behavior with Rizpah as tantamount to a claim to the throne. This resulted in Abner's entering into negotiations with David to go to his side, and he promised to bring all Israel with him. David graciously received him. Abner had not been gone long when Joab heard of the affair; believing or pretending to believe that Abner had come as a spy, Joab invited him to a friendly conversation and murdered him "to avenge the blood of his brother Asahel" (2Sa 3:6 – 27). This seems to have been a genuine grief to David, who composed a lament for the occasion (3:33 – 34). Abner dedicated spoils of war to the tabernacle (1Ch 26:27 – 28).

Cousin of Saul and commander of his army (1Sa 14:50; 17:55 – 57; 26); Made Ish-Bosheth king after Saul (2Sa 2:8 – 10); Later defected to David (2Sa 3:6 – 21)

ABOLISH

Da	11:31	and will **a** the daily sacrifice.
Hos	2:18	and sword and battle I will **a** from
Mt	5:17	come to **a** the Law or the Prophets;
	5:17	not come to **a** them but to fulfill

ABOMINATION [9199, 9359, 1007]. Activities that are offensive in a moral, religious, or even natural sense of repulsion. The word "abomination" occurs rarely in the NIV (e.g., Pr 26:25; Isa 66:3; Da 9:27; 11:31; 12:11; cf. "abominable," Isa 66:17; Jer 32:34). The idea is, however, much more widespread and often expressed in the NIV by the verb *detest* and the adjective *detestable*. Two main Hebrew words are involved: (1) *Shiqqutz*, regarding the use of idols (e.g., 2Ki 23:24; Jer 7:30), the gods represented by idols (e.g., 2Ki 23:13), forbidden practices (e.g., 23:24), and generally anything contrary to the worship and religion of the Lord (e.g., 2Ch 15:8; Isa 66:3; Jer 4:1). The related noun *sheqetz* is used of idols in animal form (Eze 8:10), forbidden foods (Lev 11:10, 13, 42), and generally anything bringing ceremonial defilement (7:21). (2) *Tô'evah*, often synonymous with *shiqqutz*, is also used in wider areas of life — things related to idols (Dt 7:25; 27:15), false gods themselves (32:16), forbidden sexual practices (e.g., Lev 18:22, 26 – 27), prophecy leading to the worship of other gods (Dt 13:13 – 14), the offering of blemished animals in sacrifice (17:1), and heathen divination (18:9, 12). Basic to the use of these words, then, is the active abhorrence the Lord feels toward that which challenges his position as the sole God of his people, or contradicts his will, whether in the way he is to be worshiped or the way his people are to live.

God's Law Regarding:
Sexual relations: incest (Lev 18:6 – 18; Dt 27:20); lying with a woman during her monthly period (Lev 18:19; 20:18); adultery (Lev 18:20); homosexuality (Lev 18:22; 20:13); bestiality (Lev 18:23; 20:15 – 16). Idolatry (Dt 7:25 – 26;

27:15; 32:16 – 42); divination, sorcery, interpretation of omens, witchcraft, casting of spells, mediums or spiritists, those who consult the dead (Dt 18:9 – 15); sacrifice of children by fire to Molech (Dt 18:10, w Lev 18:21). Wearing clothes of opposite sex (Dt 22:5). Earnings of female or male prostitute to pay a vow (Dt 23:18). Remarriage of defiled wife (Dt 24:1 – 4). Unjust weights and measures (Dt 25:13 – 16; Pr 11:1; 20:10, 23). See Law.

Idols:

(Dt 7:25 – 26; 27:15; 29:17 – 18; Eze 7:20 – 21). Solomon's devotion to, in old age (1Ki 11:1 – 12). Ashtoreth of the Sidonians, Molech of the Ammonites, Chemosh of the Moabites (1Ki 11:5 – 8; 11:33; 2Ki 23:13). No gods apart from God (Dt 6:4; 1Ch 17:20; Isa 43:10 – 13; 44:6 – 28). Turn from, and return to God (Jer 4:1 – 2), or receive disaster (Eze 5:5ff.). Worship of, and related practices (Eze 16:1 – 63; Hos 9:10). See Idol; Idolatry.

Actions and Attitudes:

A false witness who pours out lies (Dt 19:15 – 21; Pr 6:19; 21:28); perverseness (Pr 3:32; 11:20); false pride (Pr 6:17; 16:5); murder (Pr 6:17); lying (Pr 6:17, 19; 12:22); one who devises wicked schemes (Pr 6:18); wicked imaginations, i.e., the thoughts of the wicked (Pr 6:18; 15:26; 21:27); wickedness (Pr 8:7).

People, Types:

False witness (Pr 6:19; 17:15); troublemaker (Pr 6:19); mocker (Pr 24:9); dishonest (Pr 29:27).

Of Wicked:

Sacrifice (Pr 15:8; 21:27; Isa 1:13); ways (Pr 15:9); thoughts (Pr 15:26); prayer (Pr 28:9). See Wicked, Wickedness.

Pr	26:25	for seven **a** fill his heart.
Isa	66:3	and their souls delight in their **a**;
Rev	17:5	AND OF THE **A** OF THE EARTH.

ABOMINATION THAT CAUSES DESOLATION [9037+9199, 1007+2247]. An utterly abhorrent abomination (Da 9:27; 11:31; 12:11). The interpretation of the references of Daniel to some notable and frightful abomination has caused much difficulty and difference among interpreters. Daniel's prophecies may refer to one or all of three events: (1) To Antiochus's desecration of the temple in 169 – 167 BC (1Mc 1:21 – 61). Antiochus Epiphanes set up an altar in the Jerusalem temple and sacrificed a pig on it. But Mt 24:15 and Mk 13:14 make it clear that the Lord Jesus understood the "abomination" as still to come. (2) To the destruction of Jerusalem in AD 70 (Mt 24:15; Mk 13:14). These interpreters understand the Lord to refer to some horrifying act of sacrilege during the period of the Jewish revolt and the sack of Jerusalem by the Romans in AD 70. (3) To the setting up of the image of the beast (Rev 13:14 – 15). These interpreters understand the Lord to be speaking not of the fall of Jerusalem but of the end time itself, immediately prior to his own coming; they link the setting up of the abomination with the appearance and activity of the man of sin (2Th 2:3 – 4, 8 – 9).

Da	9:27	set up an **a** that causes desolation.
	11:31	set up the **a** that causes desolation.
	12:11	the **a** that causes desolation is set up.
Mt	24:15	'the **a** that causes desolation,'
Mk	13:14	'the **a** that causes desolation'

ABOUND

Ps	72:7	righteous will flourish; prosperity will **a**
	72:16	Let grain **a** throughout the land;
2Co	9:8	And God is able to make all grace **a**
	9:8	you will **a** in every good work.
Php	1:9	that your love may **a** more and more

ABRAHAM, ABRAM [90, 92, 11] (ā'bra-hăm, Heb. 'avrāhām, *father of a multitude*; earlier name Abram, Heb. 'avram, *exalted father*). The son of Terah, Abraham was the founder of the Hebrew nation and father of the people of God. His ancestry can be traced back to Noah through Shem (Ge

11:10ff.) and comes into the biblical story out of an idolatrous background (Jos 24:2). Abraham was married to Sarai (Ge 11:29) and dwelled in Ur of the Chaldeans. Terah moved Abraham and the rest of the family to the land of Canaan. On the way they stopped and settled in Haran in NW Mesopotamia, where Terah died (Ge 11:31; Ne 9:7; Ac 7:4). Abraham later received a divine call from God (Ge 12:1 – 3; Jos 24:3; Ne 9:7 – 8; Isa 51:2; Ac 7:2 – 4; Heb 11:8) in which the land of Canaan was given to him (Ge 12:1, 6 – 7; 15:7 – 21; Eze 33:24). When Abraham arrived in Canaan (12:6), God confirmed the promise that this was the land his descendants would possess (12:7) He dwelled in the hills east of Bethel and west of Ai (Ge 12:8) then relocated to Egypt because of a famine in Canaan (Ge 12:10 – 20; 26:1). Upon leaving Egypt, Abraham and his family traveled to the Negev and on to Bethel. Because there was not enough land in one place to support their large herds of sheep, Abraham gave Lot his choice of land; Lot chose the plain of Jordan, leaving Abraham to live at the great trees of Mamre the Amorite at Hebron (Ge 13; 14:13; 35:27). Later the Lord confirmed his promises of children and land in a great covenant sign (Ge 15:7 – 21), but Abraham and Sarai, tired of waiting (ch 16), turned from the way of faith to a human expedient that was permitted — even expected — by the laws of the day: a childless couple might "have children" through the medium of a secondary wife. Poor, mistreated Hagar fell into this role and Ishmael was born (Ge 16:3, 7 – 16). Yet the Lord was not diverted from his chosen course: in gentle grace he picked up the pieces of Hagar's broken life (16:7 – 16) and reaffirmed his covenant with Abraham (17:1ff.). In three ways the Lord made his promises more sure. First, he made Abraham and Sarai into new people (17:3 – 5, 15 – 16). This is the significance of the gift of new names: they were themselves made new, with new capacities. Second, the Lord restated and amplified his spoken promises so as to leave no doubt of his seriousness in making them (17:6 – 8). Third, he sealed his promises with the sign of circumcision (17:9 – 14) so that forever after Abraham and his

family would be able to look at their own bodies and say, "The Lord has indeed kept his promises to me!"

Abraham deeply loved his sons Ishmael and Isaac (17:18; 21:11 – 12), yet he was called to give them both up — in faith that the Lord would keep his promises concerning them (21:11 – 13; 22:1 – 18). The Lord did not spring these great decisions on Abraham but prepared him for them by his experience with Lot and Sodom (chs. 18 – 19). In this connection Abraham would learn two lessons: first, that it is not a vain thing to leave matters in the hand of God — he prayed, and the Lord answered prayer (18:22 – 33); second, that the Lord really meant the "family" aspect of his promises — even Lot was preserved because the Lord "remembered Abraham" (19:29). To be linked with the covenant man was to come under the sovereign hand of the covenant God. And if Lot, how much more Ishmael, and how very much more the son of promise himself, Isaac! Thus Abraham came to the maturity of faith that enabled him to say (22:5), "I and the boy [will] go ... we will worship ... we will come back" — knowing that the worship in question involved raising the knife over Isaac (Ge 22:1 – 19; Heb 11:17 – 19; Jas 2:21).

Other aspects of Abraham's life:

Dwelled in Gerar and Beersheba (Ge 20; 21:22 – 34); Defeated Kedorlaomer king of Elam (Ge 14:5 – 16; Heb 7:1); Blessed by Melchizedek (Ge 14:18 – 20; Heb 7:1 – 10); Received a new name (Ge 17:5; Ne 9:7); Circumcision of (Ge 17:10 – 14, 23 – 27); Angels appeared to (Ge 18:1 – 16; 22:11 – 12, 15; 24:7); His questions and intercession concerning the destruction of the righteous and wicked in Sodom (Ge 18:23 – 32); Witnessed the destruction of Sodom (Ge 19:27 – 29); Isaac born to Abraham at age one hundred according to the promise of Yahweh (Ge 21:1 – 5; Gal 4:22 – 30); Sent Hagar and Ishmael away (Ge 21:10 – 14; Gal 4:22 – 30); Death of Sarah, his wife (Ge 23:1 – 2); Purchased a place for her burial and buried her in a cave (Ge 23:3 – 20); Provided a wife for Isaac (Ge

24); *Married Keturah (Ge 25:1); Death of (Ge 15:15; 25:8 – 10); In paradise (Mt 8:11; Lk 13:28; 16:22 – 31); Wealth of (Ge 13:2; 24:35); Children of (Ge 16:15; 21:2 – 3; 25:1 – 4; 1Ch 1:32 – 34); Inheritance of (Ge 25:5 – 6); Age of at different periods (Ge 12:4; 16:16; 21:5; 25:7)*

Character Qualities of:
Unselfishness (Ge 13:9; 21:25 – 30). Independent character (Ge 14:23; 23:6 – 16). Faith in God (Ge 15:6; Ro 4:1 – 22; Gal 3:6 – 9; Heb 11:8 – 19; Jas 2:21 – 24). Prophet (Ge 20:7). Friend of God (2Ch 20:7; Isa 41:8; Jas 2:23). Regarded by his descendants (Mt 3:9; Lk 13:16, 28; 19:9; Jn 8:33 – 40, 52 – 59).

ABRAHAM'S SIDE In the Lukan account of the rich man and Lazarus, Lazarus is being comforted at Abraham's side [the JB, KJV, NASB, and RSV "bosom"] while the rich man is being tormented in the fires of hell (Lk 16:22 – 23). *See Lazarus.* In the Talmudic language, to sit at Abraham's side is to enter Paradise (cf. 4Mc 13:17). It is the place where the righteous go at the moment of death and where judgment is enacted as preliminary, and perhaps probationary, to the final judgment at the end of the age. The figure derives either from the Roman custom of reclining on the left side at meals, Lazarus being in the place of honor at Abraham's right, leaning on his breast, or from its appropriateness as expressing closest fellowship (Jn 1:18; 13:23). Since Abraham was the founder of the Hebrew nation, such closeness was the highest honor and bliss.

ABSALOM [94] (ăb'sa-lŏm, Heb. *'avshālôm, father [is] peace*).

1. The third son of David by Maacah, daughter of Talmai, king of Geshur, a small district NE of Lake Galilee (2Sa 3:3; 1Ch 3:2), also known as Abishalom (1Ki 15:2, 10, w 1Ch 11:20 – 21). Absalom hated Amnon, one of his stepbrothers and David's first son, because Amnon had raped his sister Tamar. After two years, Absalom avenged Tamar (2Sa 13:1 – 29) then fled to Geshur and stayed there three years (2Sa 13:37 – 38). He was permitted by David to return to Jerusalem (2Sa 14:1 – 24). After his return from exile, Absalom was not allowed to see David for two years in Geshur (2Sa 14:28), at which time he forced Joab to get him an audience with the king and was restored to favor (2Sa 14:31 – 33). He had three sons and a daughter, whom he named Tamar after his sister. Absalom now began to act like a candidate for the kingship (15:1 – 6), parading a great retinue and subtly indicating how he would improve the administration of justice in the interests of the people.

Absalom proclaimed himself king and attracted the disaffected to his standard (15:7 – 14). The armies met in the woods of Ephraim, where Absalom's forces were disastrously defeated (18:1 – 8). Absalom was caught by his hair in the branches of an oak, and the mule he was riding went on and left him dangling helpless there. Joab and his men killed him, though David, in the hearing of the whole army, had forbidden anyone to harm him. Absalom was buried in a pit and covered with a heap of stones in the woods where he fell (18:9 – 17). David's great and prolonged grief over the death of his son nearly cost him the loyalty of his subjects (2Sa 18:33 – 19:8). Absalom's rebellion was the most serious threat to David's throne, but its significance for the future lay in the weakness already existing in the kingdom in David's day. Plainly David's administration was faulty. The ease with which Absalom detached the northern tribes from allegiance to David not only exposed the fact that as a Judahite David was guilty of neglecting the Israelite section of his kingdom, but also, more seriously, showed how fragile were the bonds between Judah and Israel. Solomon's more rigorous administrative methods staved off the inevitable division that needed only the ineptitude of his son and successor Rehoboam to make it a reality (1Ki 12:1 – 19). In these ways, as much as in its more explicit predictions, the OT prepared the way for Christ. It records the golden days of David; yet the flaws in David's character and kingdom gave rise to the people's yearning for great David's greater Son.

2. Rehoboam's father-in-law (2Ch 11:20 – 21).

3. In the Apocrypha, an ambassador of Judas Maccabaeus, the father of Mattathias and Jonathan (1Mc 11:70; 13:11; 2Mc 11:17).

ABSTAIN

Ex	19:15	**A** from sexual relations."
Nu	6:3	he must **a** from wine
Ac	15:0	to **a** from food polluted by idols,
	15:29	to **a** from food sacrificed to idols,
	21:25	should **a** from food sacrificed
1Ti	4:3	order them to **a** from certain foods,
1Pe	2:11	to **a** from sinful desires,

ABSTINENCE (ăb'stĭnĕn[t]s, Gr. *apechomai*). The verb "abstain" occurs six times and means "to hold oneself away from." The noun "abstinence" occurs once in the KJV (Gr. *asitia*, Ac 27:2) and means abstinence from food. The decree of the Jerusalem council (15:20, 29) commanded abstinence from "food sacrificed to idols, from blood, from the meat of strangled animals and from sexual immorality," practices abhorrent to Jewish Christians. Paul (1Th 4:3) connects abstaining from fornication with sanctification. In 1Th 5:22 he exhorts abstinence from all appearance of evil. In 1Ti 4:3 he refers to false teachers who commanded believers "to abstain from certain foods, which God created to be received with thanksgiving by those who believe and who know the truth." In 1Pe 2:11, Peter exhorts, "Dear friends, I urge you, as aliens and strangers in the world, to abstain from sinful desires, which war against your soul."

Abstinence from eating blood antedates the Mosaic law (see Ge 9:4) but was rigorously reinforced when the Lord spoke through Moses. The sacred function of blood within the sacrificial system (Lev 17:11) made it something set apart from any common use. Israel abstained voluntarily from eating the sinew on the thigh for the reason given in Ge 32:32. Leviticus 11 defined what animals the children of Israel might not eat, "to distinguish between the unclean and the clean" (11:47), and to keep Israel separate from other nations. The priests were forbidden to drink wine while they were ministering (Lev 10:8 – 9), and the Nazirites were to abstain from the fruit of the vine absolutely. The Recabites took such a vow in deference to their ancestor Jonadab (Jer 35).

Injunctions regarding drunkenness and sobriety (1Co 5:11; 6:9 – 10; Eph 5:18; 1Ti 3:3, 8; Tit 2:2 – 4) point to the wisdom of total abstinence from alcoholic beverages if one would be at his or her best for the Lord. They are reinforced by the fact that the believer's body is the temple of the Holy Spirit (1Co 6:19; 2Co 6:16). Paul's advice to Timothy (1Ti 5:23) sanctions no more than medicinal use of wine mixed with water. While abstinence is not a virtue in itself, it can be a means to make virtue possible.

General References to:
For the sake of a weaker brother (Ac 15:20, 29; Eph 4:17 – 5:21; Col 3:1 – 11; 1Pe 2:11 – 12; Ro 14; 1Co 8). Wrongly used as a form of self-righteousness (Col 2:20 – 23; 1Ti 4:1 – 3). Appearance of evil (1Th 5:22).

From Intoxicating Beverages:
Abuse of alcohol condemned (Pr 23:20, 31 – 35; Lk 21:34). Exemplified by: Aaron and the Levitical priesthood, while on duty (Lev 10:8 – 11; Eze 44:21); Nazirites, while taking a special vow (Nu 6:2 – 4, 20); Manoah's wife, Samson's mother, during pregnancy (Jdg 13:2 – 5, 13 – 14); kings and princes (Pr 31:4 – 5); John the Baptist (Lk 1:15).

Instances of:
Israelites in the wilderness (Dt 29:6); Samson (Jdg 16:17, w 13:3 – 5, 13 – 14 & Nu 6:3 – 4); Recabites, honoring an ancestral commitment (Jer 35:1 – 14); Daniel (Da 1:8, 12); John the Baptist (Mt 11:18; Lk 1:15; 7:33).

Other Things Abstained from:
Food, in fasting (Lev 16:29; 23:27; 1Sa 7:6; Ne 9:1; Joel 2:12; Mt 6:16 – 18). Sexual contact within marriage, temporarily (Ex 19:15; 1Co 7:1 – 5). In Israel: use of blood or fat (Ge 9:4; Lev 3:17); tendon of the hip (Ge 32:32); meat not properly bled and prepared (Ex 22:31; Dt 14:21);

whole groups of animals (Lev 11); contact with unclean persons (Lev 15).

ABUNDANT

Dt	28:11	Lord will grant you **a** prosperity —
	32:2	like **a** rain on tender plants.
Job	36:28	and **a** showers fall on mankind.
Ps	68:9	You gave **a** showers, O God;
	78:15	and gave them water as **a** as the seas;
	132:15	I will bless her with **a** provisions;
	145:7	They will celebrate your **a** goodness
Pr	12:11	He who works his land will have **a** food,
	28:19	He who works his land will have **a** food,
Jer	33:9	the **a** prosperity and peace I provide
Eze	17:5	like a willow by **a** water,
	31:7	for its roots went down to **a** waters.
Joel	2:23	He sends you **a** showers,
Ro	5:17	who receive God's **a** provision of grace

ABUSE

Substance Abuse of Alcohol:

Biblical condemnation of alcohol abuse may be generalized to apply to abuse of any mind- or behavior-altering substance. Condemned (Pr 20:1; 21:17; 23:20, 30 – 35; Isa 5:22; Eph 5:18; 1Ti 3:8; Tit 2:3). Examples of (Ge 9:20 – 24; 19:30 – 36; Isa 28:7 – 8; 1Co 11:20 – 22). See Abstinence.

Abuse of Food:

(Pr 23:1 – 3, 20 – 21; 25:16; 30:22; Isa 56:10 – 11; Am 6:4 – 7; 1Co 6:12 – 13; 1Co 11:20 – 22; Php 3:18 – 19).

Sexual Abuse:

Examples of: rape (Ge 34:1 – 7; Jdg 19:25 – 20:13; 2Sa 13:1 – 20; Zec 14:2); attempted homosexual rape (Ge 19:4 – 9; Jdg 19:22 – 24). Rape punished by death (Dt 22:25 – 27).

Abuse of Persons:

Physical injury to be punished in like kind (Ex 21:22 – 25; Lev 24:19 – 20). Servants and slaves to be set free if physically abused (Ex 21:26 – 27). Unfavored wife still to be cared for (Ex 21:10 – 11; Dt 21:15 – 17). Abuse of parents punishable by death (Ex 21:15, 17; Dt 21:18 – 21). Corporal punishment not abuse if done out of love (Pr 3:11 – 12; 13:24; 29:15; Heb 12:7 – 11).

| Pr | 9:7 | rebukes a wicked man incurs **a**. |
| 1Pe | 4:4 | and they heap **a** on you. |

ABUSIVE

| Ac | 18:6 | Jews opposed Paul and became **a**, |
| 2Ti | 3:2 | lovers of money, boastful, proud, **a**, |

ABYSS [12, 5853] (a-bĭs', Gr. *abyssos, unfathomable depth*). In the NT "abyss" refers to the world of the dead (Ro 10:7) or the netherworld, the prison of disobedient spirits/demons (Lk 8:31; Rev 9:1 – 2, 11; 11:7; 17:8; 20:1 – 3). The KJV renders the Greek word as "the deep" in Lk 8:31 and Ro 10:7 and "the bottomless pit" in Revelation. The ASV and NIV uniformly have "the abyss." The RSV has "the abyss" in Lk 8:31 and Ro 10:7, "the pit" in Rev 20:3, and "the bottomless pit" elsewhere in Revelation.

In classical Greek *abyssos* was an adjective meaning "bottomless," applied to the primeval deep of ancient cosmologies, an ocean surrounding and under the earth. In the LXX it translates Hebrew *tehôm*, meaning the primal waters of Ge 1:2, once the world of the dead (Ps 71:20). In later Judaism it means also the interior depths of the earth and the prison of evil spirits.

The use of "abyss" in Ro 10:7 is parallel with the use of "the lower, earthly regions" in Eph 4:9 (see Ps 106:28); both contrast the highest heaven and the lowest depth. In Lk 8:31 the demons had a great dread of the primal abyss; even so, they may have caused themselves to go there when the pigs were drowned in the sea.

| Lk | 8:31 | not to order them to go into the **A**. |

Rev	9:1	the key to the shaft of the **A**.
	9:2	When he opened the **A**,
	9:2	by the smoke from the **A**.
	9:11	as king over them the angel of the **A**,
	11:7	up from the **A** will attack them,
	17:8	and will come up out of the **A** and go
	20:1	having the key to the **A** and holding
	20:3	He threw him into the **A**,

ACCEPT

Ge	14:23	I will **a** nothing belonging to you,
Ex	23:8	"Do not **a** a bribe,
Lev	26:23	you do not **a** my correction
Dt	16:19	Do not **a** a bribe,
2Sa	24:23	"May the LORD your God **a** you."
Job	2:10	Shall we **a** good from God,
	42:8	and I will **a** his prayer and not deal
Ps	119:108	**A**, O LORD, the willing praise of my
Pr	4:10	Listen, my son, **a** what I say,
	10:8	The wise in heart **a** commands,
	19:20	Listen to advice and **a** instruction,
Eze	43:27	Then I will **a** you,
Zep	3:7	you will fear me and **a** correction!'
Mal	1:10	I will **a** no offering from your hands.
Mt	11:14	And if you are willing to **a** it,
	19:11	"Not everyone can **a** this word,
Jn	3:11	but still you people do not **a** our testimony.
	5:41	"I do not **a** praise from men,
	14:17	The world cannot **a** him,
Ac	22:18	not **a** your testimony about me.'
Ro	14:1	**A** him whose faith is weak,
	15:7	**A** one another, then,
1Co	2:14	The man without the Spirit does not **a**
Jas	1:21	that is so prevalent and humbly **a**
1Jn	5:9	We **a** man's testimony,

ACCOUNT [ACCOUNTABLE]

Ge	2:4	the **a** of the heavens and the earth
	5:1	This is the written **a** of Adam's line.
	6:9	This is the **a** of Noah.
	10:1	This is the **a** of Shem,
	11:10	This is the **a** of Shem.
	11:27	This is the **a** of Terah.
	25:12	the **a** of Abraham's son Ishmael,
	25:19	This is the **a** of Abraham's son Isaac.
	36:1	This is the **a** of Esau (that is, Edom).
	36:9	This is the **a** of Esau the father of
	37:2	This is the **a** of Jacob.
Dt	18:19	I myself will call him to **a**.
Jos	22:23	may the LORD himself call us to **a**.
Mt	12:36	to give **a** on the day of judgment
	26:31	you will all fall away on **a** of me,
Lk	16:2	Give an **a** of your management,
Ro	14:12	each of us will give an **a** of himself
Heb	4:13	of him to whom we must give **a**.
1Jn	2:12	sins have been forgiven on **a** of his name.

ACCOUNTABLE [ACCOUNT]

Eze	3:18	and I will hold you **a** for his blood.
	3:20	and I will hold you **a** for his blood.
	33:6	but I will hold the watchman **a**
	33:8	and I will hold you **a** for his blood.
	34:10	the shepherds and will hold them **a**
Da	6:2	The satraps were made **a** to them so
Jnh	1:14	Do not hold us **a** for killing
Ro	3:19	and the whole world held **a** to God.

ACCUSATION, FALSE [H8189, H8357, H8476, G1592, G2989, G2991].

Forbidden (Ex 23:1, 7; Lev 19:16; Lk 3:14; Tit 2:3). Consolation for those falsely accused (Mt 5:11; Jn 15:19 – 21; 1Pe 4:14). People to be slanderous in the last days (2Ti 3:3).

Instances of:

Joseph by Potiphar's wife (Ge 39:7 – 20). Joseph's brothers by Joseph (Ge 42:6 – 14). Moses by Korah (Nu 16:1 – 3, 13). Ahimelech by Saul (1Sa 22:11 – 16). Abner by Joab (2Sa 3:24 – 27). Elijah by Ahab (1Ki 18:17 – 18). Naboth by Jezebel (1Ki 21:1 – 14). The Jews who returned under Ezra by the men of Trans-Euphrates (Ezr

4:6 – 16; Ne 6:5 – 9). Job by Satan (Job 1:9 – 10; 2:4 – 5). David (Ps 41:5 – 9), by the princes of Ammon (2Sa 10:1 – 4; 1Ch 19:1 – 4). Jeremiah (Jer 26:8 – 15; 37:12 – 15; 43:1 – 4). Amos (Am 7:10 – 11). Mary (Mt 1:19). Jesus (Mt 9:34; 10:25; 12:2 – 14; 26:59 – 61; Mk 3:22; 14:53 – 65; Lk 23:2; Jn 18:30). Stephen (Ac 6:11 – 14). Paul (Ac 17:6 – 7; 21:27 – 29; 24:1 – 9, 12 – 13; 25:1 – 2, 7; Ro 3:8). Paul and Silas (Ac 16:19 – 21).

ACCUSE [ACCUSER]

Ps	103:9	He will not always **a**,
Pr	3:30	Do not **a** a man for no reason —
Zec	3:1	Satan standing at his right side to **a** him.
Mt	12:10	Looking for a reason to **a** Jesus,
Lk	3:14	and don't **a** people falsely —
1Pe	2:12	though they **a** you of doing wrong,

ACCUSER

Job	31:35	let my **a** put his indictment
Isa	50:8	Who is my **a**?
Jn	5:45	Your **a** is Moses,
Rev	12:10	For the **a** of our brothers,

ACHAIA [938] (a-kā′ ya, Gr. *Achaia*). In NT times a Roman province that included the Peloponnesus and northern Greece south of Illyricum, Epirus, and Thessaly, which were districts of Macedonia; Corinth was the capital. Used together, "Macedonia and Achaia" generally mean all of Greece (Ac 19:21; Ro 15:26; 1Th 1:7 – 8). In Ac 20:2 "Greece" refers to Achaia. In Ac 18:12, Gallio is accurately called "proconsul" (RSV, NIV) of Achaia; for Claudius had just made Achaia a senatorial province, the governors of which were called proconsuls, while the governors of imperial provinces were called procurators. In Ro 16:5, KJV has "Achaia," but most other versions have "Asia." Achaia is mentioned in five other NT passages (Ac 18:27; 1Co 16:15; 2Co 1:1; 9:2; 11:10).

ACHAN [H6575] (ā′kǎn, Heb. *'ākhān*, a wordplay from Achar: *troubler*). The son of Carmi and a Juda-

hite of Zerah's clan who participated in the assault on Jericho. His tragic experience is recorded in Jos 7. Achan took a garment, silver, and gold — part of the spoil of Jericho. Joshua had devoted the metals to God (Jos 6:17 – 19). All else was to be destroyed. Because of one man's disobedience, Israel was defeated at Ai. God revealed the reason to Joshua. By a process of elimination Achan was found out. He confessed, and he and his family and possessions were brought down to the valley of Achor. In spite of some difficulty in understanding the Hebrew text in vv. 25 – 26, there is little ground for holding that Joshua's command (6:17) was not carried out in the execution of both Achan and his entourage. In the Scriptures the Lord often allows us to see the full significance of our sinful ways. Achan's experience illustrates the biblical revelation that we never sin alone: there is always a family involvement (cf. Ex 20:5 – 6) and also a wider pollution touching the whole people of God and bringing them under judgment. Joshua expressed this thought in his epitaph: "Why have you brought this disaster on us?" (7:25), allowing the name Achan to slip over into the similar-sounding verb *'achar*, "to trouble, bring disaster." This in turn became the name of the place itself, Achor, "disaster." In 2Ch 2:7 Achan's name reads "Achar," the man of disaster.

ACKNOWLEDGE

1Ch	28:9	**a** the God of your father,
Ps	79:6	on the nations that do not **a** you,
Pr	3:6	in all your ways **a** him,
Isa	59:12	and we **a** our iniquities:
Jer	3:13	Only **a** your guilt —
Jer	9:3	do not **a** me," declares the LORD.
Da	4:25	until you **a** that the Most High is sovereign
Hos	6:3	Let us **a** the LORD; let us press on to **a** him.
Mt	10:32	I will also **a** him before my Father
Lk	12:8	also **a** him before the angels of God.
2Ti	3:7	always learning but never able to **a** the truth.

| 1Jn | 4:3 | not **a** Jesus is not from God. |
| 2Jn | 1:7 | who do not **a** Jesus Christ as coming in the flesh, |

ACROPOLIS (a-krŏp′ō-lĭs, Gr. *akropolis*, *crest of city*, *high ground of city* from *akros*, *highest*, and *polis*, *city*). The upper or higher city, citadel, or castle of a Greek municipality; especially the citadel of Athens, where the treasury was located. Athens's crowning glory was the Parthenon, the finest exemplar of Greek architecture. During Paul's stay in Athens (Ac 17:15 – 18:1), "he was greatly distressed to see that the city was full of idols" (17:16). The images of gods and of heroes worshiped as gods filled Athens and were inescapably conspicuous on the Acropolis. As Paul stood on Mars Hill, before the court of the Areopagus, he could see the temples on the Acropolis directly to the east, and the Agora (marketplace) below it.

Many NT towns — e.g., Corinth, Philippi, Samaria — had an Acropolis, which served as the town's civic and religious center, while the Agora constituted the central shopping plaza.

ACROSTIC (a-krôs′tĭc, Gr. *akrostichis*, from *okros*, *topmost*, and *stichos*, *a line of poetry*). A literary device by which the first letter of each line of poetry forms either a word or successive letters of the alphabet. In the common form of acrostic found in OT poetry, each line or stanza begins with a letter of the Hebrew alphabet in order. This literary form may have been intended as an aid to memory, but more likely it was a poetic way of saying that a total coverage of the subject was being offered — as we would say, "from A to Z." Acrostics occur in Pss 111 and 112, where each letter begins a line; in Pss 25, 34, and 145, where each letter begins a half verse; in Ps 37; Pr 31:10 – 31; and La 1, 2, and 4, where each letter begins a whole verse; and in Lam 3, where each letter begins three verses. Psalm 119 is the most elaborate demonstration of the acrostic method; in each section of eight verses, the same opening letter is used, and the twenty-two sections of the psalm move through the Hebrew alphabet, letter after letter. It is the genius of Hebrew poetry to allow the demands of the sense to take precedence over the demands of form, and this accounts for "broken acrostics" (there is a letter missing in both Pss 25 and 34) or acrostics in which letters are taken out of order (as in La 2:16 – 17).

ACTS OF THE APOSTLES The book that gives the history of early Christianity from the ascension of Christ to the end of two years of Paul's imprisonment in Rome.

TITLE OF THE BOOK.

An early MS has the title "Acts" (Gr. praxeis, doings, transactions, achievements). Other early titles are "Acts of Apostles" and "Acts of the Holy Apostles." Acts narrates actions and speeches chiefly of Peter and Paul. There is some information about Judas (Ac 1:16 – 20), the man chosen to succeed him (1:21 – 26), John (3:1 – 4:31; 8:14 – 17), and James (12:12). The Twelve, except the betrayer, are listed in 1:13. Acts is not a history of all the apostles; rather, it is a selection from the deeds and words of some who illustrate the progress of first-century Christianity in those phases that interested the author as he was moved by the Holy Spirit. The title "Acts of the Holy Spirit" has often been suggested, and the contents of the book bear out the appropriateness of such a title.

AUTHOR.

Not until AD 160 – 200 did we have positive statements as to the authorship of Acts. From that time onward, all who mention the subject agree that the two books dedicated to Theophilus (Luke and Acts) were written by "Luke, the beloved physician." Only in modern times have there been attempts to ascribe both books to Titus or some other author.

By writing "we" instead of "they" in recounting events when he was present, the author indicates that he was a companion of Paul. Luke joined Paul, Silas, and Timothy at Troas during the second missionary journey and accompanied them to Philippi but did not go on with them when they left there (Ac 16:10 – 17). Luke is next mentioned as being at Philippi toward the end of the third missionary journey, when Paul was about to sail for Palestine with the contributions of the Gentile churches for the poor at Jerusalem (20:4ff.; Ro 15:25ff.). We do not know whether Luke spent the interval at Philippi. From this point Luke accompanied Paul to Jerusalem (Ac 20:5 – 21:18). Nor do we know how Luke spent the two years during which Paul was imprisoned at Caesarea, but Luke enters the narrative again in 27:1 ("when it was decided that we should sail for Italy"); he continued with Paul, giving us a vivid account of the voyage to Rome. Acts breaks off abruptly at the end of Paul's two years of ministry when he was enjoying the relative freedom of "his own rented house," where he "welcomed all who came to see him. Boldly and without hindrance he preached the kingdom of God and taught about the Lord Jesus Christ" (28:30 – 31). If a later writer had incorporated these "we" sections, he would have named their author to enhance their authority. But the style of the "we" passages cannot be distinguished from the style of the rest of Acts nor from that of Luke's gospel. The author of Luke and Acts is the author of the "we" sections of Acts and a companion of Paul.

The question remains: Which of the companions of Paul is the author of Acts? He cannot be one of those named in the "we" sections as distinct from the author. He is not likely to have been one of those named in Paul's letters written at times other than those included in the "we" sections. Of those named in Paul's letters written when the "we" author might have been with Paul, early Christian writers chose "our dear friend Luke, the doctor" (Col 4:14). Luke is not otherwise prominent in the NT. Why should he have been chosen, unless he was the author? The medical language in Acts is not sufficient to prove that the author was a physician, but it is sufficient to

confirm other evidence to that effect. Luke was with Paul shortly before his expected death (2Ti 4:11).

Luke cannot be certainly identified with Lucius of Ac 13:1 or with Lucius of Romans 16:21. There is wide and ancient support for connecting Luke with Antioch in Syria. It is not probable that he was from Philippi. The tradition that he was a painter cannot be traced earlier than the tenth century. From 2Co 8:18 it is possible to infer that Titus was Luke's brother and that Luke was "the brother who is praised by all the churches for his service to the gospel." Titus and Luke are named together in 2Ti 4:10 – 11. The conjecture that Luke was the "man of Macedonia" of Paul's vision (Ac 16:9) is attractive and inherently possible but not certain.

PLACE.

The place where Acts was written is not named, though the sudden ending of the book, while Paul is residing at Rome awaiting trial, makes Rome an appropriate choice. The question of place is tied in with that of Luke's purpose in writing and with the occasion for the publication of the book.

DATE.

Allusions to Acts in the apostolic fathers are too indefinite to compel the setting of a date much before the end of the first century AD. If Acts is dependent on Josephus for information, it cannot be earlier than 93. But such dependence is not proved and is highly unlikely. Acts must have been finished after the latest date mentioned in the book, in 28:30. The abrupt close indicates that it was written at that time, c. 61 or 62. Luke's gospel has an appropriate ending; Acts does not. We are not told how the trial of Paul came out. There is no hint of Paul's release or of his death. The attitude toward Roman officials is friendly, and that would not have been the case after the persecution under Nero in 64. The Jewish War of 66 – 70 and the destruction of Jerusalem are not referred to. Chapters 1 – 15 accurately picture conditions in Jerusalem before its destruction.

It would be attractive to think that Luke's two books were written to inform and influence well-disposed Roman officials in their handling of Paul's case.

THE SPEECHES IN ACTS.

Do the speeches report what was actually said? We do not expect stenographic reporting, but Luke is a careful writer, as a comparison of his gospel with Mark and Matthew shows. The style of the speeches in Acts is not Luke's, but that which is appropriate to each speaker: Peter, Stephen, Paul, even the minor characters such as Gamaliel (5:25ff.), the Ephesian town clerk (19:35ff.), and Tertullus (24:2ff.). Similarities between the speeches of Peter and Paul are explained by the fact that Paul explicitly preached the same gospel as Peter did. Speeches by the same person are varied in type, each suited to the occasion.

Outline:

  I. Peter and the Beginnings of the Church in Israel (chs. 1 – 12).
    A. "Throughout Judea, Galilee and Samaria" (1:1 – 9:31; see 9:31).
    B. "As far as Phoenicia, Cyprus and Antioch" (9:32 – 12:25; see 11:19).
  II. Paul and the Expansion of the Church from Antioch to Rome (chs. 13 – 28).
    A. "Throughout the region of Phrygia and Galatia" (13:1 – 15:35; see 16:6).
    B. "Over to Macedonia" (15:36 – 21; see 16:9).
    C. "To Rome" (21:17 – 28:31; see 28:14).

ADAIAH [6347, 6348] (a-dā′ya, Heb. *'ădhāyâh, Jehovah has adorned,* or *pleasing to Jehovah*).

1. A man of Boscath, father of Josiah's mother (2Ki 22:1).

2. A Levite descended from Gershom (1Ch 8:1, 21).

3. A son of Shimshi the Benjamite (1Ch 6:41 – 43).

4. A Levite of the family of Aaron, head of a family living in Jerusalem (1Ch 9:10 – 12).

5. The father of Captain Maaseiah who helped Jehoiada put Joash on the throne of Judah (2Ch 23:1).

6. A son of Bani who married a foreign wife during the exile (Ez 10:29).

7. Another son of a different Bani family who did the same (Ez 10:34).

8. A descendant of Judah by Perez (Ne 11:5).

9. A Levite of the family of Aaron. Most likely the same as no. 4 (Ne 11:12).

ADAM [134, 136, 77] (Heb. *'ādhām, of the ground* or *taken out of the red earth*). In Hebrew "Adam" is both a personal name and a general noun, "mankind." The latter meaning is found over five hundred times in the OT. Both usages are found in Ge 1 – 3, where Adam as a personal name occurs at 2:20 (for further references see 3:17, 21; 4:25; 5:2 – 5; 1Ch 1:1). As the first and representative man, Adam was made in God's image, provided with a garden and a wife, and given work to do (Ge 1 – 2). His rejection of God's authority led to the breaking of communion with God, his expulsion from the garden, and a life of toil (Ge 3). From the physical descendants of Adam and Eve the human race emerged (Dt 32:8; Mal 2:10).

Adam is mentioned nine times in the NT (Lk 3:38; Ro 5:14 [*twice*]; 1Co 15:22, 45 [*twice*]; 1Ti 2:13 – 14; Jude 14). In all these he is assumed to be the first human being to live on the earth. Paul developed a theology of the identity and role of Jesus through a comparison with the identity and role of Adam (Ro 5:12ff.; 1Co 15:20 – 22, 45 – 49). In these comparisons Paul made use of the double meaning of the Hebrew word for Adam. He also developed a theology of the submission of the woman to the man from the details of the Genesis account of Adam and Eve (1Ti 2:11ff.). Jesus referred to the union of Adam and Eve in marriage as a union of one flesh (Mt 19:4 – 6 and Mk 10:6 – 9, where Ge 1:27 and 2:24 are cited).

Adam is also a city in the Jordan Valley where the Israelites entered the Promised Land (Jos 3:16).

ADMINISTER

1Ki	3:28	wisdom from God to **a** justice.
Zec	7:9	LORD Almighty says: '**A** true justice;
2Co	8:19	which we **a** in order to honor the Lord

ADMONISH

| Col | 3:16 | and **a** one another with all wisdom, |
| 1Th | 5:12 | over you in the Lord and who **a** you. |

ADONIJAH [H153, H154] (ăd′ō-nī′ja, Heb. *'ădhō-nîyāhû, my Lord is Jehovah*).

1. The fourth son of David, by Haggith, born at Hebron (2Sa 3:2–4; 1Ch 3:2). Ammon and Absalom, David's first and third sons, had died; the second, Kileab, had not been mentioned since his birth and might have died also. Adonijah, as the eldest living son, aspired to the throne. The story of his attempt and failure to seize the crown is told in 1Ki 1:5–2:25.

He was a spoiled, handsome young man (1:6) and "got chariots and horses ready, with fifty men to run ahead of him" (1:5). He won over Joab and Abiathar the priest but failed to gain Zadok the priest and Nathan the prophet. Moreover, "David's special guard did not join Adonijah" (1:7–8). He held a great feast at En-Rogel, to which he invited "all his brothers, the king's sons, and all the men of Judah who were royal officials, but he did not invite Nathan the prophet or Benaiah or the special guard or his brother Solomon" (1:9–10). Nathan spoke to Bathsheba, Solomon's mother, and together they warned David of what Adonijah was doing. David, roused to action, had Solomon proclaimed king at Gihon (1:11–40). Adonijah and his guests heard the shout and the sound of the trumpet (1:41). Immediately Jonathan, the son of Abiathar, brought a full account of what had happened (1:42–48). The guests fled, and Adonijah sought refuge at the altar (1:49–50). Solomon pardoned him, and he returned home (1:51–53). But after the death of David, Adon-

ijah emboldened himself to ask Bathsheba to persuade King Solomon to give him Abishag, David's nurse in his last illness, for a wife (2:13–18). This revived Solomon's suspicions, for in ancient times claiming a former monarch's concubines was tantamount to claiming his throne. Solomon had Adonijah killed (2:19–25).

2. A Levite sent by Jehoshaphat to teach the law to the people of Judah (2Ch 17:8).

3. A chieftain who with Nehemiah sealed the covenant (Ne 10:14–16).

ADOPTED

Est	2:15	for Esther (the girl Mordecai had **a**,
Ps	106:35	with the nations and **a** their customs.
Eph	1:5	be **a** as his sons through Jesus Christ,

ADOPTION [1047, 4340, 5625] (Gr. *huiothesia* in the NT). The practice of adoption is exemplified in the OT: Pharaoh's daughter adopted Moses (Ex 2:10) as her son; Hadad the Edomite married the sister of the Egyptian queen, and their son Genubath was brought up "with Pharaoh's own children," whether formally adopted or not (1Ki 11:20); Esther was adopted by Mordecai (Est 2:7, 15). These cases were outside Palestine, in Egypt or Persia. Whether adoption was practiced in the Hebrews' own land is not clear. Abram thinks of Eliezer of Damascus as his heir, but God tells him this will not be (Ge 15:2–4). Sarai gave her maid Hagar to Abram that she might obtain children by her (16:1–3). Rachel (30:1–5) and Leah (30:9–12) gave Jacob their maids for a like purpose, a kind of adoption by the mother but not by the father. Jacob adopted his grandsons Manasseh and Ephraim to be as Reuben and Simeon (48:5). The case of Jair (1Ch 2:21–22) is one of inheritance rather than adoption. Levirate marriage (Dt 25:5–6) involved a sort of posthumous adoption of a brother's later-born son.

But none of the OT instances have a direct bearing on the NT usage of the term. Paul is the only writer to use it, and with him it is a metaphor derived from Hellenistic usage and Roman law. The legal situation of a son in early Roman times was little better than that of a slave, though in practice its rigor would vary with the disposition of the father. A son was the property of his father, who was entitled to the son's earnings. The father could transfer ownership of him by adoption or by a true sale and could, under certain circumstances, even put him to death. An adopted son was considered like a son born in the family. He could no longer inherit from his natural father. He was no longer liable for old debts (a loophole eventually closed). So far as his former family was concerned, he was dead. Modifications of the rigor of sonship were at intervals introduced into Roman law, and a more liberal Hellenistic view was doubtless in the mind of Paul.

In Gal 4:1 – 3 Paul states accurately the Roman law of sonship. In v. 4 he says that God sent his Son to be born into the human condition under law, and in v. 5 he gives the purpose of God in so doing: "To redeem those under law, that we might receive the full rights of sons." We were not merely children who needed to grow up; we had become slaves of sin and as such needed to be redeemed, bought out of our bondage that we might enter the new family Christ brought into being by his death and resurrection. Adoption expresses both the redemption and the new relation of trust and love, for "because you are sons, God sent the Spirit of his Son into our hearts, the Spirit who calls out, 'Abba, Father' " (4:6). The adoption brought us from slavery to sonship and heirship (4:7).

The same thought appears in Ro 8:15. Verses 1 – 14 demonstrate that the adoption is more than a matter of position or status; when God adopted us, he put his Spirit within us and we became subject to his control. This involves chastisement (Heb 12:5 – 11) as well as inheritance (Ro 8:16 – 18).

In Ro 8:23 "our adoption" is spoken of as future, in the sense that its full effects are to be consummated at the time of "the redemption of our bodies." This redemption is not the "buying out" of Gal 4:5, but a word (Gr. *apolytrosis*) emphasizing the release, the loosing from all restraints that the limitation of a mortal body imposes. We are part of a suffering cre-

ation (Ro 8:22). The spiritual body, the resurrection body, pictured in the vivid terms of 1Co 15:35 – 57, is the object of Paul's longing (2Co 5:1 – 8; Php 3:21). The present effects of God's adoption of us as sons are marvelous, yet they are only a small indication (2Co 1:22; 5:5; Eph 1:13 – 14) of what the adoption will mean when we come into our inheritance in heaven.

In Ro 9:4 Paul begins with enumeration of the privileges of Israelites with "the adoption." Although God said, "Israel is my firstborn son" (Ex 4:22); and "When Israel was a child, I loved him, and out of Egypt I called my son" (Hos 11:1); and Moses expressed the relationship in this way, "You are the children of the LORD your God" (Dt 14:1); yet Israel's sonship was not the natural relationship by creation, but a peculiar one by a covenant of promise, a spiritual relationship by faith, under the sovereign grace of God, as Paul goes on to explain in Ro 9 – 11. Thus a clear distinction is drawn between the "offspring" of God by creation (Ac 17:28) and the children of God by adoption into the obedience of faith.

With utmost compression of language Paul expresses, in Eph 1:4 – 5, God's action that resulted in his adoption of us and enumerates its effects in vv. 6 – 12. This action began with God's election: "For he chose us in him before the creation of the world," using predestination as the mode ("he predestined us"); Christ is the agent (by Jesus Christ); and he himself is the adopting parent (to himself). God's sovereign act is stressed by the concluding phrase of v. 5: "in accordance with his pleasure and will." That adoption is not a mere matter of position is made plain in the statement of the purpose of election: "He chose us … to be holy and blameless in his sight" (1:4).

Adoption is a serious matter under any system of law. As a figure of speech expressing spiritual truth, it emphasizes the sovereign and gracious character of the act of God in our salvation, our solemn obligation as adopted sons and daughters of our adopting Parent, the newness of the family relationship established, a climate of intimate trust and love, and the immensity of an inheritance that eternity alone can reveal to us.

Spiritual:

Of Israel (Ex 4:22 – 23; Nu 6:27; Dt 14:1 – 2; 26:18 – 19; 27:9; 28:9 – 10; 32:5 – 6; 2Ch 7:14; Isa 63:8, 16; Jer 3:19; 31:9, 20; Hos 1:9 – 10; 11:1; Ro 9:4). Of Solomon (2Sa 7:14; 1Ch 22:10; 28:6). Of the righteous (Pr 14:26; Isa 43:1 – 6; 63:8, 16; Mt 5:9, 44 – 45; 12:50; 13:43; Lk 6:35; Jn 11:52; Ro 9:8, 26; 2Co 6:17 – 18; Eph 2:19; Php 2:15; Heb 12:6 – 7, 9; 1Jn 3:1 – 2, 10; 4:4). Of the Gentiles: promised (Hos 2:23; Ro 9:24 – 26; Eph 3:6, 14 – 15; Heb 2:10 – 11, 13); testified to by the Holy Spirit (Ro 8:14 – 17, 19, 21, 29; Gal 4:5 – 7); through the gospel (Eph 3:6).

Means of:

By God's grace (Eze 16:3 – 6; Ro 4:16 – 17; Eph 1:5 – 6, 11). By faith (Jn 1:12 – 13; Gal 3:7, 26, 29; Eph 1:5). Through Christ (Jn 1:12 – 13; Gal 3:26; 4:4 – 5; Eph 1:5; Heb 2:10 – 11, 13). According to the promise (Ro 9:8; Gal 3:29; Eph 3:6). Through the gospel (Eph 3:6).

Holy Spirit's Role in:

(Ro 8:14 – 16; Gal 4:6).

Results of:

A new name (Nu 6:27; Isa 62:2; Ac 15:17). Discipline by the Father (Dt 8:5; 2Sa 7:14; Pr 3:11 – 12; Heb 12:5 – 11). Safety (Pr 14:26). God as Father-Redeemer (Isa 63:16). God's long-suffering mercy (Jer 31:1, 19 – 20). A desire for God's glory (Mt 5:16); likeness to God (Mt 5:44 – 45, 48). A love of peace (Mt 5:9). Avoidance of pretense (Mt 6:1 – 4). A forgiving spirit (Mt 6:14). Confidence in God (Mt 6:25 – 34). A spirit of prayer (Mt 7:7 – 11). A new inheritance (Mt 13:43; Ro 8:17). A merciful spirit (Lk 6:35 – 36). The new birth (Jn 1:12 – 13). Holiness (2Co 6:17 – 18; 7:1; Php 2:15). Following God (Eph 5:1).

Future Implications of:

Gathered as one by Christ (Jn 11:52). Will become brothers and sisters of Christ (Jn 20:17; Heb 2:11 – 12). Final consummation (Ro 8:19, 23; 1Jn 3:2).

ADULLAM [6355, 6356] (a-dŭl′ăm, Heb. *'ădhullām, retreat, refuge;* possibly *[they are] just*). A city in the Shephelah or low country, between the hill country of Judah and the sea, thirteen miles (twenty-two km.) SW of Bethlehem; very ancient (Ge 38:1, 12, 20; Jos 15:35); the seat of one of the thirty-one petty kings conquered by Joshua (Jos 12:15). It was fortified by Rehoboam (2Ch 11:7). Because of its beauty it was called "the glory of Israel" (Mic 1:15). It was reoccupied on the return from the Babylonian exile (Ne 11:30).

David hid with his family and about four hundred men in one of the many limestone caves near the city (1Sa 22:1 – 2) at a time when Saul sought his life. While David was there, three of his "mighty men" risked their lives to fulfill his expressed desire for water from the well of Bethlehem, but David refused to drink it, rightly recognizing that the extreme devotion that put life itself at risk was due only unto the Lord. For this reason he "poured it out before the LORD" (2Sa 23:13 – 17; 1Ch 11:15 – 19).

1 Sa	22:1	and escaped to the cave of **A**.
1 Ch	11:15	to David to the rock at the cave of **A**,

ADULTERER

Lev	20:10	the **a** and the adulteress must be put
Job	24:15	The eye of the **a** watches for dusk;
Heb	13:4	for God will judge the **a** and all the

ADULTERESS

Pr	2:16	It will save you also from the **a**,
	5:3	For the lips of an **a** drip honey.
	6:26	and the **a** preys upon your very life.
Hos	3:1	she is loved by another and is an **a**.
Mt	5:32	causes her to become an **a**,

ADULTERY [2388, 2393, 2424, 5537, 3655, 3656, 3657, 3658, 3659, 4518, 4519, 4521]. In the OT the word "adultery" is used in reference to sexual intercourse, usually of a man, married or unmarried, with the wife of another. One of the Ten Commandments forbids it (Ex 20:14; Dt 5:18). The punishment for both man and woman was death, probably by stoning (Dt 22:22 – 24; Jn 8:3 – 7). "Adultery" and related words translate derivatives of the Hebrew root *n'ph* (*nā'aph*), conveying the one plain meaning.

From the earliest times (Ge 39:9), even outside the people of God (26:10), adultery was regarded as a serious sin. Along with other sexual offenses (e.g., Ge 34:7; Dt 22:21; Jdg 19:23; 2Sa 13:12), it is a wicked outrage (Jer 29:23), the word being *nevalah*, behavior lacking moral principle or any recognition of proper obligation. Marriage is a covenant relationship (e.g., Mal 2:14), and for this reason it imposes obligations not only on the partners, but also on the community within which they have entered into their solemn mutual vows.

The OT finds adultery a ready figure for apostasy from the Lord and attachment to false gods, as can be seen in Isa 57:3; Jer 3:8 – 9; 13:27; Eze 23:27, 43; Hos 2:4; and similar passages.

While fornication is frequently and severely condemned in the OT, special solemnity attaches to the reproof of adultery, both in the relations of individual men and women and, figuratively, in the relations of the covenant people Israel, conceived of as a wife of God, their spiritual husband. Isaiah, Jeremiah, and Ezekiel use the figure (see references above). Hosea develops, from personal experience with an adulterous wife, an allegory of God's love for his unfaithful people. Adultery in a human marriage relationship is reprehensible; how much more serious is the infidelity of human beings toward a God who loves them with a love that can well be expressed as that of a husband for his wife! Thus the figurative use enhances the literal sense, emphasizing the divine institution and nature of marriage.

In the NT "adultery" translates Greek *moicheuo* and related words, which the LXX had already used for Hebrew *nā'aph*. The meaning throughout the Bible widens and deepens, first with the prophets, then with Jesus and his apostles.

Jesus quotes the commandment (Mt 5:27 – 30; 19:18; Mk 10:19; Lk 18:20), broadening its application to include the lustful look that betrays an adulterous heart. He teaches that such evils as adultery come from the heart (Mt 15:19; Mk 7:21). Dealing with divorce, Jesus declares remarriage of a divorced man or woman to be adultery (Mt 5:31 – 32; 19:3 – 9; Mk 10:2 – 12; Lk 16:18), with one exception (Mt 5:32; 19:9), the interpretation of which varies from one scholar to another. The Pharisee in a parable rejoices that he is not an adulterer (Lk 18:11). Jesus uses the term figuratively of a people unfaithful to God (Mt 12:39; 16:4; Mk 8:38). In Jn 8:2 – 11 the account of a woman taken in adultery reveals Jesus' insistence on the equal guilt of the man. Without belittling the seriousness of adultery, Jesus exercises the sovereign pardoning power of the grace of God, coupled with a solemn injunction against future offenses. Jesus' attitude toward adultery springs from his conception of marriage as God intended it and as it must be in the new Christian society.

Paul names adultery as one of the tests of obedience to the law (Ro 2:22), quotes the commandment (13:9), uses adultery as an analogy of our relation to God (7:3), says that adulterers "will not inherit the kingdom of God" (1Co 6:9), and lists adultery among works of the flesh (Gal 5:19). The sanctity of marriage is the point stressed in Heb 13:4. Jas 2:1 uses adultery and murder as examples of the equal obligation of all the commandments of God. In Jas 4:4 adultery is a figure of speech for unfaithfulness to God. Rev 2:20 – 23 condemns spiritual adultery.

The NT treatment of adultery, following the implications of the OT concept, supports marriage as a lifelong monogamous union. Adultery is a special and aggravated case of fornication. In the teaching of Jesus and the apostles in the NT, all sexual impurity is sin against God, against self, and against others. Spiritual adultery (unfaithfulness to God) violates the union between Christ and his own.

General References to:
(Mt 5:28, 32; 19:9; Mk 10:11 – 12; Lk 16:18; Ro 7:1 – 3). Laws concerning (Nu 5:11 – 31; Dt 22:13 – 29). Repulsive to the righteous (Job 31:1 – 12; Eze 18:5 – 6, 9). Fatal consequences of (Pr 2:16 – 19; 5:3 – 4, 5 – 23; 6:23 – 35; 7:1 – 27; 9:13 – 18;

22:14; 23:26 – 28). *Moral and spiritual corruption by (Jer 3:1 – 2; 5:7 – 8; Hos 4:1 – 2, 9 – 19). Source of: the heart (Mt 15:19; Mk 7:21 – 23); sinful nature (Gal 5:19 – 21). Forbidden (Ex 20:14; Lev 18:20; 19:29; Dt 5:18; 23:17; Pr 31:3; Mt 5:27 – 28; 19:16 – 19; Mk 10:17 – 19; Lk 18:18 – 20; Ac 15:20, 29; Ro 13:9, 13; 1Co 5:9 – 11; 6:13 – 18; 10:7 – 8; Eph 4:17 – 19; 5:3; Col 3:5; 1Th 4:3 – 7; 1Ti 1:9 – 10; Jas 2:10 – 11). Forgiveness of (Jdg 19:1 – 4; Jn 4:16 – 26, 39 – 42; 8:10 – 11). Lack of repentance in (Pr 30:20; Isa 57:3 – 4; Jer 7:9 – 15; Ro 1:28 – 32; 2Co 12:21; 1Pe 4:3 – 4; Rev 9:20 – 21).*

Instances of:

The Sodomites (Ge 19:4 – 8; Jude 7); Lot and his two daughters (Ge 19:31 – 38); Shechem (Ge 34:1 – 2); Reuben (Ge 35:22); Judah (Ge 38:1 – 26); Potiphar's wife (Ge 39:6 – 12); Israelites (Ex 32:6; Jer 23:10 – 11; 29:23; Eze 22:9 – 11; 33:26; Hos 7:4); Gilead, father of Jephthah (Jdg 11:1); Samson (Jdg 16:1); Levite's concubine (Jdg 19:1 – 2); men of Gibeah (Jdg 19:22 – 25); sons of Eli (1Sa 2:22); David (2Sa 11:1 – 5); Amnon, David's oldest son by Ahinoam (2Sa 13:1 – 20); Absalom, David's third son by Maacah (2Sa 16:22); Herod (Mt 14:3 – 4; Mk 6:17 – 18; Lk 3:19); Samaritan woman (Jn 4:17 – 18); woman brought to Jesus in the temple (Jn 8:3 – 11); Corinthians (1Co 5:1 – 5); Gentiles (Eph 4:17 – 20; 1Pe 4:3 – 4); those living in the last days (2Ti 3:6).

Penalties for:

Death (Ge 20:3, 7; 26:11; 38:24; Lev 20:10 – 12; 21:9; Dt 22:13 – 27; 2Sa 12:7 – 14; Eze 23:45 – 48; Jn 8:4 – 5). Fines (Ex 22:16 – 17; Dt 22:19, 28 – 29). Guilt offering (Lev 19:20 – 22). Curses (Nu 5:11 – 31; Dt 27:20 – 23; Job 24:15 – 18). Divine judgments (2Sa 12:10 – 12; Jer 29:22 – 23; Eze 16:38 – 41; Mal 3:5; 1Co 10:8; Heb 13:4; 2Pe 2:9 – 10, 14; Rev 2:20 – 22; 18:9 – 10). Excommunication (1Co 5:1 – 13; Eph 5:11 – 12). Exclusion from the kingdom of God (1Co 6:9 – 10; Gal 5:19, 21; Eph 5:5 – 6; Jude 7; Rev 21:8; 22:14 – 15).

Ex	20:14	"You shall not commit **a**.
Dt	5:18	"You shall not commit **a**.
Ps	51:T	after David had committed **a**
Pr	6:32	man who commits **a** lacks judgment;
Eze	23:37	They committed **a** with their idols;
Hos	1:2	vilest **a** in departing from the LORD."
Mt	5:27	'Do not commit **a**.'
	5:28	committed **a** with her in his heart.
	5:32	who marries the divorced woman commits **a**.
	15:19	murder, **a**, sexual immorality, theft,
	19:9	marries another woman commits **a**"
	19:18	"'Do not murder, do not commit **a**,
Mk	7:21	sexual immorality, theft, murder, **a**,
	10:11	marries another woman commits **a**
	10:12	marries another man, she commits **a**.
	10:19	do not commit **a**, do not steal,
Lk	16:18	marries another woman commits **a**,
	16:18	marries a divorced woman commits **a**,
	18:20	commandments: 'Do not commit **a**,
Jn	8:3	brought in a woman caught in **a**.
Ro	2:22	You who say that people should not commit **a**, do you commit **a**?
Jas	2:11	For he who said, "Do not commit **a**,"
Rev	18:3	The kings of the earth committed **a**

ADVERSITY

Pr	17:17	and a brother is born for **a**.
Isa	30:20	the LORD gives you the bread of **a**

ADVOCATE [8446, 2858, 2859] (ăd'vō-kāt, Gr. *paraklētos, counselor, comforter, supporter, backer, helper, Paraclete*). An advocate is one who pleads the case or the cause of another. The Holy Spirit is the Advocate of the Father for us, thus our Comforter (KJV, Jn 14:16, 26; 15:26; 16:7; RSV, NIV "Counselor"). As applied to the Holy Spirit, the Greek word is so rich in meaning that adequate translation by any one English word is impossible. The KJV "Comforter" is as satisfactory as any, if it is taken in the fullest sense of one who not only consoles but also strengthens, helps, and counsels, with such authority as a legal advocate has for his or her client. Jesus speaks of the Holy Spirit as "another Comforter" (NIV "Counselor," Jn 14:16), using the same Greek word, thereby implying that he himself is a "Comforter." In 1Jn 2:1 the meaning is narrowed to that of Christ being our Advocate with the Father, "one who speaks to the Father in our defense."

| Job | 16:19 | witness is in heaven; my **a** is on high |

AFFECTIONS [3137, 5883, 5073].

Of Believers:

Supremely set on God (Dt 6:5; Pss 42:1; 73:23 – 26; 119:9 – 20; Mk 12:30). To be zealous for God (Pss 69:9; 119:139; Gal 4:18). Not to grow cold (Ps 106:12 – 13; Mt 24:12; Gal 4:14 – 16; Rev 2:4). To be set on: the house and worship of God (1Ch 29:3; Pss 26:8; 27:4; 84:1 – 2); the people of God (Ps 16:3; Ro 12:10; 2Co 7:13 – 16; 1Th 2:8); the commandments and statutes of God (Pss 19:8 – 10; 119); heavenly things (Col 3:1 – 2). Blessedness of making God the object of (Ps 91:14). Christ claims first place in (Mt 10:37; Lk 14:26). Stirred up by communion with Christ (Lk 24:32). Not to be captivated by false teachers (Gal 1:9 – 10; 4:17; 2Ti 3:6; 2Pe 2:3, 18; Rev 2:14, 20).

Of the Wicked:

Not sincerely set on God (Isa 58:1 – 2; Eze 33:31 – 32; Lk 8:13). Unnatural and perverted (Ro 1:18 – 32; 2Ti 3:1 – 9; 2Pe 2:10 – 22).

| Dt | 10:15 | Yet the Lord set his **a** on your |
| 2 Co | 6:12 | not withholding our **a** from you, |

AFFLICTED

Jos	24:5	I **a** the Egyptians by what I did there,
Ru	1:21	The Lord has **a** me;
Job	2:7	**a** Job with painful sores
Job	36:6	but gives the **a** their rights.
Ps	9:12	not ignore the cry of the **a**.
	9:18	nor the hope of the **a** ever perish.
	34:2	let the **a** hear and rejoice.
	119:67	Before I was **a** I went astray,
	119:71	It was good for me to be **a** so
	119:75	and in faithfulness you have **a** me.
Isa	49:13	compassion on his **a** ones.
	53:4	smitten by him, and **a**.
	53:7	He was oppressed and **a**,
Na	1:12	Although I have **a** you, [O Judah,]

AFFLICTED, THE [1868, 1895, 2688, 2703, 5595, 5597, 5782, 6700, 6705, 6714].

General References to:

Sympathy with (Job 6:14; Mt 25:34 – 40). Help for (Job 22:29; Isa 58:6 – 7; Lk 10:30 – 37; 1Ti 5:9 – 10). Rewards for service to (Isa 53:10; Mt 25:34 – 45). Exhorted to pray (Jas 5:13). Prayer for healing (Jas 5:14 – 15).

Duty to:

Pity (Job 6:14). Comfort (Job 16:5; 29:25; 2Co 1:3 – 5; 1Th 4:18). Relieve (Job 31:19 – 20; Isa 58:9 – 12; Php 4:14; 1Ti 5:10). Protect (Ps 82:3; Pr 22:22; 31:5). Pray for (Ac 12:5; Php 1:19; Jas 5:14 – 16). Sympathize with (Ro 12:15; Gal 6:2). Remember those in prison and those who are mistreated (Heb 13:3).

AFFLICTED BELIEVERS

Attitudes and Actions of:

Should: be resigned (1Sa 3:18; 2Ki 20:19; Job 1:21; Ps 39:9); acknowledge the justice of their discipline (Ne 9:33; Job 2:10; Isa 64:5 – 7; La 3:39; Mic 7:9); not despise discipline (Job 5:17 – 18; Pr 3:11 – 12; Heb 12:5 – 6); trust in the goodness of God (Job 13:15; Ps 71:20; 2Co 1:9); avoid sin (Job 34:31 – 32; Jn 5:14; 1Pe 2:12); praise God (Pss 13:5 – 6; 56:8 – 11; 57:6 – 7; 71:20 – 23); take encouragement from former mercy (Ps 27:9; 2Co 1:10); call upon God in the day of trouble (Pss 50:15; 55:16 – 17); turn and devote themselves to God (Ps 116:7 – 9; Jer 50:3 – 5; Hos 6:1); be patient (Lk 21:19; Ro 12:12; 2Th 1:4 – 7; Jas 1:4; 1Pe 2:20); imitate Christ (Heb 12:1 – 3; 1Pe 2:21 – 23); imitate the prophets (Jas 5:10).

Examples of:

Joseph (Ge 39:20 – 23; Ps 105:17 – 19); Eli (1Sa 3:11 – 18); David (2Sa 12:15 – 23); Nehemiah (Ne 1:3 – 4); Job (Job 1:20 – 22); Paul (Ac 20:22 – 24; 21:13); the apostles (1Co 4:13; 2Co 6:4 – 10); Moses (Heb 11:24 – 29).

AFFLICTION [2716, 4316, 6411, 6700, 6715, 2568].

Consolation under:

God is the Author and Giver of (Ps 23:4; Ro 15:5; 2Co 1:3 – 4; 7:6 – 7; Col 1:11; 2Th 2:16 – 17). Christ is the Author and Giver of (Isa 61:1 – 3; Jn 14:18; 2Co 1:5). The Holy Spirit is the Author and Giver of (Jn 14:16 – 17; 15:26; 16:7; Ac 9:31). In the prospect of death (Job 19:25 – 27; Ps 23:4; Jn 14:1 – 3; 2Co 5:1; 1Th 4:12 – 13; Heb 4:9 – 10; Rev 7:14 – 17; 14:13). Through the Holy Scriptures (Ps 119:50, 76; Ro 15:4). Pray for (Ps 119:81 – 83). By ministers of the gospel (Isa 40:1 – 2; 1Co 14:3; 2Co 1:4, 6). Promised (Ps 119:76; Isa 51:3, 12; 66:13; Eze 14:22 – 23; Hos 2:14; Zec 1:17). Believers should administer to each other (1Th 4:18; 5:11, 14). Under the infirmities of age (Ps 71:9, 18). Sought in vain from the world (Ps 69:20; Ecc 4:1; La 1:2). Abundant (Ps 71:21; Isa 66:10 – 11). A cause of praise (Isa 12:1; 49:13). Everlasting (2Th 2:16 – 17). Firm and secure (Heb 6:17 – 20). To the persecuted (Dt 33:27); the poor (Pss 10:14; 34:6, 9 – 10); those deserted by friends or family (Pss 27:10; 41:9 – 12; Jn 14:18; 15:18 – 19); the sick (Ps 41:3); the troubled in mind (Pss 42; 94:19; Jn 14:1, 27; 16:20 – 22); those who mourn for sin (Ps 51:17; Isa 1:18; 40:1 – 2; 61:1 – 3; Mic 7:18 – 19; Lk 4:18 – 19); the tempted (Ro 16:17 – 20; 1Co 10:13; 2Co 12:9; Jas 1:12; 4:7 – 10; 2Pe 2:9; Rev 2:10).

Prayer under:

For the presence and support of God (Pss 10:1; 102:2). Exhortation to (Jas 5:13). That: God would consider our trouble (2Ki 19:16; Ne 9:32; Ps 9:13; La 5); we may be taught the uncertainty of life (Ps 39:4); the Holy Spirit may not be withdrawn (Ps 51:11); we may be turned to God (Pss 51:12 – 15; 80:7; 85:4 – 7; Jer 31:18). For: protection and preservation from enemies (2Ki 19:19; 2Ch 20:12; Pss 17:8 – 9; 143:11 – 12); divine teaching and direction (Job 34:32; Pss 27:11; 143:10); divine comfort (Pss 4:6; 119:76 – 77); mercy (Ps 6:2; Hab 3:2); deliverance from troubles (Pss 25:17, 22; 39:10; Isa 64:9 – 12; Jer 17:14); pardon and deliverance from sin (Pss 39:8; 51:1 – 17; 79:8 – 9); relief from troubles (Ps 39:12 – 13); restoration of joy (Pss 51:8, 12; 69:29; 90:14 – 15); increase of faith (Mk 9:24).

Dt	16:3	the bread of **a**,
Ps	107:41	he lifted the needy out of their **a**
Isa	30:20	bread of adversity and the water of **a**,
	48:10	tested you in the furnace of **a**.
La	1:9	"Look, O LORD, on my **a**,
	3:33	For he does not willingly bring **a**
Ro	12:12	Be joyful in hope, patient in **a**,

AFRAID

Ge	3:10	and I was **a** because I was naked;
	26:24	Do not be **a**, for I am with you;
	50:19	Joseph said to them, "Don't be **a**.
Ex	2:14	Then Moses was **a** and thought,
	3:6	because he was **a** to look at God.
	34:30	and they were **a** to come near him.
Lev	26:6	and no one will make you **a**.
Dt	1:21	Do not be **a**;
	1:29	do not be **a** of them.
	2:4	They will be **a** of you,
	20:3	Do not be fainthearted or **a**;
Jos	10:25	Joshua said to them, "Do not be **a**;
Ru	3:11	And now, my daughter, don't be **a**.
1Sa	15:24	I was **a** of the people and so I gave in
	18:12	Saul was **a** of David,
1Ki	19:3	Elijah was **a** and ran for his life.
2Ki	25:24	not be **a** of the Babylonian officials,"
1Ch	13:12	David was **a** of God that day
Ne	2:2	I was very much **a**,
Ps	27:1	of whom shall I be **a**?
	56:3	When I am **a**, I will trust in you.
	56:4	in God I trust; I will not be **a**.

Pr	3:24	you will not be **a**;
Isa	12:2	I will trust and not be **a**.
	44:8	Do not tremble, do not be **a**.
Jer	1:8	Do not be **a** of them,
Eze	39:26	with no one to make them **a**.
Da	4:5	I had a dream that made me **a**.
Mt	8:26	why are you so **a**?"
	10:28	not be **a** of those who kill the body
	10:28	be **a** of the One who can destroy
	10:31	So don't be **a**;
Mk	5:36	"Don't be **a**; just believe."
Lk	9:34	and they were **a** as they entered
	12:32	"Do not be **a**, little flock,
Jn	14:27	hearts be troubled and do not be **a**.
Ac	27:24	'Do not be **a**, Paul.
Ro	11:20	Do not be arrogant, but be **a**.
Heb	13:6	I will not be **a**.
2Pe	2:10	not **a** to slander celestial beings;
Rev	2:10	Do not be **a** of what you are about to suffer.

AFRICA Either the whole continent or Roman Proconsular Africa (that is, modern Tunisia, to which were added Numidia and Mauretania). In the OT there are many references to Egypt and a few to Ethiopia (e.g., Isa 45:14; Jer 13:23). In the NT, Egypt, its Greek city of Alexandria (Ac 18:24), Ethiopia (8:27), and the port of Cyrene (in modern Libya) (Mk 15:21) are mentioned primarily because of the Jewish settlements there. Jesus himself went into Egypt (Mt 2:13 – 14), and Jews from Africa were present on the day of Pentecost (Ac 2:10).

AGABUS [13] (ăg′a-bŭs). One of the prophets from Jerusalem who came to Antioch and prophesied that there would be "a severe famine ... over the entire Roman world." "This happened during the reign of Claudius." The prophecy led Christians at Antioch "to provide help for ... Judea ... by Barnabas and Saul" (Ac 11:27 – 30). Years later a "prophet named Agabus" came down from Jerusalem to Caesarea and by a dramatic action warned Paul that he would be put in bonds if he persisted in going to Jerusalem (21:10 – 11). Although we cannot prove that the two prophets are the same man, there is no reason to doubt it.

AGAG [H97] (ā′găg, Heb. *'ăghāgh*, perhaps meaning *violent*).

    1. King of Amalek, referred to by Balaam (Nu 24:2 – 3, 7). Balaam prophesied that a king of Jacob (Israel) would surpass him (24:3 – 9).

    2. Another king of Amalek. Saul spared Agag when he should have killed him. When Samuel came into the camp, he rebuked Saul and ordered that Agag be brought to him. Samuel killed Agag as Saul should have according to God's command (1Sa 15:8 – 33).

AGAPE [26, 27] (ăg′a-pā Gr. *agapē*, *love*; *volitional and self-sacrificial love*). A Greek word meaning "love" and "love feasts." The more frequent of two NT words for love, connoting the preciousness or worthiness of the one loved. It is used in Jude 12 (KJV "feasts of charity," ASV, RSV, NIV "love feasts") of common meals that cultivated brotherly love among Christians. They may be referred to in Ac 20:11; 1Co 11:21 – 22, 33 – 34; 2Pe 2:13. In Ac 2:46 "broke bread" refers to the Lord's Supper (cf. v. 42), but "ate together" requires a full meal. Paul rebukes Christians for the abuses that had crept into the love feasts and marred the Lord's Supper (1Co 11:20 – 34). The Lord's Supper properly followed, but was distinct from, the love feast.

AGE [AGED]

Mt	13:39	The harvest is the end of the **a**,
Lk	18:30	in the **a** to come, eternal life."
Tit	2:12	and godly lives in this present **a**,

AGE, OLD [1201, 2416, 2418, 2419, 2420, 2421, 3427, 3813, 6409, 8484, 1179]. Called the reward of filial obedience according to the commandment (Ex 20:12). The Mosaic legislation spelled out the respect to be shown the aged (Lev 19:32). For example, younger men would wait to speak until the the aged men had spoken (Job 32:4). God promised Abraham "a good old age" (Ge 15:15). When

Pharaoh received him, Jacob lamented that he had not lived as long as his ancestors (47:7 – 9). There are many Hebrew words relating to old age in the OT, showing the honor in which the aged were usually held; yet the gray hairs that were so much respected also had their sorrows (44:29 – 31). Official positions went to older men (elders, e.g., Ex 3:16; Mt 21:23). Elders were ordained for the early Christian churches (e.g., Ac 14:23). Aged men and women are given sound advice in Tit 2:2 – 5. There is a fine picture of old age in Ecc 12:1 – 7. Jesus Christ is portrayed with the white hair of old age in Rev 1:14.

General References to:
Promised to the righteous (Ge 15:15; Job 5:26; Pss 34:12 – 14; 91:14, 16; Pr 3:1 – 2). Wasted, is bitter (Ge 47:9; Ecc 6:3, 6; 12:1 – 7). Deference toward (Lev 19:32; Job 32:4 – 9). Vigor in (Dt 34:7; Ps 92:12 – 14). Infirmities in (2Sa 19:34 – 37; Ps 90:10). Wisdom in (1Ki 12:6 – 8; 2Ch 10:6 – 8; Job 12:12). Enjoyed by David (1Ch 29:28). Prayer not to be forsaken in (Ps 71:9, 18). The aged to join in praise to the Lord (Ps 148:12 – 13). Righteous, is glorious (Pr 16:31). God's care in (Isa 46:4). Devoutness in (Lk 2:37). Exemplary, commanded (Tit 2:2 – 3). Mentioned by Paul (Phm 9).

AGONY [H987, H1631, H2655, H7815, H8358, G990, G3849, G4506, G6047] (Gr. *agōnia, agony, anguish*). The word is derived from the Greek *agōn,* "contest, struggle," and depicts severe conflict and pain. Lk 22:44 tells us that Christ's agony was such that "his sweat was like drops of blood falling to the ground." (See also Mt 26:36 – 46; Mk 14:32 – 42; Heb 5:7 – 8.) While Luke alone records the bloody sweat and the appearance of an angel from heaven strengthening Jesus, Matthew and Mark speak of the change in his countenance and manner and record his words as he spoke of his overwhelming sorrow "even unto death." The passage in Hebrews is the only clear reference in the NT apart from the Gospels to this agonizing crisis. Jesus' struggle was

in part with the powers of darkness, which were then returning with double force, having retreated after Satan's defeat at the temptation (Lk 4:13) "until an opportune time" (Gr. "until the season," i.e., in Gethsemane, Lk 22:53). Chiefly, however, Jesus' agony was caused by the prospect of the darkness on Calvary, when he was to experience a horror never known before, the hiding of the Father's face, the climax of his vicarious suffering for our sins. The one who knew no sin was to be made sin for humankind. The hour was before him when he would cry out in wretchedness of soul, "My God, my God, why have you forsaken me?" The prospect of this dreadful cup caused the struggle in the garden. In this supreme spiritual conflict, the Captain of our salvation emerged triumphant, as is evident in the language of his final victory of faith over the sinless infirmity of his flesh: "Shall I not drink the cup the Father has given me?" (Jn 18:11).

Jer	4:19	Oh, the **a** of my heart!
Lk	16:24	because I am in **a** in this fire.'
Ac	2:24	freeing him from the **a** of death
Rev	16:10	Men gnawed their tongues in **a**

AGORA [59] (ă'gō-ra, Gr. *agora, marketplace*). In ancient cities the town meeting place, where the public met for the exchange of merchandise, information, and ideas. As centers where people congregated, the agora of Galilee and Judea were the scenes for many of the healing miracles of Christ (Mk 6:56). Here the village idlers, as well as those seeking work, would gather (Mt 20:3). Here the vain and the proud could parade in order to gain public recognition (Mt 23:7; Mk 12:38; Lk 11:43; 20:46). Here also the children would gather for play (Mt 11:16 – 17; Lk 7:32). In Gentile cities, the agora served also as forums and tribunals. The agora of Philippi was the scene of the trial of Paul and Silas following the deliverance of a "slave girl who had a spirit by which she predicted the future" (Ac 16:16ff.). In Athens Paul's daily disputations in the agora led directly to his famed message before the

Areopagus (17:17ff.), the court that met on Mars Hill, north of the Acropolis.

AGRICULTURE Though agriculture is not a Bible word, "husbandry" and "husbandman" are used for the activity and the one who practices it. In the form of horticulture, it is as old as Adam (Ge 2:5, 8 – 15). Caring for the garden of Eden became labor after the curse (3:17 – 19). Nomad and farmer began to be differentiated with Abel and Cain (4:2 – 4). As animal husbandry took its place along with tillage as part of the agricultural economy, the farmer gained in social status. Yet as late as shortly before the Babylonian exile, nomads still felt a sense of superiority over the settled agricultural people (cf. the Recabites, Jer 35:1 – 11).

"Noah, a man of the soil, proceeded to plant a vineyard" (Ge 9:20). Abraham and his descendants were nomad herdsmen in Canaan, though Isaac and Jacob at times also tilled the soil (26:12; 37:7). Recurrent famines and the sojourn in Egypt taught the Israelites to depend more on agriculture, so that the report of the spies regarding the lush growth in Canaan interested them (Nu 13:23; Dt 8:8). Agriculture became the basis of the Mosaic commonwealth, since the land of Palestine was suited to an agricultural rather than a pastoral economy. The soil is fertile wherever water can be applied abundantly. The Hauran district (Perea) is productive. The soil of Gaza is dark and rich, though porous, and retains rain; olive trees abound there. The Israelites cleared away most of the wood that they found in Canaan (Jos 17:18). Wood became scarce; dung and hay heated their ovens (Eze 4:12 – 15; Mt 6:30). Their water supply came from rain, from brooks that ran from the hills, and from the Jordan. Irrigation was made possible by ducts from cisterns hewn out of rock. As the population increased, the more difficult cultivation of the hills was resorted to and yielded abundance. Terraces were cut, one above another, and faced with low stone walls. Rain falls chiefly in autumn and winter, November and December, rarely after March, almost never as late as May. The "early" rain falls from about the September equinox to sowing time in November or December; the "latter" rain comes in January and February (Joel 2:23; Jas 5:7). Drought two or three months before harvest meant famine (Am 4:7 – 8). Wheat, barley, and rye (millet rarely) were the staple cereals. "Corn" in the KJV, according to British usage, refers to any grain, not specifically to maize (NIV renders "grain"). The barley harvest was earlier than the wheat harvest: "The flax and the barley were destroyed, since the barley had headed and the flax was in bloom. The wheat and spelt, however, were not destroyed, because they ripen later" (Ex 9:31 – 32). Accordingly, at the Passover the barley was ready for the sickle, and the wave sheaf was offered. At the Pentecost feast fifty days later, the wheat was ripe for cutting, and the firstfruit loaves were offered. The vine, olive, and fig abounded, and traces remain everywhere of wine and olive presses. Cummin, peas, beans, lentils, lettuce, endive, leek, garlic, onion, cucumber, and cabbage were also cultivated.

The Passover in the month of Nisan occurred during the green stage of produce; the Feast of Weeks in Sivan, during the ripening stage; and the Feast of Tabernacles in Tisri, during the harvest. The six months from Tisri to Nisan were occupied with cultivation; the six months from Nisan to Tisri, with gathering fruits. Rain from the equinox in Tisri to Nisan was fairly continuous but was heavier at the beginning (the early rain) and the end (the latter rain). Rain in harvest was almost unknown (Pr 26:1).

Viticulture (the cultivation of grapes) is pictured in Isa 5:1 – 7 and Mt 21:33 – 41. Some farming procedures are described in Isa 28:24 – 28. The plow was light and drawn by yokes of oxen (1Ki 19:19). Oxen were urged on with a spearlike goad, which could double as a deadly weapon (Jdg 3:31). Fallow ground was broken and cleared early in the year (Jer 4:3; Hos 10:1). Seed was scattered broadcast, as in the parable of the sower (Mt 13:1 – 8), and plowed in afterward, the stubble of the preceding crop becoming mulch by decay. In irrigated fields, the seed was trodden in by cattle (Isa 32:20). The contrast between the exclusive dependence on irrigation in Egypt and the larger dependence on rain in Palestine is drawn in Dt 11:10 – 12. To sow among thorns was deemed bad husbandry (Job 5:5; Pr 24:30 – 32). Hoeing and weeding were seldom needed in their fine tilth. Seventy days sufficed between barley sowing and the offering of the wave sheaf of ripe grain at Passover. Harvesting and harvest customs in the time of the judges are described in Ru 2 and 3. Sowing varied seed in a field was forbidden (Dt 22:9). Oxen, unmuzzled (25:4) and five abreast, trod out the grain on a threshing floor of hard beaten earth to separate the grain from chaff and straw. Flails were used for small quantities and lighter grains (Isa 28:27). A threshing sledge (41:15) was also used, probably like the Egyptian sledge still in use (a stage with three rollers ridged with iron, which cut the straw for fodder while crushing out the grain). The shovel and fan winnowed the grain afterward with the help of the evening breeze (Ru 3:2; Isa 30:24); lastly it was shaken in a sieve (Am 9:9; Lk 22:31). The fruit of newly planted trees was not to be eaten for the first three years. In the fourth it was offered as firstfruits. In the fifth year it might be eaten freely (Lev 19:23 – 25).

We have glimpses of the relations of farm laborers, steward (manager or overseer), and owner in the book of Ruth, in Mt 20:1 – 16, and in Lk 17:7 – 9.

Agriculture was beset with pests: locust, cankerworm, caterpillar, and palmerworm (Joel 2:25 KJV); God calls them "my great army," as destructive as an invasion by human enemies. Haggai speaks (2:17) of blight, mildew, and hail. Modern development of agriculture in Palestine under the British mandate and since the establishment of the State of Israel, and parallel but lesser development in the country of Jordan, is restoring the coastal plain, the plains of Esdraelon and Dothan, the Shephelah, the Negev, and the Hauran to their ancient prosperity.

Agriculture was the occupation of humans before the fall (Ge 2:15) but was rendered laborious by the curse on the earth (Ge 3:17 – 19).

Activities in:

Binding sheaves of grain or weeds into bundles (Ge 37:7; Mt 13:30); stacking (Ex 22:6); gleaning (Lev 19:9; Ru 2:3); pruning (Lev 25:3; Isa 5:6; Jn 15:2); watering (Dt 11:10; 1Co 3:6 – 8); threshing (Dt 25:4; Jdg 6:11); winnowing (Ru 3:2; Job 39:12; Mt 3:12); plowing (Job 1:14); harrowing (Job 39:10; Isa 28:24); mowing (Ps 72:6; Am 7:1; Jas 5:4); planting (Pr 31:16; Isa 44:14; Jer 31:5); sowing (Ecc 11:4; Isa 32:20; Mt 13:3); clearing out stones (Isa 5:2); hedging (Isa 5:2, 5; Hos 2:6); digging (Lk 13:8; 16:3); reaping (Isa 17:5); fertilizing (Isa 25:10; Lk 14:34 – 35); storing in barns (Mt 6:26; 13:30); weeding (Mt 13:28); grafting (Ro 11:17 – 19, 24).

Animals Used in:

Donkey (Dt 22:10); ox (Dt 22:10; 25:4); horse (Isa 28:28).

Tools of:

Sickle (Dt 16:9; 23:25); cart (1Sa 6:7; Isa 28:27 – 28); mattock (1Sa 13:20); ax (1Sa 13:20); plow (1Sa 13:20); fork (1Sa 13:21); iron pick (2Sa 12:31); hoe (Isa 7:25); pruning knives (Isa 18:5; Joel 3:10); rod (Isa 28:27); winnowing fork (Jer 15:7; Mt 3:12; Lk 3:17); shovel (Isa 30:24); threshing sledge (Isa 41:15); sieve (Am 9:9).

Illustrative of:

Cultivating the heart (Jer 4:3; Hos 10:12); cultivating the church (1Co 3:9).

AGRIPPA I [68] (a-grĭp′a). Known in history as King Herod Agrippa I or Herod Agrippa, and in the NT as Herod, 10 BC – AD 44. He was the son of Aristobulus and Bernice and the grandson of Herod the Great. Through friendship with the emperors Caligula and Claudius, he gained the rulership first of Iturea and Trachonitis, then of Galilee and Perea, and ultimately of Judea and Samaria. He ruled over this reunited domain of Herod the Great from AD 40 until his death in 44 at the age of fifty-four. While owing his position to the favor of Rome, he recognized the importance of exercising great tact in his contacts with the Jews. Thus it was that his natural humanity gave way to expediency in the severe conflict between Judaism and the growing Christian movement. He killed James, an act that "pleased the Jews," and imprisoned Peter with the intention of bringing him before the people for execution after the Passover (Ac 12:2–4). Agrippa's sudden death shortly thereafter, noted in Ac 12:20–23, is fully recorded by Josephus (*Antiq.* 19.8). On the second day of a festival held in Caesarea in honor of Claudius, Agrippa put on a silver garment of "wonderful" texture and entered the amphitheater early in the morning. When the sun's rays shone on his garment, the brilliant glare caused his flatterers to cry out that he was a god. Josephus adds that "the king did neither rebuke them nor reject their impious flattery." Almost immediately a severe pain arose in his abdomen; five days later he died in great agony.

AGRIPPA II [68] (a-grĭp′a). Known in history as King Herod Agrippa II and in the NT (where he is mentioned only in Ac 25 and 26) as Agrippa. He was the son of Agrippa I. Only seventeen at the death of his father, he was thought too young to succeed to the throne. Six years later (AD 50) he was placed over the kingdom of Chalcis, which included the right to appoint the high priest of the temple in Jerusalem. In 53 he was transferred to the tetrarchies formerly held by Philip (Iturea and Trachonitis) and Lysanias (Abilene) and given the title of king. After the death of Claudius in 54, Nero added to Agrippa's realm several cities of Galilee and Perea. When Festus became procurator of Judea, Agrippa, accompanied by his sister (and consort) Bernice, went to Caesarea to pay his respects. It was at this time that Paul appeared before him, as recorded in Ac 25:23–26:32. In the final revolt of the Jews against Rome, Agrippa sided with the Romans in the destruction of his nation in the same cynical spirit with which he met the impassioned appeal of the apostle. Following the fall of Jerusalem in 70, he retired with Bernice to Rome, where he died in 100.

AHAB [281, 282] (ā′hă̆b, Heb. *'ah'āv, father's brother*).

1. Son of Omri and seventh king of the northern kingdom of Israel. He reigned twenty-two years, 873–851 BC. Politically, Ahab was one of the strongest kings of Israel. In his days Israel was at peace with Judah and maintained its dominion over Moab, which paid a considerable tribute (2Ki 3:4). He went into battle on three different occasions in later years against Ben-Hadad, king of Syria. While he had great success in the first two campaigns, he was defeated and mortally wounded in the third. Not mentioned in the Bible is Ahab's participation in the Battle of Karkar in 854. The "Monolith Inscription" of the Assyrian king Shalmanezer III contains a description of this battle that the Assyrians fought against a Syrian coalition of twelve kings. Of these, "Hadadezer," king of Damascus, is named first. Irhuleni of Hamath follows and in third place is "Ahab, the Israelite." The inscription states that Ahab commanded two thousand chariots and ten thousand men. The number of his chariots was far greater than the number credited to any other king.

Ahab's religious corruption was equaled by his love of material wealth and display. He was well known, for example, for his elaborately ornamented ivory palace (1Ki 22:39). Not content with what he had, however, he coveted the vineyard of Naboth, which adjoined his palace at Jezreel. Naboth refused to sell the land and Ahab was utterly dejected. Seeing his state, Jezebel asked him to remember who was king in Israel and proceeded unscrupulously to charge Naboth with blasphemy, doing so in the name of the king, who weakly maintained silence. False witnesses testified against Naboth, he was stoned to death, and Ahab took possession of the vineyard. This crime sealed the doom not only of Ahab, but also of his family. The judgment of the Lord was that all of his posterity would be cut off (21:21), even as had been the case with the two previous dynasties, those of Jeroboam and Baasha. The ringing condemnatory sentence of Elijah (21:19) was fulfilled to the letter on Ahab's son Joram (2Ki 9:24–26) and in part on Ahab himself (1Ki 22:38). Execution of the sentence was, however, delayed by

Ahab's repentance (21:27 – 29). Ahab also sinned by failing to discern the Lord's will and sparing the defeated Ben-Hadad of Syria (20:20 – 43). The prediction of his own death (20:42) was fulfilled when he was killed in battle at Ramoth Gilead (22:34).

Ahab's character is succinctly summarized by the historian: "There was never a man like Ahab, who sold himself to do evil in the eyes of the Lord, urged on by Jezebel his wife" (1Ki 21:25).

2. A false prophet who deceived the Jews in Babylon. Joining with Zedekiah, another false prophet, Ahab predicted an early return to Jerusalem. For this sin and for their immoral conduct, Jeremiah prophesied that they would be burned to death by the king of Babylon and that their names would become a byword (Jer 29:21 – 23).

AHAZ [298, 937] (ā′hăz, Heb. *'āhāz, he has grasped*). Reigning over the southern kingdom of Judah, 735 – 715 BC, Ahaz was a king of great significance. Historically during his reign and as a result of his policies, the people of God became vassals of Assyria and never again did the throne of David exist in its own sovereign right. Ahaz began that prolonged period of foreign domination that continued beyond the time of the coming of Christ. The dominant political power changed — Assyria, Babylon, Persia, Greece, Rome — but the vassalage did not. In addition, Ahaz is significant theologically, for his policies involved a denial of the way of faith. The essential cause of the demeaning of the throne of David and its enslavement was unbelief. The message of the reign of Ahaz remains as Isaiah summarized it: "If you do not stand firm in your faith, you will not stand at all" (Isa 7:9).

Ahaz is often represented as a weak, ineffective king. This is not the case. He gave his country firm and resolute leadership — but in the wrong direction. In 745 BC Tiglath-Pileser gained the throne of Assyria, the contemporary superpower; at once the Assyrians threw off the lethargy of the previous years and began to pursue imperialist policies. The states of Western Palestine, particularly Syria (Aram) and Israel (the northern kingdom of the people of God), felt their security threatened and resolved to form a defensive military alliance. Desiring a united Palestinian front, these northern powers determined to coerce Judah into their anti-Assyrian bloc. From the time of Jotham, Ahaz's father, Judah had been under this pressure (2Ki 15:37), but it was not until Ahaz's day that events reached a climax. A large-scale invasion brought the northern powers the successes reported in 2Ch 28:5 – 8, though for reasons no longer clear they failed to capitalize on success by taking Jerusalem (Isa 7:1). A further incursion was planned. This time Edomite and Philistine (2Ch 28:17 – 18) armies also took the field, with the clearly defined objective of bringing the monarchy of David to an end and replacing the Davidic king, perhaps with an Aramean puppet (Isa 7:6). This threat to the dynasty of David made the events of the reign of Ahaz crucially significant. In the face of the threat, we may well ask, "What made the people of God secure? How did they keep hold of their God-given possessions and privileges?"

Isaiah answered these questions with one word: "Faith." Those who trust the Lord's promises will find that he keeps his promises. Isaiah revealed the Lord's mind in Isa 7:7 – 8. The dreaded threat from the north would come to nothing (7:7); trusting in the apparent security of its military alliance with Syria would bring Ephraim (Israel) to a total end (7:8). Only the way of faith would keep Judah secure (7:9). When Isaiah made this appeal to Ahaz, that resolute monarch was already committed to the beginning of a militarist solution. Isaiah 7:3 reveals him reviewing Jerusalem's most vulnerable point: its overground water supply that could easily be cut off by a besieging enemy. King Ahaz could not be moved to the position of simple faith. To the offer of a sign from the Lord of even cosmic proportions (7:10 – 11), he gave the sort of answer that is often the resort of the outwardly religious man (7:12), and the die was cast. Ahaz refused the way of faith and embraced instead the way of works — the military-political solution. He showed all his astute hardheadedness in the course he followed. In fear of Assyria, Syria and Israel were threatening him. What better way to deal with them than to appeal over their heads to Assyria, secure an alliance with the superpower, and leave it to Assyrian armed might to disperse the Syro-Ephraimite armies? This is exactly what Ahaz did (2Ki 16:7ff.; 2Ch 28:16ff.). But he learned the risk of taking a tiger by the tail: once Assyria had disposed of the north Palestine kingdoms, it was the turn of Judah, and Ahaz became the first vassal king in David's line.

The Bible makes it clear that Ahaz had prepared the way for his own spiritual downfall by religious apostasy long before the decisive moment came (2Ki 16:14; 2Ch 28:1 – 4). It comes as no surprise that his decisions to abandon the way of faith opened the door to further and greater religious decline (2Ki 16:10 – 18; 2Ch 28:22 – 23).

AHAZIAH [301, 302, 3370] (ā′ha-zī′a, Heb. *'ăhazyâh*, *Jehovah hath grasped* or *Yahweh has upheld*).

1. Son of Ahab and Jezebel, eighth king of Israel. His history is recorded in 1Ki 22:40, 49, 51 – 53; 2Ch 20:35 – 37; 2Ki 1. He reigned only briefly, 851 – 850 BC. Ahaziah was a worshiper of Jeroboam's calves and of his mother's idols, Baal and Ashtoreth. The most notable event of his reign was the revolt of the Moabites, who had been giving a yearly tribute of a hundred thousand lambs and a hundred thousand rams (2Ki 1:1; 3:4 – 5). Ahaziah was prevented from trying to put down the revolt by a fall through a lattice in his palace at Samaria. Injured severely, he sent messengers to inquire of Baalzebub, god of Ekron, whether he would recover. Elijah the prophet was sent by God to intercept the messengers and proclaimed to them that Ahaziah would die. The king in anger tried to capture the prophet, but two groups of fifty men were consumed by fire from heaven in making the attempt. A third contingent was sent to seize the prophet but instead implored Elijah to deliver them from the fate of their predecessors (2Ki 1:13, 14). Elijah then went down to Samaria and gave the message directly to the king,

who died shortly afterward. He was succeeded by his brother Jehoram (1:17; cf. 8:16).

2. Son of Jehoram of Judah and Athaliah; thus grandson of Jehoshaphat and Ahab and nephew of Ahaziah of Israel. He was the sixth king of Judah in the divided monarchy and reigned only one year (2Ch 22:2), 843 BC. In 2Ch 21:17 and 25:23, his name appears also as Jehoahaz (a simple transposition of the component parts of the compound name), and in 2Ch 22:6 (KJV) he is called Azariah. His history is recorderd in 2Ki 8:25 – 29; 9:16 – 29. According to 2Ki 8:26, Ahaziah was twenty-two years old when he began to reign, and his father, Jehoram, only lived to age forty (21:20). However, 2Ch 22:2 states that he was forty-two years old when he ascended the throne. Some have thought that this last reference is a scribal error, but it may indicate a co-regency. Ahaziah walked in all the idolatries of the house of Ahab, "for his mother encouraged him in doing wrong" (22:3). He sinned also in allying himself with Joram (KJV "Jehoram") of Israel against Hazael of Syria, going into battle at Ramoth Gilead (22:5). Joram was wounded and Ahaziah went to see him at Jezreel. Here judgment came on him through the hand of Jehu, who fell on Joram and all the house of Ahab. When Ahaziah saw the slaughter, he fled, but "they wounded him in his chariot … he escaped to Megiddo and died there" (2Ki 9:27). The account given in Chronicles presents different though not irreconcilable details of his death (2Ch 22:6 – 9). Ahaziah was buried with his fathers in Jerusalem (2Ki 9:28). Jehu allowed this honorable burial because Ahaziah was the grandson of Jehoshaphat, who sought the Lord with all his heart (2Ch 22:9). Following the death of Ahaziah, his mother Athaliah seized the throne. She killed all the royal sons of the house of Judah except Joash, Ahaziah's son, who was hidden by Jehosheba, sister of Ahaziah and wife of Jehoiada the high priest (22:10 – 12).

AHIJAH [308, 309] (a-hī′ja, Heb. *'ăhîyâ*, *brother of Jehovah*).

1. One of the sons of Jerahmeel, a great-grandson of Judah and brother of Caleb (1Ch 2:25).

2. A descendant of Benjamin, mentioned in connection with an intra-family conflict (1Ch 8:7).

3. Son of Ahitub. He was priestly successor to the great priest of Shiloh, Eli, and after the destruction of Shiloh served as priest under King Saul. In particular he was asked to inquire of the Lord for Saul in the course of the Philistine war recorded in 1Sa 13 – 14. See especially 14:3, 18 – 19.

4. The Pelonite, one of the valiant men of David's armies (1Ch 11:36).

5. A Levite who was in charge of the treasures of the house of God in David's reign (1Ch 26:20).

6. Son of Shisha and brother of Elihoreph and a scribe of Solomon (1Ki 4:3).

7. A prophet of Shiloh (1Ki 11:29 – 39; 12:15; 14:2; 15:29). He predicted to Jeroboam that he would reign over ten of the twelve tribes and that his dynasty would be an enduring one if he did what was right in the eyes of the Lord. However, Jeroboam ignored the condition attached to the prediction, and it fell to Ahijah to foretell not only the death of Jeroboam's son but also the end of Jeroboam's line.

8. The father of Baasha, king of Israel, of the tribe of Issachar (1Ki 15:27).

9. One of the men who set their seal to the covenant drawn up before the Lord in the days of Nehemiah (Ne 10:26).

AHIMELECH [316] (a-hĭm'ĕlĕk, Heb. 'ăhimelekh, [my] brother is king).

1. Saul's high priest serving in the priestly center of Nob, who helped David by giving him the bread of the Presence and Goliath's sword. Doeg the Edomite denounced him to Saul. Upon hearing this, Saul ordered the death of Ahimelech and the other priests with him (1Sa 21 – 22). Abiathar, son of Ahimelech, escaped.

2. A Hittite who, with Abishai, was asked to accompany David to Saul's camp (1Sa 26:6).

3. Son of Abiathar and grandson of Ahimelech (2Sa 8:17; 1Ch 18:16; 24:6). *See Abiathar.*

AI [6504] (ā'ī Heb. 'ay, ruin, the heap).

1. A royal city of the Canaanites in central Palestine, east of Bethel. Abraham pitched his tent between Ai and Bethel when he arrived in Canaan (Ge 12:8). Ai figures most prominently in the account of the conquest of the land; it was the second Canaanite city taken by the forces under Joshua (Jos 7 – 8). Having conquered Jericho, the Israelites felt that a portion of the armies would be sufficient to conquer the much smaller Ai. The Israelite contingent was routed, however. It was then disclosed that Achan had sinned in taking articles from the consecrated spoil of Jericho. After Achan had confessed his sin and he and his family had been stoned to death, the Israelites made a second attack, which resulted in the total destruction of the city and the annihilation of all its twelve thousand inhabitants. The city, the site of which belonged to the tribe of Benjamin following the partition of the land, had not been rebuilt when the book of Joshua was written (Jos 8:28). It was, however, rebuilt in later days, for men of Ai returned from Babylon with Zerubbabel (Ezr 2:28; Ne 7:32). Also called Aija (Ne 11:31) and Aiath (Isa 10:28).

2. A city of the Ammonites (Jer 49:3).

The work of Joseph Callaway (1964 – 72) at Et-Tell, generally identified with biblical Ai, has shown that no city stood there from the Early Bronze Age destruction in about 2300 BC until a pre-Israelite settlement was built in the Early Iron Age (c. 1200 BC). Thus no town existed there in the time of the conquest under Joshua during the Late Bronze Age (c. 1550 to 1200 BC). Either the biblical record may be somewhat misleading in its account of Ai's demise, or the site is not actually that of Ai. There is no certain evidence confirming this identity.

Jos	7:4	routed by the men of **A**,
	8:26	he had destroyed all who lived in **A**.

AIR In the OT and the Gospels, this word is usually found in expressions speaking of the birds or fowl of the air (Job 41:16 is the only exception) and representing words normally translated "heaven." Elsewhere in the NT it stands for *aer*, the atmosphere. An ineffective Christian is pictured as a boxer "beating the air" (1Co 9:26). "Speaking into the air" describes unintelligible utterance (14:9). Satan is called "the prince of the power of the air" (Eph 2:2) — i.e., the ruler of the demonic beings that fill the air. The rapture of the church will culminate in her meeting the Lord and Savior Jesus Christ "in the air" (1Th 4:17).

Mt	8:20	and birds of the **a** have nests,
Mk	4:32	that the birds of the **a** can perch
1 Co	9:26	not fight like a man beating the **a**.
	14:9	You will just be speaking into the **a**.
Eph	2:2	of the ruler of the kingdom of the **a**,
1 Th	4:17	the clouds to meet the Lord in the **a**.
Rev	16:17	poured out his bowl into the **a**,

AKELDAMA [192] (a-kĕl′da-ma, Gr. *Akeldama, field of blood*, ASV, NIV, RSV; Aceldama, a-sĕl′da-ma, KJV; Hakeldama, ha-kĕl′da-ma, JB, NASB). The field purchased with the money Judas received for betraying Christ (Ac 1:18–19). Matthew 27:3–10, with a fuller account of the purchase, says the priests bought it "as a burial place for foreigners." Acts 1:18–19 is a parenthesis, an explanation by Luke, not part of Peter's speech. These verses say that "with the reward he got for his wickedness, Judas bought a field." The priests apparently bought it in Judas's name, the money having been his. The field was called "the place of blood" in Aramaic. Some think the Aramaic word means "field of sleep," or "cemetery," but the meaning "field of blood" is preferable, and it is appropriate because of the manner of Judas's death, the gruesome details being given in Ac 1:18.

| Ac | 1:19 | **A**, that is, Field of Blood. |

ALEXANDER [235] (ăl′ĕg-zăn′dêr, Gr. *Alexandros, man-defending*). A common Greek name belonging to five Jews to whom reference is made in the NT:

1. Alexander, brother of Rufus and son of Simon of Cyrene, the man who carried the cross of Jesus (Mk 15:21).

2. A kinsman of the Jewish high priest Annas (Ac 4:6).

3. A Jew of Ephesus who was pushed forward to speak to a noisy crowd that had been listening to Paul (Ac 19:33).

4. A false teacher whom Paul handed over to Satan for punishment (1Ti 1:20).

5. A metalworker who did Paul harm (2Ti 4:14). It is possible that nos. 3 and 5 are identical, or nos. 4 and 5; our knowledge is too sketchy to be sure.

Ac	19:33	The Jews pushed **A** to the front,
1 Ti	1:20	Among them are Hymenaeus and **A**,
2 Ti	4:14	**A** the metalworker did me a great deal of harm.

ALEXANDER THE GREAT (ăl′ĕg-zăn′dêr, Gr. *Alexandros, man's defender*). Son of Philip, king of Macedon, and Olympias, an Epirote princess. Lived from 356 to 323 BC. He conquered the civilized world from Greece eastward to India. Although not named in the Bible, he is described prophetically in Daniel, the "goat" from the west with a notable horn between his eyes. He came against the ram with two horns, who was standing before the river, defeated the ram, and became very great until the great horn was broken and four notable ones came up from it (Da 8:5–8). The prophecy identifies the ram as the kings of Media and Persia, the goat as the king of Greece, the great horn being the first king. When he fell, four kings arose in his place (8:18–22). The historical fulfillment is striking: Alexander led the Greek armies across the Hellespont into Asia Minor in 334 BC and defeated the Persian forces at the river Granicus. Moving with amazing rapidity ("without touching the ground," 8:5), he again met and defeated the Persians at Issus. Turning south, he moved down the Syrian coast, advancing to Egypt, which fell to him without a blow. Turning again to the east, he met the armies of Darius for the last time, defeating them in the battle of Arbela, east of the Tigris River. Rapidly he occupied Babylon, then Susa and Persepolis, the capitals of Persia. The next years were spent in consolidating the new empire. Alexander took Persians into his army, encouraged his soldiers to marry Asians, and began to Hellenize Asia through the establishment of Greek cities in the Eastern Empire. He marched his armies eastward as far as India, where they won a great battle at the Hydaspes River. The army, however, refused to advance farther, and Alexander was forced to return to Persepolis. While still making plans for further conquests, he contracted a fever. Weakened by the strenuous campaign and his increasing dissipation, he was unable to throw off the fever and died in Babylon in 323 at the age of thirty-three. His empire was then divided among four of his generals. While Alexander was outstanding as a conqueror, his notable contributions to civilization came via his Hellenizing efforts. The fact that Greek became the language of literature (including the NT) and commerce throughout the "inhabited world," for example, was of inestimable importance to the spread of the gospel. The trade language had been Aramaic.

ALEXANDRIA [233] (ăl′ĕg-zăn′drĭa, Gr. *Alexanddreia*). Founded by Alexander the Great, 332 BC; successively the Ptolemaic, Roman, and Christian capital of Lower Egypt. Its harbors, formed by the island Pharos and the headland Lochias, were suitable for both commerce and war. It was the chief grain port for Rome. Its merchant ships, the largest and finest of the day, usually sailed directly to Puteoli, but at times because of the severity of the weather sailed under the coast of Asia Minor, as did the vessel that carried Paul (Ac 27:6). Alexandria was also an important cultural center, boasting an excellent university. Patterned after the great school at Athens, it soon outstripped its model. It was especially noted for the study of mathematics, astronomy, medicine, and poetry. Literature and art also flourished. The library of Alexandria became the largest and best known in the world. In different eras it reportedly possessed from 400,000 to 900,000 books and scrolls.

The population of Alexandria had three prominent elements: Jews, Greeks, and Egyptians. The Jews enjoyed equal privileges with the Greeks, so that they became established there. While they continued to regard Jerusalem as "the holy city," they looked on Alexandria as the metropolis of the Jews throughout

the world. Here the translation of the OT into Greek, known as the Septuagint, was made in the third century before Christ. It became the popular Bible of the Jews of the dispersion, generally used by the writers of the NT. At Alexandria the OT revelation was brought into contact with Greek philosophy. The consequent synthesis became of great importance in subsequent religious thought. The influence of Alexandrian philosophy on the thought of the writers of the NT is debatable, but its impact on later theological and biblical studies in the Christian church was great.

According to tradition, Mark the evangelist carried the gospel to Alexandria and established the first church there. From this city Christianity reached out into all Egypt and the surrounding countries. A theological school flourished here as early as the second century. Among its great teachers were Clement and Origen, pioneers in biblical scholarship and Christian philosophy.

> **General References to:**
> *A city of Egypt (Ac 6:9). Ships of (Ac 27:6; 28:11). Apollos born in (Ac 18:24).*

ALIVE

Ge	7:3	to keep their various kinds **a**
Dt	6:24	might always prosper and be kept **a**,
1Sa	2:6	"The LORD brings death and makes **a**;
Pr	1:12	let's swallow them **a**, like the grave,
Lk	24:23	who said he was **a**.
Ac	1:3	convincing proofs that he was **a**.
Ro	6:11	dead to sin but **a** to God in Christ
	7:9	Once I was **a** apart from law;
1Co	15:22	so in Christ all will be made a.
Col	2:13	God made you **a** with Christ.
1Th	4:17	we who are still **a** and are left
Rev	1:18	and behold I am **a** for ever and ever!

ALLEGORY [H2648] (Gr. *allēgoreuein*, from *allos*, *other*, and *agoreuein*, *to speak in the assembly*). Allegory is a literary genre that attempts to explain spiritual truths in pictorial forms. This literary device is used extensively in Scripture. To speak allegorically is to set forth one thing in the image of another, the principal subject being inferred from the figure rather than by direct statement. Some parables, for example, are a type of allegory. Allegory is also a method of interpretation that searches for a mysterious, hidden meaning beyond the literal understanding of the text.

With the exception of Gal 4:21 – 31, allegory is not used in the NT to interpret the OT. However, allegory became increasingly important during the Apostolic period and into the Ante-Nicene period. The Alexandrian Jews of this period wished to reconcile Christianity with Greek thought. Origen taught a threefold sense of Scripture, corresponding to the body, soul, and spirit. In the Middle Ages four senses were found: historical, allegorical, moral, and anagogical (mystical). Jerusalem is *literally* a city in Israel, *allegorically* the church, *morally* the believing soul, *anagogically* the heavenly Jerusalem. The conquests of Joshua have been understood to be an allegory of the soul's victory over sin and self. Many Jewish scholars understand the Song of Songs to be allegorical, depicting God's love for Israel. On the other hand, many Christian scholars understand this as Christ's love for his church.

Jesus used allegory, as in the interpretation of his parable of the sower (Mt 13:18 – 23; Mk 4:14 – 20; Lk 8:11 – 15). Paul used allegory in using Hagar and Sarah to represent the differences between the old and new covenants (Gal 4:21 – 31). Many events and characters in the book of Revelation are used allegorically; most are clear or explained in context. For example, the Lamb and the Lion of Judah are both Jesus (Rev 5:5 – 14); the dragon is Satan (Rev 12:9).

In the OT:
Of the trees seeking a king (Jdg 9:8 – 15). Israel as a vine brought from Egypt (Ps 80). Wisdom as a noble woman (Pr 1:2 – 33). Folly as a harlot (Pr 9:13 – 18). The Messiah's kingdom represented by the wolf and lamb dwelling together (Isa 11:6 – 8).

ALLIANCES [H170, H907, H2489, H6468].

Believers grieve to witness, in their brothers (Ge 26:35; Ezr 9:3; 10:6). Parents should prohibit, to their children (Ge 28:1). Believers deprecate (Ge 49:6; Pss 6:8; 15:4; 101:4, 7; 119:115; 139:19). Believers are separate from (Ex 33:16; Ezr 6:21). Believers not to make, with wicked people (Nu 16:26; 2Ch 19:2; Jer 51:6; 2Co 6:14, 16; Php 2:15; 2Jn 9 – 11; Rev 18:4). Punishment of (Nu 33:56; Dt 7:4; Jos 23:13; Jdg 2:3; 3:5 – 8; Ezr 9:7, 14; Ps 106:41 – 42; Rev 2:16, 22 – 23). A call to come out from (Nu 16:26; Ezr 10:11; Jer 51:6, 45; 2Co 6:17; 2Th 3:6; Rev 18:4). Blessedness of forsaking (Ezr 9:12; Pr 9:6; 2Co 6:17 – 18). Persons in authority should denounce (Ezr 10:9 – 11; Ne 13:23 – 27). Exhortations to shun all inducements to (Pr 1:10 – 15; 4:14 – 15; 2Pe 3:17). Means of preservation from (Pr 2:10 – 20; 19:27). Exhortations to hate and avoid (Pr 14:7; Ro 16:17; 1Co 5:9 – 11; Eph 5:6 – 7; 1Ti 6:5; 2Ti 3:5). Blessedness of avoiding (Ps 1:1). Believers hate and avoid (Pss 26:4 – 5; 31:6; 101:7; Rev 2:2). Believers grieve to meet with, in their dealings with the world (Pss 57:4; 120:5 – 6; 2Pe 2:7 – 8). Believers should be careful when accidentally thrown into (Mt 10:16; Col 4:5; 1Pe 2:12).

Exemplified by:
Solomon (1Ki 11:1 – 8); Rehoboam (1Ki 12:8 – 9); Jehoshaphat (2Ch 18:3; 19:2; 20:35 – 38); Jehoram (2Ch 21:6); Ahaziah (2Ch 22:3 – 5); Israelites (Ezr 9:1 – 2); Israel (Eze 44:7); Judas Iscariot (Mt 26:14 – 16).

Examples of Avoiding:
Man of God (1Ki 13:7 – 10); Nehemiah (Ne 6:2 – 4; 10:29 – 31); David (Pss 101:4 – 7; 119:115); Jeremiah (Jer 15:17); Joseph of Arimathea (Lk 23:51); church at Ephesus (Rev 2:6).

Examples of Forsaking:
Israelites (Nu 16:27; Ezr 6:21 – 22; 10:3 – 4, 16 – 17); sons of the priests (Ezr 10:18 – 19).

Examples of God's Judgments against:
Korah (Nu 16:32); Ahaziah (2Ch 22:7 – 8); Judas Iscariot (Ac 1:18).

ALMIGHTY

Ge	17:1	"I am God **A**;
Ex	6:3	to Isaac and to Jacob as God **A**,
Nu	24:4	who sees a vision from the **A**,
Ru	1:20	the **A** has made my life very bitter.
2Sa	7:26	'The LORD **A** is God over Israel!'
Job	6:4	The arrows of the **A** are in me,
	11:7	Can you probe the limits of the **A**?
	21:15	Who is the **A**,
	33:4	the breath of the **A** gives me life.
Ps	84:3	O LORD **A**, my King and my God.
	89:8	O LORD God **A**, who is like you?
	91:1	rest in the shadow of the **A**.
Isa	6:3	holy, holy is the LORD **A**;
	47:4	the LORD **A** is his name—
	48:2	the LORD **A** is his name:
	51:15	the LORD **A** is his name.
	54:5	the LORD **A** is his name—
Jer	11:17	The LORD **A**, who planted you,
Am	5:14	the LORD God **A** will be with you,
	5:15	the LORD God **A** will have mercy
Zec	8:22	to Jerusalem to seek the LORD **A**
Mal	3:10	Test me in this," says the LORD **A**,
Rev	4:8	holy is the LORD God **A**, who was,
	19:6	For our LORD God **A** reigns.

ALMS (ahms). Kind deeds arising out of compassion, mercy, and pity for the unfortunate. The word itself is not found in the NIV, though the practice is of Mosaic legislation and NT injunction. Greek *eleēmosynē*, also in LXX for Hebrew *tsedhāqâh*, "righteousness," and *hesedh*, "kindness." Matthew 6:1 has *dikaiosynē*, "alms" (KJV), "acts of righteousness" (NIV). The verb *poiein*, "to do, perform," is often used with the noun to convey the meaning of helping the poor and needy (cf. Mt 6:2–3; Ac 9:36; 10:2; 24:17). In the OT the law prescribed gleanings from the harvest, the vineyards, and the grain in the corners of the field for the poor (Lev 19:9–10). Deuteronomy 24:10–22 stipulated further gleanings from the orchards and olive groves. It also protected the rights of the poor and unfortunate concerning wages, working conditions, and pledges, preventing the poor from being deprived of neces-sary garments or other needs. Almsgiving is set forth in Dt 15:11: "There will always be poor people in the land. Therefore I command you to be openhanded toward your brothers and toward the poor and needy in your land."

In later Judaism the righteousness of almsgiving became somewhat legalistic and professional. The lame man at the gate called Beautiful exemplified professional begging in that daily he "asked … for money" (Ac 3:2–3 NIV; "ask alms" KJV, RSV; "beg alms" MLB, NASB). Perversion in receiving alms is seen in a beggar's cry, couching the idea "Bless yourself by giving to me." Perversion in giving alms is seen in benefactors who "announce it with trumpets," probably to be taken figuratively, and who want "to be seen" by people, involving the word from which we derive "theater" (Mt 6:1–2). Almsgiving was of two kinds: "alms of the dish" (food and money received daily for distribution) and "alms of the chest" (coins received on the Sab-bath for widows, orphans, strangers, and the poor). The practice of the NT church was foreshadowed in Jesus' admonitions to "give to the poor" (Lk 11:41; cf. 1Co 16:2) and "sell your possessions and give to the poor" (Lk 12:33; cf. 2Co 8:3). Alms in the NT church were seen in the churches of Macedonia, who in "their extreme poverty … beyond their ability … [shared] in this service to the saints" (2Co 8:1–4). True purpose and spirit were shown: "At the pres-ent time your plenty will supply what they need, so that in turn their plenty will supply what you need" (8:14). The full measure of ministry, blessings, and ability to give by God's grace is delineated in 2Co 8 and 9, to be done liberally, prayerfully, and cheer-fully. See also Jas 2:15–16 and 1Jn 3:17. A primary function of deacons was to distribute alms (Ac 6).

In the KJV "alms" is rendered "give (to the poor)" and "acts of righteousness" in the NIV.

General References to:

To be given without public show (Mt 6:1–4; Ro 12:8); freely (2Co 9:6–7). Commanded (Dt 15:7–11; Mt 5:42; 19:21; Lk 12:33; 2Co 9:5–7; Gal 2:10; 1Ti 6:18; Heb 13:16). Asked for by the unfortunate (Jn 9:8; Ac 3:2). Withholding, not of love (1Jn 3:17).

Instances of Giving:

Zacchaeus (Lk 19:8); Dorcas (Ac 9:36); Cornelius (Ac 10:2); early Christians (Ac 2:44 – 45; 4:34 – 37; 6:1 – 3; 11:29 – 30; 24:17; Ro 15:25 – 28; 1Co 16:1 – 4; 2Co 8:1 – 4; 9:1; Heb 6:10).

ALONE

Ge	2:18	"It is not good for the man to be **a**.
Ex	18:18	heavy for you; you cannot handle it **a**.
Dt	8:3	man does not live on bread **a**
Ne	9:6	You **a** are the LORD.
Ps	62:1	My soul finds rest in God **a**;
	76:7	You **a** are to be feared.
	148:13	for his name **a** is exalted;
Mt	4:4	'Man does not live on bread **a**,
Mk	2:7	Who can forgive sins but God **a**?"
	10:18	"No one is good — except God **a**.
Jas	2:24	by what he does and not by faith **a**.
Rev	15:4	For you **a** are holy.

ALPHA [270] (ăl'fa). First letter of the Greek alphabet (A). The word *alphabet*, indicating a list of elementary sounds in any language, comes from the first two Greek letters, alpha and beta. In contrast is omega, the last letter of the Greek alphabet. Combined with alpha it signifies completeness, as "from A to Z" in modern usage. So God is the Alpha and the Omega, the First and the Last, the Beginning and the End (Rev 1:8), as is also Christ (21:6; 22:13). Compare Isa 41:4; 44:6.

Rev	1:8	"I am the **A** and the Omega,"
	21:6	I am the **A** and the Omega,
	22:13	I am the **A** and the Omega,

ALTAR (Heb. *mizbēah*, *place of slaughter*, Gr. *bomos*, in Acts only, and *thysiastērion*). In OT times altars were many and varied, their importance seen in the fact that the Hebrew and Greek words appear some 360 times.

The first Hebrew altar we read about (Ge 8:20) was erected by Noah after leaving the ark. Subsequent altars were built by Abraham (12:7 – 8; 13:4, 18; 22:9), Isaac (26:25), Jacob (35:1 – 7), Moses (Ex 17:15), and Joshua (Jos 8:30 – 31). Some of these must have been very simple in structure, as the context of Ge 22:9 seems to indicate. Most of the altars were built for sacrificial purposes, but some seem to have been largely memorial in character (Ex 17:15 – 16; Jos 22:26 – 27). Sometimes God stated just how the altar was to be built and of what materials (e.g., Ex 20:24 – 26).

With the erection of the tabernacle, altars were constructed by the Hebrews for two chief purposes: the offering of sacrifices and the burning of incense. Moses was commanded to make the altar of burnt offering for the tabernacle exactly as God had commanded him (Ex 25:9). It was to be made of acacia (shittim) wood, which was to be overlaid with brass or, as is more probable, bronze. The shape was a square of five cubits, three cubits high. At each corner of the altar there was to be a projection or "horn." This feature is found outside Israel, as in the tenth-century BC altar discovered at Megiddo. The purpose of the horns is not known, and the popular belief that clinging to the horns gave security from justice is disproved by 1Ki 1:50 – 53; 2:28 – 34. A bronze grating was placed in the center of the altar that projected through the opening on two sides. Four rings were fastened to it in which two poles of the same material as the altar were to be placed to carry the altar. Steps leading up to the altar were forbidden (Ex 20:26). For seven days atonement was to be made for the altar — apparently to sanctify it for the uses to which it was to be devoted (29:37); it was to be cleansed on the Day of Atonement after the presentation of sin offerings for the high priest and the nation (Lev 16:19 – 20).

Certain bronze utensils were made in connection with the altar. There were pans to hold the ashes, shovels for removing the ashes, basins to receive the blood and to convey it to the varied places for sprinkling, three-pronged flesh hooks with which to remove the flesh, and censers for carrying coals from the altar

(Ex 27:3). Once the fire on this altar was kindled, it was required that it burn continually (Lev 6:13).

The altar of burnt offering was also in Solomon's temple, the second temple, and the temple built by Herod. Its form was altered to fit into the varying sizes of these structures. Solomon made his altar of bronze twenty cubits square and twenty cubits high (2Ch 4:1). After its construction it had a very interesting history. Because idols had polluted it, King Asa rededicated it (15:8). Later on Uriah removed it from its regular place in order, it seems, to make room for another altar that he had patterned after the one King Ahaz had seen in Damascus (2Ki 16:11 – 14). The terrible pollution of spiritual things in the reign of Ahaz led Hezekiah to cleanse the altar (2Ch 29:12 – 18). Finally, it was repaired and restored to its place by Manasseh (33:16).

In Zerubbabel's temple the altar was built first (Ezr 3:2), on the exact spot where it previously stood (*Antiq.* 11.4.1). After it had been desecrated by Antiochus Epiphanes, it was rebuilt by Judas Maccabeus, apparently with unhewn stone (1Mc 4:47).

Moses was also commanded by God to make "an altar … for burning incense" (Ex 30:1), sometimes called "the gold altar" (Ex 39:38; Nu 4:11). It was to be a cubit square and two cubits high (Ex 30:2) with horns at each corner. It was made of acacia (shittim) wood overlaid with pure gold. Around the top of this structure a crown of gold was placed, beneath which were fixed two golden rings, one on each side. Staves of the same construction as the altar were placed through these rings to carry it (30:1 – 5).

This altar was to be located before the veil that separated the Holy Place from the Most Holy Place, midway between the walls (Ex 30:6; 40:5). Because of its special location, it was referred to as "the altar before the Lord" (Lev 16:12). Elsewhere in the Bible it is referred to as "the altar that belonged to the inner sanctuary" (1Ki 6:22; cf. Heb 9:3 – 4) and "the golden altar before the throne" (Rev 8:3). Incense was burned on this altar twice each day (Ex 30:7 – 8), and the blood of the atonement was sprinkled on it (30:10). The burning of incense on this altar sym-

bolized the offering up of the believers' prayers (Rev 8:3). It was while Zechariah was officiating at this altar that the angel appeared to him (Lk 1:10).

No altars are recognized in the NT church. While Heb 13:10 is sometimes used to prove the contrary, a careful study of this passage in its context is fatal to such an idea. The concept in this passage is that Jesus Christ is the true altar of each believer. Paul mentions in Ac 17:23 the inscription on an altar, "TO AN UNKNOWN GOD," which he saw in Athens. Such inscriptions were common in pagan cultures and are referred to by a number of early writers (see Augustine, *The City of God*, 3:12).

There is good reason to believe that the need for altars was revealed to humans very early as basic in approaching God. The altar played a leading role in all OT worship of the true God, as well as a prominent part in most pagan religions. A careful study of the use of this article of furniture in Israel's worship furnishes us with many spiritual lessons today. It was the place of sacrifice where God was propitiated and where individuals were pardoned and sanctified. It looked to the great sacrifice that the Son of God was about to make on the cross. The altar of sacrifice, the first thing visible as one approached the tabernacle, spoke loudly to people that without the shedding of blood there would be no access to God and no forgiveness of sin (Heb 9:9, 22). Most scholars say that the brass or bronze speaks of divine judgment.

Ge	8:20	Noah built an **a** to the Lord and,
	12:7	So he built an **a** there to the Lord,
	13:18	where he built an **a** to the Lord.
	22:9	Abraham built an **a** there
	22:9	son Isaac and laid him on the **a**,
	26:25	Isaac built an **a** there
	33:20	an **a** and called it El Elohe Israel,
	35:1	and build an **a** there to God,
Ex	17:15	Moses built an **a** and called it
	20:24	" 'Make an **a** of earth for me
	27:1	"Build an **a** of acacia wood,
	30:1	"Make an **a** of acacia wood
	37:25	the **a** of incense out of acacia wood.

Dt	27:5	Build there an **a** to the LORD your God, an **a** of stones.
Jos	8:30	on Mount Ebal an **a** to the Lord,
	22:10	Manasseh built an imposing **a**
Jdg	6:24	Gideon built an **a** to the Lord there
	21:4	an **a** and presented burnt offerings
1Sa	7:17	he built an **a** there to the LORD.
	14:35	Then Saul built an **a** to the LORD;
2Sa	24:25	David built an **a** to the LORD there
1Ki	12:33	on the **a** he had built at Bethel.
	12:33	for the Israelites and went up to the **a**
	13:2	He cried out against the **a** by the word of the LORD: "O **a**, **a**!
	16:32	He set up an **a** for Baal in the temple
	18:30	and he repaired the **a** of the LORD,
2Ki	16:10	He saw an **a** in Damascus
1Ch	21:26	David built an **a** to the LORD there
	21:26	with fire from heaven on the **a**
2Ch	4:1	a bronze **a** twenty cubits long,
	4:19	in God's temple: the golden **a**;
	15:8	He repaired the **a** of the LORD
	32:12	'You must worship before one **a**
	33:16	Then he restored the **a** of the LORD
Ezr	3:2	began to build the **a**
Isa	6:6	taken with tongs from the **a**,
La	2:7	The LORD has rejected his **a**
Eze	40:47	And the **a** was in front of the temple.
Am	9:1	I saw the LORD standing by the **a**,
Mal	1:7	"You place defiled food on my **a**.
Mt	5:24	leave your gift there in front of the **a**.
	23:18	'If anyone swears by the **a**,
Ac	17:23	even found an **a** with this inscription:
1Co	10:18	eat the sacrifices participate in the **a**?
Heb	13:10	We have an **a** from which
Jas	2:21	offered his son Isaac on the **a**?
Rev	6:9	I saw under the **a** the souls

ALTAR OF BURNT OFFERING

Described:

Dimensions of (Ex 27:1; 38:1). Horns on the corners of (Ex 27:2; 38:2). Sacrifices bound to the horns of (Ps 118:27, n.). The blood of sacrifices put on the horns and poured at the foot of (Ex 29:12;

Lev 4:7, 18, 25; 8:15). Covered with bronze (Ex 27:2). All its vessels of bronze (Ex 27:3; 38:3). A network grating of bronze placed in (Ex 27:4 – 5; 38:4). Furnished with rings and poles (Ex 27:6 – 7; 38:5 – 7). Made after a divine pattern (Ex 27:8). Placed in the court before the door of the tabernacle (Ex 40:6, 29). Sanctified by God (Ex 29:44). Anointed and sanctified with holy oil (Ex 40:10; Lev 8:10 – 11). Cleansed and purified with blood (Ex 29:36 – 37). Was most holy (Ex 40:10). Sanctified whatever touched it (Ex 29:37). All sacrifices to be offered on (Ex 29:38 – 42; Isa 56:7). All gifts to be presented at (Mt 5:23 – 24). Nothing polluted or defective to be offered on (Lev 22:22; Mal 1:7 – 8). Offering at the dedication of (Nu 7). Jews condemned for swearing lightly by (Mt 23:18 – 19). A type of Christ (Heb 13:10).

Called:

The bronze altar (Ex 39:39; 1Ki 8:64). The altar of God (Ps 43:4). The altar of the Lord (Mal 2:13).

The Fire upon:

Came from before the Lord (Lev 9:24). Was continually burning (Lev 6:13). Consumed the sacrifices (Lev 1:8 – 9).

In Relation to the Priests:

Alone to serve (Nu 18:3, 7). Derived support from (1Co 9:13). Ahaz removed and profaned (2Ki 16:10 – 16).

ALTAR OF INCENSE

Dimensions of (Ex 30:1 – 2; 37:25). Covered with gold (Ex 30:3; 37:26). Top of, surrounded with crown of gold (Ex 30:3; 37:26). Four rings of gold under crown for poles (Ex 30:4; 37:27). Poles of, covered with gold (Ex 30:5). Called the golden altar (Ex 39:38). Placed before veil in outer sanctuary (Ex 30:6; 40:5, 26). Said to be before the Lord (Lev 4:7; 1Ki 9:25). Anointed with holy oil (Ex 30:25 – 27). Priest burned incense on, every morning and evening (Ex 30:7 – 8). No strange incense nor any sacrifice to be offered on (Ex 30:9). Atonement made on, by high priest once every year (Ex 30:10; Lev 16:18 – 19). Blood of all sin offerings put on horns of (Lev 4:7, 18). Covered by priests before removal from sanctuary (Nu 4:11). A type of Christ (Rev 8:3; 9:3). Punishment for: unauthorized fire on (Lev 10:1 – 2); unauthorized offering on (2Ch 26:16 – 19).

ALWAYS

Dt	12:28	so that it may **a** go well with you
	15:11	There will **a** be poor people
1Ch	16:11	and his strength; seek his face **a**.
Ps	16:8	I have set the LORD **a** before me.
	51:3	and my sin is **a** before me.
	119:44	I will **a** obey your law,
Pr	28:14	the man who **a** fears the LORD,
Jer	12:1	You are **a** righteous, O LORD,
Hos	12:6	and wait for your God **a**.
Mt	26:11	The poor you will **a** have with you,
	28:20	And surely I am with you **a**,
Jn	5:17	"My Father is **a** at his work
Ac	2:25	" 'I saw the Lord **a** before me.
	7:51	You **a** resist the Holy Spirit!
1Co	13:7	It **a** protects, **a** trusts, **a** hopes, **a** perseveres.
Eph	5:20	**a** giving thanks to God the Father
Php	4:4	Rejoice in the Lord **a**.
Phm	1:4	I **a** thank my God as I remember you
Heb	7:25	he **a** lives to intercede for them.
1Pe	3:15	**A** be prepared to give an answer

AMALEKITES [6667, 6668] (ămăl'ĕk-īts, ăm'a-lĕk-īts, Heb. *'ămālēqî*). An ancient and nomadic marauding people dwelling mainly in the Negev from the times of Abraham to Hezekiah, c. 2000 – 700 BC. They are first mentioned among those conquered by Kedorlaomer in the days of Abraham (Ge 14:7). Moses felt their fury in the unprovoked attack on the Israelites at Rephidim, for which God decreed continual war and ultimate obliteration (Ex 17:8ff.). Joshua and the spies encountered them in Canaan, and they and the Canaanites repulsed the Israelites at Hormah (Nu 14:45). During the period of the judges, they sided with the Ammonites and Moabites against the Israelites in the days of Ehud (Jdg 3:13) and with the Midianites and other eastern peoples against Gideon (6:3, 33). Abdon was buried "in the hill country of the Amalekites" (12:15). Saul was commissioned to destroy them utterly but failed to do so and spared Agag (1Sa 15:8ff.). An Amalekite later killed Saul (2Sa 1:8ff.). David invaded the land of the Amalekites and other ancient inhabitants from Shur to Egypt (1Sa 27:8) and struck them severely in recovering his wives and property stolen during the raid on Ziklag (30:18). They are numbered among nations subdued by him (2Sa 8:12; 1Ch 18:11). The Simeonites during the time of Hezekiah finally exterminated them (1Ch 4:43).

Distribution of the Amalekites was primarily in the Negev SW of the Dead Sea but also in the Sinai Peninsula from Rephidim (Ex 17:8) to the border of Egypt (1Sa 27:8); northward at Jezreel (Jdg 6:33), Pirathon (12:15), and at or near Jericho (3:13); and eastward to Mount Seir (1Ch 4:42). See also Nu 13:29.

The origin of the Amalekites is not known for sure. If Amalek, the grandson of Esau (Ge 36:12), is the nation's father, the note in Ge 14:7 must be seen as proleptic. Accordingly, "first among the nations" in Nu 24:20 can be first in time, first in preeminence, or first to molest liberated Israel (at Rephidim). Arab traditions, late and conflicting, have the Amalekites stem from Ham.

In character the Amalekites were warlike, usually confederate with the Canaanites (Nu 14:45) or Moabites (Jdg 3:13), but sometimes alone, as at Rephidim (Ex 17:8) and Ziklag (1Sa 10:1). They "cut off all who were lagging behind; they had no fear of God" (Dt 25:18), and they destroyed crops (Jdg 6:4).

At Rephidim the Lord said, "I will completely blot out the memory of Amalek from under heaven" (Ex 17:14), and through Balaam, "Amalek ... will come to ruin at last" (Nu 24:20). Saul failed to destroy the Amalekites, but David reduced them to inactivity, and the Simeonites at Mount Seir "killed the remaining Amalekites who had escaped" (1Ch 4:43). Archaeology has produced no evidence of them thus far.

Character of:

Wicked (1Sa 15:18). Oppressive (Jdg 10:12). Warlike and cruel (1Sa 15:33). Governed by kings (1Sa 15:20, 32). A powerful and influential nation (Nu 24:7). Possessed cities (1Sa 15:5).

Country of:

In the south of Canaan (Nu 13:29; 1Sa 27:8). Extended from Havilah to Shur (1Sa 15:7). Was the scene of ancient warfare (Ge 14:7). Some Kenites dwelled among (1Sa 15:6).

Conflict with Israel:

Were the first to oppose Israel (Ex 17:8). Beaten at Rephidim through the intercession of Moses (Ex 17:9 – 13). Doomed to utter destruction (Nu 24:20). Presumption of Israel punished by (Nu 14:45). United with Eglon against Israel (Jdg 3:13). Part of their possessions taken by Ephraim (Jdg 5:14, w Jdg 12:15). With Midian, oppressed Israel (Jdg 6:3 – 5). Saul overcame, and delivered Israel (1Sa 14:48); commissioned to destroy (1Sa 15:1 – 3); massacred (1Sa 15:4 – 8); condemned for not utterly destroying (1Sa 15:9 – 26; 28:18). Agag, king of, slain by Samuel (1Sa 15:32 – 33). Invaded by David (1Sa 27:8 – 9). Pillaged and burned Ziklag (1Sa 30:1 – 2). Pursued and slain by David (1Sa 30:10 – 20). Spoil taken from, consecrated (2Sa 8:11 – 12). Confederated against Israel (Ps 83:5 – 7). Remnant of, completely destroyed during Hezekiah's reign (1Ch 4:41 – 43).

Ex	17:8	**A** came and attacked the Israelites
Dt	25:17	Remember what the **A** did to you
1Sa	15:3	attack the **A** and totally destroy
	15:8	He took Agag king of the **A** alive,

AMBASSADOR [H7495, G4563]. The OT has three Hebrew words that express the idea of "ambassador": (1) *tzîr* (e.g., Isa 18:2), probably denoting "going," i.e., away from home in a foreign land; (2) *mal'ākh* (e.g., Isa 37:9, 14; cf. 37:36 where it is the Lord's "angel" as his ambassador), meaning "messenger," therefore one sent on higher authority; (3) *lûts* (2Ch 32:31), literally "interpreter" (e.g., Ge 42:23), i.e., one carrying an authorized understanding of his master's mind and policy. The word "ambassador(s)" in the NT — e.g., "We are therefore Christ's ambassadors" (2Co 5:20) and "I am an ambassador in chains" (Eph 6:20) — is from *presbeuein*, "to be, work, or travel as an envoy or ambassador." Today's concept of an ambassador as a personal representative of sovereigns of state, living in foreign residence, is somewhat alien to the biblical concept of a messenger as ambassador.

General References to:

(Pr 13:17; Isa 18:2; 30:4; 33:7; 36:11; 39:1 – 2; Lk 14:32).

Sent by:

Moses to Edom (Nu 20:14). Israel to the Amorites (Nu 21:21). Gibeonites to Israelites (Jos 9:4). Israelites to various nations (Jdg 11:12 – 28). Hiram: to David (2Sa 5:11); to Solomon (1Ki 5:1). Ben-Hadad to Ahab (1Ki 20:2 – 6). Amaziah to Jehoash (2Ki 14:8). Ahaz to Tiglath-Pileser (2Ki 16:7). Hoshea to So, king of Egypt (2Ki 17:4). Sennacherib to Hezekiah (2Ki 19:9). Merodach-Baladan to Hezekiah (2Ki 20:12; 2Ch 32:31). Zedekiah to Egypt (Eze 17:15).

Figurative:

(Job 33:23; Ob 1; 2Co 5:20; Eph 6:20).

Eph	6:20	for which I am an **a** in chains.

AMBITION [G2249, G5818].

Worldly:

(Jas 4:1 – 2; 1Jn 2:16). Cursed (Isa 5:8; Heb 2:9). Insatiable (Hab 2:5 – 6, 9). Perishable (Job 20:6 – 7; Ps 49:11 – 13). False accusation against Moses (Nu 16:13). Parable illustrating (2Ki 14:9). Rebuked by Jesus (Mt 16:26; 18:1 – 3; 20:20 – 28; 23:5 – 7, 12; Mk 9:33 – 37; 10:35 – 45; 12:38 – 39; Lk 9:25, 46 – 48; 11:43; 22:24 – 30; Jn 5:44). Temptation by Satan (Mt 4:8 – 10; Lk 4:5 – 8).

Instances of:

King of Babylon (Isa 14:12 – 15); Eve (Ge 3:5 – 6); Korah and his followers (Nu 16:3 – 35); Abi-

melech (Jdg 9:1 – 6); Absalom (2Sa 15:1 – 13; 18:18); Haman (Est 5:9 – 13); disciples of Jesus (Mt 18:1 – 3; 20:20 – 24; Mk 9:33 – 37; 10:35 – 45; Lk 9:46 – 48; 22:24 – 30); Diotrephes (3Jn 9 – 10).

Disappointed:
Ahithophel (2Sa 17:23); Adonijah (1Ki 1:5); Haman (Est 6:6 – 9).

Ro	15:20	It has always been my **a** to preach
Gal	5:20	fits of rage, selfish **a**, dissensions,
Php	1:17	former preach Christ out of selfish **a**,
	2:3	Do nothing out of selfish **a** or vain
1Th	4:11	Make it your **a** to lead a quiet life,
Jas	3:14	and selfish **a** in your hearts,
	3:16	where you have envy and selfish **a**,

AMEN [589, 297] (ā-mĕn, Heb. *'āmēn*, Gr. *amēn*, *so be it*). English and Greek are both transliterations of Hebrew, from the root meaning "confirm" or "support." LXX translates it *genoito*, "may it become" (KJV "verily"). In the NT it is found as assent of the congregation to utterances of leaders (1Co 14:16); it is also equated with certainty of the promises of God (2Co 1:20). The general sense is "so let it be," "truly," "indeed." In the OT it appears with doxologies (1Ch 16:36; Ne 8:6; Ps 41:13) as an assent by the congregation to laws (Nu 5:22; Dt 27:15 – 26), with oaths (Ne 5:13), with appointments (1Ki 1:36), and as a call to divine witness (Jer 28:6). In the NT it is used to introduce a solemn saying of Jesus, always in the sense of "I tell you the truth" (KJV, "Verily I say," Jn 3:5; cf. Ps 41:13). It is also used following a doxology (Ro 11:36); following a benediction (15:33); as a concluding particle at the end of a writing (all but Acts, James, and 3 John end with "Amen" — fifteen are with benedictions, three are with doxologies, and six are unrelated); as an assent to forebodings (Rev 1:7; 22:20); in reverence to God (Ro 1:25; 9:5; Rev 1:18); and as a title of God (Rev 3:14; cf. Isa 65:15).

Dt	27:15	Then all the people shall say, "**A**!"
1Co	14:16	who do not understand say "**A**"
2Co	1:20	so through him the "**A**" is spoken
Rev	3:14	the words of the **A**,

22:20   I am coming soon." **A**.

AMMINADAB [6657, 300] (ă-mĭn′a-dăb, Heb. *'ammînādhāv, my people are willing*, or *my kinsman is generous*).

1. A Levite, Aaron's father-in-law (Ex 6:23).

2. A prince of Judah (Nu 1:7; 2:3; 7:12, 17; 10:14; Ru 4:19 – 20; 1Ch 2:10).

3. A son of Kohath, son of Levi (1Ch 6:22). Perhaps the same as 1.

4. A Kohathite who assisted in the return of the ark from the house of Obed-Edom (1Ch 15:10 – 11).

AMMONITES [1201+6648, 6648, 6649] (ăm′ŏn-īts, Heb. *'ammônîm*). The name given to the descendants of Ben-Ammi or Ammon (Ge 19:38). They were related to the Moabites by ancestry and often appear in Scripture in united effort with them. Because by ancestry they were related to Israel, "children of my people" (see NIV note to Ge 19:38), the Israelites were told by the Lord not to enter into battle with them as they journeyed toward the land of Canaan (Dt 2:19). Lot fled from the destruction of the cities of Sodom and Gomorrah and dwelled in the mountains to the east of the Dead Sea. The land God gave the Ammonites stretched to the north as far as the Jabbok River and to the south to the hills of Edom. Many years later the Ammonites made war with Israel in order to extend their borders farther west. Although this land never really belonged to the Ammonites, they claimed it and gave this as a reason for their aggression (Jdg 11:13).

Unable to expand westward and not desiring the desert tract of land on the east, the Ammonites were confined to a small area. Although they were a nomadic people, they did have a few cities, their capital Rabbath-Ammon being the most famous.

The people were fierce in nature and rebellious and, apart from the period when Nahash was a friendly ally of David's (2Sa 10:1ff.), hostile to Israel. They threatened to gouge out the right eyes of all in Jabesh Gilead (1Sa 11:2). They were given to brutal murder (Jer 40:14; 41:5 – 7; Am 1:14). Though related to Israel, they refused to help them when asked, and they joined with Moab in securing Balaam to curse them (Dt 23:3 – 4). Later in Israel's history they united with Sanballat to oppose the work of Nehemiah in restoring the walls of Jerusalem (Ne 2:10 – 19). In religion the Ammonites were a degraded, idolatrous people. Their chief idol was Molech, to whom they offered human sacrifices (1Ki 11:7).

Because of their sins and especially because they constantly opposed Israel, Ezekiel predicted their complete destruction (Eze 25:1 – 7). Their last stand seems to have been against Judas Maccabeus (1Mc 5:6).

History of:

Character of (Jdg 10:6; 2Ki 23:13; 2Ch 20:22 – 23; Jer 27:3, 9; Eze 25:1 – 7; Am 1:13; Zep 2:10). Territory of (Nu 21:24; Dt 2:19; Jos 12:2; 13:10, 25; Jdg 11:13). Israelites forbidden to disturb (Dt 2:19, 37). Excluded from the congregation of Israel (Dt 23:3 – 6). Confederated with Moabites and Amalekites against Israel (Jdg 3:12 – 13). Defeated by the Israelites (Jdg 10:7 – 18; 11:32 – 33; 12:1 – 3; 1Sa 11; 2Sa 8:12; 10; 11:1; 12:26 – 31; 17:27; 1Ch 18:11; 20:1 – 3; 2Ch 20; 26:7 – 8; 27:5). Conspired against the Jews (Ne 4:7 – 8). Solomon took wives from (1Ki 11:1; Ne 13:26). Rehoboam took wives from (2Ch 12:13). Jews intermarried with (Ezr 9:1, 10 – 12; 10:10 – 44; Ne 13:23).

Prophecies Concerning:

(Isa 11:14; Jer 9:25 – 26; 25:15 – 21; 27:1 – 11; 49:1 – 6; Eze 21:20, 28 – 32; 25:1 – 11; Da 11:41; Am 1:13 – 15; Zep 2:8 – 11).

Ge	19:38	the father of the **A** of today.
Dt	2:19	When you come to the **A**,
Jdg	11:4	when the **A** made war on Israel,
1Ki	11:5	Molech the detestable god of the **A**.
Jer	49:6	I will restore the fortunes of the **A**,"
Eze	25:10	the **A** will not be remembered among
Zep	2:9	the **A** like Gomorrah —

AMNON [H578, H596] (ăm'nŏn, *trustworthy*).

1. Son of David by Ahinoam. By contrivance he raped his half sister Tamar as she tended him during a pretended sickness; for this he was later murdered by Tamar's brother Absalom (2Sa 13:1 – 29).

2. Son of the Judahite Shimon (1Ch 4:20).

AMON [571, 572, 321] (ā'mŏn, Heb. *'āmôn, trustworthy*).

1. The successor and son of King Manasseh and father of the illustrious King Josiah. Since this name was identical with that of the Egyptian deity, it is thought that perhaps Manasseh named him while he was still in idolatry. He was an evil king and after two years of reign (642 – 640 BC) was slain by officials of his household (2Ki 21:19 – 26; 2Ch 33:21 – 25).

2. The governor of Samaria to whom Micaiah the prophet was committed by Ahab, king of Israel, because he had predicted the king's death (1Ki 22:15 – 28).

3. One of Solomon's servants (Ne 7:57 – 59), though sometimes he is called Ami (Ezr 2:57).

4. The name of an Egyptian deity that appears in the OT linked with his city, No (Jer 46:25; Na 3:8, see NIV note). Better known by its Greek name, Thebes, No was 318 miles (530 km.) south of Cairo and is now known by the names Karnak and Luxor and is famed for its huge necropolis. Little is known of Amon for sure. During the period of the Theban Dynasties (from 1991 BC), Amon became the state god of the Egyptian empire. His city and priesthood came to such glory that Nahum was able to recall its downfall as evidence to great Nineveh that its time of desolation surely would come also.

AMORITES [616] (ăm'ō-rīts, Heb. *'ĕmōrî, mountain dwellers*). Although this word in the Hebrew is always in the singular, it is used collectively of that tribe of people who, according to Ge 10:16, descended from Canaan. They probably were east Semites and although not Akkadians were very closely akin to them.

They were a prominent people in pre-Israelite days, for it is believed that at one time their kingdom occupied the larger part of Mesopotamia and Syria, with their capital at Haran. The Mari tablets throw a flood of light on them, and it is now thought that Amraphel of Shinar (Ge 14:1) was one of their kings. When people from the north drove them from this region, they settled Babylonia and brought the entire area under their control, giving to Babylonia one of the richest periods in her history. After several hundred years they were defeated by the Hittites, and they settled throughout a large portion of Canaan. They may even have ruled in Egypt for a time.

We do know that during their supremacy in Canaan they marched on the kingdom of Moab and under the leadership of King Sihon subdued a large portion of this land, in which they settled (Nu 21:13, 26 – 31). Joshua speaks of their land as east of the Jordan (Jos 24:8), but Moses describes it as being on the western shore of the Dead Sea (Ge 14:7), on the plain of Mamre (14:13), and around Mount Hermon (Dt 3:8). They were apparently a very wicked people, for God told Abraham that his descendants would mete out divine vengeance on them when their iniquity was full (Ge 15:16). Under Moses' leadership this judgment was dealt to Og, king of Bashan, and to Sihon, king of Heshbon — the kings of the Amorites east of the Jordan. Their territory was subdued and given to Reuben, who held it for five hundred years until it fell to Moab. This land was very rich, attractive to both farmers and herdsmen. Joshua met these people in battle in the united campaign of the five Amorite kings of Jerusalem, Hebron, Marmuth, Lachish, and Eglon (Jos 10:1 – 43). These battles (11:1 – 14), fought by Joshua under divine leadership, ended forever Amorite hostilities against Israel (1Sa 7:14; 1Ki 9:20 – 21).

General References to:

Descendants of Canaan (1Ch 1:13 – 14). Were giants (Am 2:9). Conquered by Kedorlaomer and rescued by Abraham (Ge 14). Territory of (Ge 14:7; Nu 13:29; 21:13; Dt 1:4, 7, 19; 3:8 – 9; Jos 5:1; 10:5; 12:2 – 3; Jdg 1:35 – 36; 11:22); given to descendants of Abraham (Ge 15:21; 48:22; Dt 1:20; 2:26 – 36; 7:1; Jos 3:10; Jdg 11:23; Am 2:10); allotted to Reuben, Gad, and Manasseh (Nu 32:33 – 42; Jos

13:15 – 21); conquest of (Nu 21:21 – 30; Jos 10:11; Jdg 1:34 – 36). Chiefs of (Jos 13:21). Wickedness of (Ge 15:16; 2Ki 21:11; Ezr 9:1). Idolatry of (Jdg 6:10; 1Ki 21:26). Judgments denounced against (Ex 23:23 – 24; 33:2; 34:10 – 11; Dt 20:17 – 18). Hornets sent among (Jos 24:12). Not exterminated (Jdg 1:34 – 36; 3:1 – 3, 5 – 8; 1Sa 7:14; 2Sa 2:2; 1Ki 9:20 – 21; 2Ch 8:7). Intermarriage with Jews (Ezr 9:1 – 2; 10:18 – 44). Kings of (Jos 10:3 – 26).

Ge	15:16	the sin of the **A** has not yet reached
Nu	21:31	So Israel settled in the land of the **A**,
Jdg	6:10	not worship the gods of the **A**,

AMOS [6650, 322] (ā'mŏs, Heb. *'āmôs*, Gr. *amos*, *burden-bearer*). One of the colorful personalities in an era that saw the rise of several towering prophetic figures (Am 1:1). His ministry occurred in the reign of Jeroboam II (c. 786 – 746 BC), son of King Jehoash of the Jehu dynasty of Israel. Due to the removal of Benhadad III of Syria as a military threat, the northern kingdom had been able to consolidate its hold on Damascus and extend its borders northward to the pass of Hamath. To the south and east, its territorial acquisitions equaled those of the early kingdom period under David and Solomon. While Assyria was becoming an increasingly serious political threat, its military might under Tiglath-Pileser III was still a distant prospect when Jeroboam II began to rule Israel.

Jeroboam's forty-year reign was one of great prosperity for the northern kingdom, approaching in character the "golden age" of David and Solomon. With the threat of war removed, a cultural, social, and economic revival took place. The expansion of trade and commerce resulted in a steady drift from country to city, and the small towns in the northern kingdom gradually became overcrowded. But prosperity was accompanied by an almost unprecedented degree of social corruption (Am 2:6 – 8; 5:11 – 12), caused principally by the demoralizing influence of Canaanite Baal worship, which had been fostered at the local shrines from the time when the northern kingdom had assumed a separate existence.

Archaeological discoveries in Palestine have furnished a dramatic picture of the extent to which this depraved, immoral religion exerted its corrupting influences over the Israelites. Characteristic of the ritual observances were drunkenness, violence, gross sensuality, and idolatrous worship. The effect was seen in the corruption of justice, in wanton and luxurious living, and in the decay of social unity in Hebrew society. The rich manifested no sense of responsibility toward the poor and instead of relieving their economic distress seemed bent on devising new means of depriving them of their property.

To this perilous situation Amos brought a message of stern denunciation. Although he was not an inhabitant of the northern kingdom, he was painfully aware of its moral, social, and religious shortcomings. Amos lived in the small mountain village of Tekoa, which lay to the south of Jerusalem on the borders of the extensive upland pastures of Judah. By trade he was a herdsman of sheep and goats (Am 7:14) and was also engaged in dressing the sycamore-fig tree, whose fruit must be incised about four days before the harvest to hasten the ripening process. His background was of a strictly agricultural nature, and his work afforded him ample time for meditating on God's laws and their meaning for wayward Israel.

On receiving his call, Amos protested vigorously against the luxurious and careless lifestyle characteristic of Samaria, castigated the elaborate offerings made at the shrines of Beersheba and Gilgal, and stated flatly that ritual could never form an acceptable substitute for righteousness. He asserted the moral jurisdiction of God over all nations (Am 1:3, 6, 9, 11, 13; 2:1, 4, 6) and warned the Israelites that unless they repented of their idolatry and, following a renewed spiritual relationship with God, commenced to redress social inequalities, they would fall victim to the invader from the east. So great was the impact of this vigorous personality that Amos was accused of sedition by Amaziah, the idolatrous high priest of Bethel (7:10ff.). In reply, Amos pointed out that he had no connection with any prophetic order, nor was he linked in any way politically with the house of David. Instead he was called by God to prophesy the captivity of an unrepentant Israel.

The style of his book, though simple, is picturesque, marked by striking illustrations taken from his rural surroundings. His work as a herdsman was clearly not incompatible either with a knowledge of history (Am 9:7) or with an ability to assess the significance of contemporary political and religious trends. The integrity of his book has suffered little at the hands of modern critical scholars.

AMOS, BOOK OF The book of Amos was written by Amos, a shepherd of Tekoa, probably between 760 and 750 BC.

Outline:

ANANIAS [G393] (ăn'a-nī'ăs, Gr. form of Heb. *hă-nanyâh, Jehovah has been gracious*).

1. The husband of Sapphira (Ac 5:1 – 11). He and his wife pretended to give to the church all they received from a sale of property but kept back part of the money. When Peter denounced his deceit, Ananias fell down dead. The generosity of others (4:32 – 37) accentuates the meanness of Ananias. Yet lying to the Holy Spirit, rather than exhibiting greed, was the sin for which he was punished. That his was the first gross act of disobedience within the church justifies the severity of the punishment. Peter prophesied rather than decreed his death, which was a penalty God inflicted.

2. A disciple at Damascus who, obeying a vision, was the means of healing the sight of Saul of Tarsus and of introducing him to the Christians of Damascus (Ac 9:10 – 19). In Ac 22:12 – 16 Paul recalls Ananias's part in his conversion and speaks of him as "a

devout observer of the law and highly respected by all the Jews living" in Damascus.

3. A high priest before whom Paul was tried in Jerusalem (Ac 23:1 – 5). Paul, whether because of poor eyesight or momentary forgetfulness or Ananias's unpriestly behavior, reviled him, was rebuked, and promptly apologized. Ananias came down to Caesarea in person to accuse Paul before the Roman governor Felix (24:1).

ANATHEMA [353] (a-năth′ĕma, Gr. *anathema*, the rendering in the LXX and NT of the Hebrew *herem*, *anything devoted*, *devoted to destruction*). An anathema was a thing irrevocably devoted to God and thus withdrawn from common use. A person so devoted was doomed to death — a death implying moral worthlessness (Lev 27:28 – 29; Ro 3:9; 1Co 12:3; 16:22; Gal 1:9). The word "anathema" is used in the KJV. In the NIV it is rendered "curse" or "cursed."

ANCIENT OF DAYS A title of Yahweh. In Da 7:9, 13, 22 the reference is to God, as he appeared in a vision to the prophet.

ANDREW [436] (ăn′drŭ Gr. *Andreas*, *manly*). An apostle. The brother of Simon Peter and son of Jonas of Bethsaida on the Sea of Galilee (Jn 1:44). He was a fisherman, like his brother, with whom he lived at Capernaum (Mk 1:29). He was a disciple of John the Baptist, who directed him to Jesus as the Lamb of God. Convinced that Jesus was the Messiah, he quickly brought his brother Peter to Jesus (Jn 1:25 – 42). Subsequently Jesus called the two brothers to abandon their fishing and take up permanent fellowship with him (Mt 4:18 – 19); later Jesus appointed Andrew an apostle (Mt 10:2; Mk 3:18; Lk 6:14; Ac 1:13). In the lists of the apostles his name always appears next to that of Philip, who was also from Bethsaida. He is associated with the feeding of the five thousand, where he expressed doubt that the multitude could be fed with the boy's five loaves and two fishes (Jn 6:6 – 9), and also with the request of the Greeks to see Jesus (12:22). Andrew was one of the four who asked Jesus about the destruction of the temple and the time of the second coming. After Ac 1:13 he is never mentioned again. According to tradition he preached in Scythia and suffered martyrdom in Achaia, crucified on an X-shaped cross, now called a St. Andrew's cross.

ANGEL [H52, H466+H1201, H466+H1201+H2021, H4855, G34, G2694] (Gr. *angelos, messenger*). A supernatural, heavenly being, a little higher in dignity than humans. Angels are created beings (Ps 148:2 – 5; Col 1:16). Scripture does not tell us the time of their creation, but it was certainly before the creation of humankind (Job 38:7). They are described as "spirits" (Heb 1:14). Although without a bodily organism, they have often revealed themselves in bodily form to people. Jesus said that they do not marry and do not die (Lk 20:34 – 36). They therefore constitute a company, not a race developed from one original pair. Scripture describes them as personal beings, not mere personifications of abstract good and evil. Although possessed of superhuman intelligence, they are not omniscient (Mt 24:36; 1Pe 1:12); and although stronger than people, they are not omnipotent (Ps 103:20; 2Th 1:7; 2Pe 2:11). They are not glorified human beings but are distinct from humans (1Co 6:3; Heb 1:14). There is a vast multitude of them. John said, "I … heard the voice of many angels, numbering thousands upon thousands, and ten thousand times ten thousand" (Rev 5:11). They are of various ranks and endowments (Col 1:16), but only one — Michael — is expressly called an archangel in Scripture (Jude 9). The great hosts of angels, both good and bad, are highly organized (Ro 8:38; Eph 1:21; 3:10; Col 1:16; 2:15).

Angels were created holy (Ge 1:31; Jude 6), but after a period of probation some fell from their state of innocence (2Pe 2:4; Jude 6). Scripture is silent regarding the time and cause of their fall, but it is clear that it occurred before the fall of man (for Satan deceived Eve in the garden of Eden) and that it was due to a deliberate, self-determined rebellion against God. As a result these angels lost their original holiness, became corrupt, and were confirmed in evil.

Some were "sent ... to hell," where they are held in chains until the day of judgment (2Pe 2:4); others were left free, and they oppose the work of God.

The work of the angels is varied. Good angels stand in the presence of God and worship him (Mt 18:10; Heb 1:6; Rev 5:11). They assist, protect, and deliver God's people (Ge 19:11; Ps 91:11; Da 3:28; 6:22; Ac 5:19). The author of Hebrews says (1:14), "Are not all angels ministering spirits sent to serve those who will inherit salvation?" They sometimes guide God's children, as when one told Philip to go into the desert near Gaza (Ac 8:26); and they bring encouragement, as when one spoke to Paul in Corinth (27:23 – 24). Sometimes they interpret God's will to people (Da 7:16; 10:5, 11; Zec 1:9, 13 – 14, 19). They execute God's will toward individuals and nations (Ge 19:12, 13; 2Sa 24:16; Eze 9:2, 5, 7; Ac 12:23). The affairs of nations are guided by them (Da 10:12 – 13, 20). God uses them to punish his enemies (2Ki 19:35; Ac 12:23).

Angels had a large place in the life and ministry of Christ. At his birth they made their appearance to Mary, Joseph, and the shepherds. After the wilderness temptation of Christ, they ministered to him (Mt 4:11); an angel strengthened him in the garden (Lk 22:43); an angel rolled away the stone from the tomb (Mt 28:2 – 7); and angels were with him at the ascension (Ac 1:10 – 11).

As for the evil angels, it is clear that their principal purpose is to oppose God and try to defeat his will and frustrate his plans. Evil angels endeavor to separate believers from God (Ro 8:38). They oppose good angels in their work (Da 10:12 – 13). They hinder humans' temporal and eternal welfare by exerting a limited control over natural phenomena (Job 1:12 – 13, 19; 2:7), by inflicting disease (Lk 13:11, 16; Ac 10:38; 2Co 12:7), by tempting individuals to sin (Mt 4:3; Jn 13:27; 1Pe 5:8), and by spreading false doctrine (1Ki 22:21 – 23; 2Th 2:2; 1Ti 4:1). They cannot, however, exercise over people any moral power independent of the human will, and whatever power they have is limited by the permissive will of God. The word *Satan* means "adversary," and Scripture shows him to be the adversary of both God and humankind. All of his many other names show his extremely wicked character.

Scripture shows that good angels will continue in the service of God in the future age, whereas evil angels will have their part in the eternal fire (Mt 25:41).

Elect:

Created by God and Christ (Ne 9:6; Col 1:16). Worship God and Christ (Ne 9:6; Php 2:9 – 11; Heb 1:6). Are ministering spirits (1Ki 19:5; Pss 68:17; 104:4; Lk 16:22; Ac 12:7 – 11; 27:23; Heb 1:7, 14). Communicate the will of God and Christ (Da 8:16 – 17; 9:21 – 23; 10:11; 12:6 – 7; Mt 2:13, 20; Lk 1:19, 28; Ac 5:20; 8:26; 10:5; 27:23; Rev 1:1). Obey the will of God (Ps 103:20; Mt 6:10). Execute the purposes of God (Nu 22:22; Ps 103:21; Mt 13:39 – 42; 28:2; Jn 5:4; Rev 5:2). Execute the judgments of God (2Sa 24:16; 2Ki 19:35; Ps 35:5 – 6; Ac 12:23; Rev 16:1). Celebrate the praises of God (Job 38:7; Ps 148:2; Isa 6:3; Lk 2:13 – 14; Rev 5:11 – 12; 7:11 – 12). Law given by the mediation of (Ps 68:17; Ac 7:53; Heb 2:2). Announced: conception of Christ (Mt 1:20 – 21; Lk 1:31); birth of Christ (Lk 2:10 – 12); resurrection of Christ (Mt 28:5 – 7; Lk 24:23); ascension and second coming of Christ (Ac 1:11); conception of John the Baptist (Lk 1:13, 36). Ministered to Christ (Mt 4:11; Lk 22:43; Jn 1:51). Are subject to Christ (Eph 1:21; Col 1:16; 2:10; 1Pe 3:22). Shall execute the purposes of Christ (Mt 13:41; 24:31). Shall attend Christ at his second coming (Mt 16:27; 25:31; Mk 8:38; 2Th 1:7). Know and delight in the gospel of Christ (Eph 3:9 – 10; 1Ti 3:16; 1Pe 1:12). Mediation of, in response to prayer (Mt 26:53; Ac 12:5, 7). Rejoice over every repentant sinner (Lk 15:7, 10). Have charge over the children of God (Pss 34:7; 91:11 – 12; Da 6:22; Mt 18:10). Are of different orders (Isa 6:2; 1Th 4:16; 1Pe 3:22; Jude 9; Rev 12:7). Not to be worshiped (Col 2:18; Rev 19:10; 22:9). Are wise (2Sa 14:20); innumerable (Job 25:3; Heb 12:22);

mighty (Ps 103:20); holy (Mt 25:31); elect (1Ti 5:21); meek (2Pe 2:11; Jude 9).

Fallen:

(Job 4:18; Mt 25:41; 2Pe 2:4; Jude 6; Rev 2:9). See Demons.

Ge	16:7	The **a** of the LORD found Hagar
	21:17	and the **a** of God called to Hagar
	22:11	the **a** of the LORD called out to him
	24:7	he will send his **a** before you
	31:11	The **a** of God said to me
	48:16	the **A** who has delivered me
Ex	3:2	the **a** of the LORD appeared to him
	14:19	Then the **a** of God,
	23:20	an **a** ahead of you to guard you along
	32:34	and my **a** will go before you.
	33:2	an **a** before you and drive out
Nu	20:16	an **a** and brought us out of Egypt.
	22:22	the **a** of the LORD stood in the road
Jdg	2:1	The **a** of the LORD went up
	6:12	**a** of the LORD appeared to Gideon,
	6:22	I have seen the **a** of the LORD face
	13:3	The **a** of the LORD appeared to her
1Sa	29:9	as pleasing in my eyes as an **a**
2Sa	14:17	like an **a** of God in discerning good
	19:27	My lord the king is like an **a** of God;
	24:16	When the **a** stretched out his hand
1Ki	13:18	And an **a** said to me by the word of
	19:7	The **a** of the LORD came back
2Ki	1:3	the **a** of the LORD said to Elijah
	19:35	the **a** of the LORD went out and put
Job	33:23	"Yet if there is an **a** on his side as
Ps	34:7	The **a** of the LORD encamps
Da	3:28	who has sent his **a** and rescued
	6:22	My God sent his **a**,
Hos	12:4	struggled with the **a** and overcame
Zec	1:11	they reported to the **a** of the LORD
	3:1	the high priest standing before the **a**
Mt	1:20	an **a** of the Lord appeared to him
	2:13	an **a** of the Lord appeared to Joseph
	28:2	for an **a** of the Lord came down
Lk	1:11	an **a** of the Lord appeared to him,
	1:26	God sent the **a** Gabriel to Nazareth,
	2:9	An **a** of the Lord appeared to them,
	22:43	An **a** from heaven appeared to him
Jn	12:29	an **a** had spoken to him.
Ac	5:19	an **a** of the Lord opened the doors of
	6:15	like the face of an **a**.
	7:30	an **a** appeared to Moses in the flames
	8:26	Now an **a** of the Lord said to Philip,
	10:3	He distinctly saw an **a** of God,
	12:7	Suddenly an **a** of the Lord appeared
	27:23	an **a** of the God whose I am
1Co	10:10	and were killed by the destroying **a**.
2Co	11:14	masquerades as an **a** of light.
Gal	1:8	an **a** from heaven should preach
	4:14	you welcomed me as if I were an **a**
Rev	1:1	by sending his **a** to his servant John,
	2:1	the **a** of the church in Ephesus write:
	5:2	And I saw a mighty **a** proclaiming in
	7:2	Then I saw another **a** coming up
	8:3	Another **a**, who had a golden censer,
	9:11	as king over them the **a** of the Abyss,
	14:6	I saw another **a** flying in midair,
	16:2	The first **a** went and poured
	17:3	the **a** carried me away in the Spirit
	19:17	And I saw an **a** standing in the sun,

ANGEL OF GOD (Ge 21:11; 31:11; Ex 14:19; Jdg 6:20; 13:6, 9; 1Sa 29:9; 2Sa 14:17, 20; 19:27; Ac 10:3; Gal 4:14).

ANGEL OF THE LORD In the OT we often find the phrase "the angel of the LORD." In almost every case, this messenger is regarded as deity and yet is distinguished from God (Ge 16:7 – 14; 22:11 – 18; 31:11, 13; Ex 3:2 – 5; Nu 22:22 – 35; Jdg 6:11 – 23; 13:2 – 25; 1Ki 19:5 – 7; 1Ch 21:15 – 17). These references show that the Angel is the Lord himself adopting a visible form (and therefore a human appearance) for the sake of speaking with people (e.g., Jdg 13:6, 10, 21). While himself holy as God is holy (e.g., Ex 3:2 – 5), the Angel expresses the Holy One's condescension to walk among sinners (32:34; 33:3). He is also the executant of divine wrath (e.g., 2Sa 24:16; 2Ki 19:35). In all these ways, as we can see from the NT perspective, the Angel is part of the OT preparation for the Lord Jesus Christ.

ANGER [678, 2405, 2779, 3019, 4087, 4088, 4089, 5757, 6301, 6939, 7287, 7861, 7863, 7911, 7912, 8074, 8120, 2596, 3973, 3974]. The English rendering of at least ten biblical words, of which the most common is Heb. 'aph, which could also mean "snorting." The OT condemns anger because it encourages folly and evil (Ps 37:8; Pr 12:16; 14:29; 27:3; Ecc 7:9) and because vengeance belongs to God (Dt 32:35). Elsewhere it calls for restraint from those confronted by anger (Pr 16:14; Ecc 10:4). In the NT anger is among those emotions that provoke God's wrath (Eph 5:6) and is regarded as alien to godliness (Gal 5:20; 1Ti 2:8; Jas 1:19 – 20). There is righteous anger, however, as when Jesus condemned the misuse of the temple (Jn 2:12 – 17), the corruption of children (Mk 9:42), and lack of compassion (3:5).

General References to:
Brings its own punishment (Job 5:2; Pr 19:19; 25:28). Grievous words stir up (Jdg 12:4; 2Sa 19:43; Pr 15:1). Should not lead into sin (Ps 37:8; Eph 4:26). In prayer be free from (1Ti 2:8). May be averted by wisdom (Pr 29:8). Pacified by meekness (Pr 15:1; Ecc 10:4). Children should not be provoked to (Eph 6:4; Col 3:21). Be slow to (Pr 15:18; 16:32; 19:11; Tit 1:7; Jas 1:19). Avoid those given to (Ge 49:6; Pr 22:24).

Connected with:
Pride (Pr 21:24). Cruelty (Ge 49:7; Pr 27:3 – 4). Clamor and evil speaking (Eph 4:31). Malice and blasphemy (Col 3:8). Strife and contention (Pr 21:19; 29:22; 30:33).

Justifiable, Exemplified by:
Jacob (Ge 31:36); Moses (Ex 11:8; 32:19; Lev 10:16; Nu 16:15); Nehemiah (Ne 5:6; 13:17, 25); Jesus (Mk 3:5).

Sinful, Exemplified by:
Cain (Ge 4:5 – 6); Esau (Ge 27:45); Simeon and Levi (Ge 49:5 – 7); Moses (Nu 20:10 – 11); Balaam (Nu 22:27); Saul (1Sa 20:30); Ahab (1Ki 21:4); Naaman (2Ki 5:11); Asa (2Ch 16:10); Uzziah (2Ch 26:19); Haman (Est 3:5); Nebuchadnezzar (Da 3:13); Jonah (Jnh 4:4); Herod (Mt 2:16); Jews (Lk 4:28); high priest (Ac 5:17; 7:54).

Ex	4:14	Then the LORD's **a** burned
	15:7	You unleashed your burning **a**;
	22:24	My **a** will be aroused,
	32:10	that my **a** may burn against them and
	32:11	"why should your **a** burn
	32:12	Turn from your fierce **a**;
	32:19	his **a** burned and he threw
	34:6	gracious God, slow to **a**
Lev	26:28	in my **a** I will be hostile toward you,
Nu	11:1	he heard them his **a** was aroused.
	11:33	the **a** of the LORD burned against
	12:9	The **a** of the LORD burned
	14:18	'The LORD is slow to **a**,
	25:11	has turned my **a** away from
	32:10	The LORD's **a** was aroused
Dt	6:15	is a jealous God and his **a** will burn
	9:19	the **a** and wrath of the LORD,
	29:28	In furious **a** and in great wrath
Jos	7:1	LORD's **a** burned against Israel.
	7:26	the LORD turned from his fierce **a**.
Jdg	2:12	They provoked the LORD to **a**
	14:19	Burning with **a**,
1Sa	20:30	Saul's **a** flared up at Jonathan
2Sa	12:5	David burned with **a** against the man
1Ki	16:13	to **a** by their worthless idols.
2Ki	22:13	the LORD's **a** that burns against us
	24:20	the LORD's **a** that all this happened
Ne	9:17	slow to **a** and abounding in love.
Ps	4:4	In your **a** do not sin;
	30:5	For his **a** lasts only a moment,
	37:8	Refrain from **a** and turn from wrath;
	78:38	after time he restrained his **a** and did
	86:15	gracious God, slow to **a**

	90:7	We are consumed by your **a**
	103:8	slow to **a**, abounding in love.
	103:9	nor will he harbor his **a** forever;
	145:8	slow to **a** and rich in love.
Pr	15:1	but a harsh word stirs up **a**.
	29:8	but wise men turn away **a**.
	29:11	A fool gives full vent to his **a**,
	30:33	so stirring up **a** produces strife."
Ecc	7:9	for **a** resides in the lap of fools.
Isa	63:6	I trampled the nations in my **a**;
Da	9:16	turn away your **a** and your wrath
Joel	2:13	slow to **a** and abounding in love,
Jnh	3:9	compassion turn from his fierce **a**
	4:2	slow to **a** and abounding in love,
Na	1:3	The LORD is slow to **a** and great
Mk	3:5	He looked around at them in **a** and,
2Co	12:20	jealousy, outbursts of **a**, factions,
Eph	4:26	"In your **a** do not sin":
Col	3:8	of all such things as these: **a**,
Jas	1:20	for man's **a** does not bring about

ANGER OF GOD

Is turned away: by Christ (Lk 2:11, 14; Ro 5:9; 2Co 5:18 – 19; Eph 2:14, 17; Col 1:20; 1Th 1:10); from those who believe (Jn 3:14 – 18; Ro 3:25; 5:1); upon confession of sin and repentance (Job 33:27 – 28; Ps 106:43 – 45; Jer 3:12 – 13; 18:7 – 8; 31:18 – 20; Joel 2:12 – 14; Lk 15:18 – 20). Is slow (Ps 103:8; Isa 48:9; Jnh 4:2; Na 1:3); righteous (Ps 58:10 – 11; La 1:18; Ro 2:6, 8; 3:5 – 6; Rev 16:6 – 7). Justice of, not to be questioned (Ro 9:18, 20, 22). Manifested: in terrors (Ex 14:24; Ps 76:6 – 8; Jer 10:10; La 2:20 – 22); in judgments and afflictions (Job 21:17; Pss 78:49 – 51; 90:7; Isa 9:19; Jer 7:20; Eze 7:19; Heb 3:17). Cannot be resisted (Job 9:13; 14:13; Ps 76:7; Na 1:6). Aggravated by continual provocation (Nu 32:14). Specially reserved for the day of wrath (Zep 1:14 – 18; Mt 25:41; Ro 2:5, 8; 2Th 1:8; Rev 6:17; 11:18; 19:15). Folly of provoking (Jer 7:19; 1Co 10:22). To be dreaded (Pss 2:12; 76:7; 90:11; Mt 10:28); deprecated (Ex 32:11; Pss 6:1; 38:1; 74:1 – 2; Isa 64:9); borne with submission (2Sa 24:17; La 3:39, 43;

Mic 7:9). Removal of, should be prayed for (Pss 39:10; 79:5; 80:4; Da 9:16; Hab 3:2). Tempered with mercy to believers (Ps 30:5; Isa 26:20; 54:8; 57:15 – 16; Jer 30:11; Mic 7:11). Should lead to repentance (Isa 42:24 – 25; Jer 4:8).

Against:

The wicked (Pss 7:11; 21:8 – 9; Isa 3:8; 13:9; Na 1:2 – 3; Ro 1:18; 2:8; Eph 5:6; Col 3:6). Those who forsake him (Ezr 8:22; Isa 1:4). Unbelief (Ps 78:21 – 22; Jn 3:36; Heb 3:18 – 19). Impenitence (Ps 7:12; Pr 1:30 – 31; Isa 9:13 – 14; Ro 2:5). Apostasy (Heb 10:26 – 27). Idolatry (Dt 29:20, 27 – 28; 32:19 – 20, 22; Jos 23:16; 2Ki 22:17; Ps 78:58 – 59; Jer 44:3). Sin, in believers (Pss 89:30 – 32; 90:7 – 9; 99:8; 102:9 – 10; Isa 47:6). Those who oppose the gospel (Ps 2:2 – 3, 5; 1Th 2:16).

ANIMALS [H989, H2651, H3274, H7366, H8802, H10263, G4465, G5488].

Creation of (Ge 1:24 – 25; 2:19; Jer 27:5). Food of (Ge 1:30). Named (Ge 2:20). Under the curse (Ge 3:14; 6:7, 17). Two of every kind preserved in the ark (Ge 6:19 – 20; 7:2, 9, 14 – 15; 8:19). Seven clean of every kind preserved in the ark (Ge 7:2 – 3). Clean and unclean (Ge 7:2, 8; 8:20; Lev 7:21; 11; 20:25; Dt 14:3 – 20; Ac 10:11 – 15; 1Ti 4:3 – 5). Ordained as food for man (Ge 9:2 – 3; Lev 11:3, 9, 21 – 22; Dt 14:4 – 6, 9, 11, 20). Suffered the plagues of Egypt (Ex 8:17; 9:9 – 10, 19; 11:5). Perish at death (Ecc 3:21). Suffer under divine judgments sent upon humankind (Jer 7:20; 14:4; 21:6; Eze 14:13, 17, 19 – 21; Joel 1:18 – 20). Possessed by demons (Mt 8:31 – 32; Mk 5:13; Lk 8:33).

In Relation to God:

God's care of (Ge 9:9 – 10; Dt 25:4; Job 38:41; Pss 36:6; 104:11, 21; 145:15 – 16; 147:9; Jn 4:11; Mt 6:26; 10:29; Lk 12:6, 24; 1Co 9:9). Instruments of God's will (Ex 8; 10:4 – 15, 19; Nu 21:6; 22:28; Jos 24:12; Joel 1:4). Sent in judgment (Lev 26:22; Nu 21:6 – 7; Dt 8:15; Eze 5:17; 14:15; Rev 6:8). God's ownership of (Ps 50:10 – 12). God's control of (Ps 91:13; Lk 10:19).

Nature of:

(Job 41; Ps 32:9; Jas 3:7). Habits of (Job 12:7 – 8; 37:8; 39; 40:20 – 21; Ps 104:20 – 25; Isa 13:21 – 22; 34:14). Instincts of (Dt 32:11; Job 35:11; 39; 40:15 – 24; Ps 104:11 – 30; Pr 6:5 – 8; 30:25 – 28; Isa 1:3; Jer 2:24; 8:7; La 4:3; Mt 24:28). Breeding of (Ge 30:35 – 43; 31:8 – 9). Abodes of (Job 24:5; 37:8; 39:5 – 10, 27 – 29; Ps 104:20, 22, 25; Isa 34:14 – 15; Jer 2:24; 50:39; Mk 1:13).

Cruelty to:

Balaam in beating his donkey (Nu 22:22 – 33). In hamstringing horses (2Sa 8:4; 1Ch 18:4).

Kindness to:

By the righteous (Pr 12:10). In not muzzling an ox while threshing (Dt 25:4; 1Ti 5:18). In relieving the overburdened (Ex 23:5; Dt 22:4). In rescuing from pits (Mt 12:11; Lk 13:15; 14:5). In feeding (Ge 24:32; 43:24; Jdg 19:21). Instances of: Jacob in making shelters for his cattle (Ge 33:17); people of Gerar in providing tents for cattle (2Ch 14:15).

Laws Concerning:

Sabbath rest for (Ex 20:10; Dt 5:14). Treatment of vicious (Ex 21:28 – 32, 35 – 36). Penalty for injury of (Ex 21:33 – 34). Hybridizing of, forbidden (Lev 19:19). Working of (Dt 22:10). Mother birds and their young (Dt 22:6 – 7).

ANNA [483] (ăn'a, Gr. form of *Hannah, grace*). Daughter of Phanuel of the tribe of Asher. Widowed after seven years of marriage, she became a prophetess. At the age of eighty-four, when the infant Jesus was brought into the temple to be dedicated, she recognized and proclaimed him as the Messiah (Lk 2:36 – 38).

ANNAS [483, 484] (ăn'as, Gr. for Hanan, contraction for Hananiah, *merciful, gracious*; called "Ananos" by Josephus). In his thirty-seventh year (c. AD 6), he was appointed high priest by Quirinius, governor of Syria. He was deposed in c. AD 15 by Valerius Gratus, governor of Judea. His five sons became high priests, and he was father-in-law of Caiaphas (Jn 18:13). He and Caiaphas are described as the high priests when John the Baptist began his public ministry (Lk 3:2), perhaps because as family head Annas was the most influential priest and still bore the title. Therefore when Jesus was arrested, he was led first to Annas (Jn 18:13) and only later was sent bound to Caiaphas (18:24). Similarly, Annas is called the high priest in Ac 4:6 when Peter and John were arrested, although Caiaphas was probably the actual high priest.

ANNIHILATION The belief that there is no existence after death or that there is no existence for the wicked after death. Some texts seem to imply death as final (Job 14:12, 18 – 22; Pss 6:5; 88:10; Isa 26:14). The resurrection is the hope of all believers (Ps 16:9 – 11; Isa 53:11; Da 12:1 – 3). In the teaching of Jesus (Mt 22:23 – 32; Lk 14:14; Jn 11:24 – 26) and of the apostles (Ac 4:1 – 4, 33; 23:6 – 8; 24:10 – 21; 1Co 15), eternal punishment of the wicked is also clearly taught (Da 12:2; Mt 18:8 – 9; Jn 3:36; 2Th 1:9; Rev 14:11; 20:4 – 15).

ANNUAL FEASTS All but Purim and Dedication were instituted by Moses.

General References to:

Designated as: holy convocations (Lev 23:4); solemn feasts (Nu 15:3; 2Ch 8:13; La 2:6; Eze 46:9); set feasts (Nu 29:39; Ezr 3:5) appointed feasts (Isa 1:14). First and last days Sabbatic (Lev 23:39 – 40; Nu 28:18 – 25; 29:12, 35; Ne 8:1 – 18). Kept with rejoicing (Lev 23:40; Dt 16:11 – 14; 2Ch 30:21 – 26; Ezr 6:22; Ne 8:9 – 12, 17; Ps 122:4; Isa 30:29; Zec 8:19). Divine protection given during (Ex 34:24). All males required to attend (Ex 23:17; 34:23; Dt 16:16; Eze 36:38; Lk 2:41 – 42; Jn 4:45; 7). Aliens permitted to attend (Jn 12:20; Ac 2:1 – 11). Attended by women (1Sa 1:3, 9; Lk 2:41).

Observed by:

Jesus (Mt 26:17 – 20; Lk 2:41 – 42; 22:15; Jn 2:13, 23; 5:1; 7:10; 10:22). Paul (Ac 20:6, 16; 24:11, 17).

New Moon:

(Nu 10:10; 28:11 – 15; 1Ch 23:31; 2Ch 31:3; Ezr 3:5). Buying and selling at time of, suspended (Am 8:5).

Passover:

Institution of (Ex 12:3 – 49; 23:15 – 18; 34:18; Lev 23:4 – 8; Nu 9:2 – 5, 13 – 14; 28:16 – 25; Dt 16:1 – 8, 16; Ps 81:3, 5). Design of (Ex 12:21 – 28). Special, for those who were unclean or on journey, to be held in second month (Nu 9:6 – 12; 2Ch 30:2 – 4). Lamb killed by Levites for those ceremonially unclean (2Ch 30:17; 35:3 – 11; Ezr 6:20). Strangers authorized to celebrate (Ex 12:48 – 49; Nu 9:14). Observed at place designated by God (Dt 16:5 – 7). With unleavened bread (Ex 12:8, 15 – 20; 13:3, 6; 23:15; Lev 23:6; Nu 9:11; 28:17; Dt 16:3 – 4; Mk 14:12; Lk 22:7; Ac 12:3; 1Co 5:8). Penalty for neglecting to observe (Nu 9:13). Reinstituted by Ezekiel (Eze 45:21 – 24). Observation of, renewed: by Israelites on entering Canaan (Jos 5:10 – 11); by Hezekiah (2Ch 30:1); by Josiah (2Ki 23:22 – 23; 2Ch 35:1, 18); after return from captivity (Ezr 6:19 – 20); by Jesus (Mt 26:17 – 20; Lk 22:15; Jn 2:13, 23; 13). Jesus, when twelve years old, in temple at time of (Lk 2:41 – 50). Jesus crucified at time of (Mt 26:2; Mk 14:1 – 2; Jn 18:28). Lord's Supper ordained at (Mt 26:26 – 28; Mk 14:12 – 25; Lk 22:7 – 20). Lamb of, a type of Christ (1Co 5:7). Prisoners released at, by Romans (Mt 27:15; Mk 15:6; Lk 23:16 – 17; Jn 18:39). Peter imprisoned at time of (Ac 12:3). Christ called our Passover lamb (1Co 5:7; see also Jn 1:36; Rev 5:6 – 14).

Pentecost:

Called: Feast of Weeks (Ex 34:22; Dt 16:10); Feast of Harvest (Ex 23:16); Day of Firstfruits (Nu 28:26). Day of (Ac 2:1; 20:16; 1Co 16:8). Institution of (Ex 23:16; 34:22; Lev 23:15 – 21; Nu 28:26 – 31; Dt 16:9 – 12, 16). Holy Spirit given to apostles on day of (Ac 2).

Purim:

Instituted by Esther and Mordecai to commemorate deliverance of Jews from Haman's plot (Est 9:20 – 32).

Tabernacles:

Also called Feast of Ingathering. Institution of (Ex 23:16; 34:22; Lev 23:34 – 43; Nu 29:12 – 40; Dt 16:13 – 16). Design of (Lev 23:42 – 43). Law read in connection with, every seventh year (Dt 31:10 – 12; Ne 8:18). Observance of: after captivity (Ezr 3:4; Ne 8:14 – 18); neglected (Ne 8:17); by Jesus (Jn 7:2, 14). Penalty for not observing (Zec 14:16 – 19). Jeroboam's institution of idolatrous feast parallel to (1Ki 12:32 – 33).

Trumpets:

When and how observed (Lev 23:24 – 25; Nu 29:1 – 6). Celebrated after captivity with joy (Ne 8:2, 9 – 12).

Dedication or Hanukkah:

Instituted in intertestamental era to commemorate dedication of temple by Judas Maccabeus (1Mc 4:59). Observed by Jesus (Jn 10:22 – 39).

ANNUNCIATION (from Lat. *annuntiatio, an announcement*). The word itself is not found in Scripture but is the name given to the announcement made by the angel Gabriel to Mary that she would conceive and give birth to a son to be called Jesus (Lk 1:26 – 38). Mary, a virgin, was betrothed but not yet married to Joseph. They lived in Nazareth, a town of Galilee. In his message Gabriel assured the frightened Mary that she was highly favored and that the Lord was with her. The young woman was overcome with surprise and fear, not only by the presence of the angel, but also by his message. Gabriel, however, assured her that she had no need to fear. God had chosen her to be the mother of a unique boy: "He will be great and will be called the Son of the Most High" (1:32). Her son would be God's Son, and like David, he would reign over the people of God; yet unlike David's kingdom, his would be an everlasting kingdom. When Mary asked how this could occur since she was not yet married, Gabriel explained that she would conceive through the direct agency of the Holy Spirit. Like her relative Elizabeth (who had conceived in her old age and was carrying John the Baptist), she would know the power of God in her life. Overwhelmed by this amazing message, Mary submitted to the will of the Lord, and the angel left her.

The word is used also of the festival held on March 25 (nine months before Chrismas Day) to celebrate the visit of Gabriel to the Virgin Mary.

ANOINT To apply oil to a person or thing, a practice common in the East. Anointing was of three kinds: ordinary, sacred, and medical. Ordinary anointing with scented oils was a common operation (Ru 3:3; Ps 104:15; Pr 27:9). It was discontinued during a time of mourning (2Sa 14:2; Da 10:3; Mt 6:17). Guests were anointed as a mark of respect (Ps 23:5; Lk 7:46). The dead were prepared for burial by anointing (Mk 14:8; 16:1). The leather of shields was rubbed with oil to keep it from cracking (Isa 21:5), but this could be called also a sacred anointing—i.e., consecration to the war in the name of whatever god was invoked to bless the battle.

The purpose of sacred anointing was to dedicate the thing or person to God. Jacob anointed the stone he had used for a pillow at Bethel (Ge 28:18). The tabernacle and its furniture were anointed (Ex 30:22–29). Prophets (1Ki 19:16; 1Ch 16:22), priests (Ex 28:41; 29:7; Lev 8:12, 30), and kings (Saul—1Sa 9:16; 10:1; David—1Sa 16:1, 12–13; 2Sa 2:7; Solomon—1Ki 1:34; Jehu—1Ki 19:16) were anointed, the oil symbolizing the Holy Spirit. They were thus set apart and empowered for a particular work in the service of God. "The Lord's anointed" was the common term for a theocratic king (1Sa 12:3; La 4:20).

Messiah, from the Hebrew word *mashach*, and Christ, from the Greek *chrein*, mean "the anointed one." The word is twice used of the coming Redeemer in the OT (Ps 2:2; Da 9:25–26). Jesus was anointed with the Holy Spirit at his baptism (Jn 1:32–33), marking him as the Messiah of the OT (Lk 4:18, 21; Ac 9:22; 17:2–3; 18:5, 28). His dis-

ciples, through union with him, are anointed with the Holy Spirit too (2Co 1:21; 1Jn 2:20).

Medical anointing, not necessarily with oil, was customary for the sick and wounded (Isa 1:6; Lk 10:34). Mark 6:13 and Jas 5:14 speak of the use of anointing oil by disciples of Jesus.

Ex	30:26	Then use it to **a** the Tent of Meeting,
	30:30	"**A** Aaron and his sons
Jdg	9:15	'If you really want to **a** me king
1Sa	9:16	**A** him leader over my people Israel;
	15:1	to **a** you king over his people Israel;
1Ki	1:34	and Nathan the prophet **a** him king
	19:16	**a** Elisha son of Shaphat
2Ki	9:3	the Lord says: I **a** you king
Ps	23:5	You **a** my head with oil;
Ecc	9:8	and always **a** your head with oil.
Da	9:24	and prophecy and to **a** the most holy.
Mk	16:1	that they might go to **a** Jesus' body
Jas	5:14	to pray over him and **a** him with oil

ANOINTED [ANOINT]

Ge	31:13	where you **a** a pillar and
Lev	7:36	On the day they were **a**,
1Sa	2:10	and exalt the horn of his **a**."
	10:1	"Has not the Lord **a** you leader
	16:13	took the horn of oil and **a** him
	24:6	for he is the **a** of the Lord."
2Sa	1:14	to destroy the Lord's **a**?"
	2:4	and there they **a** David king over
	5:3	and they **a** David king over Israel
	19:21	He cursed the Lord's **a**."
1Ki	1:39	from the sacred tent and **a** Solomon.
1Ch	16:22	"Do not touch my **a** ones;
2Ch	6:42	do not reject your **a** one.
Ps	2:2	the Lord and against his **A** One.
	105:15	"Do not touch my **a** ones;
Isa	61:1	because the Lord has **a** me
Da	9:26	the **A** One will be cut off
Hab	3:13	to save your **a** one.
Zec	4:14	the two who are **a** to serve the Lord
Lk	4:18	because he has **a** me

Ac	4:26	the Lord and against his **A** One.'
	10:38	how God **a** Jesus of Nazareth with
2Co	1:21	He **a** us,

ANOINTED ONE (1Sa 2:35; 2Ch 6:42; Pss 2:2; 28:8; 84:9; 89:38, 51; 132:10, 17; Da 9:25, 26; Hab 3:13; Ac 4:26).

ANOINTING [H5417, H5418, H5431, G230, G5987, G5984].

Of: the body (Dt 28:40; Ru 3:3; Est 2:12; Pss 92:10; 104:15; 141:5; Pr 27:9, 16; Ecc 9:8; SS 1:3; 4:10; Isa 57:9; Am 6:6; Mic 6:15); guests (2Ch 28:15; Lk 7:46); the sick (Isa 1:6; Mk 6:13; Lk 10:34; Jas 5:14; Rev 3:18); the dead (Mt 26:12; Mk 14:8; 16:1; Lk 23:56); Jesus, as a token of love (Lk 7:37 – 38, 46; Jn 11:2; 12:3). Omitted in mourning (2Sa 12:20; 14:2; Isa 61:3; Da 10:3). God preserves those who receive (Pss 18:50; 20:6; 89:20 – 23). Believers receive (Isa 61:3; 1Jn 2:20).

In Consecration:
Of high priests (Ex 29:7, 29; 40:13; Lev 6:20; 8:12; 16:32; Nu 35:25; Ps 133:2). Of priests (Ex 28:41; 30:30; 40:15; Lev 4:3; 8:30; Nu 3:3). Of kings (Jdg 9:8, 15); Saul (1Sa 9:16; 10:1; 15:1); David (1Sa 16:3, 12 – 13; 2Sa 2:4; 5:3; 12:7; 9:21; 1Ch 11:3); Solomon (1Ki 1:39; 1Ch 29:22); Jehu (1Ki 19:16; 2Ki 9:1 – 3, 6, 12); Hazael (1Ki 19:15); Joash (2Ki 11:12; 2Ch 23:11); Jehoahaz (2Ki 23:30); Cyrus (Isa 45:1). Of prophets (1Ki 19:16). Of the tabernacle (Ex 30:26; 40:9; Lev 8:10; Nu 7:1); altars of (Ex 30:26 – 28; 40:10; Lev 8:11; Nu 7:1); vessels of (Ex 30:27 – 28; 40:9 – 10; Lev 8:10 – 11; Nu 7:1). Jacob's pillar at Bethel (Ge 28:18; 31:13; 35:14).

Figurative:
Of Christ's kingly and priestly office (Pss 45:7; 89:20; Isa 61:1; Da 9:24; Lk 4:18; Ac 4:27; 10:38; Heb 1:9). Of spiritual gifts (2Co 1:21; 1Jn 2:20, 27). Of God's choice and enabling of leaders (Ex 40:13 – 15; Lev 8:12; 1Sa 16:13; 1Ki 19:16). Symbolic of Jesus' death (Mt 26:7 – 12; Jn 12:3 – 7).

Ex	30:25	It will be the sacred **a** oil.
Lev	8:12	of the **a** oil on Aaron's head
1Ch	29:22	**a** him before the LORD to be ruler
Ps	45:7	above your companions by **a** you
Heb	1:9	above your companions by **a** you
1Jn	2:20	you have an **a** from the Holy One,
	2:27	the **a** you received from him remains
	2:27	as his **a** teaches you about all things and as the **a** is real,

ANOINTING OIL Formula of, given by Moses (Ex 30:22 – 25, 31 – 33).

ANTHROPOMORPHISMS Figures of speech that attribute human anatomy, acts, and affections to God.

Anatomy:
Arm (Ps 89:13); body or form (Nu 11:25); ear (Ps 34:15); eye (2Ch 16:9; Isa 1:15); mouth (Ps 33:6); voice (Eze 1:24, 28); wings (Pss 36:7; 57:1). See terms for body parts, e.g., Arm, Hand.

Intellectual Facilities:
Knowing (Ge 18:17 – 19); remembering (Ge 9:16; 19:29; Ex 2:24; Isa 43:26; 63:11); understanding (Ps 147:5); reason (Isa 1:18); will (Ro 9:19).

Actions:
Breathing (Ps 33:6); grasping with hand (Ps 35:2); hearing (Ps 94:9); laughing (Pss 2:4; 37:13; 59:8; Pr 1:26); not tiring (Isa 40:28); resting (Ge 2:2 – 3, 19; Ex 20:11; 31:17; Dt 5:14; Heb 4:4, 10); seeing (Ge 18:21; Ex 14:24; Ps 94:9); sleeping (Pss 44:23; 78:65; 121:4); speaking (Ge 18:33; Nu 11:25; Ps 33:6); standing (Ps 35:2); walking (Ge 3:8; Lev 26:12; Dt 23:14; Job 22:14; Hab 3:15).

Affections and Emotions:
Amazement (Isa 59:16; 63:5; Mk 6:6); grief (Ge 6:6; Jdg 10:16; Ps 95:10; Heb 3:10, 17); jealousy (Ex 20:5; 34:13 – 14; Nu 25:11; Dt 29:20; 32:16, 21; 1Ki 14:22; Pss 78:58; 79:5; Isa 30:1 – 2; 31:1, 3; Eze 16:42; 23:25; 36:5 – 6; 38:19; Zep 1:18; 3:8; Zec 1:14; 8:2; 1Co 10:22); swearing an oath (Isa 62:8; Heb 6:16 – 17; 7:21, 28).

ANTICHRIST [532] (Gr. *antichristos*, *against* or *instead of Christ*; *substitute Christ*). The word *antichrist* may mean either an enemy of Christ or one who usurps Christ's name and rights. The word is found in only four verses of Scripture (1Jn 2:18, 22; 4:3; 2Jn 7), but the idea conveyed by the word appears throughout Scripture. It is evident from the way John and Paul refer to the Antichrist that they took for granted a tradition well known at the time (2Th 2:6, "you know"; 1Jn 4:3, "you have heard").

The OT gives evidence of a belief in a hostile person or power who in the end time will bring an attack against God's people — an attack that will be crushed by the Lord or his Messiah. Psalm 2 gives a picture of the rebellion of the world kingdoms "against the LORD and against his Anointed One." The same sort of contest is described in Eze 38 – 39 and Zec 12 – 14. The book of Daniel contains vivid descriptions of the Antichrist that find their echo in the writings of the apostles (cf. 2Th 2:4, w Da 11:36 – 37; and cf. Rev 13:1 – 8, w Da 7:8, 20 – 21; 8:24; 11:28, 30).

In his eschatological discourse Christ warns against the "false Christs" and "false prophets" who would lead astray, if possible, even the elect (Mt 24:24; Mk 13:22). In Mt 24:15 he refers to "the abomination that causes desolation" spoken of by Daniel.

In 2Th 2:1 – 12 Paul gives us a very full description of the working of the Antichrist, under the name of "the man of lawlessness," in which he draws on the language and imagery of the OT. The Thessalonian Christians seem to have been under the erroneous impression that the "day of the Lord" was at hand, and Paul told them that before that day could come, two things would have to take place: an apostasy and the revelation of the man of lawlessness, the son of perdition. The "secret power of lawlessness" (2:7) is already at work, he said, but is held in check by some restraining person or power. With the removal of this restraining force, the man of lawlessness is revealed. He will oppose and exalt himself above God and will actually sit in the temple of God and claim to be God. With satanic power he will perform signs and deceitful wonders, bringing great deception to people who reject God's truth. In spite of his extraordinary power, however, "the Lord Jesus will overthrow [him] with the breath of his mouth" (2:8).

In 1Jn 2:18 John shows that the coming of the Antichrist was an event generally expected by the church. It is apparent, however, that he is more concerned about directing the attention of Christians to anti-Christian forces already at work ("Even now many antichrists have come"). He says that teachers of erroneous views of the person of Christ (evidently Gnostic and Ebionite) are antichrists (1Jn 2:22; 4:3; 2Jn 7).

In the book of Revelation, the beast of Rev 17:8 recalls the horned beast of Da 7 – 8. He claims and is accorded divine homage and makes war on God's people. For a period of three and one-half years he rules over the earth and is finally destroyed by the Lord in a great battle. With his defeat the contest of good and evil comes to its final decision.

1Jn	2:18	heard that the **a** is coming.
	2:22	Such a man is the **a**
	4:3	This is the spirit of the **a**,
2Jn	1:7	the deceiver and the **a**.

ANTIOCH [G522, G523] (ăn′tĭ·ŏk, Gr. *Antiocheia*).

1. Antioch in Syria, the capital of Syria, built in 301 BC by Seleucus Nicator, founder of the Seleucid Empire, which had been the Asiatic part of the vast empire of Alexander the Great. It was the greatest of sixteen Antiochs he founded in honor of his father Antiochus. It was a great commercial center. Caravan roads converged on it from the east, and its situation on the Orontes River, fifteen navigable miles (twenty-five km.) from the Mediterranean, made it readily available to ships as well. The city was set in a broad and fertile valley, shielded by majestic snow-covered mountains, and was called "Antioch the Beautiful and the Golden." In 65 the Romans took the city and made it the capital of the Roman province of Syria. Seleucid kings and early Roman emperors extended and adorned the city until it became the third largest in the Roman Empire (after Rome and Alexandria), with a population in the first century AD of about 500,000. A

cosmopolitan city from its foundation, its inhabitants included many Jews, who were given privileges similar to those of the Greeks. Its citizens were a vigorous and aggressive race, famous for their commercial aptitude, licentiousness, and biting wit.

Antioch has an important place in the early history of Christianity. One of the original deacons of the apostolic church was Nicolas, a proselyte of Antioch (Ac 6:5). The first Gentile church, the mother of all the others, was founded there. Many fugitive Christians, scattered at the death of Stephen, went to Antioch and inaugurated a new era by preaching not only to the Hellenist Jews but to "Greeks also" (11:20). The Jerusalem church sent Barnabas to assist in the work; after laboring there for a while, Barnabas summoned Paul from Tarsus to assist him. After they had worked there for a year, they were sent with relief to the famine-stricken saints in Jerusalem. The disciples were called Christians first in Antioch (11:19 – 26), a designation probably coming from the populace, who were well known for their invention of nicknames. The church at Antioch sent Paul and his companions out on his three missionary journeys (13:1ff.; 15:36ff.; 18:23), and he reported to it on his return from the first two (14:26ff.; 18:22). It submitted the question of the circumcision of Gentile converts to a council at Jerusalem (Ac 15), winning for the church at large a great victory over Judean narrowness.

Antioch gave rise to a school of thought distinguished by literal interpretation of the Scriptures. Between AD 252 and 380, ten church councils were held there. The city was taken and destroyed in 538 by the Persians, rebuilt by the Roman emperor Justinian shortly afterward, and in 635 was taken by the Muslims, by whom it has since, except for a brief period, been retained. The place, now called Antakiyeh, is unimportant today, with a population of about 42,000.

In 1916 an announcement was made that Arabs in or near Antioch had found what has come to be known as "the Chalice of Antioch." It is a plain silver cup surrounded by an outer shell decorated with vines and the figures of Christ and the apostles and is set on a solid silver base. The cup was vigorously claimed to be the Holy Grail, used by Jesus at the Last Supper, the figures on the shell interpreted as first-century portraits. But the authenticity of the chalice has been called into question. Serious scholars have virtually proved that at most the cup is a piece of early Christian silver from the fourth or fifth century and had nothing to do with the Last Supper in Jerusalem.

2. Antioch near Pisidia, a town in southern Asia Minor, founded also by Seleucus Nicator, and named in honor of his father Antiochus. It was situated in Phrygia, not far from Pisidia, and was therefore called Antioch toward Pisidia and Pisidian Antioch to distinguish it from the other cities of the same name. In 25 BC it became a part of the Roman province of Galatia. Soon after, it was made the capital of southern Galatia, and a Roman colony. The Romans made it a strong garrison center to hold down the surrounding wild tribes. Paul and Barnabas preached in the synagogue there on their first missionary journey; but the Jews, jealous of the many new Gentile converts, drove the missionaries from the city to Iconium and followed them even to Lystra (Ac 13:14 – 14:19). On Paul's return journey he revisited Antioch to establish the disciples and probably returned on his second (16:6) and third journeys as well (18:23).

Ac	11:26	were called Christians first at **A**.
	13:1	the church at **A** there were prophets
Gal	2:11	When Peter came to **A**,

ANTIOCHUS (ăn-tī′ŏ́kŭs, Gr. *withstander* or *opposer*). A favorite name of the Seleucid kings of Syria, referred to as the kings of the North in Da 11.

1. Antiochus II Theos (286 – 246 BC) married Berenice, daughter of Ptolemy II, the "king of the South" (Da 11:6).

2. Antiochus III, the Great (223 – 187 BC), king of Syria and sixth ruler of the Seleucid dynasty. By his victory over the Egyptians in 198, Syria gained control of Palestine. He was decisively defeated by the Romans in 190 and thereby lost control over

Asia Minor. He was murdered by a mob while plundering a temple.

3. Antiochus IV (Epiphanes), son of Antiochus III and eighth ruler of the Seleucid Dynasty, 175 – 163 BC (1Mc 1:10; 6:16). In his attempt to Hellenize the Jews, he had a pig sacrificed on the altar in Jerusalem, forbade circumcision, and destroyed all the OT books he could find. These outrages involved him in the Maccabean war in which the Syrian armies were repeatedly defeated by the brilliant Judas Maccabeus (Da 8:9 – 12, 23 – 25; 11:21 – 35; see also 1 and 2 Mc).

4. Antiochus V (Eupator), son of no. 3. He reigned as a minor for two years and then was assassinated.

ANTIPAS [525] (ăn′tĭ·pas, Gr. *Antipas*). A contraction of Antipater.

1. An early Christian martyr of Pergamum, described as "my faithful witness" (Rev 2:13).

2. Herod Antipas, son of Herod the Great and brother of Philip the Tetrarch and of Archelaus; ruled Galilee and Perea from 4 BC to AD 39. *See Herod.*

APHEK [707] (ā′fěk, Heb. *'ăpēk, strength, fortress*).

1. A city NE of Beirut, identified with Afqa (Jos 13:4).

2. A city in the territory of Asher, never wrested from its Canaanite inhabitants (Jos 19:30; Jdg 1:31).

3. A town in the Plain of Sharon (Josh 12:18), probably within twenty-five miles (forty-two km.) of Shiloh (1Sa 4:1, 12). The Philistines may have encamped here before the first battle with Israel at Ebenezer.

4. A town west of the Jordan in the Plain of Jezreel. The Philistines used it as a base in two important campaigns against Israel (1Sa 4:1; 29:1). It also may have been the town where a wall fell and killed 27,000 of Ben-Hadad's soldiers (1Ki 20:26 – 30) and where, according to prophecy, the Syrians were to be destroyed (2Ki 13:14 – 19).

APOCRYPHA Interspersed among the canonical books of the OT in the old Latin Vulgate Bible are certain additional books and chapters. It is to these that Protestant usage generally assigns the term *Apocrypha*. In English versions the Apocrypha are usually presented as fifteen separate books. (See below for individual treatment of these.) The Jewish people, who produced them, and Protestants do not consider them canonical.

At the Council of Trent (AD 1546) the Roman Catholic Church received as canonical all the additional materials in the Vulgate except for 1 and 2 Esdras and the Prayer of Manasseh. That decision was made in contradiction of the best tradition of even the Roman Catholic Church itself. It was a reaction to the Reformers, who recognized as divinely inspired and as their infallible rule of faith and practice only those books that were in the canon of the Jews (cf. esp. Josephus, *Contra Apionem* 1.8), the canon sanctioned by the Lord Jesus Christ.

The apocryphal literature includes the following titles: *1 Esdras, 2 Esdras, Tobit, Judith, Additions to Esther, Wisdom of Solomon, Ecclesiasticus, Baruch, Epistle of Jeremy, The Prayer of Azariah and the Song of the Three Children, Susanna, Bel and the Dragon, The Prayer of Manasseh, 1 Maccabees,* and *2 Maccabees.*

APOLLOS [663] (a-pŏl′ŏs, Gr. *Apollōs*). The short form of Apollonius, an Alexandrian Jew, described in Ac 18:24 – 25 as a man mighty in the Scriptures, eloquent, fervent in the Spirit, instructed in the way of the Lord, but knowing only the baptism of John. He came to Ephesus after Paul had visited that city on his second missionary journey. There he met Aquila and Priscilla, who had been left there to minister pending the apostle's return. They heard Apollos speak boldly in the synagogue and, observing that he was deficient in his knowledge of the gospel, "explained to him the way of God more adequately" (18:26). It is not easy to determine from the brief account in Acts the precise character of his religious knowledge. Before long he went to Achaia with letters of recommendation from the Ephesian brothers. When he arrived in Corinth, "he was a great help to those who by grace had believed. For he vigorously refuted the Jews in public debate, proving from the Scriptures that Jesus was the Christ" (18:27 – 28).

Apollos's gifts and methods of presenting the gospel were undoubtedly different from those of Paul, and he put the impress of his own mode of thinking on many who heard him. Before long a party arose in the Corinthian church with the watchword, "I follow Apollos" (1Co 1:12; 3:4 – 7). There does not, however, appear to have been any feeling of rivalry between Paul and Apollos. Paul urged Apollos to revisit Corinth (16:12), and he also asked Titus to help Apollos, apparently then or when he was on his way to Crete (Tit 3:13).

Luther suggested the theory, since accepted by some scholars, that Apollos wrote the letter to the Hebrews.

APOSTASY (a-pŏs′ta-sē Gr. *apostasia, a falling away, a withdrawal, a defection*). The word is seldom found in English translations of the Bible, but it is a description of Israel's rebellion against God (Josh 22:22; 2Ch 29:19; Jer 2:19). In Greek, where it has the implication of deserting a post, it refers generally to the abandonment of Christianity for unbelief (1Ti 4:1; 2Ti 2:18), perhaps on the part of those who had never truly believed (1Jn 1:19; cf. Jn 15:6). The writer of the letter to the Hebrews declares apostasy to be irrevocable (Heb 6:4 – 6; 10:26), and Paul applies it eschatologically to the coming of a time of great rebellion against God (2Th 2:3).

Described:

(Dt 13:13, 32; 32:15; Isa 65:11 – 12; Mt 12:45; Lk 11:24 – 26; Ac 7:39 – 43; 1Ti 4:1 – 3; 2Ti 3:6 – 9; 4:3 – 4; Heb 3:12; 2Pe 2:15 – 22; Jude 8). Foretold (Mt 24:12; 2Th 2:3; 1Ti 4:1 – 3; 2Ti 3:1 – 9; 4:3 – 4; 2Pe 2:1). Admonitions against (Mt 24:4 – 5; Mk 13:5 – 6; Heb 3:12; 2Pe 3:17; 2Jn 8; Jude 4 – 6). No remedy for (Heb 6:4 – 8; 10:26 – 29). Punishment of (1Ch 28:9; Isa 1:28; 65:12 – 15; Jer 17:5 – 6; Eze 3:20; 18:24, 26; 33:12 – 13, 18; Zep 1:4 – 6; Jn 15:6; 2Th 2:11 – 12; Heb 10:25 – 31, 38 – 39; 2Pe 2:17 – 22; Jude 6).

Caused by:

Persecution (Mt 13:20 – 21; 24:9 – 12; Mk 4:5 – 17; Lk 8:13). Worldliness (2Ti 4:10).

Instances of, by:

Israelites (Ex 32; Nu 14; Ac 7:39 – 43); Saul (1Sa 15:26 – 29; 18:12; 28:15, 18); Amaziah (2Ch 25:14, 27); disciples (Jn 6:66); Judas (Mt 26:14 – 16; 27:3 – 5; Mk 14:10 – 11; Lk 22:3 – 6, 47 – 48; Ac 1:16 – 18); Hymenaeus and Alexander (1Ti 1:19 – 20); Phygelus and Hermogenes (2Ti 1:15).

APOSTLE [692, 693] (a-pŏs′l, Gr. *apostolos, messenger, envoy, ambassador*). This title is used to describe various men in the NT. It describes Jesus himself — "Jesus, the apostle and high priest ..." (Heb 3:1), pointing to Jesus' role on earth as the ambassador of the Father. Second, the twelve disciples whom Jesus chose to be with him and whom he commissioned and sent out to preach are also called "apostles" (Mt 10:2; Mk 3:14; 6:30; Lk 6:13; 9:10; 11:49; 17:5; 22:14; 24:10). These men (without Judas but with Matthias, Ac 1:26) were primary witnesses of the resurrection of Jesus, and their task was to proclaim the gospel of God, establish churches, and teach sound doctrine (Ac 4:33; 5:12; 5:29; 8:1, 14 – 18). They did this as they lived in spiritual union with the exalted Jesus through the Holy Spirit promised by Jesus in Jn 14 – 16.

Since Paul met the resurrected and glorified Jesus and was given a commission by him to be the messenger to the Gentiles and the planter of churches in Gentile cities, he called himself an apostle (Ro 1:1; Gal 1:1), defended his right to be known as an apostle (2Co 11 – 12; Gal 1), and was described as an apostle by Luke (Ac 14:14). He believed suffering was an inescapable part of his apostolic role (1Co 4:9 – 13; 2Co 4:7 – 12; 11:23 – 29) and held that the church of God was built on Christ as the chief cornerstone and on the apostles as primary foundational stones (Eph 2:20).

Further, and this information prevents neat and tidy definitions of an apostle, there are others who are called "apostles" in the NT. James, brother of the Lord Jesus (Gal 1:19; 2:9); Barnabas, a fellow worker with Paul (Ac 14:4, 14); Andronicus and Junias (Ro 16:7); and Silas (1Th 2:6) were probably known as "apostles" within the early church. But they were not of the Twelve (Rev 21:14) and not on the same footing as Paul, who was uniquely *the* apostle to the Gentiles.

The teaching contained within the pages of the NT is apostolic teaching, and its authority rests on the relation of the apostles to Christ.

Ro	1:1	be an **a** and set apart for the gospel
	11:13	as I am the **a** to the Gentiles,
1Co	1:1	to be an **a** of Christ Jesus by the will
	9:1	Am I not an **a**?
	15:9	not even deserve to be called an **a**,
2Co	12:12	The things that mark an **a** —
Gal	2:8	Peter as an **a** to the Jews,
	2:8	my ministry as an **a** to the Gentiles.
1Ti	1:1	an **a** of Christ Jesus by the command
	2:7	appointed a herald and an **a**
2Ti	1:11	a herald and an **a** and a teacher.
Heb	3:1	**a** and high priest whom we confess.
1Pe	1:1	Peter, an **a** of Jesus Christ,

APOSTLES [G693, G6013].

The Twelve:

In the Gospels, a title distinguishing the twelve disciples, whom Jesus selected to be intimately associated with himself (Lk 6:13). Names of (Mt 10:2 – 4; Mk 3:16 – 19; Lk 6:13 – 16; Ac 1:13, 26). Selection of (Mt 4:18, 22; 9:9 – 10; 10:2 – 4; Mk 3:13 – 19; Lk 6:13 – 16; Jn 1:43). Commission of (Mt 10; 28:19 – 20; Mk 3:14 – 15; 6:7 – 11; 16:15; Lk 9:1 – 5; 22:28 – 30; Jn 20:23; 21:15 – 19; Ac 1; 2; 10:42). Uneducated (Mt 11:25; Ac 4:13). Miraculous power given to (Mt 10:1; Mk 3:15; 6:7; 16:17; Lk 9:1 – 2; 10:9, 17; Ac 2:4, 43; 5:12 – 16; 1Co 14:18; 2Co 12:12). Authority of (Mt 16:19; 18:18; 19:28). Inspiration of (Mt 10:27; 16:17 – 19; Lk 24:45; Ac 1:2; 13:9). Duties of (Lk 24:48; Jn 15:27; Ac 1:8, 21 – 22; 2:32; 3:15; 4:33; 5:32; 10:39 – 41; 13:31; 2Pe 1:16, 18; 1Jn 1:1 – 3). Moral state of, before Pentecost (Mt 17:17; 18:3; 20:20 – 22; Lk 9:54 – 55). Slow to receive Jesus as Messiah (Mt 14:33). Forsake Jesus (Mk 14:50). Fail to comprehend Jesus' mission and the nature of the kingdom he came to establish (Mt 8:25 – 27;

15:23; 16:8 – 12, 21 – 22; 19:25; Mk 4:13; 6:51 – 52; 8:17 – 18; 9:9 – 10, 31 – 32; 10:13 – 14; Lk 9:44 – 45; 18:34; 24:19, 21; Jn 4:32 – 33; 10:6; 11:12 – 13; 12:16; 13:6 – 8; 14:5 – 9, 22; 16:6, 17 – 18, 32; 20:9; 21:12; Ac 1:6).

Other Than the Twelve:

Matthaias (Ac 1:26); Paul and Barnabas (Ac 14:1 – 4, 14); Paul (Ro 1:1); Andronicus and Junias (Ro 16:7). As a spiritual gift (1Co 12:28 – 31; Eph 4:11 – 13).

Mt	10:2	These are the names of the twelve **a**:
Mk	3:14	twelve — designating them **a**
Lk	6:13	whom he also designated **a**:
	11:49	'I will send them prophets and **a**,
Ac	1:26	so he was added to the eleven **a**,
	2:43	miraculous signs were done by the **a**.
	5:18	the **a** and put them in the public jail.
	8:1	and all except the **a** were scattered.
	14:14	**a** Barnabas and Paul heard of this,
Ro	16:7	They are outstanding among the **a**,
1Co	12:28	God has appointed first of all **a**,
	15:9	For I am the least of the **a** and do not
2Co	11:13	For such men are false **a**,
	11:13	masquerading as **a** of Christ.
Eph	2:20	the foundation of the **a** and prophets,
	4:11	It was he who gave some to be **a**,
Rev	2:2	who claim to be **a** but are not,
	21:14	names of the twelve **a** of the Lamb.

APOSTOLIC AGE The period in the history of the Christian church when the apostles were alive, beginning with the day of Pentecost and ending with the death of the apostle John near the end of the first century. Our only source for the period is the NT, especially Acts and the Epistles.

APPEAL [2011, 2704, 7924, 2126, 4151, 4155]. No provision was made in the OT for the reconsideration from a lower to a higher court of a case already tried. Exodus 18:26 shows, however, that Moses provided for lower and higher courts: "The difficult cases they brought to Moses, but the simple ones they decided themselves." In Dt 17:8 – 13 provision was made for a lower court, under certain conditions, to seek instructions as to procedure from a higher court; but the decision itself belonged to the lower court.

In NT times the Roman government allowed each synagogue to exercise discipline over Jews, but only the Romans had the power of life and death. A Roman citizen could, however, claim exemption from trial by the Jews and appeal to be tried by a Roman court. Paul did this when he said, "I appeal to Caesar!" (Ac 25:11). In such cases the litigant either pronounced the word *appellō*, as Paul did, or submitted the appeal in writing. In either case the presiding magistrate was under obligation to transmit the file, together with a personal report, to the competent higher magistrate.

Ac	25:11	I **a** to Caesar!"
2Co	5:20	God were making his **a** through us.
Phm	1:9	yet I **a** to you on the basis of love.
1Pe	5:1	I **a** as a fellow elder.

APPEAR

Ge	1:9	and let dry ground **a**."
Ex	23:15	to **a** before me empty-handed.
Lev	16:2	because I **a** in the cloud over
Da	11:3	Then a mighty king will **a**,
Mt	24:30	the sign of the Son of Man will **a** in
Mk	13:22	and false prophets will **a**
Lk	19:11	the kingdom of God was going to **a**
2Co	5:10	**a** before the judgment seat of Christ,
Col	3:4	you also will **a** with him in glory.
Heb	9:24	now to **a** for us in God's presence.
	9:28	and he will **a** a second time,

APPIAN WAY (ăp′ĭăn). Oldest of the Roman roads, begun in 312 BC, which originally ran from Rome to Capua and was later extended to Brundisium. Parts of the road are still in use. Paul must have traveled by it from Puteoli to Rome (Ac 28:13 – 16).

APPOINTED

Lev	23:2	the **a** feasts of the LORD,
Dt	1:15	**a** them to have authority over you —
1Ki	1:35	I have **a** him ruler over Israel
Ezr	1:2	he has **a** me to build a temple
Pr	8:23	I was **a** from eternity,
Da	11:27	an end will still come at the **a** time.
Mic	6:9	the rod and the One who **a** it.
Hab	2:3	For the revelation awaits an **a** time;
Mk	3:16	These are the twelve he **a**:
Lk	10:1	the LORD **a** seventy-two others
Jn	15:16	and **a** you to go and bear fruit —
Ac	15:2	So Paul and Barnabas were **a**,
Ro	9:9	"At the **a** time I will return,
1Co	12:28	And in the church God has **a** first
Heb	1:2	whom he **a** heir of all things,

AQUEDUCT [9498] (*water channel*). A channel, covered or open, cut in the rock; a waterway built of stone and sometimes faced with smooth cement. Aqueducts convey water from reservoirs, pools, cisterns, or springs to the places where it is to be used. They may have existed even in pre-Israelite times and continued to be developed until the excellent work of the Nabatean period (100 BC – AD 100). The Roman period shows many fine examples. Hezekiah excavated the Siloam Tunnel (conduit) to bring water into Jerusalem by a way that could not be stopped up in time of siege (2Ki 18:17; 20:20; 2Ch 32:30; Isa 7:3; 36:1), and this served the purpose of an aqueduct. Many fine Roman aqueducts survive.

AQUILA [217] (ăk′wĭla, Gr. *Akylos*, Latin for "eagle"). A Jewish Christian whom Paul found at Corinth on his arrival from Athens (Ac 18:2, 18, 26; Ro 16:3 – 4; 1Co 16:19; 2Ti 4:19). A characteristic feature of Aquila and his wife Priscilla is that their names are always mentioned together. All that they accomplished was the result of their unity of spiritual nature and purpose in Christ. Having been expelled from Rome, they opened a tentmaking business in Corinth. Because Paul followed the same trade, he was attracted to them. Being in full sympathy with Paul, they hospitably received him into their home, where he remained for a year and a half. Their willingness to "risk their lives" for him earned the gratitude of all the churches. Apollos and many others were helped by their spiritual insight. Aquila and Priscilla had a "church that [met] at their house." Priscilla is usually named first; whether because she became a Christian first or was more active or for some other reason is a matter of conjecture.

ARABAH [6858] (ăr′a-ba, Heb. *'ărāvâh, desert plain, steppe*). The remarkable rift running from Mount Hermon to the Gulf of Aqabah. Its northern portion drains into the Dead Sea, and from above the Sea of Gennesaret (Kinnereth) it is below sea level. South of the Dead Sea it is higher and drains into the Gulf of Aqabah at Ezion Geber. The southern portion is referred to in Dt 1:1; 2:8. It is associated with the Dead Sea and the Sea of Galilee in Dt 3:17; 4:49; Jos 3:16, 12:3; 2Ki 14:25. It was used in the most extended sense, as appears from Dt 11:30; Jos 8:14; 12:1; 18:18; 2Sa 2:29; 4:7; 2Ki 25:4; Jer 39:4; 52:7. The Arabah represents one of the major natural divisions of Palestine in Jos 11:16; 12:8. It is a narrow valley of varying breadth; the productivity of various sections depends on the availability of water. Populated intermittently from early ages, it lay in the path of caravan traffic between the Arabian and Sinai deserts and Canaan to the north. The Israelites made stops here in their wilderness wanderings. Solomon got iron and copper from the mines of the Arabah, which was part of the extended kingdom of David and Solomon when they ruled over Edom. The name Arabah itself signifies that which is arid or even waste, as references such as Isa 33:9 indicate.

Dt	4:49	as far as the Sea of the **A**,
Zec	14:10	will become like the **A**.

ARABIA [6851, 728] (a-rā′bĭ̆a, Heb. *'ărāv, desert* or *steppe*). The large peninsula consisting of (1) Arabia Petraea, including Petra and the peninsula of Sinai; (2) Arabia Deserta, the Syrian desert, between the Jordan Valley and the Euphrates; and (3) Arabia Felix to the south. Arabia is bounded east, south, and west by the Persian Gulf, Indian Ocean, and Red Sea; north by the Fertile Crescent. Arabia is an arid steppe, a rocky tableland with enough rainfall in the interior and south to support considerable population, yet with resources so meager as to encourage emigration. With water barriers on three sides, expansion was toward the more fertile lands northward, in successive waves of Canaanites, Israelites, Amorites, Babylonians, Assyrians, Arameans (called Syrians in the Bible, except NIV), Idumeans, and Nabateans, all Semitic peoples. They collided with Indo-Europeans pressing down from Asia Minor and Iran. The proximity of Arabia, with a border ill-defined and difficult to defend, and with a "have-not" population ready to plunder, was a major factor influencing the history of Israel.

The first mention of Arabia in the Bible by name is in the reign of Solomon, when its king brought gold and spices, either as tribute or in trade (1Ki 10:15; 2Ch 9:14). Arabians brought tribute to Jehoshaphat (2Ch 17:11). They joined the Philistines against Jehoram, defeating him disastrously (21:16 – 22:1). At desolate Babylon not even the Arabian nomad would pitch his tent (Isa 13:20). Isaiah 21:13 – 17 laid a burden on Arabia. Moral depravity is indicated in Jer 3:2. The kings of Arabia were involved in judgment on the nations after the Babylonian captivity (Jer 25:24). Arabia sold cattle to Tyre (Eze 27:21), gave Nehemiah trouble when he was rebuilding the walls of Jerusalem (Ne 2:19; 4:7; 6:1), and were among those present at Pentecost (Ac 2:11). Paul went into Arabia (Gal 1:17). The belief that he went to Mount Sinai is based on the experiences of Moses and Elijah there and on his mention of "Mount Sinai in Arabia" (4:25).

Isa	21:13	An oracle concerning **A**:
Gal	1:17	but I went immediately into **A**
	4:25	Hagar stands for Mount Sinai in **A**

ARAD [6865, 6866] (ā′răd, Heb. *'ărādh, wild donkey*).

1. A descendant of Benjamin, the son of Beriah (1Ch 8:15).

2. A city, now Tell Arad, about seventeen miles (twenty-eight km.) south of Hebron. Its king opposed Israel and his city was destroyed and renamed Hormah (Nu 21:1 – 3; 33:40; cf. Jos 12:14). According to Jdg 1:16, Kenites settled in the area.

ARAM [806] (āʹrăm, Heb. *ʹărām*).

1. Son of Shem (Ge 10:22 – 23; 1Ch 1:17).

2. Son of Kemuel, Abraham's nephew (Ge 22:21).

3. Son of Shamer, of the tribe of Asher (1Ch 7:34).

4. In the KJV, for the Greek form of Ram (Mt 1:3 – 4 ASV, RSV, NIV), called Arni in ASV, RSV of Lk 3:33.

5. A district of the hill country belonging to Gilead (1Ch 2:23).

6. Usually appearing as "Syria" in English Bibles, Aram broadly describes the area north of Israel and extending eastward to Mesopotamia. The latter was itself Aram Naharaim, i.e., Aram of the two rivers (Ge 24:10). In the title of Ps 60 we hear of the two divisions, Aram Naharaim and Aram Zobah, conquered by David. The Aramean kingdom of Damascus, though once conquered by David, was able later to reassert itself and was continually hostile to the northern kingdom of Israel until it fell before the westward thrust of Assyria in 732 BC.

Jdg	10:6	and the gods of **A**, the gods of Sidon,
2Ki	13:3	under the power of Hazael king of **A**
2Ch	16:7	"Because you relied on the king of **A**

ARAMAIC [811, 1365+1579, 1580] (ârʹa-māʹĭk, Heb. *ʹărāmîth*). A West Semitic language, closely related to Hebrew, that developed various dialects. Genesis 31:47 calls attention to Laban's use of Aramaic in contrast to Jacob's use of Hebrew. That Aramaic had become the language of Assyrian diplomacy is clear from 2Ki 18:26; Isa 36:11 (see the NIV). Aramaic and Hebrew were so different that the people of Jerusalem did not understand the former. Jeremiah 10:11 is in Aramaic, an answer by the Jews to their Aramaic-speaking conquerors who would seduce them to worship idols. Daniel 2:4 – 7:28 is in Aramaic, also Ezra 4:8 – 6:18 and 7:12 – 26. It is not surprising that men in government circles in their period of history should write in Aramaic, but why these particular parts of their books should be in Aramaic is not clear. Some Aramaic place names and personal names occur in the OT, as Tabrimmon (1Ki 15:18) and Hazael (2Ki 8:8ff.). There are sev-

eral Aramaic words and phrases in the NT, such as *Talitha koum* (Mk 5:41), *Ephphatha* (7:34), *Eloi, Eloi, lama sabachthani* (Mt 27:46; Mk 15:34), *Maranatha* (1Co 16:22, n.), *Abba* (Mk 14:36; Ro 8:15; Gal 4:6), and more. It has been generally assumed as proven that Aramaic was the colloquial language of Palestine from the time of the return of the exiles from Babylon. But some believe that Hebrew was spoken in Galilee in NT times. It is probably safe to assert that our Lord habitually spoke Aramaic and occasionally Greek and could read and speak Hebrew.

2Ki	18:26	"Please speak to your servants in **A**,
Ezr	4:7	The letter was written in **A** script and
Da	2:4	astrologers answered the king in **A**
Jn	19:20	and the sign was written in **A**,
Ac	21:40	he said to them in **A**:
	26:14	I heard a voice saying to me in **A**,

ARARAT [827] (ârʹa-răt, Heb. *ʹărārāt*). An area in eastern Armenia, a mountainous tableland from which flow the Tigris, Euphrates, Aras (Araxes), and Choruk rivers. Near its center lies Lake Van, which, like the Dead Sea, has no outlet. Its general elevation is about 6,000 feet (1,875 m.), above which rise mountains to as high as 17,000 feet (5,313 m.), the height of the extinct volcano that in modern times is called Mount Ararat and on which the ark is supposed to have rested, though Ge 8:4 is indefinite: "on the mountains of Ararat" (plural). There the sons of Sennacherib fled after murdering their father (2Ki 19:37; Isa 37:38). Jeremiah 51:27 associates the kingdoms of Ararat, Minni, and Ashkenaz with the kings of the Medes as prophesied conquerors of Babylonia. The region is now part of Turkey. The Babylonian name was Urartu, having the same consonants as the Hebrew *ʹărārāt*. Its meaning cannot be determined with certainty.

| Ge | 8:4 | to rest on the mountains of **A**. |

ARCHAEOLOGY (*study of ancient things*). Study of the material remains of the past by excavating ancient buried cities and examining their remains; deciphering inscriptions; and evaluating the language, literature, art, architecture, monuments, and other aspects of human life and achievement. Biblical archaeology is concerned with Israel and the countries with which the Hebrews and early Christians came into contact

THE MEANING OF ARCHAEOLOGY.

By definition archaeology is the study of antiquity. In modern times it has graduated from a treasure hunt into a highly scientific discipline, a branch of history that works with the unwritten material remains of antiquity. W. F. Albright once wrote that next to nuclear science, archaeology has become the fastest-growing discipline in the country. Excavation is only one aspect of the total effort of an archaeological enterprise. Geographical regional surveys, geological analyses, evaluation of artifacts, translation of inscriptions, reconstruction of architecture, examination of human remains, identification of art forms, construction of ceramic pottery typology for chronological purposes, and many other highly complex scientific endeavors constitute a major part of the expedition's work. The end result of it all is to enrich our understanding of unknown aspects of ancient civilizations.

BIBLICAL ARCHAEOLOGY.

G. E. Wright has insisted that biblical archaeology is an armchair variety of general archaeology, but William Dever has correctly emphasized that archaeology is biblical only where and when the scientific methodology of general archaeology uncovers something relative to the Bible. There is no special science or technique available to the biblical scholar. One who digs a biblical site is a biblical archaeologist in the same way that one who digs a classical site is a classical archaeologist. The methods are the same. There are no special methods or aims for biblical archaeology. Special emphasis should be given to the fact that all reputable archaeology strives for the same total reconstruction of the past and presupposes the same standards of objectivity. As Roland de Vaux

pointed out, archaeology cannot prove the Bible. Spiritual truth is of such a nature that it cannot be proven or disproven by the material discoveries of archaeology. The truths of the Bible do not need proving; they are self-evident. But as Israeli scholar Gaalyah Cornfeld has commented, "The net effect of archaeology has been to support the general trustworthiness and substantial historicity of the biblical tradition where data are available." The study of the Bible and the pursuit of archaeology belong together. When Middle-Eastern archaeology began about a century ago, the majority of the excavators were biblical scholars. They recognized the fact that the greatest contribution archaeology could make to biblical studies would be to illuminate our understanding of the cultural settings in which the various books of the Bible were written and which they reflect. That information will, at times, significantly affect our interpretation of relevant sections of the text.

ARCHANGEL [G791] (*ruling angel*).

A high order of angels (1Th 4:16). Michael called a "prince" (Da 10:13, 21; 12:1; Jude 9; Rev 12:7). *See Angels.*

1Th	4:16	voice of the **a** and with the trumpet
Jude	1:9	But even the **a** Michael,

ARCHIPPUS [800] (ar-kǐp'ŭs, *master of the horse*). A Christian at Colosse, conspicuous as a champion of the gospel, a close friend (perhaps the son) of Philemon, and an office-bearer in the church (Col 4:17; Phm 2). Because of the spiritual laxity at Colosse (like Laodicea, Rev 3:14 – 19), it is not surprising to find that Paul exhorts his fellow soldier to maintain his zeal and fidelity.

AREOPAGUS [740, 741] (âr'ē-ŏp'a-gŭs, Gr. *Areios pagos, hill of the Greek god Ares*). The rocky hill of the god Ares, or Mars; a spur jutting out from the western side of the Acropolis at Athens, separated from it by a short saddle. To the north directly below was the Agora or marketplace.

Areopagus is also the name of the council that met on Mars Hill, a court dating back to legendary times, in NT days still charged with questions of morals and the rights of teachers who lectured in public. Its importance was enhanced under the Romans. Paul was brought to the Areopagus (Ac 17:19) to be examined regarding his teaching. The KJV says that "Paul stood in the midst of Mars hill," where the ASV and RSV have "in the midst [middle] of the Areopagus," referring to the court, not the hill (17:22). The NIV, even more specific, says that Paul stood up "in the meeting of the Areopagus." Before these "solid citizens," the bulwark of civic and religious conservatism, Paul met the mocking taunts of adherents of two of that day's most popular philosophies, Epicureanism and Stoicism. His address is today more widely read than any of the writings of the philosophers and is almost the only means by which we remember the Council of Areopagus. Paul's mission in Athens produced numerically scant results, and the founding of no church is recorded; but Dionysius the Areopagite, one of the members of this honorable court, was among those who "became followers of Paul and believed" (17:34).

Ac	17:19	to a meeting of the **A**,
	17:22	then stood up in the meeting of the **A**
	17:34	Dionysius, a member of the **A**,

ARGUE

Job	13:3	and to **a** my case with God.
	13:8	Will you **a** the case for God?
Pr	25:9	If you **a** your case with a neighbor,
Isa	43:26	let us **a** the matter together;
Ac	6:9	These men began to **a** with Stephen,

ARIMATHEA [751] (âr′ĭ-ma-thē′a). The city of the Joseph who buried the body of Jesus in his own new tomb near Jerusalem (Mt 27:57; Mk 15:43; Lk 23:51; Jn 19:38). The location of Arimathea is in doubt but is conjectured to be Ramathaim-Zophim, the Ramah of Samuel's residence, in the hill country of Ephraim, about twenty miles NW of Jerusalem and six miles (ten km.) SE of Antipatris.

| Jn | 19:38 | Joseph of **A** asked Pilate for the body |

ARK [778, 9310, 3066] (Heb. *tēvâh, a chest* or *a vessel to float*). A boat. It is used of the vessel that God directed Noah to build (Ge 6:14 – 16). God told Noah what to bring into it (6:18 – 21), and Noah obeyed (6:22 – 7:10). The ark floated during the flood (7:11 – 8:3) then came to rest "on the mountains of Ararat" (8:4). After Noah abandoned the ark (8:18 – 19), what happened to it is unknown, despite many traditions and expeditions. We do not even know on which peak of the mountains in the land of Ararat the ark grounded.

The ark of Noah is referred to in Mt 24:38 and Lk 17:27 in a warning of coming judgment; in Heb 11:7 its construction is an example of faith; and in 1Pe 3:20 "the days of Noah while the ark was being built" are held up as an example of the long-suffering of God, followed by disaster for the disobedient and salvation for the few who entered the ark. The same Hebrew word is used of the basket of bulrushes in which Moses was cast out to float on the Nile (Ex 2:2 – 5).

Ge	6:14	make yourself an **a** of cypress wood;
Ex	25:16	Then put in the **a** the Testimony,
	37:1	Bezalel made the **a** of acacia wood —
Nu	10:35	Whenever the **a** set out, Moses said,
Dt	10:5	the tablets in the **a** I had made,
Jos	3:3	"When you see the **a** of the covenant
1Sa	4:11	The **a** of God was captured,
	6:3	you return the **a** of the god of Israel
	7:2	that the **a** remained at Kiriath Jearim,
2Sa	6:17	They brought the **a** of the LORD
1Ki	8:9	in the **a** except the two stone tablets
1Ch	13:9	his hand to steady the **a**,
2Ch	35:3	the sacred **a** in the temple
Lk	17:27	up to the day Noah entered the **a**.
Heb	9:4	This **a** contained the gold jar
	11:7	built an **a** to save his family.
Rev	11:19	and within his temple was seen the **a**

ARK OF THE COVENANT, ARK OF THE TESTI-MONY (Heb. *'ărôn haberîth, chest of the covenant*). The word used for "ark" is the same as that used of the coffin (mummy case) of Joseph (Ge 50:26); elsewhere of the chest containing the tables of the law, resting in the tabernacle or temple. God directed Moses (Ex 25:10 – 22; Dt 10:2 – 5) to make the ark of acacia (shittim) wood, of precise dimensions, and to overlay it with pure gold within and without, with a crown of gold about it. Rings of gold at the corners and staves covered with gold to slide through the rings were made to carry the ark. Moses placed inside the ark the stone tablets on which the commandments were written. An atonement cover of gold, with two winged cherubim of gold, covered the top of the ark. There God promised to meet and talk with Moses. Moses made the ark after the golden calf was destroyed (Dt 10:1, "at that time") and set it up in the tabernacle (Ex 40:20).

The ark went before Israel in the wilderness journeys "to find them a place to rest" (Nu 10:33). The ark was instrumental in the crossing of the Jordan on dry land under Joshua (Jos 3) and in the capture of Jericho (4:7 – 11). Joshua prayed before the ark after the defeat at Ai (7:6) and after the subsequent victory at Mount Ebal with the ark present (8:33). In the days of Eli the ark was in the tabernacle at Shiloh (1Sa 3:3). Eli's sons took it into battle against the Philistines, who captured it; as a result, it was said, "The glory has departed from Israel" (4:3 – 22). The Philistines held the ark until a plague convinced them that it was too dangerous to keep, and they ceremoniously sent it back to Beth Shemesh (5:1 – 6:16). The men of this place also suffered a plague for looking into the ark, and it was removed to Kiriath Jearim (6:19 – 21). Here it was treated with due respect and kept in the house of Abinadab under the care of his son Eleazar (7:1 – 2).

David brought the ark to Jerusalem after some misadventures (2Sa 6; 1Ch 13; 15). When Uriah said to David, "The ark and Israel and Judah are staying in tents" (2Sa 11:11), he may have meant that the ark had been taken by the army into the field or merely that the ark was in a tent (the tabernacle) just as the armies of Israel and Judah were in tents. At the time of Absalom's rebellion, Zadok and the Levites carried the ark out of Jerusalem, but David had them take it back (15:24 – 29). The priests brought the ark into Solomon's temple (1Ki 8:3 – 9). There was nothing in it at this time "except the two stone tablets that Moses had placed in it at Horeb" (8:9).

Before the ark was made, Moses directed that a pot of manna be kept before the Lord (Ex 16:32 – 34), and Heb 9:4 says that the "ark contained the gold jar of manna, Aaron's staff that had budded, and the stone tablets of the covenant," though it need not be understood to imply that these were the contents of the ark throughout its history. Jeremiah, writing after the destruction of Jerusalem by Nebuchadnezzar, prophesied that in times to come the ark would no longer be of significance for worship (Jer 3:16). Psalm 132:8 speaks of the ark poetically as representing the strength of the Lord. Hebrews 9 uses the tabernacle and all its furnishings, including the ark, in explaining by analogy salvation by the high priesthood of Christ. After the destruction of the first temple, there is no evidence as to what happened to the ark, but only highly speculative tradition and conjecture. Synagogues, from our earliest knowledge of them to the present, have had arks in the side wall toward Jerusalem; the scrolls of the law are stored in them behind a curtain.

The ark was set in the very heart of the tabernacle, the Most Holy Place (Ex 26:34), symbolizing its central significance in Israel. When the high priest, once each year (Lev 16:15; Heb 9:7), entered the innermost shrine, he came into the very presence of the God of Israel (Ex 30:6; Lev 16:1 – 2). But that presence was not visibly expressed in any image form (Dt 4:12), but by the presence of the law of the Lord (the stone tablets) and the atonement cover that was over the law. In other words, the ark by its contents declared the divine holiness by which all stand condemned and by its form (specifically the atonement cover) declared the divine redeeming mercy through the shed blood. *See Atonement.*

Description of:

Dimensions of (Ex 25:10; 37:1). Entirely covered with gold (Ex 25:11; 37:2). Surrounded with crown of gold (Ex 25:11). Furnished with rings and poles (Ex 25:12 – 15; 37:3 – 5). Tables of testimony alone placed in (Ex 25:16, 21; 1Ki 8:9, 21; 2Ch 5:10; Heb 9:4). Atonement cover laid upon (Ex 25:21; 26:34). Placed in Most Holy Place (Ex 26:33; 40:21; Heb 9:3 – 4). Pot of manna and Aaron's rod laid up before (Heb 9:4, w Ex 16:33 – 34; Nu 17:10). Copy of the law laid in side of (Dt 31:26). Anointed with sacred oil (Ex 30:26). Covered with veil by priests before removal (Nu 4:5 – 6). Symbol of presence and glory of God (Nu 14:43 – 44; Jos 7:6; 1Sa 14:18 – 19; Ps 132:8). Considered the glory of Israel (1Sa 4:21 – 22). Sanctified its resting place (2Ch 8:11). Israelites inquired of the Lord before (Jos 7:6 – 9; Jdg 20:27; 1Ch 13:3). Holiness of (2Ch 35:3). Profanation of, punished (Nu 4:5, 15; 1Sa 6:19; 1Ch 15:13). Protection of, rewarded (1Ch 13:14).

Was Called the:

Ark of God (1Sa 3:3); ark of God's might (2Ch 6:41; Ps 132:8); ark of the covenant of the Lord (Nu 10:33); ark of the testimony (Ex 30:6; Nu 7:89).

Was Carried:

By priests or Levites alone (Dt 10:8; Jos 3:14; 2Sa 15:24; 1Ch 15:2). Before the Israelites in their journeys (Nu 10:33; Jos 3:6). Sometimes to the camp in war (1Sa 4:4 – 5).

History and Miracles Connected with:

Jordan divided (Jos 4:7). Fall of the walls of Jericho (Jos 6:6 – 20). Captured by Philistines (1Sa 4:11). Fall of Dagon (1Sa 5:1 – 4). Philistines plagued (1Sa 5:6 – 12). Restoration of (1Sa 6:1 – 18). At Kiriath Jearim twenty years (1Sa 7:1 – 2). Removed from Kiriath Jearim to the house of Obed-Edom (2Sa 6:1 – 11). David made tent for (2Sa 6:17; 1Ch 15:1). Brought into city of David (2Sa 6:12 – 15; 1Ch 15:25 – 28). Brought

into temple by Solomon (1Ki 8:1 – 6; 2Ch 5:2 – 9). A type of Christ (Ps 40:8; Rev 11:19).

ARM [274, 2432, 2741, 3338, 4190, 7396, 1098, 3959].

Used as a figure for personal, active power and for divine providence and salvation (Ex 6:6; 15:16; Dt 4:34; 5:15; 7:19; 9:29; 11:2; 26:8; 33:27; 1Ki 8:42; 2Ki 17:36; 2Ch 6:32; Pss 77:15; 89:10, 13, 21; 98:1; 136:12; SS 2:6; Isa 33:2; 40:10 – 11; 51:5, 9; 52:10; 53:1; 59:16; 62:8; 63:5, 12; Jer 21:5; 27:5; 32:17; Eze 20:33; Lk 1:51; Ac 13:17). *See Anthropomorphisms.*

Ex	6:6	redeem you with an outstretched **a**
Nu	11:23	"Is the LORD's **a** too short?
Dt	4:34	a mighty hand and an outstretched **a**,
	7:19	the mighty hand and outstretched **a**,
1Ki	8:42	mighty hand and your outstretched **a**
2Ch	32:8	With him is only the **a** of flesh,
Job	40:9	Do you have an **a** like God's,
Ps	44:3	nor did their **a** bring them victory;
	44:3	your **a**, and the light of your face,
	98:1	and his holy **a** have worked salvation
SS	8:3	His left **a** is under my head and his right **a** embraces me.
Isa	40:10	and his **a** rules for him.
Jer	27:5	and outstretched **a** I made the earth
1Pe	4:1	**a** yourselves also with the same

ARMAGEDDON [762] (ar-ma-gĕd′ŏn, Gr. *Armagedōn*, from Heb., *har-mĕgiddôn*; ASV, Mount Megiddo). A word found only in Rev 16:16 for the final battleground between the forces of good and evil. The Valley of Jezreel and the Plain of Esdraelon at the foot of Mount Megiddo were the scene of many decisive incidents in the history of Israel: the victory over Sisera sung by Deborah and Barak (Jdg 5:19 – 20); Gideon's defeat of Midian (6:33); Saul's death at the hands of the Philistines (1Sa 31; cf. 2Sa 4:4); Josiah's death in battle with Pharaoh Neco (2Ki 23:29 – 30); Ahaziah's death when he fled there (9:27). The town of Megiddo guarded the pass that formed the easiest caravan route between the

Plain of Sharon and the Valley of Jezreel, and the low mountains around were silent witnesses of perhaps more bloody encounters than any other spot on earth, continuing down to recent times. Hence the appropriateness of this place for the vast conflict pictured in Rev 16.

Rev   16:16   the place that in Hebrew is called **A**.

ARMIES [H2657, H4722, H5120, H7372, G4213, G5128, G5136].

General References to:

Fortifications (Jdg 9:31; 2Sa 5:9; 2Ki 25:1; 2Ch 11:11; 26:9; Ne 3:8; 4:2; Isa 22:10; 25:12; 29:3; 32:14; Jer 6:6; 32:24; 33:4; 51:53; Eze 4:2; 17:17; 21:22; 26:8; 33:27; Da 11:15, 19; Na 2:1; 3:14). Machines used (2Ch 26:15; Jer 6:6; Eze 26:9). Standards (Nu 2:2 – 3, 10, 17 – 18, 25, 31, 34; 10:14, 18, 22, 25). Standing armies (1Sa 13:2; 1Ch 27; 2Ch 1:14; 17:12 – 19; 26:11 – 15). Uniforms of (Eze 23:6, 12; Na 2:3).

How Commanded:

Commander in chief (1Sa 14:50; 2Sa 2:8; 8:16; 17:25; 19:13; 20:23). Generals of corps and divisions (Nu 2:3 – 31; 1Ch 27:1 – 22; 2Ch 17:12 – 19). Captains of thousands (Nu 31:14, 48; 1Sa 17:18; 1Ch 28:1; 2Ch 25:5); of hundreds (Nu 31:14, 48; 2Ki 11:15; 1Ch 28:1; 2Ch 25:5); of fifties (2Ki 1:9; Isa 3:3). See Cavalry.

Mustering of:

Methods employed in: sounding a trumpet (Nu 10:9; Jdg 3:27; 6:34; 1Sa 13:3 – 4); cutting oxen in pieces and sending pieces throughout Israel (1Sa 11:7). Refusal to obey summons, instance of (Jdg 21:5 – 11, w Jdg 20).

Tactics:

Camp and march (Nu 2). Decoy (Jos 8:4 – 22; Jdg 20:29 – 43; Ne 6). Delay (2Sa 17:7 – 14). Flanks called wings (Isa 8:8). Forced marches (Isa 5:26 – 27). March in ranks (Joel 2:7). Move in attack in three divisions (Jdg 7:16; 9:43; 1Sa 11:11; 13:17, 18; 2Sa 18:2; Job 1:17). Night attacks

(Ge 14:15; Jdg 7:16 – 22). Orders delivered with trumpets (2Sa 2:28; 18:16; 20:1, 22; Ne 4:18, 20).

Ambushes:

At Ai (Jos 8:2 – 22); at Shechem (Jdg 9:25, 34); at Gibeah (Jdg 20:29 – 43); at Zemaraim (2Ch 13:4, 13); by Jehoshaphat (2Ch 20:20 – 22).

Reconnaissances:

Of Jericho (Jos 2:1 – 24); Ai (Jos 7:2 – 3); Bethel (Jdg 1:23 – 24); Laish (Jdg 18:2 – 10).

Sieges:

(Jer 39:1). Of Jericho (Jos 6); Samaria (2Ki 6:24 – 33:7); Jerusalem (2Ki 25:1 – 3).

Religious Ceremonies Attending:

Ark taken to battle (Jos 6:6 – 7, 13; 1Sa 4:4 – 11). Army choir and songs (2Ch 20:21 – 22). Counsel sought from God before battle (Nu 27:21; Jdg 1:1; 1Sa 14:19, 37 – 41; 23:2 – 12; 30:8; 2Sa 2:1; 5:19, 23; 1Ki 22:7 – 28; 2Ki 3:11 – 19; 1Ch 14:10, 14; Jer 37:7 – 10). Holiness required (Dt 23:9). Officers consecrated to God (2Ch 17:16). Prophecy (2Ch 20:14 – 17). Purifications (Nu 31:19 – 24). Sacrifices (1Sa 13:11 – 12).

Divine Assistance to:

When Aaron and Hur held up Moses' hands (Ex 17:11 – 12). In siege of Jericho (Jos 6). Sun stands still (Jos 10:11 – 14). Gideon's victory (Jdg 7). Samaria's deliverances (1Ki 20; 2Ki 7). Jehoshaphat's victories (2Ki 3; 2Ch 20). Angel of the Lord puts to death Assyrians (2Ki 19:35). To determine royal succession (2Sa 2:8 – 10; 1Ki 16:16; 2Ki 11:4 – 12). Composed of insurgents (1Sa 22:1 – 2); mercenaries (2Sa 10:6; 1Ch 19:6 – 7; 2Ch 25:5 – 6). Confederated (Jos 10:1 – 5; 11:1 – 5; Jdg 1:3; 2Sa 10:6, 15 – 16, 19; 1Ki 15:20; 22:1 – 4; 2Ki 16:9; 18:19 – 21; 1Ch 19:6 – 7; 2Ch 16:2 – 9; 18:1, 3; 20:1; 22:5; 28:16, 20; Ps 83:1 – 12; Isa 7:1 – 9; 8:9 – 12; 54:15). Exhorted before battle (Dt 20:1 – 9). Battle shouts (Jdg 7:18; 1Sa 17:20, 52).

ARMOR-BEARER [3998+5951]. An attendant who carried a soldier's equipment. Of Abimelech (Jdg 9:54); Jonathan (1Sa 14:6 – 7, 12, 14, 17); Saul (1Sa 16:21; 31:6); Goliath (1Sa 17:7); Joab (2Sa 18:15).

1Sa	14:6	Jonathan said to his young **a**,
	31:4	Saul said to his **a**,

ARMS AND ARMOR These are mentioned often in the Bible, both literally and as illustrative of spiritual conflicts. Here only hand weapons and body armor are considered, not chariots or machines used in siege.

OFFENSIVE WEAPONS.

(1) *Sword* is the first offensive weapon mentioned in the Bible: "A flaming sword flashing back and forth to guard the way to the tree of life" (Ge 3:24). Hebrew *hereb*, a weapon for killing, is the common sword (Ge 27:40; Ex 17:13); a sword for punishment is ascribed to God (Ex 5:3; 22:24). Figurative and literal are united in "a sword for the LORD and for Gideon" (Jdg 7:20). Gideon's men were executing the judgment of God. In NT Greek the more common word is *machaira*, short sword, dagger, or saber (Mt 26:27 – 53; Ro 8:35; 13:4); figuratively "the sword of the Spirit" (Eph 6:17). *Rhomphaia*, once a large, broad sword, occurs with symbolic meaning once in Lk 2:35 and six times in the book of Revelation (e.g., Rev. 1:16). (2) *Rod*, a stick loaded at one end. It could be for reassurance (Ps 23:4), to count sheep (Lev 27:32), or as a weapon (Ps 2:9). (3) *Sling*, a band of leather, wide in the middle to receive a stone. With the ends held together, it was swung around the head; then one end was released so that the stone could fly to its mark (1Sa 17:40, 49; Jdg 20:16; 2Ki 3:25). (4) *Bow*, sometimes of bronze (2Sa 22:35; Job 20:24; Ps 18:34), and *arrows*. First mentioned (Ge 27:3) as used in hunting, except that the same word is used for the rainbow in Ge 9:13 – 16. The practice of archery is described in 1Sa 20:20 – 22, 35 – 40. The bow is mentioned only once in the NT (Rev 6:2). (5) *Spear, lance, javelin, or dart*, sharp-pointed instruments to be thrust or thrown (Jos 8:18; Jdg 5:8; 1Sa 17:7; 18:11; Ps 68:30, different Heb. words). Spearmen are mentioned in Ac 23:23, and a Roman lance pierced the body of Jesus on the cross (Jn 19:34). Flame-tipped darts were used also (Eph 6:16).

DEFENSIVE ARMOR.

(1) *Shields* were either small and round, Hebrew *maghēn* (Ge 15:1; Jdg 5:8), or large, Hebrew *tsinnâh* (1Sa 17:7, 41), and were sometimes used for display (2Ch 9:16), called *thyreos*, "like a door" in Greek (Eph 6:16). (2) *Helmet* (1Sa 17:5; Isa 59:17), sometimes of bronze (1Sa 17:38), surrounding the head (Eph 6:17; 1Th 5:8). (3) *Coat of mail*, only in 1Sa 17:5, 38, called "breastplate" in Isa 59:17. In the NT, Greek *thorax* (Eph 6:14; 1Th 5:8, figuratively; Rev 9:9, 17, symbolic). (4) *Greaves*, for the legs, only in 1Sa 17:6. (5) *Girdle*, or belt from which the sword hung (2Sa 20:8). Ephesians 6:14 implies it as part of the equipment of a heavily armed soldier; the description of this equipment in Eph 6:11 – 18 is evidently drawn from Paul's intimate contact, as a prisoner, with Roman guards. "The whole armor," Greek *panoplia*, is a technical term for such armament. Note also the detailed description of the armor of Goliath (1Sa 17:4 – 7).

ARNON [818] (ar'nŏn). The swift "roaring stream" and the valley of the same name that descend to the east side of the Dead Sea a little north of its center. The river begins in the hills of northern Arabia, flows NW awhile, and then turns westward to descend precipitously into the Dead Sea, emptying at about the lowest point on the earth's surface. It is now a "wadi," implying that it is dry most of the year. It is mentioned (Nu 21:13 – 14, 26; 22:36; Dt 2:24, 36; 3:8, 16; Jos 12:1) as the boundary between the Moabites and Amorites in the time of Moses; Israel encamped on its north side so as not to invade Moab. In Jdg 11:18–26 Jephthah tells the Ammonites how Israel had held the land north of the Arnon for three hundred years previous to this time (c. 1560–1260 BC). For all those years, and for a long time after, the Arnon was the southern boundary of the tribe of Reuben. In the days of Jehu (ninth century), Hazael, king of Syria, overpowered Israel east of the Jordan as far as Arnon (2Ki 10:32–33). The Arnon now flows through the kingdom of Jordan.

Nu	21:13	The **A** is the border of Moab,
Jer	48:20	by the **A** that Moab is destroyed.

ARREST [9530, 2095+3836+5931, 3195, 4140, 4389, 5197].

Of Jesus (Mt 26:57; Mk 14:46; Lk 22:54; Jn 18:12); apostles (Ac 5:17–18; 6:12); Paul and Silas (Ac 16:19); Paul (Ac 21:30). Paul authorized to arrest Christians (Ac 9:2).

ARROGANT

Ne	9:16	became **a** and stiff-necked,
Ps	5:5	The **a** cannot stand in your presence;
	73:3	envied the **a** when I saw the prosperity
	119:78	May the **a** be put to shame
Pr	17:7	**A** lips are unsuited to a fool —
	21:24	The proud and **a** man —
Hab	2:5	indeed, wine betrays him; he is **a**
Zep	3:4	Her prophets are **a**;
Mal	3:15	But now we call the **a** blessed.
Ro	1:30	God-haters, insolent, **a** and boastful;
	11:20	Do not be **a**, but be afraid.
1Co	4:18	Some of you have become **a**,
1Ti	6:17	rich in this present world not to be **a**
2Pe	2:10	Bold and **a**, these men are not afraid

ARTAXERXES [831, 10078] (ar-ta-zûrk′sēz, *kingdom of righteousness*). A proper name or possibly a title, like *Pharaoh* or *Caesar* for several kings of Persia. The name is variously derived by scholars, but perhaps "strong king" (Gesenius) is as good as

any. Herodotus said it meant "great warrior." Three kings bore the name Artaxerxes.

1. Artaxerxes I (465–425 BC), son of Xerxes I; known as Macrocheir or Longimanus. He overcame revolts in Egypt, where, with Athenian support, unrest started in 460 and lasted until 454, and in other parts of the Persian Empire. During that time some of the eastern possessions were lost. By the peace treaty of Callias (449), signed at Susa, the relations between Athens and Persia were stabilized on a status quo antebellum basis. Artaxerxes I temporarily halted the reconstruction of Jerusalem (Ezr 4:7–23) but later authorized Ezra's mission to Jerusalem in 458 (7:8, 11–26). Nehemiah's two missions were under his reign and with his permission, the first in 445 (Ne 2:1ff; 13:6). Artaxerxes I was buried at Naqsi Rustam next to the tombs of his father and grandfather.

2. Artaxerxes II (404–359 BC), son of Darius II and grandson of Artaxerxes I; known as Mnemon. He crushed the rebellion of his brother Cyrus (Battle of Cunaxa, 401), as related by Xenophon in his *Anabasis*. He lost Egypt probably in 402 or 401, repelled the meddling of Sparta in the affairs of Asia Minor (Peace of Antalcidas, 386), and suppressed other rebellious movements led by local satraps. Several of his inscriptions refer to his building activities. The palace he built at Susa is considered by some authorities to be identical with the palace described in Esther (Est 1:5–6).

3. Artaxerxes III (359–338 BC), son of Artaxerxes II; known as Ochus. By the use of skillful diplomacy and military force, he succeeded in maintaining a superficially strong empire until he was murdered as the result of a conspiracy led by Bagoas (338).

ARTEMIS [783] (Gr. *Artemis*, Lat. *Diana*). Diana was the Roman goddess of the moon. A daughter of Jupiter, she was a twin sister of Apollo, who was associated with the sun. Diana was represented as a virgin huntress and was widely worshiped. When Greek worship penetrated Italy in c. 400 BC, the Italians identified Diana with their Artemis, her Greek counterpart. Her worship was pure compared with the sensual worship of eastern gods and goddesses.

"Artemis of the Ephesians" is mentioned only in Ac 19:24–35 ("Diana" in the JB, KJV, NEB), and her myths were of a very different sort. Her silver "shrines" (19:24) were little "temples" containing an image of Artemis as imagined by the Asiatics, a combination of the Greek virgin goddess with the many-breasted and lewd Semitic moon goddess Ashtoreth. For the Ephesians, Artemis was the great Asiatic nursing mother of gods, men, animals, and plants and was the patroness of the sexual instinct. Her images, instead of being artistically beautiful like those of the Greeks, were ugly, more like the lascivious images of India and Tyre and Sidon. Her special worship was centered in the great temple at Ephesus, probably because of the discovery of a very interesting aerolite that supposedly fell from heaven (19:35). The feasts of Diana, "who is worshiped throughout the province of Asia and the world" (19:27), were commercialized, and among the silversmiths there was a large industry in making shrines and idols for the worship of this goddess. Paul's preaching interfered with this commerce and aroused violent opposition. It seems that Paul and his companions had preached the gospel from the positive side instead of directly attacking the idolatry, for the city clerk testified that they "neither robbed temples nor blasphemed our goddess" (19:37).

Ac   19:27   temple of the great goddess **A**

ARTS AND CRAFTS

Armorer (1Sa 8:12). Baker (Ge 40:1; 1Sa 8:13). Blacksmith (Ge 4:22; 1Sa 13:19). Brickmaker (Ge 11:3; Ex 5:7–8, 18). Carpenter (2Sa 5:11; Mk 6:3). Carver (Ex 31:5; 1Ki 6:18). Caulker (Eze 27:9, 27). Dyer (Ex 25:5). Embalmer (Ge 50:2–3, 26). Embroiderer (Ex 35:35; 38:23). Engraver (Ex 28:11; Isa 49:16; 2Co 3:7). Gardener (Ge 4:2; 9:20; Jer 29:5; Jn 20:15). Goldsmith (Isa 40:19; Jer 10:9). Launderer (2Ki 18:17; Mk 9:3). Mariner (Eze 27:8–9). Mason (2Sa 5:11; 2Ch 24:12). Musician (1Sa 18:6; 1Ch 15:16). Perfumer (Ex 30:25, 35; 1Sa 8:13). Potter (Isa 64:8; Jer 18:3; La 4:2; Zec 11:13). Refiner of metals (1Ch 28:18; Mal 3:2–3). Rope maker (Jdg 16:11). Shipbuilder (1Ki 9:26). Silversmith (Jdg 17:4; Ac 19:24). Smelter of metals (Job 28:2). Spinner (Ex 35:25; Pr 31:19). Stonecutter (Ex 20:25; 1Ch 22:15). Tailor (Ex 28:3). Tanner (Ac 9:43; 10:6). Tentmaker (Ge 4:20; Ac 18:3). Toolmaker (Ge 4:22; 2Ti 4:14). Weaver (Ex 35:35; Jn 19:23). Wine maker (Ne 13:15; Isa 63:3).

ASA [654, 809] (ā'sa, Heb. *'āsā', healer* BDB; *myrtle* KB).

1. The third king of Judah, reigning from 911/10–870/69 BC (1Ki 15:9–24; 2Ch 14–16). He was the first of the five kings of Judah (Asa, Jehoshaphat, Joash, Hezekiah, Josiah) who were outstanding for godliness, and he deserves special credit considering his idolatrous ancestors. He was the son of Abijah and grandson of Rehoboam. Asa's grandmother was Maacah, a daughter of Absalom and a confirmed idolatress who greatly influenced Judah toward idolatry. She is spoken of as "mother" of both her son (1Ki 15:2) and her grandson (15:10) in the KJV and RSV. Asa began his reign by deposing his wicked and powerful grandmother and by destroying a fearful, impure image that she had set up. He then drove out the male shrine prostitutes and destroyed idols that his fathers had worshiped (15:12), commanding Judah to seek the Lord God of their fathers (2Ch 14:4).

In the early peaceful days of his reign, he gathered into the temple the things that he and his father had dedicated to the Lord (1Ki 15:15). Then in c. 897 BC Zerah the Ethiopian came against him with an immense force. The Lord helped Judah defeat them at Mareshah in the west-central part of Judah, because Asa trusted the Lord (2Ch 14:9–15). In 2Ch 15:1–13 we see how the Lord approved and encouraged Asa in his faith and in his work of reformation. Later in c. 895/94 Baasha of the northern kingdom made war against Judah. This time the people did not put their whole trust in the Lord, but Asa bribed Ben-Hadad of Syria to break his league with Baasha so as to draw off the forces of Israel. This Ben-Hadad did, but the Lord, through his prophet Hanani, rebuked Asa for trusting in politics rather than in God (1Ki 15:16–22; 2Ch 16:1–10). In the thirty-ninth year of his reign, Asa was taken with a severe disease of the feet, and because he trusted his physicians rather than the Lord, he died two years later (2Ch 16:11–14).

2. A Levite among those who had returned from captivity (1Ch 9:16).

ASAPH [666] (āʹsăf, *gatherer*).

1. A Levite of the Gershonite family, appointed over the service of praise in the time of David and Solomon (1Ch 16:5; 2Ch 5:12). He led the singing and sounded cymbals before the ark and apparently set up a school of music (Ne 7:44). Twelve psalms are credited to Asaph (Pss 50, 73–83). This accreditation does not necessarily imply authorship (*see Psalms*) and may mean no more than that these psalms constituted an Asaphic collection, begun by the great man and then prolonged over the years by the Asaph singers. The psalms themselves cover a long span of time, for psalms like 74 are best understood in an exilic context. The psalms of Asaph have certain points in common: God as Judge (50:3–4; 75:8; 76:8–9), a call to true spirituality reminiscent of the prophets (50:7, 14–15, 22–23; 81:8–10), the use of history to teach spiritual lessons (78), and the Lord as Shepherd (74:1; 77:20; 79:13; 80:1). These psalms have a deep and contemplative nature.

2. The father of Hezekiah's recorder (2Ki 18:18).

3. An official (keeper of the king's forest) under Artaxerxes Longimanus, king of Persia (Ne 2:8).

4. A Kohath Levite; in 1Ch 26:1 read Ebiasaph (cf. 9:19).

5. A Levite whose descendants lived in Jerusalem after the exile (1Ch 9:15).

ASCENSION OF CHRIST The movement of the eternal Son, in his assumed and glorified humanity, from earth to heaven in order to sit at the right hand of the Father as co-regent. The witness of the NT to the ascension is of three kinds. First, there is the descriptive material in Mk 16:19; Lk 24:51; Ac 1:9–11. Second, there is the prophetic or anticipatory reference found in Jn 6:62; 20:17. Third, there is the reference that assumes that Christ is ascended and exalted and therefore proclaims his present exalted position or future coming in glory (Eph 4:8–11; Heb 4:14; 6:19–20; Rev 12:1–6). Much of the latter teaching is molded in the light of Ps 110:1, 4. Ascension presupposes bodily resurrection, for it was in his body that Jesus went up (*anabaino*). "Exaltation" covers both resurrection and ascension, while "session" means his sitting at the Father's right hand. The position of the exalted Jesus has often been portrayed in biblical imagery as that of King (= Lord) of the universe and church, Priest of the people of God, and Prophet to the people of God and the world. The Holy Spirit is sent by the Father in the name of the Lord Jesus so that he comes bearing the virtues and characteristics of Christ and so is the Paraclete (Jn 16:5–14). As Jesus ascended into heaven, so he will return from heaven to judge the world (Ac 1:11).

General References to:
Prophecies regarding (Pss 24:7; 68:18, w Eph 4:7–8). Foretold by Jesus (Jn 6:62; 7:33; 14:28; 16:5; 20:17). Forty days after his resurrection (Ac 1:3). Described (Ac 1:9). From Mount of Olives (Lk 24:50; w Mk 11:1; Ac 1:12). While blessing his disciples (Lk 24:50). When he had atoned for sin (Heb 9:12; 10:12). Was triumphant (Ps 68:18). Was to supreme power and dignity (Lk 24:26; Eph 1:20–21; 1Pe 3:22). As forerunner of his people (Heb 6:20). To intercede (Ro 8:34; Heb 9:24). To send the Holy Spirit (Jn 16:7; Ac 2:33). To receive gifts for people (Ps 68:18, w Eph 4:8–11). To prepare a place for his people (Jn 14:2). Second coming shall be in like manner as (Ac 1:10–11). Typified (Lev 16:15, w Heb 6:20; 9:7, 9, 12).

ASCENTS (Heb. *maʻălâh*, *a going up* or *ascent*, Gr. *tapeinos*, *low*). The word "ascent" (KJV "degrees") occurs in the titles of fifteen psalms (120–134), which are called songs of ascents (KJV "songs of degrees"). The common opinion regarding the meaning is that they were sung by the pilgrims as they went up to Jerusalem (cf. 1Sa 1:3; Pss 42:4; 122:4; Isa 30:29). The word is also used in 2Ki 20:9–10 (NIV "steps," KJV "degrees"), where Hezekiah is told that his sundial would go back ten degrees as a sign that the Lord would heal him. It is also used in a secondary sense of rank or order (1Ch 15:18; 17:17; Ps 62:9; Lk 1:52; Jas 1:9).

ASCENTS, SONGS OF The title given to Pss 120–34. There is uncertainty about the origin of the title. Some Jewish authorities attributed it to the use made of fifteen steps leading from the court of men to the court of women in the temple. The Levitical musicians performed with these steps as the stage. Some scholars attribute the title to the way in which the thought advances from step to step, as seen in 121:4–5; 124:1–4, but not all these songs do this. Because Ezra (7:9) used the word *hamma'lah,* meaning "a going up from Babylon," some have thought the title originated when exiles were returning to Jerusalem during the reign of Artaxerxes in Babylon. The most logical explanation is that the title was given the series of hymns because they were used by pilgrims *going up* to the three annual pilgrimage feasts of Jerusalem (*see Feasts*).

These pilgrim songs should be studied in groups of three: in each triad the first finds the pilgrim far away (e.g., in Ps 120, he feels himself an alien in Kedar; in Ps 129, he is still among enemies); the second in each triad concentrates on the Lord's power to preserve, whatever the vicissitudes of the way; and the third is a psalm of arrival and security in Zion. In this way the whole "pilgrim hymnbook" is vibrant with the theme of going up and going home to Zion.

ASHAMED

Isa	29:22	"No longer will Jacob be **a**;
Jer	48:13	Then Moab will be **a** of Chemosh,
Eze	43:10	that they may be **a** of their sins.
Mk	8:38	If anyone is **a** of me and my words
	8:38	the Son of Man will be **a** of him

Ro	1:16	I am not **a** of the gospel,
	6:21	from the things you are now **a** of?
Php	1:20	and hope that I will in no way be **a**,
2Ti	1:8	do not be **a** to testify about our Lord,
	1:8	or **a** of me his prisoner.
	2:15	workman who does not need to be **a**
Tit	2:8	that those who oppose you may be **a**
Heb	2:11	Jesus is not **a** to call them brothers.
	11:16	God is not **a** to be called their God,

ASHDOD [846, 847, 848] (ăsh'dŏd, *stronghold, fortress*). One of the five chief cities of the Philistines: Ashdod, Gaza, Ashkelon, Gath, and Ekron (Josh 13:3; 1Sa 6:17; Am 3:9). They were assigned to Judah, but Judah failed to drive out the inhabitants "because they had iron chariots" (Jdg 1:19). Ashdod was a center of Dagon worship, but when the Philistines thought to honor the ark of the Lord by placing it in the house of Dagon (1Sa 5:1–7), God cast down and destroyed their idol. The Philistines found by careful testing that their plagues (1Sa 5–6) were from God, so they sent back the ark with a guilt offering. Uzziah, king of Judah early in the eighth century BC, conquered the city (2Ch 26:6). Amos predicted Ashdod's destruction (Am 1:8). In c. 711 Sargon II of Assyria took it (Isa 20:1). In Jeremiah's prophecy (Jer 25:15–29) Ashdod was to drink with the nations "this cup filled with the wine" of God's wrath. Zephaniah prophesied the destruction of the Philistines (Zep 2:4), and Zechariah said that "foreigners will occupy Ashdod" (Zec 9:6). In Nehemiah's time (c. 444) the men of Ashdod combined with others to hinder the Jews (Ne 4:7–9). Failing in this, they tried intermarrying with them (13:23–24) to produce a mongrel race, but Nehemiah foiled them. In the LXX and NT Ashdod is "Azotus." Philip the evangelist found himself there after the Holy Spirit had taken him away from the Ethiopian eunuch (Ac 8:40).

Jos	13:3	**A**, Ashkelon, Gath and Ekron —
1Sa	5:1	they took it from Ebenezer to **A**.

| Ne | 13:23 | of Judah who had married women from **A**, |

ASHER, ASER [888, 888+1201, 896, 818] (ăsh′êr, ă′sêr, *happy*).

1. The second son of Zilpah, the handmaid whom Laban gave to Leah his daughter and whom she gave to Jacob; named "Happy" by Leah in her happiness at his birth. He was born at Padan-Aram (in the plain of Mesopotamia) during Jacob's service with Laban (Ge 30:13; 35:26; 49:20; Ex 1:4; 1Ch 2:2). We know little of his personal history except the names of his five children (Ge 46:17; Nu 26:44 – 47; Lk 2:36).

2. The tribe that descended from Asher (Josh 19:24 – 31). It was given the territory along the Mediterranean in the NW corner of Palestine, but failed to drive out the inhabitants of Sidon, Acco, and other Canaanite towns and settled down to dwell among them. By David's time Asher seems to have become insignificant, for this tribe is omitted in the list of David's chief rulers (1Ch 27:16 – 22).

> **General References to:**
>
> *Tribe of, blessed (Ge 49:20; Dt 33:24 – 25). Census of, by families (Nu 1:40 – 41; 26:44 – 47; 1Ch 7:40; 12:36). Station of, in camp (Nu 2:25, 27). Prophecies concerning, by Moses (Dt 33:24 – 25); by John (Rev 7:6). Allotment to, of land in Canaan (Jos 19:24 – 31; Eze 48:2). Fail to fully possess land (Jdg 1:31 – 32). Criticized by Deborah (Jdg 5:17). Summoned by Gideon (Jdg 6:35; 7:23). Support David (1Ch 12:36). Men of, join Hezekiah (2Ch 30:11). Represented by 12,000 from (Rev 7:6).*

ASHERAH [H895] (a-shē′ra).

1. Canaanite goddess, sometimes identified with Anath and Ashtoreth. *See Ashtoreth.*

2. Asherah poles: images of or trees planted to the goddess Asherah. Forbidden to be established (Ex 34:13; Dt 7:5; 16:21; Isa 1:29; 17:8; 27:9; Mic 5:14). Worshiped by Israelites (Jdg 3:7; 1Ki 14:15, 23; 15:13; 2Ki 13:6; 17:10, 16; 21:3 – 7; 2Ch 24:18; Jer 17:2). Destroyed by Gideon (Jdg 6:28); Hezekiah (2Ki 18:4);

Josiah (2Ki 23:14; 2Ch 34:3 – 4); Asa (2Ch 14:3); Jehoshaphat (2Ch 17:6; 19:3). *See High Places; Idolatry.*

Ex	34:13	and cut down their **A** poles.
Jdg	6:25	and cut down the **A** pole beside it.
1Ki	14:15	to anger by making **A** poles.
	18:19	and the four hundred prophets of **A**,
2Ch	34:4	and smashed the **A** poles,

ASHES [709, 2014, 2016, 6760, 5075, 5491]. The expression "dust and ashes" (e.g., Ge 18:27) is a play on words (*aphar* and *epher*) and signifies the origin of the human body from the ordinary chemical elements. It contrasts the lowliness of humankind with the dignity of God. Ashes were sprinkled over a person, or a person sat among ashes, as a sign of mourning (2Sa 13:19; Job 2:8). The word is often united with "sackcloth" to express mourning (Jer 6:26).

The expression "beauty for ashes" (Isa 61:3) is also a play on words. Another word for ashes, *deshen*, is used for the remains of the burnt offering (e.g., Lev 6:10 – 11).

> **General References to:**
>
> *Uses of, in purification (Nu 19:9 – 10, 17; Heb 9:13). A symbol of mourning (2Sa 13:19; Est 4:1, 3). Sitting in (Job 2:8; Isa 58:5; Jer 6:26; Eze 27:30; Jnh 3:6; Lk 10:13). Repenting in (Job 42:6; Da 9:3; Jnh 3:6; Mt 11:21; Lk 10:13). Disguises of (1Ki 20:38, 41).*

Ge	18:27	though I am nothing but dust and **a**,
Est	4:1	put on sackcloth and **a**,
Job	42:6	and repent in dust and **a**."
Ps	102:9	For I eat **a** as my food
Isa	61:3	a crown of beauty instead of **a**,
Mt	11:21	repented long ago in sackcloth and **a**.

ASHKELON [884, 885] (ăsh′kĕ-lŏn). One of the five chief cities of the Philistines, located on the seacoast about twelve miles (twenty km.) NE of Gaza. It was taken by the tribe of Judah shortly after the death of Joshua (Jdg 1:18) but was retaken by the Philistines and remained in their hands through much of the OT period. In the eighth century BC Amos denounced the city for its complicity with Phoenicia and Edom in their warfare on Israel (Am 1:6 – 8). Zephaniah, writing in the dark days before the captivity of Judah (Zep 2:4, 7) and looking far into the future, saw the restoration of Judah and the Jews occupying the desolate ruins of Ashkelon. Zechariah, writing in c. 518 BC, prophesied that Ashkelon would see the destruction of Tyre and that Ashkelon itself would then be destroyed (Zec 9:5). Apparently it was rebuilt, for Herod the Great was born there and Roman ruins have been found. During the Crusades it came to life again, and Richard Coeur de Lion held court there. Later the town reverted to the Saracens.

Archaeological remains are sparse: a ruined and overgrown Byzantine church, a quadrangle with some preserved columns and foundation walls of an odeum (tiered council chamber) attributed to Herod the Great by the excavators, some statues belonging to the façade of the odeum, and a third-century AD painted tomb. The oldest evidence of occupation here is from the area near the beach and dates to c. 2000 BC.

Jdg	1:18	men of Judah also took Gaza, **A**
2Sa	1:20	proclaim it not in the streets of **A**,

ASHTORETH [6956] (ăsh'tō-rĕth). A goddess of the Canaanites, worshiped all along the seacoast from Ras Shamra (Ugarit) southward through Phoenicia and Philistia. The plural Ashtaroth (NIV "the Ashtoreths") is found commonly and refers to the idols representing her. Her male consort was apparently Baal, and the two were worshiped with lewd rites. In Jdg 2:11 – 23; 10:6; 1Sa 7:3 – 4; 12:10; 1Ki 11:5, 33; 2Ki 23:13 we are told that Israel forsook their God and served "Baal and the Ashtoreths." The prophet Samuel brought about a great revival, but before Israel could be saved from the Philistines, they had to give up Ashtoreth and turn to the Lord (1Sa 7:3 – 4). Israel kept fairly close to the Lord through the times of Samuel, Saul, and David and the early days of Solomon, until that "wise" man lost his wisdom by marrying various heathen women for political reasons. They

succeeded in turning his heart from the Lord to worship of the Ashtoreth and other idols (1Ki 11:4 – 8). These idols remained more than three and a half centuries until Josiah defiled and demolished them (2Ki 23:13 – 14). Biblical scholar Gesenius related the name Ashtoreth to the Persian word *sitarah* or *star* and connected it with Venus, goddess of love.

1Ki	11:5	**A** the goddess of the Sidonians,

ASHURBANIPAL [10055] (ă-shĕr-bă'nĕ-păl, *Ashur creates a son*). King of Assyria. He was grandson of the famous Sennacherib and son of Esarhaddon. Ashurbanipal, or, as he was known to the Greeks, Sardanapalus, reigned from 668 to 626 BC and therefore was contemporary with Manasseh, Jotham, and Josiah of Judah. Modern scholars have reason to be grateful to Ashurbanipal because he was a lover of learning and collected a great library of cuneiform tablets (more than 22,000 in number) that have given to us most of what we know of Babylonian and Assyrian literature. In Ezr 4:10 his name is also rendered "Asnapper" (KJV, MLB, NEB) and Osnapper (NASB, RSV); see the NIV note to this passage.

ASIA [823, 824]. Proconsular Asia in NT times was the Roman province that contained the SW part of Asia Minor, and in particular "the seven churches in the province of Asia" addressed in the first three chapters of Revelation. In the NT the word "Asia" occurs nineteen times and always refers to this division, not to the whole continent, nor even to Anatolia. Its capital was Ephesus, where both Paul and John labored. Most of its cities have disappeared, but Smyrna (Rev 2:8 – 11) remains a great city even now (called Izmir, in modern Turkey).

Ac	2:9	and Cappadocia, Pontus and **A**,
	16:6	the word in the province of **A**.
Rev	1:4	seven churches in the province of **A**:

ASSEMBLY

Nu	14:10	whole **a** talked about stoning them.
	16:21	"Separate yourselves from this **a**
Dt	23:1	may enter the **a** of the LORD.

2Ch	29:28	The whole **a** bowed in worship,
Ps	1:5	nor sinners in the **a** of the righteous.
	35:18	I will give you thanks in the great **a**;
	82:1	God presides in the great **a**;
	149:1	his praise in the **a** of the saints.
Joel	1:14	Declare a holy fast; call a sacred **a**.
Heb	12:22	upon thousands of angels in joyful **a**,

ASSHUR [855] (ăsh′ûr, Heb. *'ashshûr*). The god of the Assyrians; their reputed human founder; the ancient capital of the country; often the nation Assyria. Asshur is the builder of Nineveh and nearby cities (Ge 10:11 JB, KJV). He comes from the kingdom of Nimrod, a descendant of Ham, but may not be of his race, for in Ge 10:22 and 1Ch 1:17 Asshur is a descendant of Shem. The ASV, NIV, and RSV render Ge 10:11 to read that Nimrod went into Assyria and founded Nineveh. In Balaam's prophecy (Nu 24:22, 24) Asshur appears to be Assyria. Assur (KJV) in Ezr 4:2 is translated "Assyria" in the ASV, NIV, and RSV. In Ps 83:8, in a list of enemies of Israel, the ASV, NIV, and RSV have "Assyria," while the JB, KJV, and NEB have "Assur." In Eze 27:23 Asshur is in a list of nations with whom Israel traded; but in 32:22, in a list of nations to be destroyed, the ASV and KJV retain "Asshur," while the NIV and RSV have "Assyria." The KJV, NIV, and RSV all have "Assyria" in Hos 14:3. For most occurrences of the Hebrew word, the KJV has "Assyria," which is the probable meaning in every case.

ASSOCIATION-SEPARATION

Evil Associations:
Warnings concerning (Ex 23:2; 34:12; Ps 1:1; Pr 4:14; 24:1; 1Co 5:11; 2Co 6:14). Results of (Nu 33:55; 1Ki 11:2; 2Ch 19:2; Pr 28:7; Jn 18:18, 25; 1Co 15:33). Contact with impurity (Lev 5:2; 15:11; Nu 19:13; Isa 52:11; 2Co 6:17; Col 2:21). Separation from unclean (Lev 13:5, 21, 33, 46; Nu 5:3). Israel from nations (Lev 20:26; Nu 23:9; Dt 7:2; Jos 23:7; Jdg 2:2; Ezr 9:12; 10:11; Isa 52:11; Jer 15:19). Believers from (Jn 15:19; Ac 2:40; Eph 5:11; 2Th 3:6). Final separation of evil from good (Mt 13:30, 49; 25:32; Lk 16:26; 17:34).

Good Associations:
Companionship (Ps 119:63; Pr 2:20; 13:20; 2Th 3:14). Personal contact with Jesus (Mt 9:20, 25; 14:34 – 36; Mk 3:10; 9:27; Lk 6:19); with Peter (Ac 3:7; 9:41). Produced by faith (Eph 3:12; 2Ti 1:12; Heb 10:22). Made full by hope (Heb 6:11, 19). Confirmed by love (1Jn 3:14, 19; 4:18). Effect of righteousness (Isa 32:17). Abundant in the understanding of the gospel (Col 2:2; 1Th 1:5).

ASSURANCE [586, 622, 6859, 4244, 4443]. The internal and external evidence by which Christians may have confidence to believe that God is their Father and Christ their Savior and Lord. Thus they know that what the gospel declares about Jesus is true and that in Jesus they have a new relationship with God.

Faith (*pistis*) as belief in, trust of, and commitment to God through Jesus Christ carries with it a certain assurance. This is because true faith includes the acceptance of God's own testimony concerning himself and his relation to a sinner (Ac 17:31; 1Co 2:10 – 13; 1Th 2:13). Thus the believer approaches the Father in prayer and worship with *plerophoria* (humble conviction and "full assurance" — Col 2:2; Heb 6:11; 10:22 KJV). In fact, the Christian is "fully persuaded" that God is what he says he is and does what he claims to do (Ro 4:21; 8:38; 2Ti 1:12 KJV).

There is also the internal witness of the Holy Spirit bringing the knowledge that the believer is truly a child of God (Ro 8:15 – 16), as well as the external testimony of a changed life (1Jn 2:3 – 5, 29; 3:9 – 14, 18 – 19; 4:7). Because of the presence of the indwelling Spirit, assurance in the new covenant is of a much deeper order than in the old covenant. However, assurance was a reality for believers within the Mosiac covenant (Isa 32:17).

Believers Privileged to Have:
Election (Ps 4:3; 1Th 1:4); redemption (Job 19:25); adoption (Ro 8:16; 1Jn 3:2); salvation (Isa 12:2); eternal life (1Jn 5:13); unalienable love of God (Ro 8:38 – 39); union with God and Christ (1Co 6:15; 2Co 13:5; Eph 5:30; 1Jn 2:5; 4:13); peace with God by Christ (Ro 5:1); preservation

(Pss 3:6, 8; 27:3 – 5; 46:3); answers to prayer (1Jn 3:22; 5:14 – 15); continuance in grace (Php 1:6); comfort in affliction (Ps 73:26; Lk 4:18 – 19; 2Co 4:8 – 10, 16 – 18); support in death (Ps 23:4); a glorious resurrection (Job 19:26; Ps 17:15; Php 3:21; 1Jn 3:2); a kingdom (Heb 12:28; Rev 5:10); a crown (2Ti 4:7 – 8; Jas 1:12). Believers should give diligence to attain to (2Pe 1:10 – 11); strive to maintain (Heb 3:14, 18). Confident hope in God restores (Ps 42:11).

Exemplified by:

David (Pss 23:4; 73:24 – 26); Paul (2Ti 1:12; 4:18).

ASSYRIA [824+855, 855] (a-sĭr′ĭa, Heb. *'ashshûr*). Originally a land between the upper Tigris and Zab rivers, with its capital first at Assur, later at Nineveh. Assyria was taken over in the third millennium BC by Semites from Arabia. First mentioned in the Bible in Ge 2:14, Assyria and the Assyrians are frequently named, sometimes as Asshur or Assur. By 1900 Assyrian traders had a colony in Hittite territory, at Kanish in Asia Minor. In the thirteenth century Assyrian military expeditions crossed the Euphrates, and by 1100 they reached the Mediterranean. But Assyria was not strong enough to maintain their advance. By 1000 the Aramean kingdom of Zobah reached the Euphrates, but David conquered Zobah and stopped its invasion of Assyria, an irony of history enabling Assyria to become strong. The tenth century was one of powerful and systematic advance. Assyria rounded out its borders north and east, conquered Babylonia, and advanced westward through Aramean territory to the Mediterranean. Under Shalmaneser III the Assyrians turned toward Palestine. In 853 they were defeated at Karkar but claimed a victory over Ben-Hadad of Damascus and a coalition incuding Ahab, king of Israel. They failed to follow up their effort.

After the religious revival under Elijah and Elisha, the coalition of Israel with Syria broke up. When Jehu gained the throne (2Ki 9 – 10), Shalmaneser III seized the opportunity to claim tribute from Jehu and to weaken Damascus. Internal difficulties kept Assyria from further Palestinian inroads for nearly a century, until shortly after the middle of the eighth century BC, when Tiglath-Pileser III invaded the west, divided the territory into subject provinces, and exchanged populations on a large scale to make rebellion more difficult. In 733 – 732 he conquered Galilee, the Plain of Sharon, and Gilead and made both Israel and Judah pay tribute (15:29; 16:9). Isaiah prophesied that this attempt to subjugate Judah would eventually fail. Shalmaneser V besieged Samaria for three years. He died during the siege, and his successor, Sargon II (now called Sargon III), took the city in 721 and carried its more prosperous citizens into exile, replacing them with colonists from other provinces of his empire (17:6 – 41).

For nearly a century thereafter, Assyria was troubled from all sides — from Babylon, Elam, the Medes, Phrygia, and Egypt. Yet Sennacherib nearly captured Jerusalem in 701 – 700 BC (2Ki 18:13 – 19:37; Isa 36 – 37), the danger ending only when "the angel of the LORD went out and put to death a hundred and eighty-five thousand men in the Assyrian camp," followed by the assassination of Sennacherib. Manasseh, king of Judah, paid tribute to Assyria, except during a short rebellion for which he was carried to Babylon but released after he sought the Lord (2Ch 33:11 – 13). The last quarter of the seventh century saw the fall and decline of the Assyrian Empire and its subjugation by the Chaldean conquerors of Babylonia with the Medes. Nineveh was taken in 612. For a short time Babylonia replaced Assyria as the great power. The prophets Elijah, Elisha, and Isaiah are largely concerned with Assyria; several other prophets — Jeremiah, Ezekiel, Hosea, Micah, Nahum, Zephaniah, and Zechariah — refer to it. Jonah was actually sent to prophesy to Nineveh, and the revival he unwillingly promoted saved the city from destruction for a long period of time.

Assyrian art, architecture, and technology were successively influenced by Sumerians, Akkadians, and Babylonians and early attained high levels, excit-

ing the admiration and imitation of Ahaz, king of Judah (2Ki 16:10 – 13). Literature was largely utilitarian — legal, historical, commercial, scientific, pseudo-scientific, and religious — but it exists in abundance, notably the library of Ashurbanipal, consisting of thousands of clay tablets. The Assyrians early added to their worship of the primitive national god Asshur the Babylonian deities with their cultic apparatus. Wherever they influenced Israel and Judah, the effort was demoralizing, as the historical books of the Bible and the prophets bear abundant witness.

General References to:

(Ge 10:8 – 11). Situated beyond the Euphrates (Isa 7:20). Watered by the Tigris (Ge 2:14). Governed by kings (2Ki 15:19, 29). Invaded Israel (2Ki 15:19). Bought off by Menahem (2Ki 15:19 – 20). Idolatry of, brought into Samaria (2Ki 17:29). Condemned for oppressing God's people (Isa 52:4). Judah condemned for trusting (Jer 2:18, 36). Israel condemned for trusting (Hos 5:13; 7:11; 8:9). Jews condemned for following idolatries of (Eze 16:28; 23:5, 7). Greatness, extent, duration, and fall of, illustrated (Eze 31:3 – 17).

Called:

Land of Nimrod (Mic 5:6). Shinar (Ge 11:2; 14:1). Asshur (Nu 24:22, 24). Nineveh, chief city of (Ge 10:11; 2Ki 19:36).

Celebrated for:

Fertility (2Ki 18:32; Isa 36:17). Extent of conquests (2Ki 18:33 – 35; 19:11 – 13; Isa 10:9 – 14). Extensive commerce (Eze 27:23 – 24). Idolatry, the religion of (2Ki 19:37).

Described:

Most formidable (Isa 28:2). Intolerant and oppressive (Na 3:19). Cruel and destructive (Isa 10:7). Selfish and reserved (Hos 8:9). Unfaithful (2Ch 28:20 – 21). Proud and haughty (2Ki 19:22 – 24; Isa 10:8). An instrument of God's vengeance (Isa 7:18 – 19; 10:5 – 6). Chief men of, described (Eze 23:6, 12, 23). Armies of, described (Isa 5:26 – 29).

Predictions Regarding:

Conquest of Kenites by (Nu 24:22). Invasion of Judah by (Isa 5:26; 7:17 – 20; 8:8; 10:5 – 6, 12). Conquest of Syria by (Isa 8:4). Conquest and captivity of Israel by (Isa 8:4; Hos 9:3; 10:6; 11:5). Destruction of (Isa 10:12 – 19; 14:24 – 25; 30:31 – 33; 31:8 – 9; Zec 10:11). Restoration of Israel from (Isa 27:12 – 13; Hos 11:11; Zec 10:10). Participation in the blessings of the gospel (Isa 19:23 – 25; Mic 7:12).

Ge	10:11	From that land he went to **A**,
2Ki	15:29	and deported the people to **A**.
	18:11	The king of **A** deported Israel to **A**
	19:10	not be handed over to the king of **A**.'
Isa	30:31	of the LORD will shatter **A**;
Jer	50:18	as I punished the king of **A**.
Hos	14:3	**A** cannot save us;

ASTROLOGER, ASTROLOGY [2042+9028, 4169, 10373]. One who tries to find out the influence of the stars upon human affairs or to foretell events by their positions and aspects (Isa 47:12 – 13; Jer 10:1 – 2; Da 1:20; 2:27; 4:7; 5:7, 11). In warning his people against Canaanite superstition (Dt 18:10 – 13), Moses made no reference to astrology or any sort of fortune-telling by means of the stars, for, though it later came into western Palestine, it was essentially a Babylonian or Mesopotamian study. Although the translation "astrologer" appears several times in the English Bible (e.g., Da 2:2; 5:7 NIV), the only unequivocal reference to the practice and its practitioners is found in Isa 47:13 ("those stargazers who make predictions month by month") and Jer 10:2 (where people are urged not to be "terrified by signs in the sky"). It was a characteristic of Babylonian wisdom, as well as Egyptian, to ponder the movement of the stars, taking note of variations and conjunctions so as to predict events on earth. The Hebrew word 'ashshāph (e.g., in Da 1:20; 2:2, 10, 17; 4:7; 5:7, 11, 17) has often been translated "astrologer," though not by the NIV. It refers to the general practice of magic or the casting of spells and pronouncing of charms. The NIV does, however, use "astrologer" to represent "Chaldean" in some of these same verses as well as others (e.g., Da 2:2, 4 – 5, 10; 5:7, 11), a needless restriction of meaning for a word that covers, for example, philosophy as well as astrology and, in general, refers to educated or knowledgeable people.

| Isa | 47:13 | Let your **a** come forward, |
| Da | 2:2 | **a** to tell him what he had dreamed. |

ASTRONOMY While the word *astronomy* is not found in the Bible, there are many passages that refer to some aspect of the subject. God is recognized as the maker of the stars (Ge 1:16) as well as the one who knows their number and names (Ps 147:4). Psalm 19 contains a poem telling how the heavenly bodies (referring to the stars) show forth the glory of their Creator. A reference is made also to the sun as another of the heavenly bodies.

Phenomena Concerning the Universe:

God the creator of (Job 9:6 – 9; 26:7, 13; 37:18; Pss 8:3; 136:5 – 9; Isa 40:22, 26). God the ruler of (Job 38:31 – 33; Ps 68:33; Eze 32:7 – 8; Am 5:8). Immeasurable (Jer 31:37; 33:22). Laws of, permanent (Ecc 1:5; Jer 31:35 – 36). Declares God's glory (Ps 19:1 – 6). Destruction of (Isa 34:4; Mt 24:35; 2Pe 3:10; Rev 6:12 – 14; 21:1).

Celestial Phenomena:

Fire from heaven: on cities of the plain (Ge 19:24 – 25); on the two captains and their fifties (2Ki 1:10 – 14); on the flocks and servants of Job (Job 1:16). Thunder and lightning on Mount Sinai (Ex 19:16, 18; 20:18). Pillar of cloud and fire (Ex 13:21 – 22; 14:19, 24; 40:38; Nu 9:15 – 23; Ps 78:14). Sun seemingly rotating (Ecc 1:5). Sun and moon standing still (Jos 10:12 – 14). Hail on Egyptians (Ex 9:22 – 34). Darkness on Egyptians (Ex 10:21 – 23); at Jesus' crucifixion (Mt 27:45; Lk 23:44 – 45). Wandering stars (Jude 13).

Signs in the Sun, Moon, and Stars:

(Joel 2:30 – 31; Isa 13:10). Foretold by Jesus as part of his second coming (Mt 24:29, 35; Mk 13:24 – 25; Lk 21:25; Ac 2:19 – 20). In the final judgments (Rev 8:10 – 12; 9:1 – 2; 10:1 – 2; 12:3 – 4; 13:13; 16:8 – 9; 19:11 – 14).

Constellations:

Glory of (1Co 15:41). Darkened (Isa 13:10). The serpent (Job 26:13). Bear, Orion, and Pleiades (Job 9:9; 38:31; Am 5:8).

ATHEISM Instances of (Pss 10:4; 14:1; 53:1). Arguments against (Job 12:7 – 25; Ro 1:19 – 20).

ATHENS [121, 122] (ăth'ĕnz, Gr. *Athēnai*). In ancient times the famous capital of Attica, one of the Greek states; now the capital of Greece. The city was named after its patron goddess Athene. It centered around a rocky hill called Acropolis and was 4.5 miles (7.5 km.) from the sea. Two walls, 250 feet (78 m.) apart, connected the city with its harbor (Peiraeus). According to tradition, the city was founded by Cecrops, who came from Egypt about 1556 BC. Athens sent fifty ships to the Trojan War. The city was ruled by kings until about 1068, when archons (magistrates) began to rule. Two of the most famous archons were Draco, who in c. 620 issued laws "written in blood," and Solon, who in 594 gave the state a constitution. The Athenians defeated the Persians at Marathon in 490 and again in 480 at Salamis. They then built a small empire, with a powerful fleet for its support. The period of Athens's greatest glory was during the rule of Pericles (459 – 431), who erected many beautiful public buildings in the city and under whose administration literature and art flourished. The Peloponnesian War (431 – 404) ended with the submission of Athens to Sparta. Later wars sapped the strength of Athens. Philip of Macedon crushed the city in 338. In 146 the Romans made it a part of the province of Achaea. The Roman general Sulla sacked the city in 86. It subsequently came into the hands of the Goths, the Byzantines, and other peoples. The Turks ruled it from AD 1458 until the emancipation of Greece in 1833.

In ancient times Athens had a population of at least a quarter of a million. It was the seat of Greek art, science, and philosophy and was the most important university city in the ancient world, even under Roman sway. Although politically conquered, it conquered its conquerors with its learning and culture.

Paul visited the city on his second missionary journey and spoke to an interested but somewhat disdainful audience (Ac 17). He reminded them of their altar inscribed with the words "TO AN UNKNOWN GOD," which he had seen in the city, and declared that he could tell them about this God. He made some converts in the city, but there is no record of his establishing a church there or of his returning on any later occasion. From Athens he went to Corinth, where he remained for a year and a half, establishing a strong church.

Ac   17:16   Paul was waiting for them in **A**,

ATONEMENT [4105, 4113, 4114, 2661, 2662, 2663] (ătō̆n′mĕnt). The root meaning in English, "reparation," leads to the secondary meaning of reconciliation, or "at-one-ment," the bringing together into harmony of those who have been separated, enemies. This double meaning brings a basic biblical concept into focus. Atonement is the divine act of grace in which God accepts an offering as a substitute for the punishment for sin. In the OT, the shed blood of sacrificial offerings effected atonement. The blood shed in the sacrifices was sacred. It epitomized the life of the sacrificial victim. Since life was sacred, blood (a symbol of life) had to be treated with respect (Ge 9:5 – 6). Eating blood was therefore strictly forbidden (Lev 7:26 – 27; Dt 12:16, 23 – 25; 15:23; 1Sa 14:32 – 34). Leviticus 17:14 stresses the intimate relationship between blood and life by twice declaring that "the life of every creature is its blood." Life is the precious and mysterious gift of God, and people are not to seek to preserve it or increase their life-force by eating "life" that is "in the blood" (Lev 17:11) — as many pagan peoples throughout history have thought they could do (Ge 9:4). Practically every sacrifice included the sprinkling or smearing of blood on the altar or within the tabernacle (Lev 1:5; 3:2; 4:6, 25; 7:2; 17:6), thus teaching that atonement involves the substi-

tution of life for life. The blood of the OT sacrifice pointed forward to the blood of the Lamb of God, who obtained for his people "eternal redemption" (Heb 9:12). "Without the shedding of blood there is no forgiveness" (Heb 9:22).

In the OT, atonement is mainly expressed by the verb *kāphar*, whose root meaning is "to cover over." In secular use, for example, Noah "covered over" the woodwork of the ark with pitch (Ge 6:14). The noun related to this verb, *kōpher*, while it has its secular use (6:14; NIV "pitch"), is mainly used of the ransom price that "covers" an offense — not by sweeping it out of sight but by making an equivalent payment so that the offense has been actually and exactly paid for (e.g., Ex 30:12, "ransom"; Nu 35:31; Ps 49:7; Isa 43:3). Arising from this use of the noun, one whole section of the verb (in Heb. the piel and pual forms, *kippēr* and *kuppar*) came to be set aside to express only the idea of removing offense by equivalent payment and so bringing the offender and the offended together. The only secular uses of this word (in Ge 32:20; Lev 5:16; 16:30, 33; 17:11) show also that the means of atonement — the actual price paid as equivalent to the sin committed — was the sacrificial blood, the life laid down in death. *See Blood.*

The ritual of the Day of Atonement should be studied, and in particular the part played by the two goats (Lev 16:15 – 17, 20 – 22). The Lord wanted his people to know the significance of what happened in secret when the high priest sprinkled the blood on the "atonement cover" (Heb. *kappōreth*). Therefore he commanded the ceremony of the live goat so that they might actually see their sins being laid on another and borne away, never to return again.

In Christian theology, atonement is the central doctrine of faith and can properly include all that Jesus accomplished for us on the cross. It was a vicarious (substitutionary) atonement. On the Day of Atonement, the goat that was substituted was in some sense not as valuable as a person, though the goat had never sinned; but God in his matchless grace provided a Substitute who was *infinitely* better than the sinner, absolutely sinless and holy, and dearer to the Father than all creation. "The wages of sin is death" (Ro 6:23), and "God made him who had no sin to be sin for us, so that in him we might become the righteousness of God" (2Co 5:21).

There are two opposite facts that the ingenuity of the theologians could not have reconciled without God's solution: First, that God is holy and he hates sin, and that by his holy law sin is a capital crime; and second, that "God is love" (1Jn 4:8). So the problem was this: "How can God be just and at the same time justify the sinner?" (cf. Ro 3:26). John 3:16 tells us that God so loved that he gave — but our blessed Lord was not just a means to an end, not a martyr to a cause. In the eternal counsels of the Trinity, he offered himself to bear our sins (Rev 13:8). He voluntarily emptied himself of the divine trappings of omnipotence, omniscience, and glory (Php 2:5 – 8) that he might be truly human, becoming the babe of Bethlehem. For some thirty-three years he perfectly fulfilled the law on our behalf (Mt 5:18) and then paid the penalty for our sins in his death for us on the cross. Our Lord's work of atonement looks in three directions: toward sin and Satan (1Pe 1:18 – 19), toward us (Ro 5:6 – 11), and toward the holy Father (1Jn 2:2).

Means of:

Meat offerings (Lev 5:11 – 13); jewels (Nu 31:50); money (Ex 30:12 – 16; Lev 5:15 – 16; 2Ki 12:16); incense (Nu 16:46 – 50). Animals. See below, Made by Animal Sacrifices. Jesus. See below, Made by Jesus.

Day of:

Time of (Ex 30:10; Lev 23:27; 25:9; Nu 29:7). How observed (Ex 30:10; Lev 16:2 – 34; 23:27 – 32; Nu 29:7 – 11; Heb 5:3; 9:7).

Made by Animal Sacrifices:

In the blood shed (Lev 17:11). In sin offerings (Ex 29:36; Lev 4:20). In burnt offerings (Lev 1:4). For unintentional sin (Lev 4:13 – 21; Nu 15:22 – 28; 28:27 – 31; 29); of a leader (Lev 4:22 – 35); of the descendants of Aaron (Lev 9:7; 10:17; 16:6 – 9). In guilt offerings for sin (Lev 5:6 – 10; 6:7). Forgiveness of sins through (Lev 5:10; 19:22). For

purification after childbirth (Lev 12:6 – 8). For cleansing from a skin disease (Lev 14:12 – 32). The scapegoat (Lev 16:10 – 34). On festival days (Nu 28:22; 29).

Made by Jesus:

(Ge 4:4, w Heb 11:4; Ge 22:2, w Heb 11:17, 19; Ex 12:5, 11, 14, w 1Co 5:7; Ex 24:8, w Heb 9:10; Lev 16:30, 34, w Heb 9:7, 12, 28; Lev 17:11, w Heb 9:22). Through his blood shed (Lk 22:20; 1Co 1:23; Eph 2:13 – 15; Heb 9:12 – 15, 25 – 26; 12:24; 13:12, 20 – 21; 1Jn 5:6; Rev 1:5; 5:9; 7:14; 12:11); his death (Ro 3:24 – 26; 5:11 – 15; 1Th 1:10; Heb 13:12; 1Jn 2:2; 3:5; 4:10; Rev 5:6, 9; 13:8). Typified in the Passover lamb (Ex 12:5, 11, 14; 1Co 5:7); in sacrifices (Ex 24:8; Lev 16:30, 34; 17:11; 19:22; Heb 9:11 – 28). Divinely inspired (Lk 2:30 – 31; Gal 4:4 – 5; Eph 1:3 – 12, 17 – 22; 2:4 – 10; Col 1:19 – 20; 1Pe 1:20; Rev 13:8). A mystery (1Co 2:7; 1Pe 1:8 – 12). Once for all (Heb 7:27; 9:24 – 28; 10:10, 12, 14; 1Pe 3:18). Made on our behalf (Isa 53:4 – 12; Mt 20:28; Jn 6:51; 11:49 – 51; Gal 3:13; Eph 5:2; 1Th 5:9 – 10; Heb 2:9; 1Pe 2:24). For reconciliation (Da 9:24 – 27; Ro 5:1 – 21; 2Co 5:18 – 21; Eph 2:16 – 17; Col 1:20 – 22; Heb 2:17). For remission of sins (Zec 13:1; Mt 26:28; Lk 22:20; 24:46 – 47; Jn 1:29; Ro 4:25; 1Co 15:3; Gal 1:3 – 4; Eph 1:7; Col 1:14; Heb 1:3; 10:1 – 20; 1Jn 1:7; 3:5). For redemption (Mt 20:28; Ac 20:28; Gal 3:13; 1Ti 2:6; Heb 9:12; Rev 5:9).

Ex	25:17	"Make an **a** cover of pure gold —
	29:36	Purify the altar by making **a** for it,
	30:10	Once a year Aaron shall make **a**
	32:30	perhaps I can make **a** for your sin."
Lev	17:11	to make **a** for yourselves on the altar;
	17:11	the blood that makes **a** for one's life.
	23:27	seventh month is the Day of **A**.
Nu	25:13	the honor of his God and made **a** for
1Ch	6:49	making **a** for Israel,
Ro	3:25	God presented him as a sacrifice of **a**
Heb	2:17	and that he might make **a** for the sins

ATONEMENT COVER [4114, 2663] (KJV "mercy seat").

> *Description of (Ex 25:17 – 22). Where God met with his people (Ex 25:22; 30:6, 36; Lev 16:2; Nu 7:89; 17:4; 1Sa 4:4; 2Sa 6:2; 2Ki 19:15; 1Ch 13:6; Pss 80:1; 99:1; Isa 37:16; Heb 4:16). Placed on the ark of the testimony (Ex 26:34; 30:6; 31:7; 40:20; Heb 9:5). Materials of, to be a freewill offering (Ex 35:4 – 12). Made by Bezalel (Ex 37:1, 6 – 9). Sprinkled with blood (Lev 16:14 – 15). In Solomon's temple (1Ch 28:11). See Tabernacle.*

ATONEMENT, DAY OF An annual Hebrew feast when the high priest offered sacrifices for the sins of the nation (Lev 23:27; 25:9). It was the only fast period required by Mosaic law (Lev 16:29; 23:31). The day marked the only entry of the high priest into the Most Holy Place (Lev 16). It was observed on the tenth day of the seventh month and was a day of great solemnity and strictest conformity to the law.

Theologically and spiritually, the Day of Atonement is the center of Leviticus, "the book of holiness." The sixteenth chapter gives the law for the Day of Atonement. The divinely inspired commentary on this chapter is found in Heb 9:1 – 10:25. Israel had two beginnings for its years, six months apart. In the first month on the fourteenth day, they ate the Passover as a memorial of the events leading to the exodus from Egypt; half a year later, in the seventh month on the tenth day (Lev 16:29), they denied themselves and the priest made atonement for them. The Jews now celebrate their New Year's Day (Rosh Hashanah) on the first day of the seventh month (September), and the Day of Atonement (Yom Kippur), properly *yom hakkippurim*, on the tenth.

The purpose of the Day of Atonement seems to have been at least fourfold: first, to show God's hatred of sin, that the "wages of sin is death" (Ro 6:23) and that "without the shedding of blood there is no forgiveness" (Heb 9:22); second, to show the contagious nature of sin, for even the Most Holy Place had to be cleansed "because of the uncleanness and rebellion of the Israelites, whatever their sins have been" (Lev 16:16); third, to point forward by three types to the death of "the Lamb of God," our blessed Savior; and fourth, by its repetition year after year to signify that the way into the very presence of God had not been made manifest before the death of Christ (Heb 9:7 – 9). When our Lord offered himself on Calvary, the veil of the temple was torn (Mk 15:38), and God signified that from that moment on we were under a new covenant — a covenant of grace, not of law. "For the law was given through Moses; grace and truth came through Jesus Christ" (Jn 1:17). The OT ceremonies were but symbols and types and shadows: the NT records the realities. In OT times God was teaching his people by "kindergarten" methods — godliness brought health, long life, and prosperity; sin brought quick, visible, corporeal punishment. Today, under grace, we look back to Calvary, when the great Day of Atonement took place once for all.

ATTENTION

Ex	4:8	or pay **a** to the first miraculous sign,
	15:26	if you pay **a** to his commands
	16:20	some of them paid no **a** to Moses;
Dt	28:13	If you pay **a** to the commands of
1Ki	18:29	no one answered, no one paid **a**.
Ne	8:13	to give **a** to the words of the Law.
Pr	4:1	to a father's instruction; pay **a**
	4:20	My son, pay **a** to what I say;
	5:1	My son, pay **a** to my wisdom,
	17:4	a liar pays **a** to a malicious tongue.
	22:17	Pay **a** and listen to the sayings of
Ecc	7:21	not pay **a** to every word people say,
Isa	42:20	but have paid no **a**;
Jer	44:5	But they did not listen or pay **a**;
Tit	1:14	and will pay no **a** to Jewish myths or
Heb	2:1	We must pay more careful **a**,
Jas	2:3	If you show special **a** to
2Pe	1:19	and you will do well to pay **a** to it,
3Jn	1:10	I will call **a** to what he is doing,

AUGUSTUS CAESAR (ô-gŭs'tŭs sē´zêr). Gaius Octavius, whose male ancestors for four generations had the same name, was born in Rome in 63 BC and early became influential through his great-uncle Julius Caesar. He was studying quietly in Illyria when he heard of Caesar's murder in 44. Hastening to Italy, he learned that Caesar had adopted him and made him his heir. Thus in his early manhood by skillful manipulation of his friends, he conquered his rival Antony at Actium. The beginning of the Roman Empire may be reckoned from that date — September 2, 31. By his adoption he had become "Caesar," and now the Roman senate added the title "Augustus." Although he preserved the forms of a republic, he gradually took all the power into his hands. He reigned until AD 14. Some of the secular histories omit the most important event in his reign — a Baby was born in Bethlehem! Augustus Caesar is mentioned just once in the NT (Lk 2:1).

Lk   2:1   In those days Caesar **A** issued

AUTHORITY (Gr. *exousia*). The legal and/or moral right to exercise power, or power that is rightly possessed. In the Bible God is presented as the ultimate, personal authority and the source of all authority. All exercise of authority in the created order, by angels or humans, is therefore subordinate and derivative. The important statements of Daniel (4:34 – 35; cf. 2:21; 7:13 – 14) and Paul (Ro 13:1) point to the sovereign, final, and incontestable authority of God, Creator, Judge, and Redeemer over and in his creation. Thus the Lord exercises power as the one with authority.

In the life of the people of Israel, the Lord exercised his authority through the authority he gave to king, priest, and prophet. It was the duty of the king to reign in righteousness and justice, of the priest rightly to order the worship and service of God, and of the prophet to declare the word of the sovereign Lord, whether the people would or would not hear. When the word of the Lord came to be written down as Scripture, it was seen as authoritative because of its source (see Ps 119).

Since Jesus is uniquely sent by God, he has authority; and since he is anointed by the Holy Spirit to perform the ministry of Messiah, he has power. Authority (*exousia*) and power (*dynamis*) are related but different (see Lk 4:36, "with authority and power he …"). Jesus is a man under authority and with authority (Mt 8:9; 7:29; Mk 1:27); he empowers his disciples to cast out demons (Mt 10:1; Mk 3:15); he does what only God can do — he forgives sins (Mt 9:6); he has control over nature (Mk 4:41); he exercises power over death (Jn 10:18); and as the resurrected Lord he has all authority in earth and heaven (Mt 28:18).

As those who believed that Jesus had been exalted to the right hand of the Father, the apostles developed the theme of the authority of Jesus, presenting him as co-regent of the Father possessing authority over the whole cosmos (Eph 1:20 – 23; Php 2:1 – 11; Col 2:9 – 10). He is the "Lord of lords and King of kings" (Rev 17:14).

The NT also recognizes other forms of authority as delegated by God and Christ. There is the authority of the state (Ro 13:1ff.), of the apostles as unique pillars of the church and recipients of divine revelation (Lk 6:13; Eph 2:20), and of the husband as head of the family (1Co 11:3). In each case the exercise of power is to be within the will of God, and the one exercising authority must be mindful that God is Judge. The possession of authority and power by Satan (Lk 22:53; Col 1:13) has been abused and will be punished.

Jer	5:31	the priests rule by their own **a**,
Da	7:6	and it was given **a** to rule.
Mt	7:29	because he taught as one who had **a**,
	9:6	that the Son of Man has **a** on earth
	28:18	"All **a** in heaven and
Mk	1:27	A new teaching — and with **a**!
	10:42	and their high officials exercise **a**
	11:28	what **a** are you doing these things?"
Lk	4:32	because his message had **a**.
	5:24	that the Son of Man has **a** on earth
	7:8	For I myself am a man under **a**,
Jn	10:18	I have **a** to lay it down and **a** to take it up again.
Ac	1:7	dates the Father has set by his own **a**.
Ro	7:1	that the law has **a** over a man only
	13:1	for there is no **a** except

	13:2	he who rebels against the **a**
1Co	11:10	the woman ought to have a sign of **a**
	15:24	destroyed all dominion, **a** and power.
2Co	10:8	the **a** the Lord gave us for building
Col	2:10	the head over every power and **a**,
1Ti	2:2	for kings and all those in **a**,
	2:12	a woman to teach or to have **a** over
Tit	2:15	Encourage and rebuke with all **a**.
Heb	13:17	and submit to their **a**
1Pe	2:13	the Lord's sake to every **a** instituted
2Pe	2:10	of the sinful nature and despise **a**.
Jude	1:6	not keep their positions of **a**
Rev	2:27	as I have received **a** from my Father.
	12:10	and the **a** of his Christ.
	13:4	the dragon because he had given **a** to

AVENGER The Hebrew word *goēl* has a two-sided application of its basic meaning. At heart it is a very gracious word: It refers to the "next of kin" who possesses the right to take on himself whatever need may have overwhelmed his kinsman or kinswoman. We see this at its human best in the book of Ruth (3:12 – 13; 4:2 – 10) and at its highest when the Lord himself is called our *goēl* (Isa 43:14). But there is a darker side. Suppose someone has committed the ultimate crime against us and we lie dead through murder. What then? The *goel* comes to take our part and to exact the vengeance that the law demands (Nu 35:11 – 34). This is how the word that means "redeemer" also means "avenger." OT law was rightly dominated by the concept of equality: an exact equivalence between crime and punishment. It expressed this in characteristically vigorous terms — for example, "an eye for an eye" (Ex 21:23 – 24; Lev 24:20; Dt 19:21). We should note that these passages all refer to punishments imposed by courts of law and are not rules for private conduct. In the case of murder, where life must be taken for life, the next of kin took up the dreadful duty, carefully circumscribed in his actions by the clear OT distinction between capital murder and accidental

manslaughter and by the limitation of vengeance to the murderer only (Dt 24:16).

Nu	35:12	be places of refuge from the **a**,
Jos	20:3	find protection from the **a** of blood.
Ps	8:2	to silence the foe and the **a**.

AWAKE

Ps	35:23	**A**, and rise to my defense!
	57:8	**A**, my soul!
Pr	6:22	when you **a**, they will speak
	20:13	or you will grow poor; stay **a**
Isa	51:9	**A**, **a**! Clothe yourself with strength
	51:9	**a**, as in days gone by
	52:1	**A**, **a**, O Zion,
Da	12:2	sleep in the dust of the earth will **a**:
1Th	5:10	whether we are **a** or asleep,
Rev	16:15	Blessed is he who stays **a**

AWAKENINGS, REFORMS

General References to:
(1Ki 18:39; 2Ch 30:11; Ezr 10:1; Lk 3:7 – 10; Jn 4:39; Ac 2:40 – 41; 8:6; 9:35; 11:21; 13:48; 18:8; 19:18).

Instances of:
Asa (1Ki 15:12); Jehu (1Ki 10:27); Jehoiada (2Ki 11:18); Josiah (2Ki 23:4); Jehoshaphat (2Ch 19:3); Hezekiah (2Ch 31:1); Manasseh (2Ch 33:15); Ezra (Ezr 10:3); Nehemiah (Ne 13:19).

AWESOME

Ge	28:17	"How **a** is this place!
Ex	15:11	**a** in glory, working wonders?
	34:10	among will see how **a** is the work
Dt	4:34	or by great and **a** deeds,
	7:21	is a great and **a** God.
	10:17	the great God, mighty and **a**,
	10:21	and **a** wonders you saw
	28:58	revere this glorious and **a** name —
	34:12	or performed the **a** deeds
Jdg	13:6	like an angel of God, very **a**.
2Sa	7:23	and **a** wonders by driving out nations

1Ch	17:21	and **a** wonders by driving out nations
Ne	1:5	God of heaven, the great and **a** God,
	4:14	who is great and **a**,
	9:32	the great, mighty and **a** God,
Job	10:16	and again display your **a** power
	37:22	God comes in **a** majesty.
Ps	45:4	right hand display **a** deeds.
	47:2	How **a** is the LORD Most High,
	65:5	with **a** deeds of righteousness,
	66:3	Say to God, "How **a** are your deeds!
	66:5	how **a** his works in man's behalf!
	68:35	You are **a**, O God, in your sanctuary;
	89:7	more **a** than all who surround him.
	99:3	praise your great and **a** name —
	106:22	and **a** deeds by the Red Sea.
	111:9	holy and **a** is his name.
	145:6	of the power of your **a** works,
Isa	64:3	**a** things that we did not expect,
Eze	1:18	Their rims were high and **a**,
	1:22	sparkling like ice, and **a**.
Da	2:31	dazzling statue, **a** in appearance.
	9:4	the great and **a** God,
Zep	2:11	be **a** to them when he destroys all

AX, AXHEAD [1366, 1749, 4172, 4477, 4490, 7935, 544].

A tool for cutting wood (Dt 19:5; 20:19; 1Sa 13:20 – 21; 2Sa 12:31; Ps 74:5 – 6). A weapon of war (Jer 46:22). Elisha causes, to float (2Ki 6:5 – 6). Figurative of judgment (Jer 46:22; Mt 3:10).

AZARIAH [6481, 6482, 10538] (ăz'a-rī'a, Heb. *'ăzaryahu, Jehovah has helped*).

1. King of Judah. *See Uzziah.*

2. A man of Judah of the house of Ethan the Wise (1Ch 2:8).

3. The son of Jehu, descended from an Egyptian through the daughter of Sheshan (1Ch 2:38).

4. The son of Ahimaaz (1Ch 6:9).

5. A Levite of the family of Kohath (1Ch 6:36).

6. The son of Zadok and the high priest under Solomon (1Ki 4:2).

7. A high priest and son of Johanan (1Ch 6:10).

8. The son of Nathan and an officer at Solomon's court (1Ki 4:5).

9. A prophet, son of Obed, in the reign of King Asa (2Ch 15:1 – 8).

10. The son of Jehoshaphat, listed with five others, of which one is called Azariahu (2Ch 21:2).

11. The son of Jehoram (2Ch 22:1).

12. The son of Jeroham. He helped to overthrow Athaliah (2Ch 23:1).

13. The son of Johanan. He helped to get the captives of Judah released (2Ch 28:12).

14. A Levite who assisted in purifying the temple in Hezekiah's reign (2Ch 29:12).

15. A high priest who rebuked Uzziah's attempt to assume priestly functions (2Ch 26:16 – 20).

16. The son of Hilkiah; a high priest not long before the exile (1Ch 6:13 – 14).

17. A man of Judah who bitterly opposed Jeremiah (Jer 43:2).

18. One of the captives taken to Babylon, whose name was changed to Abednego (Da 1:7).

19. The son of Maaseiah. He helped repair the walls of Jerusalem (Ne 3:23).

20. A Levite who assisted Ezra in explaining the Law (Ne 8:7).

21. A priest who sealed the covenant (Ne 10:2).

22. A prince of Judah who marched in the procession at the dedication of the wall of Jerusalem (Ne 12:32 – 33).

BAAL [1251, 1252, 955] (bā´ăl, Heb. *ba'al, lord, possessor, husband*).

1. The word *baal* appears in the OT with a variety of meanings. Originally it was not a proper noun, but later it came to be so used. Sometimes it is used in the primary sense of "master" or "owner" (as in Ex 21:28, 34; Jdg 19:22; Isa 16:8). Since the Hebrew husband was regarded as the literal owner of his wife, *baal* was the common term for husband (as in Ex 21:3; 2Sa 11:26; Hos 2:16). Most often, however, the word refers to the Semitic deity or deities called Baal. Baal became the proper name for the most significant god in the Canaanite pantheon, or company of gods. He was the presiding deity in many localities. The plural word, *Baalim*, may be used of the different manifestations or attributes of the one Baal or may indicate that in popular thought local Baals came to have independent existence. The Baalim were the gods of the land, owning and controlling it; and the increase of crops, fruits, and cattle was under their control. The farmer was completely dependent on the Baalim. Some Baals were greater than others. Some were in control of cities, such as Melkart of Tyre. The name Baal occurs as early as the Hyksos period (c. 1700 BC).

The struggle between Baalism and the worship of the true God came to a head on Mount Carmel when the prophet Elijah met the priests of Baal and had 450 of them killed (1Ki 16:32; 18:17–40). The cult quickly revived, however, and prospered until crushed by Jehu (2Ki 10:18–28). Jezebel's daughter Athaliah, the wife of Jehoram, gave the worship of Baal a new impulse (2Ch 17:3; 21:6; 22:2). When she was overthrown, the temple of Baal at Jerusalem was destroyed and the chief priest killed before the altar (2Ki 11:18). Before long, however, there was another revival of the worship of Baal (2Ch 28:2; 2Ki 21:3). Josiah again destroyed the temple of Baal at Jerusalem and caused the public worship of the god to cease for a time (2Ki 23:4–5). Prophets of Israel, especially Jeremiah, often denounced Baal worship (Jer 19:4–5).

Incense and sacrifice were offered to Baal (Jer 7:9) — even human sacrifice (19:5) — but the worship of Baal was chiefly marked by fertility rites. The main function of Baal was thought to be to make land, animals, and people fertile. To prompt the god to perform these functions, worshipers themselves performed human sexual acts of fertility, and the Baal shrines were staffed with male and female attendants for this purpose. They were called *gedeshim* and *gedeshoth*, "holy men" and "holy women," not because they were morally holy but because they were wholly "separated" to the service of their god. The same function of prompting Baal to do what is sought from him is seen in 1Ki 18:26, 28.

In early years the title Baal seems to have been used for the Lord (Yahweh). When the Lord's people came into Canaan, they naturally and innocently began to think of him as the "possessor" and "lord" of the land — as indeed he was. Even David described the Lord as "Baal" (2Sa 5:20). But later it was seen that this opened the door to thinking of the God of Israel as though he were only a Canaanite Baal, and the practice was dropped. We see this change in the alteration of names like Jerubaal to Jerubesheth (Jdg 6:32; 2Sa 11:21).

2. A descendant of Reuben, the firstborn son of Jacob (1Ch 5:5).

3. A Benjamite (1Ch 8:30).

4. A town somewhere on the border of Simeon (1Ch 4:33).

5. In conjunction with another name it is often the name of a man and not of Baal, e.g., Baal-Manan, a king of Edom (Ge 36:38; 1Ch 1:49).

Nu	25:3	So Israel joined in worshiping the **B**
Jdg	2:13	and served **B** and the Ashtoreths.
	6:31	If **B** really is a god,
1Ki	16:32	up an altar for **B** in the temple of **B**
	18:25	Elijah said to the prophets of **B**,
2Ki	3:2	He got rid of the sacred stone of **B**
	10:28	Jehu destroyed **B** worship in Israel.
2Ch	23:17	to the temple of **B** and tore it down.
Jer	19:5	the high places of **B** to burn their sons

	19:5	in the fire as offerings to **B**—
Hos	13:1	But he became guilty of **B** worship

BAAL-ZEBUB [1256] (bā´ăl-zē´bŭb, Heb. *ba'al zevûv*, *Baal*, or *lord of flies*). The name under which Baal was worshiped by the Philistines of Ekron (2Ki 1:2, 3, 6, 16). Elijah rebuked Ahaziah for consulting this god to find out whether he would recover from his illness. This is almost certainly the same name as Baalzebub, or Beelzebul in the Greek text. Beelzebub is the prince of the demons (Mt 1:25; 12:24; Mk 3:22; Lk 11:15, 18 – 19), and is identified with Satan (Mt 12:26; Mk 3:23; Lk 11:18). Beelzebul signifies "lord of the dwelling," a meaning that is pertinent to the argument in Mt 10:25; 12:29; Mk 3:27.

2Ki	1:2	saying to them, "Go and consult **B**,

BAASHA [1284] (bā´a-sh a, Heb. *ba'shā'*, *bold-ness*). The son of Ahijah, of the tribe of Issachar. He became the third king of Israel by assassinating Nadab, when that king, the son of Jeroboam, was directing the siege of Gibbethon in the land of the Philistines. Baasha exterminated the house of Jeroboam and made Tirzah his capital. He ascended the throne in the third year of Asa, king of Judah (1Ki 15 – 16), and carried on a long war with him. About the sixteenth year of Asa, Baasha began to fortify Ramah, five miles (eight km.) north of Jerusalem, in order to blockade the northern frontier of Judah. He was prevented from completing this work by Ben-Hadad, king of Damascus, whom Asa had hired (1Ki 15:16 – 21; 2Ch 16:1 – 6). Asa then tore down Baasha's defenses and for his own protection built up the bulwarks of Geba (between Ramah and Jerusalem). Baasha continued the calf worship begun by Jeroboam, and Jehu the prophet threatened him and his house with a worse fate than Jeroboam's. After a reign of twenty-four years, he died a natural death and was succeeded by his son Elah, who, along with every member of the house of Baasha, was killed by Zimri (1Ki 15 – 16).

BABEL [H951] (*gate of god[s]*; Ge 11:9 *confused*). A city in the plain of Shinar where a tower was built to reach the heavens and God confused the languages of humankind (Ge 11:1 – 9). *See Babylon.*

Ge	11:9	That is why it was called **B**—

BABEL, TOWER OF (bā´bĕl, *gate of God*). An expression not used as such in the OT, but found popularly for the structure built in the plain of Shinar, as the story is told in Ge 11:1 – 9. The men of Shinar intended to build a tower that reached "to the heavens," but the Lord frustrated them by confusing their tongues. The author of Genesis assumes that before this the whole human species was a single tribe moving from place to place and speaking one language. The event took place not very long after the flood.

The remains of large towers called "ziggurats" can be found at the sites of many ancient cities in Mesopotamia. These sacred temple-towers were built in steplike stages of brick and asphalt, usually with a shrine at the top. The Tower of Babel was, however, not a temple-tower but simply a tower, apparently the first one ever attempted. The ziggurats may have been imitations of this tower.

It is not known for certain whether the ruins of the Tower of Babel are still extant. There are rival claimants for the honor.

BABYLON, BABYLONIA [824+951, 824+4169, 951, 9114, 10093, 10094, 10373, 956] (Băb´ĭlŏn; *gate of god[s]*). "Babylon" is the Greek form of the Hebrew word *bavel*, which was closely allied to and probably derived from the Akkadian *babilu* or "gate of God." The name referred not only to the city itself but also to the country of which it was the capital. Though not the oldest city in Babylonia, it soon became the most important from the standpoint of both size and influence.

Babylon was situated in central Mesopotamia on the river Euphrates, some fifty miles (eighty-three km.) south of modern Baghdad, capital of Iraq. A huge plantation of palm trees added to the beauty of the ancient city, and a permanent water supply assured fertility for the surrounding areas. It was within easy reach of the Persian Gulf and, being situated on an important caravan-trade route, was in contact with all the most important cultural centers of the ancient Near East.

The date of its foundation is still disputed. The connection between Akkad, Calneh, Erech, and Babylon (Ge 10:10) indicates a period at least as early as 3000 BC. Babylon may have been founded originally by the Sumerians, and an early tablet recorded that Sargon of Akkad (c. 2400) destroyed Babylon and took some of its sacred earth to his own capital city, Akkad. Whatever the date of its foundation, the earliest archaeological levels of the mound that once was stately Babylon come from the First Dynasty period, i.e., the nineteenth to sixteenth centuries BC.

The history of Babylon is complicated by the fact that it was governed by rulers from several lands who were successively engaged in struggles for its capture and retention. It was the scene of many a decisive battle, its magnificent buildings plundered in various periods and its walls and temples leveled from time to time. Yet this apparently indestructible city rose from its ruins on each occasion more splendid than before, until during the reign of Nebuchadnezzar II (c. 605–562 BC), it was probably the largest and most elaborate city in the ancient world and included one of the seven wonders of the world, the celebrated "hanging gardens" of Babylon. They actually consisted of terraces supported on huge masonry arches, on which carefully tended gardens had been laid out at different levels. All that now remains of its former glory is a series of mounds some five miles (eight km.) in extent, lying mostly on the left bank of the Euphrates.

Described:

Origin of (Ge 10:8, 10). Origin of name (Ge 11:8–9). Land of Chaldeans (Eze 12:13). Land of Shinar in (Da 1:2; Zec 5:11, n.). Land of Merathaim (Jer 50:21). Desert of the sea (Isa 21:1, 9). Sheshach, a cryptic term for Babylon (Jer 25:12, 26, n). Lady of kingdoms (Isa 47:5). Situated beyond the Euphrates (Ge 11:31, w Jos 24:2–3). Formerly a part of Mesopotamia (Ac

7:2). Conquered by the Assyrians and a part of their empire (2Ki 17:24, w Isa 23:13). Watered by Euphrates and Tigris rivers (Ps 137:1; Jer 51:13). Composed of many nations (Da 3:4, 29). Governed by kings (2Ki 20:12; Da 5:1). Languages spoken in (Da 1:4; 2:4). With Media and Persia divided by Darius into 120 provinces (Da 6:1). Administrators placed over (Da 2:48; 6:2). Babylon chief province of (Da 3:1).

Babylon the Capital of:

Its antiquity (Ge 11:4, 9). Enlarged by Nebuchadnezzar (Da 4:30). Surrounded with a great wall and fortified (Jer 51:53, 58). Called the jewel of kingdoms and the glory of Babylonians' pride (Isa 13:19); the golden city (Isa 14:4 KJV); the city of merchants (Eze 17:4); Babylon the Great (Da 4:30).

Remarkable for:

Antiquity (Jer 5:15). Naval power (Isa 43:14). Military power (Jer 5:16; 50:23). National greatness (Isa 13:19; Jer 51:41). Wealth (Jer 50:37; 51:13). Commerce (Eze 17:4). Manufacture of garments (Jos 7:21). Wisdom of officials (Isa 47:10; Jer 50:35).

Inhabitants of:

Idolatrous (Jer 50:38; Da 3:18). Addicted to magic (Isa 47:9, 12–13; Da 2:1–2). Profane and sacrilegious (Da 5:1–3). Wicked (Isa 47:10).

As a Power Was:

Arrogant (Isa 14:13–14; Jer 50:29, 31–32). Secure and self-confident (Isa 47:7–8). Grand and stately (Isa 47:1, 5). Covetous (Jer 51:13). Oppressive (Isa 14:4). Cruel and destructive (Isa 14:17; 47:6; Jer 51:25; Hab 1:6–7). An instrument of God's vengeance on other nations (Jer 51:7; Isa 47:6). Armies of, described (Hab 1:7–9).

Represented by:

A great eagle (Eze 17:3). A head of gold (Da 2:32, 37–38). A lion with eagle's wings (Da 7:4). Figure of a woman (Rev 17). Ambassadors of, sent to Hezekiah (2Ki 20:12).

Nebuchadnezzar, King of:

Made Jehoiakim vassal (2Ki 24:1). Besieged Jerusalem (2Ki 24:10 – 11). Took Jehoiachin captive to Babylon (2Ki 24:12, 14 – 16; 2Ch 36:10). Sacked the temple (2Ki 24:13). Made Zedekiah king (2Ki 24:17). Besieged and took Jerusalem (2Ki 24:20; 25:1 – 4). Burned Jerusalem (2Ki 25:9 – 10). Took Zedekiah captive to Babylon (2Ki 25:7, 11, 18 – 21; 2Ch 36:20). Sacked and burned temple (2Ki 25:9, 13 – 17; 2Ch 36:18 – 19). Revolt of Israelites from, and their punishment illustrated (Eze 17). The Israelites exhorted to be subject to, and settle in (Jer 27:17; 29:1 – 7). Treatment of Israelites in (2Ki 25:27 – 30; Da 1:3 – 7). Grief of Israelites in (Ps 137:1 – 6). Destroyed by Medes (Da 5:30 – 31). Restoration of Israelites from (2Ch 36:23; Ezr 1; 2:1 – 67). Gospel preached in (1Pe 5:13). Type of Antichrist (Rev 16:19; 17:5).

Predictions Regarding:

Conquests by (Jer 21:3 – 10; 27:2 – 6; 49:28 – 33; Eze 21:19 – 32; 29:18 – 20). Captivity of Israelites by (Jer 20:4 – 6; 22:20 – 26; 25:9 – 11; Mic 4:10). Restoration of Israelites from (Isa 14:1 – 4; 44:28; 48:20; Jer 29:10; 50:4, 8, 19). Destruction of (Isa 13; 14:4 – 22; 21:1 – 10; 47; Jer 25:12; 50; 51). Perpetual desolation of (Isa 13:19 – 22; 14:22 – 23; Jer 50:13, 39; 51:37). Acknowledgment of Yahweh (Ps 87:4).

Ge	10:10	first centers of his kingdom were **B**,
1Ch	9:1	to **B** because of their unfaithfulness.
2Ch	36:18	to **B** all the articles from the temple
	36:20	into exile to **B** the remnant,
Isa	14:4	this taunt against the king of **B**:
	21:9	gives back the answer: '**B** has fallen,
Jer	29:10	seventy years are completed for **B**,
	51:34	king of **B** has devoured us,
	51:37	**B** will be a heap of ruins,
Da	4:30	"Is not this the great **B** I have built as
1Pe	5:13	She who is in **B**,
Rev	14:8	Fallen is **B** the Great,
	17:5	written on her forehead: MYSTERY **B**
	18:2	Fallen is **B** the Great!

BABYLONIANS

Jer	32:5	If you fight against the **B**,
Da	1:4	the language and literature of the **B**.
Hab	1:6	I am raising up the **B**,

BACKBITING Evil of (Ps 15:1 – 3; Pr 25:23; Ro 1:29 – 30; 2Co 12:20).

BACKSLIDERS

Described as:

Blind (2Pe 1:9; Rev 3:17); godless (2Jn 9); idolaters (1Co 10:7); lukewarm (Rev 3:15 – 16); grumblers (Ex 17:7; 1Co 10:10); forsaking God (Jer 17:13); tempting Christ (1Co 10:9); forsaking God's covenant (Ps 78:10 – 11; Pr 2:17); turned aside to evil (Ps 125:5; 1Ti 5:15); unfit for God's kingdom (Lk 9:62).

God's Forbearance with:

(Dt 32:5 – 6, 26 – 27; Ezr 9:10, 14; Isa 42:3). God's concern for (Dt 32:28 – 29; Ps 81:13 – 14; Isa 1:4 – 9, 21 – 22; 65:2 – 3; Jer 2:5, 11 – 13, 17, 31 – 32; 18:13 – 15; 50:6; Hos 6:4 – 11; 11:1 – 4, 7 – 9; Mt 23:37). Called to repentance (Isa 30:9, 15; 31:6; Jer 3:4 – 7, 12 – 14, 21 – 22; 4:14; 6:16; Hos 14:1; Mal 3:7; Rev 2:4 – 5, 20 – 22; 3:2 – 3, 18 – 19). Promises to penitent: of finding the Lord (Dt 4:29 – 31; 2Ch 15:2 – 4); of spiritual enlightenment (Isa 29:24; Jer 3:14 – 19; Hos 6:3); of restoration (Dt 30:1 – 10; Pr 24:16; Isa 57:18 – 19; Hos 14:4; Zec 10:6); of temporal prosperity (Lev 26:40 – 42; Dt 30:1 – 5, 7 – 10; Job 22:23 – 30). Return of (Jer 31:18 – 19; 50:4 – 5; Hos 3:5; Jnh 2:4).

BALAAM [1189, 962] (bā´lăm, Heb. *bil'ām*, perhaps *Baal [lord] of the people* BDB; possibly *the clan brings forth* IDB; *devourer, glutton* KB). The son of Beor and a diviner with a remarkable history. After their victory over Sihon and Og, the Israelites pitched their tents in the plains of Moab. Balak, the king of the Moabites, sent an embassy of elders of Moab and Midian to Balaam, offering to reward him if he would curse the Israelites. After looking to God about the matter, he replied that God had forbidden him to comply with the request. Balak then sent some messengers of a higher rank with more alluring promises. This time God permitted Balaam to go, cautioning him, however, to deliver only the message God gave him. On his way to Balak, Balaam had this command strongly impressed on his mind by the strange behavior of his donkey and his encounter with the angel of the Lord.

Balak took Balaam to the high places of Baal, from which a part of the camp of the Israelites could be seen. To Balak's disappointment, Balaam pronounced a blessing on the Israelites instead of a curse. Surprised and incensed at the words of the diviner, Balak thought that a fuller view of the camp of Israel might change his disposition. He took him to the top of Mount Pisgah, but the only result was further blessing instead of cursing. Balaam compared the children of Israel to a lion who will not lie down until he has eaten his prey. In desperation Balak now suggested that the issue be tried from a third locality. They went to the top of Peor, and there the Spirit of God came on Balaam and caused him to declare not only that God would bless Israel, but that he who blessed her would be blessed and he who cursed her would be cursed. In his bitter disappointment, Balak angrily reproached Balaam and ordered him to go home without the promised reward. Before he left, Balaam reminded the king that at the very beginning he had said that no amount of money could make him give anything other than the commandment of the Lord. He then uttered a last prophecy — the most remarkable so far — in which he foretold the coming of a star from Jacob and a scepter out of Israel that would defeat Israel's enemies, including Moab.

Nothing else is said of Balaam until Nu 31. There the seer, who had failed to turn away the Lord from his people, tried before long to turn the people from the Lord. He knew that if he succeeded in this, the consequences to Israel would be just as Balak had desired, God's curse on Israel. By his advice the

Israelites were seduced into idolatry and all the vile abominations connected with it. In the judgment that followed, no fewer than 24,000 Israelites perished, until it was evident that the nation abhorred idolatry as a great crime against God. By God's command Israel brought vengeance on her seducers the Midianites, and in the universal slaughter, Balaam also perished.

In the NT Balaam is several times held up as an example of the pernicious influence of hypocritical teachers who attempt to lead God's people astray. No Bible character is more severely excoriated.

> *Son of Beor (Nu 22:5); From Mesopotamia (Dt 23:4); A soothsayer (Jos 13:22); A prophet (Nu 24:2 – 9; 2Pe 2:15 – 16); Balak sends for, to curse Israel (Nu 22:5 – 7; Jos 24:9; Ne 13:2; Mic 6:5); Anger of, rebuked by his donkey (Nu 22:22 – 35; 2Pe 2:16); Counsel of, an occasion of Israel's corruption with the Midianites (Nu 31:16; Rev 2:14 – 15); Greed of (2Pe 2:15; Jude 11); Death of (Nu 31:8; Jos 13:22)*

BALAK [1192, 963] (bā′lăk, Heb. *bālāq, devastator*). A king of Moab in Moses' day who hired Balaam, a diviner from the Euphrates, to pronounce a curse on the Israelites (Nu 22 – 24; Jos 24:9; Jdg 11:25; Mic 6:5; Rev 2:14). Frightened by the story of Israel's victory over Sihon and Og, he evidently thought that the favor of the Lord could be turned from Israel to his own nation. Instead of cursings, he heard blessings; but he achieved his end in an indirect way when he followed Balaam's advice to seduce the people of Israel to idolatry, a sin that resulted in heavy judgment on the chosen people. *See also Balaam.*

BALM [6057, 7661] (Heb. *tsŏrî*). An odoriferous resin perhaps obtained in Gilead (Ge 37:25; Jer 8:22; 46:11) and exported from Palestine. It was used as an ointment for healing wounds (Jer 51:8). It came from a small tree not now found in Gilead, and perhaps it never grew there. *See also Plants.*

Jer   8:22   Is there no **b** in Gilead?

BANK [1473, 1536, 3338, 8557, 3204]. In its modern form banking is of recent origin (seventeenth century AD), but banking of a primitive kind was known in ancient times among both Jews and Gentiles. Money was received on deposit, loaned out, exchanged for smaller denominations or for foreign money. Israelites were not permitted to charge each other interest (Ex 22:25) but could lend with interest to Gentiles (Dt 23:20). The concept of a bank as a savings institution was unknown.

BANNER [253, 1839, 1840, 5812] (Heb. *nes, deghel, banner, ensign, standard*). Banners were used in ancient times for military, national, and ecclesiastical purposes very much as they are today. In connection with Israel's wilderness journey we read, "The Israelites are to camp around the Tent of Meeting some distance from it, each man under his standard with the banners of his family" (Nu 2:2). The word occurs frequently in the figurative sense of a rallying point for God's people (Isa 5:26; 11:10; Jer 4:21).

Ex	17:15	and called it The LORD is my **B**.
SS	2:4	and his **b** over me is love.
Isa	11:10	the Root of Jesse will stand as a **b** for

BANQUET [3516+, 5492, 10389, 10447, 804, 1141, 1270, 1531]. The Hebrews, like other peoples of the ancient East, were very fond of social feasting. There were three great religious feasts that all males were expected to attend. Sacrifices were accompanied by a feast (Ex 34:15; Jdg 16:23 – 25). There were feasts for birthdays (Ge 40:20; Job 1:4; Mt 14:6), marriages (Ge 29:22; Mt 22:2), funerals (2Sa 3:35; Jer 16:7), laying of foundations (Pr 9:1 – 5), wine making (Jdg 9:27), sheep shearing (1Sa 25:2, 36), and other occasions. A banquet always included wine drinking; it was not simply a feast in our sense. At a large banquet a second invitation was often sent on the day of the feast, or a servant brought the guests to the feast (Mt 22:2ff.; Lk 14:17). The host provided robes for the guests, and they were worn in his honor and were a token of his regard. Guests were welcomed by the host with a kiss (Lk 7:45), and

their feet were washed because of the dusty roads (Ge 18:4; Jdg 19:21; Lk 7:44). The head was anointed (Ps 23:5; Lk 7:46), and sometimes the beard, the feet, and the clothes were also anointed. The head was decorated with garlands (Isa 28:1). The guests were seated according to their respective rank (1Sa 9:22; Lk 14:8), the hands were washed (2Ki 3:11), and prayers for blessing on the food were said (1Sa 9:13; Mt 15:35; Lk 22:17). The Pharisees made hand washing and the blessing of food burdensome rituals. The feast was put under the superintendence of a "governor of the feast," usually one of the guests, whose task it was to taste the food and the drinks and to organize the toasts and amusements. The most honored guests received either larger portions or more choice ones than the rest (Ge 43:34; 1Sa 9:23 – 24). Portions were sometimes sent to friends not attending the feast (2Sa 11:8; Ne 8:10). Often the meal was enlivened with music, singing, and dancing (2Sa 19:35; Lk 15:25), or with riddles (Jdg 14:12). A great banquet sometimes lasted seven days, but excess in eating and drinking was condemned by the sacred writers (Ecc 10:16 – 17; Isa 5:11 – 12).

1Sa	25:36	he was in the house holding a **b**
Est	1:3	the third year of his reign he gave a **b**
	6:14	to the **b** Esther had prepared.
SS	2:4	He has taken me to the **b** hall,
Isa	25:6	a **b** of aged wine—
Da	5:1	a great **b** for a thousand of his nobles
Mt	22:4	Come to the wedding **b**.'
Lk	14:13	But when you give a **b**,

BAPTISM [966+, 967, 968] (băp'tĭzm, *dip*, or *immerse*). A term derived from the Greek *baptisma* (antecedent, *baptizō*); the etymological significance of the word often has been obscured by a lack of exegetical clarity and by forced interpretation. Its true meaning can be found only in its usage and its theological significance. Its antecedent meaning involves the Judaic usage in the OT times and the practice of John the Baptist. Its incipient meaning lies in Christ's baptism and his interpretation of it. Its formal meaning is to be found in its apostolic interpretation, particularly by Paul. The idea of ceremonial washing, or cleansing, appears repeatedly in the Mosaic laws of purification (e.g., Ex 29:4, 17; 30:17 – 21; 40:12, 30; Lev 1:9, 13; 6:27; 9:14; 11:25; 14:8, 9, 47; 15:5 – 27; 16:4 – 28; 17:15 – 16; 22:6; Nu 8:7; 19:7 – 21; 31:23 – 24; Dt 21:6; 23:11). In the Septuagint version of the OT, translated into the Hellenistic idiom of the NT, the word *baptizō* is used twice: 2Ki 5:14 (where the meaning is cleansing) and Isa 21:4 (where its meaning is obscure). It is clear, however, that later Judaism incorporated this connotation of cleansing and purification into its idea of the new covenant relation and used baptism as a rite of initiation, as reflected in the practices of the Qumran sect and the Dead Sea Scroll communities.

While later Judaism certainly attached a deeply pietistic significance to the cleansing act, John the Baptist, who followed in this tradition, infused into the ritual act of initiation and purification an ethical quality that baptism had not had before. His was a moral community of penitent souls seeking personal righteousness, and he associated with the act of baptism the imperative necessity for a thorough change in the condition of the soul, manifested in a remission of sins through repentance. His fervent exhortation to repent and flee from the wrath to come (Mt 3:7 – 8) was not a mere invitation to a religious ceremony, but was, rather, an indication of the change brought on by the act of baptism itself. The meaning of the act was deepened. Baptism was transformed from a rite to which one submitted oneself to a positive moral act initiated by the individual as a decisive commitment to personal piety.

John's baptism was, nevertheless, only transitory — his baptism of repentance was but preparatory to a baptism of identification. The meaning and efficacy of baptism can be understood only in the light of the redemptive death and resurrection of Christ. Christ referred to his death in the words "I have a baptism to undergo" (Lk 12:59) and "Can you drink the cup I drink or be baptized with the baptism I am baptized with?" (Mt 20:22; Mk 10:38). Here the word *baptisma*, which indicates the state or condition, is used instead of *baptismos*, which applies to Jewish rites and refers only to the act itself. *Baptisma*, used only in the NT and in Christian writings, never refers to the act alone but always incorporates into its meaning the entire scope of the redemptive significance of the incarnate person of Christ.

John's baptism of Jesus, therefore, connects the act of water baptism with the meaning of the salvation events through his own person and work. To the act of water baptism Jesus added the promise of the baptism with the Spirit, the means by which his redemptive work is applied to human beings (Mt 3:11; Mk 1:8; Lk 3:16; Ac 1:4ff.; 11:16). Using the initiatory and purificatory meaning found in water baptism, Christ made spiritual baptism (by the Holy Spirit) synonymous with the actual application of the virtues of his death and resurrection to sinners.

The apostolic writers, particularly Paul, related Spirit baptism to the whole of the redemptive act. The act of water baptism symbolizes cleansing, but Spirit baptism gives the believer entry into the righteousness of Christ through an identification with Christ himself. Through Spirit baptism the redeemed sinner is incorporated into the spiritual body of Christ, not merely as an act of initiation but as a state or condition of personal righteousness. It is, therefore, the only access to identification with the redeeming Christ.

While much recent emphasis among evangelicals has been on the "symbol only" concept of baptism, and while the NT pointedly abstains from ascribing a sacramental value to the act itself, a renewed emphasis on Spirit baptism will restore to its proper place a much neglected aspect of this doctrine. No statement of the doctrine can be a truly biblical one if it fails to emphasize that beyond the symbolic and commemorative act performed by a person there is also the Holy Spirit's inward operation. Spirit baptism brings the regenerated person into a redemptive relationship through his participation in and identification with the death, burial, and resurrection of Christ and the subsequent infusion of the merits of that death and resurrection into the life of the believer, by which he may live as one dead to sin but alive to God (Ro 6:11).

General References to:

Baptism as administered by John (Mt 3:5 – 12; Jn 3:23; Ac 13:24; 19:4). Sanctioned by Christ's submission to it (Mt 3:13 – 15; Lk 3:21). Adopted by Christ (Jn 3:22; 4:1 – 2). Appointed an ordinance of the Christian church (Mt 28:19 – 20; Mk 16:15 – 16). To be administered in the name of the Father, the Son, and the Holy Spirit (Mt 28:19). Water, the outward and visible sign in (Ac 8:36; 10:47). Regeneration, the inward and spiritual grace of (Jn 3:3, 5 – 6; Ro 6:3 – 4, 11). Remission of sins, signified by (Ac 2:38; 22:16). Unity of the church effected by (1Co 12:13; Gal 3:27 – 28). Confession of sin necessary to (Mt 3:6). Repentance necessary to (Ac 2:38). Faith necessary to (Ac 8:37; 18:8). There is but one (Eph 4:5). Administered to: individuals (Ac 8:38; 9:18); households (Ac 16:15; 1Co 1:16). Emblematic of the influences of the Holy Spirit (Mt 3:11; Tit 3:5). Typified (1Co 10:2; 1Pe 3:20 – 21).

Mt	21:25	John's **b** — where did it come from?
Mk	1:4	a **b** of repentance for the forgiveness
	10:38	with the **b** I am baptized with?"
	11:30	John's **b** — was it from heaven,
Lk	3:3	a **b** of repentance for the forgiveness
	12:50	But I have a **b** to undergo,
Ac	1:22	beginning from John's **b** to the time
	10:37	after the **b** that John preached —
	13:24	John preached repentance and **b**
	18:25	though he knew only the **b** of John.
	19:3	"Then what **b** did you receive?"
Ro	6:4	therefore buried with him through **b**
Eph	4:5	one Lord, one faith, one **b**;
Col	2:12	with him in **b** and raised with him
1Pe	3:21	and this water symbolizes **b** that

BAPTIST

Mt	3:1	In those days John the **B** came,
	11:11	anyone greater than John the **B**;
	14:8	on a platter the head of John the **B**."
	16:14	"Some say John the **B**;

BAPTIZE

Mt	3:11	" I **b** you with water for repentance.
Lk	3:16	"I **b** you with water.
	3:16	He will **b** you with the Holy Spirit
Jn	1:25	"Why then do you **b** if you are not
	1:33	except that the one who sent me to **b**
1Co	1:14	I am thankful that I did not **b** any
	1:17	For Christ did not send me to **b**,

BAPTIZED

Mt	3:6	they were **b** by him in the Jordan
	3:13	from Galilee to the Jordan to be **b**
	3:14	saying, "I need to be **b** by you,
	3:16	As soon as Jesus was **b**,
Mk	1:5	they were **b** by him in the Jordan
	1:9	from Nazareth in Galilee and was **b**
	10:38	the cup I drink or be **b** with the baptism I am **b** with?"
	16:16	Whoever believes and is **b** will
Lk	3:7	to the crowds coming out to be **b**
	3:12	Tax collectors also came to be **b**.
	3:21	Jesus was **b** too.
	7:29	because they had been **b** by John.
Jn	3:22	he spent some time with them, and **b**.
	3:23	were constantly coming to be **b**.
	4:2	in fact it was not Jesus who **b**,
Ac	1:5	For John **b** with water,
	1:5	but in a few days you will be **b** with
	2:38	Peter replied, "Repent and be **b**,
	2:41	who accepted his message were **b**,
	8:12	they were **b**, both men and women.
	8:36	Why shouldn't I be **b**?"
	8:38	into the water and Philip **b** him.
	9:18	He got up and was **b**,
	10:47	from being **b** with water?
	10:48	be **b** in the name of Jesus Christ.

	11:16	'John **b** with water, but you will be **b** with the Holy Spirit.'
	16:15	members of her household were **b**,
	16:33	he and all his family were **b**.
	19:5	**b** into the name of the Lord Jesus.
	22:16	be **b** and wash your sins away,
Ro	6:3	that all of us who were **b** into Christ Jesus were **b** into his death?
1Co	1:13	Were you **b** into the name of Paul?
	10:2	They were all **b** into Moses in
	12:13	For we were all **b** by one Spirit
	15:29	who are **b** for the dead?
	15:29	why are people **b** for them?
Gal	3:27	for all of you who were **b**

BAR An Aramaic word for the Hebrew *ben*, "son." In the NT it is used as a prefix to the names of persons, e.g., Bar-Jonah, "son of Jonah" (Mt 16:17); Barabbas; Bar-Jesus; Barnabas; Barsabbas; Bartholomew; Bartimaeus.

BARABBAS (bar-ăb'ăs, Gr. *Barabbas*, for Aramaic *Bar-abba, son of the father*, or *teacher*). A criminal chosen by the Jerusalem mob, at the instigation of the chief priests, in preference to Christ, to be released by Pilate on the feast of the Passover. Matthew calls him a notorious prisoner, and the other evangelists say he was arrested with others for robbery, sedition, and murder (Mt 27:16; Mk 15:15; Lk 23:18; Jn 18:40). The custom here mentioned of releasing a prisoner on the Passover is otherwise unknown. The reading "Jesus Barabbas" for his full name in Mt 27:16 – 17 was found by Origen in many MSS and is still found in some early versions and a few cursives. It is probably due to a scribe's error in transcription.

BARAK [H1399, G973] (bâr'ăk, Heb. *bārāq, lightning*). The son of Abinoam of Kedesh, a refuge city in Mount Naphtali. He was summoned by Deborah the judge and prophetess to lead the Israelites to war against the Canaanites who were under the leadership of Sisera, the commander in chief of Jaban, king of Canaan. For twenty years Israel had been oppressed by the Canaanites. The farmlands were plundered; traffic almost ceased; and the fighting men of Israel were disarmed, so that not a shield nor spear was to be seen among them. Barak raised an army of one hundred thousand men, mostly from a few faithful tribes. They encamped on Mount Tabor where wooded slopes would protect them against the chariots of the Canaanites. The army of Israel routed Jabin's eight hundred iron chariots and heavily armed host in the plain of Jezreel (Esdraelon). A heavy rainfall caused the alluvial plain to become a morass in which the Canaanite army found it impossible to move. Sisera abandoned his chariot and ran away on foot. Barak pursued him and found him killed by Jael in her tent. A peace of forty years followed (Jdg 4 – 5). In Heb 11:32 Barak's name appears among those who achieved great things through faith. The period of the judges is probably to be dated from 1200 BC, with Deborah and Barak c. 1125.

BARBARIAN [975] (bar-bâr'ĭăn). Originally anyone who did not speak Greek. Paul uses it in this strict sense in Ro 1:14 (KJV; "non-Greeks" in NIV), where "Greeks" and "barbarians" mean the whole human race. Romans and Jews did not mind being called barbarians in this sense. In 1Co 14:11 (KJV) Paul uses the word to describe one who spoke in an unintelligible foreign tongue; and in Ac 28:2, 4 (KJV) the inhabitants of Malta are called barbarians (they spoke a Punic dialect). In Col 3:11 the word refers to those who did not belong to the cultivated Greek race.

| Col | 3:11 | circumcised or uncircumcised, **b**, |

BAR-JESUS [G979] (Gr. *Bariesous, son of Jesus*). A Jewish magician and false prophet in the court of Sergius Paulus when the latter was proconsul of Cyprus. He was struck blind for interfering with Paul's work (Ac 13:6 – 12).

| Ac | 13:6 | sorcerer and false prophet named **B**, |

BARNABAS [982] (bar'na-băs, Gr. *Barnabas*, explained in Ac 4:36 to mean *son of exhortation* or *consolation*). The surname of Joseph, a Levite from Cyprus, who was an early convert to Christianity.

He sold a field and gave the proceeds to the support of the poorer members of the church in Jerusalem (4:36ff.). In Ac 11:24 he is described as "a good man and full of the Holy Spirit and faith," traits that early brought him into leadership. When the church in Jerusalem hesitated to receive Paul into their fellowship, Barnabas removed their fears by speaking in the apostle's behalf (9:27).

After the start of the work at Antioch, the church in Jerusalem sent Barnabas there to give the work direction; after laboring there for some time, he went to Tarsus and brought back Paul as his associate (Ac 11:22 – 26). At the end of a year the two men were sent to carry alms from the infant church to the believers at Jerusalem, who were suffering from famine (11:27 – 30). Returning with John Mark from Jerusalem, they were ordained as missionaries and proceeded on a mission to the Gentiles (13:2 – 3). Barnabas as well as Paul is called an "apostle" (14:14). Together the two men labored at Cyprus, Antioch in Pisidia, Iconium, Lystra, and Derbe. Up to Ac 13:43 the leadership is ascribed to Barnabas; after that, Paul takes the lead. At Lystra, after a crippled man was healed, the inhabitants worshiped Barnabas as Jupiter, and Paul, the chief speaker, as Mercury (13:3 – 14:28). After their return to Antioch, the church sent them to the council at Jerusalem (15:2). They were commissioned to carry the decrees of the council to the churches in Syria and Asia Minor (15:22 – 35).

The beginning of a difference between the two men is suggested by Paul in Gal 2:13, where he says that Barnabas went along with Peter in the latter's inconsistent course. This was followed by a more serious break when, after Paul had suggested a second missionary journey, he refused to take along Barnabas's cousin Mark on the ground that he had left them on their first journey. The two men separated, Barnabas going with Mark to Cyprus, and Paul to Asia Minor (Ac 15:36 – 41). The mutual affection of the two evangelists did not cease, however. Paul's allusions to Barnabas in his letters shows that he continued to hold his former associate in high esteem (1Co 9:6; Gal 2:1, 9, 13; Col 4:10).

Some early church leaders attributed the authorship of the letter to the Hebrews to Barnabas.

BARRENNESS [1678, 4497, 6808, 6829, 9039, 9155, 9332, 5096]. Inability of women to bear children. A reproach (Ge 30:22 – 23; 1Sa 1:6, 7; 2:1 – 11; Isa 4:1; Lk 1:25).

Sent as a Judgment:
(Ge 20:17 – 18).

Barrenness Miraculously Removed:
Sarai (Ge 17:15 – 21); Rebekah (Ge 25:21); Manoah's wife (Jdg 13); Hannah (1Sa 1:6 – 20); Elizabeth (Lk 1:5 – 25).

BARTHOLOMEW [978] (bar-thŏl'ŏ·mū̄ Gr. from Aram., *son of Tolmai* or *Talmai*, Gr. *Bartholomaios*). One of the twelve apostles. He is mentioned in all four of the lists of the apostles in the NT (Mt 10:3; Mk 3:18; Lk 6:14; Ac 1:13). There is no further reference to him in the NT, and the traditions concerning him are not trustworthy. Some scholars think that Bartholomew is the surname of Nathanael, who was led to Christ by Philip (Jn 1:45 – 46). The reason for this is that in the list of the apostles in the Gospels the name of Bartholomew immediately follows that of Philip, and the Synoptic Gospels never mention Nathanael, while John never mentions Bartholomew. This view has, however, not been conclusively established.

BARTIMAEUS [985] (bar'tĭ·mē̄'ŭs, Gr. *Bartimaios*, *son of Timaeus*, or *son of uncleanness*). A blind man healed by Jesus as he went out from Jericho on his way to Jerusalem shortly before Passion Week (Mk 10:46 – 52). A similar account is given by Luke (18:35 – 43), except that the miracle occurred as Jesus drew near to Jericho, and the blind man's name is not given. Matthew (20:29 – 34) tells of Jesus healing two blind men on the way out of Jericho. On the surface the stories seem irreconcilable, but there is no doubt that if we knew some slight circumstance not mentioned, the difficulty would be cleared up. Various explanations, which may be found in the standard commentaries, have been suggested.

BARUCH [1358] (bâr'ŭk, Heb. *bārûkh', blessed*).

1. Son of Neriah and brother of Seraiah (Jer 36:32), of a princely family. He was the trusted friend (32:12) and secretary (36:4ff.) of the prophet Jeremiah. A man of unusual qualities, he might have risen to a high position if he had not thrown in his lot with Jeremiah (45:5). Jeremiah dictated his prophecies to Baruch, who read them to the people (ch. 36). King Jehoiakim, on hearing the opening sentences of the prophecy, became greatly angered and burned the scroll. He ordered the arrest of Baruch and Jeremiah, but they escaped. Baruch rewrote the prophet's oracles with additions (36:27–32). In the reign of Zedekiah, during the final siege of Jerusalem, Jeremiah bought his ancestral estate in Anathoth. Since he was at that time a prisoner, he placed the deed in Baruch's hands and testified that Israel would again possess the land (ch. 32). Josephus (*Antiq.* 10.9.1) says that Baruch continued to live with Jeremiah at Mizpah after the fall of Jerusalem. After the murder of Gedaliah, the leaders accused him of unduly influencing Jeremiah when the latter urged the people to remain in Judah (43:3), a fact that shows how great Baruch's influence was thought to be over his master. He was taken to Egypt with Jeremiah (43:6). After that, all reliable records about him cease. Jerome preserves a tradition that he died in Egypt soon after his arrival. Other traditions say that he was taken by Nebuchadnezzar to Babylon after this king conquered Egypt and that he died there twelve years later. The high regard in which Baruch was held is shown by the large number of spurious writings that were attributed to him, among them *The Apocalypse of Baruch*, the *Book of Baruch*; *The Rest of the Words of Baruch*, the *Gnostic Book of Baruch*, and others.

2. A man who helped Nehemiah in rebuilding the walls of Jerusalem (Ne 3:20).

3. A priest who signed the covenant with Nehemiah (Ne 10:6).

4. The son of Colhozeh, a descendant of Perez (Ne 11:5).

BARUCH, BOOK OF Jewish pseudepigraphal book found in the Apocrypha; alleging to be a treatise by Jeremiah's scribe Baruch to Jewish exiles in Babylon. (*See Apocrypha.*)

BASHAN [824+1421, 1421] (bā'shăn, Heb. *bāshān, smooth, fertile land*). The broad, fertile region east of the Sea of Galilee, extending roughly from Gilead in the south to Mount Hermon in the north. Josephus identifies Bashan with Gaulonitis and Batanea (cf. *Antiq.* 4.5.3 with 1Ki 4:13; *Antiq.* 9.8.1 with 2Ki 10:33). In the days of Abraham it was occupied by a people called the Rephaites (Ge 14:5). Og, the last king of the race, was defeated and killed by the Israelites at Edrei in the time of Moses (Nu 21:33–35; Dt 3:1–7). The entire district was assigned to the half-tribe of Manasseh (Dt 3:13). Edrei, Ashtaroth, Golan, and Salecah were its chief cities (1:4; 3:1, 10; 4:43). Solomon taxed the land (1Ki 4:13). It was lost to Israel in the Syrian wars (1Ki 22:3ff.; 2Ki 8:28; 10:32, 35). Tiglath-Pileser incorporated it into the Assyrian Empire (2Ki 15:29). The Nabateans held it in the second century BC. It was included in the kingdom of Herod the Great and then belonged to Philip, Herod's son.

General References to:
Fertility and productivity of (Isa 33:9; Jer 50:19; Na 1:4). Forests of, famous (Isa 2:13; Eze 27:6; Zec 11:2). Distinguished for its fine cattle (Dt 32:14; Ps 22:12; Eze 39:18; Am 4:1; Mic 7:14)

Nu	21:33	and Og king of **B**
Jos	13:30	the entire realm of Og king of **B** —
	22:7	Moses had given land in **B**,
Ps	22:12	strong bulls of **B** encircle me.
Am	4:1	you cows of **B** on Mount Samaria,

BASTARD (Heb. *mamzēr*, Gr. *nothos, bastard,* specifically, *child of incest*). In Dt 23:2 the word probably means a "child of incest," not simply an illegitimate child (NIV "one born of a forbidden marriage"). There it says that a bastard and his descendants to the tenth generation are excluded from the assembly of the Lord. Jephthah, the "son of a strange woman" (KJV), a "prostitute" (NIV), was called to be a judge of Israel (Jdg 11:1 – 2). In Zec 9:6 the KJV reads, "And a bastard shall dwell in Ashdod," but the NIV renders it, "Foreigners will occupy Ashdod." In Heb 12:8 the word is used in its later sense of born out of wedlock. Bastards had no claim to paternal care or the usual privileges and discipline of legitimate children.

BATHSHEBA [1444] (băth-shē′ba, Heb. *bath-sheva'*, *daughter of Sheba*). The daughter of Eliam (2Sa 11:3) or Ammiel (1Ch 3:5); both names have the same meaning. She was the wife of Uriah the Hittite, a soldier in David's army. During Uriah's absence in the wars, David forced her to commit adultery with him (2Sa 11). Uriah was then treacherously killed by David's order (11:6ff.). She became David's wife and lived with him in the palace. They had four sons, including Solomon (2Sa 5:14; 1Ch 3:5), after the first child had died (2Sa 12:14ff.). With the help of the prophet Nathan, she defeated the plot of Adonijah to usurp the kingdom and succeeded in having David choose Solomon as his successor. Adonijah was ultimately put to death. She was a woman of resourcefulness and energy, and she retained her influence over David until his death. Her sons Nathan and Solomon were both ancestors of Jesus Christ (Mt 1:6; Lk 3:31).

BATTLE [4309, 4878, 5120, 7372, 7930, 8131, 9558, 4483]. In ancient times a trumpet signal by the commander opened each battle (Jdg 7:18) and, when it was over, called the soldiers away from the fight (2Sa 2:28; 18:16). Priests accompanied the army into war to ascertain God's will (Jdg 6:36ff.; 1Sa 14:8ff.). To make the Lord's help in battle more certain, the ark was taken along. When the army drew near the battle, a priest or the commander encouraged the soldiers by reminding them of God's presence and help. The fainthearted were exempted (Dt 20:8). Military science was relatively simple. A force was usually divided into two attacking divisions, the one in the rear serving as a reserve or as a means of escape for the leader in case of defeat. Spearmen probably formed the first line, bowmen or archers

the second, and slingers the third. Horses and chariots were not used by Israel until quite late. Most of the fighting was done by footmen. Sometimes the battle was preceded by duels between individuals, and these on occasion determined the outcome of the battle (1Sa 17:3ff.; 2Sa 2:14ff.).

> **The Spiritual Battle:**
> *An inward battle (Ro 7:23). Spiritual weapons (2Co 10:4). Invisible foes (Eph 6:12). Young soldiers enlisted (1Ti 1:18). A fight of faith (1Ti 6:12). Demands entire consecration (2Ti 2:4).*

Ex	13:18	went up out of Egypt armed for **b**.
Jos	4:13	for **b** crossed over before the LORD
1Sa	17:47	for the **b** is the LORD's,
2Sa	22:35	He trains my hands for **b**;
1Ki	22:30	"I will enter the **b** in disguise,
2Ch	20:15	For the **b** is not yours, but God's.
Ps	24:8	the LORD mighty in **b**.
Ecc	9:11	or the **b** to the strong,
Isa	31:4	down to do **b** on Mount Zion and
Eze	13:5	so that it will stand firm in the **b**
Ob	1:1	"Rise, and let us go against her for **b**
Jas	4:1	from your desires that **b** within you?
Rev	16:14	to gather them for the **b** on
	20:8	to gather them for **b**.

BEATITUDES [H897, H1385, G2328, G3421] (bē-ăt′ĭ-tūds, Lat. *beatitudo, blessedness, divine favor*). A word not found in the English Bible, but referring to either (1) the joys of heaven or (2) a declaration of blessedness. Beatitudes occur frequently in the OT (Pss 32:1 – 2; 41:1). The Gospels contain isolated beatitudes by Christ (Mt 11:6; 13:16; Jn 20:29), but the word is most commonly used of those in Mt 5:3 – 11 and Lk 6:20 – 22, which set forth the qualities that should characterize his disciples. Scholars are not agreed whether we have here two different records of the same discourse or records of two different but similar discourses.

The Beatitudes do not describe separate types of Christian character. Rather, they set forth qualities and experiences that are combined in the ideal character. In Matthew there are nine beatitudes and no woes; Luke has four beatitudes and four corresponding woes. In Matthew all the sayings except the last are in the third person; in Luke they are in the second. In Matthew all the blessings except the last are attached to spiritual qualities; in Luke they relate to outward conditions of poverty and suffering. The general declarations in Matthew require certain spiritual conditions, whereas the special declarations in Luke, since they were addressed to Jesus' disciples, do not. Luke omits the third, fifth, sixth, and seventh beatitudes of Matthew. Some scholars profess to find a gradation in the order in which the beatitudes are recorded. Much has been written on the grouping of the Beatitudes, but no grouping is generally accepted.

BEEROTH [H940, H943] (be͞-ê'rŏth, Heb. *be'ērôth, wells*). A Canaanite town whose inhabitants succeeded in deceiving Israel by making a covenant with them (Jos 9:3ff.). When the deceit was discovered, they were made slaves by the Israelites (9:22–23). They were apparently Hivites (9:7), their village located in the territory assigned to Benjamin (Jos 18:25; 2Sa 4:2). The murderers of Ish-Bosheth (2Sa 4:2) and Naharai, Joab's armor-bearer (23:37), came from Beeroth; and Beerothites returned from Babylon after the exile (Ezr 2:25).

BEERSHEBA [H937] (be͞'êr-she͞'ba, Heb. *be'ēr shēva', well of seven* or *the seventh well*).

1. The most southerly town in the kingdom of Judah (Jdg 20:1); hence, its practical boundary line, with only the Wadi el Arish (the river of Egypt, Ge 15:18) some sixty miles (one hundred km.) to the south. In the days of the conquest of Canaan, it was allotted to the tribe of Simeon (Jos 19:2). The familiar expression "from Dan to Beersheba" is used to designate the northern and southern extremities of the nation of Israel (2Sa 3:10; 17:11; 24:2).

General References to Beersheba:
Named by Abraham, who dwelt there (Ge 21:31–33; 22:19). The dwelling place of Isaac (Ge 26:23). Jacob went out from, toward Haran (Ge 28:10). Sacrifices offered at, by Jacob when traveling to Egypt (Ge 46:1). In the inheritance of Judah (Jos 15:20, 28; 2Sa 24:7). Afterward assigned to Simeon (Jos 19:2, 9; 1Ch 4:28). Two sons of Samuel were judges at (1Sa 8:2). Became a seat of idolatrous worship (Am 5:5; 8:14).

2. Well of, belonged to Abraham and Isaac (Ge 21:25–26).

3. Wilderness in which Hagar miraculously sees a well (Ge 21:14–19). A place where an angel fed Elijah (1Ki 19:5, 7).

BEHEMOTH [H990]. The word is a Hebrew plural and means "beast par excellence," referring to a large land animal, possibly the hippopotamus or the elephant (Job 40:15, n.). Much of the language used to describe it in vv. 16–24 is highly poetic and hyperbolic (Job 40:15–24).

BELIAL [G1016] (be͞'lĭ-ăl, Heb. *beliya'al*, Gr. *Beliar, wicked, without use*). A word meaning "worthlessness," "wickedness," "lawlessness" translated as a proper noun in the KJV (Dt 13:13; Jdg 19:22; 1Sa 25:25). Belial is a KJV epithet of scorn and disdain that appears often throughout the OT, either as such or in its associate variation, "Sons of Belial" (Dt 13:13; Jdg 19:22; 1Sa 2:12 KJV). The spelling of the word in the Hebrew text is plainly intended to mean "worthlessness" (*beli, without* and *ya-al, profit*), and "son of" is an idiom meaning "in the condition of." It is therefore equivalent to our "good-for-nothing." But it is also suggested that originally it may have had some link with Baal or with the Hebrew verb *bala*, "to swallow down," "to engulf," metaphorical of Sheol or destruction. A "son of destruction" would be one set on a disasterous course and meriting the outcome of it. Nabal (1Sa 25:25 KJV) receives such a description from the lips of Abigail, his wife (cf. "Raca," Mt 5:22). The apostle Paul employs the term once (2Co 6:15; the only place where the term appears in the NIV) where Belial (Beliar) stands as opposed to Christ, thus approaching the diabolical status of Antichrist. In this later usage it is often used by Jewish apocalyptic writers for both Satan and the Antichrist.

BELSHAZZAR [1157, 10105, 10109] (bĕl-shăz′ar, Heb. *bĕlsha′tstsar, may Bel protect the king*). This was for many years regarded as a fictitious literary creation of a postcaptivity author assuming the pen name of Daniel (c. 165 BC). Now, however, it is well authenticated through archaeological studies that Belshazzar was a historic personage. In Da 5 he is referred to as the son of Nebuchadnezzar (vv. 2, 11, 13, 18, 22). This conforms with general Semitic usage where one's descendant is often referred to as his "son." Nebuchadnezzar died in 562 BC, after a forty-two-year reign, and was followed in quick succession by Amel-Marduk (562 – 560), the Evil-Merodach of Jer 52:31 and 2Ki 25:27. He was replaced by Nergal Shar-usar (Nergal-Sharezer) who reigned from 560 to 556. He was succeeded by Labashi-Marduk, his weak son, who reigned but a few months and was then overthrown by revolution.

One of the conspirators, Nabonidus (Nabonaid), then ascended the throne. Though a revolutionary, he was still a man of culture and religious zeal for the gods of Babylon. He is sometimes styled "the world's first archaeologist." Nabonidus is thus the last true king of Babylon and the father of Belshazzar. Nabonidus made Belshazzar coregent when he retired to Arabia, presumably to consolidate the weakening empire. The Nabonidus chronicle was written after the capture of Babylon in 539 BC. Cyrus of Persia declares how he was able to take the city without a struggle. He describes his leniency toward the population, regarding himself as an "Enlightened Despot" and executioner of the will of the gods. His estimation of the character of Belshazzar is exceedingly low, not at all out of harmony with that represented by the biblical account.

Regarding the latter account, Belshazzar's miserable doom came about at the end of, and largely as a consequence of, a drunken orgy held October 29, 539 BC (Da 5). Suddenly the fingers of a man's hand appeared, writing in fiery letters a message that Belshazzar could not decipher but which he still recognized as ominous. After the failure of his advisers to decipher the "cryptogram," he followed the sugges-

tion of the queen mother and summoned the venerable Hebrew prophet Daniel. After verbally castigating Belshazzar, Daniel interpreted the message ("You have been weighed on the scales and found wanting"). The judgment was swift and inevitable. Babylon fell to the Medo-Persians, Belshazzar was killed, and Darius in the name of Cyrus took the throne.

BELTESHAZZAR [1171, 10108] (bĕl′tĕ-shăz-ar, Heb. *beltsha tstsar, may Bel protect his life*). His Hebrew name was Daniel. He was taken as a captive to Babylon with Hananiah, Mishael, and Azariah, where each one was given a Babylonian name by Nebuchadnezzar's steward (Da 1:6 – 20; 2:17, 49; 3:12 – 30). Daniel was given the name Belteshazzar. Not to be confused with Belshazzar (5:1ff.). *See Daniel.*

BEN (Heb. *ben*).

1. In Semite usage a term used to designate a male descendant, without being limited to the father-son association of the west. Thus, Uzziah (Azariah) can be represented as Joram's son, despite the intervening generations (Mt 1:8). The term Ben is also used in connection with a clan, in plural only, as in the children of (sons of) Israel, children of (sons of) Ammon, etc. It is used also in prefixes of proper names such as Benjamin, Ben-Hadad, etc. It is found also connoting a class, as "sons of the prophets" (2Ki 2:15; NIV "company of the prophets").

2. A Levite appointed by David to serve in a musical capacity before the ark of the Lord (1Ch 15:18). The text is doubtful, because Ben is not mentioned in v. 20 and receives no reference at all in the LXX. The NIV omits it.

BENAIAH [1225, 1226] (bē-nā′ya, Heb. *benāyâh, Jehovah has built*).

1. According to 1Ch 27:5, the son of Jehoiada the priest, and so of the tribe of Levi; probably from the village of Kabzeel in the south of Judah (2Sa 23:30). He was appointed over David's personal bodyguard, the Kerethites and the Pelethites (1Ki 1:38). He was a man of exceptional prowess and bravery. He earned this reputation by killing two "lionlike"

men of Moab and killing a lion trapped in a pit in a snowstorm (2Sa 23:20). Although outstanding for these achievements, Benaiah never gained the status of David's "original three" but is always listed as being next in order of rank (23:23). One of the special duties imposed on Benaiah by the rapidly failing monarch was the oversight of the coronation of his son Solomon (1Ki 1:38 – 39). Benaiah played no part in the rebellion of Adonijah but remained faithful to the cause of Solomon. He thus succeeded Joab as captain of the host (2:35; 4:4).

2. One of David's "valiant Thirty," the Pirathonite, tribe of Ephraim (2Sa 23:30).

3. A prince from the tribe of Simeon who drove the Amalekites from the pastureland of Gedor (1Ch 4:39 – 40).

4. A Levite who played with the psaltery "according to *alamoth*" at the return of the ark to Jerusalem (1Ch 15:20).

5. A priest appointed to blow the trumpet on the same occasion (1Ch 15:24).

6. Ancestor of Jahaziel the prophet who prophesied for Moab and Ammon in the days of Jehoshaphat, the good king (2Ch 20:14).

7. One of the overseers for the offerings in the temple in the days of Hezekiah (2Ch 31:13).

8. Father of Pelatiah who died as a judgment for false teaching in the days of Ezekiel (Eze 11:13).

9. The name of four men, each of whom had taken a foreign wife in the time of Ezra (Ezr 10:25, 30, 35, 43).

BEN-AMMI [1214] (bĕn-ăm′ī̆ Heb. *ben‛ammî, son of my people*). Son of the younger daughter of Lot (Ge 19:38), whom she conceived through her own father following the destruction of Sodom. The progenitor of the Ammonites. Moab shares a like origin through the older sister (19:37).

BEN-HADAD [1207] (bĕn-hā′dăd, Heb. *ben hăd-hadh, son of Hadad*). The name is titular, as opposed to a proper name. As the rulers in Egypt bore the title Pharaoh, so the rulers of Syria bore the designation Ben-Hadad, "son of [the god] Hadad." The Syrians believed their rulers were lineal descendants of the Syrian god Hadad, the deity of storm and thunder, to be identified with Rimmon (2Ki 5:18). There are three individuals in the OT called Ben-Hadad.

Ben-Hadad I was a contemporary with Asa, king of Judah (1Ki 15:18). It is plausible (913 – 873 BC) that he is to be identified with Rezon, the founder of the kingdom of Damascus (11:23 – 25). At the request of Asa of Judah, Ben-Hadad severed his alliance with Baasha of Israel and aligned himself with the southern kingdom (15:16ff.). Though his assistance was of temporary value, the price that Asa was obliged to pay for such aid was tremendous, as Ben-Hadad not only gained control of the treasures of Asa's kingdom but was able through his alliance to extend his territory into the Hebrew kingdoms themselves. Asa was sternly reprimanded by the prophet Hanani for this unfortunate alliance (2Ch 16:7ff.).

Ben-Hadad II was in all probability the son of Ben-Hadad I. He is the Hadadezer of the monuments. He was contemporary with Ahab of Israel (873 – 853 BC), against whom he waged war, laying siege to the newly constructed capital, Samaria. Because of the ungracious terms of surrender demanded by Ben-Hadad, Ahab refused to capitulate. With divine aid, Ahab was able to rout the Syrian army utterly at the battle of Aphek (1Ki 20:26ff.). Ahab spared the life of Ben-Hadad, thus never fully realizing the victory that otherwise would have been his.

Ben-Hadad III (796 – 770 BC) was son of the usurper Hazael, hence not in direct line. His name was adopted from the illustrious name before him. He was a contemporary of Amaziah, king of Judah, and Jehoahaz of Israel. He reduced the fighting personnel of Israel till it was "like the dust at threshing time" (2Ki 13:7). It was at this time that God raised up a deliverer for Israel, most likely Ramman-Mirari III, as shown from an inscription. Joash was able to defeat Ben-Hadad on three different occasions and to recover the cities of Israel (13:25). Under Jeroboam II the northern kingdom restored its prestige, but Amos had already prophesied of the time when

Israel and Samaria would go into captivity beyond Damascus (Am 1:4ff.; 5:27).

BENEDICTIONS (*pronouncements of blessing*). Divinely appointed (Nu 6:23 – 26; Dt 10:8; 21:5).

By God:

On creatures he had made (Ge 1:22); on humankind (Ge 1:28); on Noah (Ge 9:1 – 2).

Instances of:

By Melchizedek on Abraham (Ge 14:19 – 20; Heb 7:7). By Bethuel's household on Rebekah (Ge 24:60). By Isaac on Jacob (Ge 27:23 – 29, 37; 28:1 – 4); Esau (Ge 27:39 – 40). By Jacob on Pharaoh (Ge 47:7 – 10); on Joseph's sons (Ge 48); on his own sons (Ge 49). By Moses on tribes of Israel (Dt 33). By Aaron (Lev 9:22 – 23) on half the tribes who stood on Mount Gerizim (Dt 11:29 – 30; 27:11 – 13; Jos 8:33). By Joshua on Caleb (Jos 14:13); on the Reubenites, Gadites, and half-tribe of Manasseh (Jos 22:6 – 7). By Naomi on Ruth and Orpah (Ru 1:8 – 9). By elders and people on Ruth (Ru 4:11 – 12). By Eli on Hannah (1Sa 1:17); on Elkanah (1Sa 2:20). By David on the people (2Sa 6:18); on Barzillai (2Sa 19:39). By Araunah on David (2Sa 24:23). By Solomon on the people (1Ki 8:14, 55 – 58; 2Ch 6:3). By Simeon on Jesus (Lk 2:34). By Jesus (Lk 24:50).

Levitical:

(Nu 6:23 – 26).

Apostolic:

(Ro 1:7; 15:5, 13, 33; 16:20; 1Co 1:3; 16:23; 2Co 1:2; 13:14; Gal 1:3; 6:16, 18; Eph 1:2; 6:23 – 24; Php 1:2; 4:23; Col 1:2; 1Th 1:1; 5:23; 2Th 1:2; 3:16, 18; 1Ti 1:2; 6:21; 2Ti 1:2; 4:22; Tit 3:15; Phm 3, 25; Heb 13:20 – 21, 25; 1Pe 1:2; 5:10 – 11, 14; 2Pe 1:2 – 4; 2Jn 3; Jude 2; Rev 22:21).

BENEFACTOR [2309]. A title of honor bestowed by ancient states on those famous for notable deeds of benevolence (Lk 22:25).

BENEFICENCE (*goodness, kindness*).

Commanded:

(Lev 25:35 – 43; Dt 15:7 – 15, 18; Pr 3:27 – 28; 25:21 – 22; Mt 5:42; 19:21; 25:35 – 45; Mk 10:21; Lk 3:11; Ro 15:27; 1Co 13:3; 16:1 – 3; 2Co 8:7 – 15, 24; 9:1 – 15; Gal 2:10; 1Ti 5:8, 16; Heb 13:16; Jas 2:15 – 16; 1Jn 3:17).

Results:

Blessed (Ps 41:1; Pr 22:9). Rewarded (Ps 112:9; Pr 11:25; 28:27; Isa 58:6 – 11; Eze 18:5 – 9; Mt 19:21; Mk 9:41; 10:21; Heb 6:10).

Examples:

(Mt 25:35 – 45; Ac 11:29 – 30; Ro 15:25 – 27; 2Co 8:1 – 15; Php 4:10 – 18; 1Ti 6:18). See Alms; Poor, The, Duty to; Rich, The; Riches.

Instances of:

Old man of Gibeah (Jdg 19:16 – 21); Boaz (Ru 2); Jews returned from exile (Ne 5:8 – 12; 8:10 – 11); Job (Job 29:11 – 17; 31:16 – 23); Temanites (Isa 21:14); Good Samaritan (Lk 10:33 – 35); Zacchaeus (Lk 19:8); first Christians (Ac 2:44 – 46; 4:32 – 37); Cornelius (Ac 10:2, 4); Onesiphorus (2Ti 1:16 – 18).

BENJAMIN [278+2157, 408+, 1228+, 1229, 3549, 1021] (běn'ja-mĭn, Heb. *binyamîn, son of [the] right hand* BDB; *southerner* KB).

1. The youngest son of the patriarch Jacob whom his wife Rachel bore in her dying agony; named Ben-oni ("son of my sorrow") by Rachel, his mother, but renamed Benjamin ("son of my right hand") by his father Jacob (Ge 35:18, 24; 46:19). Of all the children of Jacob, he alone was born in Palestine, between Ephrathah and Bethel. Together with his elder brother Joseph, he appears as a special object of parental love and devotion, no doubt, in part at least, because of the sad circumstances surrounding his birth. He seems to have played no part in the sale of Joseph into Egypt. The intercession on the part of Judah in behalf of Benjamin (Ge 44:18 – 34) is one of the most moving speeches in all of literature. No doubt the brothers had been softened in their

attitude as they had observed the continued suffering of their father over the fate of Joseph, whom he believed irrevocably lost. Prophecy concerning (Ge 49:27). Descendants of (Ge 46:21; Nu 26:38 – 41).

2. A great-grandson of Benjamin, son of Jacob (1Ch 7:10).

3. A son of Harim (Ezr 10:32). Probably identical with the man mentioned in Ne 3:23.

4. A Jew who assisted in purifying the wall of Jerusalem (Ne 12:34).

5. A gate of Jerusalem (Jer 20:2; 37:13; 38:7; Zec 14:10).

BENJAMIN, TRIBE OF Named for Jacob's youngest son. On the basis of the first census taken after the exodus, the tribe numbered 35,400; at the second census, it numbered 45,600 (Nu 1:37; 26:41).

In the division of territory by Joshua among the twelve tribes, Benjamin was assigned the portion between Judah on the south and Ephraim on the north (Jos 11:18ff.). Benjamin thus occupied a strategic position commercially and militarily. Benjamin loyally participated in Deborah's rebellion against Sisera (Jdg 5:14). The civil war with Benjamin constitutes a sad and strange story (Jdg 19 – 20).

Saul, son of Kish, came from this tribe (1Sa 9:1ff.). After the death of Saul there was tension and actual fighting between the forces of David and the men of Benjamin. Ish-Bosheth, Saul's weak son, was set up as David's rival (2Sa 2:8). Shimei of Bahurim, who cursed David, was a Benjamite (2Sa 16:5, 11). At the time of the schism after the death of Solomon, however, the Benjamites threw in their lot with the tribe of Judah and followed the Davidic house as represented by Rehoboam, against Jeroboam, the son of Nebat to the north. Benjamin was included in the restoration. Saul of Tarsus (Paul) was a member of the tribe of Benjamin (Php 3:5).

General References to:

Census of, at Sinai (Nu 1:37); in the plain of Moab (Nu 26:41). Clans of (Nu 26:38 – 40; 1Ch 7:6 – 12; 8). Position of, in camp and march (Nu 2:18, 22). Moses' benediction on (Dt 33:12).

Allotment in the land of Canaan (Jos 18:11 – 28). Reallotment (Eze 48:23). Did not exterminate the Jebusites (Jdg 1:21). Join Deborah in the war against Sisera (Jdg 5:14). Territory of, invaded by the Ammonites (Jdg 10:9). Did not avenge the crime of the Gibeonites against the Levite's concubine, the war that followed (Jdg 19 – 20). Saul, the first king of Israel, from (1Sa 9:1, 17; 10:20 – 21). Its rank in the time of Samuel (1Sa 9:21). Jerusalem within the territory of (Jer 6:1). A company of, joins David at Ziklag (1Ch 12:1 – 2, 16). Not enrolled by Joab when he took a census of the military forces of Israel (1Ch 21:6). Loyal to Ish-Bosheth, the son of Saul (2Sa 2:9, 15, 31; 1Ch 12:29). Subsequently joins David (2Sa 3:19; 19:16 – 17). Loyal to Rehoboam (1Ki 12:21; 2Ch 11:1). Military forces of, in the reign of Asa (2Ch 14:8); of Jehoshaphat (2Ch 17:17). Skill in archery and as slingers of stones (Jdg 3:15; 20:16; 1Ch 8:40; 12:2). Return to Israel from the exile in Babylon (Ezr 1:5). Saints of, seen in John's vision (Rev 7:8). Paul, of the tribe of (Ro 11:1; Php 3:5). See Israel.

BEREA, BEROEA [1023, 1024] (bêr-ē′a, Gr. *Beroia*). A city in SW Macedeonia (Ac 17:10 – 15; 20:4). Lying at the foot of Mount Bermius, situated on a tributary of the Haliacmon, its origins appear lost in the mists of time. The Berea mentioned by Thucydides in all likelihood refers to another place. It is, however, twice mentioned by Polybius. Following the battle of Pynda in 168 BC, it surrendered to the Romans and was counted in the third of the four divisions of the empire of Alexander the Great. In the NT, Paul and his party visited Berea on the second missionary journey. Here they found some open-minded people who were willing to study the teachings of Paul in the light of the Scripture. They are important as an example of comparing new teaching to the received Scriptures. This happy situation was disrupted, however, when Jews from Thessalonica arrived, turning the Bereans against the message and forcing Paul to flee to Athens. Silas and Timothy remained there briefly instructing the true believers.

BEREAVEMENT [8892, 8897, 8898].

From God (Hos 9:12). Mourning in, forbidden to Aaron, on account of his son's wickedness (Lev 10:6); to Ezekiel, for his wife (Eze 24:16 – 18).

Instances of:

Abraham, of Sarah (Ge 23:2). Jacob, of Joseph (Ge 37:34 – 35). Joseph, of his father (Ge 50:1, 4). The Egyptians, of their firstborn (Ex 12:29 – 33). Naomi, of her husband (Ru 1:3, 5, 20 – 21). David, of his child by Bathsheba (2Sa 12:15 – 23); of Absalom (2Sa 18:33; 19:4).

Resignation in:

Job (Job 1:18 – 21). David (2Sa 12:22, 30). Solomon (Ecc 7:2 – 4). Christians (1Th 4:13 – 18). See Affliction, Consolation under, Prayer under.

BERYL [1403, 1404, 1039] (*yellow jasper*). A precious stone (Eze 28:13) set in the priestly breastplate (Ex 28:17; 39:10) and seen by John in the foundation of the new Jerusalem (Rev 21:20).

BESTIALITY (*Sexual relations between a human and an animal*). (Ex 22:19; Lev 18:23; 20:16).

BETH (*beth, house*). The name by which the second letter of the Hebrew alphabet is known. The Hebrew uses it also for the number two. It is the most common OT word for house. It designates a more permanent dwelling than tent. It is used often in connection with other words to form proper names, the most common of which are Bethel and Bethlehem.

BETHABARA (bĕth'ăb'a-ra, *house of the ford*). A place on the east bank of the Jordan where John baptized (Jn 1:28 KJV). The later and more reliable Greek manuscripts have rendered this word "Bethany." Care must be taken, however, not to confuse this with the city of the same name near Jerusalem, the home of Mary, Martha, and Lazarus. Its exact location is uncertain. Some identify it with Beth Barah (Jdg 7:24).

BETHANY [1029] (bĕth'a-nē Gr. *Bethania, house of unripe dates or figs*).

1. Town mentioned in Jn 1:28, Bethabara being its name as given in the KJV. Nothing certain is known about it except what is found in this passage: it is beyond the Jordan, and it is where John the Baptist was accomplishing his work.

2. Another city of this name — the home of Mary, Martha, and Lazarus (Lk 10:38 – 41), situated about two miles (three km.) SE of Jerusalem (Jn 11:18) on the eastern slope of Mount Olivet. Some refer to this as the Judean home of Jesus. It was here that he raised Lazarus (Jn 11) and attended the feast at Simon's house (Mt 26; Mk 14; Lk 7). The ascension took place in the region of this city (Lk 24:50 – 51). It is known today as El-Azariyeh. The modern city contains the supposed tomb of Lazarus and house of Simon the leper.

BETHEL [1078, 1088] (bĕth'ĕl, Heb. *bêth'el, house of God*).

1. A town originally known as Luz, twelve miles (twenty km.) north of Jerusalem (Ge 28:19), west of Ai. Abraham stopped near this spot on his way to the Negev and offered a sacrifice (12:8; 13:3). Jacob called Luz "Bethel" (28:10 – 22), since God met him here and confirmed the Abrahamic covenant to him. Jacob revisited this town when he returned from Paddan Aram in response to the command of God (35:1). He built an altar and worshiped, calling the place El Bethel (35:7). Here Jacob buried Deborah, the nurse of Rebekah who had died (35:8). It was a logical stopping place, for it lay on a well-known route running from the Plain of Esdraelon to Beersheba.

Bethel seems to have been a Canaanite city originally, and after the conquest by Joshua was given to the tribe of Benjamin (Jos 18:21 – 22). Joseph's descendants, under the guidance of the Lord, went up against Bethel and took it (Jdg 1:22 – 26). It remained on the southern border of Ephraim. During the period of the judges, because of the wickedness of the tribe of Ephraim, the Israelites marched against them. They stopped at Bethel to ascertain God's will (20:18). The

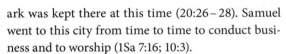

ark was kept there at this time (20:26 – 28). Samuel went to this city from time to time to conduct business and to worship (1Sa 7:16; 10:3).

At a later period when the kingdom was divided, Jeroboam, in order to nullify the influence of Jerusalem as the center of religious activity for the people, chose Bethel as one of the two centers in which he set up golden calves (1Ki 12:26 – 30). Here he sacrificed to the calves and placed priests to minister in the high places (12:32). Because of these and other sins, Amos cried out against this city (Am 3:14; 4:4 – 6). Hosea too pronounced judgment on Bethel, even calling it "Beth Aven," "the house of wickedness" (Hos 4:15). An Israelite priest returned here to teach the people resettled here by Assyria about the Lord (2Ki 17:27 – 28). They combined worship of their heathen gods with worship of the Lord (17:33). It was not until Josiah became king that this idolatry was removed from Bethel and the true worship of the Lord established (23:15 – 23). When the Jews returned from the Babylonian captivity, Ezra and Nehemiah both record that some returned to Bethel (Ezr 2:28; Ne 7:32), and as one might suppose, they are listed as Benjamites (Ne 11:31).

Bethel is mentioned in the apocryphal books as being fortified by Bacchides (1Mc 9:50).

Modern Beitin, Bethel was excavated by Albright and Kelso intermittently from 1934 to 1961. City walls from the Middle Bronze Age (2200 to 1550 BC), the time of the patriarchs, were found. In the Late Bronze Age (1550 – 1200) there were well-built houses here with much imported pottery. In the thirteenth century a destruction layer of ashes and burned bricks testifies to its demise that some attribute to Joshua.

2. Another city mentioned in southern Judah (1Sa 30:27) is also called Bethel. Joshua refers to it as Bethul (Jos 19:4). It is noted again as "Bethuel" (1Ch 4:30). This site has not yet been identified.

3. A mountain (1Sa 13:2).

BETHESDA [1031] (bĕthĕs′da, Gr. *Bēthesda, house of grace or mercy*). A spring-fed pool at Jerusalem,

surrounded by five porches and mentioned only in Jn 5:2. Sick people waited to step down into these waters that were thought to have healing properties. Here Jesus healed a man who had been sick for thirty-eight years (Jn 5:1 – 16). John 5:4, though appearing in most Greek MSS and in some versions (e.g., JB, KJV, MLB, MOF), is omitted by most other modern versions because some early MSS and versions omit it.

In AD 1888, while the church of St. Anne in NE Jerusalem was being repaired, a reservoir was discovered. On the wall is a faded fresco that depicts an angel troubling the water. It is thought, therefore, that this best fits the description in the NT. The reservoir is cut from the rock and is rain-filled. It is about fifty-five feet long and twelve feet wide. It is approached by a flight of steps both steep and winding.

BETHLEHEM [1095, 1107, 1033] (bĕth′lĕ·hĕm, Heb. *bêth-lehem, house of bread*).

1. A town five miles SW of Jerusalem, 2,550 feet above sea level, in the hill country of Judea on the main highway to Hebron and Egypt. In Jacob's time it was called Ephrath ("fruitful") and was the burial place of Rachel (Ge 35:16, 19; 48:7). After the conquest of Canaan, it was called Bethlehem in Judah (Ru 1:1) to distinguish it from Bethlehem no. 2 (see below). It was the home of Ibzan, the tenth judge (Jdg 12:8 – 10); of Elimelech, father-in-law of Ruth (Ru 1:1 – 2), as well as of her husband Boaz (2:1, 4). Here their great-grandson David kept his father's sheep and was anointed king by Samuel (1Sa 16:13, 15). Hence it was known as "the city of David" (Lk 2:4, 11). It was once occupied by a Philistine garrison (2Sa 23:14 – 16), later fortified by Rehoboam (2Ch 11:6).

In Jeremiah's time (Jer 41:17) the caravan inn of Kimham (see 2Sa 19:37 – 40) near Bethlehem was the usual starting place for people traveling to Egypt. The inn mentioned in Lk 2 was a similar one and may have been the same. Here the Messiah was born (Mt 2:1; Lk 2:1 – 7), for whom this town that was "small among the clans of Judah" (Mic 5:2) achieved its great fame. Its male children under two years of age were murdered in Herod's attempt to kill the king of the Jews (Mt 2:16).

Justin Martyr, second century AD, said that our Lord's birth took place in a cave close to the village. Over this traditional manger site the emperor Constantine (AD 330) and Helena his mother built the Church of the Nativity. Rebuilt more sumptuously by Justinian in the sixth century, it still has part of the original structure and is a popular attraction for tourists today. The grotto of the nativity is beneath a crypt, thirty-nine feet (twelve m.) long, eleven feet (three and one-half m.) wide, and nine feet (three m.) high, hewn out of the rock and lined with marble. A rich altar is over the supposed site of the Savior's birth. In a part of this cave Jerome, the Latin scholar, spent thirty years translating the Bible into Latin.

Modern Bethlehem is a village of fewer than ten thousand inhabitants. The slopes abound in figs, vines, almonds, and olives. The shepherds' fields are still seen to the NE.

2. A town of Zebulun (Jos 19:15), now the village of Beit Lahm, seven miles NW of Nazareth.

BETH PEOR [1121] (bĕth' pē'ôr, Heb. *bêth pe'ôr, house of Peor*). One of Israel's last campsites (Dt 3:29; 4:46). Moses was buried here (34:6). It was also a possession of Reuben (Jos 13:20).

BETHPHAGE [1036] (bĕth'fa-jē Heb. *bêth paghah, house of unripe figs*). A village on the Mount of Olives, on the road going east from Jerusalem to Jericho. The traditional site is NW of Bethany, and it is mentioned twice in the NT (Mk 11:1 – 11; Lk 19:28 – 40). Here the colt was obtained for the Palm Sunday entry into Jerusalem (Mt 21:1 – 11). Jesus cursed the fruitless fig tree in the vicinity of Bethphage (Mt 21:18 – 20; Mk 11:12 – 14, 20 – 21).

BETHSAIDA [1034] (bĕth'sā'ĭ·da, Gr. *Bēthsaida, house of fishing*).

1. A village close to the west side of the Sea of Galilee in the land of Gennesaret, where Jesus sent his disciples by boat after he had fed the five thousand (Mk 6:45 – 53). John says that they headed for Capernaum (6:17), but when they were blown off their course they landed in Gennesaret and then went to Capernaum. Possibly, therefore, this Bethsaida was close to Capernaum and may have been its fishing district next to the lake. This would explain how Peter and Andrew are said to be of Bethsaida (Jn 1:44; 12:21), whereas Mark mentions their house close to the synagogue in Capernaum (Mk 1:29). Along with Chorazin and Capernaum, Jesus rebuked Bethsaida for unbelief (Mt 11:20 – 23; Lk 10:13 – 15).

2. Another Bethsaida, NE of the Sea of Galilee and the scene of the feeding of the five thousand (Lk 9:10). Jesus restored sight to a blind man in Bethsaida (Mk 8:22), which is on the east side of the lake, since Jesus had just come from Dalmanutha (Magdala, Mt 15:39) on the west side (Mk 8:10 – 13). This Bethsaida was a village in Gaulanitis (now Jaulan). Philip the tetrarch enlarged it to be the capital and called it Julias, after Julia, the daughter of Emperor Augustus. Its site is uncertain, but some identify it with et Tel, east of the Jordan and one mile from the Sea of Galilee, from which it rises to a height of one hundred feet.

BIBLE The collection of books recognized and used by the Christian church as the inspired record of God's revelation of himself and of his will to humankind.

NAMES.

The word Bible is from Greek biblia, plural of biblion, diminutive of biblos ("book"), from byblos ("papyrus"). In ancient times papyrus was used in making the paper from which books were manufactured. The words biblion and biblia are used in the OT (LXX) and the Apocrypha for the Scriptures (Da 9:2; 1Mc 1:56; 3:48; 12:9). By about the fifth century AD, the Greek church fathers applied the term biblia to the whole Christian Scriptures. Later the word passed into the Western church, and although it is really a plural neuter noun, it came to be used in the Latin as a feminine singular. Thus "The Books" became by common consent "The Book."

In the NT the OT is usually referred to as "the Scriptures" (Mt 21:42; 22:29; Lk 24:32; Jn 5:39; Ac 18:24). Other terms used are "Scripture" (Ac 8:32; Gal 3:22), the "holy Scriptures" (Ro 1:2; 2Ti 3:15), and "sacred writings" (2Ti 3:15 RSV).

The plural term *biblia* stresses the fact that the Bible is a collection of books. That the word came to be used in the singular emphasizes that behind these many books there lies a wonderful unity. That no qualifying adjective stands before it points to the uniqueness of this book.

The names Old Testament and New Testament have been used since the close of the second century AD to distinguish the Jewish and Christian Scriptures. The Old Testament is composed of books produced by writers under God's covenant with Israel; the New Testament contains writings of the apostles (members of God's new covenant people). The term *Novum Testamentum* occurs first in Tertullian (AD 190 – 220). "Testament" is used in the NT (KJV) to render the Greek word *diatheke* (Latin *testamentum*), which in classical usage meant "a will" but in the LXX and in the NT was used to translate the Hebrew word *berith* ("a covenant").

LANGUAGES.

Most of the OT was written in Hebrew, the language spoken by the Israelites in Canaan before the Babylonian captivity. After the return from exile, Hebrew gave way to Aramaic, a related dialect generally spoken throughout SW Asia. A few parts of the OT are in Aramaic (Ezr 4:8 – 7:18; 7:12 – 26; Jer 10:11; Da 2:4 – 7:28). The ancient Hebrew text consisted only of consonants, since the Hebrew alphabet had no written vowels. Vowel signs were invented by the Jewish Masoretic scholars in the sixth century AD and later.

Except for a few words and sentences, the NT was composed in Greek, the language of ordinary conversation in the Hellenistic world. The difference of NT Greek from classical Greek and the Greek of the LXX used to be a cause of bewilderment to scholars, but the discovery, since the 1890s, of many thousands of papyri documents in the sands of Egypt has shown that the Greek of the NT is identical with the Greek generally spoken in the Mediterranean world in the first century. The papyri have thrown a great deal of light on the meaning of many NT words.

COMPASS AND DIVISIONS.

The Protestant Bible in general use today contains sixty-six books, thirty-nine in the OT and twenty-seven in the NT. The thirty-nine OT books are the same as those recognized by the Palestinian Jews in NT times. The Greek-speaking Jews of this period, on the other hand, recognized as Scripture a larger number of books, and the Greek OT (LXX), which passed from them to the early Christian church contained, in addition to the thirty-nine books of the Hebrew canon, a number of others, of which seven — Tobit, Judith, Wisdom, Ecclesiasticus, Baruch, 1 and 2 Maccabees, plus the two so-called additions to Esther and Daniel — are regarded as canonical by the Roman Catholic Church, which therefore has an OT canon of forty-six books. Jews today consider canonical only the thirty-nine books accepted by Protestants.

The books in the Hebrew Bible are arranged in three groups: the Law, the Prophets, and the Writings. The Law comprises the Pentateuch. The Prophets consist of eight books: the Former Prophets (Joshua, Judges, Samuel, and Kings) and the Latter Prophets (Isaiah, Jeremiah, Ezekiel, and the Minor Prophets). The Writings are the remaining books: Psalms, Proverbs, Job, Song of Songs, Ruth, Lamentations, Ecclesiastes, Esther, Daniel, Ezra-Nehemiah, and Chronicles. The total is traditionally reckoned as twenty-four, but these correspond to the Protestant thirty-nine, since in the latter reckoning the Minor Prophets are counted as twelve books, and Samuel, Kings, Chronicles, and Ezra-Nehemiah as two each.

In ancient times there were also other enumerations, notably one by Josephus, who held twenty-two books as canonical (after the number of letters in the Hebrew alphabet), but his twenty-two are the same as the twenty-four in the traditional reckoning.

In the LXX both the number of books and the arrangement of them differ from the Hebrew Bible. It is evident that the NT writers were familiar with the LXX, which contained the Apocrypha, but no quotation from any book of the Apocrypha is found in their pages. The books of the Apocrypha are all late in date and are in Greek, though at least one (Sirach) had a Hebrew origin. The more scholarly of the church fathers (Melito, Origen, Athanasius, Jerome) did not regard the Apocrypha as canonical, although they permitted their use for edification.

The Protestant OT does not follow the grouping of either the Hebrew canon or the LXX. It has, first, the five books of the Pentateuch; then the eleven historical books, beginning with Joshua and ending with Esther; after that what are often called the poetical books: Job, Psalms, Proverbs, Ecclesiastes, and the Song of Songs; and finally the prophets, first the major and then the minor.

All branches of the Christian church are agreed on the NT canon. The grouping of the books is a natural one: first the four gospels; then the one historical book of the NT, the Acts of the Apostles; after that the letters to the churches, first the letters of Paul and then the general letters; and finally the Revelation.

TEXT.

Although the Bible was written over a period of approximately 1,400 years, from the time of Moses to the end of the first century AD, its text has come to us in a remarkable state of preservation. It is of course not identical with the text that left the hands of the original writers. Scribal errors have crept in. Until the invention of printing in the middle of the fifteenth century, all copies of the Scriptures were made by hand. There is evidence that the ancient Jewish scribes copied the books of the OT with extreme care. The recently discovered Dead Sea Scrolls, some going as far back as the second and third centuries BC, contain either whole books or fragments of all but one (Esther) of the OT books; and they bear witness to a text remarkably like the Hebrew text left by the Masoretes (from AD 500 on). The Greek translation of the OT, the Septuagint, was begun about 250 BC and completed about one hundred years later. Although it differs in places from the Hebrew text current today, it is also a valuable witness to the accuracy of the OT text.

In the NT the evidence for the reliability of the text is almost embarrassingly large and includes about 4,500 Greek manuscripts, dating from AD 125 to the invention of printing; various versions, the Old Latin and Syriac going back to about AD 150; and quotations of Scripture in the writings of the church fathers, beginning with the end of the first century. The superabundance of textual evidence for the NT may be appreciated when it is realized that very few manuscripts of ancient Greek and Latin classical authors have survived, and those that have survived are all late in date. Among the oldest manuscripts of the Greek NT that have come down to us are the John Rylands fragment of the gospel of John (c. 125); Papyrus Bodmer II, a manuscript of the gospel of John dating c. 200; the Chester Beatty Papyri, consisting of three codices containing the Gospels and Acts, most of Paul's letters, and the Revelation, dating from c. 200; and codices Vaticanus and Sinaiticus, both written about c. 350.

CHAPTERS AND VERSES.

The books of the Bible originally had no chapters or verses. For convenience of reference, Jews of pre-Talmudic times divided the OT into sections like our chapters and verses. The chapter divisions we use today were made by Stephen Langton, archbishop of Canterbury, who died in 1228. The division of the NT into its present verses is found for the first time in an edition of the Greek NT published in 1551 by a printer in Paris, Robert Stephens, who in 1555 also brought out an edition of the Vulgate that was the first edition of the entire Bible to appear with our present chapters and verses. The first English Bible to be so divided was the Genevan edition of 1560.

TRANSLATIONS.

The Old and New Testaments appeared very early in translations. The OT was translated into Greek (the LXX) between 250 and 150 BC, and other translations in Greek appeared soon after the beginning of the Christian era. Parts, at least, of the OT were rendered into Syriac as early as the first century AD, and a Coptic translation appeared probably in the third century. The NT was translated into Latin and Syriac c. 150 and into Coptic c. 200. In subsequent centuries versions appeared in the Armenian, Gothic, Ethiopic, Georgian, Arabic, Persian, and Slavonic languages. The Bible, in whole or in part, is now available in more than 1,100 different languages and dialects. Many languages have been reduced to writing in order that the Bible might be translated into them in written form, and this work still goes on in many lands.

MESSAGE.

Although the Bible consists of many different books written over a long period of time by a great variety of writers, most of whom did not know one another, it has an organic unity that can be explained only by assuming, as the book itself claims, that its writers were inspired by the Holy Spirit to give God's message to humans. The theme of this message is the same in both Testaments: the redemption of humankind. The OT tells about the origin of man's sin and the preparation God made for the solution of this problem through his own Son the Messiah. The NT describes the fulfillment of God's redemptive plan; the four gospels telling about the Messiah's coming; the Acts of the Apostles describing the origin and growth of the church, God's redeemed people; the Epistles giving the

meaning and implication of the incarnation; and the Revelation showing how some day all of history will be consummated in Christ. The two Testaments form two volumes of one work. The first is incomplete without the second; and the second cannot be understood without the first. Together they are God's revelation to people of the provision he has made for their salvation.

General References to:

(2Sa 22:31; Pss 12:6; 119:9, 50; 147:15; Mk 12:24; Lk 8:11; Eph 6:17). The book of the ages (Ps 119:89; Mt 5:18; 24:35; 1Pe 1:25). Food for the soul (Dt 8:3; Job 23:12; Ps 119:103; Jer 15:16; 1Pe 2:2). Divinely inspired (Jer 36:2; Eze 1:3; Ac 1:16; 2Ti 3:16; 2Pe 1:21; Rev 14:13). Precepts written in the heart (Dt 6:6; 11:18; Ps 119:11; Lk 2:51; Ro 10:8; Col 3:16). Furnishes a light (Pss 19:8; 119:105, 130; Pr 6:23; 2Pe 1:19). Loved by believers (Ps 119:47, 72, 82, 97, 140; Jer 15:16). Mighty in its influence: a devouring flame (Jer 5:14); a crushing hammer (Jer 23:29); a life-giving force (Eze 37:7); a saving power (Ro 1:16); a penetrating sword (Eph 6:17; Heb 4:12). Blessings to those who reverence it (Jos 1:8; Ps 19:11; Mt 7:24; Lk 11:28; Jn 5:24; 8:31; Rev 1:3). Purifies the life (Ps 119:9; Jn 15:3; 17:17; Eph 5:26; 1Pe 1:22). Written with a purpose (Jn 20:31; Ro 15:4; 1Co 10:11; 1Jn 5:13). The standard of faith (Pr 29:18; Isa 8:20; Jn 12:48; Gal 1:8; 1Th 2:13). Its words sacred (Dt 4:2; 12:32; Pr 30:6; Rev 22:19). Study of it commanded (Dt 17:19; Isa 34:16; Jn 5:39; Ac 17:11; Ro 15:4). Contains seed for the sower (Ps 126:6; Mk 4:14 – 15; 2Co 9:10). Absolutely trustworthy (1Ki 8:56; Ps 111:7; Eze 12:25; Mt 5:18; Lk 21:33). Profitable for instruction (Dt 4:10; 11:19; 2Ch 17:9; Ne 8:13; Isa 2:3). Ignorance of, dangerous (Mt 22:29; Jn 20:9; Ac 13:27; 2Co 3:15). See Word of God.

BIBLE, ENGLISH VERSIONS In the earliest days of English Christianity, the only known Bible was the Latin Vulgate, made by Jerome between AD

383 and 405. This could be read by the clergy and by monks, the only ones who were familiar with the language. In 670 Caedmon, a monk at Whitby, produced in Old English a metrical version of some of the more interesting narratives of the OT. The first straightforward translation of any part of the Bible into the language of the people was the Psalter, made in about 700 by Aldhelm, the first bishop of Sherborne in Dorset. Some parts of the NT were translated into English by Bede, the learned monk of Jarrow, author of the famous *Ecclesiastical History of the English Nation.* According to a letter of his disciple Cuthbert, Bede was still engaged in translating the gospel of John into English on his deathbed. It is not certain whether he completed it, but, unfortunately, his translation has not survived. King Alfred (871 – 901) produced during his reign English versions of parts of the Old and New Testaments, including a part of the Psalter. Some Latin gospels that survive from this period have written between the lines what are known as "glosses," a word-for-word translation of the text into English, without regard to the idiom and usage of the vernacular. From the same period as these glosses come, what are known as the Wessex Gospels, the first independent Old English version of the Gospels. Toward the end of the tenth century, Aelfric, archbishop of Canterbury, translated parts of the first seven books of the OT, as well as parts of other OT books.

For nearly three centuries after the Norman Conquest in 1066, the uncertain conditions of the language prevented any real literary progress, but some manuscripts of translations of parts of the Bible into Anglo-Norman French survive. About the beginning of the thirteenth century, an Augustinian monk named Orm or Ormin produced a poetical version of the Gospels and the Acts of the Apostles called the *Ormulum.* From the first half of the fourteenth century there survive two prose translations of the Psalter, done in two different dialects; and from the end of the fourteenth century, a version of the principal NT letters, apparently made,

however, not for the use of the common people but for monks and nuns. There was no thought as yet of providing ordinary laypeople with the Bible in their own tongue. It was Wycliffe who first entertained this revolutionary idea. And it was Wycliffe who first made the whole Bible available in English in the year 1382.

BIGOTRY

Condemned:

Exhibited: in self-righteousness (Isa 65:5; Mk 2:16; Lk 15:2; 18:9 – 14); in intolerance (Lk 9:49 – 50; Ac 18:12 – 13). Rebuked (Ac 10:28, 45). Paul's argument against (Ro 3:1 – 23; 4:1 – 25).

Instances of:

Joshua (Nu 11:27 – 29). The Jews with: the Samaritans (Jn 4:9, 27); Jesus (Lk 4:28; 7:39; 11:38 – 39; 15:22; 19:5 – 7; Jn 5:18); the blind man (Jn 9:29 – 34); Paul (Ac 21:28 – 29; 22:22); John (Mk 9:38 – 40; Lk 9:49 – 50); James and John (Lk 9:51 – 56); the early Christians (Ac 10:45; 11:2 – 3; 15:1 – 10, 24; Gal 2:3 – 5); Paul (Ac 9:1 – 2; 22:3 – 4; 26:9 – 11; Gal 1:13 – 14; Php 3:6). See Persecution; Respect.

BILDAD [1161] (bĭl'dăd, *Bel has loved*). One of Job's three "comforters" (cf. Job 2:11 – 13, w 42:7 – 10). He was evidently a descendant of Shuah (Ge 25:2), a son of Abraham by Keturah, who became patriarch of an Arab tribe. Bildad made three speeches (Job 8, 18, 25), and his distinctive character as a "traditionalist" can best be seen in 8:8 – 10.

BINDING AND LOOSING The carrying of a key or keys was a symbol of the delegated power of opening and closing. In Mt 16:19 our Lord gave the "power of the keys" to Peter, and Peter's use of the keys is narrated in what may be called the "three stages of Pentecost." On the day of Pentecost (Ac 2:14 – 40), Peter preached the first Christian sermon and opened "the kingdom of heaven" to what became a Hebrew-Christian church; then, with John, he went to Samaria (8:14 – 17) and opened the same "kingdom" to

the Samaritans; still later in the house of Cornelius (10:44–48), he opened it to the Gentiles. Thus, the church became universal. The medieval teaching about Peter standing at the gate of heaven to receive or reject souls has no basis in biblical teaching.

BIRTH [1061, 1800, 2655, 3528, 3533, 3535, 5951, 6584+7924, 6913, 8167, 1002, 1164, 1181, 2844, 3120+3613, 4472, 5503, 5770]. The bringing forth of a separate life into the world. Although this is accompanied by rending pain, there is no evidence that such pain would have occurred had not sin entered the human race. (See Ge 3:16 where pain in childbearing is a part of the curse on Eve for her sin.) This pain is so uniquely severe that in nine-tenths of the forty-odd uses of the word "travail" in the KJV, it is used as a figure for intense suffering (e.g., Jer 13:21; Ro 8:22; Gal 4:19). Apparently the ancient Hebrew women went through travail more easily than the Egyptians did (Ex 1:19).

The day of one's birth is, in a sense, the most important day of one's life, for without it the individual would not have had life in the world; and so the celebration of birthdays goes back into very ancient times (Ge 40:20; Mt 14:6). The Hebrew ceremonies connected with childbirth are given in Lev 12. The permission to the poor to offer "a pair of turtledoves or two young pigeons" in place of a lamb (Lk 2:24) gives touching testimony to the comparative poverty of Mary, the mother of Jesus. Our Lord, in Jn 3:3–6, makes a clear distinction between the first and second births of a regenerate person; and when this distinction is applied, it seems almost to make two different species of the human race: the once-born and the regenerate. The former are depraved, and unless they repent they are destined for judgment (Heb 9:27; 10:31); the latter are being made partakers in the divine nature (2Pe 1:4) and are destined for glory.

General References to:
Pangs in giving (Ps 48:6; Isa 13:8; 21:3; Jer 4:31; 6:24; 30:6; 31:8). Giving, ordained to be in sorrow (Ge 3:16). Famous births: Cain (Ge 4:1);
Abel (Ge 4:2); Noah (Ge 5:28–29); Isaac (Ge 21:1–5); Esau and Jacob (Ge 25:24–26); the children of Jacob (Ge 29:31–30:24; 35:16–18); Moses (Ex 2:1–4); John the Baptist (Lk 1:5–25, 57); Jesus (Mt 1:18–25; Lk 1:26–38; 2:1–20). See Abortion; Children.

BIRTHRIGHT [1148]. From time immemorial a man's firstborn son has been given privileges above those of his younger sons. This is illustrated today by the order of succession to the throne (in Britain, for instance). Among the Israelites God had a special claim on the firstborn, at least from the time of the exodus, when he destroyed the firstborn of Egypt and claimed those of Israel by right of redemption (Ex 13:2, 12–16). The birthright included a double portion of the inheritance (Dt 21:15–17) and the privilege of priesthood (Ex 13:1–2; 24:5); but in Israel God later set apart the tribe of Levi instead of the firstborn for that service. (Note Nu 3:38–51, where the Levites are about the same in number as the firstborn of Israel.) Esau lost his birthright by selling it to Jacob for some stew, and no regret could undo the loss he had brought on himself. (See Ge 25:27–34; Heb 12:16; and compare the destinies of Israel and of Edom; see also Ob 17–18.) In Israel, Reuben lost his birthright through sin, and his brothers Simeon and Levi lost theirs through violence; and so the blessing came to Judah (Ge 49:3–10).

Described:
Belonged to firstborn (Dt 21:15–16). Entitled firstborn to double portion of inheritance (Dt 21:15–17); royal succession (2Ch 21:3). An honorable title (Ex 4:22; Ps 89:27; Jer 31:9; Ro 8:29; Col 1:15; Heb 1:6; 12:23; Rev 1:5).

Lost by Firstborn:
Sold by Esau (Ge 25:29–34; 27:36, w 25:33; Heb 12:16; Ro 9:12–13). Forfeited by Reuben (1Ch 5:1–2). Set aside: that of Manasseh (Ge 48:15–20); Adonijah (1Ki 2:15); Hosah's son (1Ch 26:10). See Firstborn.

BISHOP (Gr. *episkopos*, *overseer*). The same as elder or overseer (Ac 20:28; Php 1:1; 1Ti 3:1; Tit 1:7, nn.). Originally the principal officer of the local church, the other being the deacon or deacons (1Ti 3:1 – 7). The title "elder" or "presbyter" generally applied to the same man; "elder" referring to his age and dignity, and "bishop" to his work of superintendence. As the churches multiplied, the bishop of a larger church would often be given special honor, and so gradually there grew up a hierarchy, all the way from presiding elders to bishops (over groups of churches), then archbishops.

BITHYNIA [1049] (bĭ-thĭn'ĭ-a, Gr. *Bithynia*). A region along the northern edge of Asia Minor fronting on the Black Sea, the Bosphorus, and the Sea of Marmara. Paul and his companions desired to enter Bithynia with the gospel (Ac 16:6 – 10), but the Holy Spirit was leading toward Europe, and so they could not enter. However, there were Christians there in the first century (1Pe 1:1). The Roman governor Pliny the Younger complained to Trajan concerning the Christians and at the beginning of the second century asked how to deal with them.

Bithynia was settled very early, and its known history goes back past the sixth century BC when Croesus made it a part of his kingdom. A king of Bithynia in the third century BC invited the Gauls into Asia, so originating "Galatia." From the thirteenth century on, it has been Turkish or ruled by the Turks.

BLASPHEMY [1552, 5542, 5919, 7837, 1059, 1060, 1061] (blăs'fĕ-mē Gr. *blasphemia*, *speak against*, *revile*). To reproach or to bring a railing accusation against anyone is bad enough (Jude 9), but to speak lightly or carelessly of God is a mortal sin. The third commandment, "You shall not misuse the name of the LORD your God" (Ex 20:7), was observed so meticulously by the Jews that they would not speak the sacred name (Jehovah) at all, and so no one knows today for certain how it was pronounced. In the Hebrew Bible the consonants of the sacred tetragrammaton (YHWH) occur over six thousand times, always with the vowels for the Hebrew word for "Lord." Before his conversion, Paul blasphemed (1Ti 1:13) and tried to force Christians to blaspheme (Ac 26:11). The Jews, with a peculiar sense of humor, sometimes used the word "to bless" to mean "to curse" or "to blaspheme" (1Ki 21:10, 13; Job 1:5, 11; 2:5, 9). God prescribed that in Israel the punishment for blasphemy would be death by stoning (Lev 24:10 – 16). Naboth was falsely charged with blasphemy and was stoned to death (1Ki 21:10 – 13), as was Stephen (Ac 6:11). Stoning was also in the minds of those who charged Jesus with blasphemy (Mt 9:3; 26:65; Lk 5:31; Jn 10:33); what Jesus said about himself would have been blasphemy were it not true.

Described:

Reproaching God (2Ki 19:22; 2Ch 32:19; Pss 73:9, 11; 74:18; 139:20; Pr 30:9; Isa 5:19; 8:21 – 22; 37:23; 45:9; 52:5; Eze 35:12 – 13; Da 7:25; Mt 10:25). Defying God (Isa 29:15 – 16; 36:15 – 21; 37:10; Eze 8:12; 9:9; Mal 3:13 – 14). Denying God's word (Jer 17:15). Speaking lies against God (Hos 7:13). Attributing ignorance to God (Ps 10:11, 13; Isa 40:27). Exalting oneself above God (Da 11:36 – 37; 2Th 2:4). Calling Jesus accursed (1Co 12:3; Jas 2:7). Against the Holy Spirit (Mt 12:31 – 32; Mk 3:29 – 30; Lk 12:10). Occasioned by sins of believers (2Sa 12:14; Ro 2:24). Foretold by Peter (2Pe 3:3 – 4). Foretold by John (Rev 13:1, 5 – 6; 16:9, 11, 21; 17:3). Forbidden (Ex 20:7; 22:28; Lev 19:12; 22:32; Jas 3:10; 5:12). Punishment for (Lev 24:10 – 16; Isa 65:7; Heb 10:29).

Instances of:

The depraved son of Shelomith, who, in a fight with an Israelite, cursed God (Lev 24:10 – 16). Of the Israelites, in grumbling against God (Nu 21:5 – 6). Infidels who used the adultery of David as an occasion to blaspheme (2Sa 12:14). Shimei, in his malice toward David (2Sa 16:5). One of Sennacherib's field commanders, in the siege of Jerusalem (2Ki 18:22; 19; Isa 36:15 – 20; 37:10 – 33). Job's wife, when she exhorted Job to curse God and die (Job 2:9). Israel (Eze 20:27 – 28). Peter, when accused of being a disciple of Jesus (Mt 26:74; Mk 14:71). The revilers of Jesus, when he was crucified (Mt 27:40 – 44, 63). The early Christians, persecuted by Saul of Tarsus, compelled to blaspheme the name of Jesus (Ac 26:11; 1Ti 1:13). Hymenaeus and Alexander delivered to Satan that they might learn not to blaspheme (1Ti 1:20). Man of sin (2Th 2:3 – 4). Backslidden Ephesians (Rev 2:9).

False Accusations of:

Against Naboth (1Ki 21:13); against Jesus (Mt 9:3; 26:65; Mk 2:7; 14:58; Lk 5:21; 22:70 – 71; Jn 5:18; 10:33; 19:7); against Stephen (Ac 6:11, 13).

BLESS, BLESSING [887, 897, 1385, 1388, 1922, 2328, 2330, 3421] (Heb. *barakh*).

1. God blesses nature (Ge 1:22), humankind (1:28), the Sabbath (2:3), nations (Ps 33:12), classes of people (1:1 – 3), and individuals (Ge 24:1).

2. Godly people should "bless" God; i.e., they should adore him, worship him, and praise him (Ps 103:1 – 2). The same word is used for what a worshiper offers to God (blessing) and seeks from him (blessing). When we "bless" God, we bring his glories before our mind and respond in worship and adoration; when we ask him to "bless" us, we invite him to call our needs to mind and respond in meeting them.

3. Godly people by words and actions can bestow blessings on their fellows (Mt 5:44; 1Pe 3:9).

4. In Bible times, godly men under inspiration bestowed prophetic blessings on their progeny; e.g., Noah blessed Japheth and Shem (Ge 9:26 – 27), Isaac blessed Jacob and Esau (27:27 – 29, 39 – 40), Jacob blessed the tribes of Israel (ch. 49), and Moses also blessed them (Dt 33).

5. We can bless things when we set them apart for sacred use, e.g., the "communion cup" (1Co 10:16).

BLESSING, THE CUP OF (KJV, RSV, ASV, "cup of thanksgiving" in NIV). In the Communion service, the church blesses the cup when it is set apart for the Lord's Supper (1Co 10:16).

BLESSINGS, SPIRITUAL

From God:

(Dt 33:25, 27; Pss 18:28 – 36; 29:11; 37:6, 17, 24, 39; 63:8; 66:8 – 9; 68:18, 28, 35; 84:5, 11; Isa 40:11, 29, 31; 41:10, 13, 16; Ac 3:19; 1Co 2:9; Php 4:13; Jas 1:17; Jude 24). Guidance (Ex 33:16; Pss 23:2 – 3; 119:102; Isa 40:11; 58:11). Sanctification (Ex 31:13; Lev 21:8; Isa 1:25; 4:3 – 4; 6:6 – 7; 1Jn 1:9; Jude 1). The perfecting of salvation (2Co 1:21; Php 1:6; 2:13; 4:19; Col 1:11 – 12; 1Th 5:24; Heb 13:20 – 21; 1Pe 1:5; 2Pe 1:2 – 4). The deposit of the Spirit, guaranteeing what is to come (2Co 1:22; 5:5). Peace (Isa 26:12; 57:19; Mal 4:2; Php 4:7).

From Christ:

(Jn 1:16; Ro 1:7; 16:20; 1Co 1:3; 16:23; 2Co 1:2; 13:14; Gal 1:3; 6:16, 18; Eph 1:2; 6:23 – 24; Php 1:2; 4:23; 1Th 5:28; 2Th 1:2; 3:16, 18; 1Ti 1:2; 2Ti 1:2; Phm 3, 25; 2Pe 1:1; 2Jn 3).

Contingent on Obedience; Resulting in:

Divine favor (Ex 19:5; Jer 7:23); mercy (Ex 20:6; Dt 5:10, 16; 7:9; 1Ki 8:23; 2Ch 30:9); holiness (Dt 28:9; 30:1 – 3, 6; Col 1:22 – 23); eternal salvation (Mt 10:22; 24:13; Mk 13:13; Heb 3:6, 14; 10:36; Rev 2:10). See Faithfulness; Regeneration; Salvation.

BLESSINGS, TEMPORAL

From God:

Rain (Dt 11:14; 28:12; Job 37:6; 38:25 – 27; Pss 68:9; 135:7; 147:8; Jer 10:13; 14:22; 51:16; Joel 2:23; Am 4:7; Zec 10:1, 12; Mt 5:45; Ac 14:17). Seedtime and harvest (Ge 8:22; Lev 25:20 – 22; 26:4 – 5; Ps 107:35 – 38; Isa 55:10; Jer 5:24; Eze 36:30; Mal 3:11; Ac 14:17). Food and clothing (Ge 9:1 – 3; 28:20 – 21; Dt 8:3 – 4; 10:18; 29:5; Ru 1:6; 2Ch 31:10; Pss 65:9; 68:1 – 10; 81:16; 104:14 – 15, 27 – 28; 111:5; 132:15; 136:25; 145:15 – 16; 146:7; Ecc 2:24; 3:13; Isa 33:15 – 16; Joel 2:26; Mt 6:26, 30 – 33; Lk 12:22 – 31; Jn 6:31). Preservation of life (Dt 4:1, 40; 5:33; 7:15; Pss 21:4; 23:6; 91:16; 103:2 – 5; Da 6:20, 22). Children (Pss 113:9; 127:3 – 5). Prosperity (Ge 24:56; 26:24; 49:24 – 25;

Nu 10:29; Dt 8:7 – 10, 18; 1Sa 2:7 – 8; 1Ch 29:12, 14, 16; 2Ch 1:12; Ezr 8:22; Ps 147:13 – 14; Ecc 5:19; Isa 30:23; Hos 2:8). National greatness (Ge 22:17; 26:3 – 4; Dt 1:10; 7:13 – 14; 15:4, 6; 26:18 – 19; 32:13 – 14; Job 12:23; Ps 69:35 – 36; Isa 51:2; Jer 30:19; Eze 36:36 – 38; Da 5:18). Social peace (Lev 26:6; 1Ch 22:9). Victory over enemies (Ex 23:22; Lev 26:6 – 9; Dt 28:7; Ps 44:3). Worldly honors (2Sa 7:8 – 9; 1Ch 17:7 – 8).

Received by:

Noah at the time of the flood (Ge 7:1). Abraham (Ge 24:1). Isaac (Ge 26:12 – 24, 28). Jacob (Ge 35:9 – 15). Israelites in Egypt (Ex 11:3); in the wilderness, supplying water (Ex 17:1 – 7; Nu 20:10 – 11; Pss 78:15 – 20; 105:4), manna (Ex 16:14, 31; Nu 11:7 – 9; Ne 9:15; Ps 78:23 – 24), quail (Nu 11:31 – 33; Pss 78:23 – 30; 105:40). David (2Sa 5:10; 1Ch 14:17). Obed-Edom (2Sa 6:11). Solomon (1Ki 3:13; 1Ch 29:25; 2Ch 1:1). Elijah, fed by ravens (1Ki 17:2 – 7); by an angel (1Ki 19:5 – 8). The widow of Zarephath (1Ki 17:12 – 16). Hezekiah (2Ki 18:6 – 7; 2Ch 32:29); restored to health (2Ki 20:1 – 7). Asa (2Ch 14:6 – 7). Jehoshaphat (2Ch 17:3 – 5; 20:30). Uzziah (2Ch 26:5 – 15). Jotham (2Ch 27:6). Job (Job 1:10; 42:10, 12). Daniel (Da 1:9).

Prayer for:

Rain (1Ki 8:36; 2Ch 6:27); plentiful harvests (Ge 27:28; Dt 26:15; Dt 33:13 – 16); daily bread (Mt 6:11; Lk 11:3); prosperity (Ge 28:3 – 4; 1Ch 4:10; Ne 1:11; 3Jn 2); providential guidance (Ge 24:12 – 14, 42 – 44; Ro 1:10; 1Th 3:11).

Instances of Prayer for:

Abraham (Ge 15:2 – 4); Abraham's servant (Ge 24:12); Laban (Ge 24:60); Isaac (Ge 25:21); Hannah (1Sa 1:11); Elijah (1Ki 17:20 – 21; 18:42, 44; Jas 5:17 – 18); Ezra (Ezr 8:21 – 23); Nehemiah (Ne 1:11; 2:4; 6:9).

Contingent on Obedience; Resulting in:

Longevity (Ex 20:12; Dt 4:40; 5:16; 1Ki 3:14; Pr 3:1 – 2); deliverance from enemies (Ex 23:22; Lev 26:6 – 8; Dt 28:7; 30:1 – 4; Pr 16:7; Jer 15:19 – 21);

prosperity (Lev 26:3 – 5; Dt 7:12 – 14; 15:4 – 5; 28:2 – 12; 29:9; 30:1 – 5, 9 – 20; Jos 1:8; 1Ki 2:3 – 4; 9:3 – 9; 1Ch 22:13; 28:7 – 8; 2Ch 7:17 – 22; 26:5; 27:6; 31:10; Job 36:11; Isa 1:19; Jer 7:3 – 7; 11:1 – 5; 12:16; 17:24 – 27; 22:4 – 5, 15 – 16; Mal 3:10 – 12); favors to children (Dt 4:1, 40; 5:29; 7:9; 12:25, 28); preeminent honors (Dt 28:1, 13; Zec 3:7); averted judgments (Ex 15:26; Dt 7:15). See God, Goodness of, Providence of; Prosperity.

BLOOD [408+1460, 1414+8638, 1414, 1947, 2446, 2743+3655+4946, 3655+3870+4946, 5906, 6795, 135+, 136]. The word occurs more than four hundred times in the Bible and is especially frequent in Leviticus. The circulation of the blood was not known until long after Scripture was written, and for the most part Bible references are directed toward the practical observation that loss of blood leads to loss of vitality and that a draining away of the blood leads to death. Genesis 9:5 says (literally), "Your blood, belonging to your lives, I will seek … from the hand of man … I will seek the life of man." "Seek" in this verse means "seek requital." In this verse "seeking your blood" is parallel with "seeking the life," and both mean exacting the death penalty. When blood is shed, life is terminated, and the Lord seeks requital for the shedding of blood by demanding the life of the murderer (cf. Ge 37:26; Pss 30:9; 58:10). The statement "Your blood be on your own head" (e.g., 2Sa 1:16) witnesses to the same understanding of things: a person guilty of murder must pay with his life. Our concern here is not the question of the death penalty, but the way in which the Bible uses "blood" as a metaphor for "death." When blood is spoken of as the life of the flesh (Ge 9:4; cf. Lev 17:11), the meaning is the practical one that flesh and blood in their proper union constitute a living creature, beast or man, but that when they are separated death takes place. The bearing of this on the use of blood in the sacrifices is most important.

General References to:

Blood is the life (Ge 9:4; Lev 17:11, 14; 19:16; Dt 12:23; Mt 27:4, 24). Forbidden to be used as food (Ge 9:4; Lev 3:17; 7:26 – 27; 17:10 – 14; 19:26; Dt 12:16, 23; 15:23; Eze 33:25; Ac 15:20, 29; 21:25). Plague of (Ex 7:17 – 25; Pss 78:44; 105:29).

Sacrificial:

Sprinkled on altar and people (Ex 24:6 – 8; Eze 43:18, 20). Sprinkled on doorposts (Ex 12:7 – 23; Heb 11:28). Without shedding of, no remission of sins (Heb 9:22).

Of Sin Offering:

Sprinkled seven times before veil (Lev 4;5 – 6, 17); on horns of altar of sweet incense and at bottom of altar of burnt offering (Ex 30:10; Lev 4:7, 18, 25, 30; 5:9; 9:9, 12). Of bull of sin offering, put on horns of altar (Ex 29:12; Lev 8:15); poured at bottom of altar (Ex 29:12; Lev 8:15). See Offerings.

Of Trespass Offering:

Sprinkled on altar (Lev 7:2). See Offerings.

Of Burnt Offering:

Sprinkled round about and on altar (Ex 29:16; Lev 1:5, 11, 15; 8:19; Dt 12:27). Used for cleansing of leprosy (Lev 14:6 – 7, 17, 28, 51 – 52). See Offerings.

Of Peace Offering:

Sprinkled about altar (Lev 3:2, 8, 13; 9:19). Blood of ram of consecration put on tip of right ear, thumb, and large toe of, and sprinkled on, Aaron and his sons (Ex 29:20 – 21; Lev 8:23 – 24, 30). See Offerings.

Blood of the Covenant:

(Ex 24:5 – 8; Zec 9:11; Mt 26:28; Heb 9:18 – 19, 22; 10:29; 13:20). See Offerings.

Of Atonement:

Sprinkled on atonement cover (Lev 16:14 – 15, 18 – 19, 27; 17:11).

Figurative:

Of victories (Ps 58:10); oppression and cruelty (Hab 2:12); destruction (Eze 35:6); guilt (Lev 20:9; 2Sa 1:16; Eze 18:13); judgments (Eze 16:38; Rev 16:6).

Of Jesus:

Shed on the cross (Jn 19:18, 34). Atoning (Mt 26:28; Mk 14:24; Lk 22:20; Ro 3:24 – 25; 5:9; Eph 2:13, 16; Heb 10:19 – 20; 12:24; 13:20; 1Jn 5:6, 8). Redeeming (Ac 20:28; Eph 1:7; Col 1:14, 20; Heb 9:12 – 14; 1Pe 1:18 – 19; Rev 1:5; 5:9; 7:14). Sanctifying (Heb 10:29; 13:12). Justification through (Ro 3:24 – 25; 5:9). Victory through (Rev 12:11). Eternal life by (Jn 6:53 – 56). Typified by blood of sacrifices (Heb 9:6 – 28). Symbolized by wine of the Lord's Supper (1Co 10:16; 11:25). See Atonement; Jesus the Christ.

BLOOD, AVENGER OF Genesis 9:6 states the biblical law of equity that the taking of life by murder requires the taking of the life of the murderer as a judicial penalty. The OT recognizes in this connection both the function of the courts (e.g., Ex 24:12; Dt 19:15 – 21) and the rights of the family of the murdered person. The next of kin was permitted to exact the death penalty. The word that is questionably translated "avenger" (e.g., Nu 35:12) is properly "next of kin" or "redeemer" (*go'el*). Not only in capital cases but in all the vicissitudes of life, the *go'el* was at hand to take on himself whatever need oppressed his close relative. For this reason "redeemer" became one of the most beautiful and theologically significant descriptions of the Lord in relation to his people (e.g., Isa 43:14; *see also Redemption*). To prevent the work of the "avenger" from becoming a family vendetta, OT law appointed cities of refuge to which one guilty of manslaughter (not of murder) could flee for safety and where the avenger was not permitted to enter; also the OT insisted that children could not be punished for a parent's crime or vice versa (Dt 24:16).

BOAZ [1244, 1245, 1067, 1078] (bō′ăz, Heb. *bō′az*, perhaps *in him is strength*).

1. A well-to-do Bethlehemite in the days of the judges who became an ancestor of Jesus by marrying Ruth, the Moabitess, widow of one of the sons of Elimelech (Ru 2 – 4). This was in accordance with the levirate law of Dt 25:5 – 10; Boaz could marry Ruth only after the nearer kinsman (Ru 3:12; 4:1 – 8) had refused the privilege — or the duty. The other refused, because if he had married Ruth and had had a son, a portion of his property would have gone to the credit of Elimelech's posterity instead of to his own by a former marriage. It is impossible to date Boaz exactly, because the genealogy of Ru 4:18 – 22 (given in Mt 1:4 – 6) is almost certainly a partial list, giving ten names to cover eight hundred years. The list in Mt 1 is demonstrably schematic, as it omits names of four kings, and this one in Ruth is almost as surely partial also. They are both accurate but, like most genealogies, partial. Salmon (or Salmah), given here as the father of Boaz, lived at the time of the conquest, for he married Rahab; but the general setting of the story is that of a later period of settled life.

2. One of Solomon's bronze pillars erected at the temple. It stood on the left (north) side of the porch (1Ki 7:21; 2Ch 3:17).

BODY [1061, 1414, 1581, 2728, 5055, 5516, 5577, 5883, 6795, 7007, 10151, 3517, 4773, 4922, 5393] (Gr. *sōma*). The word has a wide range of meaning in the NT. It can refer to a corpse (Mt 27:52), one's physical body (Mk 5:29), and the human self expressed in and through a body (Heb 10:10; 1Pe 2:24). As a Jewish thinker, Paul saw the body not merely as an outer shell to house the soul/spirit, but as the expression of the whole person (Ro 12:1). So he warned against the misuse of the body (1Co 6:13ff.), especially since it is the temple of the Holy Spirit in the case of the believer (6:15, 19). However, the body is affected by sin and so may be called the "body of sin" (Ro 6:6) and "body of death" (7:24). Even so, Paul's use of "body" must be distinguished from his use of "flesh." The latter always points to the principle of sin endemic in human nature.

As there is a physical body for this life, so there is a spiritual body for the life of the age to come after the resurrection (1Co 15:38ff.). The present body, which is affected by sin, will be replaced by a body whose nature is spirit and which is pure and glorious — like Christ's resurrection body.

In the Lord's Supper the bread symbolizes the body of Jesus offered as a sacrifice for sin (Mk 14:22; 1Co 11:24). Further, the local church, which meets for the Lord's Supper as believing disciples, is called by Paul a "body" (Ro 12:4 – 5; 1Co 12:12ff.), as is the universal church, "the body of Christ" (Eph 4:12). The OT does not have one word that has the range of meaning possessed by *sōma*.

> **General References to:**
> *The body is called a house of clay (Job 4:19); golden bowl (Ecc 12:6); earthen vessel (2Co 4:7); house (2Co 5:1); tabernacle (2Pe 1:13); temple of God (1Co 3:16 – 17; 6:19); member of Christ (1Co 6:15). Perishable (Job 17:14; 1Co 15:53 – 54). To be consecrated to God (Ro 12:1). To be kept unto holiness (1Co 6:13 – 20). Resurrection of, to a spiritual body (1Co 15:19 – 54; 2Co 5:14; Php 3:21).*

BODY OF CHRIST. Within the NT this may be understood in three ways:

1. As the natural, human body of Jesus that the eternal Son made his own in the womb of Mary, and in which he offered himself as a sacrifice for the sin of the world (Heb 10:10). This body was transformed from a physical into a spiritual body in resurrection and then taken to heaven in ascension. Yet it remains a human body, and thus he who sits at the right hand of the Father as coregent is still the God-man.

2. As the people of God or the church (local and universal) united to Christ in grace by faith and through baptism. Believers are "one body in Christ" (Ro 12:5) in each locality and, as a universal community, are the "body of Christ" (Eph 4:12) ruled and sustained by Christ, the head (5:23).

3. As the bread used at the Last Supper by Jesus and then as the bread used in Holy Communion by believers. "This is my body," said Jesus (Mt 26:26). As his body (bread) was broken on the cross and as by eating the Passover meal the Israelites had been associated with delivery from Egypt and bondage, so the believers participate in the saving work of Christ on the cross by taking this bread (and wine).

BOLDNESS OF THE RIGHTEOUS

Exemplified:
(Pr 28:1; Ac 18:26; 19:8; Heb 13:6). In prayer (Heb 4:16; 10:19; 1Jn 3:21 – 22; 5:14 – 15). Inspired by fear of the Lord (Pr 14:26). Through faith in Christ (Eph 3:12).

Instances of, in prayer:
Abraham (Ge 18:23 – 32). Moses (Ex 33:12 – 18). In day of judgment (1Jn 2:28; 4:17). Effect on others (Ac 4:13). See Courage.

BOOTH [6109, 5468].
Made for shelter (Jnh 4:5); cattle (Ge 33:17); watchmen (Job 27:18; Isa 1:8; 24:20). Prescribed for the Israelites to dwell in during the Feast of Tabernacles to remember their wanderings in the wilderness (Lev 23:40 – 43; Ne 8:15 – 16).

BOOTY [1023, 8965]. Spoils of war. Goods taken from a defeated enemy. Property and persons were sometimes preserved and sometimes completely destroyed (Jos 6:18 – 21; Dt 20:14, 16 – 18). Abraham gave a tenth (Ge 14:20), David ordered that booty be shared with baggage guards (1Sa 30:21 – 25). In the law as given through Moses, very different arrangements were made for varying circumstances.

BORN AGAIN *See New Birth.*

BORROWING [4278, 928+5957, 6292, 8626, 1247]. Several times in the OT the Hebrew word *sha'al* is translated by the verb "borrow." This occurs three times in the context of the people of Israel "borrowing" extensively from the Egyptians (Ex 3:22; 11:2; 12:35). The fact is that the Egyptians, thoroughly cowed by the rigors of the ten plagues, were willing to give generously in order to get rid of their troublesome "guests"; and God, in his providence, allowed Israel to despoil the Egyptians (Ex 12:36) in order to provide gold and silver for the tabernacle that was to be constructed. "Surely your wrath against men brings you praise" (Ps 76:10).

The law of Moses gives careful direction concerning the responsibility of those who borrow or who hold property in trust or who are criminally careless in regard to the property of another (Ex 22:1 – 15). Among the blessings promised Israel on condition of obedience is that they would be lenders, not borrowers (Dt 15:6; 28:12). Also, Jesus instructed his followers to not turn away those who wanted to borrow from them (Mt 5:42). Generally the borrower is the servant of the lender (Pr 22:7), but God's judgment can erase differences (Isa 24:2).

General References to:
Dishonesty in (Ps 37:21). Obligations in (Ex 22:14 – 15). Distress from (Ne 5:1 – 5; Pr 22:7). Compassion toward debtors commanded (Ne 5:6 – 13). Christ's rule concerning (Mt 5:42). Israelites from Egyptians (Ex 3:22; 11:2; 12:35). Iron axhead (2Ki 6:5). Returned exiles from each other (Ne 5:1 – 13). Borrowing trouble. See Security, for Debt.

BOSOM [1843, 2668]. Although in English the word means the part of the body between the arms, in Scripture it is generally used in an affectionate sense, e.g., "the only Son, who is in the bosom of the Father" (Jn 1:18 RSV), carrying the lambs in his bosom (Isa 40:11 KJV), or Lazarus resting in Abraham's bosom (Lk 16:22 – 23 KJV). It can be almost synonymous with "heart" as the center of one's life (cf. Ps 35:13; Ecc 7:9 KJV). Quite commonly, of course, it refers to conjugal love, as in Pr 5:20; Eze 23:8, 21; Mic 7:5 (KJV; NIV "embrace"). In Pr 17:23, KJV and RSV, we read of the bosom as a place of hiding money (NIV, "accepts a bribe in secret").

BOUNDARY STONES [1473, 1474]. Stones used to mark the boundary of property (Jos 13:21). To remove them was forbidden (Dt 27:17). Figuratively, the expression implies a decent regard for ancient institutions (Pr 22:28; 23:10).

BOWELS [5055]. In the KJV the word occurs thirty-six times and in three principal senses:

1. Literally (2Ch 21:15 – 19; Ac 1:18).

2. As the generative parts of the body, whether male or female (Ge 15:4; Ps 71:6).

3. The seat of the emotions, as we use the word "heart." See La 1:20 (ASV, NIV "heart"); Php 1:8 (ASV "tender mercies"; NIV "affection").

BREAD [4312, 5121, 5174, 6314, 109, 788, 6040].

Kinds of:

Bread of affliction (1Ki 22:27; Ps 127:2; Hos 9:4; Isa 30:20); leavened (Lev 7:13; 23:17; Hos 7:4; Am 4:5; Mt 13:33); unleavened (Ge 19:3; Ex 29:2; Jdg 6:19; 1Sa 28:24); wheat (Ex 29:2; 1Ki 4:22; 5:11; Ps 81:16); manna (Nu 11:8); meal (1Ki 17:12); barley (Jdg 7:13).

How Prepared:

Mixed with oil (Ex 29:2, 23); honey (Ex 16:31); yeast. See above, Kinds of. Kneaded (Ge 18:6; Ex 8:3; 12:34; 1Sa 28:24; 2Sa 13:8; Jer 7:18; Hos 7:4). Made into loaves (1Sa 10:3; 17:17; 25:18; 1Ki 14:3; Mk 8:14); cakes (2Sa 6:19; 1Ki 14:3; 17:12); wafers (Ex 16:21; 29:23). Baked in ovens (Ex 8:3; Lev 2:4; 7:9; 11:35; 26:26; Hos 7:4); in pans (Lev 2:5, 7; 2Sa 13:6 – 9); on hearths (Ge 18:6); on coals (1Ki 19:6; Isa 44:19; Jn 21:9). Made by men (Ge 40:2); women (Lev 26:26; 1Sa 8:13; Jer 7:18). Trade in (Jer 37:21; Mk 6:35 – 37). Offered in sacrifice (Lev 21:6, 8, 17, 21 – 22; 22:25; 1Sa 2:36; 2Ki 23:9). By idolaters (Jer 7:18; 44:19). See Bread, Consecrated; Offerings.

Figurative:

(Isa 55:2; 1Co 10:17; 2Co 9:10). Christ, the Bread of Life (Jn 6:32 – 59).

Symbolic:

Of the body of Christ (Mt 26:26; Ac 20:7; 1Co 11:23 – 24).

BREAD, CONSECRATED (1Sa 21:4, 6; 1Ch 28:16; 2Ch 2:4; 29:18; Mt 12:4; Mk 2:26; Lk 6:4; Heb 9:2). Required to be kept before the Lord continually (Ex 25:30; 2Ch 2:4). Placed on table in the Tent of Meeting (Ex 40:22 – 23). See Table of, below. Ordinance concerning (Lev 24:5 – 9). Unlawfully eaten by David (1Sa 21:6; Mt 12:3 – 4; Mk 2:25 – 26; Lk 6:3 – 4). Prepared by the Levites (1Ch 9:32; 23:29). Provided by a yearly per capita tax (Ne 10:32 – 33).

Table of:

(Heb 9:2). Ordinances concerning (Ex 25:23 – 28; 37:10 – 15). Its situation in the tabernacle (Ex 26:35; 40:22). Furniture of (Ex 25:29 – 30; 37:16; Nu 4:7). Consecration of (Ex 30:26 – 27, 29). How removed (Nu 4:7, 15). For the temple (1Ki 7:48, 50; 2Ch 4:19, 22).

BREATH [678, 2039, 3640, 5883, 5972, 8120, 4460, 4466].

Of life (Ge 2:7; 7:22; Ac 17:25). Of God (2Sa 22:16; Job 4:9; 15:30; 33:4; 37:10; Pss 18:15; 33:6; Isa 30:33). Figurative (Eze 37:9).

BRIBERY [H4111, H5510, H8815, H8816, H8936, H9556, G5975].

General References to:

(Ps 26:9 – 10; Pr 15:27; Isa 33:15 – 16). Corrupts conscience (Ex 23:8; Dt 16:18 – 19; Ecc 7:7). Perverts justice (1Sa 8:1 – 3; 12:3; Pr 17:23; 28:21; Isa 1:23; 5:22 – 23; Eze 22:12; Am 5:12; Mic 7:3). Destroys national welfare (Pr 29:4). Profanes God (Eze 13:19). Condemnation of (Job 15:34; Eze 22:12 – 13). Punishment for (Dt 27:25; Am 2:6).

Instances of:

Delilah (Jdg 16:4 – 5); Samuel's sons (1Sa 8:1 – 3); the false prophet, Shemaiah (Ne 6:10 – 13); Ben-Hadad (1Ki 15:18 – 19). Haman bribes Xerxes to destroy the Jews (Est 3:8 – 9). Chief priests bribe Judas (Mt 26:15; 27:3 – 9; Mk 14:11; Lk 22:5).

Soldiers bribed to declare that the disciples stole the body of Jesus (Mt 28:12 – 15). Felix seeks a bribe from Paul (Ac 24:26).

BRIDE [3987, 3994, 4558, 8712, 1222, 3811].

Presents for (Ge 24:53). Maids of (Ge 24:59, 61; 29:24, 29). Ornaments of (Isa 49:18; 61:10; Jer 2:32; Rev 21:2). Figurative (Ps 45:10 – 17; Eze 16:8 – 14; Rev 19:7 – 8; 21:2, 9; 22:17).

BRIDEGROOM [1033, 3163, 3812, 3813].

Ornaments of (Isa 61:10). Exempt from military duty (Dt 24:5). Companions of (Jdg 14:11). Joy with (Mt 9:15; Mk 2:19 – 20; Lk 5:34 – 35). Parable of (Mt 25:1 – 13; SS 4:7 – 16). Figurative (Eze 16:8 – 14).

BRIMSTONE More properly translated "sulfur" in the NIV, the Hebrew word is related to *gopher*, a resinous wood that was used in the construction of the ark. Its root meaning is "resinous" or "highly combustible." It is generally connected with judgment, as when the Lord rained brimstone and fire on Sodom and Gomorrah (Ge 19:24; cf. Ps 11:6 KJV) or as when the dust of Edom was to be turned into brimstone (Isa 34:9 KJV). In the NT "fire and brimstone" are principal elements in the punishment of the wicked in Gehenna, or the "lake of fire" (Rev 20:10; 21:8 KJV). In Rev 9:17 KJV, "fire, jacinth, brimstone" refer to colors, as indicated in NIV: "fiery red, dark blue, and yellow as sulfur."

BRONZE SNAKE Numbers 21:4 – 9 records how the people of Israel complained against Moses and against God, who in judgment sent venomous snakes against them. When the people confessed their sin, Moses made a "bronze snake" (KJV "serpent of brass"), set it on a pole, and in effect said, "Look and live." Those who looked recovered. This bronze snake later was worshiped, but Hezekiah scornfully called it "Nehushtan" (which 2Ki 18:4 NIV footnote describes as sounding like the Hebrew for "bronze" and "snake" and "unclean thing") and destroyed it. This bronze snake was a type of our Lord bearing our sins on the cross (Jn 3:14 – 16).

BROTHER [H278+, H288, H408, H3303, H3304, H10017, G81, G82, G5789, G5790, G6012].

Signifies a relative (Ge 14:16; 29:12); a neighbor (Dt 23:7; Jdg 21:6; Ne 5:7); any Israelite (Jer 34:9; Ob 10); a companion (2Sa 1:26; 1Ki 13:30; 20:33). An inclusive term for all humankind (Ge 9:5; Mt 18:35; 1Jn 3:15). Love of (Pr 17:17; 18:24; SS 8:1). Unfaithful (Pr 27:10). Reuben's love for Joseph (Ge 37:21 – 22); Joseph's, for his brothers (Ge 43:30 – 34; 45:1 – 5; 50:19 – 25). A fraternal title, especially among Christians. Instituted by Christ (Mt 12:50; 25:40; Heb 2:11 – 12). Used by disciples (Ac 9:17; 21:20; Ro 16:23; 1Co 7:12; 2Co 2:13); Peter (1Pe 1:22). Used among the Israelites (Lev 19:17; Dt 22:1 – 4). Brother's widow, law concerning Levirate marriage of (Dt 25:5 – 10; Mt 22:24; Mk 12:19; Lk 20:28).

BURDEN [3877, 5362, 6024, 6268, 6673, 6701+6721, 976, 983, 2096, 2915, 5845]. That which is laid on an animal or person in order to be carried. The word translates eight different words in the OT and three in the NT. When it is literally used, it is easily understood and needs no special comment. Figuratively, it is used in the sense of "responsibility" (Nu 11:11; Mt 11:30) or of a "sorrow" (Ps 55:22 KJV; NIV "cares"). The KJV translates "burden" where the NIV has "oracle" (Isa 15:1; 19:1; 22:1). These are generally "dooms," though in Zec 12:1 and in Mal 1:1 the word is used simply for a "message" (NIV "oracle").

BURIAL [3243, 7690, 7699, 7700, 1946, 1947, 2507, 5313]. The act of placing a dead body in a tomb, in the earth or in the sea, generally with appropriate ceremonies; as opposed to exposure to the beasts, or abandonment or burning. Various peoples, notably the Egyptians, who believed that their dead would live and practice ordinary human occupations in "the land of the dead," often went to great lengths to preserve the bodies of their departed loved ones. They sometimes placed with the mummy tools or instruments or weapons, and occasionally killed and buried a wife or a servant to accompany the one whom they had buried. Partly because of God's declaration to fallen man, "For dust you are and to dust you will return" (Ge 3:19), the people of Israel almost always buried their dead; and because the land of Canaan had so many caves, these places were very frequently used as places of burial. Probably the prevailing motive for our respect for the dead, and even for the place of burial, is the sense of decency and our feeling of love for the person, often without regarding the fact that the real person has gone and that only his former "residence" remains. The story of the treatment of the bodies of Saul and of his sons sheds light on the subject. The Philistines beheaded the bodies, exhibiting the heads throughout their land and fastening Saul's body to the wall of Beth Shan (1Sa 31:8 – 13). The men of Israel rescued the bodies, burned them, reverently buried the bones under a tree, and mourned seven days.

It is remarkable that although God had given to Abraham the deed of the land of Canaan (Ge 15:18 – 21), the only land that the patriarchs possessed before Joshua's time was the burial places for the original family: a cave at Hebron and a field at Shechem (cf. Ge 23 — the burial of Sarah; 49:29 – 32 — Jacob's final request; and Jos 24:32 – 33 — the burial of the mummy of Joseph and the body of Eleazar). In Canaan, in ancient times and in the more primitive parts of the land even today, there was (and is) no embalming in most cases but immediate burial to avoid unpleasant odors (Ac 5:5 – 10) and ceremonial uncleanness (Nu 19:11 – 22). In the time of Christ, the bodies were wrapped in clean linen (Mt 27:57 – 60), and spices and ointments were prepared (Lk 23:56).

General References to:

Rites of (Jer 34:5). Soon after death (Dt 21:23; Jos 8:29; Jn 19:38 – 42; Ac 5:9 – 10). With spices (2Ch 16:14; Mk 16:1; Lk 23:56). Bier used at (2Sa 3:31; Lk 7:14). Attended by relatives and friends: of Jacob (Ge 50:5 – 9); Abner (2Sa 3:31); child of Jeroboam (1Ki 14:13); son of widow of Nain (Lk 7:12 – 13); Stephen (Ac 8:2). Lack of, a disgrace (2Ki 9:10; Pr 30:17; Jer 16:4; 22:19; Eze 39:15). Directions given about, before death, by Jacob (Ge 49:29 – 30); Joseph (Ge 50:25). Burial of Gog (multitude) requiring seven months (Eze 39:12 – 13).

BURNING [202, 430, 836+, 1277, 1624, 1730, 2779, 3013, 3019, 3081, 3675, 3678, 3918, 4003, 4805, 6590, 6592, 7787, 8596, 8599, 9462, 2794, 2876, 3906, 4786, 4792, 4796]. God's judgments have often been accompanied with fire, as e.g., with Sodom and Gomorrah (Ge 19:24 – 28), Nadab and Abihu (Lev 10:1 – 6), and the 250 rebels in the wilderness (Nu 16:2, 35). The final dissolution of "this present evil world" is to be with fierce fire (2Pe 3:7 – 10, 12).

BURNING BUSH A thorny bush that Moses saw burning and from which he heard the Lord speak (Ex 3:2 – 3; Dt 33:16; Mk 12:26). Many attempts have been made to identify the bush, but without success. The incident is important because it is the first direct statement in the Bible linking holiness with the very life of God and making fire the symbol of that holiness. The flame that needs no fuel to maintain it ("the bush … did not burn up") represents the eternal, self-sufficient life of God. Where this God is, holiness is, and sinners can draw near only by meeting the conditions God imposes ("take off your sandals"). This is the seed from which the whole Mosaic system grows. The unapproachable fire is seen in all its majesty on Mount Sinai (Ex 19:18), and this in turn is reflected in the undying fire on the altar (Lev 6:9). The same God who made the simple provision for Moses to draw nigh (Ex 3:5; cf. Jos 5:13) provided the sacrifices.

BURNT OFFERING See *Offerings, Burnt.*

BUSINESS LIFE

Virtues Found in:

Diligence (Pr 10:4; 13:4; 22:29; 2Pe 3:14). Fidelity (Ge 39:6; 2Ch 34:11 – 12; Ne 13:13; Da 6:4; 1Co 4:2; Heb 3:5). Honesty (Lev 19:35 – 36; Dt 25:15; Pr 11:1; Ro 12:17; 13:8). Industry (Ge 2:15; Pr 6:6; 10:5; 12:11; 13:11; 20:13; Ro 12:11). Giving of just weights (Lev 19:36; Dt 25:13; Pr 11:1; 16:11; 20:10; Eze 45:10; Mic 6:11). Integrity (Ps 41:12; Pr 11:3; 19:1; 20:7).

Vices Found in:

Breach of trust (Lev 6:2; SS 1:6; Eze 16:17; Lk 16:12). Dishonesty (Dt 25:13; Pr 11:1; 20:14; 21:6; Hos 12:7). Extortion (Isa 10:2; Eze 22:12; Am 5:11; Mt 18:28; 23:25; Lk 3:13). Fraud (Lev 19:13; Mk 10:19; 1Co 6:8). Unjust gain (Pr 16:8; 21:6; 22:16; Jer 17:11; 22:13; Eze 22:13; Jas 5:4). Slothfulness (Pr 18:9; 24:30 – 31; Ecc 10:18; 2Th 3:11; Heb 6:12).

CAESAR [2790] (sē′zêr).

1. The name of a Roman family prominent from the third century BC, of whom Caius Julius Caesar (c. 102 – 44) was by far the most prominent.

2. The title taken by each of the Roman emperors; e.g., Augustus Caesar, who reigned when Jesus was born (Lk 2:1); his successor Tiberius Caesar, who reigned AD 14 – 37 (3:1); Claudius Caesar, 41 – 54 (Ac 11:28; 18:2); and Nero, under whom Peter and Paul were martyred, 54 – 68 (Ph 4:22). Domitian was "Caesar" from 81 to 96, and it was under him that John was exiled to Patmos. "Caesar" is mentioned by our Lord (Lk 20:22 – 25) both literally as referring to Tiberius and figuratively as meaning any earthly ruler. The name Caesar came to be used as a symbol of the state in general and is often used in this sense in the NT (Mt 22:17, 21; Mk 12:14, 16 – 17; Lk 20:22, 25).

Caesars in the Bible: (1) Augustus (Lk 2:1), (2) Tiberius (Lk 3:1; 20:22), (3) Claudius (Ac 11:28), and (4) Nero (Php 4:22).

Mt   22:21   "Give to **C** what is Caesar's,

CAESAREA [2791] (sĕs′a-rē′a). A seaport city in Israel built between 25 and 13 BC by Herod "the Great" at a vast cost and named in honor of his patron Augustus Caesar. It lay on the coast of the Mediterranean about twenty-five miles (forty-two km.) NW of the town of Samaria, which Herod had rebuilt and renamed Sebaste, also in honor of Augustus. Herod intended it as the port of his capital, and a splendid harbor was constructed. Great stone blocks were used to top the reefs that helped to form the harbor. Being the military headquarters for the Roman forces and the residence of the procurators, it was the home of Cornelius in whose house Peter first preached to the Gentiles (Ac 10). It was the place of residence of Philip the evangelist with his four unmarried prophesying daughters (8:40; 21:8 – 9),

who entertained Paul and Luke and their party on their return from the third missionary journey. Later it was the enforced residence of Paul while he was a prisoner for two years, and where he preached before King Agrippa (23:31 – 26:32). The Jewish war that Josephus described with such power and pathos, and that culminated in the destruction of Jerusalem, had its origin in a riot in Caesarea. Here Vespasian was proclaimed emperor of Rome in the year AD 69, while he was engaged in the Jewish war. Caesarea became the birthplace of Eusebius (c. 260) and the seat of his bishopric. It is still called Kaysariyeh.

CAESAREA PHILIPPI [2791+5805] (sĕs′a-rē′a fĭ-lĭp′ī, *Caesarea of Philip*). A town at the extreme northern boundary of Israel, about thirty miles (fifty km.) inland from Tyre and fifty miles (eighty-three km.) SW of Damascus. It lies in the beautiful hill country on the southern slopes of Mount Hermon and was probably near the scene of Jesus' transfiguration (cf. Mt 16:13 – 17:8; Mk 8:27 – 9:8). The town was very ancient, being perhaps the Baal Gad of Joshua 12:7; 13:5, and for centuries it was a center of worship of the heathen god Pan, whence it was known as Paneas and whence the modern name Banias (because there is no *p* in the Arabic alphabet). Augustus Caesar presented it, with the surrounding country, to Herod the Great, who built a temple there in honor of the emperor. Herod's son, Philip the tetrarch, enlarged the town and named it Caesarea Philippi to distinguish it from the other Caesarea. It lies at the easternmost of the four sources of the Jordan, and nearby these streams unite to form the main river. It was at a secluded spot near here that the Lord began to prepare his disciples for his approaching sufferings and death and resurrection, and that Peter made his famous confession (Mt 16:13 – 17).

CAIAPHAS [2780] (kā′ya-făs). In the hundred years from 168 BC, when Antiochus Epiphanes desecrated the temple, to 66, when the Romans took over, the high priesthood was almost a political office, the priests still coming from the descendants of Aaron but being generally appointed for worldly considerations.

From 66 BC the Roman rulers appointed not only the civil officers (e.g., Herod) but the high priests also, with the result that the office declined spiritually. Annas, father-in-law of Caiaphas (Jn 18:13), had been high priest by appointment of the Roman governor from AD 7 to 14 (see Lk 3:2), and though three of his sons succeeded for a short period, Caiaphas held the office from 18 to 36, with Annas still a sort of "high priest emeritus." After Jesus had raised Lazarus from the dead (Jn 11), many of the Jews believed in him (11:45 – 46), but some through jealousy reported the matter to the Pharisees. With the chief priests they gathered a council, fearing, or pretending to fear, that if Jesus were let alone, many would accept him and the Romans would destroy what was left of Jewish autonomy. Caiaphas (11:41 – 53) declared that it would be better for Jesus to die than for the whole nation to be destroyed. When our Lord was betrayed into the hands of his enemies, the Roman soldiers and the Jewish officers took him first to the house of Annas, where by night he was given the pretense of a trial (18:12 – 23). Then Annas sent him bound to Caiaphas before whom the "trial" continued (18:24 – 27). Afterward he was delivered to Pilate because the Jews could not legally execute him. Peter and other disciples were accused before Caiaphas (Ac 4:1 – 22).

CAIN (kān, *metal worker* BDB KB; *brought forth, acquired* Ge 4:1).

1. The first son of Adam and Eve, and a farmer by occupation. As an offering to God, he brought some of the fruits of the ground, while his brother brought an animal sacrifice (Ge 4). Angry when his offering was not received (Heb 11:4 shows that he lacked a right disposition toward God), he murdered his brother. He added to his guilt before God by denying the act and giving no evidence of repentance. He fled to the land of Nod (Ge 4:16) and there built a city, becoming the ancestor of a line that included Jabal, forefather of tent-dwelling

cattle-keepers; Jubal, forefather of musicians; Tubal-Cain, forefather of smiths; and Lamech, a man of violence. His wife must have been one of his own sisters — not an impropriety in those days.

2. The progenitor of the Kenites (Nu 24:22).

3. A village in Judah (Jos 15:57, NIV "Kain").

CALEB [3979, 3992] (kā'lĕb, *dog* BDB; *snappish, warding off* KB).

1. The son of Jephunneh the Kenezite; the prince of Judah whom Moses sent with eleven others to spy out the Promised Land (Nu 13:6). Also spelled Kelubai (1Ch 2:9). Most of the spies brought back a pessimistic report. Their names are almost forgotten; but two heroes of faith, Caleb and Joshua, who encouraged the people to go up and take the land, are still remembered. Because Israel in cowardice adopted the majority report, God imposed on them forty years of "wandering" in the wilderness until that generation died out. Caleb was forty years old when the spies were sent (Jos 14:7). At the age of eighty-five, when the land of Canaan was being distributed, he asked for, and received, Hebron and the hill country. There lived the fearful Anakim who had terrorized ten of the spies. Later he became father-in-law of Othniel, the first of the "judges," by giving him Acsah his daughter (Jdg 1:12 – 15, 20).

> One of the two survivors of the Israelites permitted to enter the land of promise (Nu 14:30, 38; 26:63 – 65; 32:11 – 13; Dt 1:34 – 36; Jos 14:6 – 15); Sent to Canaan as a spy (Nu 13:6); Brings favorable report (Nu 13:26 – 30; 14:6 – 9); Assists in dividing Canaan (Nu 34:19); Life of, miraculously saved (Nu 14:10 – 12); Leader of the Israelites after Joshua's death (Jdg 1:11 – 12); Age of (Jos 14:7 – 10); Inheritance of (Jos 14:6 – 15; 15:13 – 16); Descendants of (1Ch 4:15)

2. A son of Hezron, son of Judah. Ancestor of Bezalel (1Ch 2:18 – 19, 42).

3. Brother of Jerahmeel (1Ch 2:42, 50), possibly the same as 1.

CALENDAR Calendars are devised as a trustworthy means for recording history and determining dates in advance for social, civic, and religious anniversaries, and for economic planning. Comparatively little is known of the calendar of the early Israelites from the patriarchs to the exile, but a critical study of the biblical records and archaeological discoveries is rewarding.

During the Bible period, time was reckoned solely on astronomical observations. The early Chaldean and Egyptian astrologers became quite learned in the movements of astronomical bodies. Their discoveries, as well as those of other Near Eastern neighbors, made their impact on the Jewish calendar. From earliest times the sun and moon were determinants of periods: days, months, and years.

CALF [1201+1330, 5309, 6319, 8802, 3674, 3675].

Offered in sacrifice (Mic 6:6). Golden idol, made by Aaron (Ex 32; Dt 9:16; Ne 9:18; Ps 106:19; Ac 7:41). Images of, set up in Bethel and Dan by Jeroboam (1Ki 12:28 – 33; 2Ki 10:29). Worshiped by Jehu (2Ki 10:29). Prophecies against the golden calves at Bethel (1Ki 13:1 – 5, 32; Jer 48:13; Hos 8:5 – 6; 10:5 – 6, 15; 13:2; Am 3:14; 4:4; 8:14). Altars of, destroyed (2Ki 23:4, 15 – 20).

Ex	32:4	into an idol cast in the shape of a **c**,
Pr	15:17	than a fattened **c** with hatred.
Lk	15:23	Bring the fattened **c** and kill it.
Ac	7:41	made an idol in the form of a **c**.

CALL (Gr. *kaleo*, to call). One of the most common verbs in the Bible, representing over twenty words in the Hebrew and Greek text, but principally with four different meanings:

1. To speak out in the way of prayer: "Call to me and I will answer you" (Jer 33:3).

2. To summon or appoint: "I am about to summon all the peoples of the northern kingdoms" (Jer 1:15).

3. To name a person or thing: "God called the light 'day'" (Ge 1:5).

4. To invite people to accept salvation through Christ. This last is a call by God through the Holy Spirit; it is heavenly (Heb 3:1) and holy (2Ti 1:9). This call comes to people in all situations and occupations (1Co 1:26; 7:20).

Personal:

By Christ (Isa 55:5; Ro 1:6); his Spirit (Rev 22:17); his works (Ps 19:2 – 3; Ro 1:20); his ministers (Jer 35:15; 2Co 5:20); his gospel (2Th 2:14). Is from darkness to light (1Pe 2:9). Addressed to all (Isa 45:22; Mt 20:16). Most reject (Pr 1:24; Mt 20:16). Effective to believers (Ps 110:3; Ac 13:48; 1Co 1:24). Not to many wise by human standards (1Co 1:26). To repentance (Isa 55:1). To believers is of grace (Gal 1:6; 2Ti 1:9); according to the purpose of God (Ro 8:28; 9:11, 23 – 24); irrevocable (Ro 11:29); high (Php 3:14); holy (2Ti 1:9); heavenly (Heb 3:1); to fellowship with Christ (1Co 1:9); to holiness (1Th 4:7); to a prize (Php 3:14); to liberty (Gal 5:13); to peace (1Co 7:15; Col 3:15); to glory and virtue (2Pe 1:3); to the eternal glory of Christ (2Th 2:14; 1Pe 5:10); to eternal life (1Ti 6:12). Partakers of, justified (Ro 8:30). Walk worthy of (Eph 4:1; 2Th 1:11). Blessedness of receiving (Rev 19:9). Is to be made sure (2Pe 1:10). Praise God for (1Pe 2:9). Illustrated (Pr 8:3 – 4; Mt 23:3 – 9). Rejected (Jer 6:16; Mt 22:3 – 7). Rejection of leads to judicial blindness (Isa 6:9, w Ac 28:24 – 27; Ro 11:8 – 10); delusion (Isa 66:4; 2Th 2:10 – 11); withdrawal of the means of grace (Jer 26:4 – 6; Ac 13:46; 18:6; Rev 2:5); temporal judgments (Isa 28:12; Jer 6:16, 19; 35:17; Zec 7:12 – 14); rejection by God (Pr 1:24 – 32; Jer 6:19, 30); condemnation (Jn 12:48; Heb 2:1 – 3; 12:25); destruction (Pr 29:1; Mt 22:3 – 7).

To Special Religious Duty:

Abraham (Ge 12:1 – 3; Isa 51:2; Heb 11:8); Moses (Ex 3:2, 4, 10; 4:1 – 16; Ps 105:26; Ac 7:34 – 35); Aaron and his sons (Ex 4:14 – 16; 28:1; Ps 105:26; Heb 5:4); Joshua (Nu 27:18 – 19, 22 – 23; Dt 31:14, 23; Jos 1:1 – 9); Gideon (Jdg 6:11 – 16); Samuel (1Sa 3:4 – 10); Solomon (1Ch 28:6, 10); Jehu (2Ki 9:6 – 7; 2Ch 22:7); Cyrus (Isa 45:1 – 4); Amos (Am

7:14 – 15); apostles (Mt 4:18 – 22; 9:9; Mk 1:16 – 17; 2:14; 3:13 – 19; Lk 5:27; 6:13 – 16; Jn 15:16); the rich young ruler (Mk 10:21 – 22); Paul (Ac 9:4 – 6, 15 – 16; 13:2 – 3; Ro 1:1; 1Co 1:1; 2Co 1:1; Gal 1:1, 15 – 16; Eph 1:1; Col 1:1; 1Ti 1:1; 2Ti 1:1).

To All Believers:

(Ro 8:30; 1Co 1:2, 9, 24; 1Th 2:11 – 12; 2Th 2:13 – 14; 2Ti 1:9; Heb 3:1 – 2, 3:7 – 8; 1Pe 5:10; 2Pe 1:3, 10; Jude 1; Rev 17:14). See Backsliders.

1Ki	18:24	I will **c** on the name of the LORD.
2Ki	5:11	**c** on the name of the LORD his
1Ch	16:8	to the LORD, **c** on his name;
Ps	116:13	and **c** on the name of the LORD.
	145:18	near to all who **c** on him,
Pr	31:28	children arise and **c** her blessed;
Isa	5:20	Woe to those who **c** evil good
	12:4	to the LORD, **c** on his name;
	55:6	**c** on him while he is near.
Jer	33:3	'C to me and I will answer you
Zep	3:9	that all of them may **c** on the name
Zec	13:9	They will **c** on my name
Mt	9:13	come to **c** the righteous,
Lk	5:32	I have not come to **c** the righteous,
Ac	2:39	all whom the Lord our God will **c**."
	9:14	to arrest all who **c** on your name."
	9:21	among those who **c** on this name?
Ro	10:12	and richly blesses all who **c** on him,
	11:29	gifts and his **c** are irrevocable.
1Co	1:2	with all those everywhere who **c**
1Th	4:7	For God did not **c** us to be impure,
2Ti	2:22	along with those who **c**

CALLING

Isa	40:3	A voice of one **c**:
Mk	1:3	"a voice of one **c** in the desert,
	10:49	Cheer up! On your feet! He's **c** you
Jn	1:23	I am the voice of one **c** in the desert
Ac	22:16	wash your sins away, **c** on his name
Eph	4:1	worthy of the **c** you have received.
2Pe	1:10	all the more eager to make your **c**

CALLING, THE CHRISTIAN (1Co 1:26; Eph 1:18; 4:1; Php 3:14; 1Th 2:12; 2Th 2:14; 2Ti 1:9; Heb 3:1; 1Pe 5:10; 2Pe 1:10).

CALVARY (kăl′va-rē Lat. calvaria, skull). A place not far from the walls of Jerusalem where Christ was crucified and near which he was buried (Lk 23:33). The Latin calvaria is a rendering of the Greek kranion, "skull," which renders the Hebrew Gulgoleth and the Aramaic Gulgulta. The common explanation is that the name was due to the cranial shape of the hill.

The exact site of Calvary is a matter of dispute. Two sites contend for acceptance, the Church of the Holy Sepulchre, which is within the walls of the modern city; and the Green Hill, or Gordon's Calvary, in which is Jeremiah's Grotto, a few hundred feet NE of the Damascus Gate. The first is supported by ancient tradition; but the second, suggested for the first time in 1849, has much to be said in its favor.

CANA (kā′n a). Cana of Galilee is mentioned four times in the gospel of John (2:1, 11; 4:46; 21:2) and nowhere else in Scripture. It was in the highlands of Galilee, as one had to go "down" from there to Capernaum, but opinions differ as to its exact location. It may have been at Kefr Kenna, about five miles (eight km.) NE of Nazareth, or at Khirbet Kana, a little farther north. Here Jesus performed his first miracle, graciously relieving the embarrassment caused by the shortage of wine at a marriage feast. It was here, too (Jn 4:46), that he announced to the nobleman from Capernaum the healing of his apparently dying son. Nathanael came from Cana (Jn 21:2).

CANAAN [4046, 4050, 5913] (kā′năn, land of purple hence merchant, trader).

1. Canaan was the son of Ham in the genealogical lists in Ge 9 – 10. His descendants occupied Canaan and took their name from that country (Ge 9:18, 22, 25 – 27; 10:6). Descendants of (Ge 10:6, 15; 1Ch 1:8, 13).

2. Canaan was one of the old names for Palestine, the land of the Canaanites dispossessed by the Israelites. The etymology of the name is unknown, as is also the earliest history of the name; but Egyptian inscriptions of c. 1800 BC use it for the coastland between Egypt and Asia Minor. In the Amarna Letters of c. 1400 BC, the name is applied to the Phoenician coast.

General References to:

Land of (Ge 11:31; 17:8; 23:2). Called: Israel (Ex 15:14); land of Israel (1Sa 13:19); land of the Hebrews (Ge 40:15); land of the Jews (Ac 10:39); land of promise (Heb 11:9); Beautiful Land (Da 8:9); holy land (Zec 2:12); the Lord's land (Hos 9:3); Immanuel's land (Isa 8:8); Beulah (Isa 62:4). Promised to Abraham and his seed (Ge 12:1 – 7; 13:14 – 17; 15:18 – 21; 17:8; Dt 12:9 – 10; Ps 105:11). Promise renewed to Isaac (Ge 26:3). Extent of: according to the promise (Ge 15:18; Ex 23:31; Dt 11:24; Jos 1:4; 15:1); after the conquest by Joshua (Jos 12:1 – 8); in Solomon's time (1Ki 4:21, 24; 2Ch 7:8; 9:26). Prophecy concerning, after the restoration of Israel (Eze 47:13 – 20). Fertility of (Dt 8:7 – 9; 11:10 – 13). Fruitfulness of (Nu 13:27; 14:7 – 8; Jer 2:7; 32:22). Products of: fruits (Dt 8:8; Jer 40:10, 12); minerals (Dt 8:9); exports (Eze 27:17). Famines in (Ge 12:10; 26:1; 47:13; Ru 1:1; 2Sa 21:1; 1Ki 17). Spies sent into, by Moses (Nu 13:17 – 29). Conquest of, by the Israelites (Nu 21:21 – 35; Dt 3:3 – 6; Jos 6 – 12; Ps 44:1 – 3). Divided by lot among the twelve tribes and families (Nu 26:55 – 56; 33:54; 34:13); by Joshua, Eleazar, and a prince from each tribe (Nu 34:16 – 29; 35:1 – 8; Jos 14 – 19). Divided into twelve provinces by Solomon (1Ki 4:7 – 19); into two kingdoms, Judah and Israel (1Ki 11:29 – 36; 12:16 – 21). Roman provinces of (Lk 3:1; Jn 4:3 – 4).

Ge	10:15	**C** was the father of Sidon his
Lev	14:34	"When you enter the land of **C**,
	25:38	of Egypt to give you the land of **C**
Nu	13:2	men to explore the land of **C**,

	33:51	'When you cross the Jordan into **C**,
Jdg	4:2	a king of **C**, who reigned in Hazor.
1Ch	16:18	"To you I will give the land of **C**
Ps	105:11	"To you I will give the land of **C**
Ac	13:19	he overthrew seven nations in **C**

CANAANITE(S) [4046, 4050, 5914] (kā′năn-īts, *land of purple*, hence *merchant, trader*). According to Jdg 1:9 – 10, Canaanites lived throughout the land. In Ge 12:6; 24:3, 37; Jos 3:10 the Canaanites included the whole pre-Israelite population, even east of the Jordan. The language of Canaan (Isa 19:18) refers to the group of West Semitic languages of which Hebrew, Phoenician, and Moabite were dialects. The Canaanites were of Semitic stock and were part of a large migration of Semites (Phoenicians, Amorites, Canaanites) from NE Arabia in the third millennium BC. They came under Egyptian control c. 1500. The Israelites were never able to exterminate the Canaanites completely, and many were undoubtedly absorbed by their Israelite conquerors. Their continued presence with their heathen practices created serious religious problems for the Israelites.

General References to:

Eleven nations descended from Canaan (Ge 10:15 – 19; Dt 7:1; 1Ch 1:13 – 16). Territory of (Ge 10:19; 12:6; 15:18; Ex 23:31; Nu 13:29; 34:1 – 12; Jos 1:4; 5:1); given to the Israelites (Ge 12:6 – 7; 15:18; 17:8; Ex 23:23; Dt 7:1 – 3; 32:49; Ps 135:11 – 12). Wickedness of (Ge 13:13; Lev 18:25, 27 – 28; 20:23). To be expelled from the land (Ex 33:2; 34:11). To be destroyed (Ex 23:23 – 24; Dt 19:1; 31:3 – 5). Not expelled (Jos 17:12 – 18; Jdg 1:1 – 33; 3:1 – 3). Defeat Israelites (Nu 14:45; Jdg 4:1 – 3). Defeated by Israelites (Nu 21:1 – 3; Jos 11:1 – 16; Jdg 4:4 – 24); by Egyptians (1Ki 9:16). Chariots of (Jos 17:18). Isaac forbidden by Abraham to take a wife from (Ge 28:1). Judah marries a woman of (Ge 38:2; 1Ch 2:3). Jews intermarry with after the exile (Ezr 9:2). Prophecy concerning (Ge 9:25 – 27).

Ge	10:18	Later the **C** clans scattered
	28:1	"Do not marry a **C** woman.

Ex	33:2	before you and drive out the **C**,
Jos	5:1	all the **C** kings along the seacoast
Jdg	1:32	lived among the **C** inhabitants

CANONICITY (kăn′ŏn-ĭc′i-tē). The word *canon* originally meant "measuring rule," hence "standard." In theology its chief application is to those books received as authoritative and making up our Bible. The Protestant canon includes thirty-nine books in the OT, twenty-seven in the NT. The Roman Catholic and Orthodox canons add seven books and some additional pieces in the OT. The Jews accept as authoritative the same thirty-nine books of the OT as do Protestants.

It is commonly said that the Protestant test of canonicity is inspiration. That is, Protestants accept into their canon those books they believe to be immediately inspired by God and therefore true, infallible, and inerrant, the very Word of God. Creeds of the Reformation era often listed the books accepted as inspired, but the Protestant churches have accepted these books not because of the decision of a church or council, but because the books themselves were recognized as true and inspired, having God for their author. The history of the acceptance of these books and the study of the principles on which this acceptance occurred is an important phase of Bible introduction.

CAPERNAUM [3019] (ka-pŭr′nā-ŭm, Gr. *Kapernaoum*, from Heb. *Kaphar-Nahum, village of Nahum*). A town on the NW shore of the Sea of Galilee where Jesus made his headquarters during his ministry in Galilee (Mt 4:13; Mk 2:1). In Scripture it is mentioned only in the Gospels, and perhaps did not arise until after the captivity. That it was a town of considerable size in the days of Christ is shown by a number of facts: a tax collector had his office there (Mk 2:14); a high officer of the king (Herod Antipas) had his residence there and built a synagogue for the people (Mt 8:5 – 13; Lk 7:1 – 10). Jesus performed many striking miracles there, among them the healing of the centurion's palsied servant (Mt 8:5 – 13), the paralytic who was lowered through a

roof by four friends (Mk 2:1 – 13), and a nobleman's son (Jn 4:46 – 54). It was there that Jesus called Matthew to the apostleship as he was sitting at the tax collector's booth (Mt 9:9 – 13). The discourse on the Bread of Life, which followed the feeding of the five thousand, and many other addresses were delivered at Capernaum (Mk 9:33 – 50). In spite of Jesus' remarkable works and teachings, the people did not repent, and Jesus predicted the complete ruin of the place (Mt 11:23 – 24; Lk 10:15). His prophecy was so completely fulfilled that the town has disappeared and its very site is a matter of debate. There are two main claimants, about two and one-half miles (four km.) apart, for the honor of being the site: Tell Hum, which is about two and one-half miles (four km.) SW of the mouth of the Jordan, and Khan Minyeh, which is SW of Tell Hum. The present trend of opinion is in favor of Tell Hum.

| Mt | 4:13 | Nazareth, he went and lived in **C**, |
| Jn | 6:59 | teaching in the synagogue in **C**. |

CAPPADOCIA [G2838] (kăp′a-dō′shĭa). A large inland region of Asia Minor that apparently was given this name by the Persians, though its people were called "Syrians" by the Greeks. In the latter time of the Persian Empire, the region was divided into two territories of which the more northerly was later named Pontus and the southerly Cappadocia, the name it retained in NT times. Jews from Cappadocia (Ac 2:9) were among the hearers of the first Christian sermon along with men from other Anatolian provinces; and Peter directed his first letter (1Pe 1:1) in part to "God's elect … scattered throughout" various provinces in the north. It is almost certain that many of these Cappadocian Jews were converted on the day of Pentecost, and so had the honor of being among the very earliest Christians.

CAPSTONE [7157+8031, 74+8036, 1224+3051]. The keystone of an arch or the last stone put in place to complete a building. Figurative of Jesus: first rejected; finally taking his rightful place of supremacy (Ps

118:22; Zec 4:7; Mt 21:42; Mk 12:10; Lk 20:17; Ac 4:11; 1Pe 2:7). *See Cornerstone.*

Ps	118:22	has become the **c**;
Zec	4:7	he will bring out the **c** to shouts
Mt	21:42	has become the **c**;
Mk	12:10	has become the **c**;
Lk	20:17	has become the **c**'?
Ac	4:11	which has become the **c**.'
1Pe	2:7	has become the **c**,"

CAPTIVE [659, 660, 673, 1655, 4334, 4374, 8647, 8660, 8664, 9530, 168, 5197].

Prisoner of war (Ge 14:12; 1Sa 30:1 – 2). Cruelty to: Putting to death (Nu 31:9 – 20; Dt 20:13; 21:10; Jos 8:29; 10:15 – 40; 11:11; Jdg 7:25; 8:21; 21:11; 1Sa 15:32 – 33; 2Sa 8:2; 2Ki 8:12; Jer 39:6), 20,000 by Amaziah (2Ch 25:11 – 12); ripping open of pregnant women (2Ki 8:12; 15:16; Am 1:13); enslaved or tortured with picks and axes (2Sa 12:31; 1Ch 20:3); blinded (Jdg 16:21; Jer 39:7); maimed (Jdg 1:6 – 7); ravished (La 5:11 – 13; Zec 14:2); enslaved (Dt 20:14; 2Ki 5:2; Ps 44:12; Joel 3:6); robbed (Eze 23:25 – 26); confined in pits (Isa 51:14). Other indignities to (Isa 20:4). Kindness to (2Ki 25:27 – 30; Ps 106:46). Advanced to positions in state (Ge 41:39 – 45; Est 2:8; Da 1).

Ac	8:23	full of bitterness and **c** to sin."
2Co	10:5	and we take **c** every thought
Col	2:8	See to it that no one takes you **c**
2Ti	2:26	who has taken them **c** to do his will.

CAPTIVITY [1655, 3448, 8654, 8660, 8664, 168]. When used of Israel, this term does not refer to the long series of oppressions and captivities of the Israelites by hostile peoples, beginning with the bondage in Egypt and ending with the domination of Rome, but to the captivity of the northern kingdom of Israel or Ephraim in 722 BC and the captivity of Judah in 586 BC. The practice of making large-scale deportations of people as a punishment for rebellion was introduced by Assyria, but other nations adopted it.

CAPTIVITY OF THE NORTHERN KINGDOM.

Assyria first made contact with the northern kingdom when Shalmaneser II (860 – 825 BC) routed, in the battle of Karkar (854), the combined forces of Damascus, Hamath, Israel, and other states that had united to stop his westward progress. In another campaign Shalmaneser received tribute from Jehu, king of Israel. Not many years later, Rimmon-nirari III (810 – 781) compelled Syria to let go of its hold on Israel. Tiglath-Pileser III (745 – 727), one of the greatest monarchs of antiquity, after capturing Samaria, put on the throne his vassal Hoshea, who had assassinated Pekah, king of Israel. With the death of Tiglath-Pileser III, Hoshea decided to strike a blow for independence. Help was promised by the king of Egypt, but it did not come. Hoshea was made a prisoner, and the capital was doomed to destruction as the prophets had foretold (Isa 28:1; Hos 10:7 – 8; Mic 1:5 – 6). It was, however, only after a three-year siege that the city was captured. Before it fell, Shalmaneser had abdicated or died, and Sargon, who succeeded him, completed the conquest of the city and deported the inhabitants to Assyria (2Ki 17:6 – 7; 18:11 – 12). Some time later Sargon's grandson Esarhaddon and his great-grandson Ashurbanipal imported to the region of Samaria some conquered peoples from the East (17:24). Not all of the inhabitants of the northern kingdom were taken into captivity. The very poor, who could cause no trouble in the future, were left (25:12). Intermarriage with the imported peoples resulted in the hybrid stock later known as the Samaritans. When the ten northern tribes were taken into captivity, some undoubtedly were absorbed into the pagan culture surrounding them, but for the most part they retained their identity, some returning to Judah at the end of the exile, others remaining to become part of the dispersion.

CAPTIVITY OF THE SOUTHERN KINGDOM.

The captivity of Judah was predicted 150 years before it occurred (Isa 6:11 – 12; 11:12). Isaiah (11:11;

39:6) and Micah (4:10) foretold that the place of the captivity was to be Babylonia; and Jeremiah announced that it would be for seventy years (Jer 25:1, 11 – 12). The southern kingdom rested on a firmer foundation of faith than the northern and therefore survived longer, but it too had in it the seeds of moral and spiritual decay that caused its eventual disintegration.

Sargon was followed by a number of brilliant rulers, but by 625 BC the hold of Assyria over its tributary peoples had greatly slackened. Revolts broke out everywhere, and bands of Scythians swept through the empire as far as Egypt. Nineveh fell to the Babylonians in 606, never to rise again. A great new Babylonian empire was built up by Nebuchadnezzar (604 – 562). Judah became a vassal of Nebuchadnezzar, but Jehoiakim the king, though warned by Jeremiah, rebelled. Nebuchadnezzar therefore came into Jerusalem in 605 and carried off to Babylon the vessels of the house of God and members of the nobility of Judah, among them Daniel the prophet (2Ch 36:2 – 7; Jer 45:1; Da 1:1 – 3). Jehoiakim was taken in chains to Babylon (2Ch 36:6). In 597 Nebuchadnezzar carried off Jehoiachin, his mother, his wives, three thousand princes, seven thousand men of might, and one thousand artisans (2Ki 24:14 – 16). Among them was the prophet Ezekiel. This was the first large-scale deportation of the southern kingdom into Babylonia. Eleven years later (586) Nebuchadnezzar burned the temple, destroyed the city of Jerusalem, and deported into Babylonia all but the poorest of the land (2Ki 25:2 – 21). A third group was taken into Babylonia five years after the destruction of the city (Jer 52:30).

The exiles were not heavily oppressed by their conquerors. They engaged in business, built houses (Ezr 2:65; Jer 29:5 – 7), and even held high positions in the state (Ne 1:11; Da 2:48). They were not able to continue their system of sacrifices, but they had with them their priests and teachers (Ezr 1:5; Jer 29:1); and Ezekiel gave them constant encouragement (Eze 1:1). In 539 BC Babylon fell to Cyrus king of Persia, who issued a decree permitting the Israelites to return to Jerusalem to rebuild the temple (Ezr 1:1 – 4). The next year, about 43,000 returned with Zerubbabel (Ezr 2:64). The rest preferred to remain in Mesopotamia (Zec 6:10). In 458, 1,800 returned with Ezra.

Dt	28:41	because they will go into **c**.
2Ki	25:21	So Judah went into **c**, away
Jer	30:3	Israel and Judah back from **c**
	52:27	So Judah went into **c**, away
Eze	29:14	I will bring them back from **c**

CARE [2011, 3338, 3359, 5466, 7212, 8286, 9068, 2150, 2499, 3508, 5555].

Worry:

In vain (Pss 39:6; 127:2; Mt 6:27; Lk 12:25 – 26). Proceeds from unbelief (Mt 6:26, 28 – 30; Lk 12:24, 27 – 28). Martha rebuked for (Lk 10:40 – 41). Remedy for (Pss 37:5; 55:22; Pr 16:3; Jer 17:7 – 8; Mt 6:26 – 34; Lk 12:22 – 32; Php 4:6 – 7; Heb 13:5; 1Pe 5:6 – 7). Instances of: Martha (Lk 10:40 – 41); certain people who desired to follow Jesus (Mt 8:19 – 22; Lk 9:57 – 62).

Worldly (help to others):

(Ecc 4:8; Mt 6:25 – 34; 13:22; Mk 4:19; Lk 8:14; 12:27; 14:18 – 19; 21:34; 1Co 7:32 – 33; Php 4:6; 2Ti 2:4).

Ps	8:4	the son of man that you **c** for him?
	65:9	You **c** for the land and water it;
	144:3	what is man that you **c** for him,
Pr	29:7	The righteous **c** about justice
Lk	10:34	him to an inn and took **c** of him.
	18:4	I don't fear God or **c** about men,
Jn	21:16	Jesus said, "Take **c** of my sheep."
1Ti	3:5	how can he take **c** of God's church
	6:20	what has been entrusted to your **c**.
Heb	2:6	the son of man that you **c** for him?
1Pe	5:2	of God's flock that is under your **c**,

CARMEL [4150, 4151, 4153] (kar′mĕl, *garden or orchard planted with vine and fruit trees*).

1. The mountainous promontory jutting into the Mediterranean Sea just south of the modern city Haifa and straight west of the Sea of Galilee (SS 7:5; Isa 33:9; 35:2; Jer 46:18; 50:19; Am 1:2). On the map of Palestine it forms the principal deviation from a comparatively straight coastline and forms the southern wall of the magnificent bay (or gulf) of Acre, the best natural harbor south of Beirut. When the word occurs with the definite article, it generally refers to Mount Carmel and is often used to illustrate a beautiful and fruitful place (Isa 35:2; but see 33:9, which pictures God's judgment). South of Carmel lies the fruitful Plain of Sharon, and NE of it flows the river Kishon through the Plain of Esdraelon. At Carmel, Elijah stood against 450 heathen prophets and defeated them (1Ki 18). Elisha also visited Carmel (2Ki 2:25; 4:25).

2. A very ancient town of Judah about seven miles (twelve km.) almost directly south of Hebron. First mentioned in Jos 15:55, it is best known as the residence of the very churlish Nabal, who refused kindness to David (1Sa 25:2 – 40) and whose life was saved by the tact of his beautiful wife Abigail. Abigail later became a wife of David.

> **General References to:**
> *Forests of (2Ki 19:23). Caves of (Am 9:3). An idolatrous high place on; Elijah builds an altar on, and confronts worshipers of Baal, putting to death 450 of its prophets (1Ki 18:17 – 46). Elisha's abode in (2Ki 2:25; 4:25). Saul erects memorial at (1Sa 15:12). Nabal's possessions at (1Sa 25:2). King Uzziah, who delighted in agriculture, had vineyards at (2Ch 26:10).*

CARNAL Fleshly, as opposed to spiritual, with reference to the body as the seat of the desires and appetites; usually used in Scripture in the negative sense. In 1Co 2:14 – 3:4, Paul divides humankind into two classes — the natural and the spiritual; this corresponds to the classification of people as once-born and twice-born. Then he classifies Christians as "carnal" and "spiritual" (KJV; NIV "worldly" and "spiritual") and lists the marks of carnality as "jealousy and quarreling" and undue emphasis on personalities: "I follow Paul — I follow Apollos." "Carnal" does not necessarily imply active and conscious sin but is used in contrast to that which is "spiritual" (Ro 7:14; 2Co 10:4; Heb 7:16; 9:10). It describes the dominance of the lower side of human nature apart from God's work in one's life.

The KJV OT uses the expression "lie carnally" to describe adultery (Lev 18:20) and fornication (19:20), but these words are used far more often figuratively to refer to idolatry. To take the love that belongs to husband or wife and give it to another is adultery, and to take the love that belongs to God and give it to another is idolatry (Hos 1 – 3; Rev 17:18).

CARNAL-MINDEDNESS Is in conflict with the inner being (Ro 7:14 – 22) and the Holy Spirit (Gal 5:17). Is at enmity with God (Ro 8:6 – 8; Jas 4:4). In children of wrath (Eph 2:3). To be crucified (Ro 8:13; Gal 5:24). Excludes from kingdom of God (Gal 5:19 – 21). Reaps corruption (Gal 6:8).

CARRY

Lev	16:22	goat will **c** on itself all their sins
	26:15	and fail to **c** out all my commands
Isa	46:4	I have made you and I will **c** you;
Lk	14:27	anyone who does not **c** his cross
Gal	6:2	**C** each other's burdens,
	6:5	for each one should **c** his own load.

CAST

Ex	34:17	"Do not make **c** idols.
Lev	16:8	He is to **c** lots for the two goats —
Ps	22:18	and **c** lots for my clothing.
	55:22	**C** your cares on the LORD
Pr	16:33	The lot is **c** into the lap,
Ecc	11:1	**C** your bread upon the waters,
Jn	19:24	and **c** lots for my clothing."
1Pe	5:7	**C** all your anxiety on him

CATACOMBS Subterranean burial places used by the early church. Most are in Rome, where they extend for six hundred miles.

CAUSE

Pr	24:28	against your neighbor without **c**,
Ecc	8:3	Do not stand up for a bad **c**,
Mt	18:7	of the things that **c** people to sin!
Ro	14:21	else that will **c** your brother
1Co	10:32	Do not **c** anyone to stumble,

CELEBRATE

Ex	10:9	we are to **c** a festival to the LORD
	12:14	generations to come you shall **c** it
	12:17	**C** this day as a lasting ordinance
	12:47	community of Israel must **c** it.
	12:48	to **c** the LORD's Passover must
	23:15	"**C** the Feast of Unleavened Bread;
	23:16	"**C** the Feast of Harvest
	23:16	"**C** the Feast of Ingathering
	34:18	"**C** the Feast of Unleavened Bread.
	34:22	"**C** the Feast of Weeks
Lev	23:39	**c** the festival to the LORD
	23:41	**C** this as a festival to the LORD
Nu	9:2	"Have the Israelites **c** the Passover
	9:10	they may still **c** the LORD's
	9:11	are to **c** it on the fourteenth day
	9:12	When they **c** the Passover,
Dt	16:1	**c** the Passover of the LORD your
	16:10	Then **c** the Feast of Weeks
	16:13	**C** the Feast of Tabernacles
Jdg	16:23	to Dagon their god and to **c**,
2Sa	6:21	the LORD's people Israel—I will **c**
2Ki	23:21	"**C** the Passover to the LORD your
2Ch	30:1	and **c** the Passover to the LORD,
	30:13	in Jerusalem to **c** the Feast
	30:23	to **c** the festival seven more days;
Ne	8:12	of food and to **c** with great joy,
	12:27	to **c** joyfully the dedication
Est	9:21	to have them **c** annually
Ps	145:7	They will **c** your abundant
Isa	30:29	as on the night you **c** a holy festival
Na	1:15	**C** your festivals, O Judah,
Zec	14:16	and to **c** the Feast of Tabernacles.
Mt	26:18	I am going to **c** the Passover
Lk	15:23	Let's have a feast and **c**.
	15:32	But we had to **c** and be glad,
Rev	11:10	will **c** by sending each other gifts,

CELIBACY (*abstaining from marriage and sexual activity*). The state of being unmarried, particularly when this state is deliberately chosen. The Bible lays down no definitive rules about it. John the Baptist, for example, was unmarried, but Peter was married. Jesus himself did not marry, but he contributed notably to the wedding celebrations at Cana (Jn 2:1 – 11). He realized that some "have renounced marriage because of the kingdom of heaven" (Mt 19:12), and once he warned against wrong priorities if to become married would be a hindrance to discipleship (Lk 14:20). Paul recognized the dangers of earthly ties and stressed basic principles: God has an assignment for every life, and whatever our situation, married or single, the main thing is to be able to exercise our God-given gifts to the full (1Co 7:7 – 9, 17, 32 – 38).

> **General References to:**
> *Lamented by Jephthah's daughter (Jdg 11:38 – 39). Not obligatory (1Co 7:1 – 9, 25 – 26; 9:5; 1Ti 4:1 – 3). Practiced for kingdom of heaven's sake (Mt 19:10 – 12; 1Co 7:32 – 40). The 144,000 (Rev 14:1 – 4).*

CENSUS [408+6296, 4948, 5031, 5951+8031, 6218+, 7212, 615, 616]. A numbering and registration of a people. The OT tells of three different occasions when a formal census was taken. The first was at Mount Sinai, soon after the Israelites left Egypt (Nu 1). The second was at Shittim near the end of the forty years' wilderness wandering. The third was made by David (2Sa 24:1 – 9; 1Ch 21:1 – 5). The exiles who returned from Babylonia with Zerubbabel were also numbered (Ezr 2). Shortly before the birth of Christ, Emperor Augustus ordered an enrollment in his empire (Lk 2:1).

General References to:

Numbering of Israel by Moses (Ex 38:26; Nu 1; 3:14 – 43; 26); David (2Sa 24:1 – 9; 1Ch 21:1 – 8; 27:24). A poll tax to be levied at each (Ex 30:12 – 16; 38:26). Of the Roman Empire, by Caesar (Lk 2:1 – 3).

CENTURION [1672, 3035] (cĕn-tū'rĭŏn, Lat. *centum, one hundred*). A commander of a hundred soldiers in the Roman army. The word is mentioned first in connection with the centurion of Capernaum whose beloved servant was deathly sick (Mt 8:5 – 13; Lk 7:2 – 10). This officer had built a synagogue for the Jews, who therefore appreciated him and begged Jesus to heal the servant. The centurion showed real reverence for Jesus in saying, "I do not deserve to have you come under my roof," and Jesus responded, "I have not found anyone in Israel with such great faith." A centurion who was in charge of the soldiers who crucified Jesus, testified, "Truly this was the Son of God" (Mt 27:54; Mk 15:39; Lk 23:47). Cornelius (Ac 10), another centurion, was "devout and God-fearing." Peter was sent to him and "used the keys" to open up salvation to the Gentiles, as he had at Jerusalem for the Jews (Ac 2) and at Samaria for its people (Ac 8:14 – 17). Another centurion, Julius, of the Imperial Regiment (Ac 27:1 – 43), had the duty of taking Paul to Rome. He saved Paul's life when the soldiers wished to kill all the prisoners, and Paul by his presence and counsel saved the centurion and all the ship's company. Other centurions are mentioned elsewhere (Mt 27:54; Ac 22:25; 23:17).

Mt	8:5	had entered Capernaum, a **c** came
	27:54	When the **c** and those
Mk	15:39	And when the **c**, who stood there
Lk	7:3	The **c** heard of Jesus and sent some
	23:47	The **c**, seeing what had happened,
Ac	10:1	a **c** in what was known
	27:1	handed over to a **c** named Julius,

CEPHAS [3064] (sē'făs, Gr. *Kēphas*, from Aram. *Kepha, rock, or stone*). A name given by Jesus to the apostle Peter (Jn 1:42). *See Peter.*

Jn	1:42	You will be called **C**" (which,
1Co	1:12	another, "I follow **C**"; still another,
	3:22	Paul or Apollos or **C** or the world
	9:5	and the Lord's brothers and **C**?

CEREMONIAL WASHING [H3200, G49, G968, G2752, G4778]. The Mosaic law, relative to cleansing, stresses that sin defiles. To keep this great truth constantly before the Israelites, specific ordinances concerning washings were given to Moses. The purpose was to teach, by this object lesson, that sin pollutes the soul, and that only those who were cleansed from their sins could be pure in the sight of the Lord (Heb 9:10; 10:22).

General References to:

Of garments (Ex 19:10, 14). Of priests (Ex 29:4; 30:18 – 21; 40:12, 31 – 32; Lev 8:6; 16:4, 24, 26, 28; Nu 19:7 – 10, 19; 2Ch 4:6). Of burnt offerings (Lev 1:9, 13; 9:14; 2Ch 4:6). Of the hands (Mt 15:2; Mk 7:2 – 5; Lk 11:38). Of the feet (1Ti 5:10). For defilement (Lev 11:24 – 40). Of lepers (Lev 13:6; 14:9). Of those having bodily discharge (Lev 15:5 – 13). Of those having eaten or touched that which died (Lev 11:25, 40; 17:15 – 16). Traditional forms of, not observed by Jesus (Lk 11:38 – 39). See Defile; Purification; Washing.

CERTIFICATE

Dt	24:1	and he writes her a **c** of divorce,
	24:3	and writes her a **c** of divorce,
Isa	50:1	"Where is your mother's **c**
Jer	3:8	I gave faithless Israel her **c**
Mt	5:31	divorces his wife must give her a **c**
	19:7	that a man give his wife a **c**
Mk	10:4	a man to write a **c** of divorce

CERTIFICATE OF DIVORCE [6219, 687, 1046]. Given by the husband to his wife upon divorce (Dt 24:1 – 4; Mt 5:31; 19:7; Mk 10:4). Also figurative of God's judgment on Israel (Isa 50:1; Jer 3:8). *See Divorce.*

CHAFF [3143, 5161, 7990, 10534, 949]. The refuse of the grain that has been threshed and winnowed. This is partly dust and dirt, but the real chaff is the hard and inedible coat of the grain. By threshing, most of this is separated; then on a windy day the grain is tossed into the air and the chaff and the shorter pieces of straw are blown away. In Isa 5:24 and 33:11, the word properly means "dry hay" fit for burning. The more common Hebrew word is generally used as a figure for worthless or godless men (e.g., Ps 1:4 — "Not so the wicked! They are like chaff that the wind blows away"). It is used also for godless nations (Isa 17:13). The evanescence of the wicked is likened in Hos 13:3 to the morning mist, the early dew, "chaff swirling from a threshing floor," and "smoke escaping through a window" (KJV "chimney"). In Da 2:35 the Aramaic word rendered "chaff" signifies the small chaff that can get into the eye and irritate it. The word in Jer 23:28 means the broken straw. In the preaching of John the Baptist (Mt 3:12; Lk 3:17), our Lord is to save the righteous ("gathering his wheat into his barn") and destroy the wicked ("burning up the chaff with unquenchable fire").

Ps	1:4	They are like **c**
	35:5	May they be like **c** before the wind,
Da	2:35	became like **c** on a threshing floor
Mt	3:12	up the **c** with unquenchable fire."

CHALDEANS [H4169, G5900, G10373].

1. Virtually synonymous with the Babylonians (2Ki 25:4; 2Ch 36:17; Isa 13:19, nn.). *See Babylon.*

2. Learned and wise men of the East, NIV "astrologers" (Da 2:2, 4, 5, 10; 3:8; 4:7; 5:7).

CHANGE

1Sa	15:29	of Israel does not lie or **c** his mind;
Ps	110:4	and will not **c** his mind:
Jer	7:5	If you really **c** your ways
Mal	3:6	"I the LORD do not **c**.
Mt	18:3	unless you **c** and become like little
Heb	7:21	and will not **c** his mind:
Jas	1:17	who does not **c** like shifting

CHANGERS OF MONEY Men who exchanged one currency for another at a premium. Coins issued by many governments circulated in Palestine; also Jews had to convert their currency into shekels for the temple tax. It was not the trade but the place where they plied it that led Christ to drive them out of the temple court (Mt 21:12; Mk 11:15; Jn 2:14–15); all three passages use the Greek *kollybistes*, "a changer of small coin." John 2:14 has *kermatistes*, with identical meaning. The word *trapezites*, found only in Mt 25:27, is rendered "exchangers" (KJV) or "banker" (NIV, RSV), a lender of money at interest. Both used tables (*trapezas*) and often combined the two functions.

CHARACTER [2657, 467, 1509, 2302, 2456].

Of Believers:

Attentive to Christ's voice (Jn 10:3–4); blameless and harmless (Php 2:15); bold (Pr 28:1); contrite (Isa 57:15; 66:2); devout (Ac 8:2; 22:13); faithful (Rev 17:14); fearing God (Mal 3:16; Ac 10:2); following Christ (Jn 10:4, 27); godly (Ps 4:3; 2Pe 2:9); without falsehood (Jn 1:47); holy (Dt 7:6; 14:2; Col 3:12); humble (Ps 34:2; 1Pe 5:5); hungering for righteousness (Mt 5:6); just (Ge 6:9; Hab 2:4; Lk 2:25); led by the Spirit (Ro 8:14); generous (Isa 32:8; 2Co 9:13); loathing themselves (Eze 20:43); loving (Col 1:4; 1Th 4:9); lowly (Pr 16:19); meek (Isa 29:19; Mt 5:5); merciful (Ps 37:26; Mt 5:7); new creatures (2Co 5:17; Eph 2:10); obedient (Ro 16:19; 1Pe 1:14); poor in spirit (Mt 5:3); prudent (Pr 16:21); pure in heart (Mt 5:8; 1Jn 3:3); righteous (Isa 60:21; Lk 1:6); sincere (2Co 1:12; 2:17); steadfast (Ac 2:42; Col 2:5); taught of God (Isa 54:13; 1Jn 2:27); true (2Co 6:8); undefiled (Ps 119:1); upright (1Ki 3:6; Ps 15:2); watchful (Lk 12:37); zealous of good works (Tit 2:14). See Righteous, Described.

Of the Wicked:

Abominable (Rev 21:8); alienated from God (Eph 4:18; Col 1:21); blasphemous (Lk 22:65; Rev 16:9); blinded (2Co 4:4; Eph 4:18); boastful (Pss 10:3; 49:6); conspiring against believers (Ne 4:8; 6:2; Ps 38:12); corrupt (Mt 7:17; Eph 4:22); covetous (Mic

2:2; Ro 1:29); deceitful (Ps 5:6; Ro 3:13); delighting in the iniquity of others (Pr 2:14; Ro 1:32); despising believers (Ne 2:19; 4:2; 2Ti 3:3 – 4); destructive (Isa 59:7); disobedient (Ne 9:26; Tit 3:3; 1Pe 2:7); enticing to evil (Pr 1:10 – 14; 2Ti 3:6); envious (Ne 2:10; Tit 3:3); evildoers (Jer 13:23; Mic 7:3); fearful (Pr 28:1; Rev 21:8); fierce (Pr 16:29; 2Ti 3:3); foolish (Dt 32:6; Ps 5:5); forgetting God (Job 8:13); fraudulent (Pr 21:8; Isa 57:17); glorying in their shame (Php 3:19); hardhearted (Eze 3:7); hating the light (Job 24:13; Jn 3:20); heady and conceited (2Ti 3:4); hostile to God (Ro 8:7; Col 1:21); hypocritical (Isa 29:13; 2Ti 3:5); ignorant of God (Hos 4:1; 2Th 1:8); impudent (Eze 2:4); infidels (Pss 10:4; 14:1); loathsome (Pr 13:5); lovers of pleasure; not of God (2Ti 3:4); lying (Pss 58:3; 62:4; Isa 59:4); mischievous (Pr 24:8; Mic 7:3); murderous (Pss 10:8; 94:6; Ro 1:29); persecuting (Pss 69:26; 109:16); perverse (Dt 32:5); prayerless (Job 21:15; Ps 53:4); proud (Ps 59:12; Ob 3; 2Ti 3:2); rebellious (Isa 1:2; 30:9); rejoicing in the affliction of believers (Ps 35:15); reprobate (2Co 13:5; 2Ti 3:8; Tit 1:16); selfish (2Ti 3:2); sensual (Php 3:19; Jude 19); sold under sin (1Ki 21:20; 2Ki 17:17); stiff-hearted (Eze 2:4); stiff-necked (Ex 33:5; Ac 7:51); uncircumcised in heart (Jer 9:26); unclean (Isa 64:6; Eph 4:19); unjust (Pr 11:7; Isa 26:18); ungodly (Pr 16:27); unholy (2Ti 3:2); unmerciful (Ro 1:31); unprofitable (Mt 25:30; Ro 3:12); unruly (Tit 1:10); unthankful (Lk 6:35; 2Ti 3:2); unwise (Dt 32:6); without self-control (2Ti 3:3). See Wicked, Described as.

Good:

(Pr 22:1; Ecc 7:1). Defamation of, punished (Dt 22:13 – 19). Revealed in countenance (Isa 3:9).

Steadfastness of:

(Pss 57:7; 108:1; 112:7; Mk 4:20; 2Th 3:3). Exhortations to steadfastness (1Co 7:20; 15:58; 16:13; Eph 4:14 – 15; Php 1:27; 4:1; Col 1:23; 1Th 3:8; 2Th 2:15; Heb 3:6, 14; 10:23; 13:9; 1Pe 5:9; 2Pe 3:17; Rev 3:11). Reward of steadfastness (Mt 10:22; Jas 1:25). Continuing of (Rev 22:11).

Instances of Steadfastness:

Joseph (Ge 39:12); Moses (Heb 11:24 – 26); Joshua (Jos 24:15); Daniel (Da 1:8; 6:10); three Hebrews (Da 3:16 – 18); Pilate (Jn 19:22); Peter and John (Ac 4:19 – 20); Paul (Ac 20:22 – 24; 21:13 – 14).

Instability of:

(Pr 27:8; Jer 2:36; Hos 6:4; 7:8; 10:2; Mt 13:19 – 22; Mk 4:15 – 19; Lk 8:5 – 15; 2Pe 2:14; Rev 2:4). Warnings against (Pr 24:21 – 22; Lk 9:59 – 62; Eph 4:14; Heb 6:4 – 6; 13:9; Jas 1:6 – 8; 4:8; 2Pe 2:14).

Instances of Instability:

Reuben (Ge 49:3 – 4); Pharaoh (Ex 8:15, 32; 9:34; 14:5); Israelites (Ex 32:8; Jdg 2:17 – 19; 2Ch 11:17); Saul (1Sa 18:19); Solomon (1Ki 11:4 – 8); Rehoboam (2Ch 12:1); Pilate (Jn 18:37 – 40; 19:1 – 6); Demas (2Ti 4:10).

Ru	3:11	that you are a woman of noble **c.**
Pr	12:4	of noble **c** is her husband's crown,
	31:10	A wife of noble **c** who can find?
Ac	17:11	noble **c** than the Thessalonians,
Ro	5:4	perseverance, **c**; and **c**, hope.
1Co	15:33	"Bad company corrupts good **c**."

CHARISM, CHARISMA, CHARISMATA [5922]. An inspired gift, bestowed on the apostles and early Christians without any claim of merit on the individual's part, for the good of the church (Mt 10:1, 8; Mk 16:17 – 18; Lk 10:1, 9, 17, 19; Ac 2:4; 10:44 – 46; 19:6; 1Co 12).

CHARITABLENESS ENCOURAGED

(Pr 10:12; 17:9). Commanded (Mt 5:23 – 24; 7:1 – 5; 18:21 – 22; Lk 6:36 – 42; 17:3 – 4; Jn 7:24; Ro 14:1 – 23; 15:1 – 2; 1Co 10:28 – 33; 16:14; 2Co 2:7; Gal 6:1; Eph 4:32; Col 3:13 – 14; 1Ti 1:5; 4:12; 2Ti 2:22; Jas 2:13; 4:11 – 12; 1Pe 3:9). Described (1Co 13:1 – 13). Covers sins (Pr 10:12; 17:9; 19:11; 1Pe 4:8). Pleases God (Mt 6:14 – 15; 18:23 – 35).

CHARITY The KJV translation of the Greek word agape in twenty-eight places. It is translated "love" in eighty-seven places; once it is translated "dear" (Col 1:13). Charity represents the Latin word *caritas*, which stands in the Vulgate in passages where KJV has "love." Charity in the Bible never means giving to the poor; it is always a God-given love that includes respect for, and concern for the welfare of, the one loved. See 1Co 13.

CHASTISEMENT (chăs'tĭz-ment, Heb. *mûsar*, from the verb *yāsar, discipline, chasten, admonish, correct*; Gr. *paideia, child-training, the formation of manhood*). Both are translated by many English words, exhibiting shades of meaning derived from the central concept: the widest sense (Dt 11:2; Isa 53:5); *punishment* (Jer 30:14); *discipline* (Heb 12:8). In Isa 53:5 the whole range of meaning is exhibited in the substitution of the sinless servant of the Lord for his guilty people. When *mûsar* is translated "chastening" (KJV), "discipline" (NIV) rather than punishment is meant (Job 5:17; Pr 3:11 – 12, whence Heb 12:5 – 11 is drawn; Isa 26:16); *retribution, punishment* (Lev 26:28); *instruction in wisdom* is prominent in Proverbs; *unjust chastisement, scourging* (1Ki 12:11); the prayer of Ps 6:1 is answered (Ps 94:12). The Greek word in Ac 7:22 – 23; 2Ti 3:16 (*learn, teach, instruct*) refers to education. Hebrew *yākah* means child-training (2Sa 7:14) and the meaning and value of suffering (Job 33:19; Ps 73:14). Daniel chastened himself by humility (Da 10:12, Heb. *'anâh*). "Chastisement" is chiefly a KJV term (used, however, by RSV notably in Isa 53:5). NIV prefers "discipline" or "punishment," but retains "chastened" in Job 33:19 and Ps 118:18. Chastisement is the process by which God provides a substitute to bear our sins, brings people to put their trust in him, and trains those whom he has received until they reach maturity.

CHASTISEMENT, FROM GOD [3519, 3579].

A blessing (Job 5:17; Ps 94:12 – 13; Heb 12:11). Corrective (Dt 11:2 – 9; 2Sa 7:14 – 15; 2Ch 6:24 – 31; 7:13 – 14; Job 33:19; 34:31; Pss 73:14;

118:18; 119:67, 75; Isa 57:16 – 18; Jer 24:5 – 6; 46:28; 1Co 11:32). Inflicted for sins (Lev 26:28; Pss 89:32; 107:10 – 12, 17; Isa 40:2; Jer 30:14; La 1:5; Hos 7:12; 10:10; Am 4:6). Administered in love (Dt 8:5; Pr 3:11 – 12; Heb 12:5 – 10; Rev 3:19). Repentance under (Pss 106:43 – 44; 107:10 – 13, 17 – 19; Isa 26:16; Jer 31:18 – 19). Failure to repent under (Isa 42:25; Jer 2:30; Hag 2:17). Prayer to be spared from (Pss 6:1; 38:1; 107:23 – 31). Vicariously borne by Jesus (Isa 53:4 – 5).

CHASTITY

Commanded:

(Ex 20:14; Pr 2:10 – 11, 16 – 22; 5:3 – 21; 6:24 – 25; 7:1 – 5; 31:3; Mt 5:27 – 32; Ac 15:20; Ro 13:13; 1Co 6:13 – 19; 7:1 – 2, 7 – 9, 25 – 26, 36 – 37; Eph 5:3; Col 3:5; 1Th 4:3, 7).

Instances of:

Joseph (Ge 39:7 – 20); Boaz (Ru 3:6 – 13); Job (Job 31:1, 9 – 12); Paul (1Co 7); the 144,000 (Rev 14:1 – 5). See Celibacy; Self-Control.

CHEERFUL

Pr	15:13	A happy heart makes the face **c**,
	15:15	but the **c** heart has a continual feast
	15:30	A **c** look brings joy to the heart,
	17:22	A **c** heart is good medicine,
2Co	9:7	for God loves a **c** giver.

CHERUB, CHERUBIM [4131, 5938] (chĕr'ŭb, chĕr'ŭbĭm). A kind of heavenly creature. In other than biblical usage, the English plural is cherubs. The cherubim and a flaming sword were placed at the east of Eden to guard the way to the Tree of Life after Adam and Eve were expelled from the garden of Eden (Ge 3:24). The curtains of the tabernacle were embroidered with cherubim (Ex 26:1). God directed Moses to place two cherubim of beaten gold on the mercy seat above the ark, where God would commune with Moses in the tabernacle (25:18 – 22; 37:7 – 9). God's glory rested between the cherubim (Nu 7:89; 1Sa 4:4; 2Sa 6:2; 2Ki 19:15; Pss 80:1; 99:1; Isa 37:16), in both the tabernacle and the temple. The cherubim in the temple were huge figures newly made for the purpose (1Ki 6:23 – 28; 2Ch 3:10 – 13; 5:7 – 8). Carved cherubim also ornamented the walls of the temple (1Ki 6:29). Hebrews 9:5 mentions the cherubim in the tabernacle. David sings of God riding on a cherub (2Sa 22:11; Ps 18:10). Psalm 18 pictures a storm with God riding on and speaking from the clouds.

That the cherubim were more than clouds or statues is plain from the description Ezekiel gives (Eze 9:3; 10:1 – 22), which shows that they are the "living creatures" of the first chapter.

In Rev 4:6 – 9; 5:6 – 14; 6:1 – 11; 14:3; 15:7; 19:4 are four "beasts" (Gr. *zōa, living creatures*; so ASV, RSV, NIV; these are to be distinguished from the Gr. *thēria, wild beasts*, mentioned, e.g., in Rev 13:1). They are described in terms that identify them with Ezekiel's living creatures or cherubim (Eze 1, 10). The first living creature was like a lion, the second like a calf, the third had a face as a man, the fourth was like a flying eagle (Rev 4:7). They are the bearers of the judgments that follow the breaking of the first four seals.

The cherubim are the living chariot or carriers of God when appearing to people. They are heavenly creatures, servants of God in theophany and judgment, appearing in winged human-animal form with the face of a lion, ox, man, or eagle. Their representations in the tabernacle and temple as statues and in embroidery and carving are not a breach of the second commandment (Ex 20:4). They are significant in prophecy (Ezekiel) and in the Apocalypse (Revelation). Their service is rendered immediately to God. They never came closer to humans than when one took fire in his hand and gave it into the hands of "the man in linen" (Eze 10:7). Yet because the mercy seat, on which the blood of atonement was sprinkled, lay "between the cherubim," nothing can more nearly touch our salvation. In the OT sanctuary, where everything was done and taught by visible, tangible types and symbols, physical representations of the living heavenly cherubim were essential. In Ezekiel's new temple, and in the heavenly sanctuary of Hebrews and Revelation, they are no longer needed, for the redeemed themselves stand in the presence of the living cherubim. The carvings in Eze 41:18 are memorials only.

General References to:
Eastward of the garden of Eden (Ge 3:24). In the tabernacle (Ex 25:18 – 20; 37:7 – 9). Ark rested beneath the wings of (1Ki 8:6 – 7; 2Ch 5:7 – 8; Heb 9:5). Figures of, embroidered on walls of tabernacle (Ex 26:1; 36:8); on veil (Ex 26:31; 36:35). In the temple (1Ki 6:23 – 29; 2Ch 3:10 – 13). Figures of, on veil (2Ch 3:14); walls (1Ki 6:29 – 35; 2Ch 3:7); movable stands (1Ki 7:29, 36). In Ezekiel's vision of the temple (Eze 41:18 – 20, 25). Figurative (Eze 28:14, 16). Symbolic (Eze 1; 10).

Ex	25:19	Make one **c** on one end
Eze	28:14	You were anointed as a guardian **c**,

CHERUBIM

Ge	3:24	side of the Garden of Eden **c**
1Sa	4:4	who is enthroned between the **c**.
2Sa	6:2	enthroned between the **c** that are
	22:11	He mounted the **c** and flew;
1Ki	6:23	a pair of **c** of olive wood,
2Ki	19:15	of Israel, enthroned between the **c**,
Ps	18:10	He mounted the **c** and flew;
Isa	37:16	of Israel, enthroned between the **c**,
Eze	10:1	was over the heads of the **c**.

CHILDBEARING [2228, 3528, 5349, 5450, 6048]. The pain of childbearing was increased as part of the curse (Ge 3:16). The word occurs in 1Ti 2:15 in a passage relating to the proper sphere and conduct of women. "Women will be saved through childbearing" (NIV; KJV, RSV are similar) cannot refer to salvation from sin, which is by grace through faith, but to safekeeping through the pain that became incidental to childbirth through the fall (Ge 3:16). See NIV note: "restored." Hebrew mothers had the assistance of midwives (Ex 1:15 – 21). Newborn babies had the umbilical cord cut, were washed with water, salted, and wrapped in swaddling cloths (Eze

16:4; Lk 2:7, 12). Purification rites were prescribed after childbirth (Lev 12; Lk 2:22 – 24).

CHILD, CHILDREN [1201, 2446, 3251, 3528, 3528, 3529, 5830, 5853, 6407, 6408, 6884, 8890, 8897, 3758, 4086, 5065, 5448, 5451, 5451, 5626]. Among the people of the OT and NT, as in most other cultures, children, especially male, were greatly desired (Ge 15:2; 30:1; 1Sa 1:11, 20; Pss 127:3; 128:3; Lk 1:7, 28). Among the Hebrews all the firstborn belonged to God and had to be redeemed (Nu 3:40 – 51). Children were sometimes dedicated to God for special service (Jdg 13:2 – 7; 1Sa 1:11; Lk 1:13 – 17, 76 – 79). Male descendants of Abraham were circumcised on the eighth day (Ge 17:12; 21:4; Lk 1:59; 2:21), when the name was given. Weaning often was delayed and then celebrated (Ge 21:8) with a feast. Education was primarily in the home and was the duty of parents (Ex 12:26 – 27; Dt 6:7; Jos 4:21 – 24; Pr 22:6; Eph 6:4; Col 3:21; 2Ti 3:15). Discipline was to be firm, with corporal punishment (Pr 22:15; 23:13; 29:15). Much was expected of children (Pr 20:11). Obedience and respect to parents were commanded (Ex 21:17; Eph 6:1 – 3; Col 3:20; 1Ti 3:4, 12; Tit 1:6) although favoritism was sometimes shown (Ge 25:28; 37:3). Affection for children is strikingly portrayed in many instances, as in David's love for a child who died (2Sa 12:15 – 23), and in the raising of children to life by Elijah (1Ki 17:17 – 24), by Elisha (2Ki 4:18 – 37), and by Jesus (Mt 9:23 – 26; Mk 5:35 – 43; Lk 8:49 – 56). Jesus' love and concern for children are seen in Mt 18:1 – 14; 19:13 – 15; Mk 9:35 – 37; 10:13 – 16; Lk 9:46 – 48; 18:15 – 17. There are many reports of attractive childhood — e.g., Moses (Ex 2:1 – 10), Samuel (1Sa 1:20 – 3:19), Jesus (Lk 2:7 – 40), Timothy (2Ti 1:5; 3:14 – 15).

"Children" is an affectionate address, as in 1 John, of an old man to adults, who are nevertheless expected to act their age (1Co 13:11; 14:20). The attention given to the childhood of the Messiah in prophecy (Isa 7:14; 9:6) prepares us for the infancy narratives in Mt 2 and Lk 2. The Savior came as a helpless babe and apparently had a normal childhood. A return to childlike receptiveness and trust is required of those who would enter the kingdom of heaven (Mt 18:1 – 14; 19:13 – 15; Mk 9:35 – 37; 10:13 – 61; Lk 9:46 – 48; 18:15 – 17).

A Blessing:

(Ge 5:29; 30:1; Ps 127:3 – 5; Pr 17:6). The gift of God (Ge 4:1, 25; 17:16, 20; 22:17; 28:3; 29:32 – 35; 30:2, 5 – 6, 17 – 20, 22 – 24; 48:9, 16; Ru 4:13; Job 1:21; Pss 107:38, 41; 113:9; 127:3). Promised to the righteous (Dt 7:12, 14; Job 5:25; Ps 128:2 – 4, 6). Given in answer to prayer to: Abraham (Ge 15:2 – 5; 21:1 – 2); Isaac (Ge 25:21); Leah (Ge 30:17 – 22); Rachel (Ge 30:22 – 24); Hannah (1Sa 1:9 – 20); Zechariah (Lk 1:13).

God's Care of:

(Ex 22:22 – 24; Dt 10:18; 14:29; Job 29:12; Pss 10:14, 17 – 18; 27:10; 68:5; 146:9; Jer 49:11; Hos 14:3; Mal 3:5). Blessed by Jesus (Mt 19:13 – 15; Mk 10:13 – 16; Lk 18:15 – 17). Intercessional sacrifices in behalf of (Job 1:5).

Commandments to:

To honor and obey parents (Ex 20:12; Lev 19:3, 32; Dt 5:16; Pr 1:8 – 9; 6:20 – 23; 23:22; Mt 15:4; Mk 10:19; Lk 18:20; Eph 6:1, 2 – 3; Col 3:20; 1Ti 3:4). To seek wisdom (Pr 4:1 – 11, 20 – 22; 5:1 – 2; 8:21 – 33; 27:11). To praise the Lord (Ps 148:12 – 13). To remember their Creator (Pr 23:26; Ecc 12:1). To obey (Ps 119:9; Pr 3:1 – 3; 6:20 – 25). To be pure (Ecc 11:9 – 10; La 3:27; 1Ti 4:12; 2Ti 2:22; Tit 2:6).

Miracles on Behalf of:

Raised from the dead by Elijah (1Ki 17:17 – 23); Elisha (2Ki 4:17 – 36); Jesus (Mt 9:18, 24 – 26; Mk 5:35 – 42; Lk 7:13 – 15; 8:49 – 56). Healing of (Mt 15:28; 17:18; Mk 7:29 – 30; 9:23 – 27; Lk 8:42 – 56; 9:38 – 42; Jn 4:46 – 54).

Prayer on Behalf of:

For healing (2Sa 12:16). For divine favor (Ge 17:18). For spiritual wisdom (1Ch 22:12; 29:19). For sins (Job 1:5).

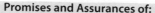

Promises and Assurances of:

Divine instruction (Isa 54:13). Long life to the obedient (Ex 20:12; Dt 5:16; Pr 3:1 – 10; Eph 6:2 – 3). Love and peace (Pr 8:17, 32; Isa 40:11; 54:13). Acceptance by Jesus (Mt 18:4 – 5, 10; 19:14 – 15; Mk 9:37; 10:16; Lk 9:48; 18:15 – 16). Joy to parents of wise children (Pr 23:15 – 16, 24 – 25; 29:3). Forgiven sins (1Jn 2:12 – 13).

The righteous, blessed by God:

In escaping judgments (Ge 6:18; 7:1; 19:12, 15 – 16; Lev 26:44 – 45; 1Ki 11:13; 2Ki 8:19; Pr 11:21; 12:7). In temporal prosperity (Ge 12:7; 13:15; 17:7 – 8; 21:13; 26:3 – 4, 24; Dt 4:37; 10:15; 12:28; 1Ki 15:4; Pss 37:26; 102:28; 112:2 – 3; Pr 13:22). In divine mercy (Ps 103:17 – 18; Pr 3:33; 20:7; Isa 44:3 – 5; 65:23; Jer 32:39; Ac 2:39; 1Co 7:14).

Parental Relationships:

Love of, for parents: Ruth (Ru 1:16 – 18); Jesus (Jn 19:26 – 27). Counsel of parents to (1Ki 2:1 – 4; 1Ch 22:6 – 13; 28:9 – 10, 20). Of ministers to their (1Ti 3:4; Tit 1:6).

Instruction of:

The law (Dt 6:6 – 9; 11:19 – 20; 31:12 – 13; Jos 8:35; Ps 78:1 – 8). The fear of the Lord (Ps 34:11). The providence of God (Ex 10:2; 12:26 – 27; 13:8 – 10, 14 – 16; Dt 4:9 – 10; Joel 1:3). Righteousness (Pr 1:1, 4; 22:6; Isa 28:9 – 10; 38:19). The Scriptures (Ac 22:3; Eph 6:4; 2Ti 3:15).

Correction and Punishment:

By discipline (Pr 19:18; 23:13; 29:15; Eph 6:4; Col 3:2). By the rod (Pr 13:24; 22:15; 23:13 – 14; 29:15). By death (Ex 21:15; 21:17; Lev 20:9; Dt 21:21; 27:16; Pr 20:20; 22:15; 30:17; Mt 15:4; Mk 7:10).

Differences and Partiality:

Differences made between male and female (Lev 12). Partiality of parents, Rebekah for Jacob (Ge 27:6 – 17). Jacob for Joseph (Ge 37:3 – 4). Partiality among, forbidden (Dt 21:15 – 17).

Death and Mistreatment:

Death, as a judgment on parents: firstborn of Egypt (Ex 12:29; Nu 8:17; Ps 78:5); sons of Eli (1Sa 3:13 – 14); sons of Saul (1Sa 28:18 – 19); David's child by Uriah's wife (2Sa 12:14 – 19). Edict to murder: of Pharaoh (Ex 1:22); Jehu (2Ki 10:1 – 8); Herod (Mt 2:16 – 18). Caused to pass through fire (2Ki 16:3; 17:7; Jer 32:35; Eze 16:21). Sacrificed (2Ki 17:31; Eze 16:20 – 21). Sold for debt (2Ki 4:1; Ne 5:5; Job 24:9; Mt 18:25). Sold in marriage, law concerning (Ex 21:7 – 11). Instance of Leah and Rachel (Ge 29:15 – 30).

Religious Involvement:

Attend divine worship (Ex 34:23; Jos 8:35; 2Ch 20:13; 31:16; Ezr 8:21; Ne 8:2 – 3; 12:43; Mt 21:15; Lk 2:46). Entitled to enjoy religious privileges (Dt 12:12 – 13). Illegitimate excluded from privilege of congregation (Dt 23:2; Heb 12:8).

Covenant Involvement:

Bound by covenants of parents (Ge 17:9 – 14). Shared benefits of parents' covenant privileges (Ge 6:18; 12:7; 13:15; 17:7 – 8; 19:12; 21:23; 26:3 – 5, 24; Lev 26:44 – 45; Isa 65:23; 1Co 7:14). Involved in guilt of parents (Ex 20:5; 34:7; Lev 20:5; 26:39 – 42; Nu 14:18, 33; 1Ki 16:12; 21:29; Job 21:19; Ps 37:28; Isa 14:20 – 21; 65:6 – 7; Jer 32:18; Da 6:24). Not punished for parents' sake (2Ki 14:6; Jer 31:29 – 30; Eze 18:1 – 30).

Pr	20:11	Even a **c** is known by his actions,
	22:6	Train a **c** in the way he should go,
	22:15	Folly is bound up in the heart of a **c**
	23:13	not withhold discipline from a **c**;
	29:15	**c** left to himself disgraces his mother.
Isa	7:14	The virgin will be with **c**
	9:6	For to us a **c** is born,
	11:6	and a little **c** will lead them.
Mt	1:23	"The virgin will be with **c**
	18:2	He called a little **c** and had him
Lk	1:42	and blessed is the **c** you will bear!
	1:80	And the **c** grew and became strong
1Co	13:11	When I was a **c**, I talked like a **c**,
1Jn	5:1	who loves the father loves his **c**

CHILDREN

Ex	20:5	punishing the **c** for the sin
Dt	4:9	Teach them to your **c**
	6:7	Impress them on your **c**.
	24:16	nor **c** put to death for their fathers;
	30:19	so that you and your **c** may live
Job	1:5	"Perhaps my **c** have sinned
Ps	8:2	From the lips of **c** and infants
	78:5	forefathers to teach their **c**,
Pr	17:6	Children's **c** are a crown
	20:7	blessed are his **c** after him.
	31:28	Her **c** arise and call her blessed;
Joel	1:3	Tell it to your **c**,
Mal	4:6	the hearts of the fathers to their **c**,
Mt	7:11	how to give good gifts to your **c**,
	11:25	and revealed them to little **c**.
	18:3	you change and become like little **c**
	19:14	"Let the little **c** come to me,
	21:16	"'From the lips of **c** and infants
Mk	9:37	one of these little **c** in my name
	10:16	And he took the **c** in his arms,
	13:12	**C** will rebel against their parents
Lk	10:21	and revealed them to little **c**.
Jn	1:12	the right to become **c** of God—
Ac	2:39	The promise is for you and your **c**
Ro	8:16	with our spirit that we are God's **c**.
1Co	14:20	Brothers, stop thinking like **c**.
2Co	12:14	parents, but parents for their **c**.
Eph	6:1	**C**, obey your parents in the Lord,
	6:4	do not exasperate your **c**; instead,
Col	3:20	**C**, obey your parents in everything,
	3:21	Fathers, do not embitter your **c**,
1Ti	3:4	and see that his **c** obey him
Heb	2:13	and the **c** God has given me."
1Jn	3:1	that we should be called **c** of God!

CHOSE

Ge	13:11	So Lot **c** for himself the whole plain
Ps	33:12	the people he **c** for his inheritance.
Jn	15:16	but I **c** you and appointed you to go
1Co	1:27	But God **c** the foolish things
Eph	1:4	he **c** us in him before the creation

2Th	2:13	from the beginning God **c** you

CHOSEN

Isa	41:8	Jacob, whom I have **c**,
Mt	22:14	For many are invited, but few are **c**
Lk	10:42	Mary has **c** what is better,
	23:35	the Christ of God, the **C** One."
Jn	15:19	but I have **c** you out of the world.
1Pe	1:20	He was **c** before the creation
	2:9	But you are a **c** people, a royal

CHRIST [5986] *(the Anointed One). See Jesus the Christ.*

Mt	1:16	was born Jesus, who is called **C**.
	16:16	Peter answered, "You are the **C**,
	22:42	"What do you think about the **C?**
Mk	1:1	of the gospel about Jesus **C**,
	14:61	"Are you the **C**, the Son
Lk	9:20	Peter answered, "The **C** of God."
Jn	1:41	found the Messiah" (that is, the **C**).
	20:31	you may believe that Jesus is the **C**,
Ac	2:36	you crucified, both Lord and **C**."
	5:42	the good news that Jesus is the **C**.
	9:22	by proving that Jesus is the **C**.
	17:3	proving that the **C** had to suffer
	18:28	the Scriptures that Jesus was the **C**.
	26:23	that the **C** would suffer and,
Ro	1:4	from the dead: Jesus **C** our Lord.
	3:22	comes through faith in Jesus **C**
	5:8	While we were still sinners, **C** died
	5:11	in God through our Lord Jesus **C**,
	5:17	life through the one man, Jesus **C**.
	6:4	as **C** was raised from the dead
	6:23	life in **C** Jesus our Lord.
	7:4	to the law through the body of **C**,
	8:1	for those who are in **C** Jesus,
	8:34	Who is he that condemns? **C** Jesus,
	8:35	us from the love of **C**?
	9:5	is traced the human ancestry of **C**,
	10:4	**C** is the end of the law
	12:5	so in **C** we who are many form one
	15:3	For even **C** did not please himself
	15:7	then, just as **C** accepted you,

	16:18	people are not serving our Lord **C**,
1Co	1:2	to those sanctified in **C** Jesus
	1:7	for our Lord Jesus **C** to be revealed.
	1:13	Is **C** divided? Was Paul crucified
	1:23	but we preach **C** crucified:
	2:2	except Jesus **C** and him crucified.
	3:11	one already laid, which is Jesus **C**.
	5:7	For **C**, our Passover lamb,
	6:15	bodies are members of **C** himself?
	10:4	them, and that rock was **C**.
	11:1	as I follow the example of **C**.
	11:3	the head of every man is **C**,
	12:27	Now you are the body of **C**,
	15:3	that **C** died for our sins according
2Co	1:5	as the sufferings of **C** flow
	2:14	us in triumphal procession in **C**
	4:5	not preach ourselves, but Jesus **C**
	5:10	before the judgment seat of **C**,
	5:17	Therefore, if anyone is in **C**,
	6:15	What harmony is there between **C**
Gal	1:7	are trying to pervert the gospel of **C**
	2:4	on the freedom we have in **C** Jesus
	2:16	but by faith in Jesus **C**.
	2:20	I have been crucified with **C**
	2:21	**C** died for nothing!" You foolish
	3:26	of God through faith in **C** Jesus,
	5:1	for freedom that **C** has set us free.
	5:4	by law have been alienated from **C**;
Eph	1:3	with every spiritual blessing in **C**.
	1:10	together under one head, even **C**.
	2:5	made us alive with **C**
	2:10	created in **C** Jesus
	2:20	with **C** Jesus himself as the chief
	3:8	the unsearchable riches of **C**,
	3:17	so that **C** may dwell in your hearts
	4:13	measure of the fullness of **C**.
	5:2	as **C** loved us and gave himself up
	5:23	as **C** is the head of the church,
	5:25	just as **C** loved the church
Php	1:21	to live is **C** and to die is gain.
	1:23	I desire to depart and be with **C**,
	3:7	now consider loss for the sake of **C**.
	3:10	I want to know **C** and the power

	4:19	to his glorious riches in **C** Jesus.
Col	1:27	which is **C** in you, the hope of glory
	1:28	may present everyone perfect in **C**.
	2:2	the mystery of God, namely, **C**,
	2:13	God made you alive with **C**.
	2:17	the reality, however, is found in **C**.
	3:1	then, you have been raised with **C**,
	3:15	Let the peace of **C** rule
1Th	5:9	through our Lord Jesus **C**.
2Th	2:1	the coming of our Lord Jesus **C**
1Ti	2:5	the man **C** Jesus, who gave himself
2Ti	1:9	us in **C** Jesus before the beginning
	1:10	appearing of our Savior, **C** Jesus,
	2:3	us like a good soldier of **C** Jesus.
	2:8	Remember Jesus **C**, raised
	3:15	salvation through faith in **C** Jesus.
	4:1	presence of God and of **C** Jesus,
Tit	2:13	our great God and Savior, Jesus **C**,
Heb	3:6	But **C** is faithful as a son
	3:14	to share in **C** if we hold firmly
	6:1	the elementary teachings about **C**
	9:11	When **C** came as high priest
	9:15	For this reason **C** is the mediator
	9:28	so **C** was sacrificed once
	10:10	of the body of Jesus **C** once for all.
	13:8	Jesus **C** is the same yesterday
1Pe	1:2	for obedience to Jesus **C**
	1:11	he predicted the sufferings of **C**
	1:19	but with the precious blood of **C**,
	2:21	because **C** suffered for you,
	3:15	in your hearts set apart **C** as Lord.
	3:18	For **C** died for sins once for all,
	4:13	participate in the sufferings of **C**,
2Pe	1:1	and Savior Jesus **C** have received
	1:16	and coming of our Lord Jesus **C**,
1Jn	2:1	Jesus **C**, the Righteous One.
	2:22	man who denies that Jesus is the **C**.
	3:16	Jesus **C** laid down his life for us.
	5:1	believes that Jesus is the **C** is born
2Jn	1:9	teaching of **C** does not have God;
Jude	1:4	deny Jesus **C** our only Sovereign
Rev	1:1	The revelation of Jesus **C**,
	1:5	from Jesus **C**, who is the faithful

| 11:15 | kingdom of our Lord and of his **C**, |
| 20:4 | reigned with **C** a thousand years. |

CHRISTIAN [5985] (Gr. *Christianos, follower of Christ*). Believers called (Ac 11:26; 26:28; 1Pe 4:16). The biblical meaning is "adherent of Christ." The disciples were formally called Christians first in Antioch (Ac 11:26). Agrippa recognized that to believe what Paul preached would make him a Christian (Ac 26:28). Peter accepted the name as in itself a basis for persecution (1Pe 4:16). Thus gradually a name imposed by Gentiles was adopted by the disciples of Jesus. Some Jews had referred to them as "the Nazarene sect" (Ac 24:5); and Paul, when he was a persecutor, referred to them as those "who belonged to the Way" (Ac 9:2). The Latin termination *-ianos*, widely used throughout the empire, often designated the slaves of the one with whose name it was compounded. This implication occurs in the NT (e.g., Ro 6:22; 1Pe 2:16). The apostles wrote of themselves as servants (slaves) of Christ (Ro 1:1; Jas 1:1; 2Pe 1:1; Jude 1; Rev 1:1). The NT calls the followers of Christ "brothers" (Ac 14:2); "disciples" (6:1–2); "saints" (Ac 9:13; Ro 1:7; 1Co 1:2); "believers" (1Ti 4:12); "the church of God" (Ac 20:28); "all who call on your name" (Ac 9:14; Ro 10:12–13). To the first Christians, their own name mattered not at all; their concern was with the one name of Jesus Christ (Ac 3:16; 4:10, 12; 5:28). Inevitably, the name that they invoked was given to them: Christians, Christ's men. Its NT meaning is alone adequate for us.

| Ac | 26:28 | you can persuade me to be a **C**?" |
| 1Pe | 4:16 | as a **C**, do not be ashamed, |

CHRISTIANITY The word does not occur in the Bible. It was first used by Ignatius, in the first half of the second century. It designates all that which Jesus Christ brings to people of faith, life, and salvation.

CHRISTMAS The anniversary of the birth of Christ and its observance. Though the date of the birth of Christ is not known, it is celebrated by most Protestants and by Roman Catholics on December 25, by Eastern Orthodox churches on January 6, and by the Armenian church on January 19. The first mention of its observance on December 25 is in the time of Constantine, c. AD 325. The word *Christmas* is formed of *Christ* plus *Mass*, meaning a religious service in commemoration of the birth of Christ. It is not clear whether the early Christians thought of or observed Christmas, but once introduced, the observance spread throughout Christendom. Some Christian groups disapprove of the festival.

CHRONICLES, 1 AND 2 These books are called in Hebrew *diverê ha-yāmîm*, "the words [affairs] of the days," meaning "the annals" (cf. 1Ch 27:24). Similar annals, now lost, are mentioned in 1 and 2 Kings (e.g., 1Ki 14:19, 29); they cannot, however, consist of our present books, which were not written until a century later. The church father Jerome (AD 400) first entitled them "Chronicles." Originally they formed a single composition but were divided into 1 and 2 Chronicles in the LXX, about 150 BC. In the Hebrew they stand as the last book of the OT canon. Christ (Lk 11:51) thus spoke of all the martyrs from Abel in the first book (Ge 4) to Zechariah in the last (2Ch 24).

Chronicles contains no statements about its own authorship or date. The last event it records is the decree of Cyrus in 538 BC that permitted the exiles to return from their Babylonian captivity (2Ch 36:22); and its genealogies extend to approximately 500 BC, as far, that is, as Pelatiah and Jeshaiah (1Ch 3:21), two grandsons of Zerubbabel, the prince who led in the return from exile. The language, however, and the contents of Chronicles closely parallel that of the book of Ezra, which continues the history of the Jews from the decree of Cyrus down to 457 BC. Both documents are marked by lists and genealogies, by an interest in priestly ritual, and by devotion to the law of Moses. The closing verses, moreover, of Chronicles (2Ch 36:22–23) are repeated as the opening verses of Ezra (1:1–3). Ancient Hebrew tradition and the modern scholarship of W. F. Albright therefore unite in suggesting that Ezra may have been the author of both volumes. His complete work would then have been finished some time around 450 BC.

Ezra's position as a "scribe" (Ezr 7:6) may also explain the care that Chronicles shows in acknowledging its written source materials. These include such records as those of Samuel (1Ch 29:29), Isaiah (2Ch 32:32), a number of other prophets (9:29; 12:15; 20:34; 33:19), and above all else, "the book of the kings of Judah and Israel" (e.g., 16:11; 25:26). This latter work cannot be equated with our present-day 1–2 Kings, for verses such as 1Ch 9:1 and 2Ch 27:7 refer to "the book of the kings" for further details on matters about which 1–2 Kings is silent. The author's source must have been a larger court record, now lost, from which the authors of both Kings and Chronicles subsequently drew much of *their* information.

The occasion for the writing of Chronicles appears to be Ezra's crusade to bring postexilic Judah back into conformity with the law of Moses (Ezr 7:10). From 458 BC, Ezra sought to restore the temple worship (7:19–23, 27; 8:33–34), to eliminate the mixed marriages of Jews with their pagan neighbors (chs. 9–10), and to strengthen Jerusalem by rebuilding its walls (4:8–16). Chronicles, accordingly, consists of these four parts: genealogies, to enable the Jews to establish their lines of family descent (1Ch 1–9); the kingdom of David, as a pattern for the ideal theocratic state (1Ch 10–29); the glory of Solomon, with an emphasis on the temple and its worship (2Ch 1–9); and the history of the southern kingdom, stressing in particular the religious reforms and military victories of Judah's more pious rulers (2Ch 10–36).

As compared with the parallel histories in Samuel and Kings, the priestly annals of Chronicles put a greater emphasis on the structure of the temple (1Ch 22) and on Israel's ark, the Levites, and the singers (1Ch 13, 15–16). They omit, however, certain individualistic, moral acts of the kings (2Sa 9; 1Ki 3:16–28), as well as detailed biographies of the prophets (1Ki 17–22:28; 2Ki 1–8:15), features that account for the incorporation of Chronicles into the third (nonprophetic) section of the Hebrew canon, as distinguished from the location of the more homiletic books of Samuel and Kings in the second (prophetic) division. Finally, the chronicler foregoes discussion of David's disputed inauguration and later shame (2Sa 1–4, 11–21), of Solomon's failures (1Ki 11), and of the whole inglorious history of Saul (1Sa 8–30, except his death, ch. 31), and of the northern kingdom of Israel. The disillusioned, impoverished Jews of 450 BC knew enough of sin and defeat; they needed an encouraging reminder of their former, God-given victories (e.g., 2Ch 13–14, 20, 25).

Because of these emphases, many modern critics have rejected Chronicles as being Levitical propaganda, a fiction of "what ought to have happened," with extensive (and conflicting) revisions as late as 250 BC. The book's high numeric totals (such as the one million invading Ethiopians, 2Ch 14:9) have been questioned despite the elucidations presented by several conservative scholars (see, e.g., E. J. Young, *An Introduction to the Old Testament*, 1949, pp. 388–90). Although Chronicles does stress the bright side of Hebrew history, it does not deny the defects (cf. 1Ch 29:22 on the successful *second* anointing of Solomon, and 2Ch 17:3 on the more exemplary *first* ways of David). The prophetic judgments of Kings and the priestly hopes of Chronicles are both true, and both are necessary. The morality of the former is invaluable, but the redemption of the latter constitutes the more distinctive feature of Christian faith.

While primarily historical in nature, the books of 1 and 2 Chronicles reflect a distinct theology. This theology is set forth in the selection and arrangement of historical events as well as in the chronicler's comments on these events.

One of the important theological themes of the books of Chronicles is the necessity of obedience for divine blessing. Another theological aspect of Chronicles is its emphasis on the Davidic theology. The Davidic covenant established the divine authority of the Davidic dynasty and guaranteed its perpetuity (1Ch 21:7). The theology of worship in

Chronicles acknowledges only one site where Israel may worship. The legitimacy of the postexilic temple and its personnel is established by virtue of its continuity with the temple built by Solomon under the sponsorship of David (1Ch 17:24; 2Ch 6:7 – 9).

CHRONOLOGY, NEW TESTAMENT The science of determining the dates of the NT books and the historical events mentioned in them. The subject is beset with serious difficulty because sufficient data are often lacking and the computations must be based on ancient documents that did not record historical events under precise calendar dates as modern historical records do. Neither sacred nor secular historians of that time were accustomed to record history under exact dates; they felt that all demands were satisfied when some specific event was related to a well-known period, as the reign of a noted ruler or the time of some famous contemporary. Luke's method of dating the beginning of the ministry of John the Baptist (Lk 3:1 – 2) is typical of the historian's method of that day. Further, the use of different local chronologies and different ways of computing years often leave the results tentative. NT chronology naturally falls into two parts: the life of Christ and the apostolic age.

CHRONOLOGICAL TABLE.

The dates for many NT events must remain tentative, but as indicated by Luke (Lk 3:1 – 2), they have a definite correlation with secular history (as shown in the accompanying diagram). The following chronological table is regarded as approximately correct.

Birth of Jesus — 7 to 4 BC
Baptism of Jesus — late AD 26 or early 27
First Passover of ministry — AD 27
Crucifixion of Jesus — AD 30
Conversion of Saul — AD 34 or 35
Death of Herod Agrippa — AD 44
Letter of James — before AD 50
First missionary journey — AD 48 – 49
Jerusalem conference — AD 49 or 50

Second missionary journey begun — spring AD 50
Paul at Corinth — AD 50 – 52
1 and 2 Thessalonians from Corinth — AD 51
Galatians from Corinth (?) — early AD 52
Arrival of Gallio as proconsul — AD May 52
Third missionary journey — begun AD 54
Paul at Ephesus — AD 54 – 57
1 Corinthians from Ephesus — spring AD 57
2 Corinthians from Macedonia — fall AD 57
Romans from Corinth — winter AD 57 – 58
Paul's arrest at Jerusalem — Pentecost AD 58
Imprisonment at Caesarea — AD 58 – 60
On island of Malta — winter AD 60 – 61
Arrival at Rome — spring AD 61
Roman imprisonment — AD 61 – 63
Colossians, Philemon, Ephesians — summer AD 62
Philippians — spring AD 63
Paul's release and further work — AD 63 – 65
1 Timothy and Titus — AD 63
Hebrews — AD 64
Synoptic Gospels and Acts — before AD 67
1 and 2 Peter from Rome — AD 64 – 65
Peter's death at Rome — AD 65
Paul's second Roman imprisonment — AD 66
2 Timothy — AD 66
Death at Rome — late AD 66 or early 67
Jude — AD 67 – 68
Writings of John — before AD 100
Death of John — AD 98 – 100

CHRONOLOGY, OLD TESTAMENT This topic presents many complex and difficult problems. The data are not always adequate or clear; they are, at times, almost completely lacking. Because of insufficient data, many of the problems are at present insoluble. Even where the data are abundant, the exact meaning is often not immediately apparent, leaving room for considerable difference of opinion and giving rise to many variant chronological reconstructions. The chronological problem is thus one of the availability of evidence, of the correct evaluation and interpretation of that evidence, and of its proper application. Only the most careful study of all the data, both biblical and extrabiblical, can hope to provide a satisfactory solution.

CHURCH [1711, 4436]. The English word derives from the Greek *kuriakos* (belonging to the Lord), but it stands for another Greek word *ekklēsia* (whence "ecclesiastical"), denoting an assembly. This is used in its general sense in Ac 19:32, but had already been applied in the LXX as an equivalent for the "congregation" of the OT. Stephen's speech makes this equation (Ac 7:38), and in this sense it is adopted to describe the new gathering or congregation of the disciples of Jesus Christ.

In the Gospels the term is found only in Mt 16:18 and 18:17. This paucity is perhaps explained by the fact that both these verses seem to envisage a situation that would follow Christ's earthly ministry. Yet the verses show that Christ has this reconstitution in view, that the church thus reconstituted will rest on the apostolic confession, and that it will take up the ministry of reconciliation.

When we turn to Acts, the situation changes. The saving work has been fulfilled, and the NT church can thus have its birthday at Pentecost. The term is now used regularly to describe local groups of believers. Thus, we read of the church at Jerusalem (Ac 5:11), Antioch (13:1), and Caesarea (18:22). At the same time the word is used for all believers (as is possibly the case in 9:31). From the outset the church has both a local and a general significance, denoting both the individual assembly and the worldwide community.

This twofold usage is also seen in Paul. He addresses his letters to specific churches, e.g., Corinth (1Co 1:2) or Thessalonica (1Th 1:1). Yet Paul also develops more fully the concept of a church that consists of all believers in all local churches, as in 1Co 10:32 and 1Ti 3:15, and with an even grander sweep in Col 1:18 and especially Ephesians. The other NT books give us mostly examples of the local usage (e.g., 3Jn 9; Rev 1:4; 2:1).

This leads us to the further consideration that the church is not primarily a human structure like a political, social, or economic organism. It is basically the church of Jesus Christ ("my church," Mt 16:18) or of the living God (1Ti 3:15). The various biblical descriptions all emphasize this. It is a building of which Jesus Christ is the chief cornerstone or foundation, "a holy temple in the Lord ... a dwelling in which God lives by his Spirit" (Eph 2:20 – 22). It is the fellowship of saints or people of God (1Pe 2:9). It is the bride of Jesus Christ, saved and sanctified by him for union with himself (Eph 5:25 – 26). Indeed, it is the body of Jesus Christ, he being the head or whole body, and Christians the members (Ro 12:5; 1Co 12:12 – 13; Eph 4:4, 12, 16 – 17). As the body, it is the fullness of Christ, who himself fills all in all (Eph 1:23). While there is an element of imagery in some of the terms used to refer to the church (Christ's temple, bride, or body), its true reality is found in the company of those who believe in Christ and are thus dead, buried, and raised in him, their Savior and substitute. The traditional marks or "notes" of the church are that it is one (Eph 4:4), for Jesus Christ has only one temple, bride, and body, and all divisions are overcome in death and resurrection with him and by endowment of his Spirit. In all its legitimate multiformity, the visible church should thus seek a unity corresponding to this reality. It is holy, for it is set apart and sanctified by himself (Gal 1:4; Eph 5:26). Even in its pilgrimage in the world, it is thus to attest its consecration by the manner of its life and the nature of its service (cf. 1Pe 1:15). It is catholic, constituted from among all people of all races, places, and ages (Eph 2:14; Col 1:6; 3:11; Rev 5:9). For all its diversity of membership and form, it is thus to maintain its universality of outreach, yet also its identity and relevance in every age and place. The church is apostolic, for it rests on the foundation of the apostles and prophets (Eph 2:20), the apostles being raised up as the first authoritative witnesses (Ac 1:8) whose testimony is basic and by whose teaching it is called, instructed, and directed. In all its activity it is thus "devoted ...

to the apostles' teaching and to the fellowship" (Ac 2:42), not finding apostolicity in mere externals but in conformity to apostolic teaching and practice as divinely perpetuated in Holy Scripture.

This brings us to the means of the church's life and its continuing function. It draws its life from Jesus Christ by the Holy Spirit; but it does so through the Word, from which it gets life (Jas 1:18) and by which it is nourished and sanctified (Eph 5:26; 1Pe 2:2). Receiving life by the Word, it also receives its function, namely, to pass on the Word that others may also be quickened and cleansed. It is to preach the gospel (Mk 16:15), to take up the ministry of reconciliation (2Co 5:19), to dispense the mysteries of God (1Co 4:1).

The ministry of the church arises in this connection. The apostles were first commissioned, and they ordained others, yet no rigid form of ministry arose in the NT. Rather, we are given patterns (notably of speech, action, and rule), historically focused in the elders, deacons, and overseers (or bishops). If it is essential that there should be the threefold pattern, there seems no biblical prescription for its discharge in a fixed order, nor for a lack of interchangeability of function, nor for the sharp isolation of an official ministry from the so-called laity or "mere" people of God. The Bible's concern is that there should be real ministry, i.e., service, not in self-assertion and pride but in humility, obedience, and self-offering that conforms to the example of him who was among us as one who serves (see Mt 23:11 – 12; Php 2:5 – 6; 1Pe 5:1 – 2).

Finally, the church's work is not merely for the salvation of people; it is primarily to the praise of God's glory (Eph 1:6; 2:7). Hence, neither the church nor its function ceases with the completion of its earthly task. There is ground, therefore, for the old distinction between the church triumphant and the church militant. All the church is triumphant in its true reality. But the warring and wayfaring church is still engaged in conflict between the old reality and the new. Its destiny, however, is to be brought into full conformity to the Lord (1Jn 3:2). Toward

this it moves hesitantly yet expectantly, confident in its future glory when it will be wholly the church triumphant as graphically depicted in Rev 7:9ff., enjoying its full reality as the bride and body of the Lord.

Mt	16:18	and on this rock I will build my **c**,
	18:17	if he refuses to listen even to the **c**,
Ac	20:28	Be shepherds of the **c** of God,
1Co	5:12	of mine to judge those outside the **c**
	14:4	but he who prophesies edifies the **c**.
	14:12	to excel in gifts that build up the **c**.
	15:9	because I persecuted the **c** of God.
Gal	1:13	how intensely I persecuted the **c**
Eph	5:23	as Christ is the head of the **c**,
Col	1:18	he is the head of the body, the **c**;
	1:24	the sake of his body, which is the **c**.

CHURCH, BODY OF BELIEVERS [1711, 4436] (*assembly*). "Church" in this entry encompasses organized bodies of believers in both Testaments. In the OT the church is a group of "gathered together" Hebrew believers, a congregation. In the NT the church (technically) is a group of "called out" Christian believers.

Discipline by:

Designed to save the sinner (Mt 18:15; 1Co 5:1 – 13; 2Th 3:14). Designed to warn others (1Ti 5:20). Designed to preserve sound doctrine (Ro 16:17; Gal 5:10; 1Ti 1:19 – 20; Tit 1:13). Exercised with kindness (2Co 2:6 – 11; Gal 6:1; Jude 22 – 23). Exercised with forbearance (Ro 15:1 – 3). Reasons for discipline: heresy (1Ti 6:3 – 5; Tit 3:10 – 11; 2Jn 10 – 11); immorality (Mt 18:17 – 18; 1Co 5:1 – 7, 11 – 13; 2Th 3:6). Reasons for schism (Ro 16:17). Discipline by reproof (2Co 7:8; 10:1 – 11; 13:2, 10; 1Th 5:14; 2Th 3:15; 1Ti 5:1 – 2; 2Ti 4:2; Tit 2:15). Witnesses required in (Mt 18:16; 2Co 13:1; 1Ti 5:19).

CHURCH, PLACE OF WORSHIP [1711, 4436]. *Note*: Nowhere in Scripture does the word "church" identify a place of worship, but rather a group (or body) of believers, and only in the NT.

CIRCUMCISED

Ge	17:10	Every male among you shall be **c**.
	17:12	who is eight days old must be **c**,
Jos	5:3	and **c** the Israelites at Gibeath
Gal	5:2	that if you let yourselves be **c**,

CIRCUMCISION [4576, 213, 4362, 4364] (sĭr′kŭm-sĭ′shŭn, Lat. *a cutting around*). The cutting off of the foreskin, a custom that has prevailed, and still prevails, among many peoples in different parts of the world — in Asia, Africa, America, and Australia. In ancient times it was practiced among the western Semites — Hebrews, Arabians, Moabites, Ammonites, Edomites, and Egyptians, but not among the Babylonians, Assyrians, Canaanites, and Philistines. Various theories are held regarding the origin and original significance of circumcision, but there can be no doubt that it was at first a religious act.

Among the Hebrews the rite was instituted by God as the sign of the covenant between him and Abraham, shortly after the latter's sojourn in Egypt. God ordained that it be performed on Abraham, on his posterity and slaves, and on foreigners joining themselves to the Hebrew nation (Ge 17:12). Every male child was to be circumcised on the eighth day. Originally the father performed the rite, but in exceptional cases a woman could do it (Ex 4:25). In later times a Hebrew surgeon was called in. The child was named at the ceremony. Today the rite is performed either in the parents' home or in the synagogue. In former times flint or glass knives were preferred, but now steel is usually used.

According to the terms of the covenant symbolized by circumcision, the Lord undertook to be the God of Abraham and his descendants, and they were to belong to him, worshiping and obeying only him. The rite effected admission to the fellowship of the covenant people and secured for the individual, as a member of the nation, his share in the promises God made to the nation as a whole. In the early history of the Christian church, Judaizing Christians argued for the necessity of circumcising Gentiles who came into the church over against Paul, who insisted that the signs of the old covenant could not be forced on the children of the new covenant. Paul's view was affirmed by the Council of Jerusalem (Ac 15).

General References to:

Institution of (Ge 17:10 – 14; Lev 12:3; Jn 7:22; Ac 7:8; Ro 4:11). A seal of righteousness (Ro 2:25 – 29; 4:11). Performed on all males on the eighth day (Ge 17:12 – 13; Lev 12:3; Php 3:5). Rite of, observed on the Sabbath (Jn 7:23). A prerequisite of the privileges of the Passover (Ex 12:48). Child named at the time of (Ge 21:3 – 4; Lk 1:59; 2:21). Neglected (Jos 5:7). Covenant promises of (Ge 17:4, 14; Ac 7:8; Ro 3:1; 4:11; 9:7 – 13; Gal 5:3). Necessity of, falsely taught by Judaizing Christians (Ac 15:1). Paul's argument against the continuance of (Ro 2:25, 28; Gal 6:13). Characterized by Paul as a yoke (Ac 15:10). Abrogated (Ac 15:5 – 29; Ro 3:30; 4:9 – 11; 1Co 7:18 – 19; Gal 2:3 – 4; 5:2 – 11; 6:12; Eph 2:11, 15; Col 2:11; 3:11).

Instances of:

Abraham (Ge 17:23 – 27; 21:3 – 4); Shechemites (Ge 34:24); Moses (Ex 4:25); Israelites at Gilgal (Jos 5:2 – 9); John the Baptist (Lk 1:59); Jesus (Lk 2:21); Paul (Php 3:5); Timothy (Ac 16:3).

Figurative:

(Ex 6:12, n.; Dt 10:16; 30:6; Jer 4:4; 6:10, n.; 9:26; Ro 2:28 – 29; 15:8, n.; Php 3:3; Col 2:11; 3:11). A designation of the Jews (Ac 10:45; 11:2; Ro 15:8, n.; Eph 2:11; Col 4:11; Tit 1:10); of Christians (Php 3:3).

Ro	2:25	**C** has value if you observe the law,
	2:29	and **c** is **c** of the heart, by the Spirit,
1Co	7:19	**C** is nothing and uncircumcision is

CITIES OF REFUGE Six cities set apart by Moses and Joshua as places of asylum for those who had accidentally committed manslaughter: Bezer (Benjamin), Ramoth Gilead (Gad), Golan (Manasseh), Hebron (Judah), Shechem (Ephraim), Kedesh (Naphtali). There they remained until a fair trial could be held. If proved innocent of willful murder, they had to remain in the city of refuge until the death of the high priest (Nu 35; Dt 4:43; 9:1 – 13; Jos 20).

CITIZENS [CITIZENSHIP]

Eph	2:19	but fellow **c** with God's people

CITIZENSHIP (Gr. *politeuma, commonwealth*). In the NT the word for citizen often means nothing more than the inhabitant of a country (Lk 15:15; 19:14). Among the ancient Jews emphasis was placed on Israel as a religious organization, not on relationship to city and state. The good citizen was the good Israelite, one who followed not just civil law but religious law. Non-Israelites had the same protection of the law as native Israelites, but they were required not to perform acts that would hurt the religious feelings of the people. The advantage of a Jew over a Gentile was thus strictly spiritual. He was a member of the theocracy.

Among the Romans, citizenship brought the right to be considered equal to natives of the city of Rome. Emperors sometimes granted it to whole provinces and cities, and also to individuals for services rendered to the state or to the imperial family, or even for a certain sum of money. Roman citizens were exempted from shameful punishments, such as scourging and crucifixion, and they had the right of appeal to the emperor with certain limitations.

Paul says he had become a Roman citizen by birth. Either his father or some other ancestor had acquired the right and had transmitted it to his son. He was proud of his Roman citizenship and, when occasion demanded, availed himself of his rights. When writing to the Philippians, who were members of a Roman colony and therefore Roman citizens, Paul emphasized that Christians are citizens of a heavenly commonwealth and ought to live accordingly (Php 1:27; 3:20).

Ac	22:28	"I had to pay a big price for my **c**."
Eph	2:12	excluded from **c** in Israel
Php	3:20	But our **c** is in heaven.

CITY OF DAVID

1. The Jebusite fortress of Zion that David captured and named the City of David (2Sa 5:7, 9; 1Ki 8:1; 1Ch 11:5, 7; 2Ch 5:2). It stood on a ridge near the later site of the temple. David made it his royal residence.

2. Bethlehem, the home of David (Lk 2:4).

CLEAN (Heb. *tahor*, Gr. *hagnos, katharos*). The division found in the OT between clean and unclean is fundamental to Hebrew/Israelite religion. The Lord is to be served and worshiped only by a clean, pure, and chaste people. They were to be physically clean (Ex 19:10ff.; 30:18 – 21), ritually and ceremonially clean (having offered the right sacrifices and been through the correct ceremonies [e.g., Lev 14:1ff.; 15:1ff.]), and morally clean in heart. David prayed, "Cleanse me with hyssop, and I will be clean" (Ps 51:7). While the NT supplies examples of the need for ritual cleansing (e.g., Mk 1:44; Ac 21:26), its emphasis is on the clean heart and pure life. Jesus condemned the obsession with external purity with no related emphasis on internal purity/wholeness (Mk 7:1 – 23). Further, by his atoning work, Jesus cleanses believers from all sin (Eph 5:25 – 26; 1Jn 1:7). As High Priest, Jesus cleanses the heart as well as the body (Heb 10:2, 21 – 22). So believers are to be pure in heart (Mt 5:8; 1Ti 1:5) and chaste in life (1Ti 4:2; 5:2). It is their duty to purify themselves (1Pe 2:22; 1Jn 3:3).

Ge	7:2	seven of every kind of **c** animal,
Lev	4:12	the camp to a place ceremonially **c**,
	16:30	you will be **c** from all your sins.
Ps	24:4	He who has **c** hands and a pure
Pr	20:9	I am **c** and without sin"?
Mt	8:2	are willing, you can make me **c**."
	12:44	the house unoccupied, swept **c**
	23:25	You **c** the outside of the cup
Mk	7:19	Jesus declared all foods "**c**.")
Jn	13:10	to wash his feet; his whole body is **c**
	15:3	are already **c** because of the word
Ac	10:15	impure that God has made **c**."
Ro	14:20	All food is **c**, but it is wrong

CLOUD

Ex	13:21	them in a pillar of **c** to guide them
1Ki	18:44	**c** as small as a man's hand is rising
Pr	16:15	his favor is like a rain **c** in spring.
Isa	19:1	See, the LORD rides on a swift **c**
Lk	21:27	of Man coming in a **c** with power
Heb	12:1	by such a great **c** of witnesses,
Rev	14:14	seated on the **c** was one "like a son

CLOUD, PILLAR OF A symbol of the presence and guidance of God in the forty-year wilderness journey of the Israelites from Egypt to Canaan (Ex 13:21 – 22). At night it became fire. When God wanted Israel to rest in any place, the cloud rested on the tabernacle above the mercy seat (29:42 – 43) or at the door of the tabernacle (33:9 – 10; Nu 12:5), or it covered the tabernacle (Ex 40:34 – 38).

> **Pillar of, with Fire:**
> *Symbolic of the Lord's presence (Ex 13:21 – 22; 16:10; 19:9, 16; 24:16 – 18; 33:9 – 10; 34:5; Lev 16:2; Nu 11:25; 12:5, 10; 14:10; 16:19, 42; Dt 31:15; 1Ki 8:10 – 11; 2Ch 7:1 – 3; Isa 6:1, 4; Mt 17:5; Lk 9:34 – 35; 1Co 10:1). A guide to Israel (Ex 14:19, 24; 40:36 – 38; Nu 9:15 – 23; 10:11 – 12, 33 – 36; Dt 1:33; Ne 9:12, 19; Pss 78:14; 105:39; Isa 4:5). In Isaiah's prophecy (Isa 4:5). In Ezekiel's vision (Eze 10:3 – 4, 18 – 19; 11:22 – 23). Figurative (Jer 4:13; Hos 6:4; 13:3). Symbolic (Rev 14:14).*

COLOSSE [3145] (kŏlŏs'ē Gr. *Kolossai*). An ancient city of Phrygia, situated on the south bank of the Lycus River. It was about eleven miles from Laodicea and thirteen from Hierapolis. Colosse stood on the most important trade route from Ephesus to the Euphrates and was a place of great importance from early times. Xerxes visited it in 481 BC, and Cyrus the Younger in 401. The city was particularly renowned for a peculiar wool, probably purple in color (*colossinus*). The church at Colosse was established on Paul's third missionary journey, during his three years in Ephesus, not by Paul himself (Col 2:1), but by Epaphras (1:7, 12 – 13). Archippus also exercised a fruitful ministry there (4:17; Phm 2). Phile-

mon was an active member of this church, and so was Onesimus (Col 4:9). During Paul's first Roman imprisonment, Epaphras brought him a report of the religious views and practices in Colosse that called forth his letter, in which he rebuked the church for its errors. Colosse lost its importance by the change of the road system. Laodicea became the greater city. During the seventh and eighth centuries AD, its openness exposed it to the terrible raids of the Saracens, and the people moved to Chonae (now called Chonas), a fortress on the slope of Mount Cadmus, about three miles farther south. In the twelfth century the Turks destroyed the city. Archaeologists have unearthed ruins of an ancient church.

COLOSSIANS, LETTER TO THE A letter written by the apostle Paul when he was a prisoner (Col 4:3, 10, 18), about the year AD 62, probably during his first imprisonment in Rome (Ac 28:30 – 31), though Caesarea (23:35; 24:27) and Ephesus have also been suggested. The external and internal evidence for its genuineness is all that can be desired. The church at Colosse was very likely founded during Paul's three-year stay in Ephesus on his third missionary journey. It appears from Col 2:1 that Paul himself had never preached in Colosse. Epaphras, a native of Colosse (Col 4:12), was probably converted under Paul's ministry at Ephesus and was then sent by the apostle to preach in his native city (1:7). He also appears to have evangelized the nearby cities of Laodicea and Hierapolis (4:13). When Paul wrote this letter, the minister of the church at Colosse was Archippus (4:17), who may have been Philemon's son (Phm 2). Epaphras had recently come to Paul with a disturbing report of the condition of the church, and this led Paul to the writing of the letter. The bearer of the letter was Tychicus (Col 4:7, 8), to whom Paul also entrusted his letter to the Ephesians (Eph 6:21), which was probably written at the same time. With him went Onesimus (Col 4:9), a runaway slave converted by Paul, bearing Paul's letter to Philemon, a resident of Colosse, who was also one of Paul's converts, perhaps becoming a believer at Ephesus.

In the few years since Paul had been in the province of Asia an insidious error had crept into the church at Colosse. Who the false teachers were we do not know; but it is clear that the trouble was different from that faced by Paul at Galatia, where Judaizers had tried to undermine his work. The teaching attacked by Paul is described in Col 2:8, 16 – 23. It was, at least in part, Judaistic, as is seen in his reference to circumcision (2:11; 3:11), ordinances (2:14), meats and drinks, feast days, new moons, and Sabbaths (2:16). There was also in it a strong ascetic element. Special self-denying rules were given (2:16, 20 – 21) that had as their purpose the mortification of the body (2:23). Some sort of worship of angels was practiced — a worship that continued for several centuries, as we know from the fact that in the fourth century AD the Council of Laodicea condemned it in one of its canons, and in the fifth century Theodoret said that the archangel Michael was worshiped in the area. This heresy claimed to be a philosophy and made much of wisdom and knowledge (2:8). Plainly, the Colossians were beguiled by this religious syncretism and even took pride in it (2:8). The exact origin of the false teaching is unknown. Some find it in Essenism; others in incipient Gnosticism or in contemporary Judaism with a syncretistic addition of local Phrygian ideas.

Paul met these errors, not by controversy or personal authority, but by presenting the countertruth that Jesus Christ is the image of the invisible God (Col 1:15), in whom are hid all the treasures of wisdom and knowledge, and in whom the fullness of the divine perfections find their perfect embodiment (1:19). He is the creator of all, and all power is from him. On the cross he revealed the impotence of all the powers that had tried to thwart his purposes (2:15). Freedom from the corruption of human nature is found in the newness of life that the death and resurrection of Christ provide. The letter to the Colossians may be divided into four parts: (1) the salutation and thanksgiving (1:1 – 8), (2) the doctrinal section (1:9 – 2:5), (3) practical exhortations (2:6 – 4:6), and (4) concluding salutations (4:7 – 18). Toward the end of the letter (4:16), Paul asks that the Colossian church exchange letters with the church at Laodicea, to which he has also written. It is likely that this letter to the Laodiceans is what we know as the letter to the Ephesians, sent as a circular letter to various churches in the Roman province of Asia.

COMFORT

Ge	5:29	"He will **c** us in the labor
	37:35	**c** him, but he refused to be comforted.
Ru	2:13	"You have given me **c**
1Ch	7:22	and his relatives came to **c** him.
Job	2:11	sympathize with him and **c** him.
Ps	23:4	rod and your staff, they **c** me.
	71:21	and **c** me once again.
	119:50	My **c** in my suffering is this:
	119:82	I say, "When will you **c** me?"
Isa	40:1	**C**, **c** my people,
	51:3	The LORD will surely **c** Zion
	57:18	I will guide him and restore **c**
	61:2	to **c** all who mourn,
La	1:2	there is none to **c** her.
	2:13	that I may **c** you,
Eze	16:54	all you have done in giving them **c**.
Na	3:7	Where can I find anyone to **c** you?"
Zec	1:17	and the LORD will again **c** Zion
Lk	6:24	you have already received your **c**.
Jn	11:19	and Mary to **c** them in the loss
1Co	14:3	encouragement and **c**.
2Co	1:3	of compassion and the God of all **c**,
	1:4	so that we can **c** those
	1:5	through Christ our **c** overflows.
	1:6	if we are comforted, it is for your **c**,
	1:7	so also you share in our **c**.
	2:7	you ought to forgive and **c** him,
	7:7	also by the **c** you had given him.
Php	2:1	if any **c** from his love,
Col	4:11	and they have proved a **c** to me.

COMFORTED

Ge	24:67	Isaac was **c** after his mother's death
	37:35	comfort him, but he refused to be **c**.
2Sa	12:24	Then David **c** his wife Bathsheba,

Job	42:11	They **c** and consoled him
Ps	77:2	and my soul refused to be **c**.
	86:17	have helped me and **c** me.
Isa	12:1	and you have **c** me.
	52:9	for the LORD has **c** his people,
Mt	2:18	and refusing to be **c**,
	5:4	for they will be **c**.
Lk	16:25	but now he is **c** here and you are
Ac	20:12	man home alive and were greatly **c**.
2Co	1:6	if we are **c**, it is for your comfort,

COMFORTER, THE *See Advocate; Holy Spirit.*

COMMAND

Ex	7:2	You are to say everything I **c** you,
Nu	14:41	are you disobeying the LORD'S **c**?
	24:13	to go beyond the **c** of the LORD —
Dt	4:2	Do not add to what I **c** you
	12:32	See that you do all I **c** you;
	30:16	For I **c** you today to love
	32:46	so that you may **c** your children
Ps	91:11	For he will **c** his angels concerning
Ecc	8:2	Obey the king's **c**, I say,
Jer	1:7	you to and say whatever I **c** you.
	7:23	Walk in all the ways I **c** you,
	26:2	Tell them everything I **c** you;
Joel	2:11	mighty are those who obey his **c**.
Mt	4:6	He will **c** his angels concerning you
	15:3	why do you break the **c** of God
Lk	4:10	"'He will **c** his angels concerning
Jn	14:15	love me, you will obey what I **c**.
	15:12	My **c** is this: Love each other
1Co	14:37	writing to you is the Lord's **c**.
Gal	5:14	law is summed up in a single **c**:
1Ti	1:5	goal of this **c** is love, which comes
	6:17	**C** those who are rich
Heb	11:3	universe was formed at God's **c**,
2Pe	2:21	on the sacred **c** that was passed
	3:2	and the **c** given by our Lord
1Jn	2:7	I am not writing you a new **c**
	3:23	this is his **c**: to believe in the name
	4:21	And he has given us this **c**:
2Jn	1:6	his **c** is that you walk in love.

COMMANDMENT [1821, 5184, 1953]. The word is used in the English Bible to translate a number of Hebrew and Greek words meaning law, ordinance, statute, word, judgment, precept, saying, charge. The idea of authority conveyed by these words comes from the fact that God as sovereign Lord has a right to be obeyed. The instruction of Jesus is full of ethical teachings that have the force of divine commandments. What he says is as authoritative as what was said by God in OT times. That is true even when he does not use the word "commandment" or its equivalents, as he often does. But what is said of God and Jesus Christ is also true of the apostles. Paul, for example, does not hesitate to say, "What I am writing to you is the Lord's command" (1Co 14:37). The Bible makes it very clear that God is not satisfied with mere external compliance with his commandments but expects willing and joyful obedience, coming from the heart.

Jos	22:5	But be very careful to keep the **c**
Mt	22:36	which is the greatest **c** in the Law?"
	22:38	This is the first and greatest **c**.
Mk	12:31	There is no **c** greater than these."
Lk	23:56	the Sabbath in obedience to the **c**.
Jn	13:34	"A new **c** I give you: Love one
Ro	7:8	the opportunity afforded by the **c**,
	7:9	when the **c** came, sin sprang to life
	13:9	and whatever other **c** there may be,
Eph	6:2	which is the first **c** with a promise
Heb	9:19	Moses had proclaimed every **c**

COMMANDMENTS [COMMAND]

Ex	20:6	who love me and keep my **c**.
	34:28	of the covenant — the Ten **C**.
Dt	4:13	to you his covenant, the Ten **C**,
	5:10	who love me and keep my **c**.
Ecc	12:13	Fear God and keep his **c**,
Mt	5:19	one of the least of these **c**
	19:17	If you want to enter life, obey the **c**
	22:40	the Prophets hang on these two **c**."
Mk	10:19	You know the **c**: 'Do not murder,
Lk	1:6	observing all the Lord's **c**

	18:20	You know the **c**: 'Do not commit
Ro	13:9	The **c**, "Do not commit adultery,"
Eph	2:15	in his flesh the law with its **c**
Rev	12:17	those who obey God's **c**
	14:12	part of the saints who obey God's **c**

COMMANDMENTS AND STATUTES OF GOD

Admonishing against:

Backsliding (Dt 8:11 – 17; 28:18; Eze 33:12 – 13, 18; Lk 9:62; 1Co 10:12; Heb 3:12 – 13; 12:15; 2Pe 2:20 – 21). Conspiracy (Ex 23:1 – 2). Hypocrisy (Mt 6:1 – 5, 16; Lk 20:46 – 47; 1Pe 2:1). Lust (Pr 31:3; Ro 13:13 – 14; Gal 5:16; 1Pe 2:11). Oppression of foreigners (Ex 22:21; 23:9; Dt 24:14; Zec 7:10). Popular corruption (Ex 23:2). Reviling rulers (Ex 22:28; Ac 23:5).

Concerning:

Children, commanding obedience to parents (Pr 6:20; Eph 6:1 – 3; Col 3:20). Debtors' protection (Dt 24:10, 12 – 13). Father's concern for children (Eph 6:4; Col 3:21). Husband's love for his wife (Eph 5:23; Col 3:19); honor for his wife (1Pe 3:7). Permanence of marriage (Ge 2:24; Mt 19:6; Mk 10:9; 1Co 7:1 – 16). Judges' justice in court (Dt 1:16). Lost property (Ex 23:4; Dt 22:1 – 3). Man's supremacy over animals (Ge 9:2). Masters' humane treatment of slaves (Col 4:1) and servants (Eph 6:9). Ministers (Ac 20:31; 1Ti 1:4; 3:2 – 13; 4:12 – 16; 5:20 – 22; 2Ti 2:1 – 3, 14 – 16, 22 – 24; Tit 1:5 – 9; 2:1 – 10, 15; 1Pe 5:2 – 3). Faithfulness (Col 4:17; 1Ti 6:11 – 12, 14; 2Ti 1:8, 13). Fortitude (2Ti 2:3). Foolish questions (2Ti 2:23). Sanctification (1Th 4:3). Strife (2Ti 2:24). Places of public worship (Dt 12:11). Restitution (Ex 21:30 – 36; 22:1 – 15; Lev 6:4 – 5; 24:18; Nu 5:7). Servants' obedience (Eph 6:5 – 8; Col 3:22 – 25; Tit 2:9 – 10; 1Pe 2:18 – 19). Vicious animals (Ex 21:28 – 32, 35 – 36). Wives' obedience (Eph 5:22; Col 3:18; 1Pe 3:1 – 4). Women (Eph 5:22, 24; Tit 2:3 – 5; 1Pe 3:1 – 3). Young men's parental obedience (Pr 6:20; 23:22).

COMMANDMENTS, TEN The OT is distinctly a religion of law, with creed, cult, and conduct prescribed minutely by God. The OT praises in the Torah (God's law or instruction as set forth in the first five books of the OT; cf. Ps 119:97) the revelational instruction that has come to the elect nation as a gift of grace and that has come to it invested with divine authority and sanction. The Torah is revered because it embodies the will and wisdom of the Creator. Expressing God's own nature, it demands of the creature only what the Creator's holiness requires for fellowship with himself. The climax of the Torah is the Decalogue, the Code of the Ten Words, received by Moses on Mount Sinai. The Decalogue is specifically the gift of grace of God the redeemer (Ex 20:2), given to his people, not to bring them into bondage but because they have been brought out of bondage. That it is unique among the several codes found in the OT can scarcely be disputed. Originally spoken by God in a context calculated to produce unforgettable awe (19:9 – 25), it was afterward inscribed by his finger on two tables of stone (31:18); in fact, it was inscribed by him a second time after Moses in anger shattered the first two tables (Dt 10:1 – 4). It was placed in the ark of the covenant (Ex 25:21) and thus enshrined at the very center of Israel's worship. All of its precepts, with the exception of Sabbathkeeping, are repeated in the NT. Hence the Code of the Ten Words is indeed *sui generis*, a statement that gives the distillation of religion and morality: these principles, so simply phrased, are remarkably comprehensive and universally valid. Mount Sinai, therefore, was the scene of an epochal event in human history; from a religious standpoint, only Mount Calvary surpasses it.

Let us now analyze briefly each of the Ten Words. The first commandment (Ex 20:3) enjoins a confession of God's singularity, his absolute and exclusive deity. It predicates faith in him as the one and only God. Though not expressly teaching monotheism, it inferentially denounces polytheism as treason and unbelief. It demonstrates that God is not a class term but a proper name.

The second commandment (Ex 20:4 – 6) enjoins the adoration of God's spirituality. Forbidding his worship by any false means, it rebukes the gross idolatry that surrounded Israel. It shows that because of his very Being (Jn 4:24), no visible or material representation of true deity is possible. Thus it prevents wrong concepts of God from taking root in an individual's mind (Ro 1:21 – 23).

The third commandment (Ex 20:7) enjoins the reverence of the Lord's name. Since in the OT name and person are equivalent, with the name practically a reification of the person, this law prohibits blasphemy and profanity. It also interdicts immorality, any conduct that causes God's honor to suffer defilement by the sinner who bears his name (Ro 2:24 – 25). With respect to the sacredness and significance of God's name, Mal 3:16 – 17 is instructive.

The fourth commandment (Ex 20:8 – 11) enjoins the observance of the Lord's Day. For both humanitarian (Am 8:5 – 6) and religious (Isa 58:13 – 14) reasons, one day of rest in every seven is a blessed necessity. A Sabbath — whether on Saturday as commemorating a finished creation or on Sunday as commemorating a finished redemption — serves man's physical and spiritual welfare simultaneously (Mk 2:27).

The fifth commandment (Ex 20:12) enjoins the honor of God's surrogates, parents to whom he grants a kind of cocreatorship in the begetting of children and to whom he grants a kind of corulership in the governing of children. Let any nation abandon respect for the mystery, dignity, and authority of parenthood, and before long the moral fiber and social fabric of that nation are bound to disintegrate. That is why the OT statutes on this score are so severe (Ex 21:15; Dt 27:16; Pr 20:20).

The sixth commandment (Ex 20:13) is a prohibition of murder. A person's life is, patently, his or her one utterly indispensable possession; but more than that, humans are God's image-bearers, and murder wantonly destroys God's image. Therefore, capital punishment is the penalty affixed to breaking this law (Ge 9:5 – 6).

The seventh commandment (Ex 20:24) is a prohibition of adultery, a stringent prohibition that safeguards the sanctity of marriage and throws a bulwark around the home. In our day we are beginning to see what happens when the home is undermined by marital infidelity.

The eighth commandment (Ex 20:15) is a prohibition of theft in any and all forms. Property is essentially an extension of a person's personality, and thus this law indicates that the rights and achievements of one's neighbor must not be ignored.

The ninth commandment (Ex 20:16) is a prohibition of falsehood in its many varieties, whether perjury, slander, or defamation. Truth is the cement of community, the sine qua non of enduring interpersonal relationships on every level. Thus the OT, like the NT, stresses the need for a sanctified tongue (Ps 5:9; 15:1 – 4; Pr 18:21; Jer 9:1 – 5).

The tenth commandment (Ex 20:17) is a prohibition of covetousness and, as such, reveals that the Ten Words are not simply a civil code, but form a moral and spiritual code that strikes beneath the surface of the overt act (which is the exclusive province of civil law), tracing evil conduct to evil desire, probing the hidden motives of people (which is the province of morality and religion, God's province). This tenth commandment, therefore, highlights the pivotal importance of wrong appetites and intentions; it agrees with Paul that covetousness is idolatry (Col 3:5), since inordinate craving means that a person's ego has become that person's god.

Except as the NT deepens and extends its principles, the Decalogue represents the high-water level of morality.

COMMIT

Ex	20:14	"You shall not **c** adultery.
Dt	5:18	"You shall not **c** adultery.
1Sa	7:3	and **c** yourselves to the LORD
Ps	31:5	Into your hands I **c** my spirit;
	37:5	**C** your way to the LORD;

Pr	16:3	**C** to the LORD whatever you do,
Mt	5:27	that it was said, 'Do not **c** adultery.'
Ac	20:32	I **c** you to God and to the word
Ro	2:22	do you **c** adultery? You who abhor
	2:22	that people should not **c** adultery,
	13:9	"Do not **c** adultery,"
1Co	10:8	We should not **c** sexual immorality,
Jas	2:11	do not **c** adultery but do **c** murder,
1Pe	4:19	to God's will should **c** themselves
Rev	2:22	I will make those who **c** adultery

COMMUNION WITH GOD (Ps 16:7; Jn 14:23; 2Co 6:16; 1Jn 1:3); with Christ (Jn 14:23; 1Jn 1:3; Rev 3:20); with the Spirit (Jn 14:16 – 18; 2Co 13:14; Gal 4:6; Php 2:1 – 2). *See Fellowship.*

> **Instances of:**
>
> *Enoch (Ge 5:22, 24); Noah (Ge 6:9, 13 – 22; 8:15 – 17); Abraham (Ge 12:1 – 3, 7; 17:1 – 2; 18:1 – 33; 22:1 – 2, 11 – 12, 16 – 18); Hagar (Ge 16:8 – 12); Isaac (Ge 26:2, 24); Jacob (Ge 28:13, 15; 31:3; 35:1, 7; 46:2 – 4); Moses (Ex 3; 4:1 – 17; 33:9, 11; 34:28 – 35; Nu 12:8); Joshua (Jos 6:11 – 24; 7:10 – 15); Gideon (Jdg 6:11 – 24); Solomon (1Ki 3:5 – 14; 2Ch 1:7 – 12).*
>
> **Of Believers:**
>
> *Unity (Pss 119:63; 133:1 – 3; Am 3:3; Jn 17:20 – 21; 1Co 10:16 – 17; 12:12 – 13). Commanded (Ro 12:15; 2Co 6:14 – 18; Eph 4:1 – 3; 5:11; Col 3:16; 1Th 4:18; 5:11, 14; Heb 3:13; 10:24 – 25; Jas 5:16). Exemplified (1Sa 23:16; Ps 55:14; Mal 3:16; Lk 22:32; 24:17, 32; Ac 2:42; 1Jn 1:3, 7). See Eucharist; Fellowship.*

COMMUNITY [824, 6337, 7736, 2681+ 4436]. Christian (Ac 2:44 – 45; 4:32 – 37; 5:1 – 10).

COMPASSION

Ex	33:19	I will have **c** on whom I will have **c**.
Dt	13:17	he will show you mercy, have **c**
	28:54	man among you will have no **c**
Jdg	2:18	for the LORD had **c** on them
2Ki	13:23	and had **c** and showed concern
2Ch	30:9	and your children will be shown **c**

Ne	9:19	of your great **c** you did not
	9:27	and in your great **c** you gave them
Ps	51:1	according to your great **c**
	77:9	Has he in anger withheld his **c**?"
	90:13	Have **c** on your servants.
	102:13	You will arise and have **c** on Zion,
	103:13	As a father has **c** on his children,
	116:5	our God is full of **c**.
	119:156	Your **c** is great, O LORD;
	135:14	and have **c** on his servants.
	145:9	he has **c** on all he has made.
Isa	1318	will they look with **c** on children.
	14:1	The LORD will have **c** on Jacob;
	49:10	He who has **c** on them will guide
	49:13	and will have **c** on his afflicted ones
	51:3	and will look with **c** on all her ruins
	54:7	with deep **c** I will bring you back.
	63:7	to his **c** and many kindnesses.
Jer	12:15	I will again have **c** and will bring
	13:14	**c** to keep me from destroying them
	15:6	I can no longer show **c**.
	21:7	show them no mercy or pity or **c**.'
	33:26	restore their fortunes and have **c**
	42:12	I will show you **c** so that he will
La	3:32	he brings grief, he will show **c**,
Eze	9:5	without showing pity or **c**.
	39:25	and will have **c** on all the people
Hos	2:19	in love and **c**.
	11:8	all my **c** is aroused.
	13:14	"I will have no **c**,
Am	1:11	stifling all **c**,
Jnh	3:9	with **c** turn from his fierce anger
Mic	7:19	You will again have **c** on us;
Zec	7:9	show mercy and **c** to one another.
Mal	3:17	as in **c** a man spares his son who
Mt	9:36	When he saw the crowds, he had **c**
	14:14	he had **c** on them and healed their
	20:34	Jesus had **c** on them and touched
Mk	1:41	with **c**, Jesus reached out his hand
	6:34	and saw a large crowd, he had **c**
Lk	15:20	and was filled with **c** for him;
Ro	9:15	and I will have **c** on whom I have **c**
2Co	1:3	the Father of **c** and the God

Php	2:1	and **c**, then make my joy complete
Col	3:12	clothe yourselves with **c**, kindness,
Jas	5:11	The Lord is full of **c** and mercy.

CONCUBINE In the Bible, not a paramour, but a woman lawfully united in marriage to a man in a relation inferior to that of the regular wife. No moral stigma was attached to being a concubine. It was a natural part of a polygamous social system. Concubinage is assumed and provided for in the law of Moses, which tried to prevent its excesses and abuses (Ex 21:7 – 11; Dt 21:10 – 14). Concubines were commonly taken from among Hebrew or foreign slave girls, or Gentile captives taken in war, although free Hebrew women might also become concubines. They enjoyed no other right but lawful cohabitation. They had no authority in the family or in household affairs. Their husbands could send them away with a small present, and their children could, by means of small presents, be excluded from the heritage (Ge 25:6). The children were regarded as legitimate, although the children of the first wife were preferred in the distribution of the inheritance. In patriarchal times, at least, the immediate cause of concubinage was the barrenness of the lawful wife, who herself suggested that her husband have children by her maidservant (Ge 16; 30). Prominent OT figures who had concubines were Nahor (22:24), Abraham (25:6), Jacob (35:22), Eliphaz (36:12), Gideon (Jdg 8:31), Saul (2Sa 3:7), David (5:13; 15:16; 16:21), Solomon (1Ki 11:3), Caleb (1Ch 2:46), Manasseh (7:14), Rehoboam (2Ch 11:21), Abijah (13:21), and Belshazzar (Da 5:2).

CONFESS

Lev	5:5	he must **c** in what way he has
Nu	5:7	must **c** the sin he has committed.
1Ki	8:33	back to you and **c** your name,
Ne	1:6	I **c** the sins we Israelites, including
Ps	32:5	I said, "I will **c**
	38:18	I **c** my iniquity;
Jn	1:20	fail to **c**, but confessed freely,
	12:42	they would not **c** their faith

Ro	10:9	That if you **c** with your mouth,
	10:10	it is with your mouth that you **c**
	14:11	every tongue will **c** to God.'"
Heb	3:1	and high priest whom we **c**.
Jas	5:16	Therefore **c** your sins to each other
1Jn	1:9	If we **c** our sins, he is faithful

CONFESSION [606, 3344, 5583, 9343, 2018, 3933, 3934, 3951] (Heb. *yādhâh*, Gr. *homologeō* and their derivatives). Both the Hebrew and Greek words are capable of the same twofold meaning as the English. To confess is openly to acknowledge the truth in anything, as in the existence and authority of God or the sins of which one has been guilty. Occasionally it also means to concede or allow (Jn 1:20; Ac 24:14; Heb 11:13), or to praise God by thankfully acknowledging him (Ro 14:11; Heb 13:15). In the Bible, confession of sin before God is recognized as a condition of forgiveness. Christ taught the necessity of confessing offenses committed against other people (Mt 5:24; Lk 17:4). The Bible gives no instruction about the mode of confession or the person to receive it, but no authority is found in it for the auricular confession practiced in the Roman Catholic Church.

General References to:
To acknowledge one's faith in anything, as in the existence and authority of God, or the sins of which one has been guilty (Mt 10:32; Lev 5:5; Ps 32:5); to concede or allow (Jn 1:20; Ac 24:14; Heb 11:13); to praise God by thankfully acknowledging him (Ro 14:11; Heb 13:15).

Of Christ:
In baptism (Ac 19:4 – 5; Gal 3:27). To salvation (Mt 10:32; Lk 12:8; Ro 10:9 – 11). Inspired by the Holy Spirit (1Co 12:3; 1Jn 4:2 – 3). Fellowship with the Father through (1Jn 2:23; 4:15). Timid believers deterred from (Jn 12:42 – 43). Those refusing to make, rejected (Mt 10:33; Mk 8:38; Lk 12:9; 2Ti 2:12). Hypocritical (Mt 7:21 – 23; Lk 13:26; 1Jn 1:6; 2:4). Commanded (2Ti 1:8). Exemplified (Mt 3:11; 14:23; 16:16; Jn 1:15 – 18; 6:29; 9:22 – 38; 11:27; Ac 8:35 – 37; 9:20; 18:5; Ro 1:16).

Ezr	10:11	Now make **c** to the LORD,
Ne	9:3	and spent another quarter in **c**
2Co	9:013	obedience that accompanies your **c**
1Ti	6:12	called when you made your good **c**
	6:13	Pontius Pilate made the good **c**,

CONGREGATION (Heb. *'ēdhâh* and *qāhāl*, Gr. *ekklēsia* and *synagōgē*). A word used in Scripture mainly to refer to the Hebrew people; in its collective capacity regarded as God's people or as an assembly of the people summoned for a definite purpose (1Ki 8:65) or on a festive occasion (Dt 23:1). Sometimes it refers to an assembly of the whole people; at other times it refers to any part of the people who might be present on a given occasion. Occasionally it conveys the idea of "horde." Every circumcised Hebrew was a member of the congregation and took part in its proceedings probably from the time he bore arms.

CONSCIENCE [4213, 4222, 4029+5323, 5287]. The OT has no separate word for "conscience," but it neither lacks the idea nor the means to express it. It is clear from Ge 3:8 that the first result of the fall was a guilty conscience, compelling Adam and Eve to hide from God. Likewise, we read that David's "heart smote him" (1Sa 24:5 KJV, MLB, RSV); NIV interprets this as "David was conscience-stricken." In everyday Greek the word *syneidesis* referred to the pain or guilt felt by persons who believed they had done wrong. Paul, who used the word more than other NT writers, refined and developed this meaning. (1) He described the universal existence of conscience (Ro 2:14–16) as the internal moral witness found in all human beings. (2) He believed that Christians should have clear and good consciences (2Co 1:12; 1Ti 1:5, 19; 3:9) because their lives are lived for the glory of God and in the light of Christian teaching. (3) He knew of and gave advice about the weak or partially formed conscience of certain Christians ("conscience" occurs nine times in 1Co 8:1–13 and 10:23–11:1); in certain cases mature Christians are to restrict their liberty of action in order not to offend the undeveloped conscience of their weaker brothers and sisters. (4) He was aware of the existence of evil consciences, corrupted by false teaching (1Ti 4:5; Tit 1:15). A person who rejects the gospel and resolutely opposes God has an evil conscience. (5) As a result of accepting the gospel, people receive a purified, or perfected, conscience (Heb 9:14; 10:22), through forgiveness and the gift of the Holy Spirit. Finally, it may be said that while Paul's use of the word *conscience* is that of the internal witness of the mind/heart judging past actions in the light of Christian teaching, he also appears to suggest that the conscience will guide present and future actions (e.g., Ro 13:3; 1Co 10:25).

General References to:

Guide (Ps 51:3; Pr 20:12; Mt 6:22–23; Lk 11:33–36; Ro 2:14–15; 7:18, 22; 2Co 5:11). Approves (Job 27:6; Pr 21:2; Ac 23:1; 24:16; Ro 9:1; 1Co 4:4; 2Co 1:12; 1Ti 1:5, 19; 3:9; 2Ti 1:3; Heb 13:18; 1Pe 2:19; 3:16, 21; 1Jn 3:20–21). Struggle with (Job 15:21, 24; Ps 51:3; Mt 6:22–23; Lk 11:33–36; Ro 7:15–23). Purged (Heb 9:14; 10:22). See Honesty; Integrity. Of another, to be respected (Ro 14:2–20; 1Co 8:7–13; 10:27–32; 2Co 4:2).

Instances of Faithful:

Pharaoh, when he took Sarah into his harem (Ge 12:18–19). Abimelech, when he took Sarah for a concubine (Ge 26:9–11). Jacob, in his care of Laban's property (Ge 31:39); in his greeting of Esau (Ge 33:1–12). Joseph, with Potiphar's wife (Ge 39:7–12). Nehemiah, with taxes (Ne 5:15). Daniel, with the king's meat (Da 1:8). Peter, in his preaching (Ac 4:19–20; 5:29).

Unfaithful:

Corrupt (Mt 6:23; Lk 11:34; Jn 16:2–3). Dead (Pr 16:25; 30:20; Jer 6:15; Am 6:1–6; Ro 1:21–25; Eph 4:17–29). Defiled (Tit 1:15). Seared (1Ti 4:2). Guilty (Job 15:21, 24; Pss 51:1–14; 73:21; Pr 28:1; Isa 59:9–14; Mt 14:1–2; 27:3–5; Mk 6:14, 16; Jn 8:9; Ac 2:37; 1Ti 4:2; Tit 1:15; Heb 9:14; 10:26–27). See Blindness, Spiritual.

Ge	20:5	I have done this with a clear **c**
	20:6	I know you did this with a clear **c**,
1Sa	25:31	have on his **c** the staggering burden
Job	27:6	my **c** will not reproach me as long
Ac	23:1	to God in all good **c** to this day."
	24:16	to keep my **c** clear before God
Ro	9:1	my **c** confirms it in the Holy Spirit
	13:5	punishment but also because of **c**.
1Co	4:4	My **c** is clear, but that does not
	8:7	since their **c** is weak, it is defiled.
	8:12	in this way and wound their weak **c**
	10:25	without raising questions of **c**,
	10:28	man who told you and for **c**' sake —
2Co	1:12	Our **c** testifies that we have
	4:2	to every man's **c** in the sight of God
	5:11	and I hope it is also plain to your **c**.
1Ti	1:5	and a good **c** and a sincere faith.
	1:19	holding on to faith and a good **c**.
	3:9	truths of the faith with a clear **c**.
2Ti	1:3	as my forefathers did, with a clear **c**
Heb	9:9	able to clear the **c** of the worshiper.
	10:22	to cleanse us from a guilty **c**
	13:18	We are sure that we have a clear **c**
1Pe	3:16	and respect, keeping a clear **c**,
	3:21	the pledge of a good **c** toward God.

CONSECRATION An act by which a person or thing is dedicated to the service and worship of God. In the KJV it translates several Hebrew and Greek words of different meanings. (1) Hebrew *hā-ram*, "devote" (Mic 4:13, NIV "devote"). (2) Hebrew *nāzar, nēzer*, "separate" (Nu 6:7, 8, 12, NIV "separation"). (3) Hebrew *qādhēsh*, "to be set apart" (i.e., from that which is common or unclean: Ex 28:3; 30:30; 2Ch 26:18; 29:33). (4) Heb. *millē' yadh*, literally, "to fill the hand," a peculiar idiom normally used for the installation of a priest into his office or of the installation offerings put into his hands (Ex 29:9, 29; Lev 8:33, NIV "ordain"). (5) Greek *teleioō*, "to make perfect" (Heb. 10:20, NIV "opened").

CONTENT

Jos	7:7	If only we had been **c** to stay

Pr	13:25	The righteous eat to their hearts' **c**,
	19:23	one rests **c**, untouched by trouble.
Ecc	4:8	yet his eyes were not **c**
Lk	3:14	don't accuse people falsely — be **c**
Php	4:11	to be **c** whatever the circumstances
	4:12	I have learned the secret of being **c**
1Ti	6:8	and clothing, we will be **c** with that.
Heb	13:5	and be **c** with what you have,

CONVERSION (Heb. *shûv*, Gr. *epistrophē*). The words commonly used in the English Bible as equivalent to the Hebrew and Greek words are "turn," "return," "turn back," "turn again." Thus conversion is synonymous with "turning." The turning may be in a literal or in a figurative, ethical, or religious sense, either from God or, more frequently, to God. It is significant that when the turning refers to a definite spiritual change, it almost invariably denotes an act of man: "Turn! Turn from your evil ways!" (Eze 33:11; cf. Mt 18:3). Since the word implies both a turning *from* and a turning *to* something, it is not surprising that in the NT it is sometimes associated with repentance (Ac 3:19; 26:20) and faith (11:21). That is, conversion on its negative side is turning from sin and on its positive side is faith in Christ ("they must turn to God in repentance and have faith in our Lord Jesus," 20:21). Although conversion is an act of man, Scripture makes clear that it has a divine ground. The turning of sinful people is done by the power of God (3:26). In the process of salvation, conversion is the first step in the transition from sin to God. It is brought about by the Holy Spirit operating on the human mind and will, so that the course of one's life is changed. It is not the same as justification and regeneration, which are purely divine acts. It may come as a sudden crisis or as a more or less prolonged process.

CONVICTION (Gr. *elencho, to convince or prove guilty*). Conviction is the first stage of repentance, experienced when in some way the evil nature of sin has been brought home to the penitent, and it has been proved to him that he is guilty of it. Although the word "conviction" is never used in the KJV, both

Testaments give many illustrations of the experience. In the OT one of the most notable is found in Ps 51, where David, realizing he has sinned against God, is overwhelmed with sorrow for his transgression and cries out to God for forgiveness and cleansing. In the NT the central passage bearing on this theme is Jn 16:7 – 11, where Jesus says that when the Holy Spirit comes "he will reprove the world of sin, and of righteousness, and of judgment" (KJV). Here the word "reprove" (NIV "convict") means "convince" (so RSV) or "prove guilty." The thought is that the Holy Spirit addresses the heart of the guilty and shows how inadequate ordinary standards of righteousness are. The purpose of conviction is to lead to godly repentance.

CORINTH [3172] (Gr. *Korinthos, ornament*). A city of Greece on the narrow isthmus between the Peloponnesus and the mainland. Under the Romans, Athens was still the educational center of Greece, but Corinth was the capital of the Roman province they called Achaia and was the most important city in the country. Land traffic between the north and south of Achaia had to pass the city, and much of the commerce between Rome and the East was brought to its harbors.

Corinth occupied a strategic geographical position. It was situated at the southern extremity of the isthmus, at the northern foot of the lofty (2,000 ft. [625 m.]) and impregnable Acrocorinthus, which commanded a wonderful view over the Saronic Gulf on the east and the Corinthian Gulf on the west, as well as over central Greece and the Peloponnesus. From the Acrocorinthus it is possible on a clear day to see the Acropolis of Athens forty miles (sixty-seven km.) away. Corinth had three harbors: Lechaem to the west, Cenchreae and Schoenus to the east. Lechaeum was connected with Corinth by a double row of walls. Because of its highly favored commercial position, in ancient times the city was known as "two-sea'd Corinth."

In Roman times Corinth was a city of wealth, luxury, and immorality. It had no rivals as a city of vice. "To live like a Corinthian" meant to live a life of profligacy and debauchery. It was customary in a stage play for a Corinthian to come on the scene drunk. The inhabitants were naturally devoted to the worship of Poseidon, since they drew so much of their wealth from the sea, but their greatest devotion was given to Aphrodite, the goddess of love. Her temple on the Acrocorinthus had more than a thousand *hierodouloi* — priestesses of vice not found in other shrines of Greece, and she attracted worshipers from all over the ancient world. Besides drawing vast revenues from the sea, Corinth had many important industries, its pottery and brass especially being famous all over the world. The Isthmian games, held every two years, made Corinth a great center of Hellenic life.

At the height of its power, Corinth probably had a free population of 200,000 plus a half million slaves. Its residents consisted of the descendants of the Roman colonists who were established there in 46 BC, many Romans who came for business, a large Greek population, and many strangers of different nationalities attracted to the city for various reasons. In the last group was a considerable body of Jews and also some Gentiles brought under the influence of Judaism because of its monotheism and lofty morality.

Visited by:
Paul (Ac 18; 2Co 12:14; 13:1, w 1Co 16:5 – 7 & 2Co 1:16); Apollos (Ac 19:1); Titus (2Co 8:16 – 17; 12:18); Erastus, a Christian of (Ro 16:23; 2Ti 4:20).

Church of:
Schism in (1Co 1:12; 3:4). Immoralities in (1Co 5; 11). Writes to Paul (1Co 7:1). Alienation of, from Paul (2Co 10). Abuse of ordinances in (1Co 11:22; 14). Heresies in (1Co 15:12; 2Co 11). Lawsuits in (1Co 6). Generosity of (2Co 9). Paul's letters to (1Co 1:2; 16:21 – 24; 2Co 1:1, 13).

CORINTHIANS, 1 AND 2 The first letter to the Corinthians was written by Paul in Ephesus on his third missionary journey (Ac 19:1; 1Co 16:8, 19), probably in AD 56 or 57. He had previously written a letter to the Corinthians that has not come down to us; in it he had warned against associating with immoral persons (1Co 5:9). In reply Paul received a letter (alluded to several times in 1Co 5:10; 7:1; 8:1) in which they declared it was impossible to follow his advice without going out of the world altogether, and submitted to him a number of problems on which they asked his opinion. This letter from Corinth was probably brought by three of their number — Stephanas, Fortunatus, and Achaicus (16:17) — who came to visit Paul at Ephesus and undoubtedly told him about the condition of the church. Meanwhile, Paul had heard of factions in the church from the servants of Chloe (1:11), probably from Corinth, and this news caused him much pain and anxiety. It was these various circumstances that led to the writing of 1 Corinthians.

The following subjects are discussed in the letter, after the introductory salutation (1Co 1:1 – 9):

1. In the first four chapters the apostle takes up the reported factionalism in the church and points out the danger and scandal of party spirit. He reminds them that Christ alone is their Master, their Christian teachers being only servants of Christ and fellow workers with God.

2. In ch. 5 the apostle deals with a case of incestuous marriage and prescribes that the offender be put out of the church so that his soul may be saved.

3. In ch. 6 Paul addresses their practice of bringing disputes between themselves before heathen judges for litigation. He shows that this is morally wrong and out of harmony with the spirit of love by which they as Christians should be animated. Paul also pleads with Christians to keep their bodies pure for God's glory.

4. Various phases of the subject of marriage are considered in ch. 7. While commending a celibate life, Paul holds marriage to be wise and honorable. He forbids Christians from getting a divorce, even if they are married to unbelievers.

5. The eating of meat offered to idols was a problem of conscience to many Christians, and chs. 8 – 10 are devoted to it. Paul points out that while there is nothing inherently wrong in a Christian's eating such food, the law of love requires that it be avoided if it will offend another who regards the eating of it as sin. He illustrates this principle of self-control in his own life: lest his motives in preaching the gospel be misunderstood, he refuses to exercise his undoubted right of looking for material aid from the church. He warns against a spirit of self-confidence and urges them to be careful not to seem to countenance idolatry.

6. Paul next takes up certain abuses in public worship: the matter of appropriate head apparel for women in their assemblies (11:2 – 16) and the proper observance of the Lord's Supper (11:17 – 34), since there had been serious abuses in its administration.

7. There then follows a long discussion of the use and abuse of spiritual gifts, especially speaking in tongues (chs. 12 – 14). The apostle, while commending the careful exercise of all the gifts, bids them cultivate above all God's greatest gift, love (ch. 13).

8. In ch. 15 Paul turns to a consideration of one of the most important of their troubles — the doubt that some had concerning the resurrection of the dead. He meets the objections raised against the doctrine by showing that it is necessitated by the resurrection of Christ and that their salvation is inseparably connected with it.

9. The letter concludes with directions about the collections being made for the saints in Jerusalem, the mother church; with comments about Paul's plans; and with personal messages to various friends.

Second Corinthians was written by Paul on his third missionary journey somewhere in Macedonia, where he had just met Titus, who had brought him a report concerning the church at Corinth. The letter reveals that Judaizing teachers — perhaps recent arrivals from Jerusalem — had sought to discredit the apostle and had succeeded in turning the church as a whole against him. Paul was denounced as no minister of Christ at all. This revolt caused Paul to make a brief visit to Corinth in order to restore his authority (2Co 12:14; 13:1 – 2), but the visit did not have its expected effect.

The report Titus brought Paul was, on the whole, most encouraging. The majority had repented of their treatment of Paul and had cast out of the church the man who had led the attack on him. Paul's authority was acknowledged once more. Titus seems to have helped greatly in bringing about this happy change. It was the report of Titus that chiefly occasioned the writing of this letter.

Paul's mention of a severe letter that had caused him great sorrow of heart to write (2Co 2:3 – 4, 9; 7:8 – 12) has naturally caused scholars to wonder what he had in mind. Some think he refers to 1 Corinthians; others hold that this letter, like the one referred to in 1Co 5:9, is wholly lost; while still others believe that it is preserved in 2Co 10 – 13, which, they say, was written by Paul at Ephesus some time after the writing of 1 Corinthians.

This second letter is the least methodical and the most personal of Paul's writings. It is very auto-biographical and falls naturally into three main divisions:

1. In chs. 1 – 7 Paul, after giving thanks to God for his goodness to him in trial (1:1 – 11), shares some thoughts on the crisis through which the church has just passed.

2. In chs. 8 and 9 he admonishes the Corinthians to complete the collection for the poor in Jerusalem.

3. Chapters 10 – 13 are a defense of Paul's ministry against the attacks of his enemies and a vindication of his apostleship.

CORNERSTONE [74+7157, 7157, 214, 214+1639] (Heb. *pinnâh*, Gr. *akrogōniaios*). A term that has both a literal and figurative use in Scripture but is usually used figuratively (e.g., Job 38:6; Ps 118:22; Isa 28:16; Zec 10:4). Among the Canaanites, before the conquest of the land by Joshua, the laying of the foundation stone was accompanied by the dreadful rite of human sacrifice. Numerous skeletons have been unearthed, especially those of tiny babies in earthen jars.

Following rabbinical practice, which understood the term "cornerstone" in a messianic context, the Synoptic Gospels validate the claim of Jesus of Nazareth to messiahship by citing Ps 118:22 (Mt 21:42; Mk 12:10; Lk 20:17). Peter and Paul's use of the word must be understood in a similar fashion (see Ro 9:33, quoting Isa 28:16 and 8:14, following LXX; Eph 2:20; 1Pe 2:6).

Physically, the cornerstone determined the design and structure of a building; the most important stone in the foundation (Isa 28:16). Figurative of creation (Job 38:6); of Christ (Isa 28:16; Zec 10:4; Eph 2:20; 1Pe 2:6).

Job	38:6	or who laid its **c** —
Isa	28:16	a precious **c** for a sure foundation;
Jer	51:26	rock will be taken from you for a **c**,
Zec	10:4	From Judah will come the **c**,
Eph	2:20	Christ Jesus himself as the chief **c**.
1Pe	2:6	a chosen and precious **c**,

COURAGE [599, 1201+2657, 2616, 3338+ 8332, 4213, 4222, 5162, 5883, 8120, 437, 2313, 2510, 4244].

Of the righteous:
(Pr 28:1; 2Ti 1:7). Exhortations to (Ps 31:24; Isa 51:7, 12 – 16; Eze 2:6; 3:9; Mt 10:28; Lk 12:4; 1Co 16:13; Php 1:27 – 28).

Commanded of:
Joshua (Dt 31:7 – 8, 22 – 23; Jos 1:1 – 9); the Israelites (Lev 26:6 – 8; Jos 23:6; 1Ch 19:13; 2Ch 32:7 – 8; Isa 41:10; 51:7, 12 – 16); Solomon (1Ch 22:13; 28:20); Asa (2Ch 15:1 – 7); the disciples (Mt 10:26, 28; Lk 12:4); Paul (Ac 18:9 – 10); other Christians (1Co 16:13; Php 1:27 – 28); of judicial and executive officers by Jehoshaphat (2Ch 19:11).

Instances of the Courage of Conviction:
Abraham, in leaving his fatherland (Ge 12:1 – 9); in offering Isaac (Ge 22:1 – 14). Gideon, in destroying the altar of Baal (Jdg 6:25 – 31). Ezra, in undertaking the perilous journey from Babylon to Israel without a guard (Ezr 8:22 – 23). The Jews, in returning answer to Tattenai (Ezr 5:11). The three Hebrews who refused to bow down

to the image of Nebuchadnezzar (Da 3:16 – 18). Daniel, in persisting in prayer, regardless of the edict against praying (Da 6:10). Peter and John, in refusing to obey men rather than God (Ac 4:19; 5:29).

Instances of Personal Bravery:

Joshua and Caleb, in advising that Israel go at once and possess the land (Nu 13:30; 14:6 – 12). Othniel, in killing Kiriath Sepher (Jos 15:16 – 17). Gideon, in attacking the confederate armies of the Midianites and Amalekites with three hundred men (Jdg 7:7 – 23). Deborah, in leading Israel's armies (Jdg 4). Jael, in killing Sisera (Jdg 4:18 – 22). Agag, in the indifference with which he faced death (1Sa 15:32 – 33). David, in killing Goliath (1Sa 17:32 – 50); in entering the tent of Saul and carrying away Saul's spear (1Sa 26:7 – 12). David's captains (2Sa 23). Joab, in reproving King David (2Sa 19:5 – 7). Nehemiah, in refusing to take refuge in the temple (Ne 6:10 – 13). Esther, in going to the king to save her people (Est 4:8, 16; 5 – 7). Joseph of Arimathea, in caring for the body of Jesus (Mk 15:43). Thomas, in being willing to die with Jesus (Jn 11:16). Peter and other disciples (Ac 3:12 – 26; 4:9 – 13, 19 – 20, 31). The apostles, under persecution (Ac 5:21, 29 – 32). Paul, in going to Jerusalem, despite his impressions that bonds and imprisonments awaited him (Ac 20:22 – 24; 24:14, 25).

Jos	2:11	everyone's **c** failed because of you,
	5:1	and they no longer had the **c**
2Sa	4:1	he lost **c**, and all Israel became
1Ch	17:25	So your servant has found **c** to pray
2Ch	15:8	son of Oded the prophet, he took **c**.
	19:11	Act with **c**, and may the LORD be
Ezr	7:28	I took **c** and gathered leading men
	10:4	We will support you, so take **c**
Ps	107:26	in their peril their **c** melted away.
Eze	22:14	Will your **c** endure or your hands
Da	11:25	and **c** against the king of the South.
Mt	14:27	said to them: "Take **c**!

Mk	6:50	spoke to them and said, "Take **c**!
Ac	4:13	When they saw the **c** of Peter
	23:11	"Take **c**! As you have testified
	27:22	now I urge you to keep up your **c**,
1Co	16:13	stand firm in the faith; be men of **c**;
Php	1:20	will have sufficient **c** so that now
Heb	3:6	if we hold on to our **c** and the hope

COURAGEOUS

Dt	31:6	Be strong and **c**.
	31:7	of all Israel, "Be strong and **c**,
Jos	1:6	and **c**, because you will lead these
	1:7	Be strong and very **c**.
	10:25	Be strong and **c**.
1Ch	22:13	Be strong and **c**.
	28:20	"Be strong and **c**, and do the work.
2Ch	26:17	priest with eighty other **c** priests

COVENANT [1382, 4162, 6343, 1347] (*agreement, contract*). This translates the Hebrew noun *berîth*. The verbal root means either "to fetter" or "to eat with," which would signify mutual obligation, or "to allot" (1Sa 17:8), which would signify a gracious disposition. Compare this with the Hittite "suzerainty covenant," in which a vassal swore fealty to his king out of gratitude for favors received.

In the OT, *berîth* identifies three different types of legal relationships. (1) A two-sided covenant between human parties who both voluntarily accept the terms of the agreement (for friendship, 1Sa 18:3 – 4; marriage, Mal 2:14; or political alliance, Jos 9:15; Ob 7). God, however, never "enters in" to such a covenant of equality with humans. The closest approximation is the "covenant of redemption" between God and Christ (mentioned in certain of the Psalms: 2:7 – 8; 40:6 – 8), under which the Son agrees to undertake man's salvation. But the actual term *berîth* is not used. (2) A one-sided disposition imposed by a superior party (Eze 17:13 – 14). God the Lord thus "commands" a *berîth* that man, the servant, is to "obey" (Jos 23:16). In the original "covenant of works" (Hos 6:7 ASV), he placed Adam on probation, bestowing life, should he prove faithful

(Ge 2:17). Humanity failed; but Christ, the last Adam (1Co 15:45), did fulfill all righteousness (Mt 3:15; Gal 4:4), thereby earning restoration for all who are his. (3) God's self-imposed obligation, for the reconciliation of sinners to himself (Dt 7:6 – 8; Ps 89:3 – 4). As he said to Abraham, "I will establish my covenant … between me and you and your descendants after you for the generations to come (Ge 17:7).

Of God with People:

Salt is an emblem of (Lev 2:13; Nu 18:19; 2Ch 13:5). Confirmed with an oath (Ge 22:16; 26:3; 50:24; Ex 34:27 – 28; Nu 32:11; Pss 89:35; 105:9; Lk 1:73; Heb 6:13, 17 – 18). Binding (Lev 26; Jer 11:2 – 3; Gal 3:15). Everlasting (Ge 8:20 – 22; 9:1 – 17; Ps 105:8, 10; Isa 54:10; 61:8). God faithful to (Lev 26:44 – 45; Dt 4:31; 7:8 – 9; Jdg 2:1; 1Ki 8:23; Pss 105:8 – 11; 106:45; 111:5; Mic 7:20).
Instances of, with individuals and groups: *With Adam (Ge 2:16 – 17). Noah (Ge 6:18; 8:16; 9:8 – 17). Abraham (Ge 12:1 – 3; 15; 17:1 – 22; Ex 6:4 – 8; Ps 105:8 – 11; Ro 9:7 – 13; Gal 3). See Circumcision. Isaac (Ge 17:19). Jacob (Ge 28:13 – 15). Israel, to deliver them from Egypt (Ex 6:4 – 8); to destroy Amalek (Ex 17:14 – 16). Phinehas (Nu 25:12 – 13). Levites (Ne 13:29; Mal 2:4 – 5).*
Instances of, with Israel: *At Horeb (Ex 34:27; Dt 5:2 – 3). In Moab (Dt 29:1 – 15). Blood of (Ex 24:8). Book of (Ex 24:7). The Sabbath (Ex 31:16). The Ten Commandments (Ex 34:28; Dt 5:2 – 3; 9:9).*

Major Social Concerns in the Covenant:

(1) Personhood. Everyone's person is to be secure (Ex 20:13; 21:16 – 21, 26 – 31; Lev 19:14; Dt 5:17; 24:7; 27:18). (2) False Accusation. Everyone is to be secure against slander and false accusation (Ex 20:16; 23:1 – 3; Lev 19:16; Dt 5:20; 19:15 – 21). (3) Women. No woman is to be taken advantage of within her subordinate status in society (Ex 21:7 – 11, 20, 26 – 32; 22:16 – 17; Dt 21:10 – 14; 22:13 – 30; 24:1 – 5). (4) Punishment. Punishment for wrongdoing shall not be excessive so that the culprit is dehumanized (Dt 25:1 – 5). (5) Dignity.

Every Israelite's dignity and right to be God's freedman and servant are to be honored and safeguarded (Ex 21:2, 5 – 6; Lev 25; Dt 15:12 – 18). (6) Inheritance. Every Israelite's inheritance in the Promised Land is to be secure (Lev 25; Nu 27:5 – 7; 36:1 – 9; Dt 25:5 – 10). (7) Property. Everyone's property is to be secure (Ex 20:15; 21:33 – 36; 22:1 – 15; 23:4 – 5; Lev 19:35 – 36; Dt 5:19; 22:1 – 4; 25:13 – 15). (8) Fruit of Labor. Everyone is to receive the fruit of his labors (Lev 19:13; Dt 24:14; 25:4). (9) Fruit of the Ground. Everyone is to share the fruit of the ground (Ex 23:10 – 11; Lev 19:9 – 10; 23:22; 25:3 – 55; Dt 14:28 – 29; 24:19 – 21). (10) Rest on Sabbath. Everyone, down to the humblest servant and the resident alien, is to share in the weekly rest of God's Sabbath (Ex 20:8 – 11; 23:12; Dt 5:12 – 15). (11) Marriage. The marriage relationship is to be kept inviolate (Ex 20:14; Dt 5:18; see also Lev 18:6 – 23; 20:10 – 21; Dt 22:13 – 30). (12) Exploitation. No one, however disabled, impoverished, or powerless, is to be oppressed or exploited (Ex 22:21 – 27; Lev 19:14, 33 – 34; 25:35 – 36; Dt 23:19; 24:6, 12 – 15, 17; 27:18). (13) Fair Trial. Everyone is to have free access to the courts and is to be afforded a fair trial (Ex 23:6, 8; Lev 19:15; Dt 1:17; 10:17 – 18; 16:18 – 20; 17:8 – 13; 19:15 – 21). (14) Social Order. Every person's God-given place in the social order is to be honored (Ex 20:12; 21:15, 17; 22:28; Lev 19:3, 32; 20:9; Dt 5:16; 17:8 – 13; 21:15 – 21; 27:16). (15) Law. No one shall be above the law, not even the king (Dt 17:18 – 20). (16) Animals. Concern for the welfare of other creatures is to be extended to the animal world (Ex 23:5, 11; Lev 25:7; Dt 22:4, 6 – 7; 25:4).

General:

Repudiated by God on account of Israelite's idolatry (Jer 44:26 – 27; Heb 8:9). Broken by the Israelites (Jer 22:9; Eze 16:59; Heb 8:9). Punishment for breaking (Lev 26:25 – 46). David (2Sa 7:12 – 16; 1Ch 17:11 – 14; 2Ch 6:16); David and his house (2Sa 23:5; Ps 89:20 – 37; Jer 33:21); God's people (Isa 55:3; 59:21).

Of People with God:

Jacob (Ge 28:20 – 22); Joshua (Jos 24:25); Absalom (2Sa 15:7 – 8); Jehoiada and Joash (2Ki 11:17); Josiah (2Ki 23:3); Asa (2Ch 15:12 – 15); Nehemiah (Ne 9:38; 10); Israelites (Ex 24:3, 7; 19:8; Dt 5:27; 26:17; Jer 50:5). See Vows.

Of People with People:

Sacred (Jos 9:18 – 21; Gal 3:15). Binding (Jos 9:18 – 20; Jer 34:8 – 21; Eze 17:14 – 18; Gal 3:15); on those represented as well (Dt 29:14 – 15). Breach of, punished (2Sa 21:1 – 6; Jer 34:8 – 22; Eze 17:13 – 19). National. See Alliances. **Ratified:** by giving the hand (Ezr 10:18; La 5:6; Eze 17:18); loosing the sandal (Ru 4:7 – 11); writing and sealing (Ne 9:38; Jer 32:10 – 12); giving presents (Ge 21:27 – 30; 1Sa 18:3 – 4); making a feast (Ge 26:30); erecting a monument (Ge 31:45 – 46, 49 – 53); offering a sacrifice (Ge 15:9 – 17; Jer 34:18 – 19); salting (Lev 2:13; Nu 18:19; 2Ch 13:5); taking an oath (Ge 21:23 – 24; 25:33; 26:28 – 31; 31:53; Jos 2:12 – 14; 14:9). See Oath; Vows. **Instances of:** Abraham and Abimelech (Ge 21:22 – 32); Abimelech and Isaac (Ge 26:26 – 31); Jacob and Laban (Ge 31:44 – 54); Jonathan and David (1Sa 18:3 – 4; 20:16, 42; 2Sa 21:7); Jews with each other, to serve God (2Ch 15:12 – 15; Ne 10:28 – 32); King Zedekiah and his subjects (Jer 34:8); Ahab with Ben-Hadad (1Ki 20:34); subjects with sovereign (2Ch 23:1 – 3, 16).

New Covenant:

Prophecy concerning (Jer 31:31 – 34; Isa 59:21; 61:8 – 9; Eze 16:59 – 63; 34:25 – 31; 37:24 – 28; Heb 8:4 – 13). Characterized by the Spirit rather than the letter (2Co 3:6 – 17). Purchased or ratified by the blood of Jesus (Mt 26:28; Mk 14:24; Lk 22:20; 1Co 11:25). Jesus the mediator (Heb 12:18 – 24). Everlasting (Heb 13:20). See Covenants, Major in the Old Testament.

Ge	9:9	"I now establish my **c** with you
	17:2	I will confirm my **c** between me
Ex	19:5	if you obey me fully and keep my **c**,
	24:7	Then he took the Book of the **C**
Dt	4:13	declared to you his **c**, the Ten
Jdg	2:1	'I will never break my **c** with you,
1Sa	23:18	of them made a **c** before the LORD
1Ki	8:21	in which is the **c** of the LORD that
2Ki	23:2	the words of the Book of the **C**,
1Ch	16:15	He remembers his **c** forever,
Job	31:1	"I made a **c** with my eyes
Ps	105:8	He remembers his **c** forever,
Pr	2:17	ignored the **c** she made before God
Isa	42:6	you to be a **c** for the people
	61:8	make an everlasting **c** with them.
Jer	11:2	"Listen to the terms of this **c**
	31:31	"when I will make a new **c**
Eze	37:26	I will make a **c** of peace with them;
Da	9:27	He will confirm a **c** with many
Hos	6:7	Like Adam, they have broken the **c**
Mal	2:14	the wife of your marriage **c**.
	3:1	of the **c**, whom you desire,
Mt	26:28	blood of the **c**, which is poured out
Mk	14:24	"This is my blood of the **c**,
1Co	11:25	"This cup is the new **c** in my blood;
2Co	3:6	as ministers of a new **c**—
Gal	4:24	One **c** is from Mount Sinai
Heb	8:6	as the **c** of which he is mediator is
	8:8	when I will make a new **c**
	9:15	Christ is the mediator of a new **c**,

COVENANTS [COVENANT]

Ro	9:4	theirs the divine glory, the **c**,
Gal	4:24	for the women represent two **c**.

COVENANTS, MAJOR, IN THE OLD TESTAMENT

MAJOR TYPES

Royal Grant (Unconditional).

A king's grant (of land or some other benefit) to a loyal servant for faithful or exceptional service. The grant was normally perpetual and unconditional, but the servant's heirs benefited from it only as they continued their father's loyalty and service (1Sa 8:14; 22:7; 27:6; Est 8:1).

Parity (Conditional).

A covenant between equals, binding them to mutual friendship or at least to mutual respect for each other's spheres and interests. Participants called each other "brothers" (Ge 21:27; 26:31; 31:44 – 54; 1Ki 5:12; 15:19; 20:32 – 34; Am 1:9).

Suzerain-Vassal (Unconditional).

A covenant regulating the relationship between a great king and one of his subject kings. The great king claimed absolute right of sovereignty, demanded total loyalty and service (the vassal must "love" his suzerain) and pledged protection of the subject's realm and dynasty, conditional on the vassal's faithfulness and loyalty to him. The vassal pledged absolute loyalty to his suzerain — whatever service his suzerain demanded — and exclusive reliance on the suzerain's protection. Participants called each other "lord" and "servant" or "father" and "son" (Jos 9:6, 8; Eze 17:13 – 18; Hos 12:1).

MAJOR INSTANCES

1. Noahic: Ge 9:8 – 17.

Type: Royal grant. Participant: Made with "righteous" (Ge 6:9) Noah (and his descendants and every living thing on earth — all life that is subject to man's jurisdiction). Description: An unconditional divine promise never to destroy all earthly life with some natural catastrophe; the covenant "sign" being the rainbow in the storm cloud.

2. Abrahamic A: Ge 15:9 – 21.

Type: Royal (land) grant. Participant: Made with "righteous" (his faith was "credited to him as righteousness," v. 6) Abram (and his descendants, v. 16). Description: An unconditional divine promise to fulfill the grant of the land; a self-maledictory oath symbolically enacted it (v. 17).

3. Abrahamic B: Ge 17.

Type: Suzerain-vassal. Participant: Made with Abraham as patriarchal head of his household. Description: A conditional divine pledge to be Abraham's God and the God of his descendants (cf. "As for me," v. 4; "As for you," v. 9); the condition: total consecration to the Lord as symbolized by circumcision.

4. Sinaitic: Ex 19 – 24.

Type: Suzerain-vassal. Participant: Made with Israel as the descendants of Abraham, Isaac, and Jacob and as the people the Lord has redeemed from bondage to an earthly power. Description: A conditional divine pledge to be Israel's God (as their protector and the guarantor of their blessed destiny); the condition: Israel's total consecration to the Lord as his people (his kingdom) who live by his rule and serve his purposes in history.

5. Phinehas: Nu 25:10 – 13.

Type: Royal grant. Participant: Made with the zealous priest Phinehas. Description: An unconditionally divine promise to maintain the family of Phinehas in a "lasting priesthood" (implicitly a pledge to Israel to provide them forever with a faithful priesthood).

6. Davidic: 2Sa 7:5 – 16.

Type: Royal grant. Participant: Made with faithful King David after his devotion to God as Israel's king and the Lord's vassal had come to special expression (v. 2). Description: An unconditional divine promise to establish and maintain the Davidic dynasty on the throne of Israel (implicitly a pledge to Israel) to provide them forever with a godly king like David and through that dynasty to do for them what he had done through David — bring them into rest in the Promised Land (1Ki 4:20 – 21; 5:3 – 4).

7. New: Jer 31:31 – 34.

Type: Royal grant. Participant: Promised to rebellious Israel as they are about to be expelled from the Promised Land in actualization of the most severe covenant curse (Lev 26:27 – 39; Dt 28:36 – 37, 45 – 68). Description: An unconditional divine promise to unfaithful Israel to forgive their sins and establish his relationship with them on a new basis by writing his law "on their hearts" — a covenant of pure grace. *See Covenant.*

COVERING THE HEAD A symbol of sorrow and/or shame (2Sa 15:30; Est 6:12; Jer 14:3 – 4) and also of being under authority (1Co 11:10). In Corinth men are commanded to pray and prophesy only with uncovered heads, while women are to have their heads covered with a veil or long hair (1Co 11:3 – 16). At that time in Greece only immoral women were seen with their heads uncovered. Paul means that Christian women cannot afford to disregard social convention; it would hurt their testimony. In giving them long hair, a natural veil, "nature" teaches the lesson that women should not be unveiled in public assemblies.

COVETOUSNESS [2773, 2121, 2123, 2420] (kŭv'ĕt-ŭs-nes). The word has various shades of meaning; among the most important are the following:

1. The desire to have something (1Co 12:31; 14:39).

2. The inordinate desire to have something (Lk 12:15ff.; Eph 5:5; Col 3:5).

3. Excessive desire of what belongs to another (Ex 20:17; Ro 7:7).

A great deal of OT law was intended to counteract the spirit of covetousness. Outstanding examples of those who coveted in this sense are Achan (Jos 7), Saul (1Sa 15:9, 19), and Ananias and Sapphira (Ac 5:1 – 11).

CREATED

Ge	1:1	In the beginning God **c** the heavens
	1:21	God **c** the great creatures of the sea
	1:27	So God **c** man in his own image,
	2:4	and the earth when they were **c**.
	5:1	When God **c** man, he made him
	6:7	whom I have **c**, from the face
Dt	4:32	from the day God **c** man
Ps	89:12	You **c** the north and the south;
	89:47	what futility you have **c** all men!
	102:18	a people not yet **c** may praise
	139:13	For you **c** my inmost being;
	148:5	for he commanded and they were **c**
Isa	40:26	Who **c** all these?
	41:20	that the Holy One of Israel has **c** it.
	42:5	he who **c** the heavens and stretched
	43:7	whom I **c** for my glory,
	45:8	I, the LORD, have **c** it.
	45:18	he who **c** the heavens,
	57:16	the breath of man that I have **c**.
Eze	21:30	In the place where you were **c**,
Mk	13:19	when God **c** the world, until now —
Ro	1:25	and served **c** things rather
1Co	11:9	neither was man **c** for woman,
Eph	2:10	**c** in Christ Jesus to do good works,
	3:9	hidden in God, who **c** all things.
	4:24	**c** to be like God in true
Col	1:16	For by him all things were **c**:
	1:16	all things were **c** by him
1Ti	4:3	which God **c** to be received
	4:4	For everything God **c** is good,
Heb	12:27	**c** things — so that what cannot be
Jas	1:18	a kind of firstfruits of all he **c**.
Rev	4:11	and by your will they were **c**
	4:11	for you **c** all things,
	10:6	who **c** the heavens and all that is

CREATION [1343, 7865, 2856, 3231, 3232, 3233]. The Bible clearly teaches that the universe, "all things," came into existence through the will of the eternal God (Ge 1; 2; Jn 1:1 – 3; Heb 11:3; Rev 4:11). The Bible teaches that the universe, including all matter, had a beginning and came into existence through the will of the eternal God. In Ge 1:1 the words "the heavens and the earth" summarize all the various materials of the universe. This verse has been interpreted in various ways, but all agree in its essential significance. This is true even of the new interpretation that takes it as a mere introduction to what follows (rendering it "When God began to create heaven and earth"). For even on this interpretation, v. 2 would describe the situation that came into existence at the time God began to create, rather than contradict Heb 11:3 by implying that there was preexisting matter.

Some hold that there is a long gap between vv. 1 and 2, in which God's perfect creation came into chaos through a great catastrophe. Hebrew syntax permits such a view but does not require it.

The length of the creative days of Ge 1 is not stated in the Bible. The Hebrew word "day" may mean a period of light between two periods of darkness, a period of light together with the preceding period of darkness, or a long period of time. All three usages occur often in the Bible. Not one of them is exactly twenty-four hours, though the second usage is near it. There is no indisputable indication as to which of the three is meant. The Bible gives no specific statement as to how long ago matter was created, how long ago the first day of creation began, or when the sixth day ended.

On the seventh day (Ge 2:2–3) God ceased from his labors. God refers to this as an example for Israel to have six days of labor followed by one day of rest (Ex 20:11). No end to the rest of the seventh day is mentioned. As far as the Bible tells us, God's rest from creating still continues.

There is much discussion about the question of evolution in relation to the creation, but the word *evolution* is used in many different ways. If taken in its historic sense (the theory that everything now existing has come into its present condition as a result of natural development, all of it having proceeded by natural causes from one rudimentary beginning), such a theory is sharply contradicted by the divine facts revealed in Ge 1–2. These chapters indicate a number of specific divine commands bringing new factors into existence. God's activity is indicated throughout the entire creation narrative. It is explicitly stated several times that plants and animals are to reproduce "after their kind." Moses nowhere states how large a "kind" is, and there is no ground for equating it with any particular modern definition of "species." Yet it is clear that Genesis teaches that there are a number (perhaps a large number) of "kinds" of plants and of animals,

which cannot reproduce in such a way as to evolve from one into the other. Nothing in the Bible denies the possibility of change and development within the limits of a particular "kind."

This is exactly the relation between the two accounts. Genesis 1 describes the creation of the universe as a whole. Genesis 2:4–25 covers one special segment of that creation. The linking word (2:4) is translated in NIV as "account," but this is inadequate: it must mean "subsequent/emergent account," for the word (*toledoth*) both in its individual meaning and in its OT use tells how something emerges from what has preceded. In this way, Ge 2:4 "steps back" into Ge 1 to begin the study of "what happened next," how out of God's creative work there came the beginnings of human life and history on earth. This explains the often-alleged differences and supposed contradictions between the chapters, for Ge 2:4ff. alludes only to the creative work as a whole insofar as it is necessary to do so in recording the beginnings of human history. It is reasonable, therefore, that Ge 2:4ff. gives a more detailed account of the creation of man but says nothing about that of matter, light, heavenly bodies, or plants.

Again, it is sometimes said that Ge 1 begins with a watery chaos and Ge 2:4ff. with a dry earth. But there is no contradiction, because the two have different starting points in the creative acts of God. Genesis 2:4ff. does not describe the creation of vegetation, as some assert; it simply mentions the planting of a garden. It is hardly reasonable to insist that God created man and then put him aside while the garden was planted and given time to mature. The verbs in 2:8–9 must be understood (as is perfectly proper to do) as pluperfects, and the same is true of 2:19 where the previous creation of animals is alluded to. Genesis 2:4ff. does not contradict Ge 1 in any way; instead, it opens up our understanding of the wonder of the creation of human beings and introduces us to the beginnings of human history on earth.

Hab	2:18	he who makes it trusts in his own **c**;
Mt	13:35	hidden since the **c** of the world."
	25:34	for you since the **c** of the world.

Mk	10:6	of **c** God 'made them male
	16:15	and preach the good news to all **c**.
Jn	17:24	me before the **c** of the world.
Ro	1:20	For since the **c** of the world God's
	8:19	The **c** waits in eager expectation
	8:22	that the whole **c** has been groaning
2Co	5:17	he is a new **c**; the old has gone,
Gal	6:15	anything; what counts is a new **c**.
Eph	1:4	us in him before the **c** of the world
Col	1:15	God, the firstborn over all **c**.
Heb	4:3	finished since the **c** of the world.
1Pe	1:20	chosen before the **c** of the world,
2Pe	3:4	as it has since the beginning of **c**."
Rev	3:14	true witness, the ruler of God's **c**.
	13:8	slain from the **c** of the world.
	17:8	life from the **c** of the world will be

CREATOR [1343, 3670, 7865, 3231, 3234].

Creator of the universe, God as (Ge 1:1; Ne 9:6; Job 26:7; Ps 102:25; Ac 14:15; Heb 11:3). The Word (Jesus) as (Jn 1:1 – 3). Holy Spirit as (Ge 1:2; Job 26:13; 33:4; Ps 104:30). Creator of humankind, God as (Ge 1:26; 2:7; 5:2; Dt 4:32; Job 33:4; Pss 8:5; 100:3; Isa 51:13; Mal 2:10; Ac 17:28).

Ge	14:19	**C** of heaven and earth.
	14:22	God Most High, **C** of heaven
Dt	32:6	Is he not your Father, your **C**,
Ecc	12:1	Remember your **C**
Isa	27:11	and their **C** shows them no favor.
	40:28	the **C** of the ends of the earth.
	43:15	Israel's **C**, your King."
Mt	19:4	the beginning the **C** 'made them
Ro	1:25	created things rather than the **C**—
Col	3:10	in knowledge in the image of its **C**.
1Pe	4:19	themselves to their faithful **C**

CROSS [2005, 6015, 6296, 599, 1385, 4699, 5089] (Gr. *stauros*). There are three biblical uses of the term: first, the wooden instrument of torture; second, the cross as a symbolic representation of redemption; third, death on the cross, that is, crucifixion. Our English word is derived from the Latin *crux*. The cross existed in four different forms: (1) the *crux immissa*, the type usually presented in art in which the upright beam extends above the cross beam, traditionally held to be the cross on which the Redeemer suffered and died. (2) The *crux commissa*, or "Saint Anthony's Cross" in the form of a T. (3) The Greek cross in which the cross beams are of equal length; (4) The *crux decussata*, or "Saint Andrew's Cross," in the shape of an X. Antedating these forms, the Assyrians impaled the body with a crude pointed stick.

Because of the sacrificial death of the Savior on the cross, the cross rapidly became interwoven into the theological construction of religious thinking, especially Paul's. In 1Co 1:17 the "preaching" (*kerygma*) of the cross is set forth as the "divine folly" in sharp contrast to earthly wisdom. In Eph 2:16 it is presented as the medium of reconciliation. In Col 1:20 peace has been effected through the cross. In Col 2:14 the penalties of the law have been removed from the believer by the cross. How Paul as a pious Hebrew, to whom one hanged was accursed, and as a Roman to whom one crucified was an object of scorn (Gal 3:13), came to glory in the cross would be one of the absurdities of history were it not for the fact that the apostle held the Crucified as the Christ of God (2:20).

Crucifixion was one of the most cruel and barbarous forms of death known to humankind. It was practiced, especially in times of war, by the Phoenicians, Carthaginians, Egyptians, and later by the Romans. So dreaded was it that even in the pre-Christian era, the cares and troubles of life were often compared to a cross.

The details of the crucifixion of Christ are passed over, the evangelists content with the simple statement, "They crucified him" (Mt 27:35; Mk 15:24). Following his trial before the Jewish and Roman authorities, Christ was led forth for crucifixion. Before the actual ordeal itself, he was scourged. The prisoner was bent over and tied to a post, while the Roman soldier applied blow after blow on his bared back with a lash intertwined with pieces of bone or steel. This in itself was frequently sufficient to cause death.

The agony of the crucified victim was brought about by a number of factors. First, the painful but nonfatal character of the wounds inflicted. Although there were two distinctive methods of affixing a living victim to a cross, tying or nailing, it is well established that Christ underwent the horror of the latter, or possibly both. The second factor causing great suffering was the abnormal position of the body. The slightest movement brought on additional torture. The third factor was the traumatic fever induced by hanging for such a long period of time.

What was the physical reason for Christ's death? Recent medical studies have sought an answer to the question. When a person is suspended by his two hands, the blood sinks rapidly into the lower extremities of the body. Within six to twelve minutes the blood pressure has dropped to half, while the rate of the pulse has doubled. The heart is deprived of blood, and fainting follows. This leads to an orthorastic collapse through insufficient circulation. Death during crucifixion is due to heart failure. Victims of crucifixion did not generally succumb for two or three days. Death was hastened by the *crucifragium*, or the breaking of the legs. "But when they came to Jesus and found that he was already dead, they did not break his legs" (Jn 19:33). Sometimes a fire was built beneath the cross that its fumes might suffocate the sufferer.

Among the Jews, a stupefying potion was prepared by the merciful women of Jerusalem, a drink that Christ refused (Mk 15:23). To such a death, the one who was "in very nature God" descended (Php 2:5).

General References to:

Jesus crucified on (Mt 27:32; Mk 15:21; Lk 23:26; Ac 2:23, 36; 4:10; 1Co 1:23; 2:2, 8; Eph 2:16; Php 2:8; Col 1:20; 2:14; Heb 12:2). Borne by Simon (Mt 27:32; Mk 15:21; Lk 23:26); by Jesus (Jn 19:17). Death on, a disgrace (Gal 3:13).

Mt	10:38	and anyone who does not take his **c**
Mk	8:34	and take up his **c** and follow me.
Lk	9:23	take up his **c** daily and follow me.
	14:27	anyone who does not carry his **c**
Jn	19:17	Carrying his own **c**, he went out
Ac	2:23	to death by nailing him to the **c**.
1Co	1:17	lest the **c** of Christ be emptied
Gal	5:11	offense of the **c** has been abolished.
	6:12	persecuted for the **c** of Christ.
Eph	2:16	both of them to God through the **c**,
Php	2:8	even death on a **c**!
	3:18	as enemies of the **c** of Christ.
Col	1:20	through his blood, shed on the **c**.
	2:14	he took it away, nailing it to the **c**.
	2:15	triumphing over them by the **c**.
Heb	12:2	set before him endured the **c**,

CRUCIFIED

Mt	20:19	to be mocked and flogged and **c**.
	26:2	of Man will be handed over to be **c**
	27:35	When they had **c** him, they divided
	28:5	looking for Jesus, who was **c**.
Mk	15:15	and handed him over to be **c**.
	15:24	And they **c** him.
	15:25	the third hour when they **c** him.
	15:32	Those **c** with him also heaped
	16:6	for Jesus the Nazarene, who was **c**.
Lk	23:23	insistently demanded that he be **c**,
	24:7	be **c** and on the third day be raised
Jn	19:16	him over to them to be **c**.
	19:18	Here they **c** him, and with him two
Ac	2:36	whom you **c**, both Lord and Christ
	4:10	whom you **c** but whom God raised
Ro	6:6	For we know that our old self was **c**
1Co	1:13	Is Christ divided? Was Paul **c**
	1:23	but we preach Christ **c**: a stumbling
	2:2	except Jesus Christ and him **c**.
	2:8	they would not have **c** the Lord
2Co	13:4	to be sure, he was **c** in weakness,
Gal	2:20	I have been **c** with Christ
	3:1	Christ was clearly portrayed as **c**.
	5:24	Christ Jesus have **c** the sinful
Rev	11:8	where also their Lord was **c**.

CRUCIFY [CRUCIFIED]

Mt	23:34	Some of them you will kill and **c**;

	27:22	They all answered, "**C** him!" "Why
Mk	15:13	"**C** him!" they shouted.
Lk	23:21	they kept shouting, "**C** him! **C** him
Jn	19:6	"You take him and **c** him.
	19:10	either to free you or to **c** you?"
	19:15	Crucify him!" "Shall I **c** your king

CURSE [457, 460, 826, 1385, 4423, 7686, 7837, 7839, 353, 1059, 2129, 2800, 2932, 2933] (Heb. *'ālāh, me'ērâh, qelālâh,* Gr. *katapa*). The reverse of "to bless." On the human level, to wish harm or catastrophe. On the divine, to impose judgment. In the oriental mind the curse carried with it its own power of execution. A curse was imposed on the serpent (Ge 3:14). Noah cursed Canaan (9:25). The curse of Balaam, the pseudoprophet, turned to a blessing (Nu 24:10). A curse was placed on Mount Ebal for disobedience to the law of Moses (Dt 27:1 – 9). The cursing of one's parents is sternly prohibited by Mosaic regulations. Christ commanded those who would be his disciples to bless and not to curse (Lk 6:28). When Peter, at Christ's trial, denied that he knew him, he invited a curse on himself (Mt 26:74); this passage is often misunderstood by Western readers. Paul represents the curse of the law as borne by Christ on the cross for the believer (Gal 3:13). The modern Western practice of cursing, that is, using profane language, is never referred to in the Scriptures. *See also Blasphemy.*

General References to:

Pronounced on: the serpent (Ge 3:14 – 15); Adam and Eve (Ge 3:15 – 19); the ground (Ge 3:17 – 18); Cain (Ge 4:11 – 16); Canaan, Ham's son (Ge 9:24 – 27); the disobedient (Dt 28:15 – 68; Jer 11:3 – 17); Meroz (Jdg 5:23); Gehazi (2Ki 5:27). Barak commands Balaam to curse Israel (Nu 22:6; 23:11). Paternal (Ge 27:12 – 13; 49:5 – 7). In the covenant with Abraham (Ge 12:3). Of the Mosaic law, enforcing the covenant (Dt 11:26 – 32; 27:12 – 26; 28:15 – 68; Jos 8:30 – 34). Assumed for others (Mt 27:25). Rebekah for Jacob (Ge 27:13). Paul wishes he could assume for Israel (Ro 9:3). See Blessings. Christ assumed the curse of the Mosaic law for us (Gal 3:13).

Ge	4:11	Now you are under a **c**
	8:21	"Never again will I **c** the ground
	12:3	and whoever curses you I will **c**;
Dt	11:26	before you today a blessing and a **c**
	21:23	hung on a tree is under God's **c**.
Job	1:11	he will surely **c** you to your face."
	2:9	**C** God and die!" He replied,
Mal	2:2	and I will **c** your blessings.
Ro	12:14	persecute you; bless and do not **c**.
Gal	3:10	on observing the law are under a **c**,
Jas	3:9	with it we **c** men, who have been
Rev	22:3	No longer will there be any c.

DAGON [1837] (dā′gŏn, Heb. *damghôn*, *[god of]
grain* IDB; *fish* ISBE). Chief god of the Philistines.
Originally worshiped by the Canaanites before the
Philistine invasion of Canaan, as indicated by place
names such as Beth Dagon in Judah (Jos 15:41)
and in Asher (19:27). Either a fish god or the god
of agriculture, from *Dab*, "fish," or *Dagan*, "grain."
On a wall of a palace in Babylon he is shown as half
fish. That he was god of agriculture is supported by
the tribute that priests and diviners bade the rulers
to send when the ark was returned to Israel. Five
golden mice and five golden emerods ("tumors,"
NIV) were votive offerings expressing gratitude for
Dagon's freeing their fields of mice and their bodies
of tumors (1Sa 5).

Jdg	16:23	offer a great sacrifice to **D** their god
1Sa	5:2	Dagon's temple and set it beside **D**.

DAMASCUS [1877, 1966, 2008, 1241, 1242]
(da-măs′kŭs, Gr. *Damaskos*). For more than four
thousand years the capital of one government after
another, a prize for which nation after nation went to
war, a city whose boast for centuries has been, "The
world began at Damascus, and the world will end
there." It is a modern focal point between the Christian and the Muslim worlds, center of tourist interest
and of international unrest. Damascus is the capital of
Syria, a small region of unique geological formation,
lying between Mount Hermon and the Syrian Desert.
It is watered by the Barada and the Wadi Awaj, Abana,
and Pharpar of the OT (2Ki 5:12). A 2,000-foot (625
m.) elevation gives it a delightful climate. Its gardens
and olive groves still flourish after millennia of cultivation. Caravan routes from the east, west, and south
once crossed in the city, carrying treasures of silks,
perfumes, carpets, and foods. It was a rich city whose
merchandise was far-famed (Eze 27:16).

During NT days, Damascus was an important
center, ruled by Arabia under Aretas (2Co 11:32). A
strong Christian community had developed by Paul's
day. While en route there to arrest the believers, Saul
was converted (Ac 9:1 – 18). He escaped his Jewish
enemies of the city by being let down from a wall in a
basket (Ac 9:25; 2Co 11:33). After a checkered history
under Rome, Damascus was captured by Muslims
in AD 635 and made the seat of the Muslim world.
It remained the center of the Muslim faith until 1918
when it was put under French mandate after World
War I. In 1946 it became a free state.

General References to:

*An ancient city (Ge 14:15; 15:2). The capital
of Syria (1Ki 20:34; Isa 7:8; Jer 49:23 – 29; Eze
47:16 – 17). Laid under tribute to David (2Sa
8:5 – 6). Besieged by Rezon (1Ki 11:23 – 24).
Recovered by Jeroboam (2Ki 14:28). Taken by
the king of Assyria (2Ki 16:9). Walled (Jer 49:27;
2Co 11:33). Garrisoned (2Co 11:32). Luxury in
(Am 3:12). Paul's experiences in (Ac 9; 22:5 – 16;
26:12 – 20; 2Co 11:32; Gal 1:17). Prophecies concerning (Isa 8:4; 17:1 – 2; Jer 49:23 – 29; Am 1:3,
5; Zec 9:1). Wilderness of (1Ki 19:15).*

DAMNATION (Heb. *rasha'*, *to hold guilty*, Dt 25:1;
Isa 50:9; 54:17; Gr. *krinom*, *to put under condemnation*, Jn 3:17 – 18; Ro 14:22; *katakrinom*, *to hold
to be unpardonable*, Mt 12:41; 20:18; Ro 8:1, 3, 34;
Heb 11:7; *krima* and *krisis*, *judgment*, *eternal punishment*, Mt 23:33; Mk 12:40; Jn 5:29; Ro 3:8; 5:16;
13:2; 1Co 11:29, 34; *apomleia*, *destruction*, *damnation*, 2Pe 2:3). The penalty for unbelief (2Th 2:12);
for adulterous relations (1Ti 5:11 – 12); for hypocrisy
(Mt 23:14); and for treason (Ro 13:2). When referring to the future, the word means primarily eternal separation from God with accompanying awful
punishment (see Ps 88:10 – 12; Isa 38:18); being cast
into hell (Mt 5:29; 10:28; 23:33; 24:51; Mk 9:43). The
severity of the punishment is determined by the
degree of sin (Lk 12:36 – 48), and it is eternal (Isa
66:24; Mk 3:29; 2Th 1:9; Jude 6 – 7).

DAN, DANITE(S) [1201+1968, 1968, 1969, 1974]
(*judge*).

1. The fifth son of Jacob and Bilhah (Ge 30:6; 35:25). Descendants of (Ge 46:23; Nu 26:42 – 43). Blessed of Jacob (Ge 49:16 – 17).

2. The tribe to which Dan, the fifth son of Jacob, gave origin and the territory allotted it in Canaan. One son is mentioned among those who migrated to Egypt (Ge 46:8, 23). By the time of the exodus his offspring had increased to 62,700 men (Nu 1:39). The tribe acted as rear guard during the exodus (10:25). They were given a fertile area lying between Judah and the Mediterranean Sea, occupied by the Philistines whose lands extended from Egypt to the coast west of Shechem (Jos 13:3). Failure to conquer Philistia made the Danites move northward, where by strategy they conquered Leshem (Laish of Jdg 18:29) and renamed it Dan (Jos 19:47; Jdg 18:1 – 29).

The heritage of Dan, though small, was productive and, with the acquisition of extra lands, provided for growth. Oholiab and Samson were Danites (Ex 31:6; Jdg 13:2, 24). Jeroboam set up a golden calf in Dan and put high places throughout Israel (1Ki 12:25 – 33). Menahem stopped Pul (Tiglath-Pileser) by bribery (2Ki 15:14 – 20), but eventually Pul returned, overran Israel, and took many Danites into captivity (1Ch 5:26). Little is known of the tribe from that time. *See Israel, Israelites.*

Census of (Nu 1:39; 26:42 – 43); Inheritance of, according to the allotment of Joshua (Jos 19:40 – 47); of Ezekiel (Eze 48:1); Position of, in journey and camp, during the exodus out of Egypt (Nu 2:25, 31; 10:25); Blessed by Moses (Dt 33:22); Failure to conquer the Amorites (Jdg 1:34 – 35); Conquests by (Jos 19:47; Jdg 18:27 – 29); Deborah rebukes, for cowardice (Jdg 5:17); Idolatry of (Jdg 18); Commerce of (Jdg 5:17; Eze 27:19)

3. A city of the tribe of Dan. Northernmost city of Palestine. Called Laish (Jdg 18:7, 13, 27, 29) and Leshem (Jos 19:47) and later known as Dan.

DANCE [DANCED, DANCING]

Ecc	3:4	a time to mourn and a time to **d**,
Mt	11:17	and you did not **d**;

DANCED [DANCE]

| 2Sa | 6:14 | **d** before the LORD |
| Mk | 6:22 | of Herodias came in and **d**, |

DANCING [2565, 4159, 4688, 4703, 7174, 8376, 8471, 4004, 5962]. Dancing has formed a part of religious rites and has been associated with war, hunting, marriage, birth, and other occasions since the records of humankind began to be written. It grew out of three basic human reactions: the desire to imitate movements of beasts, birds, and even the sun and moon; the desire to express emotions by gestures; and gregarious impulses.

Throughout past ages, dancing has been linked with worship. In sacramental dance worshipers sought to express through bodily movements praise or penitence, worship or prayer. The Hebrew people developed their own type of dancing, associated in the main with worship. Basically, it was more like modern religious shouting by individuals, or processions of exuberant groups. Three things characterized it. First, the sexes never intermingled in it, except where pagan influences had crept in (cf. Ex 32:19). Second, dancing was usually done by women, with one leading, as in the case of Miriam (15:20 – 21). In this incident, as well as on other occasions, a form of antiphonal singing was used. Third, dancing usually took place out of doors. The Romans introduced the Greek dance to Palestine. Primitive Christian churches allowed dance, but it soon caused degeneracy and was banned, as is indicated by many of the early Christian writers.

General References to:
Of children (Job 21:11). Of women (Ex 15:20; Jdg 11:34; 21:19 – 21; 1Sa 18:6; 21:11). Of David (2Sa 6:14 – 16; 1Ch 15:29). In the marketplace (Mt 11:16 – 17). At feasts (Jdg 21:19 – 21; Mt 14:6; Mk 6:22; Lk 15:23 – 25). As a religious ceremony (Pss 149:3; 150:4). Idolatrous (Ex 32:19; 32:25). Figurative: of joy (Ps 30:11; Ecc 3:4; Jer 31:4; 31:13; La 5:15).

| Ps | 30:11 | You turned my wailing into **d**; |
| | 149:3 | Let them praise his name with **d** |

DANGER

Pr	22:3	A prudent man sees **d**
	27:12	The prudent see **d** and take refuge,
Mt	5:22	will be in **d** of the fire of hell.
Ro	8:35	famine or nakedness or **d** or sword?
2Co	11:26	I have been in **d** from rivers,

DANIEL [1975, 10181, 1248] (dăn′yĕl, Heb. *dam niye*m′l or *damni′em*l, *God is my judge*).

1. David's second son (1Ch 3:1; *Kileab*, 2Sa 3:3).

2. A postexilic priest (Ezr 8:2; Ne 10:6).

3. The exilic seer of the book of Daniel. The prophet was born into an unidentified family of Judean nobility at the time of Josiah's reformation (621 BC); he was among the select, youthful hostages of the first Jewish deportation, taken to Babylon by Nebuchadnezzar in 605, the third year of King Jehoiakim (Da 1:1, 3). For three years Daniel was trained in all the wisdom of the Babylonians (Da 1:4–5) and was assigned the Babylonian name Belteshazzar, "Protect his life!"—thereby invoking a pagan deity (4:8). Daniel and his companions, however, remained true to their ancestral faith, courteously refusing "the royal food and wine" (1:8, tainted with idolatry and contrary to the Levitical purity laws). God rewarded them with unsurpassed learning (1:20, qualifying them as official "wise men"; cf. 2:13). On Daniel, moreover, he bestowed the gift of visions and of interpreting dreams (1:17; cf. Daniel's wisdom in the apocryphal stories of *Susanna* and *Bel and the Dragon*).

Near the close of this second year (602 BC), Nebuchadnezzar required his fellow Babylonians, who as the ruling strata in society had assumed the position of priestly diviners (Da 2:2; cf. Herodotus, 1.191), to identify and interpret an undisclosed dream that had troubled him the preceding evening (2:5, 8). The hoax of spiritism and astrology was duly exposed; but when judgment was pronounced on the enchanters, Daniel and his companions were included under the death sentence. But the "God in heaven who reveals mysteries" (2:28; cf. 2:11) answered Daniel's prayer for illumination (2:18–19). Daniel revealed both the dream, depicting a fourfold image, and its import of four world empires (Babylon, Persia, Greece, and Rome) that would introduce God's messianic kingdom (2:44; *see also Daniel, Book of*). Nebuchadnezzar elevated Daniel to be chief over the wise men (2:48 does not, however, state that he became a pagan priest, as inferred by those who would discredit Daniel's historicity). He further offered him the governorship of the province of Babylon, though Daniel committed this latter appointment to his three friends (2:49).

In the latter years of Nebuchadnezzar's reign (604–562 BC), Daniel's courage was demonstrated (Da 4:19; cf. 4:7) when he interpreted the king's dream of the fallen tree (4:13–27). He tactfully informed his despotic master that for seven "times" pride would reduce him to beastlike madness, and reiterated that "the Most High is sovereign over the kingdoms of men" (4:24–25; cf. its historical fulfillment twelve months later, 4:28–33).

In 552 BC after the retirement of King Nabonidus to Arabian Teima and the accession of his son Belshazzar, Daniel was granted his vision of the four great beasts (Da 7) that parallels Nebuchadnezzar's earlier dream of the composite image. Then in 550, at the time of Cyrus's amalgamation of the Median and Persian states and of the growing eclipse of Babylon, Daniel received the prophecy of the ram and the goat concerning Persia and Greece (8:20–21) down to Antiochus IV (8:25). On October 12, 539, Cyrus's general, Gobryas, after having routed the Babylonian armies, occupied the city of Babylon. During the profane revelries of Belshazzar's court that immediately preceded the end, Daniel was summoned to interpret God's handwriting on the wall, and the prophet fearlessly condemned the desperate prince (5:22–23). He predicted Medo-Persian victory (5:28), and that very night the citadel fell and Belshazzar was slain.

When Darius the Mede (presumably Gobryas or another official of similar name) was made king of Babylon by Cyrus (Da 5:31; 9:1), he at once sought out Daniel as one of his three "administrators" (6:2) because of his excellency, and was considering him for the post of chief administrator (6:3). Daniel's jealous colleagues, failing to uncover a valid charge of corruption (6:4), proceeded to contrive his downfall through a royal edict prohibiting for thirty days all prayers or petitions, except to Darius himself. Daniel was promptly apprehended in prayer to God, and Darius had no recourse but to cast him into a den of lions, as had been prescribed. God, however, intervened on behalf of his faithful servant (cf. 6:16) and shut the lions' mouths, though they subsequently devoured his accusers when they were condemned to a similar fate. It was in this same first year of Darius, as the seventy years of Babylonian exile drew to a close, that the angel Gabriel answered Daniel's prayers and confessions with a revelation of the seventy "sevens" (9:24–27). "So Daniel prospered during the reign of Darius" (6:28; cf. 1:21).

The last-known event in the life of Daniel took place in the third year of Cyrus (536 BC), when he was granted an overpowering vision of the archangel Michael contending with the demonic powers of pagan society (Da 10:10–11:1); of the course of world history, through the persecutions of Antiochus IV (11:2–39); and of the eschatological Antichrist, the resurrections, and God's final judgment (11:40–12:4). The vision concluded with the assurance that though Daniel would go to his grave prior to these events, he would yet receive his appointed reward in the consummation (12:13). Thus in his mideighties, after completing his inspired autobiography and apocalyptic oracles, he finished his honored course.

The book of Daniel presents a timeless demonstration of separation from impurity, of courage against compromise, of efficaciousness in prayer, and of dedication to him whose "kingdom endures from generation to generation" (Da 4:34).

DANIEL, BOOK OF Although it stands as the last book of the Major Prophets in the English Bible, this book appears in the Hebrew OT (which consists of "the Law, Prophets, and Writings") as one of the "Writings." For though Christ spoke of Daniel's *function* as prophetic (Mt 24:15), his *position* was that of a governmental official and inspired writer rather than ministering prophet (see Ac 2:29–30).

The first half of the book (chs. 1–6) consists of six narratives on the life of Daniel and his friends: their education (605–602 BC), Daniel's revelation of Nebuchadnezzar's dream image, the trial by fiery furnace, Daniel's prediction of Nebuchadnezzar's madness, his interpretation of the handwriting on the wall (539, the fall of Babylon), and his ordeal in the lions' den. The second half consists of four apocalyptic visions predicting the course of world history.

Daniel 7 envisions the rise of four beasts: a lion, bear, leopard, and monster with iron teeth explained as representing successive kings (kingdoms, 7:23). The description parallels that of Nebuchadnezzar's image, with its head, breast, trunk, and iron legs. The first empire must therefore be contemporary Babylon (2:38). The fourth kingdom is regarded by most conservative scholars as Rome. Between them lie Persia and Greece. The vision further describes the disintegration of Rome into a tenfold balance of power (2:42; 7:24; Rev 17:12, 16), the eventual rise of the Antichrist for an indefinite period of "times" (Da 7:8, 25), and his destruction when "one like a son of man" comes with the clouds of heaven (7:13). This figure is understood by most scholars as the Messiah because Christ applied this imagery to himself (Mt 24:30). However, some understand it to symbolize the saints of the Most High (Da 7:18, 22) epitomized in Jesus Christ, the "last Adam" (Mk 14:62; 1Co 15:45). Some scholars understand the kingdom of God, represented by the rock (Da 2:34–35; cf. vv. 44–45) to be the church. Others see it as the eschatological kingdom (the millennium).

Daniel 2:4b–7:28 is composed in the international language of Aramaic. But with ch. 8, Daniel resumes his use of Hebrew, probably because of

the more Jewish orientation of the three remaining visions. The ram and the goat depict the coming victory of Greece (331 BC) over the amalgamated empire of Media and Persia (8:20 – 21) and the subsequent persecution of Judah by Antiochus IV (168 – 165 BC; Da 8:9 – 14, 23 – 26).

The prophecy of the seventy "sevens" in 9:20 – 27 was given in response to Daniel's prayer concerning the end of Jerusalem's desolations (9:16). The prophecy indicated that the desolations would cease at the end of seventy "sevens." Many scholars understand the designation "seven" to refer to a period of seven years. Sixty-nine "sevens" extend from the decree to rebuild Jerusalem (458; cf. Ezr 7:18, 25) to the Messiah. Those who do not hold to the future significance of the seventieth "seven" propose that the "cutting off" (9:26) of the Messiah is Christ's crucifixion in the midst of the seventieth "seven." Other scholars terminate the sixty-ninth "seven" with Christ's death and place the seventieth "seven" in the last days. It is in the seventieth "seven" that the Antichrist will destroy Jerusalem according to this view. If the pointing of the Masoretic tradition is observed, the first seven "sevens" are separated from the remaining sixty-two, and the seventieth "seven" witnesses either the devastations under Antiochus Epiphanes or the eschatological Antichrist.

Chapters 10 – 12, after elaborating on the succession of Persian and Greek rulers through Antiochus, then move on to "the time of the end," foretelling the Antichrist's tribulation (Da 11:40 – 12:1), the resurrections of the saved and the lost (12:2; cf. Rev 20:4 – 6, 12), and the final judgment (Da 12:2).

The authorship of the book of Daniel is nowhere expressly defined but is indicated by the autobiographical, first-person composition from 7:2 onward. Unity of style and content (as admitted by Driver, Rowley, and Pfeiffer), plus God's commitment of "the book" to Daniel (Da 12:4), imply the latter's authorship, shortly after his last vision, 536 BC (10:1).

Modern criticism, however, overwhelmingly denies the authenticity of Daniel as a product of the sixth century BC. Indeed, as early as AD 275 the neo-Platonic philosopher Porphyry categorically repudiated the possibility of Daniel's miraculous predictions. Antisupernaturalism must bring the "prophecy" down to a time after the events described (especially after Antiochus's sacrilege of 168 BC); or, if the latest possible date has been reached, it must then reinterpret the predictions to apply to other, already accomplished events. Consequently, since Daniel was extensively quoted (and misunderstood) as early as 140 BC (*Sibylline Oracles* 3:381 – 400), rationalists have no alternative but to apply the supposed coming of the Messiah and the fulfillment of the seventy weeks to Maccabean times, rather than Christ's, even though this requires "surmising a chronological miscalculation on the part of the writer" (ICC, p. 393).

DARIUS [2003, 10184] (dǎrī′ǔs, Heb. *damryamwesh*, Gr. *Darios*, Old Persian *he who upholds the good*). A common name for Medo-Persian rulers.

1. Darius the Mede (Gubaru), the son of Xerxes (Da 5:31; 9:1), made governor of Babylon by Cyrus, but he seems to have ruled for only a brief time (Da 10:1; 11:1), prominent in the book of Daniel (Da 6:1, 6, 9, 25, 28; 11:1).

2. Darius I, called the Great (spelled variously Hystaspos, Hystaspis, or Hystaspes), fourth and greatest of the Persian rulers (522 – 486 BC); reorganized the government into satraps and extended boundaries of the empire; a great builder; he was defeated by the Greeks at Marathon in 490 BC; renewed the edict of Cyrus and helped to rebuild the temple (Ezr 4:5, 24; 5:5 – 7; 6:1 – 12; Hag 1:1; 2:1, 10, 18; Zec 1:1, 7; 7:1). Died in 486 BC and was succeeded by Xerxes, the grandson of Cyrus the Great.

3. Darius, the Persian (spelled variously Codomanus or Codomannus), the last king of Persia (336 – 330 BC); defeated by Alexander the Great (330 BC) (Ne 12:22). Some scholars identify him with Darius II (Nothus), who ruled Persia and Babylon (423 – 404 BC).

DARKNESS [694, 696, 3124, 3125, 3127, 3128, 4419, 4420, 4743, 6547, 6602, 6906, 7223, 7516, 7725, 9507,

10286, 1190, 2432, 5027, 5028, 5030, 5031] (Heb. *homshekh*, *the dark*, Gr. *skotos*, *darkness*). Used in the OT and NT both in a literal and figurative sense. Humankind has long associated it with evil, danger, crime; it has also been the metaphor that describes both mystery and the place of eternal punishment. Several uses of the term are found in the Scriptures:

1. To denote the absence of light (Ge 1:2 – 3; Job 34:22; Isa 45:7).

2. To depict the mysterious (Ex 20:21; 2Sa 22:10; 1Ki 8:12; Ps 97:2; Isa 8:22; Mt 10:27).

3. As ignorance, especially about God (Job 37:19; Pr 2:13; Ecc 2:14; Jn 12:35; 1Th 5:1 – 8).

4. To describe the seat of evil (Pr 4:19; Mt 6:23; Lk 11:34; 22:53; Jn 8:12; Ro 13:12; 1Co 4:5; Eph 5:11).

5. To present supernatural events (Ge 15:12; Ex 10:21; Mt 27:45; Rev 8:12; 16:10).

6. As a sign of the Lord's return (Isa 60:2; Joel 2:2; Am 5:8; Mt 24:29).

7. As an agency of eternal punishment (Mt 22:13; 2Pe 2:4, 17; Jude 6 – 7; see also Job 2:1 – 5; 20:20).

8. To describe spiritual blindness (Isa 9:2; Jn 1:5; Eph 5:8; 1Jn 1:5; 2:8), sorrow, and distress (Isa 8:22; 13:10; Ps 23:4). It never holds sway where the Redeemer has come to shed his light (Col 1:13).

Ge	1:2	**d** was over the surface of the deep,
	1:4	he separated the light from the **d**.
Ex	10:22	and total **d** covered all Egypt
	20:21	approached the thick **d** where God
2Sa	22:29	the LORD turns my **d** into light.
Pr	4:19	the way of the wicked is like deep **d**
Joel	2:31	The sun will be turned to **d**
Mt	4:16	the people living in **d**
	6:23	how great is that **d**! "No one can
Lk	11:34	are bad, your body also is full of **d**.
	23:44	and **d** came over the whole land
Jn	1:5	The light shines in the **d**,
	3:19	but men loved **d** instead of light
Ac	2:20	The sun will be turned to **d**
2Co	6:14	fellowship can light have with **d**?
Eph	5:8	For you were once **d**, but now you
	5:11	to do with the fruitless deeds of **d**,

1Pe	2:9	out of **d** into his wonderful light.
2Pe	2:17	Blackest **d** is reserved for them.
1Jn	1:5	in him there is no **d** at all.
	2:9	but hates his brother is still in the **d**.
Jude	1:6	in **d**, bound with everlasting chains
	1:13	for whom blackest **d** has been

DAVID [1858, 1253] (dā′vĭd, Heb. *Damwîdh*, *beloved*, or as in ancient Mari, *chieftain*). Israel's greatest king, described in 1Sa 16 – 1Ki 2:11 (1Ch 11 – 29), plus many of the psalms, he ranks with Moses as one of the most commanding figures in the OT.

David was born in 1040 BC (2Sa 5:4), the youngest son of Jesse of Bethlehem (1Sa 16:10 – 11). He developed in strength, courage, and attractiveness while caring for his father's sheep (16:12; 17:34 – 36). When God rejected Saul, the prophet Samuel sought out David and secretly anointed him as Israel's next king; and God's Spirit came upon David from that time on (16:13). Saul, meanwhile, summoned David to periodic appearances at court to soothe his own troubled mind by skillful harp playing (16:18; 17:15). While still in his teens, David gained national renown and the friendship of Saul's son Jonathan (18:1 – 3; cf. 20:12 – 16; 23:16 – 17) through his faith-inspired victory over the taunting Philistine champion Goliath (17:45 – 47). Saul's growing jealousy and four insidious attempts on David's life served only to increase the latter's popularity (cf. 18:13 – 16, 27). At length, urged on by David's rivals (cf. Ps 59:12), Saul openly sought his destruction; and though frustrated by Samuel and the priests at Nob, he did succeed in driving David into exile (1Sa 19:11; 21:10).

David fled to Philistine Gath, but his motives became suspect. Only by a stratagem and by the grace of God (1Sa 21:12; Pss 56:3; 34:6 – 8) did he reach the wilderness cave of Adullam in Judah (Ps 142:6). Here David was joined by a variety of malcontents (1Sa 22:2) and by the priest Abiathar, who had escaped Saul's retaliatory attack on Nob (cf. Ps 52:1). On three separate occasions Saul attempted to seize David: when fellow Judeans from Ziph betrayed his presence; after his deliverance of Keilah

(1Sa 23; Ps 54:3); at the cave of En Gedi by the Dead Sea where Saul was caught in his own trap (1Sa 24; Pss 7:4; 57:6); and on David's return to Ziphite territory, when he again spared his pursuer's life (1Sa 26). Near the end of 1012 BC, however (27:7), David in despair sought asylum in Gath, feigning vassalage (27:8 – 28:25).

When David heard of the destruction of Saul at Mount Gilboa in 1010 BC and the Philistine domination of Israel from Beth Shan, David composed his moving lament of "The Bow" (2Sa 1:19 – 27), the authenticity of which is unquestionable. Shortly thereafter, David's forces advanced inland to Hebron, where he was declared king over Judah. His appeal, however, to the northern and eastern tribes elicited no response (2:7), and for five years most of Israel lay under Philistine control.

In 1005 BC Saul's general, Abner, enthroned Ish-Bosheth, a son of the former monarch; but in the conflict that followed, David's arms gained ascendancy. Abner himself eventually transferred his support to David, only to be treacherously murdered by David's vengeful commander Joab (2Sa 3). Only after the death of Ish-Bosheth (ch. 4) did all Israel acclaim David king in 1003 (2Sa 5:1 – 5; 1Ch 11:10; 12:38).

Realizing that their "vassal" had gotten out of hand, the Philistines undertook an all-out attack on reunited Israel. David, however, after an initial retreat to Adullam (2Sa 5:17; 23:13 – 17), expelled the enemy in two divinely directed campaigns (5:18 – 25). He next established a new capital by capturing the Jebusite stronghold of Jerusalem. This strategic site on the Benjamite border served not only as an incomparable fortress, vulnerable only to the "scaling hooks" of Joab (5:8 KJV; see NIV note), but also as a neutral location between the rival tribes of north and south. Joab, for his bravery, was appointed as commander (1Ch 11:6). Twelve corps of militia were organized under him, each with twenty-four thousand men, on periods of one-month duty annually (ch. 27). David's military organization also included the professional Kerethites and Pelethites (Cretans and Philistines) and certain elite groups: "the six hundred" mighty men (2Sa 15:18; cf. 1Sa 27:2), "the thirty" heroes, and "the three" most distinguished (2Sa 23; 1Ch 11).

David also elevated Jerusalem into his religious capital by installing Moses' ark of the covenant in a tent on Zion (2Sa 6; Ps 24; cf. Nu 4:15 on the death of Uzzah, 2Sa 6:6 – 7). He honored it, both with a dedicatory psalm (1Ch 16, from Pss 96, 105, 106) and with a permanent ministry of Levitical singers under Asaph (1Ch 16:5, 37, 42; 25:1 – 31). Once criticized as postexilic fiction, these regular *sharîm* have been authenticated by even earlier Canaanitish parallels from Ugarit. Eventually David organized thirty-eight thousand Levites under hereditary leaders, appointing them as doorkeepers, treasurers, and even district judges (chs. 23 – 26). The Aaronic priests he divided into twenty-four rotating courses, which were continued into NT times (1Ch 24:10; Lk 1:5).

From 1002 to about 995 BC, David expanded his kingdom on all sides. David reigned supreme. Rest from war followed (2Sa 7:1; 22:1 – 51; Ps 18), and David proposed a permanent temple for the Lord in Jerusalem. But while the prophet Nathan denied David the privilege of building God's house (because of excessive bloodshed, 1Ch 22:8; 28:3), he revealed that God would build David's "house," raising up his son to construct the temple (2Sa 7:13a) and establishing his dynasty (7:13), to culminate in the incarnation of God's eternal Son (7:14). This "Davidic covenant" (Pss 89:3; 132:12) mediates Christian salvation for all (Isa 55:3; Rev 22:16), climaxing God's promises begun in Ge 3:15 and accomplished in the new covenant of Jesus Christ. God's Spirit then inspired David to compose messianic psalms, depicting the deity of the Lord's anointed Son (Ps 2), his eternal priesthood (Ps 110), his atoning death (Ps 22), and his resurrection, ascension, and coming kingdom (Pss 2, 16, 68). Some of David's greatest achievements lie in this literary sphere. Of the 150 canonical psalms, 73 possess titles asserting Davidic authorship. These references, moreover, appear in the oldest MSS and warrant full acceptance. David also composed some of the titleless psalms (cf. Pss 2; 95; Ac 4:25; Heb 4:7); he stimulated Asaph and his associates to the inscripturation of others; and the king personally compiled the first book of the Psalter (Pss 1 – 41; cf. his closing doxology in 41:13). One of the world's best-loved compositions is David's heart-affirmation, "The LORD is my shepherd…." (Ps 23).

Yet soon after this, David lapsed into a series of failures (Mephibosheth's appearance [2Sa 9] could not have preceded 995 BC [4:4; 9:12], nor could Solomon's birth [12:24] have been long subsequent). He killed seven innocent descendants of Saul (but not Mephibosheth, 21:7) to enforce a promise rashly made to pagan Gibeonites (contrast Nu 35:33). He committed adultery with Bathsheba and murdered her husband to conceal his crime (2Sa 10 – 11). When exposed by Nathan, he humbly confessed his sin (the great penitential Pss 32 and 51), but the testimony of God's people had suffered compromise, and Nathan condemned the king to corresponding punishments (2Sa 12:10 – 14). David also became guilty of ineffective control over his sons. Thus in about 990 Amnon, following his father's shameful example (13:1 – 14), raped his sister Tamar; and two years later Absalom avenged Tamar by murdering Amnon (13:23 – 29). Until about 983 (13:38; 14:28) David shunned Absalom's presence; and four years later (15:7 ASV mg.) Absalom revolted, driving his father from Jerusalem (cf. Pss 3, 63) and specifically fulfilling Nathan's curses (2Sa 16:20 – 22). Through fatal delay, Absalom was defeated and killed by Joab, though only the latter's stern rebuke could shake David from irresponsible grief over the death of his son (18:33 – 19:8). Even after David's restoration to Jerusalem, intertribal jealousies led Sheba of Benjamin to prolong the disorder (ch. 20).

David's last years (975 – 970 BC) were occupied with Philistine wars (2Sa 21:15 – 22) and with a military census, motivated by David's pride in his armed forces (24:3, 9; Ps 30:6). Plague resulted. But when the destroying angel halted at Araunah's threshing floor on Mount Moriah, just north of Jerusalem (2Ch 3:1), this area became marked as David's place of sacrifice and the very house of God (1Ch 22:1; Ps 30 title). David subsequently undertook massive preparations for the temple (1Ch 22); he received (in writing) from God's Spirit the plans for its construction (28:12, 19); and he solemnly charged Solomon and the princes with their execution (chs. 22, 28, 29). As David became increasingly incapacitated by age, his oldest surviving son, Adonijah, attempted to usurp the throne from Solomon, the divinely designated heir. Nathan, however, aroused David to proclaim Solomon's coronation (1Ki 1). Thus in 970, after a final charge to his son (2:2 – 9), David died. His last words were a prophecy of the future Davidic Messiah and of his own salvation, springing from this covenant (2Sa 23:5).

DAVID, CITY OF

1. Portion of Jerusalem occupied by David in c. 1003 BC; 2,500 feet above sea level. Originally a Canaanite city (Eze 16:3), it dates back to the third millennium. Solomon enlarged the City of David for the temple and other buildings, and later kings enlarged the city still more (2Ch 32:4 – 5, 30; 2Ki 20:20; Isa 22:9 – 11).

2. Bethlehem (Lk 2:11).

DAY OF CHRIST A term used in the NT to indicate Jesus' intervention in human history. Sometimes it is called "that day" (Mt 7:22) and "the Day" (1Co 3:13). It refers to the return of Jesus for his own, and for the judgment of unbelievers (1Co 1:8; 5:5; 2Co 1:14; Php 1:6, 10; 2:16; 2Th 2:2 – 3). It will signal the completion of the redemptive work (2Th 2:1, 13), the day of triumph (Php 2:9 – 11). Paul's letters, especially, are full of the longing for this day — when Christ will manifest himself in glory and establish his kingdom.

DAY OF THE LORD An eschatological term referring to the consummation of God's kingdom and triumph over his foes and deliverance of his people. It begins at the second coming and will include the final judgment. It will remove class distinction (Isa 2:12 – 21) and abolish sins (2Pe 3:11 – 13), and it will be accompanied by social calamities and physical cataclysms (Mt 24; Lk 21:7 – 33). It will include the millennial judgment (Rev 4:1 – 19:6) and culminate in the new heaven and the new earth (Isa 65:17; 66:22; Rev 21:1).

DAY'S JOURNEY Eighteen or twenty miles (Ex 3:18; 1Ki 19:4; Jnh 3:4). Sabbath day's journey, about two thousand paces (Ac 1:12).

DEACON, DEACONESS [1354, 1356] (Gr. *diakonos, servant*). Paul used the Greek word of himself (1Co 3:5; Eph 3:7). Jesus was declared to be a *diakonos* of the Jews (Ro 15:8). Household servants were *diakonoi* (Mt 22:13). Paul told Timothy how to be good *diakonos* (1Ti 4:6). NIV usually renders "servant"; KJV, "minister."

The diaconate, as a church office, is inferred from Ac 6:1 – 8, but at least two of the seven men were evangelists. Ignatius, a contemporary of the apostle John, declared that the deacons were not mere servers of meat and drink. But the seven in Ac 6 did serve (*diakonein*) tables so that the apostles could give themselves to the ministry (*diakonia*) of the Word. Their successors came to be recognized as church officers. Qualifications given in 1Ti 3:8 – 13 show that they were not considered ordinary lay members of the church. Paul's mention of deacons in connection with bishops (Php 1:1) supports the view. Clement of Rome based the office on the two classes of synagogue workers mentioned in Isa 60:17 (LXX) — pastors and helpers.

In regard to deaconesses, the same Greek word is used of Phoebe in Ro 16:1 — translated as "servant" (KJV, NASB, NIV) or "deaconess" (JB, RSV). Certain women ministered (*diakonein*) to Jesus (Lk 8:2 – 3). The character qualities of deacons are listed in 1Ti 3:1 – 13. Verse 11 refers either to deacons' wives or to special qualities required of deaconesses. It does not appear from the Scripture or early church literature that deaconesses were ever church officers.

| 1Ti | 3:12 | A **d** must be the husband of |
| Php | 1:1 | together with the overseers and **d**: |

| 1Ti | 3:8 | **D**, likewise, are to be men worthy |
| | 3:10 | against them, let them serve as **d**. |

DEAD [6, 1588, 1775, 2222, 2728, 4637, 4638, 5577, 5782, 5877, 5883, 7007, 7516, 8327, 8619, 10625, 633, 650, 1586, 2505, 2506, 2569, 3121, 3156, 3738, 5271, 5462].

Raised to Life, Instances of:

Widow of Zarephath's son (1Ki 17:17 – 23); Shunammite's son (2Ki 4:32 – 37); young man laid in Elisha's tomb (2Ki 13:21); widow's son (Lk 7:12 – 15). Jairus's daughter (Lk 8:49 – 55); Lazarus (Jn 11:43 – 44); Dorcas (Ac 9:37 – 40); Eutychus (Ac 20:9 – 12, w Heb 11:35).

Prepared for burial:

By washing (Ac 9:37); anointing (Mt 26:12); wrapping in linen (Mt 27:59). Burnings of incense made for (2Ch 16:14; 21:19; Jer 34:5). See Burial.

Pictured as:

Rest (Job 3:13 – 19); sleep (Job 14:11 – 15, 21; Da 12:12); hopelessness (Job 17:13 – 15; Ecc 9:5 – 6; Eze 32:27, 30); separation from God (Pss 6:5; 30:9; 88:10 – 12; 115:17). Life after (Job 14:12 – 15; Ps 49:15; Da 12:2; Lk 20:35 – 36; Jn 11:25). Understanding after (Eze 32:31; Lk 16:19 – 31).

Abode of:

The pit (Job 17:13 – 15). Abraham's side (Lk 16:22). Hell (Lk 16:23). Paradise (Lk 23:43).

Dt	18:11	or spiritist or who consults the **d**.
Isa	8:19	Why consult the **d** on behalf
Mt	8:22	and let the **d** bury their own **d**."
	28:7	'He has risen from the **d**
Lk	15:24	For this son of mine was **d**
	24:46	rise from the **d** on the third day,
Ro	6:11	count yourselves **d** to sin
1Co	15:29	do who are baptized for the **d**?
Eph	2:1	you were **d** in your transgressions
1Th	4:16	and the **d** in Christ will rise first.
Jas	2:17	is not accompanied by action, is **d**.
Rev	14:13	Blessed are the **d** who die
	20:12	And I saw the **d**, great and small,

DEAD SEA Lies SE of Jerusalem. Called in Scripture the Salt Sea (Ge 14:3), Sea of the Arabah (Dt 3:17), or the "eastern sea" (Joel 2:20; Zec 14:8). It has the earth's lowest surface, 1,290 feet below sea level. Occupying a geologic fault that extends from Syria through the Red Sea into Africa, it measures forty-seven by ten miles (approximately 300 sq. mi.). Cliffs rise from 1,500 to 2,500 feet (469–781 m.) on either shore. North of Lisan, "the tongue" (Jos 15:2 ASV note), the water's depth attains 1,300 feet (406 m.), though southward it averages less than ten feet. The Dead Sea is slowly expanding, as the muddy Jordan extends its northern delta. Salt concentration reaches 25 percent, four times that of ocean water. Magnesium bromide prevents organic life; the climate is arid, and the heat extreme. The Dead Sea constituted Israel's eastern border (Nu 34:12; Eze 47:18).

DEAD SEA SCROLLS Discovered in 1947 by a Bedouin in caves a mile or so west of the NW corner of the Dead Sea, at Qumran. So far MSS have been found in eleven caves, and they are mostly dated as coming from the last two centuries BC and the first century AD. At least 382 MSS are represented by the fragments of Cave Four alone, about one hundred of which are biblical MSS. These include fragments of every book of the Hebrew Bible except Esther. Some of the books are represented in many copies. Not all the MSS are in fragments; some are complete or nearly complete. In addition to biblical books, fragments of apocryphal and apocalyptic books, commentaries, psalms, and sectarian literature have been found. Near the caves are the remains of a monastery of huge size, possibly the headquarters of a monastic sect of Jews called the Essenes. The discoveries at Qumran are important for biblical studies in general. They are of great importance for a study of the OT text, both Hebrew and the LXX. They are also of importance in relation to the NT, as they furnish the background to the preaching of John the Baptist and Jesus. There is no evidence that either John the Baptist or Jesus was a member of the group.

DEATH (Heb. *mamweth*, Gr. *thanatos*; *nekros*). Both the OT and NT present death as an event belonging to our sinful existence, but also in relation to the living God, Creator, and Redeemer. Death means the end of a human life on earth — humans are made from dust, and to dust they return (Ge 3:19). To ponder this may cause a sense of separation from God (e.g., Pss 6:5; 30:9; 88:5); but as death is faced, it is recognized that total confidence should be placed in the Lord (Job 19:25–26; Pss 73:23–24; 139:8). The hope of bodily resurrection after death leading into life everlasting, which gradually emerges in the OT (Isa 26:19; Da 12:2), is given prominence in the NT (e.g., 1Co 15).

In the NT, especially in Paul's letters, there is teaching on the cause of death; but this is death understood theologically, not biologically — not merely the end of physical existence on earth, but this together with the absence of a spiritual communion with God. (This understanding of death is also found in the OT — see, e.g., Dt 30:15; Jer 21:8; Eze 18:21–22, 31–32.) Paul declares that "the wages of sin is death" (Ro 6:23) and "sin entered the world through one man, and death through sin" (5:12); thus he exclaims, "Who will rescue me from this body of death?" (7:24). In similar vein another writer declares that it is the devil who, in this age on this fallen earth, has power over death — until Christ takes it from him (Heb 2:14–15). Thus it is not surprising that the death of Jesus for the sins of the world is greatly emphasized as is also his victory over death in bodily resurrection. As representative and substitute man, Jesus tastes death for every human being so that those who believe in him and are united to him have passed from death (separation from God) into life (that triumphs over physical death). Thus the Christian can say, "Whether we live or die, we belong to the Lord" (Ro 14:8).

The book of Revelation contains the expression "the second death" (Rev 20:6, 14; 21:8); it is defined in symbolic terms as "the fiery lake of burning sulfur" (21:8) and is the opposite of "the crown of life" (2:10–11). It will be experienced by those whose names are not written in the Lamb's Book of Life

(20:15) and means everlasting separation from God and his redeemed people.

Ex	21:12	kills him shall surely be put to **d**.
Nu	35:16	the murderer shall be put to **d**.
Dt	30:19	set before you life and **d**,
Ps	23:4	the valley of the shadow of **d**,
	44:22	for your sake we face **d** all day long
Pr	8:36	all who hate me love **d**."
	11:19	he who pursues evil goes to his **d**.
	14:12	but in the end it leads to **d**.
	18:21	tongue has the power of life and **d**,
	23:14	and save his soul from **d**.
Ecc	7:2	for **d** is the destiny of every man;
Isa	25:8	he will swallow up **d** forever.
	53:12	he poured out his life unto **d**,
Jn	5:24	he has crossed over from **d** to life.
Ro	4:25	delivered over to **d** for our sins
	5:12	and in this way **d** came to all men,
	6:3	Jesus were baptized into his **d**?
	6:23	For the wages of sin is **d**,
	7:24	me from this body of **d**?
1Co	15:21	For since **d** came through a man,
	15:26	The last enemy to be destroyed is **d**
	15:55	Where, O **d**, is your sting?"
1Jn	5:16	There is a sin that leads to **d**.
Rev	1:18	And I hold the keys of **d** and Hades
	2:11	hurt at all by the second **d**.
	20:6	The second **d** has no power

DEATH, PHYSICAL

Universal to humankind (Ecc 3:2, 19 – 21; Ro 5:12, 14; 1Pe 1:24). Time of, unknown (Ge 27:2; Ps 39:4, 13). Nearness to (Jos 23:14; 1Sa 20:3). Separates spirit and body (Ecc 12:5, 7). Does not end conscious existence (Lk 20:34 – 38; 23:39 – 43; Rev 20:12 – 13). Exemplified in the appearance of Moses and Elijah at the transfiguration of Jesus (Mt 17:2 – 3; Mk 9:4 – 5; Lk 9:30 – 33). Not to be feared by the righteous (Mt 10:28). Brings rest to the righteous (Job 3:13, 17 – 19). Dispossesses of earthly goods (Job 1:21; Ps 49:17; Lk 12:16 – 20; 1Ti 6:7). A judgment

(Ge 2:17; 3:19; 6:7, 11 – 13; 19:12 – 13, 24 – 25; Jos 5:4 – 6; 1Ch 10:13 – 14). God's power over (Dt 32:39; 1Sa 2:6; Ps 68:20; 2Ti 1:10). Christ's power over (Heb 2:14 – 15; Rev 1:18). To be destroyed (Isa 25:8; Hos 13:14; 1Co 15:21 – 22, 26, 55 – 57; Rev 20:14; 21:4). Preparation for (2Ki 20:1; Lk 12:35 – 37). By Moses (Nu 27:12 – 23); by David (1Ki 2:1 – 10); by Ahithophel (2Sa 17:23). Apostrophe to (Hos 13:14; 1Co 15:55).

DEATH PENALTY

Reasons for Infliction according to Mosaic Law:

Murder (Ge 9:5 – 6; Nu 35:16 – 21, 30 – 33; Dt 17:6); adultery (Lev 20:10; Dt 22:24); incest (Lev 20:11 – 12, 14); bestiality (Ex 22:19; Lev 20:15 – 16); sodomy (Lev 18:22; 20:13); rape of a betrothed virgin (Dt 22:25); perjury (Zec 5:4); kidnapping (Ex 21:16; Dt 24:7); immorality committed by a priest's daughter (Lev 21:9); witchcraft (Ex 22:18); offering human sacrifice (Lev 20:2 – 5); striking or cursing father or mother (Ex 21:15, 17; Lev 20:9); disobedience to parents (Dt 21:18 – 21); theft (Zec 5:3 – 4); blasphemy (Lev 24:23); Sabbath desecration (Ex 35:2; Nu 15:32 – 36); prophesying falsely or propagating false doctrines (Dt 13:10); sacrificing to false gods (Ex 22:20); refusing to abide by the decision of the court (Dt 17:12); treason (1Ki 2:25; Est 2:23); sedition (Ac 5:36 – 37). Shall not be remitted (Nu 35:31). Not inflicted on the testimony of fewer than two witnesses (Nu 35:30; Dt 17:6; 19:15).

Modes of Execution:

Burning (Ge 38:24; Lev 20:14; 21:9; Jer 29:22; Eze 23:25; Da 3:19 – 23); stoning (Lev 20:2, 27; Nu 14:10; 15:33 – 36; Dt 13:10; 17:5; 22:21, 24; Jos 7:25; 1Ki 21:10; Eze 16:40); hanging (Ge 40:22; Dt 21:22 – 23; Jos 8:29; Est 7:10); beheading (Mt 14:10; Mk 6:16, 27 – 28); crucifixion (Mt 27:35, 38; Mk 15:24, 27; Lk 23:33); the sword (Ex 32:27 – 28; 1Ki 2:25, 34, 46; Ac 12:2). Executed by: the witnesses (Dt 13:9; 17:7; Ac 7:58); the congregation (Nu 15:35 – 36; Dt 13:9).

DEBAUCHERY

Ro	13:13	not in sexual immorality and **d**,
2Co	12:21	and **d** in which they have indulged.
Gal	5:19	impurity and **d**; idolatry
Eph	5:18	drunk on wine, which leads to **d**.
1Pe	4:3	living in **d**, lust, drunkenness,

DEBORAH [1806] (*hornet, wasp, wild honeybee*).

1. A nurse to Rebekah (Ge 24:59). Buried beneath an oak below Bethel (Ge 35:8).

2. The prophetess, a judge of Israel (Jdg 4:4 – 5; 5:7) who inspired Barak to defeat Sisera (Jdg 4:6 – 16).

DEBT [2471, 4200+5957, 5391, 5963, 9024, 9023, 625, 1245, 4051, 4052, 4053] (Heb. *neshî*, Gr. *opheilema, a sum owed, an obligation*). Under Mosaic law Jews were not allowed to exact interest (usury) from other Jews (Ex 22:25) and special laws protected the poor against usurers (22:25 – 27; Dt 24:12 – 13). After the exile cruel practices arose in collecting debts (2Ki 4:1 – 7; Isa 50:1). A debtor had to make good his obligation, or land that was pledged (mortgaged) could be seized but had to be restored during the Jubilee year (Lev 25:28). A house so pledged could be sold, or held in perpetuity if not redeemed during a year, unless it was in an unwalled town (25:29 – 30). Warnings were given against becoming a guarantor for others (Pr 11:15; 22:26). In NT times the Mosaic code was disregarded. We read of bankers, money changers, interest, usury (Mt 25:16 – 27; Jn 2:13 – 17). Debtors were often thrown into prison (Mt 18:21 – 26). Jesus taught compassion toward those in debt (18:23 – 35). The prayer of Jesus, "Forgive us our debts" (6:12), implies guilt from unpaid moral obligations to God. Paul taught against debt in Ro 13:8.

Dt	15:3	must cancel any **d** your brother
Job	24:9	of the poor is seized for a **d**.
Mt	18:25	that he had be sold to repay the **d**.
	18:27	canceled the **d** and let him go.
Lk	7:43	who had the bigger **d** canceled."
Ro	13:8	Let no **d** remain outstanding,
	13:8	continuing **d** to love one another,

DEBTOR [5967, 4050, 5971].

Laws concerning (Ex 21:2 – 6; 22:10 – 15; Lev 25:14 – 17, 25 – 41, 47 – 55; Dt 24:10 – 13; Ne 10:31; Mt 5:25 – 26, 40; 18:25). Sold for debt (2Ki 4:1 – 7; Ne 5:3 – 5; Mt 18:25). Imprisoned for debt (Mt 18:30). Oppressed (2Ki 4:1 – 7; Ne 5:3 – 5; Job 20:18 – 19; Mt 18:28 – 30). Mercy toward, commanded (Mt 18:23 – 27). Wicked (Lk 20:9 – 16).

Mt	6:12	as we also have forgiven our **d**.

DEBTS [DEBT]

Dt	15:1	seven years you must cancel **d**.
	15:2	time for canceling **d** has been
2Ki	4:7	"Go, sell the oil and pay your **d**.
Ne	10:31	the land and will cancel all **d**.
Pr	22:26	or puts up security for **d**;
Mt	6:12	Forgive us our **d**,

DECALOGUE (*ten words*). Written by God (Ex 24:12; 31:18; 32:16; Dt 5:22; 9:10; Hos 8:12). Divine authority of (Ex 20:1; 34:27 – 28; Dt 5:4 – 22). Called: words of the covenant (Ex 34:28; Dt 4:13); tablets of the covenant (Ex 31:18; 34:29; 40:20). Listed (Ex 20:1 – 17; Dt 5:6 – 21). Confirmed: by Jesus (Mt 19:18 – 19; 22:34 – 40; Lk 10:25 – 28); by Paul (Ro 13:8 – 10). *See Commandments and Statutes, of God.*

DECREE [1819, 1821, 2976, 2978, 3076, 4180, 7422, 7756, 10057, 10186, 10302, 1504]. An official ruling or law. It translates various OT words such as *'esar,* "interdict" (Da 6:7); *gezerah,* "decision" (4:17); *dath,* "law" (2:9). In general it refers to any pronouncement of an official nature. In Est 1:20; Da 3:10; and Jnh 3:7, the word refers to laws governing special occasions. In Ac 16:4 the Greek *dogma* means rules for Christian living. God's decree is his settled plan and purpose (Ps 2:7 – 10; Da 4:24; see also Ex 32:32; Rev 13:8).

DEDICATION, FEAST OF An annual festival of the Jews held throughout the country for eight days, celebrating the restoration of the temple following its desecration at the hands of the Syrians under Antiochus Epiphanes (1Mc 4:52 – 59; 2Mc 10:5), of which Josephus gives a graphic picture (*Antiq.* 12.5.4). The feast came on the twenty-fifth of Kislev (December). Josephus called it the Feast of Lights. Like the Feast of Tabernacles, it was a time of pageantry and joy. It was at this feast that Jesus delivered the temple discourse recorded in Jn 10:22ff.

DEFILE A number of Hebrew and Greek words mean in general "to profane, pollute, render unclean." In the OT defilement was physical (SS 5:3), sexual (Lev 18:20), ethical (Isa 59:3; Eze 37:23), ceremonial (Lev 11:24, 17:15), and religious (Nu 35:33; Jer 3:1). In the NT it is ethical or religious (Mk 7:19; Ac 10:15; Ro 14:20). In the NT the idea of ceremonial or ritual defilement does not exist. In OT times God's purpose in issuing laws regarding ceremonial defilement was clearly an educative one — to impress the Israelites with his holiness and the necessity of their living separate and holy lives.

| Da | 1:8 | Daniel resolved not to **d** himself |
| Rev | 14:4 | are those who did not **d** themselves |

DELILAH [1935] (dē-lī'la, *dainty one or tease*). A Philistine woman from the Valley of Sorek, which extends from near Jerusalem to the Mediterranean. By her seductive wiles she learned the secret of Samson's strength and brought him to his ruin (Jdg 16:4 – 20).

DEMAS [1318] (dē'măs, Gr. *Demmas, popular*). A faithful helper of Paul during his imprisonment in Rome (Col 4:14). Paul called him a "fellow worker" (Phm 24) and was probably a citizen of Thessalonica, where he went when he deserted Paul (2Ti 4:10).

DEMONS [8717, 794, 1227, 1228, 1230] (Gr. *daimonia*). Evil spirits (Mt 8:16; Lk 10:17, 20; cf. Mt 17:18 and Mk 9:25). The immaterial and incorporeal nature of both Satan and his demon hosts is graphically set forth by the apostle Paul when he describes the believer's intense conflict as being "not against flesh and blood" but against "rulers," "authorities," "powers of this dark world," and "spiritual forces of evil in the heavenly realms" (Eph 6:12).

As purely spiritual beings or personalities, demons operate above the laws of the natural realm and are invisible. As spirit personalities, demons have an intellectual nature through which they possess superhuman knowledge. Scripture features the shrewdness of demons. They know Jesus (Mk 1:24), bow to him (5:6), describe him as "the Son of the Most High God" (5:7), entreat him (Lk 8:31), obey him (Mt 8:16), corrupt sound doctrine (1Ti 4:1 – 5), conceal the truth of Christ's incarnate deity and sole saviorhood (1Jn 4:1 – 3), and comprehend prophecy and their inevitable doom (Mt 8:29).

Because of their superhuman knowledge, demons are consulted by spiritistic mediums, who allow themselves to come under the control of evil spirits for oracular purposes (1Sa 28:1 – 25; Ac 16:16), as is seen in both ancient and modern spiritism, erroneously called "spiritualism."

In their moral nature all demons (as fallen angels) are evil and depraved, in distinction to the good spirits (the unfallen angels), who are sinless. The moral depravity of demons is everywhere evidenced in Scripture by the harmful effects they produce in their victims, deranging them mentally, morally, physically, and spiritually, and by the frequent epithet of "unclean," which often describes them (Mt 10:1; Mk 1:27; Lk 4:36; Ac 8:7; Rev 16:13 KJV; NIV renders "evil"). Fleshly uncleanness and base sensual gratification are the result of demon control of the human personality (Lk 8:27). Demons figure in the moral collapse of a people who yield to gross carnality and sexual sin, so rampant in the world today (2Ti 3:1 – 9; Rev 9:21 – 22).

In addition to their superhuman intelligence and moral depravity, demons possess terrible physical strength, imparting it to the human body (Lk 8:29) and binding their victims as with chains and with physical defects and deformities (Lk 13:11 – 17) such as blindness (Mt 12:22), insanity (8:26 – 36), dumbness (Mt 9:32 – 33), and suicidal mania (Mk 9:22).

Demons under the leadership of Satan seek to oppose God's purposes and to hinder man's welfare. Demons are of two classes — those who are free with the earth and the air as their abode (Eph 2:2; 6:11 – 12; Col 1:13) and those who are imprisoned in the Abyss (Lk 8:31; Rev 9:1 – 11; 20:1 – 3). The Abyss is only the temporary prison house of evil spirits, which must surrender its doleful inhabitants to Gehenna or the "lake of fire" (Mt 25:41), the eternal abode of Satan, demons, and unsaved human beings.

General References to:

Worship of (Lev 17:7; Dt 32:17; 2Ch 11:15; Ps 106:37; Mt 4:9; Lk 4:7; 1Co 10:20 – 21; 1Ti 4:1; Rev 13:4). Worship of, forbidden (Lev 17:7; Zec 13:2; Rev 9:20). Testify to the deity of Jesus (Mt 8:29; Mk 1:23 – 24; 3:11; 5:7; Lk 8:28; Ac 19:15). Adversaries of humans (Mt 12:45). Sent to cause trouble between Abimelech and the Shechemites (Jdg 9:23). Messages given false prophets by (1Ki 22:21 – 23). Believe and tremble (Jas 2:19). To be judged at the general judgment (Mt 8:29, w 2Pe 2:4; Jude 6). Punishment of (Mt 8:29; 25:41; Lk 8:28; 2Pe 2:4; Jude 6; Rev 12:7 – 9).

Possession by:

Instances of: Saul (1Sa 16:14 – 23; 18:10 – 11; 19:9 – 10); two men of the Gadarenes (Mt 8:28 – 34; Mk 5:2 – 20); mute man (Mt 9:32 – 33); blind and mute man (Mt 12:22; Lk 11:14); daughter of the Syrian Phoenician (Mt 15:22 – 29; Mk 7:25 – 30); child with seizures (Mt 17:14 – 18; Mk 9:17 – 27; Lk 9:37 – 42); man in the synagogue (Mk 1:23 – 26; Lk 4:33 – 35); Mary Magdalene (Mk 16:9; Lk 8:2 – 3); herd of pigs (Mt 8:30 – 32). Jesus falsely accused of being possessed of (Mk 3:22 – 30; Jn 7:20; 8:48; 10:20).

Exorcised:

Cast out: by Jesus (Mt 4:24; 8:16; Mk 3:22; Lk 4:41); by the disciples (Mk 9:38; Lk 10:17); by Peter (Ac 5:16); by Paul (Ac 16:16 – 18; 19:12); by Philip (Ac 8:7). Power over, given to disciples (Mt 10:1; Mk 6:7; 16:17). Disciples could not expel (Mk 9:18, 28 – 29). Sceva's sons exorcise (Ac 19:13 – 16). Parable of man repossessed (Mt 12:43 – 45). See Devil; Satan.

Mt	9:33	And when the **d** was driven out,
	17:18	Jesus rebuked the **d**, and it came
Mk	7:26	to drive the **d** out of her daughter.
Lk	4:33	there was a man possessed by a **d**,
	4:35	Then the **d** threw the man
	7:33	wine, and you say, 'He has a **d**.'
	8:29	driven by the **d** into solitary places.
	9:42	the **d** threw him to the ground
	11:14	When the **d** left, the man who had
Jn	8:49	"I am not possessed by a **d**,"
	10:21	Can a **d** open the eyes of the blind

DEMON-POSSESSED

Mt	4:24	those suffering severe pain, the **d**,
	8:16	many who were **d** were brought
	8:28	two **d** men coming
	9:32	man who was **d** and could not talk
	12:22	they brought him a **d** man who was
Mk	1:32	brought to Jesus all the sick and **d**.
	5:16	what had happened to the **d** man —
Lk	8:27	met by a **d** man from the town.
	8:36	the people how the **d** man had been
Jn	7:20	"You are **d**," the crowd answered.
	8:48	that you are a Samaritan and **d**?"
	10:20	Many of them said, "He is **d**
Ac	19:13	Jesus over those who were **d**.

DEMONS [DEMON]

Dt	32:17	to **d**, which are not God —
Ps	106:37	and their daughters to **d**.
Mt	7:22	and in your name drive out **d**
	9:34	prince of **d** that he drives out **d**."
	10:8	who have leprosy, drive out **d**.
	12:27	And if I drive out **d** by Beelzebub,
Mk	1:34	He also drove out many **d**,
	1:39	their synagogues and driving out **d**.
	3:15	to have authority to drive out **d**.
	6:13	They drove out many **d**
	9:38	"we saw a man driving out **d**
	16:9	out of whom he had driven seven **d**
	16:17	In my name they will drive out **d**;
Lk	4:41	**d** came out of many people,

	8:30	because many **d** had gone into him.
	9:1	and authority to drive out all **d**
	9:49	"we saw a man driving out **d**
	10:17	the **d** submit to us in your name."
	13:32	'I will drive out **d** and heal people
Ro	8:38	neither angels nor **d**, neither
1Co	10:20	of pagans are offered to **d**,
1Ti	4:1	spirits and things taught by **d**.
Jas	2:19	Good! Even the **d** believe that —
Rev	9:20	they did not stop worshiping **d**,
	16:14	of **d** performing miraculous signs,
	18:2	She has become a home for **d**

DENY

Job	27:5	till I die, I will not **d** my integrity.
Isa	5:23	but **d** justice to the innocent.
Am	2:7	and **d** justice to the oppressed.
Mt	16:24	he must **d** himself and take up his
Mk	8:34	he must **d** himself and take up his
Lk	9:23	he must **d** himself and take up his
	22:34	you will **d** three times that you
Tit	1:16	but by their actions they **d** him.
Jude	1:4	**d** Jesus Christ our only Sovereign

DEPRAVED [DEPRAVITY]

Eze	16:47	ways you soon became more **d**
	23:11	and prostitution she was more **d**
Ro	1:28	he gave them over to a **d** mind,
Php	2:15	fault in a crooked and **d** generation,
2Ti	3:8	oppose the truth — men of **d** minds,

DEPRAVITY [8845, 99, 1406, 2967, 2798, 5785].

In the Nature of Humanity:
(Ge 6:5 – 8; 8:21; Job 4:17 – 19; 9:2 – 3, 20, 29 – 31; 11:12; 14:4; 15:14 – 16; 25:4 – 6; Pss 5:9; 51:5; 58:1 – 5; 94:11; 130:3; Pr 10:20; 20:6, 9; 21:8; Isa 1:5 – 6; 51:1; Jer 13:23; 16:12; 17:9; Hos 6:7; Mic 7:2 – 4; Mt 7:17; 12:34 – 35; 15:19; Mk 7:21 – 23; Jn 3:19; 8:23; 14:17; Ro 1:21 – 32; 2:1; 6:6, 19 – 20; 7:5, 11 – 15, 18 – 25; 8:5 – 8, 13; 1Co 2:14; 3:3; 5:9 – 10; 2Co 5:14; Gal 5:17, 19 – 21; Eph 2:1 – 3,

12; 4:17 – 19, 22; Jas 4:5; 1Pe 1:18; 2:25; 1Jn 1:8, 10; 2:16).

Universal:
(Ge 6:11 – 13; 2Ch 6:36; Pss 14:1 – 3; 53:1 – 3; 143:2; Ecc 7:20; Isa 53:6; 64:6; Mic 7:2 – 4; Ro 3:9 – 19, 23; 5:6, 12 – 14; 11:32; Gal 3:10 – 11, 22; Jas 3:2; 1Jn 5:19)

Ro	1:29	of wickedness, evil, greed and **d**.
2Pe	2:19	they themselves are slaves of **d** —

DESIRE [DESIRES]

Ge	3:16	Your **d** will be for your husband,
1Ch	29:18	keep this **d** in the hearts
2Ch	1:11	"Since this is your heart's **d**
Ps	10:17	O LORD, the **d** of the afflicted;
	20:4	May he give you the **d**
	40:8	I **d** to do your will, O my God;
	73:25	earth has nothing I **d** besides you
Pr	3:15	nothing you **d** can compare
Ecc	12:5	and **d** no longer is stirred.
Isa	26:8	are the **d** of our hearts.
	53:2	appearance that we should **d** him.
	55:11	but will accomplish what I **d**
Hos	6:6	For I **d** mercy, not sacrifice,
Mt	9:13	learn what this means: 'I **d** mercy,
Jn	8:44	want to carry out your father's **d**.
Ro	7:18	For I have the **d** to do what is good,
1Co	12:31	But eagerly **d** the greater gifts.
	14:1	and eagerly **d** spiritual gifts,
Php	1:23	I **d** to depart and be with Christ,
Heb	10:5	Sacrifice and offering you did not **d**
Jas	1:14	by his own evil **d**, he is dragged
	1:15	Then, after **d** has conceived,

DESIRE, SPIRITUAL [203, 2094, 2773, 2775, 2911, 2913, 2914, 5883, 8356, 9294, 9592, 2121, 2123, 2420, 2527].

For divine piety (Pss 17:11; 51:1 – 4, 7 – 13; 119:82; Hab 3:2). For divine fellowship (Pss 62:1; 63:1, 8). For divine help (Pss 25:5, 15; 68:28; 119:77, 116 – 117). Exhortations concerning (Pss 70:4; 105:4; Isa 55:1 – 2; 55:3, 6; Hos 10:12). For God

(Pss 24:6; 27:8; 33:20; 40:1; 42:1 – 11; 69:3; 73:26; 119:10, 12, 19 – 20, 25, 40, 81, 88, 123, 131 – 132, 135 – 136, 149, 156, 174; 123:1 – 2; 130:5 – 6; 143:6 – 12; Isa 8:17, 19; 26:8 – 9; Mt 13:17; Lk 10:42; Php 3:12 – 14; 1Pe 1:10). For his holy courts (Ps 84:2). Reward of (Dt 4:29; Pss 34:10; 37:4, 9, 34; 107:9; 119:2; Pr 2:3 – 5; Isa 40:31; Jer 29:13; Mt 5:6; Lk 1:53; 6:21; Jn 6:35; Heb 11:6).

DESIRES [DESIRE]

Ge	4:7	at your door; it **d** to have you,
1Ki	11:37	rule over all that your heart **d**;
Job	17:11	and so are the **d** of my heart.
Ps	37:4	he will give you the **d** of your heart.
	103:5	who satisfies your **d** with good things,
	145:19	He fulfills the **d** of those who fear
Ecc	6:2	so that he lacks nothing his heart **d**,
SS	2:7	or awaken love until it so **d**.
Ro	1:24	over in the sinful **d** of their hearts
	6:12	body so that you obey its evil **d**.
	8:5	set on what that nature **d**;
Gal	5:16	and you will not gratify the **d**
Eph	2:3	and following its **d** and thoughts.
	4:22	being corrupted by its deceitful **d**;
1Ti	3:1	an overseer, he **d** a noble task.
	5:11	their sensual **d** overcome their
	6:9	and harmful **d** that plunge men
2Ti	2:22	Flee the evil **d** of youth,
Jas	1:20	about the righteous life that God **d**.
	4:1	from your **d** that battle within you?
1Pe	1:14	conform to the evil **d** you had
	2:11	to abstain from sinful **d**, which war
2Pe	1:4	in the world caused by evil **d**.
1Jn	2:17	The world and its **d** pass away,
Jude	1:16	they follow their own evil **d**;

DEUTERONOMY (dū-tĕr-ŏn′o-mē, Gr. *Deuteronomion, second law*). In sight of the Promise Land, which he would not be allowed to enter, Moses gathered the hosts of Israel about him for his farewell addresses. These, set within the historical framework of several brief narrative passages, constitute the book of Deu-

teronomy. Since the occasion of the renewal of the covenant made earlier at Sinai, the appropriate documentary pattern for covenant ratification supplied the pattern for Moses' speeches and thus for the book.

The English title is unfortunate, being based on the LXX's mistranslation of the phrase "a copy of this law" (Dt 17:18) as *to deuteronomion touto*, "this second law." The Jewish name *debam r̂m*, "words," derives from the opening expression, "These are the words Moses spoke" (1:1). This title is well-suited because it focuses attention on a clue to the peculiar literary character of the book; the treaties imposed by ancient imperial lords on their vassals began with such an expression. Deuteronomy is the text of "words" of a suzerainty covenant made by the Lord of heaven through the mediatorship of Moses with the servant people Israel beyond the Jordan.

The claims of Deuteronomy concerning its own authorship are plain. It consists almost entirely of the farewell speeches of Moses addressed to the new generation that had grown to manhood in the wilderness.

Outline

    I. Preamble: Covenant Mediator (1:1 – 5).
    II. Historical Prologue: Covenant History (1:6 – 4:49).
    III. Stipulations: Covenant Life (chs. 5 – 26).
    IV. Curses and Blessings: Covenant Ratification (chs. 27 – 30).
    V. Succession Arrangements: Covenant Continuity (chs. 31 – 34).

In Dt 1:1 – 5 the speaker is identified as Moses, the Lord's representative. Deuteronomy 1:6 – 4:49 is a rehearsal of God's past covenantal dealings with Israel from Horeb to Moab and serves to awaken reverence and gratitude as motives for renewed consecration. With 5:26 it is made clear that when covenants were renewed the former obligations were repeated and brought up to date. Thus chs. 5 – 11 review the Decalogue with its primary obligation of fidelity to Yahweh, while chs. 12 – 26 in considerable measure renew the stipulations of the book of the covenant (Ex 21 – 33) and other Sinaitic legislation, adapting where necessary to the new conditions awaiting Israel in Canaan. In chs. 27 – 30 directions are first given for the future and final act in this covenant renewal to be conducted by Joshua in Canaan (ch. 27). Moses then pronounces the blessings and curses as reasons for Israel's immediate ratification of the covenant, but also as a prophecy of Israel's future down to its ultimate exile and restoration (chs. 28 – 30). In chs. 31 – 34 preparations are made for the continuity of leadership through the succession of Joshua and for the continuing confrontation of Israel with the way of the covenant by periodic reading of the covenant document, which was to be deposited in the sanctuary, and by a prophetic song of covenant witness (chs. 31 – 32). The book ends with the final blessings and the death of Moses (chs. 33 – 34).

The similarity between the style of Deuteronomy and that of international suzerainty treaties is well worth noting. Deuteronomy is the Bible's full-scale exposition of the covenant concept and demonstrates that, far from being a contract between two parties, God's covenant with his people is a proclamation of his sovereignty and an instrument for binding his elect to himself in a commitment of absolute allegiance.

The covenant relation called for responsible decision: "This day I call heaven and earth as witnesses against you that I have set before you life and death, blessings and curses. Now choose life, so that you and your children may live and that you may love the LORD your God.... For the LORD is your life" (30:19 – 20).

DEVIL [1229, 1333] (Gr. *diabolos, slanderer or liar*). One of the principal titles of Satan, the archenemy of God and of man. In the NT the word refers to Satan thirty-five times. The KJV uses the same word about sixty times to render the Greek *daimonion*, which the ASV and NIV translate as "demon." Three times the word *diabolos* is used for ill-natured persons, or "slanderers" (1Ti 3:11; 2Ti 3:3; Tit 2:3); in the KJV the last two of these passages have "false accusers." The

plural word "devils" occurs four times in the OT (KJV) — twice representing *sa'îrim*, which means "he-goats" (Lev 17:7; 2Ch 11:15), and twice translating *shemdîm*, or "demons" (Dt 32:17; Ps 106:37). (Cf. NIV for these four renderings.) The LXX renders "Satan" in the OT as *diabolos* (i.e., "devil"), but the Vulgate and the English versions rightly have "Satan" as the proper name. According to Nu 22:22, the angel of the Lord stood in the way as an adversary (Heb. *Satan*) to the mad prophet Balaam, but generally the word is used in the bad sense.

How did Satan originate? The story of the beginning of sin is nowhere related explicitly in the Word; but certain passages seem to hint so strongly, that the following theory has long been held to explain them.

Apparently God first peopled the universe, or at least our part of it, with a hierarchy of holy angels, of whom one of the highest orders was (or contained) the cherubim. One of them, perhaps the highest of all, was "anointed as a guardian cherub" (Eze 28:14), who was created beautiful and perfect in his ways. This cherub knew that he was beautiful, but pride entered his heart and the first sin in the whole history of eternity occurred. Pride led to self-will (Isa 14:13 – 14) and self-will to rebellion. This great cherub became the adversary ("Satan") of God and apparently led other angels into rebellion (cf. 2Pe 2:4; Jude 6). God then created humans in his own image (innocent but with the possibility of becoming holy on condition of obedience). Because Satan already hated God, he hated humans whom God loved and tried to destroy them. It is evident that God could have destroyed Satan at the moment that he became "Satan," but God has tolerated him these many centuries and has used him for testing people until the days of testing will be over. Then Satan and all the other enemies of God will be cast into the "lake of burning sulfur" (Rev 20:10, 15). In the age-long (though not eternal) conflict between good and evil, it sometimes seems as though God has given Satan every advantage. Even so, God's victory is certain.

| Mt | 4:1 | the desert to be tempted by the **d**. |
| | 13:39 | the enemy who sows them is the **d**. |

	25:41	the eternal fire prepared for the **d**
Lk	4:2	forty days he was tempted by the **d**.
	8:12	then the **d** comes and takes away
Jn	6:70	of you is a **d**!" (He meant Judas,
	8:44	You belong to your father, the **d**,
	13:2	the **d** had already prompted Judas
Ac	10:38	were under the power of the **d**,
	13:10	"You are a child of the **d**
Eph	4:27	and do not give the **d** a foothold.
1Ti	3:6	under the same judgment as the **d**.
2Ti	2:26	and escape from the trap of the **d**,
Heb	2:14	holds the power of death — that is, the **d**
Jas	4:7	Resist the **d**, and he will flee
1Pe	5:8	Your enemy the **d** prowls
1Jn	3:8	because the **d** has been sinning
	3:8	who does what is sinful is of the **d**,
	3:10	and who the children of the **d** are:
Jude	1:9	with the **d** about the body of Moses
Rev	2:10	the **d** will put some of you in prison
	12:9	that ancient serpent called the **d**
	12:12	the **d** has gone down to you!
	20:2	that ancient serpent, who is the **d**,
	20:10	And the **d**, who deceived them,

DEVIL'S [DEVIL]

Eph	6:11	stand against the **d** schemes.
1Ti	3:7	into disgrace and into the **d** trap.
1Jn	3:8	was to destroy the **d** work.

DEVOTE [DEVOTED, DEVOTION]

1Ch	22:19	Now **d** your heart and soul
2Ch	31:4	Levites so they could **d** themselves
Col	4:2	**D** yourselves to prayer, being
1Ti	1:4	nor to **d** themselves to myths
	4:13	**d** yourself to the public reading
Tit	3:8	may be careful to **d** themselves
	3:14	people must learn to **d** themselves

DEVOTED [DEVOTE]

1Ki	11:4	and his heart was not fully **d**
Ezr	7:10	For Ezra had **d** himself to the study
Ps	86:2	Guard my life, for I am **d** to you.

Mt	6:24	or he will be **d** to the one
Ac	2:42	They **d** themselves
Ro	12:10	Be **d** to one another

DEVOTION [DEVOTE]

2Ki	20:3	and with wholehearted **d** and have
1Ch	28:9	and serve him with wholehearted **d**
	29:19	son Solomon the wholehearted **d**
2Ch	32:32	and his acts of **d** are written
Isa	38:3	and with wholehearted **d** and have
Jer	2:2	" 'I remember the **d** of your youth,
Eze	33:31	With their mouths they express **d**,
1Co	7:35	way in undivided **d** to the Lord.
2Co	11:3	from your sincere and pure **d**

DIE [DIED]

Ge	2:17	when you eat of it you will surely **d**
	3:3	you must not touch it, or you will **d**
Ex	11:5	Every firstborn son in Egypt will **d**,
Ru	1:17	Where you **d** I will **d**, and there I
2Ki	14:6	each is to **d** for his own sins."
Job	2:9	Curse God and **d**!" He replied,
Pr	5:23	He will **d** for lack of discipline,
	10:21	but fools **d** for lack of judgment.
	15:10	he who hates correction will **d**.
	23:13	with the rod, he will not **d**.
Ecc	3:2	a time to be born and a time to **d**,
Mt	26:52	"for all who draw the sword will **d**
Jn	8:21	and you will **d** in your sin.
	11:26	and believes in me will never **d**.
Ro	5:7	Very rarely will anyone **d**
	14:8	and if we **d**, we **d** to the Lord.
1Co	15:22	in Adam all **d**, so in Christ all will
	15:32	for tomorrow we **d**."
Php	1:21	to live is Christ and to **d** is gain.
Heb	9:27	Just as man is destined to **d** once,
1Pe	2:24	so that we might **d** to sins
Rev	14:13	Blessed are the dead who **d**

DIED [DIE]

1Ki	16:18	So he **d**, because of the sins he had
1Ch	10:13	Saul **d** because he was unfaithful
Lk	16:22	"The time came when the beggar **d**

Ro	5:6	we were still powerless, Christ **d**
	5:8	we were still sinners, Christ **d**
	6:2	By no means! We **d** to sin;
	6:7	anyone who has **d** has been freed
	6:8	if we **d** with Christ, we believe that
	6:10	The death he **d**, he **d** to sin once
	14:9	Christ **d** and returned to life
	14:15	brother for whom Christ **d**.
2Co	5:14	**d** for all, and therefore all **d**.
	5:15	he **d** for all, that those who live
Col	2:20	Since you **d** with Christ
1Th	4:14	We believe that Jesus **d**
	5:10	He **d** for us so that, whether we are
2Ti	2:11	If we **d** with him,
Heb	9:15	now that he has **d** as a ransom
1Pe	3:18	For Christ **d** for sins once for all,
Rev	2:8	who **d** and came to life again.

DISCIPLE [1201, 4341, 899, 3411, 3412, 3413, 5209] (Gr. *mathemtems*, *a learner* or *student*). A pupil of some teacher. The word implies the acceptance in mind and life of the views and practices of the teacher. In the NT it means, in the widest sense, those who accept the teachings of anyone — like the disciples of John the Baptist (Mt 9:14), the Pharisees (22:16), Moses (Jn 9:28). Usually, however, it refers to the adherents of Jesus. Sometimes it refers to the twelve apostles (e.g., Mt 10:1; 11:1), but more often simply to Christians (Ac 6:1 – 2, 7; 9:36). Followers of Jesus were not called "Christians" until the founding of the church at Antioch (11:26).

Disciple of: John the Baptist (Mt 9:14); the Pharisees (Lk 5:33); Jesus (Mt 10:1; 20:17; Ac 9:26; 14:20; 21:4). The Seventy sent forth (Lk 10:1). First called Christians at Antioch (Ac 11:26).

Mt	10:42	these little ones because he is my **d**,
Lk	14:26	his own life — he cannot be my **d**.
	14:27	and follow me cannot be my **d**.
	14:33	everything he has cannot be my **d**.
Jn	13:23	of them, the **d** whom Jesus loved,

DISCIPLES [DISCIPLE]

Mt	10:1	He called his twelve **d** to him
	26:56	Then all the **d** deserted him
	28:19	Therefore go and make **d**
Mk	3:7	withdrew with his **d** to the lake,
	16:20	Then the **d** went out and preached
Jn	2:11	and his **d** put their faith in him.
	6:66	many of his **d** turned back
	8:31	to my teaching, you are really my **d**
	13:35	men will know that you are my **d**
	15:8	showing yourselves to be my **d**.
Ac	6:1	the number of **d** was increasing,
	11:26	The **d** were called Christians first

DISCIPLINE [DISCIPLINES]

Job	5:17	so do not despise the **d**
Ps	6:1	or **d** me in your wrath.
	39:11	You rebuke and **d** men for their sin;
	94:12	Blessed is the man you **d**, O LORD
Pr	1:2	for attaining wisdom and **d**;
	1:7	but fools despise wisdom and **d**.
	3:11	do not despise the LORD's **d**
	5:23	He will die for lack of **d**,
	10:17	He who heeds **d** shows the way
	12:1	Whoever loves **d** loves knowledge,
	13:18	He who ignores **d** comes to poverty
	13:24	who loves him is careful to **d** him.
	15:5	A fool spurns his father's **d**,
	15:32	He who ignores **d** despises himself,
	22:15	the rod of **d** will drive it far
	23:13	Do not withhold **d** from a child;
Jer	30:11	I will **d** you but only with justice;
Heb	12:5	do not make light of the Lord's **d**,
Rev	3:19	Those whom I love I rebuke and **d**.

DISCIPLINES [DISCIPLINE]

Dt	8:5	so the LORD your God **d** you.
Pr	3:12	the LORD **d** those he loves,
Heb	12:6	because the Lord **d** those he loves,

DISHONEST

| Ex | 18:21 | trustworthy men who hate **d** gain |

193

Lev	19:35	"'Do not use **d** standards
Pr	11:1	The Lord abhors **d** scales,
	13:11	**D** money dwindles away,
Lk	16:8	master commended the **d** manager
	16:10	whoever is **d** with very little will
1Ti	3:8	wine, and not pursuing **d** gain.
Tit	1:7	not violent, not pursuing **d** gain.

DISHONESTY [1299, 2039, 5327, 6404, 8400, 94, 96, 153, 156].

> *In not paying debts (Ps 37:12, 21; Jas 5:4). In collusion with thieves (Ps 50:18). In wicked devices for gain (Job 24:2 – 11; Pr 1:10 – 14; 20:14; Isa 32:7; Jer 22:13; Eze 22:29; Hos 12:7; Am 3:10; 8:5; Mic 6:10 – 11). Denounced (Jer 7:8 – 10; 9:4 – 6; 9:8; Hos 4:1 – 2; Na 3:1). Forbidden (Lev 19:13, 35 – 36; Dt 25:13 – 16; Ps 62:10; Pr 3:27 – 28; 11:1; 20:10, 23; 1Th 4:6). Penalties for (Lev 6:2 – 7; Pr 20:17; Zep 1:9; Zec 5:3 – 4). Parable concerning (Lk 16:1 – 8).*

DISOBEDIENCE [DISOBEY]

Jos	22:22	in rebellion or **d** to the Lord,
Jer	43:7	So they entered Egypt in **d**
Ro	5:19	as through the **d** of the one man
	11:30	mercy as a result of their **d**,
	11:32	to **d** so that he may have mercy
2Co	10:6	ready to punish every act of **d**,
Heb	2:2	and **d** received its just punishment,
	4:6	go in, because of their **d**.
	4:11	fall by following their example of **d**.

DISOBEDIENCE TO GOD [4202+9048, 5286, 6296, 577, 578, 579, 4157].

> *Originated in Adam (Ro 5:19). Characteristic of all (Ro 1:32; Eph 2:2; 5:6; Col 3:6; Tit 1:16; 3:3; Heb 2:2; 1Pe 2:8). Temptation to (Ge 3:1 – 5). Denunciations against (Nu 14:11 – 12, 22 – 23; 32:8 – 13; Dt 18:19).*

DISOBEDIENT [DISOBEY]

Ne	9:26	"But they were **d** and rebelled

Lk	1:17	and the **d** to the wisdom
Ac	26:19	I was not **d** to the vision
Ro	10:21	hands to a **d** and obstinate people."
	11:30	as you who were at one time **d**
Eph	2:2	now at work in those who are **d**.
	5:6	comes on those who are **d**.
	5:12	to mention what the **d** do in secret.
2Ti	3:2	proud, abusive, **d** to their parents,
Tit	1:6	to the charge of being wild and **d**.
	1:16	**d** and unfit for doing anything
	3:3	At one time we too were foolish, **d**,
Heb	11:31	killed with those who were **d**.

DISOBEY

Dt	11:28	the curse if you **d** the commands
2Ch	24:20	'Why do you **d** the Lord's
Jer	42:13	and so **d** the Lord your God,
Ro	1:30	they **d** their parents; they are

DISPENSATION (*law or arrangement of a house*). The Greek word *oikonomia* means management or administration of a job or trust (Lk 16:2 – 4; 1Co 9:17; Eph 1:10; 3:2, 9; Col 1:25; 1Ti 1:4).

DISPENSATIONS An era of time during which humankind's obedience to God is tested according to the revelation of God available to him. From two dispensations (or covenants) to seven (innocence, conscience, human government, promise, law, grace, the kingdom) are views held by various schools of interpretation.

DIVIDING WALL [3546]. The barrier between the Court of the Gentiles and the Court of the Jews in the temple in Jerusalem. For a Gentile to go beyond it meant death (Josephus, *Antiq.* 15.11.5). The breaking down of this wall is used figuratively of Christ bringing Jews and Gentiles together as one in the church (Eph 2:14).

DIVINATION [5241, 5727, 6726, 7876, 7877, 10140]. The practice of foreseeing or foretelling future events or discovering hidden knowledge; forbidden to Jews (Lev 19:26; Dt 18:10; Isa 19:3; Ac 16:16). Various means were used: reading omens, dreams, the use of the lot, astrology, necromancy, and others.

DISPERSION (Gr. *diaspora, that which is sown*). The name applied to the Jews living outside of Palestine and maintaining their religious faith among the Gentiles. God had warned the Jews through Moses that dispersion among other nations would be their lot if they departed from the Mosaic law (Dt 4:27; 28:64 – 68). These prophecies were largely fulfilled in the two captivities, by Assyria and Babylonia, but there were other captivities by the rulers of Egypt and Syria, and by Pompey, which helped scatter the Israelites. Especially from the time of Alexander the Great, many thousands of Jews immigrated for the purposes of trade and commerce into the neighboring countries, particularly the chief cities. By the time of Christ the dispersion must have been several times the population of Palestine. As early as 525 BC there had been a temple of the Lord in Elephantine, in the early years of the Maccabean struggle. The synagogues in every part of the known world helped greatly in the spread of Christianity, for Paul invariably went to them in every city he visited. The word *diaspora* occurs three times in the NT (Jn 7:35; Jas 1:1; 1Pe 1:1).

DIVORCE [1763, 4135, 8938, 668, 687, 918, 3386] (Gr. *apostasion*). A divorce is a means whereby a legal marriage is dissolved publicly and the participants are freed from further obligations of the matrimonial relationship. It is an ancient device that has varied procedurally over the centuries, but in the main it has been instituted on the initiative of the husband.

Although the OT seems to permit divorce for rather general reasons (Dt. 24:1), it was usually either for adultery or childlessness. The bill of divorce could be a simple repudiation, such as, "She is not my wife, and I am not her husband" (Hos 2:2). Although either party could begin the divorce proceedings, it was considered a Gentile custom for the wife to do so (Mk 10:11 – 12). Because of the strength of the family unit, divorce was in actual fact not very common among the Hebrews. Nevertheless, in the postexilic period, in order for the

purity of the Hebrew faith to be maintained, wholesale divorce was required by Ezra of those Jews who had married foreign wives in Babylonia (Ezr 9:2; 10:3, 16 – 17).

The NT largely forbids divorce, and Jesus asserts that God had, under the Mosaic law, allowed divorce as a concession to the hardness of the human heart (Mt 19:8). Even the remarriage of widows was frowned upon by some in the apostolic period, though 1Ti 5:14 seems more lenient on this matter. The primary exception for divorce seems to be in the case of adultery (Mt 5:32), although some would argue against the legitimacy of this exception. A major point of counsel from Paul is to remain in whatever marital state one finds oneself in (1Co 7:10 – 15).

> **General References to:**
>
> *Mosaic laws concerning (Ex 21:7 – 11; Dt 21:10 – 14; 24:1 – 4). Authorized for marital unfaithfulness (Mt 5:31 – 32; 19:3 – 11). Unjust reproved (Mal 2:14 – 16). From Gentile wives, required by Ezra (Ezr 10:1 – 16). Disobedience, a cause for, among the Persians (Est 1:10 – 22). Final, after remarriage of either party (Jer 3:1). Christ's injunctions concerning (Mk 10:2 – 12; Lk 16:18). Paul's injunctions concerning (1Co 7:10 – 17). Figurative of God's judgment of Israel (Isa 50:1; 54:4 – 8; Jer 3:8).*

Dt	22:19	he must not **d** her as long as he lives
	24:1	and he writes her a certificate of **d**,
Isa	50:1	is your mother's certificate of **d**
Jer	3:8	faithless Israel her certificate of **d**
Mal	2:16	"I hate **d**," says the Lord God
Mt	1:19	he had in mind to **d** her quietly.
	5:31	must give her a certificate of **d**.'
	19:3	for a man to **d** his wife for any
	19:7	man give his wife a certificate of **d**
Mk	10:2	Is it lawful for a man to **d** his wife?"
	10:4	a man to write a certificate of **d**
1Co	7:11	And a husband must not **d** his wife.
	7:12	to live with him, he must not **d** her.
	7:13	to live with her, she must not **d** him
	7:27	Are you married? Do not seek a **d**.

DIVORCED [DIVORCE]

Lev	21:7	or **d** from their husbands,
	21:14	not marry a widow, a **d** woman,
	22:13	daughter becomes a widow or is **d**,
Nu	30:9	or **d** woman will be binding on her.
Dt	24:4	then her first husband, who **d** her,
Eze	44:22	not marry widows or **d** women;
Mt	5:32	marries the **d** woman commits adultery.
Lk	16:18	who marries a **d** woman commits

DOCTRINE [DOCTRINES]

1Ti	1:10	to the sound **d** that conforms
	4:16	Watch your life and **d** closely.
2Ti	4:3	men will not put up with sound **d**.
Tit	1:9	can encourage others by sound **d**
	2:1	is in accord with sound **d**.

DOCTRINES [DOCTRINE]

1Ti	1:3	not to teach false **d** any longer
	6:3	If anyone teaches false **d**

DRUNKENNESS [8893, 8913, 9275, 3494, 3886, 4232]. The Scriptures show that drunkenness was one of the major vices of antiquity, even among the Hebrews. Well-known cases of intoxication are Noah (Ge 9:21); Lot (19:33, 35); Nabal (1Sa 25:36); Uriah (2Sa 11:13); Ammon (13:28); Elah, king of Israel (1Ki 16:9); and Ben-Hadad, king of Syria, and his thirty-two confederate kings (20:16). The prophets often denounce drunkenness as a great social evil of the wealthy. Even the women were guilty (Am 4:1). The symptoms and effects of strong drink are vividly pictured in the Bible (Job 12:25; Ps 107:27; Isa 28:7; Hos 4:11). While the writers of Scripture condemn intemperance in the strongest terms, they do not prescribe total abstinence as a formal and universal rule.

Condemned:
Repugnancy of (Isa 28:7 – 8; 56:12; Hos 7:5, 14; Joel 1:5; 3:3; Am 2:8, 12; Mt 24:49; Lk 12:45). Mockery of (Ps 69:12; Pr 20:1). Consequences of (Pr 21:17; 23:21, 29 – 35; Isa 19:14; 24:9 – 11; 28:7; Hos 4:11). Death penalty for (Dt 21:20 – 21; 29:19 – 20; Jer 25:27). Excludes from the kingdom of God (1Co 6:9 – 10; Gal 5:19 – 21). Forbidden (1Sa 1:14; Pr 23:20, 31 – 32; 31:4 – 7; Lk 21:34; Ro 13:13; 1Co 11:21 – 30; Eph 5:18; 1Th 5:7 – 8; 1Pe 4:3). Woes denounced against (Isa 5:11 – 12, 22; 28:1, 3, 7 – 8; Am 6:1, 6; Na 1:10; Hab 2:15 – 16).

Figurative:
(Isa 28:8; 51:17, 21 – 23; 63:6; Jer 25:15 – 16, 27 – 28; 51:7 – 9; La 3:15; Eze 23:31 – 34; Hab 2:15 – 16).

Other Instances of:
Xerxes (Est 1:10 – 11); Belshazzar (Da 5:1 – 6); believers (1Co 11:21).

Falsely Accused of:
Hannah (1Sa 1:12 – 16); Jesus (Mt 11:19); the apostles (Ac 2:13 – 15).

Lk	21:34	weighed down with dissipation, **d**
Ro	13:13	and **d**, not in sexual immorality
Gal	5:21	factions and envy; **d**, orgies,
1Ti	3:3	not given to **d**, not violent
1Pe	4:3	living in debauchery, lust, **d**, orgies,

EARTH [141, 824, 6760, 8073, 9315, 10075, 10077, 10309, 1178, 2103, 2973, 3180, 4922, 5954] (Heb. *'ădhāmâh*, ground; *'erets, earth*; Gr. *gē, earth*; *oikoumenē, inhabited earth*; *kosmos, orderly arrangement*). The Hebrew word *'ădhāmâh* most commonly means the tilled reddish soil of Palestine. But it is also used to denote a piece of real estate (Ge 47:18ff.), earth as a material substance (2:7), a territory (28:15), and the whole earth (Ge 12:3; Dt 14:2).

The word *'erets* denotes commonly the earth as opposed to the sky (Ge 1:1; Jos 2:11); also very frequently it means "land" in the sense of a country (Ge 13:10; 45:18). In the NT, *gē* means "ground," arable and otherwise (Mt 5:18; Jn 8:6); "the earth" as opposed to the heavens (Mt 6:10; Ac 2:19); "territory" or "region" (Lk 4:25; Jn 3:22). *Oikoumenē* carries the meaning of the inhabited earth or the "world" (Mt 24:14; Lk 4:5), the Roman Empire (Lk 2:1), and all the inhabitants of the earth (Ac 17:6; Rev 3:10). *Kosmos* in a derived sense is used to denote the earth, though it is always translated "world" in our Bibles. It has more to do with the inhabitants of the earth than with the actual planet.

Sometimes it is difficult to tell whether the earth or the land is meant, particularly in the prophetic books. For example, in Isa 24:1, 3 – 5, the word "earth" may mean "land" instead. The ancient Hebrew had no idea of the shape or size of the earth, or that it was a planet. The earth was simply the area where humans lived, moved, and had their being. But Job 26:7 is a scientifically correct statement: "He spreads out the northern skies over empty space; he suspends the earth over nothing."

Creation of:

By God (Ge 1:1; Ex 20:11; 31:17; 2Ki 19:15; 2Ch 2:12; Ne 9:6; Job 38:4; Pss 90:2; 102:25; 104:5; 115:15; 124:8; 146:5 – 6; Pr 8:22 – 26; Isa 37:16; 45:18; 66:1 – 2; Jer 10:12; 27:5; 32:17; 51:15; Ac 14:15; Heb 11:3; 2Pe 3:5; Rev 10:6; 14:7). By

Christ (Jn 1:3, 10; Heb 1:10). Primitive condition of (Ge 1:2, 6 – 7; Job 26:7; 38:4 – 7; Ps 104:5 – 9; Pr 3:19 – 20; Isa 40:22; Jer 4:23 – 26). See Creation; God, Creator. Created to be inhabited (Isa 45:18). By design (Isa 45:18). Early divisions of (Ge 10 – 11; Dt 32:8; Ps 74:17). Belongs to the Lord (Ex 9:29; 19:5; Dt 10:14; 1Sa 2:8; Pss 24:1; 50:12; Isa 66:1; 1Co 10:26). God controls (Job 9:6; Rev 7:1). God's footstool (Isa 66:1; La 2:1; Mt 5:35; Ac 7:49).

Cursed:

Cursed by God (Ge 3:17 – 19; 5:29; Ro 8:19 – 22).

Future of:

Perpetuity of (Ge 49:26; Dt 33:15; Pss 78:69; 104:5; Ecc 1:4; Hab 3:6). Will be judged (1Sa 2:10; Pss 96:13; 98:9). Destruction of, foretold (Ps 102:25 – 27; Isa 24:19 – 20; 51:6; Mt 5:17 – 18; 24:3, 6, 14, 29 – 31, 35 – 42; Mk 13:24 – 37; Lk 21:26 – 36; 2Pe 3:10 – 13; Rev 20:11; 21:1). A new earth (Isa 65:17; 66:22; 2Pe 3:13; Rev 21:1).

Ge	1:1	God created the heavens and the **e**.
	1:2	Now the **e** was formless and empty,
	7:24	The waters flooded the **e**
	14:19	Creator of heaven and **e**.
1Ki	8:27	"But will God really dwell on **e**?
Job	26:7	he suspends the **e** over nothing.
Ps	24:1	**e** is the LORD's, and everything
	102:25	you laid the foundations of the **e**,
Isa	6:3	the whole **e** is full of his glory."
	40:22	enthroned above the circle of the **e**,
	65:17	new heavens and a new **e**.
	66:1	and the **e** is my footstool.
Mt	5:5	for they will inherit the **e**.
	6:10	done on **e** as it is in heaven.
	16:19	bind on **e** will be bound
	24:35	Heaven and **e** will pass away,
	28:18	and on **e** has been given to me.
Lk	2:14	on **e** peace to men
Jn	12:32	when I am lifted up from the **e**,
Ac	4:24	"you made the heaven and the **e**
1Co	10:26	The **e** is the Lord's, and everything
2Pe	3:13	to a new heaven and a new **e**,
Rev	8:7	A third of the **e** was burned up,

20:11	**E** and sky fled from his presence,
21:1	I saw a new heaven and a new **e**,
21:1	and the first **e** had passed away,

EASTER The word *Easter* occurs only once in the Bible (Ac 12:4), the only time the KJV translates *pascha* (usually "Passover") in this way. It is the day on which most Christians celebrate the resurrection of Jesus Christ.

There is no celebration of the resurrection in the NT. The Jewish Christians linked it with the Passover, and so observed it on the fourteenth day of Nisan regardless of the day of the week. But Gentile believers celebrated the resurrection on the Lord's Day, Sunday. This difference was settled by the Council of Nicea in AD 325, which ruled that Easter should be celebrated on the first Sunday after the full moon following the vernal equinox. This is the system followed today, the date of Easter varying between March 22 and April 25.

ECCLESIASTES (ĕklē-zǐ̆ăs'tē z, Gr. *Ekklēsiatēs*, Heb., *qōheleth*, meaning probably the official speaker in an assembly, rendered in English as Qoheleth). Traditionally the book has been ascribed to Solomon. This ascription is based on several factors. The superscription introduces the book as "The words of the Teacher, son of David, king of Jerusalem" (Ecc 1:1). Several allusions in the book are appropriate to Solomonic authorship, such as the reference to the author's wisdom (1:16), his interest in proverbs (12:9; cf. 1Ki 4:32), and his building projects (2:4 – 11).

From the time of Luther, however, a large number of scholars have questioned the Solomonic authorship of Ecclesiastes. The book does not actually name Solomon as its writer. The author says he *was* king of Jerusalem — past tense — (Ecc 1:12), a statement difficult to apply to Solomon, and the language of the book may incline toward a time later than King Solomon. These observations have led many to hold that Solomon serves as a literary representation of the embodiment of wisdom.

The book presents a pessimistic view of life apart from God. A positive life view emerges from the book that may be called a theology of contentment. In view of the lack of substance and meaning in life, Qoheleth urges his readers to enjoy life, for it is God who gives us that privilege (Ecc 2:24 – 25). This satisfaction does not belong to all humankind, for the work of the sinner ends in futility (2:26). Godly contentment, however, is not the ultimate good for humankind. Qoheleth reminds us of a future time when God will bring all things into judgment. This is the conclusion of his search for meaning in life (12:14).

ECOLOGY Humankind was created to care for the earth (Ge 1:28; 2:15; Pss 8:6 – 8; 115:16). The land was to enjoy rest every seven years (Lev 25:1 – 7); the land enjoyed its rest during Israel's exile (2Ch 36:20 – 21). Animals were to rest on the Sabbath (Ex 20:10). Fruit trees were not to be cut down in war time (Dt 20:19 – 20). A bird and its young were not to be caught together (Dt 22:6 – 7). Babylon was judged for violence to the forests of Lebanon and its animals (Hab 2:17, w Isa 14:8).

ECUMENICISM (*the inhabited earth*). A movement among Christian religious groups — Protestant, Eastern Orthodox, Roman Catholic — to bring about a closer unity in work and organization. The word is not found in the NIV, but backing for the movement may be found in Jn 17 where Jesus prays for the unity of his church.

EDEN [6359, 6360, 6361] (Heb. *'ēden, paradise, delight*, possibly *flat land*).

1. The district in which the Lord God planted a garden for the newly created man, Adam. In it grew every tree that was pleasant to see and good for food, including the Tree of Life and the Tree of the Knowledge of Good and Evil. A river flowed out of Eden and divided into four heads or streams: the Pishon, which went around the land of Havilah, where gold was found; the Gihon, which flowed around the whole land of Cush; the Hiddekel (or Tigris), which

flowed in front of Assyria; and the Euphrates (Ge 2:8 – 14). Adam and Eve lived there until they sinned by eating the forbidden fruit and were expelled from it (Ge 2 – 3). Later Scripture writers mention Eden as an illustration of a delightful place (Isa 51:3; Eze 28:13; 31:9, 16, 18; 36:35; Joel 2:3).

The location of Eden has been much investigated in both ancient and modern times. The data given in Genesis, however, are not sufficient to fix its site, because two of the rivers, the Pishon and Gihon, were unknown even to the ancients and still are to modern scholars.

2. An Eden mentioned by the Assyrians as conquered by them along with Gozan, Haran, and Rezeph (2Ki 19:12; Isa 37:12). Ezekiel 27:23 also mentions this region. It is believed to be the "Bit-adini" of the Assyrian inscriptions. The house of Eden, or Beth Eden (Am 1:5), was probably near Damascus, since it is mentioned in a Syrian context, but some scholars think it was the same place as Bit-adini.

3. A Gershonite who lived in Hezekiah's time and served under Kore, the porter of the east gate of the temple, in distributing the holy oblations (2Ch 29:12; 31:15).

4. A Levite (2Ch 31:15).

5. A marketplace of costly merchandise (Eze 27:23 – 24).

EDIFICATION, EDIFY, EDIFYING [3868, 3869] (Lat. *to build up*). The root of this Greek word is found in various words and compound words in the NT, i.e., "build" (Mt 23:29; 26:61), "building" (Jn 2:20), "builder" (1Co 3:10; Heb 3:3 – 4), "builds up" (1Co 8:1), "strengthen" (1Co 8:10), "edified" (1Co 14:5, 17), "edification" (Ro 14:19). Paul uses the word group frequently but never in the literal sense of "building" a building. He uses it often in the meta-phorical sense of "building" or "building up" the church, and of "building up" fellow believers (1Co 3:9; Eph 2:21). He speaks of building the church on the foundation that he and the apostles and the prophets laid (1Co 3:10, 12, 14; Eph 2:20). Paul uses

the words more frequently in the sense of "strengthening, unifying, making for peace." Christians are to build up one another in this sense (1Th 5:11). It is primarily love that "builds up" (1Co 8:1).

EDOM, EDOMITES [121+1201, 121, 122] (ē′dŏm, ē′dŏmīts, Heb. *'ĕdhōm, 'ădhômîn*, from *'ĕdhōm, red*). The nation and its people who were the descendants of Esau. He founded the country, so his name is equated with Edom (Ge 25:30; 36:1, 8). The country was also called Seir, or Mount Seir, the name of the territory in which the Edomites lived, the mountain and plateau area between the Dead Sea and the Gulf of Aqabah about 100 miles long and up to 40 miles wide. The original inhabitants of this land were the Horites or "cave dwellers" (14:6). When Esau departed from Canaan to find room for his cattle and came to Mount Seir (36:5 – 8), the Horites had some tribal chiefs reigning in the land (36:29 – 30). Esau took the daughter of one of these chiefs for a wife, Oholibamah, daughter of Anah (36:2, 25). Esau's sons and grandsons were also tribal chiefs (36:15 – 19, 40 – 43). Probably the Edomites gradually absorbed the Horites until they disappeared (Dt 2:12, 22).

Land of (Ge 32:3; Dt 2:4 – 5, 12). Descendants of Esau (Ge 36). Rulers of (Ge 36:9 – 43; Ex 15:15; 1Ch 1:51 – 54). Kings of (Ge 36:31 – 39; Nu 20:14; 1Ch 1:43 – 50; Eze 32:29; Am 2:1). Prophecies concerning (Ge 25:23; 27:29, 37 – 40; Nu 24:18; Isa 11:14; 21:11 – 12; 34; 63:1 – 6; Jer 9:25 – 26; 27:1 – 11; 49:7 – 22; La 4:21 – 22; Eze 25:12 – 14; 32:29 – 30; 36:5; Joel 3:19; Am 1:11 – 12; 9:12; Ob 1 – 21; Mal 1:2 – 5). Protected by divine command from desolation by the Israelites (Dt 2:4 – 6); from being held in abhorrence by the Israelites (Dt 23:7); Children of the third generation might be received into the congregation of Israel (Dt 23:8); Refuse the Israelites passage through their country (Nu 20:18 – 21); Saul makes war against (1Sa 14:47); Garrisons of (2Sa 8:14); David conquers (1Ki 11:14 – 16; 1Ch 18:11 – 13); writes battle songs concerning his conquest of (Pss 60:8 – 9; 108:9 – 10); Ruled by a deputy king (1Ki 22:47); Become confederates of Jehoshaphat (2Ki 3:9, 26); Revolt in the days of Jehoram (2Ki 8:20 – 22; 2Ch 21:8 – 10); Amaziah, king of Judah, invades the territory of Edom, defeating ten thousand Edomites (2Ki 14:7, 10; 2Ch 25:11 – 12; 28:17); The Lord delivers the army of, into the hands of Jehoshaphat (2Ch 20:20, 23); Jewish prophet in Babylon denounces (Ps 137:7; Eze 25:12 – 14; 35); Join Babylon in the war against the Israelites (Eze 35:5; Am 1:9 – 11; Ob 11 – 16)

EGYPT (ē′jĭpt, Gr. *Aigyptos*).

ITS NAME.

To the Israelites, Egypt was Mizraim (Heb. *mitsrayim*), a term of which the form and derivation are unknown. The Egyptians themselves had a number of names they used for their country; usually it was called "the Two Lands," which has reference to the origin of the nation in the union of Upper and Lower Egypt.

THE NILE.

"Egypt," said Hecateus, echoed by Herodotus, "is the gift of the Nile." This is a reflection of actual circumstances and of the Egyptian appreciation of the great river. The Nile, which courses like a living vein through the desiccated hills and deserts of NE Africa, laid down the black alluvium of the delta and the entire river valley. In view of the almost complete absence of rain, the annual overflow of the Nile was of great importance to the land, for it watered the soil and provided it with new alluvium and some organic fertilizer.

The awareness of the dependence of land and people on the resources of the Nile led to the deification of the river. The longest river in the world, the Nile covers some 4,000 miles (6,667 km.) from its sources in equatorial Africa to its divided mouths that open into the Mediterranean.

GEOGRAPHY.

The division of the land into Upper and Lower Egypt predates the union into one nation. Lower Egypt included the delta and a short section of the valley southward; the rest of the valley to Aswan was Upper Egypt. These areas were subdivided into administrative units that in Greek times were called "nomes," twenty in Lower Egypt and twenty-two in its southern counterpart. With the cataracts and the Nubian desert to the south and SE, the Libyan desert and the Sahara to the west, and the Arabian desert on the east, the valley was not subject to the frequent invasions that characterized less defensible lands. The biggest threat from outside was on the delta edges; even here the passage of armies was handicapped by terrain and climate. On the NE border, fronting Asia, the Egyptians made early use of fortresses and other checkpoints to control invasion from this direction. With such protection, the country was free to develop its culture in comparative security and still to retain a free exchange of goods and ideas with other peoples.

CLIMATE.

The climate of the land, along with the particular beliefs of the people, has been of great advantage to archaeology, so that it may be said that Egypt is the archaeological area par excellence. Lack of rain and frost, plenty of dry sand to form a protective cover over remains, and abundant use of stone for monumental building are helpful environmental factors. The burial customs have been of much help to the cultural historian, for the relief sculpture, tomb furniture, models, and inscriptions tell much of the daily life of antiquity.

RELIGION.

The religion of ancient Egypt is a vast and labyrinthine subject. Much of the religious literature appears as a hodgepodge of conflicting statements to the modern Western reader, to whom many of the allusions must remain obscure. In general, the religion may be described as a complex polytheism, with many local deities of varying importance. A list of these divinities would be impractical, but these may be singled out: Osiris and Isis, who are well known from their later adoption by the mystery religions of Greece and Rome; Ra (Re), a sun god, who came into prominence in the Fifth Dynasty; Horus, another sun god, the son of Osiris and Isis; Set, the rival of Osiris and Horus; Amon-Re, who became the god of empire; Ptah, the god of Memphis; Khnum, the god of Elephantine. The attempt of Akhenaton (Amenhotep IV) to reorient Egyptian religion with a primary emphasis on Aton, the sun disk, has been widely discussed as a tendency toward monotheism. There is no evidence of possible Israelite influence on his beliefs. His innovations did not long survive him, and the priests of Amon at Thebes scored a theological-political victory. Much of the religious literature has a mortuary interest; this preoccupation with death was a futile gesture to transfer earthly life to an eternal dimension.

HISTORY.

Preceding the historical or dynastic period are a number of prehistoric cultures that are known in general outline. In the late predynastic epoch, there is interesting evidence of cultural influence from Mesopotamia. The rudiments of hieroglyphic writings also appear about this time and usher in the historical period. The materials for writing the political history of Egypt are lists of kings (such as those inscribed in temples of Abydos and Karnak, that of a tomb at Sakkarah, the Turin Papyrus, and the Palermo Stone) and numerous historical records, both of kings and of lesser persons active in history making. The dynastic scheme is a historiographical convenience inherited from the priest-historian Manetho, who divided Egyptian history from Menes to Alexander into thirty-one dynasties. Egyptologists have used a somewhat standard arrangement of these dynasties into historical periods.

The Country of:

Fertility of (Ge 13:10). Imports of (Ge 37:25, 36). Productions of (Nu 11:5; Ps 78:47; Pr 7:16; Isa 19:5–10). Irrigation employed in (Dt 11:10). Called: Rahab, the poetic name for Egypt (Pss 87:4; 89:10); the land of Ham (Pss 105:23; 106:21–22). Exports of (Pr 7:16; Eze 27:7); horses (1Ki 10:28–29). Limits of (Eze 29:10). Abraham dwells in (Ge 12:10–20; 13:1). The king acquires title to land of (Ge 47:18–26). Joseph's captivity in and subsequent rule over. See Joseph, 1. Israelites in bondage in. See Israel, Israelites. Plagues in. See Plague. Civil war in (Isa 19:2). Overflowed by the Nile (Am 8:8; 9:5). Joseph takes Jesus to (Mt 2:13–20). Prophecies against (Ge 15:13–14; Isa 19; 20:2–6; 45:14; Jer 9:25–26; 43:8–13; 44:30; 46; Eze 29–32; Hos 8:13; Joel 3:19; Zec 10:11). See Egyptians. Famine in (Ge 41; Ac 7:11). See Famine. Magi of (Ge 41:8; Ex 7:11; 1Ki 4:30; Ac 7:22). See Magi. Priests of (Ge 41:45; 47:22). Army of, destroyed in the Red Sea (Ex 14:5–31; Isa 43:17). See Army. Armies of (Ex 14:7; Isa 31:1). Idols of (Eze 20:7–8).

Ge	12:10	went down to **E** to live there
	37:28	Ishmaelites, who took him to **E**.
	42:3	went down to buy grain from **E**.
	45:20	the best of all **E** will be yours.'"
	46:6	and all his offspring went to **E**.
	47:27	Now the Israelites settled in **E**
Ex	3:11	and bring the Israelites out of **E**?"
	12:40	lived in **E** was 430 years.
Nu	11:18	We were better off in **E**!"
	14:4	choose a leader and go back to **E**."
	24:8	"God brought them out of **E**;
Dt	6:21	"We were slaves of Pharaoh in **E**,
1Ki	4:30	greater than all the wisdom of **E**.
2Ch	35:20	Neco king of **E** went up to fight
Hos	11:1	and out of **E** I called my son.
Mt	2:15	"Out of **E** I called my son."
Heb	11:27	By faith he left **E**, not fearing
Rev	11:8	is figuratively called Sodom and **E**,

EL (Heb. *'ēl*, *God*). The generic word for God in the Semitic languages: Aramaic *elah*, Arabic *ilah*, Akkadian *ilu*. In the OT, *el* is used over two hundred times for "God." In the prose books it often has a modifying term with it, but in the poetic books, Job and Psalms, it occurs alone many times. El was the chief, and somewhat vague, shadowy god of the Canaanite pantheon, and the title is used in the OT to express the exalted transcendence of God. *See Elohim.* The Hebrews borrowed this word from the Canaanites. *El* has a plural, *elim*, occasionally *elhm* in Ugaritic; but the Hebrews needed no plural, though a plural term, *'elōhîm*, was their regular name for God.

ELDER [2418, 10675, 1172, 4564, 4565, 5236] (Heb. *zāqēn*, Gr. *presbyteros*). In ancient times the older men of a community were known as the elders. They governed the community and made all major decisions.

This type of society continued into NT times. The elders joined the priests and scribes against Jesus (Mt 27:12). When churches came into being, elders were appointed for each congregation (Ac 14:23). The terms *elders* and *bishops* are used interchangeably in the NT. The "elders" of Ac 20:17 are called "bishops" in v. 28 (NIV "overseers"). In Tit 1:5, "elders" in the Cretan churches are mentioned; in listing qualifications for such an office, Paul calls them "bishops" in v. 7 (NIV "overseers"). These men were required to be blameless in their lives and obedient to the truth in their faith (1Ti 3:1 – 7; Tit 1:6 – 9). Their duties involved spiritual oversight of the congregation and teaching the Word. Those who ruled well and also taught were worthy of "double honor" (1Ti 5:17). Before the first century AD had elapsed, the term *bishop* had taken on a special meaning, denoting the one leader of a church. A biblical example of this (both in the book of Acts and in Paul's letters) is James, the brother of Jesus, who was obviously the leader of the Jerusalem church.

Opinions vary regarding the twenty-four elders in heaven around the throne of God (as depicted in the book of Revelation); probably they represent the heavenly priesthood of the church associated with Christ, the Great High Priest.

In the NT Church:
Received gifts on behalf of church (Ac 11:29 – 30). Ordained (Ac 14:23; Tit 1:5 – 9). Overseers of the church (Ac 15:1 – 29; 16:4 – 5; 20:17, 28 – 32; 21:18; 1Ti 5:17 – 19; 1Pe 5:1 – 5). Performed ecclesiastical duties (1Ti 4:14; Jas 5:14 – 15).

John's Vision of the Twenty-four Elders:
(Rev 4:4, 10; 5:5 – 6, 8, 11, 14; 7:11, 13; 11:16; 14:3; 19:4).

Isa	3:2	the soothsayer and **e**,
1Ti	5:19	an accusation against an **e**
Tit	1:6	**e** must be blameless, the husband
1Pe	5:1	among you, I appeal as a fellow **e**,
2Jn	1:1	The **e**, To the chosen lady
3Jn	1:1	The **e**, To my dear friend Gaius,

ELDERS [ELDER]

1Ki	12:8	rejected the advice the **e** gave him
Mt	15:2	break the tradition of the **e**?
Mk	7:3	holding to the tradition of the **e**.
Ac	11:30	gift to the **e** by Barnabas
	14:23	and Barnabas appointed **e** for them
	15:2	the apostles and **e** about this
	16:4	and **e** in Jerusalem for the people
	20:17	to Ephesus for the **e** of the church.
	21:18	and all the **e** were present.
1Ti	4:14	when the body of **e** laid their hands
	5:17	The **e** who direct the affairs
Tit	1:5	and appoint **e** in every town,
Jas	5:14	He should call the **e** of the church
1Pe	5:1	To the **e** among you, I appeal
Rev	4:4	seated on them were twenty-four **e**.
	4:10	the twenty-four **e** fall

ELDERS, COUNCIL OF

Described:
Chosen elders of the nation, vested with representative, judicial, and executive authority (Ex 4:29; 5:15, 19; 6:14 – 25; 12:21; Nu 11:16 – 30).

Called: the council (Nu 16:2; Mk 15:43); council of the elders (Ps 107:32; Lk 22:66); elders of Israel (Ex 3:16, 18), of Judah (1Sa 30:26), of the people (Ex 19:7), of the community (Lev 4:15), of the Jews (Ezr 5:5); Sanhedrin (Mt 5:22; 26:59; Ac 4:15; 5:21 – 41). Closely associated with Moses and subsequent leaders (Ex 3:16 – 18; 4:29; 12:21; 17:5 – 6; 18:12; 19:7; 24:1, 14; Nu 16:25; Dt 5:23; 27:1; 29:10; 31:9, 28; Jos 7:6; 8:10, 33; 23:2; 24:1; Jdg 11:5 – 11; Ac 5:17 – 18, 21). Made confession of sin in behalf of the nation (Lev 4:15; 9:1). A similar council existed among the Egyptians (Ge 50:7); the Midianites and Moabites (Nu 22:4, 7 – 8); the Gibeonites (Jos 9:11).

Events Relating to:

Demands a king (1Sa 8:4 – 10, 19 – 22). Saul pleads to be honored before (1Sa 15:30). Chooses David as king (2Sa 3:17 – 21; 5:3; 1Ch 11:3). Closely associated with David (2Sa 12:17; 1Ch 15:25; 21:16). Joins Absalom in his usurpation (2Sa 17:4). David rebukes (2Sa 19:11). Assists Solomon at the dedication of the temple (1Ki 8:1 – 3; 2Ch 5:2 – 4). Counsels King Rehoboam (1Ki 12:6 – 8, 13). Counsels King Ahab (1Ki 20:7 – 8). Josiah assembles, to hear the law of the Lord (2Ki 23:1; 2Ch 34:29, 31). Legislates with Ezra in reforming certain marriages with the Gentiles (Ezr 10:8 – 14). Legislates in later times (Mt 15:2, 7 – 9; Mk 7:1 – 13). Sits as a court (Jer 26:10 – 24). Constitutes, with priests and scribes, a court for trials of both civil and ecclesiastical causes (Mt 21:23; 26:3 – 5, 57 – 68; 27:1 – 2; Mk 8:31; 14:53 – 65; 15:1; Lk 22:52 – 71; Ac 4:1 – 21; 6:12 – 15). Seeks counsel from prophets (Eze 8:1; 14:1; 20:1, 3). Corrupt (1Ki 21:8 – 14; Eze 8:11 – 12; Mt 26:14 – 15; 27:3 – 4).

ELECT [1723, 1724] (*chosen*). Those chosen by God for some special purpose (Ps 106:23; Isa 43:10; 45:4). Among the elect mentioned in Scripture are Moses, the Israelites, Christ, the angels, Christ's disciples.

Mt	24:22	the sake of the **e** those days will be
	24:31	and they will gather his **e**
Mk	13:20	sake of the **e**, whom he has chosen,
Ro	11:7	it did not obtain, but the **e** did.
1Ti	5:21	and Christ Jesus and the **e** angels,
2Ti	2:10	everything for the sake of the **e**,
Tit	1:1	Christ for the faith of God's **e**
1Pe	1:1	To God's **e**, strangers in the world,

ELECTION AND PREDESTINATION For God to predestinate (Gr. *proorizō*) is for him to decree or foreordain the circumstances and destiny of people according to his perfect will (Ro 8:29 – 30; Eph 1:11). It is, therefore, a particular aspect of the general providence of God that relates to God's superintendence of the whole cosmos and everything in it. For God to elect (Heb. *bachar*, Gr. *eklegomai*) is for him to choose for salvation and/or service a people or a person; the choice is based not on merit but on his free, sovereign love (Dt 4:37; 7:7; 14:2; Ac 13:17; 15:7; 1Th 1:4). Further, since predestination and election are both presented as acts of God, election cannot be on the basis of God's knowing in advance the reactions of people to his will. Election must be choice flowing only from God's own initiative. Believers were chosen in Christ before the foundation of the world (Eph 1:4).

Election is a prominent theme in the OT. There is the choice of Abraham and his "seed" that in him the nations of the world will be blessed (Ge 12:1ff.; 22:17 – 18); and there is the choice of (covenant with) the people Israel whom God led out of bondage into liberty (Ex 3:6 – 10; Dt 6:21 – 23). This nation was chosen by God as those to whom he could reveal himself and his will, and through whom he could exhibit and declare to the world his purposes and salvation (Dt 28:1 – 14; Isa 43:10 – 12, 20, 21). Further, there was the choice, from within the chosen people, of specific individuals — e.g., Aaron and David — for special roles and tasks (Dt 18:5; 1Sa 10:24; Pss 105:26; 106:23).

In the NT, Jesus is the Elect One (Lk 9:35), in whom the election of Israel and of the church of God of the new covenant find their meaning and center. Jesus is the elect "cornerstone" of the new building that God is constructing, composed of both Jewish and Gentile believers (1Pe 2:4–6). God destined us in love to be his sons through Jesus Christ (Eph 1:5). So the church of God is an elect race (1Pe 2:9), replacing the old Israel in the purposes of God. And this new race is mostly composed of the poor and ordinary people (1Co 1:27ff.). God's election is never presented as a cause for speculation or controversy, but rather to celebrate the free grace of God that grants salvation and also to move believers to constant worship and lives of holiness and goodness. As in the OT, there is in the NT the election of individuals for service (e.g., Ac 6:5; 15:22, 25). Further, the question as to whether the Jews are, as a people, still the elect of God is faced by Paul in Ro 9–11 in the light of the salvation of God in and through Jesus. *See Chosen; Elect; Predestination.*

General References to:
By grace (Mt 22:14; Jn 15:16; 17:6; Ro 11:5; Eph 1:4; 2:10; 2Th 2:13; 1Pe 2:9). Of Israel (Dt 7:6; Isa 45:4). Of rulers (Ne 11:1). Of Christ as Messiah (Isa 42:1; 1Pe 2:6). Of ministers (Lk 6:13; Ac 9:15). Of good angels (1Ti 5:21). Of churches (1Pe 5:13).

Ro	9:11	God's purpose in **e** might stand:
	11:28	but as far as **e** is concerned,
2Pe	1:10	to make your calling and **e** sure.

ELI [6603] (Heb. *ʿēlî, Yahweh is exalted* IDB; *[God (El)] is exalted* KB). A member of the family of Ithamar, fourth son of Aaron, who acted as both judge and high priest in Israel. He lived at Shiloh in a dwelling adjoining the tabernacle (1Sa 1–4; 14:3; 1Ki 2:27). Little is known about him until he was well advanced in age, when Hannah came to pray for a son. The conduct of Eli's sons, Phinehas and Hophni, who, although lacking their father's character, were put into the priest's office, gave him grief in his declining years. Their conduct shocked the people, for they "were treating the LORD's offering with contempt" (1Sa 2:17). While Eli warned them of their shameful ways, he did not rebuke with the severity their deeds merited. Instead, Eli mildly rea-

soned with his sons, saying, "Why do you do such things?" (2:23). But the sons no longer heeded their father, and he didn't restrain them. An old man of ninety, almost blind, Eli waited to hear the result of the battle between the Israelites and the Philistines. When the messenger came with the news of the slaughter of his sons and of the taking of the ark, Eli fell off his seat and died of a broken neck. Although a good and pure man, Eli was weak and indecisive.

Misjudges and rebukes Hannah (1Sa 1:13–14); His benediction upon Hannah (1Sa 1:17–18; 2:20); Officiates when Samuel is presented at the tabernacle (1Sa 1:24–28); High priest (1Sa 1:25; 2:11; 1Ki 2:27); Judge of Israel (1Sa 4:18, n.); Indulgent of his corrupt sons (1Sa 2:22–25, 29; 3:11–14); His concern for the ark (1Sa 4:11–18); Death of (1Sa 4:18); Prophecies of judgments upon his house (1Sa 2:27–36; 3:11–14, w 1Ki 2:27)

ELIJAH [488, 489, 2460] (ē-lī′ja, Heb. *ʿēlîyāhû, Jehovah is God*). The name of four men in the Bible, of whom three are mentioned only once each.

1. A Benjamite and son of Jeroham, resident at Jerusalem (1Ch 8:27).

2. A descendant of Harim who married a foreign wife during the exile (Ezr 10:21).

3. An Israelite induced to put away his foreign wife (Ezr 10:26).

4. The prophet Elijah (1Ki 17:1–2Ki 2:12) whose ministry was set in the days of King Ahab (c. 874–852 BC) of the northern kingdom of Israel/Ephraim. Elijah was born in Tishbe and is described as one of the settlers in Gilead (1Ki 17:1)—though some make a slight alteration in the Hebrew text (cf. NIV) that would permit the translation "from Tishbe in Gilead," thus distinguishing Elijah's birthplace from Tishbe in Naphtali. In either case, whether by emigration (as the Hebrew text says) or by birth (as the altered text says), Elijah appeared on the scene from east of Jordan.

Meets Ahab and directs him to assemble the prophets of Baal (1Ki 18:17 – 20); Derisively challenges the priests of Baal to offer sacrifices (1Ki 18:25 – 29); Slays the prophets of Baal (1Ki 18:40); Escapes to the wilderness from the fierceness of Jezebel (1Ki 19:1 – 18); Fasts forty days (1Ki 19:8); Despondency and murmuring of (1Ki 19:10, 14); Consolation given to (1Ki 19:11 – 18); Flees to the wilderness of Damascus; directed to anoint Hazael as king over Aram, Jehu son of Nimshi king over Israel, and Elisha to be a prophet in his own place (1Ki 19:9 – 21); Personal aspect of (2Ki 1:8); Piety of (1Ki 19:10, 14; Lk 1:17; Ro 11:2; Jas 5:17); His translation to heaven in a whirlwind (2Ki 2:11); Antitype of John the Baptist (Mt 11:14; 17:10 – 13; Mk 9:11 – 13; Lk 1:17; Jn 1:21 – 25); Appears to Jesus at his transfiguration (Mt 17:1 – 4; Mk 9:2 – 5; Lk 9:28 – 33)

Miracles of:

Increases widow of Zarephath's oil (1Ki 17:14 – 16). Raises son of woman of Zarephath from dead (1Ki 17:17 – 24). Causes fire to consume sacrifice (1Ki 18:24, 36 – 38). Causes rain after three-and-a-half-year drought (1Ki 18:41 – 45; Jas 5:17 – 18). Calls fire down upon soldiers of Ahaziah (2Ki 1:10 – 14; Lk 9:54, n).

Prophecies of:

Foretells: a drought (1Ki 17:1); destruction of Ahab and his house (1Ki 21:17 – 29; 2Ki 9:25 – 37); death of Ahaziah (2Ki 1:2 – 17); plague sent as a judgment in the time of Jehoram, king of Israel (2Ch 21:12 – 15).

ELISHA [515, 1811] (ē-lī′sha, called *Eliseus*, the Gr. form of Heb. *'ĕlîshā'*, in Lk 4:27 KJV; Elisha in NIV, ASV, RSV, *God [El] is [my] salvation*). At Horeb, God directed Elijah to anoint Elisha to be his successor (1Ki 19:16 – 21), who was to aid Hazael, king of Syria, and Jehu, king of Israel, in taking vengeance on the enemies of God. Elijah left Horeb and on his way north found Elisha the son of Shaphat of Abel Meholah (19:16) plowing with the last of twelve yoke of oxen. The number of oxen indicates the wealth of the family. Elijah cast his mantle on Elisha, who understood the significance of the act as the choice of himself to succeed the older prophet. Elisha ran after Elijah, who had not tarried to explain his action, and begged for permission to kiss his parents farewell. Elijah's reply, "Go back. What have I done to you?" led Elisha to go home and make his own decision to accept the prophetic call.

The successor to Elijah the prophet whom Elijah is instructed to anoint (1Ki 19:16); Called by Elijah (1Ki 19:19); Ministers to Elijah (1Ki 19:21); Witnesses Elijah's translation, receives a double portion of his spirit (2Ki 2:1 – 15; 3:11); Mocked by the children of Bethel (2Ki 2:23 – 24); Causes the king to restore the property of the hospitable Shunammite (2Ki 8:1 – 6); Instructs that Jehu be anointed the king of Israel (2Ki 9:1 – 3); Life of, sought by Jehoram (2Ki 6:31 – 33); The death of (2Ki 13:14 – 20); Bones of, restore a dead man to life (2Ki 13:21)

Miracles of:

Divides Jordan River (2Ki 2:14). Purifies waters of Jericho by casting salt into fountain (2Ki 2:19 – 22). Increases oil of woman whose sons were to be sold for debt (2Ki 4:1 – 7). Raises son of the Shunammite from dead (2Ki 4:18 – 37). Neutralizes poison in the stew (2Ki 4:38 – 41). Increases bread to feed one hundred men (2Ki 4:42 – 44). Heals Naaman the leper (2Ki 5:1 – 19; Lk 4:27). Sends leprosy as a judgment on Gehazi (2Ki 5:26 – 27). Recovers axhead that had fallen into a stream by causing it to float (2Ki 6:6). Reveals counsel of king of Syria (2Ki 6:12). Opens his servant's eyes to see the hosts of the Lord (2Ki 6:17). Brings blindness on Syrian army (2Ki 6:18).

Prophecies of:

Foretells: birth of a son to Shunammite woman (2Ki 4:16); plenty to the starving in Samaria (2Ki 7:1); death of unbelieving prince (2Ki 7:2); seven years' famine in Canaan (2Ki 8:1 – 3); death of Ben-Hadad, king of Syria (2Ki

8:7 – 10); elevation of Hazael to throne (2Ki 8:11 – 15); victory of Jehoash over Syria (2Ki 13:14 – 19). Elisha is referred to once in the NT (Lk 4:27).

ELIZABETH [1810] (Gr. *Elisabet, God is my oath,* KJV Elisabeth). The wife of the priest Zechariah, herself of the lineage of Aaron (Lk 1:5 – 57). In fulfillment of God's promise, in her old age she bore a son, John the Baptist. Her kinswoman (cousin), Mary of Nazareth in Galilee, having learned that she was to be the virgin mother of Jesus, visited Elizabeth in the hill country of Judea. Elizabeth's Spirit-filled greeting prompted Mary to reply in a song called the Magnificat. After Mary returned home, Elizabeth's son was born. She was a woman of unusual piety, faith, and spiritual gifts, whose witness to Mary must have been an incomparable encouragement. Luke, who alone tells the story, appreciated the significant role of women in the history of redemption and emphasized the agency of the Holy Spirit in the life of Elizabeth.

ELOHIM (ĕlō′hĭm, *a god, the God; Mighty One*). The most frequent Hebrew word for God (over 2,500 times in the OT). Several theories of the origin of the word have been proposed, some connecting it with Hebrew *'ēl* or *'elôah*, others distinguishing them from *'elōhîm*. The origin is prehistoric and therefore incapable of direct proof. Elohim is plural in form but singular in construction (used with a singular verb or adjective). When applied to the one true God, the plural is due to the Hebrew idiom of a plural of magnitude or majesty (Ge 1:1). When used of heathen gods (Ge 35:2; Ex 18:11; 20:3; Jos 24:20), or of angels (Job 1:6; Pss 8:5; 97:7) or judges (Ex 21:6; 1Sa 2:25) as representatives of God, Elohim is plural in sense as well as form. Elohim is the earliest name of God in the OT and persists along with other names to the latest period. Whatever its etymology, the most likely roots mean either "be strong," or "be in front," suiting the power and preeminence of God. Jesus used a form of the name on the cross (Mt 27:46; Mk 15:34).

Used of the God of Israel:

The most frequent Hebrew word for God, gods, angels, or magistrates. The plural Elohim when used for God in the OT is singular in meaning and is often called "plural of majesty." See God, Names of, Elohim; El.

Used of Pagan Gods:

The Philistine god Dagon (Jdg 16:23 – 24); the Sidonian goddess Ashtoreth (1Ki 11:5, 33); the Moabite god Chemosh (1Ki 11:33); the Ammonite god Molech (1Ki 11:33); and Baal-Zebub of Ekron (2Ki 1:2, 3, 6) are also referred to in the plural.

Used of Other Groups:

Judges (Ex 21:6; 22:8 – 9); heavenly beings (Ps 8:5); those high among people (Ps 36:7).

ELOI, ELOI, LAMA SABACHTHANI [1830+ 3316+4876] (*My God, my God, why have you forsaken me?*). One of the seven cries of Jesus from the cross (Mt 27:46; Mk 15:34, w Ps 22:1).

EL SHADDAI (ĕl shăd′a-ī -shăd′īa). The name of God (translated "God Almighty") by which, according to Ex 6:3, he appeared to Abraham, Isaac, and Jacob — recorded once to Abraham (Ge 17:1) and four times to Jacob (Ge 28:3; 35:11; 43:14; 48:3). Often "the Almighty" (*Shaddai* without *El*) is used as a name of God: in Jacob's deathbed words (Ge 49:25), in Balaam's prophecies (Nu 24:4, 16), by Naomi (Ru 1:20, 21), thirty times by Job and his friends (Job 5:17 – 37:23), by God himself (Job 40:2), and twice in the Psalms (Pss 68:14; 91:1). The name is rare in the Prophets (Isa 13:6; Eze 1:24; 10:5 ["Almighty God"]; Joel 1:15). "God (the) Almighty" (Gr. *pantokratōr*, "all-powerful") occurs nine times in the NT (2Co 6:18; eight times in Revelation). So this name for God, which was a favorite of the patriarchs, especially Jacob and Job, becomes prominent in the songs of heaven. The etymology of *El Shaddai* is in dispute, "Almighty God" being the widely accepted meaning; some who would derive the Hebrew religion from pagan cults favor "mountain god."

EMMANUEL. *See Immanuel.*

EMMAUS (ĕmā'ŭs). The village to which two disciples were going on the day of Jesus' resurrection, when he met and was recognized by them as he broke bread at supper (Lk 24:7 – 35). It was about seven miles (twelve km.) from Jerusalem, in what direction is not stated, though possibly to the NW. One site, 'Amwâs, is 20 miles (33 km.) (some MSS read 160 stadia) from the city — too far to suit Luke's narrative. Kubeibeh, Kuloniych, and other sites have their partisans.

EMPLOYEE

Rights of an Employee:

Prompt payment (Lev 19:13). Participation in consuming yields of the land (Lev 25:6 – 7). Just compensation (Mt 10:10; Lk 10:7; Ro 4:4; Col 4:1; 1Ti 5:18). Oppression of (Dt 24:14 – 15; Pr 22:16; Mal 3:5; Lk 15:15 – 17; Jas 5:4). Kindness to, exemplified (Ru 2:4; Lk 15:17, 19).

Character of Unrighteous:

(Job 7:1 – 3; 14:1, 6; Mt 20:1 – 16; 21:33 – 41; Jn 10:12 – 13). See Employer; Master; Servant; Slave, Slavery.

EMPLOYER

Required:

To grant a Sabbath rest (Ex 20:10; Dt 5:14). To make prompt payment (Lev 19:13; Dt 24:15; Jas 5:4 – 5). To be kind (Lev 25:39 – 43; Job 31:13 – 15; Eph 6:9; Phm 15 – 16). Not to oppress (Dt 24:14 – 15; Pr 22:16; Mal 3:5). To accord just compensation (Jer 22:13; Mt 10:10; 20:1 – 15; Lk 10:7; Ro 4:4; Col 4:1; 1Ti 5:18).

ENCOURAGE [ENCOURAGED, ENCOURAGEMENT]

Dt	1:38	**E** him, because he will lead Israel
	3:28	and **e** and strengthen him,
2Sa	19:7	Now go out and **e** your men.
Job	16:5	But my mouth would **e** you;
Ps	10:17	you **e** them, and you listen
	64:5	They **e** each other in evil plans,
Isa	1:17	**e** the oppressed.
Ac	15:32	to **e** and strengthen the brothers.
Ro	12:8	if it is encouraging, let him **e**;
Eph	6:22	how we are, and that he may **e** you.
Col	4:8	and that he may **e** your hearts.
1Th	3:2	to strengthen and **e** you
	4:18	Therefore **e** each other
2Th	2:17	**e** your hearts and strengthen you
2Ti	4:2	rebuke and **e** — with great patience
Tit	1:9	so that he can **e** others
	2:6	**e** the young men to be
	2:15	**E** and rebuke with all authority.
Heb	3:13	But **e** one another daily, as long
	10:25	but let us **e** one another —

ENCOURAGED [ENCOURAGE]

Jdg	20:22	But the men of Israel **e** one another
2Ch	22:3	for his mother **e** him
	32:6	and **e** them with these words:
Ac	9:31	It was strengthened; and **e**
	11:23	and **e** them all to remain true
	16:40	met with the brothers and **e** them.
Ro	1:12	and I may be mutually **e**
1Co	14:31	everyone may be instructed and **e**.
2Co	7:4	I am greatly **e**; in all our troubles
Php	1:14	brothers in the Lord have been **e**
Col	2:2	My purpose is that they may be **e**
1Th	3:7	persecution we were **e** about you
Heb	6:18	offered to us may be greatly **e**.

ENCOURAGEMENT [ENCOURAGE]

Ac	4:36	Barnabas (which means Son of **E**),
	13:15	a message of **e** for the people,
Ro	15:4	**e** of the Scriptures we might have
1Co	14:3	to men for their strengthening, **e**
Php	2:1	If you have any **e** from being united
2Th	2:16	and by his grace gave us eternal **e**
Phm	1:7	love has given me great joy and **e**,

ENDURANCE [ENDURE]

Ro	15:4	through **e** and the encouragement
2Co	1:6	which produces in you patient **e**

| | 6:4 | in great **e**; in troubles, hardships |
| Col | 1:11 | might so that you may have great **e** |

ENDURE [ENDURANCE]

Ps	72:17	May his name **e** forever;
Pr	12:19	Truthful lips **e** forever,
	27:24	for riches do not **e** forever,
Ecc	3:14	everything God does will **e** forever;
1Co	4:12	when we are persecuted, we **e** it;
2Co	1:8	far beyond our ability to **e**,
2Ti	2:3	**E** hardship with us like a good
Heb	12:7	**E** hardship as discipline; God is
1Pe	2:20	a beating for doing wrong and **e** it?
Rev	3:10	kept my command to **e** patiently,

ENEMIES [ENEMY]

Ps	23:5	in the presence of my **e**.
	110:1	hand until I make your **e**
Pr	16:7	his **e** live at peace with him.
Isa	59:18	wrath to his **e**
Mt	5:44	Love your **e** and pray
Lk	6:27	Love your **e**, do good
	6:35	But love your **e**, do good to them,
Ro	5:10	For if, when we were God's **e**,
1Co	15:25	reign until he has put all his **e**
Php	3:18	many live as **e** of the cross of Christ
Heb	1:13	hand until I make your **e**

ENEMY [67, 7640, 7675, 7756, 8533, 2398].

Kindness to:

  Commanded (Ex 23:4 – 5; Pr 25:21 – 22; Mt 5:43 – 48; Lk 6:27 – 36; Ro 12:14, 20).

Forgiveness of:

  Commanded (Mt 6:12 – 15; 18:21 – 35; Mk 11:25; Lk 17:3 – 4; Eph 4:31 – 32; Col 3:13; 1Pe 3:9). Instances of Forgiveness: Esau, of Jacob (Ge 33:4, 11); Joseph, of his brothers (Ge 45:5 – 15; 50:19 – 21); Moses, of Miriam and Aaron (Nu 12:1 – 13); David, of Saul (1Sa 24:10 – 12; 26:9, 23; 2Sa 1:14 – 17), of Shimei (2Sa 16:9 – 13; 19:23; 1Ki 2:8 – 9), of Absalom and his coconspirators (2Sa 18:5, 12, 32 – 33; 19:6, 12 – 13); the prophet

of Judah by Jeroboam (1Ki 13:3 – 6); Jesus, of his persecutors (Lk 23:34); Stephen, of his murderers (Ac 7:60).

Destruction of:

  Requested by David (Ps 35:1 – 7). The wickedness of David's enemies (Pss 56:2, 5 – 6; 57:4, 6; 62:4; 69:4; 71:10; 102:8; 109:2 – 5; 129:1 – 3). See Prayer, Imprecatory. Rejoicing at the destruction of, forbidden (Pr 24:17 – 18). Rejoicing at the destruction of, not practiced by Job (Job 31:29 – 30).

Figurative:

  Of the devil (Mt 13:25, 28, 39).

Pr	24:17	Do not gloat when your **e** falls;
	25:21	If your **e** is hungry, give him food
Lk	10:19	to overcome all the power of the **e**;
Ro	12:20	"If your **e** is hungry, feed him;
1Co	15:26	The last **e** to be destroyed is death.
1Ti	5:14	and to give the **e** no opportunity
1Pe	5:8	Your **e** the devil prowls

ENOCH [H2840, G1970] (ē'nŭk, Heb. *hănôkh*, consecrated, Gr. *Henoch*).

1. Cain's eldest son, for whom the first city was named (Ge 4:17 – 18).

2. Son of Jared (Ge 5:18) and father of Methuselah (Ge 5:21 – 22; Lk 3:37). Abram walked "before God" (Ge 17:1), but of Enoch and Noah alone it is written that they walked "*with* God" (5:24; 6:9; emphasis added). Walking with God is a relic of the first paradise when people walked and talked with God in holy familiarity, and it anticipates a new paradise (Rev 21:3; 22:3 – 4). The secret of Enoch's walk with God was faith — the ground of his pleasing God, and this was the ground of his being "taken from this life, so that he did not experience death" (Heb 11:5 – 6). After the monotonous repetition of the patriarchs who "lived … begat … and died" (Ge 5 KJV), the account of Enoch's walk with God and translation without death stands forth in bright relief. He, too, begat sons and daughters, yet family ties were no hindrance to his walking with God. Indeed, it was not until after he was sixty-five years

old, when he begat Methuselah, that it is written, "Enoch walked with God." He typifies the saints living at Christ's coming who will be removed from mortality to immortality without passing through death (1Co 15:51 – 52). His translation out of a wicked world was an appropriate testimony to the truth ascribed to him in Jude 14 – 15, "See, the Lord is coming … to judge everyone."

ENOCH, BOOKS OF A collection of apocalyptic literature written by various authors and circulated under the name of Enoch. First Enoch is an Ethiopic version made through the Greek from the original Hebrew text that was written by the Chasidim or by the Pharisees between 163 – 63 BC. It is the best source for the development of Jewish doctrine in the last two pre-Christian centuries. Jude 14 – 15 may be an explicit quotation from it. Second Enoch was written AD 1 – 50.

ENVY [7861, 7863, 8353, 2419, 2420, 4057+4505, 4143, 5784]. The Hebrew word *qin'a* is rendered in OT translations as both "envy" and "jealousy," though in English the two are not synonymous terms. Thus Saul "kept a jealous eye on David" (1Sa 18:9), "jealousy arouses a husband's fury" (Pr 6:34), and "envy slays the simple" (Job 5:2). In Isa 26:11, NIV renders "zeal," and in SS 8:6 offers the marginal reading "ardor." The same Hebrew root is used with reference to the jealousy of the Lord or for his name (Ex 20:5; Eze 39:25; Joel 2:18). In the NT two Greek words are found: *phthonos* and *zēlos*. The former always has a bad sense (e.g., Mt 27:18; Gal 5:21; Php 1:29; Jas 4:5). While *zēlos* can be used similarly (Ac 13:45), it is more often translated "zeal" (e.g., Jn 2:17; Php 3:6). The word is used by Paul in 2Co 11:2: "I am jealous for you with a godly jealousy."

Characteristic of:
Depravity (Ro 1:29; Tit 3:3). Worldliness (Ro 13:13; 1Co 3:3; 12:20; Gal 5:19 – 21; 1Ti 6:4; Jas 3:14, 16; 4:5). Not characteristic of love (1Co 13:4).

Described as:
Destructive (Job 5:2). The cause of rotting bones (Pr 14:30). All consuming (Pr 27:4; SS 8:6). Drives people to achievement (Ecc 4:4). Unyielding as the grave (SS 8:6). Where envy and selfish ambition are found, disorder and every evil practice are found (Jas 3:16).

Forbidden:
(Pss 37:1, 7; 49:16 – 20; Pr 3:31 – 32; 23:17 – 18; 24:1 – 2, 19 – 20; Ro 13:13; Gal 5:25 – 26; Jas 5:8 – 9; 1Pe 2:1 – 2). Punishment for (Eze 35:11).

Instances of:
Cain, of Abel (Ge 4:4 – 8); Sarah, of Hagar (Ge 16:5 – 6; 21:9 – 10); Philistines, of Isaac because of the large number of flocks and herds he owned (Ge 26:14); Rachel, of Leah (Ge 30:1); Leah, of Rachel (Ge 30:15); Laban's sons, of Jacob (Ge 31:1); Joseph's brothers, of Joseph (Ge 37:4 – 11, 18 – 20; Ac 7:9); Joshua, of Eldad and Medad (Nu 11:28 – 30); Miriam and Aaron, of Moses (Nu 12:1 – 10); Korah, Dathan, and Abiram, of Moses (Nu 16:3; Ps 106:16 – 18); Saul, of David (1Sa 18:8 – 9, 29; 20:31); Haman, of Mordecai (Est 5:13); Asaph, at prosperity of wicked (Ps 73:2 – 3); the wicked, at the prosperity of the righteous (Ps 112:10; Isa 26:11); the princes of Babylon, of Daniel (Da 6:3 – 4); priests, of Jesus (Mt 27:18; Mk 15:10; Jn 11:47 – 48); Jews, of Paul and Barnabas (Ac 13:45; 17:5). See Jealousy.

Pr	3:31	Do not **e** a violent man
	14:30	but **e** rots the bones.
	23:17	Do not let your heart **e** sinners,
Mk	7:22	malice, deceit, lewdness, **e**, slander
Ro	1:29	They are full of **e**, murder, strife,
	11:14	arouse my own people to **e**
1Co	13:4	It does not **e**, it does not boast,
Gal	5:21	factions and **e**; drunkenness, orgies
Php	1:15	that some preach Christ out of **e**
	3:16	where you have **e** and selfish
1Pe	2:1	**e**, and slander of every kind.

EPHESIANS, LETTER TO THE Generally acknowledged to be one of the richest and profoundest of the NT letters. The depth and grandeur of its concepts, the richness and fullness of its message, and the majesty and dignity of its contents have made the letter to the Ephesians precious to believers in all ages and in all places. Its profound truths and vivid imagery have deeply penetrated into the thought and literature of the Christian church.

Ephesians explicitly claims authorship by Paul (Eph 1:1; 3:1), and its entire tenor is eminently Pauline. The early Christian church uniformly received and treasured it as from Paul. Only within the modern era have liberal critics raised doubts as to its origin. The attacks are based solely on internal arguments drawn from the style, vocabulary, and theology of the letter. These arguments are subjective and inconclusive and offer no compelling reasons for rejecting the undeviating evidence of text and tradition.

Ephesians was written while Paul was a prisoner (Eph 3:1; 4:1; 6:20). The prevailing view has been that it was written from Rome during his first Roman imprisonment (Ac 28:30 – 31).

Along with Colossians and Philemon (Col 4:7 – 8; Phm 9, 13, 17), the letter was transmitted to its destination by Tychicus (6:21 – 22). It seems that the letter was originally addressed to the saints "at Ephesus" but was intentionally cast into a form that would make it suitable to meet the needs of the Asian churches. As transcriptions of the original to the mother church were circulated, the place of destination might be omitted, though they were uniformly recognized as the letter originally addressed to the Ephesians.

Its contents offer no clear indication as to the occasion for the writing of Ephesians. Its affinity to Colossians in time of origin and contents suggests an occasion closely related to the writing of that letter. Ephesians seems to be the after-effect of the controversy that caused the writing of Colossians. Colossians has in it the intensity, rush, and roar of the battlefield, while Ephesians has a calm atmosphere suggestive of a survey of the field after the victory. With the theme of Colossians still fresh in mind, Paul felt it desirable to declare the positive significance of the great truths set forth in refuting the Colossian heresy. A firm grasp of the truths here stated would provide an effective antidote to such philosophical speculations.

Ephesians sets forth the wealth of the believer in union with Christ. It portrays the glories of our salvation and emphasizes the nature of the church as the body of Christ. As indicated by the doxology in 3:20 – 21, its contents fall into two parts, the first doctrinal (chs. 1 – 3), the second practical and encouraging (chs. 4 – 6). An outline suggests some of its riches.

    I. Salutation (1:1 – 2).
   II. Doctrinal: Believers' Standing in Christ (1:3 – 3:21).
     A. Thanksgiving for our redemption (1:3 – 14).
     B. Prayer for spiritual illumination (1:15 – 23).
     C. The power of God manifested in our salvation (2:1 – 10).
     D. The union of Jew and Gentile in one body in Christ (2:11 – 22).
     E. The apostle as the messenger of this mystery (3:1 – 13).
     F. Prayer for the realization of these blessings (3:14 – 19).
     G. Doxology of praise (3:20 – 21).
  III. Practical: Believers' Life in Christ (4:1 – 6:20).
     A. Their walk as God's saints (4:1 – 5:21).
       1. The worthy walk, in inward realization of Christian unity (4:1 – 16).
       2. The different walk, in outward manifestation of a changed position (4:17 – 32).
       3. The loving walk, in upward imitation of our Father (5:1 – 17).
       4. The summary of the Spirit-filled life (5:18 – 21).
     B. Their duties as God's family (5:22 – 6:9).
     C. Their warfare as God's soldiers (6:10 – 20).

IV. Conclusion (6:21 – 24).

EPHESUS [1650, 2386, 2387] (ĕf′e-sŭs, Gr. *Ephesos, desirable*). An old Ionian foundation at the mouth of the Cayster. Greek colonies that surround the Mediterranean and Black Sea were primarily trading posts. Migrant communities of Greeks did not seek to dominate the hinterlands, but to secure an *emporion*, or "way in," a bridgehead for commerce and enough surrounding coast and territory to support the community. Great cities grew from such foundations from Marseilles to Alexandria, some of them royal capitals. And in all cases colonies became centers or outposts of Hellenism, distinctive and civilizing.

Ephesus displaced Miletus as a trading port; but when its harbor, like that of Miletus, in turn silted up, Smyrna replaced both as the outlet and *emporion* of the Maeander Valley trade route. In the heyday of Asia Minor, 230 separate communities, each proud of its individuality and wealth, issued their own coinage and managed their own affairs. The dominance of Persian despotism, wide deforestation, and the ravages of war on a natural bridge and highway between the continents slowly sapped this prosperity; but in early Roman times, as in the days of its Ionian independence, Ephesus was a proud, rich, busy port, the rival of Alexandria and Syrian Antioch.

Built near the shrine of an old Anatolian fertility goddess, Ephesus became the seat of an oriental cult. The Anatolian deity had been taken over by the Greeks under the name of Artemis, the Diana of the Romans. Grotesquely represented with turreted head and many breasts, the goddess and her cult found expression in the famous temple, served, like that of Aphrodite at Corinth, by a host of priestess courtesans.

Much trade clustered round the cult. Ephesus became a place of pilgrimage for tourist-worshipers, all eager to carry away talismans and souvenirs, hence the prosperous guild of the silversmiths whose livelihood was the manufacture of silver shrines and images of the meteoric stone that was said to be Diana's image "fallen from heaven."

Ephesus leaned more and more on the trade that followed the cult, and commerce declined in its silting harbor. Twenty miles (thirty-three km.) of reedy marshland now separate the old harbor works from the sea, and even in Paul's day the process was under way. Tacitus tells us that an attempt was made to improve the seaway in AD 65, but the task proved too great. Ephesus in the first century was a dying city, given to parasite pursuits, living, like Athens, on a reputation, a curious meeting place of old and new religions, of East and West. Acts 19 gives a peculiarly vivid picture of her unnatural life. The "lampstand" had gone from its place, for Ephesus's decline was mortal sickness, and it is possible to detect in the letter to Ephesus in the Apocalypse a touch of the lassitude that characterized the effete and declining community. The temple and part of the city have been extensively excavated.

> **General References to:**
>   *Paul visits and preaches in (Ac 18:19 – 21; 19; 20:16 – 38). Apollos visits and preaches in (Ac 18:18 – 28). Sceva's sons attempt to expel a demon in (Ac 19:13 – 16). Timothy directed by Paul to remain at (1Ti 1:3). Onesiphorus lives at (2Ti 1:18). Paul sends Tychicus to (2Ti 4:12). Church at (Rev 1:11). Apocalyptic message to (Rev 2:1 – 7). See Ephesians, Letter to the.*

Ac	18:19	at **E**, where Paul left Priscilla
	19:1	the interior and arrived at **E**.
Eph	1:1	To the saints in **E**, the faithful
Rev	2:1	the angel of the church in **E** write:

EPHOD [680, 681] (ē′f′ŏd, Heb. *′ēphōdh*).

1. A sacred vestment worn by the high priest. Described (Ex 25:7; 28:6 – 14, 31 – 35). Breastplate attached to (Ex 28:22 – 30). Making of (Ex 39:2 – 26). Worn by Aaron (Ex 39:5). Samuel, as a young boy, wore an ephod made by his mother while he was ministering before the Lord (1Sa 2:18). Worn by the common priests (1Sa 22:18); by David (2Sa 6:14). Used as an oracle (1Sa 23:9, 12; 30:7 – 8).

As an Idol:

Gideon made an ephod out of gold, placing it in his hometown of Ophrah, the ephod subsequently becoming an idol to Israel (Jdg 8:27). Micah from the hill country of Ephraim made one of gold (Jdg 17:5; 18:14). Prophecy concerning the absence of an ephod from Israel (Hos 3:4).

2. A man of Manasseh (Nu 34:23).

EPHRAIM [713+2394] (ē'frâ-ĭm, Heb. *'eprayim, double fruit*). The younger of two sons of Joseph and his Egyptian wife, Asenath (Ge 41:50 – 52). The aged Jacob, when he blessed his grandsons Manasseh and Ephraim, adopted them as his own sons. Despite Joseph's protest, Jacob gave the preferential blessing (signified by the right hand) to Ephraim (48:1 – 22). When Jacob blessed his own sons, he did not mention Ephraim and Manasseh, but he did give a special blessing to their father, Joseph (49:22 – 26).

Ephraim was the progenitor of the tribe called by his name, as was also Manasseh. This brought the number of the Hebrew tribes to thirteen, but the original number twelve (derived from the twelve sons of Jacob, of whom Joseph was one) continued to be referred to. The separation of the tribe of Levi from the others for the tabernacle service, and its failure to receive a separate territory in which to live, helped to perpetuate the concept of "the twelve tribes of Israel."

EPICUREANS (ĕp-ĭkū-rē'ănz, Gr. *Epikoureioi*). The followers of Epicurus, a Greek philosopher who lived 341 – 270 BC. He taught that nature rather than reason is the true reality; nothing exists but atoms and void, that is, matter and space. The chief purpose of man is to achieve happiness. He has free will to plan and live a life of pleasure. Epicurus gave the widest scope to this matter of pleasure, interpreting it as avoidance of pain, so that the mere enjoyment of good health would be pleasure. Such stress on the good things of life, while very practical, is also very dangerous. For the philosopher the highest joy is found in mental and intellectual pursuits, but for lesser souls lower goals of sensual satisfaction fulfill the greatest pleasure. Thus the high standards of the founder were not maintained, and the philosophy gained a bad reputation. Since such teaching appealed to the common person, this natural philosophy became widespread. It was widely held at the time of Christ. Paul met it at Athens when he encountered the philosophers of that city (Ac 17:16 – 33). They were not impressed by his teaching of creation, judgment, and resurrection, since all these doctrines were denied by the Epicurean philosophy.

EPIPHANY From a Greek word meaning "manifestation," the term originally marked a feast to celebrate the baptism of Christ (Mt 3:16 – 17) — and still does so in the churches of Eastern Orthodoxy. The Lord had similarly "revealed his glory" at his first miracle in Cana of Galilee (Jn 2:11). From the fourth century, however, Epiphany has been linked with Christ's manifestation of himself to the magi, the first Gentiles who believed in him (Mt 2:1 – 12). In England it has become customary for the monarch to offer gold, myrrh, and frankincense in the Chapel Royal every year on January 6, the day the feast is observed.

EPISTLE (*letter*). Formal letters containing Christian doctrine and exhortation, referring particularly to the twenty-one epistles of the NT, divided into Pauline and General Epistles. Not all the letters of the apostles have survived (1Co 5:9; Col 4:16).

ESAU [6916, 2481] (ē'saw, Heb. *'ēsāw, hairy*). The firstborn of the twin brothers, Esau and Jacob, sons of Isaac and Rebecca (Ge 25:24 – 25). Before their birth God had told their mother that the elder should serve the younger (25:23). Esau became a man of the fields. He apparently lived only for the present. This characteristic was demonstrated when he let Jacob have his birthright for a dinner of bread and stew because he was hungry (25:30 – 34).

At the age of forty, he married two Hittite women (Ge 26:34). When the time came for Isaac to give his blessing to his son, he wanted to confer it on Esau, but, through trickery, Jacob obtained the blessing instead. This loss grieved Esau very much. He begged for another blessing, and when he received it he hated it because it made him the servant of his brother. He hated Jacob for cheating him and intended to kill him (Ge 27).

When Esau saw Jacob sent away to obtain a wife from his mother's relatives, he understood that Canaanite wives did not please his father, so he went out and took for himself two additional wives of the Ishmaelites (Ge 28:6–9).

Years later, when he was living in Mount Seir, Esau heard that Jacob was returning to Canaan (Ge 32:3–5). With four hundred men, he set out to meet his brother warmly (32:7–33:15). They soon parted company, and Esau went back to Mount Seir (33:16).

In the providence of God, Esau was made subservient to Jacob. In Heb 12:16–17 he is described as a profane person. Long after Esau's death, the Lord declared he had loved Jacob and hated Esau (Mal 1:2–3). The apostle Paul used this passage to illustrate how God carries out his purposes (Ro 9:10–13).

Sometimes in Scripture Esau is used as the name of the land of Edom in which his descendants lived (Ge 36:8).

Birth of (Ge 25:19–26; 1Ch 1:34); A hunter (Ge 25:27–28); Beloved by Isaac (Ge 25:27–28); Sold his birthright for a single meal of stew (Ge 25:29–34; 27:36; Heb 12:16); Alternately called Edom because he had red coloring; Edom means red (Ge 25:25, 30); Married two Hittite women (Ge 26:34); polygamy of (Ge 26:34; 28:9; 36:2–3); His marriages a grief to Isaac and Rebekah (Ge 26:35); Was defrauded of his father's blessing by Jacob (Ge 27; Heb 11:20); Met Jacob on the return of the latter from Haran (Ge 33:1); With Jacob, buried his father (Ge 35:29); Descendants of (Ge 36; 1Ch 1:35–57); called Edom (Ge 25:30; 36:1, 8); His name used to denote his descendants and their country (Dt 2:5; Jer 49:8, 10; Ob 6); Ancestor of Edomites (Jer 49:8); Enmity of descendants of, toward descendants of Jacob (Ob 10–14); Prophecies concerning (Ob 18)

ESCHATOLOGY (ĕs-ka-tŏl'ō-gē Gr. *eschatos, last* and *logos, ordered statement, study of last events*). The study of the last things to happen on this earth in this present age. The word is used to cover the study of such important events as the second coming/parousia of Jesus Christ, the judgment of the world, the resurrection of the dead, and the creation of the new heaven and earth. Related topics include the kingdom of God (the saving rule of God exhibited in Jesus Christ and experienced now through the Holy Spirit in anticipation of its fullness in the new heaven and earth of the age to come), the nature of the millennium, the intermediate state, the concept of immortality, and the eternal destiny of the wicked.

Since the Lord is presented in Scripture as the Creator, Preserver, Redeemer, and King, that which will bring the present age to its end and inaugurate the new age is seen as being very much under his control. Thus, the believer is to have hope. However, it is helpful, in order to do justice to the tension within the NT between salvation already (but partially) experienced and salvation not yet (wholly) experienced, to speak of "inaugurated" eschatology and "fulfilled" eschatology. The people of God are living in the last days, but the Last Day has not yet arrived. The new age broke into this present evil age when Christ rose from the dead, but the new has not yet wholly replaced the old. The Spirit of Christ brings into the present age the life of the age to come; so what he makes available is "firstfruits" (Ro 8:23), and he is the "guarantee/guarantor" or "pledge" of the fullness of life to come (2Co 1:22; 5:5; Eph 1:14).

As the people of the new age yet living in the old world and age, the church is called to engage in mission and evangelism (Mt 24:14; 28:19–20) until Christ's return to earth. Signs of the times — i.e., that the end is sure and near — include the evangelization of the world, the conversion of Israel (Ro 11:25–26), the great apostasy (2Th 2:1–3), the tribulation (Mt 24:21–30), and the revelation of the

Antichrist (2Th 2:1 – 12). These signs are seen during the whole of the "last days," particularly in the last of the last days.

SECOND COMING.

Christ is now in heaven, seated at the right hand of the Father as our exalted Prophet, Priest, and King, waiting for the time appointed by the Father to return to earth. Three Greek words — *parousia* (presence, 1Th 3:13), *apokalypsis* (revelation, 2Th 1:7 – 8), and *epiphaneia* (appearance, 2:8) — are used of this event in the NT. This coming will be nothing less than the personal, visible, and glorious return of the same Jesus who ascended into heaven (Mt 24:30; Ac 1:11; 3:19 – 21; Php 3:20). It will be an event of which everyone on earth will be abruptly aware, for it will mean the end of things as they are and the universal recognition of the true identity of Jesus of Nazareth. (Note: The position adopted here is the classic position, found in the ecumenical creeds — Apostles' and Nicene — but other scholars hold that Christ will come in two stages: first, secretly, to gather his faithful people [this is called the rapture], and then, seven years later, openly to be seen by all. This is part of the system of pretribulational dispensationalism and is expounded in the *Scofield Reference Bible*.)

RESURRECTION OF THE DEAD.

Christ himself rose bodily from the dead. His body was a real, yet spiritual, body, and he is the "firstborn" from the dead (Ro 8:11, 29; Col 1:18) and the "firstfruits" of the resurrection of all believers (1Co 15:20). The resurrection (Gr. *anastasis*) of every person who has ever lived is part of God's plan for the human race (Da 12:2; Jn 5:28 – 29; Ac 24:15); but the resurrection of the wicked will be the beginning of God's judgment on them, while the resurrection of the righteous will be the beginning of their life in Christ in the fullness of the kingdom of God. At the second coming of Christ, the dead will appear in their resurrection bodies; those who are alive will find that their bodies are marvelously changed, even though they remain the same individual persons. Little is taught in Scripture concerning the new bodies of the wicked; but we learn that the resurrection bodies of the righteous will be incorruptible, glorious, and spiritual (1Co 15:35ff.), like Christ's glorious body (Php 3:21). Life in the new age of the kingdom of God in the new heaven and earth will be everlasting, abundant life in an immortal body. The NT has no doctrine of the "immortality of the soul." (Note: Again, this is the classical tradition that there is one resurrection of the dead at Christ's coming. However, premillennialists maintain that there will be two resurrections — one of believers at the beginning of the one thousand years and one of unbelievers at the end of the millennium. Those who adopt the dispensationalist premillennial approach specify two other groups that will be resurrected — saints from the tribulation at the end of the seven years and saints from the millennium at the end of the one thousand years.)

One should distinguish between (1) the resurrection to mortal life, that is, life that will involve death — as happened to the widow's son (1Ki 17:17 – 24), the son of the Shunamite woman (2Ki 4:32 – 37), the widow of Nain's son (Lk 7:11 – 17), the daughter of Jairus (Mt 9:18 – 26), and Lazarus (Jn 11:38ff.) — and (2) the resurrection to immortality, of which Jesus is the supreme example and the "prototype." The nature of the resurrected bodies of those who came to bodily life as Jesus expired on the cross (Mt 27:51 – 52) is difficult to determine.

LAST JUDGMENT.

Having returned to earth, Jesus Christ will be the judge of the nations and of every person who has ever lived. In the name of God the Father (Ro 14:10; 1Pe 1:17), Jesus the Lord acts as universal judge (Ac 17:31). This judgment, however, is not to fix but to confirm the eternal destiny of human beings according to their acceptance or rejection of the gospel. Further, it is an examination of the motives and deeds of everyone, believer and unbeliever, together with judgment based on this evidence (Mt 11:20 – 22; 12:36; 25:35 – 40; 2Co 5:10) and on the human response to the known will of God (Mt 16:27; Ro 1:18 – 21; 2:12 – 16; Rev 20:12; 22:12). True believers will, in this judgment, be shown to be those in whom faith has manifested itself in love and deeds of mercy (Mt 7:21; 25:35ff.; Jas 2:18). Therefore, there are spiritual rewards in the age to come for those in this life who have faithfully served the Lord (Lk 19:12 – 27; 1Co 3:10 – 15; cf. Mt 5:11 – 12; 6:19 – 21). Those who hold to dispensationalism refer to several judgments — of the sins of believers (at Calvary), of the works of believers (at the time of the rapture), of individual Gentiles (before the millennium), of the people Israel (before the millennium), of fallen angels, and of the wicked (after the millennium). After the second coming of Christ and the final judgment, those who are judged to be the righteous begin their life in the new heaven and earth, while those who are judged to be unrighteous are consigned to everlasting punishment.

ETERNAL HAPPINESS IN THE NEW ORDER OF EXISTENCE (NEW HEAVEN AND EARTH).

At, or following, the second coming of Christ, the old universe will be marvelously regenerated (Ac 3:19 – 21; Ro 8:19 – 21; 2Pe 3:2) in order to be reborn as the "new heaven and earth," the new cosmos/universe. This is described in Isa 65:17 – 25; 66:22, 23; 2Pe 2:13; and Rev 21:1 – 4. In Rev 21 – 22 God himself is presented as dwelling with his people in this new order of existence, and, thus they are supremely happy with Christ as the center and light of all. It is fitting that those with resurrection bodies should dwell with their God in a regenerated universe, from which heaven — as God's place and sphere — is not separated but is rather present. This is the force of the picture of the descent of the heavenly Jerusalem in Rev 21:2, to be the center of the new universe.

ETERNAL MISERY AND PUNISHMENT IN HELL.

Jesus himself had more to say about hell (*see Hell*) than any other person whose teaching is recorded in the NT (e.g., Mt 5:22, 29 – 30; 10:28; 13:41 – 42; 25:46). Through a variety of pictures and images, the NT presents a frightening portrayal of the everlasting suffering of those who have rejected the gospel. Since this is a difficult and hard teaching to accept, two alternatives have been proposed and remain popular. The first is universalism, which insists that God is love and that ultimately all people will receive God's salvation. This approach involves the denial of the commonsensical interpretation of many NT passages. The second is annihilation — the wicked cease to exist after the last judgment. This involves the view that human beings are mortal beings (like animals) who, unless they are given the gift of immortality through grace, return to nothingness.

IMMORTALITY.

God alone truly possesses immortality (*aphtharsia*, 1Ti 6:16), for he is the eternal source of life. Human beings were created for immortality (rather than created with immortal souls); and this immortality, in the sense of receiving and enjoying God's life, is given to the righteous at the resurrection of the dead, in and through the gift of an imperishable and immortal new body (1Co 15:53 – 55). This immortal/eternal life, anticipated with the gift of the Spirit in new birth in this age, is fully given at the resurrection. At all times the immortality of the redeemed sinner is dependent on the gift of God, the source of eternal life. Careless talk about the immortality of the soul can eclipse the biblical emphasis that immortality belongs to God alone and is given to believing human beings in and through a body (2Co 5:1 – 4). The wicked retain their personal existence but away from the holy love and immortal, abundant, eternal life of God. They are never said to have immortality or to exist eternally in immortal bodies, for the NT use of immortality is to denote the immunity from death and decay that results from sharing in the divine life.

INTERMEDIATE STATE.

Those who are alive at the second coming of Christ will experience the transformation of their earthly, perishable bodies. But what of those who have died and will die before the end of the age and the resurrection of the dead? We know that their bodies return to dust. Since the emphasis of the NT is on the events that bring this age to an end and inaugurate the age of the kingdom of God, little is said about the existence of those who die before the second coming. This interim period when they await the resurrection is often called the "intermediate state." The parable of the rich man and Lazarus (Lk 16:19 – 31) suggests that there is conscious existence and that this can be of misery or of rest/happiness. Certainly the NT points to the comfort and security of those who die as disciples of Jesus (Lk 23:42 – 43; 2Co 5:6 – 8; Php 1:21 – 23; 1Th 4:16; *see also Hades; Paradise; Sheol*). One of our problems in understanding this period is that it involves the great problem of the relation of time and eternity.

ESSENES

ESSENES (ĕsē̄nz′, Gr. *Essenoi* or *Essaioi*). The meaning of the name is much debated; possibly it denotes "holy ones." They constituted a sect of the Jews in Palestine during the time of Christ but are not mentioned in the NT. Our principal sources of information regarding them are Josephus and Philo (first century) and Pliny the Elder and Hippolytus (second century).

The Essenes lived a simple life of sharing everything in common. They practiced strict rules of conduct. They were mostly unmarried and were reported to number four thousand. The majority of them lived together in settlements, but some resided in the cities of the Jews. Apparently they kept their ranks filled by the adoption of other people's children. They did not participate in the temple worship but had their own purification rites. They observed the Sabbath day very strictly and greatly venerated Moses. They would take no oaths; but new members, after going through a three-year probationary period, were required to swear a series of strong oaths that they would cooperate in every way with the organization and would never reveal to outsiders any of the affairs or beliefs of the sect.

The Essenes have come into public attention in late years because of the study of the Dead Sea Scrolls and the excavation of the monastery called Khirbet Qumran where the scrolls were written. This literature and building give evidence of an organization very similar to what is known about the Essenes.

ESTHER [676] (Heb. *'estēr*, perhaps from Akkad. *Ishtar* [Venus], Gr. *aster*, star). A Jewish orphan maiden in the city of Shushan who became queen of Persia. Her Hebrew name was Hadassah (*myrtle*). Her cousin Mordecai, who was a minor official of the palace, reared her as his own daughter. Xerxes (KJV Ahasuerus), the Persian king, had divorced his wife. When he sought a new queen from among the maidens of the realm, he chose Esther. When the Jews in the empire were faced with destruction, she was able to save them. In her honor the book that bears her name is read every year at the Feast of Purim.

Called also Hadassah (Est 2:7); Cousin of Mordecai (Est 2:7, 15); Chosen to be queen (Est 2:17); Tells the king of the plot against his life (Est 2:22); Fasts on account of the decree to destroy the Israelites; accuses Haman to the king; intercedes for her people (Est 4 – 9)

ESTHER, BOOK OF The last of the historical books of the OT. It was written after the death of King Xerxes (Est 10:2; KJV "Ahasuerus"). Most scholars today agree that the KJV Ahasuerus was the Xerxes who reigned 486 BC to 465 BC. Probably the book was written about 400. The author is unknown, but it is evident from the details of the record that he was well acquainted with the Persian court life. The book of Esther has always been accepted as canonical by the Jews.

External proof of the career of Mordecai has been found in an undated cuneiform text that mentions a certain Mordecai (Marduka) who was a high official at the Persian court of Shushan during the reign of Xerxes and even before that under Darius I. This text came from Borsippa and is the first reference to Mordecai outside the Bible.

Outstanding peculiarities of the book are the complete absence of the name of God, the lack of any direct religious teaching, and no mention of prayer. These remarkable features can have occurred only by deliberate design. Probably the book was written for the Jews in the Persian Empire as an account that could be circulated without danger of offending the people of that land who ruled over many Jews.

The account contains many dramatic elements. King Xerxes gave a great feast for all the officials of his realm. Queen Vashti offended him when she refused to appear before the company at the command of the king. As a result, he divorced her (Est 1). Later, in order to procure another queen, he ordered all the beautiful maidens of the land brought together. Among them was Hadassah, who had been reared by her cousin Mordecai. Her name was changed to Esther by the Persians. This maiden was chosen by the king to be his queen. Mordecai discovered a plot against the king's life (ch. 2). The king made Haman his chief minister. Everybody bowed down to him except Mordecai. This disrespect infuriated the high official. Knowing Mordecai was a Jew, Haman decided to destroy all the Jews in revenge for his hurt feelings. Lots, called *Pur*, were cast to find an auspicious day for the destruction. The consent of the king was obtained, and an official decree was written and publicized throughout the empire, setting the date

for the slaughter of the Jews (ch. 3). Mordecai sent word to Esther that she must plead for her people before the king (ch. 4). At the risk of her life, she went in before the king. He received her favorably. Instead of pleading with him at once, she invited him and Haman to a banquet. There the king asked her to state her request, but she put it off and invited them to another banquet. Haman, rejoicing in his good fortune but incensed at Mordecai, had a gallows constructed on which to hang him (ch. 5). That night, unable to sleep, the king was listening to the reading of the royal chronicles. When the account of Mordecai's discovery of the assassination plot was read, the king asked what reward had been given him and was told none at all.

It was early morning, and Haman had come to ask permission to hang Mordecai. But the king asked him what should be done to a man he wished to honor. Being convinced that the king could have only him in mind, Haman suggested the greatest of honors he could imagine. At the king's command, he was obliged to bestow those honors on Mordecai (Est 6). At the second banquet, Esther told the king about the scheme to destroy her people and named Haman as the one responsible for it. The king became very angry and ordered Haman to be hanged on the gallows he had made (ch. 7). Another decree was sent out that enabled the Jews to save themselves (ch. 8). In two days of fighting, they were victorious everywhere. Esther and Mordecai wrote letters to the Jews instituting the commemoration of these two days in an annual Feast of Purim (ch. 9). Mordecai, being next to the king, brought blessing to the people (ch. 10).

In the Septuagint, the book of Esther contains several interpolations scattered through the account.

ETERNAL

Ge	21:33	the name of the LORD, the **E** God.
Dt	33:27	The **e** God is your refuge,
1Ki	10:9	of the LORD's **e** love for Israel,
Ps	21:6	you have granted him **e** blessings
	111:10	To him belongs **e** praise.

	119:89	Your word, O Lᴏʀᴅ, is **e**;
Isa	26:4	Lᴏʀᴅ, the Lᴏʀᴅ, is the Rock **e**.
Jer	10:10	he is the living God, the **e** King.
Da	4:3	His kingdom is an **e** kingdom;
Hab	3:6	His ways are **e**.
Mt	18:8	two feet and be thrown into **e** fire.
	19:16	good thing must I do to get **e** life?"
	25:41	into the **e** fire prepared for the devil
	25:46	but the righteous to **e** life."
	25:46	they will go away to **e** punishment,
Mk	3:29	be forgiven; he is guilty of an **e** sin."
	10:17	"what must I do to inherit **e** life?"
Lk	10:25	"what must I do to inherit **e** life?"
	16:9	will be welcomed into **e** dwellings.
Jn	3:15	believes in him may have **e** life.
	3:16	him shall not perish but have **e** life.
	4:14	spring of water welling up to **e** life."
	5:24	believes him who sent me has **e** life
	5:39	that by them you possess **e** life.
	6:54	and drinks my blood has **e** life,
	12:50	that his command leads to **e** life.
	17:3	this is **e** life: that they may know
Ac	13:48	were appointed for **e** life believed.
Ro	1:20	his **e** power and divine nature —
	2:7	and immortality, he will give **e** life.
	5:21	righteousness to bring **e** life
	6:23	but the gift of God is **e** life
2Co	4:17	for us an **e** glory that far outweighs
Gal	6:8	from the Spirit will reap **e** life.
Eph	3:11	to his **e** purpose which he
1Ti	1:16	believe on him and receive **e** life.
	1:17	Now to the King **e**, immortal,
	6:12	Take hold of the **e** life
2Ti	2:10	is in Christ Jesus, with **e** glory.
Tit	1:2	resting on the hope of **e** life,
	3:7	heirs having the hope of **e** life.
Heb	5:9	he became the source of **e** salvation
	13:20	of the **e** covenant brought back
1Pe	5:10	you to his **e** glory in Christ,
2Pe	1:11	into the **e** kingdom of our Lord
1Jn	1:2	and we proclaim to you the **e** life,
	3:15	know that no murderer has **e** life
	5:13	you may know that you have **e** life.

| Jude | 1:7 | who suffer the punishment of **e** fire. |
| Rev | 14:6 | and he had the **e** gospel to proclaim |

ETERNAL LIFE [5905, 6329, 6409, 7710, 10550, 132, 172, 173]. Participation in the life of Jesus Christ, the eternal Son of God (Jn 1:4; 10:10; 17:3; Ro 6:23), which reaches its fruition in the life to come (Mt 25:46; Jn 6:54; Ro 2:7; Tit 3:7). It is endless in its duration and divine in quality.

ETERNAL PUNISHMENT See Punishment, Everlasting.

ETERNITY [5905, 6329, 6409, 7710, 10550, 132, 172, 173, 353].

God inhabits (Isa 57:15; Mic 5:2); rules (Jer 10:10). God, adoration for (Pss 30:12; 41:13); steadfastness of (Pss 72:17; 90:2; Mt 6:13); righteousness of (Ps 119:142; 2Co 9:9). *See God, Eternity of.* Priestly order of Melchizedek (Ps 110:4). Angels (Jude 6).

EUCHARIST (*thanksgiving*). One name for the Lord's Supper, meaning "giving of thanks." *See Lord's Supper.*

Instituted (Mt 26:17 – 29; Mk 14:22 – 25; Lk 22:19 – 20; Jn 13:1 – 4). Celebrated by the early church (Ac 2:42, 46; 20:7; 1Co 11:26). Bread and cup of, symbols of the body and blood of Christ (Mt 26:26 – 28; 1Co 10:16 – 17, 21 – 22; 11:23 – 25). Profanation of, forbidden (1Co 11:20 – 22, 33 – 34). Self-examination before taking, commanded (1Co 11:27 – 32).

EUNUCH (yū′nŭk, Heb. *sārîs*, Gr. *eunouchos*). A castrated male. From the employment of such men as custodians of royal harems, the term came to designate an officer, whether physically a eunuch or not. The Heb. *sārîs* is translated variously *officer*, *chamberlain*, and *eunuch* (e.g., Ge 37:36; 2Ki 23:1; Isa 56:3; Jer 29:2). The Mosaic law forbade those blemished by castration to enter the congregation (Dt 23:1), but Isaiah prophesied of a day when this disability would be removed and their loss compensated (Isa 56:3 – 5).

EUPHRATES (yū-frā′tēz, Heb. *perāth*, from a root meaning *to break forth*, Gr. *Euphratēs*). The longest and most important river of western Asia, frequently in the OT called "the river," "the great river," as being the largest with which Israel was acquainted, in contrast to the soon dried-up torrents of Palestine (Ge 15:18; Dt 1:7; Isa 8:7). It rises from two sources in the Armenian mountains, whose branches join after having run 400 (667 km.) and 270 miles (450 km.). The united river runs SW and south through the Taurus Mountains toward the Mediterranean; but the ranges north of Lebanon prevent its reaching that sea; it turns SE and flows 1,000 miles (1,667 km.) to the Persian Gulf. The whole course is 1,780 miles (2,967 km.); for 1,200 miles (2,000 km.) it is navigable for small vessels. The melting of the snows in the Armenian mountains causes the river to flood each spring

EVANGELIST [2296] (Gr. *euangelistēs, one who announces good news*). Used in a general sense of anyone who proclaims the gospel of Jesus Christ. Sometimes in the NT, however, it designates a particular class of ministry, as in Eph 4:11: Christ "gave some to be apostles ... prophets ... evangelists ... pastors and teachers." The evangelist founded the church; the pastor-teacher built it up in the faith. The evangelist was not confined in service to one spot but moved about in different localities, preaching the good news concerning Jesus Christ to those who had not heard the message before. Once such had put their trust in the Lord, the work of the pastor-teacher began. He would remain with them, training them further in the things pertaining to Christ and building them up in the faith. Apostles (Ac 8:25; 14:7; 1Co 1:17) did the work of an evangelist, as did also bishops (2Ti 4:2 – 5). Philip, who had been set apart as one of the seven deacons (Ac 6:5), was also called "the evangelist" (21:8). The word refers to a *work* rather than an *order*. Evangelist in the sense of "inspired writer of one of the four gospels" was a later usage.

Ac	21:8	stayed at the house of Philip the **e**,
2Ti	4:5	hardship, do the work of an **e**,

EVE [2558, 2293] (Heb. *hawwâh, life, living*). The first woman, formed by God out of Adam's side. Adam designated her (Ge 2:23) as "woman" (Heb. *'ishshâh*), for she was taken out of man (Heb. *'ish*). In these words there is suggested the close relationship between man and woman, a relationship the first man could not find in the animal creation (2:20). The way in which Eve was created and the designation "woman" emphasize also the intimacy, sacredness, and inseparability of the marital state, transcending even the relationship between children and parents (2:24). The name Eve was given to her after the fall and implies both her being the mother of all living and the mother of the promised Seed who would give life to the human race now subjected to death. While the Scriptures uniformly trace the fall of the race to Adam's sin, the part Eve played in this tragedy is vividly portrayed in Ge 3. Her greater weakness and susceptibility to temptation are juxtaposed with Adam's willful act of disobedience. Deceived by Satan, she ate of the fruit. Enamored of his wife, Adam chose to leave God for the one he had given him. Paul twice refers to Eve in his letters (2Co 11:3; 1Ti 2:13).

Ge	3:20	Adam named his wife **E**,
	4:1	Adam lay with his wife **E**,
2Co	11:3	as **E** was deceived by the serpent's
1Ti	2:13	For Adam was formed first, then **E**

EVERLASTING

Ge	9:16	and remember the **e** covenant
	17:7	an **e** covenant between me and you
	48:4	**e** possession to your descendants
Nu	18:19	It is an **e** covenant of salt
Dt	33:15	and the fruitfulness of the **e** hills;
2Sa	23:5	made with me an **e** covenant,
1Ch	16:17	to Israel as an **e** covenant:
	16:36	from **e** to **e**.
Ezr	9:12	to your children as an **e** inheritance
Ps	41:13	from **e** to **e**.
	52:5	God will bring you down to **e** ruin:
	105:10	to Israel as an **e** covenant:

	106:48	from **e** to **e**.
	119:142	Your righteousness is **e**
	139:24	and lead me in the way **e**.
	145:13	Your kingdom is an **e** kingdom,
Isa	9:6	**E** Father, Prince of Peace.
	24:5	and broken the **e** covenant.
	33:14	Who of us can dwell with **e** burning
	35:10	**e** joy will crown their heads.
	40:28	The LORD is the **e** God,
	56:5	I will give them an **e** name
	60:15	I will make you the **e** pride
	60:19	for the LORD will be your **e** light,
Jer	5:22	an **e** barrier it cannot cross.
	23:40	I will bring upon you **e** disgrace —
	25:9	of horror and scorn, and an **e** ruin.
	32:40	I will make an **e** covenant
	50:5	the LORD in an **e** covenant
Eze	16:60	and I will establish an **e** covenant
Da	7:14	dominion is an **e** dominion that will
	7:27	His kingdom will be an **e** kingdom,
	9:24	to bring in **e** righteousness,
	12:2	others to shame and **e** contempt.
	12:2	some to **e** life, others to shame
Mic	6:2	you **e** foundations of the earth.
Hab	1:12	O LORD, are you not from **e**?
Jn	6:47	the truth, he who believes has **e** life.
2Th	1:9	punished with **e** destruction

EVIL [2365, 4659, 6401, 6404, 6406, 8273, 8278, 8288, 8317, 8399, 8400, 8401, 94, 176, 2123, 2798, 2803, 2805, 4504, 4505, 5765] (Heb. *ra'*, Gr. *ponēros*, *kakos*). A term designating what is not in harmony with the divine order. In the Bible, evil is clearly depicted under two distinct aspects: moral and physical. The Hebrew word *ra'* has an immensely wide coverage, ranging from what tastes "nasty" right through to intrinsic moral and spiritual evil. Its two main "blocks" of meaning, spread evenly over some six thousand occurrences, cover meanings from "calamity," "disaster," and "downfall" to "wrong," "wicked," and "pernicious." For the precise meaning, the context must always be consulted; for example, in Isa 45:7, KJV has the literal meaning of "evil"; NIV inter-

prets it as "disaster," JB and NASB choose "calamity," NEB has "trouble," and RSV takes it to mean "woe" (cf. Am 3:6, where RSV has "evil").

The reconciliation of the existence of evil with the goodness and holiness of a God infinite in his wisdom and power is one of the great problems of theism. The Scriptures indicate that evil has been permitted by God in order that his justice might be manifested in its punishment and his grace in its forgiveness (Ro 9:22 – 23). Thus the existence of evil is a reminder of the manifold perfections of God. Moral evil, or sin, is any lack of conformity to the moral law of God. According to the Bible, it is the cause of the existence of physical or natural evil in this world. Adam and Eve, the first humans, enjoyed perfect fellowship with God in the garden of Eden. The day they ate of the fruit of the tree that was in the midst of the garden, disobeying God, they fell under his condemnation and were banished from the garden. The ground was then cursed for humanity's sake, and from that time forward man has been forced to gain sustenance through arduous, sorrowful toil, even as woman has borne children only through suffering and labor (Ge 3:16 – 19). In the NT the relationship between moral and natural evil is indicated by Paul in Ro 8:18 – 22.

General References to:
Tree of the Knowledge of Good and Evil (Ge 2:9, 17). Knowledge of (Ge 3:5, 22). In the heart (Ge 6:5; 8:21; Lk 6:45). To be forsaken (Pss 34:14; 37:27; Pr 3:7; 1Pe 3:11). To be abhorred (Ps 97:10; Am 5:15; Ro 12:9). You are not to repay evil for evil done to you (Ro 12:17; 1Th 5:15; 1Pe 3:9). Appearance of, to be avoided (Ro 14:1 – 23; 1Co 8:7 – 13; 10:28 – 33; 1Th 4:11 – 12; 5:22), exemplified by Paul, refusing to eat that which was offered to idols (1Co 8:13), in supporting himself (1Co 9:7 – 23).

Ge	2:9	of the knowledge of good and **e**.
	3:5	be like God, knowing good and **e**."
	6:5	of his heart was only **e** all the time.
Ex	32:22	how prone these people are to **e**.
Jdg	2:11	Then the Israelites did **e** in the eyes

1Ki	11:6	So Solomon did **e** in the eyes
Job	1:1	he feared God and shunned **e**.
	34:10	Far be it from God to do **e**,
Ps	5:4	not a God who takes pleasure in **e**;
	23:4	I will fear no **e**,
	34:13	keep your tongue from **e**
	34:14	Turn from **e** and do good;
	97:10	those who love the Lord hate **e**,
	101:4	I will have nothing to do with **e**.
	141:4	not my heart be drawn to what is **e**,
Pr	4:27	keep your foot from **e**.
	8:13	To fear the Lord is to hate **e**;
	10:23	A fool finds pleasure in **e** conduct,
	17:13	If a man pays back **e** for good,
	24:19	Do not fret because of **e** men
	26:23	are fervent lips with an **e** heart.
	28:5	**E** men do not understand justice,
	29:6	An **e** man is snared by his own sin,
Isa	5:20	Woe to those who call **e** good
	13:11	I will punish the world for its **e**,
Jer	4:14	wash the **e** from your heart
	18:11	So turn from your **e** ways,
Eze	33:11	Turn! Turn from your **e** ways!
Am	5:13	for the times are **e**.
Hab	1:13	Your eyes are too pure to look on **e**;
Zec	8:17	do not plot **e** against your neighbor,
Mt	5:45	He causes his sun to rise on the **e**
	6:13	but deliver us from the **e** one.'
	7:11	If you, then, though you are **e**,
	12:43	"When an **e** spirit comes out
	15:19	out of the heart come **e** thoughts,
Mk	7:21	come **e** thoughts, sexual
Lk	6:45	and the **e** man brings **e** things out
Jn	3:19	of light because their deeds were **e**.
	17:15	you protect them from the **e** one.
Ro	1:30	they invent ways of doing **e**;
	2:8	who reject the truth and follow **e**,
	7:19	no, the **e** I do not want to do —
	12:9	Hate what is **e**; cling
	12:17	Do not repay anyone **e** for **e**.
	12:21	Do not be overcome by **e**,
1Co	13:6	Love does not delight in **e**
	14:20	In regard to **e** be infants,

Eph	5:16	because the days are **e**.
	6:16	all the flaming arrows of the **e** one.
1Th	5:22	Avoid every kind of **e**.
1Ti	6:10	of money is a root of all kinds of **e**.
2Ti	2:22	Flee the **e** desires of youth,
Heb	5:14	to distinguish good from **e**.
Jas	1:13	For God cannot be tempted by **e**,
	3:8	It is a restless **e**, full
1Pe	2:16	your freedom as a cover-up for **e**;
	3:9	Do not repay **e** with **e** or insult
1Jn	2:13	you have overcome the **e** one.
	2:14	and you have overcome the **e** one.
	5:19	is under the control of the **e** one.

EXALT [EXALTED]

Ex	15:2	my father's God, and I will **e** him.
Job	19:5	If indeed you would **e** yourselves
Ps	30:1	I will **e** you, O Lord,
	34:3	let us **e** his name together.
	99:5	**E** the Lord our God
	118:28	you are my God, and I will **e** you.
Pr	25:6	Do not **e** yourself in the king's
Isa	24:15	**e** the name of the Lord, the God
2Th	2:4	will **e** himself over everything that is

EXALTED [EXALT]

Ex	15:1	for he is highly **e**.
Nu	24:7	their kingdom will be **e**.
Jos	4:14	That day the Lord **e** Joshua
	22:47	**E** be God, the Rock, my Savior!
Job	36:22	"God is **e** in his power.
Ps	18:46	**E** be God my Savior!
	18:48	You **e** me above my foes;
	21:13	Be **e**, O Lord, in your strength;
	57:5	Be **e**, O God, above the heavens;
	70:4	"Let God be **e**!"
	89:13	hand is strong, your right hand **e**.
	92:8	But you, O Lord, are **e** forever.
	97:9	you are **e** far above all gods.
	99:2	he is **e** over all the nations.
Pr	30:32	have played the fool and **e** yourself,
Isa	2:11	the Lord alone will be **e**
	6:1	**e**, and the train of his robe filled

Jer	17:12	A glorious throne, **e**
La	2:17	he has **e** the horn of your foes.
Eze	21:26	The lowly will be **e** and the **e** will be
Hos	13:1	he was **e** in Israel.
Mt	23:12	whoever humbles himself will be **e**.
Ac	2:33	**E** to the right hand of God,
	5:31	God **e** him to his own right hand
Php	1:20	always Christ will be **e** in my body,
	2:9	Therefore God **e** him
Heb	7:26	from sinners, **e** above the heavens.

EXCOMMUNICATION Disciplinary exclusion from church fellowship. The Jews had two forms of excommunication, apparently alluded to in Lk 6:22 by Christ: "Blessed are you … when they exclude you [the Jewish *middûy*, for thirty, sixty, or ninety days], and … reject your name as evil [the Jewish *hērem*, a formally pronounced, perpetual cutting off from the community], because of the Son of Man." Christian excommunication is commanded by Christ (Mt 18:15 – 18), and apostolic practice (1Ti 1:20) and precept (1Co 5:11; Tit 3:10) are in agreement. "Hand this man over to Satan" (1Co 5:5; 1Ti 1:20) seems to mean casting out of the church into the world that lies in the power of the wicked one (Eph 6:12; 1Jn 5:19). The object of excommunication is the good of the offender (1Co 5:5) and the moral well-being of the sound members (2Ti 2:17). Its subjects are those guilty of heresy or great immorality (1Co 5:1 – 5; 1Ti 1:20). It is inflicted by the church and its representative ministers (1Co 5:1, 3 – 4; Tit 3:10). Paul's inspired words give no warrant for uninspired ministers claiming the same right to direct the church to excommunicate at will (2Co 2:7 – 9).

EXILE [1583, 1655, 1661, 2143, 5615, 8654, 8660, 8938, 10120+10145, 3578, 3579]. This usually refers to the period of time during which the southern kingdom (Judah) was forcibly detained in Babylon. It began with a series of deportations during the reigns of the Judean kings, Jehoiakim (609 – 598 BC), Jehoiachin (598), and Zedekiah (598 – 587). After the destruction of Jerusalem by Nebuchadnezzar (587), the kingdom of Judah ceased to exist as a political entity. Although there were settlements in Egypt, the exiles in Babylon were the ones who maintained the historic faith and provided the nucleus that returned to Judea after the decree of Cyrus (536). The northern kingdom (Israel) was earlier exiled to Assyria (722). It was the policy of the Assyrian conquerors to move the populations of captured cities, with the result that Israelites were scattered in various parts of the empire and other captives were brought to the region around Samaria (2Ki 17:24). Subsequent history knows these people as the Samaritans. Although people from the northern kingdom doubtless returned with the Judean exiles, no organized return took place from the Assyrian captivity.

EXODUS [2016] (Gr. *ex hodos*, *a going out*). The event that ended the sojourn of Israel in Egypt. The family of Jacob (Israel) voluntarily entered Egypt during a time of severe famine in Canaan. Joseph, who had been sold into slavery by jealous brothers, was then vizier of Egypt and his Israelite brothers were assigned suitable land in the NE section of Egypt known as Goshen (Ge 42 – 46). When a new dynasty arose "who did not know about Joseph" (Ex 1:8), i.e., forgot what he had done for Egypt, the Israelites were reduced to the status of slaves. Afraid that they might prove sympathetic with foreign invaders, Pharaoh ordered the male children destroyed. The infant Moses, however, was placed in an ark of bulrushes where he was rescued by Pharaoh's daughter (2:1 – 10). Raised in the royal court, Moses chose to turn his back on the possibilities of advancement in Egypt in order to lead his oppressed people into freedom.

DATE OF THE EXODUS.

There has been a lack of unanimity among Bible students concerning the date of the exodus, as well as the identity of the pharaohs who took part in the oppression of Israel. Later pharaohs are sometimes mentioned by name (e.g., Pharaoh Hophra, Pharaoh Neco), but only the title "Pharaoh" is given in the exodus account. Some biblical scholars consider that 1Ki 6:1 is decisive in furnishing the date of the exodus. That verse states that Solomon began to build the temple "in the four hundred and eightieth year after the Israelites had come out of Egypt." Since we know the approximate dates of Solomon's reign, this information can be used in calculating the date of the exodus. The date suggested by this method of computation, about 1441 BC, falls within the reign of Amenhotep II, son of Thutmose III, one of the great empire builders of New Kingdom Egypt. Paintings from the tomb of Rekhmire, vizier of Thutmose III, depict Semites working as slave laborers on building projects.

Adherents of this "early date" of the exodus (1441 BC) also find support for their position from the Amarna Letters (1400 – 1366). These cuneiform tablets discovered at the site of Akhenaton's capital contain correspondence from the kings of the city-states in Canaan, asking the help of the pharaoh against a people known as Habiru. This, it is suggested, is a description of the battles fought after the exodus by the armies of Israel when seeking to conquer Canaan.

There are, however, serious difficulties in accepting the early date. During the Eighteenth Dynasty of Egyptian history (when the early date would fall), the capital of Egypt was at Thebes, south of the delta, and the building operations of Thutmose III seem to have been centered there. Later, however (during the time of the Rameses), the pharaohs resided in the delta, where they engaged in extensive building activity. It is specifically in the delta region, adjacent to Goshen, that Moses met with Pharaoh, and it was in the city of Rameses (also known as Avaris and Tanis) in the eastern delta that the Israelites are reported to have labored (Ex 1:11). Advocates of the early date suggest that the name Rameses is a modernization of an older name.

Because of these problems in dating the exodus as early as 1441 BC, a number of biblical scholars have come to accept a date in the thirteenth century. The evidence for the historicity of the exodus account is decisive, but the evidence for specific dates is still inconclusive.

ROUTE.

The biblical record (Ex 13:17) states that Israel did not take the direct route through the Philistine country to Canaan. Had they done so, Israel would have had to pass the Egyptian wall (biblical Shur) that protected the NE highways out of Egypt. The discipline of the wilderness was a part of God's preparation for his people before they were to come into open conflict with formidable foes. Leaving Rameses (12:37) in the eastern delta, the Israelites journeyed SE to Succoth (Tell el-Mashkutah).

They then moved on to Etham "on the edge of the desert" where they were conscious of God's guidance in the pillar of cloud and pillar of fire (Ex 13:21 – 22). The word *etham* is derived from an Egyptian word meaning "wall" and was probably part of the series of fortifications built by the Egyptians to keep out the Asiatic nomads. From Etham they turned back and camped near Pi Hahiroth, described as "between Migdol and the sea" and near Baal Zephon. The location of these sites is not known with certainty. It is possible that Pi Hahiroth is Egyptian for "house of the marshes." Baal Zephon is the name of a Semitic deity who was worshiped in Egypt, doubtless at a shrine located at the town that bore his name.

After passing Pi Hahiroth, Israel arrived at the body of water designated in the English versions as the Red Sea, the Yam Suph of the Hebrew text. The geography of the exodus suggests that Yam Suph, or Sea of Reeds, formed a natural barrier between Egypt and the Sinai peninsula, the ultimate destination of the Israelites. The topography of this region has been altered since the construction of the Suez Canal, but the Yam Suph was probably north of Lake Timsah. An Egyptian document from the thirteenth century BC mentions a Papyrus Lake not far from Tanis — whose suggested location is the southern extension of the present Lake Menzaleh. The exodus from Egypt through the Yam Suph was made possible by the direct intervention of God who "drove the sea back with a strong east wind" (Ex 14:21). Israel was thus able to cross from Egypt to the Sinai peninsula. When the armies of Pharaoh attempted to pursue the Israelites, the Egyptians were destroyed by the waters that returned to their normal course.

NUMBER OF ISRAELITES.

The Bible says that 600,000 men took part in the exodus (Ex 12:37). A year later the number of male Israelites over the age of twenty was 603,550 (Nu 1:46). During the years of Israel's sojourn in Egypt, the population multiplied to the point where Pharaoh was alarmed that Israel might side with an enemy during war (Ex 1:7 – 10). It was this very fear that brought about the oppression.

MIRACLES.

The exodus period was one of the great epochs of biblical miracles. The first nine plagues may have been related to the natural phenomena of Egypt, but their timing and intensification were clearly supernatural. The last plague — the death of the firstborn — signaled the beginning of the exodus. Israel ate the Passover meal in haste, ready to depart from Egypt. The opening of the Red Sea by the "strong east wind" was the means by which God brought his people out of Egypt into the wilderness where, for a period of forty years, they were miraculously sustained.

EXODUS, BOOK OF

The second book of the Bible. The title is a Latin term derived from the Greek word *Exodos*, "a going out." The book is called *Exodos* in the LXX. The title in the Hebrew tradition is comprised of the first several words of the book, "and these are the names." It refers to the names of the Israelites who came out of Egypt. Tradition ascribes the authorship of the book to Moses. It covers the history of the Israelites from the events surrounding the exodus to the giving of the law at Sinai.

THE ISRAELITES IN EGYPT.

(Ex 1:1 – 12:36). The historical events recorded in this section flow logically from the last chapters of the book of Genesis where we are told how Jacob and his sons came to live in Egypt. The clan grew into a nation, but the lot of the Hebrew people changed when a pharaoh arose who did not remember the contributions of Jacob's son Joseph who had been elevated to prominence in the Egyptian government years before (1:8). This king forced the Hebrew people into hard servitude (1:13 – 14). The birth of Moses and his providential preservation, when the pharaoh ordered the death of every male child born to the Hebrews (1:22), is recorded in ch. 2.

The account of Moses' call to lead the Hebrews out of Egypt (Ex 3:1 – 4:17) contains the classic statement of the Lord in which he depicts his divine character in the words, "I AM WHO I AM" (3:14), or "I am the one who is." While this statement has been understood in various ways, the context emphasizes the continuity of the promise made to the forefathers (3:13, 15 – 16). It is probably best to understand the words as connoting the continuity of God's dealings with his people — "I am the God who is," or "I am the God who continues to be"; that is, the God who appeared to Moses was the same God who gave his gracious promises to their forefathers. The God of Moses was the God of Abraham.

The efforts of Moses to free his people met with no success until the firstborn in Egypt were stricken by God. Only then were the Hebrews able to escape. (*See also Exodus.*)

FROM EGYPT TO SINAI.

(Ex 12:37 – 19:2). Three important Hebrew traditions were formalized just after the flight from Egypt: the Passover (12:43 – 49), which commemorated the fact that the Lord had passed over the houses of the Israelites (12:27); the Feast of Unleavened Bread (13:3 – 10); and the consecration to God of every firstborn male, "whether man or animal"

(13:2). When the Israelites had fled from Egypt, the pharaoh realized that he had lost a major source of manpower (14:5) and pursued them to the Red Sea, where God miraculously brought about their escape (14:21 – 31).

The period of Israelite history between the exodus and the giving of the law at Sinai was marked by frequent complaining by the people against God and their leader Moses. The complaints were often due to a lack of sustenance, but the deprivation was always met by miraculous displays of God's power. The bitter waters at Marah were made sweet (Ex 15:22 – 25), the hunger of the people was satisfied by the supply of manna (16:2 – 4) and quail (16:13), and their need for water on another occasion was met when God brought water out of a rock (17:2 – 7).

THE ISRAELITES AT SINAI.

(Ex 19:3 – 40:38). One of the most momentous events in Israelite history — the giving of the law — is recorded in this section. The Law was given in three general categories: the Decalogue or the Ten Commandments (20:2 – 17), civil and societal laws (21:1 – 23:11), and ceremonial laws (23:12 – 31:18). Moses' delay in returning from the mountain where the law was given was the cause of another period of apprehension and complaining on the part of the people. This led to the construction of a golden calf that Aaron, Moses' brother, proclaimed to be Israel's god (32:4). The cult of the golden calf, which was also observed many years later in the northern kingdom of Israel (1Ki 12:25 – 30), appears not to have been an outright rejection of Yahweh, but rather a syncretistic combination of worship of Yahweh and the calf. Verse 5 makes it clear that the worship associated with the golden calf was really directed to Yahweh. In the ancient world animal forms were often used to represent the point at which the spiritual presence of a deity was localized. For example, the storm god of Mesopotamia was prefigured as a lightning bolt set on the back of a bull. This is somewhat similar to the presence of Yahweh over the cherubim on the ark of the covenant.

The remainder of the book of Exodus records the implementation of the ceremonial law in the construction of the tabernacle (Ex 35:4 – 38:31) and the fashioning of the priests' garments (39:1 – 43). When the tabernacle was completed, it was filled with the glory of the Lord (40:34 – 38).

EXORCISM (Gr. *exorkizō, to adjure*). The expelling of demons by means of magic charms, spells, and incantations. It was a common practice among ancient heathen. In Ac 19:13 – 16 the profane use of Jesus' name as a mere spell was punished when the demon-possessed man turned on the would-be exorcists; these "vagabond Jews" were pretenders. Christ, however, implies that some Jews actually cast out demons (Mt 12:27) — some probably by demonic help, others (in the name of Jesus) without saving faith in him (7:22). He gave power to cast out demons to the Twelve, to the Seventy, and to the other disciples after the ascension (Mt 10:8; Mk 16:17; Lk 10:17 – 19; Ac 16:18). The Bible never mentions Christians "exorcising."

EZEKIEL [3489] (ē-zēk′yĕl, Heb. *yehezqē'l, God strengthens*). A Hebrew prophet of the exile. A play is made on this name in connection with the prophet's call (Eze 3:7 – 8, 14). Of a priestly family (1:3), Ezekiel grew up in Judea during the last years of Hebrew independence and was deported to Babylon with Jehoiachin in 597 BC, probably early in life. He was thus a younger contemporary of the prophet Jeremiah and of Daniel who, also as a young man, was taken to Babylon in 605. Ezekiel lived with the Jewish exiles by the irrigation canal Kebar (1:1, 3; 3:15), which connected the Tigris River with the Euphrates above Babylon; Daniel carried out his quite different work in the Babylonian court. We know little more about Ezekiel, except that he was married (24:18).

Ezekiel was called to be a prophet in the fifth year of his captivity (Eze 1:1 – 2); the last date mentioned is the twenty-seventh year (29:17); his ministry therefore lasted at least twenty-two years, from about 593 to 571 BC.

The "captivity" of the Jews consisted in their deportation to a foreign land. Once arrived in Babylon, however, the exiles seem to have been completely free to settle and live their lives as they pleased. When Jerusalem was finally destroyed, some ten years after he arrived in Babylon, Ezekiel entered into the sufferings of his people. On the day on which the final siege began, the prophet's wife became suddenly sick and died. In this he became a sign to the people and was not allowed to go through the customary period of mourning, doubtless to emphasize to them the greater sorrow now coming on the nation.

Ezekiel was a powerful preacher. Possessing a deeply introspective and religious nature, he used allegory, vivid figures, and symbolic actions to clothe his message. His favorite expression to denote the divine inspiration, "the hand of the LORD was upon me" (1:3; 3:14, 22), shows how strongly he felt impelled to communicate the message given him. His preaching was directed to his fellow Jews in exile; and like Jeremiah's, it was often resented, for it held out little hope for the immediate future. No doubt his message was ultimately received, for the exile became a time of religious purging. In Babylon the Jews were cured permanently of their idolatry; and Ezekiel, their major religious leader, must be given much credit for that.

The prophet's ministry was divided into two periods. The first ends with the siege of Jerusalem in 587 BC (24:1, 27). It was a message of approaching destruction for Jerusalem and of condemnation of the sin of its inhabitants. The second period begins with the reception of the news of Jerusalem's fall, some two years later (33:21 – 22). Now the prophet's message emphasized comfort and looked forward to the coming of the kingdom of God. It would appear that during the two years between, Ezekiel ceased all public ministry.

Frequently in this book (more than seventy times), Ezekiel is referred to as "son of man." The term means a mortal, as in Ps 8:4, and is used here to emphasize the prophet's weakness and dependence on God for his success. Later the term came to be a messianic designation.

> *The time of his prophecy (Eze 1:1 – 3); Persecution of (Eze 3:25); Visions: of God's glory (Eze 1; 8; 10; 11:22), of Israelites' abominations (8:5 – 6), of their punishment (9:10), of the valley of dry bones (37:1 – 14), of a man with a measuring line (chs. 40 – 48), of the river (47:1 – 5); Teaches by pantomime: feigns muteness (Eze 3:26; 24:27; 33:22), symbolizes the siege of Jerusalem by drawings on a tile (Eze 4), shaves himself (5:1 – 4), removes his belongings to illustrate the approaching Israelite captivity (12:3 – 7), sighs (21:6 – 7), employs a boiling pot to symbolize the destruction of Jerusalem (24:1 – 14), omits mourning at the death of his wife (24:16 – 27), prophesies by parable of an eagle (17:2 – 10); other parables (15; 16; 19; 23); Prophecies of, concerning various nations (Eze 25 – 29); His popularity (Eze 33:31 – 32)*

EZEKIEL, BOOK OF Until quite recently universally accepted as written by Ezekiel. Some critics have denied the unity of the book and have attributed all or parts of it to later writers. There has been, however, no agreement among these critics. The arguments for both the unity of the book and its origin with Ezekiel are very strong. The book is autobiographical — that is, the author often uses the first person singular pronoun. The arrangement of the book shows its unity — all the parts fit together and, indeed, need each other to make the whole.

The locality of Ezekiel's ministry was Babylon, to which he had been deported in 597 BC. The book is divided into three parts: denunciation of Judah and Israel (Eze 1 – 24, dated 593 – 588 BC); oracles against foreign nations (chs. 25 – 32, dated 587 – 571 BC); and the future restoration of Israel (chs. 33 – 48, dated 585 – 573).

The prophecies of the first section were uttered before the fall of Jerusalem. Ezekiel's call to the prophetic work is described in Eze 1 – 3. Here occurs his vision of the divine glory — God's throne borne by an unearthly chariot of cherubim and wheels (1:4 – 21). The prophet eats the scroll on which his sad message is written (2:8 – 3:3); and he is commanded to be the Lord's watchman, his own life to be forfeited if he does not cry the alarm (3:16 – 21; cf. 33:1 – 9). Ezekiel then predicts the destruction of Jerusalem by symbolic acts (4:7), such as laying siege to a replica of the city (4:1 – 8) and by rationing food and drink (4:9 – 17). Next follows the famous vision of Jerusalem's iniquity, for which Ezekiel is raptured in spirit to Jerusalem (chs. 8 – 11), and sees all kinds of loathsome idolatry being practiced in the temple courts. While he watches the desecration of the house of the Lord, he beholds the divine glory — which had been manifested in the Most Holy Place (8:4) — leave the temple and city (9:3; 10:4, 19; 11:22 – 23), symbolizing God's abandonment of his apostate people. At that moment Ezekiel returns in spirit to Babylon. The rest of the first section (chs. 12 – 24) records symbolic actions and sermons of the prophet predicting the fall of Jerusalem. He enacts the departure into exile (12:1 – 7), preaches against false prophets (chs. 13), and in two deeply moving oracles (chs. 16, 23) depicts the ungrateful people's apostasy. His statement of the individual's responsibility before God (ch. 18) is famous. Finally, he announces the beginning of the siege of Jerusalem, and in the evening of the same day his wife dies and he becomes mute until the fall of the city (ch. 24).

After the prophecies of judgment against foreign nations (Eze 25 – 32) comes the climax of the prophet's vision, written after the fall of Jerusalem — the restoration of Israel (chs. 33 – 48). God will bring back the people to their land, send the son of David to reign over them, and give them a new heart (chs. 34, 36). The vision of the valley of dry bones (ch. 37) is a figurative statement of this regathering of the nation. Then follows Isra-el's defeat of the Gentile powers, Gog and Magog (chs. 38 – 39). Finally, a great restored temple is pictured (chs. 40 – 43), its holy services (chs. 44 – 46), the river of life running from it (ch. 47), and the people of Israel living in their places around the city called "The LORD is there" (ch. 48), to which the glory of the Lord has returned (43:2, 4 – 5; 44:4).

EZRA [6474, 10537] (ĕz'ra, Heb. 'ezrā', help).
1. A man of Judah mentioned in 1Ch 4:17.
2. A leading priest who returned from Babylon to Jerusalem with Zerubbabel (Ne 12:1). In Ne 10:2 the name is spelled in its full form, Azariah.
3. The famous Jewish priest and scribe who is the main character of the book of Ezra and the coworker of Nehemiah. Ezra was a lineal descendant from Eleazar, the son of Aaron the high priest, and from Seraiah, the chief priest put to death at Riblah by order of Nebuchadnezzar (2Ki 25:18 – 21). All that is really known of Ezra is what is told in Ezr 7 – 10 and Ne 8 – 10. There are various traditions about him in Josephus, 2 Esdras, and the Talmud, but they are discrepant, and consequently no reliance can be put on anything they say unless it is also found in the canonical Scriptures. According to Jewish tradition, Ezra is the author of the book of Ezra and of 1 and 2 Chronicles. Many modern scholars hold that he wrote the book of Nehemiah as well.

EZRA, BOOK OF So named because Ezra is the principal person mentioned in it; possibly also because he may be its author. It does not in its entirety claim to be the work of Ezra, but Jewish tradition says it was written by him. Supporting this view is the fact that chs. 7 – 10 are written in the first person singular, while events in which he did not take part are described in the third person. The trustworthiness of the book does not, however, depend on the hypothesis that Ezra is the author. The majority of modern critics believe that the two books of Chronicles, Ezra, and Nehemiah constitute one large work, compiled and edited by someone designated the chronicler, who has been dated from 400 to 300 BC. Ezra's ministry is to be placed during the reign of Artaxerxes I (465 – 424 BC).

The book of Ezra continues the narrative after Chronicles and records the return from Babylon and the rebuilding of the temple. The purpose of the author is to show how God fulfilled his promise given through prophets to restore his exiled people to their own land through heathen monarchs, and raised up such great men as Zerubbabel, Haggai, Zechariah, and Ezra to rebuild the temple, reestablish the old forms of worship, and put a stop to compromise with heathenism. All material that does not contribute to his purpose he stringently excludes.

As sources for the writing of the book, the author used genealogical lists, letters, royal edicts, memoirs, and chronicles. Some of these were official documents found in public records. This diversity of material accounts for the varied character of the style and for the fact that it is written in both Hebrew and Aramaic.

The order of the Persian kings of the period is Cyrus (538 – 529 BC), Darius (521 – 486), Xerxes (486 – 464), and Artaxerxes I (464 – 424). In view of this succession, Ezr 4:7 – 23 departs from the chronological order of events. The reason for this is probably that the author regarded a sequence of content more important than a chronological order. He brings together in one passage the successful attempts of the Samaritans to hinder the building of the temple and the city walls.

The period covered is from 536 BC, when the Jews returned to Jerusalem, to 458, when Ezra came to Jerusalem to carry out his religious reforms. It thus covers a period of about seventy-eight years, although the fifteen years between 535 and 520 and the fifty-eight years between 516 and 458 are practically a blank. We have a description of selected incidents, not a continuous record of the period.

FAITH [574, 575, 586, 953, 5085+5086, 5085, 9459, 601, 602, 1650+4411+4411, 1666+4411, 3898, 3899, 4409, 4411, 4412] (Heb. *'ēmûn*, Gr. *pistis*). Faith has a twofold sense in the Bible. On the one hand it means "trust," "reliance," and on the other it means "fidelity," "trustworthiness." An example of the first meaning is found in Ro 3:3, where "the faith of God" (KJV; NIV "God's faithfulness") means his fidelity to promise. In most other cases it has the second meaning.

In the OT the verb "to believe" occurs only thirty times, but this comparative infrequency does not adequately reflect the importance of the place of faith in the OT scheme of things. The NT draws all its examples of faith from the lives of OT believers (e.g., Ro 4:18ff.; Heb 11; Jas 2:14ff.), and Paul rests his doctrine of faith on the word of Hab 2:4. It would thus be true to say that the OT demands faith more than it develops an explicit doctrine of faith. It looks for, and finds in its great individuals, a true commitment of self to God, an unwavering trust in his promises, and a persistent fidelity and obedience.

In contrast with the extreme rarity with which the terms "faith" and "believe" are used in the OT, they occur with great frequency in the NT—almost five hundred times. A principal reason for this is that the NT makes the claim that the promised Messiah had finally come, and, to the bewilderment of many, the form of the fulfillment did not obviously correspond to the messianic promise. It required a real act of faith to believe that Jesus of Nazareth was the promised Messiah. It was not long before "to believe" meant to become a Christian. In the NT, faith therefore becomes the supreme human act and experience.

In his miracles and teaching, Jesus aimed at creating in his disciples a complete trust in himself as the Messiah and Savior of people. Everywhere he offered himself as the object of faith and made it plain that faith in him is necessary for eternal life, that it is what God required of OT people, and that refusal to accept his claims will bring eternal ruin. His primary concern with his own disciples was to build up their faith in him.

The record in Acts shows that the first Christians called themselves "the believers" (Ac 2:44) and that they went everywhere persuading people and bringing them into obedience to the faith that is in Jesus (6:7; 17:4; 28:24). Before long, as communities of believers arose in various parts of the Mediterranean world, the apostolic leaders had to teach them more fully the meaning and implications of the Christian faith, and so the NT books appeared.

It is in Paul's letters that the meaning of faith is most clearly and fully set forth. Faith is trust in the person of Jesus, the truth of his teaching, and the redemptive work he accomplished at Calvary, and, as a result, a total submission to him and his message, which are accepted as from God. Faith in his person is faith in him as the eternal Son of God, the God-man, the second man Adam, who died in man's stead, making possible justification with God, adoption into his family, sanctification, and, ultimately, glorification. His death brings redemption from sin in all its aspects. The truth of his claims is attested by God's raising him from the dead. Someday he will judge the living and the dead. Faith is not to be confused with a mere intellectual assent to the doctrinal teachings of Christianity, though that is obviously necessary. It includes a radical and total commitment to Christ as the Lord of one's life.

Unbelief, or lack of faith in the Christian gospel, appears everywhere in the NT as the supreme evil. Not to make a decisive response to God's offer in Christ means that individuals remain in sin and are eternally lost. Faith alone can save them.

> **Value of:**
> *People are kept secure by (2Ch 20:20; Ro 11:20; 2Co 1:24; 1Jn 5:4); are established by (Isa 7:9); are saved by (Jn 3:15; Ac 16:31; Ro 9:30 – 32; Gal 2:16; Eph 2:8 – 9; Php 3:9); are healed by (Ac 14:9; Jas 5:15); are sanctified by (Ac 26:18); receive the Holy Spirit by (Gal 3:5, 14); live by (2Co 5:7). Causes people to be a blessing to others (Jn 7:38).*

Disbelieving God is a great sin (Jn 16:9; Ro 14:23). Faith is necessary to please God (Heb 11:6).

The Gift of God:

The apostles ask Jesus to increase (Lk 17:5). God gives a certain measure of (Ro 12:3; 1Co 2:4 – 5). Given by the Spirit (1Co 12:8 – 9).

Purpose of:

To gain understanding and to grow in the truth (Pss 119:97 – 105, 129 – 131; Jn 8:31 – 32; 2Ti 2:15; 1Jn 2:5, 14). To grow in the grace of God (Ac 2:42 – 47; Ro 4:4 – 5; 5:2; 1Co 15:10; Eph 4:15; Heb 4:16). To help us to rejoice through our faith (Ro 5:2 – 5, 11; 15:13; Php 1:18 – 19; 2:17 – 18). To strengthen the person of faith (Ro 6:12 – 14; 11:20; 1Co 9:27; Php 4:6 – 7; 2Th 3:3; 2Ti 4:7 – 8; 1Pe 1:3 – 5). To be transformed into the image of Christ (Ro 8:29; 1Co 15:49; 2Co 3:18; 4:3 – 6). To become strong people of faith (Eph 4:1 – 3, 11 – 13, 15 – 16).

Effect of:

Faith not works (Gal 5:5 – 6). Produces good works (1Th 1:3; 2Th 1:11); internal changes (1Th 2:13); perseverance (Jas 1:3).

Righteousness of:

The true righteousness of God comes from (Ro 1:17; 3:21 – 30; 4:3, 11; 9:31 – 33; 10:4 – 11; Gal 2:16; Php 3:9; Heb 11:7).

Biblical Position Concerning:

Credited as righteousness (Ge 15:6; Ro 4:3; Gal 3:6; Jas 2:23). Inspired by God's goodness (Ps 36:7, 9). Inspired by the Holy Spirit (1Co 12:8 – 9). Explained (Ps 118:8 – 9; Lk 17:6; 18:8; 1Ti 4:12; Heb 11:1 – 3, 6). Worry, doubt, and the lack of faith (Mt 6:25 – 34; 14:31; Lk 9:40; 17:5). Prayer for increase of faith (Mk 9:24; Lk 17:5). The gift of God (Ro 12:3). The righteous live by (Hab 2:4; Ro 1:17; Gal 3:11; Heb 10:38). Miracles accomplished by (Mt 17:18 – 20; 21:21 – 22; Mk 9:23; 11:23 – 24). Secures salvation (Col 2:12; 2Th 2:13; Heb 4:1 – 11; 6:1, 12, 18).

Strengthened by Miracles:

Of Abraham (Ge 15:8 – 18); of Gideon (Jdg 6:17, 36 – 40); of Hezekiah (2Ki 20:8 – 11); of Zechariah (Lk 1:18 – 20, 64).

In Affliction:

Exemplified by Job (Job 13:15 – 16; 14:15; 16:19; 19:25 – 27).

In Adversity:

Exemplified by Hagar (Ge 16:15); Moses (Nu 14:8 – 9); Asa (2Ch 14:11); Jehoshaphat (2Ch 20:12); Hezekiah (2Ch 32:7 – 8); Nehemiah (Ne 1:10; 2:20); the psalmist (Pss 3:3, 5 – 6; 4:3, 8; 6:8 – 9; 7:1, 10; 9:3 – 4; 11:1; 13:5; 17:6; 20:5 – 7; 31:1, 3 – 6, 14 – 15; 32:7; 33:20 – 22; 35:10; 38:9, 15; 42:5 – 6, 8; 43:5; 44:5, 8; 46:1 – 3, 5, 7; 54:4; 55:16 – 17, 23; 56:3 – 4, 8 – 9; 57:1 – 3; 59:9, 17; 60:9 – 10, 12; 61:2, 4, 6 – 7; 62:1, 5 – 7; 63:6 – 7; 69:19, 35 – 36; 70:5; 71:1, 3, 5 – 7, 14, 16, 20 – 21; 73:23 – 24, 26, 28; 86:2, 7; 89:18, 26; 91:1 – 2, 9 – 10; 92:10, 15; 94:14 – 15, 17 – 18, 22; 102:13; 108:10 – 13; 118:6 – 7, 10, 14, 17; 119:42, 57, 74, 81, 114, 166; 121:2; 138:7 – 8; 140:6 – 7, 12; 142:3, 5; 143:8 – 9); Jeremiah (La 3:24); Daniel (Da 3:16 – 17); Jonah (Jnh 2:2); Micah (Mic 7:7 – 9, 20); Paul (Ac 27:25; 2Co 1:10; 4:8 – 9, 13, 16 – 18; Php 1:19 – 21; 1Ti 4:10; 2Ti 1:12 – 13; 4:7 – 8, 18); the author of the letter to the Hebrews (Heb 10:34).

Commanded:

(Pss 4:5; 115:9, 11; Ecc 11:1; Isa 26:4; Mt 6:25 – 34; Mk 1:15; 11:22; Lk 12:32; 1Ti 6:11 – 12, 17; Jas 1:6). In time of public danger (Ex 14:13; Nu 21:34; Dt 1:21, 29 – 30; 3:2, 22; 7:17 – 21; 20:1; 31:8, 23; Jos 10:25; Jdg 6:14 – 16; 2Ki 19:6 – 7; 2Ch 20:15, 17, 20; 32:7 – 8; Ne 4:14; Isa 37:6; Jer 42:11). In time of adversity (Pss 37:3, 5, 7; 55:22; 62:8; Isa 43:1 – 2, 5, 10; 44:2, 8). Upon public leaders (Jos 1:5 – 9; 2Ch 15:7); upon the young (Pr 3:5 – 6, 24 – 26); upon the discouraged (Isa 35:3 – 4; 41:10, 13 – 14; 50:10); upon widows (Jer 49:11).

Ex	21:8	because he has broken **f** with her.
2Ch	20:20	Have **f** in the Lord your God
Isa	7:9	If you do not stand firm in your **f**,

Hab	2:4	but the righteous will live by his **f**—
Mal	2:10	by breaking **f** with one another?
Mt	6:30	O you of little **f**? So do not worry,
	8:10	anyone in Israel with such great **f**.
	9:2	When Jesus saw their **f**, he said
	9:22	he said, "your **f** has healed you."
	13:58	there because of their lack of **f**.
	15:28	"Woman, you have great **f**!
	17:20	if you have **f** as small as a mustard
	21:21	if you have **f** and do not doubt,
	24:10	many will turn away from the **f**
Mk	2:5	When Jesus saw their **f**, he said
	4:40	still have no **f**?" They were
	6:6	he was amazed at their lack of **f**.
	11:22	"Have **f** in God," Jesus answered.
	16:14	he rebuked them for their lack of **f**
Lk	7:9	I have not found such great **f**
	7:50	the woman, "Your **f** has saved you;
	12:28	will he clothe you, O you of little **f**!
	17:5	"Increase our **f**!" He replied,
	18:8	will he find **f** on the earth?"
	22:32	Simon, that your **f** may not fail.
Jn	2:11	and his disciples put their **f** in him.
	7:31	in the crowd put their **f** in him.
	11:45	had seen what Jesus did, put their **f**
	12:11	to Jesus and putting their **f** in him.
	14:12	anyone who has **f** in me will do
Ac	3:16	By **f** in the name of Jesus, this man
	6:5	full of **f** and of the Holy Spirit;
	6:7	of priests became obedient to the **f**.
	14:9	saw that he had **f** to be healed
	14:22	them to remain true to the **f**.
	14:27	the door of **f** to the Gentiles.
	15:9	for he purified their hearts by **f**.
	26:18	those who are sanctified by **f**
Ro	1:5	to the obedience that comes from **f**.
	1:12	encouraged by each other's **f**.
	1:17	"The righteous will live by **f**."
	3:3	What if some did not have **f**?
	3:3	lack of **f** nullify God's faithfulness?
	3:22	comes through **f** in Jesus Christ
	3:25	a sacrifice of atonement, through **f**
	4:5	his **f** is credited as righteousness.
	4:13	the righteousness that comes by **f**.
	4:16	Therefore, the promise comes by **f**,
	5:1	we have been justified through **f**,
	5:2	access by **f** into this grace
	9:30	a righteousness that is by **f**;
	10:6	the righteousness that is by **f** says:
	10:17	**f** comes from hearing the message,
	11:20	of unbelief, and you stand by **f**.
	12:3	measure of **f** God has given you.
	14:1	Accept him whose **f** is weak,
	14:23	that does not come from **f** is sin.
1Co	2:5	so that your **f** might not rest
	13:2	and if I have a **f** that can move
	13:13	And now these three remain: **f**,
	15:14	is useless and so is your **f**.
	16:13	stand firm in the **f**; be men
2Co	1:24	Not that we lord it over your **f**,
	5:7	We live by **f**, not by sight.
	10:15	as your **f** continues to grow,
	13:5	to see whether you are in the **f**;
Gal	1:23	now preaching the **f** he once tried
	2:16	Jesus that we may be justified by **f**
	2:20	I live by **f** in the Son of God,
	3:14	by **f** we might receive the promise
	5:5	But by **f** we eagerly await
Eph	2:8	through **f**—and this not
	3:12	through **f** in him we may approach
	4:5	one Lord, one **f**, one baptism;
	4:13	up until we all reach unity in the **f**
	6:16	to all this, take up the shield of **f**,
Php	1:25	for your progress and joy in the **f**,
	3:9	comes from God and is by **f**.
Col	1:23	continue in your **f**, established
	2:5	and how firm your **f** in Christ is.
	2:7	in the **f** as you were taught,
1Th	1:8	your **f** in God has become known
	3:10	supply what is lacking in your **f**.
	5:8	on **f** and love as a breastplate,
1Ti	1:4	than God's work—which is by **f**.
	1:14	along with the **f** and love that are
	1:19	and so have shipwrecked their **f**.
	2:15	if they continue in **f**, love
	3:9	of the **f** with a clear conscience.

	3:13	assurance in their **f** in Christ Jesus.
	4:1	later times some will abandon the **f**
	5:8	he has denied the **f** and is worse
	6:11	pursue righteousness, godliness, **f**,
	6:12	Fight the good fight of the **f**.
2Ti	1:13	with **f** and love in Christ Jesus.
	2:18	and they destroy the **f** of some.
	4:7	finished the race, I have kept the **f**.
Tit	1:1	Christ for the **f** of God's elect
	2:2	self-controlled, and sound in **f**,
	3:15	Greet those who love us in the **f**.
Phm	1:5	because I hear about your **f**
	1:6	may be active in sharing your **f**,
Heb	4:2	heard did not combine it with **f**.
	4:14	firmly to the **f** we profess.
	10:22	heart in full assurance of **f**,
	10:38	But my righteous one will live by **f**.
	11:1	**f** is being sure of what we hope for
	11:4	And by **f** he still speaks, even
	11:4	By **f** Abel offered God a better
	11:39	were all commended for their **f**,
	12:2	the author and perfecter of our **f**,
	13:7	way of life and imitate their **f**.
Jas	1:3	of your **f** develops perseverance.
	2:14	has no deeds? Can such **f** save him?
	2:18	I will show you my **f** by what I do.
	2:26	so **f** without deeds is dead.
	5:15	in **f** will make the sick person well;
1Pe	1:7	These have come so that your **f** —
	1:9	you are receiving the goal of your **f**,
	5:9	Resist him, standing firm in the **f**,
2Pe	1:5	effort to add to your **f** goodness;
1Jn	5:4	overcome the world, even our **f**.
Jude	3	to contend for the **f** that was once
	20	up in your most holy **f**
Rev	2:13	You did not renounce your **f** in me,

FAITHFULNESS [573, 574, 575, 586,622, 2874, 2876, 2883, 9068, 4411, 4412] (Heb. *ĕmûnâh*). An attribute or quality applied in the Bible to both God and humans. When used of God, it has in the OT a twofold emphasis, referring first to his absolute reliability, firm constancy, and complete freedom from arbitrariness or fickleness, and also to his steadfast love toward his people and his loyalty. God is constant and true in contrast to all that is not God. He is faithful in keeping his promises and is therefore worthy of trust. He is unchangeable in his ethical nature. God's faithfulness is usually connected with his gracious promises of salvation. Faithful people are dependable in fulfilling their responsibilities and in carrying out their word. In the NT there are frequent exhortations to faithfulness. It is one of the fruits of the Spirit in Gal 5:22.

Described:
   Scarce (Ps 12:1; Pr 20:6). Tested (Lk 16:10 – 12). A fruit of the Spirit (Gal 5:22). Rewards of (Ps 31:23; Pr 28:20; Mt 10:22; 13:12; 25:29; Mk 13:13; Heb 10:34; Rev 2:10).

Required:
   (Mt 24:45 – 51, w Lk 12:36 – 48; Mt 25:14 – 30, w Lk 19:12 – 27). Of those who are trusted (1Co 4:2). Of servants (Eph 6:5 – 9; Col 3:22).

Instances of:
   Abraham's servant (Ge 24:33); Moses (Nu 12:7; Heb 3:3, 5); Ruth (Ru 1:15 – 18); Ittai the Gittite (2Sa 15:19 – 22); David (2Sa 22:22 – 25); Elijah (1Ki 19:10, 14); workmen in temple repairs (2Ki 12:15; 2Ch 34:12); Josiah (2Ki 22:2); Abijah (2Ch 13:10 – 12); Jehoshaphat (2Ch 20:1 – 30); Hanani and Hananiah (Ne 7:2); Abraham (Ne 9:7 – 8; Gal 3:9); Nehemiah's treasurer (Ne 13:13); Job (Job 1:21 – 22; 2:9 – 10); the three Hebrew captives (Da 3:16 – 18); Daniel (Da 6:10); Jesus (Jn 4:34; Heb 3:2); Abraham (Gal 3:9); Paul (1Ti 1:12; 2Ti 4:7).

Ge	47:29	you will show me kindness and **f**.
Ex	34:6	**f**, maintaining love to thousands,
Jos	24:14	the Lord and serve him with all **f**.
Ps	30:9	Will it proclaim your **f**?
	36:5	your **f** to the skies.
	40:10	I speak of your **f** and salvation.
	85:10	Love and **f** meet together;
	86:15	to anger, abounding in love and **f**.

	88:11	your **f** in Destruction?
	89:1	mouth I will make your **f** known
	89:8	and your **f** surrounds you.
	89:14	love and **f** go before you.
	91:4	his **f** will be your shield
	98:3	and his **f** to the house of Israel;
	100:5	**f** continues through all
	115:1	because of your love and **f**.
	117:2	the **f** of the Lord endures forever.
	119:75	and in **f** you have afflicted me.
	138:2	name for your love and your **f**,
Pr	3:3	Let love and **f** never leave you;
	16:6	Through love and **f** sin is atoned for
Isa	11:5	and **f** the sash around his waist.
	16:5	in **f** a man will sit on it —
	42:3	In **f** he will bring forth justice;
	61:8	In my **f** I will reward them
La	3:23	great is your **f**.
Hos	2:20	I will betroth you in **f**,
Mt	23:23	of the law — justice, mercy and **f**.
Ro	3:3	lack of faith nullify God's **f**?
Gal	5:22	patience, kindness, goodness, **f**,
3Jn	3	and tell about your **f** to the truth
Rev	13:10	and **f** on the part of the saints.

FALL, THE The fall of man is narrated in Ge 3 as a historical fact, not as a myth. It stands in a context of historical facts. Though not alluded to again in the OT, it is regarded as historical in the NT (Ro 5:12 – 13; 1Co 15:22; 1Ti 2:14). Some philosophers and theologians think the account is an allegory describing the awakening of man from a brute state of self-consciousness and personality — a fall upward rather than downward — but such an explanation conflicts radically with biblical teaching. There is no doubt that Paul takes the account literally and sees in the fall the origin of sin in the human race. The scriptural view of sin and of redemption takes the fall for granted.

The Scriptures teach us that humans were created in the image of God, with a rational and moral nature like God's, with no inner impulse or drive to sin, and with a will free to do God's will. There was, moreover,

nothing in their environment to compel them to sin or to make sin excusable. In these circumstances, solicitation to sin could come only from outside. The Bible does not allow us to probe the mystery of the presence of sin in God's fair universe; as in so many other things, it faces us with the practical reality, the voice of the Tempter coming to humans from outside themselves, the voice of the serpent that the rest of the Bible recognizes as the voice of Satan.

The sin that constituted the fall involved Adam and Eve in disobeying the word of God (Ge 3:1 – 4) and challenging the goodness of God by imputing to him an ill motive (3:5). But chiefly it consisted in disobeying the law of God. Such was the bounty of the Creator that the whole lavish richness of the garden was open to Adam and Eve with only a single condition (2:16 – 17). The fall was thus the breaking of the whole law of God. Equally involved in the fall was the whole nature of humankind. Eve was first emotionally attracted to the forbidden fruit (3:6, "good for food and pleasing to the eye"); second, she was led into sin by the logic of her mind that contradicted the mind of God. He had said, "You must not eat from the tree of the knowledge of good and evil, for … you will surely die" (2:17). Eve appears to have said to herself that a tree of knowledge was bound to make those who partake wise. It was a question of God's logic or man's. Third, the fall was an act of will: "She took some and ate it" (3:6). Emotions, mind, and will combined in the first sin. The whole law of God was broken by the whole nature of the sinner.

The effect of the fall, as Ge 4 and the remainder of the Bible explicitly and implicitly bring out, was not merely immediate alienation from God for Adam and Eve, but guilt and depravity for all their posterity and the cursing of the earth. Redemption from the fall and its effects is accomplished through the Lord Jesus Christ (cf. Ro 5:12 – 21; 1Co 15:21 – 22, 45 – 49).

FALSE

Ex	23:1	"Do not spread **f** reports.
Dt	5:20	"You shall not give **f** testimony

Pr	12:17	but a **f** witness tells lies.
	13:5	The righteous hate what is **f**,
	19:5	A **f** witness will not go unpunished,
Jer	23:16	they fill you with **f** hopes.
Mt	19:18	not steal, do not give **f** testimony,
Mk	13:22	For **f** Christs and **f** prophets will
Lk	6:26	their fathers treated the **f** prophets.
Jn	1:47	in whom there is nothing **f**."
1Co	15:15	found to be **f** witnesses about God,
2Co	11:13	For such men are **f** apostles,
Gal	2:4	some **f** brothers had infiltrated our
Php	1:18	whether from **f** motives or true,
Col	2:18	anyone who delights in **f** humility
1Ti	1:3	not to teach **f** doctrines any longer
2Pe	2:1	also **f** prophets among the people,
Rev	16:13	out of the mouth of the **f** prophet.

FALSE APOSTLES [6013]. Paul speaks of false apostles in 2 Corinthians only. These people "masquerade as apostles of Christ" (2Co 11:13). Paul denounces them as servants of Satan (2Co 11:14), "masquerading as servants of righteousness," which is not surprising, since their master "masquerades as an angel of light" (2Co 11:14 – 15). Yet they claim to be servants of Christ (2Co 11:23). Apparently they boasted of their Jewish heritage, using this to help justify their self-proclaimed position as "apostles of Christ" (see 2Co 11:22).

FALSE CHRISTS [6023]. These are people who make a false claim to be the Messiah. Jesus warned his disciples that imitators and pretenders would follow him who would try to deceive his followers (Mt 24:5 – 11, 23 – 25; Mk 13:6, 21, 23; Lk 21:8). False Christs are to be distinguished from the Antichrist. The false Christ is an impostor, while the latter is one who opposes Christ. His opposition is mainly through the doctrines about Jesus' person and work that are contrary to the truth.

FALSE PROPHET [967, 6021]. Any person pretending to possess a message from God, but not possessing a divine commission (Jer 29:9). Test for (Dt 13:1 – 5; 18:20 – 22).

FALSE WITNESS [8736, 9214, 6018, 6019, 6020].

Described:
Punishment for (Dt 19:16 – 20; Pr 19:5, 9; 21:28; Zec 5:3 – 4). Innocent suffer from (Pss 27:12; 35:11). Proverbs concerning (Pr 6:16 – 19; 12:17; 14:5, 8, 25; 19:5, 9; 21:28; 24:28; 25:18). God hates (Pr 6:16 – 19). Results from a corrupt heart (Mt 15:19). See Evidence; Falsehood; Perjury; Witness.

Forbidden:
(Ex 20:16; 23:1 – 3; Lev 6:1 – 5; 19:11 – 12, 16; Dt 5:20; Pr 24:28; Mt 19:18; Lk 3:14; 18:20; 1Ti 1:9 – 10).

Instances of:
Witnesses against Naboth (1Ki 21:13); Jesus (Mt 26:59 – 61; Mk 14:54 – 59); Stephen (Ac 6:11 – 13); Paul (Ac 16:20 – 21; 17:5 – 7; 24:5; 25:7 – 8).

FAMILY [3, 1074, 278, 1074, 1215, 2446, 3509, 4580, 5476, 5476, 9352, 1169, 3836, 3858, 3875]. The concept of the family in the Bible differs from the modern institution. The Hebrew family was larger than families today, including the father of the household, his parents (if living), his wife or wives and children, his daughters and sons-in-law, slaves, guests, and foreigners under his protection. Marriage was arranged by the father of the groom and the family of the bride, for whom a dowry or purchase money was paid to her father (Ge 24). Polygamy and concubinage were practiced, though not favored by God. A husband could divorce his wife, but she could not divorce him. The father of a family had the power of life and death over his children. To dishonor a parent was punishable by death (Ex 21:15, 17). The NT concept followed that of the OT. Parents and children, husbands and wives, masters and slaves were commanded to live together in harmony and love (Eph 5:22 – 6:9; Col 3:18 – 4:1).

Pr	15:27	greedy man brings trouble to his **f**
	31:15	she provides food for her **f**
Mk	5:19	to your **f** and tell them how much
Lk	9:61	go back and say good-by to my **f**."

	12:52	in one **f** divided against each other,
Ac	10:2	He and all his **f** were devout
	16:33	and all his **f** were baptized.
1Ti	3:4	He must manage his own **f** well
	5:4	practice by caring for their own **f**
	5:8	and especially for his immediate **f**,

FARMING [438, 3086, 4494, 6268, 6275, 1175, 1177, 5062]. Was the chief occupation of the people of Israel after the conquest of Canaan. Each family received a piece of ground marked by boundaries that could not be removed (Dt 19:14). Plowing took place in the autumn when the ground was softened by the rain. Grain was sown during the month of February; harvest began in the spring and usually lasted from Passover to Pentecost. The grain was cut with a sickle, and gleanings were for the poor (Ru 2:2). The grain was threshed out on the threshing floor, a saucer-shaped area of beaten clay 25 or more feet in diameter, on which animals dragged a sledge over the sheaves to beat out the grain. The grain was winnowed by tossing it into the air to let the chaff blow away and was then sifted to remove impurities (Ps 1:4). Wheat and barley were the most important crops, but other grains and vegetables were cultivated as well.

FASTING [7426, 7427, 3763, 3764] (Heb. *tsûm*, Gr. *nesteia*, *nestis*). Fasting, meaning abstinence from food and drink for a long or short period, is frequently mentioned in the Scriptures. Sometimes, instead of the single word "fast," the descriptive phrase "to afflict the soul" is used, the reference being to physical fasting rather than to spiritual humiliation. This term is used in various parts of the OT in the KJV, but is the only one used to denote the religious observance of fasting in the Pentateuch (Lev 16:29 – 31; 23:27; Nu 30:13; Isa 58:3, 5, 10). NIV generally renders "deny" oneself or "humble" oneself.

Described:

Accompanied by self-denial (Dt 9:18; Ne 9:1); confession of sin (1Sa 7:6; Ne 9:1 – 2); reading of Scripture (Jer 36:6); prayer (Da 9:3; Mt 17:21). Commanded (Joel 1:14; 2:12 – 13). Precepts concerning (Mt 6:16 – 18). Of the disobedient, unacceptable (Isa 58:3 – 7; Jer 14:12; Zec 7:5; Mt 6:16).

Observed:

In times of bereavement, of the people of Jabesh Gilead, for Saul and his sons (1Sa 31:13; 1Ch 10:12); of David, at the time of Saul's death (2Sa 1:12); of Abner's death (2Sa 3:35); of his child's sickness (2Sa 12:16, 21 – 23). On occasions of, public calamities (2Sa 1:12; Ac 27:33); private afflictions (2Sa 12:16); approaching danger (Est 4:16; Ac 27:9, 33 – 34); afflictions (Ps 35:13; Da 6:18); religious observances (Zec 8:19); ordination of ministers (Ac 13:3; 14:23). Habitual, of the Israelites (Zec 8:19); by John's disciples (Mt 9:14); by Pharisees (Mt 9:14; Mk 2:18; Lk 18:12); by Anna (Lk 2:37); by Cornelius (Ac 10:30); by Paul (2Co 6:5; 11:27). Prolonged, forty days and nights, by Moses (Ex 24:18; 34:28; Dt 9:9, 18); forty days and nights, by Elijah (1Ki 19:8); three weeks, by Daniel (Da 10:2 – 3); forty days and nights, by Jesus (Mt 4:2; Mk 1:12 – 13; Lk 4:1 – 2). See Humility.

Ps	35:13	and humbled myself with **f**.
Ac	13:2	were worshiping the Lord and **f**,
	14:23	and **f**, committed them to the Lord

FATHER [3, 408, 587, 3528, 8037, 10003, 574, 1164, 4252, 4257, 4260, 4262] (Heb. *'āv*, Gr. *patēr*).

1. The originator of a way of life (Ge 4:20).

2. A male ancestor, immediate or remote, the father of nations or peoples (Ge 17:4; Ro 9:5).

3. An immediate male progenitor (Ge 42:13).

4. An adviser (Jdg 17:10) or a source (Job 38:28).

5. A spiritual ancestor (Jn 8:44; Ro 4:11). God is the Creator of the human race (Mal 2:10) and is called the Father of the universe (Jas 1:17).

Ge	2:24	this reason a man will leave his **f**
	17:4	You will be the **f** of many nations.
Ex	20:12	"Honor your **f** and your mother,
Lev	18:7	"'Do not dishonor your **f**

Dt	1:31	carried you, as a **f** carries his son,
	21:18	son who does not obey his **f**
	32:6	Is he not your **F**, your Creator,
Ps	2:7	today I have become your **F**.
	27:10	Though my **f** and mother forsake
	68:5	A **f** to the fatherless, a defender
Pr	3:12	as a **f** the son he delights in.
	10:1	A wise son brings joy to his **f**,
	17:25	A foolish son brings grief to his **f**
	23:22	Listen to your **f**, who gave you life,
	29:3	loves wisdom brings joy to his **f**,
Isa	9:6	Everlasting **F**, Prince of Peace.
	45:10	Woe to him who says to his **f**,
	63:16	But you are our **F**,
Eze	18:19	the son not share the guilt of his **f**?'
Mt	3:9	'We have Abraham as our **f**.'
	5:16	and praise your **F** in heaven.
	6:9	" 'Our **F** in heaven,
	6:26	yet your heavenly **F** feeds them.
	10:37	"Anyone who loves his **f**
	11:27	no one knows the **F** except the Son
	15:4	'Honor your **f** and mother'
	19:5	this reason a man will leave his **f**
	19:29	or brothers or sisters or **f** or mother
Lk	9:59	"Lord, first let me go and bury my **f**
	12:53	**f** against son and son against **f**,
	14:26	and does not hate his **f** and mother,
	23:34	Jesus said, "**F**, forgive them,
Jn	3:35	The **F** loves the Son and has placed
	5:20	For the **F** loves the Son
	6:44	the **F** who sent me draws him,
	6:46	No one has seen the **F**
	8:41	The only **F** we have is God himself
	8:42	God were your **F**, you would love
	8:44	You belong to your **f**, the devil,
	10:17	reason my **F** loves me is that I lay
	10:30	I and the **F** are one."
	10:38	and understand that the **F** is in me,
	14:6	No one comes to the **F**
	14:9	who has seen me has seen the **F**.
	15:23	He who hates me hates my **F**
	20:17	'I am returning to my **F** and your **F**,
Ac	13:33	today I have become your **F**.'

Ro	4:11	he is the **f** of all who believe
	8:15	And by him we cry, "Abba, **F**."
2Co	6:18	"I will be a **F** to you,
Php	2:11	to the glory of God the **F**.
Heb	12:7	what son is not disciplined by his **f**?
1Jn	1:3	And our fellowship is with the **F**
	2:15	the love of the **F** is not in him.
	2:22	he denies the **F** and the Son.

FEAR [399, 1593, 1796, 3006, 3010, 3328, 3707, 3710, 3711, 4570, 4616, 5022, 6907, 7064, 7065, 925, 5828, 5832] (Heb. *yir'âh*, Gr. *phobos*). This word in English has two principal meanings: (1) that apprehension of evil that normally leads one either to flee or to fight and (2) that awe and reverence that a person of sense feels in the presence of God and, to a lesser extent, in the presence of a king or other dread authority. A child feels the first of these in the presence of a cruel parent and feels the second before one who is good but who must also be just. Fifteen different Hebrew nouns are rendered "fear" in the KJV; the Greek word for "fear" is *phobos*. The word "reverend," which occurs only in the KJV of Ps 111:9 (NIV has "awesome"), means literally "to be feared" and is used only for God.

Dt	6:13	**F** the LORD your God, serve him
	31:12	and learn to **f** the LORD your God
1Sa	12:14	If you **f** the LORD and serve
Ps	2:11	Serve the LORD with **f**
	19:9	The **f** of the LORD is pure,
	23:4	I will **f** no evil,
	27:1	whom shall I **f**?
Pr	1:7	**f** of the LORD is the beginning
	8:13	To **f** the LORD is to hate evil;
	19:23	The **f** of the LORD leads to life:
	29:25	**F** of man will prove to be a snare,
	31:21	she has no **f** for her household;
Ecc	12:13	**F** God and keep his
Isa	11:3	delight in the **f** of the LORD.
	35:4	"Be strong, do not **f**;
	41:10	So do not **f**, for I am with you;
2Co	5:11	we know what it is to **f** the Lord,
Php	2:12	to work out your salvation with **f**
1Jn	4:18	But perfect love drives out **f**,

Jude   23   to others show mercy, mixed with **f**
Rev   14:7   "**F** God and give him glory,

FEAR OF GOD

Described:

As wisdom (Job 28:28; Pr 15:33); pure (Ps 19:9); the beginning of wisdom (Ps 111:10; Pr 9:10; 15:33); the beginning of knowledge (Pr 1:7); hating evil (Pr 8:13); adding length to life (Pr 10:27); a fountain of life (Pr 14:27); leading to life (Pr 19:23). Commanded (Lev 19:14, 32; 25:36, 43; Dt 6:13; 10:20; 13:4; Jos 24:14; 1Sa 12:24; 2Ki 17:36; 1Ch 16:30; 2Ch 19:7, 9; Ne 5:9; Pss 2:11; 22:23; 34:9; 96:4; Pr 3:7; 23:17; 24:21; Ecc 5:7; 12:13; Isa 8:13; 29:23; Ro 11:20 – 21; Col 3:22; 1Pe 2:17; Rev 14:7). Cultivated by God (Ex 3:5; 19:12 – 13; Heb 12:18 – 24). Deters from sin (Ex 20:18 – 20; Pr 16:6; Jer 32:39 – 40). Averts temporal calamity (Dt 28:47 – 49; 28:58 – 68; 2Ki 17:36 – 39). Secures divine blessing (Dt 5:29; Pss 25:12 – 14; 31:19 – 20; 33:18 – 19; 34:7, 9; 85:8 – 9; 103:11, 13, 17; 111:5; 112:1; 115:11, 13; 128:1 – 4; 145:18 – 19; Pr 22:4; Ecc 7:18; 8:12 – 13; Mal 4:2; Lk 1:50; Ac 10:34 – 35). Universality of, foretold (Pss 76:11 – 12; 102:15). A bond of fellowship among righteous (Mal 3:16 – 18).

Instances of Godly Fear:

Noah, in preparing ark (Heb 11:7). Abraham, tested in offering of Isaac (Ge 22:12). Jacob, in vision of stairway, and covenant of God (Ge 28:16 – 17; 42:18). Midwives of Egypt, in refusing to take lives of Hebrew children (Ex 1:17, 21). Egyptians, at time of plague of thunder, hail, and fire (Ex 9:20). Phinehas, in turning away God's anger at time of plague (Nu 25:11, w 25:6 – 15). Nine and a half tribes of Israel west of Jordan, for building an altar there (Jos 22:15 – 20). Obadiah, in devotion to God, sheltered one hundred prophets against Jezebel because he feared God more than wrath of Jezebel (1Ki 18:3 – 4). Jehoshaphat, in proclaiming a fast when land was about to be invaded by armies of Ammonites and Moabites (2Ch 20:3).

Nehemiah, in his reform of the public administration that had heavily taxed the people and lorded their rule over the people (Ne 5:15). Hanani, which qualified him to be ruler over Jerusalem (Ne 7:2). Job, according to testimony of Satan (Job 1:8). David (Ps 119:38). Hezekiah, in his treatment of the prophet Micah, who prophesied evil against Jerusalem (Jer 26:19). Israelites, in obeying voice of the Lord (Hag 1:12). Women at the tomb (Mt 28:8). Cornelius, who feared God with all his house (Ac 10:2).

Motivates God's:

Power (Jos 4:24; Ps 99:1; Jer 5:22; Mt 10:28; Lk 12:5); providence (1Sa 12:2 – 4); power and justice (Job 37:19 – 24); wrath (Ps 90:11); forgiveness (Ps 130:4); majesty (Jer 10:7).

Motivates People:

To respect others (Lev 19:14, 30; 25:17, 36, 43); to obedience (Nu 32:15; Dt 6:13 – 15; 7:1 – 4; 8:5 – 6; 10:12 – 13, 20; 13:4, 6 – 11; 17:11 – 13; 21:18 – 21; 28:14 – 68; 31:11 – 13; 1Sa 12:24 – 25; Job 13:21; 31:1 – 4, 13 – 23; Isa 1:20; Jer 4:4; 22:5; Mt 10:28; Lk 12:4 – 5; 2Co 5:10 – 11; 2Ti 4:1 – 2; 2Pe 3:10 – 12; Rev 14:9 – 10); to truthfulness (Dt 15:9; 19:16 – 20); to filial obedience (Dt 21:21).

FEASTS [430, 2504, 4595, 5492, 109, 369, 2038] (Heb. *mô'ēdh*, an assembling, dance, or pilgrimage). The feasts, or sacred festivals, held an important place in Jewish religion. They were religious services accompanied by demonstrations of joy and gladness. In Lev 23, where they are described most fully, they are called "holy convocations." Their times, except for the two instituted after the exile, were fixed by divine appointment. Their purpose was to promote spiritual interests of the community. The people met in holy fellowship for acts and purposes of sacred worship. They met before God in holy assemblies.

FEAST OF THE WEEKLY SABBATH.

(Lev 23:3). This stood at the head of the sacred seasons. The holy meetings by which the Sabbath was distinguished were quite local. Families and other small groups assembled under the guidance of Levites or elders and engaged in common acts of devotion, the forms and manner of which were not prescribed. Little is known of where or how the people met before the captivity, but after it they met in synagogues and were led in worship by teachers learned in the law.

PASSOVER, OR FEAST OF UNLEAVENED BREAD.

(Lev 23:4 – 8). The Passover was the first of all the annual feasts, and historically and religiously it was the most important of all. It was called both the Feast of the Passover and the Feast of Unleavened Bread, the two really forming a double festival. It was celebrated on the first month of the religious year, on the fourteenth of Nisan (our April), and commemorated the deliverance of the Jews from Egypt and the establishment of Israel as a nation by God's redemptive act. The Feast of Unleavened Bread began on the day after the Passover and lasted seven days (23:5 – 8). Theologically the Passover finds its heart in the doctrine of propitiation. The Lord entered Egypt bent on judgment (Ex 12:12); but, seeing the blood, he passed over that house completely at peace with those who were sheltering there. His wrath was assuaged by the blood of the lamb. *See also Substitution.*

FEAST OF PENTECOST.

(Lev 23:15 – 21). Other names for this are the Feast of Weeks, the Day of the Firstfruits, and the Feast of Harvests. It was celebrated on the sixth day of the month of Sivan (our June), seven weeks after the offering of the wave sheaf after the Passover. The name "Pentecost," meaning "fiftieth," originated from the fact that there was an interval of fifty days between the two. The feast lasted a single day (Dt 16:9 – 12) and marked the completion of the wheat harvest. The characteristic ritual of this feast was the offering and waving of two loaves of leavened bread, made from ripe grain that had just been harvested. This was done by the priest in the name

of the congregation. In addition to these wave offerings, the people were to give the Lord an offering of the firstfruits of their produce. The amount of the offering was not designated.

FEAST OF TRUMPETS, OR NEW MOON.

(Lev 23:23 – 25). This was held on the first day of the seventh month, Tishri (our October), which began the civil year of the Jews. It corresponded to our New Year's Day, and on it, from morning to evening, horns and trumpets were blown. After the exile the day was observed by the public reading of the law and by general rejoicing.

FEAST OF THE DAY OF ATONEMENT.

(Lev 23:26 – 32). This was observed on the tenth day of Tishri. It was really less a feast than a fast, as the distinctive character and purpose of the day was to bring the collective sin of the whole year to remembrance, so that it might earnestly be dealt with and atoned for. On this day the high priest made confession of all the sins of the community and entered on their behalf into the Most Holy Place with the blood of reconciliation. It was a solemn occasion, when God's people through godly sorrow and atonement for sin entered into the rest of God's mercy and favor. In receiving his forgiveness, they could rejoice before him and carry out his commandments.

FEAST OF TABERNACLES, OR BOOTHS, OR INGATHERING.

(Lev 23:33 – 43). This was the last of the sacred festivals under the old covenant in preexilic times. It began five days after the Day of Atonement (Lev 23:34; Dt 16:13) and lasted seven days. It marked the completion of the harvest and historically commemorated the wanderings in the wilderness. During this festival people lived in booths and tents in Jerusalem to remind themselves of how their forefathers wandered in the wilderness and lived in booths. The sacrifices of this feast were more numerous than of any other. The last day of the feast marked the conclusion of the ecclesiastical year. The whole feast was popular and joyous in nature.

Besides the above feasts, which were all preexilic and instituted by God, the Jews after the captivity added two others, the Feast of Lights, or Dedication, and the Feast of Purim.

The Feast of Lights was observed for eight days beginning on the twenty-fifth day of Kislev (our December). It was instituted by Judas Maccabeus in 164 BC when the temple, which had been defiled by Antiochus Epiphanes, king of Syria, was cleansed and rededicated to the service of the Lord. During these days the Israelites met in their synagogues, carrying branches of trees in their hands, and held jubilant services. The children were told the brave and stirring deeds of the Maccabees so that they might emulate them.

The Feast of Purim was kept on the fourteenth and fifteenth days of Adar (our March), the last month of the religious year. It was instituted by Mordecai to commemorate the failure of Haman's plots against the Jews (Est 9:20 – 22, 26 – 28). The word *Purim* means "lots." On the evening of the thirteenth the whole book of Esther was read publicly in the synagogue. It was a joyous occasion.

FELIX [5772] (Gr. *Phēlix, happy, fortunate, lucky*). Born Antonius Claudius, a Greek subject, he was made a freedman by Claudius, the emperor from AD 41 to 54, and given the surname Felix, probably in congratulation. He and his brother Pallas were favorites of Claudius and later of Nero (54 – 68), and so Felix evidently thought that he could do as he pleased. Tacitus said of him that "he reveled in cruelty and lust, and wielded the power of a king with the mind of a slave." His very title of "procurator" hints at his fiscal duties of procuring funds for Rome, which he seems to have accomplished with all sorts of tyranny. He began his career as procurator of Judea by seducing Drusilla, the sister of Agrippa II and wife of the king of Emesa (modern Homs), and marrying her. Because she was Jewish

(at least in part), he learned much of Jewish life and customs.

Felix appears in the biblical account only in Ac 23:24 – 25:14. He was susceptible to flattery, as the speech of Tertullus shows, and also to conviction of sin, as is shown by his terror when Paul reasoned before him about "righteousness, self-control and the judgment to come" (24:25). His conviction faded; he procrastinated; and he held Paul for about two years (c. 58 – 60), hoping that Paul "would offer him a bribe" for his freedom (24:26). He was then replaced by Festus, a far better man.

FELLOWSHIP [6051, 8968, 3126, 3545] (Gr. *koinō-nia, that which is in common*).

1. Partnership or union with others in the bonds of a business partnership, a social or fraternal organization, or just proximity. Christians are told not to be unequally yoked together with unbelievers (2Co 6:14 – 18) because such a union, either in marriage, business, or society, is incompatible with fellowship with Christians and with God.

2. Membership in a local Christian church or in *the* church. From the very beginning of the church at Pentecost, "they devoted themselves to the apostles' teaching and to the fellowship, to the breaking of bread and to prayer" (Ac 2:42).

3. Partnership in the support of the gospel and in the charitable work of the church (2Co 8:4).

4. That heavenly love that fills (or should fill) the hearts of believers one for another and for God. For this love and fellowship, the Scriptures use the word *agape*, which seldom appears in classical Greek. This fellowship is deeper and more satisfying than any mere human love whether social, parental, conjugal, or other.

With God:

Signified in people walking with God (Ge 5:22, 24; 6:9). Signified in God dwelling with people (Ex 29:45; Ps 101:6; Isa 57:15; Zec 2:10; Jn 14:23; 2Co 6:16; 1Jn 3:24; 4:13; Rev 21:3 – 4). General (Ex 33:11, 14 – 17; Lev 26:12; Am 3:3; 2Co 13:11;

1Jn 1:3, 5 – 7). Possible only through Christ (Mk 9:37; Jn 17:21, 23). See Communion, with God.

With Christ:

Attained, by receiving Christ (Mk 9:37; Rev 3:20); by doing God's will (Mt 12:48 – 50; Lk 8:21). Through a gathering of believers (Mt 18:20; 28:20), commemorating Christ's death (1Co 10:16 – 17); by walking in the light (1Jn 1:3, 5 – 7); by abiding in Christ (1Jn 2:6, 24, 28; 3:6, 24); by keeping God's commandments (1Jn 3:6, 24); by continuing in his teaching (2Jn 9).

General References to: *(Mt 18:20; Lk 24:32; 1Co 1:9; 10:16 – 17; 1Jn 1:3, 5 – 7; Rev 3:20). Signified in Christ dwelling with people (Jn 6:56; 14:23; Eph 3:17; Col 1:27; 1Jn 3:24; 4:13). Signified in our union with Christ (Jn 15:1 – 8; 17:21 – 23, 26; Ro 7:4; 8:1, 10, 17; 11:17; 12:5; 1Co 6:13 – 15, 17; 12:12, 27; 2Co 11:2; 13:5; Eph 5:30; Col 3:3; 1Th 5:9 – 10; Heb 2:11; 1Jn 5:12, 20). Through the Spirit (Jn 14:16; 1Jn 3:6, 24; 4:13). See Communion, with the Spirit.*

With the Holy Spirit:

General (Jn 14:16 – 17; Ro 8:9; 1Co 3:16; 2Co 13:14; Gal 4:6; Php 2:1).

With the Wicked:

Abhorred by the righteous (Ge 49:6; Ex 33:15 – 16; Ezr 6:21 – 22; 9:14; Pss 6:8; 26:4 – 5). Implicating (Ps 50:18). Revelry (Ps 50:18; Pr 12:11; 29:24; 1Co 15:33; 2Pe 2:18 – 19). Impoverishing (Pr 28:19). Forbidden with those who provide bad influence (Ex 23:32 – 33; 34:12 – 16; Nu 16:26; Dt 7:2 – 3; 12:30; 13:6 – 11; Jos 23:6 – 8, 13; Ezr 9:12; 10:11; Ps 1:1; Pr 1:10 – 16; 4:14 – 17; 14:7; Mt 18:17; Ro 16:17; 1Co 5:9 – 13; 2Co 6:14 – 17; Eph 5:11; 2Th 3:6, 14 – 15; 1Ti 6:3 – 5; 2Ti 3:2 – 9; 2Pe 3:17 – 18; 2Jn 9 – 11; Rev 18:1 – 4). Punishment for fellowship with the wicked (Nu 25:1 – 8; 33:55 – 56; Dt 31:16 – 17; Jos 23:12 – 13; Jdg 3:5 – 8; Ezr 9:7, 14; Ps 106:34 – 35, 41 – 42; Rev 2:16, 22 – 23).

| Ex | 20:24 | burnt offerings and **f** offerings, |
| Lev | 3:1 | If someone's offering is a **f** offering, |

1Co	1:9	who has called you into **f**
	5:2	out of your **f** the man who did this?
2Co	6:14	what **f** can light have with darkness
	13:14	and the **f** of the Holy Spirit be
Gal	2:9	and Barnabas the right hand of **f**
Php	2:1	if any **f** with the Spirit,
	3:10	the **f** of sharing in his sufferings,
1Jn	1:3	And our **f** is with the Father
	1:6	claim to have **f** with him yet walk
	1:7	we have **f** with one another,

FERTILE CRESCENT This term does not occur in Scripture but is a modern description of the territory that may roughly be described as reaching NW from the Persian Gulf through Mesopotamia, then west to the north of Syria, then SW through Syria and Palestine. In this crescent the land is mostly rich and fertile and is watered by the Tigris, the Euphrates, the Orontes, the Jordan, and numerous rivers descending the west side of Lebanon. Various grains such as wheat and barley, and fruits such as grapes, olives, figs, oranges, lemons, and pomegranates abound. A journey in a straight line across the crescent from one end to the other would go mostly through the great Syrian Desert, with only an occasional oasis. This configuration of the land explains much of Bible history.

FESTIVALS *See Feasts.*

FESTUS PORCIUS [5776] (Gr. *Porkios Phēstos, festal, joyful*). The Roman governor who succeeded Felix in the province of Judea (Ac 24:27). The date of his accession is uncertain. Almost nothing is known of the life of Festus before his appointment by Nero as procurator of Judea. He appears in the Bible (24:27 – 26:32) principally in his relationship with his prisoner, the apostle Paul. Festus was apparently a far better and more efficient man than his predecessor. At the very beginning of his rule, he took up the case of Paul, and as King Agrippa said, Paul "could have been set free if he had not appealed to Caesar" (26:32). Paul had made this appeal when Festus, at the request of the Jews, was considering bringing Paul to Jerusalem for trial. Festus evidently knew that Paul was a good man (25:25), but he was unable to understand Paul's reasoning with King Agrippa and thought that Paul had gone mad with much study (26:24). Festus died at his post and was followed about AD 62 by Albinus.

FIRSTBORN [1144, 1147, 1148, 7081+, 7082, 1380+3616, 4758] (Heb. *bekhôr*, Gr. *prōtotokos*). The Hebrew word is used chiefly of humans, but is used also of animals (Ex 11:5). It appears that humans early felt that God had the first claim on animals (Ge 4:4). Among the ancestors of the Hebrews, the firstborn offspring of humans and animals were sacrificed to the deity. Because the firstborn of the Israelites were preserved at the time of the first Passover, every firstborn male of man and beast became consecrated to God (Ex 13:2; 34:19). Among the Israelites the firstborn son possessed special privileges. He succeeded his father as the head of the house and received as his share of the inheritance a double portion. Israel was the Lord's firstborn (Ex 4:22) and was thus entitled to special privileges, as compared with other peoples. Jesus Christ is described as the firstborn (Ro 8:29; Col 1:15; Heb 1:6), an application of the term that may be traced back to Ps 89:27, where the Messiah is referred to as the firstborn of God.

General References to:
The first male born, whether human or animal, was reserved by God for himself (Ex 13:2, 12 – 16; 22:29 – 30; 34:19 – 20; Lev 27:26; Nu 3:13; 8:17 – 18; Dt 15:19 – 23; Ne 10:36). Redemption of (Ex 13:13; 34:20; Lev 27:26 – 27; Nu 3:40 – 51; 18:15 – 17). Levites taken instead of firstborn of the families of Israel (Nu 3:12, 40 – 45; 8:16 – 18).

Birthright of:
Had precedence over other sons of the family (Ge 4:1, 5 – 7; Dt 21:15 – 17); double portion of inheritance (Dt 21:15 – 17); royal succession (2Ch 21:3). Sold by Esau (Ge 25:29 – 34; 27:36; Ro 9:12 – 13; Heb 12:16). Set aside, that of Manasseh (Ge 48:15 – 20; 1Ch 5:1); Adonijah (1Ki 2:13 – 15); Hosah's son (1Ch 26:10).

Forfeited by Reuben (Ge 49:3 – 4; 1Ch 5:1 – 2). Honorable distinction of (Ex 4:22; Ps 89:27; Jer 31:9; Ro 8:29; Col 1:15; Heb 1:6; 12:23; Rev 1:5). See Birthright.

Jesus as Firstborn:
Among many brothers (Ro 8:29); over all creation (Col 1:15); from the dead (Col 1:18; Rev 1:5); God's firstborn (Heb 1:6).

Ex	11:5	Every **f** son in Egypt will die,
	34:20	Redeem all your **f** sons.
Ps	89:27	I will also appoint him my **f**,
Lk	2:7	and she gave birth to her **f**, a son.
Ro	8:29	that he might be the **f**
Col	1:15	image of the invisible God, the **f**
	1:18	and the **f** from among the dead,
Heb	1:6	when God brings his **f**
Rev	1:5	who is the faithful witness, the **f**

FIRSTFRUITS [1137, 7262+8040, 8040, 569] (Heb. *rē'shîth, bikkûrîm*, Gr. *aparchē*). In acknowledgment of the fact that all the products of the land came from God, and to show thankfulness for his goodness, Israelites brought as an offering a portion of the fruits that ripened first. These were looked on as a pledge of the coming harvest. Such an offering was made both on behalf of the nation (Lev 23:10, 17) and by individuals (Ex 23:19; Dt 26:1 – 11). These firstfruits went for the support of the priesthood.

Jesus is the firstfruits of all who die in faith; that is, the resurrection of believers is made possible and is guaranteed by his resurrection (1Co 15:20). Believers, in turn, are "a kind of firstfruits" of all that God created (Jas 1:18); creation will share in the redemption of the children of God (Ro 8:19 – 21).

Offerings of:
First ripe of fruits, grain, oil, wine, and first of the fleece, required as an offering (Ex 22:29; Lev 2:12 – 16; Nu 18:12; Dt 18:4; 2Ch 31:5; Ne 10:35, 37, 39; Pr 3:9; Jer 2:3; Ro 11:16). Presented at the tabernacle (Ex 22:29; 23:19; 34:26; Dt 26:3 – 10); belonged to the priests (Lev 23:20; Nu 18:12 – 13; Dt 18:3 – 5); must be free from blemish (Lev

22:21; Nu 18:12). Freewill offerings of, given to the prophets (2Ki 4:42).

Ex	23:16	the Feast of Harvest with the **f**
	23:19	"Bring the best of the **f** of your soil
Ro	8:23	who have the **f** of the Spirit,
1Co	15:23	Christ, the **f**; then, when he comes,
Rev	14:4	offered as **f** to God and the Lamb.

FLESH [1414, 2693, 2743+3655+4946, 3655+3870+4946, 4695, 5055, 6425, 6889, 6913+7089, 8638, 10125, 4922] (Heb. *bāsār, shē'er*, Gr. *sarx*).

1. The physical part of the body of people or animals (Ge 17:13 – 14; 1Co 15:39).

2. Human nature, deprived of the Holy Spirit and dominated by sin (Ro 7:5, n.); usually "sinful [nature]" in the NIV. *See Body; Carnal Mindedness.*

Ge	2:23	and **f** of my **f**;
	2:24	and they will become one **f**.
2Ch	32:8	With him is only the arm of **f**,
Eze	11:19	of stone and give them a heart of **f**.
Mt	19:5	and the two will become one **f**'?
Jn	1:14	The Word became **f** and made his
	6:51	This bread is my **f**, which I will give
1Co	6:16	"The two will become one **f**."
Eph	5:31	and the two will become one **f**."
	6:12	For our struggle is not against **f**
Php	3:2	do evil, those mutilators of the **f**.
1Jn	4:2	come in the **f** is from God,

FLOOD, THE [4059, 4429, 4784, 5643, 8466, 8851, 8852, 9180, 431, 2886, 4439]. The deluge, or worldwide destruction of man and beast, except for Noah, his family, and the animals in the ark.

HISTORICAL BACKGROUND OF FLOOD INTERPRETATIONS.

The Noahic flood has been a subject for discussion among scientists and theologians for many centuries. Various geological observations over the centuries have led to many interpretations of the meaning and physical characteristics of the flood. The reality of the flood can hardly be questioned, however, because of the many references to it in both the OT and NT (Ge 6 – 8; 9:11, 28; 10:1, 32; Mt 24:38 – 39; Lk 17:27; 2Pe 2:5).

THE PURPOSE OF THE FLOOD.

An important aspect of the deluge is that God preserved some humans, for Noah and his family were saved from destruction by going into an ark that Noah made according to God's specifications, and in which he gathered animals and birds preserved to replenish the earth.

It is apparent from Ge 6:5 – 7 and other passages such as 2Pe 2:5 – 6 that the flood was brought on the earth as a judgment on the sins of the people.

THE SOURCE OF THE FLOOD.

The biblical account of the accumulation and dispersal of the waters of the flood is very brief. In Ge 7:11 the source of the water is explained: "All the springs of the great deep burst forth, and the floodgates of the heavens were opened."

The Hebrew word *tehom*, translated "great deep," is the same used in Ge 1:2. That this does not necessarily include all the oceans is shown by its use in Isa 51:10 when it refers to the escape of the Israelites in "the depths of the sea" (the Red Sea). The Hebrew word *ma'yan* means literally "place of a spring." This could mean that water rose from the ocean or from freshwater springs on the earth or both.

SUGGESTED CAUSES OF THE FLOOD.

Some would prefer to believe that the expression "the springs of the great deep burst forth" indicates that the ocean (actually the Persian Gulf, an arm of the ocean) invaded the land. Others have assumed this implies volcanic activity.

"The floodgates of the heavens were opened" has been accepted as a description of rain. Some have seen this as a torrential downpour greater than normally experienced on the earth today. A hypothesis has been proposed that the earth from the time of its creation (or at least man's creation) was surrounded by a canopy of water in some form until the time of the flood. The canopy was supposedly made of water vapor, ice, or liquid water. It is proposed that the transfer of the canopy's water from around the earth to the earth would cause rain for many days.

The canopy idea, although firmly entrenched in literature, has doubtful biblical authority, though some cite older versions of Eze 1:22 in support of it. Again it should be noted that if a miraculous explanation for the flood is accepted, physical explanations are not necessary.

THE DURATION OF THE FLOOD.

The length of the flood is generally agreed on within a few days. The Hebrews used a solar calendar in contrast to the Babylonian lunar month and the Egyptian arbitrary 365-day year. Most authorities would put the number of days from the time the rain started (Ge 7:11) to the time Noah left the ark (8:14) between 371 and 376 days.

TRADITIONS OF THE FLOOD.

The Hebrews, Assyrians, and Babylonians who lived within the area of the Tigris-Euphrates basin all had traditions of a great flood. These narratives stated the purpose of the flood to be punishment because the world was full of violence, but the Hebrew account remained simple and credible, whereas the other accounts became complex and fanciful. Only the biblical account retained a monotheistic viewpoint. Although it is not possible to affirm dogmatically that all of these three histories had a common origin, it seems probable that they did.

THE UNIVERSALITY OF THE FLOOD.

One of the great differences of opinion in describing the flood concerns its extent. Traditionally, most biblical interpreters considered the submergence to be universal; that is, it covered the entire globe including the highest mountains. The reasons proposed to defend this viewpoint include the fact that universal terms are used in the Genesis account. "All the high mountains under the entire heavens were covered" (Ge 7:19); "Every living thing that moved on the earth perished"

(7:21). It has been pointed out that if the flood were local, there would be no need for an ark to preserve Noah, for God could have directed him to move with the animals to an area that was not to be submerged.

The fact that many civilizations have flood traditions has been cited as evidence for a universal flood. The same evidence could be used to argue for a local flood because the accounts of floods in other parts of the world are less like the Hebrew tradition than those of the Assyrians and Babylonians, who lived in the same area as the Hebrews.

Today many conservative scholars defend a local flood. The crux of their argument seems to center in the covenant relation of God to humans. He deals with certain groups, such as the children of Israel. The reasoning in regard to Noah is that Noah was not a preacher of righteousness to peoples of other areas but was concerned with the culture from which Abraham eventually came. Physical arguments have also been raised against a universal flood: the origin and disposal of the amount of water necessary to make a layer six miles (ten km.) thick over the whole world, the effect on plant life of being covered for a year, the effect on freshwater life of a sea that contained salt from the ocean, and the fact that many topographic features of the earth (such as cinder cones) show no evidence of erosion by a flood and are thought to be much older than the flood could possibly be.

CHRONOLOGY OF THE FLOOD.

There is not any general agreement among conservative scholars concerning the actual date of the deluge. Although Ussher in his chronology placed the flood at 2348 BC, most scholars today hold to an earlier date. Scholars who have advocated that the earth has developed to its present condition by a series of major calamities, the flood being the greatest, have been called catastrophists. Many catastrophists believe the flood was associated in some way with the end of the Pleistocene ice age and so accept a date of about 10,000 BC.

General References to:

(Job 22:16; Mt 24:38 – 39; Lk 17:26 – 27; Heb 11:7; 1Pe 3:20; 2Pe 2:5). Foretold (Ge 6:13, 17). History of (Ge 6 – 8). The promise that it should not recur (Ge 8:20 – 22; Isa 54:9).

FOLLOW

Ex	23:2	Do not **f** the crowd in doing wrong.
Lev	18:4	and be careful to **f** my decrees.
Dt	5:1	Learn them and be sure to **f** them.
1Ki	11:6	he did not **f** the LORD completely,
2Ch	34:33	they did not fail to **f** the LORD,
Ps	23:6	Surely goodness and love will **f** me
	119:166	and I **f** your commands.
Mt	4:19	**f** me," Jesus said, "and I will make
	8:22	But Jesus told him, "**F** me,
	19:27	"We have left everything to **f** you!
Lk	9:23	take up his cross daily and **f** me.
Jn	10:4	his sheep **f** him because they know
	12:26	Whoever serves me must **f** me;
	21:19	Then he said to him, "**F** me!"
1Co	11:1	**F** my example, as I follow
	14:1	**F** the way of love and eagerly
Rev	14:4	They **f** the Lamb wherever he goes.

FOOL [211, 2147, 4067, 5571, 5572, 6118, 6119, 6618, 9438, 932, G933, 3704]. In Scripture connotes conceit and pride, or deficiency in judgment rather than mental inferiority.

1Sa	25:25	his name is **F**, and folly goes
Ps	14:1	The **f** says in his heart,
Pr	10:18	and whoever spreads slander is a **f**.
	12:15	The way of a **f** seems right to him,
	14:16	but a **f** is hotheaded and reckless.
	15:5	A **f** spurns his father's discipline,
	17:21	To have a **f** for a son brings grief;
	18:2	A **f** finds no pleasure
	20:3	but every **f** is quick to quarrel.
	24:7	Wisdom is too high for a **f**;
	26:4	Do not answer a **f** according
	26:5	Answer a **f** according to his folly,
	26:11	so a **f** repeats his folly.
	28:26	He who trusts in himself is a **f**,
	29:11	A **f** gives full vent to his anger,

FOOLISH [FOOL]

Pr	10:1	but a **f** son grief to his mother.
	14:1	her own hands the **f** one tears hers
	15:20	but a **f** man despises his mother.
	17:25	A **f** son brings grief to his father
Mt	7:26	practice is like a **f** man who built
	25:2	of them were **f** and five were wise.
Lk	11:40	You **f** people! Did not the one who
1Co	1:20	Has not God made **f** the wisdom
	1:27	God chose the **f** things of the world
Eph	5:4	should there be obscenity, **f** talk
Tit	3:9	But avoid **f** controversies

FOOLISHNESS The opposite of wisdom, with which the OT often contrasts it (Ecc 2:13). The fool exhibits many characteristics ranging from simple stupidity (Pr 7:7, 22) and a hot temper (14:17), to wickedness (Ge 34:7), atheism (Ps 14:1), and rejection of God (Job 2:9 – 10). In the NT it can mean thoughtlessness (Gal 3:3) or lack of intelligence (Ro 1:21).

1Co	1:18	of the cross is **f** to those who are
	1:25	For the **f** of God is wiser
	2:14	for they are **f** to him, and he cannot
	3:19	of this world is **f** in God's sight.

FOREKNEW

Ro	8:29	For those God **f** he
	11:2	not reject his people, whom he **f**.

FOREKNOWLEDGE

Ac	2:23	to you by God's set purpose and **f**;
1Pe	1:2	to the **f** of God the Father,

FORESKIN [6889] (Heb. *'orlâh*, Gr. *akrobystia*). The fold of skin that is cut off in the operation of circumcision. Just as the American Indians used scalps of enemies as signs of their prowess, so David presented two hundred foreskins of the Philistines (1Sa 18:25 – 27). In Dt 10:16 (KJV) the word is used figuratively meaning submission to God's law. In

Hab 2:16 (KJV) it refers to the indecent exhibitionism of a drunken man.

FOREVER

Ge	3:22	the tree of life and eat, and live **f**."
	6:3	Spirit will not contend with man **f**,
2Ch	5:13	his love endures **f**."
	20:21	for his love endures **f**."
Ps	9:7	The LORD reigns **f**;
	23:6	dwell in the house of the LORD **f**.
	44:8	and we will praise your name **f**.
	146:6	the LORD, who remains faithful **f**.
Pr	10:25	but the righteous stand firm **f**.
	27:24	for riches do not endure **f**,
Isa	25:8	he will swallow up death **f**.
	26:4	Trust in the LORD **f**,
	40:8	but the word of our God stands **f**."
	51:6	But my salvation will last **f**,
Jn	6:51	eats of this bread, he will live **f**.
	14:16	Counselor to be with you **f** —
1Co	9:25	it to get a crown that will last **f**.
1Th	4:17	And so we will be with the Lord **f**.
Heb	7:24	Jesus lives **f**, he has a permanent
	13:8	same yesterday and today and **f**.
1Pe	1:25	but the word of the Lord stands **f**."
1Jn	2:17	who does the will of God lives **f**.

FORGIVE

Ge	50:17	I ask you to **f** your brothers the sins
Ex	10:17	Now **f** my sin once more
	23:21	he will not **f** your rebellion,
	34:9	**f** our wickedness and our sin,
Nu	14:19	with your great love, **f** the sin
Dt	29:20	will never be willing to **f** him;
1Sa	15:25	**f** my sin and come back with me,
1Ki	8:34	and **f** the sin of your people Israel
2Ki	5:18	But may the LORD **f** your servant
	24:4	and the LORD was not willing to **f**.
2Ch	6:21	place; and when you hear, **f**.
	7:14	will **f** their sin and will heal their
Ps	19:12	**F** my hidden faults.
	25:11	**f** my iniquity, though it is great.
Isa	2:9	do not **f** them.

Jer	5:1	I will **f** this city.
	33:8	and will **f** all their sins of rebellion
Da	9:19	O LORD, listen! O LORD, **f**! O LORD,
	14:2	"**F** all our sins
Am	7:2	**f**! How can Jacob survive?
Mt	6:12	**F** us our debts,
	9:6	authority on earth to **f** sins.
	18:21	many times shall I **f** my brother
	18:35	you **f** your brother from your heart
Mk	2:7	Who can **f** sins but God alone?"
Lk	6:37	**F**, and you will be forgiven.
	23:34	Jesus said, "Father, **f** them,
Jn	20:23	If you **f** anyone his sins, they are
Ac	8:22	Perhaps he will **f** you
2Co	2:7	you ought to **f** and comfort him,
Col	3:13	and **f** whatever grievances you may
	3:13	**F** as the Lord forgave you.
Heb	8:12	For I will **f** their wickedness
1Jn	1:9	and just and will **f** us our sins

FORGIVENESS [4105, 5951, 6142, 6145, 6296, 912, 668, 918, 3195, 5919] (Heb. *kāphar, nāsā', sālach*, Gr. *apoluein, charizesthai, aphēsis, parēsis*). In the OT, *pardon*, and in the NT, *remission*, are often used as the equivalents of *forgiveness*. The idea of forgiveness is found in either religious or social relations, and means giving up resentment or claim to requital on account of an offense. The offense may be a deprivation of a person's property, rights, or honor; or it may be a violation of moral law.

The normal conditions of forgiveness are repentance and the willingness to make reparation or atonement; and the effect of forgiveness is the restoration of both parties to the former state of relationship. Christ taught that forgiveness is a duty and that no limit should be set to the extent of forgiveness (Lk 17:4). An unforgiving spirit is one of the most serious of sins (Mt 18:34 – 35; Lk 15:28 – 30). God forgives people's sins because of the atoning death of Christ. Jesus taught that the offended party is, when necessary, to go to the offender and try to bring him or her to repentance (Lk 17:3). God's forgiveness is conditional on people's forgiveness of the wrongs done them (Mt 5:23 – 24; 6:12; Col 1:14; 3:13). Those forgiven by God before the incarnation were forgiven because of Christ, whose death was foreordained from eternity. Christ's atonement was retroactive in its effect (Heb 11:40). God's forgiveness seems, however, to be limited. Christ speaks of the unpardonable sin (Mt 12:31 – 32), and John speaks of the sin unto death (1Jn 5:16). The deity of Christ is evidenced by his claim to the power to forgive sins (Mk 2:7; Lk 5:21; 7:49).

Of Enemies:

By showing kindness to enemy's animal (Ex 23:4 – 5). By giving (Pr 25:21 – 22; Mt 5:39 – 41; Ro 12:20). Commanded (Pr 24:17; Mt 5:38 – 48; 18:21 – 35; Mk 11:25; Lk 6:27 – 37). See Enemy.

Each Other:

(Lk 17:3 – 4; Eph 4:32; Col 3:13; Phm 10, 18). A condition of divine forgiveness (Mt 6:12 – 15; 18:21 – 35; Mk 11:25; Lk 11:4). Spirit of, disallows gloating (Pr 24:17 – 18). Disallows retaliation (Pr 24:29; Ro 12:17, 19). Blesses (Ro 12:14; 1Co 4:12 – 13; 1Pe 3:9).

Ps	130:4	But with you there is **f**;
Mt	26:28	out for many for the **f** of sins.
Lk	1:77	salvation through the **f** of their sins,
	24:47	and **f** of sins will be preached
Ac	5:31	that he might give repentance and **f**
	10:43	believes in him receives **f** of sins
	13:38	that through Jesus the **f**
Eph	1:7	through his blood, the **f** of sins,
Col	1:14	in whom we have redemption, the **f**
Heb	9:22	the shedding of blood there is no **f**.

FORNICATION (Heb. *zānâh*, Gr. *porneia*). Used in the KJV for unlawful sexual intercourse of an unwed person. It is to be distinguished from adultery, which has to do with unfaithfulness on the part of a married person, and from rape, which is a crime of violence and without the consent of the person sinned against. When these sins are men-

tioned in the Bible, they are often figurative of disloyalty. Idolatry is practically adultery against God. For the spiritualizing of this sin, see Jer 2:20 – 36; Eze 16; Hos 1 – 3 (where it applied to Israel); and Rev 17 (where it applied to Rome).

FORSAKE

Dt	31:6	he will never leave you nor **f** you."
Jos	1:5	I will never leave you nor **f** you.
	24:16	"Far be it from us to **f** the L ORD
2Ch	15:2	but if you **f** him, he will **f** you.
Ps	27:10	Though my father and mother **f** me
Heb	13:5	never will I **f** you."

FREEDOM

Ps	119:45	I will walk about in **f**,
Isa	61:1	to proclaim **f** for the captives
Lk	4:18	me to proclaim **f** for the prisoners
1Co	7:21	although if you can gain your **f**,
2Co	3:17	the Spirit of the Lord is, there is **f**.
Gal	5:13	But do not use your **f** to indulge
Jas	1:25	into the perfect law that gives **f**,
1Pe	2:16	but do not use your **f** as a cover-up

FRIEND

Ex	33:11	as a man speaks with his **f**.
Pr	17:17	A **f** loves at all times,
	18:24	there is a **f** who sticks closer
	27:6	Wounds from a **f** can be trusted
Mt	11:19	a **f** of tax collectors and "sinners.'"
Lk	11:8	him the bread because he is his **f**,
Jas	2:23	and he was called God's **f**.
	4:4	Anyone who chooses to be a **f**

FRUIT [FRUITFUL]

Ps	1:3	which yields its **f** in season
Isa	32:17	The **f** of righteousness will be peace
Jer	17:8	and never fails to bear **f**."
Hos	10:12	reap the **f** of unfailing love,
Mt	3:10	does not produce good **f** will be cut
	7:16	By their **f** you will recognize them.
	7:17	good **f**, but a bad tree bears bad **f**.

Lk	13:6	and he went to look for **f** on it,
Jn	15:2	branch in me that bears no **f**,
	15:16	and bear **f**— **f** that will last.
Ro	7:4	in order that we might bear **f**
Gal	5:22	But the **f** of the Spirit is love, joy,
Col	1:10	bearing **f** in every good work,
Rev	22:2	of **f**, yielding its **f** every month.

FRUITFUL [FRUIT]

Ge	1:22	"Be **f** and increase in number
	9:1	"Be **f** and increase in number
	35:11	be **f** and increase in number.
Ex	1:7	the Israelites were **f** and multiplied
Ps	128:3	Your wife will be like a **f** vine
Jn	15:2	prunes so that it will be even more **f**.

FRUGALITY

General References to:

Diligent (Pr 12:27). Good (Pr 13:22). Wise (Pr 21:17; 21:20). Prudent (Pr 22:3). Industrious (Eph 4:28). Mark of a virtuous woman (Pr 31:27). Admonition regarding (Pr 23:20 – 21). Commanded by Jesus (Jn 6:12). Pretense of, to cover greed (Mk 14:4 – 5).

Instances of:

Provisions made by Egyptians against famine (Ge 41:48 – 54); gathering of manna (Ex 16:17 – 18, 22 – 24); gathering of bread and fish after feeding of the multitudes (Mt 14:20; 15:37).

FULFILL [FULFILLED]

Nu	23:19	Does he promise and not **f**?
Ps	61:8	and **f** my vows day after day.
	138:8	The LORD will **f** his purpose
Ecc	5:5	than to make a vow and not **f** it.
Jer	33:14	'when I will **f** the gracious promise
Mt	3:15	us to do this to **f** all righteousness."
	5:17	come to abolish them but to **f** them.
	8:17	This was to **f** what was spoken
Jn	12:38	This was to **f** the word
	13:18	But this is to **f** the scripture:
1Co	7:3	husband should **f** his marital duty

FULFILLED [FULFILL]

Jos	21:45	of Israel failed; every one was **f**.
	23:14	Every promise has been **f**;
Mt	2:15	so was **f** what the Lord had said
	2:23	So was **f** what was said
	13:14	In them is **f** the prophecy of Isaiah:
	26:54	would the Scriptures be **f** that say it
	27:9	by Jeremiah the prophet was **f**:
Mk	13:4	that they are all about to be **f**?"
	14:49	But the Scriptures must be **f**."
Lk	4:21	"Today this scripture is **f**
	24:44	Everything must be **f** that is
Jn	18:9	words he had spoken would be **f**:
	19:36	so that the Scripture would be **f**:
Ac	1:16	to be **f** which the Holy Spirit spoke
Ro	13:8	loves his fellowman has **f** the law.
Jas	2:23	And the scripture was **f** that says,

FUNERAL [5301, 5386]. The word does not occur in the KJV and is found in the NIV only twice, both times as an adjective (Jer 16:5; 34:5). Funeral rites differed with the place, the religion, and the times; except for royal burials in Egypt, the elaborate ceremonies we use today were not held.

Generally in Palestine there was no embalmment and the body was buried a few hours after death, sometimes in a tomb but more often in a cave. Coffins were unknown. The body was washed and often anointed with aromatic spices (Jn 12:7; 19:39). The procession of mourners, made up of relatives and friends of the deceased, was led by professional mourning women, whose shrieks and lamentations pierced the air. It was an insult to a man's reputation to be refused proper burial (Jer 22:19). The "Tombs of the Kings" on the east side of Jerusalem and the "garden tomb," where our Lord's body was laid, are evidences of the two types of burial. In Egypt the bodies were embalmed so skillfully that many of them are recognizable today after the lapse of thousands of years.

GABRIEL [1508, 1120] (gā′brĭ-ebl, Heb. *gavrî′el, man of God,* Gr. *Gabriel*). An angel mentioned four times in Scripture, each time bringing a momentous message. He interpreted to Daniel the vision of the ram and the goat (Da 8:16 – 17). In Da 9:21 – 22 he explained the vision of the seventy weeks. Gabriel announced to Zechariah the birth of John, forerunner of the Messiah (Lk 1:11 – 20); and he was sent to Mary with the unique message of Jesus' birth (1:26 – 38). His credentials are the ideal for every messenger of God: "I am Gabriel. I stand in the presence of God, and I have been sent to speak to you and to tell you this good news" (1:19). The Bible does not define his status as an angel, but he appears in the book of Enoch (chs. 9, 20, 40) as an archangel.

GALATIA [1130, 1131] (ga-lā′shĭ-a). The designation in NT times of a territory in north-central Asia Minor, also a Roman province in central Asia Minor. The name was derived from the people called Galatians (*Galatia*), a Greek modification of their original name *Keltoi* or *Keltai*, Celtic tribes from ancient Gaul. After having invaded Macedonia and Greece in c. 280 BC, they crossed into Asia Minor on the invitation of Nikomedes I, king of Bithynia, to aid him in a civil war. After ravaging far and wide, they were finally confined to the north-central part of Asia Minor, where they settled as conquerors and gave their name to the territory. Their chief city-centers were Ancyra, Pessinus, and Ravium. In 189 BC the Galatians were subjugated by Rome and continued as a subject kingdom under their own chiefs, and after 63 BC under kings. On the death of King Amyntas in 25, the Galatian kingdom was converted into a Roman province called Galatia. The province included not only the area inhabited by the Galatians but also parts of Phrygia, Pisidia, Lycaonia, and Isauria. The term *Galatia* henceforth carried a double connotation: geographically, to designate the territory inhabited by the Galatians; politically, to denote the entire Roman province. That the cities of Antioch, Iconium, Lystra, and Derbe, evangelized by Paul on his first missionary journey, were in the province of Galatia is now recognized by all scholars.

GALATIANS, LETTER TO THE A short but very important letter of Paul, containing his passionate polemic against the perversion or contamination of the gospel of God's grace. It has aptly been described as "the Magna Carta of spiritual emancipation," and it remains as the abiding monument of the liberation of Christianity from the trammels of legalism.

The contents of the letter so unmistakably reveal the traces of Paul's mind and style that its genuineness has never been seriously questioned even by the most radical NT critics. The testimony of the early church to its integrity and Pauline origin is strong and unambiguous.

Written to "the churches of Galatia," it is the only letter by Paul that is specifically addressed to a group of churches. They were all founded by Paul (Gal 1:8, 11; 4:19 – 20), were all the fruit of a single mission (3:1 – 3; 4:13 – 14), and were all affected by the same disturbance (1:6 – 7; 5:7 – 9). Paul had preached to them the gospel of the free grace of God through the death of Christ (1:6; 3:1 – 14). The Galatians warmly and affectionately received Paul and his message (4:12 – 15). The converts willingly endured persecution for their faith (3:4) and "were running a good race" when Paul left them (5:7).

The startling information received by Paul that a sudden and drastic change in attitude toward him and his gospel was taking place in the Galatian churches caused the writing of the letter. Certain Jewish teachers, who professed to be Christians and acknowledged Jesus as Messiah, were obscuring the simplicity of the gospel of free grace with their propaganda. They insisted that to faith in Christ must be added circumcision and obedience to the Mosaic law (2:16; 3:2 – 3; 4:10, 21; 5:2 – 4; 6:12). Paul realized clearly that this teaching neutralized the truth of Christ's all-sufficiency for salvation and destroyed the message of justification by faith. By means of this letter Paul sought to save his converts from this fatal mixing of law and grace.

Because of the geographical and the political connotation of Galatia in NT times, two views concerning the location of the Galatian churches are advocated. The North-Galatian theory, which interprets the term in its old ethnographic sense to denote the territory inhabited by the Galatian tribes, locates the churches in north-central Asia Minor, holding that they were founded during the second missionary journey (Ac 16:6). The South-Galatian theory identifies these churches with those founded on the first missionary journey (Ac 13 – 14), located in the southern part of the Roman province of Galatia. The former was the unanimous view of the church fathers. They naturally adopted that meaning since in the second century the province was again restricted to ethnic Galatia and the double meaning of the term disappeared. The majority of modern commentators support the latter view for the following reasons: (1) it was Paul's habit to use provincial names in addressing his converts; (2) it best explains the familiar reference to Barnabas in the letter; (3) Ac 16:6 gives no hint of such a protracted mission as the older view demands; (4) the older view cannot explain why the Judaizers would bypass the important churches in South Galatia; and (5) known conditions in these churches fit the picture in the letter.

The contents of Galatians make evident Paul's purpose in writing. The first two chapters show that he was compelled to vindicate his apostolic authority. The Judaizers, in order to establish their own position, which contradicted Paul's teaching, had attempted to discredit his authority. Having vindicated his apostolic call and authority, Paul next sets forth the doctrine of justification to refute the teaching of the Judaizers. A reasoned, comprehensive exposition of the doctrine of justification by faith exposed the errors of legalism. Since the Judaizers asserted that to remove the believer from under the law opened the floodgates to immorality, Paul concluded his presentation with an elaboration of the

true effect of liberty on the Christian life, showing that the truth of justification by faith logically leads to a life of good works.

Outline:

I. Introduction (1:1 – 10).
  A. Salutation (1:1 – 5).
  B. Rebuke (1:6 – 10).
II. Vindication of His Apostolic Authority (1:11 – 2:21).
  A. Reception of his gospel by revelation (1:11 – 24).
  B. Confirmation of his gospel by the apostles at Jerusalem (2:1 – 10).
  C. Illustration of his independence (2:11 – 21).
III. Exposition of Justification by Faith (3:1 – 4:31).
  A. Elaboration of the doctrine (3:1 – 4:7).
    1. Nature of justification by faith (3:1 – 14).
    2. Limitations of the law and its relations to faith (3:15 – 4:7).
  B. Appeal to drop all legalism (4:8 – 31).
IV. Nature of the Life of Christian Liberty (5:1 – 6:10).
  A. Call to maintain their liberty (5:1).
  B. Peril of Christian liberty (5:2 – 12).
  C. Life of liberty (5:13 – 6:10).
V. Conclusion (6:11 – 17).
VI. Benediction (6:18).

GALILEE [824+1665, 1665, 1133, 1134] (găl'ĭ-lē Heb. *hā-gālîl, the ring or circuit,* Gr. *Galilaia*). The most northerly of the three provinces of Palestine (Galilee, Samaria, Judea). Measuring approximately fifty miles north to south and thirty miles east to west, it was bounded on the west by the plain of Akka to the foot of Mount Carmel. The Jordan, the Sea of Galilee, Lake Huleh, and the spring at Dan marked off the eastern border. Its northern boundary went eastward from Phoenicia to Dan. The southern border ran in a southeasterly direction from the base of Mount Carmel and the Samaritan hills along the Valley of Jezreel

(Plain of Esdraelon) to Mount Gilboa and Scythopolis (Beth Shan) to the Jordan. The Valley of Jezreel was a vital communications link between the coastal plain and the center of Palestine. For this reason, decisive battles were often fought here for possession of this desirable pass. The city of Megiddo was important for the control of the valley, and lends its name to *Har-Magedon*, the Hill of Megiddo, or Armageddon, where the conflict between Christ and the armies of the Antichrist is predicted to occur (Rev 16:16).

An imaginary line from the plain of Akka to the north end of the Sea of Galilee divided the country into Upper and Lower Galilee. "Galilee of the Gentiles" refers chiefly to Upper Galilee, which is separated from Lebanon by the Leontes River. Lower Galilee was largely the heritage of Zebulun and Issachar. Less hilly and of a milder climate than Upper Galilee, it included the rich plain of Esdraelon (or Jezreel) and was a "pleasant" land (Ge 49:15) that would yield "treasures hidden in the sand" (Dt 33:19).

The northern part of Upper Galilee was inhabited by a mixed race of Jews and pagans (Jdg 1:33). Its Israelite population was carried away captive to Assyria and was replaced by a colony of pagan immigrants (2Ki 15:29; 17:24), hence called "Galilee of the nations" or "Gentiles" (Isa 9:1; Mt 4:13, 15 – 16). During and after the captivity, the predominant mixture of Gentile races impoverished the worship of Judaism. For the same reason the Galilean accent and dialect were noticeably peculiar (Mt 26:73). This caused the southern Jews of purer blood and orthodox tradition to despise them (Jn 7:52). Nathanael asked, rather contemptuously, "Nazareth! Can anything good come from there?" (1:46). Yet its very darkness was the Lord's reason for granting more of the light of his presence and ministry to Galilee than to self-satisfied and privileged Judea. He was sent as "a light for the Gentiles" (Isa 42:6) as well as to the "lost sheep of Israel" (Mt 15:24). Wherever he found faith and repentance, he bestowed his blessing, whereas unbelief often hindered his activity (13:58). He preached his first public sermon in the synagogue at Nazareth in Lower Galilee, where he had been brought up (Lk 4:16 – 30). His disciples came from Galilee (Mt 4:18; Jn 1:43 – 44; Ac 1:11; 2:7); in Cana of Galilee he performed his first miracle (Jn 2:11). Capernaum in Galilee, the home of his manhood (Mt 4:13; 9:1), is where the first three gospels present his major ministry. Galilee's debasement made some of its people feel their need of the Savior. This and its comparative freedom from priestly and pharisaical prejudice may have been additional reasons for its receiving the larger share of the Lord's ministry.

> **General References to:**
>
> *A city of refuge in (Jos 20:7; 21:32; 1Ch 6:76). Cities in, given to Hiram (1Ki 9:11 – 12). Taken by king of Assyria (2Ki 15:29). Prophecy concerning (Isa 9:1; Mt 4:15). Called Galilee of the nations (Isa 9:1). Herod, tetrarch of (Mk 6:21; Lk 3:1; 23:6 – 7). Jesus resides in (Mt 17:22; 19:1; Jn 7:1, 9). Teaching and miracles of Jesus in (Mt 4:23, 25; 15:29 – 31; Mk 1:14, 28, 39; 3:7; Lk 4:14, 44; 5:17; 23:5; Jn 1:43; 4:3, 43 – 45; Ac 10:37). People of, receive Jesus (Jn 4:45, 53). Disciples were chiefly from (Ac 1:11; 2:7). Women from, ministered to Jesus (Mt 27:55 – 56; Mk 15:41; Lk 23:49, 55). Jesus appeared to his disciples in, after his resurrection (Mt 26:32; 28:7, 10, 16 – 17; Mk 14:28; 16:7; Jn 21). Routes from, to Judea (Jdg 21:19; Jn 4:3 – 5). Dialect of (Mk 14:70). Called Gennesaret (Mt 14:34; Mk 6:53). Churches in (Ac 9:31).*

Isa	9:1	but in the future he will honor **G**
Mt	4:15	**G** of the Gentiles —
	26:32	I will go ahead of you into **G**."
	28:10	Go and tell my brothers to go to **G**;

GALILEE, SEA OF So called from its location east of Galilee, it is also called "the Lake of Gennesaret" (Lk 5:1), since the fertile Plain of Gennesaret lies on the NW (Mt 14:34). The OT calls it "the Sea of Kinnereth" (Heb. "harp-shaped," Nu 34:11; Dt 3:17; Jos 13:27), from the town so named on its shore (Jos 19:35), of which Gennesaret is probably the corruption. "The Sea of Tiberias" is another designation (Jn 6:1; 21:10),

associated with Tiberias, the capital of Herod Antipas. All its names were derived from places on the western shore. Its present name is Bahr Tabariyeh.

Located some sixty miles (one hundred km.) north of Jerusalem, its bed is but a lower depression of the Jordan Valley. The fresh water is sweet, sparkling, and transparent, with fish in abundance. The gospel accounts picture fishing as a prosperous industry here in biblical times, but today, instead of fleets of fishing vessels, only a boat or two is seen. On these shores Jesus called his first disciples, four of whom were fishermen, and made them fishers of men (Mt 4:18; Lk 5:1 – 11).

The Sea of Galilee is noted for its sudden and violent storms caused by cold air sweeping down from the vast naked plateaus of Gaulanitis, the Hauran, and Mount Hermon through the ravines and gorges and converging at the head of the lake where it meets warm air. Jesus rebuked just such a storm (Mk 4:39). Here also Jesus walked on the tempestuous water (Mt 14:22 – 34; Mk 6:45 – 53; Jn 6:15 – 21).

The Sea of Galilee was the focus of Galilee's wealth. Nine cities of 15,000 or more stood on its shores. To the NW was Capernaum, the home of Peter and Andrew (Mk 1:29) and where Matthew collected taxes (Mt 9:9). It was the scene of much of Jesus' Galilean ministry.

GALLIO [1136] (gal'ĭ-ọ *Gr. Galliōn*). Roman proconsul of Achaia when Paul was in Corinth (AD 51). Alarmed at the inroads that the gospel was making, the Jews in Corinth brought Paul before Gallio, of whom the Roman philosopher Seneca had said, "No mortal was ever so sweet to one as Gallio was to all." The Jews hoped to convince Gallio that Paul was guilty of an offense against a lawful religion, and hence against the Roman government itself (Ac 18:12 – 17), but Gallio rejected their argument. The Greeks then beat the chief ruler of the synagogue, but Gallio remained indifferent to the incident. A sterner governor might have arrested the violence at once, but in the providence of God, Gallio's action amounted to an authoritative decision that Paul's preaching was not subversive against Rome. This gave the apostle the protection he needed to continue his preaching there. Gallio did not become a Christian; he died by committing suicide.

GARRISON (Heb. *matstsāv, netsîv*). Most of the OT occurrences of these words are translated "garrisons," but they also appear as "officer," "outpost," "pillar" (as when Lot's wife became a "pillar of salt," Ge 19:26), "place" (for the priests' feet in the crossing of the Jordan, Jos 4:3, 9), and "station." *Matstsav* (ten OT occurrences) and *netsîv* (twelve OT occurrences) primarily refer to a military post for the occupation of a conquered country such as the Philistines had when they held the land of Israel (1Sa 10:5; 13:3; 14:1, 6; 1Ch 11:16).

GATH (gắth, Heb. *gath, winepress*). One of the five great Philistine cities (Ashdod, Gaza, Ashkelon, Gath, and Ekron [Jos 13:3; 1Sa 6:17]). Its people were the Gittites, including Goliath and other giants (2Sa 21:19 – 22).

GEHENNA (gē-hĕn′a, Gr. *geenna*, a transliteration of the Aramaic form of Heb. *gê-ben-hinnôm, valley of the son of Hinnom*). In the OT it was referred to as the Valley of Ben Hinnom (NIV) or the valley of the son of Hinnom (KJV, RSV, ASV). A valley west and SW of Jerusalem that formed part of the border between Judah and Benjamin (Jos 15:8; cf. 18:16), it was still recognized as the border after the exile (Ne 11:30 – 31) and is modern Wadi er-Rababi. Here Ahaz (2Ki 16:3; 2Ch 28:3) and Manasseh (2Ki 21:6; 2Ch 33:6) sacrificed their sons to Molech (Jer 32:35). For this reason Josiah defiled the place (2Ki 23:10). After referring to these idolatrous practices (Jer 7:31 – 32), Jeremiah prophesied a great slaughter of the people there and in Jerusalem (Jer 19:1 – 13).

After the OT period, Jewish apocalyptic writers began to call the Valley of Hinnom the entrance to hell, later hell itself. In Jewish usage of the first century AD, Gehenna referred to the intermediate state of the godless dead, but there is no trace of this sense in the NT. The NT distinguishes sharply between Hades, the intermediate, bodiless state, and Gehenna, the state of final punishment after the resurrection of the body. Gehenna existed before the judgment (Mt 25:41). The word occurs twelve times in the NT, always translated "hell" (ASV, RSV margin "Gehenna"). Eleven times it is on the lips of Jesus: as the final punishment for calling one's brother a fool (5:22); for adultery, when the severest measures have not been taken to prevent commission of this offense (5:29 – 30); in a warning about whom to fear (Mt 10:28; Lk 12:5); and others (Mt 18:9; Mk 9:43, 45, 47). A hypocrite is called a "son of hell" (Mt 23:15) who cannot escape "being condemned to hell" (23:33). James 3:6 speaks of the "tongue" as "a fire … set on fire by hell." A fire was kept burning in the Valley of Hinnom to consume the garbage deposited there by the residents of Jerusalem. Terms parallel to Gehenna include "fiery furnace" (Mt 13:42, 50); "fiery lake" (Rev 19:20; 20:14 – 15); "lake of burning sulfur" (20:10); "eternal fire" (Jude 7); "hell" (2Pe 2:4), where the Greek phrase "sent … to hell" means "cast down to Tartarus," a Greek name for the place of punishment of the wicked dead. Its use by our Savior Jesus Christ warns us of the destiny that even the love of God does not avert from those who finally refuse his forgiveness.

GENEALOGY [3509, 3510, 9352, 37, 1157, 1161] (jĕn′ē-ăl′ŏ-jē, Heb. *yachas*, Gr. *genealogia*, *account of one's descent*). A list of ancestors or descendants, descent from an ancestor, or the study of lines of descent. Genealogies are compiled to show biological descent, the right of inheritance, succession to an office, or ethnological and geographical relationships. The word occurs several times in the English Bible (1Ch 4:33; 5:1, 7; 7:5, 7, 9, 40; 9:22; 2Ch 12:15; 31:16 – 19; Ezr 2:62; 8:1; Ne 7:5, 64; 1Ti 1:4; Tit 3:9), but most Bible genealogies are introduced by other words, such as "the book of the generations of," or "these are the generations of," or are given without titles.

General References to:

Of no spiritual significance (Mt 3:9; 1Ti 1:4; Tit 3:9). From Adam to Noah (Ge 4:16 – 22; 5; 1Ch 1:1 – 4; Lk 3:36 – 38); to Abraham (Ge 11:10 – 32; 1Ch 1:4 – 27; Lk 3:34 – 38); to Jesus (Mt 1:1 – 16; Lk 3:23 – 38). Of the descendants of Noah (Ge 10); Nahor (Ge 22:20 – 24); Abraham, by his wife Keturah (Ge 25:1 – 4; 1Ch 1:32 – 33); Ishmael (Ge 25:12 – 16; 1Ch 1:28 – 31); Esau (Ge 36; 1Ch 1:35 – 54); Jacob (Ge 35:23 – 26; Ex 1:5; 6:14 – 27; Nu 26; 1Ch 2 – 9); Perez to David (Ru 4:18 – 22); the Jews who returned from the captivity (Ezr 7:1 – 5; 8:1 – 15; Ne 7; 11:12); Joseph (Mt 1; Lk 3:23 – 38).

1Ti	1:4	themselves to myths and endless **g**.
Tit	3:9	avoid foolish controversies and **g**

GENEALOGY OF JESUS CHRIST Two genealogies are given in the NT (Mt 1:1 – 17; Lk 3:23 – 28). Matthew traces the descent of Jesus from Abraham and David, and divides it into three sets of fourteen generations. He omits three generations after Joram, namely Ahaziah, Joash, and Amaziah (1Ch 3:11 – 12). Contrary to Hebrew practice, he names five women: Tamar, Rahab, Ruth, Bathsheba, and Mary. The sense of "became the father of" in Hebrew genealogies is not exact; it indicated immediate or remote descent, an adoptive relation, or legal heirship. Luke's genealogy moves from Jesus to Adam, agreeing with the accounts in 1 Chronicles between Abraham and Adam (1Ch 1:1 – 7, 24 – 28). From David to Abraham he agrees with Matthew; from Jesus to David he differs from Matthew. Perhaps Matthew gives the line of legal heirship, while Luke gives the line of physical descent. Both make plain his virgin birth, and therefore his deity. The agreement of Matthew and Luke on these facts is obvious, and their differences only accentuate their value as independent witnesses, whose testimony was prompted by the Holy Spirit, not by collaboration with each other. Matthew's genealogy establishes the legal claim to the throne of David through his foster father Joseph; Luke's establishes his actual descent from David through Mary. Luke 1:32 says that Mary's child "will be called the Son of the Most High. The Lord God will give him the throne of his father David." Romans 1:3 – 4 agrees: Jesus "as to his human nature was a descendant of David," which could only be through Mary, and "was declared with power to be the Son of God by his resurrection from the dead." See also 2Ti 2:8. Isaiah 11:1 indicates that the Messiah is to be physically a descendant of David's father Jesse. The genealogies must be seen in light of this fact. See Mt 22:41 – 46 and parallels with the answer in Ro 1:4.

GENEROSITY [GENEROUS]

| 2Co | 8:2 | poverty welled up in rich **g**. |
| | 9:11 | and through us your **g** will result |

GENEROUS [GENEROSITY]

Ps	37:26	They are always **g** and lend freely;
	112:5	Good will come to him who is **g**
Pr	11:25	A **g** man will prosper;
	22:9	A **g** man will himself be blessed,
Mt	20:15	Or are you envious because I am **g**
2Co	9:5	Then it will be ready as a **g** gift,
1Ti	6:18	and to be **g** and willing to share.

GENESIS [1414] (jĕn′ĕ·sĭs, *beginning*). The first book of the Bible. In the Jewish tradition the book is named from its first word, *berēshîth* ("in the beginning"). The name Genesis, which means "beginning," derives from the LXX and is found also in the Latin tradition (*Liber Genesis*). While much of the book is concerned with origins, the name Genesis does not reflect its total scope, for the larger portion of the book consists of the history of the patriarchs and concludes with the record of Joseph's life.

AUTHORSHIP OF GENESIS.

The question of the authorship of Genesis has been the subject of debate for over two centuries. Tradition ascribes the book to Moses, but the application of source-critical methodology has partitioned Genesis into a number of sources (known as J, E, D, P, etc.) attributed to various authors writing at widely diverse times in Israelite history.

The concept of Mosaic authorship does not demand the belief that Moses was the first to write every word of each account in the book of Genesis. It is generally understood today to mean that much of his work was compilation. Many historical accounts in Genesis predate Moses by great expanses of time. There is no reason why he could not have arranged these ancient accounts into the literary structure of the book.

ARCHAEOLOGICAL BACKGROUND OF GENESIS.

Excavations at a number of sites in the ancient Near East have tended to support the antiquity and historical integrity of significant portions of the book of Genesis. For example, excavations at Yorgan Tepe, the site of ancient Nuzi, have yielded thousands of tablets, most of which have been dated to the fifteenth century BC. These tablets record several legal and societal practices that are strikingly similar to customs recorded in the patriarchal narratives.

CONTENT OF GENESIS.

The book of Genesis may be divided roughly into three parts. Chapters 1 – 11 record events from the creation to the death of Terah, the father of Abraham. Chapters 12 – 36 constitute a history of the patriarchs Abraham, Isaac, and Jacob. Chapters 37 – 50 present a sustained narrative that records the account of Joseph.

GENTILES [1580, 260, 1619, 1620, 1818] (Heb. *gôy*, plural *gôyîm*, *nation, people*). *Gentile* usually means non-Israelite people. In times of peace, considerate treatment was accorded Gentiles under OT law (e.g., Nu 35:15; Dt 10:19; 24:14 – 15; Eze 47:22). Men of Israel often married Gentile women, of whom Rahab, Ruth, and Bathsheba are notable examples, but the practice was frowned on after the return from exile (Ezr 9:12; 10:2 – 44; Ne 10:30; 13:23 – 31). Separation between Jew and Gentile became stricter, until in the NT period the hostility was complete. Persecution embittered the Jews, who retaliated with hatred of everything pertaining to

Gentiles and with avoidance, so far as was possible, of contact with Gentiles. The intensity of this feeling varied and gave way before unusual kindness (Lk 7:4 – 5).

While the teachings of Jesus ultimately broke down "the middle wall of partition" between Jew and Gentile, as is seen in the writings of Paul (Ro 1:16; 1Co 1:24; Gal 3:28; Eph 2:14; Col 3:11) and in Acts, Jesus limited his ministry to Jews, with rare exceptions (the half-Jewish Samaritans, Jn 4:1 – 42; the Syrophoenician woman, Matt 15:21 – 28; Mk 7:24 – 30; the Greeks in Jn 12:20 – 36). He instructed his twelve disciples, "Do not go among the Gentiles or enter any town of the Samaritans" (Mt 10:5); but he did not repeat this injunction when he sent out the Seventy (Lk 10:1 – 16; NIV "seventy-two"). Jesus' mission was first to "his own" (Jn 1:11), the chosen people of God, but ultimately to "all who received him" (1:12). Limitations of time held his ministry on earth within the bounds of Israel; reaching the Gentiles was left to the activity of the Holy Spirit working through his disciples.

In Acts, from the appointment of Paul as the apostle to the Gentiles (9:15), the Gentiles become increasingly prominent. Even the letters addressed particularly to Jewish Christians (Ro 9 – 11; Hebrews; James; 1 Peter) are relevant to Gentiles also. The division of all humankind into two classes, Jew and Gentile, emphasizes the importance of the Jews as the people through whom God made salvation available to all people.

General References to:

Ways of, condemned (Jer 10:2 – 3; Eph 4:17 – 19). God's forbearance toward (Ac 14:16). Impartiality toward (Ro 2:9 – 11). Ignorant worship practices of (Mt 6:7 – 8, 31 – 32; Ac 17:4, 16, 22 – 27; 1Co 10:20; 12:2). Wicked practices of (Ro 1:18 – 32; Gal 2:15; Eph 5:12; 1Th 4:5; 1Pe 4:3 – 4). Moral responsibility of (Ro 2:14 – 15).

Prophecies of the Conversion of:

(Ge 12:3; 22:18; 49:10; Dt 32:21; Pss 2:8; 22:27 – 31; 46:4, 10; 65:2, 5; 66:4; 68:31 – 32;

72:8 – 11, 16, 19; 86:9; 102:15, 18 – 22; 145:10 – 11; Isa 2:2 – 4; 9:2, 6 – 7; 11:6 – 10; 18:7; 24:16; 35:1 – 2, 5 – 7; 40:5; 42:1 – 12; 45:6, 8, 22 – 24; 49:1, 5 – 6, 18 – 23; 54:1 – 3; 55:5; 56:3, 6 – 8; 60:1 – 14; 65:1; 66:12, 19, 23; Jer 3:17; 4:2; 16:19 – 21; Da 2:35, 44 – 45; 7:13 – 14; Hos 2:23; Joel 2:28 – 32; Am 9:11 – 12; Mic 4:3 – 4; Hag 2:7; Zec 2:10 – 11; 6:15; 8:20 – 23; 9:1, 10; 14:8 – 9, 16; Mal 1:11; Mt 3:9; 8:11; 12:17 – 21; 19:30; Mk 10:31; Lk 13:29 – 30; 21:24; Jn 10:16; Ac 9:15).

Conversion of:

(Ac 10:45; 11:1 – 8; 13:2, 46 – 48; 14:27; 15:7 – 31; 18:4 – 6; 26:16 – 18; 28:28; Ro 1:5 – 7; 9:22 – 30; 10:19 – 20; 11:11 – 13, 17 – 21; 15:9 – 12; Gal 1:15 – 16; 2:2; 3:14; Eph 3:1 – 8; Col 3:11; 1Th 2:16; 1Ti 3:16; 2Ti 1:11; Rev 11:15; 15:4).

Isa	42:6	and a light for the **G**,
	49:22	"See, I will beckon to the **G**,
Lk	2:32	a light for revelation to the **G**
	21:24	on by the **G** until the times
Ac	9:15	to carry my name before the **G**
	10:45	been poured out even on the **G**.
	11:18	granted even the **G** repentance unto
	14:27	opened the door of faith to the **G**.
	18:6	From now on I will go to the **G**."
	28:28	salvation has been sent to the **G**,
Ro	2:14	when **G**, who do not have the law,
	3:9	and **G** alike are all under sin.
	3:29	Is he not the God of **G** too? Yes,
	11:11	to the **G** to make Israel envious.
	15:9	I will praise you among the **G**;
1Co	1:23	block to Jews and foolishness to **G**,
Gal	1:16	I might preach him among the **G**,
	3:8	that God would justify the **G**
Eph	3:6	the gospel the **G** are heirs together
	3:8	to the **G** the unsearchable riches
Col	1:27	among the **G** the glorious riches
1Ti	2:7	a teacher of the true faith to the **G**.

GETHSEMANE [1149] (gĕth-sĕm′a-nē̄ probably from the Aramaic for "oil press"). The place of Jesus'

agony and arrest (Mt 26:36 – 56; Mk 14:32 – 52; Lk 22:39 – 54; Jn 18:1 – 12 [John tells of the arrest only]). In Mt 26:36 and Mk 14:32 it is called "a place." Luke does not give the name but says that the place was one to which Jesus customarily went and that it was on the Mount of Olives. John 18:1, without naming it, explains that it was a garden across the Kidron Valley from Jerusalem.

GIBEON [1498, 1500] (gĭ bʹē-ŏn, Heb. *givʹôn, pertaining to a hill*). A city of Benjamin (Jos 18:25) NW of Jerusalem; in NT times Gabao; modern ej-Jib.

A city of the Hivites (Jos 9:3, 17; 2Sa 21:2); People of, deceive Joshua into a treaty (Jos 9); Made servants by the Israelites when their deception was discovered (Jos 9:27); The sun stands still over, during Joshua's battle with the five confederated kings (Jos 10:12 – 14); Allotted to Benjamin (Jos 18:25); Assigned to the Aaronites (Jos 21:17); The tabernacle located at (1Ki 3:4; 1Ch 16:39; 21:29; 2Ch 1:2 – 3, 13); Smitten by David (1Ch 14:16); Seven sons of Saul slain at, to avenge the inhabitants of (2Sa 21:1 – 9); Solomon worships at, and offers sacrifices (1Ki 3:4); God appears to Solomon in dreams at (1Ki 3:5; 9:2); Abner slays Asahel at (2Sa 2:18 – 32; 3:30); Ishmael son of Nethaniah defeated at, by Johanan (Jer 41:11 – 16); Pool of (2Sa 2:13; Jer 41:12)

GIDEON [1549, 1146] (gĭdʹē-ŏn, Heb. *Gidhʹôn, feller* or *hewer, i.e., one who cuts, hacks*). The son of Joash, an Abiezrite (Jdg 6:11) who lived in Ophrah not far from Mount Gerizim (not the Ophrah of Benjamin listed in Jos 18:23). The record about Gideon is found in Jdg 6:1 – 9:6.

Call of, by an angel (Jdg 6:11, 14); His excuses (Jdg 6:15); Promises of the Lord to (Jdg 6:16); Angel attests the call to, by miracle (Jdg 6:21 – 24); Destroys the altar of Baal and builds one to the Lord (Jdg 6:25 – 27); Tests God's word with a fleece (Jdg 6:36 – 40); Leads an army against and defeats the Midianites (Jdg 6:33 – 35; 7; 8:4 – 12); Ephraimites rebuke, for not inviting them to join in the campaign against the Midianites (Jdg 8:1 – 3); Avenges himself upon the people of Succoth (Jdg 8:14 – 17); Israel desires to make him king; he refuses (Jdg 8:22 – 23); Makes an ephod that becomes a snare to the Israelites (Jdg 8:24 – 27); Had seventy sons (Jdg 8:30); Death of (Jdg 8:32); Faith of (Heb 11:32)

GIFT, GIVING [1388, 4458, 4966, 5368, 5508, 5510, 5522, 5989, 7731, 7933, 8816, 8856, 8933, 9556, 10448, 1517, 1561, 1564, 1565, 1797, 2330, 5921, 5922]. A gift can be given as a blessing (1Sa 25:27); a way to gain a favor (Ge 34:12); an act of submission (Ps 68:29); an offering (Ex 28:38); a bribe (Pr 18:16). In the NT, anything given (Lk 21:1; Jas 1:17); a present (Mt 7:11); special spiritual endowment (Ro 1:11; 1Ti 4:14).

GIFTS FROM GOD

Himself:
   In Christ, the Savior (Isa 42:6; 55:4; Jn 3:16; 4:10; 6:32 – 33). In the Holy Spirit, the Comforter. See Holy Spirit.

Temporal:
   Food and clothing (Mt 6:25, 33). Rain and fruitful seasons (Ge 8:22; 27:28; Lev 26:4 – 5; Isa 30:23). Wisdom (2Ch 1:12). Peace (Lev 26:6; 1Ch 22:9). Gladness (Ps 4:7). Strength and power (Pss 29:11; 68:18). Wisdom and knowledge (Ecc 2:26; Da 2:21 – 23; 1Co 1:5 – 7). Talents, figurative of gifts and abilities (Mt 25:14 – 30). All good things (Pss 21:2; 34:10; 84:11; Isa 42:5; Eze 11:19; Jn 16:23 – 24; Ro 8:32; 1Ti 6:17; Jas 1:17; 2Pe 1:3). To be used and enjoyed (Ecc 3:13; 5:19 – 20; 1Ti 4:4 – 5). Should cause us to remember God (Dt 8:18). All creatures partake of (Pss 136:25; 145:15 – 16). Prayer for (Zec 10:1; Mt 6:11).

Spiritual:
   Of the Spirit (Ro 11:29; 12:6 – 8; 1Co 7:7; 12:4 – 11; 13:2; Eph 4:7; 1Pe 4:10). Eternal life (Isa 42:5; Eze 11:19; Jn 3:16 – 17, 36; 6:27; Ro

5:16 – 18; 6:23). Grace (Jas 4:6). Wisdom (Pr 2:6; Jas 1:5). Repentance (Ac 11:28). Faith (Eph 2:8; Php 1:29). Rest (Mt 11:28). Glory (Jn 17:22).

GIFTS, SPIRITUAL (Gr. *charismata*). A theological term meaning any endowment that comes through the grace of God (Ro 1:11). Paul discussed at length in 1Co 12 the spiritual gifts given for special tasks in and through the churches (Ro 12:6 – 8; 2Co 1:11; 1Pe 4:10). They include the ability to speak an unlearned tongue (1Co 14:1 – 33), the interpretation of tongues (1Co 12:30; 14:27 – 28), power to drive out evil spirits (Mt 8:16; Ac 13:7 – 12), special ability in healing the sick (1Co 12:9), prophecy (Ro 12:6), keenness of wisdom (1Co 12:8), and special knowledge (1Co 12:8). Paul told the Corinthians to diligently seek these gifts (12:31), but he pointed out that "the most excellent way" (12:31) is an emphasis on faith, hope, and love, among which love is the greatest gift (13:13). The fruit of the Spirit is described in Gal 5:22 – 23.

Everyone is accountable for any gift given to him or her (1Co 4:7; 1Pe 4:10). Claims of having such gifts are to be tested by doctrine (1Co 12:2 – 3) and on moral grounds (Mt 7:15; Ro 8:9). The ability to preach is a spiritual gift (1Co 2:4; 2Ti 1:6). To know the deep things of God requires spiritual insight (1Co 2:11 – 16). The gifts are distributed by the Holy Spirit (Heb 2:4).

GIFT [GIFTED, GIFTS]

Pr	21:14	A **g** given in secret soothes anger,
Ecc	3:13	in all his toil — this is the **g** of God.
Mt	5:23	if you are offering your **g**
Jn	4:10	"If you knew the **g** of God
Ac	1:4	wait for the **g** my Father promised,
Ro	6:23	but the **g** of God is eternal life
1Co	7:7	each man has his own **g** from God;
2Co	8:12	the **g** is acceptable according
	9:15	be to God for his indescribable **g**!
Eph	2:8	it is the **g** of God — not by works,
2Ti	1:6	you to fan into flame the **g** of God,
Heb	6:4	who have tasted the heavenly **g**,

Jas	1:17	and perfect **g** is from above,
1Pe	4:10	should use whatever **g** he has
Rev	22:17	let him take the free **g** of the water

GILEAD [824+1680, 1201+1682, 1201+1680, 1680, 1682] (gĭl'ē-ăd, Heb. *gil'ādh*, *rugged*, perhaps *monument of stones*). The name is used to indicate Israel's possession east of the Jordan River allotted to the tribes of Reuben and Gad and the half-tribe of Manasseh (Nu 32:1 – 30; Dt 3:13; 34:1; 2Ki 10:33). Josephus so understood it (*Antiq.* 12.8.3). It extended from the lower end of the Sea of Galilee to the northern end of the Dead Sea, and from the Jordan eastward to the desert, a plateau of some 2,000 feet elevation. Gilead became famous because of some of its products. Balm was exported to Tyre (Eze 27:17); Jeremiah knew of its curative power (Jer 8:22; 46:11; 51:8). The Ishmaelites who bought Joseph carried balm to Egypt (Ge 37:25).

Reubenites expel the Hagrites from (1Ch 5:9 – 10, 18 – 22); Ammonites make war against; defeated by Jephthah (Jdg 11; Am 1:13); The prophet Elijah a native of (1Ki 17:1); David retreats to, at the time of Absalom's rebellion (2Sa 17:16, 22, 24); Pursued into, by Absalom (2Sa 17:26); Absalom defeated and slain in the forests of (2Sa 18:9); Hazael, king of Syria, attacks the land of (2Ki 10:32 – 33; Am 1:3); Invaded by Tiglath-Pileser, king of Syria (2Ki 15:29); A grazing country (Nu 32:1; 1Ch 5:9); Exported spices, balm, and myrrh (Ge 37:25; Jer 8:22; 46:11); Figurative of prosperity (Jer 22:6; 50:19); A mountain (Jdg 7:3; SS 4:1; 6:5); A city (Hos 6:8; 12:11); Grandson of Manasseh (Nu 26:29 – 30; 27:1; 36:1; Jos 17:1, 3; 1Ch 2:21, 23; 7:14, 17); Father of Jephthah (Jdg 11:1 – 2); A chief of Gad (1Ch 5:14)

GILGAL [1652] (gĭl'găl, Heb. *Gilgāl*, *circle of stones*). The first camp of Israel after they had crossed the Jordan (Jos 4:19 – 20). While they were camped there, Joshua restored the Hebrew rite of circumcision in response to God's promise to "roll away the reproach of Egypt" (5:2 – 9). The town that grew up was near the northern border of Judah (15:7).

General References to:

Place of the first encampment of the Israelites west of the Jordan (Jos 4:19; 9:6; 10:6, 43; 14:6). Monument erected in, to commemorate the passage of the Jordan by the Israelites (Jos 4:19 – 24). Circumcision renewed at (Jos 5:2 – 9). Passover kept at (Jos 5:10 – 11). Manna ceased at, after the Passover (Jos 5:12). Quarries at (Jdg 3:19). Eglon, king of Moab, resides and is slain at (Jdg 3:14 – 26). A judgment seat, where Israel, in that district, came to be judged by Samuel (1Sa 7:16). Saul proclaimed king over all Israel at (1Sa 11:15; 13:4 – 15; 15:6 – 23). Agag, king of the Amalekites, slain at, by Samuel (1Sa 15:33). Tribe of Judah assembles at, to proceed to the E side of the Jordan to conduct King David back after the defeat of Absalom (2Sa 19:14 – 15, 40 – 43). A school of the prophets at (2Ki 4:38 – 40). Prophecies concerning (Hos 4:15; 9:15; 12:11; Am 4:4; 5:5). A royal city in Canaan. Conquered by Joshua (Jos 12:23).

GIVE

Ex	20:16	"You shall not **g** false testimony
	30:15	The rich are not to **g** more
Dt	5:20	"You shall not **g** false testimony
	15:10	**G** generously to him and do
2Ch	15:7	be strong and do not **g** up,
Pr	23:26	My son, **g** me your heart
	25:21	if he is thirsty, **g** him water to drink
	30:8	but **g** me only my daily bread.
Isa	42:8	I will not **g** my glory to another
Eze	36:26	I will **g** you a new heart
Mt	6:11	**G** us today our daily bread.
	7:11	know how to **g** good gifts
	10:8	Freely you have received, freely **g**.
	16:19	I will **g** you the keys
	22:21	"**G** to Caesar what is Caesar's,
Lk	6:38	**G**, and it will be given to you.

	11:13	Father in heaven **g** the Holy Spirit
	14:33	who does not **g** up everything he
Jn	10:28	I **g** them eternal life, and they shall
	13:34	"A new commandment I **g** you:
	14:16	he will **g** you another Counselor
	14:27	I do not **g** to you as the world gives.
Ac	20:35	blessed to **g** than to receive.' "
Ro	8:32	with him, graciously **g** us all things
	13:7	**G** everyone what you owe him:
	14:12	each of us will **g** an account
2Co	9:7	Each man should **g** what he has
Heb	10:25	Let us not **g** up meeting together,
Rev	14:7	"Fear God and **g** him glory,

GLEAN [4377, 4378, 4380, 6618, 6622] (Heb. *lāqat, 'ālal*). The Hebrew custom of allowing the poor to follow the reapers and gather the grain that was left behind or the grapes that remained after the vintage (Jdg 8:2; Ru 2:2, 16; Isa 17:6). This custom was backed by one of the agricultural laws of Moses (Lev 19:9; 23:22; Dt 24:19 – 21). The word is also used figuratively to describe the utter destruction of Israel (Jer 6:9).

Figurative:

(Jdg 8:2; Isa 17:6; Jer 49:9; Mic 7:1).

Instances of:

Ruth in the field of Boaz (Ru 2:2 – 3).

GLORIFYING GOD [1540, 3877, 8655, 10198, 1443+1518, 1519, 3486]. Commanded (1Ch 16:28; Ps 22:23; Isa 42:12). Due to him (1Ch 16:29) for his holiness (Ps 99:9; Rev 15:4); mercy and truth (Ps 115:1; Ro 15:9); faithfulness and truth (Isa 25:1); wondrous works (Mt 15:31; Ac 4:21); judgments (Isa 25:3; Eze 28:22; Rev 14:7); deliverances (Ps 50:15); grace to others (Ac 11:18; 2Co 9:13; Gal 1:24). Required in body and spirit (1Co 6:20). Shall be universal (Ps 86:9; Rev 5:13).

Accomplished by:

Relying on his promises (Ro 4:20); praising him (Ps 50:23); doing all to glorify him (1Co 10:31); dying for him (Jn 21:19); suffering for Christ (1Pe 4:14, 16); glorifying Christ (Ac 19:17; 2Th

1:12); bringing forth fruits of righteousness (Jn 15:8; Php 1:11); patience in affliction (Isa 24:1–3, 15); faithfulness (1Pe 4:11).

Exemplified by:

David (Ps 57:5); multitude (Mt 9:8; 15:31); virgin Mary (Lk 1:46); angels (Lk 2:14); shepherds (Lk 2:20); Jesus (Jn 17:4); paralyzed man (Lk 5:25); woman with infirmity (Lk 13:13); leper whom Jesus healed (Lk 17:15); blind man (Lk 18:43); centurion (Lk 23:47); church at Jerusalem (Ac 11:18); Gentiles at Antioch (Ac 13:48); Abraham (Ro 4:20); Paul (Ro 11:36). See Praise.

GLORIFIED [GLORY]

Isa	66:5	Let the Lord be **g**,
Eze	39:13	day I am **g** will be a memorable day
Da	4:34	and **g** him who lives forever.
Jn	7:39	since Jesus had not yet been **g**.
	11:4	glory so that God's Son may be **g**
	12:16	after Jesus was **g** did they realize
	12:23	come for the Son of Man to be **g**.
	13:31	Son of Man **g** and God is **g** in him.
Ac	3:13	our fathers, has **g** his servant Jesus.
Ro	1:21	they neither **g** him as God
	8:30	those he justified, he also **g**.
2Th	1:10	comes to be **g** in his holy people
1Pe	1:21	him from the dead and **g** him,

GLORIFY [GLORY]

Ps	34:3	**G** the Lord with me;
	63:3	my lips will **g** you.
	86:12	I will **g** your name forever.
Isa	60:13	and I will **g** the place of my feet.
Da	4:37	and exalt and **g** the King of heaven,
Jn	8:54	Jesus replied, "If I **g** myself,
	13:32	God will **g** the Son in himself,
	17:1	**G** your Son, that your Son may
	21:19	death by which Peter would **g** God.
Ro	15:6	and mouth you may **g** the God
1Pe	2:12	and **g** God on the day he visits us.
Rev	16:9	they refused to repent and **g** him.

GLORIOUS [GLORY]

1Ch	29:13	and praise your **g** name.
Ne	9:5	"Blessed be your **g** name,
Ps	45:13	All **g** is the princess
	72:19	Praise be to his **g** name forever;
	111:3	**G** and majestic are his deeds,
	145:12	the **g** splendor of your kingdom.
Isa	4:2	the Lord will be beautiful and **g**,
	12:5	for he has done **g** things;
	42:21	to make his law great and **g**.
	60:7	and I will adorn my **g** temple.
Mt	19:28	the Son of Man sits on his **g** throne,
Lk	9:31	appeared in **g** splendor, talking
Ac	2:20	of the great and **g** day of the Lord.
2Co	3:8	of the Spirit be even more **g**?
Eph	1:17	**g** Father, may give you the Spirit
	1:18	the riches of his **g** inheritance
Php	3:21	so that they will be like his **g** body.
	4:19	to his **g** riches in Christ Jesus.
Col	1:11	all power according to his **g** might
1Ti	1:11	to the **g** gospel of the blessed God,
Tit	2:13	the **g** appearing of our great God
1Pe	1:8	with an inexpressible and **g** joy,

GLORY [1540, 2086, 2146, 3877, 3883, 7382, 8655, 9514, 10331, 1518, 1519, 1901]. The Hebrew word so translated, *kabôd*, means the "weight" and therefore the "worth" of something — as we speak of someone whose word "carries weight." The glory of God is the worthiness of God, more particularly, the presence of God in the fullness of his attributes in some place or everywhere. It is in this sense that Isaiah reports the words of the seraphim, "The whole earth is full of his glory" (Isa 6:3), meaning that the Lord in his full person, deity, and majesty is present in every place. Sometimes the Lord allowed his glory to become visible. Since the cloudy-fiery pillar was the place where he was present, there were occasions (e.g., 16:10) when (whatever form it took) there was a manifestation of his presence. Possibly the same was true in Ex 40:34–35: there was either an awesome manifestation of the Lord's presence or an overwhelming sense that God was there so that Moses dared not come near. Later thought defined this indwelling presence of God as the *shekinah* (or "indwelling").

New Testament references to the shekinah glory are seen in Jn 1:14 and Ro 9:4. Glory is both physical and spiritual, as is seen in Lk 2:9 ("The glory of the Lord shone around them") and Jn 17:22, where it refers to the glory of the Father that Jesus gave to his disciples. As for the saints, glory culminates in the changing of their bodies to the likeness of their glorified Lord (Php 3:20).

Spiritual:
 Is given by God (Ps 84:11). Is the work of the Holy Spirit (2Co 3:18).

Eternal:
 Secured by the death of Christ (Heb 2:10). Accompanies salvation by Christ (2Ti 2:10). Inherited by believers (1Sa 2:8; Ps 73:24; Pr 3:35; Col 3:4; 1Pe 5:10). Believers called to (2Th 2:14; 1Pe 5:10). Enhanced by afflictions (2Co 4:17). Present afflictions not worthy to be compared with (Ro 8:18). Of the church shall be rich and abundant (Isa 60:11 – 13). The bodies of believers shall be raised in (1Co 15:43; Php 3:21). Believers shall be glory of their ministers (1Th 2:19 – 20). Afflictions of ministers are glory to believers (Eph 3:13).

Temporal:
 Is given by God (Da 2:37). Passes away (1Pe 1:24). The devil tries to seduce by (Mt 4:8). Of hypocrites turned to shame (Hos 4:7). Seek not, from others (Mt 6:2; 1Th 2:6). Of the wicked is in their shame (Php 3:19). Ends in destruction (Isa 5:14).

Of God:
 Exhibited in Christ (Jn 1:14; 2Co 4:6; Heb 1:3). Ascribed to God (Gal 1:5). Exhibited in his name (Dt 28:58; Ne 9:5); his majesty (Job 37:22; Pss 93:1; 104:1; 145:5, 12; Isa 2:10); his power (Ex 15:1, 6; Ro 6:4); his works (Pss 19:1; 111:3); his holiness (Ex 15:11). Described as great (Ps 138:5); eternal (Ps 104:31); rich (Eph 3:16); highly exalted (Pss 8:1; 113:4). Exhibited to Moses (Ex 34:5 – 7, w 33:18 – 23); Ste-phen (Ac 7:55); his church (Dt 5:24; Ps 102:16). Enlightens the church (Isa 60:1 – 2; Rev 21:11, 23). Believers desire to behold (Pss 63:2; 90:16). God is jealous of (Isa 42:8). The earth is full of (Isa 6:3). The knowledge of, shall fill the earth (Hab 2:14).

Ex	14:4	But I will gain **g** for myself
	33:18	Moses said, "Now show me your **g**
	40:34	and the **g** of the LORD filled
Nu	14:21	the **g** of the LORD fills the whole
1Sa	4:21	"The **g** has departed from Israel" —
1Ch	16:10	**G** in his holy name;
	16:28	ascribe to the LORD **g**
Ps	19:1	The heavens declare the **g** of God;
	24:7	that the King of **g** may come in.
	72:19	the whole earth be filled with his **g**.
Pr	19:11	it is to his **g** to overlook an offense.
	25:2	It is the **g** of God to conceal
Isa	26:15	You have gained **g** for yourself;
	35:2	they will see the **g** of the LORD,
	42:8	I will not give my **g** to another
	43:7	whom I created for my **g**,
	66:18	and they will come and see my **g**.
Eze	1:28	the likeness of the **g** of the LORD.
	44:4	and saw the **g** of the LORD filling
Mt	16:27	in his Father's **g** with his angels,
	24:30	of the sky, with power and great **g**.
	25:31	the Son of Man comes in his **g**,
Mk	8:38	in his Father's **g** with the holy
Lk	2:9	and the **g** of the Lord shone
	2:14	saying, "**G** to God in the highest,
	9:32	they saw his **g** and the two men
	19:38	in heaven and **g** in the highest!"
Jn	1:14	We have seen his **g**, the **g** of the One
	2:11	He thus revealed his **g**,
	8:50	I am not seeking **g** for myself;
	15:8	is to my Father's **g**, that you bear
	16:14	He will bring **g** to me by taking
Ac	7:2	The God of **g** appeared
	7:55	up to heaven and saw the **g** of God,
Ro	1:23	exchanged the **g** of the immortal
	2:7	by persistence in doing good seek **g**
	3:23	and fall short of the **g** of God,

	4:20	in his faith and gave **g** to God,
	8:17	that we may also share in his **g**.
	11:36	To him be the **g** forever! Amen.
1Co	10:31	whatever you do, do it all for the **g**
	11:7	but the woman is the **g** of man.
	11:15	it is her **g**? For long hair is given
2Co	3:10	comparison with the surpassing **g**.
	3:18	likeness with ever-increasing **g**,
	4:17	us an eternal **g** that far outweighs
Gal	1:5	to whom be **g** for ever and ever.
Eph	3:13	for you, which are your **g**.
	3:21	to him be **g** in the church
Php	1:11	to the **g** and praise of God.
Col	1:27	Christ in you, the hope of **g**.
	3:4	also will appear with him in **g**.
1Th	2:20	Indeed, you are our **g** and joy.
Heb	1:3	The Son is the radiance of God's **g**
	2:7	you crowned him with **g** and honor
1Pe	1:7	**g** and honor when Jesus Christ is
	4:11	To him be the **g** and the power
	5:4	of **g** that will never fade away.
2Pe	1:3	of him who called us by his own **g**
	3:18	To him be **g** both now and forever!
Jude	25	to the only God our Savior be **g**,
Rev	1:6	to him be **g** and power for ever
	4:9	the living creatures give **g**,
	5:12	and honor and **g** and praise!"
	11:13	and gave **g** to the God of heaven.
	14:7	"Fear God and give him **g**,
	19:1	**g** and power belong to our God,
	21:11	It shone with the **g** of God,
	21:26	**g** and honor of the nations will be

GLUTTONY [1251+5883, 2361, 1143, 5741]. Impoverishes (Pr 23:21). Deadens moral sensibilities (Am 6:4 – 7; Lk 12:19 – 20, 45 – 46; Php 3:19). Loathsome (Pr 30:21 – 22). Warnings against (Pr 30:21 – 22; Lk 21:34; Ro 13:13 – 14; 1Pe 4:2 – 3). Punished by death (Dt 21:20 – 21); plagues (Nu 11:32 – 33). Associated with drunkenness (Dt 21:20 – 21; Pr 23:21; Ecc 10:17; Lk 12:45 – 46; Ro 13:13; 1Pe 4:3). Proverb relating to (Isa 22:13; 1Co 15:32).

> **Instances of:**
> Israelites (Ex 16:20 – 21; Nu 11:4, 32 – 35; Ps 78:18). Sons of Eli (1Sa 2:12 – 17). Belshazzar (Da 5:1). Jesus falsely accused of (Mt 11:19; Lk 7:34). See Pleasure, Worldly.

GNOSTICISM (Gr. *gnosis, knowledge*). Though sometimes used of false teaching within the period when the NT was written, the word more accurately describes systems of knowledge in opposition to orthodox Christianity in the second and third centuries. It appears that some church members, embarrassed by the lowly origins of Christianity (birth in a stable, traveling teacher, death on a cross, etc.), linked aspects of traditional Christianity with attractive ideas taken from Greek philosophy and Eastern religion, magic, and astrology. We call the resulting systems Gnosticism, and they seem very complicated to modern people. Their main themes were as follows: The true God is pure spirit and dwells in the realm of pure light, totally separated from this dark world. This world is evil, for it is made of matter, and matter is evil. The true God will have nothing to do with it, for it was created by a lesser god and was a mistake. People in this world are normally made of body and mind, but in a few there is a spark of pure spirit. Such "spiritual" people need to be rescued from this evil world; thus there is need for a Savior. Jesus, who is pure spirit even though he appears to be body and mind, is the Savior who comes from the true God in light to bring knowledge (*gnosis*) of the spiritual realm of light. Therefore those who have the spark of spirit can receive the knowledge and be reunited with the true God.

Within the NT there are references to claims to knowledge and wisdom (e.g., 1Co 1:17ff.; 8:1; 13:8) that could be the roots of the growth that led to developed Gnosticism. There was a heresy in the church of Colosse (Col 2:8 – 23) and false teaching in the churches Timothy knew (1Ti 1:4ff.; 4:3ff.; 2Ti 2:18; 3:5 – 7) that may be termed a false *gnosis* (1Ti 6:20). Then in the epistles of John there are references to false teaching about the reality of the humanity of Jesus (1Jn 4:3; 2Jn 7). But there is certainly nothing in the NT of the developed kind of false doctrines that the teachers of the church had to face a century or so later.

GOD [446, 466, 468, 1425, 2006, 3051, 5822, 9199, 9359, 10033, 117, 356, 620, 1467, 1565, 2516, 2531, 2534, 2536, 2537, 4666, 5806] (Heb. *'eblōhîm, ēl, 'elyôn, shaddāy, yahweh*, Gr. *theos*). The Bible does not contain a formal definition of the word "God," yet God's being and attributes are displayed on every page. The greatest definition of the word in the history of Christendom, that is, in the culture in which the Bible has been a prevailing influence, is the one found in the Westminster Shorter Catechism (Q.4): "God is a Spirit, infinite, eternal, and unchangeable, in his being, wisdom, power, holiness, justice, goodness, and truth." It is fair to say that this definition faithfully sets forth what the Bible constantly assumes and declares concerning God.

GOD IS A SPIRIT.

These words mean that God is a nonmaterial personal being, self-conscious and self-determining.

GOD IS INFINITE.

The infinity of God is not an independent attribute. If we were to say, "God is the infinite," without specification, the meaning would be pantheistic, equal to saying, "God is everything." In using the word "infinite," we must always be specific:

Infinite in his being. This doctrine is intended to teach that God is everywhere. The omnipresence of God is vividly brought out in such Scriptures as Ps 139. The omnipresence of God means that wherever we are, even if we are like the fugitive Jacob at Bethel (Ge 28:16), God *himself* is there.

It is easier to conceive of God's omnipresence by saying, "Everything everywhere is immediately in his presence."

Infinite in his wisdom. This phrase designates God's omniscience. The Bible throughout regards God's omniscience as all-inclusive, not dependent on a step-by-step process of reasoning. God's knowledge does not increase or diminish when the temporal events of his redemptive program take place. He eternally knows what he has known in the past and what he will know in the future.

Infinite in his power. These words point to his omnipotence, his ability to do with power all that power can do, his controlling all the power that is or can be.

Infinite in his holiness, justice, and goodness. These words signify God's moral attributes. Holiness is regarded in the Bible as his central ethical character. Basic ethical principles are revealed by the will of God and derived from and based on the character of God. "Be holy because I am holy" (Lev 11:44 – 45). Justice refers to his administration of rewards and punishments among the personal beings of the universe. Goodness in this context indicates his love, his common grace toward all, and his special grace in saving sinners.

Infinite in his truth. This is the attribute that designates the basis of all logic and rationality. The axioms of logic and mathematics, and all the laws of reason, are not laws apart from God to which God must be subject. They are attributes of his own character.

Eternal. This means without temporal beginning or ending, or in a figurative sense "eternal" may designate (as in the words "eternal life") a quality of being suitable for eternity.

That God existed eternally before the creation of the finite universe does not imply a personal subject with no object, for God is triune. *See Trinity.*

Unchangeable, in Bible language, points to the perfect self-consistency of God's character throughout all eternity. This is not a static concept, but dynamic, in all his relations with his creatures. That God brings to pass, in time, the events of his redemptive program is not contradictory. The notion that God's immutability is static immobility (as in Thomism) is like the notion of timelessness and is contrary to the biblical view. The God of the Bible is intimately and actively concerned in all the actions of all his creatures.

GOD IS KNOWN BY HIS ACTS.

Supremely, "God ... has spoken to us by his Son" (Heb 1:1ff.). Further, his "invisible" being, that is, his "eternal power and divine character" (*theiotēs* as distinguished from *theotēs*) are "known" and "clearly seen" by "what has been made" (Ro 1:20). "The heavens declare the glory of God" (Ps 19; Ro 10:18). It is customary to distinguish between "natural revelation," all that God has made, and "special revelation," the Bible.

GOD IS KNOWN IN FELLOWSHIP.

That God is known by faith, beyond the mere cognitive sense, in fellowship with his people, is one of the most prominent themes throughout the Bible. The Bible abounds in invitations to seek and find fellowship with God. See Ps 27; Isa 55; and many similar gracious invitations.

Other gods are referred to in the Bible as false gods (Jdg 6:31; 1Ki 18:27; 1Co 8:4 – 6) or as demonic (1Co 10:19 – 22).

Access to:

Israel (Dt 4:7). The pure of heart (Ps 24:3 – 4). The thirsty (Isa 55:3). Gentiles (Ac 14:27). Enemies of God (Col 1:21 – 22). Believers (Heb 4:16; 1Pe 1:17). The cleansed (Jas 4:8). Through hope (Pss 27:4; 43:2); fear (Ps 145:18 – 19; 1Pe 1:17); prayer (Mt 6:6; Heb 4:10); faith (Heb 11:6); love (1Jn 4:16); Christ (Jn 10:7, 9; 14:6; Ro 5:2; Eph 2:13, 18; 3:12; Col 1:21 – 22; Heb 7:19, 25; 10:19, 22; 1Pe 1:17). Satisfying (Ps 65:4).

Creator:

(Ps 148:3 – 5; Pr 16:4; Isa 45:7; 66:2; Jer 51:19; Am 4:13; Mk 13:19; Ac 7:50; Ro 1:20; 1Co 11:12; Heb 2:10; 3:4; Rev 4:11). Of the earth (Ge 1:1 – 2, 9 – 10; 2:1 – 4; Ex 20:11; 1Sa 2:8; 2Ki 19:15; Ne 9:6; Job 38:4, 7 – 10; Pss 24:1 – 2; 89:11; 90:2; 95:5; 102:25; 104:2 – 3, 5 – 6, 24, 30; 119:90; 121:2; 124:8; 136:5 – 9; 146:5 – 6; Pr 3:19; 8:26 – 29; Isa 37:16; 40:28; 42:5; 44:24; 45:12, 18; 48:13; 51:13, 16; Jer 10:12; 27:5; 32:17; 51:15; Jnh 1:9; Ac 4:24; 14:15; 17:24 – 25; Rev 10:6; 14:7). Of the heavens (Ge 1:1, 6 – 8; 2:1 – 4; Ex 20:11; 2Ki 19:15; 1Ch 16:26; Ne 9:6; Job 9:8 – 9; 37:16, 18; Pss 8:3; 19:1, 4; 96:5; 102:25; 104:2 – 3, 5 – 6, 24, 30; 121:2; 124:8; 136:5; 146:5 – 6; Pr 3:19; 8:26 – 28; Isa 37:16; 42:5; 44:24; 45:18; Jer 32:17; Am 5:8; Ac 4:24; 14:15; Rev 10:6; 14:7). Of the sun, moon, and stars (Ge 1:14 – 19; Ps 136:7 – 9). Of the seas (Ge 1:9 – 10; Ex 20:11; Ne 9:6; Pss 95:5; 146:5 – 6; Pr 8:26 – 29; Jnh 1:9; Ac 4:24; 14:15; Rev 10:6; 14:7). Of vegetation (Ge 1:11 – 12). Of animals (Ge 1:20 – 25; Job 12:7 – 9; Jer 27:5). Creator of humankind (Ge 1:26 – 28; 2:7; 5:1 – 2; 9:6; Ex 4:11; Dt 4:32; 32:6, 15, 18; Job 10:3, 8 – 9, 11 – 12; 31:15; 33:4; 34:19; Pss 94:9; 95:6; 100:3; 119:73; 149:2; Pr 20:12; 22:2; Ecc 7:29; 12:1; Isa 17:7; 42:5; 43:1, 7, 15; 44:2, 24; 45:12; 51:13; 64:8; Jer 27:5; Zec 12:1; Mal 2:10; Mk 10:6; Ac 17:24 – 29; 1Co 12:18, 24 – 25; Heb 12:9; 1Pe 4:19). Through Christ (Ro 11:36; 1Co 8:6; Eph 3:9; Heb 1:1 – 2). See Jesus the Christ, Creator. By his word (Ps 33:6 – 7, 9; 2Co 4:6; Heb 11:3; 2Pe 3:5). By his will (Rev 4:11).

Dwells with the Righteous:

(Ex 25:8; 29:45; Lev 26:11 – 12; 1Ki 6:13; Eze 37:26 – 27; 2Co 6:16; Rev 21:3).

Eternity of:

(Ge 21:33; Ex 3:15; 15:18; Dt 32:40; 33:27; 1Ch 16:36; 29:10; Ne 9:5; Job 36:26; Pss 9:7; 41:13; 90:1 – 2, 4; 92:8; 93:2; 102:12, 24 – 27; 145:13; 146:10; Isa 40:28; 44:6; 57:15; 63:16; Jer 10:10; La 5:19; Da 4:3, 34; Hab 1:12; Ro 1:20; 16:26; Eph 3:21; 1Ti 1:17; 6:15 – 16; 2Pe 3:8; Rev 4:8 – 10; 11:17).

Faithfulness of:

(Ge 9:16; 28:15; Lev 26:44 – 45; Dt 4:31; Jdg 2:1; 1Sa 12:22; Isa 42:16; 44:21; 49:7, 14 – 16; Jer 29:10; 31:36 – 37; 32:40; 33:14, 20 – 21, 25 – 26; Eze 16:60; Hos 2:19 – 20; Ro 3:3 – 4; Heb 6:10, 13 – 19). Confidence in (Nu 23:19; Dt 32:4; 2Sa 7:28; 1Ch 28:20; Ne 1:5; Pss 36:5; 40:10; 89:1 – 2, 5, 8, 14, 24, 28, 33, 34; 92:1 – 2, 15; 94:14; 105:8, 42; 111:5, 7 – 9; 119:90 – 91; 132:11; Isa 25:1; La 3:23; Da 9:4; Mic 7:20; 1Co 1:9; 10:13; 2Co 1:18 – 20; 1Th 5:24; 2Th 3:3; 2Ti 2:13, 19; Tit

1:2; Heb 10:23; 11:11; 1Pe 4:19; 2Pe 3:9; 1Jn 1:9). Exemplified (Ge 21:1; 24:27; Ex 2:24; 6:4–5; Dt 7:8–9; 9:5; Jos 21:45; 23:14; 1Ki 8:15, 20, 23–24, 56; 2Ki 8:19; 13:23; 2Ch 6:4–15; 21:7; Ne 1:5; 9:7–8; Ps 98:3; Hag 2:5; Lk 1:54–55, 68–70, 72–73; Ac 13:32–33; Heb 6:10, 13–19).

Fatherhood of:

Taught in the Old Testament (Ex 4:22; Dt 14:1; 32:5–6; 2Sa 7:14; 1Ch 28:6; 29:10; Pss 68:5; 89:26; Isa 1:2; 9:6; 63:16; 64:8; Jer 3:19; Hos 1:10; 11:1). Taught by Jesus (Mt 5:45; 6:4, 8–9; 7:11; 10:20, 29, 32–33; 11:25–27; 12:50; 13:43; 15:13; 16:17, 27; 18:10, 14, 19; 20:23; 26:29, 39; Mk 8:38; 11:25; 13:32; Lk 2:49; 10:21–22; 11:2; 11:13; 22:29; 23:46; 24:49; Jn 1:14, 18; 2:16; 4:21, 23; 5:17–23, 36–37, 43; 6:27, 32, 44–46; 8:19, 27, 38, 41–42, 49; 10:15, 29–30, 32–33, 36–38; 12:26–28, 50; 13:1, 3; 14:2, 6–13, 20–21, 23–24, 26, 31; 15:8–10, 16, 23–24, 26; 16:3, 10, 15, 23, 25–28; 17:1, 5, 11, 21, 24; 20:17, 21). Taught by the apostles (Ac 1:4; 2:33; Ro 1:3–4, 7; 8:14–16; 1Co 1:3; 8:6; 15:24; 2Co 1:3; 6:18; Gal 1:1, 3–4; 4:4–7; Eph 1:2–3, 17; 2:18; 3:14; 4:6; 5:20; 6:23; Php 1:2; Col 1:2–3, 12; 3:17; 1Th 1:1, 3; 3:11, 13; 2Th 1:1–2; 2:16; 1Ti 1:2; 2Ti 1:2; Tit 1:4; Heb 1:5–6; 12:9; Jas 1:17, 27; 3:9; 1Pe 1:2–3, 17; 1Jn 1:2; 2:1, 13, 15, 22–24; 3:1; 4:14; 2Jn 3–4, 9; Jude 1; Rev 1:5–6; 3:5; 14:1). See Adoption, Spiritual.

Foreknowledge of:

(Ac 15:18); contingencies (1Sa 23:10–12); future events (Isa 42:9; 44:7; 45:11; 46:9–10; 48:5–6; Jer 1:5; Da 2:28–29; Ac 2:23); human needs (Mt 6:8); day of judgment (Mt 24:36; Mk 13:32); the redeemed (Ro 8:29; 11:2; 1Pe 1:2).

Glory of:

(Pss 24:8–10; 57:5, 11; 72:18–19; Isa 40:5; Php 1:11). Described (Eze 1:26–28; Hab 3:3–6). Transcendent (Ps 113:4). Shall endure forever (Ps 104:31). Ascribed by angels (Lk 2:14). To be ascribed by people (Ps 29:2; Ro 11:36). Manifested: in burning bush (Ex 3:2); in Mount Sinai (Ex 19:18; 20:18–19; 24:10, 17; 33:18–23; 34:5, 29–35; Dt 4:11–12, 33, 36; 5:5, 24–25; Heb

12:18–21); in the tabernacle (Ex 40:34–35); in the heavens (2Sa 22:10–15; Pss 18:9–14; 19:1); in his sovereignty (Pss 97:2–6; 145:5, 11–12; Isa 6:1–5; 24:23; Jude 24–25); in the church (Isa 35:2; 60:1–2, 19–21; 61:3; Eph 3:21); in Christ (Jn 13:31–32; 14:13; 17:1); to Ezekiel (Eze 3:12, 23; 8:4); to Stephen (Ac 7:55).

Goodness of:

(Ex 33:19; Dt 30:9; Pss 25:8–10; 31:19; 33:5; 36:7; 86:5; 100:5; 106:1; 119:68; Na 1:7; Mt 5:45; Ac 14:17; Jas 1:17). Enduring (Ps 52:1). Leads to repentance (Ro 2:4). Gratefully acknowledged (1Ch 16:34; 2Ch 5:13; 7:3; Pss 68:19; 107:8–9, 43; 118:29; 135:3; 136:1; 145:7, 9; Isa 63:7). Manifested: in gracious providence (Mt 7:11); to the righteous (Ps 31:19; La 3:25; Ro 11:22); to the wicked (Lk 6:35).

Grace of:

Unmerited favor (Dt 7:7–8; 2Ch 30:9; Eph 1:6; Tit 2:11; Heb 4:16). Divine help (Ps 84:11; 1Co 10:13; 2Co 1:12; 12:9; 1Pe 1:5). No warrant for sinful indulgence (Ro 6:1, 15). Intercessory prayer for (Jn 17:11–12, 15; 1Th 1:1; 5:28; 2Pe 1:2). Exhortation against rejecting (2Co 6:1–2). Exemplified with respect to Jacob and Esau (Ro 9:10–16). Manifested: in drawing people to Christ (Jn 6:44–45); in redemption (Eph 1:5–9, 11–12); in justification (Ge 15:6; Ro 3:22–24; 4:4–5, 16; 5:2, 6–8, 15–21; Tit 3:7); in passing over transgression (Nu 23:20–21; Ne 9:17; Ro 3:25); in salvation (Ro 11:5–6; Eph 2:8–9; 2Ti 1:9); in calling to service (Gal 1:15–16); in spiritual growth (Eph 3:16); in spiritual gifts (1Co 1:4–8; Eph 4:7, 11); in character and conduct (1 Co 15:10; 2Co 1:12; Php 2:13); in sustaining the righteous (1Ch 17:8; 2Co 12:9; 1Pe 1:5; Jude 24); in sustaining in temptation (1Co 10:13; Rev 3:10). Manifestation of, to Enoch (Ge 5:24); to Noah (Ge 6:8, 17–18); to Abraham (Ge 12:2; 21:22); to Ishmael (Ge 21:20); to Isaac (Ge 26:24); to Jacob (Ge 46:3–4; 48:16); to Joseph (Ge 39:2–3, 23); to Moses (Ex 3:12; 33:12–17);

to Israel (Dt 4:7); to Naphtali (Dt 33:23); to Joshua (Jos 1:5, 9); to Job (Job 10:12); to David (1Sa 25:26, 34; 2Sa 7:8–16); to Jeremiah (Jer 15:20); to the righteous (Ps 5:12; Ac 4:33).

Guidance of:

(Ge 12:1; 24:27; Pss 23:2–3; 48:14; 73:24; Pr 3:6; Jer 3:4; 32:19; Lk 1:79; Jn 10:3–4). By pillars of cloud and fire (Ex 13:21; Ne 9:19). By his presence (Ex 15:13; 33:13–15; Dt 32:10, 12; Pss 78:52; 80:1; 107:7). By the ark of the covenant (Nu 10:33). By his counsel (2Sa 22:29; Pss 5:8; 25:9; Isa 48:17). By his Spirit (Jn 16:13). Prayed for (Pss 25:5; 27:11; 31:3; 61:2). Promised (Ps 32:8; Isa 40:11; 42:16; 58:11).

Holiness of:

(Jos 24:19; 1Sa 6:20; 1Ch 16:10; Job 6:10; 15:15; 25:5; Pss 11:7; 22:3; 36:6; 47:8; 60:6; 89:35; 98:1; 105:3; 111:9; 119:142; 145:17; Pr 9:10; Isa 5:16; 6:3; 29:19, 23; 41:14; 43:14–15; 45:19; 47:4; 49:7; 52:10; 57:15; Eze 36:21–22; 39:7, 25; Da 4:8; Hos 11:9; Hab 1:12–13; Lk 1:49; Jn 17:11; Ro 1:23; 1Jn 2:20; Rev 4:8; 6:10; 15:4). Incomparable (Ex 15:11; 1Sa 2:2; Job 4:17–19). Without iniquity (Dt 32:4; 2Ch 19:7; Job 34:10; 36:23; Ps 92:15; Jer 2:5; La 3:38; Mt 19:17; Mk 10:18; Lk 18:19; Jas 1:13). A reason for personal holiness (Lev 11:44; 19:2; 20:26; 21:8; 2Ch 19:7; Mt 5:48; 1Pe 1:15–16). A reason for thanksgiving (Pss 30:4; 99:3, 5, 9; Isa 12:6). A reason for reverent approach to God (Ex 3:5; Jos 5:15). Light, figurative of. See below, Light; Perfection of; Righteousness of. See Sin, Separates from God.

Immanence of:

(Ge 26:24; 28:15; Ex 3:12; Dt 4:7; Jos 3:7; Ac 17:27–28).

Immutable:

(Nu 23:19–20; 1Sa 15:29; Ps 102:27; Isa 40:28; Jas 1:17). In purpose (Job 23:13; Ps 33:11; Pr 19:21; Ecc 3:14; 7:13; Isa 31:2; Heb 6:17–18). In faithfulness (Ps 119:89–91). In mercy (Isa 59:1; Hos 13:14; Mal 3:6; Ro 11:29).

Impartial:

(Dt 10:17). Despises none (Job 36:5). Does not show favoritism (2Ch 19:7; Job 34:19; 37:24; Ac 10:34–35; Ro 2:6, 11; Eph 6:8–9; Col 3:25; 1Pe 1:17).

Incomparable:

(Ex 16:11; Dt 33:26; 2Sa 7:22; 1Ki 8:23; Pss 35:10; 71:19; 89:6–8; 113:5; Mic 7:18).

Incomprehensible:

(Job 15:8; 37:1–24; Isa 40:12–31; 55:8–9; Mt 11:27; 1Co 2:16).

Infinite:

(1Ki 8:27; 2Ch 2:6; 6:1, 18; Ps 147:5; Jer 23:24).

Invisible:

(Ex 20:21; 33:20; Dt 4:11–12; 4:15; 5:22; 1Ki 8:12; 2Ch 6:1; Job 9:11; 23:8–9; Pss 18:11; 97:2; Jn 1:18; 5:37; 6:46; Ro 1:20; Col 1:13–15; 1Ti 1:17; 6:16; Heb 11:27; 1Jn 4:12).

Jealous:

(Ex 20:5, 7; 34:14; Dt 4:24; 5:9, 11; 6:15; 29:20; 32:16, 21; Jos 24:19; 2Ch 16:7–9; Isa 30:1–2; Eze 23:25; 36:5; 39:25; Joel 2:18; Na 1:2; Zec 1:14; 1Co 10:22).

Judge:

(Ge 16:5; Jdg 11:27; 1Sa 2:3, 10; 24:12, 15; 1Ch 16:33; Job 21:22; Pss 11:4–5; 26:1–2; 35:24; 43:1; 50:4, 6; 58:11; 75:7; 76:8–9; 82:8; 94:1–2; 135:14; Pr 16:2; 29:26; Ecc 3:17; 11:9; 12:14; Isa 3:13–14; 28:17, 21; 30:18, 27; 33:22; Jer 32:19; Da 7:9–10; Na 1:3; Mal 3:5; Ac 17:31; 1Co 5:13; Heb 10:30–31; 12:22–23; Rev 6:16–17; 11:18; 16:5; 18:8). Just Judge (Ge 18:21, 25; Nu 16:22; Dt 32:4; Ne 9:33; Job 4:17; 8:3; 34:10–12; Pss 7:9, 11; 9:4, 7–8; 67:4; 96:10, 13; 98:9; Isa 26:7; 45:21; Jer 32:19; Ro 2:2, 5–16; 3:4–6, 26; 11:22, 23; Eph 6:8–9; 1Pe 1:17; Rev 19:2). Incorruptible Judge (Dt 10:17; 2Ch 19:7; Job 8:3; 34:19).

Justice of:

(Dt 32:4; 2Sa 22:25; 1Ki 8:32; Job 31:13–15; Pss 51:4; 62:12; 89:14; 97:2; 145:17; Pr 21:2–3; 24:12;

Isa 61:8; Jer 9:24; 11:20; 20:12; 32:19; 50:7; Eze 14:23; 18:25, 29 – 30; 33:7 – 19; Da 9:7, 14; Na 1:3, 6; Zep 3:5; Ac 17:31; Ro 2:2, 5 – 16; Heb 6:10; 1Pe 1:17; 2Pe 2:9; 1Jn 1:9; Jude 6; Rev 11:18; 15:3).

Knowledge of:

(Ge 6:5; 1Sa 2:3; Job 12:13, 22; 21:22; 22:13 – 14; 26:6; 28:23 – 24; 36:4 – 5; 37:16; Ps 147:4 – 5; Pr 3:19 – 20; Isa 40:13 – 14, 26 – 28; 46:9 – 10; Mt 24:36; Mk 13:32; Ro 11:33 – 34; 1Co 1:25; 1Jn 1:5). Knows the human state and condition (Ge 16:13; Ex 3:7; Dt 2:7; 2Ki 19:27; 2Ch 16:9; Job 23:10; 31:4; 34:21, 25; Pss 1:6; 11:4; 33:13 – 15; 37:18; 38:9; 66:7; 69:19; 103:14; 119:168; 139:1 – 4, 6, 12, 14 – 16; 142:3; Pr 5:21; 15:3, 11; Isa 29:15 – 16; 37:28; 66:18; Jer 23:24; 32:19; Am 9:2 – 4; Mt 10:29 – 30; 1Co 8:3). Knows the human heart (Ge 20:6; Dt 31:21; 1Sa 16:7; 2Sa 7:20; 1Ki 8:39; 1Ch 28:9; 29:17; 2Ch 6:30; Job 11:11; Pss 7:9; 44:21; 94:9 – 11; Pr 15:11; 16:2; 17:3; 21:2; 24:12; Jer 11:20; 16:17; 17:10; 20:12; Eze 11:5; Am 4:13; Mt 6:4, 8, 18, 32; Lk 16:15; Ac 1:24; 15:8; 1Co 3:20; 1Th 2:4; Heb 4:13; 1Jn 3:20). See above, Foreknowledge of; below, Wisdom of.

Light:

(Da 2:22; Jas 1:17; 1Jn 1:5).

Longsuffering:

(Ge 6:3; 15:16; Ex 34:6; Nu 14:18; Pss 86:15; 103:8 – 10; Isa 5:1 – 4; 30:18; 48:9, 11; 57:16; Jer 7:13, 23 – 25; 9:24; Eze 20:17; Joel 2:13; Hab 1:2 – 4; Mt 21:33 – 41; Mk 12:1 – 9; Lk 20:9 – 16; Ac 14:16; Ro 3:25; 15:5; 1Pe 3:20). Abused by people (Ne 9:28 – 31; Pr 1:24 – 27; 29:1; Ecc 8:11; Isa 5:1 – 4; Jer 7:13, 23 – 25; Mt 24:48 – 51). See below, Mercy of. Manifested: in deferring judgments (Mic 7:18; Lk 13:6 – 9; Ac 17:30; Ro 9:22 – 23; 2Pe 3:9, 15); in giving time for repentance (Jer 11:7; Mt 23:37; Lk 13:34; Ro 2:4).

Love of:

(Dt 4:37; 7:7 – 8, 13; 10:15, 18; 23:5; 33:3, 12; 2Sa 12:24; Job 7:17; Pss 42:8; 47:4; 69:16; Hos 11:1; Mal 1:2; 2Co 13:11, 14; 1Jn 3:1; 4:12, 16, 19; Jude 21). Everlasting (2Ch 20:21; Jer 31:3). Better than

life (Ps 63:3). For the wicked (Mt 18:12 – 14; Lk 15:4 – 7, 11 – 27; Ro 5:8; Eph 2:4 – 5). For the righteous (Pss 103:13; 146:8; Pr 15:9; Jn 14:21, 23; 16:27; 17:10, 23, 26; Ro 1:7; 9:13; 11:28; 2Th 2:16). For the cheerful giver (2Co 9:7). Exemplified (Ex 19:4 – 6; Lev 20:24, 26; Dt 32:9 – 12; 2Sa 7:23 – 24; Ps 48:9, 14; Isa 43:1 – 4; 49:13 – 16; 54:5 – 6, 10; 62:4 – 5; 63:7 – 9; 66:13; Jer 3:14 – 15; Eze 16:8; Hos 2:19 – 20, 23; Zec 2:8); in forgiveness of sins (Isa 38:17; Tit 3:4 – 5); in the gift of his Son (Jn 3:16; 1Jn 4:8 – 10); in chastisements (Heb 12:6).

Mercy of:

(Ex 20:2, 6; Dt 5:10; Ex 33:19; Dt 4:31; 7:9; 1Ki 8:23; 2Ch 30:9; Ezr 9:9; Pss 18:50; 25:6, 8; 31:7; 32:10; 36:5; 57:10; 62:12; 69:16; 98:3; 108:4; 111:4; 116:5; 117:2; 119:64, 156; 138:2; 146:7 – 8; Isa 60:10; Jer 9:24; 31:20; 32:18; Da 9:4; Hos 2:23; Zec 10:6; Lk 6:36; Ac 17:30; Ro 9:15; 11:32; 15:9; 2Co 1:3; Heb 4:16; 1Pe 1:3; 2Pe 3:9). Everlasting (1Ch 16:34, 41; 2Ch 5:13; 7:3, 6, 14; Ezr 3:11; Pss 89:1 – 2, 28; 100:5; 103:17; 106:1; 107:1; 118:1 – 4, 29; 136:1 – 26). Manifested: in withholding punishment (Ge 8:21; 18:26, 30 – 32; Ex 32:14; Nu 16:48; 2Sa 24:14, 16; 2Ki 13:23; Ezr 9:13; Job 11:6; Isa 12:1; 54:9; Eze 16:6, 42, 63; 20:17; Hos 11:8 – 9; Joel 2:13, 18; Jnh 4:2, 10 – 11; Mal 3:6); in rescuing from destruction (Ge 19:16; Nu 21:8; Jdg 2:18; 2Ki 14:26 – 27; Ne 1:10; 9:17 – 20, 27 – 31); in leading his people (Ex 15:13); in comforting the afflicted (2Co 12:9); in hearing prayer (Ex 22:27; Heb 4:16); in desire to save sinners (Dt 5:29; 32:29; Jdg 10:16; 2Ch 36:15; Isa 65:2, 8; Jer 2:9; 7:25; Eze 18:23, 31 – 32; 33:11; Mt 18:12 – 14; Lk 15:4 – 7; 1Ti 2:4, 6); in forbearance toward sinners (2Ch 24:18 – 19; Ps 145:8 – 9; La 3:22 – 23, 31 – 33; Da 4:22 – 27; Na 1:3); in granting forgiveness (Ex 34:6 – 7; Nu 14:18 – 20; 2Sa 12:13; 2Ch 7:14; Job 33:14 – 30; Pss 32:1 – 2, 5; 65:3; 78:38 – 39; 85:2 – 3; 86:5, 13, 15; 99:8; 103:3, 8 – 14; 130:3 – 4; 130:7 – 8; Pr 16:6; 28:13; Isa 55:7 – 9; Jer 3:12, 22; 31:20, 34; 33:8, 11; 36:3; 50:20; Eze 36:25; Da 9:9; Hos 14:4; Mic 7:18 – 19; Mt 6:14; 18:23 – 27; Lk 1:50, 77 – 78; Ac

3:19; 26:18; Ro 10:12–13; 2Co 5:19; Eph 1:6–8; 2:4–7; 1Ti 1:13; Tit 3:5; Heb 8:12; 1Jn 1:9). Symbolized: in the atonement cover (Ex 25:17–22; 37:6–9; Lev 16:1–14; Nu 7:89; Heb 9:5).

Name of:

To be revered (Ex 20:7; Dt 5:11; 28:58; Ps 111:9; Mic 4:5; 1Ti 6:1). To be praised (Pss 34:3; 72:17). Not to be profaned (Ex 20:7; Lev 18:21; 19:12; 20:3; 21:6; 22:2, 32; Dt 5:11; Ps 139:20; Isa 52:5; Ro 2:24; Rev 16:9). Profaned (Ps 139:20).

Names of:

In the ancient world a name was not merely a label but the meaning of the name was virtually equivalent to whoever or whatever bore it (1Sa 25:25). Giving a name to anyone or anything was tantamount to owning or controlling it (Ge 1:5, 8, 10; 2:19–20; 2Sa 12:28). Changing a name could signify a promotion to a higher status (Ge 17:5; 32:28) or a demotion (2Ki 23:34–35; 24:17), and blotting out or cutting off the name of a person or thing meant that that person or thing was destroyed (2Ki 14:27; Isa 14:22; Zep 1:4; cf. Ps 83:4). The name and being of God are often used in parallelism with each other (Pss 18:49; 68:4; 74:18; 86:12; 92:1; Isa 25:1; Mal 3:16), which stresses their essential identity. Believing in Jesus' name (Jn 3:18) is therefore the same as believing in Jesus himself. Prayer in his name would be prayer in concert with his character, mind, and purpose. The name Jesus is the Greek form for the Hebrew Joshua or "salvation of Yahweh." As Yahweh's Savior his name accurately describes his work and purpose (Mt 1:21).

El and Its Compounds: El [H446] is the generic Semitic name for "God" or "deity." El is one of the oldest designations for deity in the ancient world.

Yahweh, Yâh, and Compounds: Yahweh [H3378] is the personal covenant name of Israel's God, the most common name for God in the OT (6829 times). Yâh [H3363] is its shortened form. The NIV consistently renders Yahweh as Lord.

The name sounds like and may be derived from the Hebrew for the word "I AM" (Ex 3:14–15). The basic meaning of his name is "He who is" or "He who is truly present." or "I will be to you all that I am." For Israel, Yahweh is not merely one god among many; he is the Creator and Ruler of heaven and earth, who is worthy of and demands the exclusive homage of his people. It is important to understand that this is God's intensely personal name. The respect with which it was treated bears witness to the national feeling of Israel and also their fear of the God who is among them. This was recognized by the scribes who even avoided pronunciation of the name. They would use circumlocutions and alternate names where possible.

'Âdôn, 'Âdônāy, and Kurios 'Âdôn [H123] or 'Âdônāy [H151] is a title for God that emphasizes his sovereignty, that is "Lord." 'Âdôn is basically a title of honor. Out of respect one might address a superior with this title in the same way that we would say "sir" or "Your Honor." It would be used by a subject addressing a king (1Sa 24:8), a wife to her husband (Ge 18:12), a daughter or son to their father (Ge 31:35), a slave to his master (Ge 24:12; Ex 21:5), a subordinate to his leader (Nu 11:28). It therefore refers to one's position of authority and prestige (Ge 23:6; 45:8). The special spelling 'Âdônāy belongs preeminently to Yahweh, because he alone is the "Lord of the earth" (Jos 3:11, 13; Ps 97:5; Mic 4:13; Zec 4:14; 6:5.

Shaddai [H8724] is used forty-eight times as a name of God, thirty-two times in Job (Job 5:17; 6:4, 14; etc.), seven times in the compound name El Shaddai. See above, El. It probably means "[God] the Mountain," similar to "God the Rock" (Dt 32:4). Older etymology defined it as "[God] the Provider," understanding Shaddai to be derived from the word for "breast." The NIV consistently translates Shaddai as "Almighty" (Ge 17:1; Ps 91:1).

Elyon and Hupsistos Elyon [H6610] means "the Most High" or "the exalted One" (Ge 14:17–20;

Ps 18:13; Isa 14:13 – 14). The NT Greek uses the form hupsistos [G5736], meaning "highest," or "most exalted."

Omnipotent:

(Ge 17:1; 18:14; Job 42:2; Ac 26:8; Rev 19:6; 21:22). See below, Power of.

Omnipresent:

(Ge 28:16; 1Ki 8:27; 2Ch 2:6; Pss 139:3, 5, 7 – 10; Jer 23:23 – 24; Ac 7:48 – 49; 17:24, 27 – 28). See below, Presence of.

Omniscient:

See above, Knowledge of; below, Wisdom of.

Perfection of:

(Dt 32:4; 2Sa 22:31; Ps 18:30; Mt 5:48; Ro 12:2; Jas 1:17; 1Jn 1:5; Rev 15:3). See above, Holiness of; below, Righteousness of.

Personality of:

See below, Unity of.

Power of:

(Ex 9:16; 15:6 – 7, 11 – 12; Nu 11:23; Dt 7:21; 11:2; Job 37:1 – 23; Pss 21:13; 29:3 – 9; 62:11; 68:34 – 35; 74:13, 15; 77:14, 16, 18; 78:12 – 51; 79:11; 89:8, 13; 93:1, 4; 105:26 – 41; 106:8; 111:6; 135:6, 8 – 12; 147:5, 16 – 18; Isa 26:4; 40:12, 22, 24, 26, 28; 51:10, 15; 63:12; Jer 5:22; 27:5; 32:17, 27; Da 2:20; Mt 19:26; Mk 10:27; 14:36; Lk 1:49, 51; 18:27; 22:29; 1Co 6:14; Rev 19:1). Supreme (Dt 32:39; Jos 4:24; 1Sa 2:6 – 7; 14:6; 1Ch 29:11 – 12; 2Ch 14:11; 25:8 – 9; Job 5:9; 23:13 – 14; 26:7 – 14; 36:5, 22, 27 – 33; 38:8, 11; 40:9; 42:2; Ps 104:7, 9, 29 – 30, 32; Da 4:35). Irresistible (Dt 32:39; Job 10:7; 1Sa 2:10; 2Ch 20:6; Job 9:4 – 7, 10, 12 – 13, 19; 11:10; 12:14 – 16; 14:20; 41:10 – 11; Pss 66:3, 7; 76:7; Isa 14:24, 27; 31:3; 43:13, 16 – 17; 46:10 – 11; 50:2 – 3; Na 1:3 – 6). Incomparable (Dt 3:24; Job 40:9; Ps 89:8). Omnipotent (Ge 18:14; Jer 32:27; Mt 19:26). Everlasting (Ro 1:20). Creation by (Jer 10:12). The resurrection of Christ by (1Co 6:14; 2Co 13:4). The resurrection of believers by (1Co 6:14). Manifested: in behalf of believers (Dt 33:26 – 27; 2Ch 16:9; Ezr 8:22; Ne 1:10; Jer 20:11;

Da 3:17); in his works (Dt 3:24; Pss 33:9; 107:25, 29; 114:7 – 8; Pr 30:4; Isa 48:13; Jer 10:12 – 13; 51:15; Ro 1:20). See above, Omnipotent.

Presence of:

(Ge 16:13; 28:16; Ex 20:24; 29:42 – 43; 30:6; 33:14; Dt 4:34 – 36, 39; 1Ki 8:27; Ps 139:3, 5, 7 – 10; Isa 57:15; 66:1; Jer 23:23 – 24; 32:18 – 19; Jnh 1:3 – 4; Ac 17:24, 27 – 28; 1Co 12:6). Manifested above the atonement cover. See Shekinah.

Preserver:

(Ne 9:6; Job 33:18; Pss 3:3; 12:7; 17:7; 68:6; 73:23; Isa 27:3; 49:8; Jer 2:6; Da 5:23; Mt 10:29 – 31; Lk 12:6 – 7; 21:18; Jn 17:11, 15; 1Pe 3:12 – 13; 2Pe 2:9). Of the righteous (Ge 15:1; 28:15; 49:24 – 25; Ex 8:22 – 23; 9:26; 11:7; 12:13, 17, 23; 15:2, 13, 16 – 17; 19:4; 23:20 – 31; Dt 1:30 – 31; 32:10; 33:12, 25 – 28; Jos 23:10; 1Sa 2:9; 2Sa 22:1 – 51; 2Ch 16:9; Job 1:10; 5:11, 18 – 24; 10:12; Pss 9:9; 18:14; 23:1 – 6; 31:20, 23; 32:6, 8; 34:7, 15, 17, 19 – 22; 37:17, 23 – 24, 28, 32 – 33; 41:1 – 3; 46:1, 7; 50:15; 84:11; 91:1, 3 – 4, 7, 9 – 10, 14 – 15; 102:19 – 20; 103:2 – 5; 107:9 – 10, 13; 116:6; 118:13; 121:3 – 4, 7 – 8; 125:1 – 3; 145:14, 19 – 20; 146:7 – 8; Pr 2:7 – 8; 10:3, 30; Isa 25:4; 30:21, 26; 33:16; 40:11, 29, 31; 42:16; 43:2; 46:3 – 4; 52:12; 58:11; 63:9; Jer 31:9 – 10, 28; Eze 11:16; 34:11 – 16, 22, 31; Da 3:27 – 28; Joel 2:18; Zec 2:5, 8; Mt 4:6; 1Co 10:13; 2Ti 4:17 – 18; 2Th 3:3; Jas 4:15).

Providence of:

(Ge 24:7, 40 – 50, 56; 26:24; Lev 26:4 – 6, 10; Dt 8:18; 11:12 – 15; 15:4 – 6; 32:11 – 14; 1Sa 2:6 – 9; 1Ki 11:14 – 40; 1Ch 29:14, 16; Pss 23:1 – 6; 34:7, 9 – 10; 71:6 – 7, 15; 107:1 – 43; 127:1 – 5; 136:5 – 25; 144:12 – 15; 147:8 – 9, 13 – 14; Pr 16:33; Ecc 2:24; 3:13; 5:19; Isa 46:4; 51:2; 55:10; Eze 36:28 – 38; Joel 2:18 – 26; Mt 5:45; Ro 8:28; Jas 4:15). In providing for temporal necessities (Ge 1:29 – 30; 2:16; 8:22; 9:1 – 3; 28:20 – 21; 48:15 – 16; 49:24 – 25; Ex 16:15; Lev 25:20 – 22; Dt 2:7; 7:13 – 15; 8:4; 10:18; 28:2 – 13; 29:5; Ru 1:6; Ne 9:24 – 25; Job 5:8 – 11; 22:18, 25; Pss 36:6 – 7; 37:3, 19, 22, 25, 34; 65:9 – 13; 67:6; 85:12; 104:10 – 15; 111:5; 136:25;

145:15 – 16; Isa 43:20; 48:21; Jer 5:24; 27:6; Hos 2:8; Jnh 4:6; Zec 10:1; Mt 6:26, 30 – 33; 10:29 – 31; Lk 12:6 – 7, 24 – 28; 22:35; Jn 6:31; Ac 14:17; 2Co 9:10). *In sending prosperity* (Pss 75:7; 127:1 – 2; Isa 48:14 – 15; 54:16 – 17; Eze 29:19 – 20). *In sending adversity* (1Sa 2:6 – 9; 2Sa 17:14; Ps 75:7; Ecc 3:10). *In saving from adversity* (Ge 7:1; Ex 9:26; 15:26; 23:25 – 26; Pss 103:3 – 5; 116:1 – 15; 118:5 – 6, 13 – 14; 146:7 – 9; Da 6:20 – 22). *In delivering from enemies* (Ge 14:20; Ex 3:17; 6:7; 14:29 – 30; 23:22; 34:24; Dt 20:4; 23:14; 30:4, 20; 31:3, 8; 2Ki 20:6; 2Ch 20:3 – 30; 32:8; Ezr 8:22 – 23; Pss 18:17, 27; 44:1 – 3; 61:3; 78:52 – 55; 97:10; 105:14 – 45; Pr 16:7; Ac 7:34 – 36; 12:1 – 12). *In thwarting evil purpose* (Ge 37:5 – 20, w 45:5 – 7 & Ps 105:17 & Ac 7:9 – 10; Ex 14:4; Nu 23:7 – 8, 23, w 22:12 – 18; 24:10 – 13; Ezr 5:5; Ne 6:16; Est 7:10, w 6:1 – 12 & 9:25; Job 5:12 – 13, w Isa 8:9 – 10; Ps 33:10; Ac 5:38 – 39). *In turning the curse into blessing* (Dt 23:4, 6; Php 1:12, 19). *In exalting the lowly* (2Sa 7:8 – 9; 1Ch 17:7 – 8; Pss 68:6; 113:7 – 8). *In leading people to repentance* (Am 4:7 – 12). *In punishing evildoers* (Dt 2:30; Jos 10:10 – 11, 19; Jdg 9:23 – 24; 1Ch 5:26; Isa 41:2, 4). *In punishing rulers* (Da 5:18, 22). *In punishing nations* (Dt 9:4 – 5; Job 12:23; Eze 29:19 – 20). *In ordaining instruments of discipline* (Isa 13:3 – 5). *In using the Gentiles to execute his purpose* (Ezr 6:22; Isa 44:28; 45:1 – 6, 13). *In fulfilling prophecy* (1Ki 12:15; 2Ch 10:15; 36:22 – 23; Ezr 1:1; Ac 3:17 – 18). *In nature* (Job 12:7 – 20; 37:6 – 24; 38:25 – 27, 41; 39:5 – 6; Pss 104:16 – 19, 24 – 30; 135:7; Jer 10:13; 14:22; 31:35; 51:16). *Instances of: Saving Noah* (Ge 7:1; 2Pe 2:5). *The call of Abraham* (Ge 12:1). *Protecting Abraham, Sarah, and Abimelech* (Ge 20:3 – 6). *Deliverance of Lot* (Ge 19). *Care of Isaac* (Ge 26:2 – 3); *of Jacob* (Ge 31:7). *The mission of Joseph* (Ge 37:5 – 10; 39:2 – 3, 21, 23; 45:7 – 8; 50:20; Ps 105:17 – 22). *Warning Pharaoh of famine* (Ge 41). *Delivering the Israelites* (Ex 3:8; 11:3; 13:18; Ac 7:34 – 36). *The pillar of cloud* (Ex 13:21; 14:19 – 20). *Dividing the Red Sea* (Ex 14:21). *Delaying and destroying Pharaoh* (Ex 14:25 – 30). *Purifying the waters of*

Marah (Ex 15:25). *Supplying manna and quail* (Ex 16:13 – 15; Nu 11:31 – 32). *Supplying water at Meribah* (Nu 20:7 – 11; Ne 9:10 – 25). *Protection of homes while at feasts* (Ex 34:24). *In the conquest of Canaan* (Ps 44:2 – 3). *Saving David's army* (2Sa 5:23 – 25). *The revolt of the ten tribes* (1Ki 12:15, 24; 2Ch 10:15). *Fighting the battles of Israel* (2Ch 13:12, 18; 14:9 – 14; 16:7 – 9; 20:15, 17, 22; 23; 32:21 – 22). *Restoring Manasseh after his conversion* (2Ch 33:12 – 13). *Feeding Elijah and the widow* (1Ki 17; 19:1 – 8). *Prospering Hezekiah* (2Ki 18:6 – 7; 2Ch 32:29); *Asa* (2Ch 14:6 – 7); *Jehoshaphat* (2Ch 17:3, 5; 20:30); *Uzziah* (2Ch 26:5 – 15); *Jotham* (2Ch 27:6); *Job* (Job 1:10; 42:10, 12); *Daniel* (Da 1:9). *Turning the heart of the king of Assyria to favor the Jews* (Ezr 6:22). *Rescuing Jeremiah* (La 3:52 – 58; Jer 38:6 – 13). *Restoring the Jews* (2Ch 36:22 – 23; Ezr 1:1). *Rescuing the Jews from Haman's plot* (Esther). *Rebuilding walls of Jerusalem* (Ne 6:16). *Warning Joseph in dreams* (Mt 1:20; 2:13, 19 – 20). *Warning wise men of the east* (Mt 2:12 – 13). *Deliverance of Paul* (2Co 1:10). *Restoring Epaphroditus* (Php 2:27). *Banishment of John to Patmos* (Rev 1:9).

Mysterious and Misinterpreted: *Silence of God* (Job 33:13). *Adversity of the righteous* (Ecc 7:15; 8:14). *Prosperity of the wicked* (Job 12:6; 21:7; 24:1; Ps 73:2 – 5, 12 – 17; Ecc 7:15; 8:14; Jer 12:1 – 2; Mal 3:14 – 15). *Likeness in the lot of the righteous and wicked* (Ecc 9:2, 11). *Permitting violence of the wicked toward the righteous* (Job 24:1 – 12; Hab 1:2 – 3, 11, 13 – 14).

Rejected:

By Israel (1Sa 8:7 – 8; Isa 65:12; 66:4); by Saul (1Sa 15:26).

Repentance Attributed to:

(Ge 6:6 – 7; Ex 32:14; Jdg 2:18; 1Sa 15:35; 2Sa 24:16; 1Ch 21:15; Ps 106:45; Jer 26:19; Am 7:3; Jnh 3:10). *See Anthropomorphisms; Relent.*

Righteousness of:

(Ge 18:25; Jdg 5:11; Pss 7:9; 72:1; 88:12; 89:16; 119:40; 143:1; Isa 41:10; 56:1; Jer 4:2; 9:24; Mic

7:9; Ac 17:31). *Ascribed by: people (Ex 9:27; Ezr 9:15; Job 36:3; Pss 5:8; 48:10; 71:15, 19; 89:14; 97:2; 116:5; 145:7, 17; Jer 12:1; Da 9:7, 14; 2Ti 4:8); Jesus (Jn 17:25); the angel (Rev 16:5). Revealed in the heavens (Ps 50:6). Revealed in the gospel (Ro 1:17; 3:4–6, 21–22; 10:3–4; 2Pe 1:1). Endures forever (Ps 119:142, 144; Isa 51:8). See above, Holiness of; Perfection of.*

Savior:

(Ex 6:6–7; Pss 3:8; 18:30; 28:8; 31:5; 33:18–19; 34:22; 37:39–40; 74:12; 76:8–9; 85:9; 96:2; 98:2–3; 111:9; 118:14; 121:7; 149:4; Isa 26:1; 33:22; 35:4; 43:3, 11–12, 14; 45:15, 17, 21–22; 46:12–13; 49:25; 50:2; 59:1; 60:16; 63:8, 16; Jer 3:23; 14:8; 33:6; Eze 37:23; Hos 1:7; 13:4; Joel 3:16; Jnh 2:9; Lk 1:68; Jn 3:16–17; Ro 8:30–32; 1Ti 2:3–4; 4:10; Tit 1:2–3; 2:10–11; 3:4–5; 1Jn 4:9–10). Called Redeemer (Ps 19:14; Isa 41:14; 47:4; 48:17; Jer 50:34). Salvation (Pss 27:1; 62:1–2; 62:6–7; Isa 12:2). God of salvation (Pss 25:5; 65:5; 68:19–20; 88:1). Rock of salvation (Dt 32:15, 31). Shield (Dt 33:29). Salvation from national adversity (Ex 15:2; Isa 25:4, 9; 52:3, 9–10); from sin (Job 33:24, 27–30; 44:22–24; Ro 1:16); through Christ (2Ti 1:9).

Self-Existent:

Has life in himself (Jn 5:26). Is the "I am who I am" (Ex 3:14). Is the first and the last (Isa 44:6). Is the living God (Jer 10:10). Lives forever (Dt 32:40). Needs nothing (Ac 17:24–25).

Sovereign:

(Ex 20:3; Job 25:2; 33:13; 41:11; Pss 44:4; 47:8; 59:13; 74:12; 82:1, 8; 83:18; 93:1–2; 95:3–5; 96:10; 97:1, 5, 9; 98:6; 103:19; 105:7; 113:4; 115:3, 16; 136:2–3; Isa 24:23; 33:22; 40:22–23; 43:15; 44:6; 52:7; 66:1; La 3:37; Mic 4:7, 13; Mal 1:14; Jn 10:29; 19:11; Ac 7:49; Ro 9:19; 11:36; Eph 4:6; 1Ti 6:15–16; Heb 1:3; Jas 4:12; Rev 4:11; 19:6). Over heaven (2Ch 20:6). Over earth (Ex 9:29; Jos 3:11; Pss 24:1, 10; 47:2, 7–8; 50:10–12; Isa 54:5; Jer 10:10; 1Co 10:26). Over heaven and earth (Ge 14:18–20, 22; 24:3; Ex 19:5; Dt 4:39;

10:14, 17; Jos 2:11; 2Ki 19:15; 1Ch 29:11–12; Ne 9:6; Pss 89:11; 135:5–6; Mt 6:10; 11:25; Lk 10:21; Ac 17:24–26; Rev 11:4, 13, 17). *Over the spirits of all humankind (Nu 27:16; Dt 32:39; Job 12:9–10, 16–17; Ps 22:28–29; Ecc 9:1; Isa 45:23; Jer 18:1–23; Eze 18:4; Ro 14:11). In human affairs (Ps 75:6–7; Jer 27:5–7; 32:27–28; Eze 16:50; 17:24; Da 2:20–21, 47; 4:3, 17, 25, 34–35, 37; 5:18, 26–28). Everlasting (Ex 15:18; Pss 10:16; 29:10; 66:7; 145:11–13; 146:10; La 5:19; Da 6:26).*

Spirit:

(Jn 4:24; Ac 17:29). See Holy Spirit.

Teacher:

(Job 36:22; Pss 94:10, 12; 119:135, 171; Isa 28:26; 54:13; Jn 6:45; 1Th 4:9).

Truth:

(Ge 24:27; Ex 34:6; Nu 23:19; 1Sa 15:29; Pss 25:10; 31:5; 33:4; 43:3; 57:3, 10; 71:22; 86:11, 15; 89:14; 108:4; 132:11; 138:2; Isa 25:1; 65:16; Da 4:37; Jn 8:26; Ro 3:4, 7; Tit 1:2; Rev 6:10; 15:3). Endures to all generations (Pss 117:2; 146:6).

Unity of:

(Dt 4:35; 6:4; 2Sa 7:22; Isa 42:8). Taught by Jesus (Mk 12:29, 32; Jn 17:3); Paul (1Co 8:4, 6; Gal 3:20; Eph 4:6; 1Ti 2:5). Disbelieved in by Syrians (1Ki 20:28). Believed in by demons (Jas 2:19).

Unsearchable:

(Dt 29:29; Job 5:8–9; 9:10; 11:7–9; 26:9, 14; 36:26; 37:5, 23; Pss 77:19; 139:6; 145:3; Pr 30:4; Ecc 3:11; 11:5; Isa 40:28; 45:15; 55:8–9; Ro 11:33–34; 1Co 2:10–11, 16). Symbolized by darkness (Ex 20:21; Dt 4:11; 5:22; 1Ki 8:12; Pss 18:11; 97:2); by the cloud over the atonement cover (Lev 16:2). Name of, secret (Jdg 13:18). Dwells in thick darkness (1Ki 8:12; Ps 97:2). Known only to Christ and those to whom Christ reveals him (Mt 11:27). See Mysteries.

Wisdom of:

(Ezr 7:25; Job 9:4; 12:13, 16; Isa 31:2; Da 2:20–22, 28; Ro 11:33; 16:27; 1Co 1:24–25). Infinite (Ps

147:5). Manifold (Eph 3:10). Ascribed by angels (Rev 7:12). Works made in (Pss 104:24; 136:5; Pr 3:19–20; Jer 10:12). See above, Knowledge of.

GODLESSNESS [2866, 2868, 813, 815, 1013].

Described as:

Destitute of the love of God (Jn 5:42, 44). Forgetting God (Job 8:11–13; Pss 9:17; 50:22; Isa 17:10; Jer 2:32). Ignoring God (Job 35:10; Pss 28:5; 52:7; 53:2–3; 54:3; 55:19; 86:14; Isa 5:12; 22:11; 30:1; 31:1; Hos 7:2–4). Forsaking God (Dt 32:15). Despising God (1Sa 2:30; Ps 36:1; Pr 14:2; Jn 15:23–25). Loving deceit (Isa 30:9–11). Devoid of understanding (Pss 14:2–3; 53:4; Isa 1:3; Ro 1:21–22; 3:11; Eph 4:18). Rebellious (Ps 2:2; Isa 30:2; Da 5:23). Haters of God (Dt 7:10). Enemies of God (Col 1:21; Jas 4:4). Sinfulness (Ro 8:6–8). Impugning God's justice (Eze 33:17–20; Mal 2:17). Atheistic; rejecting God (Pss 10:4; 14:1; 53:1). Willfully sinning (Heb 10:26–27).

GODLINESS [466, 2883, 2327, 2354, 2356, 2357, 2536+2848, 2536, 2538] (Gr. *eusebeia, theosebeia*). The piety toward God and the proper conduct that springs from a right relationship with him. It is not belief in itself, but the devotion toward God and love toward others that result from that belief. Religious faith is empty without godliness, for it is then but an empty form (2Ti 3:5). The Greek *eusebeia* is found fifteen times in the NT. It is the sum total of religious character and actions, and it produces both a present and future state of happiness. It is not right action that is done from a sense of duty, but is the spontaneous virtue that comes from the indwelling Christ and reflects him.

1Ti	2:2	and quiet lives in all **g** and holiness.
	4:8	but **g** has value for all things,
	6:6	**g** with contentment is great gain.
	6:11	and pursue righteousness, **g**, faith,
2Pe	1:6	and to perseverance, **g**;

GODLY

| Ps | 4:3 | that the Lord has set apart the **g** |

2Co	7:10	**G** sorrow brings repentance that
	11:2	jealous for you with a **g** jealousy.
2Ti	3:12	everyone who wants to live a **g** life
2Pe	3:11	You ought to live holy and **g** lives

GOG AND MAGOG *See Magog.*

GOLDEN RULE (Mt 7:12; Lk 6:31; also Lev 19:18; Ro 13:9; Gal 5:14).

GOLGOTHA [1201] (gol'go-th a, Gr. *Gŏlgŏtha*, from Aram. *Gulgaltā', skull*). The place of our Lord's crucifixion. From the Hebrew *gulgoleth*, which implies a bald, round, skull-like mound or hillock. The Latin name, *Calvarius* ("bald skull"), has been retained in the form *Calvary* (Lk 23:33). In NIV, following RSV, it is simply, "The Skull." Two explanations of the name are found: (1) it was a place of execution and therefore abounded in skulls; (2) the place had the appearance of a skull when viewed from a short distance. The Gospels and tradition do not agree as to its location. Both Matthew (27:33) and Mark (15:22) locate it outside the city, but close to it (Jn 19:20) on the public highway, which was the type of location usually chosen by the Romans for executions. Tradition locates it within the present city.

Mt	27:33	to a place called **G** (which means
Mk	15:22	to the place called **G** (which means
Jn	19:17	(which in Aramaic is called **G**).

GOLIATH [1669] (gō-lī'ăth, Heb. *golyāth, exile*). A gigantic warrior of the Philistine army, probably one of the Anakites (Nu 13:33; Jos 11:22). Goliath's size was extraordinary. If a cubit is twenty-one inches (fifty-four cm.), he was over eleven feet (three and one-half m.) in height; if about eighteen inches (forty-six cm.), he was over nine feet (almost three m.). The only mention made of Goliath is his appearance as a champion of the Philistines (1Sa 17). The Philistines had ventured into Israel's territory and had taken a firm position on the slope of a hill, with Israel camped on the opposite hill. From the Philistine camp Goliath made daily challenges to personal combat, but after forty days no one had accepted. David had been sent to his brothers with provisions. When he heard Goliath's challenge, he inquired about its meaning. After being told, he went to face Goliath, armed only with a sling and five stones. Hit in the forehead, Goliath fell, and David cut off his head. When the Philistines saw that their champion was dead, they fled, pursued by victorious Israel. The Goliath of 2Sa 21:19 was probably the son of the giant whom David killed. He was killed by Elhanan, one of David's men.

GOMER [1699, 1700] (gō'měr, Heb. *gōmer*, possibly meaning *God accomplishes it* or *completion*).

1. Gomer was the oldest son of Japheth (Ge 10:2 – 3; 1Ch 1:5 – 6) and the father/ancestor of a people (Eze 38:6). The latter are probably to be equated with the Indo-European tribes, the Cimmerians (Gimirrai) of classical history who settled in Cappadocia.

2. Gomer was the wife of the prophet Hosea, and the daughter of Diblaim (Hos 1:3). She bore Jezreel, Lo-Ruhamah, and Lo-Ammi. God used the unfaithfulness of Gomer in her marriage to illustrate the unfaithfulness of Israel in their covenant relationship to himself. *See also Hosea, Book of.*

GOMORRAH [6686, 1202] (gō-mŏr'r a, Heb. *'ămō-râh*, Gr. *Gomorra*, *submersion*, *to overwhelm with water*). One of the five "cities of the plain" located in the Vale of Siddim at the south end of the Dead Sea. Zoar alone escaped the destruction by fire from heaven in the time of Abraham and Lot. The district where the five cities were located was exceedingly productive and well-peopled, but today traces of the punitive catastrophe abound. There are great quantities of salt, with deposits of bitumen, sulphur, and niter on the shores of the Dead Sea. The location was long a contention, but it reportedly was established in AD 1924 by an archaeological expedition led by M. G. Kyle that placed it beneath the shallow waters of the Dead Sea south of the Lisan promontory.

General References to:

One of the "cities of the plain" (Ge 10:19; 13:10). Its king defeated by Kedorlaomer (Ge 14:2, 8 – 11). Wickedness of (Ge 18:20). Destroyed (Ge 19:24 – 28; Dt 29:23; 32:32; Isa 1:9 – 10; 13:19; Jer 23:14; 49:18; 50:40; Am 4:11; Zep 2:9; Mt 10:14 – 15; Mk 6:11; Lk 9:5; Ro 9:29; 2Pe 2:6; Jude 7).

Ge	19:24	sulfur on Sodom and **G**—
Mt	10:15	and **G** on the day of judgment
2Pe	2:6	and **G** by burning them to ashes,
Jude	7	**G** and the surrounding towns gave

GOOD

Ge	1:4	God saw that the light was **g**,
	1:31	he had made, and it was very **g**.
	2:9	and the tree of the knowledge of **g**
	2:18	"It is not **g** for the man to be alone.
	3:22	become like one of us, knowing **g**
	50:20	but God intended it for **g**
2Ch	7:3	"He is **g**; his love endures
Job	2:10	Shall we accept **g** from God,
Ps	14:1	there is no one who does **g**.
	34:8	Taste and see that the LORD is **g**;
	34:14	Turn from evil and do **g**;
	84:11	no **g** thing does he withhold
	147:1	How **g** it is to sing praises
Pr	13:22	A **g** man leaves an inheritance
	15:30	**g** news gives health to the bones.
	17:22	A cheerful heart is **g** medicine,
	18:22	He who finds a wife finds what is **g**
	19:2	It is not **g** to have zeal
	22:1	A **g** name is more desirable
Isa	5:20	Woe to those who call evil **g**
	52:7	the feet of those who bring **g** news,
	61:1	me to preach **g** news to the poor.
Mt	5:45	sun to rise on the evil and the **g**,
	7:11	Father in heaven give **g** gifts
	7:17	Likewise every **g** tree bears **g** fruit,
	12:35	The **g** man brings **g** things out
	13:8	Still other seed fell on **g** soil,
	19:17	"There is only One who is **g**.
	25:21	'Well done, **g** and faithful servant!

Mk	1:15	Repent and believe the **g** news!"
	8:36	What **g** is it for a man
	10:18	"No one is **g** — except God alone.
	16:15	preach the **g** news to all creation.
Lk	2:10	I bring you **g** news
	6:27	do **g** to those who hate you,
	14:34	"Salt is **g**, but if it loses its saltiness,
Jn	10:11	"I am the **g** shepherd.
Ro	3:12	there is no one who does **g**,
	7:18	I have the desire to do what is **g**,
	8:28	for the **g** of those who love him,
	12:2	his **g**, pleasing and perfect will.
	12:9	Hate what is evil; cling to what is **g**.
1Co	7:1	It is **g** for a man not to marry.
	10:24	should seek his own **g**, but the **g**
	15:33	Bad company corrupts **g** character
Gal	6:9	us not become weary in doing **g**,
Eph	2:10	in Christ Jesus to do **g** works,
Php	1:6	that he who began a **g** work
Col	1:10	bearing fruit in every **g** work,
1Ti	3:7	have a **g** reputation with outsiders,
	6:12	Fight the **g** fight of the faith.
2Ti	3:17	equipped for every **g** work.
	4:7	I have fought the **g** fight, I have
Tit	1:8	loves what is **g**, who is
Heb	5:14	to distinguish **g** from evil.
	10:24	on toward love and **g** deeds.
	12:10	but God disciplines us for our **g**,
Jas	4:17	who knows the **g** he ought to do
1Pe	2:3	you have tasted that the Lord is **g**.
	2:12	Live such **g** lives among the pagans

GOSHEN [824+1777, 1777] (gō'shĕn, Heb. *gōshĕn*, probably *mound of earth*).

1. The NE section of the Nile delta region is usually termed "the land of Goshen." The Israelites under Jacob settled here while Joseph was prime minister of Egypt (Ge 46). The district is not large, an area of some 900 square miles, but because of irrigation it is considered some of the best land of Egypt, excellent for grazing and for certain types of agriculture. The district had two principal cities, both built for the pharaohs by the Hebrews. The one of greater importance had, at various times, at least three and possibly four names. Zoan, Avaris, and Tanis were certainly its names, and archaeologists do not agree as to whether it also bore the name of Rameses. Some indicate a different location for Rameses. Under the name of Avaris, it was for five hundred years the capital of the Hyksos Empire. The other city, Pithom, is particularly interesting to the student of biblical archaeology because here is found a proof of Ex 5:7 – 13. The labor overseers were told not to give the Hebrew workers straw for making bricks, yet with no diminishing of the assigned quota. In a building at Pithom three types of bricks are found. At its foundation straw was used. After Pharaoh refused to supply straw any longer, the Hebrews desperately gathered all bits of straw and stubble they could find, and such bricks are found higher in the building. It was completed with bricks devoid of straw, as the uppermost bricks indicate.

2. A district of south Palestine, lying between Gaza and Gibeon, its name probably given in remembrance of Egypt (Jos 10:41).

3. A town mentioned with Debir, Socoh, and others, in the SW part of the mountains of Judah (Jos 15:51).

GOSPEL [2294, 2295, 4603] (Gr. *euangelion*, *good news*). The English word *gospel* is derived from the Anglo-Saxon *godspell*, which meant "good tidings" and, later, the "story concerning God." As now used, the word describes the message of Christianity and the books in which the record of Christ's life and teaching is found. This message is the good news that God has provided a way of redemption through his Son Jesus Christ. Through the gospel, the Holy Spirit works for the salvation of human beings (Ro 1:15 – 16). In the NT the word never means a book (one of the four gospels); instead, it always refers to the good tidings that Christ and the apostles announced. It is called "the gospel of God" (Ro 1:1; 1Th 2:2, 9); "the gospel about Jesus Christ" (Mk 1:1; Ro 15:19); "the gospel of God's grace" (Ac 20:24); "the gospel of peace" (Eph 6:15); "the gospel of your salvation" (1:13); and "the gospel of the glory of Christ" (2Co 4:4). The gospel has to do entirely with Christ. It was preached by him (Mt 4:23; 11:5), by the apostles (Ac 16:10; Ro 1:15), and by the evangelists (Ac 8:25). Not until about AD 150 was the word applied to the writings concerning the message of Christ.

General References to:

From God (Jn 17:7 – 8, 14; 2Th 2:14). Contrasted with the law (Lk 16:16; Jn 1:16 – 17; Ac 12:24; 19:20; 2Co 3:6 – 11). Called the new covenant (Jer 31:31 – 34; Heb 7:22; 8:6 – 13; 9:8 – 15; 10:9; 12:22 – 24). Dissemination of (Ac 14:3; 16:17; 20:24), commanded (Mt 24:14; 28:18 – 20; Mk 13:10; 16:15; Ac 5:20; Ro 10:15 – 18; 16:25 – 26; 1Co 1:18, 21, 24 – 25; 9:16 – 18; Eph 3:8 – 11). Desired by prophets, righteous (Mt 13:17; Lk 23:34). Hid from the lost (2Co 4:3 – 4). Comes in power, word, assurance (1Th 1:5). Proclaimed to Abraham (Gal 3:8); by angels (Lk 2:10 – 11; Rev 14:6). Preached by Jesus (Mt 4:23; Mk 1:14 – 15); by Peter (Ac 10:36); by Paul (Ac 13:32 – 33; 20:24; Ro 15:29; 1Co 9:16 – 18; Gal 2:2; Col 1:5 – 6, 23); to the Gentiles (Gal 2:2; Eph 3:8; Col 1:23, 26 – 29); to both Jews and Gentiles (Ro 1:16; 1Co 1:24); to the poor (Mt 11:4 – 6; Lk 7:22); to the dead (1Pe 3:19; 4:6); to every nation (Lk 2:10 – 11; Ro 16:26; Rev 14:6). Life and immortality brought to light in (2Ti 1:10). Salvation through (Ro 1:16 – 17; 1Co 15:1 – 2; Eph 1:13 – 14; Jas 1:21; 1Pe 1:23).

Described as:

Dispensation of grace (Eph 3:2). Doctrine according to godliness (1Ti 6:3). Everlasting gospel or eternal good tidings (Rev 14:6). The faith (Jude 3). Glorious gospel (1Ti 1:11). Pattern of sound teaching (2Ti 1:13). Gospel of the glory of Christ (2Co 4:4). Good tidings or good news (Isa 40:9; 41:27; 52:7; 61:1; Mt 11:5; Lk 7:22; Ac 13:32 – 33; 1Pe 1:25). Gospel of Christ (Ro 1:16; 1Co 9:12, 18; Gal 1:7; Php 1:27; 1Th 3:2); of God (Ro 1:1; 15:16; 1Th 2:8; 1Pe 4:17); of grace of God (Ac 20:24); of Jesus Christ (Mk 1:1); of the kingdom (Mt 4:23; 24:14); of peace (Eph 6:15); of salvation (Eph 1:13). The kingdom of God (Lk 16:16). The law of liberty (Jas 1:25). Ministration of the Spirit (2Co 3:8). Mystery of Christ (Eph 3:4); of the gospel (Eph 6:19). Power of God (Ro 1:16; 1Co 1:18). Preaching of Jesus Christ (Ro 16:25). Word of Christ (Col 3:16); of faith (Ro 10:8); of God (1Th 2:13; 1Pe 1:23); of life (Php 2:16); of the Lord (1Pe 1:25); of reconciliation (2Co 5:19); of salvation (Ac 13:26); of truth (Eph 1:13). Words of this life (Ac 5:20).

Likened to:

A mustard seed (Mt 13:31 – 32; Mk 4:30 – 33; Lk 13:18 – 19); good seed (Mt 13:24 – 30, 36 – 43); yeast (Mt 13:33); a pearl of great price (Mt 13:45 – 46; Lk 13:20 – 21); treasure hidden in a field (Mt 13:44); a householder (Mt 20:1 – 16); a feast (Lk 14:16 – 24).

Prophecies concerning:

(Isa 2:3 – 5; 4:2 – 6; 9:2, 6 – 7; 25:7 – 9; 29:18, 24; 32:3 – 4; 35:5 – 10; 40:9; 41:27; 42:6 – 7; 46:13; 49:13; 51:4 – 6; 52:7; 55:1 – 5; 60:1 – 22; 61:1 – 3; Jer 31:31 – 34; Eze 34:23 – 31; 47:1 – 12; Joel 2:28 – 32; Mic 4:1 – 7; Mt 24:14; Lk 1:67 – 79; 2:12 – 14, 34). Fulfilled by Christ (Lk 4:18 – 19).

Ro	1:16	I am not ashamed of the **g**,
	15:16	duty of proclaiming the **g** of God,
	15:20	to preach the **g** where Christ was
1Co	9:12	rather than hinder the **g** of Christ.
	15:2	By this **g** you are saved,
2Co	4:4	light of the **g** of the glory of Christ,
	9:13	your confession of the **g**
Gal	1:7	a different **g** — which is really no **g**
Eph	6:15	comes from the **g** of peace.
Php	1:27	in a manner worthy of the **g**
Col	1:23	This is the **g** that you heard
1Th	2:4	by God to be entrusted with the **g**.
2Ti	1:10	immortality to light through the **g**.

GOSPEL: THE FOUR GOSPELS The word *gospel* is derived from the Anglo-Saxon *godspell*, meaning "good tidings," and is a literal translation of the

Greek *euangelion*, which meant originally a reward for bringing good news, and finally the good news itself. In the NT the term is applied to the revelation of God's plan for reconciling humans to himself by forgiving their sin and transforming their character. The gospel is the message of God's gift of salvation through the person and work of Christ that the church has been commissioned to proclaim (Mk 16:15; Ac 20:24; Eph 1:13). The impact of the life, death, and resurrection of Christ compelled his disciples to present his message to the public. By repeating the significant features of his ministry and his accompanying precepts, following the general order of his biography, they formulated a body of teaching that may have varied in detail with each recital but maintained the same general content.

From such samples of apostolic preaching one may conclude that the facts of Jesus' life constituted the gospel, which was interpreted and applied to suit the occasion on which it was preached.

This gospel, which was initially proclaimed in oral form, has been transmitted through the writings called "the Gospels." Although Matthew, Mark, Luke, and John differ considerably in detail, they agree on the general outline of Jesus' career, on the supernatural character of his life, and on the high quality of his moral precepts. From the earliest period of the church they have been accepted as authoritative accounts of his life and teachings.

The three gospels of Matthew, Mark, and Luke are called *synoptic* from the Greek word *synoptikos*, which means "to see the whole together, to take a comprehensive view." They present similar views of the career and teaching of Christ and resemble each other closely in content and in phraseology. The numerous agreements between these gospels have raised the question whether the relationship between them can be traced to common literary sources. Each gospel, however, was shaped to its own purpose and audience, so that the variations in wording reflected the differences of interest and environment. Matthew was written for Christians with a Jewish background; Mark, for active Gen-

tiles, probably Romans; Luke, for a cultured and literary Greek. All three, however, bear united witness to the supernatural character and saving purpose of Jesus Christ.

The fourth gospel, John, differs markedly in character and in content from the Synoptics. Excluding the feeding of the five thousand and the passion narrative, there are few points of agreement with the others. So radical are the differences that the veracity of John has been challenged on the grounds that if it is historical, it should coincide more nearly with the Synoptics. The gospel of John is the account of an eyewitness writing in his later years and interpreting the person of Christ in the perspective of his Christian experience.

The Gospels were among the first writings to be quoted as sacred and authoritative. Individual passages are quoted or alluded to in Ignatius of Antioch (c. AD 116), the *Epistle of Barnabas*, and the *Shepherd of Hermas*, which were written in the early part of the second century. Justin Martyr (c. 140) mentions the Gospels explicitly, calling them "Memoirs of the Apostles" (*First Apology*, 66).

GOSSIP [2143+8215, 8087, 5826, 5827, 6030, 6031]. Proverbs concerning (Pr 11:13; 16:28; 17:9; 26:20). Forbidden (Lev 19:16; Ps 50:20; Pr 11:3; 20:19; Eze 22:9).

Pr	11:13	A **g** betrays a confidence,
	16:28	and a **g** separates close friends.
	18:8	of a **g** are like choice morsels;
	20:19	A **g** betrays a confidence;
	26:20	without **g** a quarrel dies down.
2Co	12:20	slander, **g**, arrogance and disorder.

GOVERNMENT [5385, 6269, 10424]. Paternal functions of (Ge 41:25 – 57). Civil service school provided by (Da 1:3 – 20). Maintains a system of public instruction (2Ch 17:7 – 9).

Constitutional:

It was provided in the law of Moses that in the event of the establishment of a monarchy a copy of the law of Moses should be made and the king should be required to study this law all the days of his life and conform his administration to it (Dt 17:18 – 20). This constituted the fundamental law and had its likeness to the constitution of modern governments.

Corruption in:

(1Ki 21:5 – 13; Pr 25:5; Mic 3:1 – 4, 9 – 11). Instances of: Pilate, in delivering Jesus to death to please the noisy crowd (Mt 27:24; Jn 19:12 – 16); Felix, who hoped for money from Paul (Ac 24:26). See Church, the Body of Believers.

Duty of Citizens to:

To pay taxes (Mt 22:17 – 21; Lk 20:22 – 25). To render obedience to civil authority (Ro 13:1 – 7; Tit 3:1; 1Pe 2:13 – 17).

God in:

(2Ch 22:7; Jer 18:6; Eze 21:25 – 27; 29:19 – 20). In appointment of Saul as king (1Sa 9:15 – 17; 10:1). In Saul's rejection (1Sa 15:26 – 28; Ac 13:22). In appointment of David (1Sa 16:1, 7, 13; 2Sa 7:13 – 16; Ps 89:19 – 37; Ac 13:22); of Solomon (1Ki 2:13 – 15). In counseling Solomon (1Ki 9:2 – 9). In magnifying Solomon (1Ch 29:25). In reproving Solomon's wickedness (1Ki 11:9 – 13). In raising adversaries against Solomon (1Ki 11:14, 23). In tearing the nation of Israel in two (1Ki 11:13; 12:1 – 24; 2Ch 10:15; 11:4). In blotting out the house of Jeroboam (1Ki 14:7 – 16; 15:27 – 30). In appointment of kings (1Ki 14:14; 16:1 – 2; 1Ch 28:4 – 5; Da 2:20 – 21, 37; 4:17; 5:18 – 23). In destruction of nations (Jer 25:12 – 17; Am 9:8; Hag 2:22).

Mosaic:

Administrative and judicial system (Ex 18:13 – 26; Nu 11:16 – 17, 24 – 25; Dt 1:9 – 17). See Elders, Council of.

Ecclesiastical: *See Church, the Body of Believers*
Imperial: *(Ge 14:1; Jos 11:10; 1Ki 4:21; Est 1:1; Da 4:1; 6:1 – 3; Lk 2:1).*
Monarchical: *Tyranny in: by Pharaoh (Ex 1:8 – 22; 2:23 – 24; 3:7; 5:1 – 10); by Saul (1Sa 22:6, 12 – 19); by David (2Sa 11:14 – 17); by Sol-*

omon (1Ki 2:23 – 25, 28 – 34, 36 – 46); by Rehoboam (1Ki 12:1 – 16); by Ahab and Jezebel (1Ki 21:7 – 16); by Jehu (2Ki 10:1 – 14); by Xerxes (Est 1:11 – 12, 19 – 22; 3:6 – 15; 8:8 – 13); by Nebuchadnezzar (Da 1:10; 2:5 – 13; 5:19); by Herod (Mk 6:27 – 28).

Municipal: *Based on a local council and executive officers (Dt 19:12; 21:2 – 8, 18 – 21; 22:13 – 21; 25:7 – 9; Jos 20:4; Jdg 8:14 – 16; 11:5 – 11; Ru 4:2 – 11; 1Sa 11:3; 16:4; 30:26; 1Ki 21:8 – 14; 2Ki 10:1 – 7; Ezr 10:8, 14; Ne 3:9, 12, 16, 18 – 19; La 5:14).*
Patriarchal: *(Ge 27:29, 37).*
Provincial: *(Ezr 4:8 – 9; 5:3, 6; 6:6; 8:36; Ne 2:7, 9; 5:14; Da 6:1 – 3; Mt 27:2; 28:14; Lk 2:2; 3:1; Ac 24:1).*
Representative: *(Dt 1:13 – 15; Jos 9:11).*
Theocratic: *(Ex 19:3 – 8; Dt 26:16 – 19; 29:1 – 13; Jdg 8:23; 1Sa 8:6 – 7; 10:19; 12:12; Isa 33:22).*

GRACE [2834, 2858, 2876, 5919, 5921] (Heb. *hēn*, Gr. *charis*). A term used by the biblical writers with a considerable variety of meaning: (1) Properly speaking, that which affords joy, pleasure, delight, charm, sweetness, loveliness; (2) goodwill, lovingkindness, mercy, etc.; (3) the kindness of a master toward a slave. Thus by analogy, grace has come to signify the kindness of God to humankind (Lk 1:30). The NT writers, at the end of their various letters, frequently invoke God's gracious favor on their readers (Ro 16:20; Php 4:23; Col 1:19; 1Th 5:28). In addition, the word *grace* is often used to express the concept of kindness given to someone who doesn't deserve it: hence, undeserved favor, especially that kind or degree of favor bestowed on sinners through Jesus Christ (Eph 2:4 – 5). Grace, therefore, is that unmerited favor of God toward fallen humanity whereby, for the sake of Christ — the only begotten of the Father, full of grace and truth (Jn 1:14) — he has provided for people's redemption. He has from all eternity determined to extend favor toward all who have faith in Christ as Lord and Savior.

The relationship between law and grace is one of the major themes of Paul's writings (Ro 5:1, 15 – 17;

8:1–2; Gal 5:4–5; Eph 2:8–9). Grace is likewise without equivocation identified as the medium or instrument through which God has effected the salvation of all believers (Tit 2:11). Grace is also regarded as the sustaining influence enabling the believer to persevere in the Christian life (Ac 11:23; 20:32; 2Co 9:14). Thus, grace is not merely the initiatory act of God that secures the believer's eternal salvation, but also that which maintains it throughout all of the Christian's life. It is also used as a token or proof of salvation (2Co 1:5). A special gift of grace is imparted to the humble (Jas 4:6; 1Pe 5:5). Grace can also refer to the capacity for the reception of divine life (1Pe 1:10). There are secondary senses in which "grace" is used: as a gift of knowledge (1Co 1:4) and also as thanksgiving or gratitude expressed for favor (1Co 10:30; 1Ti 1:1–2).

Ps	45:2	lips have been anointed with **g**,
Pr	3:34	but gives **g** to the humble.
Isa	26:10	Though **g** is shown to the wicked,
Jnh	2:8	forfeit the **g** that could be theirs.
Zec	12:10	of Jerusalem a spirit of **g**
Lk	2:40	and the **g** of God was upon him.
Jn	1:14	who came from the Father, full of **g**
Ac	4:33	and much **g** was upon them all.
	6:8	a man full of God's **g** and power,
	11:23	saw the evidence of the **g** of God,
	13:43	them to continue in the **g** of God.
	18:27	to those who by **g** had believed.
	20:24	testifying to the gospel of God's **g**.
Ro	3:24	and are justified freely by his **g**
	5:2	access by faith into this **g**
	5:15	came by the **g** of the one man,
	5:20	where sin increased, **g** increased all
	6:1	on sinning so that **g** may increase?
	6:14	you are not under law, but under **g**.
	11:5	there is a remnant chosen by **g**.
	15:15	because of the **g** God gave me
1Co	1:4	of his **g** given you in Christ Jesus.
	3:10	By the **g** God has given me,
2Co	1:2	**G** and peace to you
	1:12	wisdom but according to God's **g**.
	6:1	not to receive God's **g** in vain.
	12:9	"My **g** is sufficient for you,
	13:14	May the **g** of the Lord Jesus Christ,
Gal	1:3	**G** and peace to you
	2:21	I do not set aside the **g** of God,
	3:18	God in his **g** gave it to Abraham
	5:4	you have fallen away from **g**.
Eph	1:6	to the praise of his glorious **g**,
	2:5	it is by **g** you have been saved.
	2:8	For it is by **g** you have been saved,
	4:7	to each one of us **g** has been given
	6:24	**G** to all who love our Lord Jesus
Php	1:7	all of you share in God's **g** with me.
	4:23	The **g** of the Lord Jesus Christ be
Col	4:6	conversation be always full of **g**,
2Th	2:16	and by his **g** gave us eternal
	3:18	The **g** of our Lord Jesus Christ be
1Ti	1:14	The **g** of our Lord was poured out
2Ti	1:9	because of his own purpose and **g**.
	2:1	be strong in the **g** that is
Tit	2:11	For the **g** of God that brings
	3:7	having been justified by his **g**,
Heb	2:9	that by the **g** of God he might taste
	4:16	find **g** to help us in our time of need
	4:16	the throne of **g** with confidence,
	10:29	and who has insulted the Spirit of **g**
	12:15	See to it that no one misses the **g**
	13:9	hearts to be strengthened by **g**,
Jas	4:6	but gives **g** to the humble."
1Pe	1:13	fully on the **g** to be given you
	4:10	faithfully administering God's **g**
	5:5	but gives **g** to the humble."
	5:12	and testifying that this is the true **g**
2Pe	3:18	But grow in the **g** and knowledge
Jude	4	who change the **g** of our God

GRACE OF GOD [2834, 2858, 2876, 5919, 5921]. Unmerited favor (Dt 7:7–8; 2Ch 30:9; Eph 1:6; Tit 2:11; Heb 4:16). Abundant (1Ti 1:14). Divine help (Ge 20:6; Job 10:12; Pss 84:11; 94:17–19; 138:3; 1Co 10:13; 2Co 1:12; 12:9; 1Pe 1:5). Growth in (Ps 84:7; Pr 4:18; Php 1:6, 9–11; 3:12–15; Col 1:10–11; 2:19; 1Th 3:10, 12–13; 2Th 1:3; Heb 6:1–3; 1Pe 2:1–3; 2Pe 3:18). Believers to be stewards of (1Pe 4:10). Intercessory prayer for (Ps 143:11; Da 9:18; Jn 17:11–12, 15; 1Th 1:1;

5:28; 2Pe 1:2). No warrant for sinful indulgence (Ro 6:1, 15). Exhortation against rejecting (2Co 6:1 – 2). With respect to Jacob and Esau (Ro 9:10 – 16).

Manifested:

In drawing people to Christ (Jn 6:44 – 45); in redemption (Eph 1:5 – 9, 11 – 12); in justification (Ge 15:6; Ro 3:22 – 24; 4:4 – 5, 16; 5:2, 6 – 8, 15 – 21; Tit 3:7); in passing over transgressions (Nu 23:20 – 21; Ne 9:17; Ro 3:25); in salvation (Ro 11:5 – 6; Eph 2:8 – 9; 2Ti 1:9); in calling to service (Gal 1:15 – 16); in spiritual growth (Eph 3:16); in spiritual gifts (1Co 1:4 – 8; Eph 4:7, 11); in the character and conduct of the righteous (1Co 15:10; 2Co 1:12; Php 2:13); in sustaining the righteous (1Ch 17:8; Da 10:18 – 19; 2Co 12:9; 1Pe 1:5; 5:10; Jude 24); in sustaining against temptation (Ge 20:6; 1Co 10:13; Rev 3:10).

Manifested to:

Enoch (Ge 5:24); Noah (Ge 6:8, 17 – 18); Abraham (Ge 12:2; 21:22); Ishmael (Ge 21:20); Isaac (Ge 26:24); Jacob (Ge 46:3 – 4; 48:16); Joseph (Ge 39:2 – 3, 23); Moses (Ex 3:12; 33:12 – 17); Israel (Dt 4:7); Naphtali (Dt 33:23); Joshua (Jos 1:5, 9); Job (Job 10:12); David (1Sa 25:26, 34; 2Sa 7:8 – 16); Daniel (Da 10:18 – 19); Jeremiah (Jer 15:20); the righteous (Ps 5:12; Ac 4:33).

GREED [1298, 1299, 5883, 8143, 154, 771, 4431, 4432].

Described:

As idolatry (Col 3:5). Insatiable (Pr 1:19; 21:26; Ecc 1:8; 4:8; 5:10 – 11; Isa 56:11). Root of evil (1Ti 6:9 – 11). Tends to poverty (Pr 11:24, 26; 22:16). Gains of, unstable (Job 20:15; Pr 23:4 – 6; Jer 17:11). Disqualifies from sacred office (Ex 18:21; 1Ti 3:3; Tit 1:7, 11; 1Pe 5:2). Disqualifies from kingdom of God (Mt 19:23 – 24; 22:25; Lk 18:24 – 25; 1Co 6:10; Eph 5:3, 5; Php 3:18 – 19). Denounced (Ps 10:3; Pr 1:19; Isa 5:8; Jude 11).

Forbidden:

Warnings against (Dt 15:9 – 10; Pr 1:19; 15:27; Hos 4:18; Hab 2:5 – 9; Mt 6:19 – 21, 24 – 25,

31 – 33; 13:22; 16:26; Mk 4:19; 7:21 – 23; Lk 8:14; 12:16 – 21; Jn 6:26 – 27; 1Co 5:11; 1Th 2:5; 1Ti 6:5 – 8; 2Ti 3:2, 5; Heb 13:5; Jas 4:2; 1Jn 2:15 – 17). Commandments against (Ex 20:17; Dt 5:21; Ro 13:9; Col 3:2; 1Ti 3:8). Prayer against (Ps 119:36). Reproof for (Ne 5:7; Isa 1:23; Jer 6:13; 22:17; Eze 33:31; Hos 10:1; Mic 2:2; 3:11; 7:3; Hag 1:6; Ro 1:29). Punishment for (Ex 18:21; Job 31:24 – 25, 28; Isa 57:17; Jer 8:10; 51:13; Eze 22:12 – 13; Col 3:5 – 6; 2Pe 2:3, 14 – 17).

Instances of:

Eve, in desiring the forbidden fruit (Ge 3:6). Lot, in choosing the plain of the Jordan (Ge 13:10 – 13). Laban, in giving Rebekah to be Isaac's wife (Ge 24:29 – 51); in deceiving Jacob when he served him seven years for Rachel (Ge 29:15 – 30); in deceiving Jacob in wages (Ge 31:7, 15, 41 – 42). Jacob, in defrauding Esau of his father's blessing (Ge 27:6 – 29); in defrauding Laban of his flocks and herds (Ge 30:35 – 43); in buying Esau's birthright (Ge 25:31). Balaam, in loving the wages of unrighteousness (2Pe 2:15, w Nu 22). Achan, in hiding the treasure (Jos 7:21). Eli's sons, in taking the flesh of the sacrifice (1Sa 2:13 – 17). Samuel's sons, in taking bribes (1Sa 8:3). Saul, in sparing Agag and the booty (1Sa 15:8 – 9). David, of Bathsheba (2Sa 11:2 – 5). Ahab, in desiring Naboth's vineyard (1Ki 21:2 – 16). Gehazi, in taking a gift from Naaman (2Ki 5:20 – 27). Israelites, in exacting usury of their brothers (Ne 5:1 – 11); in keeping back the portion of the Levites (Ne 13:10); in building fine houses while the house of the Lord lay in ruins (Hag 1:4 – 9); in following Jesus for the loaves and fishes (Jn 6:26). Money changers in the temple (Mt 21:12 – 13; Lk 19:45 – 46; Jn 2:14 – 16). Rich young ruler (Mt 19:16 – 22). Rich fool (Lk 12:15 – 21). Judas, in betraying Jesus for thirty pieces of silver (Mt 26:15 – 16; Mk 14:10 – 11; Lk 22:3 – 6; Jn 12:6). The unjust steward (Lk 16:1 – 8). The Pharisees (Lk 16:14). Simon Magus, in trying to buy the gift of the Holy Spirit (Ac 8:18 – 23). The sorcerers, in filing complaint against Paul and Silas (Ac 16:19). Demetrius, in raising a riot against Paul and Silas (Ac 19:24, 27). Felix, in hoping for a bribe from Paul (Ac 24:26). Demas, in forsaking Paul for love of the world (2Ti 4:10).

Lk	12:15	on your guard against all kinds of **g**
Ro	1:29	kind of wickedness, evil, **g**
Eph	5:3	or of any kind of impurity, or of **g**,
Col	3:5	evil desires and **g**, which is idolatry
2Pe	2:14	experts in **g** — an accursed brood!

GREEDY [GREED]

Pr	15:27	A **g** man brings trouble
1Co	6:10	nor thieves nor the **g** nor drunkards
Eph	5:5	No immoral, impure or **g** person —
1Pe	5:2	not **g** for money, but eager to serve;

GREEK LANGUAGE A branch of the Indo-European family from which most of the languages of Europe are descended. The Attic dialect spoken in Athens and its colonies on the Ionian coast was combined with other dialects in the army of Alexander the Great and was spread by his conquests through the East. A kind of "Jewish Greek," influenced by Semitic thought and culture, was widely spoken in Israel and became the chief language of the early church (Ac 21:37).

GREEK VERSIONS There were several early translations of the Hebrew OT into Greek. Some of the major versions were the following: (1) The Septuagint, originating in Alexandria in the third and second centuries BC. This was the Bible of the early church. (2) The version of Aquila in the early second century (AD 125) was a word-for-word rendering of the Hebrew produced for the Jewish people when Christians took over the Septuagint. (3) The version of Theodotion, a late second-century revision of the Septuagint. (4) The version of Symmachus, an idiomatic translation probably of the second century.

GROW

Pr	13:11	by little makes it **g**.

	20:13	not love sleep or you will **g** poor;
Isa	40:31	they will run and not **g** weary,
Mt	6:28	See how the lilies of the field **g**.
1Co	3:6	watered it, but God made it **g**.
2Pe	3:18	But **g** in the grace and knowledge

GUIDE

Ex	13:21	of cloud to **g** them on their way
	15:13	In your strength you will **g** them
Ps	25:5	**g** me in your truth and teach me,
	43:3	let them **g** me;
	48:14	he will be our **g** even to the end.
	67:4	and **g** the nations of the earth.
	73:24	You **g** me with your counsel,
	139:10	even there your hand will **g** me,
Pr	4:11	I **g** you in the way of wisdom
	6:22	When you walk, they will **g** you;
Isa	58:11	The LORD will **g** you always;
Jn	16:13	comes, he will **g** you into all truth.

GUILT [870, 871, 873, 1947, 2628, 2631, 5927, 5929, 6404, 6411, 7322, 281, 1794]. The deserving of punishment because of the violation of a law or a breach of conduct. In the OT, the concept of guilt is largely ritualistic and legalistic; it entails obligation. A person could be guiltless before both God and the nation (Nu 32:22); on the other hand, one could be guilty because of unwitting sin (Lev 5:17). Israel, moreover, was viewed as an organic whole: what one does affects all. There is collective responsibility for sin; when Achan sinned, all Israel suffered. The prophets stressed the ethical and personal aspects of sin and of guilt. God is less interested in ritual correctness than in moral obedience.

In the NT, Jesus stressed the importance of right heart attitude over against outwardly correct acts and taught that there are degrees of guilt, depending on a person's knowledge and motive (Lk 11:29 – 32; 12:47 – 48; 23:34). Paul likewise recognized differences of degree in guilt (Ac 17:30; Eph 4:18), though also stating that the law makes everyone guilty before God (Ro 3:19). Theologians differ as to what Paul taught in Ro 5:12 – 21, both as to whether Adam's guilt was imputed to all his posterity and, if it was, as to just how it was done.

Lev	5:15	It is a **g** offering.
Ps	32:5	the **g** of my sin.
	38:4	My **g** has overwhelmed me
Isa	6:7	your **g** is taken away and your sin
Jer	2:22	the stain of your **g** is still before me
Eze	18:19	'Why does the son not share the **g**

GUILTY [GUILT]

Ex	34:7	does not leave the **g** unpunished;
Mk	3:29	Spirit will never be forgiven; he is **g**
Jn	8:46	Can any of you prove me **g** of sin?
1Co	11:27	in an unworthy manner will be **g**
Heb	10:2	and would no longer have felt **g**
	10:22	to cleanse us from a **g** conscience
Jas	2:10	at just one point is **g** of breaking all

HABAKKUK [2487] (ha-băk′ŭk, Heb. *hăvaqqûq, embrace or garden plant* KB). The name of a prophet and of the eighth book of the Minor Prophets, which is entitled "The oracle that Habakkuk the prophet received" (Hab 1:1). Of the man Habakkuk nothing is known outside of the book that bears his name. Legendary references to him (in the apocryphal *Bel and the Dragon* and elsewhere) appear to have no historical value. The musical references in ch. 3 have led some to believe that he was a member of a Levitical musical guild, but even this is uncertain. Habakkuk wrote when the temple was still standing (Hab 2:20; 3:19), between c. 605 – 587 BC, probably during the reign of the Judean king Jehoiakim.

HABAKKUK, BOOK OF Most traditional scholars believe the book to be a unity, the work of one author, Habakkuk, produced in Judah during the Chaldean period. The reasons for this view are found in the book itself. The temple still stands (Hab 2:20; 3:19) and the rise of the Chaldean power is predicted (1:5 – 6). The Neo-Babylonian or Chaldean Empire first came to prominence when the Babylonian king Nebuchadnezzar defeated the Egyptians at the battle of Carchemish in 605 BC and reestablished Babylon as the seat of world power. The prophecy of Habakkuk could hardly have been given before 605. Jerusalem fell to Nebuchadnezzar in 587. The book must be placed somewhere between these dates, probably during the reign of the Judean king Jehoiakim. Some date the book earlier, believing that the Chaldeans were known to Judah before Carchemish and emphasizing the unexpectedness of the attack mentioned by Habakkuk (Hab 1:5). Still, a date soon after 605 seems to be preferred.

The first two chapters set forth Habakkuk's prophetic oracle, or burden. Twice the prophet is perplexed and asks for divine enlightenment; twice he is answered. First he is concerned over the violence and sin of his people, the Judeans. Why are these wicked people not punished (Hab 1:2 – 4)? God answers that he is about to send the Babylonians (Chaldeans) to judge Judah (1:5 – 11). This answer plunges Habakkuk into a greater perplexity: How can a righteous God use the wicked Babylonians to punish Judah, which, though it has become apostate, is still better than the Babylonians (1:12 – 17)? God's answer is that the proud conquerors will themselves be punished (2:2 – 20). The Babylonians are puffed up with self-sufficient pride, but in this hour of national calamity, the righteous will live by their faithfulness, that is, by their constancy. The prophet sees only two ways of looking at life: in faith or in unbelief. This statement naturally becomes important to the NT writers and is quoted in Ro 1:17; Gal 3:11; and Heb 10:38. The second answer to Habakkuk concludes with a series of woes against the Babylonians (Hab 2:5 – 20).

Habakkuk 3 is called "a prayer of Habakkuk the prophet" (3:1). In a moving lyric poem, the prophet records his final response to God's message of judgment. He describes the divine revelation in terms of a story theophany (3:2 – 15) but concludes that no matter what comes, he will trust in God (3:16 – 19). *See Prophets, The Minor.*

Outline:

    I. Title (1:1).

    II. Habakkuk's First Complaint (1:2 – 4).

    III. God's Answer (1:5 – 11).

    IV. Habakkuk's Second Complaint (1:12 – 2:1).

    V. God's Answer (2:2 – 20).

    VI. Habakkuk's Prayer (ch. 3).

HADAD [119, 2060, 2524] (hā′dăd, *sharpness, fierceness, thunder* [Semitic storm god]).

    1. Grandson of Abraham (Ge 25:15).

    2. A king of Edom (Ge 36:35 – 36; 1Ch 1:46 – 47).

    3. Another king of Edom (Ge 36:39, n.; 1Ch 1:50 – 51).

    4. A member of the royal house of Edom who escaped to Egypt when David conquered Edom and then later returned to his homeland to revolt against

Solomon (1Ki 11:14 – 25). The Hebrew actually reads "Adad" for the first "Hadad" in 1Ki 11:17, and it has been conjectured that 1Ki 11:14ff. combines two accounts, one of Hadad the Edomite and the other of Adad the Midianite. Convincing reasons have been given for identifying this Hadad with 3 above.

5. The ancient Semitic storm god who as the great Baal of the Ugaritic pantheon figured in the struggle of the religion of Israel against Canaanite religion.

HADES [87] (hā′dēz, Gr. *Hades, haidēs, not to be seen, the underworld*). The place or state of the dead, as contrasted with the final punishment of the wicked. In the NT Greek the word occurs ten times and is uniformly translated "hell" in the KJV. In the TR, from which the KJV was translated, the word occurs also in 1Co 15:55 and is rendered "grave"; but other manuscripts have the Greek *thanate*, and both ASV and NIV render it "death." The NT word is taken over from Greek mythology, in which *Hades* was the god of the lower regions. Although the word was taken from pagan myths, the concept is from the OT word *Sheol. Sheol* occurs sixty-five times in the Hebrew OT and is rendered in the KJV as "hell" thirty-one times, "the grave" thirty-one times, and "the pit" three times; but in the ASV it is uniformly transliterated *Sheol*, even as *Hades* in the ASV is a transliteration rather than an attempt to translate the Greek. The word *hell* in English always has an unpleasant connotation and is properly thought of as the final destiny of the wicked when it translates *geenna*, which occurs twelve times and is always rendered "hell."

The NT generally does not give definite light on Hades. In Mt 11:23 (cf. Lk 10:15) our Lord says that Capernaum will go down into Hades. The preposition "down" points to the OT teaching that Sheol is inside the earth (Ps 139:8; Am 9:2), and the following verse (Mt 11:24) puts the day of judgment for both Sodom and Capernaum later than the stay in Hades. In the parable of the rich man and Lazarus (Lk 16:19 – 31) the rich man is pictured as being

tormented in Hades but able to see in the distance Abraham with Lazarus by his side. He asks for a drop of water to cool his tongue and for a message to be sent to his five brothers who are still alive on earth, and in each case his request is denied. In the first Christian sermon, Peter quotes (Ac 2:25 – 31) from Ps 16:8 – 11, proving from it that our Lord arose from the dead and was not left in Hades. In the book of Revelation, death and Hades are four times associated (1:18; 6:8; 20:13 – 14), being treated as almost synonymous terms. In the last verse mentioned, death and Hades are to be cast into the lake of fire, i.e., doomed to utter destruction.

> **General References to:**
> *The unseen world (Mt 11:23; 16:18; Lk 10:15; 16:23; Ac 2:27, 31; Rev 1:18; 6:8; 20:13 – 14). The realm (or state) of the dead is usually expressed in Hebrew by sheol [H8619] and in Greek by hades [G87] (2Sa 22:6; Job 26:5; Pss 6:5; 17:15; 30:9; 49:15; 86:13; 88:10 – 12; 115:17; 116:3; Pr 15:24; 21:16; 27:20; Ecc 9:4 – 6; Isa 5:14; Jnh 2:2; Lk 23:42 – 43; Jn 8:22; 2Co 12:4).*

Mt	16:18	the gates of **H** will not overcome it.
Rev	1:18	And I hold the keys of death and **H**
	6:8	**H** was following close behind him.
	20:13	and **H** gave up the dead that were
	20:14	**H** were thrown into the lake of fire.

HAGAR [2057, 29] (hā′g ar, Heb. *hāghār, emigration, flight*). An Egyptian handmaid to Sarai, wife of Abram. God had promised him a son and heir (Ge 15:4), but Sarai was barren. Following the marital customs of the times, she gave Hagar to her husband as her substitute (16:1 – 16). When Hagar saw that she had conceived, she despised her mistress, causing trouble in the household. Hagar was driven out, but the angel of the Lord appeared and sent her back to her mistress (16:7 – 14). When her son Ishmael was fourteen years old, his father one hundred, and Sarah ninety, Isaac was born. At a great feast held in connection with Isaac's weaning, Ishmael scoffed at the proceedings (21:9), so Sarah insisted that Hagar and her son be cast out, and Abraham unwillingly complied. God told Abraham that Ishmael's descendants would become a nation. Hagar is last seen taking a wife for her son out of the land of Egypt, her own land (21:1 – 21). Paul made Hagar's experience an allegory of the difference between law and grace (Gal 4:21 – 5:1).

HAGGAI [2516, 10247] (hăg′ā-ī Heb. *haggay; festal* BDB; *born on the feast day* KB). Prophet of the Lord to the Jews in 520 BC. Little is known of his personal history. He lived soon after the captivity and was contemporary with Zechariah (cf. Hag 1:1 with Zec 1:1). They encouraged the returned exiles to rebuild the temple (Ezr 5:1 – 2; 6:14). The prophet's name ("festal") may indicate he was born during one of the three pilgrimage feasts (Unleavened Bread, Pentecost or Weeks, or Tabernacles; cf. Dt 16:16). Based on Hag 2:3, Haggai may have witnessed the destruction of Solomon's temple. If so, he must have been in his early seventies during his ministry.

HAGGAI, BOOK OF The messages of Haggai were given during a four-month period in 520 BC, the second year of King Darius. The first message was delivered on the first day of the sixth month (Aug. 29), the last on the 24th day of the ninth month (Dec. 18).

After the return from the captivity, the Israelites set up the altar on its base, established daily worship, and laid the foundation for the second temple; then they were compelled to cease building for some years. However, although times were hard, the people were able to build finely paneled houses for themselves (Hag 1:4). Meanwhile kings succeeded one another in Persia. Cyrus, favored of God and friend of the Jews (2Ch 36:22; Isa 44:28), passed away in 529 BC; his son Cambyses (the "Xerxes" of Ezr 4:6) reigned 529 – 522, followed for only seven months in 522 by the Pseudo-Smerdis (a usurper); then arose Darius Hystaspes (Ezr 4 – 6; Haggai; Zec 1 – 6), who helped and encouraged the Jews to go ahead and who allowed no opposition. In the second year of Darius (520), Haggai fulfilled

his brilliant mission of rebuking and encouraging the Jews. The five short messages that make up his book are all dated, occupying only three months and twenty-three days; and in those few weeks the whole situation changed from defeat and discouragement to victory. Zechariah assisted Haggai in the last month of his recorded ministry (Zec 1:1 – 6). *See Prophets, The Minor*

Outline:

    I. First Message: The Call to Rebuild the Temple (1:1 – 11).

    II. Response of Zerubbabel and the People (1:12 – 15).

    III. Second Message: The Temple to Be Filled with Glory (2:1 – 9).

    IV. Third Message: A Defiled People Purified and Blessed (2:10 – 19).

    V. Fourth Message: The Promise to Zerubbabel (2:20 – 23).

HALLEL (hă-lāl, *praise*). Psalms 113 – 118, which were read on Passover day, were called the "Egyptian Hallel"; Ps 136 is an antiphonal psalm of praise and is sometimes called "The Hallel." Psalms 120 – 136 are often called "The Great Hallel."

HALLELUJAH [252] (hăl′-lē-lū′ya, Heb. *halellû-yâh*, Gr. *allēlouia, praise ye Jehovah*). A word of praise found in most of the languages into which the Bible has been translated. The word is often translated "Praise the Lord" and is used by the writers of various psalms to invite all to join them in praising God (Pss 104:35; 105:45; 106:1, 48; 111:1; 112:1; 113:1, 9; 115:18; 116:19; 117:2; 135:1, 21; first and last verses of Pss 146 to 150). The term in Rev 19:1, 3, 4, 6 is borrowed from these psalms.

HAM [2154, 2769] (Heb. *hām*, perhaps *hot*).

1. The youngest son of Noah, born probably about ninety-six years before the flood, and one of the eight persons to live through the flood. He became the progenitor of the dark-skinned races — the Egyptians, Ethiopians, Libyans, and Canaanites (Ge 10:6 – 20). His indecency when his

father lay drunk brought a curse on Canaan (Ge 9:20 – 27).

2. The descendants of Ham (1Ch 4:40; Pss 78:51; 105:23; 106:22). In these passages "Ham" is used as another name for Egypt as representing Ham's principal descendants.

3. A city of the Zuzites, east of the Jordan where Kedorlaomer killed the Zuzites (Ge 14:5).

HAMAN [2172] (hā′măn, Heb. *hāmān*). Prime minister of Xerxes, king of Persia (Est 3:1, 10; 7:7 – 10). The great enemy of the Jews in the days of Esther. He is called "the Agagite," undoubtedly because he came from Agag, a territory adjacent to Media. Xerxes (KJV Ahasuerus) had promoted Haman to a high position in the court, but Mordecai, the noble Jew, refused to bow down to him. Therefore, Haman plotted to destroy the Jewish race, but God intervened. Esther foiled Haman's plot (Est 7) and Haman died on the gallows he had made for Mordecai.

Agagite nobleman honored by Xerxes (Est 3:1 – 2); Plotted to exterminate the Jews because of Mordecai (Est 3:3 – 15); Forced to honor Mordecai (Est 5 – 6); Plot exposed by Esther (Est 5:1 – 8; 7:1 – 8); Hanged (Est 7:9 – 10)

HAMATH [2828] (hā′măth, Heb. *hamath, fortification*). One of the most ancient surviving cities on earth, located in upper Syria on the Orontes River, from which it derives its water by means of immense undershot water wheels driven by the current. The "entrance to Hamath" (Nu 34:8; NIV "Lebo Hamath," but see note) was to be the northern limit of Israel, but God left some of the Hivites in that neighborhood to be a test to the faithfulness of Israel (Jdg 3:3 – 4). In the days of David, Hamath had a king of its own (2Sa 8:9). Jeroboam II, the last powerful king of the northern tribes (2Ki 14:23 – 28), recovered Hamath for Israel. The city has had a checkered history for thousands of years. For a time it was under the power of Assyria (18:34), later under the power of Babylonia (Jer 39:5). Still later Antiochus Epiphanes of Syria (c. 175 – 164

BC) renamed it Epiphaneia after himself. Today it is largely Muslim but has a large admixture of Christians. The city is dominated by its citadel hill, which no doubt contains layers of many different civilizations.

HAMMURABI (ham′ū-ra′bē). The king of the city of Babylon who brought that city to its century-and-a-half rule over southern Mesopotamia, known as the Old Babylonian Kingdom. He was an Amorite, the name given to a Semitic group that invaded the Fertile Crescent about 2000 BC, destroying its civilization and establishing their own Semitic culture. There has been considerable difference of opinion about the date of his reign, recent scholars favoring 1728 – 1686.

Hammurabi made Babylon one of the great cities of the ancient world. Archaeologists have discovered that in his city the streets were laid out in straight lines that intersect approximately at right angles, an innovation that bears witness to city planning and strong central government, both little known in Babylon before this time. Marduk, the god of Babylon, now became the head of the pantheon, and his temple, Etemenanki, became one of the wonders of the ancient world. Many letters written by Hammurabi have been found. These show his close attention to the details of his realm and enable us to call him an energetic and benevolent ruler. By far Hammurabi's most famous claim to fame is his law code. Hammurabi began the first golden age of Babylon — the second being that of Nebuchadnezzar, over a thousand years later.

HAND [2908, 3338, 4090, 10311, 1288, 942, 3638, 4140, 5931, 5935]. One of the most frequently used words in Scripture, occurring over sixteen hundred times. Besides its literal use, it occurs in many figurative senses as well. It very often stands for power, as in Ge 9:2. "They are given into your hands" would make no sense if taken literally. To put one's hand under another's thigh as in Ge 24:2, 9 and 47:29 meant to take a solemn oath, evidently related to covenant obligations; to put one's hand on the head meant blessing, as in Ge 48:14, and signified ordination, as in 1Ti 4:14 and 2Ti 1:6. To kiss the hand of another is one of the usual marks of respect in the East; however, this custom is not mentioned in Scripture.

In the OT the hand is also the symbol of personal agency. When the Lord stretches out his hand, it means that he is taking personal action in whatever case or situation is involved, and this usage carries over into the NT (e.g., 1Sa 5:11; Jn 10:29; Ac 4:30).

Ex	13:3	out of it with a mighty **h**.
	15:6	Your right **h**, O LORD,
	33:22	and cover you with my **h**
Dt	12:7	in everything you have put your **h**
1Ki	8:42	and your mighty **h** and your
Ps	16:8	Because he is at my right **h**,
	37:24	the LORD upholds him with his **h**.
	44:3	it was your right **h**, your arm,
	98:1	his right **h** and his holy arm
	109:31	at the right **h** of the needy one,
	110:1	"Sit at my right **h**
	137:5	may my right **h** forget [its skill].
	139:10	even there your **h** will guide me,
Pr	27:16	or grasping oil with the **h**.
Isa	40:12	the waters in the hollow of his **h**,
La	3:3	he has turned his **h** against me
Mt	5:30	if your right **h** causes you to sin,
	6:3	know what your right **h** is doing,
	12:10	a man with a shriveled **h** was there.
	18:8	If your **h** or your foot causes you
	22:44	"Sit at my right **h**
Mk	16:19	and he sat at the right **h** of God.
Jn	10:28	one can snatch them out of my **h**.
	20:27	Reach out your **h** and put it
Ac	7:55	Jesus standing at the right **h** of God
1Co	12:15	I am not a **h**, I do not belong
Heb	1:13	"Sit at my right **h**
Rev	13:16	to receive a mark on his right **h**

HANDS, LAYING ON OF Ceremony having the idea of transference, identification, and devotion to God (Ex 29:10, 15, 19; Lev 16:21; Ac 8:14 – 17; 2Ti 1:6).

HANNAH [2848] (Heb. *hannâh, grace, favor*). One of the two wives of Elkanah, a Levite who lived at Ramah (1Sa 1:19), a village of Ephraim, otherwise known as Ramathaim (1:1). Peninnah, the other wife of Elkanah (1:2), had children; but Hannah was barren for a long time and, as is common in polygamous households, "her rival kept provoking her" (1:6). The fact that Elkanah loved Hannah and gave her a double portion (1:5) only increased the hatred and jealousy in Peninnah's heart. Hannah, however, was a godly woman, and she prayed for a son and vowed to give him to the Lord as a perpetual Nazirite (1:11). The priest Eli saw Hannah's lips moving in silent prayer and rebuked her for what he thought was drunkenness. She replied very humbly, and Eli apologized. The family returned home; Hannah conceived and became the mother of Samuel, the great prophet of Israel and the last of the judges. Hannah's praise (2:1 – 10) shows that she was a deeply spiritual woman. Mary's song, "the Magnificat," resembles Hannah's (Lk 1:46 – 55). Mary, like Hannah, praised God when she was expecting a baby by miraculous conception. Each woman rejoiced in the Lord; each expressed in marvelous fashion God's way of dealing with the proud and with the humble. See also Ps 113:7 – 9.

HANUKKAH [1589] (*dedication*). The Feast of Rededication. After Judas Maccabeus had cleansed the temple from the pollution of pagan worship (c. 165 BC), the twenty-fifth of Kislev (December) was kept annually in memory of this.

HAPPINESS [245, 897, 3202, 8523, 8524, 8525, 5915].

Of the Wicked:

Limited to this life (Ps 17:14; Lk 16:25); short (Job 20:5); uncertain (Lk 12:20); vain (Ecc 2:1; 7:6). Is derived from their wealth (Job 21:13; Ps 52:7); power (Job 21:7; Ps 37:35); worldly prosperity (Pss 17:14; 73:3 – 4, 7); gluttony (Isa 22:13; Hab 1:16); drunkenness (Isa 5:11; 56:12); vain pleasure (Job 21:12; Isa 5:12); successful oppres-

sion (Hab 1:15). Marred by jealousy (Est 5:13); often interrupted by judgments (Nu 11:33; Job 15:21; Ps 73:18 – 20; Jer 25:10 – 11). Leads to sorrow (Pr 14:13); recklessness (Isa 22:12). Sometimes a stumbling block to saints (Ps 73:3, 16; Jer 12:1; Hab 1:13). Saints often permitted to see the end of (Ps 73:17 – 20); envy not (Ps 37:1). Woe against (Am 6:1; Lk 6:25). Illustrated (Ps 37:35 – 36; Lk 12:16 – 20; 16:19 – 25). Exemplified: Israel (Nu 11:33). Haman (Est 5:9 – 11). Belshazzar (Da 5:1). Herod (Ac 12:21 – 23).

Of the Righteous:

In the Lord, through abundance (Ps 36:8; Ecc 2:24 – 26; 3:12 – 13, 22); in chastisement (Job 5:17 – 27); in fellowship (Ps 133:1); in good works (Pr 14:21; Ecc 3:12; Mt 5:3 – 9); in hope (Ro 5:2); in obedience (Pss 40:8; 128:1 – 2; 144:15; 146:5; Pr 16:20; 28:14; 29:18); in peace (Php 4:7); in persecution (Mt 3:10 – 11; 2Co 12:10; 1Pe 3:14; 4:12); in protection (Dt 33:29; Isa 12:2 – 3); in satisfaction (Ps 63:5); in trust (Pr 16:20); in wisdom (Pr 3:13 – 18). Beatitudes (Mt 5:3 – 12). See Joy; Peace; Praise.

HAPPY

Ge	30:13	The women will call me **h**."
	30:13	Then Leah said, "How **h** I am!
1Ki	4:20	they drank and they were **h**.
	10:8	How **h** your men must be!
Est	5:9	Haman went out that day **h**
	5:14	the king to the dinner and be **h**."
Ps	10:6	I'll always be **h** and never have
	68:3	may they be **h** and joyful.
	113:9	as a **h** mother of children.
	137:8	**h** is he who repays you
Pr	15:13	A **h** heart makes the face cheerful,
Ecc	3:12	better for men than to be **h**
	5:19	to accept his lot and be **h**
	7:14	When times are good, be **h**;
	11:9	Be **h**, young man, while you are
Jnh	4:6	Jonah was very **h** about the vine.
Zec	8:19	and glad occasions and **h** festivals
1Co	7:30	those who are **h**, as if they were not

| 2Co | 7:9 | yet now I am **h**, not because you |
| Jas | 5:13 | Is anyone **h**? Let him sing songs |

HARMONY

Zec	6:13	there will be **h** between the two.'
Ro	12:16	Live in **h** with one another.
2Co	6:15	What **h** is there between Christ
1Pe	3:8	live in **h** with one another;

HARVEST [658, 665, 668, 1292, 1305, 3292, 3823+3824, 7811, 7907, 7917, 8040, 9311, 1163, 2545, 2546, 2843] (har-věst, Heb. *qātsîr*, Gr. *therismos*). The economy of the Israelites was strictly agricultural. Harvesttime was a very significant event for them. They had three each year. The barley reaping (Ru 1:22) came in April – May; the wheat harvest (Ge 30:14) was about six weeks later, in June – July; and the ingathering of the fruits of tree or vine took place in September – October.

Grain crops were reaped with sickles, and the cut stalks were laid in bunches that were carried to the threshing floor. Some laws governed these simple harvest operations. The corners of the fields were not to be reaped, and the scatterings of the cut grain were not to be picked up. The part of the crop thus left was for the poor people to use (Lev 23:22). The owner was required each year to present the firstfruits of the crop as an offering to God before he could take any of it for his own use (23:10, 14). Stalks of grain that grew up without being sown were not to be harvested (25:5). With a new orchard or vineyard, the fruit was not to be gathered for three years, and the fourth year's crop had to be given entirely to the Lord. So the owner had to wait until the fifth year to get any fruit for himself (19:23 – 25).

The Lord fitted the three main religious feasts that he prescribed for the people into this agricultural economy. The Passover came in the season of the barley harvest (Ex 23:16). Seven weeks later at time of the wheat harvest the Feast of Pentecost occurred (34:22). The Feast of Tabernacles was observed in the seventh month, which was the period of the fruit harvest (34:22).

In the NT, most of the time the term "harvest" is used figuratively for the gathering in of the redeemed saints at the end of the age (Mt 13:39).

Ge	8:22	seedtime and **h**,
Ex	23:16	the Feast of **H** with the firstfruits
Dt	16:15	God will bless you in all your **h**
Pr	10:5	during **h** is a disgraceful son.
Joel	3:13	for the **h** is ripe.
Mt	9:37	**h** is plentiful but the workers are
Lk	10:2	He told them, "The **h** is plentiful,
Jn	4:35	at the fields! They are ripe for **h**.
1Co	9:11	if we reap a material **h** from you?
2Co	9:10	the **h** of your righteousness.
Gal	6:9	at the proper time we will reap a **h**
Heb	12:11	it produces a **h** of righteousness
Jas	3:18	in peace raise a **h** of righteousness.
Rev	14:15	for the **h** of the earth is ripe."

HATE [HATES, HATRED]

Lev	19:17	"'Do not **h** your brother
Ps	5:5	you **h** all who do wrong.
	36:2	too much to detect or **h** his sin.
	45:7	righteousness and **h** wickedness;
	97:10	those who love the LORD **h** evil,
	119:104	therefore I **h** every wrong path.
	119:163	I **h** and abhor falsehood
	139:21	Do I not **h** those who **h** you,
Pr	8:13	To fear the LORD is to **h** evil;
	9:8	rebuke a mocker or he will **h** you;
	13:5	The righteous **h** what is false,
	25:17	too much of you, and he will **h** you.
Ecc	3:8	a time to love and a time to **h**,
Isa	61:8	I **h** robbery and iniquity.
Eze	35:6	Since you did not **h** bloodshed,
Am	5:15	**H** evil, love good;
Mal	2:16	"I **h** divorce," says the LORD God
Mt	5:43	your neighbor and **h** your enemy.'
	10:22	All men will **h** you because of me,
Lk	6:22	Blessed are you when men **h** you,
	6:27	do good to those who **h** you,
	14:26	does not **h** his father and mother,
Ro	12:9	**H** what is evil; cling to what is good

HATES [HATE]

Pr	6:16	There are six things the LORD **h**,
	13:24	He who spares the rod **h** his son,
	26:28	A lying tongue **h** those it hurts,
Jn	3:20	Everyone who does evil **h** the light,
	12:25	while the man who **h** his life
1Jn	2:9	**h** his brother is still in the darkness.
	4:20	"I love God," yet **h** his brother,

HATRED [8533, 8534, 3631].

Is blinding (1Jn 2:9, 11). Carnal (Gal 5:19 – 20). Murderous (1Jn 3:15). Unforgiving (Mt 6:15). Leads to deceit (Pr 26:24 – 26). Opposite of love (Pr 15:17). Prevents from loving God (1Jn 4:20). Produces strife (Pr 10:12). Toward the righteous (Pss 25:19; 35:19; Mt 10:22; Jn 15:18 – 19, 23 – 25; 17:14). Forbidden (Eph 4:31; Col 3:8). Toward a brother (Lev 19:17). Toward an enemy (Mt 5:43 – 44). Justified against iniquity (Pss 97:10; 101:3; 119:104, 128, 163; 139:21 – 22). Of God (Pss 5:5; 45:7; Isa 61:8; Mal 2:16).

Pr	10:12	**H** stirs up dissension,
	15:17	than a fattened calf with **h**.
Jas	4:4	with the world is **h** toward God?

HAZAEL [2599] (hăz'-ā-ĕl, Heb. *hăzā'ēl, God sees*).

A high official of Ben-Hadad, king of Syria. When the king was sick, he sent Hazael to inquire of the prophet Elisha concerning his recovery from this illness. Elisha told Hazael to tell the king that he would certainly recover, but he would in fact die (2Ki 8:7 – 15). Previously God had instructed Elijah to anoint Hazael king of Syria (1Ki 19:15). Hazael pretended to be surprised by Elisha's statement that he would become king. He returned and suffocated Ben-Hadad and seized the throne for himself (2Ki 8:7 – 15).

This usurpation is confirmed by an inscription of Shalmaneser III that states that Hadadezer of Damascus (that is, Ben-Hadad) perished and Hazael, a son of nobody, seized the throne. The phrase "a son of nobody" means he was not in the royal line of descent.

The date of Hazael's reign can be ascertained as at least forty-three years in length (841–798 BC); very likely it was a few years longer. Ahaziah, king of Judah, reigned only one year (2Ki 8:26), namely, 841. During that year he fought with Joram, king of Israel, against Hazael (8:28). The annals of Shalmaneser III, king of Assyria (858–824), in his fourteenth year (844), record a battle against Hadadezer (Ben-Hadad) of Damascus. In his eighteenth year (840), Shalmaneser said he encountered Hazael at Damascus. So Hazael usurped the throne during the period 844–841. He reigned at least until 798, the date of the death of Jehoahaz, king of Israel, for Hazael oppressed Israel all the days of this king (13:22). He died shortly afterward (13:24).

HEAD [5265, 7721, 7949, 8031, 8484, 8553, 8569, 8672, 10646, 3051, 5092] (Heb. *rō'sh*, Gr. *kephalē*). The OT uses *rō'sh* 592 times, translated "chief," "leader," "top," "company," "beginning," "captain," and "hair" but most often "head," sometimes used figuratively: Almost all the NT uses of *kephalē* refer to the upper part of the body, but eight verses use it figuratively for the God-ordained order of authority — (1) the husband as head of the wife (1Co 11:3; Eph 5:23), (2) Christ as head of the church (Eph 4:15; 5:22, 23; Col 1:18; 2:19), (3) Christ as head over all people and power (1Co 11:3; Col 2:10; 1Pe 2:7), and (4) God the Father as head of Christ (1Co 11:3).

Ge	3:15	he will crush your **h**,
Nu	6:5	no razor may be used on his **h**.
Jdg	16:17	If my **h** were shaved, my strength
2Sa	18:9	Absalom's **h** got caught in the tree.
Ps	23:5	You anoint my **h** with oil;
Pr	10:6	Blessings crown the **h**
	25:22	will heap burning coals on his **h**,
Isa	59:17	and the helmet of salvation on his **h**
Eze	33:4	his blood will be on his own **h**.
Mt	8:20	of Man has no place to lay his **h**."
Jn	19:2	crown of thorns and put it on his **h**.
Ro	12:20	will heap burning coals on his **h**."
1Co	11:3	and the **h** of Christ is God.

	11:5	her **h** uncovered dishonors her **h** —
	12:21	And the **h** cannot say to the feet,
Eph	1:22	him to be **h** over everything
	5:23	For the husband is the **h** of the wife
Col	1:18	And he is the **h** of the body,
2Ti	4:5	keep your **h** in all situations,
Rev	14:14	with a crown of gold on his **h**
	19:12	and on his **h** are many crowns.

HEAL [HEALING]

Nu	12:13	please **h** her!" The LORD replied
2Ch	7:14	their sin and will **h** their land.
Job	5:18	he injures, but his hands also **h**.
Ps	41:4	**h** me, for I have sinned against you
Ecc	3:3	a time to kill and a time to **h**,
Jer	17:14	**H** me, O LORD, and I will be
	33:6	I will **h** my people and will let them
Hos	6:1	but he will **h** us;
Zec	11:16	or seek the young, or **h** the injured,
Mt	8:7	said to him, "I will go and **h** him."
	10:1	to **h** every disease and sickness.
	10:8	**H** the sick, raise the dead,
	12:10	"Is it lawful to **h** on the Sabbath?"
	17:16	but they could not **h** him."
Mk	3:2	if he would **h** him on the Sabbath.
	6:5	on a few sick people and **h** them.
Lk	4:23	to me: 'Physician, **h** yourself!
	5:17	present for him to **h** the sick.
	8:43	years, but no one could **h** her.
Jn	4:47	begged him to come and **h** his son,
	12:40	nor turn — and I would **h** them."
Ac	4:30	Stretch out your hand to **h**
	28:27	and turn, and I would **h** them.'

HEALING [776, 5340, 8324, 9499, 1407, 2542, 2543, 2611, 2615, 2617, 5392]. *See also Miracles.*

In the OT:

The Lord the healer (Ge 20:17; Ex 15:26; Pss 6:2; 30:2; 103:3; Ac 4:30). In answer to prayer: (Jas 5:14–16); of Miriam (Nu 12:10–15); of Jeroboam (1Ki 13:1–6); of Hezekiah (2Ki 20:1–7); of Naaman by Elisha (2Ki 5:1–14).

By Jesus:

The nobleman's son (Jn 4:46 – 53). The disabled man (Jn 5:2 – 9). A leper (Mt 8:2 – 4; Mk 1:40 – 45; Lk 5:12 – 13). Peter's mother-in-law (Mt 8:14 – 15). Paralyzed man (Mt 9:2 – 8; Mk 2:1 – 12; Lk 5:17 – 26). Man with withered hand (Mt 12:9 – 13; Mk 3:1 – 5; Lk 6:6 – 10). Centurion's servant (Mt 8:5 – 13; Lk 7:1 – 10). Demoniacs (Mt 8:28 – 34, w Mk 5:1 – 20, & Lk 8:26 – 36; Mt 12:22; 17:14 – 18; Mk 9:14 – 27; Lk 9:38 – 42; 11:14). Blind and mute (Mt 9:27 – 33; 12:22; 20:30 – 34; Mk 8:22 – 25; 10:46 – 52; Lk 18:35 – 43). Woman with issue of blood (Mt 9:20 – 22; Mk 5:25 – 34; Lk 8:43 – 48). Many sick (Mt 8:16; 9:35; 14:14, 35 – 36; 15:30 – 31; 19:2; Mk 6:5, 53 – 56; Lk 4:40; 9:11). Daughter of Syrian Phoenician woman (Mt 15:22 – 28; Mk 7:25 – 30). Woman with an infirmity (Lk 13:10 – 13). Ten lepers (Lk 17:12 – 14). See Miracles, of Jesus. Power of, given to the apostles (Mt 10:1, 8; Mk 3:13 – 15; 6:7, 13; Lk 9:1 – 2, 6), to the Seventy (Lk 10:9, 17), to all believers (Mk 16:18). Special gifts of (1Co 12:9, 28, 30).

By the Apostles:

Lame man, in Jerusalem (Ac 3:2 – 10); in Lystra (Ac 14:8 – 10). Sick, in Jerusalem (Ac 5:15 – 16); on Malta (Ac 28:8 – 9). Aeneas (Ac 9:34).

Figurative:

Healing of disease as a metaphor for forgiving of sins (Ps 103:3; Hos 7:1).

2Ch	28:15	food and drink, and **h** balm.
Pr	12:18	but the tongue of the wise brings **h**.
	13:17	but a trustworthy envoy brings **h**.
	15:4	The tongue that brings **h** is a tree
	16:24	sweet to the soul and **h** to the bones
Isa	58:8	and your **h** will quickly appear;
Jer	30:13	no **h** for you.
	33:6	I will bring health and **h** to it;
Mal	4:2	rise with **h** in its wings.
Mt	4:23	and **h** every disease and sickness

Lk	6:19	coming from him and **h** them all.
	9:6	gospel and **h** people everywhere.
Jn	7:23	angry with me for **h** the whole man
Ac	3:16	him that has given this complete **h**
	10:38	**h** all who were under the power
1Co	12:9	to another gifts of **h**
	12:28	also those having gifts of **h**,
	12:30	Do all have gifts of **h**? Do all speak
Rev	22:2	are for the **h** of the nations.

HEART [1061, 789, 2668, 2693, 4000, 4213, 4220, 4222, 5055, 5570, 5883, 7931, 8120, 9348, 10381, 1571, 1591, 2426, 2510, 2840, 2841, 5016, 5073, 6034] (Heb. *lēv, lēvāv,* Gr. *kardia*). Scripture uses the word *heart* more than nine hundred times, almost never literally; the principal exception is in Ex 28:29 – 30, which speaks of the breastplate of decision over the heart of Aaron. The heart is regarded (as in the modern usage) as the seat of the affections (e.g., "comfort ye your hearts," 18:5 KJV; "though your riches increase, do not set your heart on them," Ps 62:10 NIV) but also as the seat of the intellect (e.g., "every inclination of the thoughts of his heart," Ge 6:5 NIV) and of the will ("seek him with all their heart," Ps 119:2 NIV). Often it signifies the innermost being (e.g., "his heart was filled with pain," Ge 6:6 NIV).

Both in ancient times and today, different parts of the body are used figuratively as the seat of different functions of the soul; and the ancient usage often differs from the modern. In expressing sympathy, we might say, "This touches my heart," where the ancients might say, "My bowels were moved for him" (SS 5:4 KJV; cf. Ps 7:9 KJV ["the righteous God trieth the hearts and reins"] with NIV ["... minds and hearts"]). This reflects a difference in common figurative usage; it is not a question of truth and error in ancient or modern psychology. The NT was written mostly by Jews and so is colored by Hebrew thinking and usage; for example, "they do always err in their heart" (Heb 3:10 KJV) may mean that they are wrong in both their thinking and their affections. Often the word *heart* implies the whole moral nature of fallen humanity (e.g., "The heart is deceitful above all things, and beyond cure" [Jer 17:9; cf. 17:10]; "search the heart ... try the reins" [KJV]; "search the mind ... try the heart" [ASV]; "search the heart and examine the mind" [NIV]).

General references to:

Seat of affection and source of action (Dt 5:29; 6:5 – 6; 2Ch 12:14; Pss 57:7; 112:7; Pr 4:23; 14:30; 15:13 – 15; 16:1; Mt 9:4; 12:33, 35; 15:18 – 20; 23:26; Mk 7:21 – 23). Lives forever (Ps 22:26). Of the Gentiles, taught of God (Ro 2:14 – 16).

Changed:

(Ps 51:10). Instances of: Saul (1Sa 10:9); Solomon (1Ki 3:11 – 12); Paul (Ac 9:1 – 18).

Hardening of:

Forbidden (Heb 3:8, 15; 4:7). Instances of: Pharaoh (Ex 4:21; 7:3, 13, 22; 8:15, 32; 9:12, 35; 10:1; 14:8); Sihon (Dt 2:30); king of Canaan (Jos 11:20); Philistines (1Sa 6:6).

Known to God:

(Dt 31:21; 1Sa 16:7; 2Sa 7:20; 1Ki 8:39; 1Ch 28:9; 2Ch 6:30; Job 11:11; 16:19; 31:4; Pss 1:6; 44:21; 51:10; 94:11; 139:1 – 12; Pr 5:21; 16:2; 21:2; Isa 66:18; Jer 12:13; 17:10; Eze 11:5, 19 – 21; 36:25 – 26; Lk 16:15; Ac 1:24; 15:8; Ro 8:27; 1Co 3:20; Heb 4:12; Rev 2:23). To Christ (Ro 8:27; Rev 2:23).

Regenerate:

Penitent (Pss 34:18; 51:10, 17; 147:3; Pr 15:3). Renewed (Dt 30:6; Ps 51:10; Eze 11:19; 18:31; 36:26; Jn 3:3, 7; Ro 2:29; Eph 4:22 – 24; Col 3:9 – 10; Heb 10:22; Jas 4:8). Pure (Pss 24:4; 66:18; Pr 20:9; Mt 5:8; 2Ti 2:22; 1Pe 3:15). Enlightened (2Co 4:6). Established (Pss 57:7; 108:1; 112:7 – 8; 1Th 3:13). Refined by affliction (Pr 17:3). Tried or tested (1Ch 29:17; Pss 7:9; 26:2; Pr 17:3; Jer 11:20; 12:3; 20:12; 1Th 2:4; Heb 11:17; Rev 2:2, 10). Strengthened (Pss 27:14; 112:8; 1Th 3:13). Graciously affected of God (1Sa 10:26; 1Ch 29:18; Ezr 6:22; 7:27; Pr 16:1; 21:1; Jer 20:9; Ac 16:14).

Should Be:

Joyful (1Sa 2:1; Pss 4:7; 97:11; Isa 65:14; Zec 10:7); perfect (1Ki 8:61; Ps 101:2); upright (Pss 97:11; 125:4); clean (Pss 51:10; 73:1); pure (Ps 24:4; Pr 22:11; Mt 5:8; 1Ti 1:5; 2Ti 2:22; Jas 4:8; 1Pe 1:22); sincere (Lk 8:15; Ac 2:46; Eph 6:5; Col 3:22; Heb 10:22); repentant (Dt 30:2; Pss 34:18; 51:17); devout (1Sa 1:13; Pss 4:4; 9:1; 27:8; 77:6; 119:10, 69, 145); wise (1Ki 3:9, 12; 4:29; Job 9:4; Pr 8:10; 10:8; 11:29; 14:33; 23:15); tender (1Sa 24:5; 2Ki 22:19; Job 23:16; Ps 22:14; Eph 4:32); holy (Ps 66:18; 1Pe 3:15); compassionate (Jer 4:19; La 3:51); lowly (Mt 11:29).

The Unregenerate Heart:

Full of iniquity (Ge 6:5; 8:21; 1Sa 17:28; Pr 6:14, 18; 11:20; Pr 20:9; Ecc 8:11; 9:3; Jer 4:14, 18; 17:9; Ac 8:21 – 23; Ro 1:21). Loves evil (Dt 19:18; Ps 95:10; Jer 17:5). Fountain of evil (Mt 12:34 – 35; Mk 7:21). See Depravity. Wayward (2Ch 12:14; Ps 101:4; Pr 6:14; 11:20; 12:8; 17:20; Jer 5:23; Heb 3:10). Blind (Ro 1:21; Eph 4:18). Double (1Ch 12:33; Ps 12:2; Pr 28:14; Isa 9:9; 10:12; 46:12; Hos 10:2; Jas 1:6, 8). Hard (Ps 76:5; Eze 2:4; 3:7; 11:19; 36:26; Mk 6:52; 10:5; 16:14; Jn 12:40; Ro 1:21; 2:5). Deceitful (Jer 17:9). Proud (2Ki 14:10; 2Ch 25:19; Ps 101:5; Pr 18:12; 28:25; Jer 48:29; 49:16). See Pride. Subtle (Pr 7:10). See Hypocrisy. Sensual (Eze 6:9; Hos 13:6; Ro 8:7). Worldly (2Ch 26:16; Da 5:20; Ac 8:21 – 22). Judicially hardened (Ex 4:21; Jos 11:20; Isa 6:10; Ac 28:26 – 27). Malicious (Pss 28:3; 140:2; Pr 24:2; Ecc 7:26; Eze 25:15). See Malice. Impenitent (Ro 2:5). Diabolical (Jn 13:2; Ac 5:3). Covetous (Jer 22:17; 2Pe 2:14). See Covetousness. Foolish (Pr 12:23; 22:15; Ecc 9:3). Under wrath of God (Ro 1:18 – 19, 31; 2:5 – 6). See Regeneration; Sanctification.

Ge	6:5	of his **h** was only evil all the time.
Ex	4:21	But I will harden his **h**
Lev	19:17	Do not hate your brother in your **h**.
Dt	4:9	or let them slip from your **h** as long
	6:5	Lord your God with all your **h**
	11:13	and to serve him with all your **h**

	26:16	observe them with all your **h**
Jos	22:5	and to serve him with all your **h**
1Sa	10:9	God changed Saul's **h**,
	13:14	sought out a man after his own **h**
	16:7	but the LORD looks at the **h**."
1Ki	3:9	So give your servant a discerning **h**
	11:4	and his **h** was not fully devoted
	15:14	Asa's **h** was fully committed
2Ki	22:19	Because your **h** was responsive
	23:3	with all his **h** and all his soul,
1Ch	28:9	for the LORD searches every **h**
2Ch	17:6	His **h** was devoted to the ways
Ezr	1:5	everyone whose **h** God had moved
Ne	4:6	the people worked with all their **h**.
Ps	9:1	you, O LORD, with all my **h**;
	14:1	The fool says in his **h**,
	16:9	Therefore my **h** is glad
	19:14	and the meditation of my **h**
	24:4	who has clean hands and a pure **h**,
	26:2	examine my **h** and my mind;
	37:4	will give you the desires of your **h**.
	51:10	Create in me a pure **h**, O God,
	51:17	a broken and contrite **h**,
	66:18	If I had cherished sin in my **h**,
	86:11	give me an undivided **h**,
	109:22	and my **h** is wounded within me.
	119:10	I seek you with all my **h**;
	119:11	I have hidden your word in my **h**
	119:32	for you have set my **h** free.
	139:23	Search me, O God, and know my **h**
Pr	2:2	applying your **h** to understanding,
	3:1	but keep my commands in your **h**,
	3:5	Trust in the LORD with all your **h**
	4:23	Above all else, guard your **h**,
	13:12	Hope deferred makes the **h** sick,
	15:30	A cheerful look brings joy to the **h**,
	16:23	A wise man's **h** guides his mouth,
	17:22	A cheerful **h** is good medicine,
	23:15	My son, if your **h** is wise,
	23:26	My son, give me your **h**
SS	3:1	I looked for the one my **h** loves;
	8:6	Place me like a seal over your **h**,
Jer	4:14	wash the evil from your **h**

	9:26	of Israel is uncircumcised in **h**."
	17:9	The **h** is deceitful above all things
	32:39	I will give them singleness of **h**
	51:46	Do not lose **h** or be afraid
Eze	11:19	I will give them an undivided **h**
	18:31	and get a new **h** and a new spirit.
	36:26	I will give you a new **h**
Joel	2:12	"return to me with all your **h**,
	2:13	Rend your **h**
Zep	3:14	Be glad and rejoice with all your **h**,
Mt	5:8	Blessed are the pure in **h**,
	5:28	adultery with her in his **h**.
	6:21	treasure is, there your **h** will be
	11:29	for I am gentle and humble in **h**,
	12:34	of the **h** the mouth speaks.
	13:15	For this people's **h** has become
	15:18	out of the mouth come from the **h**,
	18:35	forgive your brother from your **h**."
	22:37	the Lord your God with all your **h**
Mk	11:23	and does not doubt in his **h**
	12:30	the Lord your God with all your **h**
Lk	2:19	and pondered them in her **h**.
	2:51	treasured all these things in her **h**.
	8:15	for those with a noble and good **h**,
Jn	12:27	"Now my **h** is troubled,
Ac	2:37	they were cut to the **h**
	4:32	All the believers were one in **h**
	8:21	your **h** is not right before God.
	16:14	The Lord opened her **h** to respond
Ro	1:9	with my whole **h** in preaching
	2:29	is circumcision of the **h**,
	10:9	in your **h** that God raised him
	10:10	is with your **h** that you believe
2Co	2:4	anguish of **h** and with many tears,
	4:1	this ministry, we do not lose **h**.
	9:7	give what he has decided in his **h**
Eph	1:18	eyes of your **h** may be enlightened
	5:19	make music in your **h** to the Lord,
	6:5	and with sincerity of **h**, just
Col	3:22	but with sincerity of **h**
	3:23	work at it with all your **h**,
1Ti	1:5	which comes from a pure **h**
	3:1	If anyone sets his **h**

2Ti	2:22	call on the Lord out of a pure **h**.
Phm	1:12	who is my very **h** — back to you.
	1:20	in the Lord; refresh my **h** in Christ.
Heb	4:12	the thoughts and attitudes of the **h**.
1Pe	1:22	one another deeply, from the **h**.

HEATHEN, PAGAN [1620] (Heb. *gôy*, pl. *gôyim*, Gr. *ethnos*, *people*, *nation*). In the OT *gôy* is rendered "Gentiles," "heathen," and "nation," but it is usually used for a non-Israelitish people, and thus has the meaning of "Gentiles." Sometimes, however, it refers to the Israelites, as in Ge 12:2; Dt 32:28, but the word ordinarily used for the people of God is *'ām*. In the NT *ethnos* is the equivalent of OT *gôy*, while *laos* corresponds to *'ām*. Sometimes in the KJV the Greek *Hellenes* is translated "Gentiles" (Jn 7:35; Ro 2:9 – 10).

The differentiation between Israelites and Gentiles was more sharply accentuated in NT times than in OT times, because the Jews had suffered so much from Gentile hands. Gentiles were looked on with aversion and hatred. This is evident in the NT (Jn 18:28; Ac 10:28; 11:3).

God's interest in and concern for the heathen is seen in the OT, especially in the book of Jonah. In the NT Jesus commanded the apostles to preach the gospel to all the world; and we find them proclaiming it to Gentile nations throughout the Mediterranean world.

Described:

Cast out of Canaan (Lev 18:24 – 25; Ps 44:2) and their land given to Israel (Pss 78:55; 105:44; 135:12; 136:21 – 22; Isa 54:1 – 3). Excluded from the temple (La 1:10). Wicked practices of. See Idolatry.

Divine Revelations Given to:

Abimelech (Ge 20:3 – 7); Nebuchadnezzar (Da 4:1 – 18); Belshazzar (Da 5:5, 24 – 29); Cyrus (2Ch 36:23; Ezr 1:1 – 4); magi (Mt 2:1 – 11), centurion (Mt 8:5 – 13; Lk 7:2 – 9); Cornelius (Ac 10:1 – 7).

Pious People among:

(Isa 65:5; Ac 10:35). Melchizedek (Ge 14:18 – 20); Abimelech (Ge 20); Balaam (Nu 22); Jethro (Ex 18); Cyrus (Ezr 1:1 – 3); Eliphaz (Job 4); Bildad (Job 8); Zophar (Job 11); Elihu (Job 32); Nebuchadnezzar, after his restoration (Da 4); Ninevites (Jnh 3:5 – 10); magi (Mt 2:1 – 12); centurion of Capernaum (Mt 8:5 – 13; Lk 7:2 – 9), of Caesarea (Ac 10). Believed in Christ (Mt 8:5 – 13; Lk 7:2 – 9). See Gentiles.

HEAVEN [5294, 9028, 10723, 1479, 2230, 4039, 4040, 4041, 5734, 5737] (Heb. *shāmayim*, Gr. *ouranos*).

1. Cosmologically, one of the two great divisions of the universe, the earth and the heavens (Ge 1:1; 14:19); or one of the three — heaven, earth, and the waters under the earth (Ex 20:4). In the visible heavens are the stars and planets (Ge 1:14 – 17; Eze 32:7 – 8). Later Jews divided the heavens into seven strata, but there is no evidence for this in the Bible, though Paul spoke of being caught up into the third heaven (2Co 12:2). The term "heaven of heavens" (Dt 10:14; 1Ki 8:27; Ps 148:4) is "highest heavens" in NIV.

2. The abode of God (Ge 28:17; Ps 80:14; Isa 66:1; Mt 5:12) and of the good angels (Mt 24:36). It is the place where the redeemed will someday be (Mt 5:12; 6:20; Eph 3:15), where the Redeemer has gone and intercedes for the saints, and from where he will someday come for his own (1Th 4:16).

3. The inhabitants of heaven (Lk 15:18; Rev 18:20).

God's Dwelling Place:

(Dt 26:15; 1Ki 8:30, 39, 43, 49; 1Ch 16:31; 21:26; 2Ch 2:6; 6:21, 27, 30, 33, 35, 39; 7:14; 30:27; Ne 9:27; Job 22:12, 14; Pss 2:4; 11:4; 20:6; 33:13; 102:19; 103:19; 113:5 – 6; 123:1; 135:6; Ecc 5:2; Isa 57:15; 63:15; 66:1; Jer 23:24; La 3:41, 50; Da 5:23; Zec 2:13; Mt 5:34, 45; 6:9; 10:32 – 33; 11:25; 12:50; 16:17; 18:10, 14; Mk 11:25 – 26; 16:19; Ac 7:49, 55 – 56; Ro 1:18; Heb 8:1; Rev 8:1; 12:7 – 9; 21:22 – 27; 22:1 – 5).

Figurative:

*Of divine government (Mt 16:19; 18:18; 23:22).
Of God (Mt 21:25).*

Future Home of the Righteous:

*(2Ki 2:11; Mt 5:12; 13:30, 43; Lk 16:22; Jn 12:8,
26; 13:36; 17:24; 2Co 5:1; Php 3:20; Col 1:5 – 6,
12; 3:9; 1Th 4:17; Heb 10:34; 11:10, 16; 12:22;
1Pe 1:4; Rev 2:7; 3:21).*

Called:

*City (Heb 11:10, 16); garden (Mt 3:12); house (Jn
14:2 – 3; 2Co 5:1); kingdom (Mt 25:34; Lk 12:32;
22:29 – 30); kingdom of Christ and of God (Eph
5:5); heavenly country (Heb 11:16); rest (Heb 4:9;
Rev 14:13); glory (Col 3:4); paradise (Lk 23:43;
2Co 12:2, 4; Rev 2:7); everlasting (2Co 5:1; Heb
10:34; 13:14; 1Pe 1:4; 2Pe 1:11). Allegorical representatives of (Rev 4:1 – 11; 5:1 – 14; 7:9 – 17;
14:1 – 3; 15:1 – 8; 21; 22:1 – 5). No marriage in
(Mt 22:30; Lk 20:34 – 36). Names of righteous
written in (Lk 10:20; Heb 12:22 – 24). Treasures
in (Mt 6:20; 19:21; Lk 12:33). Joy in (Ps 16:11;
Lk 15:6 – 7, 10). Righteousness dwells in (2Pe
3:13). No sorrow in (Rev 7:16 – 17; 21:4). Wicked
excluded from (Gal 5:21; Eph 5:5; Rev 22:15).
See Righteous, Promises to and Comfort of.*

Ge	14:19	Creator of **h** and earth.
Ex	20:22	that I have spoken to you from **h**:
Dt	26:15	from **h**, your holy dwelling place,
1Ki	8:27	the highest **h**, cannot contain you.
2Ki	2:1	up to **h** in a whirlwind,
	19:15	You have made **h** and earth.
2Ch	7:14	then will I hear from **h**
Isa	14:12	How you have fallen from **h**,
	66:1	"**H** is my throne,
Da	7:13	coming with the clouds of **h**.
Mt	3:2	for the kingdom of **h** is near."
	3:16	At that moment **h** was opened,
	5:12	because great is your reward in **h**,
	5:19	great in the kingdom of **h**.
	6:9	"'Our Father in **h**,
	7:21	Lord,' will enter the kingdom of **h**,
	16:19	bind on earth will be bound in **h**,

	19:23	man to enter the kingdom of **h**.
	24:35	**H** and earth will pass away,
	26:64	and coming on the clouds of **h**."
	28:18	"All authority in **h**
Mk	1:10	he saw **h** being torn open
	10:21	and you will have treasure in **h**.
	16:19	he was taken up into **h**
Lk	3:21	**h** was opened and the Holy Spirit
	10:18	saw Satan fall like lightning from **h**.
	10:20	that your names are written in **h**."
	15:7	in **h** over one sinner who repents
	18:22	and you will have treasure in **h**.
Jn	3:13	No one has ever gone into **h**
	6:38	down from **h** not to do my will
	12:28	Then a voice came from **h**,
Ac	7:55	looked up to **h** and saw the glory
	9:3	a light from **h** flashed around him.
	26:19	disobedient to the vision from **h**.
Ro	10:6	'Who will ascend into **h**?'" (that is,
1Co	15:47	the earth, the second man from **h**.
2Co	5:1	an eternal house in **h**, not built
	12:2	ago was caught up to the third **h**.
Eph	1:10	to bring all things in **h**
Php	2:10	**h** and on earth and under the earth,
	3:20	But our citizenship is in **h**.
Col	1:16	things in **h** and on earth, visible
	4:1	that you also have a Master in **h**.
1Th	1:10	and to wait for his Son from **h**,
	4:16	himself will come down from **h**,
Heb	8:5	and shadow of what is in **h**.
	9:24	he entered **h** itself, now to appear
	12:23	whose names are written in **h**.
1Pe	1:4	spoil or fade — kept in **h** for you,
	3:22	who has gone into **h** and is
2Pe	3:13	we are looking forward to a new **h**
Rev	5:13	Then I heard every creature in **h**
	11:19	God's temple in **h** was opened,
	12:7	And there was war in **h**.
	15:5	this I looked and in **h** the temple,
	19:1	of a great multitude in **h** shouting:
	21:1	Then I saw a new **h** and a new earth
	21:10	coming down out of **h** from God.

HEAVEN OPENED (Mt 3:16; Ac 7:56; 10:11; Rev 19:11).

HEAVENS, NEW To be created (Isa 65:17; 66:22; 2Pe 3:13; Rev 21:1 – 4).

HEBREW, HEBREWS These are traditionally considered designations for Abraham and his descendants, especially through Jacob, the equivalent of Israelite(s); 1Sa 14:21 may suggest that the terms are to be equated. Jews quite uniformly have used "Israel" and "the children of Israel" (later "Jews") in referring to themselves, finding in such terminology treasured religious and national associations. Foreigners thought of them as "Hebrews" (Ex 1:16; 2:6), and they so identified themselves in speaking to non-Jews (Ge 40:15; Ex 10:3; Jnh 1:9). Also, in contexts involving contrasts between Israelites and people of other nations, the same phenomenon appears (Ge 43:32; Ex 1:15; 2:11; 1Sa 13:3; 14:21).

There is the possibility, however, that in OT times the names "Hebrews," "Habiru," "Khapiru," "Apiru," and "pr" were forms of the same word (equivalent to the Akkadian SA.GAZ), a designation without national significance. Rather, they indicated wandering peoples greatly restricted as regards financial means and without citizenship and social status. Ancient records show the "Habiru" to be scattered over western Asia for centuries until about 1100 BC. Nomadic peoples, mostly Semitic — sometimes raiders, sometimes skilled artisans — they frequently offered themselves as mercenaries and slaves, with individuals occasionally rising to prominence. In Egypt the Israelites were reduced to a lowly position and later moved about in the wilderness. Conceivably they could, therefore, have been known as "Hebrews." It is noteworthy that, in taking oaths, the Habiru swore by "the gods of the Habiru," whereas similar phraseology, "the God of the Hebrews," is found in Ex 3:18; 5:3; 7:16. "Hebrews" and "Habiru" were terms used prior to the name "Israel," and both were discontinued generally about the time of the judges.

New Testament "Hebrews" references contrast people (Ac 6:1) and language (Jn 5:2; 19:13, 17, 20; 20:16) to differentiate between the Greeks and Hellenistic culture on the one hand and Jews and their traditional life and speech on the other. What is called "Hebrew language" may in John's gospel refer to Aramaic, but in the Apocalypse to Hebrew proper (Rev 9:11; 16:16).

Etymologically, it has been debated whether "Hebrew" is to be traced to Eber, the father of Peleg and Joktan (Ge 10:24 – 25; 11:12 – 16) or is derived from the Hebrew root "to pass over" and has reference to "a land on the other side," as the dweller east of the Euphrates might think of Canaan. However, the possible equating of the Hebrews and the Habiru might suggest that the Hebrews were "those who crossed over" in the sense of trespassing, i.e., "trespassers."

HEBREW LANGUAGE With the exception of Aramaic in Ezr 4:8 – 6:18; 7:12 – 26; Da 2:4 – 7, 28; and Jer 10:11, Hebrew is the language of the OT. The term *Hebrew* was first used as a designation for individuals or a people and only later denoted a language. The OT refers to the language not as "Hebrew" but as "the language of Canaan" (Isa 19:18) or "the Jews' language" (2Ki 18:26, 28 KJV and parallel passages; also Ne 13:24). Josephus, Ecclesiasticus, and the NT (Rev 9:11; 16:16), however, speak of it as "Hebrew." With close affinity to Ugaritic, Phoenician, Moabitic, and the Canaanite dialects, Hebrew represents the northwest branch of the Semitic language family. Its sister languages include Arabic, Akkadian, and Aramaic.

HEBREWS, BOOK OF

AUTHORSHIP.

The writer of Hebrews does not attach his name to his letter. First John is the only other letter in the NT to which a name is not attached. Because of this fact, there has been much discussion since the first century as to who wrote Hebrews. Speculation includes Paul, Barnabas, Apollos, and Priscilla. It was written before the destruction of the temple in AD 70.

ORIGINAL READERS.

The letter was first known in Rome and the West. Its first readers were Jewish Christians who spoke and wrote Greek. Although we cannot be absolutely certain, it seems best to regard the original readers as being located somewhere in Italy. Many roads led to Rome. These believers may have been in one of the cities nearer or farther from the capital.

SUMMARY OF CONTENT AND OUTLINE.

Although God spoke to the fathers by the prophets, he has now spoken by his Son. In the prologue we see the distinctiveness of the Son. He is before history, in history, above history, the goal of history, and the agent who brings about a cleansing of people from sins committed in history. He shares the essence of deity and radiates the glory of deity. He is the supreme revelation of God (Heb 1:1 – 3).

The writer's first main task is to make clear the preeminence of Christ (Heb 1:4 – 4:13). He is superior to angels. They assist those who will be heirs of salvation. Christ, by virtue of who he is, of God's appointment, and of what he has done, stands exalted far above them. Unbelief kept one entire generation of Israelites from Canaan. Christians are warned of such unbelief. Faith is emphasized as well as zeal to enter into the eternal rest of God. Both the gospel of God and God himself scrutinize people.

The second major emphasis in the letter falls on the priesthood of Christ (Heb 4:14 – 10:18). Qualifications, conditions, and experiences of the Aaronic priesthood are listed in comparison to Christ as a priest. Before further developing this theme, the writer warns his readers of their unpreparedness for advanced teaching. Only earnest diligence in things of God will bring them out of immaturity. Christ as a priest, like Melchizedek, is superior to the Levitical priesthood, because his life is indestructible. He is both priest and sacrifice. His priesthood is eternal. His sanctuary is in heaven, and his blood establishes the validity of the new covenant, which is also an eternal covenant. His one offering on behalf of sins is final; i.e., it is for all time. Likewise, he has made perfect for all time those who are in the process of being sanctified.

The last main section of Hebrews deals with the response of Christians (10:19 – 12:29). Perseverance on the part of Christians springs out of fellowship with God, activity for God, faith in God, and a consciousness of what lies ahead.

In concluding the letter the writer puts stress on the cross as the Christian altar and the resurrection of the Shepherd of the sheep as the basis for God's action. Such redemptive-historical events move the believer to action (Heb 13:1 – 25).

Outline:

I. Prologue: The Superiority of God's New Revelation (1:1 – 4).
II. The Superiority of Christ to Leaders of the Old Covenant (1:5 – 7:28).
III. The Superior Sacrificial Work of Our High Priest (chs. 8 – 10).
IV. Final Plea for Persevering Faith (chs. 11 – 12).
V. Conclusion (ch. 13).

HEBRON [2496, 2497 (hĕ'brŏn, Heb. *hevrôn, league, confederacy, association*).

1. One of the oldest cities of the world, and one that has had several names at different times. It is located nineteen miles (thirty-two km.) SW of Jerusalem on the main road to Beersheba and has one of the longest records of continuous occupation. Though lying in a shallow valley, it is about 3,000 feet (940 m.) above sea level and 4,300 feet (1,340 m.) above the Dead Sea, which lies a few miles east of Hebron. The hills about the city still bear choice grapes, and the Jewish people there make a fine wine. The Valley of Eshcol, from which the spies brought an immense cluster of grapes (Nu 13:22 – 24), runs quite near Hebron. Hebron's original name was Kiriath Arba, that is, "fourfold city" (Jos 14:15; 15:13).

2. Third son of Kohath, and so an uncle of Moses, Aaron, and Miriam (Ex 6:18). His descendants, 1,700 men of valor in the days of David, had

the responsibility for the Lord's business and for the service of the king west of the Jordan (1Ch 26:30).

3. A town in Asher (Jos 19:28 KJV). ASV, NASB, and RSV, as well as most Hebrew MSS, have "Ebron," but "Abdon" (21:30, copied in 1Ch 6:74) is found in JB and NIV.

4. A descendant of Caleb, son of Hezron, son of Perez, son of Judah (1Ch 2:42 – 43), not to be confused with Caleb, the faithful spy, who was a distant cousin.

HEIR [3769, 3772, 3101, 5169, 5626].

Literal:

Mosaic law relating to inheritance of (Nu 27:8 – 11; 36:1 – 8; Jos 17:3 – 6). Prescribing right of, to redeem alienated land (Lev 25:25; Ru 4:1 – 12). To inherit slaves (Lev 25:45 – 46). First-born son to have double portion (Dt 21:15 – 17). Children of wives and concubines are (Ge 15:3; 21:10; 25:5 – 6; Gal 4:30). All possessions left to (Ecc 2:18 – 19). Minor, under guardians (Gal 4:1 – 2). See Birthright; Firstborn; Inheritance; Orphan; Will.

Figurative:

Of spiritual adoption (Ro 8:14 – 17; Gal 3:29; 4:6 – 7; Tit 3:7; Jas 2:5). See Adoption.

Gal	4:7	God has made you also an **h**.
Heb	1:2	whom he appointed **h** of all things,

HEIRS [INHERIT]

Ro	8:17	then we are **h** — **h** of God
Gal	3:29	and **h** according to the promise.
Eph	3:6	gospel the Gentiles are **h** together
1Pe	3:7	as **h** with you of the gracious gift

HELL [87, 1147, 5434].
The real existence of hell is irrefutably taught in Scripture as both a *place* of the wicked dead and a *condition* of retribution for unredeemed people. It is plain that "to die in sin" is a dreadful thing (e.g., Eze 3:18; NIV note). Sheol, which is in one sense the undifferentiated place of all the dead (cf. Job 3:13 – 22), is in another sense the special doom of the wicked (Ps 49:14). It is necessary to follow the NIV footnotes in such references, for if the KJV was inaccurate in translating Sheol as "hell" (e.g., Ps 9:17), NIV is equally inaccurate in formalizing it as "the grave." Daniel 12:2 takes the matter as far as the OT will go, with its reference to "shame and everlasting contempt."

In the intertestamental period, both apocryphal literature and rabbinical teaching continued the development of the association of immortality and retribution until, during NT times, two words were used: Hades and Gehenna (see separate entry on each).

The *nature* of hell is indicated by the repeated reference to eternal punishment (Mt 25:46), eternal fire (Mt 18:8, Jude 7), everlasting chains (Jude 6), the pit of the Abyss (Rev 9:2, 11), outer darkness (Mt 8:12), the wrath of God (Ro 2:5), second death (Rev 21:8), eternal destruction from the face of God (2Th 1:9), and eternal sin (Mk 3:29). While many of these terms are symbolic and descriptive, they connote real entities, about whose existence there can be no doubt.

The *duration* is explicitly indicated in the NT. The word "eternal" (*aiōnios*) is derived from the verb *aiōn*, signifying an "age" or "duration." Scripture speaks of two *aeons*, or ages: the present age and the age to come (Mt 12:32; Mk 10:30; Lk 18:30; Eph 1:21). The present age — this world — is always contrasted with the age to come as temporal, while the future age will be endless. As the everlasting life of the believer is to be endless, just so the retributive aspect of hell refers to the future infinite age. In every reference in which *aiōnios* applies to the future punishment of the wicked, it indisputably denotes endless duration (Mt 18:8; 25:41, 46; Mk 3:29; 2Th 1:9; Heb 6:2; Jude 7).

Hell is, therefore, both a *condition* of retribution and a *place* in which the retribution occurs. In both of these aspects, the three basic ideas associated with the concept of hell are reflected: absence of righteousness, separation from God, and judgment.

The absence of personal righteousness, with its correlative of the presence of personal unrighteousness, renders the individual unable to enter a right relationship with the holy God (Mk 3:29). The eternal state of the wicked, therefore, will involve a separation from the presence of God (Jn 3:36). The concept of judgment is heightened by the note of finality in the warnings against sin (Mt 8:12). It is a judgment, however, against the sinful nature of humans — still unredeemed though Christ died — (25:31 – 46) and is decisive and irreversible.

When all else has been said about hell, however, there is still the inescapable fact taught by Scripture that it will be a retributive judgment on the *spirit* of man, the inner essence of his being. The severity of the judgment will be on the fixed character of a person's essential nature — his soul, which will involve eternal loss in exclusion from Christ's kingdom and fellowship with God.

In the NIV, "hell" usually translates the Greek *geenna* and *hādēs*, but is conceptually the same as the Hebrew *Sheol*, usually rendered "grave," the unseen world and abode of the dead (Ge 37:35; 42:38; 44:29, 31; Dt 32:22; 1Sa 2:6; 2Sa 22:6; 1Ki 2:6, 9; Job 7:9; 11:8; 14:13; 17:13; 21:13; 24:19; 26:6; Pss 9:17; 16:10; 18:5; 55:15; 86:13; 116:3; 139:8; Pr 5:5; 7:27; 9:18; 15:11, 24; 23:14; 27:20; Isa 5:14; 14:9, 15; 28:15, 18; 57:9; Eze 31:16 – 17; 32:21, 27; Am 9:2; Jnh 2:2; Hab 2:5). In the NT hell is the unseen world (Mt 11:23; 16:18; Lk 10:15; 16:23; Ac 2:27, 31; Rev 1:18; 6:8; 20:13 – 14), a place of torment (Mt 5:22, 29 – 30; 10:28; 18:9; 23:15, 33; Lk 12:5; Jas 3:6) and of captivity for fallen angels (2Pe 2:4).

Figurative:

Of divine judgments (Dt 32:22; Eze 31:15 – 17).

The Future State, or Abode, of the Wicked:

(Ps 9:17; Pr 5:5; 9:18; 15:24; 23:14; Isa 30:33; 33:14; Mt 3:12; 5:22, 29 – 30; 7:13; 8:11 – 12; 10:28; 13:30, 38 – 42, 49 – 50; 16:18; 18:8 – 9, 34 – 35; 22:13; 25:30, 41, 46; Mk 9:43 – 48; Lk 3:17; 16:23 – 28; Ac 1:25; 2Th 1:9; 2Pe 2:4; Jude 6, 23; Rev 2:11; 9:1 – 2; 11:7; 14:10 – 11; 19:20; 20:10, 15; 21:8).

Mt	5:22	will be in danger of the fire of **h**.
	10:28	destroy both soul and body in **h**.
	18:9	and be thrown into the fire of **h**.
	23:15	as much a son of **h** as you are.
	23:33	you escape being condemned to **h**?
Mk	9:43	than with two hands to go into **h**,
Lk	12:5	has power to throw you into **h**.
	16:23	In **h**, where he was in torment,
Jas	3:6	and is itself set on fire by **h**.
2Pe	2:4	but sent them to **h**, putting them

HERESY [146] (hăr′ĕ·sē̆ Gr. *hairēsis*, *sect*, *heretical group or opinion*, from *haireō*, *to choose*). A doctrine or group considered contrary to correct doctrine — from the Jewish (Ac 24:14; cf. 28:22) or Christian (2Pe 2:1) perspective.

HERMES [2258] (possibly *rock*, *cairn*).

1. Greek god (messenger), the same as Mercury in Latin, whom Paul was mistaken for (Ac 14:12).

2. Friend of Paul in the church at Rome (Ro 16:14).

HEROD [2476]. Idumean rulers of Israel (37 BC to AD 100). Line started with Antipater, whom Julius Caesar made procurator of Judea in 47 BC.

1. Herod the Great, first procurator of Galilee, then king of the Jews (37 – 4 BC); built Caesarea, temple at Jerusalem; slaughtered children at Bethlehem (Mt 2:1 – 18). At his death his kingdom was divided among his three sons: Archelaus, Herod Antipas, and Philip.

2. Archelaus ruled over Judea, Samaria, and Idumea (4 BC to AD 6), and was removed from office by the Romans (Mt 2:22).

3. Herod Antipas ruled over Galilee and Perea (4 BC to AD 39); killed John the Baptist (Mt 14:1 – 12); called "fox" by Jesus (Lk 13:32).

4. Philip, tetrarch of Batanaea, Trachonitis, Gaulanitis, and parts of Jamnia (4 BC to AD 34). Best of the Herods.

5. Herod Agrippa I; grandson of Herod the Great; tetrarch of Galilee; king of Israel (AD 37 – 44); killed James the apostle (Ac 12:1 – 23).

6. Herod Agrippa II. King of territory east of Galilee (AD 50 – 100); Paul appeared before him (Ac 25:13 – 26:32).

HERODIAS [2478] (hĕrō'dĭ-ăs, Gr. *Hērōdias*; feminine form of Herod). A wicked granddaughter of Herod the Great who married her uncle Philip; but his brother Antipas saw her at Rome, desired her, and married her. John the Baptist reproved Herod Antipas for his immoral action (Lk 3:19 – 20) and was put in prison for his temerity (Mt 14:3 – 12; Mk 6:14 – 29). This did not satisfy Herodias, so by a sordid scheme she secured his death. Later Antipas was banished to Spain. Herodias accompanied him and died there.

HEZEKIAH [2624, 2625, 3490, 3491, 1614] (hĕz'ē-kī'a, Heb. *hizqîyâh*, *Jehovah has strengthened*). King of Judah for twenty-nine years, from c. 724 to 695 BC. The record of his life is found in 2Ki 18 – 20; 2Ch 29 – 32; and Isa 36 – 39. He lived in one of the great periods of human history. The first Olympiad from which the Greeks dated their history occurred in 776; Rome was reputed to have been founded in 753; Assyria, though approaching its end, was still a mighty power; and Egypt, though weak, was still strong enough to oppose Assyria. Judah's position, on the main road between Egypt and Assyria, was a very precarious one. Hezekiah's grandfather Jotham reigned at Jerusalem (755 – 739) when Hezekiah was a child, and though he was in some ways a good king, he allowed the people to sacrifice and burn incense in the high places. Because of Judah's growing apostasy, the Lord permitted the Syrians and the northern kingdom to trouble Jerusalem. In Hezekiah's youth and early manhood, his weak and wicked father Ahaz was king. He went so far as to follow the abominable rites of the Moabites by burning children in the fire (2Ch 28:3), in spite of the warnings of the prophets Hosea, Micah, and Isaiah. At this time, when Israel and Syria were threatening Judah, God gave through Isaiah the famous "virgin birth" prophecy (Isa 7:14). For a while Hezekiah was associated in the government with his father, but because of his father's incapaci-

tation he was made active ruler. He began his reign, at the age of twenty-five, in troubled and threatening times. Some counseled him to side with Egypt against Assyria; others favored surrender to Assyria to save themselves from Egypt. Isaiah warned against trusting in foreign alliances. One of the first acts of Hezekiah was the cleansing and reopening of the temple, which his father had left closed and desecrated. After this was accomplished, the Passover feast was celebrated (2Ch 30). The idolatrous altars and high places were destroyed

From the fourth to the sixth year of Hezekiah's reign, the northern kingdom was in trouble. Sargon finally destroyed Samaria and deported the people to Assyria. Hezekiah became ill, probably from a carbuncle, and almost died; but God granted him a fifteen-year extension of life (2Ki 20:1 – 11). After Hezekiah's recovery, Merodach-Baladan of Babylon sent an embassy ostensibly to congratulate him, but actually to persuade him to join a secret confederacy against the Assyrian power. This was the great crisis for Hezekiah, and indeed for Judah. During his illness he had received from God not only the promise of recovery, but also the pledge that the Lord would deliver Jerusalem from the Assyrians (Isa 38:6 – 7). The ambassadors of Merodach-Baladan were intent also on freeing Jerusalem from the Assyrians — but by force of arms and the power of a military alliance. The question facing Hezekiah was therefore whether to walk the way of faith that the Lord would keep his promise or to take the way of "works," setting out to liberate the city by his own abilities and clever policies. When Isaiah learned that Hezekiah had entertained the ambassadors and their suggestion, he knew that all was over for Judah and immediately (39:5 – 7) predicted the Babylonian captivity. Hezekiah paid a high price for dabbling in rebellion. Assyria compelled Judah to pay heavy tribute; and to obtain it, Hezekiah even had to strip the plating from the doors and pillars of the temple. Shortly after, Assyria decided to destroy Jerusalem, but God saved the city by sending a sudden plague that in one night killed 185,000 soldiers. After Hezekiah's death, his son Manasseh succeeded him (2Ki 20:21).

> *Religious zeal of (2Ch 29; 30; 31); Purges the nation of idolatry (2Ki 18:4; 2Ch 31:1; 33:3); Restores the true forms of worship (2Ch 31:2 – 21); His piety (2Ki 18:2, 5 – 6; 2Ch 29:2; 31:20 – 21; 32:32; Jer 26:19); Military operations of (2Ki 18:19; 1Ch 4:39 – 43; 2Ch 32; Isa 36; 37); Sickness and restoration of (2Ki 20:1 – 11; 2Ch 32:24; Isa 38:1 – 8); His psalm of thanksgiving (Isa 38:9 – 22); His lack of wisdom in showing his resources to commissioners of Babylon (2Ki 20:12 – 19; 2Ch 32:25 – 26, 31; Isa 39); Prospered of God (2Ki 18:7; 2Ch 32:27 – 30); Conducts the Brook Gihon into Jerusalem (2Ki 18:17; 20:20; 2Ch 32:4, 30; 33:14; Ne 2:13 – 15; 3:13, 16; Isa 7:3; 22:9 – 11; 36:2); Scribes of (Pr 25:1); Death and burial of (2Ki 20:21; 2Ch 32:33); Prophecies concerning (2Ki 19:20 – 34; 20:5 – 6, 16 – 18; Isa 38:5 – 8; 39:5 – 7; Jer 26:18 – 19); One of the exiles (Ezr 2:16; Ne 7:21; 10:17); An ancestor of the prophet Zephaniah (Zep 1:1)*

HIGH PLACES [1195] (Heb. *bāmâh, rāmâh, elevation*). It seems to be inherent in human nature to think of God as dwelling in the heights. From earliest times people have tended to choose high places for their worship, whether of the true God or of the false gods people have invented. The reason for this is that the so-called gods were in fact the barely personified forces of nature; they were empty of moral character, and therefore one could not appeal to them in the same sense as one could appeal to the God of Israel. They had made no promises and extended no covenant to their people. All, therefore, that the worshipers could do was choose an exposed site where the "god" was likely to see what they were doing and to perform there some act comparable to what they wished their god to do for them. *See also Baal.* In Canaan the high places had become the scenes of orgies and human sacrifice connected with the idolatrous worship of

these imaginary gods; and so, when Israel entered the Promised Land, they were told, "Drive out all the inhabitants of the land before you. Destroy all their carved images and their cast idols, and demolish all their high places" (Nu 33:52). Figured stones were covered with crude carvings, sometimes more or less like geometrical figures, or with talismans or other signs presumably understood by the priests and used to mystify or terrorize the worshipers. Israel partly obeyed but largely failed in this work.

> **General References to:**
> *Term used to describe places of worship (Ge 12:8; 22:2, 14; 31:54; 1Sa 9:12; 2Sa 24:25; 1Ki 3:2, 4; 18:30, 38; 1Ch 16:39; 2Ch 1:3; 33:17). Term used to signify a place of idolatrous worship (Nu 22:41; 1Ki 11:7; 12:31; 14:23; 15:14; 22:43; 2Ki 17:9, 29; Jer 7:31). Licentious practices at (Eze 16:24 – 43). The idolatrous, to be destroyed (Lev 26:30; Nu 33:52). Destroyed by Asa (2Ch 14:3); Jehoshaphat; (2Ch 17:6); Hezekiah (2Ki 18:4); Josiah (2Ki 23:8).*

HIGH PRIEST *See Priest.*

HINNOM, VALLEY OF [2183]. More properly, "the valley of the son of Hinnom," running southward from the Jaffa Gate at the west side of Jerusalem, then turning eastward and running south of the city until it joined the valley of the Kidron. It was a part of the boundary between Judah on the south (Jos 15:8) and Benjamin on the north (18:16). Nothing is known of the "son of Hinnom" except that he lived before Joshua's time and presumably owned the valley. It seems to have been a dumping ground and a place for burning. Topheth was here (2Ki 23:10), where human sacrifices had been offered to Molech, and so it was later to be called "the Valley of Slaughter" (Jer 19:6). The Hebrew name, transliterated into Greek as *geenna* (or *gehenna*), becomes the word for "hell." Jesus uses it in referring to the final destination of the wicked; and probably "the fiery lake of burning sulfur" (Rev 19:20; 20:10, 14 – 15; 21:8) is a description of the same terrible place. That the mythological name Tartarus was also used is implied in 2Pe 2:4, where Peter uses a verb derived from Tartarus to mean "to cast down to hell." *See also Gehenna.*

General References to:
A valley west and SW of Jerusalem (Jos 15:8; 18:16; 2Ki 23:10; Ne 11:30). Children offered in sacrifice in (2Ch 28:3; 33:6; Jer 7:31 – 32; 19:2, 4, 6; 32:35). Possibly valley of vision identical with (Isa 22:1, 5).

HITTITES [3147, 3153] (hĭt'ïts, Heb. *hittîm, descendants of Heth*). With the Mesopotamians and Egyptians (2Ki 7:6), they were one of the three great powers confronting early Israel. The biblical portrayals of Hittite dominance, once held to be unreliable, were first substantiated by discoveries at Carchemish on the Euphrates in AD 1871 and then totally vindicated by Hugo Winckler's excavations at Khattusa (Boghaz-köy) in Turkey, 1906 – 07. Ten thousand tablets from this ancient Hittite capital served to confirm Joshua's description of the entire western Fertile Crescent as "all the Hittite country" (Jos 1:4).

The original Hittites, or "Hattians," sprang from Ham, through Canaan's second son, Heth (Ge 10:15; 1Ch 1:13), and became established by the mid-third millennium BC along the Halys River in what is now central Turkey. The Hittite dress of heavy coats and turned-up-toed shoes reflected the rugged cold of this Anatolian plateau. From some time after 2200 the Hattians were overrun by a vigorous Indo-European – speaking people from the north. They became Heth's ruling class, while adapting the older and often immoral Hittite culture.

Ancient monuments depict the Hittites as a stocky people with prominent noses, retreating foreheads, and thick lips. The Hittite strain became widely diffused throughout Palestine along with that of the Hurrians, whose Aryan rulers had assumed the leadership of upper Mesopotamia at about this same time. Scripture thus regularly lists "Hittites" among the peoples of Canaan (Ge 15:20; Ex 3:8, 17; Dt 7:1;

20:17). They were "the people of the land" (Ge 23:7), especially in the central hills (Nu 13:29; Jos 11:3).

A tribe of Canaanites. Sons of Heth (Ge 10:15; 23:3 n., 5, 7, 10, 16, 18); Sell a burial site to Abraham (Ge 23); Esau intermarries with (Ge 26:34; 36:2); Hill country dwelling place of (Ge 23:17 – 20; Nu 13:29; Jos 1:4; Jdg 1:26); Their land given to the Israelites (Ex 3:8; Dt 7:1; Jos 1:4); Conquered by Joshua (Jos 9:1 – 2; 10; 11; 12; 24:11); Intermarry with Israelites (Jdg 3:5 – 7; Ezr 9:1); Solomon intermarries with (1Ki 11:1; Ne 13:26); Pay tribute to Solomon (1Ki 9:20 – 21); Retain their own kings (1Ki 10:29; 2Ki 7:6; 2Ch 1:17); Officers from, in David's army (1Sa 26:6; 2Sa 11:3; 23:39)

HOLINESS, HOLY [7705, 7727, 7731, 10620, 39, 40, 41, 42, 43, 605, 4008, 4009, 4949]. Usually translations of words derived from a Hebrew root *qadash* and Greek *hag-*. The basic meaning of *qadash* is "separateness, withdrawal." It is first applied to God and is early associated with ideas of purity and righteousness. Long before the prophetic period the ethical content is plain. Greek *hag-* is an equivalent of *qadash*, and its history is similar. Beginning as an attribute of deity, the *hag-* family of words developed two stems, one meaning "holy," the other "pure." The use of words of this family in the LXX to translate the *qadash* family resulted in a great development of their ethical sense, which was never clear in classical Greek. What became increasingly evident in the OT is overwhelmingly explicit in the NT: that holiness means the pure, loving nature of God, separate from evil, aggressively seeking to universalize itself; that this character is inherent in places, times, and institutions intimately associated with worship; and that holiness is to characterize human beings who have entered into personal relationship with God.

Attribute of God:
(Jos 24:19; 1Sa 6:20; Job 6:10; Pss 22:3; 47:8; 60:6; 89:35; 111:9; 145:17; Isa 5:16; 6:3; 29:19, 23; 41:14; 43:14 – 15; 47:4; 49:7; 57:15; Eze 36:21 – 22;

39:7, 25; Hos 11:9; Hab 1:12 – 13; Lk 1:49; Jn 17:11; Ro 1:23; Rev 4:8; 6:10; 15:4).

Described:

(Ro 14:17). As walking in uprightness (Isa 57:2); as a highway (Isa 35:8); as departing from evil (Pss 34:14; 37:27); as satisfying (Jn 6:35); as crucifying the sinful nature (Gal 5:24); as a new creature (Gal 6:15); as a new self (Eph 4:24; Col 3:10); as a rest (Heb 4:3, 9); as pure, peaceable, gentle (Jas 3:17).

Commanded:

(Ge 17:1; Ex 22:31; Lev 10:8 – 10; 11:44 – 45; 19:2; 20:7, 26; Nu 15:40; Dt 13:17; 18:13; Jos 7:13; 2Ch 20:21; Job 5:24; Pss 4:4; 97:10; Isa 52:1, 11; Mic 6:8; Zep 2:3; Mt 5:19 – 30, 48; 12:33; Jn 5:14; Ro 6:1 – 23; 1Co 3:16; 5:7; 15:34; 2Co 6:14 – 17; 7:1; Eph 1:4; 5:1, 3, 8 – 11; 1Th 4:3 – 4, 7; 5:22 – 23; 2Th 2:13; 1Ti 4:12; 5:22; 6:11 – 12; 2Ti 2:19, 21 – 22; 1Pe 1:5; 2Pe 1:5 – 8; 1Jn 2:1, 5, 29; 2Jn 4; Rev 18:4). Commanded upon Israel (Ex 19:6; 22:31; Dt 7:6; 26:19; 28:9; Isa 4:3; 52:1, 11; 60:1, 21; Zec 8:3; 14:20 – 21). Commanded upon the church (2Co 11:2; 1Pe 2:5, 9; Rev 19:8).

Exhortations to:

(Mt 5:30; Jn 5:14; Ro 6:13, 19; 12:1 – 2; 13:12 – 14; 1Co 6:13, 19 – 20; 10:31; 2Co 13:7 – 8; Eph 4:22 – 24; Col 3:5, 12 – 15; 1Th 2:12; 3:13; 1Ti 4:12; Tit 2:9 – 10, 12; 1Pe 4:1; 2Pe 3:11 – 12, 14; 3Jn 11).

Motives to:

God's holiness (Ge 17:1; Lev 11:44 – 45; 19:2; 20:26; Isa 6:1 – 8; Mt 5:48; 1Pe 1:15 – 16). God's mercies (Ro 12:1).

Taught:

By figures (Isa 61:9 – 11; Mt 12:33; 1Co 3:17; Eph 2:21). By inscriptions (Ex 28:36; Zec 14:20). By disfellowship: of the uncircumcised (Ge 17:14); of those who violated the law, of unleavened bread (Ex 12:15); of sacrifices (Lev 17:9; 19:5 – 7); of purification (Nu 19:20); of those who were defiled (Lev 7:25, 27; 13:5, 21, 26; 17:10; 18:29; 19:8; 20:3 – 6; Nu 5:2 – 3; 19:13); of

those who were guilty of blasphemy (Nu 15:31). As a condition of fellowship (Heb 12:14).

Typified:

In unblemished offerings (Ex 12:5; Lev 1:3, 10; 3:1, 6; 4:3, 23; 5:15; 6:6; 9:2 – 3; 22:19, 21; Nu 28:3, 9, 11, 19, 31; 29:2, 8, 13, 17, 20, 23, 26, 29, 32, 36); in washing of offerings (Lev 1:9, 13); in washing of priests (Ex 29:4; Lev 8:6; 1Ch 15:14); in washing of garments (Lev 11:28, 40; 13:6, 34; 14:8 – 9, 47; 15:5 – 13; Nu 19:7 – 8, 10, 19, 21); in purifications (Lev 12:4, 6 – 8; 15:16 – 18, 21 – 22, 27; 16:4, 24, 26, 28; 17:15 – 16). By differentiating between clean and unclean animals (Lev 11:1 – 47; 20:25; Dt 14:3 – 20).

Ex	15:11	majestic in **h**,
Dt	32:51	because you did not uphold my **h**
1Ch	16:29	the Lord in the splendor of his **h**.
Ps	29:2	in the splendor of his **h**.
	89:35	Once for all, I have sworn by my **h**
Isa	29:23	they will acknowledge the **h**
	35:8	it will be called the Way of **H**.
Eze	36:23	I will show the **h** of my great name,
Am	4:2	Lord has sworn by his **h**:
Lk	1:75	fear in **h** and righteousness
Ro	1:4	the Spirit of **h** was declared
	6:19	to righteousness leading to **h**.
1Co	1:30	our righteousness, **h**
2Co	1:12	in the **h** and sincerity that are
Eph	4:24	God in true righteousness and **h**.
1Ti	2:2	quiet lives in all godliness and **h**.
	2:15	love and **h** with propriety.
Heb	12:10	that we may share in his **h**.
	12:14	without **h** no one will see the Lord.

HOLY

Ge	2:3	the seventh day and made it **h**,
Ex	3:5	you are standing is **h** ground."
	19:6	kingdom of priests and a **h** nation.'
	26:33	Place from the Most **H** Place.
	31:13	I am the Lord, who makes you **h**.
Lev	10:3	I will show myself **h**;
	11:44	and be **h**, because I am **h**.

	19:8	he has desecrated what is **h**
	20:7	" 'Consecrate yourselves and be **h**,
	22:32	Do not profane my **h** name.
	25:12	For it is a jubilee and is to be **h**
	27:9	given to the LORD becomes **h**.
Dt	5:12	the Sabbath day by keeping it **h**,
	23:14	Your camp must be **h**,
	26:15	from heaven, your **h** dwelling place
Jos	5:15	place where you are standing is **h**."
	24:19	He is a **h** God; he is a jealous God.
1Sa	2:2	"There is no one **h** like the LORD;
1Ch	16:10	Glory in his **h** name;
	29:3	I have provided for this **h** temple:
2Ch	30:27	heaven, his **h** dwelling place.
Ezr	9:2	and have mingled the **h** race
Ne	11:1	the **h** city, while the remaining nine
Job	6:10	not denied the words of the **H** One.
Ps	2:6	King on Zion, my **h** hill."
	11:4	The LORD is in his **h** temple;
	16:10	will you let your **H** One see decay.
	30:4	praise his **h** name.
	78:54	to the border of his **h** land,
	111:9	**h** and awesome is his name.
Pr	9:10	of the **H** One is understanding.
Isa	5:16	the **h** God will show himself **h**
	6:3	H, **h**, **h** is the LORD Almighty;
	54:5	**H** One of Israel is your Redeemer;
Eze	20:41	I will show myself **h** among you
Hab	2:20	But the LORD is in his **h** temple;
Zec	14:5	and all the **h** ones with him.
	14:20	On that day **h** to the LORD
Mt	24:15	in the **h** place 'the abomination
Lk	1:35	the **h** one to be born will be called
Jn	6:69	and know that you are the **H** One
Ac	2:27	will you let your **H** One see decay.
Ro	1:2	prophets in the **H** Scriptures
	7:12	and the commandment is **h**,
	12:1	as living sacrifices, **h** and pleasing
1Co	1:2	in Christ Jesus and called to be **h**,
	7:14	be unclean, but as it is, they are **h**.
Eph	1:4	the creation of the world to be **h**
	2:21	and rises to become a **h** temple
	3:5	by the Spirit to God's **h** apostles

	5:3	improper for God's **h** people.
	5:26	up for her to make her **h**,
Col	1:22	death to present you **h** in his sight,
1Th	2:10	and so is God, of how **h**,
	4:7	us to be impure, but to live a **h** life.
2Th	1:10	to be glorified in his **h** people
1Ti	2:8	to lift up **h** hands in prayer,
2Ti	1:9	saved us and called us to a **h** life —
	2:21	for noble purposes, made **h**,
	3:15	you have known the **h** Scriptures,
Heb	2:11	Both the one who makes men **h**
	7:26	one who is **h**, blameless, pure,
	10:10	we have been made **h**
	10:19	to enter the Most **H** Place
	13:12	gate to make the people **h**
1Pe	1:15	But just as he who called you is **h**,
	2:5	house to be a **h** priesthood,
	3:5	For this is the way the **h** women
2Pe	3:11	You ought to live **h** and godly lives
Jude	1:14	upon thousands of his **h** ones
Rev	3:7	are the words of him who is **h**
	4:8	"**H**, **h**, **h** is the Lord God
	15:4	For you alone are **h**.
	20:6	and **h** are those who have part

HOLY OF HOLIES *See Tabernacle.*

HOLY SPIRIT [7731+8120, 41+4460] (Gr. *pneuma hagion*; in KJV of NT, Holy Ghost). The third person of the triune Godhead (Mt 28:19; 2Co 13:14).

There is a rich revelation of the Spirit of the Lord in the OT, running along the same lines as that in the NT and directly preparatory to it. Customarily we think of the Spirit of God in the OT as powerfully endowing chosen individuals for great tasks, but actually his work ranges much more widely. First, we notice that the Spirit is God's agent in creation (e.g., Ge 1:1; Pss 33:6; 104:30). For animals (Isa 34:16) and humans (Job 27:3) alike (cf. Isa 42:5), created life is the work of the Holy Spirit. Second, the Spirit is the agent in the providential work of God in the moral sphere, the areas of history and ethical relationships. Though the actual translation of Ge 6:3 is uncertain, it is by his Spirit that God senses and reacts to wickedness on earth. In Eze 1:14, 20 the Spirit is the power by which the sovereign God controls the complexities of life on earth (cf. Isa 4:4; 30:1; 63:14). Godly people know that their sin offends the Holy One, and they fear quenching the Spirit (Ps 51:11) — this is the form that the Lord's judgment on the disobedient Saul took (1Sa 16:14). Third, the Spirit is known in the OT as a personal endowment. He indwells the people of God as a whole (Hag 2:5), just as he was among them at the exodus (Isa 63:11). He endowed Bezalel for artistic skill (Ex 31:3) and many others for mighty deeds (Jdg 3:10 and 6:34, literally "clothed himself with Gideon"; 11:29; 13:25; 1Sa 11:6). These references correspond to what the NT speaks of as the "filling" of the Spirit, that is, special endowment for a special task (cf. Ac 4:8); but there is also the constant endowment of individuals (Nu 11:17, 29; 27:18; 1Sa 16:13), especially those individuals who stood directly in the great messianic line (Isa 11:2; 42:1; 48:16; 61:1). The OT, indeed, looks forward to the messianic day as a time of special enjoyment of the Spirit of God (Isa 32:15; 44:3; 59:21; Eze 36:27; 39:29; Joel 2:28 – 29). The verb "to pour out" is notable in these references and points to a hitherto unknown abundance. Fourth, the Spirit inspired the prophets (Nu 11:29; 24:2; 1Sa 10:6, 10; 2Sa 23:2; 1Ki 22:24; Ne 9:30; Hos 9:7; Joel 2:28 – 29; Mic 3:8; Zec 7:12). In all these references the personality of the Spirit is notable.

Moreover, the Spirit is wise (Isa 40:13; cf. 11:2; Da 4:8 – 9, 18), he is vexed by sin and rebellion (Isa 63:10), and he is at rest when sin has been dealt with (Zec 6:8). He is holy (Ps 51:13; Isa 63:10) and good (Ne 9:20; Ps 143:10). We note that this is the same sort of evidence that we would adduce from the NT for holding that the Spirit of God is "he," not "it." But like the NT, the OT goes further. Psalm 139:7 shows that the Spirit is the very presence of God himself in all the world. The Spirit of God is God himself actually present and in operation. In Isa 63:10, when the people vex the Spirit, God becomes their enemy; in 63:14 the work of the Spirit giving rest is parallel to the act of God leading his people.

The ascription of holiness (e.g., Ps 51:13) accords to the Spirit the character and personality of God.

That the Holy Spirit has power and influence is plain from Ac 1:8; that he is a person, the NT makes clear in detail: he dwells with us (Jn 14:17), teaches and brings to remembrance (14:26), bears witness (15:26), convinces of sin (16:8), guides, speaks, declares (16:13, 15), inspires the Scriptures and speaks through them (Ac 1:16; 2Pe 1:21), speaks to his servants, (Ac 8:29), calls ministers (13:2), sends out workers (13:4), forbids certain actions (16:6 – 7), and intercedes (Ro 8:26). He has the attributes of personality: love (Ro 15:30), will (1Co 12:11), mind (Ro 8:27), thought, knowledge, words (1Co 2:10 – 13). The Holy Spirit can be treated as one may treat a human person: he can be lied to and tempted (Ac 5:3 – 4, 9), resisted (7:51), grieved (Eph 4:30), outraged (Heb 10:29 RSV), blasphemed against (Mt 12:31). The Holy Spirit is God, equated with the Father and the Son (Mt 28:19; 2Co 13:14). Jesus speaks of him as of his other self (Jn 14:16 – 17), whose presence with the disciples will be of greater advantage than his own (16:7). To have the Spirit of God is to have Christ (Ro 8:9 – 12). God is spirit in essential nature (Jn 4:24) and sends his Holy Spirit to live and work in people (14:26; 16:7).

The Hebrew and Greek words translated "spirit" are *rûach* and *pneuma*, both meaning literally "wind, breath." Both came to be used for the unseen reality of living beings, especially God and humans. Therefore, breath and wind are symbols of the Holy Spirit (Ge 2:7; Job 32:8; 33:4; Eze 37:9 – 10; Jn 20:22). Other symbols are the dove (Mt 3:16; Mk 1:10; Lk 3:22; Jn 1:32), oil (Lk 4:18; Ac 10:38; 1Jn 2:20), fire for purification (Mt 3:11; Lk 3:16; Ac 2:3 – 4), living water (Isa 44:3; Jn 4:14; 7:37 – 39), and earnest or guarantee of all that God has in store for us (2Co 1:22; Eph 1:13 – 14). In the OT the Spirit of God appears from the beginning (Ge 1:2); God calls him his Spirit (6:3); and the Spirit of God comes on certain people for special purposes (e.g., Bezalel, Ex 31:3; some judges, Jdg 3:10; 6:34; 11:29; David, 1Sa 16:13). This kind of endowment was temporary (e.g., Saul, 1Sa 10:10; 16:14); so David, repentant, prayed, "Do not … take your Holy Spirit from me" (Ps 51:11). The Spirit of God came "upon" the Messiah (Isa 11:2; 42:1; 61:1). God acts by his Spirit (Zec 4:6). (For the meaning of "holy" *see Holiness*.)

In the Gospels, as in the OT, the Holy Spirit comes upon certain people for special reasons: John the Baptist and his parents (Lk 1:15, 41, 67), Simeon (2:25 – 27), and Jesus as a man (Mt 1:18, 20; 3:16; 4:1; Mk 1:8, 10; Lk 1:35; 3:16, 22; 4:1, 14, 18; Jn 1:32 – 33). Jesus promises the Holy Spirit in a new way to those who believe in him (Jn 7:37 – 39; cf. 4:10 – 15); also as "what my Father has promised" in Lk 24:49; covered in fuller detail in Ac 1:1 – 8. Jesus taught the nature and work of the Holy Spirit in Jn 14:16, 26; 15:26; 16:7 – 15. This work is to dwell in the disciples as Comforter, Counselor, Advocate (Greek *paraklētos*); to teach all things; to help believers remember what Jesus said; to testify of Jesus; to reprove the world of sin, righteousness, and judgment; to guide the disciples into all truth; not to speak on his own initiative, but to speak only what he hears; to show the disciples things to come; and to glorify Jesus by showing the things of Jesus to the disciples. On the evening of the resurrection, Jesus "breathed on" the disciples (Thomas being absent) and said, "Receive the Holy Spirit" (Jn 20:22). This was not the complete enduement of the Holy Spirit that Jesus had taught and promised and that occurred at Pentecost, but it was provisional and enabled the disciples to persevere in prayer until the promised day.

At Pentecost a new phase of the revelation of God to people began (Ac 2) — as new as when the Word became flesh in the birth of Jesus. With the rushing of a mighty wind and what appeared to be tongues of fire, the disciples were all filled with the Holy Spirit and spoke in foreign languages (listed in 2:9 – 11). The excitement drew a crowd of visitors to the feast, to whom Peter explained that the prophecy of Joel 2:28 – 32 was being fulfilled in accordance with the salvation that Jesus of Nazareth had accomplished by dying on the cross. Another 3,000 souls were added by baptism to the 120 disciples,

and thus began the fellowship of apostolic teaching, of breaking of bread and of prayer, the fellowship that is the church. When the first crisis that threatened the extinction of the early church was passed, again "they were all filled with the Holy Spirit" (Ac 4:31), binding them more closely together. When the first Gentiles were converted, the Holy Spirit was poured out on them and they spoke in tongues (10:44 – 48); likewise when Paul met a group of John the Baptist's disciples, the Holy Spirit came on them (19:1 – 7).

The NT is full of the work of the Holy Spirit in the lives of believers (Ro 8:1 – 27); for example, he gives gifts (1Co 12:14), our "body is a temple of the Holy Spirit" (6:19), and he works in us "the fruit of the Spirit" (Gal 5:22 – 23). Being "filled with the Spirit" (Eph 5:18) means that one experiences Christ living within (Ro 8:9 – 10). As the heavenly Father is God and his Son Jesus Christ is God, so the Holy Spirit is God. The Holy Spirit as well as the Son was active in creation; he was active on certain occasions in his own person in OT times and more intensively in the Gospels; and in Acts and the Epistles he becomes the resident divine agent in the church and in its members. Teaching concerning the Holy Spirit has been both neglected and distorted, but the subject deserves careful attention as one reads the NT.

Activities:

Convinces of sin (Ge 6:3; Jn 16:8 – 11). Comforts (Jn 14:16 – 17, 26; 15:26; 16:7 – 14; Ac 9:31). Guides (Jn 16:13; Ac 13:2 – 4; 15:8, 28; 16:6 – 7; Ro 8:4, 14; Gal 5:16, 18, 25). Helps our infirmities (Ro 8:26). Regenerates (Jn 3:5 – 6; 2Co 3:3, 18; Tit 3:5 – 6). Sanctifies (Ro 15:16; 1Co 6:11; 2Th 2:13; 1Pe 1:2). Dwells in believers (Ro 8:11). Invites to salvation (Rev 22:17). Communion with (2Co 13:14; Php 2:1). Given to every Christian (1Co 12:7). Given in answer to prayer (Lk 11:13; Ac 8:15); through laying on of hands (Ac 8:17 – 19; 19:6). Access to the Father by (Eph 2:18). Prayer in (Eph 6:18; Jude 20). Wisdom and strength from (Ne 9:20; Zec 4:6; Eph 3:16). Liberty from (2Co 3:17). Love of God given by (Ro 5:5). Ministers commissioned by (Ac 20:28). Christian baptism in the name of, with the name of Father and Son (Mt 28:19). Gospel preached in power of (1Co 2:4, 10; 1Th 1:5; 1Pe 1:12). Word of God, sword of (Eph 6:17). Water, a symbol of (Jn 7:38–39). Demons cast out by (Mt 12:28). Power to bestow, not for sale (Ac 8:18–20). Poured upon: Israel (Isa 32:15; Eze 39:29); the Gentiles (Ac 10:19–20, 44–47; 11:15–16); all people (Joel 2:28–29; Ac 2:17).

Jesus and the Spirit:

Conception of Jesus by (Mt 1:20; Lk 1:35). Jesus anointed and led by (Isa 61:1; Mt 3:16; 4:1; Mk 1:10; Lk 3:22; 4:18; Jn 1:32–33; Ac 10:38; Heb 9:14). Sent in Jesus'name (Jn 14:15–17; 15:26).

Christians:

Are temples of (1Co 3:16; 6:19). Are filled with (Ac 2:4, 33; 4:8, 31; 6:5; 8:17; 11:24; 13:9, 52; Eph 5:18; 2Ti 1:14). Have fellowship with (Ro 8:9, 11; 1Co 3:16; 6:19; 2Co 13:14; Php 2:1). Receive deposit of (2Co 1:22; 5:5; Eph 1:13–14). Are sealed with (2Co 1:22; Eph 1:13; 4:30). Have righteousness, peace, and joy in (Ro 14:17; 15:13; 1Th 1:6). Are unified by (1Co 12:13). Testifiy that Jesus is Lord by (Jn 15:26; 16:14; 1Co 12:3).

Baptism of:

(Mt 3:11; Mk 1:8; Lk 3:16; Jn 1:33; 20:22; Ac 1:5; 11:16; 19:2–6; 1Jn 2:20, 27).

Deity of:

See Trinity, Holy.

Emblems of:

Water: (Jn 3:5; 7:38–39); watering (Ps 1:3; Isa 27:3; 44:3–4; 58:11); refreshing (Ps 46:4; Isa 41:17–18); freely given to those who are thirsty (Isa 55:1; Jn 4:14; Rev 22:17); cleansing (Eze 16:9; 36:25; Eph 5:25–27; Heb 10:22); abundant (Jn 7:37–38).

Fire: as a guiding light as the Israelites traveled at night (Ex 13:21; Ps 78:14); purifying (Isa 4:4; Mal 3:2–3); searching (Zep 1:12, w 1Co 2:10).

Wind: powerful (1Ki 19:11, w Ac 2:2); reviving (Eze 37:9–10, 14); independent (Jn 3:8); the coming of the promised Holy Spirit at Pentecost (Ac 2:2).

Oil: consecrating (Isa 61:1); comforting (Isa 61:3; Heb 1:9); illuminating (Mt 25:3–4; 1Jn 2:20, 27); healing (Lk 10:34; Jas 5:14).

Rain and dew: blessing (Ps 133:3; Hos 14:5); righteousness (Hos 10:12).

A dove (Mt 3:16).

A voice: guiding (Isa 30:21, w Jn 16:13); speaking through the Twelve as they were to go out (Mt 10:20); warning (Heb 3:7–11).

A seal: (Rev 7:2): authenticating (Jn 6:27; 2Co 1:22); securing (Eph 1:13–14; 4:30).

Tongues of fire: (Ac 2:3–4, 6–11).

Fruit of:

(Ro 8:23; Gal 5:22–23).

Gifts of:

Foretold (Isa 44:3; Joel 2:28–29). Of different kinds (1Co 12:4–6, 8–10, 28). Bestowed for the confirmation of the gospel (Ro 15:19; Heb 2:4). See Gifts from God.

Inspiration of:

(Mt 10:20; Mk 13:11; Lk 12:12; 1Co 2:4, 10–14; 1Ti 4:1). Instances of: Joseph (Ge 41:38); Bezalel (Ex 31:3; 35:31); seventy elders (Nu 11:17); Balaam (Nu 24:2); judges Othniel (Jdg 3:10), Gideon (Jdg 6:34), Jephthah (Jdg 11:29); King Saul (1Sa 11:6); King David (1Ch 28:11–12); the prophets (2Pe 1:21); Azariah (2Ch 15:1); Zechariah (2Ch 24:20); Zechariah (Lk 1:67); Elizabeth (Lk 1:41); Simeon (Lk 2:25–26); John the Baptist (Lk 1:15); the disciples (Ac 6:3; 7:55; 8:29; 9:17; 10:45).

Intercession of:

(Ro 8:26–27).

Power of:

Promised (Lk 24:49; Ac 1:8; 2:38); on Christ (Mt 12:28; Lk 4:14); on ministers (Ac 2:4; Ro 15:19); on the righteous (Ro 15:13; Eph 3:16).

Revelations from:

(Mk 12:36; Lk 2:26 – 27; Jn 16:13; 1Co 2:10 – 11; Eph 3:5; 1Ti 4:1; Heb 3:7; 2Pe 1:21; Rev 2:7, 11, 29; 14:13).

Sin against:

(Ac 8:18 – 22; 1Jn 5:16). By grieving (Isa 63:10 – 11, 14; Eph 4:30); bBy resisting (Ac 5:9; 7:51; Eph 4:30; 1Th 5:19; Heb 10:29); by blaspheming (Mt 12:31 – 32; Mk 3:29; Lk 12:10); by lying to (Ac 5:3).

Withdrawn from Unrepentant Sinners:

(Ge 6:3; Dt 32:30; Jer 7:29; Hos 4:17 – 18; 9:12; Ro 1:24, 26, 28). Instances of: Antediluvians (Ge 6:3 – 7); Israelites (Dt 1:42; 28:15 – 68; 31:17 – 18); Saul (1Sa 16:14; 18:12; 28:15 – 16; 2Sa 7:15).

Witness of:

(Ac 5:32; Ro 8:15 – 16; 9:1; 2Co 1:22; 5:5; Gal 4:6; Eph 1:13 – 14; Heb 10:15; 1Jn 3:24; 4:13; 5:6 – 8).

See Titles and Names: Of the Holy Spirit.

HONOR

Ex	20:12	"**H** your father and your mother,
Nu	20:12	trust in me enough to **h** me
	25:13	he was zealous for the **h** of his God
Dt	5:16	"**H** your father and your mother,
1Ch	29:12	Wealth and **h** come from you;
Ps	8:5	and crowned him with glory and **h**.
	45:11	**h** him, for he is your lord.
	84:11	the LORD bestows favor and **h**;
Pr	3:9	**H** the LORD with your wealth,
	3:35	The wise inherit **h**,
	15:33	and humility comes before **h**.
	20:3	It is to a man's **h** to avoid strife,
	25:27	is it honorable to seek one's own **h**.
Isa	29:13	and **h** me with their lips,
Jer	33:9	and **h** before all nations
Mt	13:57	own house is a prophet without **h**."
	15:4	'**H** your father and mother'
	15:8	These people **h** me with their lips,
	23:6	they love the place of **h** at banquets
Mk	6:4	own house is a prophet without **h**."
Lk	14:8	do not take the place of **h**,
Jn	5:23	that all may **h** the Son just
	7:18	does so to gain **h** for himself,
	12:26	My Father will **h** the one who
Ro	12:10	**H** one another above yourselves.
1Co	6:20	Therefore **h** God with your body.
Eph	6:2	"**H** your father and mother" —
1Ti	5:17	well are worthy of double **h**,
Heb	2:7	you crowned him with glory and **h**
Rev	4:9	**h** and thanks to him who sits

HOMOSEXUAL [3879, 780, 3434]. Sexual activity between members of the same sex is universally condemned in Scripture. Male homosexuality forbidden by law and punished by death (Lev 18:22; 20:13). Male and female homosexuality condemned (Ro 1:26). With other sexually immoral persons, excluded from the kingdom of God (1Co 6:9 – 11). Male shrine prostitution was practiced even in the temple (1Ki 14:24; 15:12; 2Ki 23:7). Male prostitutes also translates the derogatory term "dog" (Dt 23:17 – 18; possibly Rev 22:15). Instances of: the men of Sodom (Ge 19:4 – 5; Jude 7) and Gibeah (Jdg 19:22).

HOPE [344, 1059, 2675, 3498, 4438, 4440, 5223, 7595, 7747, 8432, 8433, 9214, 9347, 9536, 1623, 1639+1827, 1827, 1828, 2671, 3607, 4054, 4598]. A gift of the Holy Spirit that, with faith and love, is an essential characteristic of the Christian when prophecies, tongues, and knowledge pass away (1Co 13:8, 13). The Greek noun *elpis* and its related verb *elpizo*, usually rendered "hope," occur in the NT fifty-four and thirty-one times respectively. The biblical concept of hope is not mere expectation and desire, as in Greek literature, but includes trust, confidence, refuge in the God of hope (Ro 15:13). Christ in you is the hope of glory (Col 1:27). All creation hopes for redemption (Ro 8:19 – 25 RSV). Christ Jesus is our hope (1Ti 1:1 RSV, NIV). In 2Co 5:1 the first house (RSV, NIV "tent"; Greek "tent-house") is the physical body, the second house the resurrection body. The related Greek *oikos* also refers to a building (Mt 9:6 – 7, RSV, NIV "home"), but often to its inhabitants (Lk 19:9;

Ac 11:14, RSV, NIV "household") or to descendants (Mt 10:6; Lk 1:33) or to the temple (Mt 12:4; 21:13; Mk 2:26; 11:17; Lk 6:4; 11:51; 19:46; Jn 2:16, 17; Ac 2:47, 49).

Godly:

In God (Pss 31:24; 33:22; 38:15; 39:7; 43:5; 71:5, 14; 78:7; 130:7; 146:5; Jer 17:7; La 3:21, 24, 26; 1Pe 1:21). A helmet (1Th 5:8). An anchor (Heb 6:18 – 19). Joy in (Pr 10:28; Ro 5:2; 12:12; Heb 3:6). Of God's calling (Eph 1:18; 4:4). Of eternal life (Col 1:5 – 6, 23, 27; Tit 1:2; 2:13; 3:7; 1Pe 1:3, 13; 1Jn 3:3). Of the resurrection (Ac 23:6; 24:14 – 15; 26:6 – 7; 28:20). Deferred (Pr 13:12). Of wicked shall perish (Job 8:13; 11:20; 27:8; Pr 10:28; 11:7, 23).

Grounds of:

God's Word (Ps 119:74, 81; Ro 15:4). God's mercy (Ps 33:18). Jesus Christ (1Th 1:3; 1Ti 1:1).

Instances of:

(Job 31:24, 28; Pss 9:18; 16:9; 119:116; Pr 14:32; 23:18, 22; 24:14; Hos 2:15; Zec 9:12; Ro 4:18; 5:3 – 5; 15:13; 1Co 13:13; 2Co 3:12; Gal 5:5; Eph 2:12; Php 1:20; 2Th 2:16; Heb 6:11; 1Pe 3:15). See Faith.

Job	13:15	Though he slay me, yet will I **h**
Ps	25:3	No one whose **h** is in you
	33:17	A horse is a vain **h** for deliverance;
	33:18	on those whose **h** is
	42:5	Put your **h** in God,
	62:5	my **h** comes from him.
	119:74	for I have put my **h** in your word.
	130:7	O Israel, put your **h** in the LORD,
	146:5	whose **h** is in the LORD his God,
	147:11	who put their **h** in his unfailing love
Pr	13:12	**H** deferred makes the heart sick,
	23:18	There is surely a future **h** for you,
Isa	40:31	but those who **h** in the LORD
Jer	29:11	plans to give you **h** and a future.
La	3:21	and therefore I have **h**:
Ro	5:4	character; and character, **h**.
	12:12	Be joyful in **h**, patient in affliction,

	15:4	of the Scriptures we might have **h**.
	15:13	May the God of **h** fill you
1Co	13:13	now these three remain: faith, **h**
	15:19	for this life we have **h** in Christ,
Eph	2:12	without **h** and without God
Col	1:27	Christ in you, the **h** of glory.
1Th	1:3	and your endurance inspired by **h**
	5:8	and the **h** of salvation as a helmet.
1Ti	4:10	that we have put our **h**
	6:17	but to put their **h** in God,
Tit	1:2	resting on the **h** of eternal life,
	2:13	while we wait for the blessed **h** —
Heb	6:19	We have this **h** as an anchor
	10:23	unswervingly to the **h** we profess,
	11:1	faith is being sure of what we **h** for
1Jn	3:3	Everyone who has this **h**

HOPHNI (hŏf′nī, Heb. *hophnî*). A son of Eli, the high priest and judge who proved unworthy of his sacred offices (1Sa 1:3; 2:34; 4:4, 17). Hophni is always associated with his brother Phinehas. The two were partners in evil practices and brought a curse on their heads (2:34; 3:14). Both were killed at the battle of Aphek, and their death, coupled with the loss of the ark, caused the death of Eli (4:17 – 18). Both sons disgraced their priestly office by claiming and appropriating more than their share of the sacrifices (2:13 – 17) and by their immoral actions in the tabernacle (1Sa 2:22; Am 2:6 – 8).

HOREB (hō′rĕb, *drought, desert*). The mountain where Moses received his commission (Ex 3:1), where he brought water out of the rock (17:6), and where the people stripped off their ornaments in token of repentance (33:6). It was eleven days' journey from Kadesh Barnea (Dt 1:2) and was mentioned also in Dt 1:6, 19; 4:10, 15; 5:2; 9:8; 18:16; 1Ki 8:9; 2Ch 5:10; Ps 106:19; Mal 4:4, in connection with the journeys of Israel, the giving of the law, and events of the year in which the Israelites stayed nearby. Elijah fled here (1Ki 19:8). It is geographically indistinguishable from Sinai.

HOSANNA [6057] (hō-zăn'a, Heb. *hôsa'-nā'*, Gr. *hōsanna, save now*). Originally a prayer, "Save now, pray" (Ps 118:25), which had lost its primary meaning and become an exclamation of praise (Mt 21:9, 15; Mk 11:9 – 10; Jn 12:13). That it is transliterated instead of translated in three of the gospels (Luke omits it) is evidence of the change of meaning. Not that the Hebrew word no longer had any connection with salvation: the context, which is a reminiscence of Ps 118:25 – 26, if not a direct quotation from or allusion to it, shows that in its application to God the Father and to Jesus, hosanna was concerned with the messianic salvation.

Mt	21:9	"**H** in the highest!"
Mk	11:9	"**H**!"
Jn	12:13	"**H**!"

HOSEA [2107, 6060] (Heb. *hôshēa', salvation*). Of all the prophetic material contained in the OT, the writings of Hosea were the only ones to come from the northern kingdom of Israel. This notable eighth-century BC prophet lived during a period of great national anxiety. He was born during the reign of Jeroboam II (c. 786 – 746), the last great king of Israel, and according to the superscription of his book (Hos 1:1), he exercised his prophetic ministry in Israel when Uzziah (c. 783 – 743), Jotham (c. 742 – 735), Ahaz (c. 735 – 715), and Hezekiah (c. 715 – 686) reigned in Judah. While Hosea did not mention the events referred to in Isa 7:1 and 2Ki 16:5, in 733 he certainly experienced the raids of the Assyrian ruler Tiglath-Pileser III on Galilee and Transjordan.

The catalyst of Hosea's prophetic message is his marriage to a woman named Gomer. There are two major views of this relationship. The proleptic view holds that Gomer was pure when she married Hosea but later proved unfaithful. Another major view holds that she was a harlot when the prophet married her. Either way, the shock effect of Hosea's marital difficulties would have had telling impact on the people of his community. The children born of this marriage were given symbolic names indicating divine displeasure with Israel. After Gomer had pursued her paramours, she was to be brought back and with patient love readmitted to Hosea's home, there to await in penitence and grief the time of restoration to full favor. This was a clear picture of wayward Israel in its relationship with God and showed the unending faithfulness of the Almighty.

The remainder of the prophecy (Hos 4 – 14) is an indictment of Israel, delivered at various times from the later days of Jeroboam II up to about 730 BC. The style of this section is vigorous, though the Hebrew text has suffered in transmission, making for difficulties in translation. The first three chapters have been regarded by some as allegorical. Though the book is generally held to be a unity, critical writers have maintained that interpolations and editorial material occur throughout the work.

> Chs. 1 – 3: Hosea's unhappy marriage and its results
> Ch. 4: The priests condone immorality
> Ch. 5: Israel's sin will be punished unless she repents
> Ch. 6: Israel's sin is thoroughgoing, her repentance halfhearted
> Ch. 7: Inner depravity and outward decay
> Ch. 8: The nearness of judgment
> Ch. 9: The impending calamity
> Ch. 10: Israel's guilt and punishment
> Ch. 11: God pursues Israel with love
> Chs. 12 – 14: An exhortation to repentance, with promised restoration

HOSPITALITY [3827, 3828, 5696, 5810, 5811, 5819] (Gr. *philoxenia, loving strangers*). Although the word occurs only a few times in the Bible (e.g., Ro 12:13; 16:23; 1Ti 3:2; 5:10; Tit 1:8; 1Pe 4:9; 3Jn 8), the idea appears as early as Abraham (Ge 14:17 – 19).

Commanded:
> (Isa 58:6 – 7; Mt 25:34 – 39; Ro 12:13; 1Ti 3:2; 5:10; Tit 1:7 – 8; Heb 13:2; 1Pe 4:9 – 11; 3Jn 5 – 8). Toward strangers (Ex 22:11; 23:9; Lev 19:10, 33 – 34; 24:22; Dt 10:18 – 19; 26:12 – 13; 27:19).

Instances of:

Pharaoh to Abraham (Ge 12:16); Melchizedek to Abraham (Ge 14:18); Abraham to angels (Ge 18:1 – 8); Lot to an angel (Ge 19:1 – 11); Abimelech to Abraham (Ge 20:14 – 15); Hittites, to Abraham (Ge 23:3 n., 6, 11); Laban, to Abraham's servant (Ge 24:31 – 33), to Jacob (Ge 29:13 – 14); Isaac to Abimelech (Ge 26:30); Joseph to his brothers (Ge 43:31 – 34); Pharaoh to Jacob (Ge 45:16 – 20; 47:7 – 12); Jethro to Moses (Ex 2:20); Rahab to the spies (Jos 2:1 – 16); man of Gibeah to Levite (Jdg 19:16 – 21); Pharaoh to Hadad (1Ki 11:17, 22); Jeroboam to prophet of Judah (1Ki 13:7); widow of Zarephath to Elijah (1Ki 17:10 – 24); Shunammite to Elisha (2Ki 4:8); Elisha to Syrian spies (2Ki 6:22); Job to strangers (Job 31:32); David to Mephibosheth (2Sa 9:7 – 13); king of Babylon to Jehoiachin (2Ki 25:29 – 30); Nehemiah to rulers and Jews (Ne 5:17 – 19); Martha to Jesus (Lk 10:38; Jn 12:1 – 2); Pharisees to Jesus (Lk 11:37 – 38); Zacchaeus to Jesus (Lk 19:1 – 10); disciples to Jesus (Lk 24:29); tanner to Peter (Ac 10:6, 23); Lydia to Paul and Silas (Ac 16:15); barbarians to Paul (Ac 28:2); Publius to Paul (Ac 28:7); Phoebe to Paul (Ro 16:2); Onesiphorus to Paul (2Ti 1:16); Gaius (3Jn 5, 8).

Rewarded:

Rahab (Jos 6:17, 22 – 25); widow of Zarephath (1Ki 17:10 – 24).

Ro	12:13	Practice **h**.
	16:23	whose **h** I and the whole church
1Ti	5:10	as bringing up children, showing **h**,
1Pe	4:9	Offer **h** to one another
3Jn	1:8	therefore to show **h** to such men

HUMBLE [HUMILITY]

Nu	12:3	(Now Moses was a very **h** man,
2Ch	7:14	will **h** themselves and pray
Ps	18:27	You save the **h**
	25:9	He guides the **h** in what is right
	149:4	he crowns the **h** with salvation.

Pr	3:34	but gives grace to the **h**.
Isa	66:2	he who is **h** and contrite in spirit,
Mt	11:29	for I am gentle and **h** in heart,
Eph	4:2	Be completely **h** and gentle;
Jas	4:6	but gives grace to the **h**."
	4:10	**H** yourselves before the Lord,
1Pe	5:5	but gives grace to the **h**."
	5:6	H yourselves,

HUMILITY [6708, 7560, 4246+5425, 4559, 5425] (Heb. *'ănāwâh*, Gr. *tapeinophrosynē*). Humility and the related substantive and verb *humble* translate several OT Hebrew words and the NT Greek *tapeinoō* family. The meaning shades off in various directions, but the central thought is freedom from pride — lowliness, meekness, modesty, mildness. There is a "false humility" (Col 2:18, 23) called "self-abasement" in RSV. God humbles people to bring them to obedience (Dt 8:2). To humble ourselves is a condition of God's favor (2Ch 7:14) and his supreme requirement (Mic 6:8). God dwells with the humble (Isa 57:15). Humility is encouraged (Pr 15:33; 18:12; 22:4). To the Greeks humility was weak and despicable, but Jesus made it the cornerstone of character (Mt 5:3, 5; 18:4; 23:12; Lk 14:11; 18:14). Jesus by his humility drew people to himself (Mt 11:28 – 30; Jn 13:1 – 20; Rev 3:20). Paul emphasized the humility of Jesus (2Co 8:9; Php 2:1 – 11), commanded us to be humble toward one another (Ro 12:10; 1Co 13:4 – 6; Php 2:3 – 4), and spoke of himself as an example (Ac 20:19). Peter exhorted humility before the brethren and before God (1Pe 5:5 – 6). The above and other passages show that humility is an effect of the action of God, circumstances, other people, ourselves, or of any or all of these on our lives.

Commanded:

(Dt 15:15; Pr 25:6 – 7 a; 27:2; 30:32; Ecc 5:2; Jer 45:5; Mic 6:8; Mt 18:2 – 4; 20:26 – 27; Mk 9:33 – 37; 10:43 – 44; Lk 9:46 – 48; 14:10; 17:10; 22:24 – 27; Jn 13:14 – 16; Ro 11:18 – 20, 25; 12:3, 10, 16; 1Co 3:18; 4:6; 10:12; Gal 5:26; Eph 4:1 – 2; 5:21; Php 2:3 – 11; Col 3:12; Jas 1:9 – 10; 4:10; 1Pe 5:3, 5 – 6). Feigned, forbidden (Col 2:18 – 23).

Rewards of:

(Job 5:11; 22:29; Ps 138:6; Pr 15:33; 18:12; 22:4; 29:23; Mt 5:3; 23:12; Lk 1:52; 14:11; 18:13 – 14).

Exemplified in:

Abraham (Ge 18:27, 32); Jacob (Ge 32:10); Joseph (Ge 41:16); Moses (Ex 3:11; 4:10); David (1Sa 18:18 – 23; 23:14; 26:20; 2Sa 7:18 – 20; 1Ch 17:16 – 18; 29:14); the psalmist (Pss 8:3 – 4; 73:22; 131:1 – 2; 141:5; 144:3); Solomon (1Ki 3:7; 2Ch 1:10; 2:6); Mephibosheth (2Sa 9:8); Ahab (1Ki 21:29); kings and princes of Israel (2Ch 12:6 – 7, 12); Josiah (2Ki 22:18 – 19; 2Ch 34:26, 27); Job (Job 7:17 – 18; 9:14 – 15; 40:4 – 5; 42:2 – 6); Elihu (Job 32:4 – 7; 33:6); Ezra (Ezr 9:13, 15); Agur (Pr 30:2 – 3); Isaiah (Isa 6:5); Hezekiah (Isa 38:15); Jeremiah (Jer 1:6; 10:23 – 24); Daniel (Da 2:30); Ezra and the Jews (Ezr 8:21, 23); Elizabeth (Lk 1:43); John the Baptist (Mt 3:14; Mk 1:7; Lk 3:16; Jn 1:27; 3:29 – 30); Jesus (Mt 11:29; 13:4 – 16); woman of Canaan (Mt 15:27); the righteous (Mt 25:37 – 40); tax collector (Lk 18:13); centurion (Mt 8:8; Lk 7:6 – 7); Peter (Ac 2:12); Paul (Ac 20:19; Ro 7:18; 1Co 2:1 – 3; 15:9 – 10; 2Co 3:5; 11:30; 12:5 – 12; Eph 3:8; Php 3:12 – 13; 4:12; 1Ti 1:15).

Ps	45:4	of truth, **h** and righteousness;
Pr	11:2	but with **h** comes wisdom.
	15:33	and **h** comes before honor.
	22:4	**H** and the fear of the LORD
Zep	2:3	Seek righteousness, seek **h**;
Ac	20:19	I served the Lord with great **h**
Php	2:3	but in **h** consider others better
Col	2:18	let anyone who delights in false **h**
	3:12	**h**, gentleness and patience.
Tit	3:2	and to show true **h** toward all men.
Jas	3:13	in the **h** that comes from wisdom.
1Pe	5:5	clothe yourselves with **h**

HUSBAND [408, 1249, 1251, 8276,467, 476].

Relation to His Wife:

In general (Ge 2:23 – 24; Mt 19:5 – 6; Mk 10:7; 1Co 7:3 – 5). Love for (Eph 5:22 – 33; Col 3:19).

Headship of (1Co 11:3). Chastity of (Pr 5:15 – 20; Mal 2:14 – 16). Rights of (1Co 7:3, 5). Sanctified in the wife (1Co 7:14, 16). May give wife certificate of divorce (Dt 24:1 – 4). Law relating to, in cases where wife's virtue is questioned (Nu 5:11 – 31; Dt 22:13 – 21). Exemptions for (Dt 24:5). Duties of (Ecc 9:9; Col 3:19; 1Pe 3:7). Family provider (Ge 30:30; 1Ti 5:8).

Examples:

Faithful: Isaac (Ge 24:67); Joseph (Mt 1:19 – 20). Unreasonable and oppressive (Est 1:10 – 22).

Figurative:

(Isa 54:5 – 6; Jer 3:14; 31:32; Hos 2:19 – 20). See Family; Marriage.

Pr	31:11	Her **h** has full confidence in her
	31:23	Her **h** is respected at the city gate,
	31:28	her **h** also, and he praises her:
Isa	54:5	For your Maker is your **h** —
Jer	3:14	the LORD, "for I am your **h**.
	3:20	like a woman unfaithful to her **h**,
Jn	4:17	"I have no **h**," she replied.
Ro	7:2	a married woman is bound to her **h**
1Co	7:2	and each woman her own **h**.
	7:3	The **h** should fulfill his marital duty
	7:10	wife must not separate from her **h**.
	7:11	And a **h** must not divorce his wife.
	7:13	And if a woman has a **h** who is not
	7:14	For the unbelieving **h** has been
	7:39	A woman is bound to her **h** as long
	7:39	But if her **h** dies, she is free
2Co	11:2	I promised you to one **h**, to Christ,
Gal	4:27	woman than of her who has a **h**."
Eph	5:23	For the **h** is the head of the wife
	5:33	and the wife must respect her **h**.
1Ti	3:2	the **h** of but one wife, temperate,
	3:12	A deacon must be the **h** of
	5:9	has been faithful to her **h**,
Tit	1:6	An elder must be blameless, the **h**

HYPOCRISY [6623, 5347, 5694, 5695] (hĭpŏk'rĭsē pretender, pretentious). From a Hebrew root hnph, "pollute," correctly translated "profane," "godless," "ungodly" in ASV, RSV, NIV (Job 8:13; 13:16; Ps 35:16; Pr 22:9; Isa 9:17; 10:6; 32:6; 33:14). The LXX used Greek *hypokrinomai*, "act a part in a play." The thought in the NT lies close to the literal meaning "play-acting," with special reference to religion: "having a form of godliness, but denying its power" (2Ti 3:5), as Mt 6:1 – 18 and 23:13 – 36 plainly show.

Described:

(Job 31:33 – 34; Pss 5:6, 9; 52:4; 78:34 – 37; Isa 29:13; 32:5 – 6; 48:1 – 2; 58:2 – 5; Jer 12:2; 17:9; Eze 33:30 – 32; Hos 6:4; 10:1, 4; Zec 7:5 – 6; Mt 15:3 – 9; 21:28 – 32; Mk 7:5 – 13; 9:50; 14:34 – 35; Lk 18:11 – 12; Ro 9:6 – 7; 1Co 5:8; 13:1; 2Co 4:2; 1Jn 1:6, 10; 2:4, 9, 19; 4:20; Rev 3:1). Betrays friends (Pss 55:12 – 14, 20 – 23; Pr 11:9; 25:19; Ob 7; Zec 13:6). Hypocrisy of prostitutes (Pr 7:10 – 21); of false teachers (Mic 3:11; Ro 16:17 – 18; 2Pe 2:1 – 3, 17, 19); of dishonest buyers (Pr 20:14).

Condemned:

Abhorred by God (Job 13:16; Ps 50:16 – 17; Pr 15:8; 21:27; Isa 1:9 – 15; 9:17; 10:6; 58:2 – 5; 61:8; 65:2 – 5; 66:3 – 5; Jer 5:2; 6:20; 7:4, 8 – 10; Eze 5:11; 20:39; Hos 8:13; 9:4; 11:12; Am 5:21 – 27; Zec 7:5 – 6; Mal 1:6 – 14; 2:13). Rebuked by Jesus (Mt 3:7 – 8; 7:7 – 8; 9:13; 15:7 – 9; 16:3; 23:2 – 33; Lk 6:46; 11:39, 42, 44; 12:54 – 56; 13:13 – 17; Jn 6:26, 70; 7:19; 15:2, 6; Rev 2:9; 3:9). Exposed by Paul (Ro 2:1, 3, 17 – 29; 2Co 5:12; Gal 6:3; Php 3:2, 18 – 19; 1Ti 4:2; 2Ti 3:5, 13; Tit 1:16). Warning to (Job 15:31, 33 – 34; 17:8; 20:4 – 5; 27:8 – 10; 34:30). Warning against (Pr 23:6 – 8; 26:18 – 19, 23 – 26; Jer 9:8; Mic 7:5; Mt 6:1 – 2, 5, 16, 24; 7:5, 15, 21 – 23; 16:6; 23:14; Mk 8:15; 12:38 – 40; Lk 12:1 – 2; 13:26 – 27; 16:13, 15; 20:46 – 47; Jas 1:8, 22 – 24, 26; 3:17; 4:8; 1Pe 2:1, 16; Jude 12 – 13). Punishment for (Job 8:13 – 15; 36:13 – 14; Pss 55:23; 101:7; Isa 29:15 – 16; 33:14; 42:21 – 22; Eze 5:11; 14:3 – 4, 7 – 8; Hos 8:13; 9:4; Mt 22:12 – 13; 24:50 – 51; 25:41 – 45; Ro 1:18).

Instances of:

Jacob, in impersonating Esau and deceiving his father (Ge 27); Jacob's sons, in deception of their father concerning Joseph (Ge 37:29 – 35); Joseph's deception of his brothers (Ge 42 – 44), Pharaoh (Ex 8:15, 28 – 29, 32; 9:27 – 35; 10:8 – 29); Balaam (Jude 11, w Nu 22 – 24); Delilah, the wife of Samson (Jdg 16); Jael (Jdg 4:8 – 21); Ehud (Jdg 3:15 – 25); Assyrian field commander (2Ki 18:17 – 37); Ahaz (Isa 7:12, w 17 – 25); Johanan (Jer 42:1 – 12, 20, 22); Ishmael (Jer 41:6 – 7); false prophets (Eze 13:1 – 23); Herod (Mt 2:8); Judas (Mt 26:25, 48; Jn 12:5 – 6); Pilate (Mt 27:24); Pharisees (Mt 15:1 – 9; 22:18; Mk 12:13 – 14; Jn 8:4 – 9; 9:24; 19:15); ruler (Lk 13:14 – 17); spies sent to entrap Jesus (Lk 20:21); priests and Levites (Lk 10:31 – 32); chief priests (Jn 18:28); Ananias and Sapphira (Ac 5:1 – 10); Simon (Ac 8:18 – 23); Peter and others at Antioch (Gal 2:11 – 14); Judaizing Christians in Galatia (Gal 6:13); false teachers at Ephesus (Rev 2:2).

Mt	23:28	but on the inside you are full of **h**
Mk	12:15	we?" But Jesus knew their **h**.
Lk	12:1	yeast of the Pharisees, which is **h**.
Gal	2:13	The other Jews joined him in his **h**,
	2:13	by their **h** even Barnabas was led
1Pe	2:1	**h**, envy, and slander of every kind.

HYPOCRITE [HYPOCRISY]

Mt	7:5	You **h**, first take the plank out
Lk	6:42	You **h**, first take the plank out

HYPOCRITES [HYPOCRISY]

Ps	26:4	nor do I consort with **h**;
Mt	6:2	as the **h** do in the synagogues
	6:5	when you pray, do not be like the **h**
	6:16	do not look somber as the **h** do,
	15:7	You **h**! Isaiah was right
	23:13	of the law and Pharisees, you **h**!
	23:27	you **h**! You are like whitewashed
	24:51	and assign him a place with the **h**,
Mk	7:6	when he prophesied about you **h**;
Lk	12:56	**H**! You know how
	13:15	The Lord answered him, "You **h**!

ICHABOD (ī k′a-bŏd, Heb. *'ikhā vôdh, inglorious*). Son of Phinehas, Eli's son, who was killed by the Philistines at the battle of Aphek when the ark was taken. Ichabod was born after his father's death and was given this name by his mother on her deathbed because, she said, "The glory has departed from Israel" (1Sa 4:19 – 22). His nephew Ahijah was one of those who remained with Saul and his men at Gibeah just before Jonathan attacked the Philistines (14:2ff.).

ICONIUM (ī-cō′nĭ-ŭm, Gr. *Ikonion*). A city of Asia Minor that Paul and Barnabas visited on Paul's first missionary journey after they had been expelled from Antioch in Pisidia, which lay to the west. They revisited the city on their return journey to Antioch (Ac 13:51ff.). On his second missionary journey, Paul, with Silas, stopped off at Iconium to read the letter sent out by the Jerusalem Council on the Judaizing question, and at nearby Lystra he took young Timothy with him as his associate (16:1 – 5). In 2Ti 3:11 Paul alludes to persecutions endured by him at Antioch, Iconium, and Lystra.

In the first century it was one of the chief cities in the southern part of the Roman province of Galatia. It was a city of immemorial antiquity and was situated near the western end of a vast, level plain, with mountains a few miles toward the west, from which streams flowed that made it a veritable oasis. Two important trade routes passed through it, and it was on the road leading to Ephesus and Rome. Its geographical position makes it the natural capital of Lycaonia. Archaeological inscriptions found there in AD 1910 show that the Phrygian language was spoken there for two centuries after the time of Paul, though at neighboring Lystra the natives spoke "the Lycaonian language" (Ac 14:11). Hadrian made the city a Roman colony. The city has had a continuing history and is now known as Konia, still the main trading center of the Lycaonian plain.

IDOL [IDOLATRY, IDOLS]

Ex	20:4	make for yourself an **i** in the form
	32:4	made it into an **i** cast in the shape
Isa	40:19	As for an **i**, a craftsman casts it,
	41:7	He nails down the **i**
	44:15	he makes an **i** and bows down to it.
	44:17	From the rest he makes a god, his **i**;
Hab	2:18	"Of what value is an **i**,
1Co	8:4	We know that an **i** is nothing at all

IDOLATRY [496, 1658, 2393, 3913, 4024, 9572, 1629, 1630] (ī-dŏl′a-trē Gr. *eidōlolatria, image*). Idolatry in ancient times included two forms of departure from the true religion: the worship of false gods, whether by means of images or otherwise; and the worship of the Lord by means of images. All the nations surrounding ancient Israel were idolatrous, though their idolatry assumed different forms. The early Semites of Mesopotamia worshiped mountains, springs, trees, and blocks of stone — things in which the deity was supposed to be in some sense incarnate. A typical example of such wooden representations is the sacred pole or Asherah pole. This was the idol of Gideon's clan; Gideon destroyed it (Jdg 6:25 – 32). The religion of the Egyptians centered mostly on the veneration of the sun and of the Nile as sources of life. They also had a number of sacred animals: the bull, cow, cat, baboon, crocodile, etc. Some of the deities were represented with human bodies and animal heads. Among the Canaanites, religion took on a very barbarous character. The chief gods were personifications of life and fertility. The gods had no moral character whatsoever, and worship of them carried with it demoralizing practices, including child sacrifice, prostitution, and snake worship. Human and animal images of the deities were worshiped. When the Israelites conquered the land, they were commanded to destroy these idols (Ex 23:24; 34:13; Nu 33:52; Dt 7:5).

For an Israelite, idolatry was the most heinous of crimes. In the OT the relation between God and his covenant people is often represented as a marriage bond (Isa 54:5; Jer 3:14), and the worship of false gods was regarded as religious harlotry. The penalty was death (Ex 22:20). To attempt to seduce others to false worship was a crime of equal enormity (Dt 13:6 – 10). The God of Israel was a jealous God who brooked no rivals.

In the NT, references to idolatry are understandably few. The Maccabean war resulted in the Jews becoming fanatically opposed to the crass idolatry of OT times. The Jews were never again tempted to worship images or gods other than the Lord. Jesus, however, warned that to make possessions central in life is also idolatry, and said, "You cannot serve both God and Money" (Mt 6:24). The OT conception of idolatry is widened to include anything that leads to the dethronement of God from the heart, as, for example, covetousness (Eph 5:5; Col 3:5). *See High Places; Idol; Prostitute*

Wicked Practices of:

Human sacrifices (Lev 18:21; 20:2 – 5; Dt 12:31; 18:10; 2Ki 3:26 – 27; 16:3; 17:17 – 18; 21:6; 23:10; 2Ch 28:3; 33:6; Ps 106:37 – 38; Isa 57:5; Jer 7:31; 19:4 – 7; 32:35; Eze 16:20 – 21; 20:26, 31; 23:37, 39; Mic 6:7); practices of, relating to the dead (Dt 14:1); licentiousness of (Ex 32:6, 25; Nu 25:1 – 3; 1Ki 14:24; 15:12; 2Ki 17:30; 23:7; Eze 16:17; 23:1 – 44; Hos 4:12 – 14; Am 2:8; Mic 1:7; Ro 1:24, 26 – 27; 1Co 10:7 – 8; 1Pe 4:3 – 4; Rev 2:14, 20 – 22; 9:20 – 21; 14:8; 17:1 – 6).

Other Customs of:

Offered burnt offerings (Ex 32:6; 1Ki 18:26; Ac 14:13). Offerings of libations (Isa 57:6; 65:11; Jer 7:18; 19:13; 32:29; 44:17, 19, 25; Eze 20:28); of wine (Dt 32:38); of blood (Ps 16:4; Zec 9:7). Meat offerings (Isa 57:6; Jer 7:18; 44:17; Eze 16:19). Peace offerings (Ex 32:6). Incense burned on altars (1Ki 12:33; 2Ch 30:14; 34:25; Isa 65:3; Jer 1:16; 11:12, 17; 44:3; 48:35; Eze 16:18; 23:41; Hos 11:2). Prayers to idols (Jdg 10:14; Isa 44:17; 45:20; 46:7; Jnh 1:5). Praise (Jdg 16:24; Da 5:4). Singing and dancing (Ex 32:18 – 19). Music (Da 3:5 – 7). Cutting the flesh (1Ki 18:28; Jer 41:5). Kissing (1Ki 19:18; Hos 13:2; Job 31:27). Bowing

(1Ki 19:18; 2Ki 5:18). Tithes and gifts (2Ki 23:11; Da 11:38; Am 4:4 – 5).

Annual Feasts:

(1Ki 12:32; Eze 18:6, 11 – 12, 15; 22:9; Da 3:2 – 3).

Objects of:

Sun, moon, and stars (Dt 4:19; 2Ki 17:16; 21:3, 5; 2Ch 33:3, 5; Job 31:26 – 28; Jer 7:17 – 20; 8:2; Eze 8:15 – 16; Zep 1:4 – 5; Ac 7:42). Images of angels (Col 2:18); animals (Ro 1:23). Gods of Egypt (Ex 12:12). Golden calf (Ex 32:4). Bronze serpent (2Ki 18:4). Net and dragnet (Hab 1:16). Pictures (Nu 33:52; Isa 2:16). Pictures on walls (Eze 8:10). Earrings (Ge 35:4). See Artemis; Shrine.

Folly of:

(Dt 4:28; 32:37 – 38; Jdg 6:31; 10:14; 1Sa 5:3 – 4; 12:21; 1Ki 18:25 – 29; 19:18; 2Ch 25:15; Pss 106:19 – 20; 115:4 – 5, 8; 135:15 – 18; Isa 37:19; 44:9 – 20; 45:20; 46:1 – 2, 6 – 7; Jer 2:28; 11:12; 16:19 – 20; 48:13; 51:17; Hos 8:5 – 6; Zec 10:2; Ac 14:13, 15; 17:22 – 23, 29; Ro 1:22 – 23; 1Co 8:4; 10:5; 12:2; Gal 4:8; Rev 9:20). Illustrated by contrast of idols with the true God (Ps 96:5; Isa 40:12 – 26; 41:23 – 29; Jer 10:5; 14:22; Da 5:23; Hab 2:18 – 20). Exemplified in the ruin of Israel (2Ch 28:22 – 23).

Forbidden:

(Ge 35:2; Ex 20:3 – 6, 23; 23:13, 24, 32 – 33; 34:14, 17; Lev 19:4; 26:1, 30; Dt 4:15 – 28; 5:7 – 9; 7:2 – 5, 16; 11:16 – 17; 16:21 – 22; Ps 81:9; Eze 8:8 – 18; 14:1 – 8; 16:15 – 63; 20:7 – 8, 16, 18, 24, 27 – 32, 39; 23:7 – 49; Ac 15:20 – 29; 1Co 10:14, 20 – 22; 1Jn 5:21).

Prophecies Relating to:

(Isa 46:1 – 2). Punishments of (Nu 33:4; Dt 31:16 – 21, 29; Isa 21:9; Jer 51:44, 47, 52). End of (Isa 2:8, 18, 20; 17:7 – 8; 27:9; Jer 10:11, 15; Hos 10:2; 14:8; Mic 5:13 – 14; Zep 2:11; Zec 13:2).

Punishment of:

(Dt 8:19; 11:28; 13:6 – 9; 17:2 – 5; 28:14 – 18; 30:17 – 18; 32:15 – 26; Jdg 2:3; 1Ki 9:6 – 9; Ne

9:27 – 37; Pss 16:4; 59:8; 78:58 – 64; 106:34 – 42; Isa 1:29 – 31; 2:6 – 22; 30:22; 65:3 – 7; Jer 1:15 – 16; 5:1 – 17; 7; 8:1 – 2, 19; 13:9 – 27; 16; 17:1 – 6; 18:13 – 17; 19; 22:5 – 9; 44; Eze 6; 8:8 – 18; 9; 14:1 – 8; 16:15 – 63; 20:7 – 8, 24 – 39; 22:4; 23:9 – 10, 22 – 49; 44:10 – 12; Hos 8:5 – 14; 10; 13:14; 5:5; Mic 1:1 – 9; 5:12 – 14; 6:16; Zep 1; Mal 2:11 – 13; Rev 21:8; 22:15).

1Sa	15:23	and arrogance like the evil of **i**.
1Co	10:14	my dear friends, flee from **i**.
Gal	5:20	and debauchery; **i** and witchcraft;
Col	3:5	evil desires and greed, which is **i**.
1Pe	4:3	orgies, carousing and detestable **i**.

IDOLS [IDOL]

Dt	32:16	angered him with their detestable **i**.
Ps	78:58	aroused his jealousy with their **i**.
Isa	44:9	All who make **i** are nothing,
Eze	23:39	sacrificed their children to their **i**,
Ac	15:20	to abstain from food polluted by **i**,
	21:25	abstain from food sacrificed to **i**,
1Co	8:1	Now about food sacrificed to **i**:
1Jn	5:21	children, keep yourselves from **i**.
Rev	2:14	to sin by eating food sacrificed to **i**

IMAGE OF GOD [7512, 1635]. Two fundamental truths about humans taught in Scripture are that they are created by God and that God made them in his own image. Humans came into being as the result of special deliberation on the part of God. They are God's creatures, and there is therefore an infinite qualitative difference between God and humans; but humans have been made like God in a way that the rest of creation has not. Humankind is created in God's image (Ge 1:26 – 27; 5:1, 3; 9:6; 1Co 11:7; Eph 4:24; Col 3:10; Jas 3:9). The image is not corporeal but rational, spiritual, and social. The fall distorted but did not obliterate the image. Restoration of the image begins with regeneration.

IMMANUEL [6672, 1842] (ĭ-măn′ū-ĕl, Heb. 'immānû'ēl, God is with us). The name of a child (occurring three times in the Bible — Isa 7:14; 8:8; Mt 1:23) whose birth was foretold by Isaiah and who was to be a sign to Ahaz during the Syro-Ephraimitic war (Isa 7). At this time, 735 BC, Judah was threatened by the allied forces of Syria and Israel. They were trying to compel Judah to form an alliance with them against Assyria, whose king, Tiglath-Pileser, was attempting to bring the whole of western Asia under his sway. Isaiah directed Ahaz to remain confident and calm in the Lord and not to seek aid from Tiglath-Pileser. To overcome the king's incredulity, he offered him a sign of anything in heaven or earth; but when the king evasively refused the offer, Isaiah bitterly chided him for his lack of faith and gave him a sign, the sign of "Immanuel."

Isaiah's words have led to much controversy and have been variously interpreted, chiefly because of the indefinite terms of the prediction and the fact that there is no record of their fulfillment in any contemporary event.

1. The traditional Christian interpretation is that the emphasis should be laid on the virgin birth of our Immanuel, Jesus Christ, as Matthew does (Mt 1:22 – 23). *See Virgin Birth.*

2. Another explanation is that the event of the birth of the child is intended as a sign to Ahaz and nothing more. At the time of Judah's deliverance from Syria and Ephraim, some young mothers who give birth to sons will spontaneously name them "Immanuel." Children bearing this name will be a sign to Ahaz of the truth of Isaiah's words concerning deliverance and judgment.

3. A third view, somewhat similar to the preceding one, is that Isaiah has a certain child in mind, the *almah* being his own wife or one of Ahaz's wives or perhaps someone else. Before the child has emerged from infancy, Syria and Ephraim will be no more (Isa 7:16); and later in his life Judah will be a country fit only for the pastoral life (7:15).

4. There are semimessianic interpretations that apply the prophecy to a child of Isaiah's time and also to Jesus Christ.

5. Perhaps the most widely held view among evangelicals is that Isaiah has in mind Israel's Messiah. When the prophet learns of the king's cowardice, God for the first time gives to him a revelation of the true King, who would share the poverty and affliction of his people and whose character and work would entitle him to the great names of Isa 9:6. In this interpretation the essential fact is that in the coming of Immanuel people will recognize the truth of the prophet's words. He would be Israel's deliverer, and the government would rest on his shoulders (9:6). The messianic idea was prevalent in Judah at this time (e.g., 2Sa 7:12; Mic 5:3).

IMMORAL [IMMORALITY]

Pr	6:24	keeping you from the **i** woman,
1Co	5:9	to associate with sexually **i** people
	5:10	the people of this world who are **i**,
	5:11	but is sexually **i** or greedy,
Eph	5:5	No **i**, impure or greedy person —
Heb	12:16	See that no one is sexually **i**,
	13:4	the adulterer and all the sexually **i**.
Rev	21:8	the murderers, the sexually **i**,
	22:15	the sexually **i**, the murderers,

IMMORALITY [IMMORAL]

Nu	25:1	in sexual **i** with Moabite women,
Jer	3:9	Because Israel's **i** mattered so little
Mt	15:19	murder, adultery, sexual **i**, theft,
Ac	15:20	from sexual **i**, from the meat
	15:29	animals and from sexual **i**.
Ro	13:13	not in sexual **i** and debauchery,
1Co	5:1	reported that there is sexual **i**
	6:13	The body is not meant for sexual **i**,
	6:18	Flee from sexual **i**.
	7:2	But since there is so much **i**,
	10:8	We should not commit sexual **i**,
Gal	5:19	sexual **i**, impurity and debauchery;
Eph	5:3	must not be even a hint of sexual **i**,
Col	3:5	sexual **i**, impurity, lust, evil desires
1Th	4:3	that you should avoid sexual **i**;
Jude		4 grace of our God into a license for **i**
Rev	2:14	and by committing sexual **i**.

	2:20	misleads my servants into sexual **i**
	9:21	their sexual **i** or their thefts.

IMMORTALITY [440+4638, 114, 914, 915]. The biblical concept of immortality is not simply the survival of the soul after bodily death, but the self-conscious continuance of the whole person, body and soul together, in a state of blessedness, due to the redemption of Christ and the possession of "eternal life." The Bible nowhere attempts to prove this doctrine but everywhere assumes it as an undisputed postulate. The condition of believers in their state of immortality is not a bare, endless existence but a communion with God in eternal satisfaction and blessedness. Exemption from death and annihilation.

Apparently Understood:

By David (2Sa 12:23; Pss 21:4; 22:26; 23:6; 37:18, 27; 86:12; 133:3; 145:1 – 2); by Nehemiah (Ne 9:5); by Job (Job 14:13); by the psalmists (Pss 49:7 – 9; 73:26; 121:8); by Moses (Ex 3:6; Mt 22:32; Mk 12:26 – 27; Lk 20:36 – 38; Ac 7:32); by Abraham (Heb 11:10).

Implied:

In the translation of Enoch (Ge 5:24; Heb 11:5); in the translation of Elijah (2Ki 2:11); in redemption from Sheol (Ps 16:10 – 11); in the spirit returning to God (Ecc 3:21; 12:7); in the soul surviving the death of the body (Mt 10:28); in the appearance of Moses and Elijah at the transfiguration of Jesus (Mt 17:2 – 9; Mk 9:2 – 10; Lk 9:29 – 36); in the abolition of death (Isa 25:8); in the Savior's promise to his disciples (Jn 14:2 – 3); in the resurrection (Isa 26:19; Da 12:2 – 3; Jn 6:40; 1Co 15:12 – 25; 1Th 4:13 – 18; 5:10); in eternal inheritance (Ac 20:32; 26:18; Heb 9:15; 1Pe 1:3 – 5); in the everlasting punishment of the wicked (2Th 1:7 – 9); in the judgment (2Pe 3:7).

Taught:

By Christ (Mt 16:26; 19:16 – 17; 25:46; Mk 10:30; Lk 9:25; 10:25 – 28; Jn 3:14 – 16, 36; 5:39 – 40; 6:39 – 40, 44, 47, 50 – 58; 10:28; 11:25 – 26; 14:19; 17:2 – 3; Rev 3:4); by Paul (Ro 2:7; 6:22 – 23; 1Co

15:12 – 25; 2Co 5:1; Gal 6:8; Col 1:5 – 6; 2Th 2:16; 1Ti 4:8; 6:12, 19; 2Ti 1:9 – 10; Tit 1:2; 3:7); by John (1Jn 2:17, 25; 5:13; Rev 1:7; 22:5); by Jude (Jude 21); in Hebrews (Heb 9:15; 10:34; 11:5, 10, 13 – 16; 13:14).

Pr	12:28	along that path is **i**.
Ro	2:7	honor and **i**, he will give eternal life
1Co	15:53	and the mortal with **i**.
	15:54	with **i**, then the saying that is
2Ti	1:10	and **i** to light through the gospel.

IMMUTABILITY (i-mū-ta-bĭl'ĭ-tē *not changeable*). The perfection of God by which he is devoid of all change in essence, attributes, consciousness, will, and promises. No change is possible in God, because all change must be to better or worse, and God is absolute perfection. No cause for change in God exists, either in himself or outside of him. The immutability of God is clearly taught in Scripture (Mal 3:6; Pss 33:11; 102:26; Jas 1:17) and must not be confused with immobility, as if there were no movement in God. Immutability is consistent with constant activity and perfect freedom. God creates, performs miracles, sustains the universe, etc. When the Scriptures speak of his repenting, as in Jnh 3:10, one should remember that this is only an anthropomorphic way of speaking. God adapts his treatment of people to the variation of their actions and characters. When the righteous do wickedly, his holiness requires that his treatment of them must change.

IMPOSSIBLE

Mt	17:20	Nothing will be **i** for you."
	19:26	"With man this is **i**,
Mk	10:27	"With man this is **i**, but not
Lk	1:37	For nothing is **i** with God."
	18:27	"What is **i** with men is possible
Ac	2:24	it was **i** for death to keep its hold
Heb	6:4	It is **i** for those who have once been
	6:18	things in which it is **i** for God to lie,
	10:4	because it is **i** for the blood of bulls
	11:6	without faith it is **i** to please God,

IMPRECATORY PSALMS A number of OT psalms, especially Pss 2, 37, 69, 79, 109, 139, and 143, contain expressions of an apparent vengeful attitude toward enemies. For some people, these expressions constitute one of the "moral difficulties" of the OT. We must note, however: (1) Imprecations are not confined to the OT, and, therefore, insofar as they constitute a moral problem, the problem pervades the Bible as a whole (cf. Lk 11:37 – 52; Gal 1:8ff.; Rev 6:10; 18:20; 19:1 – 6). We must be prepared to think, then, that what we find here is not a reprehensibly low morality but an aspect of the biblical view of the conflict between good and evil. (2) Many if not all of the imprecatory psalms contain (as well as the imprecation) theological and moral sentiments that we should wish to attain (e.g., Ps 139). We can hardly, therefore, dismiss these psalms under some blanket condemnation as "OT morality." (3) In fact, OT morality stoutly opposed a hostile and vindictive response to opponents (e.g., Lev 19:14 – 18). (4) All the imprecatory psalms except Ps 137 are prayers. They are addressed to God about opponents, and there is no suggestion in any of them that the psalmist either said any of these things to his adversary or ever intended to take vengeance into his own hands. Even if, therefore, it should be decided that these are reprehensible as prayers, the way of the psalmist is to be preferred to the modern practice of killing, maiming, bombing, and destroying those whom we think are our enemies. (5) The imprecatory psalms are full of longing for the vindication of the Lord's good name. Over and over, the psalmist's desire is not personal relief but that the Lord should be seen in his goodness and holiness (e.g., Pss 58:11; 83:16 – 18). (6) Many of the actual imprecations do no more than ask God to do what he has at any rate said that he will do in such situations (e.g., Pss 5:10; 54:5; 79:6 – 7). (7) The Bible teaches that there is a "pure anger." The fact that we do not feel it and cannot express it does not mean that God's people have never risen to such heights of holiness. Our problem may well be, also, that we have so allowed our sense of moral outrage to atrophy that we are incapable of identifying with a pure wrath. (8) The one imprecation that is not contained in a prayer is Ps 137:8, and here the Bible translators continue to choose English renderings that in fact themselves create the problem (cf. NIV "happy"). The word "concerned" (*ashre*) can mean any of three things: (a) "blessed," i.e., under God's approval and blessing; (b) "happy," i.e., personally fulfilled and enjoying well-being; and (c) "right," i.e., matching exactly the moral norms that operate in such a situation. Psalm 137:8 would better read, "How right he is...." The psalmist himself will not retaliate, for that would be an act of revenge, which the OT forbids, but he recognizes that in the outworking of moral providence, this is what will happen. He does not rejoice in it but bows before its justice.

IMPURE [IMPURITY]

Ac	10:15	not call anything **i** that God has
Eph	5:5	No immoral, **i** or greedy person —
1Th	2:3	spring from error or **i** motives,
	4:7	For God did not call us to be **i**,
Rev	21:27	Nothing **i** will ever enter it,

IMPURITY [IMPURE]

Ro	1:24	hearts to sexual **i** for the degrading
Gal	5:19	sexual immorality, **i**
Eph	4:19	as to indulge in every kind of **i**,
	5:3	or of any kind of **i**, or of greed,
Col	3:5	**i**, lust, evil desires and greed,

INCARNATION (*taking on flesh*). The doctrine of the incarnation is taught or assumed throughout the Bible and comes to explicit statement in such passages as Jn 1:14, "The Word became flesh and made his dwelling among us" (cf. 1Ti 3:16; Ro 8:3). In NT usage "flesh" means "human nature." *Incarnation* is from the Latin meaning "becoming flesh," that is, "becoming human." The doctrine of the incarnation teaches that the eternal Son of God (*see Trinity*) became human, and that he did so without in any manner or degree diminishing his divine nature. A somewhat detailed statement of the incarnation

is found in Php 2:5 – 11. Christ Jesus, "remaining" (*hyparchon*) in the "form" of God, that is, with all the essential attributes of God, took the "form" of a servant and died on the cross.

The virgin birth is necessary for our understanding of the incarnation. In the process of ordinary birth, a new personality begins. Jesus Christ did not begin to be when he was born. He is the eternal Son. The virgin birth was a miracle, wrought by the Holy Spirit, whereby the eternal Son of God "became flesh," that is, took to himself a genuine human nature in addition to his eternal divine nature. It was a *virgin* birth, a miracle. The Holy Spirit has never been thought of as the father of Jesus. Jesus was not half man and half god like the Greek mythological heroes. He was fully God, the second person of the Trinity. "In Christ all the fullness of the Deity lives in bodily form" (Col 2:9). At the same time he became genuinely a man. To deny his genuine humanity is "the spirit of the antichrist" (1Jn 4:2 – 3).

The biblical data on the incarnation came to permanent doctrinal formulation at the council of Chalcedon, AD 451. That council declared that Christ was "born of the virgin Mary" and is "to be acknowledged in two natures, inconfusedly, unchangeably, indivisibly, inseparably ... the property of each nature being preserved, and concurring in one Person."

INFIDELITY

Relating to God:

Disbelief in God (Nu 15:30 – 31; 2Ch 32:14 – 19; Isa 29:16). Prosperity tempts to (Dt 32:15). Arguments against (Job 12:7 – 25; Ps 94:8 – 9; Isa 10:15; 19:16; 45:9, 18; Ro 1:20; 9:20 – 21).

Exemplified:

In mocking God (Pss 14:1, 6; 50:21; Isa 57:4 – 11; Eze 36:2; Da 3:15; Ac 17:18; 2Pe 3:3 – 4; Jude 18 – 19). In mocking God's servants (1Ki 22:24; 2Ki 2:23; 2Ch 30:6, 10; 36:16; Jer 17:15; 43:2; Eze 20:49; Ac 2:13). In rejecting God (Ex 5:2; Job 15:25 – 26; 21:14 – 15; Pss 14:1; 53:1; 106:24 – 25;

Jer 2:31). In rejecting Christ (Mt 12:24; 27:39 – 44; Mk 3:22; Lk 11:15; 19:14, 27). By Antichrist (Da 7:25; 8:25; 11:36 – 37). In doubting God's help (Ex 17:7; Pss 3:2; 78:19 – 20, 22; 107:11 – 12). In impugning God's holiness (Job 35:3; Ps 10:11, 13; Eze 18:2, 29; Mal 1:7; 3:14); God's knowledge (Job 22:13 – 14, 17; Pss 59:7; 64:5; 73:11; Isa 29:15; Eze 8:12); God's mercy (Ps 42:3); God's righteousness (Eze 18:2, 29).

Punishment for:

(Nu 15:30 – 31; Dt 29:19 – 21; Ps 12:3 – 4; Pr 3:34; 9:12; 19:29; 24:9; Isa 3:8; 5:18 – 19, 24 – 25; 28:9 – 10, 14 – 22; 47:10 – 11; Jer 5:12, 14; 48:42; 50:24, 29; Eze 9:9 – 10; 32:20; Hos 7:5, 13, 15; Am 5:18; 7:16 – 17; Mic 7:10; Zep 1:12; Lk 19:14, 27; Heb 10:28 – 29; 2Pe 2:1).

Relating to Friends:

(Ps 41:9; Mt 26:14 – 16, 47 – 50; Mk 14:10 – 11, 43 – 46; Lk 22:3 – 6, 47 – 48; Jn 13:18; 18:2 – 5).

INHERIT

Dt	1:38	because he will lead Israel to **i** it.
Jos	1:6	people to **i** the land I swore
Ps	37:11	But the meek will **i** the land
	37:29	the righteous will **i** the land
Zec	2:12	The LORD will **i** Judah
Mt	5:5	for they will **i** the earth.
	19:29	as much and will **i** eternal life.
Lk	10:25	"what must I do to **i** eternal life?"
1Co	6:9	the wicked will not **i** the kingdom
	15:50	blood cannot **i** the kingdom of God
Rev	21:7	He who overcomes will **i** all this,

INHERITANCE [1598, 2750, 3769, 3772, 4625, 5706, 5709, 2883, 3099, 3100, 3101, 3102, 4757]. The English word in the OT is a rendering of the Hebrew words *naḥalâh, ḥēleq, yerushshâh,* and *môrashâh,* the latter two being rare. The first occurs most often — almost two hundred times — and is the common term for something inherited, an estate, a portion. A fundamental principle of Hebrew society was that real, as distinguished from personal, property belonged to the family rather than to the individual. This came from the idea that the land was given by God to his children, the people of Israel, and must remain in the family. The Mosaic law directed that only the sons of a legal wife had the right of inheritance. The firstborn son possessed the birthright, i.e., the right to a double portion of the father's possession; and to him belonged the duty of maintaining the females of the family (Dt 21:15 – 17). The other sons received equal shares. If there were no sons, the property went to the daughters (Nu 27:8), on the condition that they not marry outside of their own tribe (36:6ff.) If the widow was left without children, the nearest of kin on her husband's side had the right to marry her; and if he refused, the next of kin (Ru 3:12 – 13). If no one married her, the inheritance remained with her until her death and then reverted to the next of kin (Nu 27:9 – 11). An estate could not pass from one tribe to another. Since the land was so strictly tied up, testamentary dispositions or wills were not needed. This strong feeling regarding family hereditary privileges was chiefly responsible for the Jews' taking such care to preserve the family genealogies.

"Inheritance" is not used in Scripture only to refer to inherited property. It is used also with a definite theological significance. In the OT at first it refers to the inheritance promised by God to Abraham and his descendants — the land of Canaan, "the land you gave your people for an inheritance" (1Ki 8:36; cf. Nu 34:2; Dt 4:21, 38; 12:9 – 10; 15:4; Pss 47:4; 105:9 – 11). The conquest of the land under the leadership of Joshua was by God's help, not by Israel's military prowess (Jos 21:43 – 45). God directed the partitioning of the land among the tribes (Nu 26:52 – 56; Jos 14:1 – 5; 18:4 – 9). Israel could continue to possess the land only on condition of faithfulness to God (Dt 4:26ff.; 11:8 – 9). Disobedience to God would result in the loss of the land, which could be recovered only by repentance and a new wholehearted submission to God (Isa 57:13; 58:13 – 14).

The idea finds a further expansion and spiritualization in two other directions. Israelites came to learn that the Lord himself was the inheritance of his people (Jer 10:16) and of the individual believer (Pss 16:5 – 6; 73:26; 142:5), and that his inheritance is his elect, brought "out of Egypt, to be the people of his inheritance" (Dt 4:20; cf. 32:9). This conception was later broadened until the Lord's inheritance is seen to include the Gentiles also (Ps 2:8; Isa 19:25; 47:6; 63:17).

The conception of inheritance is very prominent in the NT too, but now it is connected with the person and work of Christ, who is the heir by virtue of being the Son (Mk 12:7; Heb 1:2). Through Christ's redemptive work believers are sons of God by adoption and fellow-heirs with Christ (Ro 8:17; Gal 4:7). As a guarantee of "the promised eternal inheritance" (Heb 9:15), Christ has given to them the Holy Spirit (Eph 1:14). The letter to the Hebrews shows that as Israel under the old covenant received its inheritance from God, so in the new covenant the new Israel receives an inheritance, only a better one. This inheritance, moreover, is not for Jews alone but for all true believers, including Gentiles (3:6). The inheritance is the kingdom of God with all its blessings (Mt 25:34; 1Co 6:9; Gal 5:21), both present and eschatological (Ro 8:17 – 23; 1Co 15:50; Heb 11:13; 1Pe 1:3 – 4). It is wholly the gift of God's sovereign grace.

General References to:

Of children (Ge 24:36; 25:5; 2Ch 21:3). Of children of concubines (Ge 15:3; 21:9 – 11; 25:6). Of children of polygamous marriages (Dt 21:15). Of daughters (Nu 27:8; Job 42:15). Of all humankind (Ecc 2:18 – 19). Of servants (Pr 17:2). Of real estate, inalienable (1Ki 21:3; Jer 32:6 – 8; Eze 46:16 – 18). Law concerning (Nu 27:6 – 11). Lesson concerning, of prodigal (Lk 15:12, 25 – 31). Proverbs concerning (Pr 17:2; 20:21). Instance of Israel to Joseph (Ge 48:21 – 22).

Figurative:

Spiritual (Mt 25:34; Ac 20:32; 26:18; Ro 8:16 – 17; Gal 4:7; Eph 1:11 – 14; Col 3:24; Tit 3:7; Heb 1:14; 9:15 – 17). See Firstborn; Heir; Will.

Lev	20:24	I will give it to you as an **i**,
Dt	4:20	to be the people of his **i**,
	10:9	the LORD is their **i**, as the LORD
Jos	14:3	two-and-a-half tribes their **i** east
Ps	16:6	surely I have a delightful **i**.
	33:12	the people he chose for his **i**.
	136:21	and gave their land as an **i**,
Pr	13:22	A good man leaves an **i**
Mt	25:34	blessed by my Father; take your **i**,
Eph	1:14	who is a deposit guaranteeing our **i**
	5:5	has any **i** in the kingdom of Christ
Col	1:12	you to share in the **i** of the saints
	3:24	you know that you will receive an **i**
Heb	9:15	receive the promised eternal **i** —
1Pe	1:4	and into an **i** that can never perish,

INIQUITIES [INIQUITY]

Ps	78:38	he forgave their **i**
	103:10	or repay us according to our **i**.
Isa	53:5	he was crushed for our **i**;
	53:11	and he will bear their **i**.
	59:2	But your **i** have separated
Mic	7:19	and hurl all our **i** into the depths

INIQUITY [INIQUITIES]

Ps	25:11	forgive my **i**, though it is great.
	32:5	and did not cover up my **i**.
	51:2	Wash away all my **i**
	51:9	and blot out all my **i**.
Isa	53:6	the **i** of us all.

I.N.R.I. The initials of the Latin superscription that Pilate had placed above the cross of Jesus in three languages (Greek, Hebrew, Latin). The Latin reads: *IESUS NAZARENUS, REX IUDAERUM,* "Jesus of Nazareth, King of the Jews" (Mt 27:37; Mk 15:26; Lk 23:38; Jn 19:19).

INSPIRATION [8120] (*breathed into*). The word "inspiration" is used twice in the KJV — in Job 32:8 (NIV "breath"), to translate the Hebrew word *neshamâh* ("to breathe"), and in 2Ti 3:16, where it translates the Greek word *theopneustos.* The latter passage has given its meaning to the word *inspiration* as commonly applied to Scripture. Literally translated, *theo-*

pneustos means "God-breathed" (so NIV). The key to its meaning may be gleaned from the OT concept of the divine breathing as producing effects that God himself is immediately accomplishing by his own will and power (see Ps 33:6). By this word, therefore, Paul is asserting that the written documents, called Holy Scripture, are a divine product.

Precisely the same idea is set forth in 2Pe 1:19 – 21. In this passage the prophetic Word (i.e., Scripture) is contrasted with mere fables devised by human cunning. Scripture is more sure and trustworthy than the testimony of any eyewitness. The explanation for its unique authority lies in its origin. It was produced not as a merely human private interpretation of the truth but by God's Spirit through the prophets.

In both 2Ti 3:16 and 2Pe 1:19 – 21, the fact of the divine productivity (spiration rather than *in*spiration) of the "Holy Writings" is thus explicitly asserted. This divine (in)spiration is further confirmed by a host of NT passages. The authors of Scripture wrote in or by the Spirit (Mk 12:36). What the Scripture states is really what God has said (Ac 4:25; Heb 3:7; and see especially Heb 1:5ff.). This is true whether or not in the particular passage cited the words are ascribed to God or are the statements of the human author. In the mind of the NT writers, any passage of Scripture was really "spoken" by God. Jesus used the same type of reference, attributing directly to God the authorship of Scripture (Mt 19:4 – 5).

Because of the character of the God of truth who "inspired" (or produced) the Holy Scriptures, the result of "inspiration" is to constitute the Bible as fully trustworthy and authoritative. Indeed, this absolute divine authority of Scripture, rather than its inspiration, is the emphasis of scriptural teaching about its own nature (see Pss 19:7 – 14; 119:89, 97, 113, 160; Zec 7:12; Mt 5:17 – 19; Lk 16:17; Jn 10:34 – 35; 1Th 2:13). Besides those passages directly teaching the authority of Scripture, such phrases as "It is written" (Mt 21:13; Lk 4:4, 8, 10), "it [or he] says" (Ro 9:15; Gal 3:16), and "Scripture says" (Ro 9:17; Gal 3:8) all clearly imply an absolute authority for the OT Scriptures.

These passages teaching the authority of Scripture indicate also the extent of inspiration. If the authority and trustworthiness of Scripture are complete, inspiration itself must also extend to all of Scripture. This completeness of inspiration and consequent authority of all Scripture is made explicit in such passages as Lk 24:25: "How foolish you are, and how slow of heart to believe all that the prophets have spoken!" (see also Mt 5:17 – 19; Lk 16:17; Jn 10:34 – 35).

Inerrancy and *infallibility* as applied to the inspiration of Scripture, though not exactly synonymous terms, are nevertheless both correctly applied to Scripture in order to indicate that inspiration and authority are complete. The word *inerrant* suggests that the Scriptures do not wander from the truth. *Infallible* is stronger, suggesting an incapability of wandering from the truth. ("Are you not in error because you do not know the Scriptures?" Mk 12:24.)

In summary, biblical inspiration (as distinguished from illumination) may be defined as the work of the Holy Spirit by which, through the instrumentality of the personality and literary talents of its human authors, he constituted the words of the Bible in all of its several parts as his written word to the human race and, therefore, of divine authority and without error.

Claims That the Scriptures Are Inspired:
(2Ti 3:16; 1Ki 13:20; 2Ch 33:18; 36:15; Ne 9:30; Job 33:14 – 16; Isa 51:16; Jer 7:25; 17:16; Da 9:6, 10; Hos 12:10; Joel 2:28; Am 3:7 – 8; Zec 7:12; Lk 1:70; Ac 3:18; Ro 1:1 – 2; 1Co 12:7 – 11; Heb 1:1; 2Pe 1:21; Rev 10:7; 22:6, 8).

INTEGRITY [575, 622, 3841, 4797, 7406, 7407, 9447, 9448, 9450, 239, 917].

Essential (Ex 18:21; Lk 16:10; 2Co 8:21). Commanded (Dt 16:19 – 20; Pr 4:25 – 27; Isa 56:1; Mic 6:8; Zec 7:9; Lk 3:13 – 14; 6:31; 11:42; Ro 13:5; 14:5, 14, 22; Eph 6:6; Php 4:8; Col 3:22 – 23; 1Ti 1:5; 3:9; Tit 1:7 – 8; 1Pe 2:12; 3:16). Rewards of (2Sa 22:21; Pss 15:1 – 5;

18:20; 24:3 – 5; Pr 10:9; 20:7; 28:20; Isa 26:7; 33:15 – 16; Jer 7:5, 7; Eze 18:5, 7 – 9). Proverbs concerning (Pr 2:2, 5, 9; 3:3 – 4; 4:25 – 27; 10:9; 11:3, 5; 12:22; 14:30; 15:21; 16:11; 19:1; 20:7; 21:3, 15; 22:11; 28:6, 20).

Instances of:

Pharaoh, when he learned that Sarah was Abraham's wife (Ge 12:18 – 20). Abraham, in instructing his family (Ge 18:19). Abimelech, when warned of God that the woman he had taken into his household was Isaac's wife (Ge 26:9 – 11). Jacob, in the care of Laban's property (Ge 31:39). Joseph, in resisting Potiphar's wife (Ge 39:8 – 12); in his innocence of the charge on which he was cast into the dungeon (Ge 40:15). Moses, in taking nothing from the Israelites in consideration of his services (Nu 16:15). Samuel, in exacting nothing from the people on account of services (1Sa 12:4 – 5). Workmen, who repaired the temple (1Ki 12:15; 22:7). Priests who received the offerings of gold and other gifts for the renewing of the temple under Ezra (Ezr 2:24 – 30, 33 – 34). Nehemiah, in his reforms and in receiving no compensation for his own services (Ne 5:14 – 19). Job (Job 1:8; 10:7; 13:15; 16:17; 27:4 – 6; 29:14; 31:1 – 40). The psalmist (Pss 7:3 – 5, 8; 17:3; 26:1 – 3; 69:4; 73:15; 119:121). The Recabites, in keeping the Nazirite vows (Jer 35:12 – 19). Daniel, in maintaining uprightness of character (Da 6:4). The three Hebrews, who refused to worship Nebuchadnezzar's idol (Da 3:16 – 21, 28). Levi, in his life and service (Mal 2:6). Joseph, the husband of Mary, in not jealously accusing her of immorality (Mt 1:19). Zacchaeus, in the administration of his recompense (Lk 19:8). Nathanael, in whom was no guile (Jn 1:47). Joseph, a counselor (Lk 23:50 – 51). Peter, when offered money by Simon (Ac 8:18 – 23). Paul and Barnabas (Ac 14:12 – 15). Paul (Ac 23:1; 24:16; Ro 9:1; 2Co 4:2; 5:11; 7:2; 1Th 2:4). The author of Hebrews (Heb 13:18).

Dt	9:5	or your **i** that you are going
1Ki	9:4	if you walk before me in **i** of heart
1Ch	29:17	the heart and are pleased with **i**.
Ne	7:2	because he was a man of **i**
Job	2:3	And he still maintains his **i**,
	2:9	"Are you still holding on to your **i**?
	27:5	till I die, I will not deny my **i**.
Ps	7:8	according to my **i**, O Most High.
	25:21	May **i** and uprightness protect me,
	78:72	David shepherded them with **i**
Pr	10:9	The man of **i** walks securely,
	11:3	The **i** of the upright guides them,
	13:6	Righteousness guards the man of **i**,
	17:26	or to flog officials for their **i**.
	29:10	Bloodthirsty men hate a man of **i**
Isa	45:23	my mouth has uttered in all **i**
	59:4	no one pleads his case with **i**.
Mt	22:16	"we know you are a man of **i**
Mk	12:14	we know you are a man of **i**.
Tit	2:7	your teaching show **i**, seriousness

ISAAC [3663, 3773, 2693] (ī′z ak, Heb. *yitshāk*, Gr. *Isaak, one laughs*). The only son of Abraham by Sarah, and the second of three Hebrew patriarchs (with Abraham and Jacob) who were the progenitors of the Jewish race. He was born in the south country, probably Beersheba (Ge 21:14, 31), when Abraham was a hundred and Sarah ninety years old (17:17; 21:5). He was named Isaac because both Abraham and Sarah had laughed incredulously at the thought of having a child at their age (17:17 – 19; 18:9 – 15; 21:6). His birth must be regarded as a miracle. Twenty-five years after God had promised the childless Abraham and Sarah a son, the promise was fulfilled. He is thus rightly called the child of promise, in contrast with Ishmael, who was born of Hagar (Sarah's maid) and Abraham. Isaac married Rebekah. They had two sons, Jacob and Esau. Isaac died at 180 years of age.

The NT refers to Isaac almost a score of times. Abrhama's sacrifice of Isaac is twice mentioned, in Heb 11:17 – 18 and Jas 2:21; but while the submission of Isaac is referred to, the stress is on the triumph of Abraham's faith. Isaac is contrasted with Ishmael, as the child of promise and the progenitor of the children of promise (Ro 9:7, 10; Gal 4:28;

Heb 11:18). In Jesus' argument with the Sadducees on the matter of resurrection, he represents Isaac, although dead in human terms, as still living to God (Lk 20:37). In the Sermon on the Mount, Jesus proclaimed that many would come from the east and the west to sit down with Abraham, Isaac, and Jacob in the kingdom of heaven (Mt 8:11).

Of the three patriarchs, Isaac was the least conspicuous, traveled the least, had the fewest extraordinary adventures, but lived the longest. He was free from violent passions; quiet, gentle, dutiful; less a man of action than of thought and suffering. His name is always joined in equal honor with Abraham and Jacob.

Miraculous son of Abraham (Ge 17:15 – 19; 18:1 – 15; 21:1 – 8; Jos 24:3; 1Ch 1:28; Gal 4:28; Heb 11:11); Ancestor of Jesus (Mt 1:2); Offered in sacrifice by his father (Ge 22:1 – 19; Heb 11:17; Jas 2:21); Is provided a wife from among his kindred (Ge 24; 25:20); Abrahamic covenant confirmed in (Ge 26:2 – 5; 1Ch 16:15 – 19); Dwells in the south country at the well Beer Lahai Roi (Ge 24:62; 25:11); With Ishmael, buries his father in the cave of Machpelah (Ge 25:9); Esau and Jacob born to (Ge 25:19 – 26; 1Ch 1:34; Jos 24:4); Dwells in Gerar (Ge 26:7 – 11); Prospers (Ge 26:12 – 14); Possesses large flocks and herds (Ge 26:14); Digs wells, and is defrauded of them by the herdsmen of Abimelech (Ge 26:15, 21); Removes to the Valley of Gerar, afterward called Beersheba (Ge 26:22 – 33); His old age, last blessing upon his sons (Ge 27:18 – 40); Death and burial of (Ge 35:27 – 29; 49:31); His filial obedience (Ge 22:9); His peaceableness (Ge 26:14 – 22); His blessings/ prophecies (Ge 27:28 – 29, 39 – 40; Heb 11:20); His devoutness (Ge 24:63; 25:21; 26:25; Mt 8:11; Lk 13:28); Prophecies concerning (Ge 17:16 – 21; 18:10 – 14; 21:12; 26:2 – 5, 24; Ex 32:13; 1Ch 16:16; Ro 9:7)

ISAIAH [3833, 2480] (*Yahweh saves*). Little is known about the prophet Isaiah except what his own words reveal. His name Isaiah (*salvation of Jehovah*) is almost identical in meaning with Joshua (*Jehovah is salvation*), which appears in the NT as Jesus, the name of the Messiah whom Isaiah heralded. That his name played a formative role in his life is not improbable, since it expresses the great theme of his prophetic ministry. His father Amoz may have been a person of prominence, since the prophet is so often called (thirteen times) "the son of Amoz"; but nothing is known about him. Isaiah was married and had two children to whom he gave significant names (Isa 7:3; 8:3). Isaiah prophesied during reigns of four kings of Judah, from Uzziah to Hezekiah (Isa 1:1).

The Prophet:

Son of Amoz (Isa 1:1). Prophecies in the days of Uzziah, Jotham, Ahaz, and Hezekiah, kings of Judah (Isa 1:1; 6:1; 7:1, 3; 14:27; 20:1; 36:1; 38:1; 39:1), at the time of the invasion by the Assyrian supreme commander (Isa 20:1). Symbolically wears sackcloth and walks barefoot as a sign to Israel (Isa 20:2 – 3). Comforts and encourages Hezekiah and the people in the siege of Jerusalem by Sennacherib, king of Assyria (2Ki 18; 19; Isa 37:6 – 7). Comforts Hezekiah in his affliction (2Ki 20:1 – 11; Isa 38). Performs the miracle of the returning shadow to confirm Hezekiah's faith (2Ki 20:8 – 11). Reproves Hezekiah's folly in exhibiting his resources to the commissioners from Babylon (2Ki 20:12 – 19; Isa 39). Is chronicler of the times of Uzziah and Hezekiah (2Ch 26:22; 32:32).

The Prophecies:

Foretells punishment of the Jews for idolatry and reproves self-confidence and distrust of God (Isa 2:6 – 20). Foretells the destruction of the Jews (Isa 3). Promises to the remnant restoration of divine favor (Isa 4:2 – 6; 6). Delineates in the parable of the vineyard the ingratitude of the Jews and reproves it (Isa 5:1 – 10). Denounces existing corruption (Isa 5:8 – 30). Foretells the ill success of the plot of the Israelites and Syrians against

Judah (Isa 7:1 – 6). Pronounces calamities against Israel and Judah (Isa 7:16 – 25; 9:2 – 6). Foretells prosperity under Hezekiah and the manifestation of the Messiah (Isa 9:1 – 7). Pronounces vengeance upon the enemies of Israel (Isa 9:8 – 12). Denounces the wickedness of Israel, and foretells the judgments of God (Isa 9:13 – 21). Pronounces judgments against false prophets (Isa 10:1 – 4). Foretells the destruction of Sennacherib's armies (Isa 10:5 – 34), the restoration of Israel, and the triumph of the Messiah's kingdom (Isa 11). The burden of Babylon (Isa 13; 14:1 – 28). Denunciation against the Philistines (Isa 14:9 – 32). Burden of Moab (Isa 15 – 16). Burden of Damascus (Isa 17). Obscure prophecy, supposed by some authorities to be directed against the Assyrians, by others against the Egyptians, and by others against the Ethiopians (Isa 18). The burden of Egypt (Isa 19 – 20). Denunciations against Babylon (Isa 21:1 – 10). Prophecy concerning Seir (Isa 21:11 – 12); Arabia (Isa 21:13 – 17); the conquest of Jerusalem, the captivity of Shebna, and the promotion of Eliakim (Isa 22:1 – 22); the overthrow of Tyre (Isa 23); the judgments on the land, but that a remnant of the Jews would be saved (Isa 25 – 27). Reproves Ephraim for his wickedness and foretells the destruction by Shalmaneser (Isa 28:1 – 5). Declares the glory of God on the remnant who are saved (Isa 28:5 – 6). Exposes the corruption in Jerusalem and exhorts to repentance (Isa 28:7 – 29). Foretells the invasion of Sennacherib, the distress of the Jews, and the destruction of the Assyrian army (Isa 29:1 – 8). Denounces the hypocrisy of the Jews (Isa 29:9 – 17). Promises a reformation (Isa 29:18 – 24). Reproves the people for their confidence in Egypt and their contempt of God (Isa 30:1 – 17; 31:1 – 6). Declares the goodness and patience of God toward them (Isa 30:18 – 26; 32 – 35). Reproves the Jews for their spiritual blindness and infidelity (Isa 42:18 – 25). Promises ultimate restoration of the Jews (Isa 43:1 – 13). Foretells the ultimate destruction of Babylon (Isa 43:14 – 17; 47). Exhorts the people to repent (Isa 43:22 – 28). Comforts the church with promises, exposes the folly of idolatry, and predicts their future deliverance from captivity by Cyrus (Isa 44; 45:1 – 5; 48:20). Foretells the conversion of the Gentiles and triumph of the gospel (Isa 45:5 – 25). Denounces the evils of idolatry (Isa 46). Reproves the Jews for their idolatries and other wickedness (Isa 48). Exhorts to sanctification (Isa 56:1 – 8). Foretells calamities to Judah (Isa 57 – 58; 59:9 – 12). Foreshadows the person and the kingdom of the Messiah (Isa 32 – 35; 42; 45; 49 – 56; 59:15 – 21; 60 – 66).

ISAIAH, BOOK OF Isaiah is preeminently the prophet of redemption. The greatness and majesty of God, his holiness and hatred of sin and the folly of idolatry, his grace and mercy and love, and the blessed rewards of obedience are constantly recurring themes. No wonder that the NT writers quote so often from Isaiah and that so much of Handel's *Messiah* is taken from it. *Redeemer* and *Savior* (*save, salvation*) are among Isaiah's favorite words. The names and words that describe the character of the promised Messiah (9:6) are frequently on his lips: Wonderful (25:1; 28:29; 29:14), Counselor (19:17; 25:1; 28:29; 40:13 – 14, 16 – 17), Mighty God (30:29; 33:13; 40:26 – 28; 49:20 – 26; 60:16), Everlasting Father (26:4; 40:28; 45:17; 55:3; 57:15; 60:19 – 20; 63:16; 64:8), Prince of Peace (26:12; 45:7; 52:7; 53:5; 55:12; 57:19; 66:12). Isaiah had a deep appreciation of beauty and wonder of the world of nature (e.g., ch. 35). A striking figure that he uses repeatedly is the "highway," the pathway (11:16; 19:23; 33:8; 35:8; 36:2; 40:3; 49:11; 57:14; 62:10). All the barriers that separate nation from nation and delay the coming of the King to his kingdom will be removed, and "the glory of the LORD will be revealed, and all mankind together will see it" (40:5).

The importance of the book is indicated by how frequently it is quoted in the NT. Isaiah is quoted by name twenty-one times, slightly more than all the other writing prophets taken together; and there are many more allusions and quotations where his name is not given. He has been called the evangelist of the OT, and many of the most precious verses in the Bible come to us from his lips. The fact that the Lord began his public ministry at Nazareth by reading from Isa 61 and applying its prophetic words to himself is significant of the place that this book would come to hold in the Christian church.

Outline:

PART 1: THE BOOK OF JUDGMENT (CHS. 1 – 39)

    I. Messages of Rebuke and Promise (chs. 1 – 6).

    II. Prophecies Occasioned by the Aramean and Israelite Threat against Judah (chs. 7 – 12).

    III. Judgment against the Nations (chs. 13 – 23).

    IV. Judgment and Promise (the Lord's Kingdom) (chs. 24 – 27).

    VI. More Prophecies of Judgment and Promise (chs. 34 – 35).

    VII. A Historical Transition from the Assyrian Threat to the Babylonian Exile (chs. 36 – 39).

PART 2: THE BOOK OF COMFORT (CHS. 40 – 66)

    VIII. The Deliverance and Restoration of Israel (chs. 40 – 48).

    IX. The Servant's Ministry and Israel's Restoration (chs. 49 – 57).

ISHMAEL [3817] (ish'mā-ĕl, Heb. *yishmā'ēl, God hears,* Gr. *Ismaēl*).

1. The son of Abraham by Hagar, the Egyptian maid of his wife Sarah. Sarah was barren (Ge 16:1) and in accordance with the custom of the age, she gave to Abraham her handmaid Hagar as his concubine, hoping that he might obtain a family by her. Abraham was then eighty-six years old and had been in Canaan for ten years (16:3). When Hagar saw that she had conceived, she began to despise her mistress, so that Sarah complained bitterly to Abraham, who told her that since Hagar was her slave, she could do anything she wanted with her. Sarah made things so difficult for Hagar that she fled, and somewhere on the road to Egypt, the angel of the

Lord met her and told her to return to her mistress and submit herself to her. He encouraged her with a promise of many descendants. Ishmael was circumcised when he was thirteen (17:25). Abraham loved him, and even after God had promised him a son by Sarah, he fervently exclaimed, "If only Ishmael might live under your blessing!" (17:18).

At the weaning of Isaac, the customary feast was held; and Sarah saw Ishmael, now a boy of sixteen, mocking Isaac. Jealous, and probably fearing future trouble if the boys were brought up together, Sarah urged Abraham to get rid of Ishmael and his slave mother, but he was unwilling until he was encouraged to do so by God. Sent away with bread and a bottle of water, Ishmael and his mother wandered about in the wilderness of Beersheba. When he became faint for thirst and was on the verge of death, she put him in the shade of a shrub and sat nearby, "for she thought, 'I cannot watch the boy die'" (21:16). For the second time in Hagar's life, the angel of the Lord appeared to her. He directed her to some water and renewed his former promise of Ishmael's future greatness (Ge 21:19 – 20). Ishmael grew up and became famous as an archer in the wilderness of Paran. His mother gave him in marriage to an Egyptian wife. When Abraham died, Ishmael returned from exile to help Isaac bury their father (25:9). He became the father of twelve sons and a daughter, whom Esau took for his wife. He died at the age of 137 (25:17). In Gal 4:21 – 31 Paul uses the lives of Ishmael and Isaac allegorically. Hagar represents the old covenant, and Sarah, the new; the rivalry between Ishmael and Isaac foreshadows the conflict in the early church between those who would cling to the ordinances of the law, which must pass away, and those who realize that through the grace of Christ there is freedom from the law.

Son of Abraham (Ge 16:11, 15 – 16; 1Ch 1:28); Prayer of Abraham for (Ge 17:18, 20); Circumcised (Ge 17:23 – 26); Promised to be the father of a nation (Ge 16:11 – 12; 17:20; 21:12 – 13, 18);

Sent away by Abraham (Ge 21:6–21); With Isaac buries his father (Ge 25:9); Children of (Ge 25:12–18; 1Ch 1:29–31); Daughter of, marries Esau (Ge 28:9; 36:2–3); Death of (Ge 25:17–18)

2. A descendant of Jonathan (1Ch 8:38; 9:44).

3. The father of Zebadiah, a ruler in the house of Judah in the reign of Jehoshaphat (2Ch 19:11).

4. The son of Jehohanan. He helped Jehoiada to restore Jehoash to the throne of Judah (2Ch 23:1).

5. The son of Nethaniah, a member of the royal house of David. (2Ki 25:25; Jer 40:7–41:18).

ISRAEL (ĭz′rā̆ĕl). Used in Scripture to designate: (1) an individual man, the son of Isaac (*see Jacob*); or (2) his descendants, the twelve tribes of the Hebrews; or (3) the ten northern tribes, led by the tribe of Ephraim, as opposed to the southern, under the tribe of Judah.

Before the year 2100 BC, the God who directs all history chose the patriarch Abraham and called him out of Ur of the Chaldees (Ge 11:31; Ne 9:7). The Lord's redemptive purpose was to bring Abraham and his descendants into a saving (covenant) relationship with himself (Ge 17:7) and also to make of Abraham's seed a nation in Palestine (17:8) and through them to some day bring salvation to the entire world (12:3; 22:18). God accordingly blessed Abraham's grandson Jacob with many children. Furthermore, when Jacob returned to Palestine in 1909 BC, God "wrestled" with him and brought him to a point of total submission (32:25; Hos 12:4). By yielding his life to God's purpose, Jacob achieved victory; and God changed his name to Israel. Hebrew *Yisra'el*, which means, "He strives with God and prevails" (Ge 32:28; 35:10). Jacob's twelve sons were, literally, the children of "Israel" (42:5; 45:21). Israel, however, was aware that God would build each of them into a large tribe (49:7, 16). The term "children of Israel" came to signify the whole body of God's chosen and saved people (32:32; 34:7). It included Jacob's grandchildren and all subsequent members of the household, as they proceeded to Egypt for a stay of 430 years, 1876–1446 (46:8; Ex 1:7).

MOSAIC PERIOD.

In the space of approximately ten generations, God increased Israel from a clan of several hundred (Ge 14:14; 46:27) to a nation of almost 3 million souls (Ex 12:37; Nu 1:46), equipped with all the material and cultural advantages of Egypt (Ex 2:10; 12:36; Ac 7:22). God, however, still remembered his covenant promises with Abraham (Ex 2:24–25). At the death of the great pharaoh (2:23), God appeared to Moses in a burning bush at Mount Sinai and commissioned him to deliver the enslaved people (3:10). The exodus took place in the spring of 1446 BC (Ex 12:37–40). Israel reached Mount Sinai at the beginning of summer in 1446 (Ex 19:1). Here God extended the covenant offer of reconciliation that he had made with Abraham and Jacob (Ge 12:1–3; 28:13–15), so as to embrace the whole nation of the sons of Israel, promising, "Now if you obey me fully and keep my covenant, then out of all nations you will be my treasured possession. Although the whole earth is mine, you will be for me a kingdom of priests and a holy nation" (Ex 19:5–6). God, on his part, provided the objective way of salvation by officially "adopting" Israel as his own sons and daughters (cf. 4:22) on the basis of the atoning death that Jesus Christ, the unique Son of God, would someday suffer to redeem all of God's people (24:8; Heb 9:15–22). God's choosing Israel involved a universal goal, that they would become a "kingdom of priests," to bring salvation to others (cf. Isa 56:6–7). God provided Israel with his fundamental moral law, the Decalogue, or Ten Commandments (Ex 20:3–17), together with elaborations in the various other codes of the Pentateuch. God also furnished them with his ceremonial law, to depict Israel's reconciliation with their heavenly Father (e.g., Lev 23:39–40) and to provide a symbolic way of forgiveness, should they transgress his moral requirements (e.g., Lev 6:1–3, 6–7). The ceremonials, however, gained their true effectiveness because they foreshadowed the ultimate redemptive work of Jesus Christ (Heb 9:9 – 14, 23 – 24).

In May 1445 BC Israel broke up camp (Nu 10:11) and marched northeast to Kadesh on the southern border of the promised land of Canaan. But after taking forty days to spy out the land, all the tribal representatives except Caleb and Joshua reported unfavorably on attempting any conquest of Canaan: "But the people who live there are powerful, and the cities are fortified and very large" (13:28). Impetuous Israel then refused to advance into the Promised Land and prayed for a return to Egypt (14:4). Moses' intercession did save them from immediate divine wrath, but the Lord still condemned them to wander for forty years in the wilderness, one year for each day of spying, until that entire generation died away (14:32 – 34).

In the late summer of 1407 BC (Nu 20:28; 33:38), the advance of the Hebrews on Canaan was resumed. Moses anointed Joshua as his successor (27:23), spoke the final two addresses that constitute most of the book of Deuteronomy, chs. 1 – 4 and 5 – 30, and ascended Mount Pisgah to view the Promised Land. There Moses died and was buried by God's own hand (Dt 34:5 – 6). He had been the founder of the Hebrews as a nation.

THE CONQUEST.

At Joshua's accession, the land of Canaan lay providentially prepared for conquest by the Hebrews. In the spring of 1406 BC, the Jordan River was in its annual flood stage (Jos 3:15). But Joshua anticipated a miracle of divine intervention (3:13), and the Lord did indeed open a gateway into Canaan. For "the water from upstream stopped flowing. It piled up in a heap a great distance away, at a town called Adam," some fifteen miles (twenty-five km.) north of Jericho (3:16). Israel marched across the dry riverbed, led by the ark of God's testament (3:13).

Joshua's war of conquest developed in three major campaigns: in central, southern, and north-

ern Canaan. After these campaigns, much land still remained to be possessed (Jos 13:1), but at this point Joshua was compelled by advancing age to divide the land among the twelve Hebrew tribes (Jos 13 – 22). He then charged his people with faithfulness to the Lord (24:15) and died.

JUDGES.

Moses had ordered the "devotion" (extermination) of the Canaanites (Dt 7:2), both because of their longstanding immoralities (9:5; cf. Ge 9:22, 25; 15:16) and because of their debasing religious influence on God's people (Dt 7:4; 12:31). In the years immediately following Joshua's death, Judah accordingly accomplished an initial capture of Jerusalem (Jdg 1:8; though the city was not held, 1:21); Ephraim and western Manasseh killed the men of Bethel (1:25) because the city had begun to reassert itself. But then came failure: Israel ceased to eradicate the Canaanites, no more cities were taken (1:27 – 34), and the tribe of Dan actually suffered eviction themselves (1:34). Israel's tolerance of evil had to be rectified by national chastening (2:3).

The next three and one-half centuries were used of God to impress on his people three major lessons: (1) The Lord's wrath because of sin. When Israel yielded to temptation, God "sold them to their enemies all around, whom they were no longer able to resist" (Jdg 2:14). (2) God's mercy when people repented. The Lord would then raise "up a judge for them, [and] he was with the judge and saved them out of the hands of their enemies" (2:18). (3) Man's total depravity. "When the judge died, the people returned to ways even more corrupt than those of their fathers" (2:19). The period of the fourteen judges (twelve in Judges, plus Eli and Samuel in 1 Samuel) demonstrates a repeated cycle of human sin, of servitude or supplication, and then of salvation.

THE UNITED KINGDOM.

The United Kingdom of Israel was precipitated by the demand of the people themselves. Despite God's directive that they be holy and separate (Lev 20:26), they still wished to be like "all the other nations" (1Sa 8:5), with a human king to fight their battles (8:20), rather than having God acting through a theocratic judge (8:7). They conveniently forgot that it was faithlessness that brought them under attack in the first place. Still, their rebellion served to accomplish God's purpose (see Ps 76:10), for he had long before decreed a kingdom in Israel over which Jesus the Messiah would someday reign (Ge 49:10; Nu 24:17). The Lord accordingly authorized Samuel to anoint a king (1Sa 8:22) and directed him to Saul of Benjamin (ch. 9).

Saul's accession proceeded in three steps. He was first privately anointed by Samuel (1Sa 10:1) and filled with God's Spirit (10:10), then publicly selected at Mizpah (10:24), and at last popularly confirmed at Gilgal, after having delivered the town of Jabesh Gilead from Ammonite attack (Jdg 11). The primary concern of his forty-year reign (1050 – 1010 BC, cf. Ac 13:21) was the Philistines. These oppressors had already occupied much of his territory, and open war was provoked when one of their garrisons was destroyed by Saul's son Jonathan (1Sa 13:3). In the ensuing battle at Micmash, Jonathan's personal bravery (14:14), plus the Philistines' own superstitious reaction to a heaven-sent earthquake (14:15, 20), brought about their total defeat. Saul thus terminated the second oppression but, by his failure to submit to Samuel (13:8 – 9), suffered the rejection of his dynasty from the throne of Israel (13:14).

From his capital in Gibeah of Benjamin, Saul "fought valiantly" and pushed back the enemies of Israel on every side (1Sa 14:47 – 48). In about 1025 BC, however, having been ordered to destroy Israel's implacable enemies the Amalekites (15:1 – 3; cf. Ex 17:14), Saul disobeyed and spared both the king and the best of the spoils, under pretext of making offerings to God (1Sa 15:15). Samuel stated that "to obey is better than sacrifice" (15:22) and declared Saul's personal deposition from the kingship (15:23, 28). Samuel then privately anointed David, a son of Jesse of Judah, as king over Israel (16:13). David was about fifteen at the time (cf. 2Sa 5:4), but by God's providence, he gained rapid promotion at court, first as a minstrel (1Sa 16:21 – 23) and then by his victory over the Philistine champion Goliath (ch. 17). Even Saul's growing jealousy, which removed David from court to the dangers of battle, augmented the latter's popularity (18:27 – 30). Saul's overt hostility finally drove David and his followers into exile, first as outlaws in Judah (1Sa 20 – 26) and then as vassals to the Philistine king of Gath (1Sa 27 – 30). But while Saul was diverting his resources in the futile pursuit of David, the Philistines prepared for a third, all-out attack on Israel in 1010. David barely escaped engaging in war against his own people (29:4; cf. v. 8); and Saul, routed at Mount Gilboa, committed suicide rather than suffering capture (31:4). Israel's sinful demand for a king had brought about their own punishment.

Having learned of the death of Saul, David moved to Hebron and was there proclaimed king over his own tribe of Judah (2Sa 2:4). With Philistia broken, Israel remained free from foreign threat for 150 years. From about 1002 to 995 BC, David extended his power on every side, from the Euphrates River on the north (2Sa 8:3) to the Red Sea on the south (8:14).

David sought to construct a "house," or temple, in Jerusalem that would be fitting for the Lord. This plan was denied him because of his excessive bloodshed (1Ch 22:8; cf. 2Sa 8:2); but God's prophet did inform him, "The LORD himself will establish a house for you" (2Sa 7:11). He explained, "When your days are over and you rest with your fathers, I will raise up your offspring to succeed you, who will come from your own body; ... he is the one who will build a house for my Name." God's promise, moreover, extended beyond Solomon and climaxed in that One in whom Israel's ultimate purpose would be fulfilled: "And I will establish the throne of his kingdom forever. I will be his [the Messiah's] father, and he will be my son" (7:13 – 14; Heb 1:5). The eternal Christ would indeed suffer a "testator's" death (Ps 22:16 – 18) but would rise in power to give everlasting life to his own (16:10 – 11; 22:22, 26). In the Lord's promises to him (89:3; 132:12), David experienced fundamental clarifications of God's former redemptive revelation on Mount Sinai.

Solomon, after a bloody accession (1Ki 2:25, 34, 36), reigned in peace, culture, and luxury, experiencing only one military campaign in forty years (2Ch 8:3). His greatest undertaking was the building of the Jerusalem temple, erected from 966 to 959 BC (1Ki 6) out of materials lavishly provided by David (1Ch 22). Like the tabernacle before it, the temple symbolized the abiding presence of God with his people (1Ki 8:11).

But Solomon also engaged in a number of luxurious building projects of his own (1Ki 7:1 – 12), so that despite his great commercial revenues (9:26 – 28; 10:14 – 15), indebtedness forced him to surrender territory (9:11 – 12) and to engage in excessive taxation and labor conscription. Unrest grew throughout the empire; and while the tribute continued during his lifetime (4:21), surrounding subject countries, such as Edom and Damascus, became increasingly independent (11:14, 23). More serious was Solomon's spiritual failure, induced by wanton polygamy (11:1 – 8). "The LORD became angry with Solomon because his heart had turned away from the LORD.... So the LORD said to Solomon 'Since this is your attitude and you have not kept my covenant,... I will most certainly tear the kingdom away from you and give it to one of your subordinates.... Yet I will not tear the whole kingdom from [your son], but will give him one tribe for the sake of David my servant and for the sake of Jerusalem, which I have chosen' " (11:9 – 12).

THE DIVIDED KINGDOM.

Early in 930 BC Solomon died, and his son Rehoboam went to Shechem to be confirmed as king. The people, however, were led by Jeroboam of Ephraim to demand relief from Solomon's tyranny (1Ki 12:4), and when Rehoboam spurned their pleas, the ten northern tribes seceded to form an independent kingdom of Israel (or Ephraim). Underlying causes for the rupture include the geographical isolation of the tribes (compare the phrase "to your tents," 12:16) and their longstanding social tensions (2Sa 2:7 – 9; 19:43). But the basic reason lay in God's decision to punish Israel for Solomon's apostasy (1Ki 11:31; 12:15, 24). Israel and Judah were ruled by various kings of varied character and quality. Eventually, they led them away from the Lord, which brought discipline in the form of captivity. The final blows were delivered by Babylon. The Babylonians advanced, and Jerusalem fell in 586. The city and temple were burned (2Ki 25:9), the walls were dismantled (25:10), and most of the people were carried into exile in Babylon (25:11). A small, fourth deportation in 582 removed even some of the poor that were left (25:12; Jer 52:30). Israel had "mocked God's messengers, despised his words and scoffed at his prophets until the wrath of the LORD was aroused against his people and there was no remedy" (2Ch 36:16). But though the external kingdom of Israel ceased to exist, it did so because it had accomplished its divine purpose. A remnant, albeit small, had been nurtured to the point of profiting from the fiery trial of Babylon (see Exile) so as to be ready for that ultimate day: " 'The time is coming,' declares the LORD, 'when I will make a new covenant with the house of Israel.... I will put my law in their minds and write it on their hearts. I will be their God, and they will be my people.... For I will forgive their wickedness and will remember their sins no more' " (Jer 31:31 – 34; See also Heb 8:6 – 13; 10:15 – 22).

JABESH GILEAD [3316] (ja′bĕsh gĭl′ē-ăd, Heb. *yavēsh gil‘ādh, dry*). The metropolis of the Gileadites (*Antiq.* 6.5.1). It lay a night's journey across the Jordan from Beth Shan (1Sa 31:11 – 12) and was in the area given to the half-tribe of Manasseh (Nu 32:33). When the citizens refused to attend the sacred assembly at Mizpah, an army was sent to destroy them (Jdg 21:8 – 15). The city was not destroyed and grew again in power and wealth. During Saul's reign over Israel, Nahash, king of Ammon, besieged the city. When appealed to for a treaty, Nahash proposed to grant peace only if every able-bodied man would have his right eye put out. Granted a seven-day truce, the city sought Saul's help. Saul killed a pair of oxen and sent the pieces throughout his land, indicating what would happen to those who refused to help in his battle for Jabesh. His army defeated Nahash; the city was saved and the nation reunited (1Sa 11:1 – 15). One of the purposes behind this military aid was to secure wives for Benjamites, since Israel had sworn never to allow Benjamites to marry their daughters (Jdg 21:1). Later, when Saul's forces had been routed by the Philistines and he and his sons had been killed, men of Jabesh Gilead rescued their bodies, cremated them, and buried the remains in Jabesh (1Sa 31:1 – 13). After becoming king, David sent thanks for the act (2Sa 2:4 – 6) and had the remains of Saul and Jonathan exhumed and interred in the tomb of Kish in the land of Benjamin (21:12 – 14).

It is probable that the stream Wady-Yabish received its name from the city. Al-Dair (ed Dair) is now thought to be the probable site of the ancient city. It was ten miles (seventeen km.) east of the Jordan and about twenty-five miles (forty-two km.) south of the Sea of Galilee.

Jdg	21:8	that no one from **J** had come to
2Sa	2:4	the men of **J** who had buried Saul,
1Ch	10:11	the inhabitants of **J** heard

JACOB [3620, 2609] (ja′kŭb, Heb. *ya‘ăqōv, follower, replacer, one who follows the heel*). One of the great names of history, a person about whom a multitude of traditions gathered and about whose record scholars have a wide diversity of opinion.

Jacob's name was an old one among the Semitic people. As early as 2000 BC it occurs among writings of Hammurabi as *Yakibula*. That it was a well-known name among the Canaanites of pre-Abraham days is attested by records in the temple at Karnak. Two cities captured by Thotmes III — Joseph-el and Jakob-el — are similar to the Hebrew word.

Isaac and Rebekah had twin sons, Jacob and Esau. They were children of faith, as was their father (Heb 11:20). However, the continuing influence of Aramean paganism that Abraham had left behind is seen in Rachel's act of taking her father's idols when Jacob was leaving the home of Laban (Ge 31:19). From ancient Assyrian culture came the cunning and creative abilities that enabled Jacob to raise a family that shaped the destiny of the human race. He would have his name changed to Israel and become the father of the twelve tribes of Israel.

Son of Isaac and twin brother of Esau (Ge 25:24 – 26; Jos 24:4; 1Ch 1:34; Ac 7:8). Ancestor of Jesus (Mt 1:2). Given in answer to prayer (Ge 25:21). Obtains Esau's birthright for a bowl of stew (Ge 25:29 – 34; Heb 12:16). Fraudulently obtains his father's blessing (Ge 27:1 – 29; Heb 11:20). Esau seeks to kill, escapes to Paddan Aram (Ge 27:41 – 46; 28:1 – 5; Hos 12:12). Has vision of a stairway (Ge 28:10 – 22). God confirms covenant of Abraham to (Ge 28:13 – 22; 35:9 – 15; 1Ch 16:13 – 18). Lives in Haran with his uncle Laban (Ge 29; 30; Hos 12:12). Serves fourteen years for Leah and Rachel (Ge 29:15 – 30; Hos 12:12). Gains experience in animal husbandry with flocks and herds of Laban (Ge 30:32 – 43). Dissatisfied with Laban's treatment, returns to land of Canaan (Ge 31). Meets angels of God on the journey and calls the place Mahanaim (Ge 32:1 – 2). Dreads to meet Esau; sends him presents; wrestles with an angel (Ge 32). Name of, changed to Israel (Ge 32:28; 35:10). *See Israel.* Reconciliation of, with Esau (Ge 33:4). Journeys to

Succoth (Ge 33:17); to Shechem where he purchases a parcel of ground from Hamor and erects an altar (Ge 33:18 – 20). Daughter Dinah raped and avenged (Ge 34). Returns to Bethel, where he builds an altar and dedicates a pillar (Ge 35:1 – 7). Deborah, Rebekah's nurse, dies and is buried at Bethel (Ge 35:8). Journeys to Ephrath; Benjamin is born to; Rachel dies and is "buried on the way to Ephrath (that is, Bethlehem)" (Ge 35:16 – 19; 48:7). Erects a monument at Rachel's grave (Ge 35:20). Incest of his son Reuben and concubine Bilhah (Ge 35:22). List of the names of his twelve sons (Ge 35:23 – 26). Returns to Kiriath Arba, city of his father (Ge 35:27). Lives in land of Canaan (Ge 37:1). Partiality for his son Joseph and consequent jealousy of other sons (Ge 37:3 – 4). Joseph's prophetic dream concerning (Ge 37:9 – 11). Grief over the loss of Joseph (Ge 37:34 – 35). Sends sons into Egypt to buy grain (Ge 42:1 – 2; 43:1 – 14). Grief over detention of Simeon, and demand for Benjamin to be taken into Egypt (Ge 42:36). Love for Benjamin (Ge 43:14; 44:29). Hears that Joseph still lives (Ge 45:26 – 28). Moves to Egypt (Ge 46:1 – 7; 1Sa 12:8; Ps 105:23; Ac 7:14 – 15). List of children and grandchildren who went down into Egypt (Ge 46:8 – 27). Meets Joseph (Ge 46:28 – 34). Pharaoh receives him and is blessed by Jacob (Ge 47:1 – 10). Land of Goshen assigned to (Ge 47:11 – 12, 27). Lives in Egypt seventeen years (Ge 47:28). Exacts promise from Joseph to bury him with his fathers (Ge 47:29 – 31). Benediction upon Joseph and his two sons (Ge 48:15 – 22). Gives the land of the two Amorites to Joseph (Ge 48:22; Jn 4:5). Final prophetic benedictions upon his sons: Reuben (Ge 49:3 – 4); Simeon and Levi (Ge 49:5 – 7); Judah (Ge 49:8 – 12); Zebulun (Ge 49:13); Issachar (Ge 49:14 – 15); Dan (Ge 49:16 – 18); Gad (Ge 49:19); Asher (Ge 49:20); Naphtali (Ge 49:21); Joseph (Ge 49:22 – 26); Benjamin (Ge 49:27). Charges sons to bury him in field of Machpelah (Ge 49:29 – 30). Death of (Ge 49:33). Body of, embalmed (Ge 50:2). Forty days mourning for (Ge 50:3). Burial of (Ge 50:4 – 13). Descendants of (Ge 29:31 – 35; 30:1 – 24; 35:18, 22 – 26; 46:8 – 27; Ex 1:1 – 5; 1Ch 2 – 9). Prophecies concerning himself and descendants (Ge 25:23;

27:28 – 29; 28:10 – 15; Ge 31:3; 35:9 – 13; 46:3; Dt 1:8; Ps 105:10 – 11). His wealth (Ge 36:6 – 7).

JACOB'S WELL Modern *Bir Ya'kub* is doubtless the well mentioned in Jn 4:6 as the well of Jacob. For more than twenty-three centuries, Samaritans and Jews have believed that this is true. The ground mentioned by John had been purchased by Jacob (Ge 33:19). The area was later wrested by force from the Amorites (48:22). The well is near the base of Mount Gerizim, whose bluffs may have been meant in Jesus' phrase "this mountain" (Jn 4:21). A narrow opening four feet (one and one-fourth m.) long led from the floor of the vault into the well, which was dug through limestone. The depth of the well has not been determined. One explorer in AD 670 claimed it was 240 feet (75 m.). Another reported in 1697 that it was 105 feet (33 m.). In 1861 a Major Anderson found it only 75 feet (23 m.) deep. For centuries, tourists cast pebbles into it until Greek Catholics bought the site and put it under guard.

JAMES [2610] (Gr. *Iakōbos, follower, replacer, one who follows the heel*; same as Jacob). The English form of Jacob. The name occurs thirty-eight times in the NT, mostly in the Synoptic Gospels. Apart from no. 1 below, the identities of those bearing this name have been much debated. They may have been as many as four in number, though some scholars argue for two or three. In the absence of clear biblical connection between one and another, it is convenient to list the occurrence of the name in the maximum number of categories (five) as follows:

1. James, the son of Zebedee. He was a Galilean fisherman whose circumstances we can suppose to have been comfortable (Mk 1:20; cf. 15:41; Lk 8:3) and who was called to be one of the twelve apostles at the same time as his brother John (Mt 4:21; Mk 1:19 – 20). It is reasonable to assume that he was older than John, both because he is nearly always mentioned first and because John is sometimes identified as "the brother of James" (Mt 10:2; 17:1; Mk 3:17; 5:37).

James, John, and Simon (Peter), who were part of a fishing partnership that included Andrew,

Simon's brother (Lk 5:10), came to comprise also a trio that attained in some sense a place of primacy among the disciples. James and John were given by Jesus the name "Boanerges" or "Sons of Thunder" (Mk 3:17) when they were rebuked by the Lord for impetuosity and for having totally misconceived the purpose of his coming. This may have been the result of a suggestion made by them that they should pray for the destruction of a Samaritan village, whose inhabitants had repulsed Jesus' messengers (Lk 9:54; cf. Mk 9:38; Lk 9:49 – 50).

Their presumption and ill-considered thinking were obvious also when James, after asking with his brother for a place of honor in the kingdom, was told that they would drink the cup their Master was to drink (Mk 10:35ff.; cf. Mt 20:20ff.). The two sons of Zebedee are also recorded as having been among those present when the risen Christ appeared to the disciples (Jn 21:1ff.), though it is curious to note that James's name is nowhere mentioned in the fourth gospel.

We know nothing about James's career after the crucifixion until Jesus' prophecy was fulfilled when James was "put to death with the sword" by Herod Agrippa I about AD 44 (Ac 12:2). James thus became the first of the Twelve whose martyrdom was referred to in the NT.

The wife of Zebedee was Salome (Mt 27:56; cf. Mk 15:40) who appears to have been a sister of the Virgin Mary (cf. Jn 19:25). If this was so, James and John were cousins of Jesus and thus may have felt themselves in a privileged position.

2. James, the son of Alphaeus. Another of the apostles (Mt 10:3; Mk 3:18; Lk 6:15; Ac 1:13). Nothing is known for certain about him. Since Levi or Matthew is also described as "the son of Alphaeus" (Mk 2:14), he and James may have been brothers.

3. James "the younger," the son of a Mary (Mt 27:56; Mk 15:40; Lk 24:10) who might have been the wife (or the daughter) of Clopas. Assuming that she was Clopas's wife, some go on to conclude from a superficial word resemblance that Clopas and Alphaeus are two forms of the same name. This in turn has led to a suggested identification of James, son of Mary, with no. 2 above. The description "the younger" seems to have been given to distinguish him from the son of Zebedee.

4. James, the brother of Jesus. The only two references to him in the Gospels mention him with his brothers Joses, Simon, and Judas (Mt 13:55; Mk 6:3). This James may have been, after Jesus, the oldest of the brothers. Like the other brothers, James apparently did not accept Jesus' authority during Jesus' earthly life (Jn 7:5).

There is no specific mention of his conversion; he may have been included in the group to which Jesus appeared after the resurrection (1Co 15:7). He became head of the Jewish Christian church at Jerusalem (Ac 12:17; 21:18; Gal 2:9). Although Jesus had always taught the relative subordination of family ties (Mt 12:48 – 50; Mk 3:33 – 35; Lk 8:21), it is hard to believe that James's authority was not somehow strengthened because of his relationship to the Master.

This James was regarded as an apostle (Gal 1:19), although he was not one of the Twelve. Some suggest he was a replacement for the martyred son of Zebedee; others infer his apostleship by widening the scope of that term to embrace both the Twelve and "all the apostles" (see the two separate categories cited in 1Co 15:5, 7).

Tradition stated that James was appointed the first bishop of Jerusalem by the Lord himself and the apostles. What is certain is that he presided over the first Council of Jerusalem, called to consider the terms of admission of Gentiles into the Christian church, and he may have formulated the decree that met with the approval of all his colleagues and was circulated to the churches of Antioch, Syria, and Cilicia (Ac 15:19ff.).

His name occurs again in the NT as the traditional author of the Letter of James, where he describes himself as "a servant of God and of the Lord Jesus Christ" (Jas 1:1).

According to Hegesippus (c. AD 180), James's faithful adherence to the Jewish law and his austere lifestyle led to the designation "the just." It seems clear that he suffered martyrdom; Josephus places his death in the year 61 when there was a Jewish uprising after the death of Festus the procurator and before his successor had been appointed.

5. James, a relative of the apostle Judas. This Judas (not Judas Iscariot, Jn 14:22) is called Thaddaeus in Matthew and Mark. The elliptical text in two passages ("Judas of James" — Lk 6:16; Ac 1:13) has been interpreted in two ways: Judas was the brother (KJV) or the son (most other versions) of James.

JAMES, LETTER OF This letter is among the last to become firmly established in the NT canon. While traces of it seem to be found in the writings of the apostolic fathers (AD 90 – 155), the oldest author to mention it by name is Origen (250), who considers it canonical, although he is aware that its canonicity is not universally acknowledged. Eusebius (323) lists it among the disputed books but says it is read in most churches. In the East the church accepted it from a very early period, but in the West it was not received into the canon until the end of the fourth century.

The author of the letter refers to himself as "James, a servant of God and of the Lord Jesus Christ" (Jas 1:1). The NT mentions five who bore the name of James. *See James.* All the characteristics of the letter support the traditional attribution of it to James the brother of the Lord. The author speaks with the authority of one who knew he did not need to justify or defend his position. There is no more Jewish book in the NT than this letter; and this is to be expected from a man whom both tradition and the rest of the NT show was distinguished by a greater attachment to the law of Moses than Paul had. The whole of the letter, moreover, bears a striking resemblance to the Sermon on the Mount, both in the loftiness of its morality and in the simple grandeur of its expression.

The letter is addressed to "the twelve tribes scattered among the nations." There is no doubt that the letter is intended for Jewish Christians, although its message is applicable to all Christians. The object of the author was to rebuke and correct the error and sins into which his readers had fallen and to encourage them in the heavy trials through which they were going.

Outline:
    I. Greetings (1:1).
    II. Trials and Temptations (1:2 – 18).
    III. Listening and Doing (1:19 – 27).
    IV. Favoritism Forbidden (2:1 – 13).
    V. Faith and Deeds (2:14 – 26).
    VI. Taming the Tongue (3:1 – 12).
    VII. Two Kinds of Wisdom (3:13 – 18).
    VIII. Warning against Worldliness (ch. 4).
    IX. Warning to Rich Oppressors (5:1 – 6).
    X. Miscellaneous Exhortations (5:7 – 20).

JAPHETH [3651] (jā′fĕth, Heb. *yepheth, God will enlarge,* Ge 9:27). A son of Noah. He was older than Shem (Ge 10:21) but comes third in some lists of the three sons (6:10; 9:18). Shem is usually named first (5:32; 11:10). Japheth and his wife were saved in the ark (7:7). Japheth aided Shem in covering the naked body of their drunken father (9:20 – 27). He is the progenitor of the more remote northern peoples of SE Europe. That he was to occupy the tents of Shem (9:27) is thought to refer to conquests of the Greeks, who were descendants of Japheth. This he did during the days of Assyrian power. He had seven sons whose descendants occupied the isles of the Gentiles, Hellenes, or Greeks (10:5), an area including Asia Minor and upper Greece.

JASHAR, BOOK OF (jā′shar). Quoted in Jos 10:13; 2Sa 1:18; and in the LXX of 1Ki 8:53, this ancient book is thought to have been a collection of poetry, probably odes and psalms in praise of Israel's heroes and exploits. Many ideas about the book have been advanced: (1) It continued the Song of Deborah (Jdg 5). (2) It contained the book of the law. (3) It vanished during the Babylonian captivity. It was certainly a well-known bit of Hebrew literature. KJV spells the name "Jasher."

JEALOUSY [6523, 7861, 7862, 7863+, 7868, 2419, 2420, 4143] (Pr 6:34; 27:4; Ecc 4:4; SS 8:6).

Law concerning, when husband is jealous of his wife (Nu 5:12 – 31). Image of (Eze 8:3 – 4). Forbidden (Ro 13:13). Attributed to God (Ex 20:5; 34:13 – 14; Nu 25:11; Dt 29:20; 32:16, 21; 1Ki 14:22; Pss 78:58; 79:5; Isa 30:1 – 2; 31:1, 3; Eze 16:42; 23:25; 36:5 – 6; 38:19; Zep 1:18; 3:8; Zec 1:14; 8:2; 1Co 10:22). A desire to emulate (Ro 10:19; 11:11). See Envy.

Instances of:

Cain, of Abel (Ge 4:5 – 6, 8); Sarah, of Hagar (Ge 16:5). Joseph's brothers, of Joseph (Ge 37:4 – 11, 18 – 28); Saul, of David (1Sa 18:8 – 30; 19:8 – 24; 20:24 – 34); Joab, of Abner (2Sa 3:24 – 27); Nathan, of Adonijah (1Ki 1:24 – 26); Ephraimites, of Gideon (Jdg 8:1); of Jephthah (Jdg 12:1); brother of prodigal son (Lk 15:25 – 32). Sectional, between Israel and the tribe of Judah (2Sa 19:41 – 43).

Ps	79:5	How long will your **j** burn like fire?
Pr	6:34	for **j** arouses a husband's fury,
SS	8:6	its **j** unyielding as the grave.
Zep	1:18	In the fire of his **j**
Zec	8:2	I am burning with **j** for her."
Ro	13:13	debauchery, not in dissension and **j**
1Co	3:3	For since there is **j** and quarreling
	10:22	trying to arouse the Lord's **j**?
2Co	11:2	I am jealous for you with a godly **j**.
	12:20	**j**, outbursts of anger, factions,
Gal	5:20	hatred, discord, **j**, fits of rage,

JEBUSITES [3294] (jĕb'ū-zīts, Heb. *Yebûsi, of Jebus*).

A Canaanite tribe, descended from Canaan according to the table of nations in Ge 10, and dwelling in the land before the Israelite conquest (Ge 10:15 – 16; Ex 3:8, 17; Dt 7:1; 20:17; Jos 3:10; 10:1 – 5; Jdg 1:8). Their king, Adoni-Zedek, was one of the five who conspired against Gibeon and was killed by Joshua. The Jebusites lived many years at the site of Jerusalem (Jebus) and were not dislodged until David sent Joab and his men into the city (2Sa 5:6 – 7). David then bought the threshing floor of Araunah (or Ornan) the Jebusite as a site for the temple (24:18ff.). This large flat rock where the altar

of burnt offering stood is now said to be visible in the Dome of the Rock (Mount Moriah) at Jerusalem.

JEHOAHAZ [3370, 3407] (jē-hō'a-hăz, Heb. *yehô'āhāz, Jehovah has grasped*).

1. The son and successor of Jehu, and eleventh king of Israel. He is said to have reigned seventeen years, c. 815 – 800 BC (2Ki 10:35; 13:1). Like his father, he maintained the calf worship begun by Jeroboam; and as a result of his apostasy, God permitted the Syrians to inflict heavy defeats on his armed forces until he had almost none left. His kingdom became involved in such awful straits that he in desperation called on the Lord for help. God answered his prayers after his death in the persons of his two successors, Jehoash and Jeroboam II, through whom Israel's ancient boundaries were restored. The life of Elisha extended through his reign. When he died he was succeeded by his son Jehoash (13:2 – 9, 22 – 25).

2. King of Judah, 608 BC. He was the third son of Josiah, and at his father's death he succeeded to the throne. However, he reigned only three months and was then deposed and taken in chains into Egypt by Pharaoh Neco, who had defeated Josiah in battle. The throne was given to Jehoahaz's elder brother (2Ki 23:30 – 35). Two times he is called Shallum (1Ch 3:15; Jer 22:10 – 12). He died in Egypt.

3. A variant form of the name of Ahaziah, king of Judah (2Ch 21:17, see footnote; cf. 22:1).

4. The full name of Ahaz, king of Judah, according to an inscription of Tiglath-Pileser III.

JEHOASH, JOASH [3371, 3409] (jē-hō'ăsh, Heb. *yehô'āsh*; jō'ăsh, Heb. *yô'āsh, Yahweh bestows* ISBE; *man of Yahweh* KB).

1. A son of Beker and grandson of Benjamin, probably born soon after the descent into Egypt (1Ch 7:8).

2. An early descendant of Judah through Shelah, who with his brother Saraph ruled in Moab (1Ch 4:22).

3. A descendant of Abiezer son of Manasseh (Jos 17:2; Jdg 6:11). Evidently his family had become insignificant, for Gideon his son said, "My clan is the

weakest in Manasseh, and I am the least in my family" (Jdg 6:15); but in spite of that Gideon could call on ten of his servants for help (6:27). This Joash, though "Jehovah" was a part of his name, had succumbed to the polytheism around him and had built an altar to Baal; but when the men of his city demanded the death of Gideon for destroying the altar, Joash, truer to his family than to his god, stood by his son and said, "Jerubbaal," i.e., "Let Baal plead!" This exclamation became a nickname for Gideon, whom many called "Jerubbaal" thereafter (6:30 – 32). Gideon was later buried in Joash's sepulchre (8:32).

4. The keeper of David's cellars of oil (1Ch 27:28).

5. One of the relatives of King Saul who fell away to David while he was in voluntary exile at Ziklag and became one of the commanders of his forces (1Ch 12:3).

6. A son of King Ahab who was ordered to imprison Micaiah the prophet and to feed him "nothing but bread and water" till Ahab would return to deal with him — but Ahab never returned, and Joash presumably freed Micaiah (1Ki 22:26; 2Ch 18:25 – 26).

7. King of Judah from 884 to 848 BC (2Ki 11 – 13; 2Ch 24 – 25). As an infant he was rescued from Athaliah's massacre of the royal line after the death of Ahaziah in the revolt of Jehu (2Ch 22:8 – 9). Jehosheba (2Ki 11:2; 2Ch 22:11 – 12), sister of King Ahaziah and wife of the priest Jehoiada, hid the baby Joash in the house of God for six years, after which Jehoiada showed him to the people and made a covenant with them. Joash became king, living a godly and useful life all the time that his uncle instructed him. See 2Ki 12 and 2Ch 24 for the details of his reign. He was succeeded by his son Amaziah.

8. The king of Israel from 848 to 832 BC (2Ki 13:10 – 13; 14:8 – 16; 2Ch 25:17 – 24). He was son of Jehoahaz, son of Jehu, and was father of Jeroboam II. These four comprised the dynasty of Jehu (2Ki 10:30 – 31). Jehoash, like the other kings of the north, was an idolater.

JEHOIACHIN [3382, 3422, 3526, 3527, 4037] (jĕ hoi'a-kĭn, Heb. *yehôyākhîn, Jehovah establishes or*

supports). Next to the last king of Judah, reigning at Jerusalem three months and ten days (2Ch 36:9) in the year 597 BC. He is called Coniah three times (Jer 22:24, 28; 37:1 JB, KJV, MLB, NASB, NEB; Jehoiachin NIV), Jeconiah seven times, and Jechonias (the Hellenized name) once (Mt 1:11 – 12 KJV).

Jehoiachin was born to Jehoiakim and his wife Nehushta during the reign of the godly Josiah, his grandfather. According to 2Ki 24:8, he was eighteen when he came to the throne, but 2Ch 36:9 (see NIV note) gives his age as eight. Probably an early scribe made a mistake of ten years in copying one of these two books. The evidence favors the record in 2Kings, for 24:15 speaks of his wives, and he would hardly have been married at eight years of age. Jehoiakim displayed his contempt for the Word of God by cutting up and burning the prophecies of Jeremiah (Jer 36:23, 32), thereby adding to the curses that the Lord pronounced on Jerusalem.

In Eze 19:5 – 9, Jehoiachin is characterized as "a strong lion. He learned to tear the prey and he devoured men." The prophet announced that the "strong lion" would be taken to Babylon, and this was literally fulfilled later. Although Jeremiah was prophesying with mighty power all through the youth of Jehoiachin, the influences of the palace were stronger than those of the prophet. Jehoiakim had been rapacious, violent, and oppressive. He had "the burial of a donkey — dragged away and thrown outside the gates of Jerusalem" (Jer 22:18 – 19). In these sad conditions and under the threatening shadow of Nebuchadnezzar, Jehoiachin became king; and in his three months of power, "he did evil in the eyes of the LORD, just as his father had done" (2Ki 24:9). "In the spring King Nebuchadnezzar sent for him and brought him to Babylon" (2Ch 36:10), where he remained a captive the rest of his life, though apparently not under extremely hard conditions. Nebuchadnezzar died in 561 BC, and his son Evil-Merodach, who succeeded almost immediately, took Jehoiachin from prison and "spoke kindly to him and gave him a seat of honor higher than those of the other kings who were with him in Babylon. So Jehoiachin put aside his prison clothes" and after thirty-seven years of captivity was given a daily allowance of food the rest of his life (2Ki 25:27 – 30).

JEHOIAKIM [3383] (jē-hoi′a-kĭm, Heb. *yehôyā qîm, Jehovah sets up*). Second son of the godly Josiah, king of Judah. He was originally named "Eliakim" (*whom God sets up*). In 607 BC, Pharaoh Neco of Egypt marched northward, intending to fight the king of Assyria at the Euphrates River. Josiah imprudently intercepted him and was mortally wounded at Megiddo near Mount Carmel. The people of Judah passed by Eliakim and made his youngest brother, Shallum, or Jehoahaz, king after Josiah (1Ch 3:15; 2Ch 36:1). Jehoahaz reigned for three months in Jerusalem, when Neco in displeasure "put him in chains at Riblah" in the north of Syria, then sent him to Egypt, where he died (2Ki 23:33 – 34). The king of Egypt next took Eliakim, elder half brother of Jehoahaz, changed his name to Jehoiakim, put the land under heavy tribute, and made Jehoiakim king over Jerusalem, where he reigned from 607 – 597. Jehoiakim was an oppressive and thoroughly godless king (2Ki 23:36 – 24:7; 2Ch 36:4 – 8; cf. Jer 22 – 36).

The prophecies of Jer 22:1 – 23 were uttered (if all at one time) soon after the death of Josiah and the taking away of Jehoahaz (22:10 – 12). They describe the wrongdoing and oppression by Jehoiakim (22:13 – 23). The prophet wrote about the dooms of Judah and the other nations at the direction of the Lord. When the princes heard these words, they let Jeremiah and his clerk Baruch hide themselves; then when the king heard the words of the book, he cut out the passages that displeased him and burned them, with the result that the book of Jeremiah was rewritten and enlarged (Jer 36). Jehoiakim died in disgrace and had "the burial of a donkey" (22:19).

JEHOSHAPHAT [3398, 3399, 2734] (jē-hŏsh′a-făt, Heb. *yehôshāphat, Jehovah is judge*; shortened to *Joshaphat* in 1Ch 15:24; Gr. *Jōsaphat* [Mt 1:8, KJV *Josaphat*]).

1. One of the seven priests who blew trumpets before the ark of the Lord in David's time (1Ch 15:24, NIV Joshaphat).

2. Son of Ahilud, and recorder or chronicler in the time of David (2Sa 8:16; 20:24).

3. Son of Paruah, appointed by Solomon as officer of the commissariat over the tribe of Issachar (1Ki 4:17). He had to provide the household of the king with food one month of every year.

4. Son and successor of King Asa on the throne of Judah. He reigned for twenty-five years, including five years of rule with his father. He began to reign about 871 BC. His mother was Azubah, the daughter of Shilhi. For the account of his reign, see 1Ki 22; 2Ch 17 – 20. Jehoshaphat was the second of the five kings of Judah who were outstanding for godliness, the later ones being Joash, Hezekiah, and Josiah. He took away the high places and Asherah poles from Judah (2Ch 17:6), though he apparently was not able to keep the people from using certain high places in worshiping the Lord (1Ki 22:43). One of the first men to sense the importance of religious education for the people, he sent out in the third year of his reign princes and priests and Levites to teach the people the law of the Lord. They went throughout the cities of Judah in doing this work (2Ch 17:7 – 9). Because of Jehoshaphat's godliness, "the fear of the LORD" fell on the surrounding nations, and even the Philistines and the Arabs brought him tribute. With all this godliness, he seems, however, to have been lacking in spiritual discernment, for he made the great and almost fatal mistake of associating with the wicked King Ahab of the northern kingdom; so much so that his son Jehoram married Athaliah, who was almost as wicked as her mother Jezebel. Jehoshaphat died at the age of sixty, about the year 850 BC. His son Jehoram succeeded to the throne.

5. The son of Nimshi, and father of Jehu who destroyed the house of Ahab (2Ki 9:2, 14).

JEHOSHAPHAT, VALLEY OF (jē-hŏsh′a-făt, Heb. *yehôshāphāt, Jehovah judges*). A name used in Joel 3:2, 12 as the scene where all nations will be gathered by the Lord for judgment. Since the fourth century the Kidron Valley has been named the Valley of Jehoshaphat, but there is no real reason for believing that this is the spot referred to by Joel. He may have spoken of an ideal spot only. There is no evidence that any valley ever actually bore this name.

JEHOVAH A misleading representation in English of the only name (as distinct from titles) of God in the OT. Since it is uncertain what vowels should be attached to the Hebrew consonants YHWH that make up the divine name, actual pronunciation must remain hypothetical, but there are reasonable grounds for thinking that the name was Yahweh. At a late date it became a matter of binding scruple not to pronounce the divine name, and Jews (in reading the Scriptures) customarily substituted the noun *adhonai*, which means "Lord." LXX followed this lead, using the Greek *kyrios*, "Lord," to stand for the divine name — a significant thing in the light of the usual NT designation of Jesus as *kyrios*. But the formulation "Jehovah" arose by inserting the vowels of *adhonai* into the consonants YHWH, thus producing a name that never was!

JEHOVAH-JIREH (jē-hō′va-jī′rĕ *Jehovah will provide*). The name Abraham gave to the place where God provided a ram to offer in place of his son Isaac (Ge 22:14 KJV, MLB, MOF, NEB).

JEHOVAH-NISSI (jē-hō′va-nĭs′ī *Jehovah is my banner*). The name Moses gave to an altar he built as a memorial of Israel's victory over the Amalekites at Rephidim (Ex 17:15 JB, KJV, NEB).

JEHOVAH-SHALOM (jē-hō′v a-shā′lŏm, *Jehovah is peace*). The name Gideon gave to an altar he built at Ophra to commemorate the word spoken to him by the Lord, "The Lord is Peace" (Jdg 6:24 KJV).

JEHOVAH-SHAMMAH (jē-hō′va-shā′ma, *Jehovah is there*). The name of the heavenly Jerusalem as seen in the vision of Ezekiel (48:35 KJV, note).

JEHOVAH-TSIDKENU (jē-hō′va-tsĭd-kē′nu *Jehovah is our righteousness*). The symbolic name given to the king who is to rule over restored Israel (Jer 23:6) and to the state or capital (33:16).

JEHU [3369] (jē′hū Heb. *yēhû'*, probably *Jehovah is he*).

1. Son of Obed and father of Azariah, mentioned only in the genealogy of Elishama (1Ch 2:38).

2. A Simeonite mentioned only in 1Ch 4:35.

3. A Benjamite of Anathoth who joined David at Ziklag (1Ch 12:3).

4. Son of Hanani, and a prophet of Israel who pronounced the curse of the Lord on Baasha in almost the same words used against Jeroboam (cf. 1Ki 14:11; 16:4). Several years later he went out to denounce Jehoshaphat (2Ch 19:1 – 3) for helping Ahab. Jehu's account of the reign of Jehoshaphat was inserted in the lost "book of the kings of Israel" (20:34).

5. Tenth king of Israel and founder of its fourth dynasty. Son of Jehoshaphat, but more often called "son of Nimshi," perhaps because Nimshi, his grandfather, was better known than Jehoshaphat. Jehu appears first as a soldier in the service of Ahab (2Ki 9:25). Ahab and Jezebel were rejected for their crimes. God commanded Elijah to anoint Jehu king over Israel, a command that Elisha fulfilled. He executed God's judgments on the house of Ahab and thoroughly exterminated the worship of Baal, killing all its devotees who gathered together in response to Jehu's pretended interest in worshiping Baal with them; but he did not depart from the sins of Jeroboam. Jehu reigned in Samaria twenty-eight years (c. 842 – 814 BC). Because of his zeal for the Lord in the matter of Ahab's house, God allowed him to set up a dynasty that lasted just over one hundred years (Jehu, Jehoahaz, Joram, and Jeroboam II).

JEPHTHAH [3653, 2650] (jĕf′tha, Heb. *yiphtâh*, *opened* or *opener*). Eighth judge of the Israelites. His history is given in Jdg 10:6 – 12:7. He was the son of Gilead, a Gileadite, and of a woman who was a harlot. Because of his illegitimacy, his brothers born in wedlock drove him from the paternal home and refused him any share in the inheritance. Their action was confirmed by the elders of Gilead. He fled to the land of Tob, probably a region in Syria or the Hauran. There he made a name for himself by his prowess and gathered about him a band of men without employment, like David's men (1Sa 22:2). He must not be thought of as just a captain of a band of freebooters, for he was a God-fearing man, with a high sense of justice and of the sacredness of vows made to God. At the time of his expulsion by his brothers, Israel had been for many years under bondage to the Ammonites. In the course of time, when these oppressors of Israel were planning some new form of humiliation, the elders of Gilead offered to anyone who was willing to accept the office of captain the headship over all the inhabitants of Gilead. When no one volunteered, the elders in desperation went to Jephthah and urged him to become a captain of Israel's army. He accepted, and he and the elders made vows before the Lord to keep all promises. On assuming the headship of Gilead, Jephthah's first effort was to secure the cooperation of the tribe of Ephraim, one of the most influential of the tribes during the period of the judges, but they refused to help. He then sent messengers to the king of the Ammonites, asking for the grounds of his hostile action and requesting that he desist, but the king refused to listen to reason. Endued with the Spirit of the Lord, Jephthah prepared for war. Before going out to battle, he made a vow that if he was victorious he would offer to God as a burnt offering whatever first came to him out of his house. He defeated his enemies with a very great slaughter and recovered twenty cities from them. The Ephraimites then came to him with the complaint that he had slighted them in the preparation for the Ammonite campaign, but he answered their false accusation and defeated them in battle. Forty-two thousand Ephraimites were killed. Jephthah judged Israel for six years. Samuel cited him as one proof of God's faithfulness in raising up deliverers for Israel in time of need (1Sa 12:11). He is listed among the heroes of faith in Heb 11 (v. 32).

The great point of interest in his history is his vow (Jdg 11:29 – 40) and the way it was fulfilled. On his return home after the victory over the Ammonites, his own daughter was the first to meet him from his house. A man of the highest integrity, he knew that he could not go back on his vow to the Lord, and his daughter agreed with him. She asked only that she and her companions be allowed to go for two months to the mountains to bewail her virginity. When she returned to her father, he "did to her as he had vowed. And she was a virgin" (11:39). After that she was lamented by the daughters of Israel four days every year.

How was this vow fulfilled? Did Jephthah actually sacrifice his daughter as a burnt offering, or did he redeem her with money and doom her to perpetual celibacy? The ancient Jewish authorities and the early church fathers, as well as many in modern times, like Martin Luther, hold that she was actually sacrificed, as a first reading of the narrative suggests. Leviticus 27:1 – 8 contemplates the possibility of someone's vowing to give himself or some person of his household to the Lord and makes provision for the redemption of such a person by the payment of money. We know, too, from the experience of Samuel that sometimes persons coming under a vow were handed over for the service of the sanctuary (1Sa 1:11). It is therefore thought by some that Jephthah redeemed his daughter with money and gave her up to the service of the Lord as a perpetual virgin. That may be the meaning of her request that she be allowed to bewail her virginity for two months, and of the statement that "she knew no man" (Jdg 11:39 KJV). The fact is, however, that we cannot be absolutely certain of the mode of fulfillment of Jephthah's vow.

JEREMIAH [3758, 3759, 2635] (jĕr′ĕmī′a, Heb. *yirmeyâhû*, *Yahweh loosens [the womb]* BDB; *Yahweh lifts up* IDB; possibly *Yahweh shoots*, *establishes* KB). Jeremiah was one of the greatest Hebrew prophets. He was born into a priestly family of Anathoth, a Benjamite town two and one-half miles (four km.) NE of Jerusalem. His father was Hilkiah (Jer 1:1), not to be confused with the high priest Hilkiah mentioned in 2Ki 22 – 23. Because of the autobiographical nature of his book, it is possible to understand his life, character, and times better than those of any other Hebrew prophet.

Jeremiah was called to prophesy in the thirteenth year of King Josiah (626 BC), five years after the great revival of religion described in 2Ki 23. This was a time of decision, a time filled with both hope and foreboding. Looking back, we can know it as the last religious awakening in a series that only slowed down the idolatry and apostasy of the Hebrews. Their apostasy finally plunged the nation into destruction.

> *Prophesied during reigns of last five kings of Judah (Josiah, Jehoahaz II, Jehoiakim, Jehoia-chin, Zedekiah), probably helped Josiah in his reforms (2Ki 23), warned Jehoiakim against Egyptian alliance, and saw his prophetic role destroyed by the king (Jer 36); Persecuted by nobility in days of the last king (Jer 36 – 37); Nebuchadnezzar kind to him after destruction of Jerusalem (Jer 39:11 – 12); Compelled to go to Egypt with Israelites who slew Gedaliah, and died there (Jer 43:6 – 7)*

Six other Jeremiahs are briefly mentioned in the OT: (1) a Benjamite who came to David at Ziklag (1Ch 12:4); (2) a Gadite (1Ch 12:10); (3) a Gadite (1Ch 12:13); (4) a Manassite (1Ch 5:24); (5) father of the wife of King Josiah (2Ki 23:30 – 31); (6) a Recabite (Jer 35:3).

JEREMIAH, BOOK OF Jeremiah is a book of prophetic oracles or sermons, together with much autobiographical and historical material that gives the background of these oracles. Jeremiah was called to be a prophet at a most unhappy time. With the failure of Josiah's revival, the final decline of the nation was

under way. When God called Jeremiah, he intimated to him that his message would be one of condemnation rather than salvation (Jer 1:10, 18 – 19). Yet he was also given a message of hope (30:1 – 3, 18 – 22; 31:1 – 14, 23 – 40). Throughout his long ministry of more than forty years, his preaching reflected this theme of judgment. God had risen early and sent his servants the prophets, but Israel would not hear (7:25; 44:4). Now the fate predicted for an apostate nation in Dt 28 – 30 was inevitable. Babylon would capture Judah, and it would be better for the people to surrender and so to save their lives.

This message, coming to people whose desperate nationalism was all they had to cling to, was completely rejected, and the bearer was rejected with his message. Jeremiah was regarded as a meddler and a traitor; and leaders, nobles, and kings tried to put him to death. Although he needed the love, sympathy, and encouragement of a wife, he was not permitted to marry; and in this prohibition he became a sign that normal life was soon to cease for Jerusalem (Jer 16:1 – 4). Because his book is full of autobiographical sections — Jeremiah's "confessions" — Jeremiah's personality can be understood more clearly than that of any other prophet. These outpourings of the human spirit are some of the most poignant and pathetic statements of the tension of a man under divine imperative to be found anywhere in Scripture.

Outline:

I. Jeremiah's Oracles against the Theocracy (1:1 – 25:38).

II. Events in the Life of Jeremiah (26:1 – 45:5).

III. Jeremiah's Oracles against Foreign Nations (46:1 – 51:64).

IV. Appendix: The Fall of Jerusalem and Related Events (52:1 – 34).

JERICHO [3735, 2637] (jĕr′ĭkō Heb. *yerēhô, yerîhô*, Gr. *Ierichō, moon city*).

THE SITE.

Jericho, also called the City of Palms (Dt 34:3), is located five miles west of the Jordan and seven miles north of the Dead Sea, some 800 feet below sea level.

There are actually three Jerichos. The OT city was situated on a mound now called Tell es-Sultan, a mile NW of the modern town. NT Jericho is on a higher elevation nearby. Modern Jericho, called Er Riha by the Arabs, has a population of about ten thousand people of very mixed racial descent.

Jericho is probably the oldest city in the world. Its strategic site by a ford of the Jordan controlled the ancient trade routes from the East. After crossing the river these branched out, one going toward Bethel and Shechem in the north, another westward to Jerusalem, and a third to Hebron in the south. Thus Jericho controlled the access to the hill country of Palestine from Transjordan.

JERICHO IN THE BIBLE.

Jericho first entered the biblical record when it was captured by Joshua and the invading Hebrews as the opening wedge of their campaign to take Canaan (Jos 6). The city's location made its capture the key to the invasion of the central hill country. It was regarded as a formidable obstacle by the Hebrews. After the two spies had searched it (Jos 2), Joshua led the Hebrew forces against the city, marching around it daily for six days. On the seventh day they circled it seven times, then shouted and blew their trumpets, and "the wall collapsed; so every man charged straight in, and they took the city" (6:20). The city was devoted to God, totally destroyed and burned except for metal objects found in it (6:17 – 19). Only Rahab and her family, who had cared for the spies, was saved (6:22 – 23, 25). Joshua placed a curse on the place, that it might not be rebuilt (6:26). The site seems to have remained a ruin for centuries.

General References to:

City east of Jerusalem and near the Jordan (Nu 22:1; 26:3; Dt 34:1). Called City of Palms (Dt 34:3). Situation of, pleasant (2Ki 2:19). Rahab the harlot lived in (Jos 2; Heb 11:31). Joshua sees "captain of the host" of the Lord

near (Jos 5:13 – 15). Besieged by Joshua seven days; fall and destruction of (Jos 6; 24:11). Situated within territory allotted to Benjamin (Jos 18:12, 21). Kenites lived at (Jdg 1:16). King of Moab makes conquest of and establishes his capital at (Jdg 3:13). Rebuilt by Hiel (1Ki 16:34). Company of "the sons of the prophets" lived at (2Ki 2:4 – 5, 15, 18). Captives of Judah, taken by the king of Israel, released at, on account of the denunciation of the prophet Obed (2Ch 28:7 – 15). Inhabitants of, taken captive to Babylon, return to, with Ezra and Nehemiah (Ezr 2:34; Ne 7:36); assist in repairing walls of Jerusalem (Ne 3:2). Blind men healed at, by Jesus (Mt 20:29 – 34; Mk 10:46; Lk 18:35). Zacchaeus lived at (Lk 19:1 – 10). Plain of (2Ki 25:5; Jer 52:8). Waters of (Jos 16:1). Purified by Elisha (2Ki 2:18 – 22).

JEROBOAM I [3716] (jĕr′ō-bō′ăm, Heb. *yārov′ām*, *the people contend*, or *the people become numerous*). Son of Nebat, of the tribe of Ephraim, and of Zeruah, a widow (1Ki 11:26 – 40). He founded the kingdom of Israel when the nation was split following the death of Solomon. His father was an official under Solomon and came from the village of Zeredah in the Jordan. As a young man Jeroboam showed such ability that Solomon put him in charge of the fortifications and public works at Jerusalem and made him overseer of the levy from the house of Joseph (1Ki 11:28). However, he used his position to stir up dissatisfaction against the government. This was not difficult to do, as the people were already filled with bitterness because of the enforced labor and burdensome taxation imposed on them by Solomon. One day as he was walking outside Jerusalem, Jeroboam was met by the prophet Ahijah of Shiloh. Ahijah tore a new mantle into twelve pieces and gave ten of them to Jeroboam, informing him that because of the idolatrous nature of Solomon's reign the kingdom would be torn apart. Two of the tribes would remain with David's house, while Jeroboam would become the head of the other ten. He also told him that if as king he walked in the fear of the Lord and kept his commandments, the kingdom would be his and that of his descendants for many years. When news of these happenings reached Solomon, he tried to kill Jeroboam, but the latter escaped to Egypt, where he was kindly received by Shishak, the pharaoh who had succeeded (and, it is thought, dethroned) the pharaoh whose daughter Solomon had married. As soon as Solomon died, Jeroboam returned from Egypt. When the people met at Shechem to proclaim Solomon's son Rehoboam king, they invited Jeroboam to come and take the lead in presenting their grievances. As spokesman of the people, he urged that their burdens be alleviated, but the protest was contemptuously rejected; therefore the ten tribes revolted from the house of David and made Jeroboam their king (12:1 – 16). In this way Ahijah's prophecy that the ten tribes would form a separate kingdom with Jeroboam as king was fulfilled (12:15).

Although he had been divinely set apart for his task, and although he had been raised to the throne with the full approval of the people, Jeroboam failed to rise to the greatness of his opportunities.

He sacrificed the higher interests of religion to politics. To establish his throne firmly, he led the people into the immoralities of heathenism, which led eventually to the destruction of the nation. The successive kings, with possibly one exception (Jehu), supported this idolatrous worship until Israel fell.

Promoted by Solomon (1Ki 11:28); Ahijah's prophecy concerning (1Ki 11:29 – 39; 14:5 – 16); Flees to Egypt to escape from Solomon (1Ki 11:26 – 40); Recalled from Egypt by the ten tribes on account of disaffection toward Rehoboam, and made king (1Ki 12:1 – 20; 2Ch 10:12 – 19); Subverts the religion of Moses (1Ki 12:25 – 33; 13:33 – 34; 14:9, 16; 16:2, 26, 31; 2Ch 11:14; 13:8 – 9); Hand of, paralyzed (1Ki 13:1 – 10); His wife sent to consult the prophet Ahijah concerning her child (1Ki 14:1 – 18); His wars with Rehoboam (1Ki 14:19, 30; 15:6; 2Ch 11:1 – 4);

His war with Abijah (1Ki 15:7; 2Ch 13); Death of (1Ki 14:20; 2Ch 13:20)

JERUSALEM [3731, 10332, 2643, 2647] (*foundation of Shalem [peace]*). The most important city on earth in the history of God's revelation to humankind in those divine acts by which redemption has been accomplished. It was the royal city, the capital of the only kingdom God has (thus far) established on earth. Here the temple was erected, and here, during the kingdom age, sacrifices were legitimately offered. This was the city of the prophets, as well as the kings of David's line. Here occurred the death, resurrection, and ascension of Jesus Christ, David's greatest Son. The Holy Spirit descended at Pentecost on an assembled group in this city, giving birth to the Christian church; and here the first great church council was held. Rightly did the chronicler refer to Jerusalem as "the city the LORD had chosen out of all the tribes of Israel in which to put his Name" (1Ki 14:21). Even the first-century Roman historian Pliny referred to Jerusalem as "by far the most famous city of the ancient Orient." This city has been the preeminent objective of the pilgrimages of devout men and women for over two thousand years, and it was in an attempt to recover the Church of the Holy Sepulchre in Jerusalem that the Crusades were organized.

While the word *Jerusalem* is Semitic, it apparently was not a name given to the city for the first time by the Hebrew people. Far back in the time of the Amarna Letters (1400 BC), it was called *U-ru-sa-lim*, that is, a city of Salim, generally taken to mean "city of peace." In the Hebrew Bible the word first appears in Jos 10:1 where it is spelled *Yerushalayim*. The name Jerusalem itself occurs about six hundred times in the OT, though it is not found in Job, Hosea, Jonah, Nahum, Habakkuk, and Haggai. The name most often used for this city, apart from Jerusalem itself, is *Zion*, which occurs more than a hundred times in the OT.

Called:

Jebus (Jos 18:28; Jdg 19:10); Zion (1Ki 8:1; Zec 9:13); City of David (2Sa 5:7; Isa 22:9); Salem

(Ge 14:18; Ps 76:2); Ariel (Isa 29:1); *city of God* (Ps 46:4); *city of the Great King* (Ps 48:2); *City of Judah* (2Ch 25:28); *the perfection of beauty, the joy of the whole earth* (La 2:15); *the throne of the Lord* (Jer 3:17); *holy mountain* (Da 9:16, 20); *holy city* (Ne 11:1, 18; Mt 4:5); *city of our festivals* (Isa 33:20); *city of truth* (Zec 8:3), *to be called "The LORD Our Righteousness"* (Jer 33:16), *Yahweh Shammah* (Eze 48:35; see God, Names of: Yahweh Shammah). *New Jerusalem* (Rev 21:2, 10–27). Situation and appearance of (Pss 122:3; 125:2; SS 6:4; Mic 4:8). Walls of (Jer 39:4).

Gates of:

Benjamin Gate (Jer 37:13; 38:7; Zec 14:10); Corner Gate (2Ki 14:13; 2Ch 25:23; 26:9; Jer 31:38; Zec 14:10); Dung Gate (Ne 2:13; 3:13, 14; 12:31); East Gate (1Ch 26:14; 2Ch 31:14; Ne 3:29); Ephraim Gate (2Ki 14:13; 2Ch 25:23; Ne 8:16; 12:39); First Gate (Zec 14:10); Fish Gate (2Ch 33:14; Ne 3:3; 12:39; Zep 1:10); Fountain Gate (Ne 2:14; 3:15; 12:37); Foundation Gate (2Ch 23:5); Gate of Joshua (2Ki 23:8); Gate of the guards (2Ki 11:19); Horse Gate (2Ch 23:15; Ne 3:28; Jer 31:40); Inspection Gate (Ne 3:31); Jeshanah [Old] Gate (Ne 3:6; 12:39); King's Gate (1Ch 9:18); Middle Gate (Jer 39:3); New Gate (Jer 26:10; 36:10); North Gate (1Ch 26:14); Potsherd Gate (Jer 19:2); Shalleketh Gate (1Ch 26:16); Sheep Gate (Ne 3:1, 32; 12:39; Jn 5:2); South Gate (1Ch 26:15); Sur Gate (2Ki 11:6); Upper Gate (2Ki 15:35; 2Ch 23:20; 27:3); Upper Gate of Benjamin (Jer 20:2); Valley Gate (2Ch 26:9; Ne 2:13, 15; 3:13); Water Gate (Ne 3:26; 8:1, 3, 16; 12:37); West Gate (1Ch 26:16). Gates of the twelve tribes in Ezekiel's vision (Eze 48:31–34). Measurement of (Eze 45:6).

History of:

Melchizedek, ancient king and priest of (Ge 14:18). Adoni-Zedek, king of, confederated with the four other kings of the Amorites, against Joshua and the hosts of Israel (Jos 10:1–5). Confederated kings defeated, and the king of Jerusalem slain by Joshua (Jos 10:15–26). Fell to Benjamin in the allotment of the land of Canaan (Jos 18:28). Conquest of, made by David (2Sa 5:7). The inhabitants of, not expelled (Jos 15:63; Jdg 1:21). Conquest of Mount Zion in, made by David (1Ch 11:4–6). Citadel of Mount Zion, occupied by David and called City of David (2Sa 5:5–9; 1Ch 11:7). Ark brought to, by David (2Sa 6:12–19). Threshing floor of Araunah within the citadel of (2Sa 24:16). David purchased and built an altar upon it (2Sa 24:16–25). City built around the citadel (1Ch 11:8). Capital of David's kingdom by divine appointment (1Ki 15:4; 2Ki 19:34; 2Ch 6:6; 12:13). Fortified by Solomon (1Ki 3:1; 9:15). Temple built within the citadel. See Temple. Chief Levites lived in (1Ch 9:34). High priest lived at (Jn 18:15). Annual feasts kept at (Eze 36:38, w Dt 16:16, & Ps 122:3–5; Lk 2:41; Jn 4:20; 5:1; 7:1–14; 12:20; Ac 18:21). Prayers of Israelites made toward (1Ki 8:38; Da 6:10). Beloved (Pss 122:6; 137:1–7; Isa 62:1–7). See Patriotism. Oaths taken in the name of (Mt 5:35). Captured and pillaged by: Shishak, king of Egypt (1Ki 14:25–26; 2Ch 12:9); Jehoash, king of Israel (2Ki 14:13–14; 2Ch 25:23–24); Nebuchadnezzar, king of Babylon (2Ki 24:8–16; 25:1–17; 2Ch 36:17–21; Jer 1:3; 32:2; 39; 52:4–7, 12–24; La 1:5–8). Walls of, restored and fortified by: Uzziah (2Ch 26:9–10); Jotham (2Ch 27:3); Manasseh (2Ch 33:14). Water supply brought in from the Gihon by Hezekiah (2Ki 18:17; 20:20; 2Ch 32:3–4, 30; Ne 2:13–15; Isa 7:3; 22:9–11; 36:2). Besieged by: Pekah (2Ki 16:5); the Philistines (2Ch 21:16–17); Sennacherib (2Ki 18:13–37; 19:20–37; 2Ch 32). Rebuilding of ordered by proclamation of Cyrus (2Ch 36:23; Ezr 1:1–4). Rebuilt by Nehemiah under the direction of Artaxerxes (Ne 2–6). Wall of, dedicated (Ne 12:27–43). Temple restored. See Temple. Roman rulers resided at: Herod I (Mt 2:3); Pontius Pilate (Mt 27:2; Mk 15:1; Lk 23:1–7; Jn 18:28–29); Herod III

(Ac 12:1 – 23). Life and miracles of Jesus connected with: See Jesus the Christ, History of. Gospel first preached at (Mic 4:2; Lk 24:47; Ac 1:4; 2:14). Day of Pentecost at (Ac 2). Stephen martyred at (Ac 6:8 – 7:60). Disciples persecuted and dispersed from (Ac 8:1 – 4; 11:19 – 21). For personal incidents occurring there, see biographies of individuals; Israel, Israelites.

Prophecies Concerning:

Prophecies against (Isa 3:1 – 8; Jer 9:11; 19:6, 15; 21:10; 26:9, 11; Da 9:2, 27; Mic 1:1; 3:12). Pestilence, famine, and war in (Jer 34:2; Eze 5:12; Joel 3:2 – 3; Am 2:5). Destruction of (Jer 7:32 – 34; 26:18; 32:29, 31 – 32; Da 9:24 – 27). Destruction of, foretold by Jesus (Mt 23:37 – 38; 24:15; Mk 13:14 – 23; Lk 13:35; 17:26 – 37; 19:41 – 44; 21:20 – 24). Prophecies of the rebuilding of (Isa 44:28; Jer 31:38 – 40; Eze 48:15 – 22; Da 9:25; Zec 14:8 – 11). Of final restoration of (Joel 3:20 – 21; Zec 2:2 – 5; 8).

JERUSALEM, NEW A name found twice in the Bible (Rev 3:12; 21:2) where the new Jerusalem is described as coming down out of heaven from God. In Rev 21:2 it is also called "the Holy City," and in Rev 21:10 "the Holy City, Jerusalem." In Rev 21:10 – 22:5 the city is described in material terms, as though it were literal. It is in the form of a cube, 1,500 miles (2,500 km.) square; its walls are of jasper; its streets, of gold; the foundations of the walls are precious stones; its twelve gates are of pearls. For light it needs neither moon nor sun. A pure river of water of life flows through it; and in the midst of it there is the tree of life, whose leaves are for the healing of the nations.

Views on the nature of the city, whether it is literal or symbolic, and on when it comes into existence are legion. Hardly any two expositors fully agree, but in general there are two main views. Some hold that the city is a symbol of the ideal church as conceived in the purpose of God and to be fully realized in his own time. The church, allegorically depicted by the city, is of course already in

existence, but God's ideal for it will not be reached until the new age has been ushered in by the Lord's return. The great size of the city denotes that the church is capable of holding almost countless numbers. The fact that the city descends "out of heaven from God" means that it is the product of God's supernatural workmanship in the historic process of redemption. In support of this view, it is said that in Rev 21:9 – 10, when John is told that he would be shown the bride, the Lamb's wife, he is actually shown the new Jerusalem; and, moreover, as Jerusalem and Zion often refer to the inhabitants and faithful worshipers of the Lord, so the new Jerusalem is symbolic of the church of God.

Those who consider the new Jerusalem a literal city usually regard it as the eternal dwelling place of God. Premillennialists see it as a special creation of God at the beginning of the millennium, to be inhabited by the saints, first during the millennium and then, after the creation of the new heaven and new earth, throughout eternity. It would seem, however, that the city will not be in sight during the millennium but will be above the earthly Jerusalem. The saints in the city will have the privilege of seeing the face of God and of having his name on their foreheads. Some expositors hold that the new Jerusalem as a literal city does not appear above Jerusalem during the millennium, and that the description in Rev 21:10 – 22:5 has reference to the eternal state.

Rev	3:12	the new **J**, which is coming
	21:2	I saw the Holy City, the new **J**,
	21:10	and showed me the Holy City, **J**,

JESSE [414, 3805, 2649] (jĕs′ē, Heb. *yishay*, meaning uncertain). Son of Obed, of the family of Perez. He was descended from Nahshon, chief of the tribe of Judah in the days of Moses, and was the grandson of Boaz, whose wife was Ruth the Moabitess (Ru 4:18 – 22). From his descent and from the fact that when Saul pursued David he entrusted his parents to the care of the king of Moab (1Sa 22:3 – 4), we can assume that he was the chief man of his village. He had eight sons, of whom the youngest was David (17:12 – 14), and two daughters, the latter being by a different wife from David's mother (1Ch 2:16; cf. 2Sa 17:25). Jesse lived at Bethlehem and probably had land outside the town wall, as Boaz did. When Samuel went to Jesse to anoint a king from among his sons, neither of them at first discerned God's choice. Jesse had not even thought it worthwhile to call his youngest son to the feast (1Sa 16:11). He is almost always mentioned in connection with his son David. After Saul had quarreled with David, he usually called him the son of Jesse (20:31; 22:7; 25:10), undoubtedly in derision of David's relatively humble origin. We are not told when Jesse died. The contrast between his small beginnings and future glory is brought out in Isa 11:1, 10; and Mic 5:2.

Ancestor of Jesus (Mt 1:5 – 6); Samuel visits, under divine command, to select from his sons a successor to Saul (1Sa 16:1 – 13); Saul sends for David to become a member of his court (1Sa 16:19 – 23); Sons in Saul's army (1Sa 17:13 – 28); Lives with David in Moab (1Sa 22:3 – 4); Descendants of (1Ch 2:13 – 17)

JESUS THE CHRIST [2652] (jē'zŭs the krīst, Gr. *Iēsous*, for Heb. *Jeshua, Jehoshua, Joshua, Jehovah is salvation; Yahweh saves*; Heb. *māshîah*, Gr. *Christos, anointed; Anointed One*).

COMPREHENSIVE LIFE AND WORK.

Although the life of Christ, as ordinarily understood, embraces the years our Lord spent on this earth, as described in the four gospels, his full career spans the ages and invites reflection on its several aspects. Fundamental to the various "I Am" sayings of Jesus is his assertion of absolute existence (Jn 8:58). Therefore it is reasonable to think of him as belonging to eternity. Scripture, in fact, affirms his preexistence and does so in terms of fellowship with the Father (1:1), glory (17:5), and designation in advance as the Savior of the world (1Pe 1:20). His more immediate rela-

tion to the realm of people and things belongs to his activity in creation. All things came into being through him (Jn 1:3; 1Co 8:6; Heb 1:2) and in him continue to have their cohesive principle (Col 1:17). Evidence is not lacking for his presence also in the OT. The manifestations of God in this period are apparently connected with the preincarnate Christ. When Isaiah glimpsed the glory of God, he was seeing Christ (Jn 12:41). Moses and the prophets spoke of him (Lk 24:27, 44; Jn 5:46), with special reference to his sufferings and the glories that would follow (1Pe 1:11). Some of the more important passages of a predictive nature are Ge 3:15; Dt 18:15, 18; Pss 2, 16, 22, 110; Isa 7:14; 9:6, 7, 11; 42:1 – 4; 52:13 – 53:12; 61:1, 2; Jer 23:5 – 6; Mic 5:2.

By the incarnation, the Christ of God took on himself human nature in order to reveal God to people in a way they could grasp (1:14, 18), to become their Savior by ransoming them from their sins (Mk 10:45), and to deal sympathetically with their needs (Heb 2:17 – 18). Today, in glory, he is still the God-man. The incarnation persists.

The present ministry of Christ is being carried on in heaven, where he represents the saints before the throne of God (Heb 7:25; 1Jn 2:1). By the successful completion of his work on earth, he is exalted to be the head of the church (Eph 1:22; 4:15); and by the Spirit he directs the life and service of his saints on earth (Mt 28:20).

One purpose of the incarnation was not achieved during the earthly ministry of our Lord but is reserved for his second coming. His kingly rule will then be introduced following his work as Judge (Mt 25:31 – 34). This future coming is one of the major truths set forth in the epistles (Php 3:20 – 21; 2Th 1:7 – 10) and is the leading theme of the Revelation. After the millennial kingdom, Christ will enter with his people the blessedness of the eternal state, which will be unmarred by the inroads of sin or death.

EARTHLY MINISTRY.

The long-heralded Christ came in the fullness of time (Gal 4:4). God providentially supplied the proper background for his appearing and mission. The world had become to a great extent homogeneous through the spread of the Greek language and culture and through the organizing genius of Rome. The means were thus provided for the spread of the gospel once it had been forged out in the career of the Son of God. His advent occurred at a point in human history when the law of Moses had done its work of demonstrating the sinfulness of man and the impossibility of achieving righteousness by human effort. People here and there were looking with longing for spiritual deliverance.

Entirely in keeping with this divine control of the circumstances surrounding the incarnation is the careful selection of the Virgin Mary as the mother of Jesus. The birth of the Savior was natural, but his conception was supernatural by the power of the Holy Spirit (Mt 1:18; Lk 1:35). Augustus, too, was drawn into the circle of the instruments chosen by God when he ordered a universal enrollment for taxation, not realizing that by doing so he would make possible the birth of Jesus in the place appointed by prophetic announcement (Mic 5:2; Lk 2:1 – 7). The shepherds, by their readiness to seek out the babe in the manger and by their joy at seeing him, became prototypes of the humble souls in Jewry who in coming days would recognize in Jesus their Savior. An intimation of Gentile desire to participate in the Christ may be seen in the coming of the magi from the East. In darker perspective appears the figure of Herod, emblematic of the hatred and opposition that would meet Jesus of Nazareth and work for his death. In the scribes, who are conversant with the Scriptures but apathetic about seeking the one who fulfilled them, we see the shape of things to come — the leaders of a nation refusing to receive him when he came to his own.

In more theological terms the Christ-event is an incarnation. God was manifest in flesh. The one who was in the form of God took the form of a servant and was made in the likeness of men (Php 2:6 – 7). Therefore, when the Scriptures assert from time to time that God sent his Son into the world, this affirmation is not to be treated as though Christ is merely a messenger of God, like the ancient prophets. Rather, he is the eternal Son of God now clothing himself with human nature to accomplish the salvation of people. Though the expression "God-man" is not found in the sacred records, it faithfully expresses the truth regarding the person of Jesus Christ. God did not appropriate a man who already existed and make of him an instrument for the working out of the divine purposes. He took what is common to us all, our human nature, yet free from any taint of sin, and combined it with deity to become an actual person with his own individuality. This is the mystery of the incarnation. The gulf between the Creator and the creature is bridged, first by the person of Christ and then by his mediatorial work.

The boyhood of Jesus should be approached from the standpoint of the truth revealed about the incarnation. Deity did not eclipse humanity so as to render the process of learning unnecessary. Christ grew in body and advanced in knowledge and in the wisdom that enabled him to make proper use of what he knew. He did not command his parents but rather obeyed them, fulfilling the law in this matter as in all others. The scriptural accounts have none of the fanciful extravagances of the apocryphal gospels, which present the boy Jesus as a worker of wonders during his early years. They emphasize his progress in the understanding of the OT and affirm his consciousness of a special relation to his Father in heaven (Lk 2:49).

At his baptism Jesus received divine confirmation of the mission now opening out before him and also the anointing of the Holy Spirit for the fulfillment of it. The days of preparation were definitely at an end, so that retirement was put aside and contact begun with his people Israel. By the baptism he was fulfilling all righteousness (Mt 3:15) in the sense that he was identifying himself with those he came to redeem.

Closely related to the baptism is the temptation, for it also includes this representative character. The first Adam failed when put to the test; the last Adam succeeded, though weakened by hunger and harried by the desolation of the wilderness. In essence, the temptation was the effort of Satan to break Christ's dependence on the Father, so that he would desert the standpoint of man and rely on special consideration as the Son of God. But Christ refused to be moved from his determined place of chosen identification with the human race. "Man does not live on bread alone" was his first line of defense. He maintained it in the two following episodes, quoting the obligation of Israel in relation to God as his own reason for refusing to be moved from a place of trustful dependence on the Almighty (Mt 4:7, 10).

Only when equipped by the baptism and seasoned by the ordeal of temptation was Jesus ready for his life and work. No word of teaching and no work of power is attributed to him prior to these events, but immediately afterward he began moving in the power of the Spirit to undertake the work the Father had given him to do (Lk 4:14).

The public ministry of Jesus was brief. Its length has to be estimated from the materials recorded in the Gospels. John gives more information on this point than the other Evangelists. Judging from the number of Passovers mentioned there (Jn 2:23; 5:1; 6:4; 13:1), the period was at least somewhat in excess of two years and possibly more than three.

John supplements the Synoptic Gospels also in the description of the place of ministry. Whereas the synoptic writers put chief stress on Galilee, plus notice of a visit to the regions of Tyre and Sidon (Mt 15:21 – 28), Caesarea-Philippi (16:13ff.), the Gentile cities of the Decapolis (Mk 7:31; cf. also Mk 5:1 – 20), Samaria (Lk 9:51 – 56; 17:11), and the region east of the Jordan River known as Perea (Mk 10:1), John reports several visits to Jerusalem. In fact, most of his record is taken up with accounts of Jesus' ministry in Judea. The synoptic writers hint at such a ministry (e.g., Mt 23:37; Lk 10:38 – 42) but give little information.

During his Galilean mission, Jesus made the city of Capernaum his headquarters. From this center he went out, usually in the company of his disciples, to challenge the people in city and town and village with his message. Several such tours are indicated in the sacred text (Mk 1:38, 6:6; Lk 8:1). A part of his ministry consisted in healings and exorcisms, for many had diseases of various sorts and many were afflicted with demon possession. These miracles were not only tokens of divine compassion but also signs that in the person of Jesus of Nazareth the Promised One had come (cf. Mt 11:2 – 6; Lk 4:16 – 19). They were revelations of the mercy and power of God at work in God's Anointed. Jesus found fault with the cities of Galilee for rejecting him despite the occurrence of so many mighty works in their midst (Mt 11:20 – 24).

The message proclaimed by Jesus during these journeys was epitomized in the phrase "the kingdom of God." Fundamentally, this means the rule of God in human life and history. The phrase may have a more concrete significance at times, for Jesus spoke now and again about entering into the kingdom. In certain passages he spoke of the kingdom as future (Mt 25:31ff.), but in others of the kingdom as present (Lk 11:20). This last reference is of special importance, for it connects the kingdom with the activity of Jesus in casting out demons. To the degree that Jesus invades the kingdom of Satan in this fashion, the kingdom of God has already come. But in the more spiritual and positive aspects of kingdom teaching, where the individual life is concerned, the emphasis does not fall on invasion of personality or compulsive surrender to the power of God. The laws of discipleship are demanding indeed, but for their application they await the consent of the individual. No disciple is to be forced but is rather to be persuaded by the power of love and grace.

If we inquire more definitely into the relation of Jesus himself to the kingdom, we are obliged to conclude that he not only introduced the kingdom (in a sense, John the Baptist did that also) but also was its perfect embodiment. The appropriate response to the preaching of the kingdom is committal to the will of God (Mt 6:10), and it is clear that doing the will of God was the mainspring of Jesus' ministry (Mt 12:50; Mk 14:36; Jn 4:34). It is evident, of course, that Jesus will also inaugurate the final phase of the kingdom when he comes again in power and glory. Entrance into the present aspect of the kingdom comes through faith in the Son of God and the successful completion of his mission. This could be done during his earthly ministry by anticipation of this redeeming work and thereafter by acceptance of the gospel message.

Much of our Lord's teaching was conveyed through parables. These were usually comparisons taken from various phases of nature or human life. "The kingdom of God is like …" This method of teaching preserved the interest of the hearers until the spiritual application could be made. If the truth so taught was somewhat veiled by this method, this served to seal the spiritual blindness of the unrepentant and at the same time created a wholesome curiosity on the part of those who were disposed to believe, so that they could be led on to firm faith by more direct teaching.

The ministry of the Savior was predominantly to the multitudes during its earlier phase, as he sought out the people where they were, whether in the synagogue or on the city street or by the lakeside. "He went around doing good" is the way Peter described it (Ac 10:38). But much of Jesus' last year of ministry was given over to instruction of the twelve disciples whom he had chosen (for the two phases, see Mt 4:17 and 16:21). This shift of emphasis was not due primarily to the lack of response on the part of the multitudes, although his following faded at times (Jn 6:15, 66), but principally to his desire to instruct his disciples concerning himself and his mission. These men, nearly all Galileans and many of them fishermen, had been able to learn much through hearing Jesus address the crowds and through watching him heal the sick and relieve the distressed, and especially through being sent out by him to minister in his name (Lk 9:1 – 6). However, they needed more direct teaching to prepare them for the part they would play in the life of the church after the ascension.

Christ's investment of time and patience with these men was well rewarded, for when the Spirit took up the work of instruction begun by him and gave them his own power for witness, they became effective instruments for declaring the Word of God and for the leadership of the Christian church. The record of the book of Acts vindicates the wisdom of Christ and his understanding of the future.

In contrast to the Twelve in their attitude to Jesus are the scribes and Pharisees. The former were experts in the law and the traditions that had grown up around it, and the latter were men dedicated to a meticulous devotion to this heritage of Judaism. These groups usually worked together, and they collided with Jesus on many occasions over many issues. They were shocked that he would declare people's sins forgiven and claim a special relation to God as Son that others did not have. They resented his rejection of the traditions that they kept so carefully, and stood aghast at his willingness to break the Sabbath (in their way of thinking) by doing deeds of mercy on that day. It was tragic that people who held to the Scriptures as God's Word should fail to see in Jesus Christ the one of whom that Word spoke. They refused to put their trust in him despite all his miracles and the matchless perfection of his personal life. Because tradition meant more to them than truth, they stumbled in their apprehension of the Christ of God. In the end they plotted with their opponents the Sadducees in order to do away with Jesus.

Even as Christ was engaged in teaching his disciples from the days of the transfiguration on, he was ever moving toward Jerusalem to fulfill his course at the cross (Lk 9:51). In those latter days some stirring events were unfolded — the triumphal entry into Jerusalem, the cleansing of the temple, the institution of the Lord's Supper, the soul conflict in the garden of Gethsemane, the arrest and trial, the crucifixion, the resurrection, the appearances, the ascension into heaven. In all of them Jesus remained the central figure. In all of them he received testimony to himself or gave it. Nothing was unimportant. All contributed to the working out of the plan of God. The cross was humankind's decision respecting Christ, but it had already been his own decision and that of the Father. It underscored the sins of some people even as it removed the sins of others. In the cross, humankind's day erupted in violence and blasphemy. In the resurrection, God's day began to dawn. It was his answer to the world and to the powers of darkness. In it Christ was justified and his claims illuminated.

History of:

Birth and Childhood: Genealogy of (Mt 1:1 – 17; Lk 3:23 – 38). Angel Gabriel appears to Mary (Lk 1:26 – 38). Mary visits Elizabeth (Lk 1:39 – 56). Mary's magnificat (Lk 1:46 – 55). Angel appears to Joseph concerning Mary (Mt 1:18 – 25). Birth of (Lk 2:1 – 7). Angels appear to shepherds (Lk 2:8 – 20). Magi visit (Mt 2:1 – 12). Circumcision of (Lk 2:21). Is presented in temple (Lk 2:21 – 38). Flight into and return from Egypt (Mt 2:13 – 23). Disputes with doctors in temple (Lk 2:41 – 52).

Ministry: Baptized by John (Mt 3:13 – 17; Mk 1:9 – 11; Lk 3:21 – 23). Temptation of (Mt 4:1 – 11; Mk 1:12 – 13; Lk 4:1 – 13). John's testimony concerning him (Jn 1:1 – 18). Testimony of John the Baptist concerning (Jn 1:19 – 34). Disciples adhere to (Jn 1:35 – 51). Miracles at Cana of Galilee (Jn 2:1 – 12). Drives money changers from temple (Jn 2:13 – 25). Nicodemus comes to (Jn 3:1 – 21). Baptizes (Jn 3:22; 4:2). Returns to Galilee (Mt 4:12; Mk 1:14; Lk 4:14; Jn 4:1 – 3). Visits Sychar and teaches Samaritan woman (Jn 4:4 – 42). Teaches in Galilee (Mt 4:17; Mk 1:14 – 15; Lk 4:14 – 15; Jn 4:43 – 45). Heals nobleman's son of Capernaum (Jn 4:46 – 54). Rejected by people of Nazareth, so

lives at Capernaum (Mt 4:13 – 16; Lk 4:16 – 31). Chooses Peter, Andrew, James, and John as disciples, and performs miracle of the catch of fish (Mt 4:18 – 22; Mk 1:16 – 20; Lk 5:1 – 11). Preaches throughout Galilee (Mt 4:23 – 25; Mk 1:35 – 39; Lk 4:42 – 44). Heals a demoniac (Mk 1:21 – 28; Lk 4:31 – 37). Heals Peter's mother-in-law (Mt 8:14 – 17; Mk 1:29 – 34; Lk 4:38 – 41). Heals leper in Galilee (Mt 8:2 – 4; Mk 1:40 – 45; Lk 5:12 – 16). Heals paralytic (Mt 9:2 – 8; Mk 2:1 – 12; Lk 5:17 – 26). Calls Matthew (Mt 9:9; Mk 2:13 – 14; Lk 5:27 – 28). Heals invalid at pool of Bethesda on Sabbath, is persecuted and makes his defense (Jn 5:1 – 47). Defines law of the Sabbath when his disciples pick heads of grain (Mt 12:1 – 14; Mk 3:1 – 6; Lk 6:6 – 11). Withdraws from Capernaum to Sea of Galilee, where he heals many (Mt 12:15 – 21; Mk 3:7 – 12). Goes up onto a mountain, and calls and ordains twelve disciples (Mt 10:2 – 4; Mk 3:13 – 19; Lk 6:12 – 19). Delivers Sermon on the Mount (Mt 5 – 7; Lk 6:20 – 49). Heals centurion's servant (Mt 8:5 – 13; Lk 7:1 – 10). Raises from dead son of widow of Nain (Lk 7:11 – 17). Receives message from John the Baptist (Mt 11:2 – 19; Lk 7:18 – 35). Rebukes unbelieving cities surrounding Capernaum (Mt 11:20 – 30). Anointed by sinful woman (Lk 7:36 – 50). Preaches in cities of Galilee (Lk 8:1 – 3). Heals demoniac and denounces scribes and Pharisees (Mt 12:22 – 37; Mk 3:19 – 30; Lk 11:14 – 20). Replies to scribes and Pharisees who seek a sign from him (Mt 12:38 – 45; Lk 11:16 – 36). Denounces Pharisees and other hypocrites (Lk 11:37 – 54). Discourses to his disciples (Lk 12:1 – 59). Parable of barren fig tree (Lk 13:6 – 9). Parable of sower (Mt 13:1 – 23; Mk 4:1 – 25; Lk 8:4 – 18). Parable of weeds, and other teachings (Mt 13:24 – 53; Mk 4:26 – 34). Crosses Sea of Galilee and stills tempest (Mt 8:18 – 27; Mk 4:35 – 41; Lk 8:22 – 25). Casts out legion of demons (Mt 8:28 – 33; Mk 5:1 – 21; Lk 8:26 – 40). Returns to Capernaum (Mt 9:1; Mk 5:21; Lk 8:40). Eats with tax collectors and sinners, and speaks on fasting (Mt 9:10 – 17; Mk 2:15 – 22; Lk 5:29 – 39).

Raises to life daughter of Jairus and heals woman with issue of blood (Mt 9:18 – 26; Mk 5:22 – 43; Lk 8:41 – 56). Heals two blind men and casts out mute spirit (Mt 9:27 – 34). Returns to Nazareth (Mt 13:53 – 58; Mk 6:1 – 6). Teaches in various cities in Galilee (Mt 9:35 – 38). Instructs his disciples and empowers them to heal diseases and cast out unclean spirits (Mt 10; Mk 6:6 – 13; Lk 9:1 – 6). Herod falsely supposes him to be John, whom he had beheaded (Mt 14:1 – 2, 6 – 12; Mk 6:14 – 16, 21 – 29; Lk 9:7 – 9). The Twelve return; he goes to desert; multitudes follow him; he feeds five thousand (Mt 14:13 – 21; Mk 6:30 – 44; Lk 9:10 – 17; Jn 6:1 – 14). Walks on the water (Mt 14:22 – 36; Mk 6:45 – 56; Jn 6:15 – 21). Teaches in synagogue in Capernaum (Jn 6:22 – 65). Disciples forsake him (Jn 6:66 – 71). He justifies his disciples in eating without washing their hands (Mt 15:1 – 20; Mk 7:1 – 23). Heals daughter of Syrian Phoenician woman (Mt 15:21 – 28; Mk 7:24 – 30). Heals mute man (Mt 15:29 – 31; Mk 7:31 – 37). Feeds four thousand (Mt 15:32 – 39; Mk 8:1 – 9). Refuses to give a sign to Pharisees (Mt 16:1 – 4; Mk 8:10 – 12). Cautions his disciples against yeast of hypocrisy (Mt 16:4 – 12; Mk 8:13 – 21). Heals blind man (Mk 8:22 – 26). Foretells his death and resurrection (Mt 16:21 – 28; Mk 8:31 – 38; 9:1; Lk 9:21 – 27). Is transfigured (Mt 17:1 – 13; Mk 9:2 – 13; Lk 9:28 – 36). Heals a demoniac (Mt 17:14 – 21; Mk 9:14 – 29; Lk 9:37 – 43). Foretells his death and resurrection (Mt 17:22 – 23; Mk 9:30 – 32; Lk 9:43 – 45). Miracle of tribute money in fish's mouth (Mt 17:24 – 27). Reproves ambition of his disciples (Mt 18:1 – 35; Mk 9:33 – 50; Lk 9:46 – 50). Reproves intolerance of his disciples (Mk 9:38 – 39; Lk 9:49 – 50). Journeys to Jerusalem to attend Feast of Tabernacles, passing through Samaria (Lk 9:51 – 62; Jn 7:2 – 11). Commissions the Seventy (Lk 10:11 – 19). Heals ten lepers (Lk 17:11 – 19). Teaches in Jerusalem at Feast of Tabernacles (Jn 7:14 – 53; 8). Answers lawyer, who tests his wisdom with the question "What must I do to inherit eternal life?" with parable of the good Samaritan (Lk 10:25 – 37). Hears the report of the Seventy (Lk 10:17 – 24). Teaches in house of Mary, Martha, and Lazarus in Bethany (Lk 10:38 – 42). Teaches his disciples to pray (Lk 11:1 – 13). Heals blind man, who, because of his faith in Jesus, was excommunicated (Jn 9). Teaches in Jerusalem (Jn 9:39 – 41; 10:1 – 21). Teaches in temple at Jerusalem during Feast of Dedication (Jn 10:22 – 39). Goes across the Jordan to escape violence from rulers (Jn 10:40 – 42; 11:3 – 16). Returns to Bethany and raises Lazarus from dead (Jn 11:1 – 46). Escapes to Ephraim from conspiracy led by Caiaphas, the high priest (Jn 11:47 – 54). Journeys toward Jerusalem to attend the Passover; heals many who are diseased, and teaches (Mt 19:1 – 2; Mk 10:1; Lk 13:10 – 35). Dines with Pharisee on Sabbath (Lk 14:1 – 24). Teaches multitude the conditions of discipleship (Lk 14:25 – 35). Tells parables of lost sheep, lost piece of silver, prodigal son, unjust steward (Lk 15:1 – 32; 16:1 – 13). Reproves hypocrisy of Pharisees (Lk 16). Tells parable of rich man and Lazarus (Lk 16:19 – 31). Teaches his disciples concerning offenses, meekness, and humility (Lk 17:1 – 10). Teaches Pharisees concerning coming of his kingdom (Lk 17:20 – 37). Tells parables of unjust judge, and Pharisee and tax collector praying in the temple (Lk 18:1 – 14). Interprets law concerning marriage and divorce (Mt 19:3 – 12; Mk 10:2 – 12). Blesses little children (Mt 19:13 – 15; Mk 10:13 – 16; Lk 18:15 – 17). Receives rich young ruler, who asks what he must do to inherit eternal life (Mt 19:16 – 22; Mk 10:17 – 22; Lk 18:18 – 24). Tells parable of the vineyard (Mt 20:1 – 16). Foretells his death and resurrection (Mt 20:17 – 19; Mk 10:32 – 34; Lk 18:31 – 34). Listens to mother of James and John in behalf of her sons (Mt 20:20 – 28; Mk 10:35 – 45). Heals two blind men at Jericho (Mt 20:29 – 34; Mk 10:46 – 50; Lk 18:35 – 43). Visits Zacchaeus (Lk 19:1 – 10). Tells parable of the minas (Lk 19:11 – 28).

Final Week in Jerusalem: Goes to Bethany six days before the Passover (Jn 12:1 – 9). Triumphal entry into Jerusalem while people throw palm branches (Mt 21:1–11; Mk 11:1–11; Lk 19:29–44; Jn 12:12–19). Enters temple (Mt 21:12; Mk 11:11; Lk 19:45). Drives money changers out of temple (Mt 21:12–13; Lk 19:45–46). Heals the sick in temple (Mt 21:14). Teaches daily in temple (Lk 19:47–48). Causes barren fig tree to wither (Mt 21:17–22; Mk 11:12–14, 20–22). Tells parable of the two sons (Mt 21:28–31); parable of the wicked farmers (Mt 21:33–46; Mk 12:1–12; Lk 20:9–19); parable of the wedding banquet (Mt 22:1–14; Lk 14:16–24). Tested by the Pharisees and Herodians and enunciates the duty of the citizen to government (Mt 22:15–22; Mk 12:13–17; Lk 20:20–26). Tried by the Sadducees concerning the resurrection of the dead (Mt 22:23–33; Mk 12:18–27; Lk 20:27–40) and by a lawyer (Mt 22:34–40; Mk 12:28–34). Exposes the hypocrisies of the scribes and Pharisees (Mt 23; Mk 12:38–40; Lk 20:45–47). Extols widow who casts two small copper coins into treasury (Mk 12:41–44; Lk 21:1–4). Verifies prophecy of Isaiah concerning unbelieving Jews (Jn 12:37–50). Foretells destruction of temple and of Jerusalem (Mt 24; Mk 13; Lk 21:5–36). Laments over Jerusalem (Mt 23:37; Lk 19:41–44). Tells parables of the ten virgins and of the talents (Mt 25:1–30). Foretells scenes of day of judgment (Mt 25:31–46). Anointed with precious ointment (Mt 26:6–13; Mk 14:3–9; Jn 12:1–8). Last Passover and institution of the Lord's Supper (Mt 26:17–30; Mk 14:12–25; Lk 22:7–20). Washes disciples' feet (Jn 13:1–17). Foretells his betrayal (Mt 26:23; Mk 14:18–21; Lk 22:21; Jn 13:18). Accuses Judas of his betrayal (Mt 26:21–25; Mk 14:18–21; Lk 22:21–23; Jn 13:21–30). Teaches his disciples and comforts them with promises, including the gift of the Holy Spirit (Jn 14–16). Last prayer (Jn 17). Arrest, Crucifixion, Resurrection: Moves to Gethsemane (Mt 26:30, 36–46; Mk 14:26, 32–42; Lk 22:39–46; Jn 18:1). Is betrayed and apprehended (Mt 26:47–56; Mk 14:43–54, 66–72; Lk 22:47–53; Jn 18:2–12). Trial of, before Caiaphas (Mt 26:57–58, 69–75; Mk 14:53–54, 66–72; Lk 22:54–62; Jn 18:13–18, 25–27). Led by the council to Pilate (Mt 27:1–2, 11–14; Mk 15:1–5; Lk 23:1–5; Jn 18:28–38). Arraigned before Herod (Lk 23:6–12). Tried before Pilate (Mt 27:15–26; Mk 15:6–15; Lk 23:13–25; Jn 18:39–40; 19:1–16). Mocked by soldiers (Mt 27:27–31; Mk 15:16–20). Led away to be crucified (Mt 27:31–34; Mk 15:20–23; Lk 23:26–32; Jn 19:16–17). Crucified (Mt 27:35–56; Mk 15:24–41; Lk 23:33–49; Jn 19:18–30). Taken from the cross and buried (Mt 27:57–66; Mk 15:42–47; Lk 23:50–56; Jn 19:31–42). Arises from dead (Mt 28:2–15; Mk 16:1–11; Lk 24:1–12; Jn 20:1–18). Seen by Mary Magdalene (Mt 28:1–10; Mk 16:9; Jn 20:11–17); by Peter (Lk 24:34; 1Co 15:5). Appears to two disciples who journey to Emmaus (Mk 16:12–13; Lk 24:13–35). Appears in disciples' midst when Thomas is absent (Mk 16:14–18; Lk 24:36–49; Jn 20:19–23); when Thomas is present (Jn 20:26–29); at the Sea of Galilee (Mt 28:16; Jn 21:1–14); to the apostles and five hundred believers on a mountain in Galilee (Mt 28:16–20, w Ac 10:40–42; 13:31; 1Co 15:6–7). Appears to James, and also to all the apostles (Ac 1:3–8; 1Co 15:7). Ascension and Additional Appearances: Ascends to heaven (Mk 16:19–20; Lk 24:50–53; Ac 1:9–12). Appears to Paul (Ac 9:3–17; 18:9; 22:14, 18; 23:11; 26:16; 1Co 9:1; 15:8). Stephen's vision of (Ac 7:55–56). Appears to John on Patmos (Rev 1:10–18).

Ac	2:32	God has raised this **J** to life,
	9:5	"I am **J**, whom you are persecuting
	9:34	said to him, "**J** Christ heals you.
	15:11	of our Lord **J** that we are saved,
	16:31	"Believe in the Lord **J**,
	20:24	the task the Lord **J** has given me —
Ro	3:24	redemption that came by Christ **J**.
	5:17	life through the one man, **J** Christ.
	8:1	for those who are in Christ **J**,
1Co	1:7	for our Lord **J** Christ to be revealed
	2:2	except **J** Christ and him crucified.

	6:11	in the name of the Lord **J** Christ
	8:6	and there is but one Lord, **J** Christ,
	12:3	and no one can say, "**J** is Lord,"
2Co	4:5	not preach ourselves, but **J** Christ
	13:5	Do you not realize that Christ **J** is
Gal	2:16	but by faith in **J** Christ.
	3:28	for you are all one in Christ **J**.
	5:6	in Christ **J** neither circumcision
	6:17	bear on my body the marks of **J**.
Eph	1:5	as his sons through **J** Christ,
	2:10	created in Christ **J**
	2:20	with Christ **J** himself as the chief
Php	1:6	until the day of Christ **J**.
	2:5	be the same as that of Christ **J**:
	2:10	name of **J** every knee should bow,
Col	3:17	do it all in the name of the Lord **J**,
1Th	1:10	whom he raised from the dead — **J**,
	4:14	We believe that **J** died
	5:23	at the coming of our Lord **J** Christ.
2Th	1:7	when the Lord **J** is revealed
	2:1	the coming of our Lord **J** Christ
1Ti	1:15	Christ **J** came into the world
2Ti	1:10	appearing of our Savior, Christ **J**,
	2:3	us like a good soldier of Christ **J**.
	3:12	life in Christ **J** will be persecuted,
Tit	2:13	our great God and Savior, **J** Christ,
Heb	2:9	But we see **J**, who was made a little
	2:11	So **J** is not ashamed to call them
	3:1	fix your thoughts on **J**, the apostle
	4:14	through the heavens, **J** the Son
	6:20	where **J**, who went before us,
	7:22	**J** has become the guarantee
	7:24	but because **J** lives forever,
	8:6	But the ministry **J** has received is
	12:2	Let us fix our eyes on **J**, the author
	12:24	to **J** the mediator of a new
1Pe	1:3	the resurrection of **J** Christ
2Pe	1:16	and coming of our Lord **J** Christ,
1Jn	1:7	and the blood of **J**, his Son,
	2:1	**J** Christ, the Righteous One.
	2:6	to live in him must walk as **J** did.
	4:15	anyone acknowledges that **J** is
Rev	1:1	The revelation of **J** Christ,

| | 22:16 | **J**, have sent my angel |
| | 22:20 | Come, Lord **J**. |

JETHRO [3858, 3861] (jĕth'rō, Heb. *yithrô, excellence*). A priest of Midian and father-in-law of Moses (Ex 3:1). Reuel, which means "friend of God," seems to have been his personal name (2:18; 3:1), and Jethro his honorary title. When Moses fled from Egypt to Midian, he was welcomed into the household of Jethro because of his kindness to the priest's seven daughters, whom he helped water their flocks. Moses married Zipporah, one of the daughters, and kept his father-in-law's flocks for about forty years (3:1 – 2). After the Lord commanded Moses to return to Egypt to deliver the enslaved Israelites, Jethro gave him permission to depart. Moses took with him his wife Zipporah and their two sons (4:18 – 20), but later he sent the three back to stay with Jethro temporarily. After the deliverance from Egypt, before the Israelites reached Sinai, Jethro came to see Moses, bringing back to him his daughter and her two sons (18:1 – 7). We are told that "Jethro was delighted to hear about all the good things the LORD had done for Israel," and that he offered a burnt offering to the Lord. When he saw how occupied Moses was in deciding disputes among his people, he suggested the appointment of judges of various grades to help him decide cases of minor importance. Moses acted on his advice. Jethro then returned to his own country.

JEW [3373, 3374, 10316, 2678, 2679, 2680, 2681+, 4364] (Heb. *yehûdî*, Gr. *Ioudaios*, Lat. *Judaeus; from Judah*). This word does not occur before the period of Jeremiah in OT literature. Originally it denoted one belonging to the tribe of Judah or to the two tribes of the southern kingdom (2Ki 16:6; 25:25). Later its meaning was extended, and it was applied to anyone of the Hebrew race who returned from the captivity. As most of the exiles came from Judah, and as they were the main historical representatives of ancient Israel, the term *Jew* came finally to comprehend all of the Hebrew race throughout the world (Est 2:5; Mt 2:2). As early as the days of

Hezekiah, the language of Judah was called Jewish (NIV Hebrew). In the OT the adjective applies only to the Jews' language or speech (2Ki 18:26, 28; Ne 13:24; Isa 36:11, 13). In the Gospels, *Jews* (always plural, except for Jn 4:9; 18:35) is the usual term for Israelites; and in the NT, Jews (Israelites) and Gentiles are sometimes contrasted (Mk 7:3; Jn 2:6; Act 10:28). Paul warns against Jewish myths (Tit 1:14) and speaks of the Jews' religion (Gal 1:13 – 14, lit., KJV; Judaism NIV, RSV).

Est	2:5	of Susa a **J** of the tribe of Benjamin,
Zec	8:23	of one **J** by the hem of his robe
Ac	21:39	"I am a **J**, from Tarsus in Cilicia,
Ro	1:16	first for the **J**, then for the Gentile.
	2:28	A man is not a **J** if he is only one
	10:12	there is no difference between **J**
1Co	9:20	To the Jews I became like a **J**,
Gal	2:14	"You are a **J**, yet you live like
	3:28	There is neither **J** nor Greek,
Col	3:11	Here there is no Greek or **J**,

JEZEBEL [374, 2630] (jĕz′ă̇bĕl, Heb. *'îzevel*, meaning uncertain, perhaps *unexalted, unhusbanded*).

1. Daughter of Ethbaal, king of the Zidonians, and queen of Ahab, king of Israel (c. 874 – 853 BC). She had been brought up a zealous worshiper of Baal, and as the wife of Ahab, she not only continued her ancestral religion but tried to impose it on the people of Israel. To please her, Ahab built a temple and an altar to Baal in Samaria (1Ki 16:32). Four hundred fifty prophets of Baal ate at her table (18:19). She killed all the prophets of the Lord on whom she could lay her hands (18:4 – 13). When she was told of the slaughter of the prophets of Baal by Elijah, she threatened Elijah's life, and he was obliged to flee. In 2Ki 9:7 we are told that the killing of Ahab's family was a punishment for the persecution of the prophets of the Lord by Jezebel. Later she secured Naboth's vineyard for Ahab by having its owner unjustly executed (1Ki 21). When Elijah heard of this crime, he told Ahab that God's vengeance would fall on him and that dogs would eat Jezebel's body by the wall of Jezreel. The prophecy

was fulfilled when, eleven years after the death of Ahab, Jehu executed pitiless vengeance on the royal household. Jezebel "painted her eyes and arranged her hair," looked out an open window, and taunted Jehu for being his master's murderer. Jehu asked those who were on his side to throw her down, and this was unhesitatingly done by some eunuchs. Jehu drove over her body with his chariot, and her blood spattered the horses and the wall. Later he gave directions that she be buried, but it was found that dogs had left nothing of her but skull, feet, and hands (2Ki 9:7, 30 – 37).

2. In Rev 2:20, in the letter to Thyatira, we read of "that woman Jezebel, who calls herself a prophetess," and led some members of the Christian church there to commit spiritual fornication. This may be a symbolic name, given because of the resemblance between her and the idolatrous wife of Ahab.

> *Worshiped idols and persecuted the prophets of God (1Ki 18:4, 13, 19; 2Ki 3:2, 13; 9:7, 22); Vowed to kill Elijah (1Ki 19:1 – 3); Wickedly accomplished the death of Naboth (1Ki 21:5 – 16); Death of, foretold (1Ki 21:23; 2Ki 9:10); Death of, at the hand of Jehu (2Ki 9:30 – 37); Figurative (Rev 2:20)*

JOAB [3405] (jō′ăb, Heb. *yô'āv, Jehovah is father*).

1. The second of the three sons of Zeruiah, the half sister of David, the two others being Abishai and Asahel (2Sa 8:16; 1Ch 2:16). He first appears in public life in the narrative of David's war with Ish-Bosheth for the throne left vacant by Saul's death. He was David's captain of the army, while Abner led the forces of Ish-Bosheth. When the two armies met, a tournament took place between twelve men from each side, followed by a general engagement in which, after Joab's men were routed, Asahel was killed in his pursuit of Abner (2Sa 2:12 – 32). When Abner transferred his allegiance to David, Joab treacherously killed him, with the connivance of Abishai, for killing Asahel at the battle of Gibeon, though Abner had done so in self-defense. David

declared himself innocent of this murder, and after composing a lament for Abner, commanded that there be a period of public mourning for the dead man (3:31). David pronounced a curse on Joab and his descendants, but he did not bring him to justice, perhaps because he was politically too weak to do so.

2. Son of Seraiah and descendant of Kenaz of the tribe of Judah. He was father of Ge Harashim (1Ch 4:14).

3. Founder of a family of returned exiles (Ezr 2:6; 8:9; Ne 7:11).

4. A village, apparently in Judah (1Ch 2:54 RV). KJV has the translation "Ataroth, the house of Joab"; and NIV, "Atroth Beth Joab."

JOB [373, 6275, 3873] (jōb, Heb. *'iyôv*, meaning uncertain; *where is my father*, or perhaps *where is my father, O God?*).

> *A man who lived in Uz (Job 1:1); Righteousness of (Job 1:1, 5, 8; 2:3; Eze 14:14, 20); Riches of (Job 1:3); Trial of, by affliction of Satan (Job 1:13 – 19; 2:7 – 10); Fortitude of (Job 1:20 – 22; 2:10; Jas 5:11); Visited by Eliphaz, Bildad, and Zophar as comforters (Job 2:11 – 13); Complaints of, and replies by his three friends (Job 3 – 37); Replied to by God (Job 38 – 41); Submission of, to God (Job 40:3 – 5; 42:1 – 6); Later blessings and riches of (Job 42:10 – 16); Death of (Job 42:16 – 17)*

JOB, BOOK OF This book has a definite kinship with eastern *chokmâ* (wisdom) literature. OT Wisdom books (cf. Proverbs, Ecclesiastes, and, in a sense, Song of Songs) applied foundational Mosaic revelation to the problems of human existence and conduct as they were being formulated in the philosophical circles of the world of that day. A figure like Job, standing outside the Abrahamic and Mosaic covenants, was an ideal vehicle for biblical wisdom doctrine, concerned as it was with the common ways and demands of God rather than with his peculiarly theocratic government of Israel.

Even an approximate date for the anonymous author is uncertain. The events he narrates belong to the early patriarchal period, as is evident from features such as Job's longevity, revelation by theophany (God visibly manifesting himself), the nomadic status of the Chaldeans, and early social and economic practices. But the question is, when was the tradition of Job transformed by the inspired author into the canonical book of Job? Dates have been assigned by twentieth-century critics all the way from the Mosaic to the Maccabean ages.

The particular purpose of the book of Job as Wisdom Literature is to articulate and point the direction for a true apologetic for the faith. The doctrine of God as incomprehensible Creator and sovereign Lord is offered as the fundamental reality people must reckon with as religious beings serving God amid the historical tensions of life. It is also the presupposition with which a philosophical being bent on interpretative adventure must begin. This enterprise is illustrated by the debate of Job and his friends over the problem of theodicy (God's goodness versus evil). The folly of depending for answers on human observation and speculation is portrayed by the silencing of the trio who represent it. The book of Job identifies the way of the covenant with the way of wisdom (cf. Job 28:28) and so brings philosophy under the authority of divine revelation.

No comprehensive answer is given to the problem of suffering since theodicy is not the book's major theme; nevertheless, considerable light is given. Elihu traces the mystery to the principle of divine grace: sufferings are a sovereign gift, calling to repentance and life. Moreover, impressive assurance is given that God, as a just and omnipotent covenant Lord, will ultimately visit both the curses and blessings of the covenant on his subjects according to righteousness. Especially significant are the insights Job himself attains into the role God will play as his heavenly vindicator, redeeming his name from all slander and his life from the king of terrors. Job utters in raw faith what is later revealed in the doctrines of eschatological theophany: resurrection of the dead and the final judgment. This vision does not reveal the why of the particular sufferings of Job or any other believer, but it does present the servants of God with a framework for hope.

Outline:

    I. Desolation: The Trial of Job's Wisdom (1:1 – 2:10)

    II. Complaint: The Way of Wisdom Lost (2:11 – 3:26)

    III. Judgment: The Way of Wisdom Darkened and Illuminated (4:1 – 41:34)

    IV. Confession: The Way of Wisdom Regained (42:1 – 6)

    V. Restoration: The Triumph of Job's Wisdom (42:7 – 17)

JOEL [3408, 2727] (jō'ĕl, Heb. *yô'ēl*, *Jehovah is God*).

1. The prophet, son of Pethuel and author of the second book of the Minor Prophets. We know nothing of the man, his life, or times.

2. Samuel's firstborn son (1Sa 8:2; 1Ch 6:33).

3. A Simeonite prince (1Ch 4:35).

4. A Reubenite chief (1Ch 5:4, 8).

5. A Gadite chief (1Ch 5:12).

6. An ancestor of Samuel, of the tribe of Levi (1Ch 6:36).

7. A chief of Issachar (1Ch 7:3).

8. One of David's mighty men (1Ch 11:38).

9. A Levite (1Ch 15:7, 11, 17), probably also mentioned in 1Ch 23:8; 26:22.

10. David's officer over half of Manasseh (1Ch 27:20).

11. A Levite of Hezekiah's time (2Ch 29:12).

12. A Jew who had married a foreign wife (Ezr 10:43).

13. A Benjamite overseer (Ne 11:9).

JOEL, BOOK OF (jō'ĕl, Heb. *yô'ēl*, *Jehovah is God*). The book of Joel is without the customary dating formula used by the prophets (Hos 1:1; Am 1:1) and nowhere indicates the date either of the ministry of the prophet Joel or of the writing of the book.

Indirect references throughout the book have been claimed in support of dates that have differed from each other by as much as half a millennium.

Scholars who follow the traditional viewpoint believe the book to be preexilic, written perhaps during the reign of the boy king Joash (837 – 800 BC).

The occasion of the book was a devastating locust plague. Those who have not experienced such a calamity can hardly appreciate its destruction. An article with convincing photographs appeared in *National Geographic* in December 1915 describing a locust attack on Jerusalem in that year. This description of a visitation similar to that which occasioned Joel's prophecy provides an excellent background for understanding the book of Joel. The prophet, after describing the plague and its resulting chaos, urges the nation to repent of its sins and then goes on to predict a worse visitation, the future day of the Lord.

Outline:

    I. The Locust Plague and Its Removal (1:1 – 2:27).

    II. The Future Day of the Lord (2:28 – 3:21).

        A. The Spirit of God to be poured out (2:28 – 32).

        B. The judgment of the nations (3:1 – 17).

        C. Blessing on Israel following judgment (3:18 – 21).

JOHN [2722] (Gr. *Iōannēs*, from Heb. *Yôhānān*, *Yahweh is gracious*).

1. John the Baptist. *See John the Baptist.*

2. The apostle, the son of Zebedee, and brother of James. *See John, the Apostle.*

3. John Mark. *See Mark.*

4. Father of Simon Peter (Jn 1:42; 21:15, 17).

5. Jewish religious dignitary who called Peter and John to account for their preaching about Jesus (Ac 4:6).

6. Father of Mattathias (1Mc 2:1).

7. Eldest son of Mattathias (1Mc 9:36).

8. Father of Eupolemus (2Mc 4:11).

9. John Hyrcanus, son of Simon (1Mc 13:53; 16:1).

10. Jewish envoy (2Mc 11:17).

JOHN, THE APOSTLE The sources for the life of John are relatively meager. All that exists is what is found in the NT and what has been preserved by tradition. One can, therefore, give no more than a fragmentary account of his life. He was the son of Zebedee and the brother of James the apostle, who was put to death by Herod Agrippa I about AD 44 (Mt 4:21; Ac 12:1 – 2). It may be reasonably inferred that his mother was Salome (cf. Mt 27:56 with Mk 15:40) and that she was the sister of Mary the mother of Jesus. Jesus and John would then have been cousins. The family lived in Galilee, probably at Bethsaida. The father and the two sons were fishermen on the Sea of Galilee (Mk 1:19 – 20). There are reasons for thinking that the family was not poor. They had hired servants and thus belonged to the employer class. Salome was one of the women who ministered to Jesus of her own funds (Mk 15:40; Lk 8:3) and was also one of the women who bought spices and came to anoint the body of Jesus (Mk 16:1). In addition, the fact that John knew the high priest well enough to gain entrance to the court where Jesus was tried and could get permission for Peter to enter also suggests that the family was not poor.

Five books of the NT are attributed to him — the fourth gospel, three letters, and Revelation. The only one in which his name actually appears is the last. According to tradition, he spent his last years in Ephesus. Very likely the seven churches of Asia enjoyed his ministry. The book of Revelation was written on the island of Patmos, where he was exiled "because of the word of God and the testimony of Jesus" (Rev 1:9). Tradition says that he wrote the gospel of John in Asia at the request of Christian friends and that he agreed to do so only after the church had fasted and prayed about the matter for three days. He apparently died in Ephesus about the end of the century.

It is evident from all we know of John that he was one of the greatest of the apostles. He is described as the disciple whom Jesus loved, no doubt because of his understanding of and love for his Lord. The defects of character with which he began his career as an apostle — an undue vehemence, intolerance, and selfish ambition — were in the course of time brought under control, until he became especially known for his gentleness and kindly love.

Lived in Galilee, probably in Bethsaida (Lk 5:10; Jn 1:44); Fisherman (Mk 1:19 – 20); Became disciple of Jesus through John the Baptist (Jn 1:35); Called as an apostle (Mk 1:19 – 20; Lk 5:10); One of three apostles closest to Jesus (the others are Peter and James), at raising of Jairus's daughter (Mk 5:37; Lk 8:51), transfiguration (Mt 17:1; Mk 9:2; Lk 9:28), and Gethsemane (Mt 26:37; Mk 14:33); Asked Jesus to call down fire on Samaritans, and given name Boanerges ("sons of thunder") (Mk 3:17; Lk 9:54); Mother requested that John and James be given places of special honor in coming kingdom (Mk 10:35); Helped Peter prepare Passover (Lk 22:8); Lay close to Jesus' breast at Last Supper (Jn 13:25); Present at Jesus' trial (Jn 18:15 – 16). Witnessed crucifixion of Jesus (Jn 19:26 – 27); Recognized Jesus at Sea of Galilee (Jn 21:1 – 7); Active with Peter in apostolic church (Ac 3:1 – 4:22; 8:14 – 17)

JOHN THE BAPTIST The immediate forerunner of Jesus, sent by God to prepare the way for the coming of the Messiah. John was of priestly descent on the side of both his parents. His father Zechariah (KJV Zacharias) was a priest of the course of Abijah, while his mother Elizabeth belonged to the family of Aaron. They are described as being "upright in the sight of God, observing all the Lord's commandments and regulations blamelessly" (Lk 1:6). John was born in a city of the hill country of southern Judea, about six months before the birth of Jesus. His parents were then old. His birth had been foretold by an angel to Zechariah while he was serving in the temple. The angel told him that his prayer for a child would be answered and that his wife would give birth to a son who was to be named John and who was to prepare the way for the coming of the Messiah. About his childhood and youth we know only that he lived as a Nazirite in the desert and that he was filled with the Holy Spirit even from birth (1:15). It is thought by some that he was a member of a Jewish sect of monks called the Essenes, but there is no clear evidence that this was so.

His first public appearance is carefully dated by Luke (3:1 – 2), according to the way time was then reckoned. This was somewhere about AD 26 or 27. His early ministry took place in the wilderness of Judea and in the Jordan Valley. The main theme of his preaching was the near approach of the messianic age and the need for adequate spiritual preparation to be ready for it. His mission was to prepare the people for the advent of the Messiah so that when he made his appearance, they would recognize and accept him. His message did not harmonize with what many of his hearers expected, for while they looked for deliverance from and judgment on the foreign oppressor, John said that the Messiah would separate the good from the bad and would cast into the fire any tree that did not bring forth good fruit. Many of the Jews, especially the Pharisees, thought that they would enter the kingdom of God automatically, simply because they were physically descended from Abraham; but John declared in no uncertain terms that this was not so at all. He called on them to repent sincerely of their sins and to be baptized. The baptism by water that he administered signified a break with and cleansing from sin. His baptism was not something utterly new to the Jews; it had its roots in practices already familiar to them: in the various washings required by the Levitical law (Lev 11 – 15), in the messianic cleansing foretold by the prophets (Jer 33:8; Eze 36:25 – 26; Zec 13:1), and in the proselyte baptism of the Jewish church. His baptism, however, differed essentially from these in that while the Levitical washings brought restoration to a former condition, his baptism prepared for a new condition; the Jews baptized

only Gentiles, but he called on Jews themselves to be baptized; and his baptism was a baptism of water only in preparation for the messianic baptism of the Spirit anticipated by the prophets.

While the multitudes of common people flocked to the Jordan, Jesus also came to be baptized. Although Jesus and John were cousins, it appears that John did not know that Jesus was the Messiah until he saw the Holy Spirit descend on him at his baptism (Jn 1:32 – 34). Shortly after, John said to two of his disciples as they saw Jesus pass by, "Look, the Lamb of God, who takes away the sin of the world!" (1:29), and they left him to follow Jesus. He recognized the subordinate and temporary character of his own mission. For some unexplained reason, some of his disciples did not leave him to follow Jesus; and when some of them came to John with the complaint that all people were coming to Jesus, he said to them, "He must become greater; I must become less" (3:30), saying also that he was not the Messiah but only the forerunner of the Messiah. The exact time of John's imprisonment or the length of time he was in prison is not known. It is clear, however, that Jesus began his ministry in Galilee after John was put in prison and that John was in prison approximately seven months when he sent two of his disciples to Jesus to inquire whether he really was the Messiah. This inquiry seems strange in view of his previous signal testimonies and is probably to be explained either in the interest of his disciples, who needed assurance that Jesus was really the Messiah; or in some misgivings of his own because the messianic kingdom was not being ushered in as suddenly and as cataclysmically as he had expected; or perhaps because he thought he was being forgotten while others were being helped. When the two disciples returned to John, Jesus expressed the frankest appreciation of John, declaring him to be more than a prophet, and that he was indeed God's messenger sent to prepare the way for him (Mt 11:10 – 19).

The Gospels tell that John met his death through the vindictiveness of Herodias, whom John had denounced for her sin of living in adultery with Herod. Josephus, on the other hand, attributes John's death to Herod's jealousy of his great influence with the people. He also says that the destruction of Herod's army, in the war with his spurned wife's father-in-law, was regarded by the Jews as God's punishment on him for the murder of John. Josephus undoubtedly gives, not the real reason, which he would not dare to give to the public, but the reason Herod chose that the public be given.

Forerunner of Jesus; son of Zechariah and Elizabeth, both of priestly descent (Lk 1:5 – 25, 56 – 58); Lived as Nazirite in desert (Lk 1:15; Mt 11:12 – 14, 18); Began ministry beyond Jordan in the fifteenth year of Tiberias Caesar (Lk 3:1 – 3); Preached baptism of repentance in preparation of coming of Messiah (Lk 3:4 – 14); Baptized Jesus (Mt 3:13 – 17; Mk 1:9 – 10; Lk 3:21; Jn 1:32); Bore witness to Jesus as Messiah (Jn 1:24 – 42); Imprisoned and put to death by Herod Antipas (Mt 14:6 – 12; Mk 6:17 – 28); Praised by Jesus (Mt 11:7 – 14; Lk 7:24 – 28); Disciples loyal to him long after his death (Ac 18:25)

JOHN, GOSPEL OF

AUTHORSHIP, DATE, PLACE.

Never was there a book written that made higher claim for its "hero." To the Jesus of history its author gives the most exalted titles. In fact, in the very opening verse he calls him "God." This becomes even more remarkable when we note that the author describes himself as one who belongs to the same race, stock, and family as Jesus — in fact, as an eyewitness of the scenes that he so vividly portrays. No one knew Jesus better than he did. John walked with Jesus from day to day. Tradition holds the apostle John to be this author and that the date and place of authorship was sometime toward the close of the first century AD, Asia Minor.

PURPOSE.

The author states his purpose as follows: "Jesus did many other miraculous signs in the presence of his disciples, which are not recorded in this book. But these are written that you may believe that Jesus is the Christ, the Son of God, and that by believing you may have life in his name" (Jn 20:30 – 31). The faith of believers was being undermined by the errors of men like Cerinthus, who taught that Jesus was not really God and that Christ had not actually come in the flesh (i.e., had not adopted human nature). The apostle, seeing this danger and being guided by the Holy Spirit, wrote this gospel in order that the church might abide in the true faith. The readers for whom this gospel was primarily intended (though in the final analysis it was composed for the church of the entire NT period, cf. Jn 17:20 – 21) were living in Ephesus and surrounding areas. They were Gentile Christians mostly. This explains why the evangelist adds explanatory notes to some of his references to Jewish customs and conditions (2:6; 4:9; 7:2; 10:22; 18:28; 19:31, 41 – 42). It also explains the circumstantial manner in which he locates places that were situated in Palestine (4:5; 5:2; 6:1; 11:1, 18; 12:21).

Outline:

I. During Jesus' Public Ministry
   A. Revealing himself to ever-widening circles, *rejected* (chs. 1 – 6).
   B. Making his tender appeal to sinners, *bitterly resisted* (chs. 7 – 10).
   C. Manifesting himself as the Messiah by two mighty deeds, *repulsed* (chs. 11 – 12).
II. During Jesus' Private Ministry
   A. Issuing and illustrating his new commandment (ch. 13).
   B. Tenderly instructing his disciples and committing them to the Father's care (chs. 14 – 17).
   C. Dying as a substitute for his people (chs. 18 – 19).
   D. Triumphing gloriously (chs. 20 – 21).

JOHN, LETTERS OF

THE FIRST LETTER OF JOHN.

Evidently written by the author of the fourth gospel. The author does not give his name in the letter or the gospel, but the early church attributed both works to the apostle John. This attribution is supported by internal evidence of both books. The writer of the letter speaks with authority, as an apostle would (1Jn 1:2; 2:1; 4:6, 14). He claims to have firsthand knowledge of the facts that underlie the gospel message (1:1 – 3; 4:14). The tone and teaching of the letter are such as we would expect from the aged apostle, writing to his disciples a last message regarding the truths he had taught throughout his life. When the gospel and the letter are compared, the conclusion is well-nigh irresistible that the two books are by the same person. There are striking resemblances in style, language, and thought. Among these resemblances are characteristic words used in a peculiar sense (e.g., life, light, darkness, and world), characteristic expressions (e.g., eternal life, a new commandment, and abide in Christ), and identical phrases (e.g., walks in darkness and that your joy may be full). The few divergencies are easily explainable on the basis of differences of purpose and of subject.

We cannot be sure whether the letter was written before or after the gospel. Tradition says that the gospel was written late in the life of John, toward the end of the first century. Evidences of a late date for the letter are that Christianity has been so long in existence that its precepts may be spoken of as an "old commandment" (1Jn 2:7) and signs that the Gnostic movement had begun, though it had not yet grown to its developed form.

The purpose of the author is to warn the readers against false teachers who are trying to mislead them, to exhort them to hold fast to the Christian faith they have received and to fulfill conscientiously the duties, especially brotherly love, that flow from it.

THE SECOND LETTER OF JOHN.

Both 2 and 3 John are similar in wording, style, ideas, and character to 1 John, and must have been written by the same author, who refers to himself simply as "the elder" (2Jn 1; 3Jn 1). Both are very brief, containing just the number of words that could conveniently be written on one sheet of papyrus. Although written to different people and for different purposes, there are striking resemblances of wording in them. The opening address is almost identical, and in both letters the writer expresses joy in the spiritual progress of those to whom he writes, and does so in almost the same words. The conclusion of the letters is the same in both thought and words.

Second John is addressed to "the chosen lady and her children" (2Jn 1). Many suppose that the reference is to a church and its spiritual children, while others hold that a particular individual named Kyria (Gr. for *lady*) is meant. The introductory greeting is followed by an exhortation to hold fast to the commandments they had received, especially brotherly love, a warning against false teachers who deny that Christ is come in the flesh, and a prohibition against receiving them. The author concludes with a promise to visit them soon.

THE THIRD LETTER OF JOHN.

This is addressed to Gaius, "my dear friend" (3Jn 1), who is eulogized for walking in the truth and being hospitable to evangelists sent, apparently by John, to the church of which Gaius is a member. The author then censures another member of the church, the talkative, overbearing Diotrephes, who for some unexplained reason, probably jealously, not only refused to receive the itinerant preachers but did all he could to get the whole church to follow his course, even to the length of threatening excommunication for those who took a different view of their duty. The elder adds that he had written a letter to the church also, but apparently he has little hope that it will overcome the headstrong opposition of Diotrephes. He threatens a speedy visit to the church, when he will call Diotrephes to account for his bad conduct. There is in this letter no suggestion of heretical tendency in the church.

JONAH [3434, 980, 2731] (Heb. *yônâh, dove*). A prophet of Israel. He was the son of Amittai and came from the town of Gath Hepher in the tribe of Zebulun (2Ki 14:25). He predicted the restoration of the land of Israel to its ancient boundaries through the efforts of Jeroboam II. The exact words of the prophet are not given, nor are we told the specific time when the prophecy was uttered; but we may be certain that it was pronounced sometime before the conquests of Jeroboam, either about the start of Jeroboam's reign or toward the close of the preceding reign. Jeroboam ruled for a period of forty years (790 – 750 BC).

The identity of the prophet with the prophet of the book of Jonah cannot reasonably be doubted. Jonah 1:1 reads, "The word of the LORD came to Jonah son of Amittai." It is extremely unlikely that there were two prophets with the same name. While the author of the book of Jonah does not identify himself, the likelihood is that he is the same as the book bearing his name. It is sometimes objected that he writes in the third person; but this is true of the OT prophets in general. In all probability the book was written not long after the events took place, in the latter part of Jeroboam's reign.

The spirit and teaching of the book of Jonah rank with the highest of the OT prophetical books. Not as much can be said for the prophet himself, who ranks low in the catalog of OT prophets. He was a proud, self-centered egotist: willful, pouting, jealous, bloodthirsty; a good patriot and lover of Israel, without proper respect for God or love for his enemies.

JONAH, BOOK OF Fifth in the canonical order of the Minor Prophets. It differs from them in that while they for the most part contain prophetic discourses, with a minimum of narrative material, the book of Jonah is mainly occupied with a narrative,

and the prophetic message in it is almost incidental. The chapter divisions mark the natural divisions of the book: ch. 1, Jonah's disobedience; ch. 2, Jonah's prayer; ch. 3, Jonah's preaching to the Ninevites; ch. 4, Jonah's complaints. Chapter 1 records Jonah's call to preach at Nineveh because of its great wickedness. Instead of obeying, he took a ship in the opposite direction, to Tarshish, probably in SW Spain. His disobedience undoubtedly arose from his fear that the Ninevites would heed his message and repent, and that God would forgive the city that had for many years grievously oppressed his own land. During a violent storm at sea, the heathen sailors prayed to their own gods who, they thought, must be offended with some person on board. They cast lots to discover the culprit, and when the lot fell on Jonah, he confessed that he was fleeing from the Lord and volunteered to be thrown overboard for their sakes. This was done, the storm subsided, and the sailors offered a sacrifice to God.

The Lord prepared a great fish to swallow Jonah. Surprised to find himself alive in the body of the fish, the prophet gave thanks to God and expressed the confident hope that he would ultimately be delivered. After three days and three nights, the fish vomited him onto the dry land.

Commanded a second time to go to Nineveh, Jonah obeyed and delivered his message, "Forty more days and Nineveh will be overturned" (Jnh 3:4). The effect of his message was undoubtedly greatly heightened by the account of his deliverance, which had either preceded him or been told by himself. The people of Nineveh repented in sackcloth and ashes, and God spared the city.

When Jonah learned that Nineveh was to be spared, he broke out into loud and bitter complaint, not because he felt discredited as a prophet on account of the failure of his prediction, but because he was sure that the sparing of Nineveh sealed the doom of his own country. By the withering of a vine, the Lord taught the prophet that if a perishable plant could come to have such value to him, how much greater should be the estimate put on the lives of thousands of children and cattle in the great city of Nineveh. These meant more to God than Jonah's vine could ever mean to Jonah.

The purpose of the book is primarily to teach that God's gracious purposes are not limited to Israel but extend to the Gentile world. The author wishes to enlarge the sympathies of Israel, so that as God's missionaries they will lead the Gentiles to repentance and to God. The ready response of the Ninevites shows that the heathen are capable of genuine repentance. The book of Jonah may be regarded as a great work of foreign missions. It anticipates the catholicity of the gospel program of Jesus and is the OT counterpart of Jn 3:16, "For God so loved the world."

The book is anonymous, and its authorship is in dispute. The traditional view is that the prophet Jonah is the author, and his book is a record of his own experiences. A more recent view is that the book was written long after Jonah's time by some anonymous author and that it is a work of fiction with a moral lesson.

Outline:

I. Jonah Flees His Mission (chs. 1 – 2).
   A. Jonah's commission and flight (1:1 – 3).
   B. The endangered sailors' cry to their gods (1:4 – 6).
   C. Jonah's disobedience exposed (1:7 – 10).
   D. Jonah's punishment and deliverance (1:11 – 2:1; 2:10).
   E. Jonah's prayer of thanksgiving (2:2 – 9).

II. Jonah Reluctantly Fulfills His Mission (chs. 3 – 4).
   A. Jonah's renewed commission and obedience (3:1 – 4).
   B. The endangered Ninevites' repentant appeal to the Lord (3:5 – 9).
   C. The Ninevites' repentance acknowledged (3:10 – 4:4).
   D. Jonah's deliverance and rebuke (4:5 – 11).

JONATHAN [3387, 3440] (jŏn′a-thăn, Heb. *yehônāthān*, *yônāthān*, *Jehovah has given*). While various Jonathans appear in the Bible, one stands out in significance. Jonathan, the oldest son of Saul the first king of Israel (1Sa 14:49). He comes on the scene soon after his father was crowned king, gaining an important victory over the Ammonites. But great as Jonathan's military qualities were, he is best remembered as the friend of David. He exemplified all that is noblest in friendship — warmth of affection, unselfishness, helpfulness, and loyalty. His love for David began the day the two first met after the killing of Goliath (1Sa 18:1 – 4), and it remained steadfast despite Saul's suggestion that David would someday be king in their stead (20:31). When Jonathan first realized his father's animosity toward David, he interceded for his friend (19:1 – 7); and later, more than once, he risked his life for him. Once Saul, angered by what he regarded as unfilial conduct, threw a javelin at Jonathan, as he had done several times at David. The last meeting of the two friends took place in the desert of Ziph, where Jonathan "helped his friend find strength in God" (23:16). He would not take part in the proceedings of his father against David, who was forced to live in hiding and from whom he was separated for many years. His disinterestedness and willingness to surrender all claims to the throne for the sake of his friend gives evidence of a character that is unsurpassed. While always holding to his own opinion of David, he conformed as much as he could to his father's views and wishes, and presents a noble example of filial piety. There was one temporary estrangement between Saul and Jonathan, provoked when Saul impugned the honor of Jonathan's mother (20:30). Jonathan died with Saul and his brothers on Mount Gilboa in battle against the Philistines (31:2). Their bodies were hung on the walls of Bethshan, but under cover of night the men of Jabesh Gilead, out of gratitude for what Saul had done for them at the beginning of his career (11:1 – 11), removed them and gave them honorable burial. One son, Mephibosheth, survived. David showed him kindness, and Saul's posterity through him may be traced for several generations. These descendants, like their ancestors, were famous soldiers, especially distinguished in the use of the bow (1Ch 8:3ff.; 9:40ff.).

> *Victory of, over the Philistine garrison of Geba (1Sa 13:3 – 4, 16); over Philistines at Micmash (1Sa 14:1 – 18); Under Saul's curse pronounced against any who might take food before he was avenged of his enemies (1Sa 14:24 – 30, 43); Rescued by the people (1Sa 14:43 – 45); Killed in battle with Philistines (1Sa 31:2, 6; 2Sa 21:12 – 14; 1Ch 10:2); Buried by inhabitants of Jabesh Gilead (1Sa 31:11 – 13); Mourned by David (2Sa 1:12, 17 – 27); Son of, cared for by David (2Sa 4:4; 9; 1Ch 8:34)*

JOPPA [3639, 2673] (jŏp′pa, Heb. *yāphô*, Gr. *Ioppē*, *beautiful*). An ancient walled town on coast of Israel, about thirty-five miles NW of Jerusalem; assigned to Dan; mentioned in Amarna Letters; seaport for Jerusalem. In NT times Peter raised Dorcas to life there (Ac 9:36ff.) and received the vision of a sheet filled with animals (Ac 10:1ff; 11:5ff). Modern-day Jaffa.

JORDAN RIVER The only large flowing body of water in Palestine and, as such, it played a significant part in the history of Israel, as well as in the earlier days of our Lord's ministry. The word *Jordan* derives from a Hebrew word, *hayyardēn*, meaning "flowing downward," or "the descender," and one with any knowledge of its course can easily see the appropriateness of the name. Four rivers in Syria are recognized as the source of what later becomes the Jordan River proper. They are the Bareighit; the Hasbany, at the western foot of Mount Hermon, twenty-four miles (forty km.) long; the Leddan; and, the most famous of all, though the shortest, the Banias, five and one-half miles (nine km.) long.

By far the most significant single event relating to the Jordan River in the entire history of Israel is the crossing on the part of the Israelites after the death of Moses, a crossing anticipated by Moses in Dt 3:20, 25, 27. While the Jordan is now and then referred to as a boundary, it was not a boundary for Israel or even for the specific tribes, for Manasseh occupied a huge territory on both sides of the river. Nevertheless, Israel was told that until this river was crossed and the territory on the western side possessed, they would not be occupying the land flowing with milk and honey (Nu 35:10; Dt 3:20; 11:31; 31:13; Jos 1:2). The Promised Land more generally refers to the territory on the western side of the Jordan than to all of the land occupied by Israel. The account of the crossing of the Jordan is given in detail in the third and fourth chapters of Joshua.

The Jordan is important in only one particular way in the NT. It was here that John the Baptist carried on his ministry (Mt 3:6; Mk 1:5; Jn 1:28; 3:26), and thus in this river Jesus himself was baptized (Mt 3:13; Mk 1:9; Lk 4:1).

General References to:
> *Empties into the Dead Sea (Jos 15:5). Fords of (Ge 32:10; Jos 2:7; Jdg 3:28; 7:24; 8:4; 10:9; 12:5 – 6; 2Sa 2:29; 17:22, 24; 19:15, 31; 1Ch 19:17). Swelling of, at harvesttime (Jos 3:15; Jer 12:5); in the early spring (1Ch 12:15). The waters of, miraculously separated for the passage of the Israelites (Jos 3; 4; 5:1; Ps 114:3); of Elijah (2Ki 2:6 – 8); of Elisha (2Ki 2:14). Crossed at a ford (2Sa 19:18). Naaman washes in, for the healing of his leprosy (2Ki 5:10 – 14). John the Baptist baptizes in (Mt 3:6; Mk 1:5); baptizes Jesus in (Mt 3:13; Mk 1:19).*

JOSEPH [3388, 3441, 2736, 2737] (jō′zĕf, Heb. *yôsēph, may God add*).

1. The eleventh of Jacob's twelve sons, and the firstborn son of Rachel, who said when he was born, "May the LORD add to me another son," and therefore called his name Joseph (Ge 30:24). The account of his birth is told in Ge 30:22 – 24, and the account of the rest of his life is found in Ge 37 – 50. He became the ancestor of the two tribes Manasseh and Ephraim, the latter being the most powerful and important in northern Israel. Joseph presents a noble ideal of

character, remarkable for his gentleness, faithfulness to duty, magnanimity, and forgiving spirit, so that he is often regarded as an OT type of Christ.

2. The father of Igal of Issachar, one of the twelve spies (Nu 13:7).

3. A son of Asaph and head of a course of musicians in the reign of David (1Ch 25:2, 9).

4. A son of Bani, who had married a foreign wife and was induced by Ezra to put her away (Ezr 10:42).

5. A priest of the family of Shecaniah in the days of the high priest Joiakim (Ne 12:14).

6. The name of three ancestors of Jesus, according to the KJV (Lk 3:24, 26, 30); the NIV reads "Josech" in 3:26.

7. The husband of Mary, the mother of Jesus (Mt 1:16; Lk 3:23). He was a carpenter (Mt 13:55) living in Nazareth (Lk 2:4). He was of Davidic descent (Mt 1:20; Lk 2:4), the son of Heli (Lk 3:23) or Jacob (Mt 1:16), and thought by many of that day to be the father of Jesus (Mt 13:55; Lk 3:23; 4:22; Jn 1:45; 6:42). After learning that Mary was pregnant before marriage, he had in mind to divorce her quietly, but an angel assured him in a dream that the child to be born had been conceived by the Holy Spirit, so he made her his wife (Mt 1:18 – 25). When the emperor Augustus decreed that a census should be taken of the entire Roman world, Joseph and Mary went to Bethlehem to enroll, and there Jesus was born. Joseph was with Mary when the shepherds came to pay homage to Jesus (Lk 2:8 – 20) and when, forty days after his birth, Jesus was presented in the temple. Warned by the Lord in a dream that Herod was plotting the murder of the child, he fled with Mary and Jesus to Egypt (Mt 2:13 – 19), returning to Nazareth after the death of Herod. Every year Joseph attended the Passover Feast in Jerusalem (Lk 2:41); and when Jesus was twelve, he too went with Joseph and Mary. Joseph undoubtedly taught Jesus the carpenter trade (Mk 6:3). It is likely that he was alive after the ministry of Jesus had well begun (Mt 13:55), but as we do not hear of him in connection with the crucifixion, and as Jesus commended Mary

to John at the crucifixion (Jn 19:26 – 27), it may be inferred that he had died prior to that event.

8. One of the brothers of Jesus (Mt 13:55). KJV has "Joses."

9. A Jew of Arimathea, a place probably to the NW of Jerusalem. He is described as a rich man, a member of the Sanhedrin (Mt 27:57; Mk 15:43), and a righteous man looking for the kingdom of God (Mk 15:43; Lk 23:50). A secret disciple of Jesus because of his fear of the Jews (Jn 19:38), he did not take part in the resolution of the Sanhedrin to put Jesus to death. After the crucifixion he secured permission from Pilate to remove the body of Jesus from the cross, and he laid it in his own new tomb (Mt 27:57 – 60; Lk 23:50 – 53; Jn 19:38).

10. A Christian also called Barsabbas, or son of Sabas, and surnamed Justus (Ac 1:23). He was one of those who had accompanied Jesus and the apostles from the time of Jesus' baptism and was one of the two candidates considered by the apostles as a replacement for Judas Iscariot. However, the lot fell to Matthias (1:21, 26).

11. The personal name of Barnabas (Ac 4:36; in KJV "Joses").

JOSHUA [2107, 3397, 3800, 2652] (jŏsh'ū-a, *Yahweh saves*). A son of Nun, an Ephraimite (1Ch 7:22 – 27). Although born in Egyptian bondage c. 1500 BC, he was named, significantly, Hoshea (Oshea), "salvation" (Nu 13:8; Dt 32:44). Two months after Israel's exodus, he was appointed Moses' commander and successfully repulsed an Amalekite attack (Ex 17:9). Moses changed Hoshea's name to Jehoshua, *yehôshûaʻ*, "Jehovah is salvation" (Nu 13:16; 1Ch 7:27), or Joshua, later forms of which are Jeshua (*yēshûaʻ*, Ne 8:17) and, in Greek, Jesus (*Iēsous*, Ac 7:45; Heb. 4:8); compare Mt 1:21. Joshua attended Moses on Sinai (Ex 24:13; 32:17) and guarded both his tent (33:11) and position (Nu 11:28). Later he represented Ephraim in spying out Canaan. Joshua opposed the majority report, insisting that Israel, if faithful to God, could conquer Canaan. He almost suffered stoning for his trust in God (14:7 – 10).

Subsequently, however, for having "followed the Lord wholeheartedly" (32:12), he not only escaped destruction (14:38) but also received assurance, unique to himself and Caleb (13:30; 14:24), of entering the Promised Land (14:30; 26:65).

About forty years later, east of the Jordan River, God designated Joshua as Moses' successor (Nu 27:18). Moses charged him to be faithful (Nu 27:23; Dt 31:23), committed the "song of admonition" and other writings to him (Ex 17:14; Dt 32:44), counseled him on procedures (Nu 32:28; 34:17), and encouraged both new leader and people (Dt 3:21; 31:3, 7). God himself warned Joshua of coming apostasy (31:14) but promised that Joshua would be successful in the conquest of the Promised Land (1:38; 3:28; 31:23).

After Moses' death, Joshua, as the oldest man in Israel, must have been in his nineties (Caleb was eighty-five, Jos 13:1; 14:7 – 11). Yet God assured him of victory, as he relied on the inspired book of the law (1:6 – 9). From this point onward, Joshua's history is that of Israel's occupation of Canaan.

As death approached, Joshua first summoned Israel's leaders, urging them to faithfulness in conquest (Jos 23), and then assembled the tribal heads to Shechem, charging them, "Choose for yourselves this day whom you will serve" (24:15). Having renewed their covenant with the Lord, he inserted it in the book of the law (24:25 – 26) and died at the age of 110 (24:29 – 30; Jdg 2:8 – 9). Throughout his days, and even afterward, his influence caused Israel to remain faithful to their Lord (Jos 24:31; Jdg 1:1; 2:7)

JOSHUA, BOOK OF Standing sixth in Scripture, this book describes how Moses' successor, after whom the book is named, conquered Canaan (Jos 1:1; 24:31; *see Joshua*). But while Joshua is the first of "the historical books" in English (and Greek), it introduces "the prophets" in the original Hebrew canon of Law, Prophets, and Writings. These prophetic books include the "former prophets" — Joshua, Judges, Samuel, and Kings — since biblical prophets, as God's spokesmen (Ex 7:1 – 2), enforced their

messages using the past as well as the future. Joshua exemplifies historical "prophetic" preaching, in respect of authorship as well as of content.

Joshua's prophetic author is not named; but his statements about the death of Joshua and his colleagues (Jos 24:29 – 31), plus his allusions to Othniel, the migration of the Danites (15:17; 19:47), and the name Hormah (12:14; 15:30; 19:4) indicate that he lived after the rise of Israel's judges, c. 1380 BC (Jdg 1:12 – 13, 17). At the same time, his designation of Jerusalem as Jebusite (Jos 15:8, 63; 18:16, 28) and his writing before its choice as the site of God's temple (9:27), indicate that he wrote before the time of David, 1000 (1Ch 11:4 – 6; 22:1). His references, moreover, to Sidon rather than to Tyre as Phoenicia's leading city (Jos 11:8; 13:4 – 6; 19:28) suggest a date prior to 1200. Indeed, the writer must have been an eyewitness of the events he describes. He speaks, for example, of the Lord's blocking Jordan "until *we* had crossed over" (5:1). Since the writer follows Moses' Deuteronomic style and seemingly had access to Joshua himself (cf. 5:13 – 15), a proposed author has been Phinehas, the son and successor of high priest Eleazar, the son of Aaron. He ministered at Peor in 1406 (Nu 25:7 – 13; 31:6 – 8) and thereafter (Jos 22:13 – 20; Jdg 20:28). Someone, then, of his standing composed the book of Joshua about 1375 BC.

Most modern critics, however, attribute Joshua to four mutually contradictory source documents, brought together over a millennium after the time of Phinehas.

Outline:
    I. Entrance into the Land (1:1 – 5:12).
       A. Exhortations to conquer (ch. 1).
       B. Reconnaissance of Jericho (ch. 2).
       C. Crossing of the Jordan (chs. 3 – 4).
       D. Consecration at Gilgal (5:1 – 12).
    II. Conquest of the Land (5:13 – 12:24).
       A. Initial battles (5:13 – 8:35).
          1. Victory at Jericho (5:13 – 6:27).
          2. Failure at Ai because of Achan's sin (ch. 7).

3. Victory at Ai (8:1 – 29).
4. Covenant renewed at Shechem (8:30 – 35).
B. Campaign in the south (chs. 9 – 10).
1. Treaty with the Gibeonites (ch. 9).
2. The long day of Joshua (10:1 – 15).
3. Southern cities conquered (10:16 – 43).
C. Campaign in the north (ch. 11).
D. The defeated kings of Canaan (ch. 12).
III. Distribution of the Land (chs. 13 – 21).
A. Areas yet to be conquered (13:1 – 7).
B. Land east of the Jordan for Reuben, Gad, and half of Manasseh (13:8 – 33).
C. Lands given to Judah and "Joseph" at Gilgal (chs. 14 – 17).
D. Lands given to the remaining tribes at Shiloh (chs. 18 – 19).
1. The tabernacle at Shiloh and the allotments for Benjamin (ch. 18).
2. The allotments for Simeon, Zebulun, Issachar, Asher, Naphtali, and Dan (19:1 – 48).
3. The town given to Joshua (19:49 – 51).
E. The cities assigned to the Levites (chs. 20 – 21).
1. Six cities of refuge (ch. 20).
2. Forty-eight cities of the priests (ch. 21).
IV. Epilogue: Tribal Unity and Loyalty to the Lord (chs. 22 – 24).
A. The altar of witness by the Jordan (ch. 22).
B. Joshua's farewell exhortation (ch. 23).
C. Renewal of the covenant at Shechem (24:1 – 28).
D. Death and burial of Joshua and Eleazar (24:29 – 33).

JOSIAH [3287, 3288, 2739] (jō-zī′a, Heb. *yō'shîyāhû*, *Jehovah supports him*). Son of Amon and Jedidah and the grandson of Manasseh, the son of Hezekiah

(2Ki 22:1). Josiah's reign on the Davidic throne for thirty-one years was the last surge of political independence and religious revival before the disintegration of the southern kingdom that ended with the destruction of Jerusalem in 586 BC.

When palace officials murdered King Amon in 642 BC (2Ki 21:23), the eight-year-old Josiah was crowned king of Judah. While the boy-king grew to manhood, the imposing international influence of Assyria declined rapidly. Insurrections and rebellions in the East and the death of Ashurbanipal (c. 633) provided an opportunity for a rising tide of nationalism in Judah. By 612 the coalition of Media under Cyaxares and Babylon under Nabopolassar converged on Nineveh to destroy Assyria's famous capital. Within three years the Babylonians had routed the last of the great Assyrian army. These decades gave Josiah the political advantage not only to assert Judah's independence but also to extend its influence into the northern tribes — perhaps even kindling fond hopes of claiming the boundaries as established by David and Solomon.

Josiah's religious leadership ranks him with Jehoshaphat and Hezekiah as an outstanding righteous ruler. In 609 BC Josiah's leadership was abruptly ended. In an effort to interfere with Pharaoh Neco's plans to aid the Assyrians, Josiah was fatally wounded at Megiddo (2Ch 35:20 – 24). National and religious hopes vanished with the funeral of this thirty-nine-year-old king so that all Judah had reason to join Jeremiah in lamenting for Josiah (35:25).

1. King of Judah (2Ki 21:24 – 26; 22:1; 1Ch 3:14; 2Ch 33:25). Ancestor of Jesus (Mt 1:10 – 11). Slain in battle with Pharaoh Neco (2Ki 23:29 – 30; 2Ch 35:20 – 24). Lamentations for (2Ch 35:25). Piety of, exemplified in his repairing the temple (2Ki 22:3 – 7; 2Ch 34:1 – 4). Anxiety, when the copy of the law was discovered and read to him (2Ki 22:8 – 20; 2Ch 34:14 – 33), in keeping a solemn Passover (2Ki 23:21 – 23; 2Ch 35:1 – 19). Prophecies concerning (1Ki 13:1 – 3). Destroys the altar and high places of idolatry (2Ki 23:3 – 20, 24 – 25).

2. Son of Zephaniah (Zec 6:10).

JOY [5375, 8131, 8523, 8525, 8262, 8264, 8607, 9558, 5897, 5915] (Pss 30:5, 11; 33:21; 97:11; 132:16; Pr 29:6). In the OT, joy is commonly a group expression, often associated with dancing (Ps 96:11) or the blessings of prosperity (Isa 60:15). God's praise is shouted or sung even in more formal public worship (Ezr 3:10 – 11; Ps 100:1 – 2). Linked with this concept also are musical instruments, clapping, leaping, or footstamping. Feasting or offering sacrifice (Dt 12:12; Isa 56:7), celebration of harvest or victory (1Sa 18:6; Joel 1:16), enjoying prosperity or personal triumph (Ps 31:7; Isa 61:3ff.) are all occasions of joy.

In the NT, the word is often found in connection with salvation (1Pe 1:6), or with eating, drinking, and feasting (Lk 12:19; Ac 7:41). Most often found in the NT, however, are the meanings "to boast, take pride, or rejoice in." Thus, Paul contrasts man's inclination to boast in himself (Ro 3:27) with his right to boast in Christ and his cross (Gal 6:14; Php 3:3). The NT applies joy to suffering as well as to salvation. When reviled or persecuted or lied about, the Christian is to "rejoice and be glad," knowing that this is traditionally part of the believer's portion (Mt 5:11 – 12). Joy comes from the Holy Spirit (Gal 5:22).

General References to:

From God (Ecc 2:26; Ro 15:13). In the Lord (Pss 9:2; 104:34; Isa 9:3; 29:19; 41:16; 61:10; Lk 1:47; Ro 5:11). In Christ (Php 3:3; 4:4; 1Pe 1:8). In the word of God (Pss 19:8; 119:14, 16, 111, 162; Jer 15:16). In worship (2Ch 7:10; Ezr 6:22; Ne 12:43; Pss 42:4; 43:4; 71:23; Isa 56:7; Zep 3:14; Zec 2:10; 9:9). A fruit of the Spirit (Gal 5:22; Eph 5:18 – 19). For salvation (Pss 13:5; 20:5; 21:1, 6; 35:9; Isa 12:2 – 3; 25:9; 35:1 – 2, 10; 55:12; Ro 5:2; 14:17). On account of a good conscience (2Co 1:12). Over a sinner's repentance (Lk 15:6 – 10, 22 – 32). Under adversity (Ps 126:5 – 6; Isa 61:3; Mt 5:12; Ac 5:41; 2Co 6:10; 7:4; 8:2; 12:10; Col 1:11; 1Th 1:6; Heb 10:34; Jas 1:2; 1Pe 4:13). Fullness of (Pss 16:11; 36:8; 63:5; Jn 15:11; 16:24; Ac 2:28; 1Jn 1:4). Everlasting (Isa 51:11; 61:7).

In heaven (Mt 25:21; Lk 15:7, 10). Attributed to God (Dt 28:63; 30:9; Jer 32:41).

Commanded:

(Dt 12:18; Ne 8:10; Pss 2:11; 5:11; 32:11; 68:3; 97:12; 100:1 – 2; 105:3, 43; 149:2, 5; Joel 2:23; Lk 2:10; 6:23; 10:20; Ro 12:12; 1Th 5:16).

Of the Wicked:

Brief (Job 20:5). Meaningless (Ecc 2:10; 7:6; 11:8 – 9). Shallow (Pr 14:13; 15:21). Overshadowed by impending judgment and sorrow (Pr 14:13; Ecc 11:8 – 9; Isa 16:10; Jas 4:10).

Lev	9:24	shouted for **j** and fell facedown.
Dt	16:15	and your **j** will be complete.
1Ch	16:33	sing for **j** before the LORD,
2Ch	30:26	There was great **j** in Jerusalem,
Ezr	3:12	while many others shouted for **j**.
Ne	8:10	for the **j** of the LORD is your
Est	8:16	a time of happiness and **j**,
	9:22	their sorrow was turned into **j**
Job	6:10	my **j** in unrelenting pain —
	33:26	he sees God's face and shouts for **j**;
Ps	4:7	have filled my heart with greater **j**
	16:11	me with **j** in your presence,
	20:5	We will shout for **j**
	81:1	Sing for **j** to God our strength;
	86:4	Bring **j** to your servant,
	97:11	and **j** on the upright in heart.
	100:1	for **j** to the LORD, all the earth.
	119:111	they are the **j** of my heart.
Pr	10:1	A wise son brings **j** to his father,
	15:30	A cheerful look brings **j**
	17:21	there is no **j** for the father of a fool.
	29:3	A man who loves wisdom brings **j**
Isa	9:3	and increased their **j**;
	44:23	Sing for **j**, O heavens,
	54:1	burst into song, shout for **j**,
	56:7	give them **j** in my house of prayer.
Jer	15:16	they were my **j** and my heart's
	31:12	shout for **j** on the heights of Zion;
	48:33	**J** and gladness are gone
Mt	13:20	and at once receives it with **j**.
	13:44	in his **j** went and sold all he had

	28:8	afraid yet filled with **j**,
Mk	4:16	and at once receive it with **j**.
Lk	1:14	He will be a **j** and delight to you,
	1:44	the baby in my womb leaped for **j**.
	2:10	news of great **j** that will be
	6:23	"Rejoice in that day and leap for **j**,
	8:13	the word with **j** when they hear it,
	10:17	The seventy-two returned with **j**
	10:21	full of **j** through the Holy Spirit,
	24:52	returned to Jerusalem with great **j**.
Jn	3:29	That **j** is mine, and it is now
	15:11	and that your **j** may be complete.
	16:20	but your grief will turn to **j**.
	17:13	measure of my **j** within them.
Ac	2:28	with **j** in your presence.'
	8:8	So there was great **j** in that city.
	13:52	And the disciples were filled with **j**
	14:17	and fills your hearts with **j**."
Ro	14:17	peace and **j** in the Holy Spirit,
	15:13	the God of hope fill you with all **j**
2Co	1:24	but we work with you for your **j**,
	2:3	that you would all share my **j**.
	7:4	our troubles my **j** knows no
	8:2	their overflowing **j** and their
Gal	4:15	What has happened to all your **j**?
	5:22	**j**, peace, patience, kindness,
Php	1:4	I always pray with **j**
	1:25	for your progress and **j** in the faith,
	2:2	then make my **j** complete
1Th	1:6	with the **j** given by the Holy Spirit.
	2:19	For what is our hope, our **j**,
2Ti	1:4	so that I may be filled with **j**.
Phm	1:7	Your love has given me great **j**
Heb	1:9	by anointing you with the oil of **j**."
	12:2	for the **j** set before him endured
	13:17	them so that their work will be a **j**,
Jas	1:2	Consider it pure **j**, my brothers,
	4:9	to mourning and your **j** to gloom.
1Pe	1:8	with an inexpressible and glorious **j**
1Jn	1:4	this to make our **j** complete.
2Jn	1:4	It has given me great **j** to find some
	1:12	so that our **j** may be complete.
Jude	1:24	without fault and with great **j** —

JUBILEES, BOOK OF A Jewish apocalyptic book written in the intertestamental period. It gives a history of the world from the creation to the giving of the law and defends Pharisaical views against liberal Hellenistic tendencies. *See also Apocalyptic Literature.*

JUDAH [3373+, 3374, 3376, 10315, 2683] (jū'd a, Heb. *yehûdhâh, praised*).

1. The fourth son of Jacob; his mother was Leah (Ge 29:35). Few details of his life are known. He saved Joseph's life by persuading his brothers to sell him to the Midianites at Dothan (37:26 – 28). His disgraceful actions recorded in Ge 38 left a stain on his memory. He gradually appears to have achieved leadership among his brothers (43:3; 46:28; 49:8 – 12), and no doubt it was during his own lifetime that there arose among them the rivalry that was much later to give rise to the division of the kingdom. Through his son Perez, Judah became an ancestor of David (Ru 4:18 – 22) and of Jesus Christ (Mt 1:3 – 16). The blessing of dying Jacob to Judah (Ge 49:9 – 10) is usually understood as being a messianic prophecy.

2. The Hebrew tribe descended from the man Judah described above. Judah was one of the largest tribal territories. During the rule of the judges, Judah tended to be separated from the rest of the Hebrew tribes, which were to the north, by the pagan people who lived between them (Gibeonites, Jos 9; Jebusites, Jdg 19:10 – 13), and also by rough and wild land, with deep east-west valleys. The Simeonites, who lived in southern Judean cities, tended to become assimilated into Judah and thus to lose their tribal identity.

3. Judah is also the name of five individuals who are mentioned in Ezra and Nehemiah. Three were Levites (Ezr 3:9 KJV; 10:23; Ne 12:8), one a Benjamite (Ne 11:9), and the fifth probably a prince of Judah (12:34). NIV has "Hodaviah" in Ezr 3:9 (cf. note). A Judah other than the son of Jacob is also named in Lk 3:30 as an ancestor of Jesus (KJV "Juda").

JUDAISM The religious system held by the Jews. Its teachings come from the OT, especially from the law of Moses as found from Exodus 20 through Deuteronomy; but also from the traditions of the elders (Mk 7:3 – 13), some of which our Lord condemned. The principal elements of Judaism include circumcision, a strict monotheism, an abhorrence of idolatry, and Sabbath-keeping.

JUDAS ISCARIOT The archtraitor who betrayed the Lord. He and his father Simon were both surnamed "Iscariot" (Jn 6:71), a word thought to be from the Hebrew *Ish Kerioth*, that is, "a man of Kerioth." Kerioth is almost certainly in southern Judah (Jos 15:25). Nothing is known of his early life. He may have joined the disciples of Jesus from pure motives and probably showed evidence of business acumen and so was appointed treasurer for the disciples (Jn 12:6; 13:29), but after his hopes for a high place in an earthly kingdom of Jesus were dashed (6:66), he became a thief. His indignation when Jesus was anointed at Bethany was hypocritical. His pretended zeal for the poor was really covetousness, and is so interpreted by John (12:6), though the disciples of Jesus apparently trusted him to the end (13:21 – 30). Jesus, however, was not deceived (6:64) but knew from the beginning who would betray him. It was only at the Last Supper that Jesus revealed that one of them "was later to betray him" (6:71). Then Satan entered into Judas; Jesus dismissed Judas, and Judas went out to do the dastardly deed that he had already planned (Mk 14:10). He sold the Lord for thirty pieces of silver, betrayed him with a kiss, then in remorse threw down the money before the chief priests and elders (Mt 27:3 – 10) and went out and committed suicide. Matthew (27:5) says he hanged himself, and Acts (1:18) says that "he fell headlong, his body burst open." He is always mentioned last among the apostles.

Chosen as an apostle (Mt 10:4; Mk 3:19; Lk 6:16; Ac 1:17); Treasurer of the disciples (Jn 12:6; 13:29); His greed exemplified by his pro-test against the breaking of the box of ointment (Jn 12:4 – 6), and by his bargain to betray Jesus for a sum of money (Mt 26:14 – 16; Mk 14:10 – 11; Lk 22:3 – 6; Jn 13:2); His apostasy (Jn 17:12); His betrayal of the Lord (Mt 26:47 – 50; Mk 14:43 – 45; Lk 22:47 – 49; Jn 18:2 – 5; Ac 1:16 – 25); His return of the money to the rulers of the Jews (Mt 27:3 – 10); His hanging of himself (Mt 27:5; Ac 1:18); Prophecies concerning (Zec 11:12 – 13; Mt 26:21 – 25; Mk 14:18 – 21; Lk 22:21 – 23; Jn 13:18 – 26; 17:12; Ac 1:16, 20, w Pss 41:9; 109:8)

JUDE [2683] (Gr. *Ioudas Judah*). Writer of the last of the letters in the NT. Both James and Jude in the opening of their letters show their Christian humility and their faith in the deity of Jesus by referring to themselves as servants of Jesus Christ, rather than as his brothers in the flesh. Beyond this we know of Jude from Scripture only that, like his brothers, he did not believe in Jesus during his earthly ministry (Jn 7:5) but became his follower after the resurrection (Ac 1:14). Hegesippus (c. AD 110 – c. 180) says that two of his grandsons were brought before Domitian as descendants of David but were dismissed as harmless peasants.

JUDE, LETTER OF One of the General Epistles included in the earliest-known list (probably second century AD) of NT writings, although not otherwise cited or even mentioned by any of the early church fathers until Clement of Alexandria (c. 150 – c. 215). It was regarded in the following generation by Origen as "of but few verses yet full of mighty words of heavenly wisdom."

AUTHORSHIP AND DATE.

The opening verse describes the author as "Jude, a servant of Jesus Christ and a brother of James." This may be the same person as "Judas," brother of James and Jesus (Mt 13:55; Mk 6:3). Nothing more is known about him or about his place of writing, nor is precise dating of the letter possible. We do know that the problems it discusses were common during the last quarter of the first century when heresy was increasing.

PURPOSE.

Here there is no doubt: the writer is directing to his readers an urgent appeal "to contend for the faith that was once for all entrusted to the saints" (Jude 3). The very basis of Christianity was in jeopardy.

CONTENT.

Jude goes on to deal with the new heresy threatening the churches from within. What it was and who its supporters were are not clear; but we are told something about their appalling lifestyle and its baneful influence on the church. Jude reminds Christians of the inevitability of opposition, of the need for compassion toward sinners, and of the ineffable attributes of God. As he denounces those who would undermine the true faith, his voice seems to rise in righteous anger: this was a time for holy intolerance. There is no place in the church for those who divide the people of God (Jude 4 – 16). Jude 17 – 25 exhorts to continued perseverance. There is a reminder that the apostles had foretold the coming of the "scoffers" (cf. 2Pe 3:3) who love worldly things and sow dissension among believers.

Outline:

    I. Salutation (vv. 1 – 2).
   II. Occasion for the Letter (vv. 3 – 4).
      A. The change of subject (v. 3).
      B. The reason for the change: the presence of godless apostates (v. 4).
  III. Warning against the False Teachers (vv. 5 – 16).
      A. Historical examples of the judgment of apostates (vv. 5 – 7).
        1. Unbelieving Israel (v. 5).
        2. Angels who fell (v. 6).
        3. Sodom and Gomorrah (v. 7).
      B. Description of the apostates of Jude's day (vv. 8 – 16).
        1. Their slanderous speech deplored (vv. 8 – 10).

        2. Their character graphically portrayed (vv. 11 – 13).
        3. Their destruction prophesied (vv. 14 – 16).
  IV. Exhortation to Believers (vv. 17 – 23).
   V. Concluding Doxology (vv. 24 – 25). *See General Letters.*

JUDEA, JUDAEA [3373, 3374, 2677, 2681, 2683] (jū-dē´a, Heb. *yehûdhâh*, Gr. *Ioudaia; land of the Judahites, Jews*). A geographical term that first appears in the Bible in Ezr 5:8 (KJV, NIV "district of Judah"), where it designates a province of the Persian Empire. The land of Judea is also mentioned in the apocryphal books 1 Esdras (1:30) and 1 Maccabees (5:45; 7:10). Since most of the exiles who returned from the Babylonian exile belonged to the tribe of Judah, they came to be called Jews, and their land, Judea.

Under the Persian Empire, Judea was a district administered by a governor who was usually a Jew (Hag 1:14; 2:2). Under Rome, with the banishment of Herod's son Archelaus, Judea became annexed to the Roman province of Syria, but its governors were procurators appointed by the Roman emperor. Their immediate superior was the proconsul of Syria, who ruled from Antioch (Lk 3:1). The official residence of the procurators was Caesarea. This was true during the ministry of Christ.

JUDGE

Ge	16:5	May the LORD **j** between you
	18:25	Will not the **J** of all the earth do
Lev	19:15	but **j** your neighbor fairly.
Dt	1:16	between your brothers and **j** fairly,
	17:12	man who shows contempt for the **j**
	32:36	The LORD will **j** his people
Jdg	2:18	Whenever the LORD raised up a **j**
1Sa	24:12	May the LORD **j** between you
1Ch	16:33	for he comes to **j** the earth.
2Ch	19:7	**J** carefully, for with the LORD our
Job	9:15	plead with my **J** for mercy.
Ps	7:8	**J** me, O LORD, according
	7:11	God is a righteous **j**,

	9:8	He will **j** the world in righteousness
	50:6	for God himself is **j**.
	82:8	Rise up, O God, **j** the earth,
	96:10	he will **j** the peoples with equity.
	96:13	He will **j** the world in righteousness
Pr	31:9	Speak up and **j** fairly;
Isa	2:4	He will **j** between the nations
Jer	11:20	Almighty, you who **j** righteously
Eze	7:3	I will **j** you according
	7:27	by their own standards I will **j** them
Mt	7:1	Do not **j**, or you too will be judged.
Lk	6:37	"Do not **j**, and you will not be
	18:2	there was a **j** who neither feared
Jn	5:27	And he has given him authority to **j**
	5:30	By myself I can do nothing; I **j** only
	8:16	But if I do **j**, my decisions are right,
	12:47	For I did not come to **j** the world,
	12:48	There is a **j** for the one who rejects
Ac	10:42	as **j** of the living and the dead.
	17:31	a day when he will **j** the world
Ro	2:16	day when God will **j** men's secrets
	3:6	how could God **j** the world?
	14:10	then, why do you **j** your brother?
1Co	4:3	indeed, I do not even **j** myself.
	6:2	that the saints will **j** the world?
Gal	2:6	not **j** by external appearance —
Col	2:16	Therefore do not let anyone **j** you
2Ti	4:1	who will **j** the living and the dead,
	4:8	which the Lord, the righteous **J**,
Heb	10:30	"The Lord will **j** his people."
	12:23	come to God, the **j** of all men,
	13:4	for God will **j** the adulterer
Jas	4:12	There is only one Lawgiver and **J**,
	4:12	who are you to **j** your neighbor?
1Pe	4:5	to him who is ready to **j** the living
Rev	20:4	who had been given authority to **j**.

JUDGES, BOOK OF The seventh book of the OT takes its name from the title of the men who ruled Israel during the period from Joshua to Samuel. They are called judges (*shophetim*, Jdg 2:16), their principal function being that of military deliverers of the oppressed Hebrews.

The book makes no clear claim to authorship or date of composition. The purposes of the book of Judges are (1) to bridge in some manner the historical gap between the death of Joshua and the inauguration of the monarchy, (2) to show the moral and political degradation of a people who neglected their religious heritage and compromised their faith with the surrounding paganism, and (3) to show the need of the people for the unity and leadership by a strong central government in the person of a king.

In its structure the book falls into three easily recognizable parts: (1) introduction: the state of things at the death of Joshua (Jdg 1:1 – 2:10); (2) main body: the judges' cycles (Jdg 2:11 – 16:31); (3) appendix: life in Israel in the days of the judges (Jdg 17 – 21).

INTRODUCTION.

(Jdg 1:1 – 2:10). This section gives a description of the state of the conquest of Canaan when Joshua died. It is a record of incomplete success. The less desirable hill country had been taken, but the fertile plains and the cities were still largely in Canaanite hands. This culture and religion were often largely Canaanite and pagan. This is the reason for the moral and spiritual degradation of the Hebrew people during the period of the judges.

MAIN BODY OF THE BOOK.

(Jdg 2:11 – 16:31). Here occur the accounts of the judges, the cycles of failure, oppression, and relief by a judge. The cycle is set forth in the abstract in 2:11 – 3:6, and the accounts of the judges follow. It will be noted that these men were not principally civil magistrates. Rather, they were military deliverers who led the people of Israel to freedom against their enemies and seem frequently to have been singularly unfit to be what we would today call *judges*.

APPENDIX.

(Jdg 17 – 21). The events recorded here seem to have occurred, not after the judges mentioned in the main part of the book, but during their judgeships. They are relegated to the appendix probably because they are narratives in their own right and if inserted in the main body would have marred the symmetry of the judge cycles there.

JUDGMENT [466, 1906, 1907, 3248, 3519, 4213, 5477, 6885, 7132, 7213, 9149, 9150, 9370, 10170, 10171, 10188, 373, 1037, 1191, 1359, 1471, 3210, 3212, 3213, 3216] (Heb. *dhîn*, *mishpāt*, Gr. *krima*, *krisis*). A word found many times in Scripture. Sometimes it refers to the pronouncing of a formal opinion or decision by human beings, but more often it indicates either a calamity regarded as sent by God for punishment or a sentence of God as the Judge of all. Among the more important judgments of God prior to the exodus are those on Adam, Eve, and the serpent after the fall (Ge 3), the flood (6:5), Sodom and Gomorrah (18:20), and the confusion of tongues (11:1 – 9). God brings judgment to his creatures when they rebel against his will.

In the OT, the relationship between the Lord and Israel is thought of under the form of a covenant. Of his own will, the Lord brought first Noah (Ge 6:17), then Abraham and his sons (15:18; 17:1ff.), into a close relationship with himself. He bound himself to them by covenant and looked in return for their responsive devotion. The purpose of the judgment of God's people is not their total destruction but their purification. A remnant will survive, and this will be the nucleus of the new Israel (Am 5:15). In the later prophets there are expressions of a hope of an ultimate victory of the Divine Judge, of a final or last judgment. Here God's judgment is not thought of so much in terms of his intervention in history but of a last judgment of all human beings at the end of time. Perhaps the clearest expression of this is found in Da 12:1 – 3, where the dead are described as being raised, some for everlasting life, others for shame and everlasting contempt.

In the NT the idea of judgment appears in both human and divine contexts. Jesus warns against uncharitable judgments (Mt 7:1). Paul says that the spiritual man cannot be judged by unbelievers (1Co 2:15), and in Ro 14 and 1Co 8 – 10 he warns against judging those who are "weak" in the faith.

In the NT judgment is one of the aspects of the coming of the kingdom of God. God's judgment, says John the Baptist, will fall on those who do not make ready the way of the Lord (Lk 3:9). Jesus declares that someday he will come to judge both the living and the dead (Mt 25:31ff.).

In the NT, as in the OT, judgment is an aspect of the deliverance of believers (Lk 18:1 – 8; 2Th 1:5 – 10; Rev 6:10). God is long-suffering in meting out judgment so that people may be able to come to repentance (Lk 13:6 – 9; Ro 2:4; 2Pe 3:9). This present world will be shaken and destroyed (Mt 24:29, 35), and a new world will replace the present one (2Pe 3:13; Rev 21:2). God will entrust the administration of this final judgment to his Son at his appearance in glory (Mt 3:11 – 12; Jn 5:22; Ro 2:16).

General References to:
Forewarned (Ecc 11:9; 12:14; Mt 8:29 w 2Pe 2:4 & Jude 6; Mt 13:30, 40 – 43, 49 – 50; 25:31 – 46; Mk 8:38; Ac 24:25; 2Th 1:7 – 8; Heb 6:2). Fierce and fiery (Mt 3:12; 10:15; 11:22; 12:36 – 42; Lk 3:17; 10:10 – 14; 11:31 – 32; 13:24 – 29; Ac 2:19 – 20). According to opportunity and works (Ge 4:7; 1Sa 26:23; Job 34:11 – 12; Ps 62:12; Pr 12:14; 24:11 – 12; Isa 3:10 – 11; 59:18; Jer 17:10; 32:19; Eze 7:3 – 4, 27; 18:4 – 9, 19 – 32; 33:18 – 20; Hos 4:9; 12:2; Zec 1:6; Mt 25:1 – 30; Lk 12:47 – 48; 13:6 – 9; 19:12 – 27; Jn 3:19 – 20; Ro 2:5 – 12; 1Co 3:8, 12 – 15; 2Co 11:15; Gal 6:7 – 8; Eph 6:7 – 8; Col 3:25; Heb 10:26 – 30; 12:25; Jas 2:13; 1Pe 1:17; 2Pe 2:20 – 21; Rev 2:23; 20:12 – 13).

Design of:
To exhibit a basis for rewards and punishments (2Co 5:10; 2Ti 4:8; Rev 11:18; 22:12). To reveal secrets (Ecc 12:14; Lk 12:2 – 3; Ro 2:16; 1Co 3:13).

Who Will Be the Judge:
God as Judge (1Ch 16:33; Pss 9:7; 50:4, 6; 96:13; 98:9; Ecc 12:14; Da 7:9 – 10; Ro 2:5, 16; 3:6; 2Ti 4:8; Heb 10:30; 12:23; 13:4; 1Pe 4:5; Rev 20:11 – 15). Jesus Christ as Judge (Mt 7:22 – 23; 13:30, 40 – 43, 49 – 50; 16:25, 27; 25:31 – 46; Mk

8:38; Jn 5:22; 12:48; Ac 10:42; 17:31; Ro 2:16; 14:10; 1Co 4:5; 2Co 5:10; 2Th 1:7 – 8; 2Ti 4:1; 2Pe 2:9; 3:10; Rev 1:7; 6:15 – 17). *The saints as judges (Mt 19:28; 1Co 6:2; Jude 14).*

Time of:

Appointed (Mt 13:30; Ac 17:31; Heb 9:27; 2Pe 3:7, 10 – 12). Known to God only (Mk 13:32).

Who Will Be Judged:

The righteous and wicked (Ecc 3:17; Mt 25:31 – 46; Jude 14 – 15; Rev 11:18). The wicked (Job 21:30; Eze 18:20 – 28; 2Pe 2:9; 3:7). The living and the dead (Ac 10:42; 2Ti 4:1; 1Pe 4:5). All must be made manifest (Mk 4:22; Ac 17:31; 2Co 5:10). Kings and princes, slaves and freemen (Rev 6:15 – 16). Fallen angels (2Pe 2:4; Jude 6). See God, Judge; Jesus the Christ, Judge; Punishment, According to Deeds.

Nu	33:4	for the LORD had brought **j**
Dt	1:17	of any man, for **j** belongs to God.
1Sa	25:33	May you be blessed for your good **j**
Ps	1:5	the wicked will not stand in the **j**,
	119:66	Teach me knowledge and good **j**,
	143:2	Do not bring your servant into **j**,
Pr	6:32	man who commits adultery lacks **j**;
	10:21	but fools die for lack of **j**.
	12:11	but he who chases fantasies lacks **j**.
	28:16	A tyrannical ruler lacks **j**,
Ecc	12:14	God will bring every deed into **j**,
Jer	2:35	But I will pass **j** on you
	25:31	he will bring **j** on all mankind
Da	7:22	pronounced **j** in favor of the saints
Am	7:4	Sovereign LORD was calling for **j**
Zec	8:16	and sound **j** in your courts;
Mal	3:5	"So I will come near to you for **j**.
Mt	5:21	who murders will be subject to **j**.'
	12:36	have to give account on the day of **j**
Jn	5:22	but has entrusted all **j** to the Son,
	8:26	"I have much to say in **j** of you.
	9:39	"For **j** I have come into this world,
	12:31	Now is the time for **j** on this world;
	16:8	to sin and righteousness and **j**:
Ac	24:25	self-control and the **j** to come,

Ro	2:1	you who pass **j** on someone else,
	5:16	The **j** followed one sin
	12:3	rather think of yourself with sober **j**
	14:10	stand before God's **j** seat.
	14:13	Therefore let us stop passing **j**
1Co	11:29	body of the Lord eats and drinks **j**
2Co	5:10	appear before the **j** seat of Christ,
1Ti	3:6	fall under the same **j** as the devil.
	5:12	Thus they bring **j** on themselves,
Heb	6:2	of the dead, and eternal **j**.
	9:27	to die once, and after that to face **j**,
Jas	2:13	**j** without mercy will be shown
	4:11	are not keeping it, but sitting in **j**
1Pe	4:17	For it is time for **j** to begin
2Pe	2:9	the unrighteous for the day of **j**,
	3:7	being kept for the day of **j**
1Jn	4:17	have confidence on the day of **j**,
Jude	1:6	bound with everlasting chains for **j**
Rev	14:7	because the hour of his **j** has come.

JUDGMENT SEAT (Gr. *bēma*, *a raised place, platform, tribune*). The bench or seat where a judge sits to hear arguments and pleas and to deliver sentence. Although the word is used principally in the NT in connection with the trials of Christ (Mt 27:19; Jn 19:13) and of Paul (Ac 18:12), its main association is with the judgment seat of Christ before which all believers will stand (Ro 14:10; 2Co 5:10).

JUST [JUSTIFIED]

Ge	18:19	LORD by doing what is right and **j**,
Dt	32:4	and all his ways are **j**.
2Sa	8:15	doing what was **j** and right
2Ch	12:6	and said, "The LORD is **j**."
Ne	9:13	and laws that are **j** and right,
Ps	37:28	For the LORD loves the **j**
	111:7	of his hands are faithful and **j**;
Pr	2:8	for he guards the course of the **j**
	8:8	All the words of my mouth are **j**;
	12:5	The plans of the righteous are **j**,
Jer	4:2	if in a truthful, **j** and righteous way
	22:3	what the LORD says: Do what is **j**
Eze	18:5	who does what is **j** and right.

	18:25	'The way of the Lord is not **j**.'
Da	4:37	does is right and all his ways are **j**.
Jn	5:30	as I hear, and my judgment is **j**,
Ro	3:26	as to be **j** and the one who justifies
2Th	1:6	God is **j**: He will pay back trouble
Heb	2:2	received its **j** punishment,
1Jn	1:9	and **j** and will forgive us our sins
Rev	15:3	**J** and true are your ways,
	19:2	for true and **j** are his judgments.

JUSTICE [1906, 1907, 2006, 4793, 4797, 5477, 5742, 7405, 7406, 7407, 8190, 9149, 10169, 1466, 1472, 1688, 1689, 3213].

> *From God (Ps 72:1 – 2; Pr 29:26). Commanded (Ex 23:1 – 3, 6 – 8; Lev 19:13 – 15; Dt 16:18 – 20; 25:1 – 4; Pss 82:3 – 4; 106:3; Pr 18:5; Isa 1:17; Jer 7:5, 7; La 3:35 – 36; Mic 6:8; Zec 7:9; 8:16; Jn 7:24, 51). Must be impartial (Pr 24:23; 28:21). Can be perverted (Ecc 3:16; 5:8; Isa 59:14 – 15; Jer 22:3; Am 5:7, 11 – 12; Mic 7:3; Hab 1:4; Mt 12:7). Will be rewarded (Jer 22:4, 15 – 16; Eze 18:5 – 9).*

Ex	23:6	"Do not deny **j** to your poor people
Dt	16:20	Follow **j** and **j** alone,
	27:19	Cursed is the man who withholds **j**
1Ki	3:28	wisdom from God to administer **j**.
Job	8:3	Does God pervert **j**?
	19:7	though I call for help, there is no **j**.
	34:5	but God denies me **j**.
	36:3	I will ascribe **j** to my Maker.
	40:8	"Would you discredit my **j**?
Ps	9:8	he will govern the peoples with **j**.
	9:16	The Lord is known by his **j**;
	11:7	he loves **j**;
	89:14	**j** are the foundation of your throne;
	103:6	and **j** for all the oppressed.
	106:3	Blessed are they who maintain **j**,
Pr	16:10	and his mouth should not betray **j**.
	17:23	to pervert the course of **j**.
	19:28	A corrupt witness mocks at **j**,
	21:15	When **j** is done, it brings joy
	28:5	Evil men do not understand **j**,

	29:7	The righteous care about **j**
Isa	1:17	Seek **j**,
	10:2	and withhold **j** from the oppressed of
	28:6	He will be a spirit of **j**
	42:1	and he will bring **j** to the nations.
	51:4	my **j** will become a light
Jer	9:24	**j** and righteousness on earth,
	10:24	Correct me, Lord, but only with **j**
	46:28	I will discipline you but only with **j**;
Eze	22:29	mistreat the alien, denying them **j**.
	34:16	I will shepherd the flock with **j**.
Hos	2:19	you in righteousness and **j**,
	12:6	maintain love and **j**,
Am	2:7	and deny **j** to the oppressed.
	5:15	maintain **j** in the courts.
	5:24	But let **j** roll on like a river,
Hab	1:4	and **j** never prevails.
Zec	7:9	'Administer true **j**; show mercy
Mal	2:17	or "Where is the God of **j**?"
Mt	12:18	he will proclaim **j** to the nations.
	23:23	important matters of the law — **j**,
Lk	11:42	you neglect **j** and the love of God.
Ac	8:33	humiliation he was deprived of **j**.
	28:4	**J** has not allowed him to live."
Ro	3:25	He did this to demonstrate his **j**,
2Co	7:11	what readiness to see **j** done.
Heb	11:33	administered **j**, and gained what
Rev	19:11	With **j** he judges and makes war.

JUSTIFICATION [2342, 7136, 7405, 8750, 1466+1650, 1467, 1468, 1470] (Heb. *tsedheq, tsādhēq*; Gr. *dikaioō, to make valid, to absolve, to vindicate, to set right*). Justification may be defined as "that judicial act of God by which, on the basis of the meritorious work of Christ, imputed to the sinner and received through faith, God declares the sinner absolved from sin, released from its penalty, and restored as righteous." Expressed simply, it is being placed by God in a right relationship with himself. The doctrine is found in Paul's letters, chiefly those to Galatia and Rome.

General References to:

Not imputing guilt to the sinner (Ps 32:2; Isa 53:11; Zec 3:4; Jn 5:24; Ro 4:6; 8:1). Comes from God (Isa 45:24 – 25; 50:8; 54:17; 61:10; Ro 3:25; 8:30, 33; 2Co 5:19, 21; Tit 3:7). Achieved through Christ (Isa 53:11; Jer 23:6; Ac 13:39; Ro 3:20 – 25; 5:9, 11, 16 – 18, 21; 1Co 1:30; 6:11; Col 2:13 – 14). Is based on his righteousness (Pss 71:16; 89:16; Isa 42:21; 46:12 – 13; 51:5 – 6; 56:1; Ro 1:16 – 17; Gal 5:4 – 6). Is not by the law (Ro 3:20; Gal 2:16; 3:11; 5:4 – 6). Is by faith (Ge 15:6; Hab 2:4; Ro 1:16 – 17; 3:20 – 22, 24, 28, 30; 4:2 – 25; 5:1; 9:30 – 32; 10:4, 6, 8 – 11; Gal 2:14 – 21; 3:6, 8 – 9, 21 – 22, 24; 5:4 – 6; Php 3:8 – 9; Heb 11:4, 7; Jas 2:20 – 23, 26). Fruits of: peace (Ro 5:1); holiness (Ro 6:22). Example of: Abraham (Ge 15:6; Ro 4:3).

Eze	16:52	for you have furnished some **j**
Ro	4:25	and was raised to life for our **j**.
	5:16	many trespasses and brought **j**.
	5:18	of righteousness was **j** that brings

JUSTIFIED [JUST]

Ps	51:4	and **j** when you judge.
Lk	18:14	rather than the other, went home **j**
Ac	13:39	from everything you could not be **j**
	13:39	him everyone who believes is **j**
Ro	3:24	and are **j** freely by his grace
	4:2	If, in fact, Abraham was **j** by works,
	5:1	since we have been **j** through faith,
	5:9	Since we have now been **j**
	8:30	those he called, he also **j**; those he **j**,
	10:10	heart that you believe and are **j**,
1Co	6:11	you were **j** in the name
Gal	2:16	in Christ Jesus that we may be **j**
	3:11	Clearly no one is **j** before God
	3:24	to Christ that we might be **j** by faith
	5:4	to be **j** by law have been alienated
Tit	3:7	so that, having been **j** by his grace,
Jas	2:24	You see that a person is **j**

KADESH, KADESH BARNEA [7729] (kā´dĕsh bar´nē-a, Heb. *qādhēsh*, from *qādhôsh, be holy; sacred place*). Also known as En Mishpat (Ge 14:7). A place about seventy miles south of Hebron, in the vicinity of which Israel wandered for thirty-seven years (Dt 1:46; Nu 33:37 – 38; Dt 2:14). Miriam died there (Nu 20:1), and Moses sent spies to Israel from there (Nu 13:21 – 26; Dt 1:19 – 25) and displeased God there by striking the rock instead of speaking to it (Nu 20:2 – 13). Often called Kadesh Barnea (Nu 32:8; Dt 2:14).

KIDRON [7724, 3022] (kĭd´rŏn, kī´drŏn, Heb. *qidhrôn*, Gr. *Kedrŏn*). The valley along the east side of Jerusalem, where the Pool of Gihon is located, whose water was brought by an aqueduct into the Pools of Siloam within the walls. South of the city the Kidron joins the Valley of Hinnom near the Pool of En Rogel, and the united valley, Wadi en-Nar, runs down to the Dead Sea. Through the Kidron Valley a winter torrent runs, the Brook Kidron, but the stream bed is dry much of the year. David's crossing of the Kidron (2Sa 15:23) in his escape from his rebellious son Absalom marked the decisive abandonment of his throne. When Solomon spared Shimei, he warned him that to cross the Kidron would bring him death (1Ki 2:37). Asa burned idols at the brook (1Ki 15:13; 2Ch 15:16), as did Josiah (2Ki 23:4, 6, 12) and Hezekiah (2Ch 29:16; 30:14). It is called "the stream" (32:4) that Hezekiah stopped, to deny the attacking Assyrians a water supply. Nehemiah went up it by night to view the state of the walls of Jerusalem (Ne 2:15 KJV, ASV "brook," RSV, NIV "valley"). Jeremiah mentions it in prophesying the permanent rebuilding of Jerusalem (Jer 31:38 – 40). After the Last Supper, Jesus and his disciples crossed it on their way out of the city to reach the garden of Gethsemane on the slopes of the Mount of Olives (Jn 18:1, KJV Cedron). He must often have looked across this valley as he "was sitting on the Mount of Olives" (e.g., Mt 24:3;

Mk 13:3), and he must have crossed it on his triumphal entry into the city of Jerusalem (Mt 2:1 – 11; Mk 11:1 – 10; Lk 19:28 – 44; Jn 12:12 – 19).

KILL

Ecc	3:3	a time to **k** and a time to heal,
Mt	10:28	**k** the body but cannot **k** the soul.
	17:23	They will **k** him, and on the third
Mk	9:31	will **k** him, and after three days
	10:34	spit on him, flog him and **k** him.

KIND [KINDNESS]

Ge	1:24	animals, each according to its **k**."
2Ch	10:7	"If you will be **k** to these people
Pr	11:17	A **k** man benefits himself,
	12:25	but a **k** word cheers him up.
	14:21	blessed is he who is **k** to the needy.
	14:31	whoever is **k** to the needy honors
	19:17	He who is **k** to the poor lends
Da	4:27	by being **k** to the oppressed.
Lk	6:35	because he is **k** to the ungrateful
1Co	13:4	Love is patient, love is **k**.
Eph	4:32	Be **k** and compassionate
1Th	5:15	but always try to be **k** to each other
2Ti	2:24	instead, he must be **k** to everyone,
Tit	2:5	to be busy at home, to be **k**,

KINDNESS [1691, 2858, 2876, 3512, 14, 2307, 5789, 5792, 5982, 5983].

> *Commanded (Zec 7:9 – 10; Mt 5:42; Lk 6:30, 34 – 35; Ac 20:35; Ro 12:15; 15:1 – 2; Gal 6:1 – 2, 10; Eph 4:32; Col 3:12; 1Pe 3:8 – 9; 1Jn 3:17 – 18). To enemies (Ex 23:4 – 5; Lk 6:34 – 35). To strangers (Lev 19:34). To a brother (Dt 22:1). Inspired by love (1Co 13:4 – 7). Commends ministers (2Co 6:6). Rewards of (Pr 14:21; Mt 5:7; 25:34 – 35). Of God (Lk 6:35). Of good women (Pr 31:26; 1Ti 5:9 – 10). Of good men (Ps 112:5; Heb 5:2).*

Ge	24:12	and show **k** to my master Abraham
	32:10	I am unworthy of all the **k**
Jdg	8:35	failed to show **k** to the family

Ru	2:20	has not stopped showing his **k**
2Sa	9:3	to whom I can show God's **k?**"
	22:51	he shows unfailing **k**
Isa	54:8	but with everlasting **k**
Jer	9:24	I am the LORD, who exercises **k**,
Hos	11:4	I led them with cords of human **k**,
Ac	14:17	He has shown **k** by giving you rain
Ro	11:22	Consider therefore the **k**
2Co	6:6	understanding, patience and **k**;
Gal	5:22	peace, patience, **k**, goodness,
Eph	2:7	expressed in his **k** to us
Col	3:12	yourselves with compassion, **k**,
Tit	3:4	But when the **k** and love
2Pe	1:7	brotherly **k**; and to brotherly **k**,

KING [3782, 4482, 4887, 4889, 4930, 10421, 995, 996, 5203]. A male ruler, usually hereditary, of a city, tribe, or nation. Hebrew *melekh* may mean "possessor," stressing physical strength, or "counselor, decider," stressing intellectual superiority. Some combination of the two ideas probably was in the minds of most people, the latter predominating in better governed societies. Greek *basileus* is of obscure origin but always denoted a ruler and leader of a people, city, or state. Kings often had priestly functions in the maintenance of the religion of the group, though most of these were separated from the kingly office in the Hebrew monarchy: the king was expected to further religion but not to act as its priest.

Several times we are told that in the time of the judges there was no king in Israel (Jdg 17:6; 18:1; 19:1; 21:25); everyone did what was right in his own eyes. Moses had foreseen that the people would demand a king as a strong human ruler (Dt 17:14 – 15; 28:36), not content with a theocracy, the direct rule of God as King over them (33:5). Hannah looked forward to a time when there would be a king of Israel who was appointed and anointed by God (1Sa 2:10). Toward the end of Samuel's judgeship, however, Israel was unwilling to wait for a messianic king and demanded one "such as all the other nations have" (1Sa 8:5, 22; 12:1 – 25; 19:19, 24; cf. Hos 13:10). Samuel duly warned the people what to expect of a king, then selected Saul, whose choice they ratified. The reigns of Israelite kings are recorded as follows: Saul (1Sa 12 – 31; 1Ch 10); David (2Sa; 1Ki 1; 1Ch 11 – 29); Solomon (1Ki 1 – 11; 1Ch 28 – 2Ch 9); later kings of Israel and Judah (1Ki 12 – 2Ki 25; 2Ch 10 – 36). Ezra, Nehemiah, and Esther deal with kings of Persia.

Jeremiah refers to God as King (Jer 8:19; 10:7, 10; 46:18; 48:15; 51:57) and to the messianic king (23:5). Ezekiel 37:22, 24 refers to the Davidic king of restored Israel whom the context shows to be messianic. The messianic king enters Jerusalem riding on a colt (Zec 9:9), and God is king (14:9, 16 – 17; Mal 1:14).

Among God's chosen people a rightful king was designated by God and anointed by his representative (1Sa 9:15 – 16; 16:1 – 13) with the approval of the people. He ruled by virtue of a covenant between God and his people, to which the king was a party (2Sa 7). This covenant was extended and renewed as the basis of the NT kingdom of God or of heaven, of which Jesus is sovereign until at the resurrection when he delivers the kingdom to his Father (1Co 15:24 – 28).

Kings in Israel:

Israel warned against seeking (1Sa 8:9 – 18). Sin of Israel in seeking (1Sa 12:17 – 20). Israel, in seeking, rejected God as their king (1Sa 8:7; 10:19). Israel asked for, that they might be like other nations (1Sa 8:5, 19 – 20). First given to Israel in anger (Hos 13:11). God reserved to himself the choice of (Dt 17:14 – 15; 1Sa 9:16 – 17; 16:12). When first established in Israel, not hereditary (Dt 17:20, w 1Sa 13:13 – 14; 15:28 – 29). Rendered hereditary in the family of David (2Sa 7:12 – 16; Ps 89:35 – 37). Of Israel not to be foreigners (Dt 17:15). Laws for the government of the kingdom by, written by Samuel (1Sa 10:25). Forbidden to accumulate: horses (Dt 17:16); wives (Dt 17:17); treasure (Dt 17:17). Required to write and keep a copy of the divine law (Dt 17:18 – 20). Had power to make war and peace (1Sa 11:5 – 7). Often exercised power arbitrarily (1Sa 22:17 – 18; 2Sa 1:15; 4:9 – 12; 1Ki 2:23, 25, 31). Sometimes nominated their successors (1Ki 1:33 – 34; 2Ch 11:22 – 23).

Punished for transgressing the divine law (2Sa
12:7–12; 1Ki 21:18–24). Called the Lord's
anointed (1Sa 16:6; 24:6; 2Sa 19:21).

Dt	17:14	"Let us set a **k** over us like all
Jdg	17:6	In those days Israel had no **k**;
1Sa	8:5	now appoint a **k** to lead us,
	12:12	the Lᴏʀᴅ your God was your **k**.
2Sa	2:4	and there they anointed David **k**
Ps	2:6	"I have installed my **K**
	24:7	that the **K** of glory may come in.
	44:4	You are my **K** and my God,
	47:7	For God is the **K** of all the earth;
Isa	32:1	See, a **k** will reign in righteousness
Jer	30:9	and David their **k**,
Hos	3:5	their God and David their **k**.
Zec	9:9	See, your **k** comes to you,
Mt	2:2	is the one who has been born **k**
	27:11	"Are you the **k** of the Jews?" "Yes,
Lk	19:38	"Blessed is the **k** who comes
Jn	1:49	of God; you are the **K** of Israel."
	12:13	"Blessed is the **K** of Israel!"
Ac	17:7	saying that there is another **k**,
1Ti	1:17	Now to the **K** eternal, immortal,
	6:15	the **K** of kings and Lord of lords,
Heb	7:1	This Melchizedek was **k** of Salem
1Pe	2:13	to the **k**, as the supreme authority,
	2:17	of believers, fear God, honor the **k**.
Rev	15:3	**K** of the ages.
	17:14	he is Lord of lords and **K** of kings —

KINGDOM OF GOD, OF HEAVEN [806, 4867, 4889, 4895, 4930, 4931, 4939, 10424, 993, 2026] (Gr. *basileia tou theou*). The word *kingdom* is capable of three different meanings: (1) the realm over which a monarch reigns, (2) the people over whom he or she reigns, and (3) the actual reign or rule itself. In English the third use of the word is archaic and so is not always given its rightful place in discussion of the term; but in Greek and Hebrew, this is the primary meaning. All three meanings are found in the NT.

1. The kingdom of God is sometimes the people of the kingdom. In Rev 5:10 the redeemed are a kingdom, not, however, because they are the people over whom God reigns, but because they will share his reign. The same usage appears in Rev 1:6.

2. The kingdom of God is the realm in which God's reign is experienced. This realm is sometimes something present, sometimes future. It is a realm introduced after the ministry of John the Baptist; people enter it with violent determination (Lk 16:16). John did not stand within this new realm but only on its threshold; but so great are the blessings of God's kingdom that the least in it is greater than John (Mt 11:11). Jesus offered the kingdom to Israel, for they were its proper heirs (8:12); but the religious leaders, followed by most of the people, not only refused to enter its blessings but tried to prevent others from entering (23:13). Nevertheless, many tax collectors and prostitutes did enter the kingdom (21:31; see also Col 1:13). In all of these verses, the kingdom is a present realm where people may enjoy the blessings of God's rule. Elsewhere the kingdom is a future realm inaugurated by the return of Christ. The righteous will inherit this kingdom (Mt 25:34) and will shine like the sun in God's kingdom (13:43). Entrance into this future kingdom is synonymous with entering the eternal life of the age to come (Mt 19:16, 23–30; Mk 10:30).

3. The kingdom is also God's reign or rule. *Basileia* is used of kings who have not received "royal power" (RSV) or authority to rule as kings (Rev 17:12). Later these kings give their "kingdoms," i.e., their authority, to the beast (Rev 17:17). In Lk 19:12 a nobleman went into a distant country to receive the crown (*basileia*) that he might be king over his country.

This "abstract" meaning of kingdom is evident in many passages. Only those who "receive the kingdom of God," i.e., accept God's rule here and now, enter into the realm of its blessings in the future (Mk 10:15). When we seek God's kingdom and righteousness, we seek God's rule in our lives (Mt 6:33).

God's kingdom is, however, not merely an abstract rule. The kingdom is God's rule *dynamically* defeating evil and redeeming sinners. Christ must reign as King until he has destroyed (*katargeō*) all enemies, the last of which is death, and that he will then deliver the kingdom to God (1Co 15:24–26). Thus, the kingdom of God is the dynamic rule of God manifested in Christ to destroy his (spiritual) enemies and to bring to men and women the blessings of God's reign. Both death and Satan will be destroyed at Christ's second coming to raise the dead and to judge the world.

Entrance into the kingdom is by the new birth (Jn 3:3–5). There are two stages in the kingdom of God, present and future in an eschatological sense. Jesus said that his ability to cast out demons was evidence that the kingdom of God had come among humans (Mt 12:28).

Ex	19:6	you will be for me a **k** of priests
Dt	17:18	When he takes the throne of his **k**,
2Sa	7:12	body, and I will establish his **k**.
1Ki	11:31	to tear the **k** out of Solomon's hand
Ps	103:19	and his **k** rules over all.
	145:11	They will tell of the glory of your **k**
Da	2:39	"After you, another **k** will rise,
	7:27	His **k** will be an everlasting **k**,
Ob	:21	And the **k** will be the LORD's.
Mt	3:2	Repent, for the **k** of heaven is near
	4:23	preaching the good news of the **k**,
	5:3	for theirs is the **k** of heaven.
	5:20	you will certainly not enter the **k**
	6:10	your **k** come,
	6:33	But seek first his **k** and his
	9:35	preaching the good news of the **k**
	11:11	least in the **k** of heaven is greater
	12:25	"Every **k** divided against itself will
	12:28	then the **k** of God has come
	13:11	knowledge of the secrets of the **k**
	13:24	"The **k** of heaven is like a man who
	13:31	**k** of heaven is like a mustard seed,
	13:33	"The **k** of heaven is like yeast that
	13:44	**k** of heaven is like treasure hidden
	13:45	the **k** of heaven is like a merchant
	13:47	**k** of heaven is like a net that was let
	16:19	the keys of the **k** of heaven;
	16:28	the Son of Man coming in his **k**."
	18:4	the greatest in the **k** of heaven.

	18:23	the **k** of heaven is like a king who
	19:14	for the **k** of heaven belongs to such
	19:23	man to enter the **k** of heaven.
	19:24	for a rich man to enter the **k** of God
	20:21	the other at your left in your **k**."
	21:31	the prostitutes are entering the **k**
	22:2	"The **k** of heaven is like a king who
	24:7	rise against nation, and **k** against **k**.
	25:34	the **k** prepared for you
	26:29	anew with you in my Father's **k**."
Mk	1:15	"The **k** of God is near.
	4:11	"The secret of the **k**
	4:30	"What shall we say the **k**
	6:23	I will give you, up to half my **k**."
	9:1	before they see the **k** of God come
	9:47	better for you to enter the **k** of God
	10:15	anyone who will not receive the **k**
	11:10	"Blessed is the coming **k**
	12:34	"You are not far from the **k** of God
	15:43	who was himself waiting for the **k**
Lk	1:33	Jacob forever; his **k** will never
	4:43	of the **k** of God to the other towns
	6:20	for yours is the **k** of God.
	7:28	in the **k** of God is greater than he."
	8:1	proclaiming the good news of the **k**
	9:2	out to preach the **k** of God
	9:11	spoke to them about the **k** of God,
	9:62	fit for service in the **k** of God."
	10:9	'The **k** of God is near you.'
	11:17	"Any **k** divided against itself will
	12:32	has been pleased to give you the **k**.
	13:18	"What is the **k** of God like?
	13:28	all the prophets in the **k** of God,
	13:29	places at the feast in the **k** of God.
	16:16	the good news of the **k**
	17:20	when the **k** of God would come,
	17:21	because the **k** of God is within you
	18:29	for the sake of the **k** of God will fail
	19:11	and the people thought that the **k**
	21:10	rise against nation, and **k** against **k**.
	21:31	you know that the **k** of God is near.
	22:16	until it finds fulfillment in the **k**
	22:18	the vine until the **k** of God comes."

	22:29	And I confer on you a **k**, just
	22:30	and drink at my table in my **k**
	23:42	me when you come into your **k**."
	23:51	he was waiting for the **k** of God.
Jn	3:3	no one can see the **k** of God.
	3:5	no one can enter the **k** of God.
	18:36	now my **k** is from another place."
Ac	1:3	and spoke about the **k** of God.
	1:6	going to restore the **k** to Israel?"
	8:12	he preached the good news of the **k**
	14:22	hardships to enter the **k** of God,"
	19:8	arguing persuasively about the **k**
	20:25	about preaching the **k** will ever see
	28:23	and declared to them the **k** of God
	28:31	hindrance he preached the **k**
1Co	4:20	For the **k** of God is not a matter
	6:9	the wicked will not inherit the **k**
	15:24	hands over the **k** to God the Father
	15:50	blood cannot inherit the **k** of God,
Gal	5:21	live like this will not inherit the **k**
Eph	2:2	and of the ruler of the **k** of the air,
	5:5	has any inheritance in the **k**
Col	1:12	of the saints in the **k** of light.
	4:11	among my fellow workers for the **k**
1Th	2:12	who calls you into his **k** and glory.
2Th	1:5	will be counted worthy of the **k**
2Ti	4:1	in view of his appearing and his **k**,
Heb	1:8	will be the scepter of your **k**.
	12:28	we are receiving a **k** that cannot be
Jas	2:5	to inherit the **k** he promised those
2Pe	1:11	into the eternal **k** of our Lord
Rev	1:6	has made us to be a **k** and priests
	1:9	companion in the suffering and **k**
	11:15	of the world has become the **k**
	12:10	the power and the **k** of our God,
	16:10	his **k** was plunged into darkness.
	17:12	who have not yet received a **k**,

KINGS, 1 AND 2 These are named in English, as in Hebrew, by subject matter. They cover four centuries of Israelite kings, from David (his death in 930 BC) to Jehoiachin (in Babylon, after 561). They thus provide a sequel to the books of Samuel, which cover the reigns of Saul and David. The LXX actually entitles 1 and 2 Samuel "Books A and B of the Kingdoms" (Latin Vulgate and KJV subtitle: "I and II Books of the Kings"), so that 1 and 2 Kings become, correspondingly, "III and IV King(dom)s." Like Samuel, Kings was written as a unit but was divided in two at the time of the LXX translation, about 200 BC. In the original Hebrew canon (the Law, Prophets, and Writings), Kings preceded Isaiah-Malachi as the concluding volume of the "former prophets," following Joshua, Judges, and Samuel. For though listed among the "historical books" in English (and Greek), these four works possess an essentially prophetic character (contrast the priestly volumes of Chronicles), employing the events of past history as a vehicle for contemporary preaching (cf. Da 9:6). Thus, even as Isaiah scanned the future to motivate his people's obedience (Isa 1:19 – 20), so the anonymous author of Kings drove home lessons, born of previous disasters, "because they had not obeyed the LORD their God" (2Ki 18:12).

The date of composition is not specified; but the author refers repeatedly to conditions that continued to exist in his day (e.g., the presence of the ark within the temple, 1Ki 8:8; cf. 9:21; 12:19), indicating that he wrote prior to the destruction of Judah in 586 BC (2Ki 8:22; 16:6; 17:41 are less definite).

Outline:

    I. The Solomonic Era (1:1 – 12:24).

    II. Israel and Judah from Jeroboam I/Rehoboam to Ahab/Asa (12:25 – 16:34).

    III. The Ministries of Elijah and Elisha and Other Prophets from Ahab/Asa to Joram/Jehoshaphat (17:1 – 2Ki 8:15).

    IV. Israel and Judah from Joram/Jehoram to the Exile of Israel (2Ki 8:16 – 17:41).

    V. Judah from Hezekiah to the Babylonian Exile (2Ki 18 – 25).

KINSMAN [278, 1457, 4530, 4531, 7940]. Family or friends (Job 19:14); of same tribe (1Ch 12:2, 29; 2Ch 29:34; Ezr 8:17); fellow Israelites (2Ch 28:8). Figurative of wisdom (Pr 7:4).

KINSMAN-REDEEMER [1457] (Heb. *gō'ēl, one who has the right to redeem*). A close relative responsible for: protecting the interests of needy members of the extended family and for providing an heir for a brother who had died (Ge 38:6 – 11; Dt 25:5 – 10; Ru 3 – 4). *See Levirate Marriage.* Expected to: redeem land that a poor relative had sold outside the family (Lev 25:25 – 28); to redeem a relative who had been sold into slavery (Lev 25:47 – 49); to avenge the killing of a relative (Nu 35:19 – 21).

KNOWLEDGE [1978, 1981, 3359, 4529, 5795, 7924, 8011, 10313, 10430, 1182, 1192, 1194, 1196, 2105, 2106, 2179, 2813, 3857].

Of good and evil (Ge 2:9, 17; 3:22). Is power (Pr 3:20; 24:5). Desire for (1Ki 3:9; Ps 119:66; Pr 2; 3; 12:1; 15:14; 18:15). Rejected (Hos 4:6). Those who reject are destroyed (Hos 4:6). Fools hate (Pr 1:22, 29). A divine gift (1Co 12:8). Is pleasant (Pr 2:10). Shall be increased (Da 12:4). The earth shall be full of (Isa 11:9). Fear of the Lord is the beginning of (Pr 1:7). Of more value than gold (Pr 8:10). The priest's lips should keep (Mal 2:7). Of salvation (Lk 1:77). Key of (Lk 11:52). Now we know in part (1Co 13:9 – 12). Of God more than burnt offering (Hos 6:6). Of Christ (Php 3:8).

Ge	2:9	the tree of the **k** of good and evil.
Job	21:22	"Can anyone teach **k** to God,
	38:2	counsel with words without **k**?
Ps	94:10	Does he who teaches man lack **k**?
	119:66	Teach me **k** and good judgment,
Pr	1:7	of the LORD is the beginning of **k**,
	2:6	from his mouth come **k**
	8:10	**k** rather than choice gold,
	9:10	**k** of the Holy One is understanding
	10:14	Wise men store up **k**,
	12:1	Whoever loves discipline loves **k**,
	12:23	A prudent man keeps his **k**
	13:16	Every prudent man acts out of **k**,
	14:6	**k** comes easily to the discerning.
	15:7	The lips of the wise spread **k**;
	17:27	A man of **k** uses words
	19:2	to have zeal without **k**,
	20:15	lips that speak **k** are a rare jewel.
	23:12	and your ears to words of **k**.
Ecc	7:12	but the advantage of **k** is this:
Isa	11:2	the Spirit of **k** and of the fear
	11:9	full of the **k** of the LORD
Hos	4:6	are destroyed from lack of **k**.
Mt	13:11	The **k** of the secrets of the kingdom
Ac	18:24	with a thorough **k** of the Scriptures
Ro	1:28	worthwhile to retain the **k** of God,
	10:2	but their zeal is not based on **k**.
	11:33	riches of the wisdom and **k** of God!
1Co	8:1	**K** puffs up, but love builds up.
	12:8	to another the message of **k**
2Co	8:7	in **k**, in complete earnestness
Eph	3:19	to know this love that surpasses **k**
	4:13	and in the **k** of the Son of God
Php	1:9	and more in **k** and depth of insight,
Col	1:9	God to fill you with the **k** of his will
	3:10	which is being renewed in **k**
1Ti	2:4	and to come to a **k** of the truth.
	6:20	ideas of what is falsely called **k**,
Tit	1:1	and the **k** of the truth that leads
Heb	10:26	after we have received the **k**
2Pe	1:5	and to goodness, **k**; and to **k**,
	3:18	grow in the grace and **k** of our Lord

LABAN [4238, 4239] (lā′băn, Heb. *lāvān, white*).

1. The nephew of Abraham who lived in Haran on a tributary of the Euphrates River in Mesopotamia. He belonged to that branch of the family of Terah (Abraham's father) that came from Abraham's brother Nahor and his niece Milcah (Ge 22:22 – 24), and is first mentioned as Rebekah's brother when she is introduced (24:29). In ancient Semitic custom, the brother was the guardian of the sister, and thus Laban takes a prominent place in the account of Rebekah's leaving for Canaan to be Isaac's bride. His grasping nature is hinted at in Ge 24:30 – 31, where his invitation to Abraham's servant follows immediately after his appraisal of the servant's expensively equipped party.

> *Son of Bethuel (Ge 28:5); Brother of Rebekah (Ge 22:23; 24:15, 29); Receives the servant of Abraham (Ge 24:29 – 33); Receives Jacob and gives him his daughters in marriage (Ge 29:12 – 30); Jacob becomes his servant (Ge 29:15 – 20, 27; 30:27 – 43); Outwitted by Jacob (Ge 30:37 – 43; 31:1 – 21); Pursues Jacob and overtakes him in the hill country of Gilead, then covenants with him (Ge 31:22 – 55)*

2. Laban is also the name of an unidentified place in the Plains of Moab, or perhaps in the Sinai peninsula (Dt 1:1).

LABOR [2655, 3330, 3333, 4989, 5126, 6025, 6026, 6268, 6275, 6661, 6662, 7189, 7674, 8492, 3159, 3160]. The noun is today confined to the abstract use — the act of laboring (Ge 31:42; Ro 16:6). Formerly it expressed also the fruit of labor, as in Ex 23:16, "When thou hast gathered in thy labours out of the field," or Jn 4:38, "Ye are entered into their labours" (both KJV). The word is used also of labor in childbirth (Ge 35:16 KJV).

In Bible times there was no class of men known as "labor" in contrast with "management." All but a favored few labored, and hard work was looked on as the common lot of man and a result of the curse (Ge 3:17 – 19), a bitter servitude. Slavery was commonly practiced in the Bible world; the conscription of freemen for labor on government building projects was practiced by Solomon (1Ki 5:13 – 17) and Asa (15:22).

Although most workers in the simple culture of OT times were what we today would call "unskilled," there were certain skilled occupations such as potter or stone mason. By NT times things had changed, and the more complex civilization of the Roman world, with its skilled and more diversified occupations and better standards of living, had come to Palestine.

> **General References to:**
> *Honorable (Ps 128:2; Pr 21:25; 1Th 4:11). Laborers protected by laws (Dt 24:14). Creative work of God described as labor (Ge 2:2). Difficult labor the result of the curse (Ge 3:17 – 19). Sleep of labor sweet (Ecc 5:12). Labor commanded (Ge 3:19; Ex 20:9 – 11; 23:12; 34:21; Lev 23:3; Lk 13:14; Ac 20:35; Eph 4:28; 1Th 4:11; 2Th 3:10 – 12). Compensation for (Lev 19:13; Dt 25:4; 1Co 9:9; 1Ti 5:18; Jer 22:13; Mal 3:5; Mt 20:1 – 15; Lk 10:7; Jas 5:4). Of servants must not be oppressive (Dt 24:14 – 15). Paul, an example (2Th 3:8 – 13).*

Ex	1:11	to oppress them with forced **l**,
	20:9	Six days you shall **l** and do all your
Ps	127:1	its builders **l** in vain.
	128:2	You will eat the fruit of your **l**;
Pr	12:24	but laziness ends in slave **l**.
Isa	55:2	and your **l** on what does not satisfy
Mt	6:28	They do not **l** or spin.
Jn	4:38	have reaped the benefits of their **l**."
1Co	3:8	rewarded according to his own **l**.
	15:58	because you know that your **l**
Gal	4:27	you who have no **l** pains;
Php	2:16	day of Christ that I did not run or **l**
Rev	14:13	"they will rest from their **l**,

LAKE OF FIRE [3349]. Place of final judgment (Rev 19:20; 20:10, 14 – 15; 21:8).

LAMB [3231, 3897, 3898, 4166, 4167, 7175, 8445+, 303, 768, 4247]. A translation of several Hebrew words in the English Bible, most of them referring to the young of the sheep. One, however (*sheh*, used in Ex 12:3 – 6), refers to the young of either sheep or goats (cf. 12:5) and seems to include adult specimens at times. The meat of lambs was considered a delicacy among the ancient Hebrews (Dt 32:14; 2Sa 12:3 – 6; Am 6:4). Meat was scarce among them, and the killing of a lamb would mark an important occasion. Lambs were used for sacrifices from the earliest times (Ge 4:4; 22:7).

The lamb was a staple in the Mosaic sacrificial system. A lamb was offered for the continual burnt offering each morning and evening (Ex 29:38 – 42), and on the Sabbath the number was doubled (Nu 28:9). On the first day of each month (28:11), during the seven days of the Passover (28:16, 19), at the Feast of Weeks (28:26 – 27) and the Feast of Trumpets (29:1 – 2), on the Day of Atonement (29:7 – 8), and on the Feast of Tabernacles (29:13 – 36) lambs were offered. The lamb was one of the sacrifices accepted for the ceremonial cleansing of a woman after childbirth (Lev 12:6) or for the cleansing of a recovered leper (14:10 – 18).

General References to:

Used for food (Dt 32:14; Am 6:4); for sacrifices (Ge 4:4; 22:7), especially at Passover (Ex 12:3 – 5). Sacrificial lambs typical of Christ (Jn 1:29; Rev 5:6, 8). Offering of (Lev 3:7; 5:6; 22:23; 23:12; Nu 7:15, 21; 28:3 – 8); at the daily morning and evening sacrifices (Ex 29:38 – 42). Offering of, at the Feast of Passover (Ex 12:15); Pentecost (Lev 23:18 – 20); Tabernacles (Nu 29:13 – 40); the New Moon (Nu 28:11); Trumpets (Nu 29:2). Offering of, on the Sabbath day (Nu 28:9); at purifications (Lev 12:6; 14:10 – 25); by the Nazirite (Nu 6:12); for sin of ignorance (Lev 4:32).

Figurative:

The wolf living with, a figure of Messiah's reign (Isa 11:6; 65:25). A type of young believers (Jn 21:15). A name given to Christ (Jn 1:29, 36; Rev 5:6, 8, 12 – 13; 6:1, 16; 7:9 – 10, 14; 12:11; 13:8; 14:4, 10; 17:14; 19:7, 9; 21:9, 14, 22 – 23, 27; 22:1, 3). Jesus compared to (Isa 53:7; Ac 8:32; 1Pe 1:19).

Ge	22:8	"God himself will provide the **l**
Ex	12:21	and slaughter the Passover **l**.
Nu	9:11	are to eat the **l**, together
Isa	11:6	The wolf will live with the **l**,
	53:7	he was led like a **l** to the slaughter,
Mk	14:12	to sacrifice the Passover **l**,
Jn	1:29	**L** of God, who takes away the sin
Ac	8:32	as a **l** before the shearer is silent,
1Co	5:7	our Passover **l**, has been sacrificed.
1Pe	1:19	a **l** without blemish or defect.
Rev	5:6	Then I saw a **L**, looking
	5:12	"Worthy is the **L**, who was slain,
	7:14	white in the blood of the **L**.
	14:4	They follow the **L** wherever he
	15:3	of God and the song of the **L**:
	17:14	but the **L** will overcome them
	19:9	to the wedding supper of the **L**!' "
	21:23	gives it light, and the **L** is its lamp.

LAMB OF GOD Jesus was called the Lamb of God by John the Baptist (Jn 1:29, 36). The expression emphasizes the redemptive character of the work of Christ. More than a score of times in the book of Revelation the lamb is used as a symbol of Christ, and in Christian art of the succeeding centuries, the motif is continued, as it is also in the Communion service of many churches when they use these words: "Lamb of God, Son of the Father, that takest away the sins of the world, have mercy upon us."

The OT has numerous references to the lamb as a sacrificial victim (*see Lamb*). Of special interest is the Passover lamb (Ex 12:3 – 6) through whose sacrifice deliverance from Egypt was achieved. This deliverance became in time a picture of redemption from sin (Lk 9:31; 1Co 5:7). The substitutionary use of the unblemished lamb in sacrifice led to the idea of the Suffering Servant, who as a lamb died in the place of sinners (Isa 53:4 – 7).

A title of Jesus (Jn 1:29; Rev 6:16; 7:9 – 10, 14, 17; 12:11; 13:8; 14:1, 4; 15:3; 17:14; 19:7; 21:9, 14, 22 – 23, 27; 22:1, 3).

LAMENTATIONS This book, entitled in most English versions The Lamentations of Jeremiah, is placed between Jeremiah and Ezekiel in the LXX, Vulgate, and the English Bible. In the Hebrew text, however, it occurred in the Sacred Writings as one of the Megilloth or "five scrolls," of which it is the third. Its Hebrew title *êkhâh* ("Oh, how") is derived from the word with which the book commences. The Talmud renamed the book *Qinoth* ("Lamentations" or "elegies") as a more accurate designation of its true contents. The book comprises five poems lamenting the desolation that had overtaken the Holy City in 586 BC.

Although in the Hebrew no name was attached to the book, the authorship was uniformly ascribed by ancient authorities to Jeremiah. The LXX added an introductory note stating that "Jeremiah lamented this lamentation over Jerusalem," but the traditional view of the authorship appears to be rooted in the elegy composed for the mourning period of the deceased Josiah (c. 609 BC). Many modern critics have envisaged several authors at work in the book, or else have assumed that Baruch, Jeremiah's secretary, was responsible for the work in its final form.

The book bewails the siege and destruction of Jerusalem and sorrows over the sufferings of the inhabitants during this time. It makes poignant confession of sin on behalf of the people and their leaders, acknowledges complete submission to the divine will, and prays that God will once again favor and restore his people.

Analysis:

1. The fallen city admits its sin and the justice of divine judgment (chs. 1 – 2).
2. Lamentation; reassertion of divine mercy and judgment; prayer for divine intervention (chs. 3 – 4).
3. Further confession and prayers for mercy (ch. 5).

LAODICEA [3293] (lā-ŏd′ĭse̅′a, Gr. *Laodikia*). A wealthy city in Asia Minor founded by Antiochus II (261 – 246 BC), and head of the "circuit" of "the seven churches in the province of Asia" (Rev 1:4). The city lay on one of the great Asian trade routes, and this insured its commercial prosperity. Laodicea was a leading banking center. In 51 BC Cicero, en route to his Cilician province, cashed drafts there. It was no doubt the rich banking firms that in AD 60 financed the reconstruction of the city after the great earthquake that destroyed it. Laodicea refused the senate's earthquake relief. She was "rich and increased with goods" and had "need of nothing" (3:17 KJV). The Lycus Valley produced a glossy black wool, the source of black cloaks and carpets, for which the city was famous. Laodicea was also the home of a medical school and the manufacture of collyrium, a famous eye salve. The scornful imagery of the apocalyptic letter to Laodicea is obviously based on these activities. It also has reference to the emetic qualities of the soda-laden warm water from nearby Hierapolis, whose thermal springs ran into the Maeander. Laodicea's water supply also came from Hierapolis, and Sir William Ramsay suggests that its vulnerability, together with the city's exposed position and its easy wealth, caused the growth in the community of that spirit of compromise and worldly mindedness castigated in the book of Revelation. Under Diocletian, Laodicea, still prosperous, was made the chief city of the province of Phrygia.

LAODICEANS, EPISTLE TO Letter mentioned by Paul (Col 4:16). This is probably a letter of Paul that was not preserved for the canon. Some theorize it may be the letter to the Ephesians as a circular letter. An apocryphal epistle to the Laodiceans exists in Latin.

LAST

Ex	14:24	During the **l** watch of the night
Isa	2:2	and Jerusalem: In the **l** days
	44:6	I am the first and I am the **l**;
Hos	3:5	and to his blessings in the **l** days.

Mic	4:1	In the **l** days
Mt	19:30	But many who are first will be **l**,
	20:8	beginning with the **l** ones hired
Mk	9:35	must be the very **l**, and the servant
	15:37	a loud cry, Jesus breathed his **l**.
Jn	6:40	and I will raise him up at the **l** day."
	15:16	and bear fruit — fruit that will **l**.
Ac	2:17	" 'In the **l** days, God says,
1Co	15:26	**l** enemy to be destroyed is death.
	15:52	of an eye, at the **l** trumpet.
2Ti	3:1	will be terrible times in the **l** days.
2Pe	3:3	in the **l** days scoffers will come,
Jude	1:18	"In the **l** times there will be
Rev	1:17	I am the First and the **L**.
	22:13	the First and the **L**, the Beginning

LAST DAYS [344, 2274]. The days before the final judgment (Jn 12:48), when God's kingdom is established on earth (Isa 2:2 – 4; Mic 4:1 – 8) and Israel is restored to her God (Hos 3:5). Began with the coming of Jesus and of the Spirit (Ac 2:16 – 21; Heb 1:2; 1Pe 1:20). The time of the resurrection (Jn 6:39 – 44, 54; 11:24). A time of great trouble and deception (1Ti 3:1 – 17; 2Pe 3:3 – 17; Jude 18 – 19), culminating in the second coming of Christ (1Pe 1:5). *See Day of the Lord; Eschatology.*

LATIN [4872]. The language of the Romans and, in Palestine, used primarily by the Romans. The official superscription on the cross was written in Hebrew, Greek, and Latin (Jn 19:20). The NT contains about twenty-five administrative and military Latin words translated into Greek.

LAUGHTER [6600, 7464, 7465, 8468, 8471, 1151, 1152, 2860].

1. Laughter cannot satisfy (Pr 14:13; Ecc 2:2; 7:3, 6; 10:19).

2. God's laughter: he laughs at his enemies (Pss 2:4; 37:13; 59:8).

3. The believers' laughter: they sometimes laugh incredulously (Ge 17:17; 18:12 – 15; 21:6), but they can laugh for real joy (Ps 126:2; Lk 6:21) and in derision of the wicked (Job 22:19; Ps 52:6; Isa 37:22).

4. The unbelievers' laughter: they laugh at Christ (Ps 22:7; Mt 9:24), at believers (Ne 2:19; Job 12:4; Ps 80:6), and at God's ordinances (2Ch 30:10); but their laughter will vanish (Pr 1:26; Lk 6:25; Jas 4:9).

Ge	21:6	Sarah said, "God has brought me **l**,
Ps	126:2	Our mouths were filled with **l**,
Pr	14:13	Even in **l** the heart may ache,
Jas	4:9	Change your **l** to mourning

LAW [2017, 2976, 2978, 5477, 9368, 10186, 492, 491, 1208, 2003, 3788, 3791, 3795].

TERMS OF SCRIPTURE.

Of Hebrew words, the one most often used, *tôrāh*, may refer to human instruction (Pr 1:8), to divine instruction (Isa 1:10), to a regulation (Lev 7:7), to the law of Moses (1Ki 2:3), or to custom (2Sa 7:19). Other words that may be so translated include *dāth*, *hôq*, *mitswâh*, and *mishpat*. The common Greek word *nomos* is occasionally used of law(s) in the most general sense (Ro 3:27) of a principle that governs one's actions (7:23), of the Pentateuch (Gal 3:10), and of the other portions of Holy Scripture (as Jn 10:34; 1Co 14:21), but most often for the Mosaic law (Ac 15:5). English synonyms include *commandment*, *direction*, *judgment*, *ordinance*, *precept*, *statute*, and *testimony*.

MORAL LAW.

It is plain from the Decalogue (Ex 20:3 – 17; Dt 5:7 – 21) that morality is not to be derived from human standards and the verdict of society but from God and his declarations and one's relationship of subordination to him. Right and wrong are not determined by the voice of society but by the voice of God. The Ten Commandments declare the broad principles of God's moral law. As the expression of the character and will of God, it sets forth the only standard of righteousness acceptable to him; but humans were without power to conform to that perfect standard. The law made them aware of their sinfulness (Ro 7:7, 13), condemned them as unrighteous (7:9 – 11; Gal 3:13;

Jas 2:9), and having removed any hope of salvation through their own righteousness, brought them to the place where they would cast themselves on the grace of God and trust only in the righteousness and merit of the atoning Savior, Jesus Christ (Gal 3:24).

Christians are free from the condemnation of the law (Ro 8:2) since the righteousness of him who kept the law perfectly and who vicariously paid the penalty for the transgression of the law on the part of his people has been imputed to them. The goal of the Christian is conformity to the moral image of God as manifested to them by the incarnate Son (Eph 4:13). So it is that Christians are under obligation to keep the moral law (cf. Mt 5:19ff.; Eph 4:28; 5:3; 6:2; Col 3:9; 1Pe 4:15), not as a condition of salvation, but that they may become more and more like their Father in heaven (Ro 8:1 – 9; Eph 4:13), and this because of love for the One who redeemed them (Ro 13:8 – 10; 1Jn 5:2 – 3).

SOCIAL LEGISLATION.

In the giving of the law at Sinai, Moses first communicated to the people the body of principles, the Ten Words, and then the applicatory precepts. Careful study of the individual statutes shows the specific commands to be rooted in the basic principles set out in the Decalogue.

OT laws of judicial, civil, or political nature are to be found in the block of legislative material known as the book of the covenant (Ex 20:23 – 23:33), in the so-called Holiness Code (Lev 17 – 26), and here and there throughout most of the book of Deuteronomy, especially Dt 21 – 25.

The dignity of the individual was to be preserved. A high premium was set on selflessness and consideration of others. God's wisdom and grace were manifest in the legislation given the Israelites through his servant Moses.

RELIGIOUS LEGISLATION.

Embodied in the OT are many laws governing the worship of God. Some are very general in nature, having to do with purity of worship. Large numbers of the laws concern the sanctuary, its priesthood, and the rites and ceremonies connected with it and the covenant relationship between the Israelites and their God. Some consist of prescriptions pertaining to special occasions of the religious year. Basic principles of worship are outlined in the first table of the Decalogue (Ex 20:3 – 11). They are then worked out into detailed applicatory legislation.

PURPOSE OF THE LAW.

Under the old covenant, believers manifested their faith in Yahweh by observing the law for their own good (Dt 6:4 – 9; 10:12 – 13; 30:1 – 16). Christ fulfilled the law; respected it, loved it, and showed its deeper significance (Mt 5:17 – 48). The law prepared the way for the coming of Christ (Gal 3:24). The law could not bring victory over sin (Ro 3 – 8; Gal). Jesus' summary of the law: it demands perfect love for God and love for one's neighbor comparable to that which one has for oneself (Mt 22:35 – 40). Made for the lawless (1Ti 1:8 – 10). Must be obeyed (Mt 22:21; Lk 20:22 – 25).

Law of God:
(Ps 119:1 – 8; Jas 1:25). Spiritual (Ro 7:14). Must be obeyed (1Jn 5:3). Love, the fulfilling of (Ro 13:10; 1Ti 1:5).

Law of Moses:
Contained in the books of Exodus, Leviticus, Numbers, and Deuteronomy.

Lev	24:22	are to have the same **l** for the alien
Dt	1:5	Moses began to expound this **l**,
	6:25	to obey all this **l** before the LORD
	31:26	"Take this Book of the **L**
Jos	1:8	of the **L** depart from your mouth;
2Ch	6:16	walk before me according to my **l**,
Ezr	7:6	versed in the **L** of Moses,
Ne	8:2	Ezra the priest brought the **L**
Ps	1:2	and on his **l** he meditates day

	37:31	The **l** of his God is in his heart;
	119:77	for your **l** is my delight.
	119:97	Oh, how I love your **l**!
Pr	28:9	If anyone turns a deaf ear to the **l**,
	29:18	but blessed is he who keeps the **l**.
Jer	31:33	"I will put my **l** in their minds
Mic	4:2	The **l** will go out from Zion,
Hab	1:7	they are a **l** to themselves
Mt	5:17	that I have come to abolish the **L**
	7:12	sums up the **L** and the Prophets.
	22:36	greatest commandment in the **L**?"
	22:40	All the **L** and the Prophets hang
Lk	11:52	"Woe to you experts in the **l**,
	16:17	stroke of a pen to drop out of the **L**.
Jn	1:17	For the **l** was given through Moses;
Ac	13:39	justified from by the **l** of Moses.
Ro	2:12	All who sin apart from the **l** will
	2:15	of the **l** are written on their hearts,
	3:28	by faith apart from observing the **l**.
	4:15	worthless, because **l** brings wrath.
	6:15	we are not under **l** but under grace?
	7:1	that the **l** has authority
	7:6	released from the **l** so that we serve
	7:12	**l** is holy, and the commandment is
	7:14	We know that the **l** is spiritual;
	8:3	For what the **l** was powerless to do
	9:31	who pursued a **l** of righteousness,
	10:4	Christ is the end of the **l**
	13:8	his fellowman has fulfilled the **l**.
	13:10	love is the fulfillment of the **l**.
1Co	9:21	I became like one not having the **l**
	15:56	and the power of sin is the **l**.
Gal	2:16	justified by observing the **l**,
	2:19	For through the **l** I died to the **l**
	3:2	the Spirit by observing the **l**,
	3:17	The **l**, introduced 430 years later,
	3:19	then, was the purpose of the **l**?
	3:24	So the **l** was put in charge to lead us
	5:3	obligated to obey the whole **l**.
	6:2	and in this way you will fulfill the **l**
Eph	2:15	flesh the **l** with its commandments
Php	3:9	of my own that comes from the **l**,
1Ti	1:8	We know that the **l** is good

Heb	7:12	there must also be a change of the **l**.
	10:1	The **l** is only a shadow
Jas	1:25	intently into the perfect **l** that gives
	2:8	If you really keep the royal **l** found
1Jn	3:4	Everyone who sins breaks the **l**;

LAYING ON OF HANDS In the OT the act symbolizes (1) the parental bestowal of inheritance rights (Ge 48:14 – 20); (2) the gifts and rights of an office (Nu 27:18, 23; Dt 34:9); and (3) substitution: of an animal for one's guilt (Ex 29:10, 15, 19; Lev 1:4; 3:2, 8, 13; 4:4, 15, 24, 29, 33; 8:14, 18, 22; 16:21; cf. Ge 22:9 – 13), of the Levites for the firstborn of the other tribes (Nu 8:10 – 19), and of one's innocence for another's guilt (Lev 24:13 – 16; Dt 13:9; 17:7).

In the NT the act symbolizes (1) the bestowal of blessings and benediction (Mt 19:13, 15; cf. Lk 24:50), (2) the restoration of health (Mt 9:18; Ac 9:12, 17), (3) the reception of the Holy Spirit in baptism (Ac 8:17, 19; 19:6), and (4) the gifts and rights of an office (Ac 6:6; 13:3; 1Ti 4:14; 2Ti 1:6).

LAZARUS [3276] (lăz′a-rus, Lat. from Gr., for Heb. *Eleazar, one whom God helps*).

1. Lazarus, the brother of Martha and Mary, who lived in Bethany. Lazarus became sick and died; Christ, after some delay, returned and raised him from death (Jn 11:1 – 12:19). The following factors enhance the importance of this miracle: (1) the number of days (four) between death and resurrection (11:39); (2) the number of witnesses involved (11:45; 12:17 – 18); (3) the evident health of Lazarus after the event (12:1, 2, 9); and (4) the significance of the event among the Jews (11:53; 12:10 – 11).

This miracle (1) illustrates Christ's sympathy (Jn 11:5, 11, 34 – 35) and power (11:40ff.); (2) manifests the purposiveness of his miracles (11:4, 40; 20:31); (3) gives concrete backing to the truth of Lk 16:30 – 31; (4) affords opportunity for eschatological teaching (Jn 11:23 – 25); and (5) precipitates the crucifixion (11:45 – 53; 12:9 – 19).

2. Lazarus, a beggar who died and went to Abraham's bosom (Lk 16:19 – 31). The passage illustrates these truths: (1) destiny is settled at death; (2) no purgatory awaits the righteous; and (3) people have sufficient warning now.

LAZINESS [4206, 6790, 6792, 8244, 8332, 734, 3821, 3891].

(Pr 12:27; 18:9; 19:24; 21:25; 22:13; 26:13 – 16). Brings adversity (Pr 12:24; Ecc 10:18); destruction (Pr 13:4; 19:15; 20:4; 23:21; 24:30 – 34). Admonitions against (Pr 6:6 – 11; 10:4 – 5, 26; 15:19). Denounced (Mt 25:26 – 27). Of ministers, denounced (Isa 56:10). Forbidden (Ro 12:11; Heb 6:12).

| Pr | 12:24 | but **l** ends in slave labor. |
| | 19:15 | **L** brings on deep sleep, |

LEAH [4207] (lē′a, Heb. *lē'âh*, meaning uncertain; possibly *wild cow* BDB; *wild cow, gazelle* IDB; *cow* KB). Laban's daughter and Jacob's first wife (Ge 29:21 – 30); mother of Reuben, Simeon, Levi, Judah, Issachar, Zebulun, and Dinah (29:31 – 35; 30:17 – 21). Loyal to Jacob (31:14 – 16), she returned with him to Canaan, where, at her death, she was buried in Machpelah (49:31). Two of her sons (Levi and Judah) became progenitors of prominent tribes in Israel, and through Judah, Jesus Christ came (49:10; Mic 5:2; Mt 2:6; Heb 7:14; Rev 5:5; cf. Ru 4:11).

LEARN

Dt	4:10	so that they may **l** to revere me
	5:1	**L** them and be sure to follow them.
	31:12	and **l** to fear the LORD your God
Ps	119:7	as I **l** your righteous laws.
Isa	1:17	**l** to do right!
	26:9	of the world **l** righteousness.
Mt	11:29	yoke upon you and **l** from me,
Jn	14:31	world must **l** that I love the Father
1Th	4:4	that each of you should **l**
1Ti	2:11	A woman should **l** in quietness

LEAVEN [2809] (lĕv′ĕn, Heb. *se'ōr, hāmēts*, Gr. *zymē*; *piece of fermented dough*). The answer to seven questions will cover most of the biblical material.

1. Why was leaven so rigorously excluded from meal offerings in the Sinaitic legislation (Ex 29:2, 23, 32; Lev 2:1 – 16; 6:14 – 23; 7:9 – 10; 8:2, 26, 31; 10:12; Nu 15:1 – 9, 17 – 21; 18:9, cf. Ex 23:18; 34:15)? The answer seems to lie in the fact that leaven represented corruption and therefore symbolized evil.

2. Why was leaven permitted in certain other offerings (Ex 23:15 – 16; 34:22 – 23; Lev 2:11; 7:13 – 14; 23:17 – 18; Nu 15:20)? The answer seems to be that leaven, a part of the daily food, is included in the offerings of thanks. Some hold that leaven here symbolizes the evil that still inheres in the worshiper.

3. Why was leaven excluded from the Passover (Ex 12:14 – 20; 23:15; 34:18; Dt 16:2 – 4)? The record indicates that Israel's haste in leaving Egypt prompted this exclusion (Ex 12:11, 29; Dt 16:3). However, the Passover as a type of Christ, who was wholly free of corruption, must be taken into account here (cf. 1Co 5:7 – 8).

4. Does Lot's use of unleavened bread (Ge 19:3) anticipate the symbolism of the Sinaitic legislation? Haste may have been the reason; but the latent symbolism of evil (as inconsistent with angels) cannot be entirely ruled out.

5. What does Am 4:5 indicate? That the degenerate northern kingdom mixed the permitted (Lev 7:13; 23:17) with the forbidden (Ex 23:18; 34:25; Lev 2:11).

6. What about the NT significance of leaven? Apart from Mt 13:33 (see below), leaven symbolizes either Jewish legalism (Mt 16:6, 12; Gal 5:9) or moral corruption (1Co 5:6ff.).

7. What, then, about Mt 13:33? This is a much-disputed passage. Some interpret leaven as symbolizing the final apostasy of the professing church; others explain leaven as symbolizing the permeating effect of the gospel in Christianizing the world.

LEBANON [4248] (lĕb′anŏn, Heb. *levānôn, white, snow*). A snow-clad mountain range extending in a

NE direction for 100 miles along the Syrian coast, from Tyre to Arvad, and the country that bears its name. The name signifies the whiteness either of the fossil-bearing limestone cliffs or the snowy crests of this mountain system.

> **General References to:**
>
> *Northern boundary of the land of Canaan (Dt 1:7; 3:25; 11:24; Jos 1:4; 9:1). Early inhabitants of (Jdg 3:3). Snow of (Jer 18:14). Streams of (SS 4:15). Cedars of (Jdg 9:15; 2Ki 19:23; 2Ch 2:8; Pss 29:5; 104:16; Isa 2:13; 14:8; Eze 27:5). Other trees (2Ki 19:23; 2Ch 2:8). Flower of (Na 1:4). Beasts of (Isa 40:16). Fertility and productiveness of (Hos 14:5 – 7). "Palace of the Forest of," (1Ki 7:2 – 5). Valley of (Jos 11:17; 12:7). Tower of (SS 7:4). Solomon had store cities (1Ki 9:19). Figurative (Isa 29:17; Jer 22:6).*

LED

Dt	8:2	the LORD your God **l** you all
1Ki	11:3	and his wives **l** him astray.
2Ch	26:16	his pride **l** to his downfall.
Ne	13:26	he was **l** into sin by foreign women.
Ps	68:18	you **l** captives in your train;
	78:52	he **l** them like sheep
Pr	7:21	persuasive words she **l** him astray;
Isa	53:7	he was **l** like a lamb to the slaughter
Mt	4:1	Then Jesus was **l** by the Spirit
	27:31	they **l** him away to crucify him.
Ac	8:32	"He was **l** like a sheep
Ro	8:14	those who are **l** by the Spirit
2Co	7:9	your sorrow **l** you to repentance.
Gal	5:18	But if you are **l** by the Spirit,
Eph	4:8	he **l** captives in his train

LEGALISTIC [1877+3795]. Seeking God's favor by keeping the letter of the law without keeping its spirit (Mt 23:23 – 24). Legalists in the early church required circumcision for salvation (Ac 15:1 – 29). Paul's first letter, Galatians, was written to combat legalistic teaching about the Christian life (Gal 3:2, 10 – 14; 4:9 – 11). The Christian lives a life of grace, not works (Eph 2:8 – 9), and is not judged by ritual observance of special diet or holy days (Ro 14:1 – 18; Col 2:16 – 19; Heb 13:9).

LEGION [3305] (Gr. *legiōn*, or *legeōn*, Lat. *Legio, military company*). The largest single unit in the Roman army, including infantry and cavalry. A division of infantry at full strength consisted of about six thousand Roman soldiers. Each division was divided into ten cohorts, and each cohort was further divided into six centuries. Each subdivision, as well as the large whole, had its own officers and its own standards. The term "legion" in the NT represents a vast number (Mt 26:53; Mk 5:9, 15; Lk 8:30).

LEPROSY [7665, 7669, 3319, 3320]. The word is used for various diseases affecting the skin — not necessarily leprosy (Hansen's disease).

> **General Reference to:**
>
> *Law concerning (Lev 13 – 14; 22:4; Nu 5:1 – 3; 12:14; Dt 24:8; Mt 8:4; Lk 5:14; 17:14). Entailed (2Ki 5:27). Isolation of lepers (Lev 13:46; Nu 5:2; 12:14; 2Ki 15:5; 2Ch 26:21). Separate burial (2Ch 26:23). Sent as a judgment: on Miriam (Nu 12:1 – 10); Gehazi (2Ki 5:27); Azariah/Uzziah (2Ki 15:5; 2Ch 26:20 – 21). Other instances: four lepers outside Samaria (2Ki 7:3); Simon (Mk 14:3).*
>
> **Healed:**
>
> *Miriam (Nu 12:13 – 14); Naaman (2Ki 5:8 – 14); by Jesus (Mt 8:3; Mk 1:40 – 42; Lk 5:13; 17:12 – 14). Disciples empowered to heal (Mt 10:8).*

LEVI [4290, 4291, 3322] (lē′vī, Heb. *lēwî, joined,* perhaps *wild cow* or *person pledged for a debt or vow*).

1. Jacob's third son by Leah (Ge 29:34; 35:23). Levi, born in Haran, accompanied his father on his return to Canaan. He joined his brothers in sinister plots against Joseph (37:4, 28); and, with them, eventually bowed before Joseph (42:6). A predicted famine caused Jacob's entire family to migrate to Egypt, where Levi died at age 137 (Ex 6:16). His three sons — Gershon, Kohath, and Merari (Ge 46:11) — later became heads

of families. Three things deserve special attention. (1) His mother named him "Levi," hoping that Jacob, his father, would now be "attached" to her (29:34). (2) His part in the massacre of the Shechemites because of Shechem's raping of Dinah, his sister, showed two facets of his character: duplicity and righteous indignation (34:25 – 31). (3) Jacob, facing death, pronounced a curse on Simeon and Levi because of their iniquitous deed at Shechem (cf. 34:25 – 31 with 49:5 – 7); but because of holy zeal manifested at Sinai (Ex 32:25 – 29) and in his descendant Phinehas (Nu 25:6 – 13), Levi's curse was turned into a blessing (Dt 33:8 – 11) for his descendants. *See also Levites.*

LEVIATHAN [H4293] (*coiled one [like a serpent]*). Possibly a crocodile (Job 41; Ps 104:26). A sea monster figurative of forces of chaos opposed to Yahweh (Job 3:8; Ps 74:14; Isa 27:1). *See Serpent.*

Job	41:1	pull in the **l** with a fishhook
Ps	74:14	you who crushed the heads of **L**
Isa	27:1	**L** the gliding serpent,

LEVIRATE MARRIAGE Jewish custom according to which when an Israelite died without male heirs, his nearest relative married the widow, and their firstborn son became the heir of the first husband (Dt 25:5 – 10; Ru 3 – 4). *See Kinsman-Redeemer.*

LEVITES [278, 4290+, 4291+, 10387, 3324, 3325] (lē'vīts, *of Levi*). The name given to the descendants of Levi.

THEIR ORIGIN.

Levi was the third son of Jacob by Leah (Ge 29:34; 35:22 – 26).

THEIR APPOINTMENT.

Several discernible factors undoubtedly influenced the selection of Levi's descendants for their special place in Israel's religion. (1) The divine selection of Moses and Aaron, who were descendants of Kohath, one of Levi's three sons (Ex 2:1 – 10; 6:14 – 27; Nu 26:59), obviously conferred on the Levites an honor that was recognized by the other tribes. (2) However, an event of transcending importance at Mount Sinai (Ex 32:25 – 29) gave to the Levites as a tribe their place of privilege and responsibility in God's plan. (3) Moreover, this choice was undoubtedly confirmed by a very similar event when an individual Levite, Phinehas by name, stayed the plague that was about to decimate the Israelites (Nu 25:1 – 13).

THEIR ORGANIZATION.

A threefold organization is discernible: (1) The top echelon was occupied by Aaron and his sons; these alone were priests in the restricted sense. The priests belonged to the family of Kohath. (2) The middle echelon included all the other Kohathites who were not of Aaron's family; to them were given certain privileges in carrying the most sacred parts of the tabernacle (Nu 3:27 – 32; 4:4 – 15; 7:9). (3) The bottom echelon comprised all members of the families of Gershon and Merari; to them lesser duties were prescribed (3:21 – 26, 33 – 37).

PRIESTS AND LEVITES.

The Mosaic legislation made a sharp distinction between the priests and nonpriests or ordinary Levites. (1) The priests must belong to Aaron's family; the Levites belonged to the larger family of Levi. A priest was a Levite, but a Levite was not necessarily a priest. (2) Priests were consecrated (Ex 29:1 – 37; Lev 8); Levites were purified (Nu 8:5 – 22). (3) Levites were considered a gift to Aaron and his sons (3:5 – 13; 8:19; 18:1 – 7). (4) The fundamental difference consisted of this: only the priest had the right to minister at the altar and to enter the sanctuary (Ex 28:1; 29:9; Nu 3:10, 38; 4:15, 19 – 20; 18:1 – 7; 25:10 – 13).

Three Divisions of:
Each having the name of one of its progenitors: Gershon, Kohath, and Merari (Nu 3:17). Gershonites and their duties (Nu 3:18 – 26; 4:23 – 26; 10:17). Ruling chief over the Gershonites was the second son of the ruling high priest (Nu 4:28). Kohathites, consisting of the families of the

Amramites, Izharites, Hebronites, Uzzielites (Nu 3:27; 4:18 – 20). Of the Amramites, Aaron and his family were set apart as priests (Ex 28:1; 29:9; Nu 3:38; 8:1 – 14; 17; 18:1), the remaining families were appointed to take charge of the ark, table, lampstand, altars and vessels of the sanctuary, the hangings, and all the service (Nu 3:27 – 32; 4:2 – 15). The chief over the Kohathite was the oldest son of the ruling high priest (Nu 3:32; 1Ch 9:20). Merarites (Nu 3:20, 33 – 37; 4:31 – 33; 7:8; 10:17; 1Ch 6:19, 29 – 30; 23:21 – 23). The chief over the Merarites was the second son of the ruling high priest (Nu 4:33). Place of, in camp and march (Nu 1:50 – 53; 2:17; 3:23 – 35). Cities assigned to, in the land of Canaan (Jos 21). Lodged in the chambers of the temple (1Ch 9:27, 33; Eze 40:44). Resided also in villages outside of Jerusalem (Ne 12:29). Age of, when inducted into office (Nu 4:3, 30, 47; 8:23 – 26; 1Ch 23:3, 24, 27; Ezr 3:8), and when retired from office (Nu 4:3, 47; 8:25 – 26).

Functions of:

Had charge of the tabernacle in camp and on the march (Nu 1:50 – 53; 3:6 – 9, 21 – 37; 4:1 – 15, 17 – 49; 8:19, 22; 18:3 – 6), and of the temple (1Ch 9:27 – 29; 23:2 – 32; Ezr 8:24 – 34). Bore the ark of the covenant (Dt 10:8; 1Ch 15:2, 26 – 27). Ministered before the ark (1Ch 16:4). Custodians and administrators of the tithes and other offerings (1Ch 9:26 – 29; 26:28; 29:8; 2Ch 24:5, 11; 31:11 – 19; 34:9; Ezr 8:29 – 30, 33; Ne 12:44). Prepared the bread of the Presence (1Ch 23:28 – 29). Assisted the priests in preparing the sacrifice (2Ch 29:12 – 36; 2Ch 35:1 – 18). Killed the Passover lamb for the children of the captivity (Ezr 6:20 – 21). Teachers of the law (Dt 33:10; 2Ch 17:8 – 9; 30:22; 35:3; Ne 8:7 – 13; Mal 2:6 – 7). Were judges (Dt 17:9; 1Ch 23:4; 26:29; 2Ch 19:8 – 11; Ne 11:16). See Judge. Were scribes of the sacred books. See Scribe. Pronounced the blessings of the law in the responsive service at Mount Gerizim (Dt 27:12; Jos 8:33). Were gatekeepers of the temple. Were overseers in building and the repairs of the temple (1Ch 23:2 – 4; Ezr 3:8 – 9). Were musicians of the temple service. See Music. Supervised weights and measures (1Ch 23:29). List of those who returned from the captivity (Ezr 2:40 – 63; 7:7; 8:16 – 20; Ne 7:43 – 73; 12). Sealed the covenant with Nehemiah (Ne 10:9 – 28).

Privileges of:

In lieu of landed inheritance, forty-eight cities with suburbs were assigned to them (Nu 35:2 – 8, w 18:24 & 26:62; Dt 10:9; 12:12, 18 – 19; 14:27 – 29; 18:1 – 8; Jos 13:14; 14:3; 18:7; 1Ch 6:54 – 81; 13:2; 2Ch 23:2; Eze 34:1 – 5). Assigned to, by families (Jos 21:4 – 40). Suburbs of their cities were inalienable for debt (Lev 25:32 – 34). Tithes and other offerings (Nu 18:24, 26 – 32; Dt 18:1 – 8; 26:11 – 13; Jos 13:14; Ne 10:38 – 39; 12:44, 47). Firstfruits (Ne 12:44, 47). Spoils of war, including captives (Nu 31:30, 42 – 47). See Tithes. Tithes withheld from (Ne 13:10 – 13; Mal 3:10). Pensioned (2Ch 31:16 – 18). Owned lands (Dt 18:8, w 1Ki 2:26). Land allotted to, by Ezekiel (Eze 48:13 – 14). Enrollment of, at Sinai (Nu 1:47 – 49; 2:33; 3:14 – 39; 4:2 – 3; 26:57 – 62; 1Ch 23:3 – 5). Degraded from the Levitical office by Jeroboam (2Ch 11:13 – 17; 13:9 – 11). Loyal to the ruler (2Ki 11:7 – 11; 2Ch 23:7). Intermarry with Canaanites (Ezr 9:1 – 2; 10:23 – 24). Exempt from enrollment for military duty (Nu 1:47 – 54, w 1Ch 12:26). Subordinate to the sons of Aaron (Nu 3:9; 8:19; 18:6).

Prophecies Concerning:

(Jer 33:18; Eze 44:10 – 14; Mal 3:3), of their repentance of the crucifixion of the Messiah (Zec 12:10 – 13). John's vision concerning (Rev 7:7).

Nu	1:53	The **L** are to be responsible
	3:12	"I have taken the **L**
	8:6	"Take the **L** from among the other
	18:21	I give to the **L** all the tithes in Israel
	35:7	must give the **L** forty-eight towns,
2Ch	31:2	assigned the priests and **L**
Mal	3:3	he will purify the **L** and refine them

LEVITICAL CITIES The plan set out in Nu 35:1 – 8 (fulfilled in Jos 21) gave the Levites forty-eight cities. This plan involved a threefold purpose: (1) Such cities caused the Levites to be "scattered" in Israel and thus fulfilled Jacob's dying prophecy (Ge 49:7). (2) Thus "scattered," they could carry out their teaching ministry better (Dt 33:10). (3) Since six of their cities were to be "cities of refuge" (Nu 35:6), they would thereby become more accessible to those seeking legal protection (Dt 19:1 – 3, 7 – 10, 17ff.). Negative criticism finds three problems: (1) The Levites were given "no inheritance" in Israel (Nu 18:20). However, although these cities were not an inheritance, they were a gift from the other tribes (35:2, 4, 6 – 8). (2) No substantial evidence exists in preexilic history for such cities. True, but Israel also failed to carry out fully other Mosaic legislation (cf. 2Ch 35:18; 36:21). (3) Nu 35:2 – 8 is only an ideal theory never realized until Eze 48:8 – 14. Not so; Ezekiel's symbolic idealization is based on Nu 35:1 – 8 (and Jos 21), though not literally confined to the earlier legislation.

LEVITICUS (lĕvĭt′ĭkŭs, Gr. *Levitikon*, *relating to the Levites*). The designation in the English Bible of the third book of the Pentateuch, derived from the Latin rendering (*Liber Leviticus*) of the Greek title *Levitikon*. The Hebrew title merely consists of the first word of the text (*wayyiqrāʾ*), "and he called." The book is closely associated with Exodus and Numbers in historical continuity but differs from them in that the purely historical element is subordinate to legal and ritual considerations. Although the emphasis in Leviticus is more on priests than on Levites, the English title is not inappropriate, since the Jewish priesthood was essentially Levitical (cf. Heb 7:11). Leviticus enshrines the laws by which the religious and civil organization of the primitive theocracy in Canaan was to be regulated.

ANALYSIS.

The first seven chapters of Leviticus give the detailed sacrificial procedures showing how the various kinds of burnt offerings, the meal offering, the sin and guilt offerings, and other sacrifices avail for the removal of sin and defilement under the covenant. A subsequent liturgical section (8:1 – 10:20) describes the consecration of Aaron and the priesthood, followed by the designation of clean and unclean beasts and certain rules of hygiene (11:1 – 15:33). The ritual of the Day of Atonement occurs in ch. 16, followed by a section (17:1 – 20:27) treating sacrificial blood, ethical laws, and penalties for transgressors. The theme of 21:1 – 24:23 is priestly holiness and the consecration of seasons, while the following chapter deals with the legislation surrounding the sabbatical and Jubilee years. A concluding chapter outlines promises and threats (26:1 – 46), and an appendix covers vows (27:1 – 34). Man as sinner, substitutionary atonement, and divine holiness are prominent throughout Leviticus.

Outline:

I. The Five Main Offerings (chs. 1 – 7).
   A. Their content, purpose, and manner of offering (1:1 – 6:7).
   B. Additional regulations (6:8 – 7:38).
II. The Ordination, Installation, and Work of Aaron and His Sons (chs. 8 – 10).
III. Laws of Cleanness — Food, Childbirth, Infections, etc. (chs. 11 – 15).
IV. The Day of Atonement and the Centrality of Worship at the Tabernacle (chs. 16 – 17).
V. Moral Laws Covering Incest, Honesty, Thievery, Idolatry, etc. (chs. 18 – 20).
VI. Regulations for the Priests, the Offerings, and the Annual Feasts (21:1 – 24:9).
VII. Punishment for Blasphemy, Murder, etc. (24:10 – 23).
VIII. The Sabbath Year, Jubilee, Land Tenure, and Reform of Slavery (ch. 25).
IX. Blessings and Curses for Covenant Obedience and Disobedience (ch. 26).
X. Regulations for Offerings Vowed to the Lord (ch. 27).

LIBERTINES (Gr. *Libertinoi*). Probably originally captive Jews brought to Rome by Pompey in 63 BC, liberated subsequently, and repatriated to Palestine, where, presumably, they built a synagogue still occupied by their descendants a century after Pompey's Palestinian campaign (Ac 6:9). These people were Roman citizens. There seems to be some evidence for a synagogue of Libertines at Pompeii. There is no substance in the conjectural alternative explanation that the Libertines were natives of "Libertum" near Carthage. The place is unknown to history or geography. The explanation adopted goes back to Chrysostom.

LIBERTY [2002]. Freedom, the opposite of servitude or bondage, whether physical, moral, or spiritual. The term is used of slaves or captives being set free from physical servitude or imprisonment (Lev 25:10; Jer 34:8, 15 – 17; Ac 26:23; Heb 13:23), or the granting of certain privileges while imprisoned (Ac 24:23; 27:3). In Eze 46:17 reference is made to "the year of freedom," which is the Year of Jubilee. The term has a legal and moral tone in 1Co 7:39 in asserting the right of a widow to remarry. The special concern of Christianity is the spiritual liberty of believers in Christ. Found in union with Christ, it carries with it freedom from the ceremonial law (Gal 5:1; 2:4) and must be valued and guarded. The essence of Christian liberty lies not in external freedom but in deliverance from the bondage of sin and its consequent inner corruption (Jn 8:34 – 36; Ro 6:20 – 22).

Spiritual liberty is the result of the Spirit's regenerating work, for his presence and work within produces liberty (2Co 3:17), giving a sense of freedom through a filial relation with God (Ro 8:15 – 16). Godly men of the OT knew a measure of this spiritual liberty (Ps 119:45), but the gospel reveals and offers it in its fullness.

LIE, LYING (Heb. *seqer*, Gr. *pseudos*). Since God is truth and truthful, he cannot lie as humans do (Nu 23:19). The source of lies is the devil (Jn 8:44; Ac 5:3). Christians must not lie to one another (Eph 4:25; Col 3:9), for Christ is the truth, and those who lie are not one with him. Therefore those who are redeemed by the Lamb are those with no lie on their lips (Rev 14:5).

Connected with the idea of a lie are those who live a lie or convey a lie — a false brother (2Co 11:26), a false apostle (11:13), a false teacher (2Pe 2:1), a false witness (Mt 26:60), a false prophet (7:15), and a false Christ (24:24). In each of these cases, the Greek word begins with *pseudo* ("lying" or "false").

Lev	18:22	" 'Do not **l** with a man
	19:11	" 'Do not **l**.
Nu	23:19	God is not a man, that he should **l**,
Dt	6:7	when you **l** down and when you get
1Sa	15:29	the Glory of Israel does not **l**
Ps	23:2	me **l** down in green pastures,
Isa	11:6	leopard will **l** down with the goat,
Jer	9:5	They have taught their tongues to **l**
	23:14	They commit adultery and live a **l**.
Eze	13:6	are false and their divinations a **l**.
Ro	1:25	exchanged the truth of God for a **l**,
Col	3:9	Do not **l** to each other,
2Th	2:11	so that they will believe the **l**
Tit	1:2	which God, who does not **l**,
Heb	6:18	which it is impossible for God to **l**,
1Jn	2:21	because no **l** comes from the truth.
Rev	14:5	No **l** was found in their mouths;

LIFE [344, 1414, 2006, 2644, 2649, 2652, 3427, 5883, 6409, 419, 482, 1053, 1586, 2409, 2437, 2443, 2461, 4344, 6034]. A complex concept with varied shades of meaning, rendering several Hebrew and Greek terms. It may denote *physical* or natural life, whether animal (Ge 1:20; 6:17; Rev 8:9) or human (Lev 17:14; Mt 2:20; Lk 12:22). It is the vital principle or breath of life, which God imparted to man, making him a living soul (Ge 2:7). This life is a precious gift, and the taking of life is prohibited (Ge 9:5; Ex 20:13; Lev 24:17). It is propagated through physical generation and is subject to physical death. It may signify the period of one's earthly existence, one's lifetime (Ge 23:1; 25:7; Lk 16:25), or the relations, activities, and experiences that make up life (Ex 1:14; Dt 32:47; Job 10:1; Lk 12:15). Occasionally it means one's manner of life (1Ti 2:2; 1Jn 2:16) or the means for sustaining life (Dt 24:6; 1Jn 3:17). But the primary concern of the Scriptures is *spiritual* or *eternal* life for the human race. It is the gift of God, mediated through faith in Jesus Christ (Jn 3:36; 5:24; Ro 5:10; 6:23; 1Jn 5:12). It is not synonymous with endless existence, which is also true of the unsaved. It is qualitative, involving the impartation of a new nature (2Pe 1:3 – 4). It is communicated to the believer in this life, resulting in fellowship with God in Christ, and is not interrupted by physical death (1Th 5:10). It will find its perfection and full reality of blessedness with God in the life to come (Ro 2:7; 2Co 5:4). As "the living God" (Dt 5:26; Ps 42:2; 1Th 1:9; 1Ti 3:15), the eternal and self-existent one, God has *absolute* life in himself (Jn 5:26) and is the source of all life (Ps 36:9; Jn 1:4; 17:3; 1Jn 1:1 – 2; 5:20). *See Immortality.*

Length of:

Long life promised: (Ge 6:3; Ps 91:16) to Solomon (1Ki 3:11 – 14); to the wise (Pr 3:16; 9:11); to the obedient (Dt 4:40; 22:7; Pr 3:1 – 2); to those who honor parents (Ex 20:12; Dt 5:16); to those who show kindness to animals (Dt 22:7); to those who fear God (Pr 10:27; Isa 65:20). Brevity of (Ge 47:9; Job 10:9, 20 – 21; 13:12, 25, 28; Pss 89:47 – 48; 90:10; 146:4; Isa 2:22). Compared: to a shadow (1Ch 29:15; Job 8:9; 14:1 – 2; Pss 102:11; 144:3 – 4; Ecc 6:12); to a weaver's shuttle (Job 7:6 – 10); to a courier (Job 9:25 – 26); to a handbreadth (Ps 39:4 – 5, 11); to a wind (Ps 78:39); to grass (Pss 90:3, 5 – 6, 9 – 10; 102:11; 103:14 – 16; Isa 40:6 – 8, 24; 51:12; Jas 1:10 – 11; 1Pe 1:24); to a leaf (Isa 64:6); to a vapor (Jas 4:14). Weary of: Job (Job 3; 7:1 – 3; 10:18 – 19); Jeremiah (Jer 20:14 – 18); Elijah (1Ki 19:1 – 4); Jonah (Jnh 4:8); Paul (Php 1:21 – 24). See Suicide. Hated (Ecc 2:17). To be hated for Christ's sake (Lk 14:26). What shall a man give in exchange for (Mt 16:26; Mk 8:37). He that loses it for Christ's sake shall save it (Mt 10:39; 16:25 – 26; Lk 9:24; Jn 12:25). Uncertainty of

(1Sa 20:3; Job 4:19 – 21; 17:1; Pr 27:1; Lk 12:20). End of, certain (2Sa 14:14; Ps 22:29; Ecc 1:4; Isa 38:12). See Death, Physical.

Comes from God:

(Ge 2:7; Dt 8:3; 30:20; 32:39; 1Sa 2:6; Job 27:3; Pss 30:3; 104:30; Ecc 12:7; Isa 38:16; Ac 17:25, 28; Ro 4:17; 1Ti 6:13; Jas 4:15).

Spiritual Life:

(Dt 8:3). From Christ (Jn 1:4; 6:27, 33, 35; 10:10; 17:2 – 3; Ro 6:11; 8:10; Col 3:4). Through faith (Jn 3:14 – 16; 5:24 – 26, 40; 6:40, 47; 11:25 – 26; 20:31; Gal 2:19 – 20). Signified, in figure of new birth (Jn 3:3 – 8; Tit 3:5). In figure of death, burial, and resurrection (Ro 6:4 – 8).

Everlasting Life:

(Pss 21:4; 121:8; 133:3; Isa 25:8; Da 12:2; Mt 19:16 – 21, 29; 25:46; Mk 10:17 – 21, 29 – 30; Lk 18:18 – 22, 29 – 30; 20:36; Jn 3:14 – 16, 36; 4:14; 5:24 – 25, 29, 39; 6:27, 40, 47, 50 – 58, 68; 10:10, 27 – 28; 12:25, 50; 17:2 – 3; Ac 13:46, 48; Ro 2:7; 5:21; 6:22 – 23; 1Co 15:53 – 54; 2Co 5:1; Gal 6:8; 1Ti 1:16; 4:8; 6:12, 19; 2Ti 1:10; Tit 1:2; 3:7; 1Jn 2:25; 3:15; 5:11 – 13, 20; Jude 21; Rev 1:18).

Ge	1:30	everything that has the breath of **l**
	2:7	into his nostrils the breath of **l**,
	2:9	of the garden were the tree of **l**
	6:17	to destroy all **l** under the heavens,
Ex	21:23	you are to take **l** for **l**, eye for eye,
Lev	17:14	the **l** of every creature is its blood.
Nu	35:31	a ransom for the **l** of a murderer,
Dt	30:15	I set before you today **l**
	30:19	Now choose **l**, so that you
	30:20	For the LORD is your **l**,
Job	2:6	hands; but you must spare his **l**."
	33:4	of the Almighty gives me **l**.
Ps	16:11	known to me the path of **l**;
	23:6	all the days of my **l**,
	27:1	LORD is the stronghold of my **l** —
	63:3	Because your love is better than **l**,
	69:28	they be blotted out of the book of **l**

	119:25	preserve my **l** according to your word
Pr	1:3	a disciplined and prudent **l**,
	4:23	for it is the wellspring of **l**.
	6:23	are the way to **l**,
	8:35	For whoever finds me finds **l**
	10:11	of the righteous is a fountain of **l**,
	13:3	He who guards his lips guards his **l**,
	19:23	The fear of the LORD leads to **l**:
Isa	53:10	LORD makes his **l** a guilt offering,
	53:11	he will see the light [of **l**]
	53:12	he poured out his **l** unto death,
Jer	10:23	that a man's **l** is not his own;
La	3:58	you redeemed my **l**.
Da	12:2	some to everlasting **l**, others
Jnh	2:6	you brought my **l** up from the pit,
Mal	2:5	a covenant of **l** and peace,
Mt	6:25	Is not **l** more important than food,
	7:14	and narrow the road that leads to **l**,
	10:39	Whoever finds his **l** will lose it,
	16:21	and on the third day be raised to **l**.
	18:8	better for you to enter **l** maimed
	19:16	thing must I do to get eternal **l**?"
	20:28	to give his **l** as a ransom for many."
Mk	8:35	but whoever loses his **l** for me
	10:30	and in the age to come, eternal **l**.
	10:45	to give his **l** as a ransom for many."
Lk	12:15	a man's **l** does not consist
	12:22	do not worry about your **l**,
	12:25	can add a single hour to his **l**?
	14:26	even his own **l** — he cannot be my
Jn	1:4	In him was **l**, and that **l** was
	3:15	believes in him may have eternal **l**.
	3:36	believes in the Son has eternal **l**,
	5:21	raises the dead and gives them **l**,
	5:24	him who sent me has eternal **l**
	6:27	for food that endures to eternal **l**,
	6:35	Jesus declared, "I am the bread of **l**
	6:53	and drink his blood, you have no **l**
	6:68	You have the words of eternal **l**.
	8:12	but will have the light of **l**."
	10:10	I have come that they may have **l**,
	10:15	and I lay down my **l** for the sheep.
	11:25	"I am the resurrection and the **l**.
	13:37	I will lay down my **l** for you."
	14:6	am the way and the truth and the **l**.
	15:13	lay down his **l** for his friends.
	17:3	Now this is eternal **l**: that they may
	20:31	that by believing you may have **l**
Ac	2:32	God has raised this Jesus to **l**,
	3:15	You killed the author of **l**,
	11:18	the Gentiles repentance unto **l**."
	13:48	appointed for eternal **l** believed.
Ro	2:7	immortality, he will give eternal **l**.
	4:25	was raised to **l** for our justification.
	5:21	righteousness to bring eternal **l**
	6:4	the Father, we too may live a new **l**.
	6:13	have been brought from death to **l**;
	6:23	but the gift of God is eternal **l**
	8:38	convinced that neither death nor **l**,
2Co	3:6	letter kills, but the Spirit gives **l**.
Gal	2:20	The **l** I live in the body, I live
	6:8	from the Spirit will reap eternal **l**.
Eph	4:1	I urge you to live a **l** worthy
Php	2:16	as you hold out the word of **l** —
Col	1:10	order that you may live a **l** worthy
	3:3	your **l** is now hidden with Christ
1Ti	1:16	on him and receive eternal **l**.
	4:8	for both the present **l** and the **l**
	4:16	Watch your **l** and doctrine closely.
	6:12	Take hold of the eternal **l**
	6:19	hold of the **l** that is truly **l**.
2Ti	1:9	saved us and called us to a holy **l** —
	1:10	destroyed death and has brought **l**
Tit	1:2	resting on the hope of eternal **l**,
	3:7	heirs having the hope of eternal **l**.
Heb	7:16	of the power of an indestructible **l**.
Jas	1:12	crown of **l** that God has promised
	3:13	Let him show it by his good **l**,
2Pe	1:3	given us everything we need for **l**
1Jn	3:14	we have passed from death to **l**,
	3:16	Jesus Christ laid down his **l** for us.
	5:11	has given us eternal **l**, and this **l** is
Jude	1:21	Christ to bring you to eternal **l**.
Rev	2:7	the right to eat from the tree of **l**,
	2:10	and I will give you the crown of **l**.

3:5	name from the book of **l**,	
20:12	was opened, which is the book of **l**.	
20:15	not found written in the book of **l**,	
21:27	written in the Lamb's book of **l**.	
22:2	side of the river stood the tree of **l**,	

LIFE, THE BOOK OF A figurative expression denoting God's record of those who inherit eternal life (Php 4:3; Rev 3:5; 21:27). From the human point of view, individuals may be blotted out of that book (Ps 69:28; Mt 25:29); but from God's point of view it contains only the names of the elect, which will not be blotted out (Rev 3:5; 13:8; 17:8; 20:15).

LIGHT [239, 240, 4401, 5585, 5586, 5944, 847, 3290, 5766, 5890, 5894, 5895]. The first recorded utterance of God in the Bible is "Let there be light" (Ge 1:3), the first sign of divine operation in the world of chaos and darkness. Dawn indicates the sure dispelling of darkness, the essence of all God's gifts. God is the creator of both light and darkness (Isa 45:6 – 7) and watches over their orderly succession (Ps 104:20; Am 4:13), yet light is superior (Ecc 2:13). It is virtually impossible to distinguish between natural and metaphorical uses of light in the Bible. Light is above all the source of life (11:7). The word is often used in synonyms for being alive (Job 3:20), being born (3:16), for the pleasures of life (Ps 97:11) or good days for the righteous (112:4), or for an essential in man's happiness (36:9). Light brings order to the world. Light and truth are coupled biblically (Ps 43:3; cf. Ps 19; Pr 6:23; Isa 51:4). Truth and law give knowledge (Pss 19:8; 139:11 – 12) and guidance (Dt 28:29; Job 22:28; Pr 4:18; cf. Mic 7:8). The recipient of light himself becomes a light, shining outwardly (Ps 34:5; Ecc 8:1) and inwardly (Pr 20:27; Da 5:11). The manifestations of light are the work of "the Father of the heavenly lights" (Jas 1:17), he who dwells in light (Ex 13:21; Ps 104:2; 1Ti 6:16) and who imparts light as a divine gift. The OT concept of Scripture as a lamp or a light is taken over in the NT (2Pe 1:19). Conversion is spoken of as illumination (Heb 6:4; 10:32). Believers are "people of the light" (Lk 16:8; 1Th 5:5) and the "light of the world" (Mt 5:14). Because the

gift may be lost through inactivity (Jn 5:35; 1Th 5:5 – 6), the heavenly light must be used as armor or a weapon (Eph 6:12; Ro 13:12) in the fight against darkness. The light is permanently present in Christ (Jn 1:7 – 9; Heb 1:3) and in the gospel (Ac 26:23; 2Co 4:4). In the new age there will be no more night (Rev 21:23). John stresses that "God is light" (1Jn 1:5), and he who hates his brother is in darkness (2:11).

Physical:

> Created (Ge 1:3 – 5; Ps 74:16; Isa 45:7; 2Co 4:6). Miraculous (Ex 13:21; Dt 1:33; Mt 17:2; Mk 9:3; Lk 9:29; Ac 9:3; 12:7; 26:13).

Figurative:

> (1Ki 11:36); of the Lord (Ps 27:1; Isa 60:19 – 20; Jas 1:17; 1Jn 1:5, 7; 2:8 – 10); of the Lord's word (Ps 119:105; Pr 6:23); of personal influence for righteousness (Mt 5:14 – 16; Mk 4:21; Lk 8:16); of the righteous (Lk 16:8; Eph 5:8, 14; Php 2:15; 1Th 5:5); of John the Baptist (Jn 5:35); of spiritual understanding (Isa 8:20; Lk 1:33 – 36; 2Co 4:6); of the gospel (2Co 4:4, 6); of spiritual wisdom (Ps 119:130; Isa 2:5; 2Pe 1:19); of righteousness (Mt 5:16; Ac 26:18; 1Pe 2:9); of heavenly glory (Rev 21:23); of Christ's heavenly glory (1Ti 6:16); of Christ's kingdom (Isa 58:8); of the Savior (Isa 49:6; Mal 4:2; Mt 4:16; Lk 2:32; Jn 1:4 – 5, 7 – 9; 3:19 – 21; 8:12; 9:5; 12:35 – 36, 46; Rev 21:23).

Ge	1:3	"Let there be **l**," and there was **l**.
Ex	13:21	in a pillar of fire to give them **l**,
2Sa	22:29	LORD turns my darkness into **l**.
Ps	4:6	Let the **l** of your face shine upon us
	18:28	my God turns my darkness into **l**.
	56:13	God in the **l** of life.
	89:15	who walk in the **l** of your presence,
	104:2	He wraps himself in **l**
	119:105	and a **l** for my path.
Isa	2:5	let us walk in the **l** of the LORD.
	9:2	have seen a great **l**;
	42:6	and a **l** for the Gentiles,
	53:11	he will see the **l** [of life]
	60:1	"Arise, shine, for your **l** has come,

Mic	7:8	the LORD will be my **l**.
Mt	4:16	have seen a great **l**;
	5:14	"You are the **l** of the world.
	5:16	let your **l** shine before men,
	6:22	your whole body will be full of **l**.
	11:30	yoke is easy and my burden is **l**."
Lk	2:32	a **l** for revelation to the Gentiles
	8:16	those who come in can see the **l**.
Jn	1:4	and that life was the **l** of men.
	1:5	The **l** shines in the darkness,
	1:7	witness to testify concerning that **l**,
	3:19	but men loved darkness instead of **l**
	8:12	he said, "I am the **l** of the world.
	9:5	in the world, I am the **l** of the world
	12:35	Walk while you have the **l**,
Ac	13:47	"'I have made you a **l**
Ro	13:12	darkness and put on the armor of **l**.
2Co	4:6	made his **l** shine in our hearts
	6:14	Or what fellowship can **l** have
	11:14	masquerades as an angel of **l**.
Eph	5:8	but now you are **l** in the Lord.
1Th	5:5	You are all sons of the **l**
1Ti	6:16	and who lives in unapproachable **l**,
1Pe	2:9	of darkness into his wonderful **l**.
1Jn	1:5	God is **l**; in him there is no
	1:7	But if we walk in the **l**,
	2:9	Anyone who claims to be in the **l**

LIVE [ALIVE, LIFE]

Ge	3:22	tree of life and eat, and **l** forever."
Ex	20:12	so that you may **l** long
	33:20	for no one may see me and **l**."
Dt	6:2	as you **l** by keeping all his decrees
Job	14:14	If a man dies, will he **l** again?
Ps	119:175	Let me **l** that I may praise you,
Pr	21:9	Better to **l** on a corner of the roof
	21:19	Better to **l** in a desert
Isa	55:3	hear me, that your soul may **l**.
Eze	20:11	for the man who obeys them will **l**
	37:3	can these bones **l**?" I said,
Am	5:6	Seek the LORD and **l**,
Hab	2:4	but the righteous will **l** by his faith
Lk	4:4	'Man does not **l** on bread alone.'"

Jn	14:19	Because I **l**, you also will **l**.
Ac	17:24	does not **l** in temples built by hands
	17:28	'For in him we **l** and move
Ro	1:17	"The righteous will **l** by faith."
2Co	5:7	We **l** by faith, not by sight.
Gal	2:20	The life I **l** in the body, I **l** by faith
	5:25	Since we **l** by the Spirit, let us keep
Php	1:21	to **l** is Christ and to die is gain.
Col	1:10	order that you may **l** a life worthy
1Th	4:1	we instructed you how to **l** in order
2Ti	3:12	who wants to **l** a godly life
Tit	2:12	and to **l** self-controlled, upright
Heb	10:38	But my righteous one will **l** by faith
1Pe	1:17	**l** your lives as strangers here
	3:8	**l** in harmony with one another;

LOGOS (Gr. *logos*). Usually rendered "word," in the Johannine writings, it also appears as a title of Jesus: "The Word" (Jn 1:1ff; 1Jn 1:1; Rev 19:13). In the OT God creates by the word (Ge 1:3; Ps 33:9). In the Judaism of NT times, *word* was used as a way of referring to God himself. In Greek philosophy, *word* refers to the dynamic principle of reason operating in the world and forming a medium of communion between God and man.

LONG-SUFFERING [678+800] (Heb. *'erekh*, *'appayim*, *slow to anger*, Gr. *makrothymia*). The noun preferred by KJV (other versions use "forbearance") to account for the delay of the Lord in inflicting punishment or exercising his anger/wrath. The idea is that God delays his exercise of wrath to give time for repentance and amendment of life (Ex 34:6; Nu 14:18; Ps 86:15; Jer 15:15; Ro 2:4; 2Pe 3:9). In a similar manner, Christ is said to be long-suffering (1Ti 1:16; 2Pe 3:15).

The KJV also uses the noun to describe human beings (other versions use "patience" and "forbearance"). As so used, it refers to being patient, especially when being faced with evil.

LORD [1484, 8606, 10437, 3259, 3261]. The KJV translation for a variety of Hebrew and Greek terms. It is applied to both men and God and expresses varied degrees of honor, dignity, and majesty. The Hebrew *'ădhōnay*, often translated "lord" or "master," may be a term of respect (Ge 23:11; 24:18), but its meaning of *owner* indicates one who has absolute control, as an owner of slaves, or a king. When applied to God, it denotes the owner and governor of the whole earth (Pss 97:5; 114:7; Isa 1:24). The term *'adonai*, perhaps the plural of *'adhôn* ("the Lord"), is always used where God is submissively and reverently addressed (Ex 4:10; Jos 7:8; Ne 1:11). In the KJV, *'ădhōnay* is given as "Lord," and Jehovah (Heb. *Yahweh*, "the self-existent one") is printed "LORD." The Jews, due to their interpretation of Lev 24:16, read *'ădhōnay* to avoid pronouncing *Yahweh* (the supreme name of God alone). Of the four Greek terms rendered "lord," *megistanes* is used in Mk 6:21 and means (pl.) "great men, courtiers." *Rabbouni*, "my Lord" (heightened form of Heb. *rab*), occurs in Mk 10:51 KJV and Jn 20:16 (transliterated). *Despotēs*, implying absolute ownership or power, is rendered "Lord" in Lk 2:29; Ac 4:24; 2Pe 2:1; Jude 4; Rev 6:10. The prevailing Greek term rendered "lord" is *kyrios*, "master or owner," one who has power or authority over some property (Mt 20:8; Lk 10:2), animals (Lk 19:34), or persons (Mt 13:27). It may be used as a term of respect (Mt 21:30; Jn 4:15; 12:21). It is frequently used of God (Mt 1:22; Mk 5:19; Ac 7:33) as well as of Jesus as Messiah, who by his resurrection and ascension was exalted to lordship (Ac 2:36; Ro 1:4; 14:8; Php 2:9 – 11). At times it is difficult to determine whether "the Lord" refers to the Father or to the Son (Ac 1:24; 9:31; 16:14; Ro 14:11; 1Co 4:19; 2Th 3:16).

Lord. (*'ădhōnay*, master, Lord)

Ex	15:17	O **L**, your hands established.
Nu	16:13	now you also want to **l** it over us?
Dt	10:17	God of gods and **L** of lords,
Jos	3:13	the **L** of all the earth — set foot
Ne	4:14	Remember the **L**, who is great
Job	28:28	'The fear of the **L** — that is wisdom,
Ps	37:13	but the **L** laughs at the wicked,
	38:22	O **L** my Savior.
	54:4	the **L** is the one who sustains me.
	86:5	You are forgiving and good, O **L**,
	147:5	Great is our **L** and mighty in power
Isa	6:1	I saw the **L** seated on a throne,
Da	2:47	and the **L** of kings and a revealer
Mt	3:3	'Prepare the way for the **L**,
	4:7	'Do not put the **L** your God
	7:21	"Not everyone who says to me, '**L**,
	9:38	Ask the **L** of the harvest, therefore,
	20:25	of the Gentiles **l** it over them,
	22:37	" 'Love the **L** your God
Mk	12:11	the **L** has done this,
	12:29	the **L** our God, the **L** is one.
Lk	2:9	glory of the **L** shone around them,
	6:46	"Why do you call me, '**L**, **L**,'
	11:1	one of his disciples said to him, "**L**,
	24:34	The **L** has risen and has appeared
Ac	2:21	on the name of the **L** will be saved.'
	8:16	into the name of the **L** Jesus.
	9:5	"Who are you, **L**?" Saul asked.
	10:36	through Jesus Christ, who is **L**
	16:31	replied, "Believe in the **L** Jesus,
Ro	4:24	in him who raised Jesus our **L**
	6:23	life in Christ Jesus our **L**.
	10:9	with your mouth, "Jesus is **L**,"
1Co	1:31	Let him who boasts boast in the **L**."
	3:5	the **L** has assigned to each his task.
	8:6	and there is but one **L**, Jesus Christ,
	15:57	victory through our **L** Jesus Christ.
2Co	2:12	found that the **L** had opened a door
	3:17	Now the **L** is the Spirit,
	4:5	but Jesus Christ as **L**, and ourselves
	8:5	they gave themselves first to the **L**
	10:17	Let him who boasts boast in the **L**."
Gal	6:14	in the cross of our **L** Jesus Christ,

Eph	4:5	one **L**, one faith, one baptism;
	5:8	but now you are light in the **L**.
	5:19	make music in your heart to the **L**,
	5:22	submit to your husbands as to the **L**
	6:1	obey your parents in the **L**,
	6:7	as if you were serving the **L**,
Php	2:11	confess that Jesus Christ is **L**,
	3:1	my brothers, rejoice in the **L**!
	4:4	Rejoice in the **L** always.
Col	1:10	you may live a life worthy of the **L**
	2:6	as you received Christ Jesus as **L**,
	3:13	Forgive as the **L** forgave you.
	3:23	as working for the **L**, not for men,
	3:24	receive an inheritance from the **L**
1Th	3:12	May the **L** make your love increase
	4:6	The **L** will punish men
	5:2	day of the **L** will come like a thief
	5:23	at the coming of our **L** Jesus Christ.
2Th	1:7	when the **L** Jesus is revealed
1Ti	6:15	the King of kings and **L** of lords,
2Ti	1:8	ashamed to testify about our **L**,
	2:19	"The **L** knows those who are his,"
Heb	1:10	O **L**, you laid the foundations
	10:30	"The **L** will judge his people."
	13:6	**L** is my helper; I will not be afraid.
Jas	3:9	With the tongue we praise our **L**
	4:10	Humble yourselves before the **L**,
	5:11	The **L** is full of compassion
1Pe	1:25	the word of the **L** stands forever."
	2:3	you have tasted that the **L** is good.
	3:15	in your hearts set apart Christ as **L**.
2Pe	1:11	into the eternal kingdom of our **L**
	2:1	the sovereign **L** who bought
	3:9	The **L** is not slow in keeping his
Jude	1:14	the **L** is coming with thousands
Rev	4:8	holy, holy is the **L** God Almighty,
	19:16	KINGS AND **L** OF LORDS.
	22:20	Come, **L** Jesus.

LORD. [3363, 3378] (Yahweh)

Ge	2:4	When the **L** God made the earth
	3:23	So the **L** God banished him
	4:4	The **L** looked with favor on Abel

	6:7	So the **L** said, "I will wipe mankind
	11:9	there the **L** confused the language
	12:1	**L** had said to Abram, "Leave your
	15:6	Abram believed the **L**,
	15:18	On that day the **L** made a covenant
	18:14	Is anything too hard for the **L**?
	39:2	The **L** was with Joseph
Ex	4:11	Is it not I, the **L**? Now go;
	6:2	also said to Moses, "I am the **L**.
	9:12	the **L** hardened Pharaoh's heart
	13:9	For the **L** brought you out of Egypt
	13:21	By day the **L** went ahead of them
	15:3	The **L** is a warrior;
	20:5	the **L** your God, am a jealous God,
	20:10	a Sabbath to the **L** your God.
	23:25	Worship the **L** your God,
	33:11	The **L** would speak to Moses face
	34:29	because he had spoken with the **L**.
Lev	8:36	did everything the **L** commanded
	9:23	and the glory of the **L** appeared
	19:2	'Be holy because I, the **L** your God,
	20:8	I am the **L**, who makes you holy.
Nu	14:18	you have declared: 'The **L** is slow
	14:21	glory of the **L** fills the whole earth,
	21:6	Then the **L** sent venomous snakes
	30:2	When a man makes a vow to the **L**
	32:12	followed the **L** wholeheartedly.'
Dt	1:21	and take possession of it as the **L**,
	2:7	forty years the **L** your God has
	6:4	The **L** our God, the **L** is one.
	6:5	Love the **L** your God
	8:5	so the **L** your God disciplines you.
	10:20	Fear the **L** your God and serve him
	30:20	For the **L** is your life, and he will
	31:6	for the **L** your God goes with you;
Jos	24:15	my household, we will serve the **L**
Jdg	2:12	They forsook the **L**, the God
Ru	1:8	May the **L** show kindness to you,
1Sa	3:9	**L**, for your servant is listening.'"
	3:19	The **L** was with Samuel
	14:6	Nothing can hinder the **L**
	16:13	Spirit of the **L** came upon David
2Sa	6:14	danced before the **L**

	7:22	How great you are, O Sovereign **L**!
	8:6	**L** gave David victory everywhere
	22:2	"The **L** is my rock, my fortress
	22:31	the word of the **L** is flawless.
1Ki	1:30	today what I swore to you by the **L**,
	5:12	The **L** gave Solomon wisdom,
	8:11	the glory of the **L** filled his temple.
	15:14	committed to the **L** all his life.
2Ki	17:18	So the **L** was very angry with Israel
	18:5	Hezekiah trusted in the **L**,
	23:25	a king like him who turned to the **L**
	24:4	and the **L** was not willing to forgive
1Ch	10:13	because he was unfaithful to the **L**;
	16:11	Look to the **L** and his strength;
	22:5	to be built for the **L** should be
	28:9	for the **L** searches every heart
	28:20	for the **L** God, my God, is with you
2Ch	1:1	for the **L** his God was with him
	5:14	the glory of the **L** filled the temple
	13:12	do not fight against the **L**,
	19:9	wholeheartedly in the fear of the **L**.
	20:20	Have faith in the **L** your God
	26:5	As long as he sought the **L**,
	34:14	Law of the **L** that had been given
	34:31	to follow the **L** and keep his
Ezr	3:10	foundation of the temple of the **L**,
	7:6	for the hand of the **L** his God was
	9:8	the **L** our God has been gracious
	9:15	O **L**, God of Israel, you are
Ne	1:5	Then I said: "O **L**, God of heaven,
	8:1	which the **L** had commanded
Job	1:6	to present themselves before the **L**,
	1:21	**L** gave and the **L** has taken away;
	38:1	the **L** answered Job out
	42:12	The **L** blessed the latter part
Ps	1:2	But his delight is in the law of the **L**
	9:9	The **L** is a refuge for the oppressed,
	9:19	Arise, O **L**, let not man triumph;
	12:6	And the words of the **L** are flawless
	16:8	I have set the **L** always before me.
	18:1	I love you, O **L**, my strength.
	18:6	In my distress I called to the **L**;
	19:14	O **L**, my Rock and my Redeemer.

	23:1	The **L** is my shepherd, I shall
	23:6	I will dwell in the house of the **L**
	27:1	The **L** is my light and my salvation
	27:4	to gaze upon the beauty of the **L**
	32:2	whose sin the **L** does not count
	33:1	joyfully to the **L**, you righteous;
	34:7	The angel of the **L** encamps
	34:15	The eyes of the **L** are
	34:18	The **L** is close to the brokenhearted
	37:4	Delight yourself in the **L**
	55:22	Cast your cares on the **L**
	85:7	Show us your unfailing love, O **L**,
	86:11	Teach me your way, O **L**,
	94:1	O **L**, the God who avenges,
	95:3	For the **L** is the great God,
	95:6	let us kneel before the **L** our Maker
	96:1	Sing to the **L** a new song;
	99:5	Exalt the **L** our God
	100:1	Shout for joy to the **L**, all the earth.
	103:8	The **L** is compassionate
	104:1	O **L** my God, you are very great;
	104:24	How many are your works, O **L**!
	111:10	The fear of the **L** is the beginning
	118:1	Give thanks to the **L**, for he is good
	118:5	In my anguish I cried to the **L**,
	118:24	This is the day the **L** has made;
	119:89	Your word, O **L**, is eternal;
	124:1	If the **L** had not been on our side —
	127:1	Unless the **L** builds the house,
	127:3	Sons are a heritage from the **L**,
	134:3	May the **L**, the Maker of heaven
	135:6	The **L** does whatever pleases him,
	140:1	Rescue me, O **L**, from evil men;
	141:3	Set a guard over my mouth, O **L**;
	145:18	The **L** is near to all who call on him
	150:6	that has breath praise the **L**.
Pr	1:7	The fear of the **L** is the beginning
	3:5	Trust in the **L** with all your heart
	3:9	Honor the **L** with your wealth,
	3:12	the **L** disciplines those he loves,
	3:19	By wisdom the **L** laid the earth's
	6:16	There are six things the **L** hates,
	16:2	but motives are weighed by the **L**.

	16:3	Commit to the **L** whatever you do,
	16:9	but the **L** determines his steps.
	18:10	The name of the **L** is a strong tower
	18:22	and receives favor from the **L**.
	19:14	but a prudent wife is from the **L**.
	21:31	but victory rests with the **L**.
Isa	5:16	the **L** Almighty will be exalted
	6:3	holy, holy is the **L** Almighty;
	28:5	In that day the **L** Almighty
	30:18	For the **L** is a God of justice.
	40:14	Whom did the **L** consult
	40:28	The **L** is the everlasting God,
	40:31	but those who hope in the **L**
	45:5	I am the **L**, and there is no other;
	55:6	Seek the **L** while he may be found;
	59:1	the arm of the **L** is not too short
	62:4	for the **L** will take delight in you,
Jer	4:4	Circumcise yourselves to the **L**,
	16:19	O **L**, my strength and my fortress,
	17:7	is the man who trusts in the **L**,
	20:11	**L** is with me like a mighty warrior;
	42:6	we will obey the **L** our God,
	50:4	go in tears to seek the **L** their God.
	51:10	" 'The **L** has vindicated us;
	51:56	For the **L** is a God of retribution;
La	3:24	to myself, "The **L** is my portion;
	3:25	**L** is good to those whose hope is
Eze	1:28	of the likeness of the glory of the **L**.
	10:4	Then the glory of the **L** rose
	15:7	you will know that I am the **L**.
	30:3	the day of the **L** is near —
	36:23	nations will know that I am the **L**,
	37:4	'Dry bones, hear the word of the **L**!
	43:4	glory of the **L** entered the temple
Hos	6:1	"Come, let us return to the **L**.
	10:12	for it is time to seek the **L**,
Joel	1:15	For the day of the **L** is near;
	2:31	the great and dreadful day of the **L**.
	3:16	the **L** will be a refuge for his people,
Am	4:13	the **L** God Almighty is his name.
	5:6	Seek the **L** and live,
Ob	1:15	"The day of the **L** is near
Jnh	1:3	But Jonah ran away from the **L**

	1:17	But the **L** provided a great fish
	2:9	Salvation comes from the **L**."
Mic	1:1	The word of the **L** that came to Micah
	6:8	And what does the **L** require of you
Na	1:3	The **L** is slow to anger
Hab	2:14	knowledge of the glory of the **L**,
	2:20	But the **L** is in his holy temple;
Zep	1:1	The word of the **L** that came
	1:7	for the day of the **L** is near.
Zec	1:17	and the **L** will again comfort Zion
	14:9	The **L** will be king
Mal	1:1	The word of the **L** to Israel
	3:6	"I the **L** do not change.

LORD'S DAY The day especially associated with the Lord Jesus Christ. The expression occurs in the NT only in Rev 1:10. The adjective *kyriakos*, translated "the Lord's," is a possessive and means "belonging to the Lord" — to Christ. It denotes a day consecrated to the Lord (cf. the parallel expression "the Lord's Supper," 1Co 11:20). Some would equate it with the OT prophetic "day of the Lord," but clearly John is not speaking of that prophetic day. The form of his expression marks a distinction between the prophetic "day of the Lord" (1Co 5:5; 2Co 1:14; 1Th 5:2) and the first day of the week, on which Christ arose. It was the resurrection victory on that day that marked it as distinct and sacred to the Christian church. The gospel emphasis on "the first day of the week" as the day of resurrection stresses its distinctiveness. On that day the risen Christ repeatedly appeared to his disciples (Lk 24:13 – 49; Jn 20:1 – 25) and again a week later (Jn 20:26). The Pentecostal outpouring apparently also came on that day. Acts 20:7 and 1Co 16:1 – 2 show that the early church consecrated the day to worship and almsgiving (but not to earning). Sunday (the name is of pagan origin) as the day of special worship is a Christian institution and must be sharply distinguished from the Sabbath. Nor were the OT Sabbath regulations transferred to the Lord's Day as a "Christian Sabbath." The Sabbath related to the old creation (Ex 20:8 – 11; 31:12 – 17; Heb 4:4), whereas the Lord's Day commemorates the new creation in Christ Jesus. No "Sabbath" observance was stipulated in the demands on Gentile Christians in Ac 15:28 – 29. Some Jewish Christians continued to observe the Sabbath and Jewish festivals, while some members of the primitive church made no distinction between days (Ro 14:5 – 6), but it was held to be a matter of liberty (Ro 14:1), as long as the observance of a special day was not regarded as necessary for salvation (Gal 4:10; Col 2:16 – 17).

LORD'S PRAYER Properly "the Disciples' Prayer," since it was not prayed with but taught to them by Jesus (Mt 6:9 – 13; Lk 11:2 – 4). In Luke, Jesus, at the request of a disciple, gave a modified form of his earlier spontaneous presentation in the Sermon on the Mount. The earlier form is fuller and is commonly used. As a pattern prayer it is unsurpassed for conciseness and fullness, delineating the proper approach and order in prayer. It directs the disciples, as members of God's family, reverently to pray to a personal heavenly Father. The petitions are divided into two parts, the first three relating to God's interests. They are arranged in a descending scale, from himself, through the manifestation of himself in his kingdom (the coming messianic kingdom), to the complete doing of his will by his subjects. Placing God's interest first, disciples can pray for their own needs. The petitions, whether counted as three or four, are arranged in an ascending scale — from the supply of daily material needs to the ultimate deliverance from all evil. The doxology in Matthew, which constitutes an affirmation of faith, is lacking in the leading MSS and is generally regarded as a scribal addition derived from ancient liturgical usage.

LORD'S SUPPER (Gr. *kyriakon deipnon*). This expression occurs once in the NT (1Co 11:20), but there is a related expression, "Lord's table" (1Co 10:21). However, the institution of that which Paul called "the Lord's Supper" is described in four passages (Mt 26:26 – 29; Mk 14:22 – 25; Lk 22:15 – 20; 1Co 11:23 – 25). On the night before the crucifixion,

Jesus adopted the position of head of a household and ate the Passover meal with his disciples in a room within the city limits of Jerusalem. It is interesting to note that he did not give new and special significance to the special parts of that meal (e.g., lamb and bitter herbs) but to the bread and wine, common to many meals. Distributing the bread he had broken for his disciples, he said, "I am myself this bread." Later in the meal, passing to them the third cup of the four cups of the meal, he said of the wine, "This is my blood of the covenant, which is poured out for many." Then at the end of the meal Jesus refused to drink from the fourth cup, saying that he would not drink again of the fruit of the vine until he drank it anew in the kingdom of God.

There are two important themes in the words of Jesus. First he was telling them that the cup of red wine represented his own blood, shed to inaugurate a new covenant between God and "the many" (see Isa 52:15; 53:12). He was to offer himself to God as a sacrifice for sin so that a new relationship could be created by God between himself and the redeemed community of believers. Second, he was pointing toward the full realization and consummation of the kingdom of God at the end of the age, when the meal would be resumed in the "messianic banquet." Thus, it may be said that the Lord's Supper is eaten in remembrance of his atoning death by which comes redemption and in expectation of the arrival of the kingdom of God in its fullness.

At first the Supper was a part of a larger meal (see 1Co 11:17ff.); but being a special part, it could be separated and, as the years went by, it was in fact separated. It became the second half of the Sunday worship of the local church, the first part being the ministry of the Word, prayers, singing of psalms, and intercessions.

Nowhere in the NT is the Lord's Supper called a sacrifice. However, the believers are said to be offering spiritual sacrifices to God when God is worshiped, served, and obeyed (Ro 12:1; Heb 13:15 – 16; 1Pe 2:5). The Lord's Supper as a part of the worship and service offered to God is thus a sacrifice of praise and thanksgiving. Regrettably the Eucharist (ministry of Word and Lord's Supper as one service) has often been referred to in sacrificial terms as though it were a sacrifice in a unique sense — an unbloody sacrifice. While the Lord's Supper is the memorial of a sacrifice and is a sacrifice of praise offered to God, it is neither a repetition of the sacrifice of Christ made at Calvary nor a participation in the self-offering that Christ is perpetually making to the Father in heaven as the heavenly Priest. It is a proclamation of the Lord's death sacramentally until he returns to earth.

LOT [1598, 2750, 3926+4987, 5162, 7877, 3102, 3275].

1. A means of deciding an issue or of determining the divine will in a matter. The use of the lot to determine doubtful matters is very old, and the practice of casting lots was common among the nations of antiquity. It was held in religious esteem by the covenant people, and its use to determine God's will was usually accompanied by prayer (Jdg 1:1 – 3; Ac 1:24 – 26). Many scholars think that Urim and Thummim were used as lots. Only in the choice of a successor to Judas (Ac 1:26) is the use of lots by Christ's followers mentioned. As a distinctly Jewish mode of seeking divine direction, its use was appropriate for the occasion. After the coming of the Spirit at Pentecost to take direction of the affairs of the church, its use is never mentioned again.

General References to:

The scapegoat chosen by (Lev 16:8 – 10). The land of Canaan divided among the tribes by (Nu 26:55; Jos 15; 18:10; 19:51; 21; 1Ch 6:61, 65; Eze 45:1; 47:22; 48:29; Mic 2:5; Ac 13:19). Saul chosen king by (1Sa 10:20 – 21). Priests and Levites designated by, for sanctuary service (1Ch 24:5 – 31; 26:13; Ne 10:34; Lk 1:9). Used after the captivity (Ne 11:1). An apostle chosen by (Ac 1:26). Achan's guilt discovered by (Jos 7:14 – 18); Jonathan's (1Sa 14:41 – 42); Jonah's (Jnh 1:7). Used to fix the time for the execution of condemned persons (Est 3:7; 9:24). The garments of Jesus divided by (Ps 22:18; Mt 27:35; Mk 15:24; Jn 19:23 – 24).

2. That which is assigned by lot as a *portion, share,* or *inheritance* (Dt 32:9; Jos 15:1; Pss 105:11; 125:3; Isa 17:14; Ac 8:21).

LOT [4288, 3397] (Heb. *lôt, envelope, covering*). Lot's life illustrates four spiritual truths: (1) The degenerating influence of a selfish choice (Ge 13:11 – 12); (2) the effect of a wicked environment on one's family (Ge 19); (3) retribution in one's children (Ge 19:8, 31ff.); (4) God as the only true judge of a person's real state (2Pe 2:7ff.).

Accompanies Terah from Ur of the Chaldeans to Haran (Ge 11:31); Migrates with Abraham to the land of Canaan (Ge 12:4); Accompanies Abraham to Egypt; returns with him to Bethel (Ge 13:1 – 3); Rich in flocks, herds, and servants; separates from Abraham and locates in Sodom (Ge 13:5 – 14); Taken captive by Kedorlaomer; rescued by Abraham (Ge 14:1 – 16); Providentially saved from destruction in Sodom (Ge 19; Lk 17:28 – 29); Righteous (2Pe 2:7 – 8); Disobediently protests against going to the mountains, and chooses Zoar (Ge 19:17 – 22); His wife disobediently longs after Sodom and becomes a pillar of salt (Ge 19:26; Lk 17:32); Commits incest with his daughters (Ge 19:30 – 38)

LOVE [170, 171, 172, 173, 1856, 2668, 2876, 2883, 3137, 3351, 8163, 8533, 26, 27, 28, 921, 5789, 5797] (Heb. *'ahăvâh,* Gr. *agapē*). This is presented in Scripture as the very nature of God (1Jn 4:8, 16) and the greatest of the Christian virtues (1Co 13:13). It receives definition in Scripture only by a listing of its attributes (13:4 – 7). It lies at the very heart of Christianity, being essential to a person's relations to God and others (Mt 22:37 – 40; Mk 12:28 – 31; Jn 13:34 – 35). Jesus taught that on it hang all the Law and the Prophets (Mt 22:40). It is the fulfillment of the law, for its sense of obligation and desire for the welfare of the one loved impels it to carry out the demands of the law (Ro 13:8 – 10). Love found its supreme expression in the self-sacrifice on Calvary

(1Jn 4:10). All human love, whether toward God or other humans, has its source in God. Love in its true reality and power is seen only in the light of Calvary (1Jn 4:7 – 10).

Commanded:

(Lev 19:18; Mt 5:40 – 42; 7:12; 19:19; 22:39 – 40; Mk 12:30 – 33; Lk 6:30 – 38; Ro 12:9, 15; 13:8 – 10; 1Co 10:24; 16:14; Gal 6:1 – 2, 10; Eph 4:2, 32; 5:2; Php 1:9; Col 3:14; 1Th 3:12; 1Ti 1:5; 4:12; 6:11; 2Ti 2:22; Jas 2:8; 2Pe 1:7; 1Jn 4:20 – 21). Toward strangers (Lev 19:34; Dt 10:19). Toward enemies (Pr 24:17; Mt 5:43 – 48; Lk 6:35; Ro 12:14, 20). Toward fellow Christians (Jn 13:14 – 15, 34 – 35; 15:12 – 13, 17; Ro 12:9 – 10, 15 – 16; 14:19, 21; 15:1 – 2, 5, 7; 16:1 – 2; 1Co 14:1; 2Co 8:7 – 8; Gal 5:13 – 14; 6:1 – 2, 10; Eph 4:2, 32; Php 2:2; Col 2:2; 3:12 – 14; 1Th 3:12; 5:8, 11, 14; 1Ti 6:2; Phm 16; Heb 10:24; 13:13; 1Pe 1:22; 2:17; 3:8 – 9; 4:8; 2Pe 1:7; 1Jn 3:11, 14, 16 – 18, 19, 23; 4:7, 11 – 12, 20 – 21; 2Jn 5). Demonstrated by obedience (1Jn 5:1 – 2). Rewards of (Mt 10:41 – 42; 25:34 – 40, 46; Mk 9:41; 1Jn 2:10).

Instances of:

Abraham for Lot (Ge 14:14 – 16). Moses for Israel (Ex 32:31 – 32). David and Jonathan (1Sa 18:1; 20:17). Israel for David (1Sa 18:16). David's subjects for David (2Sa 15:30; 17:27 – 29). Hiram for David (1Ki 5:1). Obadiah for the prophets (1Ki 18:4). Nehemiah for Israelites (Ne 5:10 – 18). Job's friends (Job 42:11). Centurion for his servant (Lk 7:2 – 6). Good Samaritan (Lk 10:29 – 37). Stephen (Ac 7:60). Roman Christians for Paul (Ac 28:15). Priscilla and Aquila for Paul (Ro 16:3 – 4). Exemplified by Paul (Ac 26:29; Ro 1:11 – 12; 9:1 – 3; 1Co 4:9 – 16; 8:13; 2Co 1:3 – 6, 14, 23 – 24; 2:4; 3:2; 4:5; 6:4 – 6, 11 – 13; 7:1 – 4; 11:2; 12:14 – 16, 19 – 21; 13:9; Gal 4:19 – 20; Eph 3:13; Php 1:3 – 5, 7 – 8, 23 – 26; 2:19; 4:1; Col 1:3 – 4, 24, 28 – 29; 2:1, 5; 4:7; 1Th 2:7 – 8, 11 – 12, 17 – 20; 3:5, 7 – 10, 12; 2Th 1:4; 2Ti 1:3 – 4, 8; 2:10; Tit 3:15; Phm 9, 12, 16).

Love of People for God:

Defined (1Jn 5:3; 2Jn 6). Incompatible with love of the world (1Jn 2:15), with hatred of brother (1Jn 4:20 – 21), with guilty fear (2Ti 1:7; 1Jn 4:18). Reasons for (Ps 116:1; 1Jn 4:19). The gift of God (Dt 30:6; 2Ti 1:7). Through the Holy Spirit (Ro 5:5). Commanded (Dt 6:5; 10:12; 11:1, 13, 22; 19:9; 30:16, 19 – 20; Jos 22:5; 23:11; Ps 31:23; Pr 23:26; Mt 22:37 – 38; Mk 12:29 – 30, 32 – 33; Lk 11:42; 2Th 3:5; Jude 21). Tested (Dt 13:3). Obedience proof of (1Jn 2:5; 5:1 – 2; 2Jn 6). Leads to: generosity (1Jn 3:17 – 18); hate of evil (Ps 97:10); love from God (Ps 8:1 – 8). Rewards of (Ex 20:6; Dt 5:10; 7:9; Pss 37:4; 69:35 – 36; 91:14; 145:20; Isa 56:6 – 7; Jer 2:2 – 3; Ro 8:28; 1Co 8:3). Exemplified (Pss 18:1; 63:5 – 6; 73:25 – 26; 103).

Love of People for Jesus:

Commanded (Mt 10:37 – 38; Jn 15:9; 1Co 16:22). Love of God produces (Jn 8:42). Obedience results from (Jn 14:15, 21, 23; 2Co 5:6, 8, 14 – 15). Rewards of (Mt 25:34 – 40, 46; Mk 9:41; Lk 7:37 – 50; Jn 16:27; Eph 6:24; 2Ti 4:8; Heb 6:10; Jas 1:12; 2:5).

Ge	20:13	'This is how you can show your **l**
Ex	15:13	"In your unfailing **l** you will lead
	20:6	showing **l** to a thousand genera-tions
	34:6	abounding in **l** and faithfulness,
Lev	19:18	but **l** your neighbor as yourself.
Dt	6:5	**L** the LORD your God
	10:12	to walk in all his ways, to **l** him,
	10:19	you are to **l** those who are aliens,
	13:3	you **l** him with all your heart
Jos	23:11	careful to **l** the LORD your God.
Jdg	14:16	You hate me! You don't really **l** me
2Sa	7:15	But my **l** will never be taken away
	19:6	You **l** those who hate you
1Ki	10:9	of the LORD's eternal **l** for Israel,
1Ch	16:34	his **l** endures forever.
	17:13	I will never take my **l** away
Ne	1:5	covenant of **l** with those who **l** him
	9:17	slow to anger and abounding in **l**.

Job	15:34	of those who **l** bribes.
Ps	6:4	save me because of your unfailing **l**.
	11:5	wicked and those who **l** violence
	18:1	I **l** you, O LORD, my strength.
	23:6	Surely goodness and **l** will follow
	36:5	Your **l**, O LORD, reaches
	40:16	may those who **l** your salvation
	45:7	You **l** righteousness and hate
	63:3	Because your **l** is better than life,
	77:8	Has his unfailing **l** vanished forever
	86:5	abounding in **l** to all who call
	97:10	Let those who **l** the LORD hate
	103:4	crowns you with **l** and compassion.
	116:1	I **l** the LORD, for he heard my
	118:1	his **l** endures forever.
	119:97	Oh, how I **l** your law!
Pr	1:22	you simple ones **l** your simple
	5:19	you ever be captivated by her **l**.
	8:17	I **l** those who **l** me,
	8:36	all who hate me **l** death."
	9:8	rebuke a wise man and he will **l** you
	10:12	but **l** covers over all wrongs.
	17:9	over an offense promotes **l**,
	20:13	Do not **l** sleep or you will grow
Ecc	9:9	life with your wife, whom you **l**,
SS	1:2	for your **l** is more delightful
	2:4	and his banner over me is **l**.
Isa	1:23	they all **l** bribes
	55:3	my faithful **l** promised to David.
	61:8	"For I, the LORD, **l** justice;
Jer	2:25	I **l** foreign gods,
La	3:22	of the LORD's great **l** we are not
Eze	23:17	of **l**, and in their lust they defiled
Da	9:4	covenant of **l** with all who **l** him
Hos	1:6	for I will no longer show **l**
	3:1	Go, show your **l** to your wife again,
	10:12	reap the fruit of unfailing **l**,
	12:6	maintain **l** and justice,
	14:4	and **l** them freely,
Am	5:15	Hate evil, **l** good;
Mic	3:2	you who hate good and **l** evil;
	6:8	To act justly and to **l** mercy
Zec	8:17	and do not **l** to swear falsely.
Mt	3:17	"This is my Son, whom I **l**;
	5:44	**L** your enemies and pray
	5:46	you **l** those who **l** you, what reward
	6:5	for they **l** to pray standing
	6:24	he will hate the one and **l** the other,
	22:37	" '**L** the Lord your God
	22:39	'**L** your neighbor as yourself.'
	23:6	they **l** the place of honor
	23:7	they **l** to be greeted
	24:12	the **l** of most will grow cold,
Lk	6:32	Even 'sinners' **l** those who **l** them.
	6:35	**l** your enemies, do good to them,
	7:42	which of them will **l** him more?"
	11:42	you neglect justice and the **l** of God
	16:13	he will hate the one and **l** the other,
Jn	5:42	I know that you do not have the **l**
	8:42	were your Father, you would **l** me,
	11:3	"Lord, the one you **l** is sick."
	13:1	them the full extent of his **l**.
	13:34	I give you: **L** one another.
	13:35	disciples, if you **l** one another."
	14:15	"If you **l** me, you will obey what I
	14:21	I too will **l** him and show myself
	14:31	world must learn that I **l** the Father
	15:9	Now remain in my **l**.
	15:13	Greater **l** has no one than this,
	15:19	to the world, it would **l** you
	17:26	known in order that the **l** you have
	21:15	he said, "you know that I **l** you."
	21:16	do you truly **l** me?" He answered,
Ro	5:5	because God has poured out his **l**
	5:8	God demonstrates his own **l** for us
	8:28	for the good of those who **l** him,
	8:35	us from the **l** of Christ?
	12:9	**L** must be sincere.
	12:10	to one another in brotherly **l**.
	13:8	continuing debt to **l** one another,
	13:10	Therefore **l** is the fulfillment
	14:15	you are no longer acting in **l**.
1Co	2:9	prepared for those who **l** him" —
	4:17	my son whom I **l**, who is faithful
	4:21	or in **l** and with a gentle spirit?
	8:1	Knowledge puffs up, but **l** builds up

	13:1	have not **l**, I am only a resounding
	13:2	but have not **l**, I am nothing.
	13:4	Love is patient, **l** is kind.
	13:6	**L** does not delight in evil
	13:8	**L** never fails.
	13:13	But the greatest of these is **l**.
	13:13	three remain: faith, hope and **l**.
	14:1	way of **l** and eagerly desire spiritual
	16:14	Do everything in **l**.
2Co	2:4	to let you know the depth of my **l**
	5:14	For Christ's **l** compels us,
	8:24	show these men the proof of your **l**
Gal	5:6	is faith expressing itself through **l**.
	5:13	rather, serve one another in **l**.
	5:22	But the fruit of the Spirit is **l**, joy,
Eph	1:4	In **l** he predestined us
	2:4	But because of his great **l** for us,
	3:17	being rooted and established in **l**,
	3:18	and high and deep is the **l** of Christ,
	3:19	and to know this **l** that surpasses
	4:2	bearing with one another in **l**.
	4:15	Instead, speaking the truth in **l**,
	4:16	grows and builds itself up in **l**,
	5:2	loved children and live a life of **l**,
	5:25	**l** your wives, just as Christ loved
	5:28	husbands ought to **l** their wives
	6:23	**l** with faith from God the Father
Php	1:9	that your **l** may abound more
	1:16	so in **l**, knowing that I am put here
	2:1	from his **l**, if any fellowship
Col	1:5	**l** that spring from the hope that is
	1:8	also told us of your **l** in the Spirit.
	3:14	And over all these virtues put on **l**,
	3:19	**l** your wives and do not be harsh
1Th	1:3	your labor prompted by **l**,
	3:12	May the Lord make your **l** increase
	5:8	on faith and **l** as a breastplate,
2Th	1:3	and the **l** every one of you has
	2:10	because they refused to **l** the truth
	3:5	direct your hearts into God's **l**
1Ti	1:5	The goal of this command is **l**,
	6:10	For the **l** of money is a root
2Ti	1:7	of power, of **l** and of self-discipline.

	3:10	faith, patience, **l**, endurance,
Tit	2:2	in faith, in **l** and in endurance.
	2:4	women to **l** their husbands
Phm	1:9	yet I appeal to you on the basis of **l**.
Heb	6:10	and the **l** you have shown him
	10:24	may spur one another on toward **l**
	13:5	free from the **l** of money
Jas	1:12	promised to those who **l** him.
1Pe	1:22	the truth so that you have sincere **l**
	1:22	**l** one another deeply,
	2:17	**L** the brotherhood of believers,
	3:8	be sympathetic, **l** as brothers,
	4:8	Above all, **l** each other deeply,
	4:8	**l** covers over a multitude of sins.
1Jn	2:5	God's **l** is truly made complete
	2:15	Do not **l** the world or anything
	3:10	anyone who does not **l** his brother.
	3:14	Anyone who does not **l** remains
	3:16	This is how we know what **l** is:
	3:18	let us not **l** with words or tongue
	4:7	for **l** comes from God.
	4:16	God is **l**.
	4:18	But perfect **l** drives out fear,
	4:19	We **l** because he first loved us.
	4:20	anyone who does not **l** his brother,
	5:3	This is **l** for God: to obey his
Jude	1:12	men are blemishes at your **l** feasts,
	1:21	Keep yourselves in God's **l**
Rev	2:4	You have forsaken your first **l**.
	2:19	I know your deeds, your **l** and faith
	3:19	Those whom I **l** I rebuke
	12:11	they did not **l** their lives so much

LOVE FEAST [27] (Gr. *agapē*). A common meal eaten by early Christians in connection with the Lord's Supper to express and deepen brotherly love. Although often mentioned in postcanonical literature, these feasts are spoken of in the NT only in Jude 12 and the dubious footnote to 2Pe 2:13. But the situation in 1Co 11:20 – 22, 33 – 34 makes it clear that they were observed in the early Jerusalem church (Ac 2:42 – 47; 4:35; 6:1). As implied by the situation in 1Co 11, these love feasts were observed before, but in connection with the Lord's Supper (perhaps after the close relation between the first Lord's Supper and the Passover). Because of abuses, which already appeared in apostolic churches (1Co 11:23 – 29; Jude 12), they were separated from the Lord's Supper. They subsequently fell into disfavor and were ultimately forbidden to be held in churches, largely due to the growth of the sacerdotal view of the Eucharist — a view that regarded the union of the two as sacrilegious. Some Christian groups today observe them.

LUCIFER Latin for "morning star" (Isa 14:12); a title of the king of Babylon, often understood as a reference to the devil. *See Devil; Satan.*

LUKE [3371] (Gr. *Loukas*). According to the oldest extant list of NT writings, known from the name of its discoverer as the Muratorian Fragment, and dating from the latter half of the second century AD, Luke was the writer of the third gospel and the Acts of the Apostles. From the latter book his association with Paul is established. In four passages of varying length the author of Acts writes in the first person (16:10 – 17; 20:5 – 15; 21:1 – 18; 27:1 – 28:16). These so-called "we sections" constitute the major portion of the extant biographical material on Luke. Apart from this he is mentioned three times in the NT (Col 4:14; Phm 24; 2Ti 4:11). From the first reference it is evident that Luke was a physician; from the last, that he was with Paul some time after he disappears from view at the end of the Acts of the Apostles. The context of the Colossians reference also suggests that Luke was a Gentile and a proselyte.

It appears from Luke's own writings that he was a man of education and culture. He begins his gospel with an elaborate paragraph, showing that he could write in the sophisticated tradition of the Hellenistic historians, and then lapses into a polished vernacular. He uses this speech with vigor and effectiveness. He is an accurate and able historian and has contributed some of the most powerful descriptive writing in the NT. His medical knowledge and his interest in seafaring are apparent from his writings. Whatever is said beyond this is tradition and conjecture. He was obviously a man of outstanding loyalty, of unusual capacity for research, and with the scholar's ability to strip away the irrelevant and dispensable detail. A bare tradition states that he suffered martyrdom in Greece.

A physician (Col 4:14). Wrote to Theophilus (Lk 1:1 – 4; Ac 1:1 – 2). Accompanies Paul in his tour of Asia and Macedonia (Ac 16:10 – 13; 20:5 – 6); to Jerusalem (Ac 21:1 – 18); to Rome (Ac 27:28; 2Ti 4:1; Phm 24).

LUKE, GOSPEL OF

AUTHENTICITY.

The authenticity of the third gospel has not been successfully challenged. References are frequent in the second century AD (Justin, Polycarp, Papias, Hegesippus, Marcion, Heracleon, the Clementine Homilies, Theophilus of Antioch). It is probable that Clement alludes to it (95). It is mentioned as the work of Luke by the Muratorian Fragment (170) and by Irenaeus (180). Such testimony continues into the third century (Clement of Alexandria, Tertullian, Origen). Such a mass of evidence is quite decisive.

DATE.

Although uncertain, the date can be confined to fairly narrow limits. The abrupt termination of the Acts of the Apostles suggests that the author did not long survive his friend and associate Paul. Nor is it likely to have been written after the fall of Jerusalem in AD 70. The period of Paul's imprisonment in Caesarea saw Luke in Palestine, and this period (conjecturally 58 – 59) would presumably give abundant opportunity for the research that is evident in the record. Luke's gospel is thus the latest of the Synoptic Gospels.

HISTORIOGRAPHY.

W. M. Ramsay's work on the Acts of the Apostles has established the right of Luke to rank as a first-rate historian in his own capacity. He was demonstrated to have maintained a consistent level of accuracy wherever detail could be objectively tested, and the vividness of narration so evident in the second work is visible also in the gospel.

STYLE.

Luke's preface is in the elaborate style of ancient historians and demonstrates that Luke could write with facility in the literary tradition of his time. At Lk 1:5 he moves into an easy vernacular, which he employs for his whole narrative. His language is the common dialect but is used with grace and vigor and with an educated man's skill in composition.

Outline:

  I. The Preface (1:1 – 4).
  II. The Coming of Jesus (1:5 – 2:52).
  III. The Preparation of Jesus for His Public Ministry (3:1 – 4:13).
  IV. His Ministry in Galilee (4:14 – 9:9).
  V. His Withdrawal to Regions around Galilee (9:10 – 50).
  VI. His Ministry in Judea (9:51 – 13:21).
  VII. His Ministry in and around Perea (13:22 – 19:27).
  VIII. His Last Days: Sacrifice and Triumph (19:28 – 24:53).

LUST [2388+, 2393, 2773, 2801, 6311, 6312, 9373, 2123, 3979, 4079, 4432] (*evil desires*).

Sinful (Job 31:9 – 12; Mt 5:28). Worldly (1Jn 2:16 – 17). Chokes the word (Mk 4:19). Tempts to sin (Ge 3:6; Jas 1:14 – 15; 2Pe 2:18). Forbidden (Ex 20:17; Pr 6:24 – 25; Ro 13:14; Eph 4:22; Col 3:5; 1Th 4:5; Tit 2:12; 1Pe 2:11). Warnings against (1Co 10:6 – 7;

2Ti 2:22).Wicked under power of (Jn 8:44; Ro 1:24, 26 – 27; 1Ti 6:9; Jas 4:1 – 3; 1Pe 4:3; 2Pe 3:3; Jude 16, 18). Of Israelites (Ps 106:13 – 14). The righteous restrain (1Co 9:27).

Pr	6:25	Do not **l** in your heart
Eze	20:30	and **l** after their vile images?
Col	3:5	sexual immorality, impurity, **l**,
1Th	4:5	not in passionate **l** like the heathen,
1Pe	4:3	in debauchery, **l**, drunkenness,
1Jn	2:16	the **l** of his eyes and the boasting

LYDIA (lĭd′ĭa, Gr. *Lydia*). Paul's first convert in Europe. She resided in Philippi as a seller of the purple garments for which Thyatira, her native city, was famous. She was evidently well-to-do, as she owned her house and had servants. She was "a worshiper of God," meaning a proselyte. She and other women, probably also proselytes, resorted to a place by a river for prayer. She came into contact with the gospel when Paul and his company came there and spoke to the women, and she became a believer. After she and her household had been baptized, she invited the group to come to her home to stay, and they did so (Ac 16:14 – 15). Her home thus became the first church in Philippi (16:40).

As Lydia was from a city in the kingdom of Lydia, and her name was the common term to denote a woman from Lydia, some scholars have suggested that her personal name was unknown, or that she may be either Euodia or Syntyche mentioned in Php 4:2 by Paul as women who labored with him in the gospel.

MACCABEES (*hammer*). Hasmonean Jewish family of Modein (or Modin) that led revolt against Antiochus Epiphanes, king of Syria, and won freedom for the Jews. The family consisted of the father, Mattathias, an aged priest, and his five sons: Johanan, Simon, Judas, Eleazar, and Jonathan. The name Maccabee was first given to Judas, perhaps because he inflicted sledgehammer blows against the Syrian armies, and later was also used for his brothers. The revolt began in 168 BC. The temple was recaptured and sacrifices were resumed in 165 BC. The cleansing of the temple and resumption of sacrifices have been celebrated annually ever since in the Feast of Dedication. The Maccabees served as both high priests and kings. The story of Maccabees is told in two books of the Apocrypha, I and II Maccabees. The following were the most prominent of reigns of the Maccabees: Judas (166 – 160 BC), Jonathan (160 – 142 BC), Simon (142 – 134 BC), John Hyrcanus (134 – 104 BC), Aristobulus (104 – 103 BC), Alexander Jannaeus (103 – 76 BC), Alexandra (76 – 67 BC), and Aristobulus II (66 – 63 BC). In 63 BC the Romans took over when Pompey conquered the Israelites.

MACCABEES, 1 AND 2 *See Apocrypha.*

MACEDONIA [3423, 3424] (măs′ē-dō′nĭ-a, Gr. *Makedōnia*). The term is of varied import. Lying geographically between the Balkan highlands and the Greek peninsula, Macedonia was both a Greek kingdom and a Roman province.

> **General References to:**
> Paul has a vision concerning (Ac 16:9). Preaches in, at Philippi (Ac 16:12). Revisits (Ac 20:1 – 6; 2Co 2:13; 7:5). Church at, sends contributions to the poor in Jerusalem (Ro 15:26; 2Co 8:1 – 5). Timothy visits (Ac 19:22). Disciples in (Ac 19:22; 27:2).

MACEDONIAN EMPIRE, THE Called the kingdom of Greece (Da 11:2). Philippi was its chief city (Ac 16:12).

> **General References to:**
> Gospel preached in, by God's desire (Ac 16:9 – 10). Liberality of the churches of (2Co 8:1 – 5).
>
> **Illustrated by:**
> Bronze part of the image in Nebuchadnezzar's dream (Da 2:32, 39). Leopard with four wings and four heads (Da 7:6, 17). Shaggy goat with notable horn (Da 8:5 – 8, 21).
>
> **Predictions Respecting:**
> Conquest of the Medo-Persian kingdom (Da 8:6 – 7; 11:2 – 3). Power and greatness of Alexander, its last king (Da 8:8; 11:3). Division into four kingdoms (Da 8:8, 22). Divisions ruled by strangers (Da 11:4). History of four divisions (Da 11:4 – 29). Little horn to arise out of one of its divisions (Da 8:8 – 12).

MAGDALENE [3402] (*of Magdala*). *See Mary.*

MAGI [3407] (mā′jī Gr. *magoi*). Originally a religious caste among the Persians. Their devotion to astrology, divination, and the interpretation of dreams led to an extension in the meaning of the word, and by the first century BC the terms *magi* and *Chaldean* were applied generally to fortune tellers and the exponents of esoteric religious cults throughout the Mediterranean world. Magus or "sorcerer" is the name given to Simon in Ac 8:9, to Bar-Jesus in 13:6, and to Elymas in 13:8. The "wise men from the east" in Mt 2 are often referred to as "the magi." Nothing is known of their land of origin, but it is a likely theory that they came from Arabia Felix (southern Arabia). Astrology was practiced there, and a tradition of Israelite messianic expectation may have survived in the region since the days of the queen of Sheba. Many early legends connect southern Arabia with Solomon's Israel. Ancient reports, linked to later astrological study, may have prompted the famous journey.

MAGIC [2490, 3033, 4086, 10282, 3404, 5758, 5760, 5761]. The art or science of influencing or controlling the course of nature, events, and supernatural powers through occult science of mysterious arts (Ge 41:8; Ex 7:11, 22; 8:7, 18; Ac 19:19). Includes necromancy, exorcism, dreams, shaking arrows, inspecting entrails of animals, divination, sorcery, astrology, soothsaying, divining by rods, witchcraft (1Sa 28:8; Eze 21:21; Ac 16:16). Originally the word meant the science or art of the magi, the Persian priestly caste, who, like the Levites, were devoted to the practice of religion. With the wide extension of the term *magus*, the word *magic*, too, acquired broader significance. It came to mean all occult rituals or processes designed to influence or control the course of nature; to dominate men or circumstances by the alliance, aid, or use of supernatural powers; and generally to tap and to employ the forces of an unseen world. Divination, the art of forecasting the future with a view to avoiding its perils and pitfalls, might be included under the same classification. The Bible gives stern prohibitions against all forms of "wizardry" and "sorcery" (Ex 22:18; Lev 19:26; 20:27; Dt 18:10 – 11), causing security precautions like those surrounding the royal visit to "the witch of Endor" (1Sa 28).

Eze	13:20	I am against your **m** charms
Rev	21:8	those who practice **m** arts,
	22:15	those who practice **m** arts,

MAGNIFICAT The song of praise by Mary (Lk 1:46 – 55).

MAGOG (mā′gŏg, Heb. *māghôgh, land of God?*). A son of Japheth (Ge 10:2; 1Ch 1:5). Josephus and Greek writers generally applied this name to the Scythians. Some modern Christian writers indicate the Tartars of Russia and of southern Europe. The names of King Gog, "prince of Rosh, Meshech and Tubal" (Eze 38:2; see NIV note) resemble the modern Russia, Moscow, and Tobolsk. "The nations in the four corners of the earth — Gog and Magog" (Rev 20:8) refer to all the ungodly nations of the earth who oppose the people of God.

MAJESTY

Ex	15:7	In the greatness of your **m**
Dt	5:24	has shown us his glory and his **m**,
	33:26	and on the clouds in his **m**.
1Ch	16:27	Splendor and **m** are before him;
Est	7:3	if it pleases your **m**, grant me my
Job	37:22	God comes in awesome **m**.
	40:10	and clothe yourself in honor and **m**
Ps	93:1	The Lord reigns, he is robed in **m**
	110:3	Arrayed in holy **m**,
Isa	2:10	and the splendor of his **m**!
	53:2	or **m** to attract us to him,
Da	4:30	and for the glory of my **m**?"
Ac	19:27	will be robbed of her divine **m**."
	25:26	to write to His **M** about him.
2Th	1:9	and from the **m** of his power
Heb	1:3	hand of the **M** in heaven.
	8:1	of the throne of the **M** in heaven,
2Pe	1:16	but we were eyewitnesses of his **m**.
Jude	1:25	only God our Savior be glory, **m**,

MALACHI [4858] (măl′a-kī Heb. *mal'ākhî, my messenger* or *messenger of Yahweh*). Prophet of Judah who lived c. 450 – 400 BC; contemporary of Nehemiah (Mal 2:11 – 17; Ne 13:23 – 31). Author of OT book that bears his name. Nothing is known of him beyond what is said in his book.

MALACHI, BOOK OF The name given to the last book of the OT, and probably also the name of the prophet whose oracles the book contains. The book's title reads: "An Oracle: The word of the Lord to Israel through Malachi" (Mal 1:1). Thus it would seem that the prophet's name was Malachi. *Malachi* is the Hebrew expression meaning "my messenger," and it is so translated in 3:1, where there is an obvious play on the author's name. For this reason, some have supposed Malachi to be a title for the prophet, not his proper name. But since the other prophetic books of the OT always begin by stating the prophet's name, it seems more likely that here, too, the name of the prophet is given. It is not unusual to have wordplays on the names of real people (Eze 3:8 – 9). Nothing more is known about the author of this book.

The book of Malachi is believed to be one of the latest of the OT books.

The book has two principal themes: (1) the sin and apostasy of the people of Israel, emphasized in Mal 1 – 2; and (2) the judgment that will come on the faithless and the blessing in store for those who repent, predominating in chs. 3 – 4. A more detailed analysis follows:

1. Title (1:1).
2. Argument for the love of God toward Israel as shown in the contrasted experiences of Edom and Israel (1:2 – 5).
3. Protest against the negligence of the priests in worship (1:6 – 2:9).
4. Condemnation of those who divorce their wives and marry foreign women (2:10 – 16).
5. Answer to those who complain that God is indifferent to injustice: a day of judgment is at hand (2:17 – 3:5).
6. Rebuke for the neglect of tithes and offerings (3:6 – 12).
7. Reply to doubters and a promise to the faithful (3:13 – 4:3).
8. Recall to the law and prophecy of the coming of Elijah (4:4 – 6).

MALICE [224, 2095, 8273, 8288, 8534, 8624, 2798, 2799, 4504] (Gr. *kakia*). An evil desire to do harm to or act wickedly toward someone. It is an internal feeling or attitude that Christians must put away (Eph 4:31; 1Pe 2:1), for it is wholly opposed to the life in, and the fruit of, the indwelling Spirit of God. It belongs to the old nature, the "flesh" that is under the domination of sin. *See also Evil.*

Instances of:
Cain toward Abel (Ge 4:8; 1Jn 3:12). Ishmael toward Sarah (Ge 21:9). Sarah toward Hagar (Ge 21:10). Philistines toward Isaac (Ge 26:12 – 15, 18 – 21). Esau toward Jacob (Ge

27:41 – 42). Joseph's brothers toward Joseph (Ge 37:2 – 28; 42:21; Ac 7:9 – 10). Potiphar's wife toward Joseph (Ge 39:14 – 20). Ammonites toward the Israelites (Dt 23:3 – 4). Saul toward David (1Sa 18:8 – 29; 19; 20:30 – 33; 22:6 – 23; 23:7 – 28; 26:1 – 2, 18). David toward Michal (2Sa 6:21 – 23); Joab (1Ki 2:5 – 6); Shimei (1Ki 2:8 – 9). Shimei toward David (2Sa 16:5 – 8). Ahithophel toward David (2Sa 17:1 – 3). Jezebel toward Elijah (1Ki 19:1 – 2). Ahaziah toward Elijah (2Ki 1:7 – 15). Jehoram toward Elisha (2Ki 6:31). Samaritans toward the Jews (Ezr 4; Ne 2:10; 4:6). Haman toward Mordecai (Est 3:5 – 15; 5:9 – 14). Not practiced by Job (Job 31:29 – 30). The psalmist's enemies (Pss 22:7 – 8; 35:15 – 16, 19 – 21; 38:16, 19; 41:5 – 8; 55:3; 56:5 – 6; 57:4, 6; 59:3 – 4, 7; 62:3 – 4; 64:2 – 6; 69:4, 10 – 12, 26; 86:14; 102:8; 109:2 – 5, 16 – 18; 140:1 – 4). The psalmist demands retribution (Pss 10:7 – 10, 14; 70:2 – 3; 71:10 – 13, 24). Jeremiah's enemies (Jer 26:8 – 11; 38:1 – 6). Nebuchadnezzar toward Zedekiah (Jer 52:10 – 11). Daniel's enemies (Da 6:4 – 15). Herodias toward John (Mt 14:3 – 11; Mk 6:24 – 28). James and John toward the Samaritans (Lk 9:54). Jesus' enemies (Ps 22:11; Mt 27:18, 27 – 30, 39 – 43; Mk 12:13; 15:10 – 11, 16 – 19, 29 – 32; Lk 11:53 – 54; 23:10 – 11, 39; Jn 18:22 – 23). Paul's enemies (Ac 14:5, 19; 16:19 – 24; 17:5; 19:24 – 35; 21:27 – 31, 36; 22:22 – 23; 23:12 – 15; 25:3; Php 1:15 – 17).

Mk	7:22	adultery, greed, **m**, deceit,
Ro	1:29	murder, strife, deceit and **m**.
1Co	5:8	the yeast of **m** and wickedness,
Eph	4:31	along with every form of **m**.
Col	3:8	**m**, slander, and filthy language
1Pe	2:1	rid yourselves of all **m**

MALICIOUS [MALICE]

Pr	26:24	A **m** man disguises himself
1Ti	3:11	not **m** talkers but temperate
	6:4	**m** talk, evil suspicions

MAMMON (Gr. *mamōnas*, *riches*). The Aramaic word for "riches." Christ used it as a life goal opposed to God (Mt 6:24; Lk 16:13 KJV; NIV "Money"). Jesus also used the word in the phrase "mammon of unrighteousness" (NIV "worldly wealth") in commenting on his parable on the unjust steward (Lk 16:11, 13 KJV).

MAN (Heb. *'ādhām*, *'ish*, Gr. *anthrōpos*). In the Bible "man" (*see Adam*) refers both to the human species and to the male member. Thus the doctrine of man is the teaching concerning human beings in their relation to God and his creation. It includes the following truths: (1) As Creator, God made the human species, first the male and then the female (Ge 1 – 2). Human beings are a part of the created order as a single species (Ac 17:26), but they are also separate from the animal world with a special relationship both to God and to the created order. (2) God made man in the image and likeness of himself (Ge 1:26 – 27; Ps 8:5). This points to that which separates man from the animals in terms of his moral conscience, self-knowledge, and capacity for a spiritual communion with his Creator. All human beings thus have two aspects, a bodily and a spiritual (body and soul, or body and mind, or body and spirit), and so have the capacity to relate fully both to the created order and to their Creator. (3) This capacity has been seriously restricted, misdirected, and abused because of sin. Adam and Eve, the first pair of human beings, freely chose to disobey the divine command and to assert their will against that of their Creator. They lost their personal communion with God, and this had repercussions for the whole of their lives and relationships. It also had an effect on their children and their children's children (Ge 3; Ro 6:12ff.). (4) Whatever their historical and social context, human beings have found themselves capable, on the one hand, of great heroism, public service, personal kindness and goodness; and, on the other hand, of self-centeredness, pride, self-pity, and cruelty (Mk 7:20 – 23). They show signs both of being God's special creation and of being sinful creatures (Ro 7:14 – 25). (5) The eternal Son of God became man in order to provide salvation from sin and a new, permanent relationship with God both in this world and, more fully, in the world to come (Ro 5:12ff.). As such, Jesus Christ is called the "last Adam" (1Co 15:45), and the world to come is "the new heaven and earth" (Rev 21:1). (6) Thus, in Christ, human beings are restored to their right and proper relationship both with their Creator and with his created order (Col 1:15 – 20). (7) Either as unbeliever or believer, each human being is held by God to be a responsible creature, and so each person will be judged at the last judgment (Ro 2:16). *See also Woman.*

Created:

Male and female (Ge 1:26 – 27; 2:7; 5:1 – 2; Dt 4:32; Job 4:17; 10:2 – 3, 8 – 9; 31:15; 33:4; 34:19; 35:10; 36:3; Pss 8:5; 100:3; 119:73; 138:8; 139:14 – 15; Ecc 7:29; Isa 17:7; 42:5; 43:7; 45:12; 64:8; Jer 27:5; Zec 12:1; Mal 2:10; Mt 19:4; Mk 10:6; Heb 2:7). A little lower than the angels (Job 4:18 – 21; Ps 8:5; Heb 2:7 – 8); than God (Ps 8:5). Above other creatures (Mt 10:31; 12:12).

Design of:

To have dominion over all creation (Ge 1:26, 28; 2:19 – 20; 9:2 – 3; Ps 8:6 – 8; Jer 27:6; 28:14; Da 2:38; Heb 2:7 – 8; Jas 3:7). For the glory and pleasure of God (Pr 16:4; Isa 43:7). Equality of all people (Job 21:26; 31:13 – 15; Ps 33:13 – 15; Pr 22:2; Mt 20:25 – 28; 23:8 – 10; 23:11; Mk 10:42 – 44; Ac 10:28, 34 – 35; 17:26). Equality under the gospel (Gal 3:28). Mortal (Job 4:17; Ecc 2:14 – 15; 3:20; 1Co 15:21 – 22; Heb 9:27). See Immortality. A spirit (Job 4:19; 14:10; 32:8; Ps 31:5; Pr 20:27; Ecc 1:8; 3:21; 12:7; Isa 26:9; Zec 12:1; Mt 4:4; 10:28; 26:41; Mk 14:38; Lk 22:40; 23:46; 24:39; Jn 3:3 – 8; 4:24; Ac 7:59; Ro 1:9; 2:29; 7:14 – 25; 1Co 2:11; 6:20; 7:34; 14:14; 2Co 4:6 – 7, 16; 5:1 – 9; Eph 3:16; 4:4; 1Th 5:23; Heb 4:12; Jas 2:26).

Ge	1:26	"Let us make **m** in our image,
	2:7	God formed the **m** from the dust
	2:18	for the **m** to be alone
	2:20	**m** gave names to all the
	2:23	she was taken out of **m**.
	2:25	**m** and his wife were both
	3:9	God called to the **m**,
	3:22	**m** has now become like
	6:3	not contend with **m** forever,
	6:6	grieved that he had made **m**
Dt	8:3	**m** does not live on bread
1Sa	13:14	a **m** after his own heart
	16:7	at the things **m** looks at.
Ps	1:1	Blessed is the **m** who does
	8:4	what is **m** that you are
	32:2	Blessed is the **m** whose sin
	112:1	Blessed is the **m** who fears
	119:9	can a young **m** keep his
	127:5	Blessed is the **m** whose quiver
	144:3	what is **m** that you care
Pr	3:13	Blessed is the **m** who finds
	9:9	Instruct a wise **m**
	14:12	that seems right to a **m**,
Isa	53:3	a **m** of sorrows,
Mt	4:4	**M** does not live on bread
Mk	8:36	What good is it for a **m**
Ro	5:12	entered the world through one **m**
1Co	2:15	spiritual **m** makes judgments
	3:12	If any **m** builds on this
	7:1	good for a **m** not to marry.
	11:3	head of every **m** is Christ,
	11:3	head of woman is **m**
	15:21	death came through a **m**,
Eph	2:15	create in himself one new **m**
	5:31	a **m** will leave his father
Php	2:8	found in appearance as a **m**,
1Ti	2:5	the **m** Christ Jesus,
	2:12	have authority over a **m**;
2Ti	3:17	that the **m** of God may be

Heb	2:6	what is **m** that you are
	9:27	as **m** is destined to die

MANASSEH [4985, 4986, 3442] (mă-năs'sĕ, Heb. *menashsheh, one that makes to forget*).

1. The older son of Joseph, born in Egypt (Ge 41:51). Jacob claimed him and his younger brother Ephraim for his own sons, and when he blessed them he predicted Ephraim would be greater than Manasseh (48:5, 19). Manasseh had a son named Makir, and his descendants made up the tribe of Manasseh.

2. King of Judah and son of Hezekiah. He was only twelve years old when he came to the throne in 687 BC. Evidently, after the death of his father, the orthodox party was considerably weakened. The group in power around the new king was doing away with the religious reforms Hezekiah had made. Manasseh was too young to hinder them. He went along with them. No doubt the people had resented being deprived of the high places, and they rebuilt them the first chance they had after Hezekiah's death. But Manasseh went way beyond this restoration. Judah was a vassal of Assyria and paid tribute every year. The young king must have been much more impressed by the power of Assyria than by the power of God. He became a fanatical idolater, bringing a whole host of heathen practices into his realm. The subsequent reformation of Josiah could not bring the people back to true worship. Manasseh brought his country to ruin (Jer 15:4).

3. A priest of an idol at Dan (Jdg 18:30 KJV, NASB; NIV and RSV read "Moses"). The difference in Hebrew between *Manasseh* and *Moses* is one letter between the first two consonants of *Moses*. Some say that since it was thought a disgrace for one with so honored a name as Moses to be guilty of such sacrilege, someone changed the name to Manasseh.

4. One of those who married a foreign woman (Ezr 10:30).

MANASSITES [1201+4985, 4986] (m a-năs'îts, Heb. *menashshî, forgetting*). Descendants of Joseph's oldest son Manasseh (Ge 41:51). This was a tribe of noble standing, which Gilead, under Jephthah, delivered from the Ephraimites by the password *Shibboleth* (Jdg 12:4 – 6). Moses gave them a city of refuge in Bashan (Dt 4:41 – 43). Because of evil under Jehu, God caused the Manassites to be cut off (2Ki 10:31 – 33).

MANGER [17, 5764] (Gr. *phatnē, a stall*). The word was made notable by Luke's account of the birth of Jesus. The LXX used *phatnē* for the Hebrew, which is given in 2Ch 32:28 as "stalls" and in the KJV of Job 39:9 as "crib" (see Pr 14:4; Isa 1:3). Luke also gives *phatnē* as the birthplace of Jesus. Justin Martyr wrote about AD 100 that the stall was in a cave adjoining an inn. The cavern was used for livestock. Since Justin lived only forty miles (sixty-seven km.) from Bethlehem, his word may be reliable. It is more probable that the stalls were arranged around a courtyard of an inn with guest rooms and balcony above. Either kind of stall would have provided privacy for Mary and the cradle of the infant Lord.

MANKIND [MAN]

Ge	6:7	I will wipe **m**, whom I have created
Ps	33:13	and sees all **m**;
Pr	8:31	and delighting in **m**.
Ecc	7:29	God made **m** upright,
Isa	40:5	and all **m** together will see it.
Jer	32:27	"I am the LORD, the God of all **m**.
Zec	2:13	Be still before the LORD, all **m**,
Lk	3:6	And all **m** will see God's salvation

MANNA [4942, 3445] (Heb. *mān*, Gr. *manna*, *what is it?* possibly *food*). A special food provided for the Hebrews during the exodus from Egypt. The name is of uncertain meaning. The Hebrew *mān* is a question and prefixed to *hu* would be "What is it?" On the other hand, it may be an adaptation of the Egyptian *mennu*, food. Josephus and other ancient writers attribute the name to the question "Is it food?" which is in keeping with the wilderness setting. Just what it was has puzzled naturalists for ages. It came at night, resem-

bling hoarfrost, coming with the dew (Nu 11:9), and may have collected in dewdrops (Ex 16:4). It was white, of delicious flavor, and resembled seed of the coriander, a plant of the eastern Mediterranean area that was both tasty and nourishing (16:31). That it came by miraculous means is shown by its nature, its time of coming, and its preservation over the Sabbath (Ex 16:20 – 26; Dt 8:3). Being seedlike in form it had to be ground (Nu 11:7 – 8). As soon as other food was available, the manna ceased (Jos 5:12).

Called:

God's manna (Ne 9:20). Bread of heaven (Ps 105:40). Bread from heaven (Ps 78:24). Angel's food (Ps 78:25). Spiritual food (1Co 10:3). Previously unknown (Dt 8:3, 16).

Described as:

Like coriander seed (Ex 16:31; Nu 11:7). White (Ex 16:31). Like resin (Nu 11:7). Taste like wafers made with honey (Ex 16:31); oil (Nu 11:8). Like frost (Ex 16:14). Fell after the evening dew (Nu 11:9). None fell on the Sabbath (Ex 16:26 – 27). Gathered every morning (Ex 16:21). An omer of, gathered for each person (Ex 16:16). Two portions of, gathered the sixth day on account of the Sabbath (Ex 16:5, 22 – 26). He that gathered much or little had sufficient and nothing left over (Ex 16:18). Melted away by the sun (Ex 16:21).

Given:

When Israel murmured for bread (Ex 16:2 – 3). In answer to prayer (Ps 105:40). Through Moses (Jn 6:31 – 32). To exhibit God's glory (Ex 16:7). As a sign of Moses' divine mission (Jn 6:30 – 31). For forty years (Ne 9:21). As a test of obedience (Ex 16:4). To teach that man does not live by bread only (Dt 8:3, w Mt 4:4). To humble and prove Israel (Dt 8:16). If kept longer than a day (except on the Sabbath) began to spoil (Ex 16:19 – 20).

The Israelites:

At first covetous of (Ex 16:17). Ground, made into cakes, and baked in pans (Nu 11:8). Counted, *inferior to food of Egypt (Nu 11:4–6). Loathed (Nu 21:5). Punished for despising (Nu 11:10–20). Punished for loathing (Nu 21:6). Ceased when Israel entered Canaan (Ex 16:35; Jos 5:12).*

Ex	16:31	people of Israel called the bread **m**.
Dt	8:16	He gave you **m** to eat in the desert,
Jn	6:49	Your forefathers ate the **m**
Rev	2:17	I will give some of the hidden **m**.

MARA [5288] (māʹra, Heb. *mārâh, bitter*). A name adopted by Naomi instead of her own, which meant pleasant or delightful (Ru 1:20).

MARANATHA (māʹra-năthʹa, Aramaic, *māránāʹ ʹāthāh, our Lord comes!*). An expression of greeting and encouragement as well as of triumphant faith, such as is shown in 1Co 16:22, RSV margin — that is, "Our Lord comes, regardless of man's enmity!" Paul put this word over against *anathema,* the curse that befalls idolaters.

MARDUK [5281] (m arʹdūk, Heb. *merōdhākh,* Akkad. *Marduk*). Marduk, the chief god of the Babylonians (Jer 50:2).

MARITAL [MARRY]

Ex	21:10	of her food, clothing and **m** rights.
Mt	5:32	except for **m** unfaithfulness,
	19:9	except for **m** unfaithfulness,
1Co	7:3	husband should fulfill his **m** duty

MARK, GOSPEL OF The shortest of the four gospels. In comparison with Matthew and Luke, it contains relatively few of Jesus' teachings and nothing at all about his birth and childhood. Starting with the ministry of John the Baptist, it comes immediately to the public ministry of Christ, ending with his death and resurrection.

AUTHORSHIP.

On two points the tradition of the early church is unanimous: the second gospel was written by Mark and presents the preaching of Peter.

DATE.

Most scholars today place the writing of Mark between AD 65 and 70, shortly before the destruction of Jerusalem in the latter year. Conservatives commonly hold to a date in the 50s. Of course, if one accepts the tradition that Mark wrote after Peter's death, the later dates would have to be adopted.

PLACE OF WRITING.

About this there is little question. From the early church — with the exception of Chrysostom — to the present it has been held that Mark's gospel was written at Rome. Several distinctive features point in this direction. Mark uses ten Latin words, some of which do not occur elsewhere in the NT. He explains Jewish customs because he is writing to Gentiles. To his Roman readers he presents Jesus as the mighty conqueror and the suffering servant of the Lord. Because of this purpose no genealogy nor infancy narratives are given. These are found only in Matthew and Luke.

CHARACTER.

In addition to those just mentioned, there are three main characteristics of this gospel. The first is *rapidity of action.* The narrative moves quickly from one event to the next. This probably reflects the impulsive personality of Peter. Over forty times we find the Greek word *euthys,* translated (KJV) "immediately," "straightway," "forthwith." As Vincent aptly says, "His narrative runs" (*Word Studies,* 1:160). The second characteristic is *vividness of detail.* Mark often includes details omitted by the other Synoptics that make the narrative more alive. He gives special attention to the looks and gestures of Jesus. The third characteristic is *picturesqueness of description.* Mark's is preeminently the pictorial gospel. He describes, for instance, the five thousand sitting on the green grass in "groups" (literally, "flower beds"). Peter evidently was impressed with the striking scene of the groups of people in brightly colored Oriental garments of red and yellow sitting on the green hillside, and Mark has preserved the picture for us. Mark's is the gospel of action. Only one long message of Jesus is recorded, the Olivet Discourse (Mk 13). Mark includes eighteen miracles of Jesus, about the same number as Matthew or Luke. In contrast he has only four of the parables, compared with eighteen in Matthew and nineteen in Luke.

ENDING.

A word must be said about the last twelve verses of Mark (16:9 – 20). The two oldest Greek manuscripts, Vaticanus and Sinaiticus (both fourth century AD), and the Sinaitic Syriac end the gospel at 16:8. The majority of scholars now believe that these last twelve verses are not a part of the original gospel of Mark, although the matter is not settled conclusively.

PRIORITY.

Most scholars today favor the theory that Mark's gospel was written first and was used by Matthew and Luke when they composed their gospels. The fact is that about 95 percent of Mark is found in Matthew and/or Luke. The freshness and vividness of Mark's language suggest it was written first. It should be noted, however, that this position is still being challenged.

EVALUATION.

In the early church the gospel of Mark received the least attention of any of the four. This is not true today. The importance of Mark as giving us the basic message of the primitive church (cf. Ac 1:22; 2:22 – 24, 36) is increasingly recognized. The theological as well as historical value of this gospel is widely appreciated. It is the logical place to start one's study of the four gospels.

Outline:

I. The Beginnings of Jesus' Ministry (1:1 – 13).
II. Jesus' Ministry in Galilee (1:14 – 6:29).
III. Withdrawals from Galilee (6:30 – 9:32).
IV. Final Ministry in Galilee (9:33 – 50).

V. Jesus' Ministry in Judea and Perea (ch. 10).
VII. The Resurrection of Jesus (ch. 16). *See Synoptic Gospels, The.*

MARK, JOHN [3453] (Gr. *Markos*, from Lat. *Marcus*, *a large hammer*, Gr. *Iōannēs*, from Heb. *Yôhānān*, *the LORD is gracious*). Mentioned by name ten times in the NT. John was his Jewish name, Mark (Marcus) his Roman. In Acts he is twice (Ac 13:5, 13) referred to simply as John, once (15:39) as Mark, and three times (12:12, 25; 15:37) as "John, also called Mark." In the Epistles he is uniformly (four times) called simply Mark (KJV calling him Marcus three times).

He was a relative of Barnabas (Col 4:10). He accompanied and then deserted Paul on his first missionary journey (Ac 12:25; 13:13). He went with Barnabas to Cyprus after Paul refused to take him on his second missionary journey (Ac 15:36 – 39). He was a fellow worker with Paul (Phm 24) and was recommended by Paul to church at Colosse (Col 4:10). He may have been the young man of Mk 14:51 – 52. Early tradition makes him the "interpreter" of Peter in Rome and founder of the church in Alexandria.

MARRIAGE [829, 851+, 1249+, 1436, 2118+4200, 3782, 4374, 4374, 5951, 5989, 9393, 1138, 1139, 1140, 1141, 1181, 1222+, 2400, 3284, 3650]. The formalization and sanctification of the union of man and woman for the procreation of children. The common Hebrew term *lāqah*, "to take in marriage," should be seen in association with the verb *bā'al*, "to be master, rule, or possess in marriage," as well as with the noun *ba'al*, "master, lord, husband." A comparable NT verb would be *gameō*, "to marry, take to wife," along with its cognate forms *gamizō* and *gamiskō*, both meaning "to give in marriage."

Historically, as Hebrew society developed from nomadic to village settlement, more complex customs and feasts became associated with the ceremony of marriage, and in the Christian era it became regarded as a sacrament. Normally the bride left her family at marriage, and from that time she, and subsequently her children, became part of her husband's family or clan (Ge 24:58 – 61) and, as such, part of their responsibility also.

In general, marriages were arranged with relatives or with those of the same clan. In the ancient world the primary purpose of marriage was procreation rather than companionship, and as a result, large numbers of offspring were regarded as an asset. But an important secondary objective of marriage was the maintaining or increasing of family property, and in royal circles many marriages constituted the seal to what in fact were really political alliances. Despite some examples of polygamy, the most general and acceptable form of marriage was monogamy, which received the sanction of the Mosaic law (cf. Ex 20:17; 21:5; Dt 5:21; et al.). This followed the tradition of the instruction to Adam and his descendants that "a man ... shall cleave to his wife" (Ge 2:24) and Adam's fidelity to one mate. The teaching of Jesus on marriage stressed the lifetime nature of the commitment, and while recognizing that Moses had regularized an already existing practice of divorce "because of the hardness of your hearts" (Mk 10:4 – 5), he taught the traditional Hebrew monogamy and added that the remarriage of a divorced person while the spouse was still alive constituted adultery (Mk 10:11 – 12).

The betrothal (Dt 28:30; 2Sa 3:14) had a particular legal status attached to it that made it almost identical to marriage. The law required that a man committing adultery with a betrothed virgin should be stoned for violating his neighbor's wife (Dt 22:23 – 24). A one-year betrothal was considered normal, and it constituted a part of the permanent marriage relationship (Mt 1:18; Lk 1:27; 2:5). For one year after being married the groom was exempt from military service (Dt 24:5) so that the marriage might be established on a proper footing. The bride's father already used the term "son-in-law" from the time of the betrothal (Ge 19:14), a custom that enhanced the concept of family solidarity.

The wedding ceremony itself was usually brief, but from early days it became surrounded by an elaborate tradition of ceremony and feasting that was very much in vogue in the time of Christ.

The role of the wife was always subservient to that of her husband. He was the provider, decision maker, protector, and master. The wife was the legal mother of his sons and manager of his household. She obeyed his instructions, was his helper, and became his confidante. By Roman times the status of the wife had improved, particularly at the higher levels of society. In those households where menial tasks were performed by slaves, the Roman matron occupied a position of respect and was able to indulge in her own special way of life.

General References to:

Divine institution of (Ge 2:18, 20 – 24; Mt 19:4 – 6; Mk 10:7 – 8; 1Co 6:16; Eph 5:31). Based on principle of creation (Ge 2:18; 1Co 11:11 – 12). Unity of husband and wife in (Ge 2:23 – 24; Mt 19:5 – 6; Mk 10:2 – 10; 1Co 6:16; Eph 5:31, 33). Obligations under, inferior to duty to God (Dt 13:6 – 10; Mt 19:29; Lk 14:26). Indissoluble except for adultery (Mal 2:13 – 16; Mt 5:31 – 32; Mk 10:11 – 12; Lk 16:18; Ro 7:1 – 3; 1Co 7:39 – 40). Dissolved by death (Mt 22:29 – 30; Mk 12:24 – 25; Ro 7:1 – 3). Commended (Pr 18:22; Heb 13:4). Commanded of exiled Israelites (Jer 29:6). Commanded because of immorality (1Co 7:1 – 7). None in the resurrection state (Mt 22:29 – 30; Mk 12:24 – 25). Levirate (brother required to marry a brother's widow) (Ge 38:8, 11; Dt 25:5 – 10; Ru 4:5; Mt 22:24 – 27; Mk 12:19 – 23; Lk 20:28 – 33).

Mosaic Laws Concerning:

Of priests (Lev 21:1, 7, 13 – 15). Captives (Dt 21:10 – 14). Divorced persons (Dt 24:1 – 5). A virgin, not pledged to be married, who has been seduced (Ex 22:16 – 17). Within tribes (Nu 36:8). Incestuous, forbidden (Lev 18:6 – 18 w Dt 22:30; Lev 20:14, 17, 19 – 21; Mk 6:17 – 18). Among antediluvians (Ge 6:2). Among relatives: Abraham and Sarah (Ge 11:29; 12:13; 20:2, 9 – 16); Isaac and Rebekah (Ge 24:3 – 4, 67); Jacob and his wives (Ge 28:2; 29:15 – 30). Levirate (the brother required to marry a brother's widow) (Ge 38:8, 11; Dt 25:5 – 10; Ru 4:5; Mt 22:24 – 27; Mk 12:19 – 23; Lk 20:28 – 33).

Figurative:

(Isa 54:5; 62:4 – 5; Jer 3:14; 31:32; Eze 16:8; Hos 2:19 – 20; Eph 5:23 – 32; Rev 19:7 – 9) Parables of (Mt 22:2 – 10; 25:1 – 10; Mk 2:19 – 20; Jn 3:29; 2Co 11:2).

Mt	22:30	neither marry nor be given in **m**;
	24:38	marrying and giving in **m**,
Ro	7:2	she is released from the law of **m**.
Heb	13:4	by all, and the **m** bed kept pure,

MARRIED [MARRY]

Dt	24:5	happiness to the wife he has **m**.
Ezr	10:10	you have **m** foreign women,
Pr	30:23	an unloved woman who is **m**,
Mt	1:18	pledged to be **m** to Joseph,
Mk	12:23	since the seven were **m** to her?"
Ro	7:2	by law a **m** woman is bound
1Co	7:27	Are you **m**? Do not seek a divorce.
	7:33	But a **m** man is concerned about
	7:36	They should get **m**.

MARRY

Dt	25:5	brother shall take her and **m** her
Mt	22:30	resurrection people will neither **m**
1Co	7:1	It is good for a man not to **m**.
	7:9	control themselves, they should **m**,
	7:28	if you do **m**, you have not sinned;
1Ti	4:3	They forbid people to **m**
	5:14	So I counsel younger widows to **m**,

MARS HILL (Gr. *Areios pagos, Hill of Ares*). A barren hill, 370 feet high, NW of the famous Acropolis in Athens. It was dedicated to Ares, the god of war. The elevated place became the seat of the Greek council, the Areopagus. Because of the Athenians' sudden interest in his message, Paul was taken there to clarify his mysterious teachings (Ac 17:16 – 34).

MARTHA [3450] (Aram. *lady, mistress*). Sister of Lazarus and Mary of Bethany. Luke mentions a visit of Jesus to the home of Martha at a certain village (Lk 10:38). It is inferred from this that the beloved friends of Jesus had resided in Galilee before going to Bethany. Another problem grows out of the connection between the name of Martha and that of Simon the leper. Was Martha the widow of Simon? It is quite possible that she was, and that the Bethany home had been inherited from him on his death. Matthew 26:6 – 12 and Mk 14:3 may indicate this. It seems more natural to think of Martha as a near relative of Simon for whom she acted as hostess. The scriptural narrative reveals that Jesus was an intimate friend of Martha, Mary, and Lazarus. The sisters knew of his ability to work miracles (Jn 11:3, 5). He, no doubt, was a guest in their home during his last fateful days on earth (Mt 21:17; Mk 11:1, 11). Martha was a careful hostess and was familiar enough with Jesus to complain to him about her sister's conduct (Lk 10:38 – 42) and about his delay in coming when Lazarus was ill (Jn 11:1 – 3, 21). She gave the Master an occasion for presenting the great statement about the resurrection (11:25).

MARTYR [3459] (Gr. *martys, martyr, witness*). Because of its use in connection with Stephen (Ac 22:20) and others who died for Christ, the word came to mean one who paid the extreme price for fidelity to Christ. Antipas was a faithful witness (Rev 2:13). The harlot, Babylon, was drunk with the blood of martyrs (17:6).

MARTYRDOM OF PROPHETS (Mt 23:34; Lk 11:50; Rev 16:6). Followers of Jesus exposed to (Mt 10:21 – 22, 39; 23:34; 24:9; Mk 13:12; Lk 21:16 – 17). Spirit of, required by Jesus (Mt 16:25; Lk 9:24; Jn 12:25). Possessed by the righteous (Ps 44:22; Ro 8:36; Rev 12:11). Must be based on love (1Co 13:3). Prophetic reference to (Rev 6:9 – 11; 11:7 – 12; 17:6). *See Persecution.*

Instances of:

Abel (Ge 4:3 – 8). Prophets slain by Jezebel (1Ki 18:4, 13). Zechariah (2Ch 24:21 – 22). John the Baptist (Mk 6:18 – 28). Jesus. See Jesus the Christ, Death of. Stephen (Ac 7:58 – 60). James the apostle (Ac 12:2). The prophets (Mt 22:6; 23:35; Ro 11:3; 1Th 2:15; Heb 11:32 – 37).

MARY

(Gr. Maria, Mariam, from Heb. miryām). The name of several women in the NT.

1. Mary of Rome. A diligent worker in the church at Rome to whom Paul sent special greetings (Ro 16:6).

2. The mother of John Mark. She lived in Jerusalem, where she had a house in which Christians met for prayer. It was to her home that Peter immediately went when he was miraculously released from prison by an angel (Ac 12:1 – 16). She may have been a woman of some means, as she had at least one servant, a girl named Rhoda (16:13). John Mark is described as being the cousin of Barnabas (Col 4:10), but the exact relationship of Barnabas to Mary is unknown. Some scholars think the upper room in which Jesus observed the Lord's Supper was in her home, but there is no proof of this.

3. Mary of Bethany, the sister of Lazarus and Martha. She lived in Bethany (Jn 11:1), about one mile (one and one-half km.) east of the Mount of Olives. Jesus commended her for being more interested in hearing him than in providing a bounteous dinner (Lk 10:42). John relates that she joined with Martha in saying to Jesus after the death of Lazarus, "Lord,... if you had been here, my brother would not have died" (Jn 11:21). Afterward, a week before the last Passover, when Jesus was a guest in the house of Simon the leper (Mk 14:3), she showed her devotion to Jesus by anointing his head and feet with costly ointment and wiping his feet with her hair (Jn 12:3). To those who complained of this as being wasteful, Jesus said that her act would always be remembered (Mt 26:6 – 13; Mk 14:3 – 9). Jesus looked on what she did as an act of love and as a preparation, though perhaps unintentional, for his coming death (Jn 12:7 – 8).

4. The mother of James and Joses. There is uncertainty regarding this Mary. There is reason for thinking that she (Mt 27:56), the "other Mary" (Mt 27:61), and Mary the wife of Clopas (Jn 19:25) were the same person. Little is known about her except that she was very probably among the company of women who served Jesus in Galilee (Lk 8:2 – 3). She was at the cross when Jesus died (Mt 27:56; Mk 15:40). She witnessed the burial of her Lord (Mk 15:47), came to the tomb to anoint his body (16:1), and fled when told by the angel that Jesus was not in the tomb (16:8). A comparison of Mt 28:1; Mk 16:1; and Lk 24:10 seems to make it certain that the mother of James and Joses was also the wife of Clopas. That Clopas (Cleopas, Lk 24:18) and Alphaeus (Mt 10:3) were the same has not been proved.

5. Mary Magdalene. Her name probably indicates that she came from Magdala, on the SW coast of the Sea of Galilee. After Jesus cast seven demons out of her (Mk 16:9; Lk 8:2), she became one of his devoted followers. There is no real ground for thinking that she had been a woman of immoral life before Jesus healed her. The only ground for so thinking is the fact that the first mention of her (Lk 8:2) comes immediately after the account of the sinful woman who anointed Jesus (7:36 – 50). She followed the body of Jesus to the grave (Mt 27:61) and was the first to learn of the resurrection (Mt 28:1 – 8); Mk 16:9; Lk 24:1, 10). Nothing is known of her life after Christ's resurrection.

MARY, THE MOTHER OF JESUS All the authentic information we have about the Virgin Mary is found in the NT. In the opinion of many scholars, she was descended from David, because she was told that her Son would receive the throne of his father David, also because Christ "as to his human nature was a descendant of David" (Ac 2:30; Ro 1:3; 2Ti 2:8); and again because it is thought by many that Luke's genealogy of Christ is through his mother. She appears in several passages:

MARY IN THE INFANCY NARRATIVES.

(Mt 1 – 2; Lk 1 – 2). Mary lived into the apostolic period, whereas Joseph seems to have died before the crucifixion of Jesus, for there is no mention of him after the incident of Jesus in the temple when he was twelve. Luke writes about Jesus' birth from Mary's standpoint, describing her maidenly fears (1:26 – 27), her humble submission to the will of God (1:38), and her hymn of praise to God for the favor accorded her in being the mother of the Messiah (1:39 – 55). Matthew, on the other hand, writes from the standpoint of Joseph, describing his reaction when he found she was with child, his determination to protect her from shame and insult as much as possible, his obedience to God's command that he marry Mary, and his taking her and Jesus to Egypt to escape the wrath of Herod. The two accounts harmonize and dovetail perfectly. It is apparent that neither she nor Joseph fully understood her Son (2:50). In spite of their experiences with the supernatural in relation to him, he was something of an enigma to them.

MARY AT CANA IN GALILEE.

(Jn 2:1 – 11). In this episode Mary seems to have some intimation that Jesus had more than natural powers. She may have needed some correction from him regarding her notion about the use of those powers, but it is wrong to think that Jesus sharply rebuked her. It must be kept in mind that he actually did exercise his power by relieving an embarrassing situation, as she had suggested, and the word "woman" (NIV "dear woman") is the same word he used when on the cross he tenderly commended her to the beloved disciple (19:26). His words to her were a gentle suggestion that it was not for her or any other human being to determine the course of action, for that was entirely in the Father's hands.

THE EPISODE OF MATTHEW 12:46; MARK 3:21, 31FF.; LUKE 8:19 – 21.

In this incident Jesus is informed, while teaching the multitudes, that his mother and brothers desire to see him. The reason for this desire is not stated; but it appears from the context in Mark's account that they were concerned for his safety because of the bitter opposition of the authorities, who were accusing him of casting out demons in the power of Beelzebub; and they wanted to induce him to go into retirement for a time, until it was safe to teach in public again. Jesus' words "For whoever does the will of my Father in heaven is my brother and sister and mother" are meant to teach that physical relationship to him conveys no special privilege, no right of interference with him — the same lesson he taught on a later occasion (Lk 11:27).

MARY AT THE CROSS.

(Jn 19:25ff.). In this incident we find Mary, who had come to Jerusalem for the Passover, watching the crucifixion with agony. Jesus shows his appreciation of the earthly filial relation by committing her to the trustworthy keeping of the apostle who was closest to him.

THE SCENE IN THE UPPER ROOM.

(Ac 1:14). After the resurrection and ascension of Jesus, Mary appears in the midst of the Christian community, engaged with them in prayer for the baptism of the Holy Spirit, but without any discernible preeminence among them. This is the last mention of her in Scripture. It is not known how or when she died. After Mary's death, many legends grew up around her name, but none of them are trustworthy. The keen desire to know further particulars about her was partly satisfied by the writers of apocryphal gospels. There is no direct evidence of prayer being offered to Mary during the first four centuries. Augustine was among the earliest of the church fathers who thought it possible that she had never committed actual sins, though he agreed that she shared the common corruption of humanity. This led eventually to the promulgation by the pope of the dogma of the immaculate conception of Mary (AD 1854). About the middle of the fifth century, some Christian leaders, wishing to exalt her, began to invent new phrases in her honor. With the development of the idea that the celibate and virgin state is morally superior to the married state, it was suggested that she was a perpetual virgin and that the "brothers" and "sisters" of Jesus mentioned in the Gospels were not her children at all, but were either Joseph's children by a prior marriage or were the cousins of Jesus. In 1950 Pope Pius XII declared the dogma of the Assumption of Mary; that is, that Mary's body did not decompose in the grave but was reunited by God to her soul soon after she died. Roman Catholic theologians now openly refer to Mary as the "co-creator" and the "co-redemptrix" of the human race. None of these postapostolic developments has any support in Scripture.

Distinctive Roman Catholic doctrines about Mary: perpetual virginity, intercession, immaculate conception (1854), and assumption of Mary (1950).

> Wife of Joseph (Mt 1:18–25); Relative of Elizabeth, the mother of John the Baptist (Lk 1:36); Of the seed of David (Ac 2:30; Ro 1:3; 2Ti 2:8); Mother of Jesus (Mt 1:18, 20; Lk 2:1–20); Attended to ceremonial purification (Lk 2:22–38); Fled to Egypt with Joseph and Jesus (Mt 2:13–15); Lived in Nazareth (Mt 2:19–23); Took twelve-year-old Jesus to temple (Lk 2:41–50); At wedding in Cana of Galilee (Jn 2:1–11); Concerned for Jesus' safety (Mt 12:46; Mk 3:21, 31ff; Lk 8:19–21); At the cross of Jesus (Jn 19:25ff.) where she was entrusted by Jesus to the care of John (Jn 19:25–27); In the upper room (Ac 1:14)

MASTER [123, 1067, 1251, 4856+6913, 5440, 7864, 804, 1305, 1437, 2181, 3259, 3261].

Yahweh called (Jer 31:32, n.; Hos 2:16). Jesus called (Mt 8:19; 10:25; 23:8; 26:18, 25, 49; Mk 14:45; Lk 8:24; Jn 13:13–14). Jesus spoke against abuse of the title (Mt 23:8). *See Lord.*

MASTER, OF SERVANTS

Duties to Servants:

> Must allow Sabbath rest (Dt 5:14). Compensate (Jer 22:13; Ro 4:4; Col 4:1; 1Ti 5:18). Pay promptly (Lev 19:13; Dt 24:15; Jas 5:4). Forbidden to oppress (Lev 19:13; 25:43; Dt 24:14; Job 31:13–14; Pr 22:16; Mal 3:5). Forbidden to threaten (Eph 6:9). Exhorted to show kindness (Phm 10–16). Exhorted to show wisdom (Pr 29:12, 21). See Employer; Servant.

Good Masters:

> Abraham (Ge 18:19); Job (Job 31:13–15); the centurion (Lk 7:2).

Unjust Masters:

> Actions of: Sarah to Hagar (Ge 16:6); Laban to Jacob (Ge 31:7); Potiphar's wife to Joseph (Ge 39:7–20). Violent, to be punished (Ex 21:20–21, 26–27).

Ge	4:7	to have you, but you must **m** it."
Hos	2:16	you will no longer call me 'my **m**.'
Mal	1:6	If I am a **m**, where is the respect
Mt	10:24	nor a servant above his **m**.
	23:8	for you have only one **M**
	24:46	that servant whose **m** finds him
	25:21	"His **m** replied, 'Well done,
Ro	6:14	For sin shall not be your **m**,
	14:4	To his own **m** he stands or falls.
Col	4:1	you know that you also have a **M**
2Ti	2:21	useful to the **M** and prepared

MATERIALISM

Love of money:

> A root of all kinds of evil (1Ti 6:10). Insatiable (Ecc 4:7–8; 5:10–11). Forbidden in overseer (1Ti 3:2–3; Tit 1:7). Materialists do not love God (Mt 6:24; 1Jn 2:15–17; 3:17).

Treasures in Heaven versus Materialism:
(Mt 6:19 – 21; 1Ti 6:17 – 19).

MATTHEW [3414] (Gr. *Maththaios, gift of Yahweh*). Son of Alphaeus (Mk 2:14), a tax collector (*telōnēs*), also called Levi (Mk 2:14; Lk 5:27), whom Jesus met at the tax office and called to be one of his disciples (Mt 9:9; Mk 2:14; Lk 5:27). Since double names were common among the Jews (e.g., Simon became Peter, Thomas was called Didymus, Bartholomew was probably also named Nathanael, and Saul became Paul), there can be little doubt that Levi and Matthew were one and the same person. Levi probably changed his name to Matthew ("gift of Yahweh," or if a later form of Amittai, "true") when he became a disciple of Jesus.

The readiness with which Matthew responded to Jesus' call seems to indicate that he had previously come into contact with Jesus and his teachings and had already decided to dedicate his life to Jesus' cause. That Jesus should have chosen as his disciple a Jewish tax collector who was in the employ of the Roman government is indeed remarkable. Tax collectors were bitterly hated by their own countrymen and regarded as little more than traitors. However, Matthew's background and talents must have been of great value to Jesus. As a tax collector he was skilled at writing and keeping records. In addition, he must have been a man of deep spiritual convictions. This is revealed by his concern for his former colleagues whom he invited to a dinner at his own house (Luke's account alone in 5:29 – 32 makes it clear that it was Matthew's house, not Jesus'), Jesus being the honored guest. No doubt Matthew's purpose was to win these men to Christ. Apart from the mention of Matthew in the lists of the apostles (Mt 10:3; Mk 3:18; Ac 1:13), no further notices of him are found in the NT.

MATTHEW, GOSPEL OF In the early church Matthew was the most highly valued and widely read of the four gospels. This is revealed both by its position in the canon — it is found in first place in all the known lists of the Gospels except two — and by its widespread citation, for it is by far the most often quoted gospel in the Christian literature before AD 180. Among the reasons for this popularity two are particularly important:

1. The gospel's apostolic authority. Matthew's name was associated with it from at least the early second century AD.

2. Its emphasis on Christ's teaching. A growing church needed the authoritative word of Christ both to instruct converts and to refute heresy.

AUTHORSHIP.

The first gospel, as is the case with the other three, is anonymous. Nevertheless, the church, from the early second century until the rise of modern critical studies, unanimously ascribed it to Matthew, one of the Twelve (Mt 9:9; 10:3; Mk 3:18; Ac 1:13), also called Levi (Mk 2:14; Lk 5:27), a tax collector by occupation. The results of source criticism, in particular the evident dependence of Matthew on Mark's gospel, have led many, but by no means all, biblical scholars to abandon Matthew's authorship. Despite the results of source criticism, strong arguments persist for the traditional view.

DATE AND PLACE OF ORIGIN.

We do not know precisely when Matthew was written. Its dependence on Mark and its failure to mention the destruction of Jerusalem (especially in connection with Jesus' prediction of that event in ch. 24) suggest a date shortly before AD 70.

Antioch is the most likely place of origin. Early in the second century Ignatius of that city refers to Matthew as "the Gospel." Also, the Gentile-Jewish character of the Antioch church accords well with the contents of the book.

CHARACTERISTICS.

1. Matthew is the teaching gospel par excellence. In this respect it greatly supplements Mark, which is more interested in what Jesus did than in what he said.

2. Matthew is the gospel of the *church*. Matthew is the only evangelist who uses the word "church" at all (Mt 16:18; 18:17). The first occurrence is in Jesus' response to Peter's confession. Here its use is clearly anticipatory. In 18:17 the context is church discipline and seems to indicate not only the existence of a church, but also the emergence of problems within it.

3. Matthew is the gospel of *fulfillment*. It is especially concerned with showing that Christianity is the fulfillment of the OT revelation. The many OT proof texts cited by the use of the formula "that it might be fulfilled," the emphasis on the messiahship of Jesus, and the presentation of Christianity as a new "law," all reveal this basic concern of the author.

4. Matthew is the gospel of the King. The genealogy of ch. 1 traces Jesus' lineage back to David: at his birth the magi come asking, "Where is the one who has been born king of the Jews?" (Mt 2:2); eight times the regal title "Son of David" is ascribed to Christ (1:1; 9:27; 12:23; 15:22; 20:30 – 31; 21:9, 15); the triumphal entry clearly has kingly significance (21:1 – 11); in the Olivet Discourse Jesus prophesied his future kingly reign (25:31); To Pilate's question "Are you the king of the Jews?" Jesus gave the tacit answer, "Yes, it is as you say" (27:11); and over the cross were written these words: "This is Jesus, the king of the Jews" (27:37). The climax comes at the very end of the gospel, where Jesus in the Great Commission declared: "All authority in heaven and on earth has been given to me" (28:18). There can be no doubt that the author of this gospel deliberately presents Jesus as the King.

STRUCTURE.

The arrangement of the material reveals an artistic touch. The whole of the gospel is woven around five great discourses: (1) Mt 5 – 7; (2) Mt 10; (3) Mt 13; (4) Mt 18; and (5) Mt 24 – 25, each of which concludes with the refrain, "And it came to pass when Jesus ended these sayings...." In each case the narrative portions appropriately lead up to the discourses. The gospel has a fitting prologue (Mt 1 – 2) and a challenging epilogue (28:16 – 20).

Outline:

    I. Prologue: The Birth of the King (Mt 1 – 2).
    II. Narrative: The Preparation of the King (Mt 3 – 4).
    III. First Discourse: The Law of the Kingdom (Mt 5 – 7).
    IV. Narrative: The Power of the King (Mt 8 – 9).
    V. Second Discourse: The Proclamation of the Kingdom (Mt 10).
    VI. Narrative: The Rejection of the King (Mt 11 – 12).
    VII. Third Discourse: The Growth of the Kingdom (Mt 13).
    VIII. Narrative: The Mission of the King (Mt 14 – 17).
    IX. Fourth Discourse: The Fellowship of the Kingdom (Mt 18).
    X. Narrative: The King Goes to Jerusalem (Mt 19 – 23).
    XI. Fifth Discourse: The Consummation of the Kingdom (Mt 24 – 25).
    XII. Narrative: The Death and Resurrection of the King (26:1 – 28:15).
    XIII. Epilogue: The Great Challenge of the Kingdom (28:16 – 20).

MATTHIAS [3416] (mă-thī′ăs, Gr. *Matthias or Maththias, gift of the* LORD). The one chosen by lot after the death of Judas Iscariot to take his place among the twelve apostles (Ac 1:15 – 26). He had been numbered among the followers of Christ (1:21 – 22). Some number him among the Seventy, as, for instance, Clement of Alexandria and Eusebius. Nothing certain is known of him after his appointment.

MATURE [MATURITY]

Lk	8:14	and pleasures, and they do not **m**.
1Co	2:6	a message of wisdom among the **m**,

Eph	4:13	of the Son of God and become **m**,
Php	3:15	of us who are **m** should take such
Col	4:12	firm in all the will of God, **m**
Heb	5:14	But solid food is for the **m**,
Jas	1:4	work so that you may be **m**

MATURITY [MATURE]

| Heb | 6:1 | about Christ and go on to **m**, |

MEDES [4512, 4513, 10404, 3597] (mēdz, mē′dřa, Heb. *mādhî, mādhay*).

Inhabitants of Media. Israelites distributed among, when carried to Assyria (2Ki 17:6; 18:11). Palace in the Babylonian province of (Ezr 6:2). An essential part of the Medo-Persian Empire (Est 1:1 – 19). Supremacy over the Babylonian Empire (Da 5:28, 31; 9:1; 11:1).

MEDIATOR (Gr. *mesitēs, a middle man*). One who brings about friendly relations between two or more estranged people. He or she corresponds to the "umpire" ("daysman" KJV) of Job 9:33. The NT uses *mesitēs* twice in connection with Moses as the mediator of the law (Gal 3:19 – 20) and four times regarding Jesus. Jesus is the *mesitēs*, or peacemaker, between God and human beings (1Ti 2:5). He is the agent by whom the new covenant between God and the redeemed is made efficacious (Heb 8:6; 9:15; 12:24).

1Ti	2:5	and one **m** between God and men,
Heb	8:6	of which he is **m** is superior
	9:15	For this reason Christ is the **m**
	12:24	to Jesus the **m** of a new covenant,

MEDITATE [MEDITATION]

Ge	24:63	out to the field one evening to **m**,
Jos	1:8	from your mouth; **m** on it day
Ps	48:9	we **m** on your unfailing love.
	77:12	I will **m** on all your works
	119:15	I **m** on your precepts
	119:23	your servant will **m**
	119:27	then I will **m** on your wonders.
	119:78	but I will **m** on your precepts.
	119:97	I **m** on it all day long.
	119:148	that I may **m** on your promises.
	143:5	I **m** on all your works

MEDITATION [1948, 2047, 2052, 2053, 8452, 8488, 8490, 8491].

On the Lord (Pss 63:5 – 6; 104:34; 139:17 – 18). On the law of the Lord (Pss 1:2; 19:14; 49:3; 119:11, 15 – 16, 23, 48, 55, 59, 78, 97 – 99; 119:148). Commanded (Jos 1:8). On the works of the Lord (Pss 77:10 – 12; 143:5). Instances of: Isaac (Ge 24:63); David (Pss 4:4; 39:3).

| Ps | 19:14 | of my mouth and the **m** of my heart |
| | 104:34 | May my **m** be pleasing to him, |

MEDITERRANEAN SEA Because this body of water was the largest known to the Hebrews, it became known as "the Sea." The Canaanites occupied the land from Jordan to the Sea (Nu 13:29). It marked the end of the Promised Land (34:5). Joshua located it as "the Great Sea on the west" (Jos 1:4). It was the utmost sea (Dt 11:24) or western sea (34:2). It was known also as the Sea of the Philistines (Ex 23:31). Cedar for the temple was shipped by sea from Tyre to Joppa (2Ch 2:16). This sea played a big part in NT days. On one occasion Jesus may have seen its waters (Mk 7:24). Paul's missionary tours took him across the eastern half. If he did set foot in Spain, he saw most of this inland sea.

The sea was known and used by many early civilized people, and they had commercial dealings across Palestine with civilizations of the Tigris-Euphrates Valley. At one time it had been an open channel to the Red Sea. Drifting sands from the African desert and silt from the Nile River closed this and made a land route from Asia to Africa. The sea is 2,300 miles (3,833 km.) long and more than 1,000 miles (1,667 km.) across at its widest point. An elevated underwater area once reached from upper Tunisia in Africa east to Sicily. This shallow area divides the sea into the Eastern, or Levant, and the Western Sea. Its northern shore is broken by the Grecian and the Italian peninsulas. Crete and Cyprus made havens for shippers of ancient times. Paul was on both islands during his journeys (Ac 13:4; 27:7).

MEDIUM [200+, 6726].

A spiritist; one who consults the dead (Lev 19:31; 20:6; Dt 18:9 – 13; Isa 8:19 – 22). Punished by death in the law (Lev 20:27). Saul and the medium at Endor (1Sa 28:3 – 25; 1Ch 10:13 – 14).

MEEKNESS [6705, 6714, 4558, 4559] (Heb. *'ănāwâh, suffering,* Gr. *praütēs*). A quality often commended in Scripture. The meek (oppressed) are assured of divine help and ultimate victory (Pss 22:26; 25:9; 37:11). Jesus was sent to minister to the oppressed (Ps 45:4; Isa 11:4; 29:19; Zep 2:3). Meekness is a fruit of the Spirit (Gal 5:23). It is characteristic of Jesus (Mt 11:29; 2Co 10:1). Believers are commanded to be meek and to show a lowly spirit one to another (Eph 4:2; Col 3:12; Tit 3:2). A teacher should be meek (2Ti 2:25). Meekness is a mark of true discipleship (1Pe 3:15). The word does not imply a weak, vacillating, or a supine nature.

Described:

Advantageous (Ps 25:9; Pr 14:29; 17:1; 19:11; Ecc 7:8; 10:4; Am 3:3; 1Co 13:4 – 5, 7). Honorable (Pr 20:3). Potent (Pr 15:1, 18; 16:32; 25:15; 29:8). A fruit of the Spirit (Gal 5:22 – 23, 26). Commanded (Zep 2:3; Mt 5:38 – 41 w Lk 6:29; Mt 11:29; Mk 9:50; Ro 12:14, 18; 14:19; 1Co 6:7; 7:15; 10:32; 2Co 13:11; Gal 6:1; Eph 4:1 – 2; Php 2:14 – 15; Col 3:12 – 13; 1Th 5:14 – 15; 1Ti 3:3; 6:11; 2Ti 2:24 – 25; Tit 2:2, 9; 3:2; Heb 10:36; 12:14; Jas 1:4, 19, 21; 3:13; 1Pe 2:18 – 23; 3:4, 11, 15; 2Pe 1:5 – 7). Rewards of (Pss 22:26; 37:11; 76:8 – 9; 147:6; 149:4; Isa 29:19; Mt 5:5; 11:29).

Instances of:

God (La 3:22, 28 – 30); Abraham (Ge 13:8 – 9); Isaac (Ge 26:20 – 22); Moses (Ex 16:7 – 8; 17:2 – 7; Nu 12:3; 16:4 – 11); Gideon (Jdg 8:2 – 3); Hannah (1Sa 1:13 – 16); Saul (1Sa 10:27); David

(1Sa 17:29; 2Sa 16:9 – 14; Ps 38:13 – 14); psalmist (Ps 120:5 – 7); Jesus (Isa 11:4; 42:1 – 4; 53:7; La 3:28 – 30; Mt 11:29; 12:19 – 20; 26:47 – 54; 27:13 – 14; Mk 15:4 – 5; Lk 23:34; 2Co 10:1; 1Pe 2:21 – 23; see Jesus the Christ); Stephen (Ac 7:60); Paul (Ac 21:20 – 26; 1Co 4:12 – 13; 2Co 12:10; 1Th 2:7; 2Ti 4:16); the Thessalonians (2Th 1:4); Job (Jas 5:11).

MELCHIZEDEK, MELCHISEDEK [4900, 3519] (mĕl-kĭz′ĕ·dĕk, Heb. *malkî-tsedhek, king of righteousness*). A priest and king of Salem, a city identified with Jerusalem. The reference in Ge 14:18 – 20 is the first mention of Salem in the OT.

Melchizedek went out to meet Abram after his return from the slaughter of Kedorlaomer and the kings who were with him in the Valley of Siddim. He presented Abram with bread and wine and blessed him in the name of "God Most High, Creator of heaven and earth." Abram gave him "a tenth of everything." The Hebrew word for God in this instance is the same as in such phrases as "God Almighty" (Ge 17:1), "the Eternal God" (21:33), and "God of Bethel" (35:7) and is the oldest Semitic designation for God. Melchizedek was thus a monotheist and worshiped essentially the same God as Abram, who recognized him as a priest.

He appears next in Ps 110:4: "You are a priest forever, in the order of Melchizedek." This psalm is of special interest because Jesus referred to it (Mt 22:41 – 42; Mk 12:35 – 36; Lk 20:41 – 42), and it is regarded as one of the messianic psalms. The ideal ruler of the Hebrew nation would be one who combined in his person the role of both priest and king.

The author of the letter to the Hebrews uses Melchizedek (Heb 5 – 7) in his great argument showing Jesus Christ as the final and perfect revelation of God, because in his person he is Son and in his work he is Priest (1:2 – 10:18). The author cites Ps 110:4, indicating that Jesus' priesthood is of a different order from the Levitical: it is "in the order of Melchizedek."

The author of Hebrews, looking back on the history of his people, comes to the conclusion that the Levitical priesthood proved to be a failure. It was incapable of securing victory over sin and full communion with God. And so the author cites Ps 110. The ideal priest must belong to "the order of Melchizedek." To the author, Christ was the fulfillment of this prophecy, for he came out of Judah, a tribe with no connection to the Levitical priesthood. While the claims of the old priesthood were based on genealogy, Christ's were displayed in his power of an endless life. The claim of Jesus to be the real fulfillment of the psalmist's prophecy rested on the fact of his resurrection and the proof it gave that his life was indestructible. The psalmist had declared that the ideal high priest would be forever, and only one whose life could not be destroyed by death could be said to answer to the psalmist's ideal, a priest "in the order of Melchizedek."

MEMBER [408, 1201, 4632, 4946, 5883, 6830, 741, 1085, 2363, 3517, 3858, 3865, 3875, 5362] (Heb. *yātsur*, Gr. *melos*). A word usually denoting any feature or part of the body (Job 17:7; Jas 3:5 KJV, MOF, NEB, RSV), "the members" meaning "the body" (Ps 139:16). The word is used for members of the body of Christ (1Co 6:15; 12:12 – 27; Eph 4:25; 5:30).

Ro	12:5	each **m** belongs to all the others.

MEMBERS [MEMBER]

Mt	10:36	a man's enemies will be the **m**
Ro	7:23	law at work in the **m** of my body,
	12:4	of us has one body with many **m**,
1Co	6:15	not know that your bodies are **m**
	12:24	But God has combined the **m**
Eph	3:6	**m** together of one body,
	4:25	for we are all **m** of one body.
	5:30	for we are **m** of his body.
Col	3:15	as **m** of one body you were called

MENE, MENE, TEKEL, PARSIN [10428+10593+ 10770]. Four Aramaic words, probably meaning "numbered, numbered, weighed, and divided," which suddenly appeared on the walls of Belshazzar's banquet hall (Da 5:25 – 28).

MEPHIBOSHETH [5136] (mē-fĭb'ō-shĕth, Heb. *mephîvōsheth*, *from the mouth of shame* [a derogatory term for Baal]).

1. A son of King Saul and his concubine Rizpah. Together with his brother and other men, Mephibosheth was delivered to the Gibeonites to be hanged, with David's consent (2Sa 21:8).

2. A son of Jonathan and grandson of Saul. His name appears as Merib-Baal in 1Ch 8:34; 9:40. After the disaster at Mount Gilboa, where both Saul and Jonathan were killed in the battle against the Philistines (2Sa 1:4; 1Ch 10:1 – 8), Mephibosheth as a child of five was carried by his nurse to Lo Debar east of the Jordan, where they took refuge in the house of Makir, the son of Ammiel (2Sa 9:4).

On David's accession to the throne, Mephibosheth was called back to Jerusalem, given his father's inheritance, and allowed to eat at the king's table for the rest of his life. Saul's servant Ziba was commanded to serve him. The servant, however, tried to ingratiate himself with David at the expense of his master by representing Mephibosheth as a traitor (2Sa 16:1 – 4). David did not fully believe the servant's story, for later he received Mephibosheth in a friendly manner (19:24 – 30).

Mephibosheth was the father of Mica (2Sa 9:12), or Micah in 1Ch 8:35.

MERCIFUL [MERCY]

Dt	4:31	the Lord your God is a **m** God;
Ne	9:31	for you are a gracious and **m** God.
Ps	77:9	Has God forgotten to be **m**?
Jer	3:12	for I am **m**,' declares the Lord,
Da	9:9	The Lord our God is **m**
Mt	5:7	Blessed are the **m**,

Lk	1:54	remembering to be **m**
	6:36	Be **m**, just as your Father is **m**.
Heb	2:17	in order that he might become a **m**
Jas	2:13	to anyone who has not been **m**.
Jude	1:22	Be **m** to those who doubt; snatch

MERCY [2571, 2798, 2799, 2858, 2876, 8163, 8171, 9382, 9384, 10664, 447, 1796, 1799, 1799+5073, 2661, 3880, 3881] (Heb. *hesedh, kindness, raham, bowels, hanan, gracious,* Gr. *eleos, kindness, oiktirmos, compassion*).

1. Forbearance from inflicting punishment on an adversary or a lawbreaker.

2. The compassion that causes one to help the weak, the sick, or the poor. Showing mercy is one of the cardinal virtues of a true Christian (Jas 2:1 – 13) and is one of the determinants of God's treatment of us. Christian mercy is a "fruit of the Spirit" (Gal 5:22 – 23), made up in part of love, long-suffering, kindness, gentleness, and goodness. God's mercy toward sinful humans was shown most clearly and fully in his giving of his beloved Son to die in our stead; and our Lord's mercy enabled him to make willingly the awful sacrifice (Ro 5:8). The Hebrew word *raham* is the most emotional of the terms used to describe the Lord's love for his people (Ps 103:13), rightly meriting the translation "compassion." It is related to the word for "womb" and is well exemplified in the upsurging of motherly emotions in 1Ki 3:26.

General References to:

(Ps 85:10; Pr 20:28; Hos 4:1; Jas 2:13). A grace of the godly (Ps 37:25 – 26; Pr 11:17; 12:10; 14:22, 31; Ro 12:8). Iniquity atoned by (Pr 16:6). Of the wicked, cruel (Pr 12:10). Commanded (Pr 3:3; Hos 12:6; Mic 6:8; Mt 9:13; 12:7; 23:23; Lk 6:36; Col 3:12 – 13). To be shown with cheerfulness (Ro 12:8). Rewards of (2Sa 22:26; Pss 18:25; 37:25 – 26; Pr 14:21; 21:21; Mt 5:7). See God, Mercy of; Kindness. Instances of: prison keeper to Joseph (Ge 39:21 – 23); Joshua to Rahab (Jos 6:25); Israelites to man of Bethel (Jdg 1:23 – 26); David to Saul (1Sa 24:10 – 13, 17).

Ex	33:19	**m** on whom I will have **m**,
2Sa	24:14	of the LORD, for his **m** is great;
1Ch	21:13	for his **m** is very great;
Ne	9:31	But in your great **m** you did not put
Ps	28:6	for he has heard my cry for **m**.
	57:1	Have **m** on me, O God, have **m**
Pr	28:13	renounces them finds **m**.
Isa	63:9	and **m** he redeemed them;
Hos	6:6	For I desire **m**, not sacrifice,
Am	5:15	LORD God Almighty will have **m**
Mic	6:8	To act justly and to love **m**
	7:18	but delight to show **m**.
Hab	3:2	in wrath remember **m**.
Zec	7:9	show **m** and compassion
Mt	5:7	for they will be shown **m**.
	9:13	learn what this means: 'I desire **m**,
	18:33	Shouldn't you have had **m**
	23:23	justice, **m** and faithfulness.
Lk	1:50	His **m** extends to those who fear
Ro	9:15	"I will have **m** on whom I have **m**,
	9:18	Therefore God has **m**
	11:32	so that he may have **m** on them all.
	12:1	brothers, in view of God's **m**,
	12:8	if it is showing **m**, let him do it
Eph	2:4	who is rich in **m**, made us alive
1Ti	1:13	I was shown **m** because I acted
	1:16	for that very reason I was shown **m**
Tit	3:5	we had done, but because of his **m**.
Heb	4:16	so that we may receive **m**
Jas	2:13	judgment without **m** will be shown
	3:17	submissive, full of **m** and good fruit
	5:11	full of compassion and **m**.
1Pe	1:3	In his great **m** he has given us new
Jude	1:23	to others show **m**, mixed with fear

MERIBAH [5313] (mĕr'ĭ̄b a, Heb. *merîbâh, contention*).

1. A place near and to the NW of Sinai where Moses, at the Lord's command, struck the rock and water gushed out for the refreshment of the people (Ex 17:1 – 7). Moses named the place "Massah," i.e., "tempting," and "Meribah," because of the

quarreling of the children of Israel and because they tempted the Lord.

2. A place near Kadesh Barnea where the people again thirsted and where the Lord commanded Moses to speak to the rock. Moses exceeded his instructions and, apparently wanting some credit for the miracle, struck the rock, and water came forth (Nu 20:1 – 13). For this arrogance, Moses was forbidden to enter the Promised Land.

MESHACH [4794, 10415] (mē′shăk, Heb. *mēshakh*, perhaps *I have become weak*). His Hebrew name was Mishael. He was taken as a captive to Babylon with Daniel, Hananiah, and Azariah, where each one was given a Babylonian name (Da 1:6 – 20; 2:17, 49; 3:12 – 30). Mishael was given the Akkadian name Meshach. Shadrach, Meshach, and Abednego were chosen to learn the language and the ways of the Babylonians so that they could enter the king's service (Da 1:3 – 5, 17 – 20), c. 605 BC. These three were eventually thrown into Nebuchadnezzar's furnace because they refused to bow down and worship the huge golden image that he had made (Da 3:1, 4 – 6, 8 – 30).

MESOPOTAMIA [3544] (mĕs′ō-pō-tā′mǐa, from Gr. *mesos, middle,* and *potamos, river[land] between rivers*). The country located between the Tigris and the Euphrates rivers.

> **General References to:**
> Abraham a native of (Ac 7:2). Nahor lived in (Ge 24:10). People who lived in, called Syrians (Ge 25:20). Balaam from (Dt 23:4). The Israelites subjected to, eight years under the judgments of God (Jdg 3:8); delivered from, by Othniel (Jdg 3:9 – 10). Chariots hired from, by the Ammonites (1Ch 19:6 – 7). People of, present at Pentecost (Ac 2:9).

MESSAGE [MESSENGER]

Isa	53:1	Who has believed our **m**
Jn	12:38	"Lord, who has believed our **m**
Ac	10:36	You know the **m** God sent

Ro	10:16	who has believed our **m**?"
	10:17	faith comes from hearing the **m**,
1Co	1:18	For the **m** of the cross is
	2:4	My **m** and my preaching were not
2Co	5:19	to us the **m** of reconciliation.
2Th	3:1	pray for us that the **m**
Tit	1:9	firmly to the trustworthy **m**
Heb	4:2	the **m** they heard was of no value
1Pe	2:8	because they disobey the **m** —

MESSENGER [MESSAGE]

Pr	25:13	is a trustworthy **m**
Mal	3:1	I will send my **m**, who will prepare
Mt	11:10	"'I will send my **m** ahead of you,
2Co	12:7	a **m** of Satan, to torment me.

MESSIAH [5431, 3549] (*anointed*). The basic meaning of the Hebrew *māshîah* and the Greek *christos* is "anointed one." In the OT the word is used of prophets, priests, and kings who were consecrated to their office with oil. The expression "the Lord's anointed" and its equivalent are not used as a technical designation of the Messiah, but refers to the king of the line of David ruling in Jerusalem and anointed by the Lord through the priest. With the possible exception of Da 9:25 – 26, the title "Messiah" as a reference to Israel's eschatological king does not occur in the OT. It appears in this sense later in the NT, where he is almost always called "the Christ." The OT pictures the Messiah as one who will put an end to sin and war, usher in universal righteousness, and through his death make vicarious atonement for the salvation of sinful people. The NT concept of the Messiah is developed directly from the teaching of the OT. Jesus of Nazareth is the Messiah; he claimed to be the Messiah (Mt 23:63 – 64; Mk 14:61 – 62; Lk 22:67 – 70; Jn 4:25 – 26) and the claim was acknowledged by his disciples (Mt 16:16; Mk 8:29; Lk 9:20; Ac 4:27; 10:38).

MESSIANIC HOPE (Mt 13:17; Jn 8:56; Ac 9:22; Heb 11:13; 1Pe 1:10 – 12).

> *Created by prophecy (Ge 49:10; Nu 24:17; 1Sa 1:10; 2Sa 7:12 – 13; Isa 9:6 – 7; 11:1 – 9;*

33:17; 40:3 – 5; 55:3 – 5; 62:10 – 11; Jer 23:5 – 6; 33:15 – 17; Da 2:44; 7:13 – 14; 9:24 – 27; Mic 5:2; Zec 9:9; Mal 3:1 – 3; Ac 13:27); by the covenant with David to establish his throne forever (2Sa 7:12 – 16; 1Ch 17:11 – 14; 22:10; 28:7); by the messianic psalms (Pss 2; 16; 21; 22; 45; 72; 87; 89; 96; 110; 132:11, 17 – 18). Confirmed in the vision of Mary (Lk 1:30 – 33). Exemplified: by the priest Zechariah (Lk 1:68 – 79); by the prophet Simeon (Lk 2:25, 29 – 32); by the prophetess Anna (Lk 2:36 – 38); by the wise men of the East (Mt 2:1 – 12); by John the Baptist (Mt 11:3); by the people (Jn 7:31, 40 – 42; 12:34); by Caiaphas (Mt 26:63; Mk 14:61); by Joseph of Arimathea (Mk 15:43; Lk 23:51); by the disciples on the way to Emmaus (Lk 24:21); by Paul (Ac 26:6 – 7).

MICAH [4777, 4781] (mĭ′ka, Heb. *mîkkâh, who is like Yahweh?*).

1. Ephraimite whose mother made an image for which he secured a priest; both image and priest were later stolen by the tribe of Dan (Jdg 17 – 18).

2. Reubenite (1Ch 5:5).

3. Grandson of Jonathan (1Ch 8:34; 9:40).

4. Levite (1Ch 23:20).

5. Father of Abdon, one of Josiah's officers (2Ch 34:20).

6. Prophet Micah, the Moreshethite; prophesied in the reigns of Jotham, Ahaz, and Hezekiah (Mic 1:1; Jer 26:18).

MICAH, BOOK OF The fifth of the Minor Prophets, dating from the late 700s BC. The book predicts the fall of Samaria, which occurred in 722, but concerns more especially the sins and dangers of Jerusalem in the days of Hezekiah around 700. As an outline will show, the message varies between condemnation for the present sins and God's purpose of ultimate blessing for his people:

Outline:

I. Predicted Desolation of Samaria and Jerusalem (1:1 – 3:12)

II. Eventual Blessings for Zion (4:1 – 8)

III. Invasion and Deliverance by Davidic Ruler (4:9 – 5:15)

IV. Condemnation for Sins (6:1 – 7:6)

V. Eventual Help from God (7:7 – 20)

MICAIAH [4777, 4779, 4780, 4781] (*who is like Yahweh?*).

1. A prophet living in Samaria who predicted the death of King Ahab (1Ki 22; 2Ch 18).

2. Father of Acbor, one of Josiah's officers (2Ki 22:12 – 14).

3. Daughter of Uriel of Gibeah (2Ch 13:2).

4. Official of Jehoshaphat; a teacher (2Ch 17:7).

5. Ancestor of priest in Nehemiah's time (Ne 12:35).

6. Priest (Ne 12:41).

7. Grandson of Shaphan (Jer 36:11 – 13).

MICHAEL [4776, 3640] (*who is like God [El]?*).

1. An Asherite (Nu 13:13)

2. Two Gadites (1Ch 5:13 – 14).

3. A Gershonite Levite (1Ch 6:40).

4. A descendant of Issachar (1Ch 7:3).

5. A Benjamite (1Ch 8:16).

6. A captain of the thousands of Manasseh who joined David at Ziklag (1Ch 12:20).

7. Father of Omri (1Ch 27:18).

8. Son of Jehoshaphat. Slain by his brother, Jehoram (2Ch 21:2 – 4).

9. Father of Zebadiah (Ezr 8:8).

10. The archangel. His message to Daniel (Da 10:13, 21; 12:1). Contention with the devil (Jude 9). Fights with the dragon (Rev 12:7).

MICHAL [4783] (mĭ′kăl, Heb. *mîkhāl*, a contraction of *mîkhā′ēl, Michael, who is like God [El]?*). The younger daughter of King Saul of Israel (1Sa 14:49). Saul, insanely jealous of David, desired to kill him, but finding it impossible to do so by his own hands (18:11), he tried trickery. He offered David his elder daughter Merab for his service against the Philistines but changed his mind and gave her to another; then he learned that Michal loved David, so he offered her to David if he would give evidence of having killed a hundred Philistines. David killed two hundred and married Michal, but Saul hated him all the more. Once, when Saul sent some men to kill David, Michal helped him to escape (19:11 – 17), deceiving Saul's officers by putting an idol in his bed. Though Michal truly loved David, she could not comprehend him and so scoffed at him for rejoicing before the Lord (2Sa 6:16 – 23). As a result, she never had a child.

MIDIANITE(S) [4518, 4520] (mĭd′ĭăn- īt[s], Heb. *midhyān, midhānîm*).

> Descendants of Midian, son of Abraham by Keturah (Ge 25:1 – 2, 4; 1Ch 1:32 – 33)
> Called Ishmaelites (Ge 37:25, 28; Jdg 8:24)
> Were merchants (Ge 37:28)
> Bought Joseph and sold him to Potiphar (Ge 37:28, 36)
> Defeated by Israelites under Phinehas; five of their kings slain, the women taken captives, their cities burned, and rich spoils taken (Nu 31)
> Defeated by Gideon (Jdg 6 – 8)
> Owned multitudes of camels and large quantities of gold (Isa 60:6)
> A snare to the Israelites (Nu 25:16 – 18)
> Prophecies concerning (Isa 60:6; Hab 3:7)

MILLENNIUM Latin for "a thousand years," from Rev 20:1 – 15. It refers to a period when Christ rules and Satan is bound; when Jesus shall have triumphed over all forms of evil (1Co 15:24 – 28; 2Th 2:8; Rev 14:6 – 18; 19:11 – 16).

Amillenialists believe Jesus is reigning now. *Premillenialists* believe Jesus will literally reign on earth for a thousand years after his second coming. *Postmillenialists* believe the church will Christianize the world for a long period of time, after which Christ will return. *See Church, the Body of Believers; Jesus the Christ, Kingdom of, Second Coming of.*

> **General References to:**
> At the restoration of all things (Ac 3:21). When the creation shall be delivered from the corruption of evil (Ro 8:19 – 21). When the Son of Man

shall sit on the throne of his glory (Mt 19:28; Lk 22:28 – 30). The righteous shall be clothed with authority (Da 7:22; Mt 19:28; Lk 22:28 – 30; 1Co 6:2; Rev 2:5) and possess the kingdom (Mt 25:34; Lk 12:32; 22:29). Christ rules from his throne in Zion or Jerusalem (Isa 65:17 – 25; Zep 3:11 – 13; Zec 9:9 – 10; 14:16 – 21). Christ fulfills the promise of the kingdom of God on earth (Mt 16:18 – 19; 26:29; Mk 14:25; Heb 8:11).

MIND [2349, 4000, 4213, 4222, 5714, 5883, 8120, 10381, 10646, 1379, 2014, 2840, 3212, 3419, 3564, 3784, 3808, 5404, 5858, 5859, 6034]. A word for a number of Hebrew and Greek nouns in Scripture. Among the more important are the Hebrew *lebh*, "heart"; *nephesh*, "soul"; and the Greek *nous* and *dianoia*, the former denoting the faculty of reflective consciousness, of moral thinking and knowing, while the latter means "meditation, reflection." None of these words is used with any precision of meaning. In the NT the word "mind" frequently occurs in an ethical sense, as in Ro 7:25 and Col 2:18.

Nu	23:19	that he should change his **m**.
1Sa	15:29	Israel does not lie or change his **m**;
2Ch	30:12	the people to give them unity of **m**
Ps	26:2	examine my heart and my **m**;
Isa	26:3	him whose **m** is steadfast,
Jer	17:10	and examine the **m**,
Mt	22:37	all your soul and with all your **m**.'
Ac	4:32	believers were one in heart and **m**.
Ro	1:28	he gave them over to a depraved **m**
	8:6	The **m** of sinful man is death,
	12:2	by the renewing of your **m**.
	14:13	make up your **m** not
1Co	1:10	you may be perfectly united in **m**
	14:14	spirit prays, but my **m** is unfruitful.
2Co	13:11	be of one **m**, live in peace.
Php	3:19	Their **m** is on earthly things.
Col	2:18	and his unspiritual **m** puffs him up
1Th	4:11	to **m** your own business

MINISTER [2143, 6268, 6275, 6641, 9250, 692, 1354, 1355, 1356, 3302, 3311, 3313, 3364] (Heb. *shārath, shā-*

rēth, Gr. *diakonos, leitourgos, hypēretēs, servant*). Originally a servant, though distinguished from a slave who may work against his will, and a hireling, who works for wages. Joshua, as a young man, was "minister" to Moses (Ex 24:13 KJV; NIV "aide"), though in rank he was a prince of the tribe of Ephraim (Nu 13:8). As minister of Moses, he led the army of Israel against Amalek (Ex 17:8–16) and was permitted to ascend Mount Sinai with Moses. The queen of Sheba, visiting King Solomon, was amazed at the attendance (Hebrew "standing") of his ministers (1Ki 10:5 KJV). In the NT certain governmental offices are called "God's ministers" (Ro 13:6 KJV). The word *hypēretēs*, which originally meant "an under-rower," is also used for "minister": "And he closed the book and gave it back to the minister [most modern versions have "attendant"] and sat down" (Lk 4:20 KJV). The same word is used of John Mark (Ac 13:5) as an attendant of Paul and Barnabas. God himself has his ministers, the angels (Pss 103:21; 104:4 KJV; NIV "his servants"), who praise him and go about as his messengers. In Jer 33:21–22 God calls the priests of Israel his ministers, and this usage of the word for priests or religious leaders has come over into the Christian church. The Christian minister is not only a servant of God, but he should also make it his business to serve the local church to which he is attached; and lest this be thought to be a degradation of dignity, even our Lord declared, "For even the Son of Man did not come to be served, but to serve, and to give his life as a ransom for many" (Mk 10:45). The NT word *diakonos*, i.e., "deacon," means "minister" and indicates the duty as well as the privilege of the office. "Deacon" should not be confused with "elder" or "presbyter."

1. An officer in civil government. Joseph (Ge 41:40–44), Iri (2Sa 20:26), Zabud (1Ki 4:5), Ahithophel (1Ch 27:33), Zebadiah (2Ch 19:11), Elkanah (2Ch 28:7), Haman (Est 3:1), Mordecai (Est 10:3, w Est 8; 9), Daniel (Da 2:48; 6:1–3).

2. A sacred teacher.

MINISTRY [MINISTER]

Ac	6:4	to prayer and the **m** of the word."

Ro	11:13	I make much of my **m**
2Co	4:1	God's mercy we have this **m**,
	5:18	gave us the **m** of reconciliation:
	6:3	so that our **m** will not be
Gal	2:8	who was at work in the **m** of Peter
2Ti	4:5	discharge all the duties of your **m**.
Heb	8:6	But the **m** Jesus has received is

MIRACLES [4603, 7098, 7099, 1539, 2240, 4956, 5469]. The word "miracle" (Latin *miraculum*) literally means a marvelous event or an event that causes wonder. Some of the more important biblical words designating miracles are *thauma*, "wonder"; *pele'* and *teras*, "portent"; *gêvhurâh* and *dynamis*, "display of power"; *'ôth* and *sēmeion*, "sign."

The use of "miracle" in Christian theology includes, but goes beyond, the meanings of the ancient words. A miracle is (1) an extraordinary event, inexplicable in terms of ordinary natural forces, (2) an event that causes the observers to postulate a superhuman personal cause, or (3) an event that constitutes evidence (a "sign") of implications much wider than the event itself.

The majority of the miracles recorded in the Bible fall into three great epochs. First came the miracles of the exodus. The second epoch of miracles was centered in the ministry of Elijah and Elisha. The third epoch of miracles, the greatest in all recorded history, occurred in the ministry of Christ and his apostles

The purpose of miracles is revelation and edification.

General References to:
Called: marvelous things (Ps 78:12); marvelous works (Ps 105:5; Isa 29:14); signs and wonders (Jer 32:21; Jn 4:48; 2Co 12:12). Performed through the power of God (Jn 3:2; Ac 14:3; 15:12; 19:11); of the Holy Spirit (Mt 12:28; Ro 15:19; 1Co 12:9–10, 28–30); in the name of Christ (Mk 16:17; Ac 3:16; 4:30). Faith required in those who perform (Mt 17:20; 21:21; Jn 14:12; Ac 3:16; 6:8). Faith required in those for whom they were performed (Mt 9:28; Mk 9:22–24; Ac 14:9). Power to perform, given the disciples (Mk

3:14 – 15; 16:17 – 18, 20). Demanded by unbelievers (Mt 12:38 – 39; 16:1; Lk 11:16, 29; 23:8). Alleged miracles performed by magicians (Ex 7:10 – 12, 22; 8:7); by other impostors (Mt 7:22). Performed through the powers of evil (2Th 2:9; Rev 16:14). Done in support of false religions (Dt 13:1 – 2); by false Christs (Mt 24:24); by false prophets (Mt 24:24; Rev 19:20); by the medium of Endor (1Sa 28:7 – 14); by Simon (Ac 8:9 – 11). Not to be regarded (Dt 13:3). Deceive the ungodly (2Th 2:10 – 12; Rev 13:14; 19:20). A mark of apostasy (2Th 2:3, 9; Rev 13:13).

1Ch	16:12	his **m**, and the judgments he
Ne	9:17	to remember the **m** you performed
Job	5:9	**m** that cannot be counted.
Ps	77:11	I will remember your **m** of long ago
	77:14	You are the God who performs **m**;
	106:7	they gave no thought to your **m**;
Mt	7:22	out demons and perform many **m**?'
	11:20	most of his **m** had been performed,
	11:21	If the **m** that were performed
	13:58	And he did not do many **m** there
	24:24	and perform great signs and **m**
Mk	6:2	does **m**! Isn't this the carpenter?
	6:5	He could not do any **m** there,
	13:22	and **m** to deceive the elect —
Lk	10:13	For if the **m** that were performed
	19:37	for all the **m** they had seen:
Jn	7:3	disciples may see the **m** you do.
	10:25	**m** I do in my Father's name speak
	10:32	"I have shown you many great **m**
	10:38	do not believe me, believe the **m**,
	14:11	the evidence of the **m** themselves.
	15:24	But now they have seen these **m**,
Ac	2:22	accredited by God to you by **m**,
	8:13	by the great signs and **m** he saw.
	19:11	God did extraordinary **m**
Ro	15:19	by the power of signs and **m**,
1Co	12:28	third teachers, then workers of **m**,
	12:29	Are all teachers? Do all work **m**?
2Co	12:12	and **m** — were done among you
Gal	3:5	work **m** among you because you
2Th	2:9	in all kinds of counterfeit **m**,

Heb	2:4	it by signs, wonders and various **m**,

MIRACULOUS [MIRACLES]

Dt	13:1	and announces to you a **m** sign
Mt	12:39	generation asks for a **m** sign!
	13:54	this wisdom and these **m** powers?"
Jn	2:11	This, the first of his **m** signs,
	2:23	people saw the **m** signs he was
	3:2	could perform the **m** signs you are
	4:48	"Unless you people see **m** signs
	7:31	will he do more **m** signs
	9:16	"How can a sinner do such **m** signs
	20:30	Jesus did many other **m** signs
Ac	2:43	**m** signs were done by the apostles.
1Co	1:22	Jews demand **m** signs and Greeks
	12:10	to another **m** powers,

MIRIAM [5319] (mĭr′ĭ-ăm, Heb. *miryām*, various suggested meanings: *bitterness*, *plump one*, *the wished-for child*, *one who loves* or *is loved*). The daughter of Amram and Jochebed and the sister of Moses and Aaron (Nu 26:59; 1Ch 6:3). She showed concern and wisdom in behalf of her infant brother Moses when he was discovered in the Nile by the Egyptian princess (Ex 2:4, 7 – 8). Miriam first appears by name in Ex 15:20, where she is called a prophetess and is identified as the sister of Aaron. After passing through the Red Sea, she led the Israelite women in dancing and instrumental accompaniment while she sang the song of praise and victory (15:20 – 21). In Nu 12:1 Miriam and Aaron criticized Moses for his marriage to a Cushite woman. Because of this criticism, Miriam was punished by the Lord with leprosy (12:9), but on the protest of Aaron and the prayer of Moses (12:11, 13), she was restored after a period of seven days, during which she was isolated from the camp and the march was delayed. Her case of leprosy is cited in Dt 24:9. Miriam died at Kadesh and was buried there (Nu 20:1). Micah refers to her along with her brothers as leaders whom the Lord provided to bring Israel out of the Egyptian bondage (Mic 6:4).

MISSIONS [1355]. Spreading the good news throughout the world.

General References to:

Religious propagandism (2Ki 17:27 – 28; 1Ch 16:23 – 24). Commanded (Ps 96:3, 10; Mt 28:19; Mk 16:15; Lk 24:47 – 48). Prophecy concerning (Mt 24:14; Mk 13:10). Peter's vision concerning (Ac 10:9 – 20). Ordained by Jesus (Mt 24:14; 28:19; Mk 16:15 – 16; Lk 24:47 – 49). Saul and Barnabas ordained for (Ac 13:2 – 4, 47). Paul appointed to (Ac 26:14 – 18; 1Co 16:9). Practiced by the psalmist (Ps 18:49); by Jonah (Jnh 3:1 – 9). Symbolized by the flying angel (Rev 14:6 – 7). Missionary hymn (Ps 96). The first to do homage to the Messiah were Gentiles (Mt 2:11).

MOAB [824+4566, 4565, 4566, 4566+8441, 4567] (mo'ab, Heb. *mô'av, seed*).

1. Grandson of Lot by incest with his elder daughter (Ge 19:30 – 38).

2. The nation or people descended from Moab. They settled first at Ar, just east of the southern part of the Dead Sea and quite close to the site of the destroyed cities of the plain.

3. The land of the Moabites. Moab was bounded on the west by the Dead Sea, on the east by the desert, on the north by the Arnon, and on the south by Edom. It is about 3,200 feet (1,000 m.) above sea level and is chiefly rolling country, well adapted for pasturage. Machaerus, the place where John the Baptist was imprisoned and lost his life, was in Moab.

Plains of:

Israelites come in (Dt 2:17 – 18). Military forces numbered in (Nu 26:3, 63). The law rehearsed in, by Moses (Nu 35 – 36; Dt 29 – 33). The Israelites renew their covenant in (Dt 29:1). The land of promise allotted in (Jos 13:32).

MOABITE(S) [408+4566, 1201+4566, 4566, 4567].

Descendants of Lot through his son Moab (Ge 19:37).
Called the people of Chemosh (Nu 21:29).

The territory east of Jordan, bounded on the north by the Arnon River (Nu 21:13; Jdg 11:18).
Israelites commanded not to distress the Moabites (Dt 2:9).
Refuse passage of Jephthah's army through their territory (Jdg 11:17 – 18).
Balak was king of (Nu 22:4), calls for Balaam to curse Israel (Nu 22 – 24; Jos 24:9; Mic 6:5).
Snare to the Israelites (Nu 25:1 – 3; Ru 1:4; 1Ki 11:1; 1Ch 8:8; Ezr 9:1 – 2; Ne 13:23).
Land of, not given to the Israelites as a possession (Dt 2:9, 29).
David takes refuge among, from Saul (1Sa 22:3 – 4).
David conquers (2Sa 8:2; 23:20; 1Ch 11:22; 18:2 – 11).
Israelites at war with (2Ki 3:5 – 27; 13:20; 24:2; 2Ch 20).
Prophecies concerning judgments upon (Jer 48).

MOLECH, MOLOCH [4891, 4903, 4904, 3661] (mō'lĕk, mō'lŏk, Heb. *ha-mōle; "shameful" king*). Molech is the deliberate misvocalization of the name of a pagan god. The consonants for the word *king, melek,* are combined with the vowels for shame, *bosheth.* A heathen god, especially of the Ammonites, who was worshiped with gruesome orgies in which children were sacrificed. At least in some places an image of the god was heated and the bodies of children who had just been slain were placed in its arms. The worship of Molech was known to Israel before they entered Canaan, for Moses very sternly forbade its worship (Lev 18:21; 20:1 – 5). In spite of this prohibition, King Solomon, to please his numerous heathen wives, set up high places for Chemosh and for Molech on Mount Olivet (1Ki 11:7), though Molech's principal place of worship in and after Manasseh's time was the valley of Ben Hinnom (2Ch 33:6), a place of such ill repute that Gehenna ("the valley of Hinnom") became a type for hell (Mt 5:29 – 30).

General References to:

An idol of the Ammonites (Ac 7:43). Worshiped by the wives of Solomon and by Solomon (1Ki 11:1 – 8). Children sacrificed to (2Ki 23:10, w Jer 32:35; 2Ki 16:3; 21:6; 2Ch 28:3; Isa 57:5; Jer 7:31; Eze 16:20 – 21; 20:26, 31; 23:37, 39, w Lev 18:21; 20:2 – 5).

MONEY [4084, 10362, 736, 921, 2238, 3142, 3440, 5507, 5910, 5975]. Silver used as (Ge 17:12 – 13, 23, 27; 20:16; 23:9, 13; 31:15; 37:28; 42:25 – 35; 43:12 – 23; 44:1 – 8; 47:14 – 18; Ex 12:44; 21:11, 21, 34 – 35; 22:7, 17, 25; 30:16; Lev 22:11; 25:37, 51; 27:15, 18; Nu 3:48 – 51; 18:16; Dt 2:6, 28; 14:25 – 26; 21:14; 23:19; Jdg 5:19; 16:18; 17:4; 1Ki 21:2, 6, 15; 2Ki 5:26; 12:4, 7 – 16; 15:20; 22:7, 9; 23:35; 2Ch 24:5, 11, 14; 34:9, 14, 17; Ezr 3:7; 7:7; Ne 5:4, 10 – 11; Est 4:7; Job 31:39; Ps 15:5; Pr 7:20; Ecc 7:12; 10:19; Isa 43:24; 52:3; 55:1 – 2; Jer 32:9 – 10, 25, 44; La 5:4; Mic 3:11; Mt 25:18, 27; 28:12, 15; Mk 14:11; Lk 9:3; 19:15, 23; 22:5; Ac 7:16; 8:20). Gold used as (Ge 13:2; 24:35; 44:8, w 44:1; 1Ch 21:25; Ezr 8:25 – 27; Isa 13:17; 46:6; 60:9; Eze 7:19; 28:4; Mt 2:11; 10:9; Ac 3:6; 20:33; 1Pe 1:18). Copper used as (Mt 10:9; Mk 6:8; 12:42; Lk 21:2). Weighed (Ge 23:16; 43:21; Job 28:15; Jer 32:9 – 10; Zec 11:12). Image on (Mt 22:20 – 21). Conscience (Jdg 17:2; Mt 27:3, 5). Ransom atonement (Ex 30:12 – 16; Lev 5:15 – 16). Sin offering (2Ki 12:16). Value of, varied corruptly (Am 8:5). Love of, the root of evil (1Ti 6:10). *See Materialism; Shekel; Talent.*

Pr	13:11	Dishonest **m** dwindles away,
Ecc	5:10	Whoever loves **m** never has **m**
Mt	6:24	You cannot serve both God and **M**.
	27:5	Judas threw the **m** into the temple
Lk	3:14	"Don't extort **m** and don't accuse
Ac	5:2	part of the **m** for himself,
1Co	16:2	set aside a sum of **m** in keeping
1Ti	3:3	not quarrelsome, not a lover of **m**.
	6:10	For the love of **m** is a root
2Ti	3:2	lovers of **m**, boastful, proud,
Heb	13:5	free from the love of **m**
1Pe	5:2	not greedy for **m**, but eager to serve

MONEY CHANGERS [3142]. Those who changed foreign currency into sanctuary money at a profit (Mt 21:12; Mk 11:15; Jn 2:14 – 15).

MONOTHEISM (mŏn'ō-thē-ĭzm, from Gr. *monos*, one, *theos*, god). The doctrine or belief that there is but one God. *Atheism* is the belief that there is no god; *polytheism*, that there is more than one god; *monolatry*, the worship of one god as supreme, without denying there are other gods; and *henotheism*, belief in one god, though not to the exclusion of belief in others. There are three great monotheistic religions: Judaism, Christianity, and Islam, the latter two having their origin in the first. The Christian doctrine of the Trinity does not conflict with the monotheism of the OT. Rather, the manifold revelation of God contained in the OT is crystallized in the NT into the supreme doctrine of the three persons. *See also Jehovah.*

MONTH [2544, 3732, 10333, 3604, 5485, 5564]. Sun and moon serve as signs to marktime and seasons (Ge 1:14). Date marking the beginning and ending of the flood (Ge 7:11; 8:4). Twelve months reckoned to a year (1Ki 4:7; 1Ch 27:1 – 15; Est 2:12). Time computed by months (Ge 29:14; Nu 10:10; Jdg 11:37; 1Sa 6:1; Ps 81:3; Rev 22:2). Months in prophecy (Rev 11:2). The Jewish calender is as follows:

1. **Abib** (postexilic name: **Nisan**) **March – April** Month 7 in civil sequence.

2. **Ziv** (postexilic name: **Iyyar**) **April – May** Month 8 in civil sequence.

3. **Sivan** (postexilic name) **May – June** Month 9 in civil sequence.

4. **Tammuz** (postexilic name) **June – July** Month 10 in civil sequence.

5. **Ab** (postexilic name) **July – August** Month 11 in civil sequence.

6. **Elul** (postexilic name) **August – September** Month 12 in civil sequence.

7. **Ethanim** (postexilic name: **Tishri**) **September – October** Month 1 in civil sequence.

8. **Bul** (postexilic name: **Marcheshvan**) **October – November** Month 2 in civil sequence.

9. **Kislev** (postexilic name) **November – December** Month 3 in civil sequence.

10. **Tebeth** (postexilic name) **December – January** Month 4 in civil sequence.

11. **Shebat** (postexilic name) **January – February** Month 5 in civil sequence.

12. **Adar** (postexilic name) **February – March** Month 6 in civil sequence.

MORDECAI [5283] (môr′dē-kī Heb. *mordekhay*, from *Marduk*, chief god of Babylon).

1. A leader of the people of Judah during the return of Zerubbabel from exile (Ezr 2:2; Ne 7:7).

2. The deliverer of the Jews in the book of Esther. He was a Benjamite who had been deported during the reign of Jehoiachin (Est 2:5 – 6). He lived in Susa (KJV "Shushan"), the Persian capital, and brought up his cousin Esther, whose parents were dead (2:7). When Esther was taken into the royal harem, Mordecai forbade her to reveal her nationality (2:20), yet he remained in close connection with her. Mordecai discovered at the palace gate a plot against the king. By informing Esther of the plot, he secured the execution of the two eunuchs responsible (2:19 – 23). When Haman was made chief minister, Mordecai aroused his wrath by refusing to bow before him. To avenge the slight, Haman procured from the king a decree to destroy the Jews (ch. 3). Mordecai then sent Esther to the king to seek protection for her people (ch. 4). Haman meanwhile prepared a high gallows on which he planned to hang Mordecai (ch. 5). By a singular, highly dramatic series of events, Haman fell from favor and was hanged on the gallows he had prepared for Mordecai (ch. 7). Mordecai succeeded him as chief minister of the king (ch. 8). Thus the Persian officials everywhere assisted the Jews, who killed their enemies and instituted the Feast of Purim to celebrate their deliverance (ch. 9). The book of Esther ends with an account of the fame and dignity of Mordecai (ch. 10). In the apocryphal additions to Esther, Mordecai is glorified still more. He is a favorite character in rabbinical literature also.

MORIAH [5317] (mō-rī′a, Heb. *môrîyâh*). A land or district where Abraham was told to offer up Isaac (Ge 22:2). It was about a three-day journey from Beersheba where Abraham was living when given the command. Its location is not given. Jewish tradition has identified it with Jerusalem; Samaritan tradition identifies it with Mount Gerizim. According to 2Ch 3:1, Solomon built the temple on Mount Moriah where God had appeared to David (1Ch 21:15 – 22:1). Whether this is the same Mount Moriah mentioned in the account of Abraham is not certain.

MOSES [5407, 10441, 3707] (Heb. *mōseheh*, Egyp. *mes*, *drawn out*, *born*). The national hero who delivered the Israelites from Egyptian slavery, established them as an independent nation, and prepared them for entrance into Canaan. Exact dates for the life of Moses are dependent on the date of the exodus. On the basis of an early date for the exodus, c. 1440 BC, Moses was born about 1520. Some scholars date the exodus as late as 1225.

Personal History:

A Levite and son of Amram (Ex 2:1 – 4; 6:20; Ac 7:20; Heb 11:23). Hidden in a basket (Ex 2:3). Discovered and adopted by daughter of Pharaoh (Ex 2:5 – 10). Learned in all the wisdom of Egypt (Ac 7:22). Loyal to his race (Heb 11:24 – 26). Takes the life of an Egyptian; flees from Egypt; finds refuge among the Midianites (Ex 2:11 – 22; Ac 7:24 – 29). Joins himself to Jethro, priest of Midian; marries Jethro's daughter Zipporah; has two sons (Ex 2:15 – 22; 18:3 – 4). Is herdsman for Jethro in desert of Horeb (Ex 3:1). Has vision of burning bush (Ex 3:2 – 6). God reveals to him his purpose to deliver Israelites and bring them into land of Canaan (Ex 3:7 – 10). Commissioned as leader of the Israelites (Ex 3:10 – 22; 6:13). His rod miraculously turned into a serpent, his hand made leprous, and each restored (Ex 4:1 – 9, 28). With his wife and sons, he leaves Jethro to perform his mission (Ex 4:18 – 20). His controversy with his wife on account of circumcision (Ex 4:20 – 26). Meets Aaron in the wilderness (Ex 4:27 – 28). With

Aaron assembles leaders of Israel (Ex 4:29–31). With Aaron goes before Pharaoh; in name of Yahweh demands liberty of his people (Ex 5:1). Rejected by Pharaoh; hardships of the Israelites increased (Ex 5). People murmur against Moses and Aaron (Ex 5:20–21; 15:24; 16:2–3; 17:2–3; Nu 14:2–4; 16:41; 20:2–5; 21:4–6; Dt 1:12, 26–28). See Israel. Receives comfort and assurance from the land (Ex 6:1–8). Unbelief of the people (Ex 6:9). Renews his appeal to Pharaoh (Ex 6:11). Under divine direction brings plagues on land of Egypt (Ex 7–12). Secures deliverance of the people and leads them out of Egypt (Ex 13). Crosses the Red Sea; Pharaoh and his army are destroyed (Ex 14). Composes a song for the Israelites on their deliverance from Pharaoh (Ex 15). Joined by his family in wilderness (Ex 18:1–12). Institutes a system of government (Ex 18:13–26; Nu 11:16–30; Dt 1:9–18). Receives the law and ordains various statutes. See Law of Moses. Face of, transfigured (Ex 34:29–35; 2Co 3:13). Sets up tabernacle. See Tabernacle. Reproves Aaron for making golden calf (Ex 32:22–23); for irregularity in offerings (Lev 10:16–20). Jealousy of Aaron and Miriam toward (Nu 12). Rebellion of Korah, Dathan, and Abiram against (Nu 16). Appoints Joshua as his successor (Nu 27:22–23; Dt 31:7–8, 14, 23; 34:9). Not permitted to enter Canaan, but views land from top of Pisgah (Nu 27:12–14; Dt 3:17, 23–29; 32:48–52; 34:1–8). Death and burial of (Nu 31:2; Dt 32:50; 34:1–6). Body of, disputed over (Jude 9). One hundred and twenty years old at death (Dt 31:2). Mourning for, thirty days in plains of Moab (Dt 34:8). His virility (Dt 31:2; 34:7). Present with Jesus on Mount of Transfiguration (Mt 17:3–4; Mk 9:4; Lk 9:30). Type of Christ (Dt 18:15–18; Ac 3:22; 7:37).

Character of:

Murmurings of (Ex 5:22–23; Nu 11:10–15). Impatience of (Ex 5:22–23; 6:12; 32:19; Nu 11:10–15; 16:15; 20:10; 31:14). Respected and feared (Ex 33:8). Faith of (Nu 10:29; Dt 9:1–3; Heb 11:23–28). Called man of God (Dt 33:1). God

spoke to, as a man to his friend (Ex 33:11). Magnified of God (Ex 19:9; Nu 14:12–20; Dt 9:13–29, w Ex 32:30). Magnanimity of, toward Eldad and Medad (Nu 11:29). Meekness of (Ex 14:13–14; 15:24–25; 16:2–3, 7–8; Nu 12:3; 16:4–11). Obedience of (Ex 7:6; 40:16, 19, 21). Unaspiring (Nu 14:12–20; Dt 9:13–29, w Ex 32:30).

Prophecies of:

(Ex 3:10; 4:5, 11–12; 6:13; 7:2; 17:16; 19:3–9; 33:11; Nu 11:17; 12:7–8; 36:13; Dt 1:3; 5:31; 18:15, 18; 34:10, 12; Hos 12:13; Mk 7:9–10; Ac 7:37–38).

MOSES, ASSUMPTION OF Pseudonymous Jewish apocalyptic book, probably written early in first century AD; gives prophecy of future of Israel. Possibly quoted in Jude 9.

MOTHER [562, 851, 1485, 3528, 298, 1222, 1666, 3120, 3613, 3836, 5577].

Relationship with:

Reverence for, commanded (Ex 20:12; Lev 19:3; Dt 5:16; Pr 23:22; Mt 15:4; 19:19; Mk 7:10; 10:19; Lk 18:20; Eph 6:2). To be obeyed (Dt 21:18; Pr 1:8; 6:20). Love for (1Ki 19:20). Must be subordinate to love for Christ (Mt 10:37). Dishonoring of, to be punished (Ex 21:15; Lev 20:9; Pr 20:20; 28:24; 30:11, 17; Mt 15:4–6; Mk 7:10–12). Incest with, forbidden (Lev 18:7). Sanctifying influence of (1Co 7:14; 2Ti 1:5). Wicked (Ge 27:6–17; 2Ki 11:1–3).

Love of:

(Isa 49:15; 66:13). Exemplified by: Hagar (Ge 21:14–16); mother of Moses (Ex 2:1–3); Hannah (1Sa 1:20–28); Rizpah (2Sa 21:8–11); Bathsheba (1Ki 1:16–21); mother whose child was brought to Solomon (1Ki 3:16–26); woman whose sons were to be taken for debt (2Ki 4:1–7); Shunammite (2Ki 4:18–37); Mary the mother of Jesus (Lk 2:41–50); bereaved mothers of Bethlehem (Mt 2:16–18); Syrian Phoenician woman (Mt 15:21–28; Mk 7:24–30). Grieves

over wayward children (Pr 10:1; 19:26; 29:15). Rejoices over good children (Pr 23:23 – 25).

Ge	2:24	and **m** and be united to his wife,
Ex	20:12	"Honor your father and your **m**,
Lev	20:9	" 'If anyone curses his father or **m**,
Dt	5:16	"Honor your father and your **m**,
Jdg	5:7	arose a **m** in Israel.
Ps	113:9	as a happy **m** of children.
Pr	10:1	but a foolish son grief to his **m**.
	23:22	do not despise your **m**
	23:25	May your father and **m** be glad;
	29:15	a child left to himself disgraces his **m**.
	30:17	that scorns obedience to a **m**,
Isa	49:15	"Can a **m** forget the baby
	66:13	As a **m** comforts her child,
Mt	10:35	a daughter against her **m**,
	12:48	He replied to him, "Who is my **m**,
	15:4	'Honor your father and **m**'
	19:5	and **m** and be united to his wife,
Lk	11:27	"Blessed is the **m** who gave you
	18:20	honor your father and **m**.' "
Jn	19:27	to the disciple, "Here is your **m**."
Gal	4:26	is above is free, and she is our **m**.
Eph	5:31	and **m** and be united to his wife,
	6:2	"Honor your father and **m**" —
1Th	2:7	like a **m** caring for her little

MOURN, MOURNING [61, 63, 65, 1134, 5027, 5631, 5653, 6199, 7722, 9302, 4292, 4291, 3081, 3164]. The ancient Hebrews placed a much greater emphasis on external symbolic acts than do modern Western people; people in the East today still carry on this respect for symbolic actions. Ceremonies for expressing grief at the death of a relative or on any unhappy occasion are referred to frequently in the Bible. One reared in the modern West must be careful not to view these public expressions as hypocritical; they were a natural valid manifestation of grief in that culture.

For the Dead:
 Head uncovered (Lev 10:6; 21:10); lying on ground (2Sa 12:16); personal appearance neglected (2Sa 14:2); cutting the flesh (Lev 19:28; 21:1 – 5; Dt 14:1; Jer 16:6 – 7; 41:5); lamen-tations (Ge 50:10; Ex 12:30; 1Sa 30:4; Jer 22:18; Mt 2:17 – 18); fasting (1Sa 31:13; 2Sa 1:12; 3:35). Priests prohibited, except for nearest of kin (Lev 21:1 – 11). For Nadab and Abihu forbidden (Lev 10:6). Sexes separated in (Zec 12:12, 14). Hired mourners (2Ch 35:25; Ecc 12:5; Jer 9:17; Mt 9:23). Abraham mourned for Sarah (Ge 23:2); Egyptians, for Jacob seventy days (Ge 50:1 – 3); Israelites, for Aaron thirty days (Nu 20:29). David's lamentations over death of Saul and his sons (2Sa 1:17 – 27); death of Abner (2Sa 3:33 – 34); death of Absalom (2Sa 18:33). Jeremiah and the singing men and women lament for Josiah (2Ch 35:25).

For Calamities and Other Sorrows:
 Tearing the garments (Ge 37:29, 34; 44:13; Nu 14:6; Jdg 11:35; 2Sa 1:2, 11; 3:31; 13:19, 31; 15:32; 2Ki 2:12; 5:8; 6:30; 11:14; 19:1; 22:11, 19; Ezr 9:3, 5; Job 1:20; 2:12; Isa 37:1; Jer 41:5; Mt 26:65; Ac 14:14). Wearing mourning dress (Ge 38:14; 2Sa 14:2). See Sackcloth. Cutting or plucking off the hair and beard (Ezr 9:3; Jer 7:29). Covering head and face (2Sa 15:30; 19:4; Est 6:12; Jer 14:3 – 4); upper lip (Lev 13:45; Eze 24:17, 22; Mic 3:7). Laying aside ornaments (Ex 33:4, 6). Walking barefoot (2Sa 15:30; Isa 20:2). Laying hand on head (2Sa 13:19; Jer 2:37). Ashes put on head (Eze 27:30). Dust on head (Jos 7:6). Dressing in black (Jer 14:2). Sitting on ground (Isa 3:26). Caused ceremonial defilement (Nu 19:11 – 16; 31:19; Lev 21:1). Prevented offerings from being accepted (Dt 26:14; Hos 9:4).

Ecc	3:4	a time to **m** and a time to dance,
Isa	61:2	to comfort all who **m**,
Mt	5:4	Blessed are those who **m**,
Ro	12:15	**m** with those who **m**.

MURDER [1947, 2222, 4637, 5782, 8357, 5377, 5838, 5839, 5840]. From the days of Noah the biblical penalty for murder was death: "Whoever sheds the blood of man, by man shall his blood be shed" (Ge 9:6). Throughout OT times, the ancient Semitic custom of the avenger of blood was followed: a murdered man's nearest relative (the *goel*) had the duty to pursue the murderer and kill him (Nu 35:19). Since in the practice of avenging blood in this fashion men failed to distinguish between murder and manslaughter, and vicious blood feuds would frequently arise, the Mosaic law provided for cities of refuge (Nu 35). To these cities a person pursued by the avenger of blood could flee. He would be admitted and tried; if judged guilty of murder, he would be turned over to the avenger; if judged innocent, he was afforded protection in this city from the avenger. It appears likely that the advent of the monarchy began a trend away from the ancient *goel* custom, for we find the king putting a murderer to death (1Ki 2:34) and pardoning another (2Sa 14:6–8).

In a murder trial, the agreeing testimony of at least two persons was necessary for conviction (Nu 35:30; Dt 17:6). An animal known to be vicious had to be confined, and if it caused the death of anyone, it was destroyed and the owner held guilty of murder (Ex 21:29, 31).

The right of asylum in a holy place was not granted a murderer; he was dragged away even from the horns of the altar (Ex 21:14; 1Ki 2:28–34). No ransom could be accepted for a murderer (Nu 35:21). When a murder had been committed and the killer could not be found, the people of the community nearest the place where the corpse was found were reckoned guilty. To clear them of guilt, the elders of that community would kill a heifer, wash their hands over it, state their innocence, and thus be judged clean (Dt 21:1–9).

Ex	20:13	"You shall not **m**.
Pr	28:17	A man tormented by the guilt of **m**
Mt	5:21	'Do not **m**, and anyone who
	15:19	**m**, adultery, sexual immorality,
Ro	1:29	**m**, strife, deceit and malice.
	13:9	"Do not **m**," "Do not steal,"
Jas	2:11	adultery," also said, "Do not **m**."

MUSIC

Ge	31:27	singing to the **m** of tambourines
Jdg	5:3	I will make **m** to the LORD,
1Ch	6:32	They ministered with **m**
	25:7	and skilled in **m** for the LORD —
Ne	12:27	and with the **m** of cymbals,
Job	21:12	They sing to the **m** of tambourine
Ps	27:6	and make **m** to the LORD.
	33:2	make **m** to him on the ten-stringed
	57:7	I will sing and make **m**.
	81:2	Begin the **m**, strike the tambourine,
	87:7	As they make **m** they will sing,
	92:1	and make **m** to your name,
	95:2	and extol him with **m** and song.
	98:4	burst into jubilant song with **m**;
	108:1	make **m** with all my soul.
Isa	30:32	will be to the **m** of tambourines
La	5:14	young men have stopped their **m**.
Eze	26:13	**m** of your harps will be heard no
Da	3:5	lyre, harp, pipes and all kinds of **m**,
Lk	15:25	came near the house, he heard **m**
Eph	5:19	make **m** in your heart to the Lord,
Rev	18:22	The **m** of harpists and musicians,

MYRRH [4320, 5255, 3693, 5043, 5046]. A fragrant gum. A product of the land of Canaan (SS 4:6, 14; 5:1). One of the compounds in the sacred anointing oil (Ex 30:23). Used as a perfume (Est 2:12; Ps 45:8; Pr 7:17; SS 3:6; 5:13). Brought by wise men as a present to Jesus (Mt 2:11). Offered to Jesus on the cross (Mk 15:23). Used for embalming (Jn 19:39). Trade in (Ge 37:25; 43:11).

Ps	45:8	All your robes are fragrant with **m**
SS	1:13	My lover is to me a sachet of **m**
Mt	2:11	of gold and of incense and of **m**.
Mk	15:23	offered him wine mixed with **m**,
Jn	19:39	Nicodemus brought a mixture of **m**
Rev	18:13	of incense, **m** and frankincense,

MYSTERY (Gr. *mystērion*). The Greek word occurs twenty-eight times in the NT (including 1Co 2:1 where it appears in the better MSS; see NIV note). Neither the word nor the idea is found in the OT. Rather, they came into the NT world from Greek paganism. Among the Greeks, *mystery* meant not something obscure or incomprehensible, but a secret imparted only to the initiated, what is unknown until it is revealed. This word is connected with the mystery religions of Hellenistic times (*see Mystery Religions*). The mysteries appealed to the emotions rather than the intellect and offered to their devotees a mystical union with the deity, through death to life, thus securing for them a blessed immortality. Great symbolism characterized their secret ritual, climaxing in the initiation into the full secret of the cult.

The chief use of mystery in the NT is by Paul. He, as an educated man of his day, knew well the thought world of the pagans and accepted this term to indicate the fact that "his gospel" had been revealed to him by the risen Christ. This fact could best be made clear to his contemporaries by adopting the pagan term they all understood, pouring into it a special Christian meaning.

In a few passages the term refers to a symbol, allegory, or parable, which conceals its meaning from those who look only at the literal sense, but is the medium of revelation to those who have the key to its interpretation. See Mk 4:11 (NIV "secret");

Eph 5:32; and Rev 1:20; 17:5, 7, where marriage is a mystery or symbol of Christ and the church.

The more common meaning of mystery in the NT, Paul's usual use of the word, is that of a divine truth once hidden but now revealed in the gospel (Ro 16:25 – 26; Col 1:26; Eph 3:3 – 6). A mystery is thus *now* a revelation: Christian mysteries are revealed doctrines (Ro 16:26; Eph 1:9; 3:3, 5, 10; 6:19; Col 4:3 – 4; 1Ti 3:16). Christianity, therefore, has no secret doctrines, as did the ancient mystery religions.

MYSTERY RELIGIONS Greco-Roman religious movement that thrived from c. 700 BC to AD 400. To gain access to the divine mysteries, specially appointed priests carefully prepared individuals through stages of initiation, instruction, and secret revelation. The enlighted were then joined with the divine and could receive healing, success, and immortality. Though the word "mystery" is used in the NT (Ro 11:25; 16:25; 1Co 15:51; Eph 3:3 – 9), the openness of the preaching of the gospel makes it clear that Christianity is not a mystery religion. *See Mystery.*

NAHUM [5699, 3725] (nā'hŭm, Heb. *nahûm, compassionate* or *comfort*). The name is a shortened form of *Nehemiah*.

1. Nahum the Elkoshite. Of this prophet and his city of Elkosh nothing is known outside of the book that bears his name (Na 1:1). *See Nahum, Book of.*

2. One of the ancestors of Christ mentioned in Lk 3:25 (KJV "Naum").

NAHUM, BOOK OF The short book of Nahum is largely a poem, a literary masterpiece, predicting the downfall of Nineveh, the capital of Assyria. Nineveh was conquered by the Babylonians, Medes, and Scythians in 612 BC. Nahum declared that Nineveh would fall as did Thebes, which the Assyrians themselves had conquered in 663. The book therefore was written between 663 and 612 — in turbulent times. In 633 Ashurbanipal, the last great king of Assyria, died. Soon Babylon rebelled, and the Assyrian power rapidly dwindled. In Judah the wicked Manasseh reigned until about 641, followed by Amon's two-year reign and then the long reign of the good King Josiah (639 – 608). Perhaps it was in Josiah's day that Nahum prophesied the overthrow of the mighty nation that had so oppressed the Jews. Zephaniah also predicted in Josiah's time the overthrow of Nineveh (Zep 1:1; 2:13).

The book of Nahum is in two parts: First, a poem concerning the greatness of God (Na 1:2 – 15), then another and longer poem detailing the overthrow of Nineveh (2:1 – 3:19). The impassioned expressions of Nahum can be better understood when we remember how Assyria had overthrown the northern kingdom of Israel in 722 BC and had later taken forty cities of Judah captive, deporting more than 200,000 people — according to Sennacherib's own boast in his royal annals (cf. 2Ki 18:13). The cruelty of the Assyrians is almost beyond belief. Their policy seems to have been one of calculated terror. Their own pictures show captives staked to

the ground and being skinned alive. No wonder Nahum exulted at the overthrow of the proud, rich, cruel empire of Assyria.

Outline:

   I. Title (1:1).

  II. Nineveh's Judge (1:2 – 15).

    A. The Lord's kindness and sternness (1:2 – 8).

    B. Nineveh's overthrow and Judah's joy (1:9 – 15).

 III. Nineveh's Judgment (ch. 2).

    A. Nineveh besieged (2:1 – 10).

    B. Nineveh's desolation contrasted with its former glory (2:11 – 13).

 IV. Nineveh's Total Destruction (ch. 3).

    A. Nineveh's sins (3:1 – 4).

    B. Nineveh's doom (3:5 – 19).

NAME [606, 2352, 9005, 10721, 3306, 3950, 3951] (Heb. *shem*, Gr. *onoma*). In Bible times the notion of "name" had a significance it does not have today, when it is usually a personal label that does not carry significant meaning. A name was given only by a person in a position of authority (Ge 2:19; 2Ki 23:34) and signified that the person named was appointed to a particular position, function, or relationship (Ge 35:18; 2Sa 12:25). The name given was often determined by some circumstance at the time of birth (Ge 19:22); sometimes the name expressed a hope or a prophecy (Isa 8:1 – 4; Hos 1:4). When a person gave his own name to another, it signified the joining of the two in very close unity, as when God gave his name to Israel (Dt 28:9 – 10). To be baptized into someone's name therefore meant to pass into new ownership (Mt 28:19; Ac 8:16; 1Co 1:13, 15). In the Scriptures there is the closest possible relationship between a person and his or her name, the two being practically equivalent, so that to remove the name was to extinguish the person (Nu 27:4; Dt 7:24). To forget God's name is to depart from him (Jer 23:27). The name, moreover, was the person as he had been revealed; for example, the "name of the LORD" signified the Lord in the attributes he had manifested — holiness, power, love, etc. Often in the Bible the name signified the presence of the person in the character revealed (1Ki 18:24). To be sent or to speak in someone's name meant to carry that person's authority (Jer 11:21; 2Co 5:20). In later Jewish usage the name *Jehovah* was not pronounced in reading the Scriptures (cf. Wisdom 14:21), the name *Adhonai* ("my Lord") being substituted for it. To pray in the name of Jesus is to pray as his representatives on earth — in his Spirit and with his aim — and implies the closest union with Christ.

General References to:

Value of a good (Pr 22:1; Ecc 7:1). A new name given: to persons who have spiritual adoption (Isa 62:2); to Abraham (Ge 17:5); to Sarah (Ge 17:15); to Jacob (Ge 32:28); to Peter (Mt 16:18); to Paul (Ac 13:9). Intercessional influence of the name of Jesus. See Jesus the Christ. Symbolic (Hos 1:3 – 4, 6, 9; 2:1), of prestige (1Ki 1:47).

Ge	2:19	man to see what he would **n** them;
	4:26	to call on the **n** of the LORD.
	12:2	I will make your **n** great,
	32:29	Jacob said, "Please tell me your **n**."
Ex	20:7	"You shall not misuse the **n**
	34:14	for the LORD, whose **n** is Jealous,
Dt	5:11	"You shall not misuse the **n**
	12:11	choose as a dwelling for his **N** —
	18:5	minister in the LORD's **n** always.
1Sa	12:22	of his great **n** the LORD will not
2Sa	6:2	which is called by the **N**, the **n**
	7:9	Now I will make your **n** great,
1Ki	5:5	will build the temple for my **N**.'
2Ch	7:14	my people, who are called by my **n**,
Ne	9:10	You made a **n** for yourself,
Ps	8:1	how majestic is your **n**
	20:7	in the **n** of the LORD our God.
	29:2	to the LORD the glory due his **n**;
	34:3	let us exalt his **n** together.
	66:2	Sing the glory of his **n**;
	103:1	my inmost being, praise his holy **n**.
	138:2	your **n** and your word.
	147:4	and calls them each by **n**.

Pr	3:4	you will win favor and a good **n**
	18:10	**n** of the LORD is a strong tower;
	22:1	A good **n** is more desirable
	30:4	What is his **n**, and the **n** of his son?
Ecc	7:1	A good **n** is better
SS	1:3	your **n** is like perfume poured out.
Isa	12:4	thanks to the LORD, call on his **n**;
	26:8	your **n** and renown
	40:26	and calls them each by **n**.
	56:5	I will give them an everlasting **n**
	57:15	who lives forever, whose **n** is holy:
Jer	14:7	do something for the sake of your **n**
	15:16	for I bear your **n**,
Eze	20:9	of my **n** I did what would keep it
Da	12:1	everyone whose **n** is found written
Hos	12:5	the LORD is his **n** of renown!
Joel	2:32	on the **n** of the LORD will be saved
Mic	5:4	in the majesty of the **n**
Zep	3:9	call on the **n** of the LORD
Zec	6:12	is the man whose **n** is the Branch,
Mal	1:6	O priests, who show contempt for my **n**.
Mt	1:21	and you are to give him the **n** Jesus,
	6:9	hallowed be your **n**,
	18:20	or three come together in my **n**,
	24:5	For many will come in my **n**,
	28:19	them in the **n** of the Father
Mk	9:41	gives you a cup of water in my **n**
Jn	10:3	He calls his own sheep by **n**
	14:13	I will do whatever you ask in my **n**,
	16:24	asked for anything in my **n**.
Ac	2:21	on the **n** of the Lord will be saved.'
	4:12	for there is no other **n**
Ro	10:13	"Everyone who calls on the **n**
Php	2:9	him the **n** that is above every **n**,
Col	3:17	do it all in the **n** of the Lord Jesus,
Jas	5:14	him with oil in the **n** of the Lord.
1Jn	5:13	believe in the **n** of the Son of God
Rev	2:17	stone with a new **n** written on it,
	3:5	I will never blot out his **n**
	3:12	I will also write on him my new **n**.
	19:13	and his **n** is the Word of God.
	20:15	If anyone's **n** was not found written

NAOMI [5843] (nā'ō-mī, nā-ō'mǐ, Heb. *nā'ŏmî, my joy*). Wife of Elimelech of Bethlehem. Left without husband or sons, she returned from a sojourn in Moab with her Moabite daughter-in-law Ruth. In her depression she said she should no longer be called Naomi, "pleasantness," but now more appropriately Mara, "bitterness." She advised Ruth in the steps that led to Ruth's marriage to Boaz (Ru 3:1 – 6), and she nursed Ruth's child (4:16 – 17).

NAPHTALI [824+5889, 1201+ 5889, 5889, 3750] (năf'ta-lī, Heb. *naphtālî, wrestling*).

1. A son of Jacob. Naphtali was the second son of Bilhah, Rachel's handmaid. The name is a play on the word *pathal*, "fight" or "struggle." Of the patriarch himself practically nothing is known. He had four sons (Ge 46:24). Jacob's blessing for Naphtali was brief and noncommittal (49:21).

2. The tribe of Naphtali. Naphtali appears in the lists of Numbers as a tribe of moderate size. It furnished 53,400 soldiers at Kadesh Barnea (Nu 1:43) and 45,000 at the mustering of the troops across from Jericho (26:50). In the wilderness organization, Naphtali was supposed to camp on the north side of the tabernacle under the standard of Dan, and this group of tribes brought up the rear in marching. Interestingly, they settled together in Canaan. Naphtali's prince Ahira gave the last offering for the dedication of the altar (7:78). Naphtali received the next to the last lot in the final division of the land (Jos 19:32 – 39), but in many ways its inheritance was the best.

NATHAN [5990, 3718] (nā'thǎn, Heb. *nāthān, God has given, gift*).

1. The prophet at the royal court in Jerusalem during the reign of David and the early years of Solomon. David consulted him regarding the building of the temple (2Sa 7; 1Ch 17). Nathan at first approved, but that same night he had a vision directing him to advise David to leave the building of the temple to the son who would succeed him. David humbly obeyed, expressing gratitude to God for blessings bestowed and others promised. Later Nathan rebuked David for adultery with Bathsheba (2Sa 12:1 – 25). David earnestly repented. The title of Ps 51 links it with this incident. When Adonijah sought to supplant his aged father David as king, Nathan intervened through Bathsheba to secure the succession for her son Solomon (1Ki 1:8 – 53). Nathan wrote chronicles of the reign of David (1Ch 29:29) and shared in writing the history of the reign of Solomon (2Ch 9:29). He was associated with David and Gad the seer in arranging the musical services for the house of God (29:25).

2. A son of David, born to him after he began to reign in Jerusalem (2Sa 5:14; 1Ch 14:4). His mother was Bathshua, daughter of Ammiel (1Ch 3:5). He is named in the genealogy of Jesus Christ as son of David and father of Mattatha (Lk 3:31).

3. Nathan of Zobah, father of Igal, one of David's mighty men (2Sa 23:36). He may be the same as Nathan the brother of Joel (1Ch 11:38).

4. The two Nathans mentioned in 1Ki 4:5 as fathers of Azariah and Zabud may be the same man, and identified with no. 1, the prophet. If Zabad (1Ch 2:36) is the same as Zabud, his father Nathan may also be the prophet. In that case we know that the prophet's father was Attai, a descendant of Jerahmeel (2:25).

5. A leading man who returned from exile, whom Ezra sent on a mission (Ezr 8:16).

6. One of the returning exiles who had married a foreign wife and who put her away (Ezr 10:39).

Zechariah 12:12 prophesies that the house of Nathan will join on the day of the lord in mourning "the one they have pierced." It is probable that the descendants of the prophet (no. 1) are meant (12:10 – 14); but it is possible that the descendants of David's son (no. 2) are meant.

1. Prophet during reigns of David and Solomon; told David that not he but Solomon was to build the temple (2Sa 7; 1Ch 17), rebuked David for sin with Bathsheba (2Sa 12:1 – 25), helped get throne for Solomon (1Ki 1:8 – 53), wrote chronicles of reign of David (1Ch 29:29) and Solomon (2Ch 9:29), associated with David in arranging musical services for

house of God (2Ch 29:25). (2) Son of David (2Sa 5:14; 1Ch 14:4). (3) Father of Igal (2Sa 23:36). (4) Judahite (1Ch 2:36). (5) Israelite who returned from the exile (Ezr 8:16). (6) Man who put away his foreign wife (Ezr 10:39).

NATION

Ge	12:2	"I will make you into a great **n**
Ex	19:6	a kingdom of priests and a holy **n**.'
Dt	4:7	What other **n** is so great
Jos	5:8	And after the whole **n** had been
2Sa	7:23	one **n** on earth that God went out
Ps	33:12	Blessed is the **n** whose God is
Pr	11:14	For lack of guidance a **n** falls,
	14:34	Righteousness exalts a **n**,
Isa	2:4	**N** will not take up sword
	26:2	that the righteous **n** may enter,
	60:12	For the **n** or kingdom that will not
	65:1	To a **n** that did not call on my name
	66:8	a **n** be brought forth in a moment?
Mk	13:8	**N** will rise against **n**,
1Pe	2:9	a royal priesthood, a holy **n**,
Rev	5:9	and language and people and **n**.
	7:9	from every **n**, tribe, people
	14:6	to every **n**, tribe, language

NAZARENE [3716, 3717] (năz'a-rēn, Gr. *Nazarēnos*, *Nazōraios*, possibly *sprout*, *branch*).

1. A word derived from Nazareth, the birthplace of Christ. Jesus was often called a Nazarene. Used by his friends, it had a friendly meaning (Ac 2:22; 3:6; 10:38). Jesus applied the title to himself (22:8). Used by his enemies, it was a title of scorn (Mt 26:71; Mk 14:67). It is not altogether certain what Matthew intended in the words, "So was fulfilled what was said through the prophets: 'He will be called a Nazarene'" (Mt 2:23). It is usually thought that he refers to Isa 11:1, where the Messiah is called *netser*, or shoot out of the roots of Jesse. The name Nazareth was probably derived from the same root. Matthew sees a fulfillment of Isaiah's prophecy in Jesus' parents' taking up their residence in Nazareth.

2. In Ac 24:5 adherents of Christianity are called Nazarenes.

Mt	2:23	prophets: "He will be called a **N**."
Mk	14:67	"You also were with that **N**, Jesus,"
	16:6	"You are looking for Jesus the **N**,
Ac	24:5	He is a ringleader of the **N** sect and

NAZARETH [3714, 3716, 3717] (năz'a-rĕth, Gr. *Nazaret* and other forms, possibly *sprout*, *branch* or *watchtower*). A town in lower Galilee belonging to the tribe of Zebulun, nowhere referred to in the OT. It was the hometown of Mary and Joseph, the human parents of Jesus (Lk 1:26; 2:4). After their flight into Egypt to escape the ruthless hand of Herod the Great (Mt 2:13ff.), the holy family contemplated returning to Bethlehem of Judea. Hearing that Herod's son was now reigning in Judea, they withdrew to Nazareth in Galilee.

The rejection of Jesus Christ in the synagogue of Nazareth has been the cause of debate, whether indeed there were two rejections or merely one. Although the matter will never be entirely settled, it seems as if there were two such experiences in the life of Christ (cf. Lk 4:16 – 30 with Mk 6:1 – 6 and Mt 13:54 – 58). The first occurred at the beginning of the ministry of Jesus (Lk 4:14), the second on Christ's final visit to Nazareth (Mt 13:54ff.). The very exegetical structures of the accounts appear to make their own demands for two incidents, as in the first account (in Luke) there arose such great hostility that the congregation actually attempted to take his life. In the second instance a spirit of faithless apathy was the only noticeable reaction to his words. (Cf. Lk 4:29 – 31 with Mt 13:57 – 58.)

In regard to the city of Nazareth itself, the ancient site is located by the modern en-Natzirah, a Muslim village of about ten thousand inhabitants, on the most southern ranges of lower Galilee. Nazareth itself lies in a geographical basin so that not much of the surrounding countryside is in plain view. However, when one scales the edge of the basin, Esdraelon with its twenty battlefields and the place of Naboth's vineyard come into view. One can see for a distance of thirty miles (fifty km.) in three directions. Unfortunately, however, the people of Nazareth had established a rather poor reputation in morals and religion. This is seen in Nathanael's question: "Nazareth! Can anything good come from there?" (Jn 1:46).

Mt	4:13	Leaving **N**, he went and lived
Lk	4:16	to **N**, where he had been brought
Jn	1:46	"**N**! Can anything good come

NAZIRITE(S) [5687, 5693, 5694] (*one under sacred vow*). An Israelite who consecrated himself or herself and took a vow of separation and self-imposed abstinence for the purpose of some special service. The Nazirite vow included a renunciation of wine, prohibition of the use of the razor, and avoidance of contact with a dead body. The period of time for the vow was anywhere from thirty days to a lifetime (Nu 6:1 – 21; Jdg 13:5 – 7; Am 2:11, 12).

> **Instances of:**
> *Samson (Jdg 13:5, 7; 16:17). Samuel (1Sa 1:11). Recabites (Jer 35). John the Baptist (Mt 11:18; Lk 1:15; 7:33). See Abstinence; Wine.*

| Nu | 6:2 | of separation to the LORD as a **N**, |
| Jdg | 13:7 | because the boy will be a **N** of God |

NEBO (nē′bō Heb. *nevô*, Assyr. *Nabu*).

1. A god of Babylonian mythology. The special seat of his worship was the Babylonian city of Borsippa. He receives mention by Isaiah (Isa 46:1). Nebo was the god of science and learning. The thrust of Isaiah the prophet against him seems to be that Nebo himself, the imagined writer of the fate of all, is destined to go into captivity.

2. The name of the mountain from which Moses viewed the Promised Land (Dt 34:1ff.).

3. A Moabite town near or on Mount Nebo (Nu 32:3).

4. A town mentioned immediately after Bethel and Ai (Ezr 2:29; Ne 7:33).

NEBUCHADNEZZAR, NEBUCHADREZZAR [5556, 5557, 10453] (nĕb′u-kăd-nĕz′êr, nĕb′ū-kăd-rĕz′êr, *Nebo protect my boundary stone* BDB and IDB; *Nebo protect my son* KB). The great king of the Neo-Babylonian Empire who reigned from 605 to 562 BC. It was he who carried away Judah in the seventy-year Babylonian captivity. He figures prominently in the books of Jeremiah, Ezekiel, Daniel, and the later chapters of Kings and Chronicles. Until recently, not many of Nebuchadnezzar's historical records had been found, though his building inscriptions are numerous. Now the publication by Wiseman of Nebuchadnezzar's chronicle fills in some of the gaps. The name Nebuchadnezzar means "Nebo protect the boundary." The form Nebuchadrezzar is probably a minor variant.

Nebuchadnezzar is celebrated by the historians of antiquity for the splendor of his building operations as well as for the brilliance of his military exploits. With the passing of the brilliant Nebuchadnezzar, however, the Neo-Babylonian Empire soon crumbled and fell an easy prey to the Persians under Cyrus.

NEED

1Ki	8:59	Israel according to each day's **n**,
Ps	79:8	for we are in desperate **n**.
	116:6	when I was in great **n**, he saved me.
	142:6	for I am in desperate **n**;
Mt	6:8	for your Father knows what you **n**
Lk	15:14	country, and he began to be in **n**.
Ac	2:45	they gave to anyone as he had **n**.
1Co	12:21	say to the hand, "I don't **n** you!"
Eph	4:28	something to share with those in **n**.
1Ti	5:3	to those widows who are really in **n**
Heb	4:16	grace to help us in our time of **n**.
1Jn	3:17	sees his brother in **n** but has no pity

NEGEV [824+5582, 5582] (nĕg′ĕv, Nĕg′ĕb, *dry [land]*, hence *south country*). The desert region lying to the south of Judea, and hence the term has acquired the double meaning of the "south" (usually so rendered in the KJV), because of its direction from Judah, and the "desert," because of its aridity (Ge 12:9; 13:1; 20:1; Nu 13:29; 1Sa 27:5 – 6). It came to refer to a definite geographical region, as when we read concerning Abraham that he journeyed "into the south" (KJV; NIV "to the Negev") to Bethel (Ge 13:1).

NEHEMIAH [5718] (nē'hĕ-mī'a, Heb. *nehemyâh*, *Jehovah has comforted*).

1. One of the leaders of the returning exiles under Zerubbabel (Ezr 2:2; Ne 7:7).

2. The son of Azbuk, a prince of Beth Zur who helped repair the wall of Jerusalem (Ne 3:16).

3. The son of Hacaliah and governor of the Persian province of Judah after 444 BC. Of Nehemiah the son of Hacaliah little is known aside from what is in the book that bears his name. His times, however, are illuminated by the rather considerable material found in the Elephantine Papyri from Egypt, which were written in the fifth century. Nehemiah was a "cupbearer" to King Artaxerxes (Ne 1:11; 2:1). Inasmuch as some of the Elephantine Papyri that are contemporary with Nehemiah are dated, we know that this Artaxerxes must be the first, called Longimanus, who ruled 465 – 423 BC. The title "cupbearer" clearly indicates a responsible office — not merely a servile position — for the king speaks to Nehemiah as an intimate and also indicates that he regards Nehemiah's journey to Jerusalem only as a kind of vacation from official duties (2:6). Furthermore, the credentials given Nehemiah by the king and also the office of governor entrusted to him show that the king looked on him as a man of ability. Nehemiah was an officer of the palace at Susa, but his heart was in Jerusalem. Word came to him from Hanani, one of his brothers, of the ruined condition of Jerusalem. Overcome with grief, Nehemiah sought the refuge of prayer — and God answered abundantly.

Nehemiah was a man of ability, courage, and action. Arriving at Jerusalem, he first privately surveyed the scene of rubble (Ne 2:1 – 16), and he encouraged the rulers at Jerusalem with his report of answered prayer and the granting of the king's new decree (2:18). Then he organized the community to carry out the effort of rebuilding the bro-

ken-down wall. Courageously and squarely he met the opposition of men like Sanballat, Tobiah, and Geshem (who are all now known from nonbiblical documents); and at last he saw the wall completed in the brief span of fifty-two days (6:15).

Nehemiah cooperated with Ezra in numerous reforms and especially in the public instruction in the law (Ne 8). However, he left for Persia, probably on official business, in 431 BC (13:6). Later he returned to Jerusalem, but for how long we do not know. Of the end of his life we know nothing. The Elephantine Papyri indicate that a different man, Bagohi, was governor by 407 BC.

NEHEMIAH, BOOK OF The book of Nehemiah closes the history of the biblical period. Closely allied to the book of Ezra, it was attached to it in the old Jewish reckoning. It gives the history and reforms of Nehemiah the governor from 444 to about 420 BC.

Outline:

    I. Nehemiah Returns to Jerusalem (1:1 – 2:20).

    II. Building Despite Opposition (3:1 – 7:4).

    III. Genealogy of the First Returning Exiles (7:5 – 73 [= Ezr 2:2 – 70]).

    IV. The Revival and Covenant Sealing (8:1 – 10:39).

    V. Dwellers at Jerusalem and Genealogies (11:1 – 12:26).

    VI. Final Reforms (13:1 – 31).

Nehemiah's great work of restoring the wall of Jerusalem depended basically on securing permission from the king. Ezra had returned to Jerusalem with a sizable group of people and much gold and silver only a dozen years previously (*see Nehemiah*), but had been hindered in his work by adverse royal decrees secured by his enemies. In God's providence Nehemiah secured the restoration of royal favor.

The actual building of the wall was parceled out among different leaders. The opposition to Nehemiah by Sanballat and others combined ridicule, threat, and craft. Sanballat is called the governor of Samaria in the Elephantine Papyri. He was apparently not anxious to see a rival province strengthened, and there was religious antagonism as well to Nehemiah's strict reform program.

Internal difficulties also developed. The rich charged interest of 1 percent (per month, apparently, Ne 5:10), whereas the Mosaic law required outright charity to the poor. But against all opposition the wall was built by men who used both sword and trowel in the work of the Lord.

Nehemiah's reform involved the teaching of Moses' law by Ezra and others at the Feast of Tabernacles (as commanded in Dt 31:10). This led to the great prayer of confession of Ne 9, redolent with quotations from and allusions to the Pentateuch. A covenant was solemnly sealed to walk in the law of the Lord as given by Moses (10:29).

Nehemiah's final reform included the removal of Tobiah from the temple precincts. Tobiah had entered through friendship with Eliashib the high priest while Nehemiah was back in Persia. Also a grandson of Eliashib had married Sanballat's daughter (Ne 13:28). Evidently Eliashib was followed by his son Johanan in the reign of Darius II (423 – 404 BC). This Johanan is mentioned in the Elephantine Papyri as high priest in Jerusalem. The mention of him seems to indicate that Nehemiah's history continued until at least 423 BC.

NEIGHBOR [408, 824, 6017, 6660, 7940, 8276, 8907, 1150, 4340, 4341, 4446, 4489] (Heb. *rēaʿ*, *ʾāmîth*, *friend*, *qārôv*, *shākhēn*, Gr. *plēsion*, *nearby*, *geitōn*, *inhabitant*). The duties and responsibilities toward one's neighbor are varied.

General References to:
Defined (Lk 10:25 – 37). Duty to, defined in the Golden Rule (Mt 7:12). Love does no harm to (Ro 13:10). Love for, commanded (Lev 19:18; Mt 19:19; 22:39; Mk 12:31 – 33; Lk 10:25 – 37; Ro 13:9 – 10; Gal 5:14; Jas 2:8 – 9). Kindness to, commanded (Ex 23:4 – 5; Dt 22:1 – 4; Isa 58:6 – 7; Gal 6:10). Charitableness toward, commanded (Ro 15:2). Benevolence toward, commanded (Pr 3:28 – 29). Righteous treatment of, commanded (Zec 8:16 – 17). Honesty toward, commanded (Lev 19:13). Kindness to, rewarded (Isa 58:8 – 14; Mt 25:34 – 46). Righteous treatment of, rewarded (Ps 15:1 – 3). False witness against, forbidden (Ex 20:16; Lev 19:16). Hatred of, forbidden (Lev 19:17). Oppression of, denounced (Jer 22:13). Penalty for violation of the rights of (Lev 6:2 – 5). See Mankind.

Ex	20:16	give false testimony against your **n**.
	20:17	or anything that belongs to your **n**
Lev	19:13	Do not defraud your **n** or rob him.
	19:17	Rebuke your **n** frankly
	19:18	but love your **n** as yourself.
Ps	15:3	who does his **n** no wrong
Pr	3:29	Do not plot harm against your **n**,
	14:21	He who despises his **n** sins,
	24:28	against your **n** without cause,
	25:18	gives false testimony against his **n**.
	27:10	better a **n** nearby than a brother far
	27:14	If a man loudly blesses his **n**
Zec	8:17	do not plot evil against your **n**,
Mt	5:43	Love your **n** and hate your enemy.'
	19:19	and 'love your **n** as yourself.' "
Mk	12:31	The second is this: 'Love your **n**
Lk	10:27	and, 'Love your **n** as yourself.' "
	10:29	who is my **n**?" In reply Jesus said:
Ro	13:10	Love does no harm to its **n**.
	15:2	Each of us should please his **n**
Gal	5:14	"Love your **n** as yourself."
Eph	4:25	and speak truthfully to his **n**,
Heb	8:11	No longer will a man teach his **n**,

NEPHILIM [5872] (*ones falling [upon]*, hence *violent ones*, possibly *giants*). Antediluvians (Ge 6:4); aboriginal dwellers in Canaan (Nu 13:32 – 33); not angelic fallen beings (Dt 1:28).

NERO (nē´rō Gr. *Nērōn*). The fifth Roman emperor, born AD 37, commenced reign 54, died June 9, 68. The original family name of Nero was Lucius Domitus Ahenobarbus, but after he was adopted into the Claudian family line by the emperor Claudius, he assumed the name of Nero Claudius Caesar Germanicus. Nero's father was Enaeus Domitus Ahenobarbus, a man given to viciousness and vice. His mother was Agrippina, who cared little for her son's morals but was interested only in his temporal advancement.

The first years of Nero's reign were quite peaceful and gave promise of good things to come. Nero himself could boast that not a single person had been unjustly executed throughout his extensive empire. During these "rational years" of Nero's administration, the apostle Paul, in compliance with Paul's own expressed appeal (Ac 25:10–11), was brought before him as the reigning Caesar (c. AD 63). We can hardly do otherwise than infer that Paul was freed of all charges to continue his labors of evangelization.

Nero's marriage to Poppaea opened the second period of his reign. He killed his mother, his chief advisers Seneca and Burrus, and many of the nobility to secure their fortunes.

In AD 64 a large part of Rome was destroyed by fire. Whether Nero actually ordered the burning of the city is very controversial. However, justly or not, the finger of suspicion was pointed in Nero's direction. A scapegoat was provided in the Christians. Even the Roman historian Tacitus, who certainly cannot be given the name "Christian," bears testimony as to the severity of the sufferings inflicted on them. "Their death was made a matter of sport; they were covered in wild beasts' skins and torn to pieces by dogs or were fastened to crosses and set on fire in order to serve as torches by night.... Nero had offered his gardens for the spectacle and gave an exhibition in his circus, mingling with the crowd in the guise of a charioteer or mounted on his chariot. Hence,... there arose a feeling of pity, because it was felt that they were being sacrificed not for the common good, but to gratify the savagery of one man" (Tacitus, *Annals* 15, 44).

Nero's private life was a scandal. Surrendering himself to the basest of appetites, he indulged himself in the most evil forms of pleasure. Conspiracies and plots dogged his latter years. He was advised to

destroy himself but could not find the courage to do so. Learning that the senate had decreed his death, Nero's last cruel act was to put many of the senate members to death. He finally died by his own hand in the summer of AD 68. Thus perished the last of the line of Julius Caesar. Both Paul and Peter suffered martyrdom under Nero.

NEW

Ps	40:3	He put a **n** song in my mouth,
	98:1	Sing to the LORD a **n** song,
Ecc	1:9	there is nothing **n** under the sun.
Isa	62:2	you will be called by a **n** name
	65:17	**n** heavens and a **n** earth.
Jer	31:31	"when I will make a **n** covenant
La	3:23	They are **n** every morning;
Eze	18:31	and get a **n** heart and a **n** spirit.
	36:26	give you a **n** heart and put a **n** spirit
Zep	3:5	and every **n** day he does not fail,
Mt	9:17	Neither do men pour **n** wine
Mk	16:17	they will speak in **n** tongues;
Lk	22:20	"This cup is the **n** covenant
Jn	13:34	"A **n** commandment I give you:
Ac	5:20	the full message of this **n** life."
Ro	6:4	the Father, we too may live a **n** life.
1Co	5:7	old yeast that you may be a **n** batch
	11:25	"This cup is the **n** covenant
2Co	3:6	as ministers of a **n** covenant—
	5:17	he is a **n** creation; the old has gone,
Eph	4:23	to be made **n** in the attitude
	4:24	and to put on the **n** self, created
Heb	9:15	is the mediator of a **n** covenant,
	10:20	by a **n** and living way opened for us
	12:24	Jesus the mediator of a **n** covenant,
1Pe	1:3	great mercy he has given us **n** birth
2Pe	3:13	to a **n** heaven and a **n** earth,
1Jn	2:8	Yet I am writing you a **n** command;
Rev	2:17	stone with a **n** name written on it,
	3:12	the **n** Jerusalem, which is coming
	21:1	I saw a **n** heaven and a **n** earth,

NEW BIRTH The corruption of human nature requires (Jn 3:6; Ro 8:7–8). None can enter heaven without (Jn 3:3). Is of the will of God (Jas 1:18). Is of the mercy of God (Tit 3:5). Is for the glory of God (Isa 43:7).

Effected by:

God (Jn 1:13; 1Pe 1:3). Christ (1Jn 2:29). The Holy Spirit (Jn 3:6; Tit 3:5). By means of: the word of God (Jas 1:18; 1Pe 1:23); the resurrection of Christ (1Pe 1:3); the ministry of the gospel (1Co 4:15).

Described as:

A new creation (2Co 5:17; Gal 6:15; Eph 2:10). Newness of life (Ro 6:4). A spiritual resurrection (Ro 6:4 – 6; Eph 2:1, 5; Col 2:12; 3:1). A new heart (Eze 36:26). A new spirit (Eze 11:19; Ro 7:6). Putting on the new man (Eph 4:24). The inward man (Ro 7:22; 2Co 4:16). Circumcision of the heart (Dt 30:6, w Ro 2:29; Col 2:11). Partaking of the divine nature (2Pe 1:4). The washing of regeneration (Tit 3:5). All saints partake of (Ro 8:16 – 17; 1Pe 2:2; 1Jn 5:1).

Produces:

Likeness to God (Eph 4:24; Col 3:10). Likeness to Christ (Ro 8:29; 2Co 3:18; 1Jn 3:2). Knowledge of God (Jer 24:7; Col 3:10). Hatred of sin (1Jn 3:9; 5:18). Victory over the world (1Jn 5:4). Delight in God's law (Ro 7:22).

Evidenced by:

Faith in Christ (1Jn 5:1). Righteousness (1Jn 2:29). Brotherly love (1Jn 4:7). Connected with adoption (Isa 43:6 – 7; Jn 1:12 – 13). Literalistic objection to (Jn 3:4). Manner of effecting illustrated (Jn 3:8). Preserves from Satan's devices (1Jn 5:18).

NEWS

Pr	15:30	good **n** gives health to the bones.
	25:25	is good **n** from a distant land.
Isa	52:7	the feet of those who bring good **n**,
	61:1	me to preach good **n** to the poor.
Na	1:15	the feet of one who brings good **n**,
Mt	4:23	preaching the good **n**
	11:5	the good **n** is preached to the poor.
Mk	1:15	Repent and believe the good **n**!"
	16:15	preach the good **n** to all creation.
Lk	2:10	I bring you good **n**
	4:43	"I must preach the good **n**
	16:16	the good **n** of the kingdom
Ac	5:42	proclaiming the good **n** that Jesus
	10:36	telling the good **n** of peace
	17:18	preaching the good **n** about Jesus
Ro	10:15	feet of those who bring good **n**!"

NEW TESTAMENT A collection of twenty-seven documents regarded by the church as inspired and authoritative, consisting of four gospels, the Acts of the Apostles, twenty-one letters, and the book of Revelation. All were written during the apostolic period, either by apostles or by men closely associated with the apostles. The Gospels tell the story of the coming of the Messiah, God in the flesh, to become the Savior of the world. Acts describes the beginnings and growth of the church. The letters set forth the significance of the person and work of Christ and rules for the church. Revelation tells of the consummation of all things in Jesus Christ. The formation of the NT canon was a gradual process, the Holy Spirit working in the church and guiding it to recognize and choose those books God wanted brought together to form the Christian counterpart of the Jewish OT. By the end of the fourth century, the NT canon was basically settled.

NICODEMUS [3773] (nĭk′ō-dē′mŭs, Gr. *Nikodēmos, victor over the people*). A leading Pharisee, "a ruler of the Jews," and a member of the Sanhedrin. Perhaps from curiosity, and possibly under conviction, but certainly led of God, he came to Jesus by night (Jn 3:1 – 14). He must have thought of himself as quite condescending to address Jesus, the young man from Galilee, as "Rabbi," but Jesus, instead of being puffed up by the recognition, quickly made Nicodemus aware of his need by announcing the necessity of a new birth in order "to see the kingdom of God." Nicodemus did not then understand but was deeply touched, though he had not yet the courage to stand out for the Lord. Later, when at the Feast of Tabernacles (7:25 – 44) the Jewish leaders were planning to kill Jesus, Nicodemus spoke up, though timidly, in the Sanhedrin, suggesting their injustice in condemning a man without a fair trial. After the death of Jesus, however, Nicodemus came boldly with Joseph of Arimathea (19:38 – 42), provided a rich store of spices for the embalmment, and assisted in the burial of the body. After that he is not mentioned in Scripture.

NICOLAITANS [3774] (nĭk′ō-lā ′ĭ-tănz, Gr. *Nikolaitai, follower of Nicolas*). A group of persons whose works both the church at Ephesus and our Lord hated (Rev 2:6) and whose doctrine was held by some in the Pergamum church (2:15). Nothing else is surely known about them, but some have guessed that they were the followers of Nicolas of Antioch, one of the first so-called deacons (Ac 6:5), but there is no evidence for this.

NILE [3284] (nīl, Gr. *Neilos,* meaning not certainly known). The main river of Egypt and of Africa, 4,050 miles long; it begins at Lake Victoria and flows northward to the Mediterranean; the annual overflow deposits sediment that makes northern Egypt one of the most fertile regions in the world. Moses was placed on the Nile in a basket of papyrus (Ex 2:3); the turning of the Nile into blood was one of the ten plagues (Ex 7:20 – 21); on its bank grows the reed from which the famous papyrus writing material is made.

NIMROD [5808] (nĭm′rŏd, Heb. *nimrōdh,* perhaps *to rebel,* or *the Arrow, the mighty hero*). In the "Table of the Nations" (Ge 10) many of the names seem to be those of cities, e.g., Sidon (10:15); countries, e.g., Canaan (10:6, 15); or tribes, e.g., "Heth and the Jebusites" (10:15 – 18); but Nimrod stands out clearly as an individual man and a very interesting character. The beginning of his kingdom was in Babylonia, whence he moved northward and became the founder of Nineveh and other cities in or near Assyria. He became distinguished as a hunter, ruler, and builder. Many legends have grown up around the name of Nimrod, some claiming that he was identical with "Ninus," an early Babylonian

king or god. Again, some have associated Nimrod with the building of the Tower of Babel (11:1 – 9). Others have identified him with the ancient king of Babylonia, Gilgamesh, but there is no proof that the two were identical.

NINEVEH, NINEVE [5770, 3780] (nĭn′ĕ-vĕ, Heb. *nînewēh*). One of the most ancient cities of the world, founded by Nimrod (Ge 10:11 – 12), a great-grandson of Noah, and enduring till 612 BC. Nineveh lay on the banks of the Tigris above its confluence with the Greater Zab, one of its chief tributaries, and nearly opposite the site of the modern Mosul in Iraq. It was for many years the capital of the great Assyrian Empire, and its fortunes ebbed and flowed with the long strife between Babylonia and Assyria. Among the great rulers of Assyria may be mentioned Tiglath-Pileser I, who made conquests about 1100 BC, and Ashurnasirpal and Shalmaneser III, who inaugurated a system of ruthless conquest and deportation of whole populations, which greatly increased the power of Assyria and the influence of Nineveh. It was this latter king (sometimes numbered as II instead of III) who defeated Hazael of Syria and boasted of receiving tribute from Jehu of Israel. The Assyrians, instead of numbering their years, named them from certain rulers; and lists of these "eponyms" have been found, but with a gap of fifty-one years around the beginning of the eighth century, due no doubt to some great calamity and/or the weakness of her kings. It was in this space of time that Jonah was sent of the Lord to warn the people of Nineveh: "Forty more days and Nineveh will be overturned" (Jnh 3:4), but God gave Nineveh a respite for nearly two hundred years. Esarhaddon, the great king of Assyria from 680 – 668, united Babylonia to Assyria and conquered lands as far away as Egypt (Isa 19:4) and North Arabia. He was succeeded by his greater son Ashurbanipal (called by the Greeks "Sardanapalus"), who presided over Assyria in its brief climax of power and culture; but Nabopolassar of Babylon, who reigned from 625 to

605, freed it from Assyria and helped to bring about the destruction of Nineveh in 612.

> **General References to:**
>
> *A capital of the Assyrian Empire (Ge 10:11 – 12). Nineveh and its surrounding region had a population of upwards of 120,000 when Jonah preached (Jnh 4:11). Extent of (Jnh 3:4). Sennacherib in (2Ki 19:36 – 37; Isa 37:37 – 38). Jonah preaches to (Jnh 1:1 – 2; 3). Nahum prophesies against (Na 1 – 3). Zephaniah foretells the desolation of (Zep 2:13 – 15).*

NOAH [5695, 5829, 3820] (nōʹa, Heb. *nōah, rest*).

1. The son of Lamech and tenth in descent from Adam in the line of Seth (Ge 5:28 – 29). He received this name because Lamech foresaw that through him God would comfort (Heb. *naham*, same root as "Noah") the race and partially alleviate the effects of the Edenic curse. Noah was uniquely righteous (6:1 – 13). When he was 480 years old, 120 years before the flood (6:3), he was warned of God that the world would be destroyed by water (Heb 11:7). He was then given exact instructions for building the ark (Ge 6:14 – 16). While engaged in this colossal task, he warned men of the coming catastrophe, as a "preacher of righteousness" (2Pe 2:5), while God in long-suffering waited for men to repent (1Pe 3:20). Noah's three sons — Shem, Ham, and Japheth — were not born until he was 500 years old (Ge 5:32). One week before the flood, God led Noah and his family into the ark and supernaturally directed the animals also to enter. When all were safely inside, God shut the door (7:16).

The flood came in Noah's six hundredth year, increased steadily for 40 days, maintained its mountain-covering depth for 110 more days, and then subsided sufficiently for Noah to disembark in the mountains of Ararat after another 221 days (*see Flood*). During all this time, "God remembered Noah and all the wild animals ... in the ark" (Ge 8:1), implying that God did not leave the task of caring for these creatures entirely to Noah. To determine whether it was safe to disembark, Noah sent forth first a raven and then a dove at regular intervals (8:6 – 10). The freshly plucked olive leaf proved to him that such sturdy plants had already begun to grow on the mountain heights. God commanded him to disembark, and Noah built an altar and offered clean beasts as burnt offerings to God. The Lord then promised never to send another universal flood, confirming it with the rainbow sign (8:21 – 22; 9:9 – 17). God blessed Noah and his family and commanded them to multiply and fill the earth (9:1). From now on animals would fear humans, and they were given to be food for humans, except the blood (9:2 – 4). Human government was instituted by the provision of capital punishment for murderers (9:5 – 6).

Among the things preserved in the ark was sinful human nature. Noah became a husbandman, planted a vineyard, drank himself into a drunken stupor, and shamefully exposed himself in his tent (9:20 – 21). Ham, presumably led by his son Canaan, made fun of Noah. For this foul deed, Canaan was cursed and Ham received no blessing (9:25 – 27). On the other hand, Shem and Japheth showed due respect to their father (9:23) and received rich blessings for their descendants. Noah lived 350 years after the flood, dying at the age of 950 (9:29). *See Covenants, Major in the Old Testament.*

> *Righteous in a corrupt age (Ge 6:8 – 9; 7:1; Eze 14:14); Warned people of the flood 120 years (Ge 6:3); Built an ark (Ge 6:12 – 22); Saved from the flood with wife and family, together with beasts and fowl of every kind (Ge 7:8); repopulated earth (Ge 9:10); lived 950 years; God established a covenant with (Ge 9:8 – 17)*

2. One of the five daughters of Zelophehad, of the tribe of Manasseh (Nu 26:33; 27:1; 36:11; Jos 17:3), who received an inheritance in the land in their father's name, in spite of having no brothers.

NOB [5546] (nōb, Heb. *nōv*). A town of the priests in the tribe of Benjamin just north of the city of Jerusalem. The language of Isa 10:32 indicates that it was within sight of Jerusalem. In the time of King Saul the tabernacle stood here for a time, and David's visit to Ahimelech the priest (1Sa 21) was the cause or at least the occasion for the complete destruction of the city by Saul (22:19). David, fleeing from Saul, asked for provision for his young men and for a sword, all of which the priest granted; but a mischief maker, Doeg the Edomite, was a witness to the transaction and reported it to Saul who, in his insane hatred and jealousy of David, had the priests murdered and their city destroyed.

NOBLE [2657, 2985, 3202, 5618, 5619, 7312, 2302, 2819, 4948, 5507]. A word used to describe people who were renowned for deeds performed or in some other way were distinguished for skills or genius; people of high rank, position, title, or one well born (Jdg 5:13; Ezr 4:10; Est 6:9; Pr 17:26; Lk 19:12 – 27; 1Co 1:26); persons who possess high moral qualities or ideals (Ps 16:3; Isa 32:5; Ac 17:11); anything having qualities of a very high order (Eze 17:8, 23; 1Ti 3:1; Lk 21:5). A nobleman supports and defends his community. He has a generous heart (Ex 35:5, 22; Nu 21:18; 1Ch 28:21; 2Ch 29:31). He is one belonging to a king (Jn 4:46 – 53). The noble wife is praised in Pr 31:10 – 31.

Ru	3:11	you are a woman of **n** character.
Ps	45:1	My heart is stirred by a **n** theme
Pr	12:4	of **n** character is her husband's
	31:10	A wife of **n** character who can find?
	31:29	"Many women do **n** things,
Isa	32:8	But the **n** man makes **n** plans,
Lk	8:15	good soil stands for those with a **n**
Ro	9:21	of clay some pottery for **n** purposes
Php	4:8	whatever is **n**, whatever is right,
2Ti	2:20	some are for **n** purposes

NUCLEAR WAR Some see a reference to nuclear war in predictions of the fiery destruction of the earth (Zep 1:18; 2Pe 3:7, 10) and in the seven trumpets of Revelation (Rev 8:5 – 9:19).

NUMBERS, BOOK OF The fourth book of the Pentateuch, called *In the Wilderness* by the Jews after its first significant word. The Hebrew title is more meaningful than the English, for the book picks up the account of the wilderness wandering after the arrival at Sinai (Ex 19), and records the Bedouin-like travels of Israel through all the forty years of wandering.

The name *Numbers* comes from the Greek translation, which gives a misleading impression of one of the features of the book. Both at the beginning (1:2 – 46) and near the end (26:2 – 51) the number of the Israelites is given — a few more than 600,000 males above twenty years of age. The procedure sounds familiar to us. We call it a census. But the biblical censuses were not just that. Israel was not merely interested in vital statistics. This was a count of the fighting forces. Indeed, it probably was an actual mustering and organizing of the army. It is for this reason that the women, children, and Levites were not included. The numbering occurs twice because the army was called up twice for battle — first at the abortive attempt to invade the land at Kadesh Barnea, and second at the end of the forty years of wandering just before the conquest of Canaan.

The body of Numbers up to Nu 10:11 gives additional legislation and the organization of the host. From 10:11 to 12:16 is recorded the march from Sinai to Kadesh Barnea. Then comes the debacle at Kadesh recorded in chs. 13 and 14. The three leaders of this occasion — Joshua and Caleb, the believing spies, and Moses the intercessor — are forever memorialized as among God's great men. Chapters 15 to 21:11 record the repeated faithlessness on the part of the people. Apparently during much of the forty years, according to Am 5:25 – 26 and Jos 5:2ff., the people wandered far away from God, and even their national unity may have lapsed temporarily. The forty years are treated very briefly.

From Nu 21:11 on, the accounts of the conquest of Transjordan and the preparations to enter the land are given.

Outline:

    I. Israel at Sinai, Preparing to Depart for the Promised Land (1:1 – 10:10).

    II. The Journey from Sinai to Kadesh (10:11 – 12:16).

    III. Israel at Kadesh, the Delay Resulting from Rebellion (14:1 – 20:13).

    IV. The Journey from Kadesh to the Plains of Moab (20:14 – 22:1).

    V. Israel on the Plains of Moab, in Anticipation of Taking the Promised Land (22:2 – 32:42).

    VI. Appendixes Dealing with Various Matters (chs. 33 – 36).

OATH [457, 460, 8123, 8652+, 8678, 354, 2019, 2155, 3923, 3992, 3993, 4053] (ō′th, Heb. *shevû‘âh*, *’ālâh*, Gr. *horkos*). An appeal to God to witness the truth of a statement or of the binding character of a promise (Ge 21:23; 31:53; Gal 1:20; Heb 6:16). Two varieties of the oath are found in the OT — a simple one for common use and a more solemn one for cases of greater solemnity. Oaths played a very important part not only in legal and state affairs, but in the dealings of everyday life. A number of formulas were used in taking an oath, such as "the LORD is witness between you and me forever" (1Sa 20:23) and "as the LORD who rescues Israel lives" (14:39). Certain ceremonies were observed in taking an oath — in ordinary cases the raising of the hand toward heaven (Ge 14:22; Dt 32:40), in exceptional cases the putting of the hand under the thigh of the one to whom the oath was made (Ge 24:2; 47:29). Sometimes one taking an oath killed an animal, divided it into two parts, and passed between the pieces (15:8 – 18). Swearing was done by the life of the person addressed (1Sa 1:26), by the life of the king (17:55), by one's own head (Mt 5:36), by the angels and by the temple (23:16), by Jerusalem (5:35), and by God. It was forbidden to swear by a false god (Jos 23:7). A virgin could take an oath if her father did not disallow it; and a married woman, if her husband permitted it. By the time of Christ the OT law regarding oaths (Ex 22:11) was much perverted by the scribes, and our Lord therefore condemned indiscriminate and light taking of oaths, saying that people should be so transparently honest that oaths between them would be unnecessary. The lawfulness of oaths is recognized by the apostles, who called on God to witness to the truth of what they said (2Co 11:31; Gal 1:20).

Ex	33:1	up to the land I promised on **o**
Nu	30:2	or takes an **o** to obligate himself
Dt	6:18	promised on **o** to your forefathers,
	7:8	and kept the **o** he swore
	29:12	you this day and sealing with an **o**,
Ps	95:11	So I declared on **o** in my anger,
	119:106	I have taken an **o** and confirmed it,
	132:11	The LORD swore an **o** to David,
Ecc	8:2	because you took an **o** before God.
Mt	5:33	'Do not break your **o**, but keep
Heb	7:20	And it was not without an **o**!

OBADIAH [6281, 6282] (ō′b a-dī′a, Heb. *’ōvad-hyâh*, *servant of Jehovah*). The name of several men in the OT:

1. The governor of Ahab's household (1Ki 18:3 – 16) who "feared the LORD greatly" (KJV), but who seemed to fear Ahab even more.

2. The head of a household of David's descendants (1Ch 3:21).

3. A chief man of Issachar in David's time (1Ch 7:3).

4. One of the six sons of Azel, a Benjamite (1Ch 8:38 copied in 9:44).

5. A Levite who returned early from captivity (1Ch 9:16). He is called "Abda" in Ne 11:17.

6. One of the martial Gadites who joined David in the wilderness (1Ch 12:9).

7. Father of Ishmaiah, a prince of Zebulun in the days of David (1Ch 27:19).

8. One of five princes of Judah whom Jehoshaphat sent out to teach the people of Judah the law of the Lord (2Ch 17:7).

9. A Levite of the Merarite family, whom Josiah made an overseer of repairing the temple (2Ch 34:12).

10. A Jew who led back 218 men in Ezra's return from captivity (Ezr 8:9).

11. A priestly covenanter with Nehemiah (Ne 10:5).

12. A gatekeeper of Jerusalem in Nehemiah's time (Ne 12:25).

13. The prophet who wrote the book of Obadiah.

OBADIAH, BOOK OF The subject of the book is the destruction of Edom (Ob 1). From time immemorial Edom and the Edomites were hostile to Israel.

The book, like others of the Minor Prophets, is undated. The principal clue to the date of its writing is in vv. 11, 14. If "the day you stood aloof" (v. 11) alludes to the events of 2Ki 8:20 – 22 and 2Ch 21:16 – 18, when the Edomites and others rebelled against King Jehoram early in the ninth century BC, the book probably would be dated quite early; but if the reference is to Ps 137:7; 2Ch 36:20; and Eze 25:13 – 14, the prophecy would be late, later than 586. The more likely view is that 2Ch 28:16 – 18 is the apposite reference and that the time was late in the eighth century, during the reign of Ahaz of Judah. At that time Edom and the Philistines were associated in warfare against Judah, and the names of the two nations are again coupled in Ob 19.

Outline:

   I. Title and Introduction (v. 1).
   II. Judgment on Edom (vv. 2 – 14).
   III. The Day of the Lord (vv. 15 – 21).

OBEDIENCE [3682, 5915, 6913, 9048, 9068, 2848, 4272, 4275, 5498, 5633, 5634, 5675, 5875] (Heb. *shāmaʿ*, Gr. *hypakoē*). The Bible, by exhortation and commandment, requires submission and obedience to six principal authorities: (1) parents (Eph 6:1; Col 3:20; 1Ti 3:4), (2) teachers (Pr 5:12 – 13), (3) husbands (Eph 5:21 – 22, 24; Col 3:18; Tit 2:5; 1Pe 3:1, 5, 6), (4) masters — today, employers — (Eph 6:4; Col 3:22; Tit 2:9; 1Pe 2:18), (5) government (Ro 13:1 – 2, 5; Tit 3:1; 1Pe 2:13), and (6) God (Ge 26:5; Eph 5:24; Heb 5:9; 12:9; Jas 4:7). When there is a clear conflict regarding obedience to authority, Christians are to obey God, not human beings (Ac 5:29). The supreme test of faith in God is obedience (1Sa 28:18); the Bible often links obedience to faith (Ge 22:18; Ro 1:5; 1Pe 1:14). Jesus' obedience to the Father (Php 2:8) is the supreme example for Christians, who are to be "obedient children" (1Pe 1:14).

General References to:

Better than sacrifice (1Sa 15:22; Ps 40:6 – 9; Pr 21:3; Jer 7:22 – 23; Hos 6:6; Mic 6:6 – 8; Mt 9:13; 12:7; Mk 12:33; Heb 10:8 – 9). Commanded (Ge 17:9; Ex 23:22; Lev 19:19, 36 – 37; 20:8, 22; 22:31; Nu 15:38 – 40; 30:2; Dt 4:1 – 40; 5:1 – 33; 6:1 – 25; 8:1 – 6, 11 – 20; 10:12 – 13; 11:1 – 3, 8 – 9, 13 – 28, 32; 13:4; 26:16 – 18; 27:1 – 10; 32:46; Jos 22:5; 23:6 – 7; 24:14 – 15; 1Sa 12:14, 20, 24; 15:22; 2Ki 17:37 – 38; 1Ch 16:15; 28:9 – 10, 20; Ezr 7:23; Ps 76:11; Pr 7:1; Ecc 12:13; Jer 26:13; 38:20; Da 7:27; Mal 4:4; Eph 6:6 – 8; Php 2:12; 1Ti 6:14, 18; Jas 1:22 – 25; 2:10 – 12; 1Pe 1:2, 14). Proof of love (Jn 14:15, 21; 1Jn 2:5 – 6; 5:2 – 3; 2Jn 6, 9), under Mosaic law (Lev 18:5; Eze 20:11, 13, 21; Lk 10:28; Ro 10:5; Gal 3:10, 12). Proof that we know God (1Jn 2:3 – 4). Vows of (Ex 24:7; Jos 24:24; Ps 119:15, 106, 109). Prayer for guidance in (Ps 143:10). Cannot be rendered to two masters (Mt 6:24).

Rewards:

(Ge 18:19; Lev 26:3 – 13; Nu 14:24; Dt 7:12 – 15; 28:1 – 15; Jos 14:6 – 14; 2Ki 21:8; Isa 1:19). Prosperity (Dt 7:9, 12 – 15; 15:4; Jos 1:8; 1Ki 2:3 – 4; 9:3 – 5; 1Ch 22:13; 28:7 – 8; 2Ch 26:5; 27:6; Job 36:11; Pr 28:7; Jer 7:3 – 7; 11:1 – 5; 22:16; Mal 3:10 – 12; 1Jn 3:22). Long life (Dt 4:1, 40; 32:47; 1Ki 3:14; Pr 3:1 – 2; 19:16). Victory over enemies (Ex 23:22; Pr 16:7). Triumph over adversities (Mt 7:24 – 25; Lk 6:46 – 48). Divine favor (Ex 19:5; 20:6; Dt 5:10; 11:26 – 27; 12:28; 1Ki 8:23; Ne 1:5; Pss 25:10; 103:17 – 18, 20; 112:1; 119:2; Pr 1:33; Jer 7:23; 11:4; Mt 5:19; 25:20 – 23; Lk 11:28; 12:37 – 38; Jn 12:26; 13:17; Jas 1:25; Rev 22:7). Fellowship with Christ (Mt 12:50; Mk 3:35; Lk 8:21; Jn 14:23; 15:10, 14; 1Jn 3:24). Everlasting life (Mt 19:17, 29; Jn 8:51; 1Jn 2:17; Rev 2:10).

Ge	49:10	and the **o** of the nations is his.
Jdg	2:17	of **o** to the LORD's commands.
1Ch	21:19	So David went up in **o**
2Ch	31:21	in **o** to the law and the commands,
Pr	30:17	that scorns **o** to a mother,
Lk	23:56	Sabbath in **o** to the command- ment.
Ac	21:24	but that you yourself are living in **o**
Ro	1:5	to the **o** that comes from faith.
	5:19	also through the **o** of the one man
	6:16	to **o**, which leads to righteousness?

	16:19	Everyone has heard about your **o**,
2Co	9:13	for the **o** that accompanies your
	10:6	once your **o** is complete.
Phm	1:21	Confident of your **o**, I write to you,
Heb	5:8	he learned **o** from what he suffered
1Pe	1:2	for **o** to Jesus Christ and sprinkling
2Jn	6	that we walk in **o** to his commands.

OBEY

	12:24	"**O** these instructions as a lasting
Ex	19:5	Now if you **o** me fully and keep my
Lev	18:4	You must **o** my laws and be careful
	25:18	and be careful to **o** my laws,
Nu	15:40	remember to **o** all my commands
Dt	5:27	We will listen and **o**."
	6:3	careful to **o** so that it may go well
	6:24	us to **o** all these decrees
	13:4	Keep his commands and **o** him;
	21:18	son who does not **o** his father
	28:1	If you fully **o** the LORD your God
	30:2	and **o** him with all your heart
	30:10	if you **o** the LORD your God
	30:14	and in your heart so you may **o** it.
	32:46	children to **o** carefully all the words
Jos	1:7	to **o** all the law my servant Moses
	22:5	in all his ways, to **o** his commands,
	24:24	the LORD our God and **o** him."
1Sa	15:22	To **o** is better than sacrifice,
1Ki	8:61	by his decrees and **o** his commands
2Ch	34:31	and to **o** the words of the covenant
Ne	1:5	who love him and **o** his commands,
Ps	103:18	and remember to **o** his precepts.
	119:34	and **o** it with all my heart.
Pr	5:13	I would not **o** my teachers
Jer	7:23	I gave them this command: **O** me,
	11:4	'**O** me and do everything I
Da	9:4	who love him and **o** his commands,
Mt	8:27	the winds and the waves **o** him!"
	19:17	to enter life, **o** the commandments
	28:20	to **o** everything I have commanded
Lk	11:28	hear the word of God and **o** it."
Jn	14:15	you will **o** what I command.
	14:23	loves me, he will **o** my teaching.

	15:10	If you **o** my commands, you will
Ac	5:29	"We must **o** God rather than men!
Ro	2:13	it is those who **o** the law who will
	6:12	body so that you **o** its evil desires.
	15:18	in leading the Gentiles to **o** God
	16:26	nations might believe and **o** him —
Gal	5:3	obligated to **o** the whole law.
Eph	6:1	**o** your parents in the Lord,
	6:5	**o** your earthly masters with respect
Col	3:20	**o** your parents in everything,
	3:22	**o** your earthly masters
2Th	3:14	anyone does not **o** our instruction
1Ti	3:4	and see that his children **o** him
Heb	5:9	eternal salvation for all who **o** him
	13:17	**O** your leaders and submit
1Pe	4:17	for those who do not **o** the gospel
1Jn	3:24	Those who **o** his commands live
	5:3	love for God: to **o** his commands.
Rev	12:17	those who **o** God's commandments
	14:12	the saints who **o** God's

OFFENSE [6411, 7321, 7322, 4997, 4998] (ŏ·fĕns', Heb. *'āsham, hātā'*, Gr. *skandalon*). The word is used in a variety of ways in Scripture, as it is in English: injury, hurt, damage, occasion of sin, a stumbling block, an infraction of law, sin, transgression, state of being offended. In the NT it is often used in the sense of stumbling block (Mt 5:30; 11:6; 18:6; 1Co 8:13). Throughout the NT there is warning by Christ and the apostles against doing anything that would turn anyone away from the faith.

Pr	17:9	over an **o** promotes love,
	19:11	it is to his glory to overlook an **o**.
Gal	5:11	In that case the **o** of the cross has

OFFERINGS [852, 871, 2284, 2285, 2627, 2633, 2853, 4003, 4854, 4966, 5605, 5607, 5818, 5821, 6590, 6592, 7175, 7731, 7787, 7928, 7933, 8968, 9343, 9485, 9556, 10432, 1126, 3906, 4712, 4714, 5064].

Holy (Lev 2:3; 6:17, 25, 27, 29; 7:1, 6; 10:12; Nu 18:9 – 10). Offered at door of tabernacle (Lev 1:3; 3:2; 17:4, 8 – 9); of the temple (1Ki 8:62; 12:27; 2Ch 7:12). All animal sacrifices: must be eight days old or over (Lev 22:27); must be without blemish (Ex 12:5; 29:1; Lev 1:3, 10; 22:18 – 25; Dt 15:21; 17:1; Eze 43:23; Mal 1:8, 14; Heb 9:14; 1Pe 1:19). Accompanied with leaven (Lev 7:13; Am 4:5). Without leaven (Ex 23:18; 34:25). Eaten (1Sa 9:13). Ordinance relating to scapegoat (Lev 16:7 – 26).

Figurative:

(Ps 51:17; Jer 33:11; Ro 12:1; Php 4:18; Heb 13:15).

Animal Sacrifices:

A type of Christ (Ps 40:6 – 8, w Heb 10:1 – 14; Isa 53:11 – 12, w Lev 16:21; Jn 1:29; 1Co 5:7; 2Co 5:21; Eph 5:2; Heb 9:19 – 28; 10:1, 11 – 12; 13:11 – 13; Rev 5:6).

Burnt:

(Lev 9:2). Its purpose was to make an atonement for sin (Lev 1:4; 7). Ordinances concerning (Ex 29:15 – 18; Lev 1; 5:7 – 13; 6:9 – 13; 17:8 – 9; 23:18, 26 – 37; Nu 15:24 – 25; 19:9; 28:26 – 31; 29). Accompanied by other offerings (Nu 15:3 – 16). Skins of, belonged to priests (Lev 7:8). Offered daily, morning and evening (Ge 15:17; Ex 29:38 – 42; Lev 6:20; Nu 28; 29:6; 1Ch 16:40; 2Ch 2:4; 13:11; Ezr 3:3; Eze 46:13 – 15). Music with (Nu 10:10). Offered: by Noah (Ge 8:20); in idolatrous worship (Ex 32:6; 1Ki 18:26; 2Ki 10:25; Ac 14:13). For cleansing leprosy (Lev 14).

Daily:

Sacrificial (Ex 29:38 – 42; Lev 6:20; Nu 28:3 – 8; 29:6; 1Ki 18:29; 1Ch 16:40; 2Ch 2:4; 13:11; Ezr 3:3 – 6; 9:4 – 5; Ps 141:2; Eze 46:13 – 15; Da 9:21, 27; 11:31).

Drink:

Libations of wine offered with the sacrifices (Ge 35:14; Ex 29:40 – 41; 30:9; Lev 23:13, 18; Nu 6:17; 15:24; 28:5 – 15, 24 – 31; 29:6 – 11, 18 – 40; 2Ki 16:13; 1Ch 29:21; 2Ch 29:35; Ezr 7:17).

Fellowship:

Laws concerning (Ex 20:24; 24:5; Lev 3:6; 7:11 – 18; 9:3 – 4, 18 – 22; 19:5; 23:10; Nu 6:14;

10:10). Offered: by the tribal leaders (Nu 7:17, 23, 29, 35, 41, 47, 53, 59, 65, 71, 77, 83, 88); by Joshua (Jos 8:31); by David (2Sa 6:17; 24:25). Offered in idolatrous worship (Ex 32:6). Offered by harlots (Pr 7:14).

Free Will:

(Lev 23:38; Nu 29:39; Dt 12:6; 2Ch 31:14; Ezr 3:5). Must be perfect (Lev 22:17 – 25). To be eaten: at tabernacle (Dt 12:17 – 18); by priests (Lev 7:16 – 17). With meat and drink offerings (Nu 15:1 – 16). Obligatory (Dt 16:10), when signified in a vow (Dt 23:23).

Guilt:

Ordinances concerning (Lev 5; 6:1 – 7; 7:1 – 7; 14:10 – 22; 15:15, 29 – 30; 19:21 – 22; Nu 6:12; Ezr 10:19). To be eaten by the priests (Lev 7:6 – 7; 14:13; Nu 18:9 – 10). Offered by idolaters (1Sa 6:3, 8, 17 – 18). See below, Sin.

Human Sacrifices:

Forbidden (Lev 18:21; 20:2 – 5; Dt 12:31). Offered by: Abraham (Ge 22:1 – 19; Heb 11:17 – 19); Canaanites (Dt 12:31); Moabites (2Ki 3:27); Israelites (2Ki 16:3; 23:10; 2Ch 28:3; Isa 57:5; Jer 7:31; 19:5; 32:35; Eze 16:20 – 21; 20:26, 31; 23:37, 39); Sepharvites to idols (2Ki 17:31). Offered to: demons (Ps 106:37 – 38); Baal (Jer 19:5 – 6).

Meat:

Ordinances concerning (Ex 29:40 – 41; 30:9; 40:29; Lev 2; 5:11 – 12; 6:14 – 23; 7:9 – 13, 37; 9:17; 23:13, 16 – 17; Nu 4:16; 5:15, 18, 25 – 26; 8:8; 15:3 – 16, 24; 18:9; 28:5, 9, 12 – 13, 20 – 21, 26 – 31; 29:3 – 4, 14). To be eaten in the Holy Place (Lev 10:13; Nu 18:9 – 10). Offered with animal sacrifices (Nu 15:3 – 16). Not mixed with leaven (Lev 2:4, 11; 6:14 – 18; 10:12 – 13; Nu 6:15, 17). Storerooms for, in the temple (Ne 12:44; 13:5 – 6), provided for in the vision of Ezekiel (Eze 42:12).

Presentation, or Wave:

Given to the priests' families as part of their share (Lev 10:14; Nu 5:9; 18:10 – 19, 24). Consecrated by being elevated by priest (Ex 29:27).

Consisted of right thigh or hindquarter (Ex 29:27 – 28; Lev 7:12 – 14, 32, 34; 10:15); spoils, including captives and other articles of war (Nu 31:29, 41). When offered (Lev 7:12 – 14; Nu 6:20; 15:19 – 21). In certain instances this offering was brought to the tabernacle or temple (Dt 12:6, 11, 17 – 18). To be offered on taking possession of land of Canaan (Nu 15:18 – 21).

Sin:

Ordinances concerning (Ex 29:10 – 14, w Heb 13:11 – 13; Lev 4; 5; 6:1 – 7, 26 – 30; 9:1 – 21; 12:6 – 8; 14:19, 22, 31; 15:30; 23:19; Nu 6:10 – 11, 14, 16; 8:8, 12; 15:27; 28:15, 22 – 24, 30; 29:5 – 6, 11, 16 – 38). Temporary (Da 11:31; Heb 9 – 10).

Thank:

Ordinances concerning (Lev 7:11 – 15; 22:29; Dt 12:11 – 12).

Vow:

(Lev 7:16 – 17; 22:17 – 25; Dt 23:21 – 23).

Wave:

Ordinances concerning (Ex 29:22, 26 – 28; Lev 7:29 – 34; 8:25 – 29; 9:19 – 21; 10:14 – 15; 23:10 – 11, 17, 20; Nu 5:25; 6:19 – 20). Belonged to priests (Ex 29:26 – 28; Lev 7:31, 34; 8:29; 9:21; 23:20; Nu 18:11, 18). To be eaten (Lev 10:14 – 15; Nu 18:11, 18 – 19, 31).

Wood:

Fuel for temple (Ne 10:34; 13:31).

Insufficiency of:

(Heb 8:7 – 13; 9:1 – 15; 10:1 – 12, 18 – 20). Unavailing, when not accompanied by piety (1Sa 15:22; Pss 40:6; 50:8 – 14; 51:16 – 17; Pr 21:3, 27; Isa 1:11 – 14; 66:3; Jer 6:20; 7:21 – 23; 14:12; Hos 6:6; 8:13; Am 5:21 – 24; Mic 6:6 – 8; Mt 9:13; 12:7; Mk 12:33).

Ge	4:3	of the soil as an **o** to the LORD.
	22:2	a burnt **o** on one of the mountains I
	22:8	provide the lamb for the burnt **o**,
Ex	29:24	before the LORD as a wave **o**.
Lev	1:3	If the **o** is a burnt **o** from the herd,
	2:4	" 'If you bring a grain **o** baked
	3:1	" 'If someone's **o** is a fellowship **o**,
	4:3	a sin **o** for the sin he has committed
	5:15	It is a guilt **o**.
	7:37	ordination **o** and the fellowship **o**,
	9:24	and consumed the burnt **o**
	22:18	to fulfill a vow or as a freewill **o**,
1Sa	13:9	And Saul offered up the burnt **o**.
Ps	40:6	Sacrifice and **o** you did not desire,
	116:17	I will sacrifice a thank **o** to you
Isa	53:10	the LORD makes his life a guilt **o**,
Mt	5:23	if you are **o** your gift at the altar
Ro	8:3	likeness of sinful man to be a sin **o**.
Eph	5:2	as a fragrant **o** and sacrifice to God.
Php	2:17	I am being poured out like a drink **o**
2Ti	4:6	being poured out like a drink **o**,
Heb	10:5	"Sacrifice and **o** you did not desire,
1Pe	2:5	**o** spiritual sacrifices acceptable

OLD AGE [1201, 2416, 2418, 2419, 2420, 2421, 3427, 3813, 6409, 8484, 1179].

Wise (1Ki 12:6 – 8; 2Ch 10:6 – 8; Job 12:12). Devout (Lk 2:37). Exemplary, commanded (Tit 2:2 – 3). Deference toward (Lev 19:32; Job 32:4 – 9). Righteous, is glorious (Pr 16:31). Wasted, is bitter (Ge 47:9; Ecc 6:3, 6; 12:1 – 7). Promised to the righteous (Ge 15:15; Job 5:26; Pss 34:12 – 14; 91:14, 16; Pr 3:1 – 2). God's care in (Isa 46:4). Psalmist prays not to be forsaken in (Ps 71:9, 18). David enjoys (1Ch 29:28). Paul, the aged (Phm 9). Infirmities in (2Sa 19:34 – 37; Ps 90:10). Vigor in (Dt 34:7; Ps 92:12 – 14). Join in praise to the Lord in (Ps 148:12 – 13).

OLD TESTAMENT In Protestant Bibles, thirty-nine books from Genesis to Malachi: five of law, twelve of history, five of poetry, five of major prophets, and twelve of minor prophets. In the Hebrew Bible, the same contents are organized into twenty-four books from Genesis to Chronicles: Five of law, eight of the prophets, and eleven of miscellaneous writings. All of these books were regarded by Israelites as Scripture, inspired and authoritative, before the first century AD (Mt 5:17 – 20; Lk 24:44; Jn 17:17; 2Ti 3:16). They appeared over a period of c. 1000 years. The authors of many of them are unknown.

OLIVES, MOUNT OF [2339, 1777, 1779]. A ridge, about one mile long (1.6 km.), with four identifiable summits, east of Jerusalem, beyond the Valley of Jehoshaphat, through which flows the Kidron stream. Gethsemane, Bethphage, and Bethany are on its slopes (2Sa 15:30; Zec 14:4; Mt 21:1; 24:3; 26:30; Mk 11:1; 13:3; 14:26; Lk 19:29, 37; 22:39; Jn 8:1; Ac 1:12).

OMNIPOTENCE (ŏm-nĭp′ō-tĕn[t]s). The attribute of God that describes his ability to do whatever he wills. God's will is limited by his nature, and he therefore cannot do anything contrary to his nature as God, such as to ignore sin, to sin, or to do something absurd or self-contradictory. God is not controlled by his power but has complete control over it, otherwise he would not be a free being. To a certain extent, he has voluntarily limited himself by the free will of his rational creatures. Although the word *omnipotence* is not found in the Bible, the Scriptures clearly teach the omnipotence of God (Job 42:2; Jer 32:17; Mt 19:26; Lk 1:37; Rev 19:6).

OMNIPRESENCE (ŏm′nĭ-prĕz′ĕn[t]s). The attribute of God by virtue of which he fills the universe in all its parts and is present everywhere at once. Not a part, but the whole of God is present in every place. The Bible teaches the omnipresence of God (Ps 139:7 – 12; Jer 23:23 – 24; Ac 17:27 – 28). This is true of all three members of the Trinity. They are so closely related that where one is the others can be said to be also (Jn 14:9 – 11).

OMNISCIENCE (ŏm-nĭsh′ĕn[t]s). The attribute by which God perfectly and eternally knows all things that can be known — past, present, and future. God knows how best to attain to his desired ends. God's omniscience is clearly taught in Scripture (Ps 147:5; Pr 15:11; Isa 46:10).

OMRI [6687] (ŏm′rē, Heb. ′omrî, *thrive, live long* ISBE).

1. The sixth king of Israel, whose reign may be tentatively dated from 886 to 874 BC. Omri, an able if unscrupulous soldier and founder of a dynasty, is the first Hebrew monarch to be mentioned in nonbiblical records, and the fact may be some measure of his contemporary importance. It was not until 847 that Mesha included Omri's name in the inscription of the Moabite Stone, but it is a fact that Omri subdued Moab. It is of more significance that the Assyrian records after Omri's day frequently refer to northern Palestine as "the land of Humri" (the Assyrians spelled the name with an initial aspirate).

The brief but vivid account of Omri's military coup d'état and his extremely wicked reign is told in 1Ki 16:15 – 28.

2. A Benjamite, family of Beker (1Ch 7:8).

3. A man of Judah, family of Perez (1Ch 9:4).

4. A prince of the tribe of Issachar in David's reign (1Ch 27:18).

ONE ANOTHER Responsibilities of fellow believers to (1Pe 4:7 – 10). All believers members of (Ro 12:5; Eph 4:25).

ONESIMUS [3946] (ō-nĕs′ĭ-mŭs, Gr. *Onesimos, profitable or useful*). Probably a common nickname for a slave. Paul plays on the word *onesimos* in Phm 11 and again in v. 20. A plain reading of the letters to Philemon and the Colossian church leads to the conclusion that Onesimus was a slave of Philemon of Colosse. He robbed his master and made his way to Rome, the frequent goal of such fugitives, the "common cesspool of the world," as the aristocratic historian Sallust called the city. Some Ephesian or Colossian person in Rome, perhaps Aristarchus (Ac 27:2; Col 4:10 – 14; Phm 24), or Epaphras (Col 1:7; 4:12 – 13; Phm 23) seems to have recognized the man and brought him to Paul in his captivity. Onesimus became a Christian and was persuaded to return to his master. From that incident came the exquisite letter of Paul to Philemon, which demonstrates so vividly the social solvent that Christianity had brought into the world. It appears that Onesimus left Rome in company with Tychicus, carrying the letter to Philemon and also Paul's letters to the Ephesian and Colossian churches. Nothing more is known about Onesimus. The tradition that Onesimus became the martyr bishop of Berea is of doubtful authenticity.

ORACLE (ŏr′a-k′l, Heb. *dāvar*, Gr. *logion*).

1. An utterance supposedly coming from a deity and generally through an inspired medium. This is the classical usage (cf. "Sibylline Oracles").

2. In the Bible, an utterance from God. In the KJV of 2Sa 16:23 we read that Ahithophel was so highly regarded before he turned traitor to David that his words were considered oracles from God.

3. The OT was referred to as "living [KJV "lively"] oracles" or "words" (Ac 7:38). NIV has "elementary truths" in Heb 5:12 and "the very words of God" in 1Pe 4:11.

ORDAIN, ORDINATION [3338+4848, 3569, 3670, 3922, 4854, 5989, 6913, 7422, 2936]. In the KJV "ordain" is the translation of about thirty-five different Hebrew and Greek words. The word has many shades of meaning, chiefly four: (1) set in order, arrange (Ps 132:17; Isa 30:33); (2) bring into being (1Ki 12:32; Nu 28:6; Ps 8:2–3); (3) decree (Est 9:27; Ac 16:4; Ro 7:10); (4) set apart for an office or duty (Jer 1:5; Mk 3:14; Jn 15:16; Ac 14:23; 1Ti 2:7; Tit 1:5; Heb 5:1; 8:3).

Ordination in the sense of setting aside officers of the church for a certain work by the laying on of hands was practiced in apostolic times (Ac 13:2–3;1Ti 4:14; 2Ti 1:6), but it is nowhere described or enjoined. No great emphasis was placed on this rite.

ORDINANCE [2976, 2978, 5477]. A decree of the law (Ex 12:14, 24, 43; 13:10; 15:25; Nu 9:14; 10:8; 15:15; 18:8; Isa 24:5; Mal 4:4; Ro 13:2; 1Pe 2:13). Insufficiency, in salvation (Isa 1:10–17; Gal 5:6; 6:15; Eph 2:15; Col 2:14, 20–23; Heb 9:1, 8–10).

OVERCOME [OVERCOMES]

Mt	16:18	and the gates of Hades will not **o** it.
Mk	9:24	I do believe; help me **o** my unbelief
Lk	10:19	to **o** all the power of the enemy;
Jn	16:33	But take heart! I have **o** the world."
Ro	12:21	Do not be **o** by evil, but **o** evil
2Pe	2:20	and are again entangled in it and **o**,
1Jn	2:13	because you have **o** the evil one.
	4:4	are from God and have **o** them,
	5:4	is the victory that has **o** the world,
Rev	17:14	but the Lamb will **o** them

OVERCOMES [OVERCOME]

1Jn	5:4	born of God **o** the world.
	5:5	Who is it that **o** the world?
Rev	2:7	To him who **o**, I will give the right
	2:11	He who **o** will not be hurt at all
	2:17	To him who **o**, I will give some
	2:26	To him who **o** and does my will
	3:5	He who **o** will, like them, be
	3:12	Him who **o** I will make a pillar
	3:21	To him who **o**, I will give the right
	21:7	He who **o** will inherit all this,

OVERSEER [8853, 2175, 2176]. The translation of several Hebrew and Greek words, each with its distinctive meaning: Heb. *pāqadh*, "inspector, overseer" (Ge 39:4–5; 2Ch 34:12, 17); *menatstsehîm*, "foreman" (2Ch 2:18; 34:13); *shōtēr*, almost always "officer"; Greek *episkopos*, "bishop, overseer" (Ac 20:28).

General References to:
Ruler (Pr 6:7). *Office of church leadership, traditionally "bishop" (Ac 20:28; Php 1:1; 1Ti 3:1–7); same as an elder (Tit 1:5–9; 1Pe 5:1–4). A title of Christ (1Pe 2:25). See Elders.*

Pr	6:7	no **o** or ruler,
1Ti	3:1	anyone sets his heart on being an **o**,
	3:2	Now the **o** must be above reproach,
Tit	1:7	Since an **o** is entrusted
1Pe	2:25	returned to the Shepherd and **O**

PAGAN

| Mt | 18:17 | as you would a **p** or a tax collector. |
| Lk | 12:30 | For the **p** world runs |

PALESTINE (păl'ĕs-tīn, Heb. *pelesheth*). The term *Palestine* is not used in the NIV; it occurs four times in the KJV (Ex 15:14; Isa 14:29, 31; Joel 3:4). In all four contexts it refers to Philistia. The name is derived from Philistia, an area along the southern seacoast occupied by the Philistines (Ps 60:8). The original name was Canaan (Ge 12:5); after the conquest it came to be known as Israel (1Sa 13:19), and in the Greco-Roman period, Judea, Samaria, and Galilee. Physically the land is divided into five parts: the Plain of Sharon and the Philistine Plain along the coast; adjoining it, the Shephelah, or foothills region; then the central mountain range; after that the Jordan Valley; and east of the Jordan the Transjordan plateau. The varied configuration of Palestine produces a great variety of climate. Before the conquest the land was inhabited by Canaanites, Amorites, Hittites, Horites, and Amalekites. These were conquered by Joshua, the judges, and the kings. The kingdom was split in 931 BC; the northern kingdom was taken into captivity by the Assyrians in 722 BC; the southern kingdom by the Babylonians in 587 BC. From 587 BC to the time of the Maccabees the land was under foreign rule by the Babylonians, Persians, Alexander the Great, Egyptians, and Syrians. In 63 BC the Maccabees lost control of the land to the Romans, who held it until the time of Mohammed. In NT times Palestine west of the Jordan was divided into Galilee, Samaria, and Judea; and east of the Jordan into the Decapolis and Perea. *See Philistines.*

PAPYRUS [15, 1687] (*reed plant*). A reed that grows in swamps and along rivers or lakes, especially along the Nile. It is from eight to twelve feet tall and is used to make baskets, sandals, boats, and especially paper, the most common writing material of antiquity (Job 8:11; Isa 18:2). The NT books were undoubtedly all written on papyrus. Moses' basket of (Ex 2:3).

PARABLE [1948, 4886, 5442, 4130] (Gr. *parabolē*, *likeness, to be similar, to be comparable*). Derived from the Greek verb *paraballo*, composed of the preposition *para* meaning "beside" and the verb *ballō*, "to cast." A parable is thus a comparison of two objects for the purpose of teaching.

In the OT a parable is a proverbial saying used in wisdom and prophetic discourse (Ps 78:2; Pr 1:6). In the NT it is a story in which things in the spiritual realm are compared with events that could happen in the temporal realm; or an earthly story with a heavenly meaning (Eze 17; 24; Mt 13; Lk 15). Differs from a fable, myth, allegory, or proverb.

I. Didactic Parables.
   A. Nature and development of the kingdom.
      1. The sower (Mt 13:3 – 8; Mk 4:4 – 8; Lk 8:5 – 8).
      2. The tares (Mt 13:24 – 30).
      3. The mustard seed (Mt 13:31 – 32; Mk 4:30 – 32; Lk 13:18 – 19).
      4. The leaven (Mt 13:33; Lk 13:20 – 21).
      5. The hidden treasure (Mt 13:44).
      6. The pearl of great price (Mt 13:45 – 46).
      7. The drag net (Mt 13:47 – 50).
      8. The blade, the ear, and the full corn (Mk 4:26 – 29).
   B. Service and rewards.
      1. The laborers in the vineyard (Mt 20:1 – 16).
      2. The talents (Mt 25:14 – 30).
      3. The pounds (Lk 19:11 – 27).
      4. The unprofitable servants (Lk 17:7 – 10).
   C. Prayer.
      1. The friend at midnight (Lk 11:5 – 8).
      2. The unjust judge (Lk 18:1 – 8).

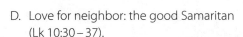

    D. Love for neighbor: the good Samaritan (Lk 10:30 – 37).

    E. Humility.

       1. The lowest seat at the feast (Lk 14:7 – 11).

       2. The Pharisee and the publican (Lk 18:9 – 14).

    F. Worldly wealth.

       1. The unjust steward (Lk 16:1 – 9).

       2. The rich fool (Lk 12:16 – 21).

       3. The great supper (Lk 14:15 – 24).

II. Evangelic Parables.

    A. God's love for the lost.

       1. The lost sheep (Mt 18:12 – 14; Lk 15:3 – 7).

       2. The lost coin (Lk 15:8 – 10).

       3. The lost son (Lk 15:11 – 32).

    B. Gratitude of the redeemed: the two debtors (Lk 7:41 – 43).

III. Prophetic and Judicial Parables.

    A. Watchfulness for Christ's return.

       1. The ten virgins (Mt 25:1 – 13).

       2. The faithful and unfaithful servants (Mt 24:45 – 51; Lk 12:42 – 48).

       3. The watchful porter (Mk 13:34 – 37).

    B. Judgment on Israel and within the kingdom.

       1. The two sons (Mt 21:28 – 32).

       2. The wicked husbandmen (Mt 21:33 – 34; Mk 12:1 – 12; Lk 20:9 – 18).

       3. The barren fig tree (Lk 13:6 – 9).

       4. The marriage feast of the king's son (Mt 22:1 – 14).

       5. The unforgiving servant (Mt 18:23 – 25).

Ps	78:2	I will open my mouth in **p**,
Mt	13:35	"I will open my mouth in **p**,
Lk	8:10	but to others I speak in **p**, so that,

PARACLETE (*comforter, exhorter*). One who pleads another's cause. Used by Christ of the Holy Spirit in John's Gospel (Jn 14:16, 26; 15:26; 16:7), and of Christ (1Jn 2:1).

PARADISE [4137] (Gr. *paradeisos, park*). A word of Persian origin, found only three times in Scripture (Lk 23:43; 2Co 12:4; Rev 2:7), referring in each case to heaven. There was a similar word in the Hebrew OT, *pardes*, translated "forest" or "orchard" or "park" (Ne 2:8; Ecc 2:5; SS 4:13). Scholars feel it was introduced into the Greek language very early and popularized by Xenophon.

The LXX uses the Greek word forty-six times, applying it to quite a wide category of places. It is used of the Adamic Eden (Ge 2:15; 3:23) and of the well-watered plains of the Jordan that Lot viewed (13:10). Since it was used to describe gardens of beauty and splendor, one is not surprised to see the NT begin to use the term to refer to the place of spiritual bliss (Lk 23:43).

The exact location of paradise is uncertain. Paul uses it in 2Co 12:4, identifying it with the third heaven. Ecclesiasticus 44:16 identifies paradise with heaven, into which Enoch was translated. Christ's single use of the term seems to establish its location best for the believer, for he uses it in reassuring the dying thief (Lk 23:43).

Lk	23:43	today you will be with me in **p**."
2Co	12:4	God knows — was caught up to **p**.
Rev	2:7	of life, which is in the **p** of God.

PARDON [4105, 5927, 5951, 6142]. Forgiveness. God demands a righteous ground for pardoning the sinner — the atoning work of Christ (Ex 34:9; 1Sa 15:25 – 26; Isa 55:7).

2Ch	30:18	**p** everyone who sets his heart
Job	7:21	Why do you not **p** my offenses
Isa	55:7	and to our God, for he will freely **p**.
Joel	3:21	I will **p**."

PARENT [3, 3+562+2256, 1204, 4252, 4591] (Gr. *goneus*). A distinctly NT word, occurring only in the plural (*goneis, parents*). Although this English word does not occur in the OT in the KJV and only infrequently in the NIV, there is much instruction there about the parent-child relationship. Children were to honor their parents (Ex 20:12) and obey and reverence them (Lev 19:3; Dt 5:16). Failure here on the child's part could be punished by death (Dt 21:18 – 21). The same high regard for parents is expected of children in the NT (Eph 6:1; Col 3:20). Parents were expected to love their children, care and provide for them, and not provoke them to wrath (2Co 12:14; Eph 6:4; Col 3:21).

General References to:

To be revered (Ex 20:12; Lev 19:3; Dt 5:16; Mt 15:4; 19:19; Mk 7:10; 10:19; Lk 18:20). Obeyed (Pr 1:8; 6:20; 23:22; Eph 6:1; Col 3:20). Covenant blessings of, entailed upon children (Ge 6:18; Ex 20:6; Ps 103:17). Curses upon, entailed upon children (Ex 20:5; Lev 20:5; Isa 14:20; Jer 9:14; La 5:7). Involved in children's wickedness (1Sa 2:27 – 36; 4:10 – 18). Cursing of, to be punished (Ex 21:17; Lev 20:9).

Beloved:

By Joseph (Ge 46:29); Rahab (Jos 2:12 – 13); Ruth (Ru 1:16 – 17); Elisha (1Ki 19:20). Mother, beloved (Pr 31:28).

Duties of:

Fathers to direct household (Ge 18:19; Lev 20:9; Pr 3:12; 13:24; 19:18; 1Ti 3:4 – 5, 12; Tit 1:6; Heb 12:7); govern with kindness (Eph 6:4; Col 3:21); provide for children (2Co 12:14; 1Ti 5:8); instruct children in righteousness (Ex 10:2; 12:27; 13:8, 14; Dt 4:9 – 10; 6:7, 20 – 25; 11:18 – 21; 32:46; Ps 78:5 – 6; Pr 22:6, 15; 27:11; Isa 38:19; Joel 1:3; Eph 6:4; 1Th 2:11); discipline children (Pr 19:8; 22:6, 15; 23:13 – 14; 29:15, 17). Prerequisite for church leadership (1Ti 3:4 – 5, 12).

Indulgent:

Eli (1Sa 2:27 – 36; 3:13 – 14); David (1Ki 1:6).

Influence of:

Evil (1Ki 15:26; 22:52 – 53; 2Ki 8:27; 21:20; 2Ch 21:6; 22:3). Good (1Ki 22:43; 2Ki 15:3, 34).

Love of:

Reflection of God's love (Ps 103:13; Pr 3:12; Isa 49:15; 66:13; Mt 7:9 – 11; Lk 11:11 – 13). Must be exceeded by love for Christ (Mt 10:37). To be taught (Tit 2:4).

Love Exemplified:

By Hagar (Ge 21:15 – 16); Rebekah's mother (Ge 24:55); Isaac and Rebekah (Ge 25:28); Isaac (Ge 27:26 – 27); Laban (Ge 31:26 – 28); Jacob (Ge 37:3 – 4; 42:4, 38; 43:13 – 14; 45:26 – 28; 48:10 – 11); Moses' mother (Ex 2); Naomi (Ru 1:8 – 9); Hannah (1Sa 2:19); David (2Sa 12:18 – 23; 13:38 – 39; 14:1, 33; 18:5, 12 – 13, 33; 19:1 – 6); Rizpah (2Sa 21:10); mother of infant brought to Solomon by harlots (1Ki 3:22 – 28); Mary (Mt 12:46; Lk 2:48; Jn 2:5; 19:25); Jairus (Mk 5:23); father of demoniac (Mk 9:24); nobleman (Jn 4:49).

PARENTS

Pr	17:6	and **p** are the pride of their children
	19:14	wealth are inherited from **p**,
Mt	10:21	children will rebel against their **p**
Lk	18:29	left home or wife or brothers or **p**
	21:16	You will be betrayed even by **p**, brothers,
Jn	9:3	Neither this man nor his **p** sinned,"
Ro	1:30	they disobey their **p**; they are
2Co	12:14	for their **p**, but **p** for their children.
Eph	6:1	Children, obey your **p** in the Lord,
Col	3:20	obey your **p** in everything,
1Ti	5:4	repaying their **p** and grandparents,
2Ti	3:2	disobedient to their **p**, ungrateful,

PAROUSIA (*presence, coming*). A Greek word frequently used in NT of our Lord's return (Mt 24:3; 1Co 15:23; 1Th 3:13; 4:15; 2Pe 1:16).

PASSION [678, 2123, 4077, 4792].

1. Lust or desire (Hos 7:6; 1Co 7:9).

2. Often used as a technical term of the suffering of Jesus. *See Jesus the Christ.*

PASSOVER [7175, 2038, 4247] (*pass over, spare*).

Institution of (Ex 12:3 – 49; 23:15 – 18; 34:18; Lev 23:4 – 8; Nu 9:2 – 5, 13 – 14; 28:16 – 25; Dt 16:1 – 8, 16; Ps 81:3, 5). Design of (Ex 12:21 – 28).

Special Passover for those who were unclean or on a journey to be held in the second month (Nu 9:6 – 12; 2Ch 30:2 – 4). Lamb killed by Levites for those who were ceremonially unclean (2Ch 30:17; 35:3 – 11; Ezr 6:20). Strangers authorized to celebrate (Ex 12:48 – 49; Nu 9:14). Observed at place designated by God (Dt 16:5 – 7) with unleavened bread (Ex 12:8, 15 – 20; 13:3, 6; 23:15; Lev 23:6; Nu 9:11; 29:17; Dt 16:3 – 4; Mk 14:12; Lk 22:7; Ac 12:3; 1Co 5:8). Penalty for neglecting to observe (Nu 9:13). Reinstituted by Ezekiel (Eze 45:21 – 24). Observation of, renewed by the Israelites on entering Canaan (Jos 5:10 – 11); by Hezekiah (2Ch 30:1); by Josiah (2Ki 23:22 – 23; 2Ch 35:1, 18); after return from captivity (Ezr 6:19 – 20). Observed by Jesus (Mt 26:17 – 20; Lk 22:15; Jn 2:13, 23; 13). Jesus in the temple at the time of (Lk 2:41 – 50). Jesus crucified at the time of (Mt 26:2; Mk 14:1 – 2; Jn 18:28). The lamb of, a type of Christ (1Co 5:7). Lord's Supper ordained at (Mt 26:26 – 28; Mk 14:12 – 25; Lk 22:7 – 20). Prisoner released at, by the Romans (Mt 27:15; Mk 15:6; Lk 23:16 – 17; Jn 18:39). Peter imprisoned at the time of (Ac 12:3). Christ called our Passover (1Co 5:7).

Ex	12:11	Eat it in haste; it is the Lord's **P**.
Nu	9:2	Have the Israelites celebrate the **P**
Dt	16:1	celebrate the **P** of the Lord your
Jos	5:10	the Israelites celebrated the **P**.
2Ki	23:21	"Celebrate the **P** to the Lord
Ezr	6:19	the exiles celebrated the **P**.
Mk	14:12	customary to sacrifice the **P** lamb,
Lk	22:1	called the **P**, was approaching,
1Co	5:7	our **P** lamb, has been sacrificed.
Heb	11:28	he kept the **P** and the sprinkling

PASTOR [4478] A leader of the church (Eph 4:11), possibly the same as elder and overseer. *See Elders; Overseer.*

Eph	4:11	and some to be **p** and teachers,

PASTORAL EPISTLES A common title for 1 and 2 Timothy and Titus, which were written by the apostle Paul to his special envoys sent on specific missions in accordance with the needs of the hour. They give instruction to Timothy and Titus concerning the pastoral care of churches. Though some date the Pastorals within the framework of Acts, most scholars believe all three were written not long after the events of Ac 28. After his imprisonment in Rome (c. AD 60 – 62), Paul most likely began his fourth missionary journey. The epistles concern church organization and discipline, including such matters as the appointment of bishops and deacons, the opposition of heretical or rebellious members, and the provision for maintenance of doctrinal purity.

PATIENCE [4206, 3428, 3429, 5705] (Gr. *hypomonē* and *makrothymia*). Both of these Greek words are translated by our English word *patience*, but they are not exactly synonymous in meaning. *Hypomonē* is the quality of endurance under trials. Those possessing this virtue are free from cowardice or despondency. It is mainly an attitude of heart with respect to things. *Makrothymia* ("long-suffering") is an attitude with respect to people. Patience is a fruit of the Spirit (Gal 5:22, KJV "longsuffering"); it is a virtue that God prizes highly in human beings and seems to be best developed under trials (Ro 5:3 – 4; Jas 1:3 – 4; 5:11 KJV; NIV perseverance). Both terms are used of God (Ro 2:4; 1Pe 3:20), apparently always in relation to persons.

General References to:
Commended (Ecc 7:8 – 9; La 3:26 – 27). Commanded (Ps 37:7 – 9; Eph 4:2; Col 3:12 – 13; 1Th 5:14; 1Ti 6:11; 2Ti 2:24 – 25; Tit 2:2; Heb 12:1; Jas 5:7 – 8; 2Pe 1:5 – 6). A fruit of tribulation (Ro 5:3 – 4; Rev 1:9). A grace of the righteous (Lk 8:15; 21:19; Ro 2:7; 8:25; 12:12; 15:4 – 5; 1Co 13:4 – 5; 2Co 6:4 – 6; 12:12; Col 1:10 – 11; 1Th 1:3; 2Th 3:5; Heb 6:12; 10:36; Jas 1:3 – 4, 19; 1Pe 2:19 – 23; Rev 14:12). Prerequisite of an overseer (1Ti 3:2). Propagates peace (Pr 15:18). Possible because of God's righteousness (Rev 13:10). Instances of: Isaac toward the people of Gerar (Ge 26:15 – 22); Moses (Ex 16:7 – 8); Job

(Job 1:21; Jas 5:11); David (Ps 40:1); Simeon (Lk 2:25); Paul (2Ti 3:10); prophets (Jas 5:10); Thessalonians (2Th 1:4); church at Ephesus (Rev 2:2 – 3); church at Thyatira (Rev 2:19); John (Rev 1:9). Of Jesus (1Pe 2:21 – 23; Rev 1:9).

Pr	19:11	A man's wisdom gives him **p**;
	25:15	Through **p** a ruler can be persuaded
Ecc	7:8	and **p** is better than pride.
Ro	2:4	and **p**, not realizing that God's
	9:22	bore with great **p** the objects
2Co	6:6	understanding, **p** and kindness;
Gal	5:22	joy, peace, **p**, kindness, goodness,
Col	1:11	may have great endurance and **p**,
	3:12	humility, gentleness and **p**.
1Ti	1:16	Jesus might display his unlimited **p**
2Ti	3:10	my purpose, faith, **p**, love,
	4:2	with great **p** and careful instruction
Heb	6:12	**p** inherit what has been promised.
Jas	5:10	as an example of **p** in the face
2Pe	3:15	that our Lord's **p** means salvation,

PATRIARCH [4252, 4256] (Gr. *patriarchēs, the father of a family, tribe,* or *race*). A title given in the NT to those who founded the Hebrew race and nation. In the NT it is applied to Abraham (Heb 7:4), the sons of Jacob (Ac 7:8 – 9), and David (2:29). The term is now commonly used to refer to the persons whose names appear in the genealogies and covenant histories before the time of Moses (Ge 5 and 11, histories of Noah, Abraham, Isaac, Jacob, et al.). In the patriarchal system the government of a clan was the right of the oldest lineal male. The patriarchal head was the priest of his own household.

While past scholars have often tended to regard the biblical accounts in the patriarchal dispensation as legendary, recent archaeological discoveries have confirmed the truthfulness of the narratives and have thrown much light on puzzling customs of the time, such as Abraham's taking Sarah's slave Hagar as a concubine, his making his steward Eliezer his heir, and Rachel's carrying away her father's household gods. Excavations at Ur, where Abraham lived,

reveal it to have been a rich commercial center, whose inhabitants were people of education and culture. *See also Abraham; Isaac; Jacob; Joseph.*

PAUL [4263] (Gr. *Paulos*, from Latin *Paulis, little*). The great apostle to the Gentiles. The main biblical source for information on the life of Paul is the Acts of the Apostles, with important supplemental information from Paul's own letters. Allusions in the letters make it clear that many events in his checkered and stirring career are unrecorded (cf. 2Co 11:24 – 28).

NAMES.

His Hebrew name was Saul (Gr. *Saulos*), and he is always so designated in Acts until his clash with Bar-Jesus at Paphos, where Luke writes, "Then Saul, who was also called Paul …" (Ac 13:9). Thereafter in Acts he is always called Paul. In his letters the apostle always calls himself Paul. As a Roman citizen, he doubtless bore both names from his youth.

BACKGROUND.

Providentially, three elements of the world's life of that day — Greek culture, Roman citizenship, and Hebrew religion — met in the apostle to the Gentiles. He had the privilege of being born a Roman citizen (22:28), though how his father had come to possess the coveted status is not known. Proud of the distinction and advantages thus conferred on him, Paul knew how to use that citizenship as a shield against injustice from local magistrates and to enhance the status of the Christian faith. His Gentile connections greatly aided him in bridging the chasm between the Gentile and the Jew. But of central significance was his strong Jewish heritage, which was fundamental to all he was and became. Born of purest Jewish blood (Php 3:5), the son of a Pharisee (Ac 23:6), Saul was cradled in orthodox Judaism. At the proper age, perhaps thirteen, he was sent to Jerusalem and completed his studies under the famous Gamaliel (22:3; 26:4 – 5). Being a superior, zealous student (Gal 1:14), he absorbed not only the teaching of the OT but also the rabbinical learning of the scholars.

At his first appearance in Acts as "a young man" (Ac 7:58), probably at least thirty years old, he was already an acknowledged leader in Judaism. His active opposition to Christianity marked him as the natural leader of the persecution that arose after the death of Stephen (7:58 – 8:3; 9:1 – 2). The persecutions described in 26:10 – 11 indicate his fanatical devotion to Judaism. He was convinced that Christians were heretics and that the honor of the Lord demanded their extermination (26:9). He acted in confirmed unbelief (1Ti 1:13).

CONVERSION.

The persecution was doubtless repugnant to his finer inner sensitivities, but Saul did not doubt the rightness of his course. The spread of Christians to foreign cities only increased his fury against them, causing him to extend the scope of his activities. As he approached Damascus, armed with authority from the high priest, the transforming crisis in his life occurred. Only an acknowledgment of divine intervention can explain it. Repeatedly in his letters Paul refers to it as the work of divine grace and power, transforming him and commissioning him as Christ's messenger (1Co 9:16 – 17; 15:10; Gal 1:15 – 16; Eph 3:7 – 9; 1Ti 1:12 – 16). The three accounts in Acts of the conversion vary according to the immediate purpose of the narrator and supplement each other. Luke's own account (Ac 9) is historical, relating the event objectively, while the two accounts by Paul (Ac 22, 26) stress those aspects appropriate to his immediate endeavor.

EARLY ACTIVITIES.

The new convert at once proclaimed the deity and messiahship of Jesus in the Jewish synagogues of Damascus, truths that had seized his soul (Ac 9:20 – 22). Three years after his conversion, Saul returned to Jerusalem with the intention of becoming acquainted with Peter (Gal 1:18). The Jerusalem believers regarded him with cold suspicion, but with the help of Barnabas, he became accepted among them (Ac 9:26 – 28).

MISSIONARY JOURNEYS.

The work of Gentile foreign missions was inaugurated by the church at Antioch under the direction of the Holy Spirit in the sending forth of "Barnabas and Saul" (Ac 13:1 – 3).

The first missionary journey, begun apparently in the spring of AD 48, began with work among the Jews on Cyprus. Paul's first three missionary journeys are captured in the remaining chapters of Acts. Acts concludes with Paul imprisoned in Rome.After his release, perhaps in the spring of AD 63, Paul went east, visited Ephesus, stationing Timothy there when he left for Macedonia (1Ti 1:3). He left Titus to complete the missionary work on Crete, and in writing to him mentions plans to spend the winter at Nicopolis (Tit 1:5; 3:12). From Nicopolis he may have made the traditional visit to Spain, working there at the outbreak of the persecution by Nero in the autumn of 64. Second Timothy makes it clear that Paul is again a prisoner in Rome, kept in close confinement as a malefactor (2Ti 1:16 – 17; 2:9). At his first appearance before the court, he escaped immediate condemnation (4:16 – 18), but to Timothy he writes of no hope for release (4:6 – 8). He was executed at Rome in late 66 or early 67. Tradition says he was beheaded on the Ostian Way.

Background and Conversion:
Also called Saul (Ac 8:1; 9:1; 13:9). Of the tribe of Benjamin (Ro 11:1; Php 3:5). Personal appearance of (2Co 10:1, 10; 11:6). Born in Tarsus (Ac 9:11; 21:39; 22:3). Educated at Jerusalem in the school of Gamaliel (Ac 22:3; 26:4). A zealous Pharisee (Ac 22:3; 23:6; 26:5; 2Co 11:22; Gal 1:14; Php 3:5). A Roman (Ac 16:37; 22:25 – 28). Persecutes the Christians; present at and gives consent to the stoning of Stephen (Ac 7:58; 8:1, 3; 9:1; 22:4). Sent to Damascus with letters for the arrest and return to Jerusalem of Christians (Ac 9:1 – 2). His vision and conversion (Ac

9:3 – 22; 22:4 – 19; 26:9 – 15; 1Co 9:11; 15:8; Gal 1:13; 1Ti 1:12 – 13). Is baptized (Ac 9:18; 22:16). Called to be an apostle (Ac 22:14 – 21; 26:14 – 21; 26:16 – 18; Ro 1:1; 1Co 1:1; 9:1 – 2; 15:9; Gal 1:1, 15 – 16; Eph 1:1; Col 1:1; 1Ti 1:1; 2:7; 2Ti 1:1, 11; Tit 1:1, 3). Preaches in Damascus (Ac 9:20, 22). Is persecuted by the Jews (Ac 9:23 – 24). Escapes by being let down from the wall in a basket; goes to Arabia (Gal 1:17), Jerusalem (Ac 9:25 – 26; Gal 1:18 – 19). Received by the disciples in Jerusalem (Ac 9:26 – 29). Goes to Caesarea and returns to Tarsus (Ac 9:30; 18:22). Brought to Antioch by Barnabas (Ac 11:25 – 26). Teaches at Antioch one year (Ac 11:26). Brings the contributions of the Christians in Antioch to the Christians in Jerusalem (Ac 11:27 – 30). Returns with John to Antioch (Ac 12:25).

First Missionary Journey:

Sent to the Gentiles (Ac 13:2 – 3, 47 – 48; 22:17:21; Ro 11:13; 15:16; Gal 1:15 – 24). Visits Seleucia (Ac 13:4); Cyprus (Ac 13:4). Preaches at Salamis (Ac 13:5); Paphos (Ac 13:6). Sergius Paulus the proconsul is converted (Ac 13:7 – 12). Contends with Elymas the sorcerer (Ac 13:6 – 12). Visits Perga in Pamphylia (Ac 13:13). John, a companion of, departs for Jerusalem (Ac 13:13). Visits Antioch in Pisidia and preaches in the synagogue (Ac 13:14 – 41). Message received gladly by Gentiles (Ac 13:42, 49). Persecuted and expelled (Ac 13:50 – 51). Visits Iconium and preaches to Jews and Greeks; is persecuted; escapes to Lystra; goes to Derbe (Ac 14:1 – 6). Heals a crippled man (Ac 14:8 – 10). People attempt to worship him (Ac 14:11 – 18). Is persecuted by Jews from Antioch and Iconium and is stoned (Ac 14:19; 2Co 11:25; 2Ti 3:11). Escapes to Derbe, where he preaches the gospel, and returns to Lystra, Iconium, and Antioch, encourages the disciples, and ordains elders (Ac 14:19 – 23). Revisits Pisidia, Pamphylia, Perga, Attalia, and returns to Antioch (Ac 14:24 – 28). Contends with Judaizing Christians against circumcision (Ac 15:1 – 2). Refers question of circumcision to apostles and elders at Jerusalem (Ac 15:2, 4). Declares to apostles at Jerusalem the miracles and wonders God had done among the Gentiles by them (Ac 15:12). Returns to Antioch, accompanied by Barnabas, Judas, and Silas, with letters to the Gentiles (Ac 15:22, 25).

Second Missionary Journey:

Makes second tour of the churches (Ac 15:36). Chooses Silas as his companion and passes through Syria and Cilicia, confirming the churches (Ac 15:36 – 41). Visits Lystra; circumcises Timothy (Ac 16:1 – 5). Goes through Phrygia and Galatia; is forbidden by Holy Spirit to preach in Asia; visits Mysia; desires to go to Bithynia, but is restrained by the Spirit; goes to Troas, where he has a vision of a man saying, "Come over to Macedonia and help us"; he immediately proceeds to Macedonia (Ac 16:6 – 10). Visits Samothrace and Neapolis; comes to Philippi, the chief city of Macedonia; visits a place of prayer at the riverside; preaches the Word; the merchant Lydia of Thyatira is converted and baptized (Ac 16:11 – 15). Exorcizes a demon from a fortune-teller (Ac 16:16 – 18). Persecuted, beaten, and cast into prison with Silas; sings songs of praise in prison; earthquake shakes the prison; he preaches to the alarmed jailer, who believes and is baptized with his household (Ac 16:19 – 34). Released by the civil authorities on the ground of his being a Roman citizen (Ac 16:35 – 39; 2Co 6:5; 11:25; 1Th 2:2). Received at the house of Lydia (Ac 16:40). Visits Amphipolis, Apollonia, and Thessalonica; preaches in the synagogue (Ac 17:1 – 4). Is persecuted (Ac 17:5 – 9; 2Th 1:1 – 4). Escapes to Berea by night; preaches in the synagogue; many honorable women and men believe (Ac 17:10 – 12). Persecuted by Jews from Thessalonica; is conducted by the brothers to Athens (Ac 17:13 – 15). Disputes on Mars' Hill with philosophers (Ac 17:16 – 34). Visits Corinth; lives with Aquila and his wife, Priscilla, tentmakers; joins in

their trade; reasons in the synagogue every Sabbath; is rejected by the Jews; turns to the Gentiles; stays there one year and six months, teaching the word of God (Ac 18:1–11). Persecuted by Jews, taken before the proconsul; accusation dismissed; takes leave after many days and sails to Syria accompanied by Aquila and Priscilla (Ac 18:12–18). Visits Ephesus where he leaves Aquila and Priscilla; enters synagogue where he reasons with Jews; starts on return journey to Jerusalem; visits Caesarea; returns to Antioch (Ac 18:19–22).

Third Missionary Journey:

Returning to Ephesus, passes through Galatia and Phrygia, strengthening the disciples (Ac 18:18–23). Baptizes disciples of John in name of the Lord Jesus; preaches in synagogue; remains in Ephesus for two years; heals the sick (Ac 19:1–12). Jewish exorcists are beaten by a demon and many Ephesians believe, bringing their books of sorcery to be burned (Ac 19:13–20; 1Co 16:8–9). Sends Timothy and Erastus into Macedonia, but he himself remains in Asia for a period of time (Ac 19:21–22). Spread of the gospel through his preaching interferes with idol makers; he is persecuted, and a great uproar is created; city clerk appeases the people, dismisses accusation against Paul, and disperses the people (Ac 19:23–41; 2Co 1:8; 2Ti 4:14). Proceeds to Macedonia after encouraging the churches in those parts; comes into Greece and stays three months; returns through Macedonia, accompanied by Sopater, Aristarchus, Secundus, Gaius, Timothy, Tychicus, and Trophimus (Ac 20:1–6). Visits Troas; preaches until the break of day; restores to life Eutychus, who fell from the window (Ac 20:6–12). Visits Assos, Mitylene, Kios, Samos, and Miletus, hurrying to Jerusalem to be there at Pentecost (Ac 20:13–16). Sends for elders of church of Ephesus; tells them of how he had preached in Asia and of his tests and afflictions; declares he was compelled by the Spirit to go to Jerusalem; exhorts them to watch over

themselves and their flock; kneels down, prays, and departs (Ac 20:17–38). Visits Cos, Rhodes, Patara; takes a ship for Tyre; stays seven days; is brought on his way by the disciples to the outskirts of the city; kneels, prays, and leaves; comes to Ptolemais; greets the brothers and stays one day (Ac 21:1–7). Departs for Caesarea; enters house of Philip the evangelist; is warned by Agabus not to go to Jerusalem; proceeds to Jerusalem (Ac 21:8–16).

Arrest and Trials:

Received warmly by the brothers; talks of the things that had been done among the Gentiles by his ministry; enters the temple; people are stirred against him by Jews from Asia; uproar ensues; he is thrown out of temple; commander of the troops interposes and arrests him (Ac 21:17–33). His defense (Ac 21:33–40; 22:1–21). Confined in the barracks (Ac 22:24–30). Brought before the Sanhedrin; his defense (Ac 22:30; 23:1–5). Returned to the barracks (Ac 23:10). Encouraged by a vision, promising him that he must testify in Rome (Ac 23:11). Jews conspire against his life (Ac 23:12–15). Thwarted by his nephew (Ac 23:16–22). Escorted to Caesarea by military guard (Ac 23:23–33). Confined in Herod's palace in Caesarea (Ac 23:35). Trial before Felix (Ac 24). Remains in custody for two years (Ac 24:27). Trial before Festus (Ac 25:1–12). Appeals to Caesar (Ac 25:10–12). Examination before Agrippa (Ac 25:13–27; 26). Taken to Rome in custody of Julius, a centurion, and guard of soldiers; boards ship, accompanied by other prisoners, and sails along coast of Asia; stops at Sidon and Myra (Ac 27:1–5). Transferred to a ship of Alexandria; sails past Cnidus, Crete, and Salmone to Fair Havens (Ac 27:6–8). Predicts loss of ship; his advice not heeded and voyage resumed (Ac 27:9–13). Ship encounters a hurricane; Paul encourages and comforts officers and crew; soldiers advise putting prisoners to death; centurion interferes; all 276 on board are saved (Ac 27:14–44). Ship is wrecked, and all on board take refuge on island of Malta (Ac 27:14 – 44). Kind treatment by island inhabitants (Ac 28:1 – 2). Bitten by a viper and miraculously preserved (Ac 28:3 – 6). Heals the chief official's father and others (Ac 28:7 – 10). Delayed in Malta three months; proceeds on voyage; delays at Syracuse; sails by Rhegium and Puteoli; meets brothers who accompany him to Rome from Forum of Appius; arrives at Rome and is permitted to live by himself in custody of a soldier (Ac 28:11 – 16). Calls chief Jews together; states his situation; is kindly received; expounds the gospel; testifies to the kingdom of heaven (Ac 28:17 – 29). Lives two years in his own hired house, preaching and teaching (Ac 28:30 – 31). Sickness of in Asia (2Co 1:8 – 11). Caught up to third heaven (2Co 12:1 – 4). Has "a thorn in the flesh" (2Co 12:7 – 9; Gal 4:13 – 14).

PEACE [1388, 4957, 5341, 5663, 5739, 8092, 8922, 8932, 8934, 8966, 9200, 457, 1644, 1645, 1646, 1647] (Heb. *shālôm*, peace, Gr. *eirēnē*, concord). The word used in the OT and still found today among Semitic peoples basically means "completeness" or "soundness." It can denote neighborliness (Ps 28:3 KJV) or well-being and security (Ecc 3:8) or the reward of a mind stayed on God (Isa 26:3). It is linked with honest dealing and true justice (Zec 8:16 KJV), and is a prominent feature of the coming Messiah (Isa 9:6).

According to the NT, peace results from God's forgiveness (Php 4:7) and is the ideal relation with one's brother or sister (2Co 13:11; cf. Mt 5:23 – 24). Peace is a mark of serenity (Jn 14:27) to be sought after (Heb 12:14), and it summarizes the gospel message (Ac 10:36). It is a fruit of the Spirit (Gal 5:22), will benefit those who practice it both now (Jas 3:18) and at the Second Coming (Ro 2:10), and is the opposite of disorder or confusion (1Co 14:33). Peace is the presence of God, not the absence of conflict. The Christian who knows peace is charged to tell others so that it may come for them, too, through Christ, who brought, preached, and is our peace (Eph 2:14ff.).

From God:

(Nu 6:26; Pss 29:11; 85:8; Isa 26:12; 57:19; 1Co 14:33).

Social:

Beneficence of (Ps 133:1; Pr 15:17; 17:1, 14; Ecc 4:6). *Honorable* (Pr 20:3). *Commanded* (Ge 45:24; Ps 34:14; Jer 29:7; Mk 9:50; Ro 12:18; 14:19; 2Co 13:11; Eph 4:3, 31 – 32; 1Th 5:13; 1Ti 2:2; 2Ti 2:22; Heb 12:14; 1Pe 3:10 – 11). *Love of, commanded* (Zec 8:19). *Promised* (Lev 26:6; Job 5:23 – 24; Isa 2:4; 11:6 – 9, 13; 60:17 – 18; Hos 2:18). *The righteous assured of* (Pr 16:7). *Broken by the gospel* (Mt 10:21 – 22, 34 – 36; Lk 12:51 – 53). *Moses' efforts in behalf of, resented* (Ex 2:13 – 14; Ac 7:26 – 29). *Promoters of peace promised: joy* (Pr 12:20); *adoption* (Mt 5:9); *fruit of righteousness* (Jas 3:17 – 18); *God's favor* (Lk 2:14). *Instances of promoters of peace: Abraham* (Ge 13:8 – 9), *Abimelech* (Ge 26:29), *Mordecai* (Est 10:3). *David* (Ps 120:6 – 7).

Spiritual:

Through Christ (Isa 2:4; 9:6 – 7; 11:6, 13; Mic 4:3, 5; Lk 1:79; Jn 7:38; 14:27; Ac 10:36; Ro 5:1; 10:15). *To the world* (Isa 2:4; 11:6 – 9; Lk 2:14). *To God's children* (Isa 54:10, 13). *From God* (Job 34:29; Pss 29:11; 72:3, 7; 85:8; Jer 33:6; Eze 34:25; Hag 2:9; Mal 2:5; Ro 15:13, 33; 16:20; 1Co 1:3; 14:33; 2Co 1:2; Gal 1:3; Php 4:7, 9; 1Th 1:1; 5:23; 2Th 3:16; 1Ti 1:2; 2Ti 1:2; Tit 1:4; Phm ; Heb 13:20; Rev 1:4). *From Christ* (Mt 11:29; Jn 14:27; 16:33; 20:19; Eph 2:14 – 17; Col 3:15; Rev 1:4 – 5). *A fruit of the Spirit* (Ro 14:17; Gal 5:22). *A fruit of righteousness* (Ro 2:10). *Assured to the righteous* (Pss 37:4, 11, 37; 125:1, 5; Pr 3:17, 24; Isa 26:3, 12; 32:2, 17 – 18; 55:2, 12; 57:1 – 2, 19; Ro 8:6). *Through the reconciliation of Christ* (Isa 53:5; Jn 7:38; Ro 5:1; Col 1:20); *acquaintance with God* (Job 22:21, 26; Pss 4:8; 17:15; 73:25 – 26; Isa 12:1 – 2; 25:7 – 8; 28:12; Lk 2:29); *loving God's law* (Pss 1:1 – 2; 119:165); *obedience* (Ps 25:12 – 13; Isa 48:18; Jer 6:16). *No peace to the wicked* (Isa 48:22; 57:21). *To be made with God* (Isa 27:5).

Lev	26:6	" 'I will grant **p** in the land,
Nu	6:26	and give you **p**.'"
	25:12	him I am making my covenant of **p**
Dt	20:10	make its people an offer of **p**.
Jdg	3:11	So the land had **p** for forty years,
1Ki	2:33	may there be the LORD's **p** forever
	22:44	also at **p** with the king of Israel.
2Ch	14:1	and in his days the country was at **p**
Job	3:26	I have no **p**, no quietness;
Ps	29:11	LORD blesses his people with **p**.
	34:14	seek **p** and pursue it.
	37:37	there is a future for the man of **p**.
	119:165	Great **p** have they who love your
	122:6	Pray for the **p** of Jerusalem:
Pr	12:20	but joy for those who promote **p**.
	14:30	A heart at **p** gives life to the body,
	16:7	his enemies live at **p** with him.
	17:1	Better a dry crust with **p** and quiet
Ecc	3:8	a time for war and a time for **p**.
Isa	9:6	Everlasting Father, Prince of **P**.
	26:3	You will keep in perfect **p**
	32:17	The fruit of righteousness will be **p**;
	48:18	your **p** would have been like a river,
	53:5	punishment that brought us **p** was
Jer	6:14	'P, p,' they say,
	30:10	Jacob will again have **p**
Eze	13:10	"P," when there is no **p**,
	34:25	" 'I will make a covenant of **p**
Mic	5:5	And he will be their **p**.
Zec	8:19	Therefore love truth and **p**."
	9:10	He will proclaim **p** to the nations.
Mal	2:5	a covenant of life and **p**,
Mt	10:34	I did not come to bring **p**,
Mk	9:50	and be at **p** with each other."
Lk	1:79	to guide our feet into the path of **p**
	2:14	on earth **p** to men on whom his
	19:38	"P in heaven and glory
Jn	14:27	P I leave with you; my **p**
	16:33	so that in me you may have **p**.
Ro	1:7	and **p** to you from God our Father
	5:1	we have **p** with God
	8:6	by the Spirit is life and **p**;
	12:18	on you, live at **p** with everyone.

	14:19	effort to do what leads to **p**
1Co	7:15	God has called us to live in **p**.
	14:33	a God of disorder but of **p**.
2Co	13:11	be of one mind, live in **p**.
Gal	5:22	joy, **p**, patience, kindness,
Eph	2:14	he himself is our **p**, who has made
	6:15	comes from the gospel of **p**.
Php	4:7	the **p** of God, which transcends all
Col	1:20	by making **p** through his blood,
	3:15	Let the **p** of Christ rule
1Th	5:3	While people are saying, "P
	5:13	Live in **p** with each other.
	5:23	the God of **p**, sanctify you through
2Th	3:16	the Lord of **p** himself give you **p**
2Ti	2:22	righteousness, faith, love and **p**,
Heb	7:2	"king of Salem" means "king of **p**."
	12:11	**p** for those who have been trained
	12:14	effort to live in **p** with all men
	13:20	May the God of **p**, who
1Pe	3:11	he must seek **p** and pursue it.
2Pe	3:14	blameless and at **p** with him.
Rev	6:4	power to take **p** from the earth

PENTATEUCH, THE (pĕn't a-tū̄k, Heb. *tôrâh, law or teaching*). The first five books of the Bible: Genesis, Exodus, Leviticus, Numbers, and Deuteronomy. These books, whose canonicity has never been called into question by the Jews, Protestants, or Catholics, head the list of the OT canon. As a literary unit they provide the background for the OT as well as the NT.

Chronologically the Pentateuch covers the period of time from the creation to the end of the Mosaic era. Since the date for the creation of the universe is not given, it is impossible to ascertain the length of this entire era.

Genesis begins with an account of creation but soon narrows its interest to the human race. Adam and Eve were entrusted with the responsibility of caring for the world about them but forfeited their privilege through disobedience and sin. In subsequent generations all humankind became so wicked that the entire human race, except Noah and his family, was destroyed. When the new civilization degenerated, God chose to fulfill his promises of redemption through Abraham. From Adam to Abraham represents a long period of time, for which the genealogical lists in Ge 5 and 10 hardly serve as a timetable.

The patriarchal era (Ge 12 – 50) narrates the events of approximately four generations — namely, those of Abraham, Isaac, Jacob, and Joseph. Scholars generally agree that Abraham lived during the nineteenth or eighteenth century BC, some dating him a century earlier and some considerably later. After the opening verses of Exodus, the rest of the Pentateuch is chronologically confined to the lifetime of Moses. Consequently, the deliverance of Israel from Egypt and their preparation for entrance into the land of Canaan is the prevailing theme.

The historical core of these books is briefly outlined as follows:

    I. From Egypt to Mount Sinai (Ex 1 – 19).
    II. Encampment at Mount Sinai, Approximately One Year (Ex 19 – Nu 10).
    III. Wilderness Wanderings, Approximately Thirty-eight Years (Nu 10 – 21).
    IV. Encampment before Canaan, Approximately One Year (Nu 22 – Dt 34).

The Mosaic law was given at Mount Sinai. As God's covenant people, the Israelites were not to conform to the idolatrous practices of the Egyptians nor to the customs of the Canaanites whose land they were to conquer and possess. Israel's religion was a revealed religion. For nearly a year they were carefully instructed in the law and the covenant. A tabernacle was erected as the central place for the worship of God. Offerings and sacrifices were instituted to make atonement for their sins and for expression of their gratitude and devotion to God. The Aaronic family, supported by the Levites, was ordained to serve at the tabernacle in the ministration of divine worship. Feasts and seasons likewise were carefully prescribed for the Israelites so that they might worship and serve God as his distinctive

people. After the entrance into Canaan was delayed for almost forty years because of the unbelief of the Israelites, Moses reviewed the law for the younger generation. This review, plus timely instructions for the occupation of Palestine, is summarized in the book of Deuteronomy.

    I. Era of Beginnings (Ge 1:1 – 11:32).
    II. Patriarchal Period (Ge 12:1 – 50:26).
    III. Emancipation of Israel (Ex 1:1 – 19:2).
    IV. Religion of Israel (Ex 19:3-Lev 27:34).
    V. Organization of Israel (Nu 1:1 – 10:10).
    VI. Wilderness Wanderings (Nu 10:11 – 22:1).
    VII. Preparations for Entering Canaan (Nu 22:2 – 36:13).
    VIII. Retrospect and Prospect (Dt 1 – 34).

PENTECOST [4300] (pĕn'tĕkŏst, Gr. *pentēcostē, fiftieth [day]*). The word derives from the Greek for "the fiftieth day." It was the Jewish Feast of Weeks (Ex 34:22; Dt 16:9 – 11), variously called the Feast of Harvest (Ex 23:16) or the Day of Firstfruits (Nu 28:26), which fell on the fiftieth day after the Feast of the Passover. The exact method by which the date was computed is a matter of some controversy.

Originally, the festival was the time when, with appropriate ritual and ceremony, the firstfruits of the corn harvest, the last Palestinian crop to ripen, were formally dedicated. The festival cannot therefore have antedated the settlement in Palestine. Leviticus 23 prescribes the sacred nature of the holiday and lists the appropriate sacrifices. Numbers 28 appears to be a supplementary list, prescribing offerings apart from those connected with the preservation of the ritual loaves. In later Jewish times, the feast developed into a commemoration of the giving of the Mosaic law. To reinforce this function, the rabbis taught that the law was given fifty days after the exodus, a tradition of which there is no trace in the OT nor in the Jewish authorities, Philo and Josephus. It was the events of Ac 2 that transformed the Jewish festival into a Christian one. Here, Pentecost marks the arrival of the Holy Spirit demonstrated by the gift of tongues and the inauguration of the church age. Some have seen a symbolic connection between the first fruits of the ancient festival and the firstfruits of the Christian dispensation. "Whitsunday" is therefore the fiftieth day after Easter Sunday. The name derives from the wearing of white garments by those seeking baptism at this festival, a practice of very ancient origin.

General References to: Ritual of the feast described (Lev 23:15 – 21). Institution of (Ex 23:16; 34:22; Lev 23:15 – 21; Nu 28:26 – 31; Dt 16:9 – 12, 16). Called in the NT the day of Pentecost (Ac 2:1; 20:16; 1Co 16:8).

Ac	2:1	of **P** came, they were all together
	20:16	if possible, by the day of **P**.
1Co	16:8	I will stay on at Ephesus until **P**,

PERFECTION, PERFECT [4003, 4005, 9459, 5455, 5457] (Heb. *shālēm*, *tāmîm*, Gr. *teleios*, *teleiotēs*). In the Bible, God alone, who lacks nothing in terms of goodness or excellence, is presented as truly perfect. Everything he is, thinks, and does has the character of perfection (Dt 32:4; 2Sa 22:31; Job 37:16; Pss 18:30; 19:7; Mt 5:48). When human beings are called perfect in the OT, it means that they are "upright" or "blameless" (Ge 6:9; Job 1:1; Ps 37:37). Sacrificial animals were deemed perfect if they were without spot or blemish and thus wholesome or sound (Lev 3:1, 6; 4:3; 14:10).

The Greek *teleios* conveys the idea of reaching the point of full growth or maturity. This meaning is intended in 1Co 14:20 and Heb 5:14 where there is a contrast between immaturity and maturity; but it is also present in 1Co 2:6; 14:20; Eph 4:13; Php 3:15; Col 1:28; 4:12. The word of Jesus in Mt 5:48 concerning the perfection of God and the perfection of the disciple of the kingdom suggests that there is a perfection appropriate to God (who is eternal) and to a disciple (who is a fallen creature in the process of being saved). The latter perfection is the highest possible maturity within the conditions of fallenness and finitude.

The theme of perfection is found in the letter to the Hebrews. Here Christ is presented as perfected (totally prepared and fitted for his priestly ministry in heaven) through suffering (Heb 2:10) and then as perfect (in his divine and human natures, 7:28) as he sits at the right hand of the Father in the perfect heavenly sanctuary (9:11). By his unique sacrifice for sin, he has made perfect forever those who are set apart as Christians for the service of God (10:14); here the idea is that Christ has perfectly consecrated those for whom he died on the cross, for there is nothing lacking in his meritorious atonement.

Major Idea:
Complete or whole, rather than without fault or shortcoming. None without sin (1Ki 8:46; 2Ch 6:36; Ecc 7:20). From God (Ps 18:32; 1Pe 5:10). Through Christ (Col 1:21 – 22, 28; 2:9 – 11; Heb 10:14; 13:20 – 21; 1Pe 5:10; 1Jn 3:6 – 10). Through God's love (1Jn 4:12).

Ascribed to:
Noah (Ge 6:8 – 9); Jacob (Nu 23:21); David (1Ki 11:4, 6); Asa (1Ki 15:14); Job (Job 1:1); Zechariah and Elizabeth (Lk 1:6); Nathanael (Jn 1:47); the peaceful (Ps 37:31, 37); the wise (1Co 2:6); man of God (2Ti 3:17); self-controlled (Jas 3:2); those who obey God's word (1Jn 2:5).

Blessings of:
(Pss 106:3; 119:1 – 3, 6; Mt 5:6). Reward of (Ps 37:31, 37; Pr 2:21; Lk 6:40; 1Jn 5:18).

Commanded:
(Ge 17:1; Dt 5:32; 18:13; Jos 23:6; 1Ki 8:61; 1Ch 28:9; Mt 5:48; 2Co 7:1; 13:11; Php 1:10; 2:15; Col 3:14; Jas 1:4). Requirements for (Dt 5:32; Jos 23:6; 1Ki 8:61; 1Ch 29:19; Mt 19:21; 2Co 7:1). Program for (Eph 4:11 – 13; Heb 6:1; 1Jn 2:5).

Desire for:
(Mt 5:6; 2Ti 3:17). In Job (Job 9:20 – 21); in David (Ps 101:2); in Paul (Php 3:12 – 15).

Prayer for:
(1Ch 29:19; 2Co 13:9; Col 4:12; 1Th 3:10, 13; Heb 13:20 – 21).

God Is Perfect:
(Dt 32:4; 2Sa 22:31; Pss 18:30; 19:7; 50:2).

Dt	32:4	He is the Rock, his works are **p**,
2Sa	22:31	"As for God, his way is **p**;
	22:33	and makes my way **p**.
Job	36:4	one **p** in knowledge is with you.
Ps	18:30	As for God, his way is **p**;
	18:32	and makes my way **p**.
	19:7	The law of the LORD is **p**,
Isa	25:1	for in **p** faithfulness
	26:3	You will keep in **p** peace
Eze	16:14	had given you made your beauty **p**,
Mt	5:48	Do not even pagans do that? Be **p**,
	19:21	answered, "If you want to be **p**,
Ro	12:2	his good, pleasing and **p** will.
2Co	12:9	for my power is made **p**
Php	3:12	or have already been made **p**,
Col	1:28	so that we may present everyone **p**
	3:14	binds them all together in **p** unity.
Heb	2:10	the author of their salvation **p**
	5:9	what he suffered and, once
		made **p**,
	7:19	useless (for the law made nothing **p**
	7:28	who has been made **p** forever.
	9:11	and more **p** tabernacle that is not
	10:1	make **p** those who draw
	10:14	he has made **p** forever those who
	11:40	with us would they be made **p**.
	12:23	spirits of righteous men made **p**,
Jas	1:17	Every good and **p** gift is from above
	1:25	into the **p** law that gives freedom,
	3:2	he is a **p** man, able
1Jn	4:18	But **p** love drives out fear,
	4:18	The one who fears is not made **p**

PERGAMUM, PERGAMOS [4307] (pûr'ga-mŭm, Gr. *Pergamos*). A city of Mysia in the Caicus Valley, fifteen miles (twenty-five km.) inland; in KJV, Pergamos (Rev 1:11; 2:12). Royally situated in a commanding position, Pergamum was the capital until the last of the Pergamenian kings bequeathed his realm to Rome in 133 BC. Pergamum became the chief town of the new province of Asia and was the site of the first temple of the Caesar cult, erected to Rome and Augustus in 29 BC. A second shrine was later dedicated to Trajan, and the multiplication of such honor marks the prestige of Pergamum in pagan Asia. The worship of Asklepios and Zeus were also endemic. The symbol of the former was a serpent, and Pausanias describes his cult image "with a staff in one hand and the other on the head of a serpent." Pergamenian coins illustrate the importance that the community attached to this cult. Caracalla is shown on one coin, saluting a serpent twined round a bending sapling. On the crag above Pergamum was a thronelike altar to Zeus (cf. Rev. 2:13) now in the Berlin Museum. It commemorated a defeat of a Gallic inroad and was decorated with a representation of the conflict of the gods and the giants, the latter shown as monsters with snakelike tails. To deepen Christian horror at Pergamum's obsession with the serpent-image, Zeus was called in this connection "Zeus the Savior." It is natural that "Nicolaitanism" should flourish in a place where politics and paganism were so closely allied (2:15), and where pressure on Christians to compromise must have been heavy.

Pergamum was an ancient seat of culture and possessed a library that rivaled Alexandria's. Parchment (*charta Pergamena*) was invented at Pergamum to free the library from Egypt's jealous ban on the export of papyrus.

PERSECUTE

Ps	119:86	for men **p** me without cause.
Mt	5:11	**p** you and falsely say all kinds
	5:44	and pray for those who **p** you,
Jn	15:20	they persecuted me, they will **p** you
Ac	9:4	why do you **p** me?" "Who are you,
Ro	12:14	Bless those who **p** you; bless

PERSECUTION [6715, 8103, 1502, 1503, 2567, 2568, 2808]. In its most common sense, this signifies a particular course or period of systematic infliction of punishment or penalty for adherence to a particular religious belief. Oppression is to be distinguished from it. Pharaoh oppressed the Hebrews; so did Nebuchadnezzar. Daniel and Jeremiah were persecuted. Systematic persecution began with the Roman imperial government. Notably tolerant toward alien religious beliefs in general, the Romans clashed with the Christians over the formalities of Caesar worship. Disregarding Claudius's anti-Semitism of AD 49 (Ac 18:2), in which the Christians were not distinguished from Jews, Nero must be regarded as the first persecutor. In 64 (Tactitus, *Annals* 15:38 – 44) this emperor used the small Christian community as a scapegoat for a disastrous fire in Rome, placing on the Christians the charge of arson that was popularly leveled against him.

Of Jesus:

(Ac 4:27; Heb 12:2 – 3; 1Pe 4:1). Meekly endured (Isa 50:6). Foretold (Ge 3:15; Isa 49:7; 50:6; 52:14; 53:2 – 10; Mic 5:1; Zec 12:10; Mt 2:13). Typified, in the persecutions of Israel's kings (Pss 2:1 – 5; 22:1 – 2, 6 – 8, 11 – 21; 69:1 – 21; 109:25; Ro 15:3). Persecution by the Jews (Mt 12:14; 22:15; 26:3 – 4; Mk 12:13; 15:14; Lk 6:11; 11:53 – 54; 20:20; 22:2 – 5, 52 – 53; 23:23; Jn 5:16; 7:1, 7, 19; 11:57; 15:18, 20 – 21; 18:22 – 23; 19:6, 15; Ac 2:23). In making false imputation (Mt 12:24; Mk 3:22; Lk 11:15; Jn 10:20). In bringing false accusation (Mt 11:19; Lk 7:34; Jn 8:29 – 30). In acts of violence (Lk 4:28 – 29; 22:63 – 65 w Mt 26:67; Mk 14:65). In seeking false testimony (Mt 26:59). In seeking his death (Mt 26:14 – 16; Mk 3:6, 21; 14:1, 48; 11:18; Lk 19:47; Jn 7:20, 30, 32; 8:37, 40, 48, 52, 59; 10:31). In crucifying him (Ac 3:13 – 15; 7:52; 13:27 – 29; 1Co 2:8). Persecution by Herod (Lk 13:31; 23:11). Persecution by Roman soldiers (Mt 27:25 – 30; Mk 15:15 – 20; Jn 19:2 – 3). Forsaken by God (Mk 15:34).

Of the Righteous:

(Ge 49:23; Pss 11:2; 37:32; 38:20; 74:7 – 8; 119:51, 61, 69, 78, 85 – 87, 95, 110, 157, 161; Pr 29:10, 27; Isa 26:20; 29:20 – 21; 59:15; Jer 11:19; 15:10; 18:18; Am 5:10; Ro 8:35; 2Co 12:10; Gal 4:29; 6:17). By mocking (Pss 42:3, 10; 69:9 – 12; 119:51; Jer 20:7 – 8). By violence (Ps 94:5; Jer 2:30; 50:7; Ac 5:29, 40 – 42; 7:52; Gal 6:12, 17; 1Th 2:2, 14 – 15; Jas 2:6). By ecclesiastical cen-sure (Jn 9:22, 34; 12:42; 2Ti 4:16 – 17). Divine permissions of, mysterious (Hab 1:13). The mode of divine chastisement (La 1:3). Done to church members (Ac 8:1, 4; 11:19 – 21; Php 1:12 – 14, 18). Powerless to separate from the love of Christ (Ro 8:17, 35 – 39). Exhortations to courage under (Isa 51:12, 16; Heb 12:3 – 4; 13:13; 1Pe 3:14, 16 – 17; 4:12 – 14, 16, 19). Courageously endured (Jer 26:11 – 14; 1Co 4:9 – 13; 2Co 4:8 – 12; 6:4 – 5, 8 – 10; 11:23 – 27; 12:10; 2Th 1:4; 2Ti 1:8, 12; 2:9 – 10; Heb 11:25 – 27; 11:33 – 38; Jas 5:6, 10). Rejoicing under (Ro 5:3; Col 1:24; 1Th 1:6; Heb 10:32 – 34). Perseverance under (Ps 44:15 – 18, 22). Prayer for deliverance from (Pss 70:1 – 5; 83:1; 140:1, 4; 142:6). Deliverance from (Pss 124; 129:1 – 2). John's vision concerning (Rev 2:3, 10, 13; 6:9 – 11; 7:13 – 17; 12:10 – 11; 17:6; 20:4). Of Christians, foretold (Mt 20:22; 23:34 – 35; 24:8 – 10; Mk 13:9 – 13; Lk 21:12 – 19; Jn 15:18 – 21; 16:1 – 2; 2Ti 3:2 – 3, 12 – 13; 1Jn 3:1, 13). Christ offers consolation (Mk 8:38; 9:42; Lk 6:22 – 23; 17:33; Jn 17:14). Promises to those who endure (Mt 5:10 – 12; 10:16 – 18, 21 – 23, 28 – 31; Lk 6:22 – 23). Should provoke love (1Co 13:3).

Instances of:

Abel (Ge 4:8; Mt 23:35; 1Jn 3:12); Lot (Ge 19:9); Moses (Ex 2:15; 17:4); David (Pss 31:13; 56:5; 59:1 – 2); prophets martyred by Jezebel (1Ki 18:4); Gideon (Jdg 6:28 – 32); Elijah (1Ki 18:10; 19; 2Ki 1:9; 2:23); Micaiah (1Ki 22:26; 2Ch 18:26); Elisha (2Ki 6:31); Hanani (2Ch 16:10); Zechariah (2Ch 24:21; Mt 23:35); Job (Job 1:9; 2:4 – 5; 12:4 – 5; 13:4 – 13; 16:1 – 4; 17:2; 19:1 – 5; 30:1 – 10); Jeremiah (Jer 11:19; 15:10, 15; 17:15 – 18; 18:18 – 23; 26; 32:2; 33:1; 36:26; 37; 38:1 – 6); Uriah (Jer 26:23); the prophets (2Ch 36:16; Mt 21:35 – 36; 1Th 2:15); the three Hebrews of the captivity (Da 3:8 – 23); Daniel (Da 6); the Jews (Ezr 4; Ne 4); John the Baptist (Mt 14:3 – 12); James (Ac 12:2); Simon (Mk 15:21); the disciples (Jn 9:22, 34; 20:19); Lazarus (Jn 9:22, 34; 12:10; 20:19); the apostles (Ac 4:3 – 16, 18; 5:18 – 42; 12:1 – 19; Rev

1:9); Stephen (Ac 6:9 – 15; 7:1 – 60); the church (Ac 8:1; 9:1 – 14; Gal 1:13); Timothy (Heb 13:23); John (Rev 1:9); Antipas (Rev 2:13); the church of Smyrna (Rev 2:8 – 10); Paul (2Ti 2:9 – 10; 4:16 – 17; Ac 9:16, 23 – 25, 29; 16:19 – 25; 21:2 – 33; 22:22 – 24; 23:10, 12 – 15; 1Co 4:9, 11 – 13; 2Co 1:8 – 10; 4:8 – 12; 6:4 – 5, 8 – 10; 11:23 – 27, 32 – 33; Col 1:24; 1Th 2:2, 14 – 15; 2Ti 1:8, 12; 3:11 – 12).

PERSEVERANCE [2846, 2152, 5702, 5705] (Gr. *proskarteresis*). This word occurs only once in the NT (Eph 6:18 KJV, RSV) and means there persistence and steadfastness in prayer. The word, however, has become an "umbrella term," especially in the expression "the perseverance of the saints." It is used to cover the biblical theme that, because God's gift of salvation is an eternal gift, believers are to persist in their Christian commitment and life, whatever their circumstances, knowing that God is on their side (Ro 8:31). As Paul told the Philippians, "Continue to work out your salvation with fear and trembling, for it is God who works in you to will and to act according to his good purpose" (Php 2:12 – 13). At all stages a believer confesses, "By the grace of God I am what I am" (1Co 15:10; see also Php 1:6; 2Th 3:3; 1Pe 1:5).

From the Lord:

(Ps 37:24, 28; Ro 8:30, 33 – 35; 1Co 1:8 – 9; 2Co 1:21 – 22). Acknowledged (Pss 73:24; 138:8; Ro 8:37 – 39; Col 2:7; 2Ti 4:18). Promised (Jer 32:40; Jn 6:34 – 40; 10:28 – 29).

Commanded:

(1Ch 16:11; Hos 12:6; 1Th 5:21; 2Th 2:15 – 17; 2Ti 2:1, 3, 12; 3:14; Tit 1:9; Jas 1:4, 25; 1Pe 4:16; 5:8 – 9; Rev 22:11). Exhortations to (Ac 11:23; 13:43; 14:21 – 22; 1Co 15:58; 16:13; Gal 5:1, 10; Eph 4:14 – 15; 6:13, 18; Php 1:27; 3:16; 4:1; Col 1:10, 22 – 23; 1Th 3:8; 2Th 3:15; 2Ti 1:13; Heb 2:1; 6:1, 11 – 12, 15; 10:23, 35 – 36; 12:5 – 15; 13:9, 13; 2Pe 3:17 – 18; Rev 16:15). A proof of discipleship (Jn 8:31 – 32). A condition of fruitfulness (Jn 15:4 – 5, 7, 9). Intercessory prayer for (Lk 22:31 – 32).

Motives to:

The example of Moses (Heb 3:5); of the prophets (Jas 5:10 – 11); of Christ (Heb 3:6, 14; 12:2 – 4). Intercession of Christ (Heb 4:14). Heavenly witnesses (Heb 12:1). Acceptance by Christ (2Co 5:9, 15; 1Pe 1:4 – 7). Rewards contingent upon (Gal 6:9; Jas 1:12; Rev 2:7, 10 – 11, 17, 25 – 28; 3:5, 11, 21; 14:12; 21:7). Eternal life contingent upon (Mt 10:22; 24:13; Mk 13:13; Ro 2:6 – 7; 2Pe 1:10 – 11).

Lacking in:

The wayside and other hearers (Mk 4:3 – 8). Churches of Asia (Rev 2:5; 3:1 – 3, 14 – 18).

Instances of:

Caleb and Joshua, in representing the land of promise (Nu 14:24, 38); the righteous (Job 17:9; Pr 4:18); in prayer, Abraham in interceding for Sodom (Ge 18:23 – 32); Jacob (Ge 32:24 – 26); Elijah for rain (1Ki 18:42 – 45); Paul for removal of thorn in his flesh (2Co 12:7 – 9).

Ro	5:3	we know that suffering produces **p**;
	5:4	**p**, character; and character, hope.
2Co	12:12	were done among you with great **p**.
2Th	1:4	churches we boast about your **p**
	3:5	into God's love and Christ's **p**.
Heb	12:1	run with **p** the race marked out
Jas	1:3	the testing of your faith develops **p**.
	1:4	**P** must finish its work
	5:11	You have heard of Job's **p**
2Pe	1:6	**p**; and to **p**, godliness;
Rev	2:2	your hard work and your **p**.
	2:19	and faith, your service and **p**,

PERSIA [7273, 7275, 10060, 10594, 10595] (pûr'zh a, Heb. *pāras*, Gr. *Persis*). As a geographical term Persia may be taken to mean the Iranian plateau, bounded by the Tigris Valley on the west and south, the Indus Valley on the east, and by the Armenian ranges and the Caspian Sea to the north, comprising in all something near one million square miles (2.5 million sq. km.). The plateau is high and saucer-shaped, rimmed by mountains rich in mineral wealth, but with wide tracts of arid desert in the interior. The land lies across the old road communications of Europe and Asia, a fact that has done much to determine Persia's ethnology and history. It is seldom possible to separate history and geography, and the term Persia has signified both less and more than the geographical and general meaning just given. The original Persia was a small area north of the Persian Gulf, known as Persis, the modern Fars. It was a rugged area with desert on its maritime borders, its chief town known to the Greeks as Persepolis. The Medes lay to the north, Elam was on the west, and Carmania to the east. This small province was the original home of the Iranian tribe that finally dominated the whole country and founded the vast Persian Empire, which at the time of its widest extent stretched from the Aegean Sea, the Dardanelles, and the Bosporus to the Indus River, and from north to south extended from the Black Sea, the Caucasus, the Caspian Sea, the Oxus, and the Jaxartes to the Persian Gulf, the Indian Ocean, and the cataracts of the Nile. This was the imperial power, described by Herodotus, that clashed with the Greeks at the beginning of the fifth century before Christ and that Alexander overthrew a century and a half later. This, too, was the imperial Persia of the OT, which rose on the ruins of Babylon, which is seen in the life of Esther, and which formed the background of the events described in the books of Ezra and Nehemiah.

In Biblical History:

An empire that extended from India to Ethiopia, comprising 127 provinces (Est 1:1; Da 6:1). Government of, restricted by constitutional limitations (Est 8:8; Da 6:8 – 12). Municipal governments in, provided with dual governors (Ne 3:9, 12, 16 – 18). The princes advisory in matters of administration (Da 6:1 – 7). Status of women in, queen sat on the throne with the king (Ne 2:6). Vashti divorced for refusing to appear before the king's courtiers (Est 1:10 – 22; 2:4). Israel captive in (2Ch 36:20), captivity

foretold (Hos 13:16). Men of in the Syrian army (Eze 27:10).

Rulers of:

Xerxes (Est 1:3); Darius (Da 5:31; 6; 9:1); Artaxerxes I (Ezr 4:7 – 24); Artaxerxes II (Ezr 7; Ne 2; 5:1); Cyrus (2Ch 36:22 – 23; Ezr 1; 3:7; 4:3; 5:13 – 14, 17; 6:3; Isa 41:2 – 3; 44:28; 45:1 – 4, 13; 46:11; 48:14 – 15); princes of (Est 1:14). System of justice (Ezr 7:25). Prophecies concerning (Isa 13:17; 21:1 – 10; Jer 49:34 – 39; 51:11 – 64; Eze 32:24 – 25; 38:5; Da 2:31 – 45; 5:28; 7; 8; 11:1 – 4). See Babylon; Chaldeans.

PETER [3064, 4377] (pḗtêr, Gr. *Petros*, *rock*). The most prominent of the twelve apostles in the Gospels and an outstanding leader in the early days of the Christian church. His original name was Simon, a common Greek name, or more properly Symeon (Ac 15:14), a popular Hebrew name.

BACKGROUND.

He was a native of Bethsaida (Jn 1:44), the son of a certain John (1:42; 21:15 – 17), apparently an abbreviation for Jonah (Mt 16:17). As a Jewish lad he received a normal elementary education. As a native of "Galilee of the Gentiles," he was able to converse in Greek, while his native Aramaic was marked with provincialisms of pronunciation and diction (26:73). The evaluation by the Sanhedrin of Peter and John as "unschooled, ordinary men" (Ac 4:13) simply meant that they were unschooled in the rabbinical lore and were laymen. He and his brother Andrew followed the hardy occupation of fishermen on the Sea of Galilee, being partners with Zebedee's sons, James and John (Lk 5:7). He was a married man (Mk 1:30; 1Co 9:5) and, at the time of Christ's Galilean ministry, lived in Capernaum (Mk 1:21, 29).

THE GOSPEL PERIOD.

Of the second period of his life, from his first encounter with Jesus until the ascension, the Gospels give a vivid picture. Simon attended the preaching ministry of John the Baptist at the Jordan and, like Andrew, probably became a personal disciple of John. When he was personally introduced to Jesus by his brother Andrew, Jesus remarked, "You are Simon son of John. You will be called Cephas" (Jn 1:42). That John translated the Aramaic Kephas into Greek Petros, both meaning "rock," indicates that it was not a proper name but rather a descriptive title (cf. "Sons of Thunder," Mk 3:17). The designation, afterward more fully explained in its prophetic import (Mt 16:18; Mk 3:16), came to be regarded as his personal name. (No other man in the NT bears the name Peter.) After a period of companionship with Jesus during his early Judean ministry (Jn 1:42 – 4:43), Peter resumed his ordinary occupation.

With the commencement of Christ's Galilean ministry, Peter and Andrew, with James and John, were called by Jesus to full-time association with him to be trained as "fishers of men" (Mk 1:16 – 20; Lk 5:1 – 11). With the growth of the work, Jesus selected twelve of his followers to be his nearest companions for special training (Mk 3:13 – 19; Lk 6:12 – 16). In the lists of these twelve designated apostles (Lk 6:13), Peter is always named first (Mt 10:2 – 4; Mk 3:16 – 19; Lk 6:14 – 16; Ac 1:13 – 14). His eminence among them was due to his being among the first chosen as well as his native aggressiveness as a natural leader. But the other disciples did not concede to Peter any authority over them, as is evident from their repeated arguments about greatness (Mt 20:20 – 28; Mk 9:33 – 34; Lk 22:24 – 27). While he was with them, Jesus alone was recognized as their leader.

THE EARLY CHURCH.

The third period in Peter's life began with the ascension of Jesus. In the early days of the church (Ac 1 – 12), Peter appeared as the spokesman of the apostolic group, but there is no hint that he assumed any authority not also exercised by the other apostles. He suggested the choice of another to fill the place of Judas (1:15 – 26), preached the Spirit-empowered sermon on Pentecost to the assembled Jews (2:14 – 40), and with John healed the lame man, the first apostolic miracle to arouse persecution (3:1 – 4:21). He was used to expose the sin of Ananias and Sapphira (5:1 – 12), was held in high esteem by the people during the miracle ministry in the church that followed (5:12 – 16), and spoke for the Twelve when arraigned before the Sanhedrin (5:27 – 41). With John he was sent to Samaria, where, through the laying on of hands, the Holy Spirit fell on the Samaritan believers and Peter exposed the unworthy motives of Simon (8:14 – 24). While on a tour through Judea, Peter healed Aeneas and raised Dorcas from the dead (9:32 – 43). Through a divinely given vision at Joppa, Peter was prepared and commissioned to preach the gospel to Cornelius at Caesarea, thus opening the door to the Gentiles (10:1 – 48). This brought on him the criticism of the circumcision party in Jerusalem (11:1 – 18). During the persecution of the church by Agrippa I in AD 44, Peter escaped death by a miraculous deliverance from prison (12:1 – 19).

HIS LATER LIFE.

With the opening of the door to the Gentiles and the spread of Christianity, Peter receded into the background and Paul became prominent as the apostle to the Gentiles. In the Acts narrative, Peter is last mentioned in connection with the Jerusalem conference, where he championed the liberty of the Gentiles (15:6 – 11, 14). The remaining NT references to Peter are scanty. Galatians 2:11 – 21 records a visit to Syrian Antioch, where his inconsistent conduct evoked a public rebuke from Paul. From 1Co 9:5 it appears that Peter traveled widely, taking his wife with him, doubtless in Jewish evangelism (Gal 2:9).

Nothing further is heard of Peter until the writing of the two letters that bear his name, apparently written from Rome. In the first letter, addressed to believers in five provinces in Asia Minor, the shepherd-heart of Peter sought to fortify the saints in their sufferings for Christ, while in the second he warns against dangers from within. A final NT reference to the closing years of Peter's life is found in Jn 21:18 – 19. John's interpretation of Christ's prediction makes it clear that the reference is to Peter's violent death. Beyond this the NT is silent about him.

Tradition uniformly asserts that Peter went to Rome and labored there, and that in his old age he suffered martyrdom there under Nero. The embellished tradition that he was bishop of Rome for twenty-five years is contrary to all NT evidence. He apparently came to Rome shortly after Paul's release from his first imprisonment there.

HIS CHARACTER.

The character of Peter is one of the most vividly drawn and charming in the NT. His sheer humanness has made him one of the most beloved and winsome members of the apostolic band. He was eager, impulsive, energetic, self-confident, aggressive, and daring, but also unstable, fickle, weak, and cowardly. He was guided more by quick impulse than logical reasoning, and he readily swayed from one extreme to the other. He was preeminently a man of action. His life exhibits the defects of his character as well as his tremendous capacities for good. He was forward and often rash, liable to instability and inconsistency, but his love for and associations with Christ molded him into a man of stability, humility, and courageous service for God. In the power of the Holy Spirit he became one of the noble pillars (Gal 2:9) of the church.

Personal History:

Also called Simon and Cephas (Mt 16:16 – 19; Mk 3:16; Jn 1:42); Simeon (Ac 15:14, n.). A fisherman (Mt 4:18; Lk 5:1 – 7; Jn 21:3). Call of (Mt 4:18 – 20; Mk 1:16 – 18; Lk 5:1 – 11). His wife's mother healed (Mt 8:14; Mk 1:29 – 30; Lk 4:38). An apostle (Mt 10:2; 16:18 – 19; Mk 3:16; Lk 6:14; Ac 1:13). An evangelist (Mk 1:36 – 37). Confesses Jesus as Christ (Mt

16:16 – 19; Mk 8:29; Lk 9:20; Jn 6:68 – 69). His presumption in rebuking Jesus (Mt 16:22 – 23; Mk 8:32 – 33); when the throng was pressing Jesus and the woman touched him (Lk 8:45); when Jesus foretold his persecution and death (Mt 16:21 – 23; Mk 8:31 – 33); in refusing to let Jesus wash his feet (Jn 13:6 – 11). Present at the healing of Jairus's daughter (Mk 5:37; Lk 8:51); at the transfiguration (Mt 17:1 – 4; Mk 9:2 – 6; Lk 9:28 – 33; 2Pe 1:16 – 18); in Gethsemane (Mt 26:36 – 46; Mk 14:33 – 42; Lk 22:40 – 46). Seeks the interpretation of the parable of the manager (Lk 12:41); of the law of forgiveness (Mt 18:21); of the law of defilement (Mt 15:15); of the prophecy of Jesus concerning his second coming (Mk 13:34). Walks on the water of the Sea of Galilee (Mt 14:28 – 31). Sent with John to prepare the Passover (Lk 22:8). Calls attention to the withered fig tree (Mk 11:21). His failure foretold by Jesus, and his profession of fidelity (Mt 26:33 – 35; Mk 14:29 – 31; Lk 22:31 – 34; Jn 13:36 – 38). Cuts off the ear of Malchus (Mt 26:51; Mk 14:47; Lk 22:50). Follows Jesus to the high priest's palace (Mt 26:58; Mk 14:54; Lk 22:54; Jn 18:15). His denial of Jesus and his repentance (Mt 26:69 – 75; Mk 14:66 – 72; Lk 22:55 – 62; Jn 18:17 – 18, 25 – 27). Visits the tomb (Lk 24:12; Jn 20:2 – 6). Jesus sends message to, after the resurrection (Mk 16:7). Jesus appears to (Lk 24:34; 1Co 15:4 – 5). Present at the Sea of Tiberias when Jesus appears to his disciples; leaps into sea and comes to land upon recognizing Jesus; commissioned to feed the flock of Christ (Jn 21:1 – 23). Remains in Jerusalem (Ac 1:13). His statement before the disciples concerning the death of Judas, and his recommendation that the vacancy in the apostleship be filled (Ac 1:15 – 22). Preaches at Pentecost (Ac 2:14 – 40). Heals crippled man in portico of temple (Ac 3). Accused by council; his defense (Ac 4:1 – 23). Foretells death of Ananias and Sapphira (Ac 5:1 – 11). Imprisoned and scourged; his defense before council

(Ac 5:17 – 42). Goes to Samaria (Ac 8:14). Prays for baptism of the Holy Spirit (Ac 8:15 – 18). Rebukes Simon, the sorcerer, who desires to purchase like power (Ac 8:18 – 24). Returns to Jerusalem (Ac 8:25). Receives Paul (Gal 1:18; 2:9). Visits Lydda; heals Aeneas (Ac 9:32 – 34). Visits Joppa; stays with Simon the tanner; raises Dorcas from dead (Ac 9:36 – 43). Has vision of sheet containing clean and unclean animals (Ac 10:9 – 16). Receives centurion's servant; goes to Caesarea; preaches and baptizes the centurion and his household (Ac 10). Advocates, in the council of the apostles and elders, the preaching of the gospel to the Gentiles (Ac 11:1 – 18; 15:7 – 11). Imprisoned and delivered by an angel (Ac 12:3 – 19). Writes two letters (1Pe 1:1; 2Pe 1:1). Miracles of. See Miracles.

PETER, FIRST LETTER OF The keynote of the first letter of Peter is suffering and the Christian method of meeting it. The writer endeavored to convey a message of hope to Christians who had been undergoing persecution and who were succumbing to discouragement because they could find no redress.

The letter was directed to members of the dispersion located in the northern Roman provinces of Asia Minor, which Paul did not visit and which may have been evangelized by Peter between the Council of Jerusalem (AD 48) and the Neronian persecution at Rome (64). First Peter was probably written about the year 64, when the status of Christians in the empire was very uncertain and when persecution had already begun in Rome.

In general arrangement 1 Peter closely resembles the letters of Paul, with a salutation, body, and conclusion. Its main subject is the Christian's behavior under the pressure of suffering. Its key is the salvation that is to be revealed at the last time (1:5).

Outline:
    I. Introduction (1:1 – 2).
    II. The Nature of Salvation (1:3 – 12).

    III. The Experience of Salvation (1:13 – 25).
    IV. The Obligations of Salvation (2:1 – 10).
    V. The Ethics of Salvation (2:11 – 3:12).
    VI. The Confidence of Salvation (3:13 – 4:11).
    VII. The Behavior of the Saved under Suffering (4:12 – 5:11).
    VIII. Concluding Salutations (5:12 – 14).

PETER, SECOND LETTER OF A general treatise, written to warn its readers of threatening apostasy. It purports to have been written by Simon Peter and contains a definite allusion to a preceding letter (2Pe 3:1).

Second Peter has the poorest external attestation of any book in the canon of the NT. Its literary style and vocabulary differ from that of 1 Peter, and its close resemblance to the book of Jude has led some scholars to believe that it is a late copy or adaptation of that work. On the other hand, the internal evidence favors authorship by Peter.

Second Peter must have been written subsequent to the publication of at least some of Paul's letters, if not of the entire collection. It cannot, therefore, have been written before AD 60; but if Paul was living and was still well known to the existing generation, it could not have been later than 70. Probably 67 is as satisfactory a date as can be established. The reference to a previous letter sent to the same group (2Pe 3:1) connects the document with 1 Peter, which was written to the Christians of northern Asia Minor. Whereas the first letter was an attempt to encourage a church threatened with official persecution and repression, the second letter deals with the peril of apostasy, which was an even greater threat.

Outline:
    I. Salutation (1:1)
    II. The Character of Spiritual Knowledge (1:2 – 21)
    III. The Nature and Perils of Apostasy (2:1 – 22)
    IV. The Doom of the Ungodly (3:1 – 7)
    V. The Hope of Believers (3:8 – 13)
    VI. Concluding Exhortation (3:14 – 18)

PETRA (pē′tra). Translates *sela*, meaning *rock*, *cliff*, or *crag*, and, as a proper noun, seems to refer to one or two places in the OT (Jdg 1:36; 2Ki 14:7; Isa 16:1; NIV "Sela"). No certain geographical identification is possible, though the second reference may be to the Petra of later history, the "rose-red city half as old as time," of Dean Burgon's sonnet, and capital city of the Nabateans from the close of the fourth century BC until AD 105, when it became part of the Roman Empire. The town lies in a basin surrounded by mountains. The town's considerable ruins are not impressive, even though Burgon's eulogy is often quoted. The main curiosities of Petra are the narrow canyons that form its approaches and the rock-hewn temples and tombs in the surrounding cliffs. Nothing is known of Petra's history before the Nabateans took over in 312 BC.

PHARAOH [7281, 5755] (fâr′ō, Heb. *par'ōh*, *the great house*). The government of Egypt, and ultimately the supreme monarch in whom all its powers were vested, was known as the "Great House," in Egyptian "Per-o," whence comes the term *pharaoh*. The recorded rulers of Egypt, twenty-six separate dynasties, extend from Menes, 3400 BC to Psamtik III, deposed at the Persian conquest in 525. The term pharaoh can be traced back to the Twenty-second Dynasty (945 – 745), since when it was commonly attached to the monarch's name. Thus "Pharaoh Neco" and "Pharaoh Hophra" are exact Hebrew translations of the Egyptian title.

Ge	12:15	her to **P**, and she was taken
	41:14	So **P** sent for Joseph, and he was
Ex	14:4	glory for myself through **P**
	14:17	And I will gain glory through **P**

PHARISEES [5757] (fâr′ĭ-sēz, Heb. *perûshûn*, Gr. *Pharisaioi*, *separate ones*). Of the three prominent parties of Judaism at the time of Christ — Pharisees, Sadducees, and Essenes — the Pharisees were by far the most influential. The origin of this strictest sect of the Jews (Ac 26:5) is shrouded in some obscurity, but it is believed the organization came out of the Maccabean revolt (165 BC). There was, however, a group of Jews resembling the Pharisees as far back as the Babylonian captivity.

The name "Pharisee," which in its Semitic form means "the separated ones, separatists," first appears during the reign of John Hyrcanus (135 BC). Generally, the term is in the plural rather than in the singular. They were also known as *chasidim*, meaning "loved of God" or "loyal to God." They were found everywhere in Palestine, not only in Jerusalem, and even wore a distinguishing garb so as to be easily recognized. According to Josephus, their number at the zenith of their popularity was more than six thousand. Because of the significant role the Pharisees played in the life of the Lord and the apostles, knowledge of the character and teachings of this group is of great importance for the understanding of the NT. They are mentioned dozens of times, especially in the Gospels, and often form the background for the works and words of Jesus.

The Pharisees bitterly opposed Jesus and his teachings. If they despised the Herods and the Romans, they hated Jesus' doctrine of equality and claims of messiahship with equal fervor (Jn 9:16, 22). He in turn condemned both their theology and life of legalism. They often became a fertile background against which he taught God's free salvation by grace through his own death and resurrection. The picture of the Pharisees painted by the NT is almost entirely negative, but the discriminating Bible student should bear in mind that not everything about every Pharisee was bad. It is perhaps not just to say that all Pharisees were self-righteous and hypocritical. Many Pharisees actually tried to promote true piety. What we know as Pharisaism from the NT was to some degree a degeneration of Pharisaism. Jesus condemned especially the Pharisees' ostentation, their hypocrisy, their salvation by works, their impenitence and lovelessness, but not always Pharisees as such. Some of the Pharisees were members of the Christian movement in the beginning (Ac 6:7). Some of the great men of the NT were Pharisees — Nicodemus (Jn 3:1), Gamaliel (Ac 5:34), and Paul (Ac 26:5; Php 3:5). Paul does not speak the name "Pharisee" with great reproach but as a title of honor, for the Pharisees were highly respected by the masses of the Jewish people. When Paul says he was, "in regard to the law, a Pharisee" (Php 3:5), he did not think of himself as a hypocrite but claimed the highest degree of faithfulness to the law. In similar manner, church leaders today might say, "We are the Pharisees." Much of modern scholarship, however, has cast the Pharisees into too favorable a light; when one reads our Lord's heated denunciation of Pharisaism in Mt 23, where he specifically lists their sins, one has not only a true but also a dark picture of Pharisaism as it was at the time of Christ.

> **General References to:**
>
> *Sect of the Jews (Ac 15:5). Doctrines of (Mt 15:9); concerning the resurrection (Ac 23:6, 8); association with tax collectors and sinners (Mt 9:11 – 13). Traditions of, in regard to fasting (Mt 9:14; Lk 18:12); the washing of hands (Mt 15:1 – 3; Mk 7:1 – 15); the duties of children to parents (Mt 15:4 – 9); the Sabbath (Mt 12:2 – 8). Denounced by Jesus (Mt 23:2 – 36; Lk 11:39 – 44). Hypocrisy of, reproved by John (Mt 3:7 – 10); by Jesus (Mt 6:2 – 8, 16 – 18; 15:1 – 9; 16:1 – 12; 21:33 – 46; 23:2 – 33; Lk 11:14 – 54; 12:1; 15:1 – 9). Reject John (Lk 7:30); Christ (Mt 12:38 – 39; 15:12; Jn 7:48). Come to Jesus with questions (Mt 19:3; 22:15 – 22). Minister to Jesus (Lk 7:36; 11:37; 14:1). Become disciples of Jesus (Jn 3:1; Ac 15:5; 22:5). Paul a Pharisee (Ac 23:6; 26:5).*

Mt	5:20	surpasses that of the **P**
	16:6	guard against the yeast of the **P**
	23:13	of the law and **P**, you hypocrites!
Jn	3:1	a man of the **P** named Nicodemus,

PHILADELPHIA [5788] (Gr. *Philadelphia, brotherly love*). A Lydian city founded by Attalus II Philadelphus (159 – 138 BC). The king was so named from his devotion to his brother Eumenes, and the city perpetuated his title. Philadelphia was an outpost of Hellenism in native Anatolia. It lies under Mount Tmolus, in a wide vale that opens into the Hermus Valley, and along which the post road ran. It is on a broad, low, easily defended hill, and this explains Philadelphia's long stand against the Turks. The district is disastrously seismic, and the great earthquake of AD 17 ruined it completely. Placed right above the fault, Philadelphia was tormented by twenty years of recurrent quakes after the disaster of 17. Hence, says Ramsay, is derived the imagery of Rev 3:12 ("Him who overcomes I will make a pillar in the temple of my God. Never again will he leave it."). The new name is certainly a reference to the proposal to rename the city Neocaesarea in gratitude for Tiberius's generous earthquake relief. The district was an area of vine growing and wine production, and therefore was a center for the worship of Dionysus, god of wine and fertility. A Christian witness, in spite of Muslim invasion and pressure, was maintained in Philadelphia through medieval and into modern times.

PHILEMON, LETTER TO (fī-lē′mŏn, Gr. *Philēmōn, loving*). Paul's letter to Philemon dates, in all probability, from the period of his Roman imprisonment. Paul's authorship is not seriously disputed. The letter is addressed: "To Philemon … Apphia … Archippus … and to the church that meets in your home." Apphia was Philemon's wife, and Archippus, not improbably, his son. Archippus appears to have been a person of some standing but was perhaps not notable for stability of character (Col 4:17).

The occasion of the letter was the return of the runaway slave Onesimus to his master. Paul appeals to Philemon for Onesimus's freedom. The approach is characteristic of early Christianity. Slavery is never directly attacked as such, but principles that must prove fatal to the institution are steadily inculcated. To speak of brotherly love between master and slave ultimately renders slavery meaningless.

> I. Greetings (vv. 1 – 3).
> II. Thanksgiving and Prayer (vv. 4 – 7).
> III. Paul's Plea for Onesimus (vv. 8 – 21).
> IV. Final Request, Greetings, and Benedictions (vv. 22 – 25).

PHILIP [5805] (*horse lover*).

1. King of Macedonia; father of Alexander the Great; founder of city of Philippi in Macedonia (1Mc 1:1).

2. Philip V, king of Macedonia (1Mc 8:5).

3. Governor of Jerusalem under Antiochus, regent of Syria (2Mc 5:22).

4. Herod Philip. Married Herodias (Mt 14:3; Mk 6:17; Lk 3:19).

5. Herod Philip II, tetrarch of Batanaea, Trachonitis, Gaulanitis, and parts of Jamnia. Best of Herods (Lk 3:1).

PHILIP THE APOSTLE (Gr. *Philippos, lover of horses*). In the lists of the apostles (cf. Mt 10:3) the fifth in the list is called simply Philip, but the church has always called him "the apostle" to distinguish him from Philip the evangelist or Philip the deacon (Ac 6:8). His hometown was Bethsaida of Galilee, and no doubt he was a close friend of Andrew and Peter who lived in the same fishing village (Jn 1:44). It is almost certain that he was first a disciple of John the Baptist, because Jesus called him directly near Bethany beyond the Jordan, where John was preaching (1:43). He is often characterized as being timid and retiring, but nonetheless, he brought Nathanael to Jesus (1:43). A more apt description appears to be that he was reluctant to believe wholeheartedly in the kingdom, and at times he seems to have had difficulty in grasping its meaning (14:8 – 14). This no doubt is why Jesus asked him the unusual question to arouse and test his faith before feeding the five thousand: "Where shall we buy bread for these people to eat?" (6:5 – 6). He served as something of a contact man for the Greeks and is familiarly known for bringing Gentiles to Jesus (12:20 – 23). The last information regarding Philip in the NT is found in Ac 1:13 where we are told that he was among the number of disciples in the upper room before Pentecost. His days after this are shrouded in legend and mystery, but the best tradition says he did mission work in Asia Minor. The historian Eusebius says that he was a "great light of Asia," and that he was buried at Hierapolis.

> Native of Bethsaida, the same town as Andrew and Peter (Jn 1:44); Undoubtedly first a disciple of John the Baptist (Jn 1:43); Brought his friend Nathanael to Jesus (Jn 1:45); Called to apostleship (Mt 10:3; Mk 3:18; Lk 6:14); Faith tested by Jesus before feeding of the 5,000 (Jn 6:5 – 6); Brought Greeks to Jesus (Jn 12:20 – 23); Asked to see the Father (Jn 14:8 – 12); In the upper room with 120 (Ac 1:13)

PHILIP THE EVANGELIST (Gr. *Philippos, lover of horses*). Although the church, beginning with the second century, often confused him with Philip the apostle, this Philip's name does not occur in the Gospels. He appears in the book of Acts as one of the famous seven deacons, said to be men "known to be full of the Spirit and wisdom" (Ac 6:3). He is second in the list, following Stephen, the first Christian martyr (6:5), so he must have been well known in the early church. Since he was a Hellenist (a Greek-speaking Jew), as a deacon he was to serve under the apostles (6:6) by taking care of the neglected Hellenist widows and the poor in general in the Jerusalem church. But after the death of Stephen the persecutions scattered the Christians abroad and, because of the great need, the deacons became evangelists or Christian missionaries. They even performed signs and wonders among the people (8:39; 6:8). In Ac 8 it is said that Philip preached in Samaria with great success: "When the crowds heard Philip and saw the miraculous signs he did, they all paid close attention to what he said." He cast out devils and healed the paralytics and the lame just as the apostles did. Some of his converts were Simon the sorcerer of Samaria (8:9 – 13) and the Ethiopian eunuch (8:26 – 40). Thus perhaps Philip was instrumental in introducing Christianity into Africa. Most of his labors seem to have been centered along the Mediterranean seaboard, where, following the Lord's command, he preached to the

Gentiles. It can easily be seen, therefore, why Paul stayed at his home (21:8 – 9), since they had much in common. Philip was a forerunner of Paul in preaching to the Gentiles. In Ac 21 it is said that Philip had four unmarried daughters who were prophets. Little else is known of his later life.

PHILIPPI [5803, 5804, 5805] (fĭ-lĭp′ī, Gr. *Philippoi*). A Macedonian town in the plain east of Mount Pangaeus. It was a strategic foundation of Philip II, father of Alexander, in 358/7 BC. The position dominated the road system of northern Greece; hence it became the center for the battle of 42 BC, in which Antony defeated Brutus and Cassius. After Actium (31), Octavian (the future Augustus) constituted the place a Roman colony, housing partisans of Antony whose presence was undesirable in Italy. Philippi had a school of medicine connected with one of those guilds of physicians that the followers of early Greek medicine scattered through the Hellenistic world. This adds point to the suggestion that Luke was a Philippian. There is a touch of pride in Luke's description of Philippi as "the leading city of that district" (Ac 16:12), though Amphipolis was the capital. Philippi was the first European city to hear a Christian missionary, as far as the records go. Paul's choice of the locality throws light on the strategy of his evangelism.

A city of Macedonia. Paul preaches in (Ac 16:12 – 40; 20:1 – 6; 1Th 2:1 – 2). Contributes to the maintenance of Paul (Php 4:10 – 18). Paul sends Epaphroditus to (Php 2:25). Paul writes a letter to the Christians of (Php 1:1).

PHILIPPIANS, LETTER TO THE (fĭ-lĭp′ĭ-ănz). One of the most personal of all the apostle Paul's letters. It was written to "all the saints in Christ Jesus at Philippi" (Php 1:1).

The church at Philippi in ancient Macedonia was the first European church founded by Paul and thus represents the first major penetration of the gospel into Gentile territory (cf. Php 4:14 – 15). The events leading to the founding of the congregation are related in Ac 16:9 – 40. Paul and his companions immediately answered the divine call of Ac 16:9 and set sail for the nearest port — Neopolis of Philippi, named for Philip II of Macedon, the father of Alexander the Great.

Philippi had been thoroughly colonized by the Romans after 30 BC, but the city was still more Greek in culture than Roman. Also the city was the first station on the Egnation Way and was the gateway to the East. Luke describes the city as follows: "From there we traveled to Philippi, a Roman colony and the leading city of that district of Macedonia. And we stayed there several days" (Ac 16:12). It is not unusual, therefore, that Paul's first convert there was a merchant woman named Lydia, a seller of purple. Her whole household was baptized and became the nucleus of the new church (16:15). The remarkable conversion of the jailer with its accompanying miraculous events also took place in Philippi (16:25 – 34). There was, therefore, a very intimate relationship between the apostle and this church. No doubt this was true also because the congregation consisted mainly of Gentiles and Paul saw in them the real future of the church. They were poor, but the fruits of faith were abundant. On several occasions they collected funds for Paul and also aided him while he was in prison (Php 4:10 – 16). He had visited this favorite congregation whenever possible. He has no rebuke for it in this letter. The members are his "joy and crown" (4:1). Before 1900 it was universally accepted that the letter to the Philippians was written at Rome where Paul was in prison after his third missionary journey. In recent years, however, scholars have developed the hypothesis that it was written during Paul's imprisonment in Caesarea, but still more recently from the prison in Ephesus.

The letter was occasioned by the gift of funds and clothing that Epaphroditus brought to Paul in prison. Paul took the opportunity to thank the Philippians for this and other favors. In doing so, as was his custom, Paul added practical Christian admonition to humility, joy, and steadfastness, which a reading of the letter will reveal. The main emphasis is joy; the concept "rejoice" appears no fewer than sixteen times in the letter. It also is a theological letter. The doctrines of the person and work of Christ, justification by faith, and the second coming of Christ are found among the practical admonitions.

Outline:

I. Salutation (1:1 – 2).

II. Thanksgiving and Prayer for the Philippians (1:3 – 11).

III. Paul's Personal Circumstances (1:12 – 26).

IV. Exhortations (1:27 – 2:18).

V. Paul's Associates in the Gospel (2:19 – 30).

VI. Warnings against Judaizers and Antinomians (3:1 – 4:1).

VII. Final Exhortations, Thanks, and Conclusion (4:2 – 23).

PHILISTINES [7148, 7149] (fĭ-lĭs'tē-nz, Heb. *pelishtîm*). The name given to the people who inhabited the Philistine plain of Palestine during the greater part of OT times. The five cities of the Philistines were Ashdod, Gaza, Ashkelon, Gath, and Ekron (Jos 13:3; 1Sa 6:17). They were situated in the broad coastal plain of southern Palestine, except for Gath, which is in the Shephelah or hill country. Our word *Palestine* is derived from the term *Philistine*.

The book of Judges mentions the Philistines as a major contender against the Hebrews for the possession of Palestine. No doubt the tribes of Judah, Simeon, and Dan felt the pressure most, for their lands were adjacent to the Philistines.

General References to:

Descendants of Mizraim (Ge 10:14; 1Ch 1:12; Jer 47:4; Am 9:7). Called Kerethites (1Sa 30:14 – 16; Eze 25:16; Zep 2:5); Casluhites (Ge 10:14; 1Ch 1:12); Caphtor (Jer 47:4; Am 9:7). Territory of (Ex 13:17; 23:31; Dt 2:23; Jos 13:3; 15:47). Rulers of (Jos 13:3; Jdg 3:3; 16:5, 30; 1Sa 5:8, 11; 6:4, 12; 7:7; 29:2, 6 – 7). Kings of: Abimelech I (Ge 20); Abimelech II (Ge 26); Achish (1Sa 21:10 – 15; 27:2 – 12; 28:1 – 2; 29). Allowed to remain in Canaan (Jdg 3:3 – 4). Shamgar

slays six hundred with an oxgoad (Jdg 3:31). For their history during the leadership of Samson (Jdg 13 – 16). Defeat Israelites, take ark, suffer plagues, and return ark (1Sa 4 – 6). Army of (1Sa 13:5). Defeated by Samuel (1Sa 7); by Saul and Jonathan (1Sa 9:16; 13 – 14). Their champion, Goliath, slain by David (1Sa 17). David slays two hundred (1Sa 18:22 – 30). David finds refuge among (1Sa 27). Defeat the Israelites and slay Saul and his sons (1Sa 31; 1Ch 10:1). Defeated by David (2Sa 5:17 – 25; 23:9 – 16; 1Ch 14:8 – 16). Pay tribute to Jehoshaphat (2Ch 17:11). Defeated by Hezekiah (2Ki 18:8). Prophecies against (Isa 9:11 – 12; 14:29 – 31; Jer 25:17 – 20; 47; Eze 25:15 – 17; Am 1:6 – 8; Zep 2:4 – 7; Zec 9:5 – 7).

Jdg	10:7	them into the hands of the **P**
	13:1	the hands of the **P** for forty years.
	16:5	The rulers of the **P** went to her
1Sa	4:1	at Ebenezer, and the **P** at Aphek.
	5:8	together all the rulers of the **P**
	13:23	a detachment of **P** had gone out
	17:1	the **P** gathered their forces for war
	23:1	the **P** are fighting against Keilah
	27:1	is to escape to the land of the **P**.
	31:1	Now the **P** fought against Israel;
2Sa	5:17	When the **P** heard that David had
	8:1	David defeated the **P** and subdued
	21:15	there was a battle between the **P**
2Ki	18:8	he defeated the **P**, as far as Gaza
Am	1:8	Ekron till the last of the **P** is dead,"

PHINEHAS [7090] (fĭn'ē-ăs, Heb. *pînehās, mouth of brass*).

1. A son of Eleazar and grandson of Aaron (Ex 6:25; 1Ch 6:4, 50; 9:20; Ezr 7:5; 8:2). He killed Zimri and Cozbi at God's command (Nu 25:6 – 15; Ps 106:30). He conducted a successful embassy to the Transjordan tribes regarding the altar they had built (Jos 22:13 – 34). These incidents evidence his great zeal and faithful service.

2. A son of Eli, unfaithful in his ministration of the priest's office (1Sa 1:3; 2:12 – 17, 22 – 25, 27 – 36;

3:11 – 13). He and his brother Hophni brought the ark into the camp of Israel, hoping its presence would bring victory against the Philistines, but the ark was taken and Hophni and Phinehas killed (ch. 4).

3. Father of Eleazar who with other priests accounted for the valuables brought back to Jerusalem with the exiles returning from the Babylonian captivity (Ezr 8:33).

PHOEBE [5833] (fē´bē, Gr. *Phoibē, pure or radiant*). A woman mentioned in the Scriptures only in Ro 16:1 – 2. She was one of the first deaconesses, if not the first, of the Christian church and was highly recommended by Paul. In a single sentence, he speaks of her Christian status ("sister"), of her position or office (*diakonos*, "servant"), of her service record ("she has been a great help to many people, including me"), and of the importance of her work ("give her any help she may need from you"). Phoebe was serving as deaconess of the church at Cenchrea, port of Corinth, when Paul arrived there at the end of his third journey, and where he wrote his letter to the Romans. Either she was on her way to Rome to serve that church or Paul sent her with this important letter to the Roman Christians.

PHOENICIA [4046, 5834] (fē-nĭsh´ĭ-a, Gr. *Phoinikē, land of purple [dye for trading]*, possibly *land of date palms*). Country along Mediterranean coast, c. 120 miles long, extending from Arvad (Arados, 1Mc 15:23) to Dor, just south of Carmel. The Semitic name for the land was Canaan. The term *Phoenicia* is from a Greek word meaning "purple-red," perhaps because the Phoenicians were the discoverers of the crimson-purple dye derived form the murex shellfish. The people were Semites who came in a migration from the Mesopotamian region during the second millennium BC. They became great seafarers, establishing colonies at Carthage and Spain, and perhaps even reached England. Inhabitants of, descended from Canaan (Ge 10:15, 18 – 19). Called Sidonians (Jdg 18:7; Eze 32:30). They were famous shipbuilders (Eze 27:9) and carpenters (1Ki 16:31; 18:19). Hiram, one of their kings, was friendly with David and Solomon (2Sa 5:11; 1Ki 5:1 – 12; 2Ch 2:3 – 16), and another Hiram helped Solomon in the building of the temple in Jerusalem (1Ki 7:13 – 47; 2Ch 2:13 – 14). Jews from Phoenicia heard Jesus (Mk 3:8) speak, and Jesus healed a Syrian Phoenician woman's daughter in its regions (Mk 7:24 – 30). Paul visited Christians there (Ac 15:3; 21:2 – 7; 27:3).

PHRYGIA [5867] (frĭj´ĭa, Gr. *Phrygia*). In Bible times an inland province of SW Asia Minor. Its tablelands, which rose to 4,000 feet (1,250 m.), contained many cities and towns considerable in size and wealth. Most historians agree that the province included greater or lesser territory at different times, and there is no common agreement on the boundaries, as they shifted almost every generation. Whatever the exact extent of the province, it receives its renown mainly from Paul's missionary journeys. Paul and his coworkers visited the fertile territory, which contained rich pastures for cattle and sheep and a heavy population in need of the gospel, during all three missionary journeys. Although a great deal of Christian activity took place in ancient Phrygia, with this reference it passes from the biblical record.

PHYLACTERY [5873] (*safeguard, means of protection*). A small box containing slips of parchment on which were written portions of the law (Ex 13:9, 16; Dt 6:4 – 9; 11:18). Worn ostentatiously on the forehead and left arm (Mt 23:5).

PIERCED

Ps	22:16	they have **p** my hands and my feet.
	40:6	but my ears you have **p**;
Isa	53:5	But he was **p** for our transgressions,
Zec	12:10	look on me, the one they have **p**,
Jn	19:37	look on the one they have **p**."
Rev	1:7	even those who **p** him;

PILATE [4397] (pī´lat, Gr. *Pilatos, family name*). The fifth procurator, or governmental representative, of imperial Rome in Palestine at the time of Christ, holding this office from AD 26 to 36. Whether it be considered an honor or a disgrace, he is the one man of all Roman officialdom who is named in the Apostles' Creed — "suffered under Pontius Pilate." To Christians, therefore, he is known almost entirely for his cowardly weakness in the condemnation of Jesus to Roman crucifixion in 30. The four Gospels relate the sad but glorious events fully, especially the gospel of John. Pilate is also mentioned in the Acts of the Apostles (3:13; 4:27; 13:28) and in 1Ti 6:13, where we are told that Jesus "before Pontius Pilate made the good confession." *Pontius* was his family name, showing that he was descended from the Roman family, or *gens*, of *pontii*. *Pilate* no doubt came from the Latin *pilatus*, meaning "one armed with a *pilum*, or javelin."

Most procurators disliked being stationed in a distant, difficult, dry outpost such as Judea. Pilate, however, seemed to enjoy tormenting the Jews, although, as it turned out, he was seldom a match for them. He never really understood them, as his frequent rash and capricious acts reveal. The Jewish historian Josephus tells us that he immediately offended the Jews by bringing the "outrageous" Roman standards into the Holy City. At another time he hung golden shields inscribed with the names and images of Roman deities in the temple itself. Once he even appropriated some of the temple tax to build an aqueduct. To this must be added the horrible incident mentioned in Lk 13:1 about "the Galileans whose blood Pilate had mixed with their sacrifices," meaning no doubt that Roman soldiers killed these men while they were sacrificing in the Holy Place. These fearful events seem to disagree with the role Pilate played in the trial of Jesus, where he was as clay in the hands of the Jews, but this may be explained by the fact that his fear of the Jews increased because of their frequent complaints to Rome.

He declared Jesus innocent after private interrogation; he sent him to Herod; he had him scourged, hoping this would suffice; and finally, he offered the Jews a choice between Jesus and a coarse insurrectionist. When he heard the words "If you let this man go, you are no friend of Caesar" and "We have no king but Caesar!" he thought of politics rather than justice and condemned an innocent man to crucifixion. Washing his hands only enhanced his guilt. Pilate is to be judged in the light of his times when one lived by the philosophy of self-aggrandizement and expediency.

Scripture is silent regarding the end of Pilate. According to Josephus, his political career came to an end six years later when he sent soldiers to Samaria to suppress a small harmless religious rebellion, and in that suppression innocent men were killed. The historian Eusebius says that soon afterward, "wearied with misfortunes," he took his own life. Various traditions conflict as to how and where Pilate killed himself.

Roman governor of Judea (Mt 27:2; Lk 3:1); Causes slaughter of certain Galileans (Lk 13:1); Tries Jesus and orders his crucifixion (Mt 27; Mk 15; Lk 23; Jn 18:28 – 40; 19; Ac 3:13; 4:27; 13:28; 1Ti 6:13); Allows Joseph of Arimathea to take Jesus' body (Mt 27:57 – 58; Mk 15:43 – 45; Lk 23:52; Jn 19:38)

PILGRIMAGE [4472, 5019] (Heb. *māghôr, a place of sojourning*, or *the act of sojourning*; see Ex 6:4 NIV, "lived as aliens"; Ps 119:54). In Ge 47:9 a lifetime is meant. The Hebrew root *ghûr* means "to dwell as a foreigner, newly come into a land in which he has no citizens' rights, such as the original inhabitants possess." The biblical usage, whether the word is translated "pilgrimage" or otherwise, began with the wanderings of Abraham and his descendants and later was applied to the status of a believer in the one true God, living on an earth unfriendly to God and to his people.

PILLAR

Ge	19:26	and she became a **p** of salt.
Ex	13:21	ahead of them in a **p** of cloud
1Ti	3:15	the **p** and foundation of the truth.
Rev	3:12	who overcomes I will make a **p**

PILLAR OF CLOUD AND FIRE God guided Israel out of Egypt and through the wilderness by a pillar of cloud by day. This became a pillar of fire by night that they might travel by night in escaping from the Egyptian army (Ex 13:21 – 22). When the Egyptians overtook the Israelites, the angel of the Lord removed this cloudy, fiery pillar from before them and placed it behind them as an effective barrier (14:19 – 20, 24). The pillar of cloud stood over the tent of meeting outside the camp whenever the Lord met Moses there (33:7 – 11). The Lord came down for judgment in the cloud (Nu 12; 14:13 – 35), and God met Moses and Joshua in the cloud at the tent of meeting to make arrangements for the succession when Moses was near death (Dt 31:14 – 23). Psalm 99:7 reminds the people that God spoke to them in the pillar of cloud. When Ezra prayed in the presence of the returning exiles at Jerusalem, he reviewed the way God had led the people by the pillar of cloud and fire (Ne 9:12, 19). First Corinthians 10:1 – 2 speaks of the Israelite forefathers being under the cloud, baptized into Moses in the cloud. No natural phenomenon fits the biblical description. The cloud and fire were divine manifestations, in a form sufficiently well-defined to be called a pillar.

PISIDIA [4407, 4408] (pĭsĭd′ĭ̵a, Gr. *Pisidia*). One of the small Roman provinces in southern Asia Minor, just north of Pamphylia and lying along the coast. It was mountainous but more densely populated than the rough coastal areas, especially because it contained the important city of Antioch. Because of this, Paul visited the city twice. On his first journey (Ac 13:14 – 50; NIV "Pisidian Antioch") he preached a lengthy sermon in the synagogue, testifying of Christ. A week later "almost the whole city gathered to hear the word of the Lord" (13:44). Then the jealous Jews stirred up both the honorable women and the chief men of the city (13:50), and Paul and Barnabas were forced out of this greatest Pisidian city. On his second journey Paul revisited Pisidia and Antioch, "strengthening the disciples and encouraging them to remain true to faith" (14:21 – 24).

PITY [365, 2571, 2798, 2858, 5714, 8163, 8171, 1796, 3091+3836+5073, 5072]. Tender, considerate, compassionate feeling for others.

> *Commanded (Job 6:14; 1Pe 3:8). For the poor (Pr 19:17; 28:8). Forbidden: to Canaanites (Dt 7:16); to idolatrous proselytizers (Dt 13:8); to murderers (Dt 19:13); to false witnesses (Dt 19:21); to wife in certain situations (Dt 25:12). Withholding of, from Jesus, prefigured in David (Ps 69:20). Of God (Ps 103:13; Isa 63:9; Joel 2:18; Jnh 4:11; Jas 5:11), withheld from reprobates (Jer 13:14; 21:7; Eze 5:11; 7:4; 8:18; 9:5, 10; Zec 11:6). Required of believers (Isa 1:17; Mt 18:28 – 35).*

Ps	72:13	He will take **p** on the weak
Ecc	4:10	But **p** the man who falls
Lk	10:33	when he saw him, he took **p** on him

PLAGUES OF EGYPT Ten in number, these were the means by which God induced Pharaoh to let the Israelites leave Egypt. A series chiefly of natural phenomena, they were unusual (1) in their severity, (2) in that all occurred within one year, (3) in their accurate timing, (4) in that Goshen and its people were spared some of them, and (5) in the evidence of God's control over them. The plagues overcame the opposition of Pharaoh, discredited the gods of Egypt (the Nile and the sun), and defiled their temples.

1. Water turned to blood (Ex 7:14 – 25).
2. Frogs (Ex 8:1 – 15).
3. Lice (Ex 8:16 – 19).
4. Flies (Ex 8:20 – 31).
5. The plague (RSV, NIV) of murrain (KJV) on cattle (Ex 9:1 – 7).
6. Boils (KJV, NIV), blains (ASV), or sores (RSV) on man and beast (Ex 9:8 – 12).
7. Hail (Ex 9:13 – 35).
8. Locusts (Ex 10:1 – 20).
9. Darkness (Ex 10:21 – 29).
10. Death of the firstborn (Ex 11:1 – 12:36).

PLAN

| Ex | 26:30 | according to the **p** shown you |

Job	42:2	no **p** of yours can be thwarted.
Pr	14:22	those who **p** what is good find love
	21:30	is no wisdom, no insight, no **p**
Am	3:7	nothing without revealing his **p**
Eph	1:11	predestined according to the **p**

PLEASURE, WORLDLY Unfulfilling (Job 21:12 – 13; Ecc 1:17; 2:1 – 13; 1Ti 5:6). Proverbs and parables concerning (Pr 9:17; 15:21; 21:17; Lk 8:14). Rejected and judged by God (Job 20:12 – 16; Isa 5:11 – 12; 22:12 – 13; 47:8 – 9; Am 6:1; Ro 1:32; 2Th 2:12). Rejected by Moses (Heb 11:25 – 26); by Paul (2Ti 3:4; Tit 3:3); by Peter (2Pe 2:13).

PLEASURE

Ps	5:4	You are not a God who takes **p**
	51:16	you do not take **p** in burnt offerings
	147:10	His **p** is not in the strength
Pr	10:23	A fool finds **p** in evil conduct,
	18:2	A fool finds no **p** in understanding
	21:17	He who loves **p** will become poor;
Jer	6:10	they find no **p** in it.
Eze	18:23	Do I take any **p** in the death
Lk	10:21	Father, for this was your good **p**.
Eph	1:5	in accordance with his **p** and will —
	1:9	of his will according to his good **p**,
1Ti	5:6	the widow who lives for **p** is dead
2Ti	3:4	lovers of **p** rather than lovers
2Pe	2:13	Their idea of **p** is to carouse

PLINY Gaius Plinius Caecilius Secundus, called "the Younger," Roman governmental official, famous as the author of literary letters covering all types of subjects, one of which contains a description of the Christian church in Bithynia, a province that Pliny governed in AD 112. The letter, together with the reply of the emperor Trajan, are important evidence for the official attitude toward the Christians.

POLYGAMY (*many marriages*).

Forbidden (Dt 17:17; Lev 18:18; Mal 2:14 – 15; Mt 19:4 – 5; Mk 10:2 – 8; 1Ti 3:2, 12; Tit 1:6). Authorized (2Sa 12:8).

Examples of:

Tolerated (Ex 21:10; 1Sa 1:2; 2Ch 24:3). Practiced by: Lamech (Ge 4:19); Abraham (Ge 16); Esau (Ge 26:34; 28:9); Jacob (Ge 29:30); Ashhur (1Ch 4:5); Gideon (Jdg 8:30); Elkanah (1Sa 1:2); David (1Sa 25:39 – 44; 2Sa 3:2 – 5; 5:13; 1Ch 14:3); Solomon (1Ki 11:1 – 8); Rehoboam (2Ch 11:18 – 23); Abijah (2Ch 13:21); Jehoram (2Ch 21:14); Joash (2Ch 24:3); Ahab (2Ki 10:1); Jehoiachin (2Ki 24:15); Belshazzar (Da 5:2, w 1Ch 2 – 8); Hosea (Hos 3:1 – 2). Mosaic law respecting the firstborn in (Dt 21:15 – 17). Sought by women [polyandry] (Isa 4:1).

The Evil Effects of:

Husband's favoritism in (Dt 21:15 – 17); Jacob's (Ge 29:30; 30:15); Elkanah's (1Sa 1:5); Rehoboam's (2Ch 11:21). Domestic infelicity, in Abraham's family (Ge 16; 21:9 – 16); Jacob's (Ge 29:30 – 34; 30:1 – 23); Elkanah's (1Sa 1:4 – 7). On Solomon (1Ki 11:4 – 8). See Marriage.

POOR [36, 1924, 1930, 3769, 4575, 4728, 5014, 6705, 8133, 8203, 8273, 1797, 4775, 4777] (Heb. *'evyôn, dal, 'ānî, rûsh,* Gr. *ptochos*).

Proverbs Concerning:

(Ps 37:16 w Isa 29:19; Pr 10:15; 13:7 – 8, 23; 18:23; 19:1, 4, 7, 17, 22; 20:13; 21:13; 22:2, 9; 23:21; 24:20 – 21, 31; 28:6, 8, 11, 19; 29:14; Ecc 4:6, 13; 6:8; 9:15 – 16). Always part of the society (Mt 26:11; Mk 14:7; Jn 12:8).

Attitudes toward:

Job (Job 30:25); Jesus and the poor widow (Mk 12:43 – 44); Lazarus (Lk 16:20 – 21); Judas (Jn 12:6); James (Jas 1:9 – 10).

Duty to:

(Ex 22:25 – 27; 23:11; Lev 19:9 – 10; 25:25 – 28, 35 – 43; Dt 14:28 – 29; 15:2 – 14; 24:12 – 21; 26:12 – 13; Ne 8:10; Pss 37:21, 26; 41:1 – 3; 112:4 – 5, 9; Pr 28:27; 29:7; 31:9, 20; Isa 1:7; 16:3 – 4; 58:7, 10; Eze 18:7; Da 4:27; Zec 7:10; Mt 5:42; 19:21; 25:35 – 36; Mk 14:7; Lk 3:11; 6:30; 11:41; 12:33; 14:12 – 14; 18:22; 19:8; Ac 20:35; Ro 12:8, 13, 20;

1Co 13:3; 16:1 – 2; 2Co 6:10; 8:9; 9:5 – 7; Gal 2:10; 6:10; Eph 4:28; 1Ti 5:9 – 10, 16; Heb 13:3; Jas 1:27; 2:2 – 9, 15 – 16; 5:4; 1Jn 3:17 – 19).

God's Care of:

(1Sa 2:7 – 8; Job 5:15 – 16; 31:15; 34:18 – 19, 28; 36:6, 15; Pss 9:18; 10:14; 12:5; 14:6; 34:6; 35:10; 68:10; 69:33; 72:2, 4, 12 – 14; 74:21; 102:17; 107:9, 36, 41; 109:31; 113:7 – 8; 132:15; 140:12; 146:5, 7; Pr 22:2, 22 – 23; 29:13; Ecc 5:8; Isa 11:4; 14:30, 32; 25:4; 29:19; 41:17; Jer 20:13; Zep 3:12; Zec 11:7; Mt 11:5; Lk 4:18; 7:22; 16:22; Jas 2:5). See *God, Goodness of, Providence of.*

Kindness to:

Commanded (Ne 8:10, 12). Rewarded (Ps 41:1 – 3; Isa 58:10; Lk 14:12 – 14). Righteous treatment of, required (Ps 82:3 – 4; Pr 22:22; 31:9; Isa 1:17). Rewarded (Pr 29:14; Jer 22:16; Eze 18:7, 16 – 17; Da 4:27). Compassion toward (Job 30:25; Pr 14:21; 29:7; Heb 13:3; Jas 1:27). Liberality to (Pr 31:20; Isa 58:7; Mt 5:42, w Lk 6:30; Lk 3:11; 19:8; Ro 12:8, 13, 20; 1Co 13:3; 16:1 – 2; 2Co 9:1 – 15; Gal 2:10; Eph 4:28; 1Ti 5:9 – 10, 16; Jas 2:15 – 16; 1Jn 3:17). Liberality to, rewarded (Pr 19:17; 22:9; 28:27; Ps 112:9; Mt 19:21; 25:34 – 36; Lk 6:35; 12:33; 18:22; Ac 20:35).

Instances of: *Ruth, to Naomi (Ru 2:2, 11); Boaz, to Ruth (Ru 2:8 – 16; 3:15); Elijah, to the widow of Zarephath (1Ki 17:12 – 24); Elisha, to the prophet's widow (2Ki 4:1 – 7); the Jews (Est 9:22); Job (Job 29:11 – 17; 31:16 – 22, 38 – 40); the Temanites (Isa 21:14); Nebuzaradan (Jer 39:10); the good Samaritan (Lk 10:33 – 35); Zacchaeus (Lk 19:8); Dorcas (Ac 9:36); Cornelius (Ac 10:2, 4). Christian church, at Jerusalem (Ac 6:1); at Antioch (Ac 11:29 – 30). Churches of Macedonia and Achaia (Ro 15:25 – 26; 2Co 8:1 – 5). By Paul (Ro 15:25).*

Oppression of:

(Ne 5:1 – 13; Job 20:19 – 21; 22:6 – 7, 9 – 11; 24:4, 7 – 12; Pss 10:2, 8 – 10; 37:14; 109:16; Pr 14:31; 17:5; 19:7; 22:7, 16; 28:3, 15; 30:14; Ecc 5:8; Isa 3:14 – 15; 10:1 – 2; 32:6 – 7; Eze 18:12; 22:29;

Am 2:6; 4:1; 5:11 – 12; 8:4 – 6; Hab 3:14; Jas 2:6; 5:4). Oppression forbidden (Dt 24:14; Zec 7:10). Instances of oppression of (2Ki 4:1; Ne 5:1 – 5).

Mosaic Laws Concerning:

Atonement money of, must be uniform with that of the rich (Ex 30:15). Inexpensive offerings authorized for (Lev 5:7; 12:8; 14:21 – 22). Discrimination, in favor of, forbidden (Ex 23:3; Lev 19:15); against, forbidden (Ex 23:6; Jas 2:2 – 9). Exactions of interest from, forbidden (Ex 22:25; Lev 25:35 – 37). Garments of, taken in pledge, to be restored (Ex 22:26; Dt 24:12 – 13). To participate triennially in the tithes (Dt 14:28 – 29; 26:12 – 13). Gleanings reserved for (Lev 19:9 – 10; 23:22; Dt 24:19 – 21). To share the products of the land in the seventh year (Ex 23:11). To be released from servitude, in seventh year (Dt 15:12); in Jubilee (Lev 25:39 – 43). Alienated lands of, to be restored in Jubilee (Lev 25:25 – 28).

Lev	19:10	Leave them for the **p** and the alien.
	27:8	If anyone making the vow is too **p**
Dt	15:4	there should be no **p** among you,
	15:7	is a **p** man among your brothers
	15:11	There will always be **p** people
	24:12	If the man is **p**, do not go to sleep
Job	5:16	So the **p** have hope,
	24:4	force all the **p** of the land
Ps	14:6	frustrate the plans of the **p**,
	34:6	This **p** man called, and the LORD
	35:10	You rescue the **p** from those too
	40:17	Yet I am **p** and needy;
	68:10	O God, you provided for the **p**.
	82:3	maintain the rights of the **p**
	112:9	scattered abroad his gifts to the **p**,
	140:12	the LORD secures justice for the **p**
Pr	10:4	Lazy hands make a man **p**,
	14:20	The **p** are shunned
	14:31	oppresses the **p** shows contempt
	19:1	Better a **p** man whose walk is
	19:17	to the **p** lends to the LORD,
	19:22	better to be **p** than a liar.

	20:13	not love sleep or you will grow **p**;
	21:13	to the cry of the **p**,
	21:17	who loves pleasure will become **p**;
	22:2	Rich and **p** have this in common:
	22:9	for he shares his food with the **p**.
	22:22	not exploit the **p** because they are **p**
	28:6	Better a **p** man whose walk is
	28:27	to the **p** will lack nothing,
	29:7	care about justice for the **p**,
	31:9	defend the rights of the **p**
	31:20	She opens her arms to the **p**
Ecc	4:13	Better a **p** but wise youth
Isa	3:14	the plunder from the **p** is
	10:2	to deprive the **p** of their rights
	14:30	of the **p** will find pasture,
	61:1	me to preach good news to the **p**.
Jer	22:16	He defended the cause of the **p**
Eze	18:12	He oppresses the **p** and needy.
Am	2:7	They trample on the heads of the **p**
Zec	7:10	or the fatherless, the alien or the **p**.
Mt	5:3	saying: "Blessed are the **p** in spirit,
	11:5	the good news is preached to the **p**.
	19:21	your possessions and give to the **p**,
	26:11	The **p** you will always have
Mk	12:42	But a **p** widow came and put
	14:7	The **p** you will always have
Lk	4:18	me to preach good news to the **p**.
	6:20	"Blessed are you who are **p**,
	11:41	is inside [the dish] to the **p**,
	14:13	invite the **p**, the crippled, the lame,
Jn	12:8	You will always have the **p**
Ac	9:36	doing good and helping the **p**.
	10:4	and gifts to the **p** have come up
	24:17	to bring my people gifts for the **p**
Ro	15:26	for the **p** among the saints
1Co	13:3	If I give all I possess to the **p**
2Co	8:9	yet for your sakes he became **p**,
Gal	2:10	continue to remember the **p**,
Jas	2:2	and a **p** man in shabby clothes
	2:5	not God chosen those who are **p**

POTIPHAR [7036] (pŏt′ĭ-fêr, Heb. *pôtîphara*ʿ, *he whom [pagan god] Ra gives*). One of the pharaoh's officers mentioned in Genesis in connection with Joseph's sojourn in that land. He purchased Joseph from the Midianites and made him head overseer over his house. When Joseph was falsely accused by the wife of Potiphar, he threw Joseph into prison (Ge 39:1 – 20).

POVERTY [2895, 2896, 3769, 4728, 8133, 8203, 4775, 5729, 5730].

Destructive (Pr 10:15). A source of temptation (Pr 30:8 – 9). To be preferred over wealth, with trouble (Pr 15:16); without right (Pr 16:8; Ecc 4:6). See Poor. Caused: by laziness (Pr 6:11; 20:13; 24:33 – 34); by drunkenness (Pr 23:21); by evil associations (Pr 28:19).

Dt	28:48	and thirst, in nakedness and dire **p**,
1Sa	2:7	The LORD sends **p** and wealth;
Pr	6:11	**p** will come on you like a bandit
	11:24	withholds unduly, but comes to **p**.
	13:18	who ignores discipline comes to **p**
	14:23	but mere talk leads only to **p**.
	1:5	as surely as haste leads to **p**.
	2:16	to the rich — both come to **p**.
	4:34	**p** will come on you like a bandit
	8:22	and is unaware that **p** awaits him.
	0:8	give me neither **p** nor riches,
	1:7	let them drink and forget their **p**
Ecc	4:14	born in **p** within his kingdom.
Mk	12:44	out of her **p**, put in everything —
Lk	21:4	she out of her **p** put in all she had
2Co	8:2	and their extreme **p** welled up
	:9	through his **p** might become rich.
Rev	2:9	I know your afflictions and your **p**

POWER [226, 600, 1475, 1476, 1524, 2432, 2616, 2617, 3338, 3946, 6434, 6437, 6786, 6793, 7502, 7756, 10130, 10717, 10768, 794, 1539, 1543, 1918, 2026, 2708, 3197].

Of Christ:
As the Son of God, is the power of God (Jn 5:17 – 19; 10:28 – 30); as man, is from the Father (Ac 10:38). Described as: supreme (Eph 1:20 – 21; 1Pe 3:22); unlimited (Mt 28:18); over all flesh (Jn

17:2); *over all things (Jn 3:35; Eph 1:22); glorious (2Th 1:9); everlasting (1Ti 6:16). Is able to subdue all things (Php 3:21). Exemplified: in creation (Jn 1:3, 10; Col 1:16); upholding all things (Col 1:17; Heb 1:3); salvation (Isa 63:1; Heb 7:25); His teaching (Mt 7:28–29; Lk 4:32); working miracles (Mt 8:27; Lk 5:17); enabling others to work miracles (Mt 10:1; Ac 5:31); giving spiritual life (Jn 5:21, 25–26); giving eternal life (Jn 17:2); raising the dead (Jn 5:28–29); rising from the dead (Jn 2:19; 10:18); overcoming the world (Jn 16:33); overcoming Satan (Col 2:15; Heb 2:14); destroying works of Satan (1Jn 3:8). Ministers should make known (2Pe 1:16). Saints made willing by (Ps 110:3); aided by (Heb 2:18); strengthened by (Php 4:13; 2Ti 4:17); preserved by (2Ti 1:12; 4:18); bodies of, shall be changed by (Php 3:21). Rests upon saints (2Co 12:9). Present in the assembly of saints (1Co 5:4). Shall be specially manifested at Jesus' second coming (Mk 13:26; 2Pe 1:16). Shall subdue all power (1Co 15:24). Wicked shall be destroyed by (Ps 2:9; Isa 11:4; 63:3; 2Th 1:9).*

Of God:

One of his attributes (Ps 62:11). Expressed by the voice of God (Pss 29:3, 5; 68:33); finger of God (Ex 9:3, 15; Isa 48:13); arm of God (Job 40:9; Isa 52:10); thunder of his power (Job 26:14). Described as, great (Ps 79:11; Na 1:3); strong (Pss 89:13; 136:12); glorious (Ex 15:6; Isa 63:12); mighty (Job 9:4; Ps 89:13); everlasting (Isa 26:4; Ro 1:20); sovereign (Ro 9:21); effectual (Isa 43:13; Eph 3:7); irresistible (Dt 32:39; Da 4:35); incomparable (Ex 15:11–12; Dt 3:24; Job 40:9; Ps 89:8); unsearchable (Job 5:9; 9:10); incomprehensible (Job 26:14; Ecc 3:11). All things possible to (Mt 19:26). Nothing too hard for (Ge 18:14; Jer 32:27). Can save by many or by few (1Sa 14:6). Is the source of all strength (1Ch 29:12; Ps 68:35). Exemplified: in creation (Ps 102:25; Jer 10:12); in establishing and governing all things (Pss 65:6; 66:7); in miracles of Christ (Lk 11:20); in resurrection of Christ (2Co 13:4; Col 2:12); in resurrection of saints (1Co 6:14); in

making gospel effectual (Ro 1:16; 1Co 1:18, 24); in delivering his people (Ps 106:8); in destruction of the wicked (Ex 9:16; Ro 9:22). Saints, long for exhibitions of (Ps 63:1–2); have confidence in (Jer 20:11); receive increase of grace by (2Co 9:8); strengthened by (Eph 6:10; Col 1:11); upheld by (Ps 37:17; Isa 41:10); supported in affliction by (2Co 6:7; 2Ti 1:8); delivered by (Nu 1:10; Da 3:17); exalted by (Job 36:22); kept by, for salvation (1Pe 1:5). Exerted in behalf of saints (1Ch 16:9). Works in and for saints (2Co 13:4; Eph 1:19; 3:20). Faith of saints stands in (1Co 2:5). Should be acknowledged (1Ch 29:11; Isa 33:13); pleaded in prayer (Ps 79:11; Mt 6:13); feared (Jer 5:22; Mt 10:28); magnified (Ps 21:13; Jude 25). Efficiency of ministers is through (1Co 3:6–8; Gal 2:8; Eph 3:7). Is a ground of trust (Isa 26:4; Ro 4:21). The wicked do not know (Mt 22:29); have it against them (Ezr 8:22); shall be destroyed by it (Lk 12:5). The heavenly host magnified (Rev 4:11; 5:13; 11:17).

Of the Holy Spirit:

Is the power of God (Mt 12:28, w Lk 11:20). Christ worked his miracles (Mt 12:28). Exemplified: in creation (Ge 1:2; Job 26:13; Ps 104:30); conception of Christ (Lk 1:35); raising Christ from dead (1Pe 3:18); giving spiritual life (Eze 37:11–14, w Ro 8:11); working miracles (Ro 15:19); making gospel efficacious (1Co 2:4; 1Th 1:5); overcoming all difficulties (Zec 4:6–7). Promised by the Father (Lk 24:49). Promised by Christ (Ac 1:8). Saints upheld by (Ps 51:12); strengthened by (Eph 3:16); enabled to speak the truth boldly by (Mic 3:8; Ac 6:5, 10; 2Ti 1:7–8); helped in prayer by (Ro 8:26); abound in hope by (Ro 15:13). Qualifies ministers (Lk 24:49; Ac 1:8–9). God's word the instrument of (Eph 6:17). See Holy Spirit.

Spiritual:

From God (Isa 40:29–31; Lk 24:49; 1Co 1:24–28; Php 2:13; 2Ti 1:7). From Christ (2Co 12:9; Eph 1:19–20). From the Holy Spirit (Jn 7:38–39; Ac 1:8; 2:2–4). On believers (Ac 6:8,

10; 1Co 4:19 – 20; Heb 6:5). In the spirit of Elijah (Lk 1:17). In preaching (Ac 4:33; 6:10; 1Th 1:5); of Christ (Lk 4:32). Through prayer (Ge 32:28; Mk 9:29; Lk 24:49; Ac 1:14; 2:1; 2:2 – 4).

Ex	15:6	was majestic in **p**.
	32:11	out of Egypt with great **p**
Dt	8:17	"My **p** and the strength
	34:12	one has ever shown the mighty **p**
1Sa	10:6	LORD will come upon you in **p**,
	16:13	the LORD came upon David in **p**.
1Ch	29:11	LORD, is the greatness and the **p**
2Ch	20:6	**P** and might are in your hand,
Job	9:4	wisdom is profound, his **p** is vast.
	36:22	"God is exalted in his **p**.
	37:23	beyond our reach and exalted in **p**;
Ps	20:6	with the saving **p** of his right hand.
	63:2	and beheld your **p** and your glory.
	66:3	So great is your **p**
	68:34	Proclaim the **p** of God,
	77:14	you display your **p**
	89:13	Your arm is endued with **p**;
	147:5	Great is our Lord and mighty in **p**;
Pr	3:27	when it is in your **p** to act.
	18:21	The tongue has the **p** of life
	24:5	A wise man has great **p**,
Isa	11:2	the Spirit of counsel and of **p**,
	40:10	the Sovereign LORD comes with **p**
Jer	10:6	and your name is mighty in **p**.
	10:12	But God made the earth by his **p**;
	27:5	With my great **p** and outstretched
	32:17	and the earth by your great **p**
Hos	13:14	from the **p** of the grave;
Na	1:3	to anger and great in **p**;
Zec	4:6	nor by **p**, but by my Spirit,'
Mt	22:29	do not know the Scriptures or the **p**
	24:30	on the clouds of the sky, with **p**
Lk	1:35	and the **p** of the Most High will
	4:14	to Galilee in the **p** of the Spirit,
	9:1	he gave them **p** and authority
	10:19	to overcome all the **p** of the enemy;
	24:49	clothed with **p** from on high."
Ac	1:8	you will receive **p** when the Holy
	4:28	They did what your **p** and will had

	4:33	With great **p** the apostles
	10:38	with the Holy Spirit and **p**,
	26:18	and from the **p** of Satan to God,
Ro	1:16	it is the **p** of God for the salvation
	1:20	his eternal **p** and divine nature —
	4:21	fully persuaded that God had **p**
	9:17	that I might display my **p** in you
	15:13	overflow with hope by the **p**
	15:19	through the **p** of the Spirit.
1Co	1:17	cross of Christ be emptied of its **p**.
	1:18	to us who are being saved it is the **p**
	2:4	a demonstration of the Spirit's **p**,
	6:14	By his **p** God raised the Lord
2Co	4:7	to show that this all-surpassing **p** is
	6:7	in truthful speech and in the **p**
	10:4	they have divine **p**
	12:9	for my **p** is made perfect
	13:4	weakness, yet he lives by God's **p**.
Eph	1:19	and his incomparably great **p**
	3:16	you with **p** through his Spirit
	3:20	according to his **p** that is at work
Php	3:10	and the **p** of his resurrection
	3:21	by the **p** that enables him
Col	1:11	strengthened with all **p** according
	2:10	who is the head over every **p**
2Ti	1:7	but a spirit of **p**, of love
	3:5	form of godliness but denying its **p**.
Heb	2:14	might destroy him who holds the **p**
	7:16	of the **p** of an indestructible life.
1Pe	1:5	by God's **p** until the coming
2Pe	1:3	His divine **p** has given us
Jude	1:25	**p** and authority, through Jesus
Rev	4:11	to receive glory and honor and **p**,
	11:17	you have taken your great **p**
	19:1	and glory and **p** belong to our God,
	20:6	The second death has no **p**

PRAETORIAN GUARD (*residence of the Praetor [leader]*). Guard of imperial palace or provincial governor; NIV "palace guard" (Php 1:13) and "Caesar's household" (Php 4:22).

PRAETORIUM [4550] (prē-tō′rĭ̆um *residence of the Praetor [leader]*). Sometimes spelled Pretorium, the

Latin term for the Greek *praitōrion*, which among the Romans could refer to a number of things. Originally it meant the general's tent in the camp of an army station. Sometimes it referred to the military headquarters in Rome itself or in the provincial capitals. It also meant the staff of men in such an establishment or even the session of a planning council. In the Gospels (Mt 27:27; Mk 15:16; Jn 18:28, 33) it refers to the temporary palace or headquarters ("judgment hall") of the Roman governor or procurator while he was in Jerusalem, which was actually Herod's palace adjacent to the temple (cf. Ac 23:35). It was the scene of the trial of Jesus before Pontius Pilate. No doubt the debated reference in Php 1:13 (cf. 4:22, "Caesar's household") means the headquarters of the emperor's bodyguard, which modern research has shown could have been either in Rome or in some of the provincial capitals.

PRAISE [1385, 2146, 2376, 3344, 9335, 10122, 10693, 140, 1518, 1519, 2018, 2046, 2047, 2328, 2329, 2330].

Examples of:

(Pss 7:17; 22:22 – 23; 28:6 – 7; 32:11; 34:1 – 3; 41:13; 42:4; 51:15; 65:1; 71:8, 14 – 15; 75:1; 79:13; 81:1; 84:4; 86:12; 89:95; 104:33 – 34; 109:30; 113:1 – 2; 115:18; 118:15; 140:13; 145:1 – 21; 146:1 – 10; 148:1 – 14; 149:1 – 9; 150; Isa 24:15 – 16; 25:1; 35:10; 38:19; 43:21; 49:13; 51:3; 52:7 – 10; Jer 31:7; Ro 11:36; 16:27; 1Co 15:57; Eph 3:20 – 21; Heb 2:12; Jude 25; Rev 1:6; 14:7). With music (Pss 33:2 – 3; 43:3 – 4; 47:1, 6 – 7; 57:7 – 9 w 108:1 – 3; 66:1 – 2, 4; 67:4; 68:4, 32 – 34; 69:30; 71:22; 81:1; 92:1 – 3; 95:1 – 2; 98:4 – 6; 104:33; 144:9; 149:2 – 3; 150:3 – 5; Jas 5:13). Daily (1Ch 23:30; Pss 92:1 – 2; 145:2). In the night (Pss 42:8; 63:5 – 6; 77:6; 92:1 – 3; 119:62; 134:1; 149:5; Ac 16:25). Seven times a day (Ps 119:164). Congregational (Pss 22:22; 26:12; 68:26; 111:1; 116:18 – 19; 134:1 – 2; 135:2; 149:1). For God's goodness and mercy (Pss 13:6; 63:3 – 6; 100:5; 101:1; 106:1, 48; 107:8 – 9, 15, 21, 31; 117:2; 118:29; 136; 138:2; 144:1 – 2; 145:7 – 9, 14 – 21; 146:7 – 9; Isa 12:1 – 6; Jer 33:11). For God's greatness (Pss 48:1; 145:3, 10 – 12; 147:1 – 20; Isa 24:14). For God's holiness (Ps 99:2, 5, 9). For God's works (Pss 9:1 – 2; 107:8 – 9, 15, 21, 31 – 32; 145:4 – 6, 10 – 13; 147:12 – 18; 150:2). For deliverance from enemies (Ge 14:20; Pss 44:7 – 8; 54:6 – 7; 69:16). For salvation (Isa 61:3).

Commanded:

(Dt 8:10; Pss 9:11; 30:4; 32:11; 33:1 – 3; 69:34; 70:4; 95:1 – 2, 6 – 7 a; 96:1 – 4, 7 – 9; 97:12; 100:1 – 5; 105:1 – 5; 117:1; 134:1 – 2; 135:1 – 3, 19 – 21; Isa 42:10 – 12; Eph 5:19; Heb 13:15; 1Pe 4:11; 5:11). All nations to praise God (Pss 69:34; 103:22; 148:1 – 14). Angels exhorted to (Pss 103:20 – 21; 148:2). In heaven (Ne 9:6; Job 38:7; Pss 103:20 – 21; 148:2 – 4; Isa 6:3; Eze 3:12; Lk 2:13 – 14; 15:7, 10; Rev 1:6; 4:8 – 11; 5:9 – 14; 7:9 – 12; 11:16 – 17; 14:2 – 3; 15:3 – 4; 19:1 – 6).

Instances of:

Song of Moses, after the passage of the Red Sea (Ex 15:1 – 19). Miriam (Ex 15:21). Deborah, after defeating the Canaanites (Jdg 5:1 – 31). Hannah (1Sa 2:1 – 10). David, celebrating his deliverance from the hand of Saul (2Sa 22 w Ps 18); on bringing ark to Zion (1Ch 16:8 – 36); at the close of his reign (1Ch 29:10 – 19). Choir when Solomon brought ark into temple (2Ch 5:13). Israelites (2Ch 7:2 – 3; Ne 9:5 – 6). Daniel (Da 2:20, 23). Nebuchadnezzar (Da 4:37). Jonah (Jnh 2:9). Mary (Lk 1:46 – 55). Shepherds (Lk 2:20). Leper (Lk 17:15). Jesus and his disciples (Mt 26:30; Mk 14:26). Disciples (Ac 2:46 – 47; 4:24). Paul and Silas in prison (Ac 16:25).

Psalms of:

For God's goodness to Israel (Pss 46; 48; 65:66; 68; 76; 81; 85; 98; 105; 124; 126; 129; 135; 136). For God's goodness to the righteous (Pss 23; 34; 36; 91; 100; 103; 107; 117; 121). For God's goodness to individuals (Pss 9; 18; 22; 30; 40; 75; 103; 108; 116; 118; 138; 144). For God's attributes (Pss 8; 19; 22; 24; 29; 33; 47; 50; 65 – 66; 76 – 77; 92 – 93; 95 – 99; 104; 111; 113 – 115; 134; 139; 147 – 148; 150).

Ex	15:2	He is my God, and I will **p** him,
Dt	10:21	He is your **p**; he is your God,
Ru	4:14	said to Naomi: "**P** be to the LORD,
2Sa	22:4	to the LORD, who is worthy of **p**,
	22:47	The LORD lives! **P** be to my Rock
1Ch	16:25	is the LORD and most worthy of **p**;
Ezr	3:10	took their places to **p** the LORD,
Ne	9:5	and **p** the LORD your God,
Ps	8:2	you have ordained **p**
	16:7	I will **p** the LORD, who counsels
	30:4	**p** his holy name.
	33:1	it is fitting for the upright to **p** him.
	42:5	for I will yet **p** him,
	45:17	the nations will **p** you for ever
	63:4	I will **p** you as long as I live,
	65:1	**P** awaits you, O God, in Zion;
	66:2	make his **p** glorious.
	68:19	**P** be to the Lord, to God our Savior
	68:26	**p** the LORD in the assembly
	69:30	I will **p** God's name in song
	71:8	My mouth is filled with your **p**,
	71:22	I will **p** you with the harp
	74:21	the poor and needy **p** your name.
	89:5	The heavens **p** your wonders,
	92:1	It is good to **p** the LORD
	100:4	and his courts with **p**;
	103:1	**P** the LORD, O my soul;
	103:20	**P** the LORD, you his angels,
	117:1	**P** the LORD, all you nations;
	119:175	Let me live that I may **p** you,
	135:20	you who fear him, **p** the LORD.
	139:14	I **p** you because I am fearfully
	144:1	**P** be to the LORD my Rock,
	145:21	Let every creature **p** his holy name
	147:1	how pleasant and fitting to **p** him!
	150:2	**p** him for his surpassing greatness.
	150:6	that has breath **p** the LORD.
Pr	27:2	Let another **p** you, and not your
	27:21	man is tested by the **p** he receives.
	31:31	let her works bring her **p**
SS	1:4	we will **p** your love more than wine
Isa	12:1	"I will **p** you, O LORD.
	61:3	and a garment of **p**

Jer	33:9	**p** and honor before all nations
Da	2:20	"**P** be to the name of God for ever
	4:37	**p** and exalt and glorify the King
Mt	5:16	and **p** your Father in heaven.
	21:16	you have ordained **p**'?"
Lk	19:37	to **p** God in loud voices
Jn	5:44	effort to obtain the **p** that comes
	12:43	for they loved **p** from men more
Ro	2:29	Such a man's **p** is not from men,
	15:7	in order to bring **p** to God.
Eph	1:3	**P** be to the God and Father
	1:6	to the **p** of his glorious grace,
	1:12	might be for the **p** of his glory.
	1:14	to the **p** of his glory.
1Th	2:6	We were not looking for **p**
Heb	13:15	offer to God a sacrifice of **p** —
Jas	3:9	With the tongue we **p** our Lord
	5:13	happy? Let him sing songs of **p**.
Rev	5:13	be **p** and honor and glory

PRAYER [606, 1819, 6983, 7137, 9525, 10114, 10612, 1255, 1289, 2263, 2377, 4666, 4667]. In the Bible prayer is the spiritual response (spoken and unspoken) to God, who is known not merely to exist but to have revealed himself and to have invited his creatures into communion with himself. Thus prayer covers a wide spectrum of addressing and hearing God, interceding with and waiting for the Lord, and contemplating and petitioning our Father in heaven. What prayer is may best be seen in the example and teaching of Jesus. This information can then be supplemented by the apostolic practice of, and teaching on, prayer as well as examples of prayer from the OT.

General References to:

Attitudes in: See Worship. Boldness in, commanded (Heb 4:16). Exemplified by Abraham in his inquiry concerning Sodom (Ge 18:23 – 32), by Moses, supplicating for assistance in delivering Israel (Ex 33:12, 18). Secret (Ge 24:63; Mt 6:6). Silent (Ps 5:1). Weeping in (Ezr 10:1). In a loud voice, satirized by Elijah (1Ki 18:27). Long: of Pharisees (Mt 23:14); scribes (Mk 12:40; Lk 20:47). Profuse, to be avoided (Ecc 5:2; Mt 6:7).

Vain repetitions of, to be avoided (Mt 6:7). In the morning (Pss 5:3; 88:13; 143:8; Isa 32:2). Morning and evening (Ps 92:2). Twice daily (Ps 88:1). Three times a day (Ps 55:17; Da 6:10). In the night (Ps 119:55, 62). All night (Lk 6:12). Without ceasing (1Th 5:17). Disbelief in (Job 21:15). Family: by Abraham (Ge 12:7 – 8; 13:4, 8); by Jacob (Ge 35:3, 7). Cornelius (Ac 10:2). Hypocritical, forbidden (Mt 6:5). Discreet (Ecc 5:2; Mt 6:6). "Lord's Prayer": a model taught to the disciples (Mt 6:9 – 12; Lk 11:2 – 4). See below, Of Jesus. Of the righteous, acceptable: (Pr 15:8, 29). Spirit of, from God (Zec 12:10). Divine help in (Ro 8:26). Postures in: bowing (Ge 24:26, 48, 52; Ex 4:31; 34:8 – 9; 2Ch 29:29); kneeling (1Ki 8:54; 2Ch 6:13; Ezr 9:5; Ps 95:6; Da 6:10; Lk 22:41; Ac 20:36; 21:5); hands uplifted (1Ki 8:22; 2Ch 6:12 – 13; Ezr 9:5; Isa 1:15; La 3:41; 1Ti 2:8); standing (Lk 18:11, 13); power of (Mk 9:28 – 29; Jas 5:16 – 18). Accompanied by works (Ne 4:9). Kept in divine remembrance (Rev 5:8; 8:3 – 4). Prayer contest proposed by Elijah (1Ki 18:24 – 39). Public, should edify (1Co 14:14 – 15). Social (Mt 18:19; Ac 1:13 – 14; 16:16, 25; 20:36; 21:5). Held in private houses (Ac 1:13 – 14; 12:12); in the temple (Ac 2:46; 3:1). Perseverance in (Ro 12:12; Eph 6:18). Evils averted by (Jer 26:19). Private commanded (Mt 6:6). Exemplified by: Lot (Ge 19:20); Eliezer (Ge 24:12); Jacob (Ge 32:9 – 12); Gideon (Jdg 6:22, 36, 39); Hannah (1Sa 1:10); David (2Sa 7:18 – 29); Hezekiah (2Ki 20:2); Isaiah (2Ki 20:11); Manasseh (2Ch 33:18 – 19); Ezra (Ezr 9:5 – 6); Nehemiah (Ne 2:4); Jeremiah (Jer 32:16 – 25); Daniel (Da 9:3, 19); Jonah (Jnh 2:1); Habakkuk (Hab 1:2); Anna (Lk 2:37); Jesus (Mt 14:23; 26:36, 39; Mk 1:35; Lk 9:18, 29); Paul (Ac 9:11); Peter (Ac 9:40; 10:9); Cornelius (Ac 10:30). Rebuked: of Moses, at the Red Sea (Ex 14:15); when he prayed to see Canaan (Dt 3:23 – 27). Of Joshua (Jos 7:10). Submissiveness in: exemplified by Jesus (Mt 26:39; Mk 14:36; Lk 22:42); David (2Sa 12:22 – 23); Job (Job 1:20 – 21). Signs asked for, as assurance of answer: by Abraham's servant (Ge 24:14, 42 – 44); by Gideon (Jdg 6:36 – 40).

Answer to:

Promised: (Ex 33:17 – 20; 1Ki 8:22 – 53; 1Ch 28:9; 2Ch 6; Job 8:5 – 6; 12:4; 22:27; 33:26; Pss 10:17; 81:10; Pr 10:24; 15:8, 29; 16:1; Isa 58:9; 65:24; Eze 36:37; Mt 6:5 – 8; 18:19 – 20; 21:22; Mk 11:24 – 25; Lk 11:9 – 13; 18:6 – 8; 21:36; 4:10, 23 – 24; Jn 16:23 – 27; Ro 8:26; 10:12 – 13; Eph 2:18; 3:20; Heb 4:16; 10:22 – 23; Jas 1:5 – 7; 1Jn 3:22; 5:14 – 15). Promised to those in adversity (Ex 6:5 – 6 w Ac 7:34; Ex 22:23, 27; Pss 9:10, 12; 18:3; 32:6; 34:15, 17; 37:4 – 5; 38:15; 50:15; 55:16 – 17; 56:9; 65:2, 5; 69:32 – 33; 86:7; 91:15; 102:17 – 20; Isa 19:20; 30:19; 31:9; Joel 2:18 – 19, 32; Zec 10:1, 6; 13:9). Promised to those who diligently seek God (2Ch 7:14; Ps 145:18 – 19; Pr 2:3, 5 – 6; Isa 55:6; Jer 29:12 – 13; 33:3; La 3:25; Am 5:4 – 6; Zep 2:3; Zec 13:9; Mt 7:7 – 11; Jn 9:31; 15:7, 16; Heb 11:6; Jas 4:8, 10; 5:16). Promised to the meek (Mk 11:25). Promised to the penitent (Dt 4:30 – 31; 2Ch 7:13 – 15).

Delayed: (Pss 22:1 – 2; 40:1; 80:4; 88:14; Jer 42:2 – 7; Hab 1:2; Lk 18:7). Withheld: of Balaam (Dt 23:5; Jos 24:10); of Job (Job 30:20, w 42:12); of the Israelites, when attacked by the Amorites (Dt 1:45). The prayer of Jesus, "Let this cup pass" (Mt 26:39, 42, 44, w 45 – 75 & Mt 27).

Differs from Request: Exceeds petition (Eph 3:20). Solomon asked for wisdom; the answer included wisdom, riches, honor, and long life (1Ki 3:7 – 14; 2Ch 1:7 – 12). Disciples prayed for Peter; the answer included Peter's deliverance (Ac 12:15, w v.5). Moses asked to see God's face; God revealed his goodness (Ex 33:18 – 20). Moses asked to be permitted to cross the Jordan; the answer was permission to view the land of promise (Dt 3:23 – 27). Martha and Mary asked Jesus to come and heal their brother Lazarus; Jesus delayed but raised Lazarus from the dead (Jn 11). Paul asked that the thorn in the flesh be removed; the answer was a promise of grace to endure it (2Co 12:8 – 9).

Answered:

(Job 34:28; Pss 3:4; 4:1; 6:8 – 9; 18:6; 21:2, 4; 22:4 – 5, 24; 28:6; 30:2 – 3; 31:22; 34:4 – 6; 40:1; 66:19 – 20; 77:1 – 2; 81:7; 99:6 – 8; 106:44; 107:6, 13; 116:1 – 8; 118:5, 21; 119:26; 120:1; 138:3; La 3:57 – 58; Hos 12:4; Jnh 2:1 – 2, 7; Lk 23:42 – 43; Ac 4:31; 2Co 12:8 – 9; Jas 5:17 – 18).

Instances of: Cain (Ge 4:13 – 15). Abraham, for a son (Ge 15); entreating for Sodom (Ge 18:23 – 33); for Ishmael (Ge 17:20); for Abimelech (Ge 20:17). Hagar, for deliverance (Ge 16:7 – 13). Abraham's servant, for guidance (Ge 24:12 – 52). Rebekah, concerning her pains in pregnancy (Ge 25:22 – 23). Jacob, for deliverance from Esau (Ge 32:9 – 32; 33:1 – 17). Moses, for help at the Red Sea (Ex 14:15 – 16); at the waters of Marah (Ex 15:25); at Horeb (Ex 17:4 – 6), in the battle with the Amalekites (Ex 17:8 – 14); concerning the murmuring of the Israelites for flesh (Nu 11:11 – 35); in behalf of Miriam's leprosy (Nu 12:13 – 15). Moses, Aaron, and Samuel (Ps 99:6). Israelites: For deliverance from bondage (Ex 2:23 – 25; 3:7 – 10; Ac 7:34); from Pharaoh's army (Ex 14:10 – 30); from the king of Mesopotamia (Jdg 3:9, 15); Sisera (Jdg 4:3, 23 – 24; 1Sa 12:9 – 11); Ammon (Jdg 10:6 – 18; 11:1 – 33), for God's favor under the reproofs of Azariah (2Ch 15:1 – 15); from Babylonian bondage (Ne 9:27). Gideon, asking the token of dew (Jdg 6:36 – 40). Manoah, asking about Samson (Jdg 13:8 – 9). Samson, asking for strength (Jdg 16:28 – 30). Hannah, asking for a child (1Sa 1:10 – 17, 19 – 20). David, asking whether Keilah would be delivered into his hands (1Sa 23:10 – 12); and Ziklag (1Sa 30:8); whether he should go into Judah after Saul's death (2Sa 2:1); whether he should go against the Philistines (2Sa 5:19 – 25). David, in adversity (Pss 118:5; 138:3). Solomon, asking for wisdom (1Ki 3:1 – 13; 9:2 – 3). Elijah, raising the widow's son (1Ki 17:22); asking fire on his sacrifice (1Ki 18:36 – 38); asking for rain (1Ki 17:1; 18:1, 42 – 45; Jas 5:17). Elisha, leading the Syrian army (2Ki 6:17 – 20). Jabez, asking for prosperity (1Ch 4:10). Abijah, for victory over Jeroboam (2Ch 13:14 – 18). Asa, for victory over Zerah (2Ch 14:11 – 15). The people of Judah (2Ch 15:15). Jehoshaphat, for victory over the Canaanites (2Ch 18:31; 20:6 – 7). Jehoahaz, for victory over Hazael (2Ki 13:4). Priests and Levites, when blessing the people (2Ch 30:27). Hezekiah and Isaiah, for deliverance from Sennacherib (2Ki 19:14 – 20; 2Ch 32:20 – 23), to save Hezekiah's life (2Ki 20:1 – 7, 11; 2Ch 32:24). Manasseh, for deliverance from the king of Babylon (2Ch 33:13, 19). Reubenites, for deliverance from the Hagrites (1Ch 5:20). The Jews, returning from captivity (Ezr 8:21, 23). Ezekiel, to have the baking of his bread of affliction changed (Eze 4:12 – 15). Daniel, for the interpretation of Nebuchadnezzar's dream (Da 2:19 – 23); interceding for the people (Da 9:20 – 23); in a vision (Da 10:12). Zechariah, for a son (Lk 1:13). The leper, for healing (Mt 8:2 – 3; Mk 1:40 – 43; Lk 5:12 – 13). Centurion, for his servant (Mt 8:5 – 13; Lk 7:3 – 10; Jn 4:50 – 51). Peter, asking that Tabitha be restored (Ac 9:40). The disciples, for Peter (Ac 12:5 – 17). Paul, to be restored to health (2Co 1:9 – 11).

Confession in:

(Lev 26:40; Ezr 10:1; Lk 15:21; 16:13). Commanded (Lev 5:5; Nu 5:6 – 7; Jer 3:13, 25). A condition of forgiveness (1Ki 8:47, 49 – 50; Pr 28:13; 1Jn 1:9).

Instances of: (Jdg 10:10, 15; 1Sa 12:10; Ne 9:2 – 3, 33 – 35; Pss 31:10; 32:5; 38:4, 18; 40:11 – 12; 41:4; 51:2 – 5; 69:5; 106:6; 119:176; 130:3). Moses for Israel (Ex 32:31 – 32; 34:9); Ezra for Judah (Ezr 9:6 – 15); Nehemiah for Judah (Ne 1:4 – 11); Isaiah for Judah (Isa 14:20 – 21; 59:12 – 15; 64:5 – 7); Jeremiah for Judah (Jer 14:7, 20; La 1:18, 20; 3:42); Daniel for Judah (Da 9:5 – 15).

Commanded:

(1Ch 16:11, 35; Ps 105:3 – 4; Isa 55:6; La 3:1; Lk 18:1; Eph 1:18; Php 4:6; Col 4:2; 1Th 5:17 – 18; 1Ti 2:8; Heb 4:16).

Exemplified:

By Eliezer (Ge 24:12); Jacob (Ge 32:9 – 12); Gideon (Jdg 6:22, 36, 39); Hannah (1Sa 1:10, 13); David (2Sa 7:18 – 29); Solomon at the dedication of the temple (1Ki 8:23 – 53; 2Ch 6:14 – 42); Hezekiah (2Ki 20:2); Isaiah (2Ki 20:11); Manasseh (2Ch 33:18 – 19); Ezra (Ezr 9:5 – 15); Nehemiah (Ne 2:4); Jeremiah (Jer 32:16 – 25); Daniel (Da 9:3 – 19); Jonah (Jnh 2:1 – 9); Habakkuk (Hab 1:2); Anna (Lk 2:37); Jesus (Mt 14:23; 26:36, 39; Mk 1:35; 6:46; Lk 5:16; 6:12; 9:18, 28 – 29); Paul (Ac 9:11); Peter (Ac 9:40; 10:9); Cornelius (Ac 10:30).

Persistence in:

(Pss 17:1 – 6; 22:1 – 2, 19; 28:1 – 2; 35:22 – 23; 55:1 – 2, 16 – 17; 57:2; 61:1 – 2; 70:5; 86:3, 6; 88:1 – 2, 9, 13; 102:1 – 28; 119:145 – 147; 130:1 – 2; 141:1 – 2; 142:1 – 2; Isa 62:7; Hos 12:4; Lk 11:5 – 8; 18:1 – 7).

Instances of: *Abraham (Ge 18:23 – 32); Jacob (Ge 32:24 – 30); Moses (Ex 32:32; 33:12 – 16; 34:9; Dt 9:18, 25); Gideon (Jdg 6:36 – 40); Samson (Jdg 16:28); Hannah (1Sa 1:10 – 11); Elijah (1Ki 18:24 – 44; Jas 5:17 – 18); Hezekiah (2Ki 19:15 – 19; Isa 38:2 – 3); Asa (2Ch 14:11); Ezra (Ezr 9:5); Nehemiah (Ne 1:4 – 11; 9:32); Isaiah (Isa 64:12); Daniel (Da 9:3, 17 – 19); sailors (Jnh 1:14); Habakkuk (Hab 1:2); two blind men of Jericho (Mt 20:30 – 31; Mk 10:48; Lk 18:39); Syrian Phoenician woman (Mt 15:22 – 28; Mk 7:25 – 30); centurion (Mt 8:5; Lk 7:3 – 4); Jesus (Mt 26:39, 42; Mk 14:36, 39; Lk 22:42 – 44; Heb 5:7); Paul (2Co 12:8); believers (Ro 8:26; Eph 6:18).*

In Adversity:

By Jacob (Ge 43:14); Moses (Ex 32:32); Israelites (Nu 20:16; Dt 26:7; Jdg 3:9); David (2Sa 22:7); Hezekiah (2Ki 19:16, 19); Jehoshaphat (2Ch 20:4 – 13); Manasseh (2Ch 33:12 – 13); psalmist

(Pss 5:1 – 12; 7:1 – 2, 6 – 7; 13:1 – 4; 22:1 – 21; 25:2, 16 – 19, 22; 27:11 – 12; 28:1; 31:1 – 4, 9, 14 – 18; 35:1 – 28; 38:1 – 22; 43:1 – 5; 44:4, 23 – 26; 54:1 – 3; 55:1 – 17; 56:1 – 13; 57:1 – 2; 59:1 – 17; 64:1 – 2; 69:1 – 36; 70:1 – 5; 71:1 – 24; 74:1 – 23; 79:1 – 13; 94:1 – 23; 102; 108:6, 12; 109:1 – 2, 21, 26 – 28; 120:2; 140:1 – 13; 142:1 – 2, 5 – 7; 143:1 – 12); Jeremiah (Jer 15:15); Jonah (Jnh 2:1 – 9); Stephen (Ac 7:59 – 60); Paul and Silas (Ac 16:25).

Intercessory:

(Ge 20:7; Jer 27:18; 29:7; Mt 5:44; Eph 6:18 – 19; 1Ti 2:1; Heb 13:20 – 21; Jas 5:14 – 16). Priestly (Ex 28:12, 29 – 30, 38; Lev 10:17). For spiritual blessing (Nu 6:23 – 26; 1Sa 12:23; Job 1:5; 42:8 – 10). To avert judgments (Ge 20:7; Ex 32:9 – 14; Nu 14:11 – 21; 16:45 – 50; Dt 9:18 – 20, 25 – 29; Isa 65:8). For deliverance from enemies (1Sa 7:5 – 9; Isa 37:4). For healing disease (Jas 5:14 – 16). For the unrepentant, unavailing (Jer 7:16; 11:14; 14:11). Of Moses for Israel (Ex 32:11 – 14, 31 – 32; 34:9; Nu 14:19; 21:7; Dt 9:18, 20, 24 – 29). Of Joshua for Israel (Jos 7:6 – 7). Of Boaz for Ruth (Ru 2:12). Of Eli for Hannah (1Sa 1:17). Of Samuel for Israel (1Sa 7:9; 12:23). Of David, for Israel (2Sa 24:17; 1Ch 29:18); for Solomon (1Ch 29:19). Of Solomon (1Ki 8:31 – 53; 2Ch 6:22 – 42). Of Hezekiah for transgressors (2Ch 30:18 – 19). Of Job for his three friends (Job 42:8 – 10). Of the psalmist for the righteous (Pss 7:9; 28:9; 36:10; 80:14 – 15). Of Daniel for Israel (Da 9:3 – 19). Of Jesus for his murderers (Lk 23:34). Of Stephen for his murderers (Ac 7:60). Of Peter and John for Samaritan believers (Ac 8:15). Of the recipients of bounty for Corinthian donors (2Co 9:14). Of Paul, for unbelieving Jews (Ro 10:1); for Roman Christians (Ro 1:9); for Ephesian Christians (Eph 1:15 – 19; 3:14 – 19); for Philippian Christians (Php 1:3 – 5, 9); for Colossian Christians (Col 1:3, 9); for Thessalonian Christians (1Th 1:2; 3:10, 12 – 13; 5:23; 2Th 1:11 – 12; 2:16 – 17; 3:5, 16); for Onesiphorus (2Ti 1:16, 18); for Philemon (Phm 4); of Philemon for Paul (Phm 22). See Mediation. Requested (Nu

21:7; Ro 15:30 – 32; 2Co 1:11; Eph 6:19; Col 4:3; 1Th 5:25; 2Th 3:1; Heb 13:18).

Of Jesus:

(Mt 6:9 – 13; 11:25 – 26; Lk 3:21; Lk 11:1 – 4; Jn 12:27 – 28). Before day (Mk 1:35). In secret (Mt 14:23; Mk 1:35; 6:46; Lk 5:16; 6:12; 9:18, 28 – 29). In a mountain (Mt 14:23; Mk 6:46; Lk 6:12; 9:28). In the wilderness (Lk 5:16). Thanksgiving before eating (Mt 14:19; 15:36; 26:26 – 27; Mk 6:41; 8:6; 1Co 11:24). In distress (Jn 12:27; Heb 5:7). In blessing children (Mt 19:13, 15; Mk 10:16). At the grave of Lazarus (Jn 11:41 – 42). For Peter (Lk 22:31 – 32). For believers (Jn 17:1 – 26). For the Comforter, the Holy Spirit (Jn 14:16). In Gethsemane (Mt 26:36 – 44; Mk 14:32 – 35; Lk 22:41 – 44; Heb 5:7). On the cross (Mt 27:46; Lk 23:34, 46). Present ministry, at the right hand of the Father (Heb 7:25). Of his apostles (Ac 1:24 – 25).

Of the Wicked, Not Heard:

(Dt 1:45; 2Sa 22:42; Job 35:12 – 13; Pss 18:41; 66:18; Pr 1:24 – 28; 15:8, 29; 21:13, 27; 28:9; Isa 1:15; 45:19; 59:2; Jer 11:11; 14:12; 15:1; 18:17; La 3:8, 44; Eze 8:18; 20:8, 31; Hos 5:6; Mic 3:4; Zec 7:12 – 13; Mal 2:11 – 13; Jn 9:31; Jas 1:6 – 7; 4:3). See Wicked, Prayers of. To idols (1Ki 18:26 – 29). See Idolatry.

Penitential:

Of David (Ps 51:1 – 17), the tax collector (Lk 18:13). See above, Confession in. See Sin, Confession of.

Pleas Offered in:

(Ex 33:13; Nu 14:13 – 19; 16:22; Dt 3:24 – 25; 9:26 – 29; Jos 7:7 – 9; 2Sa 7:25 – 29; 2Ki 19:15 – 19; 2Ch 14:11; Ne 9:32; Pss 9:19 – 20; 38:16; 71:18; 74:10 – 11, 18, 20 – 23; 79:10 – 12; 83:1 – 2, 18; 119:42, 73, 146, 149, 153; 143:11 – 12; Isa 37:15 – 20; 63:17 – 19; La 3:56 – 63; Joel 2:17). Pleas based on God's mercy (Pss 69:13, 16; 109:21, 26 – 27; 115:1; 119:124). God's providence (Pss 4:1; 27:8). God's promises (Ge 32:9 – 12; Ex 32:13; 1Ki 8:25 – 26, 59 – 60; Ne 1:8 – 9; Pss

89:49 – 51; 119:43, 49, 116; Jer 14:21). Personal consecration (Ps 119:94). Personal righteousness (Pss 86:1 – 2, 4 – 5, 17; 119:38, 145, 173 – 176; Jer 18:20).

Thanksgiving, and Before Taking Food:

(Jos 9:14; 1Sa 9:13; Ro 14:6; 1Co 10:30 – 31; 1Ti 4:3 – 5). Exemplified: by Jesus (Mt 14:19; 15:36; 26:26 – 27; Mk 6:41; 8:6 – 7; 14:22 – 23; Lk 9:16; 22:19; Jn 6:11, 23; 1Co 11:24); by Paul (Ac 27:35).

2Ch	30:27	for their **p** reached heaven,
Ezr	8:23	about this, and he answered our **p**.
Ps	4:1	be merciful to me and hear my **p**.
	6:9	the LORD accepts my **p**.
	17:1	Give ear to my **p** —
	66:20	who has not rejected my **p**
	86:6	Hear my **p**, O LORD;
Pr	15:8	but the **p** of the upright pleases him
	15:29	but he hears the **p** of the righteous.
Isa	56:7	a house of **p** for all nations."
Mt	21:13	house will be called a house of **p**,'
	21:22	receive whatever you ask for in **p**."
Mk	9:29	This kind can come out only by **p**."
Jn	17:15	My **p** is not that you take them out
Ac	1:14	all joined together constantly in **p**,
	2:42	to the breaking of bread and to **p**.
	6:4	and will give our attention to **p**
	10:31	has heard your **p** and remembered
	16:13	expected to find a place of **p**.
Ro	12:12	patient in affliction, faithful in **p**.
1Co	7:5	you may devote yourselves to **p**.
2Co	13:9	and our **p** is for your perfection.
Php	1:9	this is my **p**: that your love may
	4:6	but in everything, by **p** and petition
Col	4:2	yourselves to **p**, being watchful
1Ti	2:8	to lift up holy hands in **p**,
	4:5	by the word of God and **p**.
Jas	5:15	**p** offered in faith will make the sick
1Pe	3:12	and his ears are attentive to their **p**,

PREACHING [5752, 10452, 1877+3364, 2294, 2294+ 2295, 2295, 2859, 3060, 3062, 3281, 3364+3836,

4155]. The act of exhorting, prophesying, reproving, teaching.

General:

Noah called preacher (2Pe 2:5). Solomon called preacher (Ecc 1:1, 12). Sitting while (Mt 5:1; Lk 4:20; 5:3). Moses slow to (Ex 4:10 – 12). Appointed and practiced by Jesus as the method of promulgating the gospel (Mt 4:17; 11:1; Mk 16:15, 20; Lk 4:18 – 19, 43). Attested to by Paul (Tit 1:3). Grave responsibility of (2Co 2:14 – 17). Repentance, the subject, of John the Baptist's (Mt 3:2; Mk 1:4, 15; Lk 3:3); of Christ's (Mt 4:17; Mk 1:15); of the apostles' (Mk 6:12). The gospel of the kingdom of God, the subject of Christ's (Mk 1:14 – 15; 2:2; Lk 8:1). Christ crucified and risen, the burden of Paul's (Ac 17:3). Jesus preaches to the spirits in prison (1Pe 3:19; 4:9, w Eph 4:9).

Preaching Should:

Edify (1Co 14:1 – 25). Be skillful (2Ti 2:15 – 16). Be in power (1Th 1:5). Be with boldness (Ac 13:46; 2Co 3:12 – 13). Not be, with mere human strategy (Mt 26), with deceit or flattery (1Th 2:3 – 6).

Effective Preaching:

By Azariah (2Ch 15:1 – 15); Jonah (Jnh 3); Haggai (Hag 1:7 – 12); Peter (Ac 2:14 – 41); Philip (Ac 8:5 – 12, 27 – 38); Paul (Ac 9:20 – 22; 13:16 – 43). See Revivals.

Impenitence under:

Asa (2Ch 16:7 – 10); Ahab (2Ch 18:7 – 26); the Jews (Ac 13:46).

Lk	9:6	**p** the gospel and healing people
Ac	18:5	devoted himself exclusively to **p**,
Ro	10:14	hear without someone **p** to them?
1Co	2:4	and my **p** were not with wise
	9:18	in **p** the gospel I may offer it free
Gal	1:9	If anybody is **p** to you a gospel
1Ti	4:13	the public reading of Scripture, to **p**
	5:17	especially those whose work is **p**

PRECEPTS

| Dt | 33:10 | He teaches your **p** to Jacob |

Ps	19:8	The **p** of the Lord are right,
	103:18	and remember to obey his **p**.
	111:7	all his **p** are trustworthy.
	111:10	who follow his **p** have good
	119:15	I meditate on your **p**
	119:40	How I long for your **p**!
	119:69	I keep your **p** with all my heart.
	119:87	but I have not forsaken your **p**.
	119:100	for I obey your **p**.
	119:104	I gain understanding from your **p**;
	119:141	I do not forget your **p**.
	119:159	See how I love your **p**;

PREDESTINATION [4633]. *See also Election.*

According to the purpose of grace (Ex 33:19; Isa 44:1 – 2, 7; Mal 1:2 – 3; Ac 13:48; Ro 8:28 – 30, 33; 9:11 – 29; 11:5, 7 – 8; 1Co 1:26 – 29; Eph 1:4 – 5, 9 – 11; 3:11; 2Th 2:13; 2Ti 1:9; Tit 1:1 – 2; 1Pe 1:2, 20). Of prosperity to Abraham (Ge 21:12; Ne 9:7 – 8). Of Joseph's mission to Egypt (Ge 45:5 – 7; Ps 105:17 – 22). Of Israel as a nation (Ge 21:12; Dt 4:37; 7:7 – 8; 10:15; 32:8; 1Sa 12:22; Pss 33:12; 135:4). Of Ishmael as a nation (Ge 21:12 – 13; 25:12 – 18). Of famine in Egypt (Ge 41:30 – 32). Of judgment to Pharaoh (Ex 9:16). Of David as king (2Ch 6:6; Pss 78:67 – 68, 70 – 72). Of Jehu's dynasty (2Ki 10:30; 15:12). Of the dividing of Solomon's kingdom (1Ki 11:11 – 12, 31 – 39; 12:15). Of mercy to the widow at Sidon (Lk 4:25 – 27). Of the destruction of the Canaanites (Jos 11:20); of Ben-Hadad (1Ki 20:42); of Ahaziah (2Ch 22:7); of Amaziah and the idolatrous Israelites (2Ch 25:20). Acknowledged by Job (Job 23:13 – 14). Of agent to execute divine judgments (2Ki 19:25; 2Ch 22:7; Hab 1:12). Of Jeremiah as prophet (Jer 1:4 – 5). Of revelation to a chosen people (Mt 11:25 – 26; Lk 8:10; 1Co 2:7). Of the death of Jesus (Mt 26:24; Mk 14:21; Lk 22:22; 24:26 – 27; Ac 2:23; 3:18; 4:28; Rev 13:8). Of Paul to the ministry (Ac 9:15; Gal 1:15 – 16; 1Ti 2:7). Of the times and bounds of nations (Ac 17:26). Of times and seasons (Ac 1:7). Of the standard of righteousness (Eph 2:10). Of the kingdom prepared for the righ-

teous (Mt 25:34). Of salvation and election (Mt 20:16; 20:23; 24:22, 40; Mk 13:20, 22; Lk 10:20; 17:34 – 36; 18:7; Jn 6:37, 39, 44 – 45; 15:16, 19; 17:2, 6, 9; Ac 2:39, 47; 13:48; 22:14; Ro 1:6; 8:28 – 30, 33; 11:5, 7 – 8; 1Co 1:26 – 29; Eph 1:9 – 11; Col 3:12; 1Th 1:4; 2:12 – 13; 2Ti 1:9; Tit 1:1 – 2; Jas 1:18; 1Pe 1:2, 20; 2Pe 1:10). Of the wicked, to the day of evil (Pr 16:4); to condemnation (Jude 4). Of the day of judgment (Ac 17:31).

PREPARE

Ps	23:5	You **p** a table before me
Isa	25:6	the LORD Almighty will **p**
Am	4:12	**p** to meet your God, O Israel."
Mal	3:1	who will **p** the way before me.
Mt	3:3	'**P** the way for the Lord,
Jn	14:2	there to **p** a place for you.
Eph	4:12	to **p** God's people for works
1Pe	1:13	Therefore, **p** your minds for action;

PRESENCE

Ex	25:30	Put the bread of the **P** on this table
2Ki	17:23	LORD removed them from his **p**,
	23:27	also from my **p** as I removed Israel,
Ezr	9:15	one of us can stand in your **p**."
Ps	16:11	you will fill me with joy in your **p**,
	23:5	in the **p** of my enemies.
	51:11	Do not cast me from your **p**
	90:8	our secret sins in the light of your **p**
	139:7	Where can I flee from your **p**?
Jer	5:22	"Should you not tremble in my **p**?
Hos	6:2	that we may live in his **p**.
Mal	3:16	in his **p** concerning those who
1Th	3:9	have in the **p** of our God
	3:13	and holy in the **p** of our God
2Th	1:9	and shut out from the **p** of the Lord
Heb	9:24	now to appear for us in God's **p**.
1Jn	3:19	rest in his **p** whenever our hearts
Jude	1:24	before his glorious **p** without fault

PRIDE [1450, 1452, 1454, 1455, 1467, 1469, 1575, 2086, 2295, 5294, 8123, 8124, 8146, 3016, 3017, 3018, 5662, 5881]. One of the worst forms of sin, regarded, indeed, by many as the basis of all sin. The various Hebrew words reflect the deep-seated and far-reaching nature of pride, for they are associated with terms such as presumption, vanity, vain boasting, haughtiness, and arrogance. Pride makes impossible a right perspective toward both God and man. It deceives the heart (Jer 49:16) and hardens it (Da 5:20). It brings contention (Pr 13:10; 28:25) and destruction (16:18). It was a fundamental fault of the wandering Israelites that brought a stern warning from God (Lev 26:19) and was associated with the punishment on King Uzziah (2Ch 26:16ff.), Moab (Isa 25:11), Judah and Jerusalem (Jer 13:9), Jacob (Am 6:8), and Edom (Ob 3), among others. Nebuchadnezzar testified of the "King of heaven" that "those who walk in pride he is able to humble" (Da 4:37). The Greek words used also convey the idea of empty display, glorying, and arrogance. James quotes Pr 3:34 in pointing out God's opposition to the proud (Jas 4:6). Paul made it clear that no one has any grounds for boasting in God's sight, but he does also speak of "pride" as a legitimate attribute (e.g., 2Co 5:12; 7:4).

Condemned:

Admonitions against (Dt 8:11 – 14, 17 – 20; Pss 49:11; 75:4 – 6; Jer 9:23; Mt 23:5 – 7; Lk 14:8 – 9; 20:46 – 47; Ro 11:17 – 21, 25; 12:3, 16; 1Co 4:6 – 8, 10; 5:2, 6; 8:1 – 2; 10:12; 13:4; 14:38; 2Co 10:5, 12, 18; Gal 6:3; Eph 4:17; Php 2:3; 1Ti 2:9; 6:3 – 4, 17; 2Ti 3:2, 4; 1Pe 5:3; Rev 3:17 – 18). Prayer regarding (Pss 9:20; 10:2 – 6, 11). Prevented by divine discipline (2Co 12:7). Proceeds from the carnal mind (Mk 7:21 – 22; 1Jn 2:16). Leads: to strife (Pr 13:10; 28:25); to destruction (Pr 15:25; 16:18; 17:19; 18:11 – 12; Isa 14:12 – 16; 26:5; 28:3; Da 11:45; Zep 3:11; Mal 4:1; 1Ti 3:6; Rev 18:7 – 8). Rebuked (1Sa 2:3 – 5; 2Ki 14:9 – 10; 2Ch 25:18 – 19; Job 12:2; Jer 13:9, 15, 17; Hab 2:4 – 5, 9). Repugnant to God (Job 37:24; Pss 12:3; 18:27; 31:23; 101:5; 138:6; Pr 6:16 – 17; 8:13; 16:5; Jer 50:31 – 32; Lk 1:51; Jas 4:6). The proud shall be humbled (Lev 26:19; Ps 52:6 – 7; Pr 11:2; Isa 2:11 – 17; 3:16 – 26; 5:13; 13:11; 22:16, 19; 23:7, 9; 24:4, 21; Jer 49:4, 16; Da 4:37; Ob 3 – 4; Mt 23:12;

Mk 10:43; Lk 1:52; 9:46; 18:14; Rev 18:7 – 8). Pride discussed with Job (Job 11:12; 12:2 – 3; 13:2, 5; 15:1 – 13; 18:3 – 4; 21:31 – 32; 32:9 – 13; 37:24). Proverbs concerning (Pr 3:34; 6:16 – 17; 8:13; 10:17; 11:2, 12; 12:9, 15; 13:10; 14:21; 15:5, 10, 12, 25, 32; 16:5, 18 – 19; 17:19; 18:11 – 12; 21:4, 24; 25:14, 27; 26:5, 12, 16; 27:2; 28:11, 25; 29:8, 23; 30:12 – 13). Cited by the psalmists (Pss 10:2 – 6, 11; 49:11; 52:7; 73:6, 8 – 9; 119:21, 69 – 70, 78). See Rich, The.

Instances of:

Pharaoh (Ex 7 – 11; 12:29 – 36; 14); Ahithophel (2Sa 17:23); Naaman (2Ki 5:11 – 13); Hezekiah (2Ki 20:13; 2Ch 32:25 – 26, 31; Isa 39:2); Uzziah (2Ch 26:16 – 19); Haman (Est 3:5; 5:11, 13; 6:6; 7:10); Moab (Isa 16:6 – 7; Jer 48:7, 14 – 29; Zep 2:9); Israel (Isa 9:9 – 10; Hos 5:5; 7:10); Assyria (Isa 10:5 – 16; Eze 31:10 – 11); Jerusalem (Eze 16:56); Tyre (Eze 28:2 – 9, 17); Egypt (Eze 30:6); Nebuchadnezzar (Da 4:30 – 34; 5:20); Moab and Ammon (Zep 2:9) Nineveh (Zep 2:15); scribes and Pharisees (Mt 20:6; 23:6 – 8, 11 – 12; Mk 10:43; 12:38 – 39; Lk 9:46; 11:43; 18:14; 20:45 – 47); Herod (Ac 12:21 – 23).

Pr	8:13	I hate **p** and arrogance,
	11:2	When **p** comes, then comes
	13:10	**P** only breeds quarrels,
	16:18	**P** goes before destruction,
	29:23	A man's **p** brings him low,
Isa	25:11	God will bring down their **p**
Da	4:37	And those who walk in **p** he is able
Am	8:7	The LORD has sworn by the **P**
2Co	5:12	giving you an opportunity to take **p**
	7:4	in you; I take great **p** in you.
	8:24	and the reason for our **p** in you,
Gal	6:4	Then he can take **p** in himself,
Jas	1:9	ought to take **p** in his high position.

PRIEST, PRIESTHOOD [2424, 3912, 3913, 3914, 10347, 797, 2634, 2632, 2633, 2636]. The English word *priest* is derived from the Greek *presbyteros*, which means "elder" and suggests the priestly function of counsel. The NT word for "priest," *hiereus*, related to *hieros*, "holy," indicates one who is consecrated to and engaged in holy matters. The Hebrew *kōhēn*, "priest," is of uncertain origin. For practical Bible study, we may say simply that a priest is a minister of any religion, whether pagan (Ge 41:45; Ac 14:13) or biblical (Mt 8:4; 1Pe 2:5, 9).

THE HISTORY OF THE FORMAL PRIESTHOOD.

The formal priesthood in Israel began with the time of the exodus. In patriarchal times the heads of families offered sacrifices and intercessory prayers and performed general religious functions, but there seems to have been no specialization and no separate priestly office, as there was among the Egyptians (Ge 47:22, 26) and in the case of Melchizedek (14:18 – 20).

We read in Ex 24:5 that Moses sent young men of Israel to offer the burnt offerings at the covenant ceremony at Mount Sinai. Presumably these must be linked with the command in Ex 13:1 that the Lord's claim to all the firstborn males among the people be honored. Was it, then, the divine intention at this point that the priestly officiants should be taken from all the people, in this way reflecting the Lord's desire that his people should be a kingdom of priests? (Ex 19:4 – 5). Note, too, that Aaron is described in Ex 4:14 as "the Levite." Was there, even then, some particular significance attaching to the tribe of Levi? Furthermore, the appointment of Aaron and his sons as priests (Ex 28 – 29) precedes the events at Sinai (Ex 32) that led to the special appointment of the tribe of Levi to officiate before the Lord, and to do so instead of the firstborn (Nu 8:16). It looks, therefore, as if the Lord intended a "priestly people" who would exercise their priesthood through their firstborn sons under the rule of the house of Aaron, but that this became, through the failure of the people, the Aaronic-Levitical system familiar throughout the OT period.

CHRIST'S PRIESTHOOD.

The priestly ministry of Christ is introduced in Heb 1:3 in the words "after he had provided purification for sins." This is, of course, a reference to his death on the cross, regarded as an atoning sacrifice. But this act of sacrifice was not a mere symbol, as were all of the Aaronic priestly acts; it was of infinite intrinsic worth. He was "crowned with glory and honor because he suffered death, so that by the grace of God he might taste death [sufficiently for the offer of salvation] for everyone" (2:9).

Christ's priesthood was in no sense contrary to the Aaronic order. It fulfilled all the soteriological significance of it. But the priesthood of Christ furnished the *substance* of which the Aaronic priesthood was only the shadow (Col 2:17; Heb 8:5) and symbol.

On the Day of Atonement in Levitical ritual (Lev 16) the high priest had to go in and out past the curtain that separated the Most Holy Place from the Holy Place. By this symbolism the Holy Spirit (Heb 9:8–9) signified that "the way into the Most Holy Place had not yet been disclosed" while the Levitical mode of worship still had its proper standing. But when Jesus' body was broken on the cross, this symbolized the tearing of the curtain (10:19–22) and the clear revealing of the way into the very presence of God (Mt 27:51; Mk 15:38; Lk 23:45).

The present intercession of Christ is taught in Ro 8:34; Heb 7:25. (Cf. Ro 8:26–27 for the intercession of the Holy Spirit.) The NT word for "intercession" does not necessarily indicate any plea being offered. It suggests conferring over, or brooding over. "Who will bring any charge against those whom God has chosen?" (Ro 8:33). Satan accuses, but he has no standing in court. The case is settled, the verdict has been given. We are justified in Christ. Now our "Advocate," our great High Priest, broods over us and counsels and guides.

THE PRIESTHOOD OF BELIEVERS.

The nation of Israel was called a "kingdom of priests" (Ex 19:6) and the church (1Pe 2:5, 9, "priesthood"; Rev 1:6; 5:10), and all who have part in the first resurrection (Rev 20:6) are called priests. Paul

uses symbols of priestly ritual with reference to his own ministry (Ro 15:16; Php 2:17; and 2Ti 4:6). Neither the apostles (Mt 19:28; Lk 22:18, 28–30) nor believers in general (Rev 20:6; cf. 1Co 4:8) reign with Christ—i.e., are "kings"—until he comes to reign; but we are priests as we bring the gospel to human beings and human beings to Christ. It is significant that the priestly function of believers continues through the millennial reign of Christ (Rev 20:6) but is not mentioned as being part of the perfection of the new heavens and new earth, when mortality will have ended and sin will have been completely eliminated. There will be no need for the priesthood of believers after the great white throne judgment; "today" is the day of salvation (Heb 3:13).

Before the Mosaic Covenant:

Melchizedek (Ge 14:18; Heb 5:6, 10–11; 6:20; 7:1–21). Jethro (Ex 2:16). Priests in Israel before the giving of the law (Ex 19:22, 24).

Mosaic:

(Ex 28:1–4; 29:9, 44; Nu 3:10; 18:7; 1Ch 23:13). Hereditary descent of office (Ex 27:21; 28:43; 29:9). Consecration of (Ex 29:1–9, 19–35; 40:12–16; Lev 6:20–23; 8:6–35; Heb 7:21). Is holy (Lev 21:6–7; 22:9, 16). Washings of (Ex 40:30–32; Lev 16:24). Must be without blemish (Lev 21:17–23). Vestments of (Ex 28:2–43; 39:1–29; Lev 6:10–11; 8:13; Eze 44:17–19). Put on vestments in the temple (Eze 42:14; 44:19). Atonement for (Lev 16:6, 24; Eze 44:27). Defilement and purification of (Eze 44:25–26). Marriage of (Lev 21:7–15; Eze 44:22). Chambers for, in the temple (Eze 40:45–46). Exempt from tax (Ezr 7:24). Armed and organized for war at the time of the disaffection toward Saul (1Ch 12:27–28). Beard and hair of (Eze 44:20). Twenty-four courses of (1Ch 24:1–19; 28:13, 21; 2Ch 8:14; 31:2; 35:4–5; Ezr 2:36–39; Ne 13:30). Chosen by lot (Lk 1:8–9, 23). Usurpations of the office of (Nu 3:10; 16; 18:7; 2Ch 26:18). Jeroboam appointed priests who were not of

the sons of Levi (1Ki 12:31; 13:33). See Levites; Minister.

Compensation for: *No part of the land of Canaan allowed to (Nu 18:20; Dt 10:9; 14:27; 18:1 – 2; Jos 13:14, 33; 14:3; 18:7; Eze 44:28). Provided with cities and suburbs (Lev 25:32 – 34; Nu 35:2 – 8; Jos 21:1 – 4, 13 – 19, 41 – 42; 1Ch 6:57 – 60; Ne 11:3, 20; Eze 45:1 – 6; 48:8 – 20). Own lands sanctified to the Lord (Lev 27:21). Tithes of the tithes (Nu 18:8 – 18, 26 – 32; Ne 10:38). Part of the spoils of war, including captives (Nu 31:25 – 29). Firstfruits (Lev 23:20; 24:9; Nu 18:12 – 13, 17 – 18; Dt 18:3 – 5; Ne 10:36). Redemption money (Lev 27:23), of the firstborn (Nu 3:46 – 51; 18:15 – 16). Things devoted (Lev 27:21; Nu 5:9 – 10; 18:14). Fines (Lev 5:16; 22:14; Nu 5:8). Trespass money and other trespass offerings (Lev 5:15, 18; Nu 5:5 – 10; 18:9; 2Ki 12:16). Bread of the Presence (Ex 25:30; Lev 24:5 – 9; 2Ch 2:4; 13:11; Ne 10:33; Mt 12:4; Heb 9:2). See Bread, Consecrated. Portions of sacrifices and offerings (Ex 29:27 – 34; Lev 2:2 – 3, 9 – 10; 5:12 – 13, 16; 6:15 – 18, 26; 7:6 – 10, 31 – 34; 10:12 – 14; 14:12 – 13; Nu 6:19 – 20; 18:8 – 19; Dt 18:3 – 5; 1Sa 2:13 – 14; Eze 44:28 – 31; 45:1 – 4; 1Co 9:13; 10:18). Regulations by Hezekiah concerning compensation (2Ch 31:4 – 19). Portion of the land allotted to, in redistribution in Ezekiel's vision (Eze 48:8 – 14). For sustenance of their families (Lev 22:11 – 13; Nu 18:11, 19).*

Duties of: *Offer sacrifices (Lev 1:4 – 17; 2:2, 16; 3:5, 11, 13, 16; 4:5 – 12, 17, 25 – 26, 30 – 35; 1Ch 16:40; 2Ch 13:11; 29:34; 35:11 – 14; Ezr 6:20; Heb 10:11). See Offerings. Offer firstfruits (Lev 23:10 – 11; Dt 26:3 – 4). Pronounce benedictions (Nu 6:22 – 27; Dt 21:5; 2Ch 30:27). Teach the law (Lev 10:11; Dt 24:8; 27:14; 31:9 – 13; 33:10; Jer 2:8; Mal 2:7). Light the lamps in the tabernacle (Ex 27:20 – 21; 2Ch 13:11; Lev 24:3 – 4). Keep sacred fire burning (Lev 6:12 – 13). Furnish wood for sanctuary (Ne 10:34). Maintain sanctuary (Nu 4:5 – 15; 18:1, 5, 7). Act as scribes*

(Ezr 7:1 – 6; Ne 8:9). Be present at and supervise tithing (Ne 10:38). Sound trumpet in calling assemblies and in battle (Nu 10:2 – 10; 31:6; Jos 6; 2Ch 13:12). Examine lepers. See Leprosy. Purify the unclean (Lev 15:31). See Defilement. Value things devoted (Lev 27:8, 12). Officiate in Holy Place (Heb 9:6). Act as magistrates (Nu 5:14 – 31; Dt 17:8 – 13; 19:17; 21:5; 2Ch 19:8; Eze 44:23 – 24). Encourage army on eve of battle (Dt 20:2 – 4). Bear ark through the Jordan (Jos 3; 4:15 – 18); in battle (1Sa 4:3 – 5). Chiefs of Levites (Nu 3:9, 32; 4:19, 28, 33; 1Ch 9:20). Figurative (Ex 19:6; Isa 61:6; 1Pe 2:9; Rev 1:6; 5:10; 20:6).

High Priest:

Moses did not designate Aaron chief or high priest. The function he served was superior to that of other priests. The title appears after the institution of the office (Lev 21:10 – 15; Nu 3:32).

Qualifications of, consecration of, etc. See above, Mosaic. Clothing of (Ex 28:2 – 43; 39:1 – 31; Lev 8:7 – 9). Respect due to (Ac 23:5).

Duties of: *Had charge of sanctuary and altar (Nu 18:2, 5, 7). Offer sacrifices (Heb 5:1; 8:3). Designate subordinate priests for duty (Nu 4:19; 1Sa 2:36). Officiate in consecrations of Levites (Nu 8:11 – 21). In charge of treasury (2Ki 12:10; 22:4; 2Ch 24:6 – 14; 34:9). Light tabernacle lamps (Ex 27:20 – 21; 30:8; Lev 24:3 – 4; Nu 8:3). Burn incense (Ex 30:7 – 8; 1Sa 2:28; 1Ch 23:13). Place bread of the Presence on table every Sabbath (Lev 24:8). To offer sacrifice for his own sins of ignorance (Lev 4:3 – 12). Serve on the Day of Atonement (Ex 30:10; Lev 16; Heb 5:3; 9:7, 22 – 23). Number people (Nu 1:3). Officiate at choosing of ruler (Nu 27:18 – 19, 21). Distribute spoils of war (Nu 31:26 – 29). Judicial functions (Nu 5:15; Dt 17:8 – 13; 1Sa 4:18; Hos 4:4; Mt 26:3, 50, 57, 62; Ac 5:21 – 28; 23:1 – 5). Compensation of. See above, Compensation for. A second priest, under the high priest (Nu 3:32; 4:16; 31:6; 1Ch 9:20; 2Sa 15:24; 2Ki 25:18; Lk 3:2).*

Ge	14:18	He was **p** of God Most High,
Nu	5:10	to the **p** will belong to the **p.**'"
2Ch	13:9	and seven rams may become a **p**
Ps	110:4	"You are a **p** forever,
Heb	2:17	faithful high **p** in service to God,
	3:1	and high **p** whom we confess.
	4:14	have a great high **p** who has gone
	4:15	do not have a high **p** who is unable
	5:6	"You are a **p** forever,
	6:20	He has become a high **p** forever,
	7:3	Son of God he remains a **p** forever.
	7:15	clear if another **p** like Melchizedek
	7:26	Such a high **p** meets our need—
	8:1	We do have such a high **p**,
	10:11	Day after day every **p** stands
	13:11	The high **p** carries the blood

PRINCIPALITIES (Heb. *mera'ă-shôth*, *headparts*, Gr. *archē*, *first*). The Hebrew word is found only in Jer 13:18.

1. Rule; ruler (Eph 1:21; Tit 3:1).

2. Order of powerful angels and demons (Ro 8:38; Eph 3:10; 6:12). *See Demons.*

PRISCILLA, PRISCA [4571] (prĭ-sĭl′a, prĭs′ka, Gr. *Priskilla*, *Priska*). Priscilla (diminutive of *Prisca*, Ro 16:3, see NIV note) was the wife of the Jewish Christian Aquila, with whom she is always mentioned in the NT. They were tentmakers who seem to have migrated about the Mediterranean world, teaching the gospel wherever they went. Paul met them in Corinth (Ac 18:2); they instructed Apollos in Ephesus (18:24–26); Paul sent them greetings in Rome (Ro 16:3); and in 1Co 16:19 Paul spoke of their being in Ephesus again, where a church met in their house. In Ro 16:3–4 Paul lauded not only their service but also their courage ("they risked their lives for me"), and plainly stated that all the churches owed them a debt of gratitude. From all the scriptural references, one may easily see that Priscilla was a well-known and effective worker in the early church.

PRISON

Ps	66:11	You brought us into **p**

	142:7	Set me free from my **p**,
Isa	42:7	to free captives from **p**
Mt	25:36	I was in **p** and you came to visit me
2Co	11:23	been in **p** more frequently,
Heb	11:36	others were chained and put in **p**.
	13:3	Remember those in **p**
1Pe	3:19	spirits in **p** who disobeyed long ago
Rev	20:7	Satan will be released from his **p**

PRIZE

1Co	9:24	Run in such a way as to get the **p**.
	9:27	will not be disqualified for the **p**.
Php	3:14	on toward the goal to win the **p**
Col	2:18	of angels disqualify you for the **p**.

PROCLAIM

Ex	33:19	and I will **p** my name, the Lord,
Lev	25:10	and **p** liberty throughout the land
1Ch	16:23	**p** his salvation day after day.
Ne	8:15	and that they should **p** this word
Ps	2:7	I will **p** the decree of the Lord:
	19:1	the skies **p** the work of his hands.
	22:31	They will **p** his righteousness
	64:9	they will **p** the works of God
	68:34	**P** the power of God,
	71:16	I will come and **p** your mighty acts,
	92:2	to **p** your love in the morning
	106:2	Who can **p** the mighty acts
	118:17	will **p** what the Lord has done.
Isa	12:4	and **p** that his name is exalted.
	52:7	who **p** salvation,
	61:1	to **p** freedom for the captives
Zec	9:10	He will **p** peace to the nations.
Mt	10:27	in your ear, **p** from the roofs.
	12:18	and he will **p** justice to the nations.
Lk	4:18	me to **p** freedom for the prisoners
	9:60	you go and **p** the kingdom of God."
Ac	17:23	unknown I am going to **p**
1Co	11:26	you **p** the Lord's death
Col	1:28	We **p** him, admonishing
	4:4	Pray that I may **p** it clearly,
1Jn	1:1	this we **p** concerning the Word

PROCRASTINATION (Eze 11:2 – 3; 12:22, 27 – 28).
Rebuked (Mt 8:21 – 22; Lk 9:59, 61). Admonition against (1Th 5:2 – 3). Forbidden (Ex 22:29). Warning against (Heb 3:7 – 19). Parables of: evil servant (Mt 24:48 – 51); five foolish virgins (Mt 25:2 – 13). Instances of: Pharaoh (Ex 8:10); Elisha (1Ki 19:20 – 21); Esther (Est 5:8); disciple of Christ whose father died (Mt 8:21; Lk 9:59, 61); Felix (Ac 24:25).

PROCURATOR (pro′ku-ra′têr). The Latin term for the Greek *hegemon*, translated "governor" in KJV. Pilate, Felix, and Festus were such governors in Palestine with headquarters in Caesarea. Generally the procurators were appointed directly by the emperor to govern the Roman provinces and were often subject to the imperial legate of a large political area. It should be noted that Quirinius, "governor of Syria" (Lk 2:2), was really not a procurator but an imperial legate of the larger province of Syria.

PRODIGAL SON Parable of the (Lk 15:11 – 32).

PROFANE [2725, 2729] (Heb. *hālal, to open,* Gr. *bebēloō, to desecrate, unloose, set free*). To desecrate or defile (Ex 31:14; Lev 19:8, 12; Eze 22:26; Mt 12:5), common as opposed to holy (Eze 28:16; 42:20), godless, unholy (Heb 12:16).

Lev	19:12	and so **p** the name of your God.
	22:32	Do not **p** my holy name.
Mal	2:10	Why do we **p** the covenant

PROMISE [606, 614, 1819, 1821, 4439, 8678, 2039, 2040, 3923, 4600] (Heb. *dāvār, speaking, speech; dāvar, to speak; ′āmar, to say; ′ōmer, speech;* Gr. *epaggelia, promise*). In the OT there is no Hebrew word corresponding to "promise"; the words "word," "speak," and "say" are used instead. In the NT, however, the word "promise" is often used, usually in the technical sense of God's design to visit his people redemptively in the person of his Son. This promise was first given in the *proto-evangelium* (Ge 3:15) and was repeated to Abraham (12:2, 7). It was given also to David when God declared that his house would continue on his throne (2Sa 7:12 – 13, 28). It is found

repeatedly in the OT (Isa 2:2 – 5; 4:2; 55:5). In the NT all these promises are regarded as having their fulfillment in Christ and his disciples (2Co 1:20; Eph 3:6). Jesus' promise of the Spirit was fulfilled at Pentecost. Paul makes clear that God's promises to Abraham's seed were meant not only for the circumcision but for all who have Abraham's faith (Ro 4:13 – 16). In the NT there are many promises of blessing to believers, among them the kingdom (Jas 2:5), eternal life (1Ti 4:8), and Christ's coming (2Pe 3:9).

General References to:
(Heb 6:12; Jas 2:5; 2Pe 1:4; 3:13). Against the recurrence of universal flood (Ge 9:11). Of answer to prayer (2Ch 7:14; Job 22:27; Pss 2:8; 145:19; Isa 58:9; 65:24; Jer 29:12; 33:3; Mt 6:6; 7:7 – 8, 11; 17:20; 18:19; 21:22; Mk 11:24; Lk 11:13; Jn 14:13 – 14; 15:7, 16; 16:23 – 24; Jas 1:5; 5:15 – 16; 1Jn 5:14 – 15). Of blessings upon worshipers (Ex 20:24; Isa 40:31). Of comfort in sorrow (Pss 46:1; 50:15; 146:8; 147:3; Isa 43:2; Lk 6:21; 2Co 1:3 – 4; 7:6). Of spiritual enlightenment (Isa 29:18, 24; 35:5 – 6; 42:16; Mt 10:19; Lk 21:14 – 15; Jn 7:17; 8:12, 32; Heb 8:10). Of God's presence (Ex 3:12; Dt 31:8; 1Sa 10:7). Of Christ's presence with believers (Mt 18:20; 28:20). Of forgiveness (Ps 130:4; Isa 1:18; 43:25; 55:7; Jer 31:34; 33:8; Mt 6:14; 12:31 – 32; Mk 3:28; Lk 12:10; Ac 10:43; 13:38 – 39; Jas 5:15 – 16; 1Jn 1:9). Of healing (Jas 5:15). Of Holy Spirit (Joel 2:28; Lk 11:13; 24:49; Jn 7:38 – 39; 14:16 – 17, 26; 15:26; 16:7; Ac 2:38). Of spiritual adoption (Lev 26:12; 2Co 6:17 – 18; Heb 8:10). Of victory of the Messiah over Satan (Ge 3:15).

Given to:
Believers (Jer 17:7 – 8; Mk 16:16 – 18; Jn 3:15 – 16; 5:24; 6:35, 40, 47; 7:38; 11:25; 14:12 – 14; Ro 9:33; 10:9, 11); backsliders (Lev 26:40 – 42; Dt 30:1 – 3; 2Ch 30:9; Jer 3:12 – 15; Hos 14:4; Mal 3:7); children (Ex 20:12; Dt 5:16; Mt 19:14; Mk 10:14; Lk 18:15 – 16; Eph 6:3); the burdened (Mt 11:28 – 29); the afflicted (Job 33:24 – 28; 36:15; Pss 9:9; 12:5; 18:27; 41:3; La 3:31); orphans and widows (Dt

10:18; Pss 68:5; 146:9; Pr 15:25; Jer 49:11); seekers (Dt 4:29; 1Ch 28:9; 2Ch 15:2; Ezr 8:22; Pss 34:10; 145:18; Jer 29:13; Mt 5:6; 6:33; Lk 6:21; Jn 6:37; Ro 10:13; Heb 11:6); the faithful (Mt 25:21, 23; Lk 12:42–44; 19:16–19; Ro 2:7, 10; Rev 2:10); the forgiving, of divine forgiveness (Mt 6:14; Mk 11:25; Lk 6:37); the humble (Isa 57:15; Mt 5:3; 18:4; 23:12; Lk 6:20; 14:11; 18:14; Jas 4:6; 1Pe 5:5–6); the compassionate giver (Pss 41:1–3; 112:9; Pr 3:9–10; 11:25; 22:9; 28:27; Ecc 11:1; Isa 58:10–11; Mt 6:4; Lk 6:38; 2Co 9:6, 8); the meek (Pss 10:17; 22:26; 25:9; 37:11; 147:6; 149:4; Pr 29:23; Isa 29:19; Mt 5:5); the merciful (2Sa 22:26; Pss 18:25; 41:1–3; Mt 5:7); ministers (Ps 126:5–6; Jer 1:8; 20:11; Da 12:3; Mt 28:20; Jn 4:36–37; 1Pe 5:4); the obedient (Ex 15:26; 19:5–6; 20:6, w Dt 5:11; Ex 23:22, 25–26; Dt 4:40; 6:2–3; 12:28; 28:1–6; 30:2–10; 1Ki 3:14; Ne 1:5; Pss 1:1, 3; 25:10; 103:17–18; 119:1–2; Pr 1:33; Isa 1:19; Jer 7:23; Eze 18:19; Mal 3:10–11; Mt 5:19; 12:50; Mk 3:35; Lk 8:21; 11:28; Jn 8:51; 12:26; 14:21, 23; 15:10; 1Jn 2:5, 17; 3:24); those who fear the Lord (Pss 34:7; 103:11–13, 17; 112:1; 115:13; 128:1–6; 145:19; Pr 10:27; 19:23; Ecc 7:18; 8:12); those who have spiritual desire (Isa 55:1; Mt 5:6; Lk 6:21); those who endure to the end (Mt 10:22; 24:13; Mk 13:13; Rev 2:7, 11, 17, 26–28; 3:5, 12, 21; 21:7); those who love their enemies (Mt 5:44–45); those who rebuke the wicked (Pr 24:25); those who confess Christ (Mt 10:32; Ro 10:9; 1Jn 2:23; 4:15); peacemakers, of sonship (Mt 5:9); penitents (Lev 26:40–42; Dt 4:20–31; 2Ch 7:14; 30:9; Pss 34:18; 147:3; Isa 1:18; 55:7; Mt 5:4); the poor (Ex 22:27; Job 36:15; Pss 12:5; 35:10; 69:33; 72:2, 4, 12–14; 109:31; 132:15; Pr 22:22–23; Isa 41:17); the pure in heart (Mt 5:8); persecuted saints (Mt 5:10–11; Lk 6:22–23; 21:12–18; 1Pe 4:14); to the righteous (Job 17:9; 36:11; Pss 1:1–3; 34:7, 22; 37:4–5; 55:22; 119:1, 105; 138:8; 145:20; 146:8; Pr 25:22; Isa 58:8; Jer 17:7; Mt 6:30, 33; 10:22, 42; 24:13; Lk 6:35; 18:6–8; Ro 5:9; 8:30–31; 1Co 2:9; 3:21–22; Gal 6:9; Php 4:7; 2Th 3:3; Rev 2:17, 26, 28; 3:5; 14:13); the wise of heart (Pr 2:10–21).

Concerning:

Answer to prayer (Pr 15:29; Mk 11:23–24; Jn 14:13–14; Ac 10:4; 1Pe 3:12; 1Jn 3:22). Blessings upon their children (Pss 103:17; 112:2–3; Isa 59:21). Comfort (Isa 25:8; 66:13–14; Mt 5:4; Jn 14:16–18; Rev 21:4). Deliverance, from temptation (1Co 10:13; Jas 4:7; 2Pe 2:9), from trouble (Job 5:19–24; Pss 33:18–19; 34:15, 17; 50:15; 97:10–11; Pr 3:25–26; Isa 41:10–13; 43:2). Divine help (Ps 55:22; Isa 41:10–11, 13; 2Co 12:9; Php 4:19; Heb 13:5–6). Divine guidance (Pss 25:12; 32:8; 37:23–24; 48:14; 73:24; Pr 3:5–6; 58:11). Divine mercy (Pss 32:10; 103:17–18; Mal 3:17). Divine presence (Ge 26:3, 24; 28:15; 31:3; Ex 33:14; Dt 31:6, 8; Jos 1:5; 1Ki 6:13; Hag 1:13; 2:4–5; Mt 18:20; 28:20; Jn 14:17, 23; 2Co 6:16; 13:11; Php 4:9; Heb 13:5; Jas 4:8; Rev 21:3). Divine likeness (1Jn 3:2). The ministry of angels (Heb 1:14). Peace (Isa 26:3; Jn 16:33; Ro 2:10). Providential care (Ge 15:1; Ex 23:22; Lev 26:5–6, 10; Dt 33:27; 1Sa 2:9; 2Ch 16:9; Ezr 8:22; Job 5:15; Pss 34:9–10; 37:23–26; 121:2–8; 125:1–3; 145:19–20; Pr 1:33; 2:7; 3:6; 10:3; 16:7; Isa 49:9–11; 65:13–14; Eze 34:11–17, 22–31; Lk 12:7; 21:18; 1Pe 5:7). Overruling providence (Ro 8:28; 2Co 4:17). Spiritual enlightenment (Isa 2:3; Jn 8:12). Seeing God (Mt 5:8). Spiritual blessings (Isa 64:4; 1Co 2:9). Refuge in adversity (Pss 33:18–19; 62:8; 91:1, 3–7, 9–12; Pr 14:26; Na 1:7). Strength in adversity (Ps 29:11). Security (Pss 32:6–7; 84:11; 121:3–8; Isa 33:16). Temporal blessings (Lev 25:18–19; 26:5; Dt 28:1–13; Pss 37:9; 128:1–6; Pr 2:21; 3:1–4, 7–10; Mt 6:26–33; Mk 10:30; Lk 18:29–30). Wisdom (Jas 1:5). The rest of faith (Heb 4:9). Heavenly rest (Heb 4:9). Eternal life (Da 12:2–3; Mt 19:29; 25:46; Mk 10:29–30; Lk 18:29–30; Jn 3:15–16, 36; 4:14; 5:24, 29; 6:40; 10:28; 12:25; 17:2; Ro 2:7; 6:22–23; Gal 6:8; 1Th 4:15–17; 1Ti 1:16; 4:8; Tit 1:2; 1Jn 2:25; 5:13; Rev 22:5). Living with Christ (Jn 14:2–3; 17:24; Col 3:4; 1Th 4:17; 5:10). Everlasting remembrance (Ps 112:6). Names written in heaven (Lk 10:20).

Resurrection (Jn 5:29; 1Co 15:48 – 57; 2Co 4:14; 1Th 4:16). Future glory (Mt 13:43; Ro 8:18; Col 3:4; 2Ti 2:10; 1Pe 1:5; 5:4; Rev 7:14 – 17). Treasure in heaven (Mt 10:21; Lk 18:22). Inheritance (Mt 25:34; Ac 20:32; 26:18; Col 1:12; 3:24; Tit 3:7; Heb 9:15; Jas 2:5; 1Pe 1:4). Heavenly reward (Mt 5:12; 13:43; 2Ti 4:8; Heb 11:16; Jas 1:12; 2Pe 1:11; Rev 2:7, 10; 22:5, 12, 14). Reigning forever (Rev 22:5, w 1Co 4:8; Rev 5:10; 11:15).

Nu	23:19	Does he **p** and not fulfill?
Jos	23:14	Every **p** has been fulfilled;
2Sa	7:25	keep forever the **p** you have made
1Ki	8:24	You have kept your **p**
Ne	5:13	man who does not keep this **p**.
	9:8	have kept your **p** because you are
Ps	77:8	Has his **p** failed for all time?
	119:50	Your **p** preserves my life.
	119:58	to me according to your **p**.
Ac	2:39	The **p** is for you and your children
Ro	4:13	offspring received the **p** that he
	4:20	unbelief regarding the **p** of God,
Gal	3:14	that by faith we might receive the **p**
Eph	2:12	foreigners to the covenants of the **p**
1Ti	4:8	holding **p** for both the present life
Heb	6:13	When God made his **p** to Abraham
	11:11	him faithful who had made the **p**.
2Pe	3:9	Lord is not slow in keeping his **p**,
	3:13	with his **p** we are looking forward

PROPHECY [1821, 5547, 5363, 5553, 5566, 5752, 10451, 4460, 4735, 4736] (*speak before*). Concerning the church. *See Church, The Body of Believers.* Relating to various countries, nations, and cities. *See under their respective names.* Respecting individuals.

Concerning Jesus the Messiah:

The first messianic prophecy (Ge 3:15) concerns the announcement of the victor over Satan, the victor described as "the seed of the woman."

General References to:

Inspired (Isa 28:22; Lk 1:70; 2Ti 3:16; 2Pe 1:21). "The word of the LORD came to," Elijah (1Ki 17:8; 21:17, 28); Isaiah (Isa 2:1; 8:5; 13:1; 14:28; 38:4), Jeremiah (Jer 1:4; 7:1; 11:1; 13:8; 16:1; 18:1; 25:1 – 2; 26:1; 27:1; 29:30; 30:1, 4; 32:1, 6, 26; 33:1, 19, 23; 34:12; 35:12; 36:1; 37:6; 40:1; 43:8; 44:1; 46:1; 49:34; 50:1); Ezekiel (Eze 3:16; 6:1; 7:1; 11:14; 12:1, 8, 17, 21; 13:1; 14:12; 15:1; 16:1; 17:1, 11; 18:1; 20:45; 21:1, 8, 18; 22:1, 17, 23; 23:1; 24:1, 5, 20; 25:1; 26:1; 27:1; 28:1, 11, 20; 29:1, 17; 30:1, 20; 31:1; 32:1, 17; 33:1, 23; 34:1; 35:1; 36:16; 37:15; 38:1); Amos (Am 7:14 – 15); Jonah (Jnh 3:1); Haggai (Hag 2:1, 10, 20); Zechariah (Zec 1:7; 4:8; 6:9; 7:1, 4, 8; 8:1, 18). Publicly proclaimed (Jer 11:6). Exemplified in pantomime (Eze 4; 5:1 – 4; Ac 21:11). Written by an amanuensis (Jer 45:1), in books (Jer 45:1; 51:60). Proof of God's foreknowledge (Isa 43:9). Sure fulfillment of (Eze 12:22 – 25, 28; Hab 2:3; Mt 5:18; 24:35; Ac 13:27, 29). Cessation of (La 2:9). Of apostasy (1Jn 2:18; Jude 17 – 18), false teachers (2Pe 2:3). Tribulations of the righteous (Rev 2:10).

Miscellaneous, Fulfilled:

Birth and zeal of Josiah (1Ki 13:2; 2Ki 23:1 – 20). Death of the prophet of Judah (1Ki 13:21 – 22, 24 – 30). Extinction of Jeroboam's house (1Ki 14:5 – 17); of Baasha's house (1Ki 16:2 – 3, 9 – 13). Concerning rebuilding of Jericho (Jos 6:26; 1Ki 16:34). Drought, foretold by Elijah (1Ki 17:14). Destruction of Ben-Hadad's army (1Ki 20:13 – 30). Death of a man who refused to kill a prophet (1Ki 20:35 – 36). Death of Ahab (1Ki 20:42; 21:18 – 24; 22:31 – 38). Death of Ahaziah (2Ki 1:3 – 17). Elijah's translation (2Ki 2:3 – 11). Cannibalism among the Israelites (Lev 26:29; Dt 28:53; 2Ki 6:28 – 29; Jer 19:9; La 4:10). Death of Samaritan lord (2Ki 7:2, 19 – 20). End of famine in Samaria (2Ki 7:1 – 18). Jezebel's tragic death (1Ki 21:23; 2Ki 9:10, 33 – 37). Killing of Syria by Joash (2Ki 13:16 – 25). Conquests of Jeroboam (2Ki 14:25 – 28). Four generations of Jehu to sit on throne of Israel (2Ki 10:30, w 15:12). Destruction of Sennacherib's army, and his death (2Ki 19:6 – 7, 20 – 37). Captivity of Judah (2Ki 20:17 – 18; 24:10 – 16; 25:11 – 21). Concerning

Christ. See Jesus the Christ, Prophecies Concerning. See above, Concerning Jesus the Messiah. Concerning John (Mt 3:3). Rachel weeping for her children (Jer 31:15; Mt 2:17 – 18). Deliverance of Jeremiah (Jer 39:15 – 18). Invasion of Judah by the Chaldeans (Hab 1:6 – 11); fulfilled (2Ki 25; 2Ch 36:17 – 21). Betrayal of Jesus by Judas, prophecy (Ps 41:9); fulfillment (Jn 13:18; 18:1 – 9). Judas's self-destruction (Ps 69:25; Ac 1:16, 20); fulfilled (Mt 27:5; Ac 1:16 – 20). Outpouring of Holy Spirit (Joel 2:28 – 29); fulfilled (Ac 2:16 – 21). Spiritual blindness of Israelites (Isa 6:9; 29:13); fulfilled (Mk 7:6 – 7; Ac 28:25 – 27). Mission of Jesus (Ps 68:18); fulfilled (Eph 4:8, 10). See Jesus the Christ, Mission of. Captivity of the Israelites (Jer 25:11 – 12; 29:10, 14; 32:3 – 5; Da 9:2, w 2Ki 25:1 – 8; Ezr 1). Destruction of the ship on which Paul sailed (Ac 27:10, 18 – 44).

Da	9:24	to seal up vision and **p**
1Co	12:10	miraculous powers, to another **p**,
	13:2	of **p** and can fathom all mysteries
	14:1	gifts, especially the gift of **p**.
	14:6	or **p** or word of instruction?
	14:22	**p**, however, is for believers,
2Pe	1:20	you must understand that no **p**
Rev	22:18	the words of the **p** of this book:

PROPHESY

Eze	13:2	Say to those who **p** out
	13:17	daughters of your people who **p** out
	37:4	"**P** to these bones and say to them,
Joel	2:28	Your sons and daughters will **p**,
Mt	7:22	Lord, did we not **p** in your name,
Ac	2:17	Your sons and daughters will **p**,
1Co	13:9	know in part and we **p** in part,
	14:39	my brothers, be eager to **p**,
Rev	11:3	and they will **p** for 1,260 days,

PROPHETESS [5567, 4739] (Heb. *nevî'âh*, Gr. *prophēti*, *speak before*). A woman who exercised the prophetic gift in ancient Israel or in the early Christian church. In general she would possess the charismatic gifts and powers characterizing the prophets themselves. At least five women in the OT bear this designation: (1) Miriam, sister of Moses (Ex 15:20); (2) Deborah (Jdg 4:4); (3) Huldah (2Ki 22:14); (4) Noadiah (Ne 6:14); and (5) the unnamed wife of Isaiah, who bore him children to whom he gave prophetic names (Isa 8:3). In the NT there was Anna (Lk 2:36), and Philip the evangelist is said to have had "four unmarried daughters who prophesied" (Ac 21:8 – 9). After Pentecost the differentiation between sexes regarding prophetic gifts was removed (Ac 2:19; cf. Joel 2:28).

Prophetesses:
Miriam (Ex 15:20); Deborah (Jdg 4:4); Huldah (2Ki 22:14); false (Eze 13:17 – 19); Isaiah's wife (Isa 8:3); daughters of Israel (Joel 2:28 – 29); Noadiah (Ne 6:14); Elizabeth (Lk 1:41 – 45); Anna (Lk 2:36 – 38); daughters of Philip (Ac 21:9); Jezebel (Rev 2:20). See Women.

Ex	15:20	Then Miriam the **p**, Aaron's sister,
Jdg	4:4	a **p**, the wife of Lappidoth,
Isa	8:3	I went to the **p**, and she conceived
Lk	2:36	a **p**, Anna, the daughter of Phanuel,

PROPHETS [967, 2602, 5547, 5566, 5567, 5752, 10455, 4737, 4739, 6021] (*speak before*). Three Hebrew words are used in the OT to designate the prophets, namely *navî'*, *rō'eh*, and *hōzeh*. The last two words are participles and may be rendered "seer." They are practically synonymous in meaning. The first term, *navî'*, is difficult to explain etymologically, although various attempts have been made. The significance of these words, however, may be learned from their usage.

Each of the words designates one who is spokesman for God. The usage of *navî'* is illustrated by Ex 4:15 – 16 and 7:1. In these passages it is clearly taught that Moses stood in relation to the pharaoh as God. Between them was an intermediary, Aaron. Aaron was to speak to Pharaoh the words that Moses gave to him. "He [Aaron] will speak to the people for you, and it will be as if he were your mouth and as if you were God to him" (Ex 4:16). The man who can be designated a *navî'*, then, is one who speaks forth for God.

The two words *rō'eh* and *hōzeh* perhaps have primary reference to the fact that the person so designated sees the message God gives him. This seeing may mean that the message first came through a vision, and in some instances it did, but overall the use of these two words is as broad as the English words *perceive* and *perception*. They may refer to sight, but they usually refer to insight. Thus the words designate one who, whether by vision or otherwise, is given insight into the mind of God, and who declares what he has "seen" as a message to the people. The biblical emphasis throughout is practical. It is not the mysterious mode of reception of the prophetic revelation that is emphasized, but rather the deliverance of the message itself for God.

The biblical prophet must be distinguished from the *prophētēs* of the Greeks. The latter really acted as an *interpreter* for the muses and the oracles of the gods. The prophets, however, were not interpreters. They uttered the actual words that God had given to them, without any modification or interpretation on their part. The Bible itself gives an accurate description of the function of the true prophet: "I will put my words in his mouth, and he will tell them everything I command him" (Dt 18:18). The words were placed in the prophet's mouth by God; that is, they were revealed to the prophet, and then the prophet spoke to the nation precisely what God had commanded him.

CLASSIFICATION OF THE PROPHETS.

In the arrangement of the books of the Hebrew OT there are three parts — the Law, the Prophets, and the Writings. The division known as the Prophets is further subdivided into the former and the latter prophets. Under the first heading are included Joshua, Judges, 1 – 2 Samuel, and 1 – 2 Kings. These books are anonymous, their authors are not known. These books are rightly classified as "former prophets" because the history

they contain conforms to the biblical definition of prophecy as a declaration of the wonderful works of God (Ac 2:11, 18). This does not mean they are less than true history, but that the process of selection of things to record was performed to show how God was at work in and for his people and how the moral principles of divine providence worked out over the centuries. Against this background of interpretative history we are to understand the work of the great prophets. The former prophets cover the period from Israel's entrance into the Land of Promise until the destruction of the theocracy under Nebuchadnezzar.

The latter prophets are also called writing prophets. They are the prophets who exercised so great a ministry in Israel — Isaiah, Jeremiah, Ezekiel, and the Twelve. The designation "latter" does not necessarily have reference to historical chronology, but is simply a designation of those prophetical books that follow the "former" prophets in the Hebrew arrangement of the OT.

The "later" or "writing" prophets were not anonymous. The reason for this is that they were entrusted by God with the task and responsibility of addressing prophetical messages not only to the people of their own day but also to posterity. They must be accredited to their audience as genuine prophets, and for that reason their name is known to us. There were some prophets whose names we do not know, as, for example, the man who approached Eli and announced to him the downfall of his house. It is not necessary that we know the name of this man; it is enough that it was known to Eli. Those who received the messages of the prophets had sufficient evidence of their accreditation; they knew who spoke to them. The writing prophets, however, have uttered messages that are more relevant to us; they have spoken, for example, of the coming of the Messiah, and it is essential that we be assured that those who uttered such messages were truly accredited spokespersons of the Lord.

TRUE AND FALSE PROPHETS.

True religion has always been plagued by imitators. Alongside the faithful and true prophets of the Lord there were others, men who had not received a revelation from God. Jeremiah refused to have anything to do with these men. They were not true prophets, but men who deceived. There were those who claimed to have received messages from God, who as a matter of fact had not received such messages.

In the OT there were three tests the people could apply to discern between the true and the false prophet. First, *the theological test* (Dt 13). Through Moses there had been a revelation of the Lord who brought his people out of Egypt. Even if the prophet performed some sign to give validation to what he was saying, if his message contradicted Mosaic theology — the truth known about the Lord who brought his people out — the prophet was false. Second, *the practical test* (18:20ff.). The prediction that is not fulfilled has not come from the Lord. We ought to notice that this is a negative test. It does not say that fulfillment is proof that the Lord has spoken, for that might in fact be the evidence offered by a false prophet to validate his word. What is not fulfilled is not from the Lord. Third, *the moral test* (Jer 23:9ff.). This is a test first to be applied to the lives of the prophets themselves (23:13 – 14) and then to the tendency of the message they preach. Do they in fact strengthen the hands of evildoers, assuring them that they need not fear judgment to come (23:17)? This is a sure sign they have not stood before the Lord to hear his word (23:18 – 19). The prophet who comes fresh from the Lord's presence has a message turning people from evil (23:22).

MESSIANIC PROPHECY.

In all the prophetic messages there ran a teleological element: the prophets spoke of future deliverance to be wrought by the Messiah. It is this element of prophecy that we call "messianic prophecy."

The word *Messiah* is itself not frequently used in the OT. It means "one who is anointed," and this anointing possesses an abiding character. The Messiah is a human who came to earth to perform a work of deliverance for God. He is also a divine person, as appears from passages such as Isa 9:5 – 6. His coming to earth reveals the coming of the Lord, and so it was a supernatural coming. Furthermore, his coming represents the end of the age. It occurred in the "last days," and hence was eschatological. He came as a king, a descendant of David, and is to reign on David's throne. Lastly, the purpose of his coming is to save his people from their sins. He is a Savior and is to bear the sins of his own that they may stand in right relation with God.

Messianic prophecy must be understood against the dark background of human sin. Adam and Eve's disobedience in the garden of Eden had involved corruption of the heart and also guilt before God. Humans could not of their own efforts make themselves right with God, and hence it was necessary that God take the initiative. This God did in announcing that he would place enmity between the woman Eve and the serpent. God also announced the outcome of that enmity, in that the seed (NIV "offspring") of the woman would bruise the serpent's head (Ge 3:15). Though the point is debated, this seems to be the first definite announcement that the Messiah would come and that his work would be victorious.

All subsequent messianic prophecy is based on this Edenic prediction. To Noah it was announced that the blessing of God would be with Shem, and hence among the descendants of Shem one must look for the Messiah. The promise is then narrowed down to Abraham and after him to Isaac. For a time it seemed that Abraham would have no son, and then Ishmael was born to Abraham's concubine. Yet the promise was not to be fulfilled through Ishmael, but through Isaac. After Isaac had been born, however, Abraham was commanded to sacrifice him. Finally, when Abraham's faith was sufficiently tested, it was made clear that Isaac was after all the one through whom the Messiah was to come.

Of Isaac's two sons, Jacob was chosen and Esau rejected. Finally, Jacob called his twelve sons about him and announced to them what would take place in the "days to come" (Ge 49:1). In his prophecy he clearly pointed to the fact that redemption would come in Judah. Later Balaam, a heathen soothsayer, also prophesied, "A star will come out of Jacob; a scepter will rise out of Israel" (Nu 24:17). In Deuteronomy, in the passage in which the divine origin of the prophetic movement is revealed, we learn also of the prophet to come, who was to be like Moses. Whereas in a certain sense the entire prophetic body was like Moses, there was really only one who followed Moses, and that one was the Messiah.

In the books of Samuel, it is revealed that the throne of David was to be established permanently, and that a ruler on that throne would rule over an eternal kingdom (2Sa 7). On the basis of this prophecy, we are to understand many of the psalms that speak of a king (e.g., Pss 2, 45, 72, 110) and also many of the prophecies. The Messiah was to be the king of a kingdom that will never perish. This is taught by Isaiah, for example, who announced the supernatural birth of the Messiah and the government over which he is to rule. He was to be born of a virgin, and his supernatural birth was to be a sign to the people that God was truly with them. They did not have to fear before the growing power of Assyria. The Assyrian king would not destroy them nor render void the promises of God. They were to look to the king whom God would present to them. This king is the Messiah. His kingdom is to be eternal; it is to be built up in righteousness and justice and is to be the hope of the people.

Daniel also spoke of this kingdom as eternal. He contrasted it with the kingdoms of this world, which are both temporal and local. These kingdoms, great and powerful as they are, would nevertheless pass away; and there would be erected a kingdom that would belong to a heavenly figure, the one like a Son of Man. His kingdom alone would be universal and eternal, for he is the true Messiah. Stressing, as they do, the kingly work of the Messiah, many of these prophecies do not lay their emphasis on the actual saving work the Messiah was to perform.

There was a danger that the eyes of the people would be so attracted to the Messiah as a king that they might tend to think of him only as a political figure. This danger became very real, and the Jews more and more conceived of him as merely one who was political, who would deliver them from the yoke of foreign oppressors.

To offset this danger it was necessary that the people know full well that the Messiah's work was truly to be spiritual in nature. Hence, in the latter portion of his book, Isaiah with remarkable lucidity speaks of what the Messiah would do to save his people. It is in these great "Servant" passages that we learn that the Messiah was to be a Savior. He is set forth as one laden with griefs and sorrows, but they were not his own. They belonged to his people, and he bore them in order that people might be free and have the peace of God. The Messiah suffers and dies vicariously; that is the nature of his saving work, and Isaiah presents it with great vividness.

All the prophets were under Moses, and just as Moses was a type of Christ, so it may be said that the prophetical body as such, being under Moses, was also typical of the great prophet to come. Although they did not understand the full depth of their messages, yet they were speaking of the coming salvation and so of Jesus Christ. Through them God spoke in "divers manners" (Heb 1:1 KJV) to the children of Israel. What is so remarkable is that, when their messages are taken as a whole and in their entirety, they form such a unified picture of the work of the Messiah.

General References to:

Called seers (1Sa 9:19; 2Sa 15:27; 24:11; 2Ki 17:13; 1Ch 9:22; 29:29; 2Ch 9:29; 12:15; 29:30; Isa 30:10; Mic 3:7). Schools of (1Ki 20:35; 2Ki 2:3 – 15; 4:1, 38; 9:1). Kept the chronicles or records (1Ch 29:29; 2Ch 9:29; 12:15). Not honored in their own country (Mt 13:57; Lk 4:24 – 27; Jn 4:44). Officiate at installation of kings (1Ki 1:32 – 35). Counselors to kings (1Ki 22:6 – 28;

2Ki 6:9 – 12; Isa 37:2 – 3; Jer 27:12 – 15). *Inspired by angels* (Zec 1:9, 13 – 14, 19; Ac 7:53; Gal 3:19; Heb 2:2). *Persecutions of* (2Ch 36:16; Am 2:12). *Martyrs* (Jer 2:30; Mt 23:37; Mk 12:5; Lk 13:34; 1Th 2:15; Heb 11:37; Rev 16:6). *Compensation of: presents* (1Sa 9:7 – 8; 1Ki 14:3; 2Ki 4:42; 8:8 – 9; Eze 13:19). *Presents refused by* (Nu 22:18; 1Ki 13:7 – 8; 2Ki 5:5, 16). *Inspiration of* (1Ki 13:20; 2Ch 33:18; 36:15; Ne 9:30; Job 33:14 – 16; Jer 7:25; Da 9:6, 10; Hos 12:10; Joel 2:28; Am 3:7 – 8; Zec 7:12; Lk 1:70; Ac 3:18; Ro 1:1 – 2; 1Co 12:7 – 11; Heb 1:1; 2Pe 1:21; Rev 10:7; 22:6, 8).

Examples of Prophets:
Enoch (Jude 14); *Joseph* (Ge 40:8; 41:16, 38 – 39); *Moses* (Ex 3:14 – 15; 4:12, 15, 27; 6:13, 29; 7:2; 19:9 – 19; 24:16; 25:22; 33:9, 11; Lev 1:1; Nu 1:1; 7:89; 9:8 – 10; 11:17, 25; 12:6 – 8; 16:28 – 29; Dt 1:5 – 6; 5:4 – 5, 31; 34:10 – 11; Ps 103:7); *Aaron* (Ex 6:13; 12:1); *Eleazar* (Nu 26:1); *Balaam* (Nu 23:5, 16, 20, 26; 24:2 – 4, 15 – 16); *Joshua* (Jos 4:15); *Samuel* (1Sa 3:1, 4 – 10, 19 – 21; 9:6, 15 – 20; 15:16); *Saul* (1Sa 10:6 – 7, 10 – 13; 19:23); *Saul's men* (1Sa 19:20); *David* (2Sa 23:2 – 3; Mk 12:36); *Nathan* (2Sa 7:3 – 4; 2Sa 7:8); *Gad* (2Sa 24:11); *Ahijah* (1Ki 14:5); *Elijah* (1Ki 17:1, 24; 19:15; 2Ki 10:10); *Micaiah* (1Ki 22:14, 28; 2Ch 18:27); *Elisha* (2Ki 2:9; 3:11 – 12, 15; 5:8; 6:8 – 12, 32); *Jahaziel* (2Ch 20:14); *Azariah* (2Ch 15:1 – 2); *Zechariah, the son of Jehoiada* (2Ch 24:20; 26:5); *Isaiah* (2Ki 20:4; Isa 6:1 – 9; 8:11; 44:26; Ac 28:25); *Jeremiah* (2Ch 36:12; Jer 1:1 – 19; 2:1; 7:1; 11:1, 18; 13:1 – 3; 16:1; 18:1; 20:9; 23:9; 24:4; 25:3; 26:1 – 2, 12; 27:1 – 2; 29:30; 33:1; 34:1; 42:4, 7; Da 9:2); *Ezekiel* (Eze 1:1, 3; 2:1 – 2, 4 – 5; 3:10 – 12, 14, 16 – 17, 22, 24, 27; 8:1; 11:1, 4 – 5, 24; 33:22; 37:1; 40:1; 43:5 – 6); *Daniel* (Da 2:19; 7:16; 8:16; 9:22; 10:7 – 9); *Hosea* (Hos 1:1 – 2); *Joel* (Joel 1:1); *Amos* (Am 3:7 – 8; 7:14 – 15); *Obadiah* (Ob 1); *Jonah* (Jnh 1:1; 3:1 – 2); *Micah* (Mic 1:1; 3:8); *Habakkuk* (Hab 1:1); *Haggai* (Hag 1:13); *Zechariah, the son of Berekiah* (Zec 2:9; 7:8); *Elizabeth* (Lk 1:41); *Zechariah* (Lk 1:67); *Simeon* (Lk 2:26 – 27);

John the Baptist (Lk 3:2); *the apostles* (Ac 2:4); *Philip* (Ac 8:29); *Agabus* (Ac 11:28; 21:10 – 11); *disciple at Tyre* (Ac 21:4); *John the apostle* (Rev 1:10 – 11). See *Revelation; Word of God, Inspiration of.*

False:
(Dt 18:21 – 22; 1Ki 13:18; Ne 6:12; Jer 23:16 – 27, 30 – 32; La 2:14). *Warnings against* (Dt 13:1 – 3; Mt 24:5, 23 – 24, 26; Mk 13:6, 21 – 22; Lk 21:8). *Denunciations against* (Dt 18:20; Jer 14:15). *Punishment of* (Dt 18:20; Jer 14:13 – 16; 20:6; 28:16 – 17; 29:32; Zec 13:3). *Drunken* (Isa 28:7). *Idolatrous* (1Ki 18:19, 22, 25 – 28, 40).
Instances of: *Noadiah* (Ne 6:14); *four hundred in Samaria* (1Ki 22:6 – 12; 2Ch 18:5); *Pashhur* (Jer 20:6); *Hanani* (Jer 28; Ro 15:16).

Ex	7:1	your brother Aaron will be your **p**.
Nu	12:6	"When a **p** of the LORD is
Dt	13:1	If a **p**, or one who foretells
	18:22	If what a **p** proclaims in the name
1Sa	3:20	that Samuel was attested as a **p**
2Ki	5:8	and he will know that there is a **p**
Eze	2:5	they will know that a **p** has been
Hos	9:7	the **p** is considered a fool,
Am	7:14	"I was neither a **p** nor a prophet's
	13:4	that day every **p** will be ashamed
Mal	4:5	I will send you the **p** Elijah
Mt	10:41	Anyone who receives a **p**
	11:9	what did you go out to see? A **p**?
	12:39	except the sign of the **p** Jonah.
Lk	1:76	will be called a **p** of the Most High;
	4:24	"no **p** is accepted in his hometown.
	7:16	A great **p** has appeared among us,"
	24:19	"He was a **p**, powerful in word
Jn	1:21	"Are you the **P**?" He answered,
Ac	7:37	'God will send you a **p** like me
	21:10	a **p** named Agabus came
1Co	14:37	If anybody thinks he is a **p**
Rev	16:13	and out of the mouth of the false **p**.

PROPHETS, THE MINOR Also known as The Book of the Twelve. In Ecclesiasticus (an Apocryphal book written c. 190 BC), Jesus ben Sirach spoke of "the twelve prophets" (Sir 49:10) as a unit parallel to Isaiah, Jeremiah, and Ezekiel. He thus indicated that these twelve prophecies were at that time thought of as a unit and were probably already written together on one scroll, as is the case in later times. Josephus (*Against Apion*, 1.8.3) also was aware of this grouping. Augustine (*The City of God*, 18.25) called them the "Minor Prophets," referring to the small size of these books by comparison with the major prophetic books and not at all suggesting that they are of minor importance. In the tradition of Jewish canon these works are arranged in what was thought to be their chronological order: (1) the books that came from the period of Assyrian power (Hosea, Joel, Amos, Obadiah, Jonah, Micah), (2) those written about the time of the decline of Assyria (Nahum, Habakkuk, Zephaniah), and (3) those dating from the postexilic era (Haggai, Zechariah, Malachi). On the other hand, their order in the Septuagint (the earliest Greek translation of the OT) is: Hosea, Amos, Micah, Joel, Obadiah, Jonah, Nahum, Habakkuk, Zephaniah, Haggai, Zechariah, Malachi (the order of the first six was probably determined by length, except for Jonah, which is placed last among them because of its different character). In any event, it appears that within a century after the composition of Malachi, the Jews had brought together the twelve shorter prophecies to form a book (scroll) of prophetic writings, which was received as canonical and paralleled the three major prophetic books of Isaiah, Jeremiah, and Ezekiel. The great Greek manuscripts Alexandrinus and Vaticanus place the minor prophets before the major prophets, but in the traditional Jewish canon and in all modern versions they appear after them.

PROPITIATION (*to cover*). To appease the wrath of God so that his justice and holiness will be satisfied and he can forgive sin. Propitiation does not make God merciful; it makes divine forgiveness possible. An atonement must be provided; in OT times, animal sacrifices; now, the death of Christ for humankind's sin. Through Christ's death propitiation is made for humankind's sin (Ro 3:25; 5:1, 10–11; 2Co 5:18–19; Col 1:20–22; 1Jn 2:2; 4:10; Heb 9:5). *See Atonement.*

PROPITIATION AND EXPIATION (Gr. *hilasterion, hilasmos*). KJV and NASB used the word "propitiation" three times — "God set forth [Christ] to be a propitiation" (*hilastērion*, Ro 3:25); "[Christ] is the propitiation for our sins" (*hilasmos*, 1Jn 2:2); "God ... sent his Son to be the propitiation for our sins" (*hilasmos*, 4:10) — where RSV and NEB use *expiation* and NIV has either *sacrifice of atonement* or *atoning sacrifice*. *Propitiation* and *expiation* are not synonyms; they are very different in meaning. Propitiation is something done to a person: Christ propitiated God in the sense that he turned God's wrath away from guilty sinners by enduring that wrath himself in the isolation of Calvary. Expiation is what is done to crimes or sins or evil deeds: Jesus provided the means to cancel or cleanse them. Certainly Jesus' death provided an expiation for the sins of the world; the NT clearly affirms this. But was it necessary for Jesus to provide a propitiation (to avert the wrath of God against guilty sinners) in order to provide expiation (cleansing, forgiveness, and pardon)? Those scholars who take the biblical portrayal of the wrath of God as the description of a real, perfect attitude of God toward sin (of which genuine human righteous indignation would be an imperfect analogy) recognize that propitiation was necessary and that Christ's death was such. Those scholars who believe that the wrath of God is not the personal attitude of God toward sin and sinners but rather only a way of describing the results of evil and sin in the world, prefer to think of Christ's death as only an expiation. However, even when it is accepted that *hilastērion* and *hilasmos* point to the genuine active anger of God toward sin being appeased by the death of Jesus, the translation "propitiation" is not always used.

PROSPER

Dt	5:33	so that you may live and **p**
	28:63	pleased the Lord to make you **p**
	29:9	that you may **p** in everything you

1Ki	2:3	so that you may **p** in all you do
Ezr	6:14	and **p** under the preaching
Pr	11:10	When the righteous **p**, the city
	11:25	A generous man will **p**;
	17:20	A man of perverse heart does not **p**
	28:13	who conceals his sins does not **p**,
	28:25	he who trusts in the LORD will **p**.
Isa	53:10	of the LORD will **p** in his hand.
Jer	12:1	Why does the way of the wicked **p**?

PROSPERITY [2014, 3201, 3202, 3206, 3208, 3512, 7407, 7503, 8505, 8934, 10613, 10713, 10720].

From God (Ge 33:11; 49:24 – 26; Pss 127:1; 128:1 – 2). Design of (Ecc 7:14). Promised to the righteous (Job 22:23 – 27). Evil effects of: pride in (2Ch 32:25); forgetfulness of God in (2Ch 12:1; 26:16; Hos 4:7). The prosperous despise the unfortunate (Job 12:5). Dangers of (Dt 8:10 – 18; 31:20; 32:15; Jer 5:7; Hos 13:6).

Dt	28:11	will grant you abundant **p**—
	30:15	I set before you today life and **p**,
Job	36:11	will spend the rest of their days in **p**
Ps	73:3	when I saw the **p** of the wicked.
	128:2	blessings and **p** will be yours.
Pr	3:2	and bring you **p**.
	13:21	but **p** is the reward of the righteous.
	21:21	finds life, **p** and honor.
Isa	45:7	I bring **p** and create disaster;

PROSELYTE A person of Gentile origin who had accepted the Jewish religion, whether living in Israel or elsewhere (Mt 23:15; Ac 2:10; 6:5; 13:43). A distinction was apparently made between uncircumcised proselytes, that is, those who had not fully identified themselves with the Jewish nation and religion; and circumcised proselytes, those who identified themselves fully with Judaism.

PROSTITUTE [924, 2388, 2390, 3978, 7728, 9373, 3434, 4520]. A word that, with "whore" and "harlot," is designated by four terms in the OT: (1) *zonah*, the most frequently used; (2) *qedēshâh*, a religious harlot, a priestess of a heathen religion in which fornication was part of worship (Ge 38:21 – 22; Dt 23:17);

(3) *ishshah zarah*, or *zarah* alone, a "strange woman" (so KJV; NIV usually "wayward wife" or "adulteress"), a term found only in the book of Proverbs; (4) *nokhriyah*, "stranger," "foreigner," a word also used in Proverbs, evidently also meaning "harlot." The NT word is *pornē* ("one sold," "fornicator").

> **General References to:**
> Forbidden (Lev 19:29; Dt 23:17). Punishment of (Lev 21:9). Shamelessness of (Pr 2:16; 7:11 – 27; 9:13 – 18). Schemes of (Pr 7:10; 9:14 – 17; Isa 23:15 – 16; Hos 2:13). To be shunned (Pr 5:3 – 20; 7:25 – 27). In ancient heathen worship a special class of prostitutes was connected with shrines and temples (Ge 38:15, 21, 22). Male (1Ki 14:24; 15:12. See Shrine. Their earnings were not to be received at the temple (Dt 23:17 – 18). The term is often used in the OT to refer to religious unfaithfulness (Ex 34:15 – 16; Isa 1:21; Jer 2:20; Eze 23). Rahab (Jos 2:3 – 6; 6:17, 23, 25; Heb 11:31). Jephthah, the son of (Jdg 11:1). Gomer (Hos 1:2 – 3; 3:3). Babylon (Rev 17).

Lev	20:6	and spiritists to **p** himself
Nu	15:39	and not **p** yourselves by going
Jos	2:1	the house of a **p** named Rahab
Pr	6:26	for the **p** reduces you to a loaf
	7:10	like a **p** and with crafty intent.
	23:27	for a **p** is a deep pit
Eze	16:15	and used your fame to become a **p**.
	23:7	a **p** to all the elite of the Assyrians
Hos	3:3	you must not be a **p** or be intimate
1Co	6:15	of Christ and unite them with a **p**?
	6:16	with a **p** is one with her in body?
Rev	17:1	you the punishment of the great **p**,

PROSTITUTION

Eze	16:16	where you carried on your **p**.
	23:3	engaging in **p** from their youth.
Hos	4:10	engage in **p** but not increase,

PROVERB [5439, 5442, 4130, 4231].

Pithy saying, comparison, or question expressing a familiar or useful truth (Ge 10:9; 1Sa 10:12;

Proverbs). Design of (Pr 1:1 – 4). Written and compiled by Solomon (Pr 1:1; 25:1).

PROVERBS, BOOK OF The best representative of the so-called Wisdom Literature of ancient Israel, the book of Proverbs comprises thirty-one chapters of pithy statements on moral matters. Its text is "The fear of the LORD is the beginning of knowledge" (Pr 1:7).

The headings in Pr 1:1 and 10:1 claim a Solomonic authorship for the bulk of the book; and this claim, though often denied in recent days, has no objective evidence against it. Chapters 25 – 29 are said to be by Solomon, copied by the men of Hezekiah. This obscure reference may refer to later collecting or editing of other Solomonic material. Of the authors Agur (ch. 30) and King Lemuel (ch. 31) we know nothing. They may be poetic references to Solomon himself. Proverbs is mentioned in the apocryphal book of Ecclesiasticus (47:17), written about 180 BC. Although the canonicity of Proverbs, Ezekiel, and a few other books was questioned by individual rabbis as late as in the Council of Jamnia, AD 90, still it had long been accepted as authoritative Scripture, as the quotation in the Zadokite Document shows (col. 11, 1.19ff.). It is quoted and alluded to several times in the NT.

An outline of the book should accord with the material and style of the composition. Damage has been done by some who find in the book merely a collection of ancient maxims for success — a kind of *Poor Richard's Almanac*. Actually the book is a compendium of moral instruction. It deals with sin and holiness. And the vehicle of instruction is a favorite Semitic device — teaching by contrast. The style of Proverbs with its trenchant contrasts or more extended climactic poems can be paralleled in ancient literature in Egypt and Mesopotamia. The Hebrew author, however, has given instruction on life and holiness in proverbial form. The case is similar in Christian hymnody. There are countless examples of secular poetry and melody combined in ordinary song, but Christian hymns use the vehicles of poetry and song to express distinctively Christian thought and experience.

Outline:
    I. Introduction (1:1 – 9).
    II. Sin and Righteousness Personified and Contrasted (1:10 – 9:18).
    III. Single-Verse Contrasts of Sin and Righteousness (10:1 – 22:16).
    IV. Miscellaneous and Longer Contrasts (22:17 – 29:27).
    V. Righteousness in Poems of Climax (30:1 – 33:31).

PROVIDE

Ge	22:8	"God himself will **p** the lamb
	22:14	that place "The LORD will **P**."
Isa	43:20	because I **p** water in the desert
	61:3	and **p** for those who grieve in Zion
1Co	10:13	**p** a way out so that you can stand
1Ti	5:8	If anyone does not **p**
Tit	3:14	in order that they may **p**

PROVIDENCE [7213]. The universal providence of God is the basic assumption of all Scripture. As in English, the corresponding Hebrew and Greek words such as *rā'âh* (Ge 22:8; 1Sa 16:1) and *problepo* (Heb 11:40) in their contexts mean far more than mere foresight or foreknowledge. The meaning is "prearrangement." As used historically the theological term *providence* means nothing short of "the universal sovereign rule of God."

PRUDENCE [1067, 6874, 6891, 6893, 8505].

General References to:
(Job 34:3 – 4; Ps 112:5; Hos 14:9; Mt 7:6). In restraining speech (Ps 39:1; Pr 12:8; 21:23; 23:9; 26:4; 29:11; Am 5:13). In heeding counsel (Pr 15:5; 20:18). In restraining appetite (Pr 23:1 – 2). In avoiding strife (Pr 25:8 – 10; 29:8). In refraining from making a guarantee (Pr 6:1 – 2). Proverbs concerning (Pr 8:12; 11:13, 15, 29; 12:8, 23; 13:16; 14:8, 15 – 16, 18; 15:5, 22; 16:20 – 21; 17:2, 18; 18:15 – 16; 19:2; 20:5, 16, 18; 21:5, 20,

23; 22:3, 7, 26 – 27; 23:1 – 3, 9; 24:6, 27; 25:8 – 10; 26:4 – 5; 27:12; 29:8, 11; Ecc 7:16 – 17; 8:2 – 3; 10:1, 10). Illustration of (Lk 14:28 – 32). Injunctions concerning (Ro 14:16; 1Co 6:12; 8:8 – 13; 10:25 – 33; Col 4:5; Jas 1:19).

Instances of:

Jacob, in his conduct toward Esau (Ge 32:3 – 21); toward his sons, after Dinah's defilement (Ge 34:5, 30). Joseph, in the affairs of Egypt (Ge 41:33 – 57). Jethro's advice to Moses (Ex 18:17 – 23). The Israelites, in the threatened war with the two and a half tribes (Jos 22:10 – 34). Saul, in not slaying the Jabesh Gileadites (1Sa 11:13). David, in his overthrowing Ahithophel's counsel (2Sa 15:33 – 37). Abigail, in averting David's wrath (1Sa 25:18 – 31). Achish, in dismissing David (1Sa 29). Elijah, in his flight from Jezebel (1Ki 19:3 – 4). Rehoboam's counselors (1Ki 12:7). Jehoram, in suspecting a Syrian stratagem (2Ki 7:12 – 13). Nehemiah, in conduct of affairs at Jerusalem (Ne 2:12 – 16; 4:13 – 23). Daniel (Da 1:8 – 14). Certain elders of Israel (Jer 26:17 – 23). Jesus, in charging those who were healed not to advertise his miracles (Mt 9:30; 16:20; Mk 3:12; 5:43; 7:36; 8:30; 9:9); in going to the feast secretly (Jn 7:10); in restricting his public appearances (Jn 11:54; 12:36); in avoiding his enemies (Mt 12:14 – 16; Mk 3:7; Jn 11:47 – 54). Joseph, in his conduct toward Mary (Mt 1:19). Peter, in escaping Herod (Ac 12:17). Paul, in circumcising Timothy (Ac 16:3); in performing temple rites (Ac 21:20 – 26); in setting the Jewish sects on each other (Ac 23:6); in avoiding suspicion in administering the gifts of the churches (2Co 8:20); his lack of, in his persistence in going to Jerusalem despite the warnings of the Spirit and his friends (Ac 20:22 – 25, 37 – 38; 21:10 – 14). Paul and Barnabas, in escaping persecution (Ac 14:6). Paul and Silas, in escaping from Berea (Ac 17:10 – 15). The town clerk of Ephesus, in averting a riot (Ac 19:29 – 41).

PRUDENT

Pr	1:3	acquiring a disciplined and **p** life,
	12:16	but a **p** man overlooks an insult.
	12:23	A **p** man keeps his knowledge
	13:16	Every **p** man acts out of knowledge
	14:8	The wisdom of the **p** is
	14:15	a **p** man gives thought to his steps.
	14:18	the **p** are crowned with knowledge.
	19:14	but a **p** wife is from the LORD.
	22:3	**p** man sees danger and takes
	27:12	The **p** see danger and take refuge,
Jer	49:7	Has counsel perished from the **p**?
Am	5:13	Therefore the **p** man keeps quiet

PRUNING [2377, 4661, 2748]. To care for and increase productivity of vines (Lev 25:3 – 4; Isa 5:6; 18:5). Pruning hook (Isa 2:4; 18:5; Joel 3:10; Mic 4:3). Figurative of discipline (Jn 15:2 – 6).

PSALMS [3344, 4660, 5380, 9335, 6011].

Psalms outside the Book of:

Of Moses celebrating the deliverance at the Red Sea (Ex 15:1 – 19). Didactic songs composed by Moses, celebrating the providence, righteousness, and judgments of God (Dt 32:1 – 43; Ps 90). Song of Deborah, celebrating Israel's victory over Sisera (Jdg 5). Of Hannah, in thankfulness for a son (1Sa 2:1 – 10). Of David, celebrating his deliverance (2Sa 22); on the occasion of removing the ark (1Ch 16:7 – 36); at the close of his reign (2Sa 23:2 – 7; 1Ch 29:10 – 19). Of Isaiah (Isa 12; 25 – 26). Of Hezekiah, celebrating deliverance from death (Isa 38:9 – 20). Of Mary (Lk 1:46 – 55). Elizabeth (Lk 1:42 – 45). Zechariah (Lk 1:68 – 79).

PSALMS, BOOK OF The longest book in the Bible follows "the Law" and "the Prophets" in the Hebrew OT (Lk 24:44) and inaugurates the final division of the OT, called "the Writings" (*see* Canon). The majority of its chapters, moreover, are antedated only by Genesis-Ruth. But the basic reason why Psalms is more often quoted by the NT and more revered by Christians than any other OT book is found in its inspiring subject matter. Both for public worship — "the hymnbook of Solomon's temple" — and for individual devotional guidance, its 150 poems constitute the height of God-given literature.

NAME.

The Hebrew designation of Psalms is *Tehillîm*, meaning "praises," a term that reflects much of the book's content (cf. Ps 145, title). Its name in Latin and English Bibles, however, comes from the Greek, *Psalmoi*, which means "twangings [of harp strings]," and then, as a result, songs sung to the accompaniment of harps. This latter name originated in the LXX (cf. its NT authentication, Lk 20:42) and reflects the form of the book's poetry. The same is true of its alternate title, *Psalterion*, meaning "psaltery," a collection of harp songs, from which comes the English term *Psalter*.

AUTHORSHIP.

The individual psalms, naturally enough, make no attempt within their respective poetic framework to reveal the circumstances under which they were written. But, as might be expected, many of them do prefix explanatory titles in prose, indicating their authorship and occasion for writing, often giving poetic and musical direction as well (see below). The phrase Psalm of Moses (David, etc.), appears most commonly. The Hebrew preposition rendered by the word "of" expresses authorship (cf. Hab 3:1, "of Habakkuk the prophet") or dedication (e.g., Ps 4, "For the director of music"). But while "Psalm of David" has sometimes been interpreted to mean merely "a Psalm of Davidic character," or "... belonging to a collection entitled David," its actual usage in Scripture clearly indicates Davidic authorship (cf. Pss 7; 18). The book of Psalms thus assigns seventy-three of its chapters to David, two to Solomon (Pss 72; 127), one each to the wise men Heman and Ethan (Pss 88; 89; cf. 1Ki 4:31), one to Moses (Ps 90), and twenty-three to Levitical singing clans of Asaph (Pss 50; 73 – 83) and Korah (Pss 42 – 49; 84 – 85; 87 – 88). Forty-nine remain anonymous.

The NT repeatedly authenticates ascriptions to David: Pss 16 (Ac 2:25); 32 (Ro 4:6); 69 (Ac 1:16; Ro 11:9); 110 (Lk 20:42; Ac 2:34). Some of the anonymously titled psalms are also recognized as of Davidic composition: Pss 2 (Ac 4:25); 95 (Heb 4:7); 96; 105; 106 (underlying David's words in 1Ch 16:8 – 36, though cf. HDB, 4:148). But it is significant that no psalm that claims *other* authorship, or contains later historical allusions (as Ps 137, exilic) is ever attributed in Scripture to him.

OCCASIONS.

The titles of fourteen of the Davidic psalms designate specific occasions of composition and contribute to a historical understanding of Scripture as follows (chronologically):

Psalm 59 (1Sa 19:11) sheds light on David's envious associates (59:12).

Psalm 56 (1Sa 21:11) shows how David's fear at Gath led to faith (56:3).

Psalm 34 (1Sa 21:13) illuminates God's subsequent goodness (34:6 – 8).

Psalm 142 (1Sa 22:1) depicts David at Adullam, persecuted (142:6).

Psalm 52 (1Sa 22:9) emphasizes Saul's wickedness (52:1).

Psalm 54 (1Sa 23:19) judges the Ziphites (54:3).

Psalm 57 (1Sa 24:3) concerns En Gedi, when Saul was caught in his own trap (57:6).

Psalm 7 (1Sa 24:9) introduces slanderous Cush (7:3, 8 correspond to 1Sa 24:11 – 12).

Psalm 18 (2Sa 7:1) is repeated in 2Sa 22.

Psalm 60 (2Sa 8:13 – 14) illumines the dangerous Edomitic campaign (60:10; 1Ki 11:15).

Psalm 51 (2Sa 12:13 – 14) elaborates on David's guilt with Bathsheba.

Psalm 3 (2Sa 15:16) depicts David's faith versus Absalom's treachery (3:5).

Psalm 63 (2Sa 16:2) illumines the king's eastward flight (63:11).

Psalm 30 (2Sa 24:25; cf. 1Ch 22:1) reviews David's sin prior to his dedication of the temple area (30:5 – 6).

COMPILATION.

Psalms is organized into five books: Pss 1 – 41; 42 – 72; 73 – 89; 90 – 106; and 107 – 150; and, since the same psalm appears in more than one collection — e.g., Pss 14 and part of 40 (Book 1) as 53 and 70 (Book 2), and the latter halves of 57 and 60 (Book 2) as 108 (Book 5) — it seems likely that each compilation originally experienced independent existence.

CONTENTS.

Each of the 150 psalms exhibits the formal character of Hebrew poetry. This consists, not primarily in rhyme, or even rhythmic balance, but rather in a parallelism of thought, whereby succeeding phrases either repeat or in some way elaborate the previous line.

Collection and structure: The Hebrew Psalter is divided into five books: (1) Pss 1 – 41; (2) Pss 42 – 72; (3) Pss 73 – 89; (4) Pss 90 – 106; (5) Pss 107 – 150. The formation of psalters probably goes back to the early days of the first (Solomon's) temple or even to the time of David. The Psalter was put into its final form by postexilic temple personnel, who completed it probably in the third century BC.

Topically arranged: Psalms of affliction (Pss 3 – 5; 11; 13; 16 – 17; 22; 26 – 28; 31; 35; 41 – 42; 44; 54 – 57; 59 – 64; 69 – 71; 74; 77; 79 – 80; 83 – 84; 86; 88 – 89; 102; 109; 120; 123; 129; 137; 140 – 143). Didactic psalms (Pss 1; 5; 7; 9 – 12; 14 – 15; 17; 24 – 25; 32; 34; 36 – 37; 39; 49; 50; 52 – 53; 58; 73; 75; 82; 84; 90 – 92; 94; 101; 112; 119; 121; 125; 127 – 128; 131; 133). Historical psalms (Pss 78; 105 – 106). Imprecatory psalms *(see Imprecatory Psalms).* Intercessional psalms (Pss 20; 67; 122; 132; 144). Messianic psalms. Penitential psalms (Pss 6; 25; 32; 38; 51; 102; 130; 143). Psalms of praise (Pss 8; 19; 24; 29; 33; 47; 50; 65 – 66; 76 – 77; 93; 95 – 97; 99; 104; 111; 113 – 115; 134; 139; 147 – 148; 150). Prophetic psalms (Pss 2; 16; 22; 40; 68 – 69; 72; 87; 97; 110; 118). Psalms of thanksgiving: for God's goodness to Israel (Pss 21; 46; 48; 65 – 66; 76; 81; 85; 98; 105; 124; 126; 129; 135 – 136; 149); for God's goodness to good people (Pss 23; 34; 36; 91; 100; 103; 107; 117; 121; 145 – 146); for God's mercies to individuals (Pss 9; 18; 30; 34; 40; 75; 103; 108; 118; 138; 144).

Superscriptions and authorship: Of the 150 psalms, only 34 lack superscriptions of any kind (only 17 in the Septuagint). If the superscriptions refer to authorship, authors include Moses (Ps 90), David (Pss 3 – 9; 11 – 32; 34 – 41; 51 – 65; 68 – 70; 86; 101; 103; 108 – 110; 122; 124; 131; 133; 138 – 145), Solomon (Pss 72; 127), Asaph (Pss 50; 73 – 83), sons of Korah (Pss 42; 44 – 49; 84 – 85; 87 – 88), Heman (Ps 88), and Ethan (Ps 89). Many of the psalm titles include musical terms in Hebrew, some designating ancient melodies, others preserving musical instructions. The meaning of some of these terms is uncertain or unknown. *See Music.*

PTOLEMY Common name of the fifteen Macedonian kings of Egypt whose dynasty extended from the death of Alexander the Great in 323 BC to the murder of Ptolemy XV, son of Julius Caesar and Cleopatra in 30 BC. The time frame of their reigns includes the following: Ptolemy I, Soter (323 – 285 BC); Ptolemy II, Philadelphus (285 – 246 BC; LXX translated, Golden Age of Ptolemaic Egypt); Ptolemy III (c. 246 – 221 BC); Ptolemy IV, Philopator (221 – 203 BC); Ptolemy V, Epiphanes (203 – 181 BC); Ptolemy VI, Philometor (181 – 146 BC); Ptolemy VII, Neos Philopator (146 – 117 BC). Ptolemy XI was the last of the male line of Ptolemy I, killed by Alexandrians. Ptolemy XII (51 – 47 BC) fled to Rome. Ptolemy XIII had Cleopatra as his wife.

PUNISH

Ge	15:14	But I will **p** the nation they serve
Ex	32:34	I will **p** them for their sin."
Pr	17:26	It is not good to **p** an innocent man,
	23:13	if you **p** him with the rod, he will
Isa	13:11	I will **p** the world for its evil,
Jer	2:19	Your wickedness will **p** you;
	21:14	I will **p** you as your deeds deserve,

Zep	1:12	and **p** those who are complacent,
Ac	7:7	But I will **p** the nation they serve
2Th	1:8	He will **p** those who do not know
1Pe	2:14	by him to **p** those who do wrong

PUNISHMENT [2633, 3519, 3579, 4592, 5477, 5782, 5933, 6411, 6740, 7212, 7213, 9150, 9350, 1472, 1689, 1690, 3136, 4084, 5512].

Death Penalty:

Shall not be remitted (Nu 35:31). In the Mosaic law the death penalty was inflicted for murder (Ge 9:5 – 6; Nu 35:16 – 21, 30 – 33; Dt 17:6); adultery (Lev 20:10; Dt 22:24); incest (Lev 20:11 – 12, 14); bestiality (Ex 22:19; Lev 20:15 – 16); sodomy (Lev 18:22; 20:13); promiscuity (Dt 22:21 – 24); rape of an engaged virgin (Dt 22:25); perjury (Zec 5:4); kidnapping (Ex 21:16; Dt 24:7); a priest's daughter who became a prostitute (Lev 21:9); witchcraft (Ex 22:18); offering human sacrifice (Lev 20:2 – 5); striking or cursing father or mother (Ex 21:15, 17; Lev 20:9); disobedience to parents (Dt 21:18 – 21); theft (Zec 5:3 – 4); blasphemy (Lev 24:11 – 14, 16, 23); Sabbath desecration (Ex 35:2; Nu 15:32 – 36); prophesying falsely or propagating false doctrines (Dt 13:1 – 10); sacrificing to false gods (Ex 22:20); refusing to abide by the decision of a court (Dt 17:12); treason (1Ki 2:25; Est 2:23); sedition (Ac 5:36 – 37).

Modes of Execution of Death Penalty: *Burning (Ge 38:24; Lev 20:14; 21:9; Jer 29:22; Eze 23:25; Da 3:19 – 23); stoning (Lev 20:2, 27; 24:14; Nu 14:10; 15:33 – 36; Dt 13:10; 17:5; 22:21, 24; Jos 7:25; 1Ki 21:10; Eze 16:40); hanging (Ge 40:22; Dt 21:22 – 23; Jos 8:29); beheading (Mt 14:10; Mk 6:16, 27 – 28); crucifixion (Mt 27:35, 38; Mk 15:24, 27; Lk 23:33); the sword (Ex 32:27 – 28; 1Ki 2:25, 34, 46; Ac 12:2). Executed by the witnesses (Dt 13:9; 17:7; Ac 7:58), by the congregation (Nu 15:35 – 36; Dt 13:9). Not inflicted on testimony of less than two witnesses (Nu 35:30; Dt 17:6; 19:15).*

Minor Offenses: *Punishable by scourging (Lev 19:20; Dt 22:18; 25:2 – 3; Pr 17:10; 19:29; 20:30; Mt 27:26; Mk 15:15; Lk 23:16; Jn 19:1; Ac 22:24, 29); imprisonment (Ge 39:20; 40). See Prison. Confinement within limits (1Ki 2:26, 36 – 38).*

By God: *According to deeds (Job 34:11; Ps 62:12; Pr 12:14; 24:12; Isa 59:13; Jer 17:10; Eze 7:3, 27; 16:59; 39:24; Zec 1:6; Mt 5:22; 16:27; 25:14 – 30; Mk 12:40; Lk 12:47 – 48; 2Pe 3:7). See Judgment. See parables of the vineyard (Isa 5:1 – 7); landowner (Mt 21:33 – 41); talents (Mt 25:14 – 30); servants (Lk 12:47 – 48). Imposed on children (Ex 34:7; Jer 31:29; La 5:7). Not imposed on children (Dt 24:16; 2Ch 25:4). Delayed (Pss 50:21; 55:19; Pr 1:24 – 31; Ecc 8:11 – 13; Hab 1:2 – 4). Design of, to secure obedience (Ge 2:17; Ex 20:3 – 5; Lev 26:14 – 39; Dt 13:10 – 11; 17:13; 19:19 – 20; 21:21 – 22; Pr 19:25; 21:11; 26:3). See Judgment. No escape from (Ge 3:7 – 19; 4:9 – 11; Job 11:20; 34:21 – 22; Pr 1:24 – 31; 11:21; 16:5; 29:1; Isa 10:3; Jer 11:11; 15:1; 25:28 – 29; Eze 7:19; Am 2:14 – 16; 9:1 – 4; Zep 1:18; Mt 10:28; 23:33; Ro 2:3; 1Th 5:2 – 3; Col 3:25; Heb 2:3; 12:25 – 26; Rev 6:15 – 17). Eternal (Isa 34:8 – 10; Da 12:2; Mt 3:12; 10:28; 18:8; 25:41, 46; Mk 3:29; Lk 3:17; Jn 5:29; Heb 6:2; 10:28 – 31; Rev 14:10 – 11; 19:3; 20:10).*

Isa	53:5	the **p** that brought us peace was
Jer	4:18	This is your **p**.
Mt	25:46	Then they will go away to eternal **p**
Lk	12:48	and does things deserving **p** will be
	21:22	For this is the time of **p**
Ro	13:4	wrath to bring **p** on the wrongdoer.
Heb	2:2	disobedience received its just **p**,
2Pe	2:9	while continuing their **p**.

PUNISHMENT, EVERLASTING Is taught in Scripture for those who reject God's love revealed in Christ (Mt 25:46; Da 12:2). The final place of everlasting punishment is called the "lake of fire" (Rev 19:20; 20:10, 14 – 15), also called "the second death" (Rev 14:9 – 11; 20:6). "Hell" in Scripture translates the word *Hades,* the unseen realm where the souls of all the dead are. *Gehenna* is the place of punishment of *Hades*; *paradise* is the place of blessing of *Hades* (Lk 16:19 – 31). The reason for eternal punishment is the rejection of God's provision for the forgiveness of sin through the life and work of Jesus Christ, God's Son (Jn 3:16 – 18). *See Hades; Hell.*

PURE

2Sa	22:27	to the **p** you show yourself **p**,
Ps	19:9	The fear of the Lord is **p**,
	24:4	who has clean hands and a **p** heart,
	51:10	Create in me a **p** heart, O God,
	119:9	can a young man keep his way **p**?
Pr	15:26	those of the **p** are pleasing to him.
	20:9	can say, "I have kept my heart **p**;
Isa	52:11	Come out from it and be **p**,
Hab	1:13	Your eyes are too **p** to look on evil;
Mt	5:8	Blessed are the **p** in heart,
2Co	11:2	I might present you as a **p** virgin
Php	4:8	whatever is **p**, whatever is lovely,
1Ti	1:5	which comes from a **p** heart
	5:22	Keep yourself **p**.
2Ti	2:22	call on the Lord out of a **p** heart.
Tit	1:15	To the **p**, all things are **p**,
	2:5	to be self-controlled and **p**,
Heb	7:26	blameless, **p**, set apart from sinners
	13:4	and the marriage bed kept **p**,
Jas	1:27	that God our Father accepts as **p**
	3:17	comes from heaven is first of all **p**;
1Jn	3:3	him purifies himself, just as he is **p**.

PURIFICATION [2633, 3198, 3200, 49, 50, 2752]. In studying the Mosaic law relating to purifications, it must be kept in mind that sin defiles. To keep this great truth constantly before the mind of the Israelites, specific ordinances concerning purifications were given to Moses; the purpose being, by this object lesson, to teach that sin defiles and only the pure in heart can see God. Therefore, certain incidents, such as eating that which had died of itself, touching the dead, etc., were signified as defiling, and definite ceremonies were prescribed for persons who were defiled. During the period of defilement, and when

performing the ceremonies required of them, the defiled were expected to contemplate the defilement of sin and the need of purification of the heart.

> **Required:**
>
> *Sanitary and symbolic (Ex 19:10, 14; Heb 9:10). For women after childbirth (Lev 12:6 – 8; Lk 2:22). After menstruation (Lev 15:19 – 33; 2Sa 11:4). After intercourse (Lev 15:16 – 18). For a discharge (Lev 15:4 – 18). For those cleansed of leprosy (Lev 14:8 – 9). For eating that which died of itself (Lev 17:15). For those who had slain in battle (Nu 31:19 – 24). Of priests (Ex 29:4; 30:18 – 21; 40:12, 30 – 32; Lev 8:6; 16:4, 24, 26, 28; 22:3; Nu 19:7 – 8; 2Ch 4:6). Of Levites (Nu 8:6 – 7, 21). Of lepers. See Leprosy. Of the Jews before the Passover (Jn 11:55). By fire, for things that resist fire (Nu 31:23). By blood (Ex 24:5 – 8; Lev 14:6 – 7; Heb 9:12 – 14, 19 – 22). By abstaining from sexual intercourse (Ex 19:15). By washing in water, parts of animal sacrifices (Lev 1:9, 13; 9:14; 2Ch 4:6). Penalty to be imposed upon those who do not observe the ordinances concerning (Lev 7:20 – 21; 22:3; Nu 19:13, 20). Water of (Nu 19:17 – 21; 31:23). Washing hands in water, symbolic of innocence (Dt 21:6; Ps 26:6). Traditions of the elders concerning (Mt 15:2; Mk 7:2 – 5, 8 – 9; Lk 11:38).*

Heb	1:3	After he had provided **p** for sins,

PURIM [7052] (pūr'ĭm, Heb. *pûrîm*, lots). A Jewish festival celebrated on the fourteenth and fifteenth of the month Adar (February – March), commemorating the deliverance of the Hebrews from the murderous plans of the wicked Haman in the postexilic period (Est 3:7; 9:26). This festival is named from the casting of the lot to determine the most expeditious time for the mass murder of the Jews.

PURITY [1338, 1405, 2341, 2342, 2348, 2627, 2633, 3196, 3197, 3198, 3200, 6034, 7058, 7727, 48, 49, 54, 55, 299, 2751, 2751, 2752, 2754, 4410].

A Christian virtue (1Ti 4:12; 5:22; Tit 1:15). Word of God pure (Pss 12:6; 19:8; 119:140). Of the human heart (Pss 24:3 – 5; 65:3; Pr 15:26; 20:9; 21:8; 30:12; Isa 1:18, 25; 6:7; Mic 6:11; 1Ti 1:5; 2Ti 2:21 – 22; Heb 10:2). Blessedness of (Mt 5:8). Prayer for (Ps 51:7; Da 12:10; Heb 9:13 – 14). Through: divine discipline (Mal 3:2 – 3; Jn 15:2); the blood of Christ (Heb 9:13 – 14). Commanded (1Ti 3:9; 5:22; 2Ti 1:3; 2:21 – 22; Jas 4:8; 1Pe 1:22). Meditation upon, commanded (Php 4:8). Jesus our pattern in (1Jn 3:3). Exemplified by Paul (2Ti 1:3).

Hos	8:5	long will they be incapable of **p**?
2Co	6:6	in **p**, understanding, patience
1Ti	4:12	in life, in love, in faith and in **p**.
	5:2	as sisters, with absolute **p**.
1Pe	3:2	when they see the **p** and reverence

PURPOSE

Ex	9:16	I have raised you up for this very **p**,
Job	36:5	he is mighty, and firm in his **p**.
Pr	19:21	but it is the LORD's **p** that prevails
Isa	46:10	I say: My **p** will stand,
	55:11	and achieve the **p** for which I sent it
Ac	2:23	handed over to you by God's set **p**
Ro	8:28	have been called according to his **p**.
	9:11	in order that God's **p**
	9:17	"I raised you up for this very **p**,
1Co	3:8	the man who waters have one **p**,
2Co	5:5	who has made us for this very **p**
Gal	4:18	be zealous, provided the **p** is good,
Eph	1:11	in conformity with the **p** of his will,
	3:11	according to his eternal **p** which he
Php	2:2	love, being one in spirit and **p**.
	2:13	and to act according to his good **p**.
2Ti	1:9	but because of his own **p** and grace.

PUT [7033] (pŭt, Heb. *pût*).

1. Son of Ham (Ge 10:6; 1Ch 1:8).

2. The descendants of Put, or the country inhabited by them; Put has also been taken to signify Egypt and is often associated with the Libyans (Isa 66:19, ftn; Eze 27:10; 30:5; 38:5; Jer 46:9; Na 3:9).

PURSUE

Ps	34:14	seek peace and **p** it.
Pr	15:9	he loves those who **p** righteousness
Ro	9:30	who did not **p** righteousness,
1Ti	6:11	and **p** righteousness, godliness,
2Ti	2:22	and **p** righteousness, faith,
1Pe	3:11	he must seek peace and **p** it.

QUARREL

Pr	15:18	but a patient man calms a **q**.
	17:14	Starting a **q** is like breaching a dam;
	17:19	He who loves a **q** loves sin;
	20:3	but every fool is quick to **q**.
	26:17	in a **q** not his own.
	26:20	without gossip a **q** dies down.
2Ti	2:24	And the Lord's servant must not **q**;
Jas	4:2	You **q** and fight.

QUARRELSOME [QUARREL]

Pr	19:13	a **q** wife is like a constant dripping.
	21:9	than share a house with a **q** wife.
	26:21	so is a **q** man for kindling strife.
1Ti	3:3	not violent but gentle, not **q**,

QUEEN [1485, 1509, 4867, 4887, 4893, 4906, 8576, 8712, 10423, 999]. Dowager queens, or mothers of the monarch, are those who appear in the most influential roles in the biblical records: (1) Jezebel, princess of Tyre, who, during the twenty-two years of her husband, Ahab's, reign and during the thirteen years of the reigns of her sons Ahaziah and Joram, exercised a strong influence in favor of Phoenician pagan cults (1Ki 16:28 – 2Ki 9:37 passim). (2) Athaliah, daughter of Jezebel and of similar character, was the wife of Jehoram of Judah, son of Jehoshaphat. On the accession of her son Ahaziah (not to be confused with Ahaziah of Israel, his uncle), Athaliah exercised a dominant authority and after Ahaziah's assassination held the throne alone, securing her position by dynastic massacre (2Ki 11). (3) Bathsheba, mother of Solomon, widow of David and Uriah, demonstrated her decisive character as her husband David lay dying (1Ki 1).

The foreign queens mentioned in the OT are (1) Vashti, the queen whom Xerxes (KJV Ahasuerus) of Persia deposed (Est 1); (2) Esther, the Jewess, Vashti's successor, a brave woman whose situation, nonetheless, violated the tenets of the law and demonstrated the compromised position of those who took no part in the movements of restoration headed by Ezra and Nehemiah; (3) Balkis, legendary name of the queen of Sheba (1Ki 10); and (4) unnamed queens referred to in Ne 2:6 and Da 5:10.

Queens named in the NT include (1) Bernice, or Berenice, sister of Agrippa II and wife of her uncle, Herod, king of Chalcis (Ac 25 – 26); and (2) Drusilla, wife of Azizus, king of Emesa, whom she deserted to become the third wife of Felix, procurator of Judea (Ac 24).

General References to:
The wife of a king (1Ki 11:19). Crowned (Est 1:11; 2:17). Divorced (Est 1:10 – 22). Sits on the throne with the king (Ne 2:6). Makes feasts for the women of the royal household (Est 1:9). Exerts an evil influence in public affairs. See Jezebel. Counsels the king (Da 5:10 – 12). Queen of Sheba visits Solomon (1Ki 10:1 – 13). Candace, of Ethiopia (Ac 8:27). Queen Athaliah, only independent female ruler of Israel or Judah. See Athaliah. Queen of Heaven (Jer 7:18; 44:7 – 19, 25).

QUICKENING *(coming to life)*.

Of the church: by the Father (Pss 71:20; 80:18; Ro 4:17; 8:11; Eph 2:1; 1Ti 6:13); by the Holy Spirit (Jn 6:63; Ro 8:11; 2Co 3:6; 1Pe 3:18).

QUIET [QUIETNESS]

Ps	23:2	he leads me beside **q** waters,
Pr	17:1	Better a dry crust with peace and **q**
Ecc	9:17	The **q** words of the wise are more
Am	5:13	Therefore the prudent man keeps **q**
Zep	3:17	he will **q** you with his love,
Lk	19:40	he replied, "if they keep **q**,
1Th	4:11	it your ambition to lead a **q** life,
1Ti	2:2	we may live peaceful and **q** lives
1Pe	3:4	beauty of a gentle and **q** spirit,

QUIETNESS [QUIET]

| Isa | 30:15 | in **q** and trust is your strength, |
| | 32:17 | the effect of righteousness will be **q** |

1Ti　　2:11　　　A woman should learn in **q**

QUIRINIUS [3256] (kwĭrĭn′ĭŭs, Gr. *Kyrēnios*). Governor of Syria AD 6 – 9. His census of AD 6 at the request of the emperor Augustus is referred to in Ac 5:37. Another census, in which Joseph and Mary were registered, is mentioned in Lk 2:2. This may indicate that Quirinius served an earlier term as governor of Syria, and Luke mentions his "first" (NIV) and otherwise unknown census. Or the verse may be translated "This was *before* the census that took place while Quirinius was governor of Syria."

QUIVER (Heb. *'ashpāh, telî*). As a case for carrying arrows, a quiver was used by soldiers (Job 39:23; Isa 22:6; Jer 5:16; La 3:13) and by hunters (Ge 27:3). The man who has many children is like the quiver that is full of arrows (Ps 127:4 – 5), and the servant of Jehovah says that he has been hidden in Jehovah's quiver (Isa 49:2).

Ps　　127:5　　　whose **q** is full of them.

RA Egyptian sun god. Joseph married a daughter of the priest of On, center of the cult of Ra (Ge 41:45, 50).

RABBI, RABBONI [4806, 4808] (*[my] great one, [my] master*).

The title of a teacher (Mt 23:7 – 8; Jn 3:2). Ostentatiously used by the Pharisees (Mt 23:7). Used in addressing John the Baptist (Jn 3:26), in addressing Jesus (Mt 26:25, 49; Mk 9:5; 10:51; 11:21; 14:45; Jn 1:38, 49; 3:2; 4:31; 6:25; 9:2; 11:8). Jesus called "Rabboni" (Jn 20:16). Forbidden by Jesus as a title for his disciples (Mt 23:8).

RACA [4819] (ra′ka, Gr. *rhaka, empty, vain,* or *worthless fellow*). A term of contempt, signifying a derogatory estimate of someone's intellectual ability (Mt 5:22).

RACE (Heb. *ōrah, merôts*, Gr. *agōn, stadion,* most frequently, *a foot race*). The clearest uses of these words are in 1Co 9:24; 2Ti 4:7; and Heb 12:1. Other passages may well allude to it (Ro 9:16; Gal 5:7; Php 2:16). The Greek race was one of a series of highly competitive games. It consisted of (1) the goal, a square pillar opposite the entrance to the course, marking the end of the track; (2) the herald, whose duty it was to announce the name and the country of each competitor, as well as the name and family of the victor; (3) the prize, the crown or wreath that was awarded the winner (cf. 1Co 9:25; 2Ti 2:5); and (4) the judges (2Ti 4:8). The Lord is viewed as the righteous Judge who bestows the wreath on those who have truly run well.

Ecc	9:11	The **r** is not to the swift
Ac	20:24	if only I may finish the **r**
1Co	9:24	that in a **r** all the runners run,
Gal	2:2	that I was running or had run my **r**
	5:7	You were running a good **r**.
2Ti	4:7	I have finished the **r**, I have kept
Heb	12:1	perseverance the **r** marked out

RACHEL [8162, 4830] (rā′chĕl, Heb. *rāhēl, ewe,* Gr. *Rhachēl*). The wife of Jacob, the mother of Joseph and Benjamin (Ge 29:6, 16, 18, 31; 30:1 – 9; cf. Jer 31:15; Mt 2:18). Rachel was the younger daughter of Laban, the Aramean (ASV "Syrian"), the brother of Rebekah, Jacob's mother (Ge 28:2); thus Jacob and Rachel were full cousins.

> *Meets Jacob at the well (Ge 29:9 – 12); Jacob serves Laban fourteen years to secure her as his wife (Ge 29:15 – 30); Sterility of (Ge 29:31); gives her maid to Jacob to secure children in her own name (Ge 30:1 – 8, 15, 22 – 34); Later fertility of; becomes the mother of Joseph (Ge 30:22 – 25), of Benjamin (Ge 35:16 – 18, 24); Steals her father's household images (Ge 31:4, 14 – 19, 33 – 35); Death and burial (Ge 35:18 – 20; 48:7; 1Sa 10:2)*

RAHAB [8105, 8147, 4805, 4829] (rā′hăb, Heb. *rāhāv, broad,* Gr. *Rhachab*).

1. A woman best known for her prominent role in the capture of Jericho during the days of Joshua (Jos 2:1ff.; Mt 1:5; Heb 11:31; Jas 2:25).

According to Matthew's genealogy, she is not only one of the four women mentioned in the family tree of the Savior, but also the mother of Boaz, the husband of Ruth, and the great-grandmother of King David (Ru 4:18 – 21; Mt 1:5). The author of Hebrews speaks of her as a shining example of faith (Heb 11:31). James shows his appreciation of her as a person in whom faith was not merely "theological" but also practical (Jas 2:5).

2. A mythical monster of the deep. In such passages as Job 9:13 and Ps 89:10, the motif of the slaying of the dragon appears. In Isa 51:9 the Lord's victory is complete because he has cut Rahab, the monster, to ribbons; applied to Egypt (Ps 87:4; Isa 30:7; 51:9).

RAINBOW [8008, 2692] (Heb. *qesheth, bow*). The biblical interpretation of the rainbow is found in the record of Noah's life. God's covenant with Noah declared that he would never again send a universal flood to destroy the whole inhabited earth (Ge

9:8 – 17). The rainbow in the clouds is a sign from God to humans. God allowed Noah to understand what the bow means to him: a visible declaration that the Lord will never again destroy the earth by flood. The rainbow is the Lord's promise made visible. Thus covenant signs express covenant promises to covenant people. Ezekiel compares the glory of God to that of a rainbow (Eze 1:28). John, as a prisoner on Patmos, beheld the throne of God encircled by the rainbow (Rev 4:3).

RAISE [RISE]

| Jn | 6:39 | but **r** them up at the last day. |
| 1Co | 15:15 | he did not **r** him if in fact the dead |

RAISED [RISE]

Isa	52:13	he will be **r** and lifted up
Mt	17:23	on the third day he will be **r** to life
Lk	7:22	the deaf hear, the dead are **r**,
Ac	2:24	But God **r** him from the dead,
Ro	4:25	was **r** to life for our justification.
	6:4	as Christ was **r** from the dead
	10:9	in your heart that God **r** him
1Co	15:4	that he was **r** on the third day
	15:20	But Christ has indeed been **r**

RAMAH [8230, 4821] (*elevated spot*).

1. A city allotted to Benjamin (Jos 18:25; Jdg 19:13). Attempted fortification of, by King Baasha; destruction of, by Asa (1Ki 15:17 – 22; 2Ch 16:1 – 6). People of, return from the Babylonian captivity (Ezr 2:26; Ne 7:30; 11:33). Jeremiah imprisoned in (Jer 40:1). Prophecies concerning (Isa 10:29; Jer 31:15; Hos 5:8; Mt 2:18).

2. A city of southern Judah allotted to the tribe of Simeon (Jos 19:8).

3. A city of Asher (Jos 19:29).

4. A city of Naphtali (Jos 19:36).

5. Also called Ramathaim. A city in the hill country of Ephraim (Jdg 4:5; 1Sa 1:1). Home of Elkanah (1Sa 1:1, 19; 2:11), and of Samuel (1Sa 1:19 – 20; 7:17; 8:4; 15:34; 16:13). David flees to (1Sa 19:18). Samuel dies and is buried in (1Sa 25:1; 28:3).

RAMSES, RAMESSES (râ-am′sez). The most common royal Egyptian name in the Nineteenth and Twentieth dynasties. Ramses I was the founder of the Nineteenth Dynasty, but the most illustrious of the bearers of this name was his grandson, Ramses II. The presence in the OT of the name Rameses for a city and district in the Delta, brought about the acclamation of Ramses II as the pharaoh of the oppression, in spite of chronological complications with OT data. Among the varying interpretations of the exodus, this identification of Ramses II is not widely held at present. Although certain of these kings, such as Ramses II and III, must have had at least indirect influence on Israelite life, none of them is mentioned in the OT.

RANSOM [4105, 4111, 7009, 7014, 7018, 8815, 519, 667, 3389] (răn′sŭm, Heb. *kōpher, pidhyôn, gā′al*, Gr. *lytron, antilytron*). The price paid for the redemption of a slave (Lev 19:20); a reparation paid for injury or damages (Ex 22:10 – 12); a fee, fine, or heavy assessment laid on a person as a substitute for his own life (21:30). There was no ransom provided for the willful murderer (Nu 35:31). In the NT the term signifies the redemptive price offered by Christ on the cross for the salvation of his people (Mk 10:45; 1Ti 2:6).

> **General References to:**
> *Of a human life (Ex 21:30; 30:12; Job 36:18; Ps 49:7 – 8; Pr 6:35; 13:8; Hos 13:14). Jesus as (Mt 20:28; Mk 10:45; 1Ti 2:5 – 6; Heb 9:15). Figurative (Job 33:24; Isa 35:10; 51:10).*

RAPE [2256+6700+8886, 3359, 6700, 8711].

Law imposes death penalty for (Dt 22:25 – 27). Captives afflicted with (Isa 13:16; La 5:11; Zec 14:2). Instances of: Dinah by Shechem (Ge 34:1 – 2). The servant of a Levite by Benjamites; tribe of Benjamin nearly exterminated by the army of the other tribes as punishment for (Jdg 19:22 – 30; 20:35). Tamar by Amnon; avenged in the death of Amnon at the hand of Absalom, Tamar's brother (2Sa 13:6 – 29, 32 – 33).

RAPTURE Theological term not used in the Bible. The imminent translation or removal from earth of the church at the second coming of Christ (Mt 24:36 – 42; Mk 13:32; Ac 1:7, 11; 1Co 15:50 – 52; 1Th 4:14 – 18; Tit 2:13; 1Pe 3:12; Rev 1:7). Includes both living and dead (1Co 15:50 – 52; Php 3:20 – 21; 1Th 4:13 – 17; 1Jn 3:2). Followed by the marriage of the church to Christ (Mt 25:1 – 10; 2Co 11:2; Eph 5:23, 32; Rev 19:6 – 9) and believers being rewarded (Mt 25:19; 1Co 3:12 – 15; 2Co 5:10; 2Ti 4:8; 1Pe 5:2).

REAP [REAPER REAPS]

Job	4:8	and those who sow trouble **r** it.
Hos	10:12	**r** the fruit of unfailing love,
Jn	4:38	you to **r** what you have not worked
Ro	6:22	the benefit you **r** leads to holiness,
2Co	9:6	generously will also **r** generously.
Gal	6:8	from that nature will **r** destruction;

REAPER [REAP]

| Jn | 4:36 | and the **r** may be glad together. |

REAPING [5162, 7907, 7917, 9530, 2400, 2545] (Heb. *qātsar*, Gr. *therizō*). Reaping in ancient times consisted in either pulling up the grain by the roots or cutting it with a sickle. The stalks were then bound into bundles and taken to the threshing floor. In Bible lands cutting and binding are still practiced. The figurative usage of the term speaks of deeds that produce their own harvest (Pr 22:8; Hos 8:7; 1Co 9:11; Gal 6:7 – 8).

REAPS [REAP]

Pr	11:18	who sows righteousness **r** a sure
	22:8	He who sows wickedness **r** trouble,
Gal	6:7	A man **r** what he sows.

REBEKAH, REBECCA [8071, 4831] (rĕbĕk′a, Heb. *rivqâh*, Gr. *Rhebekka*, possibly *choice calf*). The daughter of Bethuel. Her mother's name is unrecorded. Her grandparents were Nahor and Milcah. She was the sister of Laban, the wife of Isaac, mother of Esau and Jacob, and is first mentioned in the genealogy of Nahor, the brother of Abraham (Ge 22:20 – 24).

It is in Haran, "the city of Nahor," where we are first introduced to Rebekah (Ge 24). In that incident Eliezer, the servant of Abraham, was sent out to seek a bride for Isaac. After listening to the urgings of the servant, Rebekah decided to marry Isaac. In this narrative the delineation of her character is winsome and attractive. In the narrative that follows, however, she is not only ambitious but grasping and rapacious.

> *Daughter of Bethuel, grand-niece of Abraham (Ge 22:20 – 23); Becomes Isaac's wife (Ge 24:15 – 67; 25:20); Mother of Esau and Jacob (Ge 25:21 – 28; Ro 9:10); Passes as Isaac's sister (Ge 26:6 – 11); Displeased with Esau's wives (Ge 26:34 – 35); Prompts Jacob to deceive Isaac (Ge 27:5 – 29); Sends Jacob to Laban (Ge 27:42 – 46); Burial place of (Ge 49:31)*

REBEL

Nu	14:9	Only do not **r** against the LORD.
1Sa	12:14	and do not **r** against his commands,
Mt	10:21	children will **r** against their parents

REBUKE [1721, 1722, 3519, 8189, 9349, 9350, 1791, 1794, 2203].

Cain rebukes God (Ge 4:13 – 14). Pharaoh rebukes Abraham for calling his wife his sister (Ge 12:18 – 19). Abimelech rebukes Abraham for a like offense (Ge 20:9 – 10). Abimelech rebukes Isaac for similar conduct (Ge 26:9 – 10). Isaac and Laban rebuke each other (Ge 31:26 – 42). Jacob rebukes Simeon and Levi for killing Hamor and Shechem (Ge 34:30). Reuben rebukes his brothers for their treatment of Joseph (Ge 42:22). Israelites rebuke Moses and tempt God (Ex 17:7). Deborah rebukes Israel in her poem (Jdg 5:16 – 23). David rebukes Joab for killing Abner (2Sa 3:28 – 31). Joab rebukes David for lamenting the death of Absalom (2Sa 19:5 – 7). Jesus rebukes his disciples because of their unbelief (Mt 8:26; 14:31; 16:8 – 11; 17:17; Mk 4:40; Lk 8:25); for slowness of heart (Mt 15:16; 16:8 – 9, 11; Mk 7:18; Lk 24:25; Jn 14:9); for sleeping in Gethsemane (Mt 26:40; Mk 14:27); for forbidding children to be brought to him (Mt 19:14; Mk 10:14; Lk 18:16). David prays to escape Yahweh's rebuke (Pss 6:1; 38:1). Do not rebuke a mocker (Pr 9:8); an older man (1Ti 5:1).

Lev	19:17	**R** your neighbor frankly
Pr	3:11	and do not resent his **r**,
	9:8	**r** a wise man and he will love you.
	15:31	He who listens to a life-giving **r**
	17:10	A **r** impresses a man
	19:25	**r** a discerning man, and he will gain
	27:5	Better is open **r**
	30:6	or he will **r** you and prove you a liar
Ecc	7:5	It is better to heed a wise man's **r**
Isa	54:9	never to **r** you again.
Jer	2:19	your backsliding will **r** you.
Lk	17:3	"If your brother sins, **r** him,
1Ti	5:1	Do not **r** an older man harshly,
2Ti	4:2	correct, **r** and encourage —
Tit	1:13	Therefore, **r** them sharply,
	2:15	Encourage and **r** with all authority.
Rev	3:19	Those whom I love I **r**

REBUKED [REBUKE]

| Mk | 16:14 | he **r** them for their lack of faith |
| 1Ti | 5:20 | Those who sin are to be **r** publicly, |

RECEIVE

Mk	10:15	anyone who will not **r** the kingdom
Jn	20:22	and said, "**R** the Holy Spirit.
Ac	1:8	you will **r** power when the Holy
	20:35	'It is more blessed to give than to **r**
1Co	9:14	the gospel should **r** their living
1Ti	1:16	believe on him and **r** eternal life.
Jas	1:7	should not think he will **r** anything
1Jn	3:22	and **r** from him anything we ask,
Rev	4:11	to **r** glory and honor and power,

RECONCILE

Ac	7:26	He tried to **r** them by saying, 'Men,
Eph	2:16	in this one body to **r** both of them
Col	1:20	him to **r** to himself all things,

RECONCILIATION [557, 639, 1367, 2903, 2904] (rĕk'ŏn-sĭl-ĭa'shŭn, Gr. *katallagē*). Reconciliation is a change of relationship between God and humans based on the changed status of humans through the redemptive work of Christ. Three aspects of this change are suggested by three words used for it in the NT.

1. A reconciliation of *persons* between whom there has existed a state of enmity. The Greek *katalassō* denotes an "exchange," which, when applied to persons, suggests an exchange from enmity to fellowship. Reconciliation is, therefore, God's exercise of grace toward humans who are in enmity because of sin, establishing in Christ's redemptive work the basis of this changed relationship of persons (2Co 5:19).

2. A reconciliation of *condition* so that all basis of the enmity relationship is removed and a complete basis of fellowship is established (2Co 5:18 – 20; Eph 2:16). *Apokatalassō* denotes a "movement out of" and suggests that since people are redeemed through the righteousness of Christ, they are redeemed out of their condition of unrighteousness and thus reconciled to God in this new relationship.

3. A reconciliation arising out of the change in people *induced by the action of God. Katallagē* suggests that people are not reconciled merely because their relationship has changed, but because *God* has changed them through Christ so that they can be reconciled (Ro 5:11; 11:15; 2Co 5:18; Eph 2:5).

Between People:
(Mt 5:23 – 26). Between Esau and Jacob (Ge 33:4, 11). Between Saul and David (1Sa 19:7). Between Pilate and Herod (Lk 23:12).

Between God and People:
Through atonement of animal sacrifices (Lev 8:15; Eze 45:15). After the seventy weeks of Daniel's vision (Da 9:24). Through Christ (Ro 5:1, 10; 11:15; 2Co 5:18 – 21; Eph 2:15 – 18; Col 1:20 – 22; Heb 2:17).

| Ro | 5:11 | whom we have now received **r**. |
| | 11:15 | For if their rejection is the **r** |

| 2Co | 5:18 | and gave us the ministry of **r**: |
| | 5:19 | committed to us the message of **r**. |

RED SEA [3542+6068, 2261+2498] (Heb. *yam sûph*). On the occasion of the exodus of the Israelites from Egypt, "God did not lead them on the road through the Philistine country, though that was shorter.... God led the people around by the desert road toward the Red Sea" (Ex 13:17 – 18). With Rameses as their point of departure (12:37), the nation of liberated slaves marched across the eastern boundaries of the land of Goshen toward a body of water, traditionally translated the "Red Sea." It is now quite evident that the "Red Sea" rendering is erroneous, as *Yam Sûph* should be rendered "Reed Sea" or "Marsh Sea." This newer identification in no way mitigates or militates against the miraculous deliverance by God, nor does it dissipate the awful judgment that overtook Pharaoh's armies.

> **General References to:**
> *The locusts that devastated Egypt destroyed in (Ex 10:19). Israelites cross; Pharaoh and his army drowned in (Ex 14; 15:1, 4, 11, 19; Nu 33:8; Dt 11:4; Jos 2:10; 4:23; 24:6 – 7; Jdg 11:16; 2Sa 22:16; Ne 9:9 – 11; Pss 66:6; 78:13, 53; 106:7 – 11, 22; 136:13 – 15; Isa 43:16 – 17; Ac 7:36; 1Co 10:1 – 2; Heb 11:29). Israelites camp by (Ex 14:2, 9; Nu 14:25; 21:4; 33:10 – 11; Dt 1:40; 2:1 – 3). Boundary of the Promised Land (Ex 23:31). Solomon builds ships on (1Ki 9:26).*

REDEEM

Ex	6:6	will **r** you with an outstretched arm
2Sa	7:23	on earth that God went out to **r**
Ps	44:26	**r** us because of your unfailing love.
	49:15	God will **r** my life from the grave;
Hos	13:14	I will **r** them from death.
Gal	4:5	under law, to **r** those under law,
Tit	2:14	for us to **r** us from all wickedness

REDEEMED

| Job | 33:28 | He **r** my soul from going |
| Ps | 71:23 | I, whom you have **r**. |

	107:2	Let the **r** of the Lord say this —
Isa	63:9	In his love and mercy he **r** them;
Gal	3:13	Christ **r** us from the curse
1Pe	1:18	or gold that you were **r**

REDEEMER

Job	19:25	I know that my **R** lives,
Ps	19:14	O Lord, my Rock and my **R**.
Isa	48:17	your **R**, the Holy One of Israel:
	59:20	"The **R** will come to Zion,

REDEMPTION [1453, 1460, 7009, 7012, 7014, 7017, 667, 3391] (Heb. *ge'ullâh*, Gr. *lytrōsis, apolytrōsis, to tear loose; a ransom*). A metaphor used in both OT and NT to describe God's merciful and costly action on behalf of his people (sinful human beings). The basic meaning of the word is release or freedom on payment of a price, deliverance by a costly method. When used of God, it does not suggest that he paid a price to anyone, but rather that his mercy required his almighty power and involved the greatest possible depth of suffering. Thus God redeemed Israel from Egypt by delivering the people from bondage and placing them in a new land (Ex 6:6; 15:13; Ps 77:14 – 15), and he did this by his "mighty hand." To appreciate the NT theme of redemption, the position of human beings as slaves of sin must be assumed (Jn 8:33 – 34). Thus they must be set free in order to become the liberated servants of the Lord. "For even the Son of Man did not come to be served, but to serve, and to give his life as a ransom for many" (Mk 10:45). Here again the use of the metaphor of ransom does not require that the question, "To whom was the ransom paid?" be answered. The emphasis is on costly sacrifice, the giving of a life. Paul wrote of "the redemption that came by Christ Jesus" (Ro 3:24) and claimed that in Christ "we have redemption through his blood" (Eph 1:7). Peter wrote that "it was not with perishable things ... that you were redeemed ... but with the precious blood of Christ" (1Pe 1:18 – 19; cf. Heb 9:12, 15; Rev 5:9 – 10).

Of Person or Property:

(Ex 13:13; Lev 25:25 – 34; 27:2 – 33; Ro 4:3 – 10). Redemption money paid to priests (Nu 3:46 – 51). Of the firstborn (Ex 13:13; 34:20; Lev 27:27; Nu 3:40 – 51; 18:15 – 17).

Of Land:

(Lev 27:19 – 20; Jer 32:7). In Hebrew society, any land that was forfeited through economic distress could be redeemed by the nearest of kin. If not so redeemed, it returned to its original owner in the Year of Jubilee (Lev 25:24 – 34).

Of Our Souls:

(Pss 111:9; 130:7). Through Christ (Mt 20:28; Mk 10:45; Lk 2:38; Ac 20:28; Ro 3:24 – 26; 1Co 1:30; 6:20; 7:23; Gal 1:4; 2:20; 4:4 – 5; Eph 1:7; 5:2; Col 1:14, 20 – 22; 1Ti 2:6; Tit 2:14; Heb 9:12, 15; 1Pe 1:18 – 19; Rev 5:9 – 10).

Ps	130:7	and with him is full **r**.
Lk	21:28	because your **r** is drawing near."
Ro	8:23	as sons, the **r** of our bodies.
1Co	1:30	our righteousness, holiness and **r**.
Eph	1:7	In him we have **r** through his blood
	4:30	you were sealed for the day of **r**.
Col	1:14	in whom we have **r**, the forgiveness
Heb	9:12	having obtained eternal **r**.

REFUGE

Nu	35:11	towns to be your cities of **r**,
Dt	33:27	The eternal God is your **r**,
Ru	2:12	wings you have come to take **r**."
2Sa	22:3	God is my rock, in whom I take **r**,
Ps	2:12	Blessed are all who take **r** in him.
	9:9	The Lord is a **r** for the oppressed,
	36:7	find **r** in the shadow of your wings.
	46:1	God is our **r** and strength,
Pr	14:26	and for his children it will be a **r**.
Na	1:7	a **r** in times of trouble.

REGENERATION (rē-jĕn-êr-ā′shun, Gr. *palingenesia*). Regeneration has as its basic idea "to be born again" or "to be restored." Though the word is actually used only twice in the NT (Mt 19:28; Tit 3:5), many syn-

onymous passages suggest its basic meaning. Related terms are "born again" (Jn 3:3, 5, 7), "born of God" (1:13; 1Jn 3:9), "quickened" (Eph 2:1, 5), and "renewed" (Ro 12:2; Tit 3:5). Regeneration is, therefore, an act of God through the immediate agency of the Holy Spirit operative in individuals (Col 2:13), originating in them a new dimension of moral life, a resurrection to new life in Christ. This new life is not merely a neutral state arising out of forgiveness of sin, but a positive implantation of Christ's righteousness in individuals, by which they are quickened (Jn 5:21), begotten (1Jn 5:1), made a new creation (2Co 5:17), and given a new life (Ro 6:4). The efficient cause of regeneration is God (1Jn 3:9) acting in love through mercy (Eph 2:4 – 5) to secure the new life in people through the instrument of his word (1Pe 1:23).

Also Called:

Born again or born from above (Jn 3:3 – 8; 1Pe 1:2 – 3, 22 – 23). Born of God (Jn 1:12 – 13, 16; Jas 1:18; 1Jn 2:27, 29; 3:9, 14; 4:7; 5:1, 4 – 5, 11 – 12, 18). Born by the Spirit (Jn 3:5 – 6; Gal 4:29), through the Holy Spirit (Eze 12:10; Jn 3:5 – 8; 1Co 12:13; 2Th 2:13; 1Pe 1:2 – 3, 22 – 23). Circumcision of the heart (Dt 29:4; 30:6; Eze 44:7, 9; Ro 2:28; Col 2:11 – 13). Change of heart (Ps 51:2, 7, 10; Jer 24:7; 31:33 – 34, w Heb 8:10 – 11; Jer 32:28 – 40; Eze 11:19 – 20; 18:31; 36:26 – 27, 29; Ro 12:2). New creature (2Co 5:17; Gal 6:15; Eph 4:22 – 24; Col 3:9 – 10). Spiritual cleansing (Jn 15:3; Ac 15:9; 1Co 6:11). Spiritual illumination (Jn 6:44 – 45; 8:12; Ac 26:18; 1Co 2:11 – 16; 2Co 4:6; Eph 5:14; Heb 10:16). To make spiritually alive (Heb 6:21). Spiritual resurrection (Jn 5:24; Ro 6:3 – 23; 8:2 – 4; Gal 2:20).

REHOBOAM [8154, 4850] (rē′hō-bō′ăm, Heb. *rehav′ām*, [my] people will enlarge, expand). A son of Solomon and his successor on the throne of Israel. His mother was Naamah, an Ammonitess (1Ki 14:21). He was born about 975 BC and was forty-one when he began to reign. The luxuries of his father's palace and the expenses of his diplomatic corps and of his vast building program resulted in burdensome taxation. The northern tribes turned for leadership to Jeroboam, to whom God had revealed that he was to rule ten of the tribes (11:26–40). When the coronation had been set, Jeroboam was called home from Egypt, and through him an appeal was made to Rehoboam for easier taxes. The latter, however, heeding the advice of young men, refused to heed the appeal, with the result that Israel rebelled against him. When Adoram was sent to collect the tribute, he was killed, and Rehoboam fled to Jerusalem (12:16–19). Jeroboam was then made king of the ten tribes. Rehoboam raised an army from Judah and Benjamin but was forbidden by God to attack (12:20–24). Jeroboam then fortified Shechem and Peniel, instituted pagan rites, and waged a relentless struggle against Rehoboam (12:25–28; 14:29–30). Israel was now divided into a northern and southern kingdom.

Successor to Solomon as king (1Ki 11:43; 2Ch 9:31); Refuses to reform abuses (1Ki 12:1–15; 2Ch 10:1–15); Ten tribes, under the leadership of Jeroboam, successfully revolt against Rehoboam (1Ki 12:16–24; 2Ch 10:16–19; 11:1–4); Builds fortified cities; is temporarily prosperous (2Ch 11:5–23); Invaded by king of Egypt and despoiled (1Ki 14:25–28; 2Ch 12:1–12); Death of (1Ki 14:31; 2Ch 12:16); Genealogy and descendants of (1Ch 3; Mt 1:7)

REIGN

Ex	15:18	The Lord will **r**
Isa	9:7	He will **r** on David's throne
	32:1	See, a king will **r** in righteousness
Jer	23:5	a King who will **r** wisely
Lk	1:33	and he will **r** over the house
Ro	6:12	Therefore do not let sin **r**
1Co	15:25	For he must **r** until he has put all
2Ti	2:12	we will also **r** with him.
Rev	11:15	and he will **r** for ever and ever."
	20:6	will **r** with him for a thousand years

REJECT [REJECTED]

Ps	94:14	For the Lord will not **r** his people
Ro	11:1	I ask then: Did God **r** his people?

REJECTED [REJECT]

1Sa	8:7	it is not you they have **r**,
1Ki	19:10	The Israelites have **r** your covenant
2Ki	17:15	They **r** his decrees
Ps	66:20	who has not **r** my prayer
	118:22	The stone the builders **r**
Isa	5:24	for they have **r** the law
	53:3	He was despised and **r** by men,
Jer	8:9	Since they have **r** the word
Mt	21:42	"'The stone the builders **r**
1Ti	4:4	nothing is to be **r** if it is received
1Pe	2:4	**r** by men but chosen by God
	2:7	"The stone the builders **r**

REJOICE

Dt	12:7	shall **r** in everything you have put
1Ch	16:10	of those who seek the Lord **r**.
	16:31	Let the heavens **r**, let the earth be
Ps	9:14	and there **r** in your salvation.
	118:24	let us **r** and be glad in it.
	119:14	I **r** in following your statutes
Pr	5:18	may you **r** in the wife of your youth
	24:17	stumbles, do not let your heart **r**,
Isa	62:5	so will your God **r** over you.
Zep	3:17	he will **r** over you with singing."
Zec	9:9	**R** greatly, O Daughter of Zion!
Lk	6:23	"**R** in that day and leap for joy,
	10:20	but **r** that your names are written
	15:6	'**R** with me; I have found my lost
Ro	5:2	And we **r** in the hope of the glory
Php	2:17	I am glad and **r** with all of you.
	3:1	Finally, my brothers, **r** in the Lord!
	4:4	**R** in the Lord always.
Rev	19:7	Let us **r** and be glad

RELIGION [1272, 2355, 2579] (Gr. *thrēskeia*, *outward expression of spiritual devotion*). The Latin *religare* means to hold back or restrain. It came to be applied to the services and ritual and rules by which faith in and devotion to deity were expressed. In the OT there is no word for religion. Fear (Ps 2:11; Pr 1:7) and worship (Dt 4:19; 29:26; Pss 5:7; 29:2) of God refer primarily to attitudes of the mind and acts of adoration, rather than to a ritual. *Thrēskeia* in the NT means outward expression of religion and the content of faith. James makes a distinction between the sham and the reality of religious expression (Jas 1:26 – 27). Paul was loyal to his Hebrew religion before being converted (Ac 26:1 – 5). "Religious" in Jas 1:26 (*thrēskos*) implies superstition.

False:

(Dt 32:31 – 33). See Idolatry.

National:

Supported by taxes (Ex 30:11 – 16; 38:26). Priests supported by the state (1Ki 18:19; 2Ch 11:13 – 15). Subverted by Jeroboam (1Ki 12:26 – 33; 2Ch 11:13 – 15). Idolatrous, established by Jeroboam (1Ki 12:26 – 33).

Natural:

(Job 12:7 – 16; 37:1 – 24; Pss 8:1 – 9; 19:1 – 6; Ac 14:17; 17:23 – 28; Ro 1:18 – 20; 10:16 – 18). See Revivals.

True, as Presented by:

Jesus (Mt 22:36 – 40). In the Sermon on the Mount: true blessedness (Mt 5:2 – 16); fulfillment of the law (Mt 5:17 – 48); "acts of righteousness" (Mt 6:1 – 18); service and treasure (Mt 6:19 – 21); judgment (Mt 7:1 – 6); asking (Mt 7:7 – 11); Golden Rule (Mt 7:12); wholehearted commitment to God (Mt 7:13 – 29; Mt 22:26 – 35). Paul (Ro 8:18; 10:1 – 13; 12:1 – 21; 1Co 13:1 – 13; Gal 5:22 – 25; 1Th 5:15 – 23). James (Jas 1:27; 2:8 – 26). Peter (1Pe 2:5 – 9). Jude (Jude 20 – 21).

Instances of Properly Religious Persons:

Abel (Ge 4:4 – 8; Heb 11:4); Noah (Ge 6 – 9); Abraham (Ge 12:1 – 8; 15; 17; 18:22 – 33); Jacob (Ge 28:10 – 22; 32:24 – 32); Moses (Ex 3:2 – 22; Dt 32 – 32); Jethro (Ex 18:12); Joshua (Jos 1); Gideon (Jdg 6 – 7); Samuel (1Sa 3); David (see Psalms); Solomon (1Ki 5:3 – 5; 2Ch 6); Jehu (2Ki 10:16 – 30); Hezekiah (2Ki 18:3 – 7; 19:14 – 19); Jehoshaphat (2Ch 17:3 – 9; 19 – 20); Jabez (1Ch 4:9 – 10); Asa (2Ch 14 – 15); Josiah (2Ki

22 – 23); Daniel (Da 6:4 – 22); three Hebrews (Da 3); Zechariah (Lk 1:13, 67 – 79); Simeon (Lk 2:25 – 35); Anna the prophetess (Lk 2:36 – 37); the centurion (Lk 7:1 – 10); Cornelius (Ac 10); Eunice and Lois (2Ti 1:5).

Ac	25:19	dispute with him about their own **r**
	26:5	to the strictest sect of our **r**,
1Ti	5:4	all to put their **r** into practice
Jas	1:26	himself and his **r** is worthless.
	1:27	**R** that God our Father accepts

REMEMBER

Ge	9:15	I will **r** my covenant between me
Ex	20:8	"**R** the Sabbath day
Dt	5:15	**R** that you were slaves in Egypt
1Ch	16:12	**R** the wonders he has done,
Ps	25:6	**R**, O LORD, your great mercy
Isa	46:8	"**R** this, fix it in mind,
Jer	31:34	and will **r** their sins no more."
Hab	3:2	in wrath **r** mercy.
Lk	1:72	and to **r** his holy covenant,
Gal	2:10	we should continue to **r** the poor,
Php	1:3	I thank my God every time I **r** you.
2Ti	2:8	**R** Jesus Christ, raised
Heb	8:12	and will **r** their sins no more."

REMNANT [3856, 7129, 8636, 8637, 8642, 2905, 3307, 5698]. A translation of different Hebrew words: *yether*, "what is left" (Dt 3:11; 28:54); *she'ār*, "the remainder" (Ezr 3:8; Isa 10:20; 11:16); *she'ērîth*, "residue" (2Ki 19:31; Isa 14:30). At first the word denoted a part of a family or clan left from slaughter, and later it came to be applied to the spiritual kernel of the nation that would survive God's judgment and become the germ of the new people of God. Thus Micah saw the returning glory of Israel (Mic 2:12; 5:7). Zephaniah saw the triumph of this remnant (Zep 2:4 – 7), and so did Zechariah (Zec 8:1 – 8). Isaiah named a son *She'ar-Jashub*, which means "a remnant returns" (Isa 7:3).

Ezr	9:8	has been gracious in leaving us a **r**
Isa	11:11	time to reclaim the **r** that is left

Jer	23:3	"I myself will gather the **r**
Zec	8:12	inheritance to the **r** of this people.
Ro	11:5	the present time there is a **r** chosen

REPENT [REPENTANCE]

1Ki	8:47	**r** and plead with you in the land
Job	36:10	commands them to **r** of their evil.
	42:6	and **r** in dust and ashes."
Jer	15:19	"If you **r**, I will restore you
Eze	18:30	**R**! Turn away from all your
Mt	3:2	"**R**, for the kingdom of heaven is
Mk	6:12	and preached that people should **r**.
Lk	13:3	unless you **r**, you too will all perish.
Ac	2:38	Peter replied, "**R** and be baptized,
	17:30	all people everywhere to **r**.
	26:20	also, I preached that they should **r**
Rev	2:5	**R** and do the things you did at first.

REPENTANCE [4044, 5714, 8740, 8746, 3564, 3566, 3567] (Heb. *nāham*, *sûbh*, Gr. *metanoia*). The process of changing one's mind. In the KJV of the OT, God himself is described as repenting (Ex 32:14; 1Sa 15:11; Jnh 3:9 – 10; 4:2 — using *nāham*), in the sense that he changed his attitude toward a people because of a change within the people. God as perfect Deity does not change in his essential nature; but because he is in relationship with people who do change, he himself changes his relation and attitude from wrath to mercy and from blessing to judgment as the occasion requires. His change of mind is his repentance, but there is no suggestion of change from worse to better or bad to good. In contrast, human repentance is a change for the better and is a conscious turning from evil, disobedience, sin, or idolatry to the living God (2Ki 17:13; Isa 19:22; Jer 3:12, 14, 22; Jnh 3:10 — using *shûbh*).

In the NT repentance and faith are the two sides of one coin (Ac 20:21). They are a response to grace. Jesus preached the need for the Jews to repent (Mt 4:17) and required his apostles/disciples to preach repentance to Jews and Gentiles (Lk 24:47; Ac 2:38; 17:30). Repentance is a profound change of mind involving the changing of the direction of life from that of self-centeredness or sin-centeredness to God- or Christ-centeredness. God's forgiveness is available only to those who are repentant, for only they can receive it.

Exhortations to:
(Pr 1:22 – 23; Jer 6:16 – 18; 7:3; 26:3; Hos 6:1; 14:1 – 3; Am 5:4 – 6; Mt 3:2). Commanded (Dt 32:29; 2Ch 30:6 – 9; Job 36:10; Isa 22:12; 31:6; 44:22; 55:6 – 7; Jer 3:4, 12 – 14, 19, 22; 18:11; 25:5 – 6; 26:13; 35:15; Eze 12:1 – 5; 14:6; 18:30 – 32; 33:10 – 12, 14 – 16, 19; Da 4:27; Hos 10:12; 14:1 – 2; Joel 1:14; 2:12 – 13, 15 – 17; Am 4:12; Jnh 3:8 – 9; Hag 1:7; Zec 1:3; Mt 4:17; Mk 1:4, 15; 6:12; Lk 3:3; Ac 2:38; 3:19; 8:22; 17:30; Rev 2:5, 16; 3:2 – 3, 19).

Source:
Gift of God (2Ti 2:25). Gift of Christ (Ac 5:31). Goodness of God leads to (Ro 2:4). Tribulation leads to (Dt 4:30; 30:1 – 3; 1Ki 8:33 – 50; 2Ch 6:36 – 39; Job 34:31 – 32).

Condition:
Of forgiveness (Lev 26:40 – 42; Dt 4:29 – 31; 30:1 – 3, 8; 1Ki 8:33 – 50; 2Ch 6:36 – 39; 7:14; Ne 1:9; Job 11:13 – 15; 22:23; Ps 34:18; Pr 28:13; Isa 55:7; Jer 3:4, 12 – 14, 19; 7:5 – 7; 18:7 – 8; 36:3; Eze 18:21 – 23, 27 – 28, 30 – 31; Am 5:6; Mal 3:7; Mt 5:4; Lk 13:1 – 5; 1Jn 1:9). Of divine favor (Lev 26:40 – 42; 2Ch 7:14; Isa 57:15).

Rewards of:
(Isa 59:20; Pr 1:23; Jer 7:3, 5, 7; 24:7; Eze 18:21 – 23, 27 – 28).

Preached by:
John the Baptist (Mt 3:2, 7 – 8; Mk 1:4, 15; Lk 3:3). Jesus (Mt 4:17; Mk 1:15; Lk 5:32). Peter (Ac 2:38, 40; 3:19; 8:22). Paul (Ac 17:30; 20:21; 26:20). The apostles (Mk 6:12). To be preached to all nations (Lk 24:47). Joy in heaven over (Lk 15:1 – 10). Unavailing, to Israel (Nu 14:39 – 45), to Esau (Heb 12:16 – 17).

Attributed to God:
God relents, or changes his mind, in response to change in his people (Ge 6:6 – 7; Ex 32:14;

Dt 32:36; Jdg 2:18; 1Sa 15:11, 35; 2Sa 24:16; 1Ch 21:15; Pss 106:45; 110:4; 135:14; Jer 15:6; 18:1 – 10; 26:3; 42:10; Joel 2:13; Am 7:3, 6; Jnh 3:9 – 10). *God will not repent* (Nu 23:19; 1Sa 15:29; Ps 110:4; Ro 11:29).

Exemplified:

By Job (Job 7:20 – 21; 9:20; 13:23; 40:4; 42:5 – 6); David (Pss 32:5; 38:3 – 4, 18; 40:12; 41:4; 51:1 – 4, 7 – 17); the Israelites (Nu 21:7; 2Ch 29:6; Jer 3:21 – 22, 25; 14:7 – 9, 20; 31:18 – 19; La 3:40 – 41); Daniel for the Jews (Da 9:5 – 7; 10:12); the prodigal son (Lk 15:17 – 20).

Isa	30:15	"In **r** and rest is your salvation,
Mt	3:8	Produce fruit in keeping with **r**.
Mk	1:4	a baptism of **r** for the forgiveness
Lk	5:32	call the righteous, but sinners to **r**."
	24:47	and **r** and forgiveness of sins will be
Ac	20:21	that they must turn to God in **r**
	26:20	and prove their **r** by their deeds.
Ro	2:4	kindness leads you toward **r**?
2Co	7:10	Godly sorrow brings **r** that leads
2Pe	3:9	but everyone to come to **r**.

REPROBATE (rĕp′rō-bāt, Gr. *adokimos*). The basic idea in reprobation is that of failing "to stand the test." *Adokimos*, the negative of *dokimos* ("to approve") connotes disapproval or rejection. When applied to humanity's relation to God, it suggests moral corruption, unfitness, disqualification — all arising out of a lack of positive holiness. The KJV uses it of a reprobate [disapproved] mind (Ro 1:28) and of a sinful nature (2Co 13:5, 6, 7). Its other NT uses (2Ti 3:8; Tit 1:16) bear the same disapproval quality. Human beings in sin are reprobate, disqualified, disapproved, and rejected because they cannot "stand the test" of holiness. Approval comes only in Jesus' righteousness.

REPROOF, REPROVE [3519].

Commanded:

(Lev 19:17; Ps 141:5; Pr 9:7 – 8; 10:17; 26:5; Mt 18:15 – 17; Lk 17:3 – 4; Eph 5:11; 1Th 5:14, 20;

2Ti 4:2; Tit 1:13; Heb 3:13). Of elders, forbidden (1Ti 5:1 – 2).

Profitable:

(Pr 13:18; 15:5, 31 – 32; 27:5 – 6; 28:23; Ecc 7:5). Wise profit by (Pr 17:10; 19:25; 21:11; 25:12).

Needed in the Church:

(Eph 4:15; Php 3:1; 1Th 5:14; 1Ti 5:1 – 2, 20; 2Ti 4:2; Tit 1:13; Heb 3:13).

Hated:

(Pr 10:17; 12:1; 15:10, 12; Am 5:10; Jn 7:7; Gal 4:16); by the Israelites (Nu 14:9 – 10; Jer 26:11); by Ahab (1Ki 18:17; 21:20; 22:8); by Asa (2Ch 16:10); by Herodias (Mk 6:18 – 19); by people of Nazareth (Lk 4:28 – 29); by Jews (Ac 5:33; 7:54).

Faithfulness in:

Instances of: Moses, of Pharaoh (Ex 10:29; 11:8); of the Israelites (Ex 16:6 – 7; 32:19 – 30; Nu 14:41; 20:10; 32:14; Dt 1:12, 26 – 43; 9:16 – 24; 29:2 – 4; 31:27 – 29; 32:15 – 18); of Eleazar (Lev 10:16 – 18); of Korah (Nu 16:9 – 11). Israelites, of the two and a half tribes (Jos 22:15 – 20); of the tribe of Benjamin (Jdg 20:12 – 13). Samuel, of Saul (1Sa 15:14 – 35). Jonathan, of Saul (1Sa 19:4 – 5). Nathan, of David (2Sa 12:1 – 9). Joab, of David (2Sa 19:1 – 7; 24:3; 1Ch 21:3). The prophet Gad, of David (2Sa 24:13). Shemaiah, of Rehoboam (2Ch 12:5). A prophet of Judah, of Jeroboam (1Ki 13:1 – 10; 2Ch 13:8 – 11). Elijah, of Ahab (1Ki 18:18 – 21; 21:20 – 24), of Ahaziah (2Ki 1). Micaiah, of Ahab (1Ki 22:14 – 28). Elisha, of Jehoram (2Ki 3:13 – 14); of Gehazi (2Ki 5:26); of Hazael (2Ki 8:11 – 13); of Jeroboam (2Ki 13:19). Amos, of the Israelites (Am 7:12 – 17). Isaiah, of Hezekiah (2Ki 20:17). Jehoash, of Jehoiada (2Ki 12:7). Azariah, of Asa (2Ch 15:2); of Uzziah (2Ch 26:17 – 18). Hanani, of Asa (2Ch 16:7 – 9). Jehu, of Jehoshaphat (2Ch 19:2). Zechariah, of the princes of Judah (2Ch 24:20). Oded, of the people of Samaria (2Ch 28:9 – 11). Jeremiah, of the cities of Judah (Jer 26:8 – 11). Ezra, of the men of Judah and Benjamin (Ezr 10:10). Nehemiah, of the Jews (Ne 5:6 – 13); of the corruptions in the temple and of the violation of the Sabbath (Ne 13). Daniel,

of Nebuchadnezzar (Da 4:27); of Belshazzar (Da 5:17–24). Jesus, of the Jews: when Pharisees and Sadducees came to him desiring a sign (Mt 16:1–4; Mk 8:11–12); of the scribes and Pharisees (Mt 23; Lk 11:37–54); of the Pharisees (Lk 16); of the Pharisees when they brought the woman to him who was caught in adultery (Jn 8:7). Jesus, in his parables: of the king's feast (Lk 14:16–24); of the two sons (Mt 21:28–32); of the vineyard (Mt 21:33–46; Mk 12:1–12; Lk 20:9–20); of the barren fig tree (Lk 13:6–9); of the withering of the fig tree (Mt 21:17–20; Mk 11:12–14). John the Baptist, of the Jews (Mt 3:7–12; Lk 3:7–9); of Herod (Mt 14:3; Mk 6:17; Lk 3:19–20). Peter, of Simon, the sorcerer (Ac 8:20–23). Stephen, of the high priest (Ac 7:51–53). Paul, of Elymas, the sorcerer (Ac 13:9–11); of Ananias, the high priest (Ac 23:3). Paul and Silas, of the magistrates of Philippi (Ac 16:37–40).

RESIST

Da	11:32	know their God will firmly **r** him.
Mt	5:39	I tell you, Do not **r** an evil person.
Lk	21:15	of your adversaries will be able to **r**
Jas	4:7	**R** the devil, and he will flee
1Pe	5:9	**R** him, standing firm in the faith,

RESPECT [3359, 3707, 3877, 1956, 3455, 4948, 5507, 5832].

For the aged (Lev 19:32). For rulers (Pr 25:6). For a host (Lk 14:10). For one another (Ro 12:10; Php 2:3; 1Pe 2:17).

Lev	19:3	" 'Each of you must **r** his mother
	19:32	show **r** for the elderly and revere
Mal	1:6	where is the **r** due me?" says
Eph	5:33	and the wife must **r** her husband.
	6:5	obey your earthly masters with **r**
1Th	4:12	so that your daily life may win the **r**
	5:12	to **r** those who work hard
1Ti	3:4	children obey him with proper **r**.
	3:8	are to be men worthy of **r**, sincere,
	3:11	are to be women worthy of **r**,
	6:1	their masters worthy of full **r**,

Tit	2:2	worthy of **r**, self-controlled,
1Pe	2:17	Show proper **r** to everyone:
	3:7	them with **r** as the weaker partner
	3:16	But do this with gentleness and **r**,

REST [1954, 1957, 3782, 4328, 4955, 4957, 5663, 8069, 8070, 8089, 8697, 8702, 8886, 8905, 9200, 398, 399, 2923, 2924] (Heb. *nûah, menûhâh, peace, quiet,* Gr. *anapausis, katapausis*).

A word of frequent occurrence in the Bible, in both Testaments. It is used of God as resting from his work (Ge 2:2), and as having his rest in the temple (1Ch 28:2). God commanded that the seventh day was to be one of rest (Ex 16:23; 31:15), and that the land was to have its rest every seventh year (Lev 25:4). God promised rest to the Israelites in the land of Canaan (Dt 12:9). The word is sometimes used in the sense of trust and reliance (2Ch 14:11). Christ offers rest of soul to those who come to him (Mt 11:28). Hebrews 4 says that God offers to his people a rest not enjoyed by those who died in the wilderness.

> **Divine Institution for:**
>
> *Commanded (Ex 16:23; 20:10; 23:12; 31:15; 34:21; 35:2; Dt 5:12, 14). The annual feasts added rest days: first and last days of feasts of Passover and Tabernacles (Ex 12:16; Lev 23:5–8, 39–40; Nu 28:18, 25; 29:12, 35); Pentecost (Nu 28:26); Trumpets (Lev 23:24–25; Nu 29:1); Atonement (Lev 16:29–31; 23:27–28; Nu 29:7). In seventh year (Ex 23:11; Lev 25:1–4). In Year of Jubilee (Lev 25:11–12). Recommended by Jesus (Mk 6:31–32; 7:24, w Mt 8:18, 24). Heavenly (2Th 1:7). Spiritual (Mt 11:29; Heb 4:1–11).*

Ex	31:15	the seventh day is a Sabbath of **r**,
	33:14	go with you, and I will give you **r**."
Lev	25:5	The land is to have a year of **r**.
Dt	31:16	going to **r** with your fathers,
Jos	14:15	Then the land had **r** from war.
1Ki	5:4	The LORD my god has given me **r**
Ps	62:1	My soul finds **r** in God alone;
	90:17	of the Lord our God **r** upon us;

	95:11	"They shall never enter my **r**."
Pr	6:10	a little folding of the hands to **r** —
Isa	11:2	Spirit of the LORD will **r** on him —
Jer	6:16	and you will find **r** for your souls.
Mt	11:28	and burdened, and I will give you **r**.
2Co	12:9	so that Christ's power may **r** on me
Heb	3:11	'They shall never enter my **r**.'"
	4:10	for anyone who enters God's **r**
Rev	14:13	"they will **r** from their labor,

RESTITUTION [5989, 8740, 8966].

To be made for injury to life, limb, or property (Ex 21:30 – 36; Lev 24:18); for theft (Ex 22:1 – 4; Pr 6:30 – 31; Eze 33:15); for dishonesty (Lev 6:2 – 5; Nu 5:7; Job 20:18; Eze 33:15; Lk 19:8).

Ex	22:3	"A thief must certainly make **r**,
Lev	6:5	He must make **r** in full, add a fifth
Nu	5:8	the **r** belongs to the LORD

RESTORATION [1215, 2542, 2616, 2649, 6441, 7756, 8740, 8966, 10354, 10754, 635, 2936]. Of the Jews. Of all things (Ac 3:21; Rev 21:1 – 5).

RESTORE

Ps	51:12	**R** to me the joy of your salvation
	80:3	**R** us, O God;
	126:4	**R** our fortunes, O LORD,
La	5:21	**R** us to yourself, O LORD,
Na	2:2	The LORD will **r** the splendor
Gal	6:1	are spiritual should **r** him gently.
1Pe	5:10	will himself **r** you and make you

RESTORES

Ps	23:3	he **r** my soul.

RESURRECTION [414, 1587, 1983] (Gr. *anastasis, arising, egersis, a raising*).

A return to life subsequent to death. It is a redemption of man in his whole complex personality — body and soul together. It is not that the soul does not exist in a disembodied state between death and resurrection, but in the biblical view, man in the intermediate state is incomplete and awaits "the redemption of our bodies" (Ro 8:23; cf. 2Co 5:3ff.; Rev 6:9 – 11).

In the OT the most explicit passage on the resurrection is Da 12:2, which clearly predicts the resurrection and eternal judgment of those who have died. Almost equally explicit is Isa 26:19. In its context, this verse is parallel to vv. 11 – 15. In them the voice of God's people is heard, repeating his promises and looking forward to their fulfillment; in v. 19 the voice of the Lord responds, affirming the hope that lies before his distressed people, confirming the conviction that they will rise again.

In the NT the word *anastasis*, "resurrection," signifies the arising to life of a dead body or bodies. There is one possible exception, Lk 2:34, though probably "resurrection" is the meaning here, too. In secular Greek the word may refer to any act of rising up or sitting up; but the theological interpretation of the word in the NT does not depend only on its literal meaning but on the contexts in which it is found.

The doctrine of resurrection is stated clearly in its simplest form in Paul's words before the Roman law court presided over by Felix: "There will be a resurrection of both the righteous and the wicked" (Ac 24:15). The most detailed statement of the doctrine of twofold resurrection is found in Rev 20:4 – 15.

In the OT:

As understood by Job (Job 14:12 – 15; 19:25 – 27); by the psalmists (Pss 16:9 – 10; 17:15; 49:15); by the prophets (Isa 25:8; 26:19; Da 12:2 – 3, 13; Hos 13:14).

In the NT:

Debated by the Pharisees and Sadducees (Ac 23:6, 8; 24:14 – 15; 26:6 – 8; Mt 22:23 – 32). Taught by Jesus (Mt 22:30 – 32; 24:31; Mk 12:25 – 27; Lk 14:14; 20:27 – 38; Jn 5:21, 25, 28 – 29; 6:39 – 40, 44, 54; 11:23 – 25); by the apostles (Ac 4:1 – 2; 17:18, 31 – 32; 23:6 – 8; 24:14 – 15; 26:6 – 8; Ro 4:16 – 21; 8:10 – 11, 19, 21 – 23; 1Co 6:14; 15:12 – 57; 2Co 4:14; 5:1 – 5; Php 3:10 – 11,

21; Rev 20:5 – 6; Heb 6:2; 11:35). *Error in the early church* (2Ti 2:18; 1Co 15:12 – 58).

Of Jesus:

Typified by Isaac (Ge 22:13; Heb 11:19); by Jonah (Jnh 2:10, w Mt 12:40). Foretold (Ps 16:9 – 10); by himself (Mt 16:21; 17:9, 23; 20:19; 26:61; 27:63; Mk 8:31; 9:9 – 10, 31; 10:34; Lk 9:22; 18:33; 24:7, 46; Jn 2:19 – 21; 10:17 – 18; 14:19). Appearances after the resurrection (Mt 27:53; 28:2 – 15; Mk 16:1 – 11; Lk 24:1 – 12; Jn 20:1 – 18; Rev 1:18). Denied by the Jews (Mt 28:12 – 15). Raised by the power of God (Ac 2:24, 32; 3:15, 26; 4:10; 5:30; 10:40; 15:20, 30, 33 – 34, 37; 17:31; Ro 4:24; 8:11; 10:9; 1Co 6:14; 15:15; 2Co 4:14; Gal 1:4; Eph 1:20; Col 2:12; 2Ti 1:10; 1Pe 1:21); for our justification (Ro 4:25; 1Pe 3:21). Guarantee of general resurrection (1Co 15:12 – 15; 1Pe 1:3). The theme of apostolic preaching (Ac 2:24, 31 – 32; 3:15; 4:10, 33; 5:30 – 32; 10:40 – 41; 17:2 – 3, 18). See Jesus the Christ.

Special Resurrections:

Of saints after Christ's resurrection (Mt 27:52 – 53). The two witnesses (Rev 11:11). See Dead, Raised to Life.

At Christ's Second Coming:

(1Th 4:14, 16). The first resurrection (Rev 20:4 – 6). Of all the dead (Jn 5:28 – 29; Ac 24:15; 1Co 15:20 – 21; Rev 20:13).

Figurative:

Of the restoration of Israel (Eze 37:1 – 14). Of regeneration (Ro 6:4; Eph 2:1, 5 – 6; Col 2:12; 3:1).

Mt	22:23	who say there is no **r**, came to him
	22:30	At the **r** people will neither marry
	27:53	and after Jesus' **r** they went
Lk	14:14	repaid at the **r** of the righteous."
Jn	11:24	again in the **r** at the last day."
	11:25	Jesus said to her, "I am the **r**
Ac	1:22	become a witness with us of his **r**."
	2:31	he spoke of the **r** of the Christ,
	4:33	to testify to the **r** of the Lord Jesus,

	17:18	good news about Jesus and the **r**.
	17:32	When they heard about the **r**
	23:6	of my hope in the **r** of the dead."
Ro	1:4	Son of God by his **r** from the dead:
	6:5	also be united with him in his **r**.
1Co	15:12	some of you say that there is no **r**
	15:13	If there is no **r** of the dead,
Php	3:10	power of his **r** and the fellowship
2Ti	2:18	say that the **r** has already taken
Heb	11:35	so that they might gain a better **r**.
1Pe	1:3	hope through the **r** of Jesus Christ
	3:21	It saves you by the **r** of Jesus Christ
Rev	20:5	This is the first **r**.

RESURRECTION OF JESUS CHRIST (Gr. *anastasis, egeirō, anistēmi*). There were no witnesses of the resurrection of Jesus of Nazareth. What the disciples witnessed was the appearance of the resurrected Jesus. They saw also the empty tomb. In fact, only disciples were witnesses of the appearances of Jesus; but both disciples and others saw the empty sepulchre.

In the NT there are six accounts of what followed the resurrection of Jesus. Each of the four gospels contains an account (Mt 28; Mk 16; Lk 24; Jn 20 – 21), and there are two others (Ac 1:1 – 11; 1Co 15:1 – 11).

THE NARRATIVES.

The brief accounts of the resurrection appearances contrast with the lengthy narratives of the passion and death of Jesus. The reason for this is as follows. Concerning the death of Jesus, Jews asked, "How could Jesus be the true Messiah and die on a cross when the law of Moses teaches that to die such a death is to be under God's curse?" And Gentiles asked, "If Jesus was the true King of the Jews, why was he rejected by his own people?" Thus long accounts were necessary to provide answers. But the questions concerning the resurrection were basically concerning proof. So the six accounts provide the testimony of eyewitnesses who claimed to have seen not only the empty tomb but also the resurrected Jesus. There was no need for lengthy descriptions.

WITHIN AND BEYOND HISTORY.

On the basis of the NT, Christians usually make two parallel claims concerning the resurrection of Jesus. First, it was a definite historical event and as such is open to historical investigation. Second, it was more than a historical event, for it involved a major dimension that is not open to historical investigation.

The evidence for the resurrection as an event within history may be listed as follows:

1. *The tomb of Jesus was found empty some thirty-six hours after his burial.* Despite efforts by Jews to prove that the body was stolen and buried elsewhere, the body was never located or produced by those who allegedly stole it or by anyone else. Further, the suggestion that Jesus only swooned on the cross and then revived in the cool tomb is impossible to substantiate.

2. *The disciples claimed that Jesus actually appeared.* They saw Jesus when they were fully awake and when they doubted that he was alive. What they saw was neither a subjective vision (in their imagination, a kind of hallucination) nor an objective vision (provided by God to show that the true and essential *spirit* of Jesus was alive). They actually saw Jesus on earth; they were witnesses of the resurrection.

3. *The sober nature of the narratives describing the resurrection appearances.* There is no attempt to describe the resurrection itself, and there is no obvious collusion between the various writers to doctor or adorn their material. The most amazing event in human history is described with reverential reserve.

4. *The transformation of the disciples and the existence of the church.* Men who were cowards became fearless preachers and founded the church for one reason and one alone — they believed with all their hearts that Jesus had risen from the dead and was alive forevermore. And when they preached the gospel that Jesus who was crucified now lives as Lord and Savior, they saw lives changed by that living Lord.

This century there has been a readiness within the church to discount or hold loosely to the fact of the resurrection of Jesus as an event within history. This tendency must be resisted, for if his resurrection is not an event within history (within the same physical universe and space and time in which we live), then what the NT claims that God accomplished in Jesus Christ on the cross for salvation is not applicable to us in history. The bodily resurrection of Jesus (as Paul insists in 1Co 15) is of fundamental importance and cannot be ignored or set aside.

WHAT KIND OF BODY?

There were both differences and similarities in the pre- and postresurrection body of Jesus. Yet there was a basic identity so that one may speak of "identity-in-transformation." For Jesus, bodily resurrection meant resuscitation with transformation — that is, not only resuscitation (as with Lazarus in Jn 11), but also the metamorphosis of the body so that what was a physical and mortal body became a spiritual and immortal body, transformed by the power of God, Creator of life and bodies. Apart from isolated incidents (e.g., walking on the water), the pre-Easter Jesus was subject to material, physical, and spatial limitations. He walked from one place to another, passed through doors to enter rooms, and climbed steps to get onto the roofs of houses. Yet after his resurrection he was no longer bound by these limitations. He passed through a sealed tomb, through locked doors, and appeared and disappeared without notice. He became visible here and there and from time to time. This suggests that his true or essential state as a transformed person was that of invisibility and immateriality, with the ability to be localized at will.

A THEOLOGY OF RESURRECTION.

There are various ways of stating a theology of resurrection, but perhaps that which best reflects the NT evidence is the theme of vindication.

1. *God raised Jesus from the dead and thereby vindicated him as the true Messiah.* The manner of Jesus' death gave the impression that God had rejected him, for to hang on a tree was to be under the divine curse (Dt 21:23; Gal 3:13). In resurrection, Jesus was vindicated. He was no longer implicitly claiming to be the Messiah by his teaching and deeds: he was now demonstrated to be Messiah in fact and in truth. Peter, over a year before the crucifixion, had asserted, "You are the Christ" (Mt 16:16), and fifty days after the resurrection, he told the crowd in Jerusalem: "Therefore, let all Israel be assured of this: God has made this Jesus, whom you crucified, both Lord and Christ" (Ac 2:36). Later, by means of a quotation from Ps 118, Peter explained to the Jewish leaders the vindication of Jesus; he claimed that Jesus is "the stone you builders rejected, which has become the capstone" (Ac 4:11). Then Paul wrote that Jesus "as to his human nature was a descendant of David, and who through the Spirit of holiness was declared with power to be the Son of God by his resurrection from the dead" (Ro 1:3 – 4). Jesus was always Son of God, but the resurrection was the actual vindication of this sonship.

2. *God raised Jesus from the dead and thereby vindicated his teaching and work of atonement.* The resurrection is God's "Amen" to the cry of Jesus, "It is finished." The resurrection is God's "Yes" to the ministry and teaching of Jesus. Jesus was "delivered over to death for our sins and was raised to life for our justification" (Ro 4:25). In the light of the resurrection, Paul could "boast ... in the cross of our Lord Jesus Christ" (Gal 6:14) because it revealed the eternal love of God for human sinners.

3. *God caused the new age to dawn in the resurrection.* With the raising of Jesus from death and the transformation of his body, there began a new order of existence. What belongs to the future kingdom of God, the glorious age to come, has made its appearance in this present evil age. Paul deliberately spoke of the resurrected Jesus as the "firstfruits" of the harvest of the age to come (1Co 15:20, 23).

In the NT the theology of the resurrection cannot be separated from the theology of the ascension or the theology of exaltation. Often in the NT the word "resurrection" includes the idea of ascension, while the word "exaltation" takes in both resurrection and ascension.

RETALIATION [518] (Ps 10:2).

Judicial, ordained in Mosaic law (Ex 21:23 – 25; Lev 24:17 – 22; Dt 19:19 – 21). Malicious, forbidden (Lev 19:18; Pr 20:22; 24:29; Mt 5:38 – 44; 7:1 – 2; Lk 9:54; Ro 12:17, 19; 1Co 6:7 – 8; 1Th 5:15; 1Pe 3:9). Warning against (Pr 26:27; Isa 33:1; Mt 7:1 – 2). Instances of: Israelites on the Amalekites (Dt 25:17 – 19, w 1Sa 15:1 – 9). Gideon on the princes of Succoth (Jdg 8:7, 13 – 16), the kings of Midian (Jdg 8:18 – 21), Peniel (Jdg 8:8, 17). Joab on Abner (2Sa 3:27, 30). David upon Michal (2Sa 6:21 – 23), Joab (1Ki 2:5 – 6), Shimei (1Ki 2:8 – 9). Jews on their enemies (Est 9).

RETRIBUTION [1691, 1692, 8936, 501]. The word is not found in Scripture, but the idea is expressed in reference to the wrath of God, vengeance, punishment, and judgment when God "will give to each person according to what he has done" (Ro 2:6). The concept reminds us not to be so fully engrossed in the grace of the gospel that we overlook God's judgment on the impenitent sinner (1:18). Retribution is the natural outcome of sin (Gal 6:7 – 8), the thought of which was reflected in John the Baptist's warning to "flee from the coming wrath" (Mt 3:7; Lk 3:7; cf. 1Th 1:10). One of the NT's most terrible references is to "the wrath of the Lamb" (Rev 6:16).

RETURN

Ge	3:19	and to dust you will **r**."
2Sa	12:23	go to him, but he will not **r** to me."
2Ch	30:9	If you **r** to the LORD, then your
Ne	1:9	but if you **r** to me and obey my
Ps	126:6	will **r** with songs of joy,
Isa	10:21	A remnant will **r**, a remnant
	55:11	It will not **r** to me empty,
Jer	24:7	for they will **r** to me

La	3:40	and let us **r** to the LORD.
Hos	6:1	"Come, let us **r** to the LORD.
	12:6	But you must **r** to your God;
	14:1	**R**, O Israel, to the LORD your
Joel	2:12	"**r** to me with all your heart,
Zec	1:3	'**R** to me,' declares the LORD
	10:9	and they will **r**.

REUBEN [1201+8017, 1201+8018, 8017, 8018, 4857] (rū'bĕn, Heb. *re'ûvēn, see, a son!* [Ge 29:32]; *substitute a son* IDB). The oldest son of Jacob, born to him by Leah in Paddan Aram (Ge 29:32).

Son of Jacob (Ge 29:32; 1Ch 2:1). Brings mandrakes to his mother (Ge 30:14). Commits incest with one of his father's concubines and, in consequence, forfeits the birthright (Ge 35:22; 49:4; 1Ch 5:1). Tactfully seeks to save Joseph from the conspiracy of his brothers (Ge 37:21 – 30; 42:22). Offers to become surety for Benjamin (Ge 42:37). Jacob's prophetic benediction upon (Ge 49:3 – 4). Children of (Ge 46:9; Ex 6:14; 1Ch 5:3 – 6; Nu 16:1).

REUBENITE(S) [1201+8017, 8018] (rū'bĕn-īts, *of Reuben*). The descendants of Reuben.

> Military enrollment of, at Sinai (Nu 1:20 – 21), in Moab (Nu 26:7)
> Place of, in camp and march (Nu 2:10)
> Standard of (Nu 10:18)
> Have their inheritance east of the Jordan (Nu 32; Dt 3:1 – 20; Jos 13:15 – 23; 18:7)
> Assist the other tribes in conquest of the region west of the Jordan (Jos 1:12 – 18; 22:1 – 6)
> Unite with the other tribes in building a monument to signify the unity of the tribes on the east of the Jordan with the tribes on the west of the river; monument misunderstood; explanation and reconciliation (Jos 22:10 – 34)
> Reproached by Deborah (Jdg 5:15 – 16)
> Taken captive into Assyria (2Ki 15:29; 1Ch 5:26)

REVEAL

Mt	11:27	to whom the Son chooses to **r** him.

Gal	1:16	was pleased to **r** his Son in me

REVEALED

Dt	29:29	but the things **r** belong to us
Isa	53:1	the arm of the LORD been **r**?
Mt	11:25	and **r** them to little children.
Jn	12:38	the arm of the Lord been **r**?"
Ro	1:17	a righteousness from God is **r**,
	8:18	with the glory that will be **r** in us.
	16:26	but now **r** and made known
1Co	2:10	but God has **r** it to us by his Spirit.
2Th	1:7	happen when the Lord Jesus is **r**
	2:3	and the man of lawlessness is **r**,
1Pe	1:20	but was **r** in these last times
	4:13	overjoyed when his glory is **r**.

REVELATION [1821, 2606, 2612, 636, 637]. The doctrine of God's making himself and relevant truths known to humankind. Revelation is of two kinds: general and special. General revelation is available to all people and is communicated through nature, conscience, and history. Special revelation is revelation given to particular people at particular times (although it may be intended for others as well), and comes chiefly through the Bible and Jesus Christ.

> **General References to:**
> God reveals himself to Moses (Ex 3:1 – 6, 14; 6:1 – 3). The law is revealed (Ex 20 – 35; Lev 1 – 7). The pattern of the temple (1Ch 28:11 – 19). The sonship of Jesus (Mt 3:17; 16:17; 17:5). The nature of the Father through the Son (Jn 1:18; 14:8).

2Sa	7:17	David all the words of this entire **r**.
Pr	29:18	Where there is no **r**, the people cast
Da	10:1	a **r** was given to Daniel (who was
Hab	2:3	For the **r** awaits an appointed time;
Lk	2:32	a light for **r** to the Gentiles
1Co	14:6	I bring you some **r** or knowledge
	14:26	a **r**, a tongue or an interpretation.
Gal	1:12	I received it by **r** from Jesus Christ.
Eph	1:17	you the Spirit of wisdom and **r**,
	3:3	mystery made known to me by **r**,
Rev	1:1	**r** of Jesus Christ, which God gave

REVELATION, THE BOOK OF (Gr. *apokalypsis, an unveiling*). Sometimes called "the Apocalypse." This is the last book of the Bible and the only book of the NT that is exclusively prophetic in character. It belongs to the class of apocalyptic literature in which the divine message is conveyed by visions and dreams. The title that the book itself assumes (Rev 1:1) may mean either "the revelation that Christ possesses and imparts," or "the unveiling of the person of Christ." Grammatically, the former is preferable, for this text states that God gave this disclosure to Christ that he might impart it to his servants.

THE AUTHOR.

Unlike many apocalyptic books that are either anonymous or published under a false name, Revelation is ascribed to John, evidently a well-known person among the churches of Asia Minor. He identified himself as a brother of those who were suffering persecution (Rev 1:9).

DATE AND PLACE.

There are two prevailing views regarding the date of the Apocalypse. The earlier date in the reign of Nero is favored by some because of the allusion to the temple in Rev 11:1 – 2, which obviously refers to an early structure. Had the Apocalypse been written after AD 70, the temple in Jerusalem would not have been standing. A second view, better substantiated by the early interpreters of the book, places it in the reign of Domitian (AD 81 – 96). It allows time for the decline that is presupposed by the letters to the churches, and it fits better with the historical conditions of the Roman Empire depicted in the symbolism.

The place of writing was the island of Patmos, where John had been exiled for his faith. Patmos was the site of a penal colony, where political prisoners were condemned to hard labor in the mines.

DESTINATION.

Revelation was addressed to seven churches of the Roman province of Asia, which occupied the western third of what is now Turkey. The cities where these churches were located were on the main roads running north and south, so that a messenger carrying these letters could move in a direct circuit from one to the other.

OCCASION.

Revelation was written for the express purpose of declaring "what must soon take place" (Rev 1:1), in order that the evils in the churches might be corrected and that they might be prepared for the events that were about to confront them. The moral and social conditions of the empire were deteriorating, and Christians had already begun to feel the increasing pressure of paganism and the threat of persecution. The book of Revelation provided a new perspective on history by showing that the kingdom of Christ was eternal, and that it would ultimately be victorious over the kingdoms of the world.

METHODS OF INTERPRETATION.

There are four main schools of interpretation. The *preterist* holds that Revelation is simply a picture of the conditions prevalent in the Roman Empire in the late first century, cast in the form of vision and prophecy to conceal its meaning from hostile pagans. The *historical* view contends that the book represents in symbolic form the entire course of church history from the time of its writing to the final consummation, and that the mystical figures and actions described in it can be identified with human events in history. The *futurist*, on the basis of the threefold division given in Rev 1:19, suggests that "what you have seen" refers to the immediate environment of the seer and the vision of Christ (1:9 – 19); "what is now" denotes the churches of Asia or the church age they symbolize (2:1 – 3:22); and "what will take place later" relates to those events that will attend the return of Christ and the establishment of the city of God. The *idealist* or *symbolic* school treats Revelation as purely a dramatic picture of the conflict of good and evil, which persists in every age but which cannot be applied exclusively to any particular historical period.

STRUCTURE AND CONTENT.

Revelation contains four great visions, each of which is introduced by the phrase "in the Spirit" (Rev 1:10; 4:2; 17:3; 21:10). Each of these visions locates the seer in a different place, each contains a distinctive picture of Christ, and each advances the action significantly toward its goal.

Outline:

    I. Introduction: The Return of Christ (1:1 – 8).
    II. Christ, the Critic of the Churches (1:9 – 3:22).
    III. Christ, the Controller of Destiny (4:1 – 16:21).
    IV. Christ, the Conqueror of Evil (17:1 – 21:8).
    V. Christ, the Consummator of Hope (21:9 – 22:5).
    VI. Epilogue: Appeal and Invitation (22:6 – 21).

REVENGE [5933, 5934, 5935, 1688+4932].

Forbidden (Lev 19:18; Pr 24:29; Ro 12:17, 19; 1Th 5:15; 1Pe 3:9). Jesus, an example of forbearing (1Pe 2:23). Rebuked by Jesus (Lk 9:54 – 55). Inconsistent with a Christian spirit (Lk 9:55). Proceeds from a spiteful heart (Eze 25:15). Punishment for (Eze 25:15 – 17; Am 1:11 – 12).

> **Exemplified:**
>
> *By Simeon and Levi (Ge 34:25); by Samson (Jdg 15:7 – 8; 16:28 – 30); by Joab (2Sa 3:27); by Absalom (2Sa 13:23 – 29); by Jezebel (1Ki 19:2); by Ahab (1Ki 22:27); by Haman (Est 3:8 – 15); by the Edomites (Eze 25:12); by the Philistines (Eze 25:15); by Herodias (Mk 6:19 – 24); by James and John (Lk 9:54); by the chief priests (Ac 5:33); by the Jews (Ac 7:54 – 59; 23:12). See Vengeance.*

Lev	19:18	" 'Do not seek **r** or bear a grudge
Ro	12:19	Do not take **r**, my friends,

REVERE

Lev	19:32	for the elderly and **r** your God.

Dt	4:10	so that they may learn to **r** me
	14:23	to **r** the LORD your God always.
	28:58	and do not **r** this glorious
Job	37:24	Therefore, men **r** him,
Ps	33:8	let all the people of the world **r** him
Ecc	3:14	God does it so that men will **r** him.
Isa	25:3	cities of ruthless nations will **r** you.
Jer	10:7	Who should not **r** you,
Hos	10:3	because we did not **r** the LORD.
Mal	4:2	But for you who **r** my name,

REVERENCE [1593, 3707, 3711, 10167, 2325, 5828, 5832].

For God (Ge 17:3; Ex 3:5; 19:16 – 24; 34:29 – 35; Isa 45:9). For God's house (Lev 19:30; 26:2). For ministers (1Sa 16:4; Ac 28:10; 1Co 16:18; Php 2:29; 1Th 5:12 – 13; 1Ti 5:17; Heb 13:7, 17). For kings (1Sa 24:6; 26:9, 11; 2Sa 1:14; 16:21; Ecc 10:20; 1Pe 2:17). For magistrates (Ex 22:28; 2Pe 2:10; Jude 8). For parents (Ex 20:12; Lev 19:3; Isa 45:10). For the aged (Lev 19:32; Job 32:4 – 7).

Lev	19:30	and have **r** for my sanctuary.
Ne	5:15	of **r** for God I did not act like that.
Da	6:26	people must fear and **r** the God
2Co	7:1	perfecting holiness out of **r** for God
Eph	5:21	to one another out of **r** for Christ.
Col	3:22	of heart and **r** for the Lord.
1Pe	3:2	when they see the purity and **r**
Rev	11:18	and those who **r** your name,

REVERENT

Ecc	8:12	with God-fearing men, who are **r**
Tit	2:3	women to be **r** in the way they live,
Heb	5:7	because of his **r** submission.
1Pe	1:17	as strangers here in **r** fear.

REVIVAL

> **Religious:**
>
> *(Zec 8:20 – 23). Prayer for (Hab 3:2). Prophecies concerning (Isa 32:15; Joel 2:28; Mic 4:1 – 8; Hab 3:2).*

Instances of:

Under Joshua (Jos 5:2 – 9); Samuel (1Sa 7:1 – 6); Elijah (1Ki 18:17 – 40); Jehoash and Jehoiada (2Ki 11 – 12; 2Ch 23 – 24); Hezekiah (2Ki 18:1 – 7; 2Ch 29 – 31); Josiah (2Ki 22 – 23; 2Ch 34 – 35); Asa (2Ch 14:2 – 5; 15:1 – 14); Manasseh (2Ch 33:12 – 19). In Nineveh (Jnh 3:4 – 10). At Pentecost and post-Pentecostal times (Ac 2:1 – 42, 46 – 47; 4:4; 5:14; 6:7; 9:35; 11:20 – 21; 12:24; 14:1; 19:17 – 20).

REWARD [2750, 3877, 5989, 7190, 8510, 8740, 8966, 10454, 625, 3632, 3635]. A word representing at least a dozen different Hebrew and Greek words with similar meanings. In modern English the word means something given in recognition of a good act. In the ERV, however, it generally refers to something given, whether for a good or a bad act (Ps 91:8; Jer 40:5; Mic 7:3; 1Ti 5:18). The rich meaning of the reward of faith as it is promised throughout Scripture can be seen in the beginning of the covenant of grace when God said to Abram: "I am your … very great reward" (Ge 15:1), and in the final chapter of Revelation, when Jesus says, "Behold, I am coming soon! My reward is with me, and I will give to everyone according to what he has done" (Rev 22:12).

A Motive:

To repentance (Lev 26:40 – 45; Isa 1:16 – 20; Ac 26:18); to obedience (Ex 20:6; Lev 25:18 – 19; 26:3 – 13; Dt 4:40; 6:3, 18; 11:13 – 16, 18 – 21, 26 – 29; 27:12 – 26; Jos 8:33; Isa 1:16 – 20; 3:10; Eph 6:1 – 3; Heb 12:28); to faithfulness (Mt 24:45 – 47; 25:14 – 33; Lk 12:42 – 44; 19:12 – 27; 1Co 3:8; Rev 2:10; 22:12); to righteous conduct (Ro 2:10; 1Pe 3:9 – 12); to patience (Heb 10:36); to perseverance (Mt 10:22; 24:13; Mk 13:13; Ro 2:6 – 7; Gal 6:9; Rev 2:17, 25 – 27; 3:5, 11 – 12, 21; 21:7); to honesty (Dt 25:15); to follow Christ (Mt 10:32; 16:24 – 27; 20:1 – 16; 25:34 – 46; Mk 10:21; Lk 12:8; 2Pe 1:10 – 11); to endure persecution (Lk 6:22 – 23; Heb 10:34); to endure tribulation (Rev 2:7, 10; 7:17); to love enemies (Lk 6:35); to deliver the oppressed (Jer 17:24 – 26; 22:3 – 4); to honor parents (Ex 20:12; Eph 6:1 – 3); to honor the Sabbath (Jer 17:24 – 26); to give generously (Dt 15:9 – 11; 24:19); to show kindness to animals (Dt 22:6 – 7).

Ge	15:1	your very great **r**."
1Sa	24:19	May the Lord **r** you well
Ps	19:11	in keeping them there is great **r**.
	62:12	Surely you will **r** each person
	127:3	children a **r** from him.
Pr	9:12	are wise, your wisdom will **r** you;
	11:18	sows righteousness reaps a sure **r**.
	13:21	prosperity is the **r** of the righteous.
	19:17	he will **r** him for what he has done.
	31:31	Give her the **r** she has earned,
Isa	49:4	and my **r** is with my God."
	61:8	In my faithfulness I will **r** them
Jer	17:10	to **r** a man according to his conduct
Mt	5:12	because great is your **r** in heaven,
	6:1	you will have no **r**
	6:5	they have received their **r** in full.
Lk	6:23	because great is your **r** in heaven.
	6:35	Then your **r** will be great,
1Co	3:14	built survives, he will receive his **r**.
Eph	6:8	know that the Lord will **r** everyone
Col	3:24	an inheritance from the Lord as a **r**.
Heb	11:26	he was looking ahead to his **r**.
Rev	22:12	I am coming soon! My **r** is with me

REWARDS

1Sa	26:23	The Lord **r** every man
Pr	12:14	the work of his hands **r** him.
Heb	11:6	that he **r** those who earnestly seek

RICH

Job	34:19	does not favor the **r** over the poor,
Ps	49:16	overawed when a man grows **r**,
	145:8	slow to anger and **r** in love.
Pr	22:2	**R** and poor have this in common:
	23:4	Do not wear yourself out to get **r**;
	28:20	to get **r** will not go unpunished.
	28:22	A stingy man is eager to get **r**

Ecc	5:12	but the abundance of a **r** man
Jer	9:23	or the **r** man boast of his riches,
Mt	19:23	it is hard for a **r** man
Lk	1:53	but has sent the **r** away empty.
	6:24	"But woe to you who are **r**,
	12:21	for himself but is not **r** toward God
	16:1	"There was a **r** man whose
	21:1	Jesus saw the **r** putting their gifts
2Co	6:10	yet making many **r**; having nothing
	8:2	poverty welled up in **r** generosity.
	8:9	he was **r**, yet for your sakes he
	9:11	You will be made **r** in every way
Eph	2:4	love for us, God, who is **r** in mercy,
1Ti	6:9	want to get **r** fall into temptation
	6:17	Command those who are **r**
	6:18	to do good, to be **r** in good deeds,
Jas	1:10	the one who is **r** should take pride
	2:5	the eyes of the world to be **r** in faith
	5:1	you **r** people, weep and wail
Rev	2:9	and your poverty — yet you are **r**!
	3:18	you can become **r**; and white

RICH, THE [238, 419, 2016, 2104, 2657, 2890, 3202, 3702, 3883, 5794, 6938, 6947, 6948, 9045, 4454, 4456, 4457, 4458].

Admonitions to:
(Jer 9:23; 1Ti 6:17 – 19; Jas 1:9 – 11). Not to trust riches for divine favor (Ps 49:16 – 18; Ecc 7:19; Zep 1:18).

Characteristics of:
Wicked (Job 21:7 – 15; Ps 73:3 – 9; Pr 28:8, 20, 22; Jer 5:27 – 28; Lk 12:15 – 21; 16:19 – 31; Jas 2:6 – 7). Immoral (Jer 5:7 – 8). Deluded (Pr 11:28; 13:7; 18:11). Conceited (Pr 28:11). Proud (Ps 73:3, 6, 8 – 9; Eze 28:5). Arrogant (Ps 73:8). Oppressive (Ne 5:1 – 13; Mic 6:10 – 13; Jas 2:6). Cruel to the poor (Pr 18:23). Envied (Ps 73:3 – 22). Hated (Job 27:19, 23). Denounced (Isa 5:8; Jer 17:11; 22:13 – 15; Am 6:1 – 6; Lk 6:24 – 25; Jas 5:1 – 4). Have many friends (Pr 14:20; 19:9). Made so by God (Ecc 5:19 – 20). Difficult to enter the kingdom (Mt 19:24; Mk 10:17 – 27; Lk 18:24 – 25). Unscrupulous meth-

ods of (Jer 5:26 – 28). Discrimination in favor of, forbidden in the church (Jas 2:1 – 9). Divine judgments against (Job 27:13 – 23; Pss 52:1 – 7; 73:18 – 20).

Examples of:
Abraham (Ge 13:2; 24:35); Isaac (Ge 26:12 – 14); Solomon (1Ki 10:23; 2Ch 9:22); Jehoshaphat (2Ch 18:1); Hezekiah (2Ki 20:12 – 13); Job (Job 1:3; 31:24 – 25, 28); Joseph of Arimathea (Mt 27:57); Zacchaeus (Lk 19:2). See Riches.

RICHES [238, 2104, 2657, 2776, 2890, 3702, 3883, 4759, 5794, 6217, 6948, 8214, 3353, 4458] (1Sa 2:7; Pss 37:16; 52:7; Pr 11:4; 14:24; 15:6, 16 – 17; 16:8; 19:4; Ecc 4:8; 5:11 – 14; 6:1 – 2; 7:11 – 12; 10:19; Isa 5:8; Jer 48:36).

Delusive (Pr 11:28; Lk 12:16 – 21). Unstable (Pr 23:5; 27:24). Unsatisfying to the covetous (Ecc 5:10 – 12). A snare (Dt 6:10 – 12; 8:7 – 17; 31:20; 32:15; Pr 30:8 – 9; Jer 5:7 – 8; Hos 12:8; Mt 13:22; 19:16 – 24; Mk 4:19; 10:17 – 25; Lk 16:19 – 26; 18:18 – 25; 1Ti 6:9 – 11, 17). Worthless in the day of calamity (Eze 7:17, 19; Zep 1:18). Fraudulently gotten, unprofitable (Pr 10:2; 21:6; 28:8; Jer 17:11). Admonitions against the desire for (Pr 23:4; 28:20, 22; 1Ti 6:9 – 11, 17). The heart not to be set upon (Ps 62:10; Mt 6:19 – 21). Liberality with (Pr 13:7 – 8). Benevolent use of, required (1Jn 3:17). Figurative (Rev 3:17 – 18).

Job	36:18	that no one entices you by **r**;
Ps	49:6	and boast of their great **r**?
	119:14	as one rejoices in great **r**.
Pr	3:16	in her left hand are **r** and honor.
	11:28	Whoever trusts in his **r** will fall,
	22:1	is more desirable than great **r**;
	27:24	for **r** do not endure forever,
	30:8	give me neither poverty nor **r**,
Lk	8:14	**r** and pleasures, and they do not
Ro	9:23	to make the **r** of his glory known
	11:33	the depth of the **r** of the wisdom

Eph	2:7	he might show the incomparable **r**
Col	1:27	among the Gentiles the glorious **r**
	2:2	so that they may have the full **r**

RIGHT

Ge	4:7	But if you do not do what is **r**,
	18:19	of the LORD by doing what is **r**
Ex	15:26	and do what is **r** in his eyes,
Dt	6:18	Do what is **r** and good
Jos	1:7	do not turn from it to the **r**
Ne	9:13	and laws that are just and **r**,
Ps	16:8	Because he is at my **r** hand,
	18:35	and your **r** hand sustains me;
	25:9	He guides the humble in what is **r**
	33:4	For the word of the LORD is **r**
	119:144	Your statutes are forever **r**;
	137:5	may my **r** hand forget its skill.
Pr	1:3	doing what is **r** and just and fair;
	14:12	There is a way that seems **r**
	18:17	The first to present his case seems **r**
Ecc	7:20	who does what is **r** and never sins.
Isa	1:17	learn to do **r**!
	7:15	reject the wrong and choose the **r**.
	30:10	us no more visions of what is **r**!
	41:10	you with my righteous **r** hand.
Jer	23:5	and do what is just and **r** in the land
Eze	18:5	who does what is just and **r**.
Hos	14:9	The ways of the LORD are **r**;
Mt	5:29	If your **r** eye causes you to sin,
	6:3	know what your **r** hand is doing,
	25:33	He will put the sheep on his **r**
Jn	1:12	he gave the **r** to become children
Ac	7:55	Jesus standing at the **r** hand of God
Ro	9:21	Does not the potter have the **r**
2Co	8:21	we are taking pains to do what is **r**,
Eph	1:20	and seated him at his **r** hand
Php	4:8	whatever is **r**, whatever is pure,
2Th	3:13	never tire of doing what is **r**.
Heb	1:3	down at the **r** hand of the Majesty
Jas	2:8	as yourself," you are doing **r**.
1Pe	3:14	if you should suffer for what is **r**,
1Jn	2:29	who does what is **r** has been born
Rev	2:7	I will give the **r** to eat from the tree

| | 22:11 | let him who does **r** continue to do **r** |

RIGHTEOUS [3838, 7404, 7405, 7406, 7407, 9448, 1464, 1465, 1466, 1467, 1468, 1469].

Compared with:
The sun (Jdg 5:31; Mt 13:43); stars (Da 12:3); lights (Mt 5:14; Php 2:15). Mount Zion (Ps 125:1 – 2); Lebanon (Hos 14:5 – 7). Treasure (Ex 19:5; Ps 135:4); treasured possession (Mal 3:17). Gold (Job 23:10; La 4:2); vessels of gold and silver (2Ti 2:20); stones of a crown (Zec 9:16); living stones (1Pe 2:5). Babies (Mt 11:25; 1Pe 2:2); little children (Mt 18:3; 1Co 14:20); obedient children (1Pe 1:14); members of the body (1Co 12:20, 27); soldiers (2Ti 2:3 – 4); runners in a race (1Co 9:24; Heb 12:1); wrestlers (2Ti 2:5); good servants (Mt 25:21); strangers and pilgrims (1Pe 2:11). Sheep (Ps 78:52; Mt 25:33; Jn 10); lambs (Isa 40:11; Jn 21:15); calves of the stall (Mal 4:2); lions (Pr 28:1; Mic 5:8); eagles (Ps 103:5; Isa 40:31); doves (Ps 68:13; Isa 60:8); thirsty deer (Ps 42:1); good fish (Mt 13:48). Dew and showers (Mic 5:7); watered gardens (Isa 58:11); unfailing springs (Isa 58:11); vines (SS 6:11; Hos 14:7); branches of a vine (Jn 15:2, 4 – 5); pomegranates (SS 4:13); good figs (Jer 24:2 – 7); lilies (SS 2:2; Hos 14:5); poplars by flowing streams (Isa 44:4); trees planted by rivers (Ps 1:3); cedars in Lebanon (Ps 92:12); palm trees (Ps 92:12); green olive trees (Ps 52:8; Hos 14:6); fruitful trees (Ps 1:3; Jer 17:8); grain (Hos 14:7); wheat (Mt 3:12; 13:29 – 30). Salt (Mt 5:13).

Relation to God:
(Lev 20:24 – 26). Access to God (Ps 31:19 – 20; Isa 12:6). Few (Mt 7:14; 22:14). Circumstances of righteous and wicked contrasted (Job 8; Ps 17:14 – 15).

Contrasted with the Wicked:
(Pss 1:1 – 6; 11:5; 17:14 – 15; 32:10; 37:17 – 22, 37 – 38; 73:1 – 28; 75:10; 91:7 – 8; Pr 2:21 – 22; 3:32 – 33; 4:16 – 19; 10:3, 6, 9, 11, 16, 20 – 21,

23 – 25, 28 – 32; 11:3, 5 – 6, 8 – 11, 18 – 21, 23, 31; 12:3, 5 – 7, 10, 12 – 13, 21, 26; 13:5 – 6, 9, 17, 21 – 22, 25; 14:2, 11, 19, 22 – 32; 15:6, 8 – 9, 28 – 29; 22:5, 8 – 9; 24:16; 28:1, 4 – 5, 13 – 14, 18; 29:2, 6 – 7, 27; Isa 32:1 – 8; 65:13 – 14; Ro 2:7 – 10; Eph 2:12 – 14; Php 2:15; 1Th 5:5 – 8; Tit 1:15; 1Pe 4:17 – 18; 1Jn 3:3 – 17).

Described:

(Pss 1:1 – 3; 15:1 – 5; 24:3 – 5; 37:26, 30 – 31; 84:7; 112:1 – 10; 119:1 – 3; Isa 33:15 – 16; 51:1; 62:12; 63:8; Jer 17:7 – 8; 31:12 – 14, 33 – 34; Eze 18:5 – 9; Zec 3:2, 7 – 8). Dead to sin (Ro 6:2, 11; Col 3:3). Freed from sin (Ro 6:7, 18, 22; 1Jn 3:6, 9). Good (Lk 6:45). Pure (Mt 5:8; 1Jn 3:3; 2Ti 2:21 – 22). Holy (Dt 7:6; Eph 1:4; 4:24; Col 1:22; 3:12; 2Ti 2:19; Heb 3:1; 1Pe 1:15). Sanctified (1Co 1:2; 6:11). Godly (Ps 4:3; 2Pe 2:9). Wise (Ps 37:30; Pr 2:9 – 12). Faithful (Mt 24:45; 25:21, 23; Lk 19:17; Eph 1:1; Col 1:2; Rev 17:14). Merciful (Mt 5:7). Meek (Mt 5:5; 2Ti 2:25). Industrious (Eph 4:28; 2Jn 9). Stable (Mt 7:24 – 27; Eph 4:14). Saved (Ac 2:47). Saints (Ro 1:7; 1Co 1:2; Eph 1:1). Chosen (1Pe 2:9; Rev 17:14). Spotless (Jas 1:27). Separate (Ex 33:16). Obedient (Mt 12:50; Jn 15:14; 1Jn 2:3, 5). New creature (2Co 5:17; Eph 2:10; 4:23 – 24; Col 3:9 – 10). Spiritually minded (Ro 8:4, 6). Patient, long-suffering, joyful (Col 1:11; 1Th 1:3). Peaceful, meek, gentle, patient (2Ti 2:21 – 25). Blameless, harmless, and without blemish (Eph 1:4; Php 2:15). Kind, tenderhearted, forgiving (Eph 4:32). Servants of Christ (Eph 6:6). Servants of righteousness (Ro 6:19). Children of light (1Th 5:5). Children of God (Ro 8:14, 16; 1Jn 3:2). Temple of God (2Co 6:16). Beloved of God (Ro 1:7). Poor in spirit (Mt 5:3). Hungering and thirsting after righteousness (Mt 5:6). Growing in grace (Ps 84:7; Eph 4:13). Imitators of Christ (1Pe 4:1 – 2; 1Jn 2:6). Salt of the earth (Mt 5:13). City set on a hill (Mt 5:14). Led by the Spirit (Ro 8:14; Gal 5:18). Filled with goodness and knowledge (Ro 15:14; Col 1:9 – 13). Grounded in love (Eph 3:17). Following Christ (Mt 10:38; 16:24; Mk 8:34; Lk 9:23).

Rooted in Christ (Col 2:7). Hating falsehood (Pr 13:5). Abhorring wickedness (Ps 101:3 – 4). Having renounced dishonesty (2Co 4:2). Without bitterness, wrath, anger, clamor, evil speaking, malice (Eph 4:31). Grieved by wickedness of the wicked (Ps 119:158; Ac 17:16; 2Pe 2:7 – 8).

Happiness of:

(Job 5:17 – 27; Pr 3:13 – 18; 16:20; Mt 4:3 – 12). Satisfying (Pss 36:8; 63:5). Under fiery trials (1Pe 4:12 – 13). Under persecution (Mt 5:10 – 12).

Promises to and Comfort of:

Deliverance from temptation (1Co 10:13; 2Pe 2:9). Deliverance from trouble (Job 5:19 – 24; Pss 34:15, 17; 50:15; 91:15; 97:10 – 11; Pr 3:25 – 26; Isa 41:10 – 13; 43:2). Refuge in adversity (Pss 33:18 – 19; 62:8; 91:1 – 15; Pr 14:26; Na 1:7). Strength in adversity (Ps 29:11). Security (Ps 32:6 – 7; 84:11; 121:3 – 8; Isa 33:16). Providential care (Ge 15:1; Ex 23:22; Lev 26:5 – 6, 10; Dt 33:27; 1Sa 2:9; 2Ch 16:9; Ezr 8:22; Job 5:15; Pss 34:9 – 10; 125:1 – 3; 145:19 – 20; Pr 1:33; 2:7; 3:6; 10:3; 16:7; Isa 49:9 – 11; 65:13 – 14; Eze 34:11 – 17, 22 – 31; Lk 12:7, 32; 21:18; 1Pe 5:7). Overruling providence (Ro 8:28; 2Co 4:17). Answer to prayer (Pr 15:29; Mk 11:23 – 24; Jn 14:13 – 14; Ac 10:4; 1Pe 3:12; 1Jn 3:22). Temporal blessings (Lev 25:18 – 19; 26:5; Dt 28:1 – 13; Pss 37:9; 128:1 – 6; Pr 2:21; 3:1 – 4, 7 – 10; Mt 6:26 – 33; Mk 10:30; Lk 18:29 – 30). Blessings on their children (Pss 103:17; 112:2 – 3).

Righteous Receive: Comfort in tribulation (Isa 25:8; 66:13 – 14; Mt 5:4; Jn 14:16 – 18; Rev 21:4). Joy (Isa 35:10; 51:11). Spiritual enlightenment (Isa 2:3; Jn 8:12). Peace (Isa 26:3; Ro 2:10). Seeing God (Mt 5:8). Inconceivable spiritual blessings (Isa 64:4; 1Co 2:9). The rest of faith (Heb 4:9). Wisdom (Jas 1:5). Divine help (Ps 55:22; Isa 41:10 – 13; Heb 13:5 – 6). Divine guidance (Pss 25:12; 32:8; 37:23 – 24; 48:14; 73:24; Pr 3:5 – 6). Divine mercy (Pss 32:10; 103:17 – 18; Mal 3:17). Divine presence (Ge 26:3, 24; 28:15; 31:3; Ex 33:14; Dt 31:6, 8; Jos 1:5; 1Ki 6:13; Hag 1:13; 2:4 – 5; Mt 28:20; Jn 14:17, 23; 2Co 6:16; 13:11; Php 4:9; Heb 13:5; Jas 4:8; Rev

21:3). Divine likeness (1Jn 3:2). Ministry of angels (Heb 1:14). Dwelling with Christ (Jn 14:2–3; Col 3:4; 1Th 4:17; 5:10). Everlasting remembrance (Ps 112:6). Names written in heaven (Lk 10:20). Resurrection (Jn 5:29; 1Co 15:48–57; 2Co 4:14; 1Th 4:16). Future glory (Ro 8:18; Col 3:4; 2Ti 2:10; 1Pe 5:4). Inheritance (Mt 25:34; Ac 20:32; 26:18; Col 1:12; 3:24; Tit 3:7; Heb 9:15; Jas 2:5; 1Pe 1:4). Heavenly reward (Mt 5:12; 13:43; 2Ti 4:8; Heb 11:16; Jas 1:12; 2Pe 1:11; Rev 2:7, 10; 22:5, 12, 14). Eternal life (Da 12:2–3; Mt 19:29; 25:46; Mk 10:29–30; Lk 18:29–30; Jn 3:15–18, 36; 4:14; 5:24, 29; 6:39–40; 10:28; 12:25–26; Ro 2:7; 6:22–23; Gal 6:8; 1Th 4:15–17; 1Ti 1:16; 4:8; Tit 1:2; 1Jn 2:25; 5:13; Rev 7:14–17). Contingent upon perseverance (Heb 10:36; Rev 2:7, 10–11, 17, 26–28; 3:4–5, 10, 12, 21; 21:7).

Union of:

With God (1Jn 3:24; 4:13, 15–16; 2Jn 9). With Christ (Jn 6:51–58; 14:20; 15:1–11; 17:21–23, 26; Ro 8:1; 12:5; 1Co 6:13–20; 10:16; 2Co 13:5; Gal 2:20; Col 1:27; 2:6–7; 1Jn 2:6, 24, 28; 3:6, 24; 5:12, 20; 2Jn 9).

Ge	6:9	Noah was a **r** man, blameless
Nu	23:10	Let me die the death of the **r**,
Ne	9:8	your promise because you are **r**.
Job	36:7	He does not take his eyes off the **r**;
Ps	1:5	nor sinners in the assembly of the **r**.
	5:12	O LORD, you bless the **r**;
	11:7	For the LORD is **r**,
	34:15	The eyes of the LORD are on the **r**
	37:16	Better the little that the **r** have
	37:21	but the **r** give generously;
	37:25	yet I have never seen the **r** forsaken
	55:22	he will never let the **r** fall.
	119:7	as I learn your **r** laws.
	143:2	for no one living is **r** before you.
Pr	3:33	but he blesses the home of the **r**.
	10:7	of the **r** will be a blessing,
	10:16	The wages of the **r** bring them life,
	10:24	what the **r** desire will be granted.
	13:9	The light of the **r** shines brightly,

	15:29	but he hears the prayer of the **r**.
	16:31	it is attained by a **r** life.
	20:7	The **r** man leads a blameless life;
	23:24	The father of a **r** man has great joy;
	29:7	The **r** care about justice
	29:27	The **r** detest the dishonest;
Ecc	7:20	There is not a **r** man on earth
Isa	26:7	The path of the **r** is level;
	41:10	you with my **r** right hand.
	53:11	his knowledge my **r** servant will
	64:6	and all our **r** acts are like filthy rags
Hab	2:4	but the **r** will live by his faith—
Mal	3:18	see the distinction between the **r**
Mt	5:45	rain on the **r** and the unrighteous.
	9:13	For I have not come to call the **r**,
	13:49	and separate the wicked from the **r**
	25:46	to eternal punishment, but the **r**
Ac	24:15	will be a resurrection of both the **r**
Ro	2:5	when his **r** judgment will be
	2:13	the law who will be declared **r**.
	3:10	"There is no one **r**, not even one;
	5:19	one man the many will be made **r**.
Gal	3:11	because, "The **r** will live by faith."
1Ti	1:9	that law is made not for the **r**
Tit	3:5	because of **r** things we had done,
Jas	5:16	The prayer of a **r** man is powerful
1Pe	3:12	the eyes of the Lord are on the **r**
	3:18	the **r** for the unrighteous,
1Jn	2:1	defense—Jesus Christ, the **R** One.
	3:7	does what is right is **r**, just as he is **r**.
Rev	19:8	stands for the **r** acts of the saints.)

RIGHTEOUSNESS [7404, 7405, 7406, 7407, 1465, 1466, 1468, 2319] (Heb. *sadîq, saddîq*, Gr. *dikaiosynē*). The Lord God always acts in righteousness (Ps 89:4; Jer 9:24). That is, he always has a right relationship with people, and his action is to maintain that relationship. As regards Israel, God's righteousness involved treating the people according to the terms of the covenant that he had graciously made with them. This involved acting both in judgment (chastisement) and in deliverance (Pss 68; 103:6; La 1:18). The latter activity is often therefore equated with salvation (see Isa 46:12 – 13; 51:5). The picture behind the word "righteousness" is from the law court (forensic). This comes to the surface in passages from the Prophets (e.g., Isa 1:2 – 9; Jer 2:4 – 13; Mic 6:1 – 8); there the Lord is presented as the Judge, and Israel as the accused party, with the covenant supplying the terms of reference.

As God acts in righteousness (because he is righteous), so he called Israel to be righteous as his chosen people. They were placed in his covenant, in right relationship with him through faith (Ge 15:6; Hab 2:4), and were expected to live in right relationship with others. So we see that righteousness begins as a forensic term but easily becomes an ethical term in the OT. Much the same is found in the NT.

In the teaching of Jesus, righteousness means a right relationship with God (see the parable of the Pharisee and tax collector, Lk 18:14), as well as the quality of life that involved a right relationship both with God and one's fellow human beings (Mt 5:6, 17 – 20). But it is Paul who uses the word to the greatest effect in the NT with his creation of the doctrine of justification by faith (that is, being placed by God in a right relationship with himself in and through Christ by faith). His great statement is found in Ro 1:16 – 17. The gospel is the power of God for salvation because "a righteousness from God is revealed, a righteousness that is by faith from first to last." That is, the gospel is effective because, along with the proclamation, a righteousness goes forth — a righteousness that God delights to see and accept. This righteousness is the provision of a right relationship with himself through the saving work of Jesus, substitute and representative Man. To receive this gift of righteousness is to be justified by faith. And those who receive the gift then are to live as righteous people, devoted to the service of what God declares to be right.

Required:

(Isa 28:17; Hos 10:12; Mic 6:8; Zec 7:9 – 10; 8:16 – 17; Mal 3:3; Mt 5:20; 23:23; Lk 3:10 – 14; 13:6 – 9; Ro 6:19 – 22; 7:4 – 6; 8:4; 14:17 – 19; 2Ti 2:22; 1Jn 3:10). Commanded in official administration (Jer 22:3, 6).

Imputed:

On account of obedience (Ps 106:31; Eze 18:9; Rev 6:25); on account of faith (Ge 15:6; Ro 4:3, 5, 9, 11, 13, 20, 22, 24; Gal 3:6; Jas 2:23). Proof of regeneration (1Jn 2:29). Exalts a nation (Pr 14:34). Safeguards life (Pr 10:2, 16; 11:19; 12:28; 13:6). Winning others to, rewarded (Da 12:3).

Fruits of:

(Ps 1:3; Mt 7:16 – 18; 12:35; Lk 6:43; Jn 15:4 – 8; 2Co 9:10; Gal 5:22 – 23; Php 1:11; Col 3:12 – 15; 1Th 1:3; Tit 2:2 – 6, 11 – 12; 1Pe 3:8 – 14; 2Pe 1:5 – 8; 1Jn 3:7). Generosity (Ac 11:29). Peace (Isa 32:17; Jas 3:8).

Symbolized:

(Eze 47:12; Rev 22:2). Figuratively described as a garment (Job 29:14; Isa 61:10; Zec 3:4; Mt 22:11 – 14; Rev 6:11; 7:9; 19:8).

Ge	15:6	and he credited it to him as **r**.
1Sa	26:23	LORD rewards every man for his **r**
1Ki	10:9	to maintain justice and **r**."
Ps	7:17	to the LORD because of his **r**
	9:8	He will judge the world in **r**;
	23:3	He guides me in paths of **r**
	33:5	The LORD loves **r** and justice;
	45:7	You love **r** and hate wickedness;
	71:19	Your **r** reaches to the skies, O God,
	89:14	**R** and justice are the foundation
	96:13	He will judge the world in **r**
	106:31	This was credited to him as **r**
	145:7	and joyfully sing of your **r**.
Pr	11:18	he who sows **r** reaps a sure reward.
	13:6	**R** guards the man of integrity,
	14:34	**R** exalts a nation,
	16:8	Better a little with **r**
	16:12	a throne is established through **r**.
	21:21	He who pursues **r** and love
Isa	5:16	will show himself holy by his **r**.
	11:4	but with **r** he will judge the needy,
	32:17	The fruit of **r** will be peace;
	51:6	my **r** will never fail.
	59:17	He put on **r** as his breastplate,
	61:10	and arrayed me in a robe of **r**,

Jer	9:24	justice and **r** on earth,
	23:6	The LORD Our **R**.
Eze	3:20	a righteous man turns from his **r**
	14:20	save only themselves by their **r**.
	33:12	**r** of the righteous man will not save
Da	9:24	to bring in everlasting **r**,
	12:3	and those who lead many to **r**,
Hos	10:12	Sow for yourselves **r**,
Mic	7:9	I will see his **r**.
Zep	2:3	Seek **r**, seek humility;
Mal	4:2	the sun of **r** will rise with healing
Mt	5:6	those who hunger and thirst for **r**,
	5:10	who are persecuted because of **r**,
	5:20	unless your **r** surpasses that
	6:1	to do your 'acts of **r**' before men,
	6:33	But seek first his kingdom and his **r**
Jn	16:8	world of guilt in regard to sin and **r**
Ro	3:5	brings out God's **r** more clearly,
	4:9	faith was credited to him as **r**.
	5:18	of **r** was justification that brings life
	6:13	body to him as instruments of **r**.
	6:16	or to obedience, which leads to **r**?
	6:19	in slavery to **r** leading to holiness.
	9:30	did not pursue **r**, have obtained it,
	14:17	but of **r**, peace and joy
1Co	1:30	our **r**, holiness and redemption.
2Co	5:21	that in him we might become the **r**
	6:7	with weapons of **r** in the right hand
	6:14	For what do **r** and wickedness have
Gal	2:21	for if **r** could be gained
Eph	4:24	created to be like God in true **r**
	6:14	with the breastplate of **r** in place,
Php	3:6	as for legalistic **r**, faultless.
	3:9	not having a **r** of my own that
2Ti	3:16	correcting and training in **r**,
	4:8	is in store for me the crown of **r**,
Heb	5:13	with the teaching about **r**.
	12:11	it produces a harvest of **r**
Jas	2:23	and it was credited to him as **r**,"
	3:18	sow in peace raise a harvest of **r**.
1Pe	2:24	die to sins and live for **r**;
2Pe	2:21	not to have known the way of **r**,
	3:13	and a new earth, the home of **r**.

RISE

Nu	24:17	a scepter will **r** out of Israel.
Isa	26:19	their bodies will **r**.
Mal	4:2	of righteousness will **r** with healing
Mt	27:63	'After three days I will **r** again.'
Lk	18:33	On the third day he will **r** again."
Jn	5:29	those who have done good will **r**
	20:9	had to **r** from the dead.)
Ac	17:3	had to suffer and **r** from the dead.
1Th	4:16	and the dead in Christ will **r** first.

RISEN

Mt	28:6	He is not here; he has **r**, just
Mk	16:6	He has **r**! He is not here.
Lk	24:34	The Lord has **r** and has appeared

ROCK [74, 1643, 2734, 4091, 6152, 7446, 10006, 3292, 4376, 5536+5550] (Heb. *sela'*, *a cliff* or *mass of stone*, *tsûr*, *a crag*, Gr. *petra*, any *stone*). The rock in Horeb that Moses was to strike was *tsûr* (Ex 17:6); the one he was to speak to in Kadesh was *sela'* (Nu 20:8). A *sela'* was often a natural fortress, as at Rimmon (Jdg 20:45, 47). Sometimes it was a mountain (1Sa 23:25 – 26). *Tsûr* in Nu 23:9 means a craggy height. Both terms are used to refer to God: the Lord is my rock (2Sa 22:2), my *sela'* and fortress (Pss 18:2; 71:3). In comparing God with other gods, Scripture says their *tsûr* is not like our Rock (Dt 32:31; see also Pss 61:2; 62:2; 95:1). The NT use of *petra* was both literal and figurative. Building on *petra* gave security to a house (Mt 7:24 – 25). The Lord's burial place had been cut into a *petra* (Mk 15:46). Jesus made a distinction between Simon the *petros* and the basic truth (*petra*) in Peter's confession, the truth on which the *ekklesia* was to be built (Mt 16:18). Believers are living stones being built into a spiritual house (1Pe 2:5).

General References to:
Struck by Moses for water (Dt 8:15; Ps 78:15 – 16, 20). Houses in (Jer 49:16; Ob 3; Mt 7:24 – 25). Oil from (Job 29:6; Dt 32:13). Name of God (Dt 32:4). Figurative (2Sa 22:32, 47; 23:3;

Pss 18:2; 31:2; 40:2; Isa 17:10; 32:2; Mt 16:18; 1Co 10:4).

Ge	49:24	of the Shepherd, the **R** of Israel,
Ex	17:6	Strike the **r**, and water will come
Nu	20:8	Speak to that **r** before their eyes
Dt	32:4	He is the **R**, his works are perfect,
Ps	18:2	The LORD is my **r**, my fortress
	19:14	O LORD, my **R** and my Redeemer
Isa	51:1	to the **r** from which you were cut
Mt	7:24	man who built his house on the **r**.
	16:18	and on this **r** I will build my church
Ro	9:33	and a **r** that makes them fall,
1Co	10:4	the spiritual **r** that accompanied
1Pe	2:8	and a **r** that makes them fall."

ROD [2643, 4751, 4962, 7866, 8657, 2812, 4811] (Heb. *maqqēl, matteh, shēvet*, Gr. *rhabdos*). Branch, stick, staff; symbol of authority (Ex 4:2, 17, 20; 9:23; 14:16); discipline symbolized by rod (Mic 5:1); messianic ruler (Isa 11:1); affliction (Job 9:34).

2Sa	7:14	I will punish him with the **r** of men,
Ps	23:4	your **r** and your staff,
Pr	13:24	He who spares the **r** hates his son,
	22:15	the **r** of discipline will drive it far
	23:13	if you punish him with the **r**,
	29:15	**r** of correction imparts wisdom,
Isa	11:4	the earth with the **r** of his mouth;

ROMAN EMPIRE City of Rome founded in 753 BC; a monarchy until 509 BC; a republic from 509 to 31 BC; the empire began in 31 BC, fell in the fifth century AD. Rome extended its hold over all Italy and eventually over the whole Mediterranean world, Gaul, half of Britain, the Rhine and Danube rivers, and as far as Parthia. Augustus, the first Roman emperor, divided the Roman provinces into senatorial districts, which were ruled by proconsuls (Ac 13:7; 18:12; 19:38), and imperial districts ruled by governors (Mt 27:2; Lk 2:2; Ac 23:24). Moral corruption was among the causes of the decline and fall of the Roman Empire. Roman reservoirs, aqueducts, roads, public buildings, and statues survive. Many Roman officials are referred to in the NT, including the emperors Augustus (Lk 2:1), Tiberius (Lk 3:1), Claudius (Ac 11:28), and Nero (Ac 25:11 – 12).

ROMANS, LETTER TO THE The genuineness of the letter has never been seriously questioned by competent critics familiar with first-century history. Although other NT letters have been wrongly attacked as forgeries not written by the alleged authors, this letter stands with Galatians and 1 and 2 Corinthians as one of the unassailable documents of early church history.

There can be no doubt that the author, Paul, formerly Saul of Tarsus (Ac 13:9), was a highly intellectual, rabbinically educated Jew (Ac 22:3; Gal 1:14) who had been intensely hostile to the Christian movement and had sought to destroy it (Ac 8:1 – 3; 9:1 – 2; 1Co 15:9; Gal 1:13). Even the critics who reject the supernatural cannot deny the extraordinary nature of the fact that this able enemy became the greatest exponent of the Christian faith and wrote the most powerful statements of Christian doctrine. The accounts of his conversion are given in Ac 9:3 – 19; 22:1 – 16; 26:9 – 18, and the event is alluded to in his writings (1Co 15:8 – 10; Gal 1:15).

THE TIME OF WRITING.

This cannot be discussed here in detail. Suffice it to say that the letter clearly places itself in the three-month period (Ac 20:3) that Paul spent in Corinth just before going to Jerusalem. According to the best authorities in NT chronology, this three-month period was about December AD 56 to February 57.

THE REASON FOR WRITING.

It is not difficult to know why this epistle was written. In the first place, Paul was emphatic in his claim to be "the apostle of the Gentiles" (Ro 11:13; 15:16; see also Ac 9:15; 22:15 – 21; 26:17 – 20, 23; Gal 2:7 – 9; Eph 3:2 – 8), and Rome was the capital of the Gentile world. Paul was a Roman citizen, and a visit to Rome was consistent with his regular mode of operation. He established churches in strategic centers and worked in major cities, though in Rome a church already existed. Paul planned on contributing to their spiritual welfare (Ro 1:11 – 13) while on his way to evangelize Spain (15:24). There was a great theological reason for the writing of this letter, a problem that had demanded the letter to the Galatians at an earlier juncture in Paul's ministry. It concerned the relation of (1) the OT Scriptures, (2) contemporaneous Pharisaic Judaism, and (3) the gospel implemented by the earthly work of Christ. It had been difficult for Peter to orient himself to the new day (Gal 2:6 – 14ff.), but he had made the transition (Ac 15:7 – 12; see also 2Pe 3:15 – 16). We may well marvel at Peter's humility and true vision when, in calling Paul's letters "scripture," he certainly included Galatians, in which his own short-sightedness is recalled.

Outline:

I. The Apostle Paul to the Christians in Rome.
II. The World Is Lost.
   A. The Gentile world is wretchedly lost (1:18 – 32) in spite of attempted morality (2:1 – 16).
   B. The Jewish world is equally lost, in spite of all their privileges (2:17 – 3:20).
III. Justification by Faith Is My Great Message (3:21 – 5:21).
IV. Holy Living in Principle (6:1 – 8:39).
V. God Has Not Forgotten the Jews (9:1 – 11:36).
VI. Details of Christian Conduct (12:1 – 15:13).
VII. Miscellaneous Notes.

ROME Of the Indo-European tribes who entered Italy, the Latins formed a separate branch, occupying an enclave round the mouth of the Tiber and the Latium Plain. In population the city of Rome probably passed the million mark at the beginning of the Christian era, and during the first century may have risen somewhat above this figure. It was a motley and cosmopolitan population. Early in the second century, Juvenal counted the foreign rabble as one of the chief annoyances of urban life, to be ranked with traffic dangers, fire, and falling houses.

In the third and fourth centuries, a time of urban decay all over the empire, the city declined, and the population probably fell to something near half a million by the last days of the western empire.

It is possible to roughly estimate the proportion of Christians over the imperial centuries. In the catacombs, ten generations of Christians are buried. The most conservative estimate from the evidence of the catacomb burials is that at least one-fifth were Christians, but probably the proportion was much larger. Estimates range from 175,000 to 400,000 Christians per generation on average.

Rome, like Babylon, became a symbol of organized paganism and opposition to Christianity in the Bible. In the lurid imagery of Revelation, John mingles empire and city in his symbolism of sin. Chapters 17 and 18 of the Apocalypse envisage the fall of Rome. Chapter 17, passionate, indeed shocking, in its imagery, shows Rome like a woman of sin astride the seven hills, polluting the world with her vice. The second of the two chapters reads like a Hebrew "taunt-song." It pictures, in imagery reminiscent of Ezekiel on Tyre, the galleys loading for Rome in some Eastern port. There were "cargoes of gold, silver, precious stones, and pearls; fine linen, purple, silk and scarlet cloth,… ivory, costly wood, bronze, iron and marble,… cinnamon and spice,… cattle and sheep; horses and carriages; and bodies and souls of men." The climax is bitter, as John pictures Rome under the smoke of her burning, the voice of gladness stilled.

The city appears several times in a historical context, the most notable being Paul's enforced stay there. Paul landed at Puteoli and, alerted by the little church there (Ac 28:14 – 15), members of Rome's Christian community met Paul at two stopping places. On the evidence of the Nazareth Decree, it appears that a group of believers had been established in Rome since the principate of Claudius in the late forties of the first century. Paul probably entered Rome by the Capena Gate. His "rented house" (28:30) would be in some block of flats, an "insula."

ROSETTA STONE A damaged inscribed basalt slab, found accidentally at Fort St. Julien on the Rosetta branch of the Nile, near the city of Rosetta, by a French army work crew in AD 1799. Terms of the French surrender to the British gave the French finds to the victors, and the Rosetta Stone was placed in the British Museum. The monument was originally set up in 196 BC as a formal decree of the Egyptian priesthood in honor of Ptolemy V (Epiphanes) with an identical text in three parts: hieroglyphic, demotic, and Greek. The parallel texts furnished the key for the decipherment of the Egyptian, with the proper names providing the basic clues for the achievement. Decipherment of the hieroglyphs was accomplished by Jean François Champollion in 1822.

RULE

Ge	1:26	let them **r** over the fish of the sea
	3:16	and he will **r** over you."
1Sa	12:12	'No, we want a king to **r** over us' —
Ps	2:9	You will **r** them with an iron
	67:4	for you **r** the peoples justly
	119:133	let no sin **r** over me.
Isa	28:10	**r** on **r**, **r** on **r**;
Zec	6:13	and will sit and **r** on his throne.
	9:10	His **r** will extend from sea to sea
Ro	13:9	are summed up in this one **r**:
Eph	1:21	far above all **r** and authority,
Col	3:15	the peace of Christ **r** in your hearts,
Rev	2:27	He will **r** them with an iron scepter;
	12:5	who will **r** all the nations
	19:15	He will **r** them with an iron scepter

RULER

Ps	8:6	You made him **r** over the works
Pr	29:26	Many seek an audience with a **r**,
Isa	60:17	and righteousness your **r**.
Da	9:25	the **r**, comes, there will be seven
Mic	5:2	one who will be **r** over Israel,
Mt	2:6	for out of you will come a **r**
Eph	2:2	of the **r** of the kingdom of the air,
1Ti	6:15	God, the blessed and only **R**,
Rev	1:5	and the **r** of the kings of the earth.

RUN

Ps	19:5	champion rejoicing to **r** his course.
Pr	4:12	when you **r**, you will not stumble.
	18:10	the righteous **r** to it and are safe.
Isa	10:3	To whom will you **r** for help?
	40:31	they will **r** and not grow weary,
1Co	9:24	**R** in such a way as to get the prize.
Gal	2:2	that I was running or had **r** my race
Php	2:16	on the day of Christ that I did not **r**
Heb	12:1	let us **r** with perseverance the race

RUTH [8134, 4858] (*friendship* BDB; *refreshed [as with water]* IDB; possibly *comrade, companion* ISBE). A Moabitess who married a son of Elimelech and Naomi of Bethlehem (Ru 1:1 – 4); ancestor of Christ (Mt 1:5). The book of Ruth is about her.

RUTH, BOOK OF The author of this book is unknown. The historical setting is the period of the judges (Ru 1:1), but there are certain indications that it was composed, or at least worked into its final form, at a much later time. For example, the opening words, "In the days when the judges ruled" looks back to that period; the gloss in 4:7 explains an ancient custom for later readers; and 4:22 mentions David. Thus the final editorial process could not have ended before the time of David. It is best to place its final shaping in, or immediately following, the reign of David.

The book records the circumstances that led to the marriage of Ruth, a Moabitess, to Boaz, an Israelite. A famine forced Naomi and her husband to move to Moab, where her sons married Moabite women, one of whom was Ruth. Naomi and her daughter-in-law became widows, and Ruth and Naomi settled in Bethlehem. In the course of providing food for herself and her mother-in-law, Ruth met Boaz, a prosperous farmer and a relative of Naomi. With Naomi's encouragement, Ruth tenderly reminded Boaz of the levirate obligation (Ru 3:1 – 9), a Deuteronomic law that required a man to marry his brother's widow if she was childless, the purpose being that the dead man have an heir (Dt 25:5 – 10). However, Boaz was not the nearest of kin. When the closest relative learned that there was a levirate obligation attached to the redemption of Naomi's land, he rejected it (Ru 4:1 – 6), and Boaz was free to marry Ruth.

The book of Ruth demonstrates the providence of God at work in the life of an individual, and it exalts family loyalty. It shows how a Gentile became part of the Davidic ancestry (4:17 – 21); thus Ruth is cited in the genealogy of Christ in Mt 1:5.

SABBATH [8701, 4640, 4878, 4879] (săb'ath, Heb. *shabbāth*, Gr. *Sabbaton, to desist, cease, rest*). The weekly day of rest and worship for the Jews. The Sabbath was instituted at creation. The record of creation (Ge 1:1 – 2:3) closes with an account of God's hallowing of the seventh day, because on it he rested from his creative labors. There is no express mention of the Sabbath before Ex 16:21 – 30. In the Desert of Sin, before the Israelites reached Mount Sinai, God gave them manna, a double supply being given on the sixth day of the week, in order that the seventh day might be kept as a day of rest from labor. Shortly afterward the Ten Commandments were given by the Lord at Sinai (20:1 – 17; 34:1 – 5). The fourth commandment enjoined Israel to observe the seventh day as a holy day on which no work should be done by man or beast. Everyone, including even the stranger within the gates, was to desist from all work and to keep the day holy. The reason given is that the Lord rested on the seventh day and blessed and hallowed it. It is clear that God intended the day to be a blessing to man, both physically and spiritually. The Sabbath is frequently mentioned in the Levitical legislation. It was to be kept holy for the worship of the Lord (Lev 23:3) and was to remind the Israelites that God had sanctified them (Ex 31:13). Forty years later, Moses reminded the Israelites of God's command to observe the Sabbath and told them that they were under special obligation to keep it because God had delivered them from bondage in Egypt (Dt 5:15). The sanctity of the Sabbath is shown by the offering on it of two lambs, in addition to the regular burnt offering (Nu 28:9 – 10). The twelve loaves of showbread were also presented on that day (Lev 24:5 – 9; 1Ch 9:32). A willful Sabbath-breaker was put to death (Nu 15:32 – 36). With the development of the synagogue during the exile, the Sabbath became a day for worship and the study of the law, as well as a day of rest.

Jesus came into conflict with the religious leaders of the Jews, especially on two points: his claim to be the Messiah and the matter of Sabbath observance. The rabbis regarded the Sabbath as an end in itself, whereas Jesus taught that the Sabbath was made for the benefit of people and that people's needs must take precedence over the law of the Sabbath (Mt 12:1 – 14; Mk 2:23 – 3:6; Lk 6:1 – 11; Jn 5:1 – 18). He himself regularly attended worship in the synagogue on the Sabbath (Lk 4:16).

The early Christians, most of whom were Jews, kept the seventh day as a Sabbath, but since the resurrection of their Lord was the most blessed day in their lives, they began very early also to meet for worship on the first day of the week (Ac 2:1) and designated it as the Lord's Day. Paul directed the Corinthian Christians to bring their weekly offering to the charities of the church on the first day of the week (1Co 16:1 – 2). As the split between the Jews and Christians widened, the Christians came gradually to meet for worship only on the Lord's Day and gave up the observance of the seventh day.

A Time of Rest:

(Ge 2:2 – 3; Lev 23:25; 26:34 – 35). Holy (Ex 16:23; 20:8, 11; 31:14; 35:2; Dt 5:12; Ne 9:14; Isa 58:13 – 14; Eze 44:24). A sign (Ex 31:13, 16 – 17; Eze 20:12 – 13, 16, 20 – 21, 24). The Lord is represented as resting on (Ge 2:2 – 3; Ex 31:17; Heb 4:4). Rest on, commanded (Ex 16:28 – 30; 23:12; 31:15; 34:21; 35:2 – 3; Lev 6:29 – 31; 19:3, 30; 23:1 – 3, 27 – 32; 26:2; Dt 5:12 – 15; 2Ch 36:21; Jer 17:21 – 22, 24 – 25, 27; Lk 23:56); of servants and animals (Ex 16:5, 23 – 30; 20:10; Mk 16:1; Lk 23:56).

Observation of:

Offerings prescribed for (Lev 24:8; Nu 28:9 – 10; 1Ch 9:32; 23:31; 2Ch 2:4; Eze 46:4 – 5). Song for (Pss 92:1 – 15; 118:24). Preparation for (Ex 16:5, 22; Mt 27:62; Mk 15:42; Lk 23:54; Jn 19:31). Religious usages on (Ge 2:3; Mk 6:2; Lk 4:16, 31; 6:6; 13:10; Ac 13:14). Worship on (Eze 46:1, 3; Ac 15:21; 16:13). Commanded (Eze 46:1, 3). Religious instruction on (Mk 6:2; Lk 4:16, 31;

6:6; 13:10; Ac 13:14, 27, 42, 44; 15:21; 17:2; 18:4). Apostles taught on (Ac 13:14 – 43, 44 – 48; 17:2; 18:4). Hypocritical observance, provokes divine displeasure (Isa 1:13; La 2:6; Eze 20:12 – 13, 16, 21, 24; Am 8:5). Rewards for observance of (Isa 56:2, 4 – 7; 58:13 – 14; Jer 17:21 – 22, 24 – 25). Observed by: Moses (Nu 15:32 – 34); Nehemiah (Ne 13:15, 21); the women preparing to embalm the body of Jesus (Lk 23:56); Paul (Ac 13:14); the disciples (Ac 16:13). John (Rev 1:10).

Violations of:

Punished, by death (Ex 35:2; Nu 15:32 – 36), by judgments (Jer 17:27). Instances of: gathering manna (Ex 16:27); gathering sticks (Nu 15:32). By men from Tyre (Ne 13:16). Inhabitants of Jerusalem (Jer 17:21 – 23). Profanation of (Ex 16:27 – 28; Nu 15:32 – 36; Ne 10:31; 13:15, 21; Jer 17:21 – 23; Eze 22:8; 23:38).

Christ's Interpretation of:

(Mt 12:1 – 8, 10 – 13; Lk 6:1 – 10; Mk 2:23 – 28; 13:10 – 17; 14:1 – 5; Jn 7:21 – 24; 9:14). Christ is Lord of (Mt 12:8; Mk 2:28; Lk 6:5). Christ performed miracles on (Mt 12:10 – 13; Mk 3:1 – 5; Lk 6:1 – 10; 13:10 – 17; Jn 5:5 – 14; 7:21 – 24). Christ taught on (Mk 1:21 – 22; 6:2; Lk 4:16, 31; 6:6; 13:10 – 17).

The Christian and the Sabbath:

Christian not to be judged regarding (Ro 14:1 – 12; Col 2:16). The first day of the week is called the Lord's Day (Mt 28:1, 5 – 7; Mk 16:9; Jn 20:1, 11 – 16, 19, 26; Ac 20:7; 1Co 16:2; Rev 1:10).

Ex	20:8	"Remember the **S** day
	31:14	" 'Observe the **S**, because it is holy
Lev	25:2	the land itself must observe a **s**
Dt	5:12	"Observe the **S** day
Isa	56:2	keeps the **S** without desecrating it,
Jer	17:21	not to carry a load on the **S** day
Mt	12:1	through the grainfields on the **S**.
Lk	13:10	On a **S** Jesus was teaching in one
Col	2:16	a New Moon celebration or a **S** day

SABBATH DAY'S JOURNEY A limited journey (about three thousand feet) that rabbinic scholars thought a Jew might travel on the Sabbath without breaking the law (Ac 1:12; cf. Ex 16:29; Nu 35:5; Jos 3:4).

SABBATIC YEAR A rest in every seventh year.

Called the Year of Release (Dt 15:9; 31:10). Ordinances concerning (Ex 23:9 – 11; Lev 25). Israelite servants set free in (Ex 21:2; Dt 15:12; Jer 34:14). Creditors required to release debtors in (Dt 15:1 – 6, 12 – 18; Ne 10:31). Ordinances concerning instruction in the law during (Dt 31:10 – 13; Ne 8:18). Punishment to follow a violation of the ordinances concerning (Lev 26:34 – 35, w 32 – 41; Jer 34:12 – 22).

SACKCLOTH [2520, 8566, 4884]. A symbol of mourning (1Ki 20:31 – 32; Job 16:15; Isa 15:3; Jer 4:8; 6:26; 49:3; La 2:10; Eze 7:18; Da 9:3; Joel 1:8). Worn by Jacob when it was reported to him that Joseph had been devoured by wild beasts (Ge 37:34). Animals covered with, at the time of national mourning (Jnh 3:8).

Ps	30:11	you removed my **s** and clothed me
Da	9:3	in fasting, and in **s** and ashes.
Mt	11:21	would have repented long ago in **s**

SACRAMENT (săk'r a-mĕnt, *something obligated [to do]*). Derived from the Latin *sacramentum*, which in classical times was used in two chief senses: as a technical legal term to denote the sum of money that the two parties to a suit deposited in a temple, of which the winner had his part returned, while the loser forfeited his to the temple treasury; as a technical military term to designate the oath of obedience of a soldier to his commander. In the Greek NT there is no word corresponding to "sacrament," nor do we find the word used in the earliest history of Christianity to refer to certain rites of the church. The word *sacramentum* was used with a distinctively Christian meaning for the first time in the Old Latin Bible and by Tertullian (end of the second century). In the Old Latin and in the Vulgate it was employed to translate the Greek *mystērion*, "mystery" (e.g., Eph 5:32; 1Ti 3:16; Rev 1:20; 17:7). For a long time it was used not only to refer to religious rites but to doctrines and facts.

Because of the absence of any defined sacramental concept in the early history of the church, the number of sacraments was not regarded as fixed. Baptism and the Lord's Supper were the chief sacraments. Over church history as many as thirty sacraments were listed. The Reformers saw in the NT sacraments three distinguishing marks: (1) they were instituted by Christ, (2) Christ commanded that they be observed by his followers, and (3) they are visible symbols of divine acts. Since baptism and the Lord's Supper are the only rites for which such marks can be claimed, there can be only two sacraments. There is justification for classifying them under a common name because they are associated together in the NT (Ac 2:41 – 42; 1Co 10:1 – 4).

These rites were regarded as ritual acts of faith and obedience toward God (Mt 28:19 – 20; Ac 2:38; Ro 6:3 – 5; 1Co 11:23 – 27; Col 2:11 – 12). They are symbolic rites setting forth the central truths of the Christian faith: death and resurrection with Christ and participation in the redemptive benefits of Christ's mediatorial death. They are visible enactments of the gospel message that Christ lived, died, was raised from the dead, ascended to heaven, and will some day return, and that all this is for humankind's salvation.

SACRED

Lev	23:2	are to proclaim as **s** assemblies.
Mt	7:6	"Do not give dogs what is **s**;
Ro	14:5	One man considers one day more **s**
1Co	3:17	for God's temple is **s**, and you are
2Pe	1:18	were with him on the **s** mountain.

SACRIFICE AND OFFERINGS (Heb. *zevah*, Gr. *thysia*). A religious act belonging to worship in which offering is made to God of some material object belonging to the offerer — this offering being consumed in the ceremony, in order to attain, restore, maintain, or celebrate friendly relations with the deity. The motives actuating the offerer may vary, worthy or unworthy, and may express faith, repentance, adoration, or all of these together; but the main purpose of the sacrifice is to please the deity and to secure his favor.

HISTORY OF SACRIFICE IN OT TIMES.

The sacrifices of Cain and Abel (Ge 4:4 – 5) show that the rite goes back almost to the beginnings of the human race. No priest was needed in their sacrifices, which were eucharistic and possibly expiatory. The sacrifice of Noah after the flood (8:20 – 21) is called a burnt offering and is closely connected with the covenant of God described in Ge 9:8 – 17. In the sacrifices of Abraham, several of which are mentioned (12:7 – 8; 13:4, 18; 15:4ff.), he acted as his own priest and made offerings to express his adoration of God and probably to atone for sin. In Ge 22 God reveals to him that he does not desire human sacrifices, a common practice in those days. The patriarchs Isaac and Jacob regularly offered sacrifices (26:25; 28:18; 31:54; 33:20; 35:7; 46:1). Job and his friends offered sacrifices (Job 1:5; 42:7 – 9), probably to atone for sin. The Israelites during their sojourn in Egypt no doubt were accustomed to animal sacrifices. It was to some such feast that Moses asked the pharaoh for permission to go into the wilderness (Ex 3:18; 5:3ff.; 7:16); and he requested herds and flocks for the feast to offer burnt offerings and sacrifices (10:24 – 25). The sacrifice of the Passover (12:3 – 11) brings out forcibly the idea of salvation from death. Jethro, Moses' father-in-law, a priest, offered sacrifices on meeting Moses and the people (18:12).

THE MOSAIC SACRIFICES.

Every offering had to be the honestly acquired property of the offerer (2Sa 24:24). Sacrifices had value in the eyes of the Lord only when they were made in acknowledgment of his sovereign majesty, expressed in obedience to him, and with a sincere desire to enjoy his favor. The only animals allowed for sacrifice were oxen, sheep, goats, and pigeons.

Wild animals and fish could not be offered. The produce of the field allowed for offerings was wine, oil, grain, either in the ear or in the form of meal, dough, or cakes. Sacrifices were of two kinds: animal (with the shedding of blood) and vegetable or bloodless.

Animal Sacrifices:

Sin offering (Lev 4:1 – 35; 6:24 – 30); guilt offering (Lev 5:14 – 6:7); burnt offering (Lev 1); fellowship offering (Lev 3).

Vegetable or Bloodless Sacrifices:

Grain offerings (Lev 2:1 – 16; 6:14 – 18); drink offerings (Lev 23:13).

Ge	22:2	**S** him there as a burnt offering
Ex	12:27	'It is the Passover **s** to the LORD,
1Sa	15:22	To obey is better than **s**,
1Ch	21:24	or **s** a burnt offering that costs me
Ps	51:16	You do not delight in **s**,
Pr	15:8	The LORD detests the **s**
Da	9:27	the 'seven' he will put an end to **s**
Hos	6:6	For I desire mercy, not **s**,
Mt	9:13	this means: 'I desire mercy, not **s**.'
Ro	3:25	God presented him as a **s**
Eph	5:2	as a fragrant offering and **s** to God.
Php	4:18	an acceptable **s**, pleasing to God.
Heb	9:26	away with sin by the **s** of himself.
	10:10	holy through the **s** of the body
	10:14	by one **s** he has made perfect
	10:18	there is no longer any **s** for sin.
	11:4	faith Abel offered God a better **s**
	13:15	offer to God a **s** of praise —
1Jn	2:2	He is the atoning **s** for our sins,
	4:10	as an atoning **s** for our sins.

SADDUCEES [4881] (săd′yū-sēz, Gr. *Saddoukaioi, followers of Zadok*; possibly *righteous*). One of the religious parties that existed among the Jews in the days of Christ and the early church but exercised comparatively little influence among the people. They resisted the truth of the gospel. Their origin is uncertain, but it is to be sought in the period in Jewish history between the restoration of the Jews to their own land (536 BC) and the Christian era. No evidence of Sadduceeism is to be found in Israel before the captivity.

The Sadducees had a number of distinctive beliefs, contrasting strongly with those of the Pharisees: (1) They held only to the written Law and rejected the traditions of the Pharisees. (2) They denied the resurrection of the body, personal immortality, and retribution in a future life. (3) They denied the existence of angels and spirits (Ac 23:8). (4) They differed from both the Pharisees and the Essenes on the matter of divine predestination and the freedom of the human will. According to Josephus, the Essenes held that all things are fixed by God's unalterable decree; the Pharisees tried to combine predestination and free will; and the Sadducees threw aside all ideas of divine interposition in the government of the world.

The Sadducees are mentioned by name in the NT only about a dozen times (Mt 3:7; 16:1, 6, 11 – 12; 22:23, 34; Mk 12:18; Lk 20:27; Ac 4:1; 5:17; 23:6 – 8), but it must be remembered that when mention is made of the chief priests, practically the same persons are referred to. With the destruction of Jerusalem in AD 70, the Sadducean party disappeared.

Mt	16:6	the yeast of the Pharisees and **S**."
Mk	12:18	**S**, who say there is no resurrection,
Ac	23:8	**S** say that there is no resurrection,

SAINT [2883, 7705, 10620, 41] (*unique, consecrated, holy ones*). In KJV the word "saint" is used to translate two Hebrew words: *qadôsh* and *hasîdh*. The root idea of the first is separation. In a religious sense it means that which is separated or dedicated to God, and therefore removed from secular use. The word is applied to people, places, and things — e.g., the temple, vessels, garments, the city of Jerusalem, priests. The root of the second word is personal holiness. The emphasis is on character. It has a strong ethical connotation.

In the NT the word *hagioi* is applied to OT (Mt 27:52) and NT believers (e.g., Ac 26:10; Ro 8:27;

13:12; 16:2; 2Co 1:1; Eph 1:1; 1Th 1:13; Jude 3; Rev 13:7, 10). The church is made up of people called out of the world (Ro 1:7; 1Co 1:2) by God's electing grace to be his own people. All who are in covenant relation with him through repentance and faith in his Son are regarded as saints. Objectively, the saints are God's chosen and peculiar people, belonging exclusively to him. Subjectively, they are separated from all defilement and sin and partake of God's holiness. Throughout the Bible, but especially in the NT epistles, the saints are urged to live lives befitting their position (Eph 4:1, 12; 5:3; Col 1:10; cf. 2Co 8:4).

1Sa	2:9	He will guard the feet of his **s**,
Ps	16:3	As for the **s** who are in the land,
	31:23	Love the Lord, all his **s**!
	34:9	Fear the Lord, you his **s**,
Da	7:18	the **s** of the Most High will receive
Ro	8:27	intercedes for the **s** in accordance
1Co	6:2	not know that the **s** will judge
Eph	1:15	Jesus and your love for all the **s**,
	1:18	of his glorious inheritance in the **s**,
	6:18	always keep on praying for all the **s**
Phm	1:7	have refreshed the hearts of the **s**.
Rev	5:8	which are the prayers of the **s**.
	19:8	for the righteous acts of the **s**.)

SALVATION [3802, 3828, 3829, 7407, 9591, 5401, 5403] (Heb. *yeshû'âh*, Gr. *sōtēria*). What God in mercy does for his sinful, finite human creatures is presented in the Bible through a variety of metaphors, images, and models (e.g., redemption and justification). Of these, none is more important or significant than salvation: thus God is called "Savior" (Hos 13:4; Lk 1:47) and portrayed as the "God of salvation" (Ps 68:19 – 20; Lk 3:6; Ac 28:28).

In the OT, salvation refers both to everyday, regular types of deliverance — as from enemies, disease, and danger (see 1Sa 10:24; Ps 72:4) — and to those major deliverances that are specifically interpreted as being a definite part of God's unique and special involvement in human history. There are two further aspects to salvation in the OT. First, salvation refers to the future action of God when he will deliver Israel from all her enemies and ills and create a new order of existence ("a new heaven and a new earth") in which she and all people will worship the Lord and live in peace and harmony (see Isa 49:5 – 13; 65:17ff.; 66:22 – 23; Hag 2:4 – 9; Zec 2:7 – 13). Second, intimately related to the future salvation of God is the hope of the Messiah, who will deliver his people from their sins, and will act for the Lord, who alone is Savior (Isa 43:11; 52:13; 53:12).

In the NT, Jesus is portrayed as the Savior of sinners (Lk 2:11; Jn 4:42; Ac 5:31; 13:23; Php 3:20; 2Pe 1:1, 11; 1Jn 4:14). The title reserved for God in the OT is transferred to Jesus as incarnate Son in the NT. He is the Savior or Deliverer from sin and its consequences as well as from Satan and his power. Jesus preached the arrival of the kingdom of God — the kingly, fatherly rule of God in human lives. When a person repented and believed, that person received salvation — "Today salvation has come to this house" (Lk 19:9 – 10), said Jesus to Zacchaeus.

Peter preached that "salvation is found in no one else, for there is no other name under heaven given to men by which we must be saved" (Ac 4:12). Paul wrote, "Now is the day of salvation" (2Co 6:2). The writer of Hebrews asked, "How shall we escape if we ignore such a great salvation?" (Heb 2:3). Because of the life, death, and exaltation of Jesus, salvation is a present reality and the gospel is the declaration that salvation is now accomplished and available in and through Jesus. It is deliverance from the dominion of sin and Satan; it is freedom to love and serve God now. Salvation is also, however, a future hope, for we will "be saved from God's wrath through him" at the last judgment (Ro 5:9). Salvation, which belongs to our God (Rev 19:1), includes everything that God will do for and to his people as he brings them to fullness of life in the new heaven and the new earth of the age to come.

Call to:
(Dt 30:19 – 20; Isa 55:1 – 3, 6 – 7; Lk 3:6; Ac 16:31; Heb 2:3).

From God:

(Pss 3:8; 36:8 – 9; 37:39; 68:18 – 20; 91:16; 98:2 – 3; 106:8; 121:1 – 8; Isa 46:12 – 13; 51:4 – 5; 63:9; Jer 3:23; 21:8; Eze 18:32; Joel 2:32; 1Pe 1:5; 1Jn 2:25).

Through Christ: *(Isa 61:10; Mt 1:21; Lk 19:10; 24:46 – 47; Jn 3:14 – 17; 11:51 – 52; Ac 4:12; 13:26, 38 – 39, 47; 16:30 – 31; Ro 5:15 – 21; 7:24 – 25; 9:30 – 33; 1Co 6:11; Gal 1:4; 3:13 – 14; Eph 1:9 – 10, 13; 2Ti 1:9 – 10; 2:10; Tit 3:5 – 7; Heb 2:3, 10; 5:9; 7:25; 1Jn 4:9 – 10; 5:11; Jude 3; Rev 3:20; 5:9).*

By: *the atonement (1Co 1:18, 21, 24 – 25; Gal 1:4; 3:8, 13 – 14, 21, 26 – 28; Col 1:20 – 23, 26 – 27; 1Ti 2:6; Rev 5:9); the resurrection (Ro 5:10); the gospel (Ro 1:16; Jas 1:21); the grace of God (Eph 2:8 – 9; Tit 2:11; 2Pe 3:15); the word of God (Jas 1:21); the power of God (1Co 1:18).*

Message of:

Foretold by the prophets (Isa 29:18 – 19, 24; 35:8; Lk 2:31 – 32; 1Pe 1:10). By angels (Lk 2:9 – 14). From the seed of Abraham (Ge 12:13). Proclaimed by Christ (Lk 19:10; Jn 12:32). Preached by the apostles (Ac 11:17 – 18; 16:17). Wisdom for, derived from the Scriptures (2Ti 3:15). Praise for, ascribed to God and the Lamb (Rev 7:9 – 10).

Conditions of:

Repentance (Mt 3:2; Mk 1:4; Lk 3:8; Ac 2:38; 3:19; 2Co 7:10). Faith in Christ (Mk 16:15 – 16; Jn 3:14 – 18; 5:24; 6:47; 9:35; 11:25 – 26; 12:36; 20:31; Ac 2:21; 16:30 – 31; 20:21; Ro 1:16 – 17; 3:21 – 30; 4:1 – 25; 5:1 – 2; 10:4, 8 – 13; Gal 2:16; 3:8, 26 – 28; Eph 2:8; Php 3:9; 2Th 2:13; 1Ti 1:15 – 16; Heb 4:1 – 2; 1Pe 1:9). Supreme love to Christ (Lk 14:25 – 27). Renunciation of the world (Mt 19:16 – 21; Lk 14:33; 18:18 – 26). Choice (Dt 30:19 – 20; Ps 65:4; Eph 1:4 – 5). Seeking God (Am 5:4). Fear of God (Pr 14:27; 15:23; 16:6; Mal 4:2). Not by works (Ro 3:28; 4:1 – 25; 9:30 – 33; 11:6; Gal 2:16; Eph 2:8 – 9; 2Ti 1:9 – 10; Tit 3:5 – 7). See Blessings, Spiritual, Contingent on Obedience; Faith; Obedience; Perseverance; Repentance.

Plan of:

(Jn 17:4; Heb 6:17 – 20). Foreordained (Eph 1:4 – 6; 3:11). Described as a mystery (Mt 13:11; Mk 4:11; Lk 8:10; Ro 16:25 – 26; 1Co 2:7 – 9; Eph 1:9 – 10, 13; 3:9 – 10; 6:19; Col 1:26 – 27; 1Ti 3:16; Rev 10:7).

Includes: *The incarnation of Christ (Gal 4:4 – 5). The atonement by Christ (Jn 18:11; 19:28 – 30; Ac 3:18; 17:3; Ro 16:25 – 26; 1Co 1:21 – 25; 2:7 – 9; Eph 1:7 – 11; 3:18; 6:19; Col 1:26 – 27; Heb 2:9 – 18; 10:10). Initial grace (Jn 6:37, 44 – 45, 65; Eph 2:5; Tit 2:11). The election of grace (2Th 2:13 – 14; 2Ti 1:9 – 10). Inheritance (Heb 1:14). Regeneration (Jn 3:3 – 12).*

Offered and Rejected: *(Dt 32:15; Mt 22:3 – 13; 23:37; Lk 14:16 – 24; Jn 5:40).*

Parables of:

(Lk 15:2 – 32).

Ex	15:2	he has become my **s**.
2Sa	22:3	my shield and the horn of my **s**.
1Ch	16:23	proclaim his **s** day after day.
Ps	9:14	and there rejoice in your **s**.
	27:1	The Lord is my light and my **s** —
	37:39	The **s** of the righteous comes
	51:12	Restore to me the joy of your **s**
	62:2	He alone is my rock and my **s**;
	98:2	The Lord has made his **s** known
	118:14	he has become my **s**.
	119:81	with longing for your **s**,
	119:123	My eyes fail, looking for your **s**,
	149:4	he crowns the humble with **s**.
Isa	12:2	Surely God is my **s**;
	25:9	let us rejoice and be glad in his **s**."
	26:1	God makes **s**
	33:2	our **s** in time of distress.
	45:17	the Lord with an everlasting **s**;
	46:13	I will grant **s** to Zion,
	56:1	for my **s** is close at hand
	59:17	and the helmet of **s** on his head;
Jer	3:23	is the **s** of Israel.
La	3:26	quietly for the **s** of the Lord.
Jnh	2:9	**S** comes from the Lord."

Zec	9:9	righteous and having **s**,
Lk	1:69	He has raised up a horn of **s** for us
	1:77	give his people the knowledge of **s**
	2:30	For my eyes have seen your **s**,
	3:6	And all mankind will see God's **s**
	19:9	"Today **s** has come to this house,
Jn	4:22	for **s** is from the Jews.
Ac	4:12	**S** is found in no one else,
Ro	1:16	for the **s** of everyone who believes:
	11:11	**s** has come to the Gentiles
	13:11	because our **s** is nearer now
2Co	1:6	it is for your comfort and **s**;
	7:10	brings repentance that leads to **s**
Eph	1:13	word of truth, the gospel of your **s**.
	6:17	Take the helmet of **s** and the sword
Php	2:12	to work out your **s** with fear
2Ti	2:10	they too may obtain the **s** that is
	3:15	wise for **s** through faith
Tit	2:11	of God that brings **s** has appeared
Heb	2:3	This **s**, which was first announced
	2:3	escape if we ignore such a great **s**?
	2:10	of their **s** perfect through suffering.
	5:9	of eternal **s** for all who obey him
1Pe	1:5	the coming of the **s** that is ready
	1:9	of your faith, the **s** of your souls.
	2:2	by it you may grow up in your **s**,
2Pe	3:15	that our Lord's patience means **s**,
Jude	1:3	to write to you about the **s** we share
Rev	7:10	"**S** belongs to our God,
	12:10	have come the **s** and the power
	19:1	**S** and glory and power belong

SAMARIA [9076, 9085, 10726, 4899] (sa-mâr′ĭ̆a, Heb. *shōmerôn*, Gr. *Samareia, to clan of Shemer*, 1Ki 16:24, BDB). The country of Samaria occupied a rough square of some forty miles (sixty-seven km.) north and south by thirty-five miles (fifty-eight km.) east and west. It was the territory occupied by the ten tribes led by Jeroboam, extending roughly from Bethel to Dan and from the Mediterranean to Syria and Ammon. The political and geographical frontiers are somewhat blurred. The earliest name for this section of the Palestinian uplands

was Mount Ephraim (Jos 17:15; 19:50; Jdg 3:27; 4:5). The country was too open for successful defense. Hence, too, the chariot is mentioned frequently in the annals of the northern kingdom, and the surrounding paganism poured almost unrestricted into the life of the northern kingdom.

1. City of, built by Omri (1Ki 16:24). Capital of the kingdom of the ten tribes (1Ki 16:29; 22:51; 2Ki 13:1, 10; 15:8). Besieged by Ben-Hadad (1Ki 20; 2Ki 6:24 – 33; 7). The king of Syria is led into, by Elisha, who miraculously blinds him and his army (2Ki 6:8 – 23). Ahab ruled in. (*See Ahab; Jezebel.*) Besieged by Shalmaneser, king of Assyria, three years; taken; the people carried away to Halah and Habor, cities of the Medes (2Ki 17:5 – 6; 18:9 – 11). Idolatry of (1Ki 16:32; 2Ki 13:6). Temple of, destroyed (2Ki 10:17 – 28; 23:19). Paul and Barnabas preach in (Ac 15:3). Visited by Philip, Peter, and John (Ac 8:5 – 25).

2. Country of (Isa 7:9). Foreign colonies distributed among the cities of, by the king of Assyria (2Ki 17:24 – 41; Ezr 4:9 – 10). Roads through, from Judea into Galilee (Lk 17:11; Jn 4:3 – 8). Jesus journeys through (Jn 4:1 – 42); heals lepers in (Lk 17:11 – 19). The good Samaritan from (Lk 10:33 – 35). No dealings between the Jews and the inhabitants of (Jn 4:9). Expect the Messiah (Jn 4:25). Disciples made from the inhabitants of (Jn 4:39 – 42; Ac 8:5 – 8, 4 – 17, 25). Jesus forbids the apostles to preach in the cities of (Mt 10:5).

1Ki	16:24	He bought the hill of **S**
2Ki	17:6	the king of Assyria captured **S**
Jn	4:4	Now he had to go through **S**.
	4:5	came to a town in **S** called Sychar,

SAMARITANS [4899, 4901, 4902] (sa-măr′ĭ̆tăns, Heb. *shōmerōnîm*, Gr. *Samareitai, of Samaria*). The word may signify, according to context, (1) the inhabitants of Samaria (the region rather than the town; e.g., 2Ki 17:26; Mt 10:5; Lk 9:52; 10:33; 17:16; Jn 4:9, 30, 40; Ac 8:25) or (2) the sect that derived its name from Samaria, a term of contempt with the Jews (Jn 8:48). Since the seventeenth century AD, "a good Samaritan" (Lk 10:33) has signified a generous and self-forgetful person.

Racially, the Samaritans are difficult to identify. In 721 BC Sargon of Assyria destroyed Samaria. It seems clear that the policy of deportation applied particularly to Samaria as a city and not as a region. Jeremiah 41:5, for example, seems to imply that a remnant of true Israelites remained in Shechem, Shiloh, and Samaria a century later; so a substratum, or admixture of the Hebrew stock in the later total population must be assumed. The newcomers from the north may be presumed to have intermarried with the Israelite remnant, and ultimately the population took the general name of Samaritans.

After the return from captivity, enmity became inveterate between the Samaritans and the Jewish remnant of Ezra and Nehemiah. On the strength of their worship of the LORD "since the time of Esarhaddon" (Ezr 4:2), the Samaritans sought a share in the rebuilding of the temple in Jerusalem but were firmly rebuffed; hence the policy of obstruction from Sanballat of Samaria, which was a serious hindrance to Nehemiah's work (Ne 2:10, 19; 4:6 – 7). Sanballat's son-in-law was Manasseh, grandson of the Jewish high priest, and Nehemiah's drive for racial purity led to the expulsion of this young man from Jerusalem. By his emigration with a considerable band of dissident Jews to Samaria, the rift between the peoples, politically and religiously, was made permanent. Manasseh persuaded the Samaritans, according to tradition, to abandon many of their idolatrous practices; and with Sanballat's building on Mount Gerizim of a schismatic temple for his son-in-law, the sect of the Samaritans was established. It was from this time too that Samaria became a refuge for malcontent Jews, with the consequent use of "Samaritan" as a term of abuse for a dissident rebel (Jn 8:48). John Hyrcanus destroyed the temple on Gerizim along with the city in 109 BC. When Herod provided another temple in 25 BC, the Samaritans refused to use it, continuing to worship on the mount (Jn 4:20 – 21).

Lk 10:33 But a **S**, as he traveled, came where

17:16 and thanked him — and he was a **S**.
Jn 4:7 When a **S** woman came

SAMSON [9088, 4907] (săm'sŭn, Heb. *shimshôn*, probably *little sun*, Gr. *Sampsōn*, Lat. and Eng. *Samson*). One of the judges of Israel, perhaps the last before Samuel. The record of his life is found in Jdg 13 – 16. He was an Israelite of the tribe of Dan, the son of Manoah. At the time of his birth, the Israelites had been in bondage to the Philistines for forty years because they had done evil in the sight of the Lord. After his birth "he grew and the LORD blessed him, and the Spirit of the LORD began to stir him while he was in Mahaneh Dan, between Zorah and Eshtaol" (Jdg 13:24 – 25). But almost from the beginning of his career he showed one conspicuous weakness, which was ultimately to wreck him: he was a slave to passion. Even with all of his failings, he is listed with the heroes of faith in Heb 11:32. By faith in God's gift and calling, he received strength to do the wonders he performed. Too often animal passion ruled him. He was without self-control, and accordingly he wrought no permanent deliverance for Israel.

A judge of Israel (Jdg 16:31); A Danite, son of Manoah; miraculous birth of; a Nazirite from his mother's womb; the mother forbidden to drink wine or strong drink or to eat any unclean thing during pregnancy (Jdg 13:2 – 7, 24 – 25); Desires a Philistine woman for his wife; slays a lion (Jdg 14:1 – 7); His marriage feast and the riddle propounded (Jdg 14:8 – 19); Wife of, estranged (Jdg 14:20; 15:1 – 2); Avenged for the estrangement of his wife (Jdg 15:3 – 8); His great strength exemplified (Jdg 15:7 – 14; Heb 11:32); Slays a thousand Philistines with the jawbone of a donkey (Jdg 15:13 – 17); Miraculously supplied with water (Jdg 15:18 – 19); Consorts with Delilah, a harlot, who schemes with the Philistines to overcome him (Jdg 16:4 – 20); Is blinded by the Philistines and confined to hard labor in prison; pulls down the pillars of the temple, killing himself and many Philistines (Jdg 16:21 – 31; Heb 11:32)

SAMUEL [9017, 4905] (săm′ū̆-ĕl, Heb. *shemû′ēl, name of God,* or *his name is El;* some grammarians prefer a derivation from *yishma' 'El, God hears;* others associate the name with *sha'al, to ask,* on the basis of 1Sa 1:20).

1. Samuel is often called the last of the judges (cf. 1Sa 7:6, 15 – 17) and the first of the prophets (3:20; Ac 3:24; 13:20). He was the son of Elkanah, a Zuphite, and Hannah, of Ramathaim in the hill country of Ephraim. The account of the events associated with the birth of Samuel indicates that his parents were a devoted and devout couple. Hannah's childlessness led her to pour out her complaint and supplication to God in bitterness of heart, but she trusted God to provide the answer and promised to give to the Lord the son she had requested. When Samuel was born, she kept her promise; as soon as the child was weaned, she took him to Shiloh and presented him to Eli. Then she praised the Lord in prayer (usually called her "Song," 1Sa 2:1 – 10). Samuel grew up in the Lord's house and ministered before the Lord (2:11; 3:1), and each year when his parents came to sacrifice at Shiloh, his mother brought a little robe for him (2:19). Spiritually and morally, the times were bad. The sons of Eli were unworthy representatives of the priestly office. In their greed they violated the laws of offering (2:12 – 17); they also engaged in immoral acts with the women who served at the entrance to the Tent of Meeting (2:22). Though Eli remonstrated with them, he was not firm enough, and the Lord declared that he would punish him (2:27 – 36). The Lord called to Samuel in the night and revealed to him the impending doom of Eli's house. The Lord blessed Samuel and "let none of his words fall to the ground" (1Sa 3:19), so that all Israel knew that Samuel was a prophet of the Lord.

Last of the judges (1Sa 7:15), and first of the prophets after Moses (2Ch 25:18; Jer 15:1); A seer (1Sa 9:9) and priest (1Sa 2:18, 27, 35); Son of Elkanah and Hannah (1Sa 1:19 – 20); birth the result of special providence; Brought up by

Eli (1Sa 3); Anointed Saul (1Sa 10) and David (1Sa 16:13); Traditional author of biblical books that bear his name; Died at Ramah (1Sa 25:1)

2. Descendant of Issachar (1Ch 7:2).

SAMUEL, 1 AND 2 The books are named after Samuel, the outstanding figure of the early section. Originally there was only one book of Samuel, but the LXX divided it into two. This division was followed by the Latin versions and made its appearance in the Hebrew text in Daniel Bomberg's first edition (AD 1516 – 17). In the LXX the books of Samuel and the books of Kings are called Books of Kingdoms (I – IV); the Vulgate numbers them similarly but names them Books of Kings. The title "Samuel," which appears in Hebrew manuscripts, is followed in most English translations.

AUTHORSHIP AND DATE.

There is little external or internal evidence concerning the authorship of Samuel. Jewish tradition ascribes the work to him.

PURPOSE.

The purpose of all OT history is clearly stated in the NT (Ro 15:4; 1Co 10:11): to serve as warning, instruction, and encouragement. More specifically, the books of Samuel present the establishment of the kingship in Israel. In preserving the account of Samuel, the judge and prophet, the books mark the transition from judgeship to monarchy, since Samuel filled the prophetic office and administered the divine induction into office of Israel's first two kings.

Outline:
- I. Shiloh and Samuel (1Sa 1:1 – 7:1).
- II. Samuel and Saul (1Sa 7:2 – 15:35).
- III. Saul and David (1Sa 16 – 31; 2Sa 1).
- IV. David as King of Judah (2Sa 2 – 4).
- V. David as King of All Israel (2Sa 5 – 24).

SANCTIFICATION [39, 40] (Gr. *hagiasmos* from the verb *hagiazō*). The process or result of being made holy. As the article on holiness makes clear, holiness when applied to things, places, and people means that they are consecrated and set apart for the use of God, who is utterly pure and apart from all imperfection and evil. When used of people, it can refer also to the practical realization within them of consecration to God: that is, it can have a moral dimension. Thus in the NT, believers are described as already (objectively) sanctified in Christ — "your life in Christ Jesus, whom God made our sanctification" (1Co 1:30 RSV), and "those sanctified in Christ Jesus" (1:2). Also, though set apart in Christ for God and seen as holy by God because they are in Christ, believers are called to show that consecration in their lives — "It is God's will that you should be sanctified" (1Th 4:3), and "May … the God of peace sanctify you" (5:23). The same emphasis is found in Hebrews (2:11; 9:13; 10:10, 14, 29; 13:12). Because believers are holy in Christ (set apart for God by Christ's sacrificial, atoning blood), they are to be holy in practice in the power of the Holy Spirit. They are to be sanctified because they are already sanctified.

Means:

By God (Ex 29:44; 31:13; Lev 20:8; 21:8, 15, 23; 22:9, 16; Jer 1:5; Eze 20:12; 37:28). In Christ (1Co 1:2, 30; 6:11; Eph 5:25 – 27; Heb 2:11; 10:10, 14; 13:12). By the Holy Spirit (Ro 15:16; 2Th 2:13 – 14; 1Pe 1:2). By the blood of Christ (Heb 9:14; 13:12). By faith in Christ (Ac 26:17 – 18). By the truth (Jn 17:17, 19). By confession of sin (1Jn 1:9). By intercessory prayer for (1Th 5:23). Sanctification is the will of God (1Th 4:3 – 4).

Instances of:

The altar sanctifies the gift (Ex 29:37; 30:29; Mt 23:19). The Sabbath (Ge 2:3; Dt 5:12; Ne 13:22). Mount Sinai (Ex 19:23). The tabernacle (Ex 29:43 – 44; 30:26, 29; 40:34 – 35; Lev 8:10; Nu 7:1). The furniture of the tabernacle (Ex 30:26 – 29; Nu 7:1). The altar of burnt offerings (Ex 29:36 – 37; 40:10 – 11; Lev 8:11, 15; Nu 7:1). The basin (Ex 30:23; Lev 8:11). The temple (2Ch 29:5, 17, 19). Houses (Lev 27:14 – 15).

Land (Lev 27:16 – 19, 22). Offerings (Ex 29:27). Material things by anointing (Ex 40:9 – 11). The firstborn of Israelites (Ex 13:2; Lev 27:26; Nu 8:17; Dt 15:19). Eleazar to get the ark (1Sa 7:1). Jesse to offer a sacrifice (1Sa 16:5). Job's children, by Job (Job 1:5). Of Levites (1Ch 15:12, 14; 2Ch 29:34; 30:15); commanded (1Ch 15:12; 2Ch 29:5). Of priests (1Ch 15:14; 2Ch 5:11; 30:24); commanded (Ex 19:22). Of Aaron and his sons (Ex 28:41; 29:33, 44; 40:13; Lev 8:12, 30). Of Israel (Ex 29:10, 14); commanded (Ex 19:10; Lev 11:44; 20:7; Nu 11:18; Jos 3:5; 7:13; Joel 2:16). Of the Corinthian Christians (1Co 1:2; 6:11; 7:14). Of the church (Eph 5:26; 1Th 5:23; Jude 24).

SANCTIFIED

Jn	17:19	that they too may be truly **s**.
Ac	20:32	among all those who are **s**.
	26:18	among those who are **s** by faith
Ro	15:16	to God, **s** by the Holy Spirit.
1Co	1:2	to those **s** in Christ Jesus
	6:11	But you were washed, you were **s**,
	7:14	and the unbelieving wife has been **s**
1Th	4:3	It is God's will that you should be **s**
Heb	10:29	blood of the covenant that **s** him,

SANCTUARY [185, 1074, 1808, 2121, 5219, 7163, 7164, 7731, 41, 3302, 3875] (Heb. *miqdāsh*, Gr. *hagion*, *holy place*). This refers almost exclusively to the tabernacle or temple. God's sanctuary was his established earthly abode, the place where he chose to dwell among his people. Psalm 114:2 says that "Judah became God's sanctuary, Israel his dominion." God himself is a sanctuary for his people (Isa 8:14; Eze 11:19). The word is used particularly of the Most Holy Place, whether of the tabernacle or of the temple. When it is used in the plural, it usually denotes idolatrous shrines, or high places, which Israelites who compromised with heathenism sometimes built (Am 7:9). A sanctuary was also a place of asylum, the horns of the altar especially being regarded as inviolable (cf. 1Ki 2:28 – 29). In the NT the word is used in the letter to the Hebrews (8:2; 9:1 – 2; 13:11), where the author makes clear that the earthly sanctuary was only a type of the true sanctuary, which is in heaven, of which Christ is the High Priest and in which he offers himself as a sacrifice (10:1 – 18).

Ex	25:8	"Then have them make a **s** for me,
Lev	19:30	and have reverence for my **s**,
Ps	15:1	LORD, who may dwell in your **s**?
	102:19	looked down from his **s** on high,
	150:1	Praise God in his **s**;
Eze	37:26	I will put my **s** among them forever
Da	9:26	will destroy the city and the **s**.
Heb	6:19	It enters the inner **s**
	8:2	in the **s**, the true tabernacle set up
	8:5	They serve at a **s** that is a copy
	9:24	enter a man-made **s** that was only

SANHEDRIN [5284] (săn'hē-drĭn, Talmudic Heb. transcription of the Gr. *synedrion, a council*). The highest Jewish tribunal during the Greek and Roman periods, often mentioned in the NT, where the KJV always has "council" for the Greek name. The Talmud connects the Sanhedrin with Moses' seventy elders, then with the alleged Great Synagogue of Ezra's time; but the truth is that the origin of the Sanhedrin is unknown, and there is no historical evidence for its existence before the Greek period. During the reign of the Hellenistic kings Palestine was practically under home rule and was governed by an aristocratic council of elders, which was presided over by the hereditary high priest. The council was called *gerousia*, which always signifies an aristocratic body. This later developed into the Sanhedrin. During most of the Roman period the internal government of the country was practically in its hands, and its influence was recognized even in the Diaspora (Ac 9:2; 22:5; 26:12). After the death of Herod the Great, however, during the reign of Archelaus and the Roman procurators, the civil authority of the Sanhedrin was probably restricted to Judea, and this is very likely the reason why it had no judicial authority over Jesus so long as he remained in Galilee. The Sanhedrin was abolished

after the destruction of Jerusalem (AD 70). A new court was established bearing the name Sanhedrin, but it differed in essential features from the older body: it had no political authority and was composed exclusively of rabbis, whose decisions had only a theoretical importance.

Composed of seventy members, plus the president, who was the high priest; members drawn from chief priests, scribes, and elders (Mt 16:21; 27:41; Mk 8:31; 11:27; 14:43, 53; Lk 9:22); The secular nobility of Jerusalem; final court of appeal for all questions connected with the Mosaic law; could order arrests by its own officers of justice (Mt 26:47; Mk 14:43; Ac 4:3; 5:17; 9:2); Did not have the right of capital punishment in the time of Christ (Jn 18:31 – 32)

SARAH, SARA, SARAI [8577, 8584, 4925] (sâ'ra, Heb. *sārâh, sāray*, Gr. *Sara*. Sarah means *princess*; the meaning of Sarai is doubtful).

1. The wife of Abraham, first mentioned in Ge 11:29. She was ten years younger than Abraham and was married to him in Ur of the Chaldees (11:29 – 31). According to Ge 20:12, she was Abraham's half sister, the daughter of his father but not of his mother. Marriage with half sisters was not uncommon in ancient times. Her name was originally Sarai. She was about sixty-five years old when Abraham left Ur for Haran. Still childless at the age of seventy-five, Sarah induced Abraham to take her handmaid Hagar as a concubine. According to the laws of the time, a son born of this woman would be regarded as the son and heir of Abraham and Sarah. When Hagar conceived, she treated her mistress with such insolence that Sarah drove her from the house. Hagar, however, returned at God's direction, submitted herself to her mistress, and gave birth to Ishmael. Afterward, when Sarah was about ninety, God promised her a son; her name was changed; and a year later Isaac, the child of promise, was born (17:15 – 27; 21:1 – 3). At a great feast celebrating the weaning of Isaac, Sarah observed Ishmael mock-

ing her son and demanded the expulsion of Hagar and Ishmael (ch. 21). Abraham reluctantly acceded, after God had instructed him to do so. Sarah died at Kiriath Arba (Hebron) at the age of 127 and was buried in the cave of Machpelah, which Abraham purchased as a family sepulchre (23:1 – 2). Sarah is mentioned again in the OT only in Isa 51:2, as the mother of the chosen race. She is mentioned several times in the NT (Ro 4:19; 9:9; Gal 4:21 – 5:1; Heb 11:11; 1Pe 3:6).

> *Wife of Abraham (Ge 11:29 – 31; 12:5); Near of kin to Abraham (Ge 12:10 – 20; 20:12); Abraham represents her as his sister, and Abimelech, king of Gerar, takes her; she is restored to Abraham by means of a dream (Ge 20:1 – 14); Is sterile; gives her maid, Hagar, to Abraham as a wife to bear his child (Ge 16:1 – 3); Becomes jealous of Hagar (Ge 16:4 – 6; 21:9 – 14); Miraculous conception of Isaac (Ge 17:15 – 21; 18:9 – 15); Name changed from Sarai to Sarah (Ge 17:15); Gives birth to Isaac (Ge 21:3, 6 – 8); Death and burial of (Ge 23; 25:10); Character of (Heb 11:11; 1Pe 3:5 – 6)*

2. Daughter of Asher (Ge 46:17; Nu 26:46; 1Ch 7:30).

SARDIS [4915] (sar′dĭs, Gr. *Sardeis*). The chief city of Lydia, under a fortified spur of Mount Tmolus in the Hermus Valley; near the junction of the roads from central Asia Minor, Ephesus, Smyrna, and Pergamum. It was the capital of Lydia under Croesus and the seat of the governor after the Persian conquest. Sardis was famous for arts and crafts and was the first center to mint gold and silver coins. So wealthy were the Lydian kings that Croesus became a legend for riches, and it was said that the sands of the Pactolus were golden. Croesus also became a legend for pride and presumptuous arrogance, when his attack on Persia led to the fall of Sardis and the eclipse of his kingdom. The capture of the great citadel by surprise attack by Cyrus and his Persians in 549 BC, and three centuries later by the

Romans, may have provided the imagery for John's warning in Rev 3:3. The great earthquake of AD 17 ruined Sardis physically and financially. The Romans contributed ten million sesterces in relief, an indication of the damage done, but the city never recovered.

SARGON [6236] (sar′gŏn, Heb. *sargôn, firm, faithful king* BDB; *the king is legitimate* IDB).

1. Sargon I, king and founder of early Babylonian Empire (2400 BC). Not referred to in the Bible.

2. Sargon II (722 – 705 BC), an Assyrian king (Isa 20:1); successor of Shalmaneser who captured Samaria (2Ki 17:1 – 6); defeated Egyptian ruler So (2Ki 17:4); destroyed the Hittite Empire; succeeded by his son Sennacherib.

SATAN [8477, 4928] (sā′tăn, Heb. *sātān*, Gr. *Satan* or *Satanas, an adversary* or *hostile opponent*). The chief of the fallen spirits, the grand adversary of God and humans. Without the definite article, the Hebrew word is used in a general sense to denote someone who is an opponent, an adversary — e.g., the angel who stood in Balaam's way (Nu 22:22), David as a possible opponent in battle (1Sa 29:4), and a political adversary (1Ki 11:14). With the definite article prefixed, it is a proper noun (Job 1 – 2; Zec 3:1 – 2) designating Satan as a personality. The teaching concerning evil and a personal devil finds its full presentation only in the NT. There the term *Satan*, transliterated from the Hebrew, always designates the personal Satan (but cf. Mt 16:23; Mk 8:33). This malignant foe is known in the NT by a number of other names and descriptive designations. He is often called the devil (Gr. *diabolos*), meaning "the slanderer" (Mt 4:1; Lk 4:2; Jn 8:44; Eph 6:11; Rev 12:12). ("Devils" in KJV and ERV is properly "demons.") Other titles or descriptive designations applied to him are Abaddon or Apollyon (Rev 9:11); "Accuser of our brothers" (12:10); "enemy," Gr. *antidikos* (1Pe 5:8); Beelzebub (Mt 12:24); Belial (2Co 6:15); the one who "leads the whole world astray" (Rev 12:9); "the evil one" (Mt 13:19, 38; 1Jn 2:13; 5:19); "the father of lies" (Jn 8:44); "the god of this age" (2Co 4:4); "a murderer" (Jn 8:44); "that ancient serpent" (Rev 12:9); "the prince of this world" (Jn 12:31; 14:30); "the ruler of the kingdom of the air" (Eph 2:2); "the tempter" (Mt 4:5; 1Th 3:5).

While clearly very powerful and clever, Satan is not an independent rival of God but is definitely subordinate, able to go only as far as God permits (Job 1:12; 2:6; Lk 22:31). Christ gives a fundamental description of his moral nature in calling him the evil one (Mt 13:19, 38). The origin of Satan is not explicitly asserted in Scripture, but the statement that he did not hold to the truth (Jn 8:44) implies that he is a fallen being, while 1Ti 3:6 indicates that he fell under God's condemnation because of ambitious pride. While many theologians refuse to apply the far-reaching prophecies in Isa 14:12 – 14 and Eze 28:12 – 15 to Satan, contending that these passages are strictly addressed to the kings of Babylon and Tyre, conservative scholars generally hold that they contain a clear revelation of Satan's origin. In his fall Satan drew a vast number of lesser celestial creatures with him (Rev 12:4).

Satan is the ruler of a powerful kingdom standing in opposition to the kingdom of God (Mt 12:26; Lk 11:18). As he who "leads the whole world astray" (Rev 12:9), his primary method is that of deception — about himself, his purpose, his activities, and his coming defeat. Although Satan was judged in the cross (Jn 13:31 – 33), he is still permitted to carry on the conflict, often with startling success. But his revealed doom is sure. He now has a sphere of activities in the heavenly realms (Eph 6:12); he will be cast down to the earth and will cause great woe because of his wrath, which he will exercise through "the dragon" (2Th 2:9; Rev 12:7 – 12; 13:2 – 8). With Christ's return to earth, he will be incarcerated in the bottomless pit for one thousand years. When released for a season, he will again attempt to deceive the nations but will be cast into "the eternal fire" prepared for him and his angels (Mt 25:41), to suffer eternal doom with those he deceived (Rev 20:1 – 3, 7 – 10).

General References to:

Enemy or adversary (1Sa 29:4; 1Ki 5:4; 11:14; Pss 38:20; 109:6). Chief of the fallen spirits, the

grand adversary of God and humans (Jn 1:6, 12; 2:1; Zec 3:1), hostile to everything good. Not an independent rival of God, but is able to go only as far as God permits (Job 1:12; 2:6; Lk 22:31). Basically evil; story of his origin not told, but he was originally good; fell as a star out of heaven because of pride (possibly Isa 14:12; Eze 29:12 – 19; Lk 10:18; 1Ti 3:6). Ruler of a powerful kingdom standing in opposition to God (Mt 12:26; Lk 11:18); continually seeks to defeat the divine plans of grace toward humankind (1Pe 5:8); defeated by Christ at Calvary (Ge 3:15; Jn 3:8). Steals God's word from the heart (Mt 13:19, 38 – 39; Mk 4:15; Lk 8:12). Causes spiritual blindness (2Co 4:4); physical infirmities (Lk 13:16). Devices of (2Co 2:11; 12:7; Eph 6:11 – 12, 16; 1Th 2:18; 1Ti 3:6 – 7). Hymenaeus and Alexander delivered to (1Ti 1:20). Contends with Michael (Jude 9). Ministers of, masquerade as apostles of Christ (2Co 11:15). To be resisted (Eph 4:27; Jas 4:7; 1Pe 5:8 – 9). Resistance of, effectual (1Jn 2:13; 5:18). Gracious deliverance from the power of (Ac 27:18; Col 1:13). Persecutes the church (Rev 2:10, 13 – 14). Christ accused of being (Mt 9:34; Mk 2:22 – 26; Lk 11:15, 18). Paul accuses Elymas the sorcerer of being (Ac 13:10).

Job	1:6	and **S** also came with them.
Zec	3:2	said to **S**, "The LORD rebuke you,
Mt	12:26	If **S** drives out **S**, he is divided
	16:23	**S**! You are a stumbling block to me;
Mk	4:15	**S** comes and takes away the word
Lk	10:18	"I saw **S** fall like lightning
	22:3	**S** entered Judas, called Iscariot,
Ro	16:20	The God of peace will soon crush **S**
1Co	5:5	is present, hand this man over to **S**,
2Co	11:14	for **S** himself masquerades
	12:7	a messenger of **S**, to torment me.
1Ti	1:20	handed over to **S** to be taught not
Rev	12:9	serpent called the devil, or **S**,
	20:2	or **S**, and bound him for a thousand
	20:7	**S** will be released from his prison

SATRAP [346, 10026] (sā′trăp, *protector of the land*). The official title of the viceroy who in the Persian Empire ruled several small provinces combined as one government. Each province had its own governor. Where NIV has "satrap," KJV consistently has "princes" for the Aramaic term (nine verses) and "lieutenants" for the Hebrew term (four verses).

SAUL [8620, 4910, 4930] (sôl, Heb. *shā′ûl, asked of God*, Gr. *Saulos*).

  1. A king of Edom (Ge 36:37 – 38; 1Ch 1:48 – 49).

  2. A son of Simeon.

  3. An ancestor of Samuel and descendant of Levi.

  4. A prominent apostle (*see Paul*).

  5. The first king of Israel, a son of Kish (Ac 13:21), of the tribe of Benjamin, a handsome man a head taller than his fellow Israelites. He is introduced in 1Sa 9, after the people had asked Samuel for a king (1Sa 8). Saul and Samuel met for the first time when Saul was searching for some lost donkeys of his father. Greeted by Samuel with compliments, Saul replied with becoming humility (9:21; cf. Jdg 6:15), but sadly, before the record of Saul's life is concluded we are to find that he suffered, to a chronic degree, the disability that matches his virtue: he was diffident and personally insecure more than most, making him both attractively unassuming and also (in later days) pathologically defensive and highly overreactive. Before Saul left, Samuel secretly anointed him as king of Israel, as the Lord had directed. God gave Saul a changed heart (1Sa 10:9), and Saul prophesied among a group of prophets who met him on his way home. We must not diminish the significance of Saul's new heart. It corresponds to the blessing of regeneration — Saul became a child of God. In the light of this the remainder of his life is deeply sad and pointedly relevant.

Personal History:

Sons of (1Ch 8:33). Personal appearance (1Sa 9:2; 10:23). Made king of Israel (1Sa 9; 10; 11:12 – 15; Hos 13:11). Dwells at Gibeah of Saul (1Sa 14:2; 15:34; Isa 10:29). Defeats Philistines (1Sa 13; 14:46, 52). Kills Amalekites (1Sa 15). Reproved

by Samuel for usurping the priestly functions (1Sa 13:11 – 14); for disobedience in not slaying Amalekites; loss of his kingdom foretold (1Sa 15). Dedicates spoils of war (1Sa 15:21 – 25; 1Ch 26:28). Sends messengers to Jesse, asking that David be sent to him as musician and armorbearer (1Sa 16:17 – 23). Defeats Philistines after Goliath is slain by David (1Sa 17). His jealousy of David; gives his daughter Michal to David to be his wife; becomes David's enemy (1Sa 18). Tries to slay David; Jonathan intercedes and incurs his father's displeasure; David's loyalty to him; Saul's repentance; prophesies (1Sa 19). Hears Doeg against Ahimelech and slays the priest and his family (1Sa 22:9 – 19). Pursues David to the wilderness of Ziph; the Ziphites betray David to (1Sa 23). Pursues David to En Gedi (1Sa 24:1 – 6). His life saved by David (1Sa 24:5 – 8). Saul's contribution for his bad faith (1Sa 24:16 – 22). David is again betrayed to, by the Ziphites; Saul pursues him to the hill of Hakilah; his life spared again by David; his confession and his blessing on David (1Sa 26). Slays the Gibeonites; crime avenged by the death of seven of his sons (2Sa 21:1 – 9). His kingdom invaded by Philistines; seeks counsel of the medium of Endor, who foretells his death (1Sa 28:3 – 25; 29:1). Is defeated and with his sons is slain (1Sa 31), their bodies exposed in Beth Shan; rescued by the people of Jabesh and burned; bones of, buried under a tree at Jabesh (1Sa 31, w 2Sa 1; 2; 1Ch 10). His death a judgment on account of his sins (1Ch 10:13).

SAVE

1Ch	16:35	Cry out, "**S** us, O God our Savior;
Job	40:14	that your own right hand can **s** you.
Ps	18:27	You **s** the humble
	69:35	for God will **s** Zion
	146:3	in mortal men, who cannot **s**.
Pr	2:16	will **s** you also from the adulteress,
Isa	38:20	The LORD will **s** me,
	59:1	of the LORD is not too short to **s**,

	63:1	mighty to **s**."
Eze	3:18	ways in order to **s** his life,
	34:22	I will **s** my flock, and they will no
Da	3:17	the God we serve is able to **s** us
Hos	1:7	and I will **s** them — not by bow,
Zep	1:18	will be able to **s** them
Zec	8:7	"I will **s** my people
Mt	1:21	he will **s** his people from their sins
	16:25	wants to **s** his life will lose it,
Lk	19:10	to seek and to **s** what was lost."
Jn	3:17	but to **s** the world through him.
	12:47	come to judge the world, but to **s** it.
1Co	7:16	whether you will **s** your husband?
1Ti	1:15	came into the world to **s** sinners —
Heb	7:25	to **s** completely those who come
Jas	5:20	of his way will **s** him from death

SAVIOR [3802, 3829, 4635, 9591, 5400] (sāˊvˊyôr, Gr. *sōtēr*, *savior*, *deliverer*, *preserver*). One who saves, delivers, or preserves from any evil or danger, whether physical or spiritual, temporal or eternal. A basic OT concept is that God is the Deliverer of his people; it emphatically declares that people cannot save themselves and that the Lord alone is the Savior (Ps 44:3, 7; Isa 43:11; 45:21; 60:16; Jer 14:8; Hos 13:4). The Hebrew term rendered "savior" is a participle rather than a noun, indicating that the Hebrews did not think of this as an official title of God but rather as a descriptive term of his activity. In the OT the term is not applied to the Messiah. He received salvation from God (2Sa 22:51; Pss 28:8; 144:10), but he came to offer salvation to all (Isa 49:6, 8; Zec 9:9). The term is also applied to people who are used as the instruments of God's deliverance (Jdg 3:9, 15 ASV; 2Ki 13:5; Ne 9:27; Ob 21).

The Greeks applied the title *sōtēr* (Savior) to their gods; it was also used of philosophers (e.g., Epicurus) or rulers (e.g., Ptolemy I, Nero) or men who had brought notable benefits on their country. But in the NT it is a strictly religious term and is never applied to a mere man. It is used of both God the Father and Christ the Son. God the Father is Savior, for he is the author of our salvation, which he provided through Christ (Lk 1:47; 1Ti 1:1; 2:3; 4:10; Tit 1:3; 2:10; 3:4; Jude 25). Savior is preeminently the title of the Son (2Ti 1:10; Tit 1:4; 2:13; 3:6; 2Pe 1:1, 11; 2:20; 3:2, 18; 1Jn 4:10). At his birth the angel announced him as "a Savior ... he is Christ the Lord" (Lk 2:11). His mission to save his people from their sins was announced before his birth (Mt 1:21) and was stated by Jesus as the aim of his coming (Lk 19:10). The salvation that he wrought is for all humankind; he is "the Savior of the world" (Jn 4:42; 1Jn 4:14). Believers await a future work of Christ as Savior when he will come again to consummate our salvation in the transformation of our bodies (Php 3:20).

Dt	32:15	and rejected the Rock his **S**.
2Sa	22:3	stronghold, my refuge and my **s** —
1Ch	16:35	Cry out, "Save us, O God our **S**;
Ps	18:46	Exalted be God my **S**!
	42:5	my **S** and
	79:9	Help us, O God our **S**,
	85:4	Restore us again, O God our **S**,
Isa	17:10	You have forgotten God your **S**;
	19:20	he will send them a **s** and defender,
	43:3	the Holy One of Israel, your **S**;
	43:11	and apart from me there is no **s**.
	62:11	'See, your **S** comes!
	63:8	and so he became their **S**.
Hos	13:4	no **S** except me.
Mic	7:7	I wait for God my **S**;
Hab	3:18	I will be joyful in God my **S**.
Lk	1:47	and my spirit rejoices in God my **S**,
	2:11	of David a **S** has been born to you;
Jn	4:42	know that this man really is the **S**
Ac	5:31	**S** that he might give repentance
	13:23	God has brought to Israel the **S**
Eph	5:23	his body, of which he is the **S**.
Php	3:20	we eagerly await a **S** from there,
1Ti	1:1	by the command of God our **S**
	4:10	who is the **S** of all men,
2Ti	1:10	through the appearing of our **S**,
Tit	2:13	appearing of our great God and **S**,
	3:4	and love of God our **S** appeared,
2Pe	1:11	eternal kingdom of our Lord and **S**

	2:20	and **S** Jesus Christ and are again
	3:18	and knowledge of our Lord and **S**
1Jn	4:14	Son to be the **S** of the world.
Jude	1:25	to the only God our **S** be glory,

SCAPEGOAT [6439] (Heb. *'ăzā'zēl*). The second of two goats for which lots were cast on the Day of Atonement (Lev 16:8, 10, 26). The first was sacrificed as a sin offering, but the second had the people's sins transferred to it by prayer and was then taken into the wilderness and released.

SCOURGE [3579, 5596, 8765] (skûrj, Heb. generally *shut, to whip, lash, scourge; shôt, a whip, scourge*, Gr. *mastigoō, to whip, flog, scourge; mastix, a whip, lash; phragelloō, to flog, scourge*, as a public punishment of the condemned). The act or the instrument used to inflict severe pain by beating. Scourging, well known in the East, was familiar to the Hebrews from Egypt. The Mosaic law authorized the beating of a culprit, apparently with a rod, but limited to forty the strokes given the prostrate victim (Dt 25:3). Leviticus 19:20 does not impose true scourging (*biqqoreth*, translated "due punishment" in NIV, expresses an investigation). 1 Kings 12:11, 14 apparently refers to true scourging. It was later legalized among the Jews, and a three-thonged whip was used, but the legal limitation was observed (2Co 11:24). It was administered by local synagogue authorities (Mt 10:17; Ac 22:19) or by the Sanhedrin (Ac 5:40). Among the Romans either rods were used (Ac 16:22; 2Co 11:25) or whips, the thongs of which were weighted with jagged pieces of bone or metal to make the blow more effective (Mt 27:26; Mk 15:15; Jn 19:1). It was used to wrest confessions and secrets from its victims (Ac 22:24). It was forbidden to scourge Roman citizens (22:25), that punishment generally reserved for slaves or those condemned to death.

SCRIPTURES [6219, 1207, 1210] (*writing*). The Word of God (Jer 30:2). Interpreted by doctors (Jn 3:10; 7:52). Inspired (2Ti 3:16). *See Word of God.*

Mt	22:29	because you do not know the **S**
Lk	24:27	said in all the **S** concerning himself.
	24:45	so they could understand the **S**.
Jn	5:39	These are the **S** that testify about
Ac	17:11	examined the **S** every day to see
2Ti	3:15	you have known the holy **S**,
2Pe	3:16	as they do the other **S**,

SEA OF GALILEE Called Sea of Kinnereth (Nu 34:11; Dt 3:17; Jos 12:3; 13:27); Lake of Gennesaret (Lk 5:1); Sea of Tiberias (Jn 21:1). Jesus calls disciples on the shore of (Mt 4:18–22; Lk 5:1–11). Jesus teaches from a boat on (Mt 13:13). Miracles of Jesus on (Mt 8:24–32; 14:22–33; 17:27; Mk 4:37–39; Lk 5:1–9; 8:22–24; Jn 12:1–11).

SEAL [2597, 3159, 3160, 3973, 6258, 5381, 5382] (Heb. *hôthām, seal, signet, tabb'ath, signet ring, hātham, to seal*, Gr. *sphragizō, katasphragizomai, to seal*).

1. *Literal sense.* A device bearing a design or a name made so that it can impart an impression in relief on a soft substance like clay or wax. Originally they took the form of a cylinder with a hole from end to end for a cord to pass through, but this was gradually superseded by the scarab (beetle-shaped). Some were carried by cords hung from the neck or waist; many were cone-shaped and were kept in boxes; but most were made into finger rings. Every person of any standing had a seal.

Seals were used for various purposes: (1) as a mark of authenticity and authority to letters, royal commands, etc. (1Ki 21:8; Est 3:12; 8:8, 10); (2) as a mark of the formal ratification of a transaction or covenant, as when Jeremiah's friends witnessed his purchase of a piece of property (Jer 32:11–14) or when the chief men of Jerusalem set their seal to a written covenant to keep its laws (Ne 9:38; 10:1); (3) as a means of protecting books and other documents so that they would not be tampered with (Jer 32:14; Rev 5:2, 5, 9; 6:1, 3); (4) as a proof of delegated authority and power (Ge 41:42; Est 3:10; 8:2); (5) as a means of sealing closed doors so as to keep out unauthorized persons (Da 6:17; Mt 27:66; Rev 20:3) — usually by stretching a cord across them and then sealing the cord; and (6) as an official mark of ownership, as, for example, on jar handles and jar stoppers.

2. *Figurative sense.* Scripture often uses the term metaphorically to indicate authentication, confirmation, ownership, evidence, or security. God does not forget sin, but stores it up against the sinner, under a seal (Dt 32:34; Job 14:17). Prophecies that are intended to be kept secret for a time are bound with a seal (Da 12:4, 9; Rev 5:1ff.; 10:4). Paul speaks of having sealed the offering of the Gentiles for the saints in Jerusalem (Ro 15:28 KJV). The word has the sense of authentication in 1Co 9:2, where Paul describes his converts at Corinth as the "seal" placed by Christ on his work — the proof or vindication of his apostleship. The circumcision of Abraham is described as an outward ratification by God of the righteousness of faith that he had already received before he was circumcised (Ro 4:11). Believers are said to be "marked in him with a seal, the promised Holy Spirit" (Eph 1:13), as an owner sets his seal on his property; and the same thought is conveyed in the words "with whom you were sealed for the day of redemption" (4:30). God marks off his own by putting his seal on their foreheads (Rev 7:2 – 4).

Ps	40:9	I do not **s** my lips,
SS	8:6	Place me like a **s** over your heart,
Da	12:4	and **s** the words of the scroll
Jn	6:27	God the Father has placed his **s**
1Co	9:2	For you are the **s** of my apostleship
2Co	1:22	set his **s** of ownership on us,
Eph	1:13	you were marked in him with a **s**,
Rev	6:3	the Lamb opened the second **s**,
	9:4	people who did not have the **s**
	22:10	"Do not **s** up the words

SECOND COMING OF CHRIST

Called:

Times of refreshing from the presence of the Lord (Ac 3:19). Times of restitution of all things (Ac 3:21, w Ro 8:21). Last time (1Pe 1:5). Appearing of Jesus Christ (1Pe 1:7). Revelation of Jesus Christ (1Pe 1:13). Glorious appearing of the great God and our Savior (Tit 2:13). Coming

of the day of God (2Pe 3:12). Day of our Lord Jesus Christ (1Co 1:8).

Foretold by:

Prophets (Da 7:13; Jude 14). Jesus (Mt 25:31; Jn 14:3). Apostles (Ac 3:20; 1Ti 6:14). Angels (Ac 1:10 – 11). Signs preceding (Mt 24:3). Time of, unknown (Mt 24:36; Mk 13:32).

Manner of:

In clouds (Mt 24:30; 26:64; Rev 1:7). In the glory of his Father (Mt 16:27). In his own glory (Mt 25:31). In flaming fire (2Th 1:8). With power and great glory (Mt 24:30). As he ascended (Ac 1:9, 11). With a shout and the voice of the archangel (1Th 4:16). Accompanied by angels (Mt 16:27; 25:31; Mk 8:38; 2Th 1:7). With his saints (1Th 3:13; Jude 14). Suddenly (Mk 13:36). Unexpectedly (Mt 24:44; Lk 12:40). As a thief in the night (1Th 5:2; 2Pe 3:10; Rev 16:15). As the lightning (Mt 24:27). The heavens and earth shall be dissolved (2Pe 3:10, 12). They who shall have died in Christ shall rise first at (1Th 4:16). The saints alive at, shall be caught up to meet him (1Th 4:17). Is not to make atonement (Heb 9:28, w Ro 6:9 – 10; Heb 10:14).

The Purposes of:

To complete the salvation of saints (Heb 9:28; 1Pe 1:5). Be glorified in his saints (2Th 1:10). Be marveled at among those who believe (2Th 1:10). Bring to light the hidden things of darkness (1Co 4:5). Judge (Ps 50:3 – 4, w Jn 5:22; 2Ti 4:1; Jude 15; Rev 20:11 – 13). Reign (Isa 24:23; Da 7:14; Rev 11:15). Destroy death (1Co 15:25 – 26). Every eye shall see him at (Rev 1:7). Should be always considered as at hand (Ro 13:12; Php 4:5; 1Pe 4:7). Blessedness of being prepared for (Mt 24:46; Lk 12:37 – 38).

The Saints:

Assured of (Job 19:25 – 26). Love (2Ti 4:8). Look for (Php 3:20; Tit 2:13). Wait for (1Co 1:7; 1Th 1:10). Speed its coming (2Pe 3:12). Pray for (Rev 22:20). Should be ready for (Mt 24:44; Lk 12:40). Should watch for (Mt 24:42; Mk 13:35 – 37; Lk

21:36). *Should be patient unto* (2Th 3:5; Jas 5:7–8). *Shall be preserved unto* (Php 1:6; 2Ti 4:18; 1Pe 1:5; Jude 24). *Shall not be ashamed* (1Jn 2:28; 4:17). *Shall be blameless* (1Co 1:8; 1Th 3:13; 5:23; Jude 24). *Shall be like him* (Php 3:21; 1Jn 3:2). *Shall see him as he is* (1Jn 3:2). *Shall appear with him in glory* (Col 3:4). *Shall receive a crown of glory* (2Ti 4:8; 1Pe 5:4). *Shall reign with him* (Da 7:27; 2Ti 2:12; Rev 5:10; 20:6; 22:5). *Faith of, will be praised at* (1Pe 1:7).

The Wicked:

Scoff at (2Pe 3:3–4). *Presume upon the delay of* (Mt 24:48). *Shall be surprised by* (Mt 24:37–39; 1Th 5:3; 2Pe 3:10). *Shall be punished* (2Th 1:8–9). *Man of sin to be destroyed* (2Th 2:8). *Illustrated* (Mt 25:6; Lk 12:36, 39; 19:12, 15).

SEED (Heb. *zera'*, Gr. *sperma, sporos*). There is a threefold use of this word in Scripture.

1. *Agricultural.* The farmer held his seed in his upturned garment, casting it out as he walked. Grain was sown in the early winter, after the first rains. Christ's parable of the sower is well known (Mk 4:1–20; Lk 8:5–15). Land was measured by the amount of seed that could be sown on it (Lev 27:16). The wilderness was "land not sown" (Jer 2:2).

2. *Physiological.* A "man's seed" (KJV) or "emission of semen" (NIV) is a frequent expression in the Hebrew laws of cleanness (Lev 15:16ff.). The NT speaks of Christians as having been begotten by God — "not of perishable seed, but of imperishable" (1Pe 1:23; 1Jn 3:9).

3. *Figurative.* Here seed means descendants (Ge 13:16 KJV) or genealogy (Ezr 2:59; Ne 7:61 KJV) or a class of people ("seed of evildoers," Isa 1:4 KJV). "The holy seed" (Ezr 9:2; Isa 6:13) symbolizes the people of Israel. Paul's use of "seed" ("not … 'seeds'") in Gal 3:16 had for its purpose a proof that the promises to Abraham were realized in Christ — an example of rabbinical exegesis used by Paul against his rabbinical adversaries.

Ge	1:11	on the land that bear fruit with **s**
Isa	55:10	so that it yields **s** for the sower
Mt	13:3	"A farmer went out to sow his **s**.
	13:31	of heaven is like a mustard **s**,
	17:20	have faith as small as a mustard **s**,
Lk	8:11	of the parable: The **s** is the word
1Co	3:6	I planted the **s**, Apollos watered it,
2Co	9:10	he who supplies **s** to the sower
Gal	3:29	then you are Abraham's **s**,
1Pe	1:23	not of perishable **s**,
1Jn	3:9	because God's **s** remains in him;

SEEK

Lev	19:18	Do not **s** revenge or bear a grudge
Dt	4:29	if from there you **s** the LORD your
1Ki	22:5	"First **s** the counsel of the LORD."
1Ch	28:9	If you **s** him, he will be found
2Ch	7:14	themselves and pray and **s** my face
Ps	34:10	those who **s** the LORD lack no
	119:2	and **s** him with all their heart.
Pr	8:17	and those who **s** me find me.
	28:5	those who **s** the LORD understand
Isa	55:6	**S** the LORD while he may be
Hos	10:12	for it is time to **s** the LORD,
Am	5:4	"**S** me and live;
Zep	2:3	**S** the LORD, all you humble
Mt	6:33	But **s** first his kingdom
	7:7	and it will be given to you; **s**
Lk	19:10	For the Son of Man came to **s**
Ro	10:20	found by those who did not **s** me;
1Co	7:27	you married? Do not **s** a divorce.
Heb	11:6	rewards those who earnestly **s** him.
1Pe	3:11	he must **s** peace and pursue it.

SELEUCIDS (sĕlū'sĭds, Gr. *Seleukos*). A dynasty of rulers of the kingdom of Syria (it included Babylonia, Bactria, Persia, Syria, and part of Asia Minor), descended from Seleucus I, a general of Alexander the Great. It lasted from 312 to 64 BC, when the Romans took it over. One of them, Antiochus Epiphanes, precipitated the Maccabean war by trying forcibly to Hellenize the Jews.

SELF-CONTROL [4200+5110+8120, 202, 203, 1602, 3768, 5404, 5407, 5409].

A Virtue:

Without self-control temptation and evil may freely assault a person (Pr 25:28). Of Saul (1Sa 10:27); of David (1Sa 24:1 – 15; 26:1 – 20); of Jesus (Mt 26:62 – 63; 27:12 – 14). Paul taught on self-control, in relation to righteousness (Ac 24:25); the marriage bed (1Co 7:5); a fruit of the Spirit (Gal 5:23); in contrast to the godlessness of the last days (1Th 5:8; 2Th 1:6; 2Ti 3:3). Overseers and deacons must have a life characterized by self-control (1Ti 3:2; Tit 1:8). Taught by leaders and exemplified by older believers (Tit 2:2, 5 – 6); taught by the grace of God (Tit 2:12). Peter lists self-control as one of the qualities of a godly life (2Pe 1:6). A believer should continually be prepared for Christ's return, exhibiting a self-controlled life (1Pe 1:13; 4:7). Be self-controlled and prepared for the devil, who prowls about looking for those who have a false sense of security that makes them prime candidates for his trap in the world's system (1Pe 4:7).

Sexual Self-Control:

Vow of (Job 31:1). Commanded (Mt 5:27 – 28; Ro 13:13; 1Co 7:1 – 9, 25 – 29, 36 – 38; Col 3:5; 1Ti 4:12; 5:1 – 2). Instances of: Joseph (Ge 39:7 – 12); Uriah (2Sa 11:8 – 13); Boaz (Ru 3:6 – 13); Joseph, husband of Mary (Mt 1:24 – 25); eunuchs (Mt 19:12); Paul (1Co 7:8; 9:27); believers (Rev 14:1, 4 – 5).

Pr	25:28	is a man who lacks **s**.
Ac	24:25	**s** and the judgment to come,
1Co	7:5	you because of your lack of **s**.
Gal	5:23	faithfulness, gentleness and **s**.
2Ti	3:3	slanderous, without **s**, brutal,
2Pe	1:6	and to knowledge, **s**; and to **s**,

SELF-DENIAL (Lk 21:2 – 4; 1Co 6:12; 9:12, 15, 18 – 19, 23, 25 – 27; 10:23 – 24; 2Co 6:3; Php 2:4 – 8; 3:7 – 9; 2Ti 2:4; Tit 2:12; Heb 13:13; Rev 12:11).

In Respect to:

Appetite (Pr 23:2; Da 10:3); sinful pleasures (Mt 5:29 – 30; 18:8 – 9; Mk 9:43); carnality (Ro 6:6;

8:12 – 13, 35 – 36; 13:14; 1Co 9:27; Gal 5:16 – 17, 24; Col 3:5; Tit 2:12; 1Pe 2:11 – 12, 14 – 16).

Required of Christ's Disciples:

(Mt 8:19 – 22; 10:37 – 39; 16:24 – 25; 19:12, 21; Mk 2:14; 8:34 – 35; 10:29; Lk 5:11; 9:23 – 24, 57 – 58; 12:33; 14:26 – 27, 33; 18:27 – 30; Jn 12:25; 2Ti 2:4; Heb 13:13; 1Pe 4:1; 3Jn 7). For a brother's sake (Ro 14:1 – 22; 15:1 – 5; 1Co 8:10 – 13; 10:23 – 24; Php 2:4). For the sake of the ministry (2Co 6:3). Christ's teachings concerning (Mk 12:43 – 44; Lk 21:2 – 4).

Parables of:

(Mt 13:44 – 46; 18:8 – 9; Mk 9:43).

Instances of:

Abraham, when he accorded to Lot his preference for the grazing lands of Canaan (Ge 13:9; 17:8); in offering Isaac (Ge 22:12). Moses, in choosing suffering over pleasure (Heb 11:25); in taking no compensation from the Israelites (Nu 16:15). Samuel, in his administration of justice (1Sa 12:3 – 4). The widow of Zarephath, in sharing with Elijah the last of her sustenance (1Ki 17:12 – 15). David, in paying for the threshing floor (2Sa 24:24). The psalmist (Ps 132:3 – 5). Daniel, in refusing royal food (Da 1:8); in refusing rewards from Belshazzar (Da 5:16 – 17). Esther, in risking her life for her people (Est 4:16). The Recabites, in refusing wine or fermented drink, or even to plant vineyards (Jer 35:6 – 7). Peter and other apostles, in abandoning their vocations to follow Jesus (Mt 4:20; 9:9; Mk 1:16 – 20; 2:14; Lk 5:11, 27 – 28); in forsaking all (Mt 19:27; Mk 10:28; Lk 5:28). The widow, who cast all into the treasury (Lk 21:4). The early Christians, in having everything in common (Ac 2:44 – 45; 4:34). Joseph, in selling his possessions and giving all to the apostles (Ac 4:36 – 37). Paul (1Co 10:23 – 24; Gal 2:20; 6:14); in not counting even his life valuable to himself (Ac 20:24; 21:13; Php 3:7 – 8); in laboring for his own support while he taught (Ac 20:34 – 35;

1Co 4:12; 10:33); in not exercising his authority (1Co 6:12; 9:12, 15, 18 – 19, 23 – 27).

SELF-DISCIPLINE [5406]. Needed: not to give in to sin (Ro 6:12 – 14); to "run the race" of life according to the rules (1Co 9:24 – 27; 2Ti 2:1 – 7). Contrasted to timidity (2Ti 1:7). *See Self-Control.*

SELF-EXAMINATION

Commanded:

(Ps 4:4; Hag 1:7; 1Co 11:28, 31; 2Co 13:5; Gal 6:4). By inference (Jer 17:9). Conversion as a result of (Ps 119:59; La 3:40).

Exemplified by:

Job (Job 13:23); David (Pss 19:2; 26:2; 139:23 – 24); the psalmist (Pss 77:6; 119:59); the disciples (Mt 26:22; Mk 14:19).

SELFISH

Ps	119:36	and not toward **s** gain.
Pr	18:1	An unfriendly man pursues **s** ends;
Gal	5:20	fits of rage, **s** ambition, dissensions,
Php	1:17	preach Christ out of **s** ambition,
	2:3	Do nothing out of **s** ambition
Jas	3:14	and **s** ambition in your hearts,

SELFISHNESS [1299, 9294, 2249].

Denounced:

Admonitions against (Lk 6:32 – 34; Ro 14:15; 15:1 – 3; 1Co 10:24; Gal 6:2; Php 2:4). Christ's example against (Ro 15:3; 2Co 5:15; Php 2:5 – 8). Judged (Pr 18:17; 24:11 – 12; Hag 1:4, 9 – 10).

Exemplified by:

Corrupt officials (Mic 3:11); corrupt priests and prophets (Eze 34:18; Zec 7:6); those who accumulate too much (Pr 11:26; Isa 5:8; Mt 19:21 – 22); the self-indulgent (Ro 14:15; 2Ti 3:2 – 4); those unsympathetic with the unfortunate (Pr 28:27; Jas 2:15 – 16; 1Jn 3:17); Cain (Ge 4:9); Gadites and Reubenites (Nu 32:6); David's friends (Ps 38:11); the Israelites (Hag 1:4; Mal 1:10); early Christians (Php 2:20 – 21).

SELF-RIGHTEOUSNESS

Described as:

Assertive (Pr 20:6; Mt 7:22 – 23); delusive (Pr 12:15; 16:2; 21:2; 28:26; Isa 28:20; 50:11; 64:6; Hos 12:8; Mt 7:22 – 23; 22:12 – 13; Gal 6:3).

Denounced:

(Job 12:2; Pr 25:14, 27; 26:12; 30:12 – 13; Isa 5:21; 65:3 – 5; Jer 2:13, 22 – 23, 34 – 35; 8:8; Eze 33:24 – 26; Am 6:13; Mt 9:10 – 13; Mk 2:16; 8:15; Lk 5:30; 16:14 – 15; 18:9 – 14; 22:12 – 13; 23:29 – 31; Ro 11:19 – 21). Admonitions against (Dt 9:4 – 6; 1Sa 2:9; Pr 27:2, 21; Jer 7:4; Hab 2:4; 2Co 1:9; 10:17 – 18). Judgments against (Pr 14:12; Isa 28:17; 50:11; Jer 8:8; 49:4, 16; Zep 3:11). Proverbs concerning (Pr 12:15; 14:12; 16:2; 20:6; 21:2; 25:14, 27; 26:12; 27:2, 21; 28:13, 26; 30:12 – 13). Parables concerning (Lk 7:36 – 50; 10:25 – 37; 15:25 – 32; 18:9 – 14). Paul's instruction regarding (Ro 2:17 – 20; 3:27; 10:3; 11:19 – 21; 2Co 1:9; 10:17 – 18; Gal 6:3).

Instances of:

Job accused of (Job 11:4; 32:1 – 2; 33:8 – 9; 35:2, 7 – 8); Israelites (Nu 16:3; Ro 2:17 – 20; 10:3); Saul (1Sa 15:13 – 21); the wicked (Ps 10:5 – 6); Pharisees (Mt 9:10 – 13; Mk 2:16 – 17; Lk 5:30; 7:39; 15:2; 16:14 – 15; 18:9 – 14; Jn 9:28 – 41); rich young ruler (Mt 19:16 – 22; Mk 10:17 – 22; Lk 18:18 – 23); lawyer (Lk 10:25 – 29); church of Laodicea (Rev 3:17 – 18).

SENT

Ex	3:14	to the Israelites: 'I AM has **s** me
Isa	55:11	achieve the purpose for which I **s** it.
	61:1	He has **s** me to bind up
Mt	10:40	me receives the one who **s** me.
Mk	6:7	he **s** them out two by two
Lk	4:18	He has **s** me to proclaim freedom
	9:2	and he **s** them out to preach
	10:16	rejects me rejects him who **s** me."
Jn	4:34	"is to do the will of him who **s** me
	5:24	believes him who **s** me has eternal
	16:5	"Now I am going to him who **s** me,

	17:18	As you **s** me into the world,
	20:21	As the Father has **s** me, I am
Ro	10:15	can they preach unless they are **s**?
1Jn	4:10	but that he loved us and **s** his Son

SEPTUAGINT (sĕp'tū-a-jĭnt, *seventy*). The first and most important of a number of ancient translations of the Hebrew OT into Greek, prepared in Alexandria in the second and third centuries BC. It is generally agreed that the Pentateuch was translated from Hebrew into Greek in Egypt around the time of Ptolemy II, c. 280 BC. The rest of the OT was done at a later date. Most scholars believe the whole to have been finished by 180, although some scholars (notably Kahle) disagree, believing that the LXX never contained more than the Pentateuch until the Christians took it over and added the rest of the OT books much later. The LXX came to have great authority among the non-Palestinian Jews. Its use in the synagogues of the dispersion made it one of the most important missionary aids. Probably it was the first work of substantial size ever to be translated into another language. Now the Greeks could read the divine revelation in their own tongue. When the NT quotes from the OT, as it frequently does, the form of the quotation often follows the LXX.

SERAPHS, SERAPHIM [8597] (sĕr'a-fĭm, Heb. *serāphim, burning ones, [winged] serpents*). Called seraphs (JB, NIV), seraphim (MLB, NASB, NEB, RSV, *-im* being the Hebrew plural ending), and seraphims (KJV). They were celestial beings whom Isaiah, when he was called to the prophetic ministry, saw standing before the enthroned Lord (Isa 6:2 – 3, 6 – 7). This is the only mention of these creatures in the Bible.

SERMON ON THE MOUNT The Sermon on the Mount is the first of five great discourses in Matthew (chs. 5 – 7; 10; 13; 18; 24 – 25). It contains three types of material: (1) beatitudes, or declarations of blessedness (5:1 – 12); (2) ethical admonitions (5:13 – 20; 6:1 – 7:23); and (3) contrasts between Jesus' ethical teaching and Jewish legalistic traditions (5:21 – 48). The sermon

ends with a short parable stressing the importance of practicing what has just been taught (7:24 – 27) and an expression of amazement by the crowds at the authority with which Jesus spoke (7:28 – 29). Opinion differs as to whether the sermon is a summary of what Jesus taught on one occasion or a compilation of teachings presented on numerous occasions. Matthew possibly took a single sermon and expanded it with other relevant teachings of Jesus. Thirty-four of the verses in Matthew's account of the sermon occur in different contexts in Luke than the so-called Sermon on the Plain (Lk 6:17 – 49). The Sermon on the Mount's call to moral and ethical living is so high that some have dismissed it as being completely unrealistic or have projected its fulfillment to the future kingdom. There is no doubt, however, that Jesus (and Matthew) gave the sermon as a standard for all Christians, realizing that its demands cannot be met in our own power. It is also true that Jesus occasionally used hyperbole to make his point. For example, Jesus is not teaching self-mutilation (Mt 5:29 – 30), for even a blind man can lust. The point is that we should deal as drastically with sin as necessary.

SERPENT [5729, 7352, 8597, 9490, 4058].

Satan appears in the form of, to Eve (Ge 3:1 – 15; 2Co 11:3). Subtlety of (Ge 3:1; Ecc 10:8; Mt 10:16). Curse upon (Ge 3:14 – 15; 49:17). Metaphorically feeds on dust (Ge 3:14; Isa 65:25; Mic 7:17). Unfit for food (Mt 7:10). Venom of (Dt 32:24, 33; Job 20:16; Pss 58:4; 140:3; Pr 23:31 – 32; Ac 28:5 – 6). Staff of Moses transformed into (Ex 4:3; 7:15). Poisonous, sent as a plague on the Israelites (Nu 21:6 – 7; Dt 8:15; 1Co 10:9); the wounds of miraculously healed by looking upon the bronze image set up by Moses (Nu 21:8 – 9). Charming of (Ps 58:4 – 5; Ecc 10:11; Jer 8:17). Mentioned in Solomon's riddle (Pr 30:19). Constriction of (Rev 9:19). Sea serpent (Am 9:3). The Seventy-two given power over (Lk 10:19). The apostles given power over (Mk 16:18; Ac 28:5). Figurative (Pr 23:32; Isa 14:29).

SERVANT [408, 563, 5853, 5855, 5987, 6269, 9148, 9250, 10523, 1356, 1527, 1528, 3313, 3860, 4087, 4090, 5281, 5677].

Bond Servant:

Laws of Moses concerning (Ex 20:10; 21:1 – 11, 20 – 21, 26 – 27, 32; Lev 19:20 – 22; 25:6, 10, 35 – 55; Dt 5:14; 15:12, 14, 18; 24:7). Kidnapping and slave trading forbidden (Dt 21:10 – 14; 24:7; 1Ti 1:10; Rev 18:13). Fugitive, not to be returned to master (Dt 23:15 – 16). David erroneously supposed to be a fugitive slave (1Sa 25:10). Instances of fugitive: Hagar, commanded by an angel to return to her mistress (Ge 16:9). Sought by Shimei (1Ki 2:39 – 41). Interceded for, by Paul (Phm 10 – 21). Bought and sold (Ge 17:13, 27; 37:28, 36; 39:17; Lev 22:11; Dt 28:68; Est 7:4; Eze 27:13; Joel 3:6; Am 8:6; Rev 18:13). Captives of war made (Dt 20:14; 21:10 – 14; 2Ki 5:2; 2Ch 28:8, 10; La 5:13); captive bondservants shared by priests and Levites (Nu 31:28 – 47). Thieves punished by being made (Ge 43:18; Ex 22:3). Defaulting debtors made (Lev 25:39; Mt 18:25). Children of defaulting debtors sold for (2Ki 4:1 – 7). Voluntary servitude of (Lev 25:47; Dt 15:16 – 17; Jos 9:11 – 21). Given as dowry (Ge 29:24, 29). Owned by priests (Lev 22:11; Mk 14:66). Slaves owned slaves (2Sa 9:10). The master might marry or give in marriage (Ex 21:7 – 10; Dt 21:10 – 14; 1Ch 2:34 – 35). Taken in concubinage (Ge 16:1 – 2, 6; 30:3, 9). Used as soldiers by Abraham (Ge 14:14). Rights of those born to a master (Ge 14:14; 17:13, 27; Ex 21:4; Pr 29:21; Ecc 2:7; Jer 2:14). Must be circumcised (Ge 17:13, 27; Ex 12:44). Must enjoy religious privileges with the master's household (Dt 12:12, 18; 16:11, 14; 29:10 – 11). Must have rest on the Sabbath (Ex 20:10; 23:12; Dt 5:14). Servitude threatened, as a national punishment, for disobedience of Israel (Dt 28:68; Joel 3:7 – 8). Degrading influences of bondage exemplified by cowardice (Ex 14:11 – 12; 16:3; Jdg 5:16 – 18, 23). Social status of (Mt 10:24 – 25; Lk 17:7 – 9; 22:27; Jn 13:16). Equal status of, with other disciples of Jesus (1Co 7:21 – 22; 12:13; Gal 3:28; Eph 6:8). Proverbs concerning (Pr 12:9; 13:17; 17:2; 19:10; 25:13; 26:6; 27:18, 27; 29:19, 21; 30:10, 21 – 23). Parables of (Mt 24:45 – 51; Lk 12:35 – 48; 16:1 – 13).

Cruelty to: Hagar (Ge 16:1 – 21; Gal 4:22 – 31); Joseph (Ge 37:26 – 28, 36); Israelites (Ex 1:8 – 22; 2:1 – 4; 5:7 – 9; Dt 6:12, 21; Ac 7:19, 34); sick, abandoned (1Sa 30:13); Gibeonites (Jos 9:22 – 27); Canaanites (1Ki 9:21); Jews in Babylon (2Ch 36:20; Est 1:1 – 10). Admonitions against cruelty to (Jer 22:13).

Kindness to: (Ps 123:2; Pr 29:21). Commanded (Lev 25:43; Eph 6:9). Exemplified by Job (Job 19:15 – 16; 31:13 – 14); by Boaz (Ru 2:4); by centurion (Mt 8:8 – 13; Lk 7:2 – 10); by Paul (Phm 1 – 21). Freeing of (2Ch 36:23; Ezr 1:1 – 4).

Duties of: To be faithful (1Co 4:2). To be obedient (Mt 8:9; Eph 6:5 – 9; Col 3:22 – 25; Tit 2:9 – 10; 1Pe 2:18 – 20). To honor masters (Mal 1:6; 1Ti 6:1 – 2). Warning to (Zep 1:9). Figurative (Lev 25:42, 55; Ps 116:16; Isa 52:3; Mt 24:45, 51; Lk 12:35 – 48; 16:1 – 13; 17:7 – 9; Jn 8:32 – 35; Ro 6:16 – 22; 1Co 4:1 – 2; 7:21 – 23; Gal 5:13; 1Pe 2:16; 2Pe 2:19; Rev 7:3).

Hired Workers:

Jacob (Ge 29:15; 30:26); reemployed (Ge 30:27 – 34; 31:6 – 7, 41). Parable of laborers in vineyard (Mt 20:1 – 15); of father of prodigal son (Lk 15:17, 19). Kindness to (Ru 2:4). Treatment of, more considerable than that accorded slaves (Lev 25:53). Await employment in the marketplace (Mt 20:1 – 3). Mercenary (Job 7:2). Unfaithful (Jn 10:12 – 13).

Rights of: Receive wages (Mt 10:10; Lk 10:7; Ro 4:4; 1Ti 5:18; Jas 5:4). Daily payment of wages (Lev 19:13; Dt 24:15). Share in spontaneous products of land in the seventh year (Lev 25:6). Wages of, paid in a portion of the flocks or products (Ge 30:31 – 32; 2Ch 2:10); or in money (Mt 20:2, 9 – 10). Oppression of, forbidden (Dt 24:14; Col 4:1); punished (Mal 3:5).

Ex	14:31	trust in him and in Moses his **s**.
1Sa	3:10	"Speak, for your **s** is listening."

Job	1:8	"Have you considered my **s** Job?
Ps	19:13	Keep your **s** also from willful sins;
Pr	14:35	A king delights in a wise **s**,
	22:7	and the borrower is **s** to the lender.
	31:15	and portions for her **s** girls.
Isa	41:8	"But you, O Israel, my **s**,
	53:11	my righteous **s** will justify
Zec	3:8	going to bring my **s**, the Branch.
Mal	1:6	his father, and a **s** his master.
Mt	8:13	his **s** was healed at that very hour.
	20:26	great among you must be your **s**,
	24:45	Who then is the faithful and wise **s**,
	25:21	'Well done, good and faithful **s**!
Lk	1:38	I am the Lord's **s**," Mary answered.
	16:13	"No **s** can serve two masters.
Jn	12:26	and where I am, my **s** also will be.
Ro	13:4	For he is God's **s** to do you good.
Php	2:7	taking the very nature of a **s**,
Col	1:23	of which I, Paul, have become a **s**.
2Ti	2:24	And the Lord's **s** must not quarrel;

SERVANT OF THE LORD Agent of the Lord such as the patriarchs (Ex 32:13), Moses (Nu 12:7), and the prophets (Zec 1:6). Used as a title for the Messiah in Isa 40 – 66. The NT applies Isaiah's Servant passages to Jesus (Isa 42:1 – 4; Mt 12:16 – 21).

SERVE

Dt	10:12	to **s** the LORD your God
	11:13	and to **s** him with all your heart
Jos	24:15	this day whom you will **s**,
1Sa	7:3	to the LORD and **s** him only,
	12:20	but **s** the LORD with all your heart
Ps	2:11	**S** the LORD with fear
Da	3:17	the God we **s** is able to save us
Mt	4:10	Lord your God, and **s** him only.' "
	6:24	"No one can **s** two masters.
	20:28	but to **s**, and to give his life
Ro	12:7	If it is serving, let him **s**;
Gal	5:13	rather, **s** one another in love.
Eph	6:7	**S** wholeheartedly,
1Ti	6:2	they are to **s** them even better,
Heb	9:14	so that we may **s** the living God!

| 1Pe | 4:10 | gift he has received to **s** others, |

SETH [9269, 4953] (Heb. *shēth*, "appointed," i.e., "substituted") Adam's third son; father of Enosh (Ge 4:25 – 26; 5:3 – 8). His name signifies that he was considered a "substitute" for Abel (4:25). His birth recalled humankind's tragic loss of the divine image (5:1 – 2). He became the founder of the line of faith (Ge 4:26; Lk 3:38).

SEVEN WORDS FROM THE CROSS The seven statements Jesus made from the cross. No single gospel account recounts them all: "Father, forgive them, for they do not know what they are doing" (Lk 23:34). "I tell you the truth, today you will be with me in paradise" (Lk 23:43). "Dear woman, here is your son," and to the disciple "Here is your mother" (Jn 19:26 – 27). "My God, my God, why have you forsaken me?" (Mt 27:46 – 47; Mk 15:34 – 36). "I am thirsty" (Jn 19:28). "It is finished" (Jn 19:30). "Father, into your hands I commit my spirit" (Lk 23:46; cf. Mt 27:50; Mk 15:37).

SEVENTY-TWO, THE Seventy-two (KJV seventy) disciples were sent on a preaching mission by Jesus (Lk 10:1 – 17).

SEVENTY WEEKS, THE The name applied to a period of time (probably 490 years) referred to in Daniel (Da 9:24 – 27).

SEXUAL

Ex	22:19	"Anyone who has **s** relations
Lev	18:6	relative to have **s** relations.
Mt	15:19	murder, adultery, **s** immorality,
Ac	15:20	by idols, from **s** immorality,
1Co	5:1	reported that there is **s** immorality
	6:13	body is not meant for **s** immorality,
	6:18	Flee from **s** immorality.
	10:8	should not commit **s** immorality,
2Co	12:21	**s** sin and debauchery
Gal	5:19	**s** immorality, impurity
Eph	5:3	even a hint of **s** immorality,
Col	3:5	**s** immorality, impurity, lust,

| 1Th | 4:3 | that you should avoid **s** immorality |

SHADRACH [8731, 10701] (shā′drăk, Heb. *sha-dhrakh, servant of [pagan moon god] Aku*). His Hebrew name was Hananiah. He was taken as a captive to Babylon with Daniel, Mishael, and Azariah, where each one was given a Babylonian name (Da 1:6 – 20; 2:17, 49; 3:12 – 30). Hananiah was renamed Shadrach. Shadrach, Meshach, and Abednego were chosen to learn the language and the ways of the Chaldeans (Babylonians) so that they could enter the king's service (Da 1:3 – 5, 17 – 20), c. 605 BC. These three were eventually thrown into Nebuchadnezzar's furnace because they refused to bow down and worship the huge golden image that he had made (Da 3:1, 4 – 6, 8 – 30).

SHALMANESER [8987] (shăl′măn-ē′zêr, Heb. *shal-man′-eser, the god Shulman is chief*, or *Sulmanu is leader*). The title of five Assyrian kings, of whom one is mentioned in the OT; another refers to an Israelite king.

1. Shalmaneser III (859 – 824 BC), the son of Ashurnasirpal; inscription left by him says that he opposed Ben-Hadad of Damascus and Ahab of Israel, and made Israel tributary.

2. Shalmaneser V (726 – 722 BC), the son of Tiglath-Pileser; received tribute from Hoshea; besieged Samaria and carried the northern tribes of Israel into captivity (2Ki 17:3; 18:9); "Shalman" (Hos 10:14).

SHAME

Ps	25:3	will ever be put to **s**,
	34:5	their faces are never covered with **s**
Pr	13:18	discipline comes to poverty and **s**,
	18:13	that is his folly and his **s**.
Jer	8:9	The wise will be put to **s**;
Ro	9:33	trusts in him will never be put to **s**."
1Co	1:27	things of the world to **s** the wise;
Heb	12:2	endured the cross, scorning its **s**,

SHARON [9227, 4926] (shăr′ŭn, Heb. *shārôn, plain, level country*).

1. Israel coastal plain between Joppa and Mount Carmel (1Ch 27:29; Isa 35:2; Ac 9:35).

2. Suburbs of Sharon possessed by the tribe of Gad (1Ch 5:16).

3. Figurative of fruitfulness, glory, peace (Isa 35:2; 65:10).

SHECHEM, SHECHEMITE [8901, 8902, 8903, 8904, 5374] (shē′kĕm, Heb. *shekhem*, possibly *shoulder [saddle of a hill]* BDB; *shoulders [and upper part of the back]* KB).

1. A district in the central part of the land of Canaan. The city makes its initial appearance in biblical history as the first place in Canaan to be mentioned in connection with Abram's arrival in the land. Here the Lord appeared to Abram and promised the land to his descendants; Abram responded by building an altar (Ge 12:6 – 7). Jacob buys a piece of ground in, and builds an altar (Ge 33:18 – 20). The flocks and herds of Jacob kept in (Ge 37:12 – 14). Joseph buried in (Jos 24:32). Jacob buried in (Ac 7:16, c Ge 50:13).

2. Also called Sychar, a city of refuge in Mount Ephraim (Jos 20:7; 21:21; Jdg 21:19). Joshua assembled the tribes of Israel at, with all their elders, chiefs, and judges, and presented them before the Lord (Jos 24:1 – 28). Joshua buried at (Jos 24:30 – 32). Abimelech made king at (Jdg 8:31; 9). Rehoboam crowned at (1Ki 12:1). Destroyed by Abimelech (Jdg 9:45), rebuilt by Jeroboam (1Ki 12:25). Men of, slain by Ishmael (Jer 41:5). Jesus visits; disciples made in (Jn 4:1 – 42).

3. Son of Hamor; seduces Jacob's daughter; slain by Jacob's sons (Ge 33:19; 34; Jos 24:32; Jdg 9:28).

4. Descendant of Manasseh and his clan (Nu 26:31; Jos 17:2).

5. Son of Shemida (1Ch 7:19).

SHEEP

Nu	27:17	LORD's people will not be like **s**
Dt	17:1	a **s** that has any defect or flaw in it,
Ps	44:22	we are considered as **s**
Isa	53:6	We all, like **s**, have gone astray,
	53:7	as a **s** before her shearers is silent,

Jer	50:6	"My people have been lost **s**;
Eze	34:11	I myself will search for my **s**
Zec	13:7	and the **s** will be scattered,
Mt	9:36	helpless, like **s** without a shepherd.
	10:16	I am sending you out like **s**
	12:11	"If any of you has a **s** and it falls
	18:13	he is happier about that one **s**
	25:32	as a shepherd separates the **s**
Jn	10:1	man who does not enter the **s** pen
	10:3	He calls his own **s** by name
	10:7	the truth, I am the gate for the **s**.
	10:15	and I lay down my life for the **s**.
	10:27	My **s** listen to my voice; I know
	21:17	Jesus said, "Feed my **s**.
1Pe	2:25	For you were like **s** going astray,

SHEKEL [4084, 7088, 9203] (*weight*).

A weight, equal to twenty gerahs (Ex 30:13; Nu 3:47; Eze 45:12). Used to weigh silver (Jos 7:21; Jdg 8:26; 17:2 – 3). Fractions of, used in currency (Ex 30:13; 1Sa 9:8; Ne 10:32). Used to weigh gold (Ge 24:22; Nu 7:14, 20 – 86; Jos 7:21; 1Ki 10:16); cinnamon (Ex 30:23); hair (2Sa 14:26); iron (1Sa 17:7); myrrh (Ex 30:23); rations (Eze 4:10). Fines paid in (Dt 22:19, 29). Fees paid in (1Sa 9:8). Sanctuary revenues paid in (Ex 30:13; Ne 10:32). Of different standards: of the sanctuary (Ex 30:13); of the king's weight (2Sa 14:26). Corrupted (Am 8:5).

SHEKINAH (she-kī′na, Heb. *shekhînâh, dwelling of God*). A word, though not occurring in the Bible, that is employed by some Jews and by Christians to describe the visible presence of the Lord. It is alluded to in such places as Isa 60:2 by the phrase "his glory" and in Ro 9:4 by the phrase "the glory." Moses calls this the "cloud" in Ex 14:19. Its first appearance occurred for a twofold purpose when Israel was being led by Moses out of Egypt. It hid the Israelites from the pursuing Egyptians and lighted the way at night for Israel (Ex 13:21; 14:19 – 20). To the Egyptians it was a cloud of darkness, but to Israel a cloud of light. It later covered Sinai when God spoke with Moses (24:15 – 18), filled the tabernacle (40:34 – 35), guided Israel (40:36 – 38), filled

Solomon's temple (2Ch 7:1), and was frequently seen in connection with Christ's ministry in the NT (Mt 17:5; Ac 1:9).

SHEM [9006, 4954] (shĕm, Heb. *shēm*, Gr. *Sēm*, *name, fame*). This second son of Noah and progenitor of the Semitic race was born ninety-eight years before the flood (Ge 11:10). He lived six hundred years, outliving his descendants for nine generations (except for Eber and Abraham). In the prophecy that Noah made after the episode of his drunkenness (9:25 – 27), he mentioned "the LORD, the God of Shem." The three great monotheistic religions — Judaism, Christianity, and Islam — all had Semitic origins. Noah added that Japheth's descendants would "live in the tents of Shem," indicating that the Aryan peoples to a large extent have derived their civilization from the Semites. In the "Table of the Nations" (Ge 10) Shem had five sons, of whom Arphaxad (10:22) was clearly an individual and the others were peoples or progenitors of peoples: e.g., Lud refers to the Lydians in Asia Minor; Elam points to the Elamites who lived east of the Tigris River; Aram means Arameans or Syrians who lived in Syria and Mesopotamia; and Asshur is Assyria. Critics pointed out a century ago that Asshur is mentioned also in the Hamite list (10:11), but archaeologists have found Hamitic artifacts under Semitic ruins of Assyrian cities. Shem, Ham, and Japheth probably differed only as brothers do, but their descendants are quite distinct. Listed in the genealogy of Jesus (Lk 3:36).

SHEMA [9050, 9054] (shē′ma, Heb. *shemā*ʻ, *he hears*).

1. A town in S Judah (Jos 15:26).

2. The son of Hebron (1Ch 2:43 – 44).

3. The son of Joel (1Ch 5:8).

4. A Benjamite (1Ch 8:13).

5. An assistant of Ezra (Ne 8:4).

6. The Hebrew name for, "Hear, O Israel: The LORD our God, the LORD is one" (Dt 6:4, n.), probably the most often quoted verse in the Bible, as every good Jew repeats it several times every day.

SHEOL (shē′ōl, Heb. *she'ôl*, possibly *place of inquiry [of the dead]* BDB; *desolate place, no-country under-world* KB). The OT name for the place of departed souls, corresponding to the NT word "Hades." When translated "hell," it refers to the place of punishment, but when translated "grave," the reference is to the place of the dead in general. It often means the place or state of the soul between death and resurrection. The clearest indication of different conditions in Sheol is in Christ's parable of the rich man and Lazarus (Lk 16:19 – 31). The OT makes three main points about Sheol: (1) All the dead alike go there (e.g., Ge 37:35; Isa 14:9ff.). (2) Sheol is in some unspecified sense the lot of the wicked. References such as Pss 6:5; 30:3, 9; 88:3 – 6 (cf. Job 17:13 – 16; Isa 38:18) are often quoted as allegedly showing that the OT knew of no hope after death, that the dead are cut off from the Lord and he from them. In all these references, however, the speakers believe themselves to be facing death under the wrath of God, estranged from him, without any indication of divine favor. The OT takes the matter no further; there is some undefined sense in which Sheol involves those who die under wrath in separation from God — the God their wickedness has offended. (3) On the other hand, there are those who can confidently look forward to glory (Ps 73:23 – 24), and this is seen as redemption from Sheol (49:14 – 15). But again we are not aided by further OT revelation on the point. We must wait for the One who brought life and immortality to light in the gospel (2Ti 1:10).

SHEPHERD

Ge	48:15	the God who has been my **s**
	49:24	because of the **S**, the Rock of Israel
Nu	27:17	will not be like sheep without a **s**."
2Sa	7:7	commanded to **s** my people Israel,
Ps	23:1	LORD is my **s**, I shall not be in want.
	28:9	be their **s** and carry them forever.
Isa	40:11	He tends his flock like a **s**:
Jer	31:10	will watch over his flock like a **s**.'
Eze	34:5	scattered because there was no **s**,
Zec	11:9	and said, "I will not be your **s**.

	11:17	"Woe to the worthless **s**,
Mt	2:6	who will be the **s** of my people
	9:36	and helpless, like sheep without a **s**.
Jn	10:11	The good **s** lays down his life
	10:14	"I am the good **s**; I know my sheep
	10:16	there shall be one flock and one **s**.
Heb	13:20	that great **S** of the sheep, equip you
1Pe	5:4	And when the Chief **S** appears,
Rev	7:17	of the throne will be their **s**;

SHILOH [8870, 8872, 8926, 8931] (shī′lō Heb. *shīlōh*).

1. A city in Ephraim, about twelve miles northeast of Bethel where the tabernacle remained from the time of Joshua to the days of Samuel (Jdg 21:19; 1Sa 4:3). The Benjamites kidnapped wives from there (Jdg 21:15 – 24). It was the residence of Eli and Samuel (1Sa 3:21), home of the prophet Ahijah (1Ki 14:3), a ruin in Jeremiah's time (Jer 7:12, 14).

2. A word of uncertain meaning regarded by many Jews and Christians as a reference to the Messiah; the NIV has "until he comes to whom it belongs" (Ge 49:10, n.).

SHRINE [1074, 1195, 2215, 2540, 5219, 6109, 6551, 7728, 8229, 3724, 5008] (Gr. *naos*).

Places of idolatrous worship, often a high place (Eze 16:24 – 25, 31, 39). Frequented by temple prostitutes (Ge 38:21 – 22; Dt 23:17; Hos 4:14), including male prostitutes (1Ki 14:24; 15:12; 22:46; 2Ki 23:7; Job 36:14). A shrine also refers to an idolatrous symbol, certain small idol houses, made by the silversmith Demetrius and sold to the worshipers of the temple of Diana (Ac 19:24).

SICK

Pr	13:12	Hope deferred makes the heart **s**,
Eze	34:4	or healed the **s** or bound up
Mt	9:12	who need a doctor, but the **s**.
	10:8	Heal the **s**, raise the dead, cleanse
	25:36	I was **s** and you looked after me,
1Co	11:30	many among you are weak and **s**,
Jas	5:14	of you **s**? He should call the elders

SIGN [226, 253, 4603, 5727, 5812, 7483, 9338, 1893, 4956, 5518] (Heb. *'ôth, a signal, môphēth, a miracle, omen,* Gr. *sēmeion, an indication*). In Scripture this word generally refers to something addressed to the senses to attest the existence of a divine power. Miracles in the OT were often signs (Ex 4:8; 8:23). Several specific things were given as signs, such as the rainbow (Ge 9:12 – 13), some of the feasts (Ex 13:9), the Sabbath (Ex 31:13), and circumcision (Ro 4:11). Often extraordinary events were given as a sign to insure faith or demonstrate authority. When Moses would not believe God, his rod was turned into a serpent and his hand became leprous as signs of God's divine commission (Ex 4:1 – 8). Sometimes future events were given as signs, as in the case of Ahaz (Isa 7:14). When Christ was born, the place of his birth and his dress were to be signs of his identity to the shepherds. When the scribes and the Pharisees asked Jesus for a sign, he assured them that no sign was to be given them except the sign of Jonah, whose experience in the fish portrayed Christ's burial and resurrection. Revelation tells that before Christ returns there will be signs in the heavens, in the stars, moon, and sun.

General References to:

A miracle to confirm faith (Mt 12:38; 16:4; 24:30; Mk 8:11 – 12; 13:4; Jn 2:11; 3:2; 4:48); asked for by, and given to, Abraham (Ge 15:8 – 17); Moses (Ex 4:1 – 9); Gideon (Jdg 6:17, 36 – 40); Hezekiah (2Ki 20:8); Zechariah (Lk 1:18). Given to Jeroboam (1Ki 13:3 – 5). A token of coming events (Mt 16:3 – 4; 24:3).

Ge	9:12	"This is the **s** of the covenant I am
Isa	7:14	the Lord himself will give you a **s**:
Eze	20:12	I gave them my Sabbaths as a **s**
Mt	12:38	to see a miraculous **s** from you."
	24:3	what will be the **s** of your coming
	24:30	"At that time the **s** of the Son
Lk	2:12	This will be a **s** to you: You will
	11:29	It asks for a miraculous **s**,
Ro	4:11	he received the **s** of circumcision,
1Co	11:10	to have a **s** of authority on her head
	14:22	are a **s**, not for believers

SILAS [4976, 4977] (sī'las, *asked,* possibly *dedicated to God*). A name identifying a prominent member of the Jerusalem church (Ac 15:22, 32) and a Roman citizen (Ac 16:38).

Also called Silvanus (1Th 1:1, n.); Sent to Paul in Antioch from Jerusalem (Ac 15:22 – 34); Later became Paul's companion (Ac 15:40 – 41; 2Co 1:19; 1Th 1:1; 2Th 1:1) and was imprisoned with Paul in Philippi (Ac 16:19 – 40); Driven, with Paul, from Thessalonica (Ac 17:4 – 10); Left by Paul at Berea (Ac 17:14); Rejoined Paul at Corinth (Ac 17:15; 18:5); Carried Peter's epistle to Asia Minor (1Pe 5:12)

SILOAM, POOL OF [8940, 4978] (*sent*). A reservoir located within the city walls of Jerusalem at the south end of the Tyropean Valley; receives water through a 1,780-foot tunnel from En Rogel (Ne 3:15; Lk 13:4; Jn 9:7, 11), constructed by Hezekiah in the late eighth century BC "Shiloah" (Isa 8:6). The pool today is called Birket Silwan, and a nearby village is Silwan. *See Siloam, Village of.*

SIMEON [1201+9058, 9058, 9063, 5208] (sĭm'ē-ŭn, Heb. *shim'ôn,* Gr. *Symeōn, he has heard* or *obedient one*).

1. The second son of Jacob by Leah (Ge 29:33). He and his brother Levi massacred the Hivites living in Shechem because Shechem the son of Hamor had raped their sister Dinah (34:24 – 31).

2. The tribe of which Simeon, the son of Jacob, became the founder. He had six sons, all but one of whom founded tribal families. At the distribution of the land of Canaan the extreme south of Canaan was assigned to this tribe. Eventually most of the tribe disappeared.

3. An ancestor of Jesus (Lk 3:30).

4. A righteous and devout man to whom the Holy Spirit revealed that he would not die until he had seen the Messiah. When the infant Jesus was brought into the temple, Simeon took him into his arms and praised God (Lk 2:25, 34).

5. Simon (a variant of Gr. Simeon) Peter (Ac 15:14). *See Peter.*

6. The man whose surname was Niger. He was one of the Christian leaders in the church of Antioch who set apart Paul and Barnabas for their missionary work (Ac 13:1 – 2). Nothing more is known of him.

SIMON [1639+4981, 4981, 5208] (sī'mŭn, Gr. *Simōn, hearing, he has heard,* or *obedient one*).

1. The son of Jonas and brother of Andrew, a fisherman who became a disciple and apostle of Christ. He was surnamed Peter, "stone," and Cephas, Aramaic for "rock" (Mt 4:18; 16:17 – 18). *See Peter.*

2. Another disciple of Jesus called the "Canaanite" in the KJV, a member of the party later called "the Zealots" (so NIV, Mt 10:4; Mk 3:18). The word does not mean "inhabitant of Cana." Luke properly translates the Hebrew by *Zealot* (Lk 6:15; Ac 1:13).

3. A leper of Bethany in whose house Jesus' head was anointed (Mt 26:6; Mk 14:3).

4. A brother of the Lord (Mt 13:55; Mk 6:3).

5. A man from Cyrene, father of Alexander and Rufus, who was compelled to carry the cross of Jesus (Mt 27:32; Mk 15:21; Lk 23:26).

6. A Pharisee in whose house Jesus' feet were anointed by the sinful woman (Lk 7:40, 43 – 44).

7. Judas Iscariot's father (Jn 6:71; 13:2, 26).

8. Simon Magus, a sorcerer at Samaria and a man of great power and influence among the people (Ac 8:9 – 13). He "believed" as the result of Philip's preaching there, though the real nature of his faith is not clear, as his subsequent action reveals (8:14 – 24).

9. A tanner who lived at Joppa. Peter stayed with him for a period of time (Ac 9:43; 10:6, 17, 32).

SIN [2627, 2628, 2629, 2631, 2633, 6097, 6404, 6411, 7321, 7322, 8273, 279, 280, 281, 283, 4183, 4579, 4922, 4997, 4998] (Heb. *hāttā'the, 'awôn, pesha', ra',* Gr. *adikia, hamartia, hamartēma, parabasis, paraptōma, ponēria*). The biblical writers portray sin in such a variety of terms because they have such a powerful sense of the living Lord, who is utterly pure and holy. For sin is that condition and activity of human beings that is offensive to God, their Creator. However, it is only as they are conscious of his holiness that they are truly aware of their sin (1Ki 17:18; Ps 51:4 – 6; Isa 6).

The first book of the OT reveals how human beings were created by God without sin but chose to act contrary to his revealed will and thereby caused sin to become an endemic feature of human existence (Ge 3; Ps 14:1 – 3). Sin is revolt against holiness and the sovereign will of God. Therefore, it is both a condition of the heart/mind/will/affections (Isa 29:13; Jer 17:9) and the practical outworking of that condition in thoughts, words, and deeds that offend God and transgress his holy law (Ge 6:5; Isa 59:12 – 13). For Israel, sin was a failure to keep the conditions of the covenant that the Lord graciously made with the people at Sinai (Ex 19ff.).

There is no person in Israel or the whole world who is not a sinner. However, those who have a right relationship with God, receive his forgiveness, and walk in his ways are sometimes described as righteous (Ge 6:9) and blameless (Job 1:1; Ps 18:20 – 24). This is not because they are free from sin, but because the true direction of their lives is to serve and please God in the way he requires.

The reality of sin and the need for atonement to be made (and confession of it offered to God) are clearly presupposed by the sacrifices offered to God in the temple — e.g., the regular guilt (or trespass) offering and sin offering, as well as the special annual sacrifice of the Day of Atonement (Lev 4; 6:24ff.; 7:1ff.; 16:1ff.). They are also presupposed in the prophecy of the vicarious suffering of the Servant of the Lord who acts as a "guilt offering" and bears the sin of many (Isa 53:10, 12).

The NT strengthens the OT portrayal of sin by viewing it in the light of Jesus and his atonement, which is a victory over sin. Jesus was sinless and taught that the root of sin is in the human heart: "For from within, out of men's hearts, come … evils" (Mk 7:20 – 23). The outward life is determined by the inner (Mt 7:15 – 17), and thus an outward conformity to laws and rules is not in itself a true righteousness if the heart is impure (5:17ff.).

The work of the Holy Spirit, said Jesus, is to convict "the world of … sin … because men do not believe in me" (Jn 16:8 – 9; 15:22). Further, to live without the light of God from Jesus, the Messiah, is to live in darkness and to be in the grip of evil forces (1:5; 3:19 – 21; 8:31 – 34). And to call the light darkness and the Spirit of the Messiah unclean is to commit the unforgivable sin (Mt 12:24, 31).

Paul has much to say about sin. He believed that sin is revealed by the law of God, but it is only as the Holy Spirit enlightens the mind that a person truly sees what righteousness the law demands of us (Ro 3:20; 5:20; 7:7 – 20; Gal 3:19 – 24). Thus, for Paul a person could be a devout keeper of the law (externally) and yet be a slave of sin (internally) because he knew, as Jesus also said, that sin begins in the heart (or flesh) — see Ro 6:15 – 23. The origin of sin can be traced back to the first human beings, Adam and Eve, and to their revolt against the Lord (Ro 5:12 – 19; 2Co 11:3; 1Ti 2:14).

There is a positive message in all this. In a dream Joseph was told that Mary's baby "will save his people from their sins" (Mt 1:21), and John the Baptist proclaimed that Jesus was the Lamb of God who takes away the sin of the world (Jn 1:29) — referring to Jesus as the fulfillment of the atoning sacrifices of the temple. Paul declared that God sent his only Son to be a sin offering (Ro 8:3). Jesus made himself to be the friend of sinners (Lk 7:34), and he understood that his ministry leading to death was the fulfillment of the ministry of the Suffering Servant who gives his life as a ransom for many (Mk 10:45). *See Atonement; Conviction; Offerings; Repentence.*

Adamic:

Original, of Adam (Ge 3:6; Hos 6:7; Ro 5:12, 15 – 19).

Sin Nature:

The inherited tendencies to evil (Mt 7:17 – 18; 12:33 – 35; Mk 7:20 – 23; Lk 6:45; Ro 6:6; 7:17, 20, 23, 25; 8:3, 5 – 7; Gal 5:16 – 17; Eph 2:3; Jas 1:14; 4:17).

Defined:

Transgressing the law (Hos 6:8; Mt 5:28; 1Co 8:12; Heb 12:15; Jas 2:10 – 11; 4:17; 1Jn 3:4; 5:17). Turning away from God (Dt 29:18; Ps 95:10). Not seeking God (2Ch 12:14). Foolish thoughts (Pr 24:8 – 9). Self-deception (Isa 42:20). That which is not of faith (Ro 14:23). See Atonement; Conviction; Depravity; Regeneration; Repentance; Salvation; Sanctification; Wicked, Wickedness, Punishment of. Against the body (Ecc 5:6). Against conscience (Ro 14:23). Against knowledge (Pr 26:11; Lk 12:47 – 48; Jn 9:41; 15:22; Ro 1:21, 32; 2:17 – 23; Heb 10:26; Jas 4:17; 2Pe 2:21 – 22). Attempts to cover, vain (Ge 3:10; Job 31:33; Isa 29:15; 59:6). Christ's description of (Mt 5:2 – 20; Jn 8:34, 44). Deceitful (Heb 3:13). Defiles (Ps 51:2, 7; Isa 1:18; Heb 12:15; 1Jn 1:7). Degrees in (Lk 7:41 – 47; 12:47 – 48). Dominion of (Ro 3:9). Enslaves (Jn 8:34; Ro 6:16; 2Pe 2:19). From the heart (Isa 44:20; Jer 7:24; 17:9; Eze 20:16; Mt 5:28; 7:17 – 18; 12:33 – 35; 15:8, 11, 16 – 19; Lk 6:45). Of the tongue (Ecc 5:6). In thought (Pr 24:9). Fools mock at (Pr 14:9). Little sins (SS 2:15). Magnitude of (Job 22:5; Ps 25:11). None in heaven (Rev 22:3 – 4). Parable of (Mt 13:24 – 25, 33, 39). Paul's discussion of the responsibility for (Ro 2 – 9). Pleasures of (Jn 20:12 – 16; 21:12 – 13; Lk 8:14; Heb 11:25). See Pleasure, Worldly. Reproach to God (2Sa 12:14). Secret sins (Pss 19:12; 44:22; 64:2; 90:8; Ecc 12:14; Eze 8:12; 11:5; Mt 10:26; Lk 8:17; 12:2 – 3; Jn 3:20; Ro 2:16; Eph 5:12). Sinfulness of (Job 22:5; Ps 25:11; Isa 1:18; Ro 7:13). To be hated (Dt 7:26; Ps 119:113).

Confession of:

(1Ki 8:47; Pr 28:13). Signified by placing hands on the head of the offering (Lev 3:2, 13; 4:4, 15, 24, 29, 33; 16:21; Nu 8:12). Illustrated in parables: of the prodigal son (Lk 15:17 – 21); of the Pharisee and the tax collector (Lk 18:13). To God, commanded (Lev 5:5 – 10; 16:21). Exemplified: by Israel (Nu 14:40; Jdg 10:10; 1Sa 7:6); by Saul (1Sa 15:2, 4); by David (2Sa 12:13; 24:10, 17; 1Ch 21:17); by the psalmist (Pss 32:5; 38:3 – 4, 18; 40:11 – 12; 41:4;

51:2 – 5; 69:5; 73:21 – 22; 119:59 – 60, 176); by the Jews (2Ch 29:6; Ezr 9:4 – 7, 10 – 15; Ne 9:2 – 38; Ps 106:6; Isa 26:13; 59:12 – 15; 64:5 – 7; Jer 3:21 – 22, 25; 8:14 – 15; 14:7, 20; 31:18 – 19; La 3:40 – 42; Da 9:5 – 6, 8 – 11, 15); by Job (Job 7:20; 9:20; 13:23; 40:4; 42:5 – 6); by Isaiah (Isa 6:5); by Jeremiah (La 1:18 – 20); by Paul (1Co 15:9). To believers, commanded (Jas 5:16; 1Jn 1:8 – 10).

Consequences of:

Look on the face (Isa 3:9). Guilty fear (Ge 3:7 – 10; Pr 10:24; 25:1). Depraved conscience (Pr 30:20). Judgment (Jer 5:25). Trouble (Isa 57:20 – 21; Jer 4:18). Effects on children (Ex 20:5; 34:7; Lev 26:39 – 40; Nu 14:33; Dt 5:9; Pss 21:10; 37:28; 109:9 – 10; Pr 14:11; Isa 14:20 – 22; 65:7; Jer 32:18; La 5:7; Ro 5:12 – 21). Attributed to Job's children because of Job's alleged wickedness (Job 5:4; 18:19; 21:19). Punishment for, not brought on children (Dt 24:16; 2Ki 14:6; 2Ch 25:4; Jer 31:29 – 30; Eze 18:2 – 4, 20). No escape from (Ge 3:8 – 19; Isa 28:18 – 22; Am 9:2 – 4; Mt 23:33; Heb 2:3). See Punishment; Wicked, Wickedness.

Conviction of:

Produced: by dreams (Job 33:14 – 17); by visions (Ac 9:3 – 9); by afflictions (Job 33:18 – 20; La 1:20; Lk 15:17 – 21); by adversity (Ps 107:4 – 6, 10 – 14, 17 – 20, 23 – 30); by the gospel (Ac 2:37); by religious testimony (1Co 14:24 – 25); by the conscience (Jn 8:9; Ro 2:15); by the Holy Spirit (Jn 16:7 – 11). See Conviction, of Sin; Repentance, Instances of.

Forgiveness of:

(Ac 26:18; Eph 1:7). Promised (Ex 34:6 – 7; Lev 4:20, 26, 31, 35; 5:4 – 13; Nu 14:18; 15:25; Dt 4; Ps 130:4; Isa 1:6 – 18; 43:25 – 26; 44:21 – 22; 55:6 – 7; Jer 31:34; 33:8; Eze 18:21 – 22; 33:14 – 16; Mt 12:31; Mk 3:28; Heb 8:12; 10:17; Jas 5:15; 1Jn 1:7, 9). Blessedness of (Ps 32:1 – 2; Ro 4:7 – 8). **Conditions of Forgiveness:** Repentance (Mt 3:6; Lk 3:3; 13:3, 5; Ac 2:38; 3:19). Faith (Ac 10:36, 43; 13:38 – 39; 26:16 – 18). Confession

of sins (1Jn 1:7, 9). Parable of (Mt 18:23 – 27). Through the shedding of blood (Heb 9:22). Mission of Christ to secure (Mt 1:21; 26:28; Lk 24:47; 1Jn 2:1 – 2, 12; Rev 1:5). Prayer for (Pss 19:12; 25:7, 11; 51:9; 79:9). Spirit of (Mt 6:12, 14 – 15; 18:35; Mk 11:25). Intercessory prayer for (1Ki 8:22 – 50). Apostolic (Jn 20:23).

Fruits of:

(Dt 29:18; Mk 7:21 – 23; 1Co 3:3; 6:9 – 11; Gal 5:19 – 21; Jas 5:11; 1Pe 4:3). Fruits of original sin (Ge 3:7 – 24; 4:9 – 13; Ro 5:12 – 21). God's anger (Jer 7:19). Moral insensibility (Pr 30:20). No peace (Isa 57:20 – 21). Shame (Pr 3:35). Withholding of God's goodness (Jer 7:19). Destruction and death (Ge 6:5 – 7; 1Ki 13:33 – 34; Job 5:2; Pss 5:10; 94:23; Pr 5:22 – 23; 10:24, 29 – 31; 11:18 – 19, 27, 29; Isa 3:9, 11; 9:18; 14:21; Jer 14:16; 21:14; Eze 11:21; 22:31; 23:31 – 35; Hos 12:14; 13:9; Ro 6:23). The same as sown (Job 4:8; 13:26; 20:11; Pss 9:15 – 16; 10:2; 141:10; Pr 1:31; 11:5 – 7; 12:13, 14 – 21, 26; 22:8; Isa 50:11; Jer 4:18; 21:14; Eze 11:21; Hos 8:7; 10:13; Mic 7:13; Ro 7:5; Gal 6:7 – 8). Proverbs concerning (Pr 1:31; 3:35; 5:22 – 23; 8:36; 10:24, 29 – 31; 11:5 – 7, 18 – 19, 27, 29; 12:13 – 14, 21, 26; 13:5 – 6, 15; 22:8; 28:1; 29:6; 30:20).

Love of:

(Job 15:16; 20:12 – 13; Pr 2:14; 4:16 – 17; 10:23; 16:30; 26:11; Jer 14:10; Eze 20:16; Hos 4:8; 9:10; Mic 7:3; Jn 3:19 – 20; 12:43; 1Pe 3:19 – 20; 2Pe 2:22). See Wicked, Wickedness, Described as.

National, Punishment of:

(Ge 6:5 – 7; 7:21 – 22; Lev 26:14 – 38; Dt 9:5; Job 34:29 – 30; Isa 19:4; Jer 12:17; 25:31 – 38; 46:28; Eze 16:49 – 50; Jnh 1:2). See Government.

Instances of: Sodomites (Ge 18:20); Egyptians (Ex 7 – 14) (see Egypt); Israelites (Lev 26:14 – 39; Dt 32:30; 2Sa 21:1; 24:1; 2Ki 24:3 – 4, 20; 2Ch 36:21; Ezr 9; Ne 9:36 – 37; Isa 1:21 – 23; 3:4, 8; 5; 59:1 – 15; Jer 2; 5; 6; 9; 23; 30:11 – 15; La 1:3, 8, 14; 4:6; Eze 2; 7; 22; 24:6 – 14; 28:18; 33:25 – 26; 36:16 – 20; 39:23 – 24; 44:4 – 14; Hos 4:1 – 11;

6:8 – 10; 7:1 – 7; 13; Am 2; 5; Mic 6; 7:2 – 6). Babylon (Jer 50:45 – 46; 51).

Not Imputed:

To righteous (Ps 32:2; Ro 4:6 – 8); to ignorant (Ro 4:15; 5:13); to redeemed (2Co 5:19).

Progressive:

(Dt 29:19; 1Ki 16:31; Ps 1:1; Isa 5:18; 30:1; Jer 9:3; 16:11 – 12; Hos 13:2; 2Ti 3:13; Jas 1:14 – 15). Progressiveness exemplified in Joseph's brothers, from jealousy (Ge 37:4), to conspiracy (Ge 37:18), to murder (Ge 37:20). See also Abel; Cain. Retroactive (Pss 7:15 – 16; 9:15 – 16; 10:2; 94:23; Pr 1:31; 5:22 – 23; 8:36; 11:5 – 6, 27, 29; Isa 3:9, 11; Jer 2:19; 4:8; 7:19). A root of bitterness (Dt 29:18; Heb 12:15).

Punishment of:

(Ge 2:17; 3:16 – 19; 4:10 – 14; 6:5 – 7; 18:20; 19:13; Ex 32:33 – 34; 34:7; Lev 19:8; 26:14 – 21; Nu 15:30 – 31; 32:23; Dt 28:15 – 68; 1Ki 13:33 – 34; 1Ch 21:7 – 27; Job 21:17; Ps 95:10 – 11; Pr 1:24 – 32; Jer 44:2 – 6; Eze 18:4; Mt 25:41, 46; Ro 6:23). See Punishment; Wicked, Wickedness, Punishment of.

Repentance for:

Commanded (2Ch 30:7 – 9; Job 36:10; Ps 34:14; Pr 1:22 – 23; Isa 22:12; 31:6; 44:22; 55:6 – 7; Jer 3:4, 12 – 14, 19; 6:8, 16; 18:11; 25:5; 26:13; 35:15; Eze 14:6; 18:30 – 32; 33:10 – 12; Da 4:27; Hos 6:1; 10:12; 14:1 – 2; Joel 1:14; 2:12 – 13, 15 – 18; Am 4:12; Jnh 3:8 – 9; Zec 1:3; Mt 4:17; Mk 1:15; 6:12; Ac 2:38, 40; 3:19; 8:22; 17:30; 20:21; Jas 4:8 – 10; Rev 2:5, 16; 3:2 – 3, 19). Gift, of God (2Ti 2:25), of Christ (Ac 5:31). Tribulation leads to (Dt 4:30; 1Ki 8:33 – 50; 2Ch 6:36 – 39; Ps 107:4 – 6, 10 – 14, 17 – 20, 23 – 30). Goodness of God leads to (Ro 2:4). A condition of pardon (Lev 26:40 – 42; Dt 4:29 – 31; 30:1 – 3; 2Ch 7:14; Ne 1:9; Pr 28:13; Jer 7:5 – 7; 36:3; Eze 18:21 – 23, 27 – 28, 30 – 31; Mal 3:7; 1Jn 1:9).

Repugnant:

To God (Ge 6:6 – 7; Lev 18:24 – 30; Nu 22:32; Dt 25:16; 32:19; 2Sa 11:27; 1Ki 14:22; Pss 5:4 – 6; 10:3; 11:5; 78:59; 95:10; 106:40; Pr 3:32; 6:16 – 19; 11:20; 15:8 – 9, 26; 21:27; Isa 43:24; Jer 25:7; 44:4, 21 – 22; Hab 1:13; Zec 8:17; Lk 16:15). See God, Holiness of. To Christ (Rev 2:6, 15). To the righteous (Ge 39:7 – 9; Dt 7:26; Job 1:1; 21:16; 22:18; Pss 26:5, 9; 84:10; 101:3 – 4, 7; 119:104, 113, 128, 163; 120:2, 5 – 7; 139:19 – 22; Pr 8:13; 29:27; Jer 9:2; Ro 7:15, 19, 23 – 24; 2Pe 2:7 – 8; Jude 23; Rev 2:2). See Holiness.

Separates from God:

(Dt 31:17 – 18; Jos 7:12; 2Ch 24:20; Ps 78:59 – 61; Isa 59:1 – 2; 64:7; Eze 23:18; Hos 9:12; Am 3:2 – 3; Mic 3:4; Mt 7:23; 25:41; Lk 13:27; Ro 8:7; Heb 12:14). See God, Holiness of; Wicked, Wickedness, Punishment of. Works spiritual death (Ro 5:12, 21; 6:21, 23; 7:13; Eph 2:1; Jas 1:15). By the righteous, dishonors God (2Sa 12:14); a reproach (2Sa 12:14). Against the Holy Spirit, unpardonable (Mt 12:31; Mk 3:29; Lk 12:10; 1Jn 5:16 – 17).

Words for:

Missing the mark (Ro 5:12); overstepping the boundary, or trespassing (Ro 4:15); blunder, or offense (Ro 5:15); disobedience, or disregard (Ro 5:19); unrighteousness (Ro 1:18); ungodliness (Ro 1:18); lawlessness (Tit 2:14).

Ge	4:7	**s** is crouching at your door;
Ex	32:32	please forgive their **s** — but if not,
Nu	5:7	and must confess the **s** he has
	32:23	be sure that your **s** will find you
Dt	24:16	each is to die for his own **s**.
1Ki	8:46	for there is no one who does not **s**
2Ch	7:14	and will forgive their **s** and will heal
Ps	4:4	In your anger do not **s**;
	17:3	resolved that my mouth will not **s**.
	32:2	whose **s** the Lord does not count
	38:18	I am troubled by my **s**.
	51:2	and cleanse me from my **s**.
	66:18	If I had cherished **s** in my heart,
	119:11	that I might not **s** against you.

	119:133	let no **s** rule over me.
Pr	5:22	the cords of his **s** hold him fast.
	17:19	He who loves a quarrel loves **s**;
Jer	31:30	everyone will die for his own **s**;
Eze	3:18	that wicked man will die for his **s**,
Mic	7:18	who pardons **s** and forgives
Zec	3:4	"See, I have taken away your **s**,
Mt	18:6	little ones who believe in me to **s**,
Mk	3:29	he is guilty of an eternal **s**."
	9:43	If your hand causes you to **s**,
Lk	17:1	people to **s** are bound to come,
Jn	1:29	who takes away the **s** of the world!
	8:7	"If any one of you is without **s**,
	8:34	everyone who sins is a slave to **s**.
Ro	2:12	All who **s** apart from the law will
	5:12	as **s** entered the world
	5:20	where **s** increased, grace increased
	6:2	By no means! We died to **s**;
	6:11	count yourselves dead to **s**
	6:14	For **s** shall not be your master,
	6:23	For the wages of **s** is death,
	7:7	I would not have known what **s** was
	7:25	sinful nature a slave to the law of **s**.
	14:23	that does not come from faith is **s**.
1Co	8:12	When you **s** against your brothers
2Co	5:21	God made him who had no **s** to be **s**
Gal	6:1	if someone is caught in a **s**,
1Ti	5:20	Those who **s** are to be rebuked
Heb	4:15	just as we are — yet was without **s**.
	11:25	the pleasures of **s** for a short time.
	12:1	and the **s** that so easily entangles,
Jas	1:15	it gives birth to **s**; and **s**,
1Pe	2:22	"He committed no **s**,
1Jn	1:7	his Son, purifies us from all **s**.
	1:8	If we claim to be without **s**,
	2:1	But if anybody does **s**, we have one
	3:6	No one who continues to **s** has
	3:9	born of God will continue to **s**,
	5:16	There is a **s** that leads to death.
	5:18	born of God does not continue to **s**;

SIN, DESERT OF (*desert of clay* or possibly *desert of Sin [pagan moon god]*). The wilderness through which the Israelites passed; between Elim and Mount Sinai (Ex 16:1; 17:1; Nu 33:11 – 12).

SINAI (sī′nī Heb. *sînay*, meaning uncertain). A word used in three senses in the OT.

1. It is applied to a peninsula that lay to the south of the Wilderness of Paran between the Gulf of Aqabah on the east and Suez on the west.

2. It is applied to a wilderness, the "Desert of Sinai" (Ex 19:1). It is the place where Israel came in the third month after they left Egypt.

3. Finally, there is a mountain often referred to as Mount Sinai (Ex 19:20), or Horeb. It was there that God met and talked with Moses and gave him the law (19:3).

SINFUL

Ps	51:5	Surely I was **s** at birth,
Lk	5:8	from me, Lord; I am a **s** man!"
Ro	7:5	we were controlled by the **s** nature,
	7:25	but in the **s** nature a slave to the law
	8:4	not live according to the **s** nature
	8:7	the **s** mind is hostile to God.
	8:13	if you live according to the **s** nature
	13:14	to gratify the desires of the **s** nature
1Co	5:5	so that the **s** nature may be
Gal	5:16	gratify the desires of the **s** nature.
	5:19	The acts of the **s** nature are obvious
	5:24	Jesus have crucified the **s** nature
	6:8	sows to please his **s** nature,
Col	2:11	in the putting off of the **s** nature,
1Pe	2:11	abstain from **s** desires, which war
1Jn	3:8	He who does what is **s** is

SING

Ex	15:1	"I will **s** to the LORD,
Ps	5:11	let them ever **s** for joy.
	30:4	**S** to the LORD, you saints of his;
	57:7	I will **s** and make music.
	89:1	I will **s** of the LORD's great love
	96:1	**S** to the LORD a new song;
	101:1	I will **s** of your love and justice;

1Co	14:15	also pray with my mind; I will **s**
Eph	5:19	**S** and make music in your heart
Col	3:16	and as you **s** psalms, hymns
Jas	5:13	Is anyone happy? Let him **s** songs

SINNED

Lev	5:5	confess in what way he has **s**
2Sa	12:13	"I have **s** against the LORD."
	24:10	I have **s** greatly in what I have done
2Ch	6:37	'We have **s**, we have done wrong
Job	1:5	"Perhaps my children have **s**
	33:27	'I **s**, and perverted what was right,
Ps	51:4	Against you, you only, have I **s**
Jer	2:35	because you say, 'I have not **s**.'
	14:20	we have indeed **s** against you.
Da	9:5	we have **s** and done wrong.
Mic	7:9	Because I have **s** against him,
Lk	15:18	I have **s** against heaven
Ro	3:23	for all have **s** and fall short
	5:12	all **s**—for before the law was given,
2Pe	2:4	did not spare angels when they **s**,
1Jn	1:10	claim we have not **s**, we make him

SIN OFFERING [2627, 2631, 2633, 10260, 281].

Offered:

For sins of ignorance (Lev 4:2, 13, 22, 27). At the consecration of priests (Ex 29:10, 14; Lev 8:14). At the consecration of Levites (Nu 8:8). At the expiration of a Nazirite's vow (Nu 6:14). On the Day of Atonement (Lev 16:3, 9). Was a most holy sacrifice (Lev 6:25, 29). Probable origin of (Ge 4:4, 7).

Consisted of:

A young bull for priests (Lev 4:3; 9:2, 8; 16:3, 6). A young bull or he-goat for the congregation (Lev 4:14; 16:9; 2Ch 29:23). A male goat for a ruler (Lev 4:23). A female goat or female lamb for a private person (Lev 4:28, 32). Sins of the offerer transferred to, by laying on of hands (Lev 4:4, 15, 24, 29; 2Ch 29:23). Was killed in the same place as the burnt offering (Lev 4:24; 6:25).

Blood of:

For a priest or for the congregation, brought by the priest into the tabernacle (Lev 4:5, 16). For the priest or for the congregation, sprinkled seven times before the Lord, outside the veil, by the priest with his finger (Lev 4:6, 17). For a priest or for the congregation, put upon the horns of the altar of incense (Lev 4:7, 18). For a ruler or for a private person put upon the horns of the altar of burnt offering by the priest with his finger (Lev 4:25, 30). In every case poured at the foot of the altar of burnt offering (Lev 4:7, 18, 30; 9:9). Fat, kidneys, etc., burned on the altar of burnt offering (Lev 4:8–10, 19, 26, 31; 9:10). When for a priest or the congregation, the skin and carcass burned outside the camp (Lev 4:11–12, 21; 6:30; 9:11). Sacrifice eaten by priests in a holy place when its blood had not been brought into the tabernacle (Lev 6:26, 29, w 30). Aaron's sons rebuked for burning and not eating the sin offering, its blood not having been brought into the Holy Place (Lev 10:16–18, w 9:9, 15). Whatever touched the flesh of the sacrifice was rendered holy (Lev 6:27). Garments sprinkled with the blood of a sacrifice were to be washed (Lev 6:27). Laws respecting the vessels used for boiling the flesh of the sacrifice (Lev 6:28). Typical of Christ's sacrifice (2Co 5:21; Heb 13:11–13).

SLANDER [224, 1804, 1819, 1984+5989, 4387, 8078, 8215, 8476, 8806, 1059, 1060, 2895, 2896, 3367] (Heb. *dibbâh*, slander, Gr. *diabolos*, slanderer). A malicious utterance designed to hurt or defame the person about whom it is uttered. The Scriptures often warn against it (Lev 19:16; Eze 22:9; Eph 4:31; Col 3:8; Jas 4:11).

Characteristics of:

Comes from the evil heart (Lk 6:45). Often arises from hatred (Ps 109:3). Idleness leads to (1Ti 5:13). The wicked addicted to (Ps 50:20). Hypocrites addicted to (Pr 11:9). A characteristic of the Devil (Rev 12:10). The wicked love (Ps 52:4). They who indulge in, are fools

(Pr 10:18). Women warned against (Tit 2:3). Ministers' wives should avoid (1Ti 3:11). Christ was exposed to (Ps 35:11; Mt 26:60). Rulers exposed to (Jude 8). Ministers exposed to (Ro 3:8; 2Co 6:8). The nearest relations exposed to (Ps 50:20). Saints exposed to (Ps 38:12; 109:2; 1Pe 4:4). Saints should keep their tongues from (Ps 34:13, w 1Pe 3:10); lay aside (Eph 4:31); be warned against (Tit 3:1 – 2); give no occasion for (1Pe 2:12; 3:16); return good for (1Co 4:13); blessed in enduring (Mt 5:11); characterized as avoiding (Ps 15:1, 3). Should not be listened to (1Sa 24:9). Causes anger (Pr 25:23). A fruit of wickedness (Ro 1:29 – 30; 2Co 12:20; 2Pe 2:10). Forbidden (Ex 23:1; 1Ti 3:11; Tit 2:3; 3:2; Jas 4:11; 1Pe 2:1). Punishment for (Dt 19:16 – 21; 22:13 – 19; Ps 101:5; 1Co 6:10).

Instances of:

Joseph, by Potiphar's wife (Ge 39:14 – 18). Land of Canaan misrepresented by the spies (Nu 14:36). Of Mephibosheth, by Ziba (2Sa 16:3; 19:24 – 30). Of David, by his enemies (Pss 31:13; 35:21; 41:5 – 9; 64:3; 140:3). Of Naboth, by Jezebel (1Ki 21:9 – 14). Of Jeremiah, by the Jews (Jer 6:28; 18:18). Of the Jews, of one another (Jer 9:4). Of Jesus, by the Jews falsely charging that he was a drunkard (Mt 11:19); that he blasphemed (Mk 14:64; Jn 5:18); that he had a demon (Jn 8:48, 52; 10:20); that he was seditious (Lk 22:65; 23:5); that he was a king (Lk 23:2; Jn 18:37, w 19:1 – 5). Of Paul. See Paul.

Effects of:

Separating friends (Pr 16:28; 17:9); deadly wounds (Pr 18:8; 26:22); strife (Pr 26:20); discord among brothers (Pr 6:19); murder (Ps 31:13; Eze 22:9). End of, is wicked madness (Ecc 10:13). People shall give account for (Mt 12:36).

Lev	19:16	"'Do not go about spreading **s**
Ps	15:3	and has no **s** on his tongue,
Pr	10:18	and whoever spreads **s** is a fool.
2Co	12:20	outbursts of anger, factions, **s**,
Eph	4:31	rage and anger, brawling and **s**,

1Ti	5:14	the enemy no opportunity for **s**.
Tit	3:2	to **s** no one, to be peaceable
2Pe	2:10	afraid to **s** celestial beings;

SLAVE [563, 4989, 5601, 6268, 6269, 6275, 6683, 6806, 9148, 1525, 1526, 1528, 1529, 1530, 4087] (Heb. *'evedh, servant, slave,* Gr. *doulos, bondslave, servant*). Both the OT and NT included regulations for societal situations such as slavery and divorce (Dt 24:1 – 4), which were the results of the hardness of hearts (Mt 19:8). Such regulations did not encourage or condone such situations but were divinely given, practical ways of dealing with the realities of the day. *See Servant.*

While the Hebrew and Greek words are very common in the Bible, the English word *slave* is found only twice (Jer 2:14; Rev 18:13), and the word *slavery* does not occur at all in KJV, because both the Hebrew and the Greek word involved are more often rendered "servant."

Among the Hebrews, slaves could be acquired in a number of ways: as prisoners of war (Nu 31:7 – 9), by purchase (Lev 25:44), by gift (Ge 29:24), by accepting a person in lieu of a debt (Lev 25:39), by birth from slaves already possessed (Ex 21:4), by arrest if the thief had nothing to pay for the object stolen (22:2 – 3), and by the voluntary decision of the person wanting to be a slave (21:6). Slaves among the Hebrews were more kindly treated than slaves among other nations, since the Mosaic law laid down rules governing their treatment. They could gain their freedom in a number of ways (Ex 21:2 – 27; Lev 25:25ff.; Dt 15:12 – 23). Slavery continued in NT times, but the love of Christ seemed to militate against its continued existence (Eph 6:5 – 9; Gal 3:28).

SLAVERY [SLAVE]

Ex	2:23	The Israelites groaned in their **s**
Ro	6:19	parts of your body in **s** to impurity
Gal	4:3	were in **s** under the basic principles
1Ti	6:1	of **s** should consider their masters

SLEEP [448+995, 3359, 3822, 3825, 5670, 8101, 8886, 9104, 9554, 10733, 2761, 3121] (Heb. *shēnâh, yāshēn, shākhav,* Gr. *hypnos*). A word used in a number of ways in the Bible. Its most natural use is to refer to physical rest (1Sa 26:7; Jnh 1:5 – 6). Most cases of physical sleep were natural ones, but some were supernaturally imposed to accomplish a divine purpose (Ge 2:21; 15:12). Believers' rest in sleep is considered a gift from God (Ps 127:2).

In the NT, the KJV translates *hypnos* "sleep" all six times it occurs, but the NIV only in Jn 11:13 and Ac 20:9. Sometimes "sleep" indicates the spiritually indolent (e.g., Ro 13:11, the only figurative use of *hypnos*) or believers who have died (e.g., 1Co 11:30; 15:51; 1Th 4:13).

> **General References to:**
> *From God (Ps 127:2). Of the sluggard (Pr 6:9 – 10). Of Jesus (Mt 8:24; Mk 4:38; Lk 8:23). Symbol of death (Job 14:12; Mt 9:24; Mk 5:39; Lk 8:52; Jn 11:11 – 12; 1Th 4:14).*

Ge	2:21	the man to fall into a deep **s**;
Ps	4:8	I will lie down and **s** in peace,
	121:4	will neither slumber nor **s**.
	127:2	for he grants **s** to those he loves.
Pr	6:9	When will you get up from your **s**?
Ecc	5:12	The **s** of a laborer is sweet,
1Co	15:51	We will not all **s**, but we will all be

SLOTHFULNESS Characteristic of the sluggard (Pr 10:4 – 5, 26; 13:4; 15:19; 18:9; 19:15, 24; 20:4; 21:25; 22:13; 23:21; 24:30 – 34; 26:13 – 16; Isa 56:10). Results in: poverty (Pr 10:4 – 5; 12:24, 27; 13:4; 15:19; 18:9; 19:15, 24; 20:4; 21:25; 23:21; 24:30 – 34; 26:13 – 16; Ecc 10:18), condemnation (Mt 25:26 – 27). Condemned: the ant, an example against (Pr 6:6 – 11). Christians are not to be lazy (Ro 12:11; 2Th 3:10 – 12; Heb 6:12).

SLUMBER

Ps	121:3	he who watches over you will not **s**;
Pr	6:10	A little sleep, a little **s**,
Ro	13:11	for you to wake up from your **s**,

SMYRNA [5044] (smîr′na, Gr. *Smyrna*). A port on the west coast of Asia Minor at the head of the gulf into which the Hermus River flows, a well-protected harbor and the natural terminal of a great inland trade route up the Hermus Valley. Smyrna's early history was checkered. It was destroyed by the Lydians in 627 BC and for three centuries was little more than a village. It was refounded in the middle of the fourth century before Christ, after Alexander's capture of Sardis, and rapidly became the chief city of Asia. Smyrna was shrewd enough to mark the rising star of Rome. A common danger, the aggression of Antiochus the Great of Syria, united Smyrna with Rome at the end of the third century before Christ, and the bond formed remained unbroken. Smyrna was indeed the handiest of the bridgeheads, balancing the naval power of Rhodes in the Aegean Sea. Smyrna referred to their ancient alliance with Rome when, in AD 26, they petitioned Tiberius to allow the community to build a temple to his deity. The permission was granted, and Smyrna built the second Asian temple to the emperor. The city had worshiped Rome as a spiritual power since 195 BC, hence Smyrna's historical pride in its Caesar cult. Smyrna was famous for science, medicine, and the majesty of its buildings. Apollonius of Tyana referred to Smyrna's "crown of porticoes," a circle of beautiful public buildings that ringed the summit of Mount Pagos like a diadem; hence John's reference (Rev 2:10). Polycarp, Smyrna's martyred bishop of AD 155, had been a disciple of John.

SODOM, SODOMA [6042, 1178+5047, 5047] (sŏd′ŭm, sŏ-dō′ma, Heb. *sedhōm,* Gr. *Sodoma*). One of the so-called "Cities of the Plain," along with Admah, Gomorrah, Zeboiim, and Zoar. Failing conclusive archaeological evidence, the Cities of the Plain must be listed as lost. Sodom, because of the episode of Ge 19, became a name for vice, infamy, and judgment.

> **General References to:**
> *Situated in the plain of the Jordan (Ge 13:10). The southeastern limit of the Canaanites (Ge*

10:19). Lot dwells at (Ge 13:12). The king of, joins other kings of the nations resisting the invasion of Kedorlaomer (Ge 14:1 – 12). Wickedness of the inhabitants of (Ge 13:13; 19:4 – 13; Dt 32:32; Isa 3:9; Jer 23:14; La 4:6; Eze 16:46, 48 – 49; Jude 7). Abraham's intercession for (Ge 18:16 – 33). Destroyed on account of the wickedness of the people (Ge 19:1 – 29; Dt 29:23; Isa 13:19; Jer 49:18; 50:40; La 4:6; Am 4:11; Zep 2:9; Mt 10:15; Lk 17:29; Ro 9:29; 2Pe 2:6). Figurative of wickedness (Dt 23:17; 32:32; Isa 1:10; Eze 16:46 – 56).

SOLOMON [8976, 5048] (sŏl'ō-mŭn, Heb. *shelōmōh, peaceable*). The third and last king of united Israel. He built the kingdom to its greatest geographical extension and material prosperity. Though a very intelligent man, Solomon in his later years lost his spiritual discernment and, for the sake of political advantage and voluptuous living, succumbed to apostasy. His policies of oppression and luxury brought the kingdom to the verge of dissolution, and when his son Rehoboam came to the throne, the actual split of the kingdom occurred. Solomon was the second son of David and Bathsheba, the former wife of Uriah the Hittite. When he was born, the Lord loved him, so that the child was also called Jedidiah, "because the LORD loved him" (2Sa 12:24 – 25). He did not enter the history of Israel until David's old age, when a conspiracy attempted to crown Adonijah, the son of David and Haggith, as king. Nathan and Bathsheba quickly collaborated to persuade David of the seriousness of the situation, and David had Solomon anointed king at Gihon by Zadok the priest while the conspirators were still gathered at En Rogel. As David's death drew near, he gave Solomon practical advice as to faithfulness to God, the building of the temple, and the stability of the dynasty. Solomon then began a series of marriage alliances that were his eventual undoing. Early in Solomon's reign, he loved the Lord. He sacrificed at the great high place of Gibeon, where the tabernacle was located; here he offered a thousand burnt offerings. The night he was at Gibeon the Lord appeared to him in a dream and told him to request of him of whatever he desired. Solomon chose above all else understanding and discernment. God was pleased with this choice, granted his request, and also gave him riches and honor. Solomon was a wise and learned man. Scripture says that his wisdom was greater than that of the wise men of the East and of Egypt. Expert in botany and zoology, he was also a writer, credited with three thousand proverbs and one thousand songs (1Ki 4:32) and named the author of two psalms (Pss 72 and 127) and of the books of Proverbs (Pr 1:1), Ecclesiastes (Ecc 1:1, 12), and Song of Songs, his greatest song (SS 1:1). His fame was widespread, and people came from afar to hear him. A description of the temple that Solomon built is given in some detail (1Ki 6:2 – 36). The temple was finished in seven years, and Solomon's palace was thirteen years in building.

Personal History: *Son of David by Bathsheba (2Sa 12:24; 1Ki 1:13, 17, 21). Named Jedidiah by Nathan the prophet (2Sa 12:24 – 25). Ancestor of Joseph (Mt 1:6). Succeeds David to the throne of Israel (1Ki 1:11 – 48; 2:12; 1Ch 23:1; 28; Ecc 1:12). Anointed king a second time (1Ch 29:22). His prayer for wisdom and his vision (1Ki 3:5 – 14; 2Ch 1:7 – 12). Covenant renewed in a vision after the dedication of the temple (1Ki 9:1 – 9; 2Ch 7:12 – 22). His rigorous reign (1Ki 2). Builds the temple (1Ki 5; 6; 9:10; 1Ch 6:10; 2Ch 2; 3; 4; 7:11; Jer 52:20; Ac 7:45 – 47). Dedicates the temple (1Ki 8; 2Ch 6). Renews the courses of the priests and Levites and the forms of service according to the regulations of David (2Ch 8:12 – 16; 35:4; Ne 12:45). Builds his palace (1Ki 3:1; 7:1, 8; 9:10; 2Ch 7:11; 8:1; Ecc 2:4); his Palace of the Forest of Lebanon (1Ki 7:2 – 7), and palace for Pharaoh's daughter (1Ki 7:8 – 12; 9:24; 2Ch 8:11; Ecc 2:4). Ivory throne of (1Ki 7:7; 10:18 – 20). Porches of judgment (1Ki 7:7). Builds millo, the wall of Jerusalem; the cities of Hazor, Megiddo, Gezer, Beth Horon, Baalath, Tadmor; store cities and cities for chariots and for cavalry (1Ki*

9:15 – 19; 2Ch 9:25). Provides an armory (1Ki 10:16 – 17). Plants vineyards and orchards of all kinds of fruit trees; makes pools (Ecc 2:4 – 6); imports apes and baboons (1Ki 10:22). Drinking vessels of his houses (1Ki 10:21; 2Ch 9:20). Musicians and musical instruments of his court (1Ki 10:12; 2Ch 9:11; Ecc 2:8). Splendor of his court (1Ki 10:5 – 9, 12; 2Ch 9:3 – 8; Ecc 2:9; Mt 6:29; Lk 12:27). Commerce of (1Ki 9:28; 10:11 – 12, 22, 28 – 29; 2Ch 1:16 – 17; 8:17 – 18; 9:13 – 22, 28). Presents received by (1Ki 10:10; 2Ch 9:9, 23 – 24). Visited by queen of Sheba (1Ki 10:1 – 13; 2Ch 9:1 – 12). Wealth of (1Ki 9; 10:10, 14 – 15, 23, 27; 2Ch 1:15; 9:1, 9, 13, 24, 27; Ecc 1:16). Seven hundred wives and three hundred concubines (1Ki 11:3, w Dt 17:17); their influence over him (1Ki 11:3). Marries one of Pharaoh's daughters (1Ki 3:1). Builds idolatrous temples (1Ki 11:1 – 8; 2Ki 23:13). His idolatry (1Ki 3:3 – 4; 2Ki 23:13; Ne 13:26). Extent of his dominions (1Ki 4:21, 24; 8:65; 2Ch 7:8; 9:26). Receives tribute (1Ki 4:21; 9:21; 2Ch 8:8). Officers of (1Ki 2:35; 4:1 – 19; 2Ch 8:9 – 10). His suppliers (1Ki 4:7 – 19). Divides his kingdom into subsistence departments; daily subsistence rate for his court (1Ki 4:7 – 23, 27 – 28). Military equipment of (1Ki 4:26, 28; 10:16 – 17, 26, 28; 2Ch 1:14; 9:25, w Dt 17:15 – 16). Cedes certain cities to Hiram (1Ki 9:10 – 13; 2Ch 8:2). Wisdom and fame of (1Ki 4:29 – 34; 10:3 – 4, 8, 23 – 24; 1Ch 29:24 – 25; 2Ch 9:2 – 7, 22 – 23; Ecc 1:16; Mt 12:42). Piety of (1Ki 3:5 – 15; 4:29; 8). Beloved of God (2Sa 12:24). Justice of, illustrated in his judgment of the two harlots (1Ki 3:16 – 28). Oppressions of (1Ki 12:4; 2Ch 10:4). Reigns forty years (2Ch 9:30). Death of (2Ch 9:29 – 31). Prophecies concerning (2Sa 7:12 – 16; 1Ki 11:9 – 13; 1Ch 17:11 – 14; 28:6 – 7; Ps 132:11). Type of Christ (Pss 45:2 – 17; 72).

SOLOMON'S COLONNADE A magnificent porch built by Solomon on the east side of the temple area. Christ and the apostles walked in it (Jn 10:23; Ac 3:11; 5:12).

SOLOMON'S POOLS Three in number, these were located a short distance from Jerusalem and were fed by two chief sources — surface water and springs. Cleverly engineered aqueducts carried water from the desired spring to the pools. From these pools the water was conveyed by the same means to the wells under the temple area (Ecc 2:6). The so-called Pools of Solomon outside Bethlehem were part of a sophisticated water system that carried water over forty-five miles to Jerusalem with a vertical drop of only 300 feet (see Ecc. 2:6). In the summer of AD 1962, Solomon's Pools were in the news when a severe drought made necessary an emergency pipeline from a big new well at Hebron to alleviate Jerusalem's water shortage. The eighteen miles (thirty km.) of pipe, furnished by the United States Agency for International Development, was laid within days, and the water was pumped into the ancient reservoirs eight miles (thirteen km.) south of Jerusalem. (See *Time* magazine, August 17, 1962.)

SOLOMON'S SERVANTS (Heb. *'avedhê shelōmōh*). The descendants of Solomon's servants are named among those returning from Babylon to Jerusalem under Zerubbabel (Ezr 2:55, 58; Ne 7:57, 60; 11:3). In the days of Solomon, some were appointed to care for certain temple duties, and the descendants of these servants presumably carried on the same kind of duties. Whether they were Levites or non-Israelites is not known.

SON [132, 408, 1201, 1337, 2351, 3495, 3528, 3529, 10120, 271, 980, 3666, 3836, 4757, 5451, 5626] (Heb. *bēn*, Gr. *huios*). A word with a variety of meanings in the Bible. Genetically the Hebrew word expresses any human offspring regardless of sex (Ge 3:16). In genealogical records the word "son" is often a general term expressing descendants (Da 5:22). Many times, of course, the word means a person, usually a male, who was the direct child of a given father (Ge 9:19; 16:15).

Another very common biblical use of this word is in connection with another following word to express something about the individual or individuals described. Perhaps the most familiar usage of this kind is as a title for our Lord (*see Son of Man; Son of God*). "Son of perdition" is used of Judas. Sometimes groups are thus designated (1Th 5:5). Genesis 6:4 speaks of sons of God, Dt 13:13 of children of Belial (KJV; NIV "wicked men").

Closely allied to this use is still another in which the word "son" indicates relationship in a certain group. Believers in the OT are called children (sons) of God (e.g., Dt 14:1), and believers in the NT have the same designation (e.g., 1Jn 3:2). The word is sometimes used to indicate membership in a guild or profession (2Ki 2:3, 5; Ne 3:8).

Ge	17:19	your wife Sarah will bear you a **s**,
Ex	11:5	Every firstborn **s** in Egypt will die,
Dt	6:20	In the future, when your **s** asks you,
	8:5	as a man disciplines his **s**,
Ps	2:7	He said to me, "You are my **S**;
Pr	6:20	My **s**, keep your father's
	10:1	A wise **s** brings joy to his father,
	13:24	He who spares the rod hates his **s**,
	29:17	Discipline your **s**, and he will give
Isa	7:14	with child and will give birth to a **s**,
Eze	18:20	The **s** will not share the guilt
Da	7:13	before me was one like a **s** of man,
Hos	11:1	and out of Egypt I called my **s**.
Mt	1:1	of Jesus Christ the **s** of David,
	1:21	She will give birth to a **s**,
	3:17	"This is my **S**, whom I love;
	4:3	"If you are the **S** of God, tell these
	11:27	one knows the **S** except the Father,
	13:55	"Isn't this the carpenter's **s**?
	14:33	"Truly you are the **S** of God."
	16:16	"You are the Christ, the **S**
	21:9	"Hosanna to the **S** of David!"
	24:27	so will be the coming of the **S**
	24:30	They will see the **S** of Man coming
	24:44	the **S** of Man will come at an hour
	27:54	"Surely he was the **S** of God!"
	28:19	and of the **S** and of the Holy Spirit,
Mk	8:38	the **S** of Man will be ashamed
	9:7	"This is my **S**, whom I love.
Lk	1:32	and will be called the **S**

	2:7	she gave birth to her firstborn, a **s**.
	9:35	This is my **S**, whom I have chosen;
	15:20	he ran to his **s**, threw his arms
	18:31	written by the prophets about the **S**
	19:10	For the **S** of Man came to seek
Jn	1:34	I testify that this is the **S** of God."
	3:14	so the **S** of Man must be lifted up,
	3:16	that he gave his one and only **S**,
	3:36	believes in the **S** has eternal life,
	5:19	the **S** can do nothing by himself;
	17:1	Glorify your **S**, that your **S** may
Ac	7:56	and the **S** of Man standing
	13:33	"'You are my **S**;
Ro	1:4	with power to be the **S** of God
	5:10	to him through the death of his **S**,
	8:3	did by sending his own **S**
	8:29	conformed to the likeness of his **S**,
	8:32	He who did not spare his own **S**,
1Co	15:28	then the **S** himself will be made
Gal	2:20	I live by faith in the **S** of God,
1Th	1:10	and to wait for his **S** from heaven,
Heb	1:2	days he has spoken to us by his **S**,
	2:6	the **s** of man that you care for him?
2Pe	1:17	saying, "This is my **S**, whom I love;
1Jn	1:3	is with the Father and with his **S**,
	1:7	his **S**, purifies us from all sin.
	2:23	whoever acknowledges the **S** has
	4:9	only **S** into the world that we might
	5:5	he who believes that Jesus is the **S**
	5:11	eternal life, and this life is in his **S**.
Rev	1:13	lampstands was someone "like a **s**
	14:14	on the cloud was one "like a **s**

SON OF GOD A title of Jesus referring to his equality, eternity, and consubstantiality with the Father and the Spirit in the eternal triune Godhead (Jn 5:18, 23, 36). Christ claimed to be eternal, equal, and of the same substance as the Father. He is uniquely God's Son.

SON OF MAN

1. A human being (Eze 2:1, 3, 8ff; Ps 8:4).

2. Used in a messianic sense (Da 7:13 – 14). Jesus applies the term to himself many times in

the Gospels (Mt 8:20; 9:6; 10:23; 11:19; 12:8; et al.). Sometimes he uses it in connection with his earthly mission; but he also uses it when describing his final triumph as Redeemer and Judge (Mt 16:27 – 28; 19:28; 24:30; 25:31). The phrase identifies him with humanity (cf. Heb 2:14 – 18) and with the heavenly Son of Man (Da 7:13 – 14). *See Jesus the Christ.*

SONG OF SONGS, SONG OF SOLOMON (Heb. *shîr ha-shîrîm*). This book is unique among biblical books, for it centers in the joys and distresses of the love relationship between a man and a woman.

NAME.

The Hebrew name, Song of Songs, is taken from 1:1, which introduces the book as "the song of songs which is Solomon's." This use of the Hebrew superlative declares the book the best of the 1,005 songs of Solomon (1Ki 4:32), or perhaps the greatest of all songs. It also provides the basis for the older title of the book in English versions, Song of Solomon, as well as for the title in the NIV, Song of Songs.

AUTHORSHIP AND DATE.

There is considerable range of opinion as to the authorship and date of the book. The book ascribes its authorship to Solomon, and there are lines of evidence that agree with this ascription. The book has affinities with other writings attributed to Solomon. The author's acquaintance with plants and animals is reminiscent of Solomon (1Ki 4:33). The mention of "a mare harnessed to one of the chariots of Pharaoh" (SS 1:9) accords with Solomon's involvement in horse trading with Egypt and with his being married to a daughter of the pharaoh. The lover is called "the king" (1:4), and there are other indications of his royal interests, in addition to references to Solomon by name. The place names range throughout Palestine and thus fit well with an origin predating the divided kingdom.

CONTENT.

Though the book is difficult to analyze, the divisions of Delitzsch are often followed: (1) the mutual admiration of the lovers (1:2 – 2:7); (2) growth in love (2:8 – 3:5); (3) the marriage (3:6 – 5:1); (4) longing of the wife for her absent husband (5:2 – 6:9); (5) the beauty of the Shulammite bride (6:10 – 8:4); (6) the wonder of love (8:5 – 8:14).

INTERPRETATION.

There is great diversity and much overlapping among interpretations of the Song of Songs. Various views are: (1) allegorical, (2) typical, (3) literal, (4) dramatic, (5) erotic-literary, (6) liturgical, and (7) didactic-moral.

SONS OF GOD, CHILDREN OF GOD A description of those who are in a special or intimate relationship with God. In the OT the Lord chose the people Israel and made a holy covenant with them. As a result, the people as a unit (and thus each member) were described as the son(s) of God. Moses told Pharaoh that the Israelite nation was God's "firstborn son," and that this "son" must be released in order to offer worship to his "Father" (Ex 4:22). Later the description was "children of God" and "a people holy to the Lord" (Dt 14:1). Further, the Davidic king-Messiah was described as the Son of God (see 2Sa 7:14; 23:5; Pss 2:7; 89:27 – 28). This usage is continued in the NT, where the ancient people of Israel are said to possess the "sonship" (Ro 9:4) and be God's children (Jn 11:52) and the Messiah is seen as God's "Son" (Heb 1:5; citing Ps 2:7 and 2Sa 7:14).

Building on this OT usage, members of the new covenant are also described as sons/children of God. Paul declared that "you are all sons of God through faith in Christ Jesus" (Gal 3:26), and he used the image of adoption to convey the idea of being taken into God's family, of receiving forgiveness and the gift of the indwelling Spirit (Ro 8:14ff.). John taught that by spiritual birth believers become the children of God and are thereby in an intimate spiritual/moral union with God their heavenly Father. ("How great is the love the Father has lavished on us, that we should be called children of God!" [1Jn 3:1]). Both Paul and John insisted that to be called son or child meant living in a way that reflects this relationship (Ro 8:17, 29; 1Jn 3:9). Jesus himself made a similar point (Mt 5:9, 44–45; 12:48–50). Again this continues the OT emphasis that to be the son or child of God means being god-like in behavior (Dt 32:6; Isa 1:2; Hos 1:10).

Within the OT there is at least one other way in which "sons of God" is used. That is, a few passages appear to refer to angels (Job 1:6; 2:1; 38:7; Ps 89:6). Genesis 6:1–2 may likewise involve angels (in this case they are fallen ones), or they may be demon-possessed individuals, but others view these "sons of God" as kings/rulers/princes.

SONS OF THE PROPHETS A title given to members of prophetic guilds or schools. Samuel was the head of a company of prophets at Ramah (1Sa 7:17; 28:3), and two hundred years later Elijah and Elisha were leaders of similar groups. They were men endowed with the prophetic gift (10:10; 19:20–23), who gathered around God's great leader for common worship, united prayer, religious fellowship, and instruction of the people (10:5, 10; 2Ki 4:38, 40; 6:1–7; 9:1). In the times of Elijah and Elisha, they formed a comparatively large company (2Ki 2:7, 16) and lived together at Bethel, Jericho, and Gilgal (2:3, 5; 4:38).

SONSHIP

Ro	8:15	but you received the Spirit of s.

SORCERY [4175, 4176, 4177, 5727, 5728, 6726, 3405, 3407, 4319]. Divination by an alleged assistance of evil spirits.

General References to:
Forbidden (Lev 19:26–28, 31; 20:6; Dt 18:9–14). Denounced (Isa 8:19; Mal 3:5). Practiced by: the Egyptians (Isa 19:3, 11–12); the magicians (Ex 7:11, 22; 8:7, 18); Balaam (Nu 22:6; 23:23, w chs. 22; 23); Jezebel (2Ki 9:22); the Ninevites (Na 3:4–5); the Babylonians (Isa 47:9–13; Eze 21:21–22; Da 2:2, 10, 27); Belshazzar (Da 5:7, 15); Simon the sorcerer (Ac 8:9, 11); Elymas (Ac 13:8); the young woman at Philippi (Ac 16:16); vagabond Jews (Ac 19:13); sons of

Sceva (Ac 19:14–15); astrologers (Jer 10:2; Mic 3:6–7); false prophets (Jer 14:14; 27:9; 29:8–9; Eze 13:6–9; 22:28; Mt 24:24). To cease (Eze 12:23–24; 13:23; Mic 5:12). Messages of, false (Eze 21:29; Zec 10:2; 2Th 2:9). Diviners shall be confounded (Mic 3:7). Belongs to the works of the flesh (Gal 5:20). Wickedness of (1Sa 15:23). Vainness of (Isa 44:25). Punishment for (Ex 22:18; Lev 20:27; Dt 13:5). Divining by familiar spirits (Lev 20:27; 1Ch 10:13; 2Ch 33:6; Isa 8:19; 19:3; 29:4); by entrails (Eze 21:21); by images (2Ki 23:24; Eze 21:21); by rods (Hos 4:12). Saul consulted the medium of Endor (1Sa 28:7–25). Books of, destroyed (Ac 19:19).

SORROW [16, 65, 224, 1790, 3326, 4088, 9342, 3382, 3383, 3851, 4337].

God takes notice of Hagar's (Ge 21:17–20); Israelites' (Ex 3:7–10). For sin (2Co 7:10–11). No sorrow in heaven (Rev 21:4). "Sorrow and sighing will flee away" (Isa 35:10). Of Hannah (1Sa 1:15). Of David for Absalom (2Sa 18:33; 19:1–8). Of Mary and Martha (Jn 11:19–40). Of Jeremiah (La 1:12). Of Jesus (Isa 53:11; Mt 26:37–44; Mk 14:34–42; Lk 22:42–44). From bereavement: of Jacob for Joseph (Ge 37:34–35); for Benjamin (Ge 43:14). Of the lost (Mt 8:12; 13:42, 50; 22:13; 24:51; 25:30; Lk 13:28; 16:23).

Ps	6:7	My eyes grow weak with **s**;
	116:3	I was overcome by trouble and **s**.
Isa	60:20	and your days of **s** will end.
Jer	31:12	and they will **s** no more.
Ro	9:2	I have great **s** and unceasing
2Co	7:10	Godly **s** brings repentance that

SOUL [2855+5929, 3869+4222, 3883, 5883, 6034] (Heb. *nephesh*, Gr. *psychē*). The word commonly used in the Bible to designate the nonmaterial ego of people in its ordinary relationships with earthly and physical things. It is one of a number of psychological nouns, all designating the same nonmaterial self, but each in a different functional relationship. Thus, the "mind" (*nous*) is the self in its rational functions. Again "mind" (*phronēma*) is the self as deeply comtemplating. "Heart" (*kardia*) is the self as manifesting a complex of attitudes. "Will" (*thelēsis*) is the self as choosing and deciding. "Spirit" (*pneuma*) is the self when thought of apart from earthly connections. When the blessed dead in heaven are spoken of as having been put to a martyr's death, they are called "souls" (Rev 6:9). When there is no reference to their former bodily experience, they are called "spirits" (Heb 12:23).

These functional names of the ego are not used with technical discrimination. They often overlap. The difference between humans and beasts is not that humans have a soul or spirit (Ge 1:20; 7:15; Ecc 3:21), but that humans are created in the image of God, whereas beasts are not.

The immortal, nonmaterial part of a human being (Mt 10:28; Rev 6:9; 20:4). Can represent the whole person (Jdg 5:21) or one's life (Job 33:18; Ps 26:9). Used with heart to represent the will and emotions (Dt 4:29; 6:4).

Dt	6:5	with all your **s** and with all your
2Ki	23:25	and with all his **s** and with all his
Ps	23:3	he restores my **s**.
	42:1	so my **s** pants for you, O God.
	42:11	Why are you downcast, O my **s**?
	62:5	Find rest, O my **s**, in God alone;
Pr	13:19	A longing fulfilled is sweet to the **s**,
	22:5	he who guards his **s** stays far
Isa	55:2	your **s** will delight in the richest
La	3:20	and my **s** is downcast within me.
Eze	18:4	For every living **s** belongs to me,
Mt	10:28	kill the body but cannot kill the **s**.
	16:26	yet forfeits his **s**? Or what can
	22:37	with all your **s** and with all your
Heb	4:12	even to dividing **s** and spirit,

SOVEREIGN

Ge	15:2	But Abram said, "O **S** LORD,
2Sa	7:18	O **S** LORD, and what is my family,
Ps	71:16	your mighty acts, O **S** LORD;
Isa	40:10	the **S** LORD comes with power,
	61:1	The Spirit of the **S** LORD is on me,
Da	4:25	that the Most High is **s**
2Pe	2:1	denying the **s** Lord who bought
Jude	1:4	and deny Jesus Christ our only **S**

SOVEREIGNTY OF GOD [123, 151, 10424, 10718, 1305]. The word *sovereign*, although it does not occur in any form in the English Bible, conveys the oft-repeated scriptural thought of the supreme authority of God. He is called *Pantokratōr*, "Almighty" (2Co 6:18, and nine times in Revelation); "the blessed and only Ruler, the King of kings and Lord of lords" (1Ti 6:15). He "works out everything in conformity with the purpose of his will" (Eph 1:11). His sovereignty follows logically from the doctrine that he is God, Creator, and Ruler of the universe. The sovereignty of God is sometimes presented in the Bible as an unanalyzed ultimate. "But who are you, O man, to talk back to God? Shall what is formed say to him who formed it, 'Why did you make me like this?' Does not the potter have the right to make out of the same lump of clay some pottery for noble purposes and some for common use?" (Ro 9:20 – 21; see Isa 45:9; cf. Ps 115:3; Da 4:35; and many similar passages). God is not subject to any power or any abstract rule or law that could be conceived as superior to or other than himself.

Yet the Scripture is equally emphatic that God's character is immutably holy and just and good. "He cannot disown himself" (2Ti 2:13). "It is impossible for God to lie" (Heb 6:18; cf. Tit 1:2). A person of faith may rightly stand before the Lord and plead, "Will not the Judge of all the earth do right?" (Ge 18:25). "His love endures forever" is an oft-recurring phrase (Ps 136). He assures his people of his eternal self-consistency: "I the LORD do not change. So you, O descendants of Jacob, are not destroyed" (Mal 3:6).

The inscrutable sovereignty of God is manifested, not so much in the punishment of the reprobate as in the salvation of his people. In his holy character he must logically punish moral evil (*see Sin*). But his sovereignty is most marvelously revealed in that he has graciously elected to save a people from their sin and from its consequences.

SOW

Job	4:8	and those who **s** trouble reap it.
Hos	10:12	**S** for yourselves righteousness,
Mt	6:26	they do not **s** or reap or store away
	13:3	"A farmer went out to **s** his seed.
1Co	15:36	What you **s** does not come to life
Jas	3:18	Peacemakers who **s**

SPEAKING, SPEECH [522, 606, 608, 614, 1819, 1821, 2047, 3120, 4863, 5583, 7023, 7754, 8488, 8557, 10425, 238, 2895, 3281, 3306, 3364, 3455, 4231, 4245].

Evil:

(Pss 10:8; 52:2 – 4; Isa 32:6 – 7; Jer 20:10; Jude 8, 10). Causes strife (Pr 15:1; 16:27 – 28; 17:9; 25:23). Excludes from kingdom of heaven (1Co 6:10). Hated by God (Pr 6:16 – 19; 8:13). Characteristic of humankind (Ro 1:29 – 30; 3:13 – 14). Not characteristic of a Christian (Eph 4:25, 29, 31; 5:4; Tit 3:2; Jas 1:26; 3:5 – 6, 8 – 10; 4:11; 1Pe 2:1; 3:9 – 10). Forbidden (Ex 22:28; Ps 34:13; Pr 4:24; 6:16 – 19; Mt 5:22, 37; 12:34 – 37; Ac 23:5; Eph 4:25, 29, 31; Tit 3:2; Jas 1:26; 3:5 – 6, 8 – 10; 4:11; 1Pe 2:1; 3:9 – 10). Punishment for (Pss 12:3 – 4; 52:1 – 4). Proverbs concerning (Pr 4:24; 6:16 – 19; 8:13; 10:11, 19, 31 – 32; 11:11; 12:5 – 6, 13, 17 – 19; 13:3; 14:25; 15:1, 4, 28; 16:27 – 28; 17:4, 9, 20; 18:8, 21, 23; 19:1, 22 – 23; 24:2; 25:23; 26:20 – 23, 28; Ecc 10:11, 20). Prayers for deliverance from curse of (Pss 64:2 – 5; 70:3; 120:1 – 7). Self-accusation: Solomon (Ecc 7:22); Isaiah (Isa 6:5); Paul (Ac 23:5). **Instances of:** *against Job (Job 19:18); against Lot, those of Sodom (2Pe 2:7 – 8, 10); against Moses (Ps 106:33); against the psalmists (Pss 35:21; 41:5 – 9; 69:12, 26; 102:8; 119:23); against the church, those of the circumcision (Tit 1:10 – 11). False teachers (Jude 8, 10).*

Foolish:

(Job 13:5; 16:3 – 4; 38:2). Accountable to God (Mt 12:36 – 37). Forbidden (Pr 30:18). Not char-

acteristic of a Christian (Eph 5:4). Proverbs concerning (Pr 10:14; 12:23; 13:3; 14:3; 15:2, 7, 14; 18:6 – 7, 13; 26:4, 7, 9; 29:11, 20; 30:10; Ecc 5:3, 5; 10:13 – 14).

Wise:

(Job 16:5; 27:4; Am 5:13; Zep 3:13; Zec 8:16; Rev 14:17). As good as nails (Ecc 12:11). Precious as jewels (Pr 20:16). Edifying (Eph 4:29). Rewards of (Pss 15:1 – 3; 50:23; Pr 14:3; 22:11). Of the noble woman (Pr 31:26). Admonitions concerning, to believers (Eph 4:22, 25, 29; Php 1:27; Col 4:6; Jas 1:19, 26; 3:2, 13; 1Pe 2:12; 3:15 – 16). Christ's words concerning (Mt 12:35, 37; Lk 6:45). Of psalmists (Pss 37:30; 39:1; 77:12; 119:13, 27, 46, 54, 172; 141:3; 145:5 – 7, 11 – 12). Proverbs concerning (Pr 10:11, 13, 19 – 21, 31 – 32; 11:12 – 14; 12:6, 14, 16 – 20, 23; 13:2 – 3; 14:3; 15:1 – 2, 4, 7, 23, 26, 28; 16:21, 23 – 24; 17:7, 27 – 28; 18:4, 20; 19:1; 20:15; 21:23; 22:11; 24:6; 25:11, 15; 26:5; 29:11; 31:26; Ecc 3:7; 9:17; 10:12; 12:9 – 11). Prayer concerning (Ps 141:3).

SPIRIT [200, 466, 4000, 4213, 5883, 5972, 8120, 10658, 899+3836+5858, 4460, 5249, 6035] (Heb. *rûach*, breath, spirit, Gr. *pneuma*, wind, spirit). One of the biblical nouns denoting the nonmaterial ego in special relationships. The self is generally called "spirit" in contexts where its bodily, emotional, and intellectual aspects are not prominent, but where the direct relationship of the individual to God is the point of emphasis. A typical instance is Ro 8:15b – 16, "By him we cry, . . . 'Father.' The Spirit himself testifies with *our spirit* that we are God's children" (emphasis added).

General References to:

Immortal, nonmaterial part of a human being, similar to the soul (Job 7:11). Represents one's life force or strength (Ge 45:27; Jas 2:26); character (Nu 14:24; Dt 2:30; 1Pe 3:4); desire (2Sa 13:39); heart or emotions (Pss 73:21; 77:6). The self is often called "spirit" when the direct relationship of the individual to God is the point of emphasis (2Ti 4:22; Phm 25).

Ge	1:2	and the **S** of God was hovering
	6:3	"My **S** will not contend
Ex	31:3	I have filled him with the **S** of God,
Dt	34:9	filled with the **s** of wisdom
Jdg	6:34	Then the **S** of the LORD came
1Sa	10:10	the **S** of God came upon him
	16:14	the **S** of the LORD had departed
2Sa	23:2	"The **S** of the LORD spoke
2Ki	2:9	inherit a double portion of your **s**,"
Ne	9:20	You gave your good **S**
	9:30	By your **S** you admonished them
Ps	31:5	Into your hands I commit my **s**;
	34:18	saves those who are crushed in **s**.
	51:10	and renew a steadfast **s** within me.
	51:11	or take your Holy **S** from me.
	51:17	sacrifices of God are a broken **s**;
	139:7	Where can I go from your **S**?
Isa	11:2	The **S** of the LORD will rest
	44:3	I will pour out my **S**
	57:15	him who is contrite and lowly in **s**,
	63:10	and grieved his Holy **S**.
Eze	11:19	an undivided heart and put a new **s**
	13:3	prophets who follow their own **s**
	36:26	you a new heart and put a new **s**
Joel	2:28	I will pour out my **S** on all people.
Zec	4:6	but by my S,' says the LORD
Mt	1:18	to be with child through the Holy **S**
	3:11	will baptize you with the Holy **S**
	3:16	he saw the **S** of God descending
	4:1	led by the **S** into the desert
	5:3	saying: "Blessed are the poor in **s**,
	12:31	against the **S** will not be forgiven.
	26:41	**s** is willing, but the body is weak."
	28:19	and of the Son and of the Holy **S**,
Lk	1:35	"The Holy **S** will come upon you,
	1:80	child grew and became strong in **s**;
	4:18	"The **S** of the Lord is on me,
	23:46	into your hands I commit my **s**."
Jn	3:5	a man is born of water and the **S**,
	4:24	God is **s**, and his worshipers must
	6:63	The **S** gives life; the flesh counts
	14:26	But the Counselor, the Holy **S**,
	16:13	But when he, the **S** of truth, comes,

	20:22	and said, "Receive the Holy **S**.
Ac	1:5	will be baptized with the Holy **S**."
	1:8	when the Holy **S** comes on you;
	2:4	of them were filled with the Holy **S**
	2:17	I will pour out my **S** on all people.
	2:38	will receive the gift of the Holy **S**.
	4:31	they were all filled with the Holy **S**
	5:3	that you have lied to the Holy **S**
	13:2	and fasting, the Holy **S** said,
	19:2	"Did you receive the Holy **S**
Ro	8:4	nature but according to the **S**.
	8:9	And if anyone does not have the **S**
	8:16	The **S** himself testifies
	8:23	who have the firstfruits of the **S**,
	8:26	the **S** helps us in our weakness.
1Co	2:10	God has revealed it to us by his **S**.
	2:14	man without the **S** does not accept
	6:19	body is a temple of the Holy **S**,
	12:13	baptized by one **S** into one body —
2Co	1:22	and put his **S** in our hearts
	3:3	but with the **S** of the living God,
	3:6	the letter kills, but the **S** gives life.
	5:5	and has given us the **S** as a deposit,
Gal	5:16	by the **S**, and you will not gratify
	5:22	But the fruit of the **S** is love, joy,
	5:25	let us keep in step with the **S**.
	6:8	from the **S** will reap eternal life.
Eph	1:13	with a seal, the promised Holy **S**,
	2:22	in which God lives by his **S**.
	4:4	There is one body and one **S** —
	4:30	do not grieve the Holy **S** of God,
	5:18	Instead, be filled with the **S**.
	6:17	of salvation and the sword of the **S**,
Php	2:2	being one in **s** and purpose.
2Th	2:13	the sanctifying work of the **S**
2Ti	1:7	For God did not give us a **s**
Heb	4:12	even to dividing soul and **s**,
1Pe	3:4	beauty of a gentle and quiet **s**,
2Pe	1:21	carried along by the Holy **S**.
1Jn	3:24	We know it by the **S** he gave us.
	4:1	Dear friends, do not believe every **s**
Jude	1:20	holy faith and pray in the Holy **S**.
Rev	2:7	let him hear what the **S** says

SPIRITISTS [3362]. Divination by means of communication with the spirits of the dead (necromancy) was known and practiced in the ancient Near East.

Consulting of:

Forbidden (Lev 19:31; 20:6, 27; Dt 18:10 – 11). Vain (Isa 8:19; 19:3). Those who consulted, to be cut off (Lev 20:6, 27).

Instances of Consulting of:

Saul (1Sa 28:3 – 25; 1Ch 10:13 – 14). Manasseh (2Ki 21:6; 2Ch 33:6). A slave girl (Ac 16:16 – 18). See Demons; Medium; Sorcery; Witchcraft.

SPIRITS

1Co	12:10	to another distinguishing between **s**,
	14:32	The **s** of prophets are subject
1Jn	4:1	test the **s** to see whether they are

SPIRITS IN PRISON Those who in the days of Noah refused his message (1Pe 3:18 – 20; 4:6). The exact interpretation of this passage is strongly debated.

SPIRITUAL

Ro	12:1	to God — this is your **s** act of worship.
	12:11	but keep your **s** fervor, serving
1Co	2:13	expressing **s** truths in **s** words.
	3:1	I could not address you as **s** but
	12:1	Now about **s** gifts, brothers,
	15:44	a natural body, it is raised a **s** body.
Gal	6:1	you who are **s** should restore him
Eph	1:3	with every **s** blessing in Christ.
	5:19	with psalms, hymns and **s** songs.
	6:12	and against the **s** forces of evil
1Pe	2:2	newborn babies, crave pure **s** milk,
	2:5	are being built into a **s** house

SPIRITUAL GIFTS Extraordinary gifts of the Spirit given to Christians to equip them for the service of the church (Ro 11:29; 12:6 – 8; 1Co 12:4 – 11, 28 – 30; Eph 4:7 – 11; 1Pe 4:10 – 11).

STEAL

Ex	20:15	"You shall not **s**.
Lev	19:11	"'Do not **s**.
Dt	5:19	"You shall not **s**.
Mt	19:18	do not **s**, do not give false
Ro	13:9	"Do not **s**," "Do not covet,"
Eph	4:28	has been stealing must **s** no longer,

STEPHEN [5108] (stē′vĕn, Gr. *Stephanos, crown* or *victor's wreath*). One of the seven appointed to look after the daily distribution to the poor in the early church (Ac 6:1 – 6). Stephen's ministry was not, however, limited to providing for the poor. He did "great wonders and miraculous signs among the people" (Ac 6:8). While this probably brought him into great favor with the people generally, another aspect of his ministry engaged him in bitterest conflict with the adherents of Judaism. He taught in the synagogue of the Libertines (i.e., freedmen) and there debated with Jews of the dispersion from Cyrene, Alexandria, Cilicia, and Asia. When it was evident that they could not refute Stephen's arguments in open debate, these Jews hired informers to misrepresent his arguments. Acts 7 records Stephen's remarkable *apologia* before the council. F. F. Bruce rightly points out that it was "not a speech for the defense in the forensic sense of the term. Such a speech as this was by no means calculated to secure an acquittal before the Sanhedrin. It is rather a defense of pure Christianity as God's appointed way of worship" (*The Book of Acts* [NINTC], 1956, p. 141). Stephen's exclamation at the close of his speech is particularly important to a proper understanding of it: "Look … I see heaven open and the Son of Man standing at the right hand of God" (7:56). This is the only occurrence of the title "Son of Man" in the NT on the lips of anyone other than Jesus himself. It reveals that "Stephen grasped and asserted the more-than-Jewish-Messianic sense in which the office and significance of Jesus in religious history were to be understood" (William Manson, *The Epistle to the Hebrews*, 1951, p. 31).

Such radical thinking was too much for the listening Sanhedrin. "They covered their ears and, yelling at the top of their voices, they … dragged him out of the city and began to stone him." The witnesses, whose responsibility it was to cast the first stones (cf. Dt 17:7), laid their clothes at Saul's feet (Ac 7:57 – 58).

> **General References to:**
> Appointed one of the committee of seven to oversee power of (Ac 6:5, 8 – 10). False charges against (Ac 6:11 – 15). Defense of (Ac 7). Stoned (Ac 7:54 – 60; 8:1; 22:20). Burial of (Ac 8:2). Gentle and forgiving spirit of (Ac 7:59 – 60).

STEWARD [1074+8042, 5853, 6125] (Ge 15:2; 43:19; 1Ch 28:1; Lk 8:3).

Must be faithful (1Co 4:1 – 2; Tit 1:7; 1Pe 4:10). Figurative: Faithful steward described (Lk 12:35 – 38, 42). Unfaithful, described (Lk 16:1 – 8). Parable of the minas (Lk 19:12 – 27); of the talents (Mt 25:14 – 30).

STONING [6232, 8083+, 3342, 3344]. The ordinary form of capital punishment prescribed by Hebrew law (Lev 20:2) for blasphemy (Lev 24:16), idolatry (Dt 13:6 – 10), desecration of the Sabbath day (Ex 31:15; 35:2; Nu 15:32 – 36), human sacrifice (Lev 20:2), occultism (Lev 20:27). Unlike unintentional sins, for which there are provisions of God's mercy, one who sets his hand defiantly to despise the word of God and to blaspheme his name must be punished. The one who sins defiantly (literally "with a high hand"), whether in the case of the willful blasphemer (Ex 20:7; 22:28; Lev 24:11 – 16), or the Sabbath-breaker (Ex 31:12 – 15; 35:2), was guilty of high-handed rebellion and was judged with death (Nu 15:30 – 31, 32 – 36). Execution took place outside the city (Lev 24:14; 1Ki 21:10, 13; Ac 7:58).

STOREHOUSE [238, 238, 667, 1074+]. A place for keeping treasures, supplies, and equipment. Obedience to the Lord was rewarded with full storehouses (Dt 28:8 KJV). Joseph stored grain in storehouses in Egypt against the coming famine (Ge 41:56). Hezekiah had many treasures in his storehouses and willingly showed them to visitors (2Ki 20:13). The temple storehouse was a vital link in Hebrew worship and was always guarded (1Ch 26:15 – 17; Mal 3:10).

STRENGTH

Ex	15:2	The Lord is my **s** and my song;
Dt	6:5	all your soul and with all your **s**.
Jdg	16:15	told me the secret of your great **s**."
2Sa	22:33	It is God who arms me with **s**
1Ch	16:11	Look to the Lord and his **s**;
	29:12	In your hands are **s** and power
Ne	8:10	for the joy of the Lord is your **s**."
Ps	18:1	I love you, O Lord, my **s**.
	28:7	The Lord is my **s** and my shield;
	46:1	God is our refuge and **s**,
	84:5	Blessed are those whose **s** is in you,
Pr	24:5	a man of knowledge increases **s**;
	30:25	Ants are creatures of little **s**,
Isa	40:26	of his great power and mighty **s**,
	40:31	will renew their **s**.
Jer	9:23	or the strong man boast of his **s**
Hab	3:19	The Sovereign Lord is my **s**;
Mk	12:30	all your mind and with all your **s**.'
1Co	1:25	of God is stronger than man's **s**.
Eph	1:19	is like the working of his mighty **s**,
Php	4:13	through him who gives me **s**.
Heb	11:34	whose weakness was turned to **s**;
1Pe	4:11	it with the **s** God provides,

STRIFE [4506, 5175, 8190, 2251].

> **General References to:**
> (Pss 55:9; 80:6). Domestic (Pr 19:13; 21:19; 25:24). Hated by God (Isa 58:4; Hab 1:3). Christ brings (Mt 10:34 – 36; Lk 12:51 – 53, 58 – 59). Caused by: Busybodies (Pr 26:20). Perversity (Pr 16:28). Hatred (Pr 10:12). Lusts (Jas 4:1 – 2). Pride (Pr 13:10). Scornfulness (Pr 22:10). Wrath (Pr 15:18; 29:22; 30:33). Excessive indulgence in intoxicating drinks (Pr 23:29 – 30). Destructive (Mt 12:25; Mk 3:24 – 25; Lk 11:17).

> **Exhortations against:**
> (Ge 13:8; 45:24; Ps 31:20; Pr 3:30; 17:14; 25:8; Mt 5:25, 39 – 41; Ro 12:18; 13:13; 14:1, 19, 21;

16:17 – 18; 1Co 4:6 – 7; 2Co 12:20; Gal 5:15, 20; Php 2:3, 14 – 15; 1Ti 3:2 – 3; 6:3 – 5, 20 – 21; 2Ti 2:14, 23 – 25; Tit 3:1 – 3, 9; Jas 3:14 – 16). Punishment for (Isa 41:11 – 12; Ro 2:8 – 9). Correction of (Mt 18:15 – 17). Abstinence from, honorable (Pr 20:3). Prayers concerning (Ps 55:9; 1Ti 2:8). Proverbs concerning (Pr 3:30; 6:12 – 14, 16 – 19; 10:12; 13:10; 15:18; 17:1, 14, 19; 18:6, 19; 19:13; 20:3; 21:19; 22:10; 23:29 – 30; 25:8, 24; 26:17, 20 – 21; 27:15; 28:25; 29:22; 30:33). See Anger; Envy; Jealousy; Malice.

Instances of:

Between Abraham and Lot's herdsmen (Ge 13:6 – 7); Abraham and Abimelech (Ge 21:25); Isaac's herdsmen and servants of Gerar (Ge 26:20 – 22). Laban and Jacob (Ge 31:36). Israelites (Dt 1:12). Jephthah and his brothers (Jdg 11:2); and Ephraimites (Jdg 12:1 – 6). Israel and Judah, about David (2Sa 19:41 – 43). Disciples, over who might be the greatest (Mk 9:34; Lk 22:24). Jews, concerning Jesus (Jn 10:19). Christians at Antioch, about circumcision (Ac 15:2). Paul and Barnabas, about Mark (Ac 15:38 – 39). Pharisees and Sadducees, concerning the resurrection (Ac 23:7 – 10). Christians, at Corinth (1Co 1:10 – 12; 3:3 – 4; 6:1 – 7; 11:16 – 21). At Philippi (Php 1:15 – 17).

Pr	17:1	than a house full of feasting, with **s**.
	20:3	It is to a man's honor to avoid **s**,
	22:10	out the mocker, and out goes **s**;
	30:33	so stirring up anger produces **s**."
1Ti	6:4	**s**, malicious talk, evil suspicions

STRIPES (Heb. *nākâh*, Gr. *plēgē*). Scourging by lashing was a common form of punishment in ancient times. The Jewish law authorized it for certain ecclesiastical offenses (Dt 25:2 – 3). Among the Jews a scourge consisting of three thongs was used, and the number of stripes varied from a few to thirty-nine (to make sure that the law's limit of forty was not exceeded). When scourging took place in the synagogue, it was done by the overseer, but the Sanhedrin also administered such punishment (Ac 5:40). Roman scourges had pieces of metal or bone attached to the lashes. The victim was stripped to the waist and bound in a stooping position. The body was horribly lacerated so that often even the entrails were exposed.

STRONGHOLD A place of refuge, a fortress. This can be a literal place, as in time of distress (Jdg 6:2; 1Sa 24:22), and figurative, as in Ps 27:1: "The LORD is the stronghold of my life."

2Sa	22:3	He is my **s**, my refuge and my
Ps	9:9	a **s** in times of trouble.
	18:2	the horn of my salvation, my **s**.
	27:1	The LORD is the **s** of my life —
	144:2	my **s** and my deliverer,

STUMBLE

Ps	37:24	though he **s**, he will not fall,
Pr	3:23	and your foot will not **s**;
Isa	8:14	a stone that causes men to **s**
Jer	31:9	a level path where they will not **s**,
Hos	14:9	but the rebellious **s** in them.
Mal	2:8	teaching have caused many to **s**;
Jn	11:9	A man who walks by day will not **s**,
Ro	9:33	in Zion a stone that causes men to **s**
	14:20	that causes someone else to **s**.
1Co	10:32	Do not cause anyone to **s**,
Jas	3:2	We all **s** in many ways.
1Pe	2:8	and, "A stone that causes men to **s**

SUBMIT

Ro	13:1	Everyone must **s** himself
	13:5	necessary to **s** to the authorities,
1Co	16:16	to **s** to such as these
Eph	5:21	**S** to one another out of reverence
Col	3:18	Wives, **s** to your husbands,
Heb	13:17	Obey your leaders and **s**
Jas	4:7	**S** yourselves, then, to God.
1Pe	2:18	**s** yourselves to your masters

SUCCESS

Ge	39:23	and gave him **s** in whatever he did.
1Sa	18:14	In everything he did he had great **s**,

1Ch	22:13	you will have **s** if you are careful
2Ch	26:5	the Lord, God gave him **s**.
Ecc	10:10	but skill will bring **s**.

SUFFERING [2118, 2703, 4799, 5186, 5253, 5951, 6700, 6713, 6714, 6715, 6740, 8317, 10472, 1181, 2568, 3465, 4077, 4248, 5224, 5309].

For Christ:

Promised by Christ (Mt 10:34 – 36; Lk 12:51 – 53, 58 – 59; Ac 9:16). Fellowship with Christ on account of (Php 3:10). Conditions of joint heirship with Christ (Ro 8:17 – 22, 26). A privilege (Php 1:29). Rejoicing in (Ac 5:41; Col 1:24). Motives for patient enduring of: future glory (Ro 8:17 – 18; 2Co 4:8 – – 12, 17 – 18; 1Pe 4:13 – 14); reigning with Christ (2Ti 2:12; Rev 22:5); consolations in (2Co 1:7; Php 2:27 – 30; 2Ti 2:12; 1Pe 5:10); patience in (1Co 4:11 – 13; 2Th 1:4 – 5; Jas 5:10; 1Pe 4:14).

Of Christ:

Purpose of his coming (Lk 24:46 – 47; Jn 6:51; 10:11, 15; 11:50 – 52). Reason for his coming (Ro 4:25; 5:6 – 8; 14:15; 1Co 1:17 – 18, 23 – 24; 15:3; 2Co 5:14 – 15; Gal 1:4; 2:20 – 21; Eph 5:2, 25; 1Th 5:9 – 10; Heb 2:9 – 10, 14, 18; 5:8 – 9; 9:15 – 16, 28; 10:10, 18 – 20; 1Pe 2:21, 24; 3:18; 4:1; 1Jn 3:16).

Job	36:15	who suffer he delivers in their **s**;
Ps	22:24	the **s** of the afflicted one;
Isa	53:3	of sorrows, and familiar with **s**.
	53:11	After the **s** of his soul,
La	1:12	Is any **s** like my **s**
Ac	5:41	worthy of **s** disgrace for the Name.
Ro	5:3	know that **s** produces
2Ti	1:8	But join with me in **s** for the gospel,
Heb	2:10	of their salvation perfect through **s**.
1Pe	4:12	at the painful trial you are **s**,

SUICIDE (Am 9:2; Rev 9:6).

Temptation to, of Jesus (Mt 4:5 – 6; Lk 4:9 – 11). Of the Philippian jailer (Ac 16:27). See Death, Physical. Instances of: Samson (Jdg 16:29 – 30); Saul and his armor-bearer (1Sa 31:4 – 5; 1Ch 10:4 – 5); Ahithophel (2Sa 17:23); Zimri (1Ki 16:18); Judas (Mt 27:5; Ac 1:18).

SUNDAY The first day of the week, commemorating the resurrection of Jesus (Jn 20:1 – 25), and the day of Pentecost (Ac 2:1 – 41). For a time after the ascension of Jesus, the Christians met on the seventh and the first days of the week, but as the Hebrew Christian churches declined in influence, the tendency to observe the Hebrew Sabbath slowly passed. The disciples at Troas worshiped on the first day (Ac 20:7). Paul admonished the Corinthians to lay by in store as God had prospered them, doing it week by week on the first day (1Co 16:2). The term "Lord's Day" occurs (Rev 1:10).

SUSA (sū′s a, Heb. *shûshan*). A city of the Babylonians probably named from the lilies that grow in this region in large numbers. It was famous in biblical history as one of the capitals of the Persian Empire (Ne 1:1; Est 1:2; Da 8:2) during the time of Darius the Great. Here also Persian kings came to reside for the winter, and here Daniel had a vision (Da 8:1 – 14; see v. 2). The Hebrews called this place "Shushan" (so KJV). It was located in the fertile valley on the left bank of the Choaspes River called the Ulai Canal in Da 8:2, 16. It enjoyed a very delightful climate. Many Jews lived here and became prominent in the affairs of the city as the books of Esther and Nehemiah show. From this city was sent the group who replaced those removed from Samaria (Ezr 4:9).

In the last part of the nineteenth century, the French carried on extensive excavations at Susa directed by Dieulafoy. This archaeological effort uncovered the great palace of King Xerxes (KJV Ahasuerus, 486 – 465 BC) in which Queen Esther lived.

SWEAR

Lev	19:12	" 'Do not **s** falsely by my name
Ps	24:4	or **s** by what is false.
Mt	5:34	Do not **s** at all: either by heaven,
Jas	5:12	Above all, my brothers, do not **s** —

SYNAGOGUE [697, 801, 5252] (Gr. *synagoge, place of assembly*). A Jewish institution for the reading and exposition of the Holy Scriptures. It originated perhaps as early as the Babylonian exile. It is supposed that the synagogue had its precursor in the spontaneous gatherings of the Jewish people in the lands of their exile on their day of rest and also on special feast days. Since religion stood at the very center of Jewish existence, these gatherings naturally took on a religious significance. The Jews of the exile needed mutual encouragement in the faithful practice of their religion and in the hope of a restoration to the land. These they sought and found in spontaneous assemblies, which proved to be of such religious value that they quickly spread throughout the lands of the dispersion.

By NT times the synagogue was a firmly established institution among the Jews, who considered it to be an ancient institution, as the words of James in Ac 15:21 show: "For Moses has been preached in every city from the earliest times and is read in the synagogues on every Sabbath." Josephus, Philo, and later Judaism traced the synagogue back to Moses. While this, of course, has no historical validity, it does reveal that Judaism regarded the synagogue as one of its basic institutions.

In the first Christian century, synagogues could be found everywhere in the Hellenistic world where there were sufficient Jews to maintain one. In large Jewish centers there might be numbers of them. The chief purpose of the synagogue was not public worship, but instruction in the Holy Scriptures.

General References to:
1. Primarily an assembly (Ac 13:43; Jas 2:2). Constitutes a court of justice (Lk 12:11; Ac 9:2). Had powers of criminal courts (Mt 10:17; Mt 23:34; Ac 22:19; 26:11); of ecclesiastical courts (Jn 9:22, 34; 12:42; 16:2). 2. Place of assembly. Scriptures read and expounded in (Ne 8:1 – 8; 9:3, 5; Mt 4:23; 9:35; 13:54; Mk 1:39; Lk 4:15 – 33; 13:10; Jn 18:20; Ac 9:20; 13:5 – 44; 14:1; 15:21; 17:2, 10; 18:4, 19, 26). In Jerusalem (Ac 6:9); Damascus (Ac 9:2, 20); other cities (Ac 14:1; 17:1, 10; 18:4). Built by Jairus (Lk 7:5); Jesus performed healing in (Mt 12:9 – 13; Lk 13:11 – 14). Alms given in (Mt 6:2). Of Satan (Rev 2:9; 3:9).

SYNOPTIC GOSPELS, THE A careful comparison of the four gospels reveals that Matthew, Mark, and Luke are noticeably similar, while John is quite different. The first three gospels agree extensively in language, in the material they include, and in the order in which events and sayings from the life of Christ are recorded. (Chronological order does not appear to have been rigidly followed in any of the gospels, however). Because of this agreement, these three books are called the Synoptic Gospels (*syn*, "together with"; *optic*, "seeing"; thus "seeing together").

SYRIA [5353] (Heb. *'ărām*, Gr. *Syria*). An abbreviation of Assyria or possibly from the Babylonian *Suri*. Highlands lying between the Euphrates River and the Mediterranean Sea. Called Aram, from the son of Shem (Ge 10:22 – 23; Nu 23:7; 1Ch 1:17; 2:23). In the time of Abraham, it seems to have embraced the region between the Tigris and Euphrates (Ge 24:10, w 25:20), including Paddan Aram (Ge 25:20, n.; 28:5).

SYROPHOENICIAN (sī′rō-fē-nĭsh′ăn, Gr. *Syrophoinikissa*). An inhabitant of the region near Tyre and Sidon, modern Lebanon. A Greek woman, born in Syrian Phoenicia, by persistence and humility, won from Jesus healing for her daughter (Mk 7:26; cf. Mt 15:22).

TABERNACLE [185, 5438, 6109, 5008, 5009] (Heb. *'ohel, mô'edh, tent of meeting, mishkan, dwelling,* Gr. *skene, tent*). The God of Sinai revealed himself as a supremely moral being whose leadership extended over the whole earth. He was the only true God, and he desired to enter into a special spiritual relationship with Israel as a means of his self-expression in the world. Since this relationship demanded the undivided worship of the Israelites, it was of supreme importance for a ritual tradition to be established in the wilderness so that Israel could engage in regular spiritual communion with God. The nomadic nature of the sojourn in the Sinai peninsula precluded the building of a permanent shrine for worship. The only alternative was a portable sanctuary that would embody all that was necessary for the worship of the Lord under nomadic conditions and could also serve as a prototype of a subsequent permanent building.

At Sinai Moses was given a divine revelation concerning the nature, construction, and furnishings of the tabernacle (Ex 25:40). The work was carried out by Bezaleel, Oholiab, and their workmen; and when the task was accomplished, the tent was covered by a cloud and was filled with the divine glory (40:34). The descriptions of the tabernacle in Ex 26 – 27 and 35 – 38 make it clear that the structure was a portable shrine. Particularly characteristic of its desert origins are the tent curtains, the covering of red leather, and the acacia wood used during the construction.

The ark was the meeting place of God and his people through Moses, and contained the tablets of the law (Ex 25:16, 22). In the tabernacle all the sacrifices and acts of public worship commanded by the law took place. According to Ex 40:2, 17 the tabernacle was set up at Sinai at the beginning of the second year, fourteen days before the Passover celebration of the first anniversary of the exodus. When the structure was dismantled during the wanderings, the ark and the the two altars were carried by the sons of Kohath, a Levite. The remainder of the tabernacle was transported in six covered wagons each drawn by two oxen (Nu 7:3ff.).

General References to:

One existed before Moses received the pattern authorized on Mount Sinai (Ex 33:7 – 11). The one instituted by Moses was called a sanctuary (Ex 25:8); Tent of Meeting (Ex 27:21; 33:7; 2Ch 5:5); tabernacle of the Testimony (Ex 38:21; Nu 1:50); Tent of the Testimony (Nu 17:7 – 8; 2Ch 24:6); temple of the Lord (1Sa 1:9; 3:3); house of the Lord (Jos 6:24). The pattern of, revealed to Moses (Ex 25:9; 26:30; 39:32, 42 – 43; Ac 7:44; Heb 8:5). Materials for, voluntarily offered (Ex 25:1 – 8; 35:4 – 29; 36:3 – 7). Value of the substance contributed for (Ex 38:24 – 31). Workmen who constructed it were inspired (Ex 31:1 – 11; 35:30 – 35). Description of: frame (Ex 26:15 – 37; 36:20 – 38). Outer covering (Ex 25:5; 26:7 – 14; 36:14 – 19). Second covering (Ex 25:5; 26:14; 35:7, 23; 36:19; 39:34). Curtains of (Ex 26:1 – 14, 31 – 37; 27:9 – 16; 35:15, 17; 36:8 – 19, 35, 37). Court of (Ex 27:9 – 17; 38:9 – 16, 18; 40:8, 33). Holy Place of (Ex 26:31 – 37; 40:22 – 26; Heb 9:2 – 6, 8). The Most Holy Place (Ex 26:33 – 35; 40:20 – 21; Heb 9:3 – 5, 7 – 8). Furniture of (Ex 25:10 – 40; 27:1 – 8, 19; 37; 38:1 – 8). See Altar; Ark; Atonement Cover; Bread, Consecrated; Cherubim. Completed (Ex 39:32). Dedicated (Nu 7). Sanctified (Ex 29:43; 40:9 – 16; Nu 7:1). Anointed with holy oil (Ex 30:25 – 26; Lev 8:10; Nu 7:1). Sprinkled with blood (Lev 16:15 – 20; Heb 9:21, 23). Filled with the cloud of glory (Ex 40:34 – 38). How prepared for removal during the travels of the Israelites (Nu 1:51; 4:5 – 15). How and by whom carried (Nu 4:5 – 33; 7:6 – 9). Strangers forbidden to enter (Nu 1:51). Duties of the Levites concerning. See Levites. Defilement of, punished (Lev 15:31; Nu 19:13, 20; Eze 5:11; 23:38). Duties of the priests in relation to. See Priest. Israelites worship at (Nu 10:3; 16:19, 42 – 43; 20:6; 25:6; 1Sa 2:22; Ps 27:4). Offerings brought to (Lev 17:4; Nu 31:54; Dt

12:5 – 6, 11 – 14). Tribes encamped around, while in the wilderness (Nu 2). All males required to appear before, three times each year (Ex 23:17). Tabernacle tax (Ex 20:11 – 16). Carried in front of the Israelites in the line of march (Nu 10:33 – 36; Jos 3:3 – 6). The Lord reveals himself at (Lev 1:1; Nu 1:1; 7:89; 12:4 – 10; Dt 31:14 – 15). Pitched at Gilgal (Jos 4:18 – 19); at Shiloh (Jos 18:1; 19:51; Jdg 18:31; 20:18, 26 – 27; 21:19; 1Sa 2:14; 4:3 – 4; Jer 7:12, 14); at Nob (1Sa 21:1 – 6); at Gibeon (1Ch 21:29). Renewed by David and pitched on Mount Zion (1Ch 15:1; 16:1 – 2; 2Ch 1:4). Solomon offers sacrifice at (2Ch 1:3 – 6). Brought to the temple by Solomon (2Ch 5:5, w 1Ki 8:1, 4 – 5). Symbol of spiritual things (Ps 15:1; Heb 8:2, 5; 9:1 – 12, 24).

Ex	40:34	the glory of the LORD filled the **t**.
Heb	8:2	the true **t** set up by the Lord,
	9:11	and more perfect **t** that is not
	9:21	sprinkled with the blood both the **t**
Rev	15:5	that is, the **t** of the Testimony,

TABERNACLES, FEAST OF [6109, 5009]. Also called the Feast of Ingathering.

General References to:
Instituted (Ex 23:16; 34:22; Lev 23:34 – 43; Nu 29:12 – 40; Dt 16:13 – 16). Design of (Lev 23:42 – 43). The law read in connection with, every seventh year (Dt 31:10 – 12; Ne 8:18). Observance of, after the captivity (Ezr 3:4; Ne 8:14 – 18); by Jesus (Jn 7:2, 14). Observance of, omitted (Ne 8:17). Penalty for not observing (Zec 14:16 – 19). Jeroboam institutes an idolatrous feast to correspond to, in the eighth month (1Ki 12:32 – 33; 1Ch 27:11).

TABLE OF CONSECRATED BREAD Twelve loaves of consecrated, unleavened bread were placed on a table in the Holy Place in the tabernacle and temple (Ex 25:30; Lev 24:5 – 9).

TABLETS OF THE LAW Stone tablets on which God, with his own finger, engraved the Ten Commandments (Ex 24:3 – 4, 12; 31:18; Dt 4:13; 5:22). When Moses came down from the mountain and saw the worship of the golden calf, he threw down the tablets, breaking them (Ex 32:15 – 16, 19; Dt 9:9 – 17; 10:1 – 5). At God's command, Moses again went up the mountain with two new tablets, and God wrote the law anew (Ex 34:1 – 4, 27 – 29). God gave Moses words in addition to the Ten Commandments and told him to write them down (34:10 – 27). Moses put the two tablets in the ark (Dt 10:5), where they were in the time of Solomon (1Ki 8:9; 2Ch 5:10). They are referred to in the NT (2Co 3:3; Heb 9:4).

TALENT [3971, 10352, 5419]. A weight equal to sixty minas or about seventy-five pounds (34 kg.) (1Ki 9:14, 28; 10:10, 14; Ex 25:39; 38:27). Parables of the (Mt 18:23 – 34; 25:15 – 30).

TAMAR [9470, 9471, 2500] (ta'mêr, Heb. *tamar, palm tree*).

1. The wife of Er, then becoming the levirate wife of Onan. After the death of Onan, her father-in-law Judah had twin sons by her, Perez and Zerah (Ge 38). She is remembered in Ru 4:12 and in the genealogy in 1Ch 2:4, and her name is recorded in the ancestral line of Jesus (Mt 1:3; KJV "Thamar").

2. A daughter of David and sister of Absalom, whom her half brother Amnon violated (2Sa 13:1 – 33).

3. The daughter of Absalom (2Sa 14:27).

4. A place at the SE corner of the boundary of the future Holy Land as described in Ezekiel's vision (Eze 47:18 – 19; 48:28).

5. A city in Syria, more commonly known as Tadmor, later Palmyra.

TAMMUZ [9452] (tam'uz, Heb. *tammûz*). A fertility god widely worshiped in Mesopotamia, Syria, and Palestine; equivalent to Osiris in Egypt and Adonis of the Greeks. His consort was the goddess Ishtar (Astarte or Ashtoreth). Their cult involved licentious rites. Tammuz was supposed to have been killed by a wild boar while shepherding his flocks. His wife rescued him from the underworld. His death was taken to represent the onset of winter. The long dry season was broken by spring rains when he came to life again. The fourth month of the Babylonian and later Jewish calendar was named for him (June – July). The only mention of him in the Bible occurs in connection with the custom of women mourning for him (Eze 8:14), which, being observed at the very gate of the temple of the true God, seemed to the prophet one of the most abominable idolatries. His Greek name, Adonis, is derived from the Phoenician and Hebrew word for "Lord."

TARSHISH [5432, 5433] (tar'shish, Heb. *tarshîsh*).

1. A son of Javan, great-grandson of Noah (Ge 10:4), and presumably progenitor of a Mediterranean people, as most of these names in the "Table of the Nations" refer not only to individuals but also to the people descended from them.

2. A place, presumably in the western Mediterranean region, conjecturally identified by many with Tartessus, an ancient city located on the Atlantic coast of Spain but long since lost. Jonah fled to it (Jnh 1:3).

3. "Ships of Tarshish" seems to refer to large ships of the kind and size that were used in the Tarshish trade, for Solomon had "ships of Tarshish" going from Ezion Geber through the Red Sea and on to India, making the round trip in three years (1Ki 10:22).

4. A great-grandson of Benjamin (1Ch 7:10).

5. One of the seven princes of Persia and Media who stood in the presence of Xerxes (Est 1:14).

TARSUS [5432, 5433] (tar'sus, Gr. *Tarsos*). A city of Cilicia, the capital of the province from AD 72. It was the birthplace and early residence of the apostle Paul, a fact that he himself notes with civic pride in Ac 21:39, echoing a line of Euripides applied to Athens, which the Tarsians appear to have appropriated. The city stood on the Cilician Plain, a little above sea level and some ten miles (seventeen km.) inland. The Cydnus River provided an exit to the sea, and in ancient times the river course was equipped with dock and harbor facilities. Tarsus was an ancient city, the seat of a provincial governor when Persia ruled,

and, in the days of the Greek Syrian kings, the center of a lumbering and linen industry. During the first century before Christ the city was the home of a philosophical school, a university town, where the intellectual atmosphere was colored by Greek thought.

Tarsus stood, like Alexandria, at the confluence of East and West. The wisdom of the Greeks and the world order of Rome, mingled with the good and ill of Oriental mysticism, were deep in its consciousness. A keen-minded Jew, born and bred at Tarsus, would draw the best from more than one world. The Jews had been in Tarsus since Antiochus Epiphanes' refoundation in 171 BC, and Paul belonged to a minority that had held Roman citizenship probably since Pompey's organization of the East (66 – 62).

TASSEL (Heb. *tsîtsith*, *tassel*, *lock*). The fringe of twisted cords fastened to the outer garments of Israelites to remind them of their obligations to be loyal to the Lord (Nu 15:38 – 39; Dt 22:12). Later they became distinct badges of Judaism (cf. Zec 8:23). They were common in NT times (Mt 23:5).

TAX COLLECTORS [5601, 803, 3284, 5467].

Disreputable (Isa 33:18; Da 11:20; Mt 5:46 – 47; 9:11; 11:19; 18:17; 21:31; Lk 18:11). Repent under the preaching of John the Baptist (Mt 21:32; Lk 3:12; 7:29). Matthew, the collector of Capernaum, becomes an apostle (Mt 9:9; 10:3; Mk 2:14; Lk 5:27). Parable concerning (Lk 18:9 – 14). Zacchaeus, chief among, receives Jesus into his house (Lk 19:2 – 10).

TAXES [4501, 5368, 5601, 6885, 10402, 803, 3056, 3284, 5467, 5468]. Charges imposed by governments, either political or ecclesiastical, on the persons or the properties of their members or subjects. In the nomadic period taxes were unknown to the Hebrews. Voluntary presents were given to chieftains in return for protection. The conquered Canaanites were forced to render labor (Jos 16:10; 17:13; Jdg 1:28 – 35). Under the theocracy of Israel, every man paid a poll tax of a half-shekel for the support of the tabernacle worship (Ex 30:13; 38:25 – 26), and this was the only fixed tax. It was equal for rich and poor (30:15). Under the kings, as Samuel had warned the people (1Sa 8:11 – 18), heavy taxes were imposed. They amounted to a tithe of the crops and of the flocks besides the forced military service and other services that were imposed. In the days of Solomon, because of his great building program (the magnificent temple, the king's palaces, thousands of stables for chariot horses, the navy, etc.), the burden of taxes was made so oppressive that the northern tribes rebelled against his successor, who had threatened even heavier taxation and oppression (1Ki 12).

The Ptolemies, the Seleucids, and later the Romans, all adopted the very cruel but efficient method of "farming out the taxes," each officer extorting more than his share from those under him, and thus adding to the Jewish hatred of the tax collectors, among whom were at one time Matthew and Zacchaeus, both converts later.

General References to:

Census (Ex 30:11 – 16; 38:26; Ne 10:32; Lk 2:1). Jesus pays (Mt 17:24 – 27). Land (Ge 41:34, 48; 2Ki 23:35). Land mortgaged for (Ne 5:3 – 4). Priests exempted from (Ge 47:26; Ezr 7:24). Paid in grain (Am 5:11; 7:1); in provisions (1Ki 4:7 – 28). Personal (1Ki 9:15; 2Ki 15:19 – 20; 23:35). Resisted by Israelites (1Ki 12:18; 2Ch 10:18). Worldwide, levied by Caesar. Collectors of. See Tax Collectors.

TEACH

Ex	18:20	**T** them the decrees and laws,
Lev	10:11	and you must **t** the Israelites all
Dt	4:9	**T** them to your children
	6:1	me to **t** you to observe
1Sa	12:23	I will **t** you the way that is good
1Ki	8:36	**T** them the right way to live,
Ps	32:8	**t** you in the way you should go;
	34:11	I will **t** you the fear of the LORD.
	78:5	forefathers to **t** their children,
	90:12	**T** us to number our days aright,
	119:33	**T** me, O LORD, to follow your
	143:10	**T** me to do your will,

Pr	9:9	**t** a righteous man and he will add
Mic	4:2	He will **t** us his ways,
Lk	11:1	said to him, "Lord, **t** us to pray,
	12:12	for the Holy Spirit will **t** you
Jn	14:26	will **t** you all things and will remind
Ro	15:4	in the past was written to **t** us,
1Ti	2:12	I do not permit a woman to **t**
	3:2	respectable, hospitable, able to **t**,
2Ti	2:2	also be qualified to **t** others.
	2:24	kind to everyone, able to **t**,
Tit	2:1	You must **t** what is in accord
	2:15	then, are the things you should **t**.
Heb	8:11	No longer will a man **t** his neighbor
Jas	3:1	know that we who **t** will be judged
1Jn	2:27	you do not need anyone to **t** you.

TELL (Arabic, Heb. *tel*). A mound or heap of ruins that marks the site of an ancient city and is composed of accumulated occupational debris, usually covering a number of archaeological or historical periods and showing numerous building levels or strata. Ordinarily, city sites were selected in association with certain natural features, such as a spring or other convenient water supply, a hill or similar defense advantage, or trade routes determined by local geography. In the course of the history of a town, many reconstructions would be necessary because of destruction by war, earthquake, fire, neglect, or like causes.

TEMPLE (Heb. *hêkhal*, *bayith*, Gr. *hieron*, *naos*). The name given to the complex of buildings in Jerusalem that was the center of the sacrificial cult for the Hebrews. This ritual of sacrifices was the central external service of the ancient people of God and the unifying factor of their religion, at least in OT times. By the time of Christ, the importance of the temple was somewhat lessened because of the place of the local synagogue in Jewish life.

Three temples stood successively on Mount Moriah (2Ch 3:1) in Jerusalem. This site is today called the Haram esh-Sherif and is a Muslim holy place. The first temple was built by Solomon, the second by Zerubbabel and the Jews who returned from the Babylonian exile. The third temple, which was in use in the days of Jesus, was begun and largely built by Herod the Great.

The central place of the temple in the religious life of ancient Israel is reflected throughout the Bible. The Psalms abound in references to it (42:4; 66:13; 84:1 – 4; 122:1, 9; 132:5, 7 – 8, 13 – 17). The temple was the object of religious aspiration (23:6; 27:4 – 5). Pilgrimage to the temple brought the people of Israel from the ends of the earth (Ps 122:1 – 4; Ac 2:5 – 11). The visit of Jesus to the temple at the age of twelve is well-known (Lk 2:41 – 51). Later he exercised some of his ministry there (Mt 26:55; Lk 19:45; Jn 7:28, 37; 10:23). The early Jerusalem Christians also worshiped there until the break between Israel and the church became final (Ac 3:1; 5:12, 42; 21:26 – 34).

SOLOMON'S TEMPLE.

The great economic and cultural development of the Hebrews during the reigns of David and Solomon led to David's desire to build a temple. The tabernacle, the previous sacrificial center (Ex 35 – 40), was a simple and impermanent structure brought to Palestine by the Hebrews from their desert wanderings. It was natural enough that David should wish God's house to be as grand as his own (2Sa 7:2). David, however, was not permitted to undertake the construction of this "house" (2Sa 7:5 – 7; 1Ch 22:8). He did prepare for it, however, both in plans and materials (1Ch 22:1 – 19; 28:1 – 29:9) and more especially by arranging its liturgical service (23:1 – 26:19).

The temple was noted for lavish beauty of detail rather than for great size. It was accessible only to the priests; the lay Israelites came to it but never entered it. Seven years were required to complete the temple. It was dedicated in Solomon's eleventh year, c. 950 BC (1Ki 6:38), and was destroyed when the Babylonians burned Jerusalem in 587 BC.

THE RESTORATION TEMPLE OF ZERUBBABEL.

The return from Babylonian exile (in 538 BC), made possible by the decree of Cyrus, was a small

and unpromising one. The returnees were few in number, and their resources were so meager as to need frequent strengthening from the Jews who remained in Babylon. The temple they built is a good example of this. When the foundation was laid, the old men, who had seen the "first house" (Solomon's temple), wept for sorrow (Hag 2:3), but the young men, who had been born in exile, shouted for joy (Ezr 3:12). Like most of the reconstruction in that first century of the Second Commonwealth, the temple must have been modest indeed.

Soon after the return, the community began to rebuild the temple. Joshua the high priest and Zerubbabel the governor were the leaders of the movement. Many difficulties kept the builders from completing the temple until 515 BC. At that time they were urged on in the work by the prophets Haggai and Zechariah, and the building was finished. No description of this temple exists. Its dimensions were probably the same as Solomon's, but it was much less ornate and costly.

HEROD'S TEMPLE.

Our sources of information concerning Herod's temple are Josephus, the Jewish historian and priest who flourished about AD 70, and the tract Middoth of the Mishnah written at least a century after the final destruction of the temple. Neither can be used uncritically, and many details of the Herodian building and service remain uncertain.

Herod the Great (37 – 4 BC) was an indefatigable builder. Many cities and heathen temples had been rebuilt by him, and it was natural that he should wish to show his own grandeur by replacing the modest restoration temple with a more complex and much more beautiful temple. Other motives probably moved him, especially his desire to ingratiate himself with the more religious Jews, who resented his Idumean origin and his friendliness with the Romans.

Herod began his work in his eighteenth year (20 – 19 BC). The Jews were afraid that the work would interrupt the temple service, but Herod went to great lengths to prevent this, rebuilding the old structure piecemeal, never stopping the ritual observances until an entirely new temple came into being. It was not fully complete until AD 64. All speak of the grandeur of the building, which was of white marble, its eastern front covered with plates of gold that reflected the rays of the rising sun.

The temple was burned when Jerusalem fell to the Roman armies in August AD 70. Pictures on the Triumphal Arch of Titus in Rome show the soldiers carrying off the temple furniture as loot. This destruction made complete and final the break between the temple and the church and thus helped to establish the church as a religion completely separate from Israel. The early Christians saw in this forced cessation of the Jewish ritual a proof of the validity of Christ's claims to be the Redeemer foreshadowed by the OT ceremonial law.

In the NT the term *temple* is used figuratively in a number of ways. Jesus spoke of the temple of his body (Jn 2:19, 21). The individual believer is a temple (1Co 6:19). So also is the church; but this temple, unlike the earthly one, is equally accessible to all believers (Heb 6:19; 10:20), now freed by Christ from the ritual limitations of the old covenant (Eph 2:14). The book of Hebrews (especially chs. 7 – 10) in great fullness expounds on Christ as the fulfillment of the typology of the temple and its ritual. The culmination of this idea of the "better covenant" is seen in the New Jerusalem where in his vision John "did not see a temple in the city, because the Lord God Almighty and the Lamb are its temple" (Rev 21:22).

1Ki	6:1	began to build the **t** of the LORD.
	6:38	the **t** was finished in all its details
	8:10	the cloud filled the **t** of the LORD.
	8:27	How much less this **t** I have built!
2Ch	36:19	They set fire to God's **t**
	36:23	me to build a **t** for him at Jerusalem
Ezr	6:14	finished building the **t** according
Ps	27:4	and to seek him in his **t**.
Isa	6:1	and the train of his robe filled the **t**.
Eze	10:4	cloud filled the **t**, and the court was
	43:4	glory of the LORD entered the **t**
Hab	2:20	But the LORD is in his holy **t**;
Mt	12:6	that one greater than the **t** is here.
	26:61	'I am able to destroy the **t** of God
	27:51	of the **t** was torn in two from top
Jn	2:14	In the **t** courts he found men selling
1Co	3:16	that you yourselves are God's **t**
	6:19	you not know that your body is a **t**
2Co	6:16	For we are the **t** of the living God.
Rev	21:22	I did not see a **t** in the city,

TEMPTATION, TESTING [585, 4279, 4280] (Heb. *massâh*, Gr. *peirasmos*, *trial*, *proof*). The idea of putting to the proof — from either a good or bad intention — is found throughout the Bible. Thus the Lord often tests his people with the purpose of strengthening their faith, while Satan tempts them because he wishes to undermine their faith. Jesus, true man, faced both testing from God and temptation from Satan. (Note that it is only in modern English that temptation has come to mean testing for evil purposes: testing and temptation were once synonyms.)

God tests individuals. The explanation of this testing is provided in Dt 8:2: "Remember how the LORD your God led you all the way in the desert these forty years, to humble you and to *test* you in order to know what was in your heart, whether or not you would keep his commandments" (emphasis added; cf. 8:16, "to test you so that in the end it may go well with you"). The Lord tests individuals — Abraham (Ge 22:1), Job (Job 23:10), Hezekiah (2Ch 32:31) — and nations (Dt 33:8). Sometimes his testing is severe and painful (1Co 11:32; Heb 12:4 – 11; 1Pe 1:7; 4:8 – 13), but it originates in holy love.

Satan tempts individuals. Until Jesus returns, Satan has freedom to tempt people to sin (2Sa 24:11; 1Ch 21:1). He is called the tempter (Mt 4:3; 1Th 3:5) and the adversary of Christians (1Ti 5:14; 1Pe 5:8). God sometimes uses this tempting as his own testing of believers. Satan afflicted Job within limits imposed by God (Job 1:6 – 22; 2:1 – 7). Satan deceived Eve (1Ti 2:14); Christians are urged to be constantly alert, watching for his temptation (Mk 14:38; Lk 22:40; 2Co 2:11; 1Pe 5:8). They can overcome; they need to remember God's promise: "God is faithful; he will not let you be tempted beyond what you can bear. But when you are tempted, he will also provide a way out so that you can stand up under it" (1Co 10:13).

Temptation to Evil:
(Pr 12:26; Ro 8:35 – 39). Called snares of death (Pr 13:14; 14:27). The way of escape from (1Co 10:13). Christ gives help in (Heb 2:18; 4:15; Rev 3:10). The Lord delivers from (2Pe 2:9).

Benefits of:
(Jas 1:2 – 4, 12; 1Pe 1:6 – 7).

Leading into:
To be avoided (Mt 5:29 – 30; 6:9; Mk 9:42 – 48; Lk 17:1; Ro 14:13, 15, 21; 1Co 7:5; 8:9 – 13; 10:28 – 32). Prayer against being led into (Mt 6:13; 26:41; Mk 14:38; Lk 11:4; 22:40, 46). Not to lead others into (Ro 14:13 – 15, 21; 1Co 7:5; 8:9 – 13; 10:28 – 32).

Instances of: Abraham, of Pharaoh (Ge 12:18 – 19); of Abimelech (Ge 20:9); Rebekah, of Jacob (Ge 27:6 – 14); Balak, of Balaam (Nu 22:5 – 7, 16 – 17; 23:11 – 13, 25 – 27); Eli's sons, of Israel (1Sa 2:24 – 25); Gideon, of Israel (Jdg 8:27); the old prophet of Bethel, of the prophet of Judah (1Ki 13:15 – 19); Jeroboam, of Israel (1Ki 15:30, 34).

Resistance to:
Commanded (Dt 7:25 – 26; Pr 1:10 – 19; 4:14 – 15; 5:3, 8; 19:27; Mt 24:42 – 44; 25:13; 26:41; Mk 13:21 – 22, 33 – 37; 14:37 – 38; Ro 6:12 – 14; 12:21; Eph 6:11, 13 – 17; Jas 4:7; 1Pe 5:8 – 9; 1Jn 4:4). Source of resistance (Pss 17:4; 73:2 – 25; 94:17 – 18). Rewards to those who resist (Isa 33:15 – 16; Jas 1:12; Rev 3:10).

Instances of: Joseph (Ge 39:7 – 12); Balaam (Nu 22:7 – 18, 38; 23:7 – 12, 18 – 24); David (1Sa 26:5 – 25); prophet of Judah (1Ki 13:7 – 9); Mic-

aiah (1Ki 22:13 – 28); people of Jerusalem (2Ki 18:30 – 36); Job (Job 1:6 – 21; 2:4 – 10; 31:1, 5 – 17, 19 – 34, 38 – 40); Recabites (Jer 35:5 – 9); Nehemiah (Ne 4:9); Jesus (Mt 4:1 – 11; 26:38 – 42; Lk 4:1 – 3; Heb 4:15; 12:3 – 4).

Sources of:
Cherished pleasures (Mt 5:29 – 30; 18:7 – 9; Mk 9:43 – 45); evil company (Ex 34:13 – 16; Pr 2:10 – 16); adultery and sexual desires (Pr 5:1 – 20; 6:24 – 29; 7:1 – 27; 9:15 – 18; Ecc 7:26); sinful desires (Ro 7:5; Gal 5:17; Jas 1:13 – 15; 2Pe 2:18; 1Jn 2:16 – 17); false teachers (Mt 18:6 – 7; Lk 17:1; 1Jn 2:26; 4:1 – 3; Rev 2:20); persecutions (Jn 16:1 – 2); prosperity (Dt 8:10 – 17; Lk 12:16 – 21); riches (Mt 19:16 – 24; Mk 10:17 – 30; 1Ti 6:9 – 10); cares, riches, and pleasures (Mt 13:22; Lk 8:13 – 14; 21:34 – 38); Satan (Ge 3:1 – 5; 1Ch 21:1; Mk 4:15, 17; Lk 22:3, 31 – 32; 2Co 2:11; 11:3, 14 – 15; 12:7; Gal 4:14; Eph 4:27; 6:11, 13 – 17; 1Th 3:5; 1Ti 5:15; Jas 4:7; 1Pe 5:8 – 9; Rev 12:10 – 11, 17); wicked people (Pr 16:29; 28:10; Hos 7:5; Am 2:12; Mt 5:19; 2Ti 3:13). See Demons; Faith; Satan.

Warnings against Yielding to:
(Ex 34:12 – 16; Dt 8:11 – 20; Pr 2:10 – 16; 5:1 – 21; 6:27 – 28; 7:1 – 27; 9:15 – 18; Ecc 7:26; Jer 2:25; Mt 26:31, 41; Mk 14:37 – 38; Lk 21:34 – 36; 22:40; 1Co 16:13; Eph 6:11, 13 – 17; Heb 12:3 – 4; 1Pe 4:7; 5:8 – 9; 2Pe 3:17; Rev 3:2 – 3).

Instances of: Adam and Eve (Ge 3:1 – 19); Sarah, to lie (Ge 12:13; 18:13 – 15; 20:13); Isaac, to lie (Ge 26:7); Jacob to defraud Esau (Ge 27:6 – 13); Balaam (Nu 22:15 – 22; 2Pe 2:15); Achan (Jos 7:21); David, to commit adultery (2Sa 11:2 – 5), to number Israel (1Ch 21); Solomon, to become an idolater through the influences of his wives (1Ki 11:4; Ne 13:26); prophet of Judah (1Ki 13:11 – 19); Hezekiah (2Ki 20:12 – 20; Isa 39:1 – 4, 6 – 7); Peter (Mt 26:69 – 74; Mk 14:67 – 71; Lk 22:55 – 60).

Of Jesus:

(Lk 22:28). *In all points as we are (Heb 4:15). By the devil (Mt 4:1 – 11; Mk 1:12 – 13; Lk 4:1 – 13). Before his crucifixion (Mt 26:38 – 42).*

Test of God:

Design of a test (Pss 66:10 – 13; 119:101, 110; Da 12:10; Zec 13:9; 1Pe 1:6 – 7; 4:12): of fidelity (Dt 13:1 – 3; 2Ch 32:31; Job 1:8 – 22; 2:3 – 10); of obedience (Ge 22:1 – 14; Dt 8:2, 5; Heb 11:17). Benefits of (Jas 1:2 – 4, 12; 1Pe 1:6 – 7). Rewards of (Isa 33:15 – 16; Lk 12:35 – 38; Jas 1:12; 1Jn 4:4).

Mt	6:13	And lead us not into **t**,
Mk	14:38	pray so that you will not fall into **t**.
Lk	11:4	And lead us not into **t**.'"
	22:40	"Pray that you will not fall into **t**."
	22:46	pray so that you will not fall into **t**
1Co	10:13	No **t** has seized you except what is
1Ti	6:9	want to get rich fall into **t**

TEMPTER

Mt	4:3	The **t** came to him and said,
1Th	3:5	some way the **t** might have

TENTH [TEN]

Ge	14:20	Abram gave him a **t** of everything.
Nu	18:26	you must present a **t** of that tithe
Dt	14:22	Be sure to set aside a **t**
1Sa	8:15	He will take a **t** of your grain
Lk	11:42	you give God a **t** of your mint,
	18:12	I fast twice a week and give a **t**
Heb	7:4	patriarch Abraham gave him a **t**

TERTULLUS [5472] (têr-tul'us, Gr. *Tertyllos, third*). Diminutive of Tertius; lawyer employed by the Jews to state their case against Paul before Felix (Ac 24:1).

TEST

Dt	6:16	Do not **t** the LORD your God
Jdg	3:1	to **t** all those Israelites who had not
1Ki	10:1	came to **t** him with hard questions.
1Ch	29:17	that you **t** the heart and are pleased

Ps	26:2	**T** me, O LORD, and try me,
	78:18	They willfully put God to the **t**
	139:23	**t** me and know my anxious
Jer	11:20	and **t** the heart and mind,
Lk	4:12	put the Lord your God to the **t**.'"
Ac	5:9	How could you agree to **t** the Spirit
Ro	12:2	Then you will be able to **t**
1Co	3:13	and the fire will **t** the quality
	10:9	We should not **t** the Lord,
2Co	13:5	unless, of course, you fail the **t**?
1Th	5:21	**T** everything.
Jas	1:12	because when he has stood the **t**,
1Jn	4:1	**t** the spirits to see whether they are

TESTAMENT A word the KJV uses thirteen times to translate the Greek word *diathēkē*, which signifies a testamentary disposition. KJV translates it "covenant" twenty times, as usually the NT uses *diathēkē* in the meaning of its cognate *synthēkē*, which accurately renders the OT *berith*, a binding agreement or contract between one human being and another or between a human being and God. Jesus, at the institution of the Lord's Supper, said, "This cup is the new covenant [testament] in my blood" (Lk 22:20; 1Co 11:25), referring to Ex 24:8. Jesus' death created a new relation between God and believers. The imagery in Heb 9:15 – 20 includes the notion of a testamentary disposition, operative only after the testator's death; only in 9:16 – 17 does NIV have "will" ("testament" KJV, MLB, NEB) for *diathēkē* (elsewhere NIV has "covenant").

TESTED

Ge	22:1	Some time later God **t** Abraham.
Job	23:10	when he has **t** me, I will come forth
	34:36	that Job might be **t** to the utmost
Ps	66:10	For you, O God, **t** us;
Pr	27:21	man is **t** by the praise he receives.
Isa	48:10	I have **t** you in the furnace
1Ti	3:10	They must first be **t**; and then
Heb	11:17	By faith Abraham, when God **t** him

TESTIMONY Generally "a solemn affirmation to establish some fact," and commonly among Christians the statement of one's Christian experience. In Scripture it usually refers to that which was placed in the ark of the covenant (Ex 25:21), or to the Word of God (Ps 119:14, 88, 99 KJV). In Mk 6:11, shaking off the dust of the feet in leaving an unfriendly city was to be considered as a testimony against it.

Ex	20:16	"You shall not give false **t**
	31:18	gave him the two tablets of the **T**,
Nu	35:30	only on the **t** of witnesses.
Dt	19:18	giving false **t** against his brother,
Pr	12:17	A truthful witness gives honest **t**,
Isa	8:20	and to the **t**! If they do not speak
Mt	15:19	sexual immorality, theft, false **t**,
	24:14	preached in the whole world as a **t**
Lk	18:20	not give false **t**, honor your father
Jn	2:25	He did not need man's **t** about man
	21:24	We know that his **t** is true.
1Jn	5:9	but God's **t** is greater because it is
Rev	12:11	and by the word of their **t**;

THADDAEUS [2497] (tha-de′us, Gr. *Thaddaios*, possibly *breast nipple*). One of the twelve apostles, mentioned only twice in Scripture — in two of the four lists of the apostles (Mt 10:3; Mk 3:18). In Mt 10:3, the KJV has "Lebbaeus, whose surname was Thaddaeus," the NEB has "Lebbaeus," and the NASB, NIV, and RSV have "Thaddaeus." The other two lists (Lk 6:16; Ac 1:13) insert Judas, son of (or brother of) James instead of this name. Nothing else is certainly known about him, but he may be mentioned in Jn 14:22. A spurious Gospel of Thaddaeus used to exist.

THANK

| Php | 1:3 | I **t** my God every time I remember |
| 1Th | 3:9 | How can we **t** God enough for you |

THANKFULNESS [3344, 9343, 10312, 2328, 2373, 2374, 5921]. *See also Joy; Praise; Psalms; Worship.*

To God:

Commanded or required (Ge 35:1; Ex 12:14, 17, 42; 13:3, 8–10, 14–16; 16:32; 34:26; Lev 19:24; 23:14; Dt 12:18; 16:9–15; 26:10; Jdg 5:11;

Pss 48:11; 50:14–15; 106:1; Pr 3:9–10; Ecc 7:14; Isa 48:20; Joel 2:26; Ro 2:4; 15:27; Eph 1:16; 5:4, 19–20; Php 4:6; Col 1:12; 2:7; 3:15–17; 4:2; 1Th 5:18; Heb 13:15; Jas 1:9). Exhorted (Pss 98:1; 105:1, 5, 42–45; 107:1–2, 15, 22, 42–43; 118:1, 4; Col 3:15; 1Ti 2:1; 4:3–5). Jesus set an example of (Mt 11:25; 15:36; 26:27; Mk 8:6–7; 14:23; Lk 22:17, 19; Jn 6:11, 23; 11:41).

Should Be Offered to God: *(Pss 30:4; 50:14; 75:1; 92:1; 97:12; 106:1; 118:1; 2Co 9:11; Eph 5:4, 19–20; Php 4:6; Col 1:12; 2:7; 3:15–17; 4:2; 1Th 5:18; 1Ti 2:1; Heb 13:15); through Christ (Ro 1:8; Col 3:17; Heb 13:15); in the name of Christ (Eph 5:20); in behalf of ministers (2Co 1:11); in private worship (Da 6:10); in public (1Ch 23:30; 25:3; Ne 11:17; Ps 35:18); in everything (1Th 5:18); upon the completion of great undertakings (Ne 12:31, 40); before taking food (Mt 14:19; Mk 8:9; Lk 24:30; Jn 6:11; Ac 27:35); always (Eph 1:16; 5:20; 1Th 1:2); as the remembrance of God's holiness (Pss 30:4; 97:12).*

For: *The goodness and mercy of God (Pss 68:19; 79:13; 89:1; 100:4; 106:1; 107:1; 116:12–14, 17; 136:1–3; Isa 63:7); the gift of Christ (2Co 9:15); Christ's power and reign (Rev 11:17); the reception and effectual working of the word of God in others (1Th 2:13); deliverance, from adversity (Pss 31:7, 21; 35:9–10; 44:7–8; 54:6–7; 66:8–9, 12–16, 20; 98:1); through Christ, from indwelling sin (Ro 7:23–25); providential deliverance (Ex 12:14, 17, 42; 13:3, 8–10, 14–16; Jdg 5:11; Pss 105:1–45; 107:1–2, 15, 22, 42–43; 136:1–26; Joel 2:26); victory over death and the grave (1Co 15:57); wisdom and might (Da 2:23); the triumph of the gospel (2Co 2:14); the conversion of others (Ro 6:17); faith exhibited by others (Ro 1:8; 2Th 1:3); love exhibited by others (2Th 1:3); grace bestowed on others (1Co 1:4; Php 1:3–5; Col 1:3–6); zeal exhibited by others (2Co 8:16); nearness of God's presence (Ps 75:1); appointment to the ministry (1Ti 1:12); willingness to offer our property for God's service (1Ch 29:6–14); the* supply of our bodily wants (Ro 14:6 – 7; 1Ti 4:3 – 4); all men (1Ti 2:1); all things (2Co 9:11; Eph 5:20); temporal blessings (Ro 14:6 – 7; 1Ti 4:3 – 5).

By: Ministers appointed to offer, in public (1Ch 16:4, 7; 23:30; 2Ch 31:2). Saints, exhorted to (Ps 105:1; Col 3:15); resolve to offer (Pss 18:49; 30:12); habitually offer (Da 6:10); offer sacrifices of (Ps 116:17); abound in the faith with (Col 2:7); magnify God by (Ps 95:2); come before God with (Ps 95:2); should enter God's gates with (Ps 100:4). Of hypocrites, full of boasting (Lk 18:11). The wicked averse to (Ro 1:21). The heavenly host (Rev 4:9; 7:11 – 12; 11:16 – 17).

Should be Accompanied by:

Intercession for others (1Ti 2:1; 2Ti 1:3; Phm 4); prayer (Ne 11:17; Php 4:6; Col 4:2); praise (Ps 92:1; Heb 13:15). Expressed in psalms (1Ch 16:7). Cultivated, by the Feast of Tabernacles (Dt 16:9 – 15); by thank offerings (Ex 34:26; Lev 19:24; 23:14; Dt 12:18; 26:10; Pr 3:9 – 10); by songs (1Ch 16:7 – 36; Pss 95:2; 100).

Instances of: Eve (Ge 4:1, 25); Noah (Ge 8:20); Melchizedek (Ge 14:20); Lot (Ge 19:19); Abraham (Ge 12:7); Sarah (Ge 21:6 – 7); Abraham's servant (Ge 24:27); Isaac (Ge 26:22); Leah (Ge 29:32 – 35); Rachel (Ge 30:6); Jacob (Ge 32:10; 35:3, 7; 48:11, 15 – 16); Joseph (Ge 41:51 – 52); Moses (Ex 15:1 – 18); Miriam (Ex 15:19 – 21); Jethro (Ex 18:10); Israel (Ex 4:31; 15:1 – 18; Nu 21:17; 31:49 – 54; 1Ch 29:22); Deborah (Jdg 5); Hannah (1Sa 1:27 – 28; 2:1 – 10); Samuel (1Sa 7:12); David (2Sa 6:21; 1Ch 29:13); Solomon (1Ki 8:15, 56; 2Ch 6:4); queen of Sheba (1Ki 10:9); Hiram (2Ch 2:12); Jehoshaphat's army (2Ch 20:27 – 28); The psalmist (Pss 9:1 – 2, 4; 13:6; 22:23 – 25; 26:7; 28:7; 30:1, 3, 11 – 12; 31:7, 21; 35:9 – 10, 18; 40:2 – 3, 5; 41:11 – 12; 44:7 – 8; 54:6 – 7; 56:12 – 13; 59:16 – 17; 66:8 – 9, 12 – 16, 20; 68:19; 71:15, 23 – 24; 79:13; 89:1; 92:1 – 2, 4; 98:1; 100:4; 102:18 – 20; 104:1; 116:12 – 14, 17; 119:65, 108; 136); Isaiah (Isa 63:7); Daniel (Da 2:23; 6:22); Nebuchadnezzar (Da 4:2, 34); the mariners (Jnh 1:16); Jonah (Jnh 2:9); Ezra

(Ezr 7:27); Levites (2Ch 5:12 – 13; Ne 9:4 – 38); Jews (Ne 12:31, 40, 43); shepherds (Lk 2:20); Simeon (Lk 2:28); Anna (Lk 2:38); those whom Jesus healed: paralyzed man (Lk 5:25), demoniac (Lk 8:39), woman bent with infirmity (Lk 13:13), one of the ten lepers (Lk 17:15 – 16), blind Bartimaeus (Lk 18:43), centurion for his son (Jn 4:53); lame man healed by Peter (Ac 3:8); early Christians (Ac 2:46 – 47); Paul (Ac 27:35; 28:15; Ro 1:8; 6:17; 1Co 1:4; 2Co 2:14; Php 1:3 – 5; Col 1:3 – 6; 2Th 1:3; 1Ti 1:12).

Of Person to Person:

The Israelites, to Joshua (Jos 19:49 – 50). The spies, to Rahab (Jos 6:22 – 25). Saul, to the Kenites (1Sa 15:6). Naomi, to Boaz (Ru 2:19 – 20). David, to the men of Jabesh Gilead (2Sa 2:5 – 7); to Hanun (2Sa 10:2); to Barzillai (1Ki 2:7). Paul, to Phoebe (Ro 16:1 – 4); to Onesiphorus (2Ti 1:16 – 18). The people of Malta, to Paul (Ac 28:10).

| 1Co | 10:30 | If I take part in the meal with **t**, |
| Col | 2:7 | taught, and overflowing with **t**. |

THANKS

1Ch	16:8	Give **t** to the LORD, call
Ne	12:31	assigned two large choirs to give **t**.
Ps	7:17	I will give **t** to the LORD
	28:7	and I will give **t** to him in song.
	107:1	Give **t** to the LORD, for he is good;
	118:28	are my God, and I will give you **t**;
Ro	1:21	as God nor gave **t** to him,
1Co	11:24	when he had given **t**, he broke it
	15:57	**t** be to God! He gives us the victory
2Co	2:14	**t** be to God, who always leads us
	9:15	**T** be to God for his indescribable
1Th	5:18	give **t** in all circumstances,
Rev	4:9	and **t** to him who sits on the throne

THEOCRACY (thē-ŏk′ra-sē, Gr. theokratia, rule of God). A government in which God himself is the ruler. The best and perhaps the only illustration among nations is Israel from the time that God redeemed them from the power of the pharaoh by drying the Red Sea (Ex 15:13; 19:5 – 6) and gave them his law at Mount Sinai, until the time when Samuel acceded to their demand, "Now appoint a king to lead us, such as all the other nations have" (1Sa 8:5). During this period God ruled through Moses (Ex 19 – Dt 34), then through Joshua (Jos 1 – 24), and finally through "judges" whom he raised up from time to time to deliver his people. From the human standpoint, the power was largely in the hands of the priests, who acted on the basis of laws passed by God, in which were united all the powers of the state — legislative, executive, and judicial. Such a government was, of course, possible only because of God's special revelation of himself to the nation.

General References to:
> *Established (Ex 19:8; 24:3, 7; Dt 5:25 – 29; 33:2 – 5; Jdg 8:23; 1Sa 12:12). Rejected by Israel (1Sa 8:7, 19; 10:19; 2Ch 13:8).*

THEOPHANY (*appearance of God*). A visible appearance of God, generally in human form. In the early days of humanity, before people had the written Word, before the incarnation, and before the Holy Spirit had come to make his abode in human hearts, God sometimes appeared and talked with people. Before the first humans sinned, they walked and talked with God; but after sin entered, Adam and his wife hid when they heard the voice of the Lord God (Ge 3:8). God spoke to Cain (ch. 4), Enoch and Noah "walked with God" (5:24; 6:9), and God gave Noah detailed instructions concerning the ark and the flood. One of the loveliest and most instructive of the theophanies is found in Ge 18. From Abraham's time on, theophanies generally occurred when the recipients were asleep, as in Jacob's vision at Bethel (28:10 – 17), but God addressed Moses "face to face" (Ex 33:11). There is good reason to think that theophanies before the incarnation of Christ were visible manifestations of the preincarnate Son of God. Theophanies ceased with the incarnation of our Lord.

THEOPHILUS [2541] (thē-ŏf′ĭlŭs, Gr. *Theophilos, friend of God*). It is reasonable to suppose that Theophilus, to whom Luke dedicated both his gospel (1:3) and the book of Acts (1:1), was a real person. The title "most excellent" demands this, while the name and title together suggest a person of equestrian rank who became a Christian convert. Theophilus is most probably a baptismal name (see W. M. Ramsay, *St. Paul the Traveller and Roman Citizen*, pp. 388 – 89). Nothing is known of the man.

THESSALONIANS, LETTERS TO THE With the possible exception of the letter to the Galatians, 1 and 2 Thessalonians are the earliest letters surviving from the correspondence of Paul. They were written to the church in Thessalonica, which was founded by Paul on his second journey en route from Philippi to Achaia. His preaching of Jesus as the Messiah aroused such violent controversy in the synagogue at Thessalonica that the opposing Jewish faction brought him before the city magistrates, charging him with fomenting insurrection against Caesar (Ac 17:5 – 9). Paul's friends were placed under bond for his good behavior, and to protect their own security, they sent him away from the city. He proceeded to Berea, and after a short stay interrupted by a fanatical group of Jews from Thessalonica, he went on to Athens, leaving Silas and Timothy to continue the preaching (17:10 – 14). From Athens he sent back instructions that they should join him as quickly as possible (17:15). According to 1 Thessalonians, they did so, and it is possible that he sent Timothy back again to encourage the Thessalonians while he continued at Athens (1Th 3:2). In the meantime, Paul moved on to Corinth; and there Timothy found him when he returned with the news of the growth of the Thessalonian church (3:6; Ac 18:5). The first letter was prompted by Timothy's report.

1 THESSALONIANS.

Date and Place. Paul's stay both in Thessalonica and in Athens was brief, and he probably arrived in Corinth about AD 50. According to the narrative in Acts, Paul had begun his ministry there while working at the tentmaker's trade with Aquila and Priscilla (Ac 18:1 – 3).

Occasion. Timothy brought a report concerning the problems of the church, with which Paul dealt in this letter. First Thessalonians is a friendly, personal letter. The persecution in Thessalonica and the uncertainty concerning the coming of Christ that Paul had preached had disturbed the believers. Paul devoted the first half of his letter to reviewing his relationship with them in order to counteract the attacks of his enemies. The body of teaching in the second half of the letter dealt with sexual immorality by insisting on standards of holiness. The chief doctrinal topic was the second coming of Christ. Paul assured his readers that those who had died would not perish, but that they would be resurrected at the return of Christ. In company with the living believers, who would be translated, all would enter into eternal fellowship with Christ (1Th 4:13 – 18). Since the exact time of the return was not known, they were urged to be watchful, that they might not be taken unaware.

Outline:

    I. Conversion of the Thessalonians (1:1 – 10).

    II. Ministry of Paul (2:1 – 3:13).

        A. In founding the church (2:1 – 20).

        B. In concern for the church (3:1 – 13).

    III. Problems of the Church (4:1 – 5:22).

        A. Moral instruction (4:1 – 12).

        B. The Lord's coming (4:13 – 5:11).

        C. Ethical duties (5:12 – 22).

    IV. Conclusion (5:23 – 28).

2 THESSALONIANS.

Date and Place. The second letter was probably sent from Corinth in AD 51, not more than a few months after the first letter. Since Silas and Timothy were still with Paul, it is likely that no great interval elapsed between the writing of the two.

Occasion. Evidently the Thessalonian Christians had been disturbed by the arrival of a letter purporting to come from Paul — a letter he had not authorized (2Th 2:2). Some of them were suffering harsh persecution (1:4 – 5); others were apprehensive that the last day was about to arrive (2:2); and there were still a few who were idle and disorderly (3:6 – 12). The second letter serves to clarify further the problems of the first letter and to confirm the confidence of the readers. Whereas the first letter heralds the resurrection of the righteous dead and the restoration of the living at the return of Christ, the second letter describes the apostasy preceding the coming of Christ to judgment. Paul stated that the "secret power of lawlessness" was already at work and that its climax would be reached with the removal of the "hinderer" (2Th 2:6 – 7), who has been variously identified with the Holy Spirit, the power of the Roman Empire, and the preaching of Paul himself. With the disappearance of any spiritual restraint, the "man of sin" or "lawlessness" will be revealed, who will (2:3 – 10) deceive all people and will be energized by the power of Satan himself.

In view of this prospect, Paul exhorted the Thessalonians to retain their faith and to improve their conduct. He spoke even more vehemently to those who persisted in idleness (2Th 3:6 – 12), recommending that the Christians withdraw fellowship from them.

Outline:

    I. Salutation (1:1 – 2).

    II. Encouragement in Persecution (1:3 – 12).

    III. Signs of the Day of Christ (2:1 – 17).

        A. Warning of false rumors (2:1 – 2).

        B. The apostasy (2:3).

        C. The revelation of the Man of Sin (2:4 – 12).

        D. The preservation of God's people (2:13 – 17).

    IV. Spiritual Counsel (3:1 – 15).

    V. Conclusion (3:16 – 18).

THESSALONICA [2552, 2553] (thĕs′a-lō-nī′ka, Gr. *Thessalonikē*). A Macedonian town founded by Cassander, Alexander's officer who took control of Greece after Alexander's death in 332 BC. Thessalonica was probably founded toward the end of the century by consolidating small towns at the head of the Thermaic Gulf. It dominated the junction of the northern trade route and the road from the Adriatic to Byzantium, which later became the Via Egnatia. Its comparatively sheltered harbor made it the chief port of Macedonia, after Pella yielded to the silting that was the perennial problem of Greek harbors. It was a fortress that withstood a Roman siege, surrendering only after the battle of Pydna sealed Rome's victory in the Macedonian Wars. In 147 it became the capital of the Roman province and was Pompey's base a century later in the civil war with Julius Caesar. Prolific coinage suggests a high level of prosperity. The population included a large Roman element and a Jewish colony. Paul visited Thessalonica after Philippi and appears to have worked among a composite group, comprising the Jews of the synagogue and Greek proselytes, among whom were some women of high social standing. There was a high degree of emancipation among the women of Macedonia. In Ac 17:6, 8, the "city officials" (so NIV) are called "politarchs." Its use was once dismissed as a mistake of the historian because it was a term unknown elsewhere. There are now sixteen epigraphical examples in modern Salonica, and one is located in the British Museum. It was evidently a Macedonian term, and Luke's use of it was in line with his habit of using accepted terminology.

THIRST

Ps	69:21	and gave me vinegar for my **t**.
Mt	5:6	Blessed are those who hunger and **t**
Jn	4:14	the water I give him will never **t**
2Co	11:27	I have known hunger and **t**
Rev	7:16	never again will they **t**.

THOMAS [2605] (tŏm′as, Gr. *Thōmas*, from Aram. *te'oma, twin*). One of the twelve apostles (Mt 10:3). He was called "Didymus," or "the Twin" (cf. Jn 11:16; 20:24; 21:2). The gospel of John gives the most information about him. When the other apostles tried to dissuade Jesus from going to Bethany to heal Lazarus because of the danger involved from hostile Jews,

Thomas said to them, "Let us also go, that we may die with him" (11:16). Shortly before the passion, Thomas asked, "Lord, we don't know where you are going, so how can we know the way?" (14:5). Thomas was not with the other apostles when Jesus presented himself to them on the evening of the resurrection, and he told them later that he could not believe in Jesus' resurrection (20:24–25). Eight days later he was with the apostles when Jesus appeared to them again, and he exclaimed, "My Lord and my God!" (20:28). He was with the six other disciples when Jesus appeared to them at the Sea of Galilee (21:1–8) and was with the rest of the apostles in the upper room at Jerusalem after the ascension (Ac 1:13). According to tradition, he afterward labored in Parthia, Persia, and India. A place near Madras is called St. Thomas's Mount.

> One of the twelve apostles (Mt 10:3; Mk 3:18; Lk 6:15); Present at the raising of Lazarus (Jn 11:16); Asks Jesus the way to the Father's house (Jn 14:5); Absent when Jesus first appeared to the disciples after the resurrection (Jn 20:24); Skepticism of (Jn 20:25); Sees Jesus after the resurrection (Jn 20:26–29; 21:1–2); Lives with the other apostles in Jerusalem (Ac 1:13–14); Loyalty of, to Jesus (Jn 11:16; 20:28)

THOMAS, GOSPEL OF A Gnostic gospel consisting entirely of sayings attributed to Jesus; dated c. AD 140; found at Nag Hammadi in Egypt in 1945.

THORN IN THE FLESH Paul's description of a physical ailment that afflicted him and from which he prayed to be relieved (2Co 12:7). Some hold that there are hints that it was an inflammation of the eyes. Paul generally dictated his letters but signed them with his own hand (1Co 16:21; 2Th 3:17). He wrote the end of Galatians with his own hand but apologized for the large handwriting ("what large letters," Gal 6:11). His affliction was apparently not only painful but disfiguring. The Galatians did not despise him for it and would have plucked out their own eyes and given them to the apostle, were it possible (4:13–15). He says he was unable to recognize the high priest (Ac 23:5). Ramsay thought it was some form of recurring malarial fever.

THOUGHTS

1Ch	28:9	every motive behind the **t**.
Ps	94:11	The LORD knows the **t** of man;
	139:23	test me and know my anxious **t**.
Isa	55:8	"For my **t** are not your **t**,
Mt	15:19	For out of the heart come evil **t**,
1Co	2:11	among men knows the **t** of a man
Heb	4:12	it judges the **t** and attitudes

THRESHING (Heb. *dûsh, to trample out; hāvat, to beat out* or *off; dārakh, to tread*; Gr. *aloaō, to tread down*). Threshing was done in one of two ways: (1) by beating the sheaves with a rod or flail or (2) by trampling them under the feet of oxen that pulled a wooden sledge around the threshing floor (Isa 28:27). Threshing was done out-of-doors on a hard surface of the ground. The word also had a figurative use (Isa 21:10; 41:15; Mic 4:12 – 13; 1Co 9:10).

THRESHING FLOOR (Heb. *gōren*, Gr. *halōn*). The place where grain was threshed. Usually clay soil was packed to a hard smooth surface. Sheaves of grain were spread on the floor and trampled by oxen drawing crude wooden sledges with notched rims (Dt 25:4; Isa 28:27; 1Co 9:9). A shovel and fan were used in winnowing the grain (Isa 30:24). Since robbers would visit the floor at threshing time (1Sa 23:1), the laborers slept there (Ru 3:4 – 7). Threshing floors were often on hills where the night winds could more easily blow away the chaff.

THRONE [2292, 3782, 4058, 4632, 4887, 10372, 10424, 1037, 2585] (Heb. *kissē'*, Gr. *thronos, judgment seat*). A chair of state occupied by one in authority or of high position, such as a high priest, judge, governor, or king (Ge 41:40; 2Sa 3:10; Ne 3:7; Ps 122:5; Jer 1:15; Mt 19:28). Solomon's throne was an elaborate one (1Ki 10:18 – 20; 2Ch 9:17 – 19). For ages the throne has been a symbol of authority, exalted position, and majesty (Pss 9:7; 45:6; 94:20; Pr 16:12).

Literal:

Of Pharaoh (Ge 41:40; Ex 11:5). Of David (1Ki 2:12, 24; Ps 132:11 – 12; Isa 9:7; Jer 13:13; 17:25; Lk 1:32). Of Solomon (1Ki 2:19; 2Ch 9:17 – 19). Of ivory (1Ki 10:18 – 20). Of Solomon, called the throne of the LORD (1Ch 29:23). Of Herod (Ac 12:21). Of Israel (1Ki 8:20; 10:9; 2Ch 6:10). Abdicated by David (1Ki 1:32 – 40).

Figurative:

Of God (2Ch 18:18; Pss 9:4, 7; 11:4; 47:8; 89:14; 97:2; 103:19; Isa 6:1; 66:1; Mt 5:34; 23:22; Heb 8:1; 12:2; Rev 14:3, 5); of Christ (Mt 19:28; 25:31; Ac 2:30; Rev 1:4; 3:21; 4:2 – 10; 7:9 – 17; 19:4; 21:5; 22:3).

2Sa	7:16	your **t** will be established forever
1Ch	17:12	and I will establish his **t** forever.
Ps	11:4	the LORD is on his heavenly **t**.
	45:6	Your **t**, O God, will last for ever
	47:8	God is seated on his holy **t**.
	89:14	justice are the foundation of your **t**;
Isa	6:1	I saw the Lord seated on a **t**,
	66:1	"Heaven is my **t**,
Da	7:9	His **t** was flaming with fire,
Mt	19:28	Son of Man sits on his glorious **t**,
Ac	7:49	prophet says: " 'Heaven is my **t**,
Heb	1:8	"Your **t**, O God, will last for ever
	4:16	Let us then approach the **t** of grace
	12:2	at the right hand of the **t** of God.
Rev	3:21	sat down with my Father on his **t**.
	4:2	there before me was a **t** in heaven
	4:10	They lay their crowns before the **t**
	20:11	Then I saw a great white **t**
	22:3	**t** of God and of the Lamb will be

THUNDER, SONS OF (*huioi brontēs*). The title Jesus gave James and John (Mk 3:17), apparently because of their bold and sometimes rash natures (Mt 20:20 – 23; Lk 9:54).

THYATIRA [2587] (thī′a-tī′ra, Gr. *Thyateira*). A city in the province of Asia, on the boundary of Lydia and Mysia. Thyatira has no illustrious history and is scarcely mentioned by ancient writers. Coinage suggests that, lying as it did on a great highway linking two river valleys, Thyatira was a garrison town for many centuries. Its ancient Anatolian deity was a warlike figure armed with a battle-ax and mounted on a charger. An odd coin or two shows a female deity wearing a battlemented crown. The city was a center of commerce, and the records preserve references to more trade guilds than those listed for any other Asian city. Lydia, whom Paul met in Philippi, was a Thyatiran seller of "turkey red," the product of the madder root (Ac 16:14). It is curious to find another woman, nicknamed after the princess who by marriage sealed Ahab's trading partnership with the Phoenicians, leading a party of compromise in the Thyatiran church (Rev 2:20 – 21). The necessity for membership in a trade guild invited the Christians of Thyatira to compromise and opened the door to many temptations. Thyatira played a significant part in the later history of the church.

TIBERIAS [5500] (tĭ-bē′rĭ-ăs, Gr. *Tiberias*). A city on the W shore of the Sea of Galilee; built by Herod Antipas between the years AD 16 and 22 and named for the emperor Tiberius; a famous health resort; after AD 70 it became a center of rabbinic learning. Modern Tabariya.

TIBERIUS [5501] (tĭ-bēr′ĭ-ŭs, Gr. *Tiberios*). Tiberius Julius Caesar Augustus succeeded to the principate on the death of Augustus in AD 14, becoming thus the second Roman emperor. He was born in 42 BC, son of Empress Livia, wife of Augustus, by her first husband, Tiberius Claudius Nero. He had a distinguished military career in the East and in Germany and, in the absence of direct heirs to Augustus, was the logical successor. Augustus, however, did not like Tiberius; and Tiberius for many years was the passive witness of several attempts to bypass his claims and his abilities. The experience of disapproval and rejection no doubt contributed to the dourness, secretiveness, ambiguity, and suspicious preoccupations that marred the years of Tiberius's power. A morbid fear of disloyalty led to the heavy incidence of treason trials, which were a feature of the Roman principate under its worst incumbents. There is no evidence that Tiberius was unduly tyrannous, but aristocrats and writers of their number blamed the prince for features of later tyranny and for precedents of many subsequent incidents of oppression. This, added to the natural unpopularity of a reticent and lonely man, left Tiberius with a reputation that modern scholarship (discounting Tacitus's brilliant and bitter account) has been at some pains to rehabilitate. Tiberius had great ability and some measure of magnanimity, for in spite of many unhappy memories, he sought loyally to continue Augustus's policies, foreign and domestic. The rumors of senile debauchery on Capri can be listed with the slanders of earlier years, though there is some evidence of mental disturbance in the later period of the principate. Tiberius died on March 16, AD 37. He was the reigning emperor at the time of Christ's death.

TIGLATH-PILESER [9325, 9433] (tĭg′lăth-pĭ-lē′zêr, Assyr. *Tukulti-apil-esharra*, Heb. *tiglath-pil′eser, tilleghath-pilne′ser, my trust is in the son of [the temple] Esharra*).

A famous Assyrian king (745 – 727 BC) and great conqueror. He received tribute from King Azariah of Judah and King Menahem of Samaria (2Ki 15:19 – 20). Ahaz secured his help against Pekah of Israel and Rezin of Syria. He deported Transjordanian Israelites (1Ch 5:6, 26), and Ahaz gave tribute to him (2Ch 28:20 – 21).

TIGRIS [2538] (tī′grĭs, Assyr. *idigalat, arrow*, Heb. *hiddeqel, arrow*). One of the two great rivers of the Mesopotamian area; 1,150 miles long (Ge 2:14; Da 10:4).

TIMOTHY [5510] (tĭm′ō-thē Gr. *Timotheos, honoring God*). Paul's spiritual child (1Ti 1:2; 2Ti 1:2), later the apostle's fellow traveler and official representative. His character was a blend of amiability and faithfulness in spite of natural timidity. Paul loved Timothy and admired his outstanding personality traits. One must read Php 2:19 – 22 to know how highly the apostle esteemed this young friend. None of Paul's companions is mentioned as often and is with him as constantly as is Timothy. That this relationship was of an enduring nature is clear from 2Ti 4:9, 21. Paul knew that he could count on Timothy. He was the kind of person who in spite of his youth — he was Paul's junior by several years (1Ti 4:12) — his natural reserve and timidity (1Co 16:10; 2Ti 1:7), and his frequent ailments (1Ti 5:23), was willing to leave his home to accompany the apostle on dangerous journeys, to be sent on difficult errands, and to remain to the very end Christ's faithful servant.

Parentage of (Ac 16:1); Reputation and Christian faith of (Ac 16:2; 1Co 4:17; 16:10; 2Ti 1:5; 3:15); Circumcised; becomes Paul's companion (Ac 16:3; 1Th 3:2); Left by Paul at Berea (Ac 17:14); rejoins Paul at Corinth (Ac 17:15; 18:5); Sent into Macedonia (Ac 19:22); rejoined by Paul; accompanies Paul to Asia (Ac 20:1–4); Sent to the Corinthians (1Co 4:17; 16:10–11); preaches to the Corinthians (2Co 1:19); Sent to the Philippians (Php 2:19, 23); Sent to the Thessalonians (1Th 3:2, 6); Urged to stay in Ephesus (1Ti 1:3); Joins Paul in the epistle to the Philippians (Php 1:1), to the Colossians (Col 1:1–2), to the Thessalonians (1Th 1:1; 2Th 1:1), to Philemon (Phm 1); Zeal of (Php 2:19–22; 1Ti 6:12); Power of (1Ti 4:14; 2Ti 1:6); Paul's love for (1Co 4:17; Php 2:22; 1Ti 1:2, 18; 2Ti 1:2–4); Paul writes to (1Ti 1:1–2; 2Ti 1:1–2)

TIMOTHY, LETTERS TO Released from his first Roman imprisonment, Paul, perhaps while on his way to Asia Minor, left Titus on the island of Crete to bring to completion the organization of its church(es) (Ac 2:11; Tit 1:5). At Ephesus Paul was joined by Timothy (back from Philippi? cf. Php 2:19–23). On leaving for Macedonia, Paul instructed Timothy to remain in Ephesus, which was sorely in need of his ministry (1Ti 1:3–4). From Macedonia Paul wrote a letter to Timothy in Ephesus (1 Timothy) and one to Titus in Crete (Titus).

BACKGROUND AND PURPOSE OF 1 TIMOTHY.

At Ephesus Judaizers were spreading strange and dangerous doctrines (1:4, 7; 4:7). Both men and women attended worship spiritually unprepared (ch. 2). To cope with that situation there was Timothy — timid Timothy. The letter's aim is threefold: (1) To impart guidance against error (cf. 1:3–11, 18–20; chs. 4, 6). With this in mind, proper organization is stressed: choosing the right kind of leaders (chs. 3, 5). (2) To stress the need of proper preparation and conduct (for both men and women) with respect to public worship (ch. 2). (3) To bolster Timothy's spirit (4:14; 6:12, 20).

Outline:

    I. Salutation (1:1–2).
    II. Warning against False Teachers (1:3–11).
    III. The Lord's Grace to Paul (1:12–17).
    IV. The Purpose of Paul's Instructions to Timothy (1:18–20).
    V. Instructions Concerning the Administration of the Church (chs. 2–3).
    VI. Methods of Dealing with False Teaching (ch. 4).
    VII. Methods of Dealing with Different Groups in the Church (5:1–6:2).
    VIII. Miscellaneous Matters (6:3–19).
    IX. Concluding Appeal (6:20–21).

BACKGROUND AND PURPOSE OF 2 TIMOTHY.

Emperor Nero, blamed for Rome's fearful conflagration (July AD 64), in turn blamed Christians, who suffered frightful persecution. Paul was imprisoned (second Roman imprisonment). He faced death (2Ti 1:16–17; 2:9); Luke alone was with him. Others had left him, either on legitimate missions (Crescens, Titus) or because they had become enamored of the present world (Demas; 4:6–11). Meanwhile, soul-destroying error continued in Timothy's Ephesus (1:8; 2:3, 12, 14–18, 23; 3:8–13). The letter's purpose was, accordingly, (1) to urge Timothy to come to Rome as soon as possible in view of the apostle's impending departure from this life, and to bring Mark with him, as well as Paul's cloak and books (2Ti 4:6 – 22); and (2) to admonish Timothy to cling to sound doctrine, defending it against all error (2Ti 2; 4:1 – 5).

Outline:

TITHE [5130, 6923] (tīth, Heb. ma'ăsēr, Gr. *dekatē, the tenth*). Just when and where the idea arose of making the tenth the rate for paying tribute to rulers and of offering gifts as a religious duty cannot be determined. History reveals that it existed in Babylon in ancient times, also in Persia and Egypt, even in China. It is quite certain that Abraham knew of it when he migrated from Ur (Ge 14:17 – 20). Since Melchizedek was a priest of the Most High, it is certain that by Abraham's day the giving of tithes had been recognized as a holy deed (see Heb 7:4). Dividing the spoils of war with rulers and religious leaders was widespread (1Mc 10:31). Samuel warned Israel that the king whom they were demanding would exact tithes of their grain and flocks (1Sa 8:10 – 18). When Jacob made his covenant with God at Bethel, it included payment of tithes (Ge 28:16 – 22).

It was a long time before definite legal requirements were set on tithing, therefore customs in paying it varied. At first the tither was entitled to share his tithe with the Levites (Dt 14:22 – 23). After the Levitical code had been completed, tithes belonged exclusively to the Levites (Nu 18:21). If a Hebrew lived too far from the temple to make taking his tithes practicable, he could sell his animals and use the money gained to buy substitutes at the temple (Dt 14:24 – 26). This permit eventually led to gross abuses by priests (Mt 21:12 – 13; Mk 11:15 – 17). Tithed animals were shared with the Levites (Dt 15:19 – 20).

The methods developed for paying the tithes and for their use became somewhat complicated, when to the tithes of the firstfruits (Pr 3:9) were added the firstlings of the flocks (Ex 13:12 – 13). Then when the Levitical system was established, provision for the upkeep of the sons of Levi was made by tithes (Nu 18:21 – 24). A penalty of 20 percent of the tithe was exacted from one who sold his tithes and refused to use the money to pay for a substitute (Lev 27:31). The Levites in turn gave a tenth to provide for the priests (Nu 18:25 – 32). The temple was the place to which tithes were taken (Dt 12:5 – 12). One could not partake of his tithes at home, but only when delivered at the temple (12:17 – 18).

To make sure that no deceit would be practiced regarding tithing, each Hebrew was compelled to make a declaration of honesty before the Lord (Dt 26:13 – 15). In the tithing of the flocks, every tenth animal that passed under the rod, regardless of its kind, was taken; no substitution was allowed (Lev 27:32 – 33). Malachi (3:8 – 10) railed at the Jews for refusing to bring their tithes to the temple storehouse. This did not apply to money but to grains, animals, and fowl; money was deposited in the treasury box (Lk 21:1 – 4).

By the time of Christ, Roman rule had greatly affected the economic life of Judea, therefore it was difficult for people to tithe. But that the laws regarding the tenth were still observed is shown by the fact that the Pharisees tithed even the herbs that were used in seasoning food (Mt 23:23; Lk 11:42).

Paid by Abraham to Melchizedek (Ge 14:20; Heb 7:2 – 6). Jacob vows a tenth of all his property to God (Ge 28:22). Mosaic laws instituting (Lev 27:30 – 33; Nu 18:21 – 24; Dt 12:6 – 7, 17, 19; 14:22 – 29; 26:12 – 15). Customs relating to (Ne 10:37 – 38; Am 4:4; Heb 7:5 – 9). Tithe of tithes for priests (Nu 18:26; Ne 10:38). Stored in the temple (Ne 10:38 – 39; 12:44; 13:5, 12; 2Ch 31:11 – 12; Mal 3:10). Payment of, resumed in Hezekiah's reign (2Ch 31:5 – 10). Under Nehemiah (Ne 13:12). Withheld (Ne 13:10; Mal 3:8).

Customary in later times (Mt 23:23; Lk 11:42; 18:12). Observed by idolaters (Am 4:4–5).

TITLES AND NAMES

Of Christ:

Adam, last (1Co 15:45). Almighty (Rev 1:8). Alpha and Omega (Rev 1:8; 22:13). Amen (Rev 3:14). Angel (Ge 48:16; Ex 23:20–21). Angel of his presence (Isa 63:9). Angel of the Lord (Ex 3:2; Jdg 13:15–18). Anointed One (Da 9:25; Jn 1:41). Apostle (Heb 3:1). Arm of the Lord (Isa 51:9; 53:1). Author of life (Ac 3:15). Author and perfecter of our faith (Heb 2:10; 12:2). Blessed and only Ruler (1Ti 6:15). Branch (Jer 23:5; Zec 3:8; 6:12). Bread of Life (Jn 6:35, 48). Chief Shepherd (1Pe 5:4). Chief Cornerstone (Eph 2:20; 1Pe 2:6). Chosen One of God (Isa 42:1). Christ of God (Lk 9:20). Commander (Isa 55:4). Commander of the Lord's army (Jos 5:14–15). Consolation of Israel (Lk 2:25). Counselor (Isa 9:6). David (Jer 30:9; Eze 34:23). Defender (1Jn 2:1). Deliverer (Ro 11:26). Door (Jn 10:7). The desired of all nations (Hag 2:7). Eternal life (1Jn 1:2; 5:20). Everlasting Father (Isa 9:6). Faithful witness (Rev 1:5; 3:14). First and Last (Rev 1:17; 2:8). Firstborn of all creation (Col 1:15). Firstborn of the dead (Rev 1:5). Glory of the Lord (Isa 40:5). God (Isa 40:9; Jn 20:28). God over all (Ro 9:5). Good Shepherd (Jn 10:14). Great High Priest (Heb 4:14). Guarantee (Heb 7:22). Head of the church (Eph 5:23; Col 1:18). Heir of all things (Heb 1:2). Holy One (Ps 16:10, w Ac 2:27, 31). Holy One of God (Mk 1:24). Holy One of Israel (Isa 41:14). Horn of salvation (Lk 1:69). I Am (Ex 3:14, w Rev 1:8; 22:13). Immanuel (Isa 7:14, w Mt 1:23). Israel's ruler (Mic 5:1). Jesus (Mt 1:21; 1Th 1:10). King (Zec 9:9, w Mt 21:5). King of the ages (Rev 15:3). King of the Jews (Mt 2:2). King of Israel (Jn 1:49). King of Kings (1Ti 6:15; Rev 17:14). Lamb (Rev 5:6, 12; 13:8; 21:22; 22:3). Lamb of God (Jn 1:29, 36). Lawgiver (Isa 33:22). Leader (Isa 55:4). Life (Jn 14:6; Col 3:4; 1Jn 1:2). Light of the World (Jn 8:12). Lion of the tribe of Judah (Rev 5:5). Lord of all (Ac 10:36). Lord of glory (1Co 2:8). Lord our righteousness (Jer 23:6). Lord God Almighty (Rev 15:3). Lord God of the prophets (Rev 22:6). Mediator (1Ti 2:5). Mighty God (Isa 9:6). Mighty One of Jacob (Isa 60:16). Morning Star (Rev 22:16). Nazarene (Mt 2:23). One and Only (Jn 1:14). One before us (Heb 6:20). Our Passover (1Co 5:7). Prince of Peace (Isa 9:6). Prophet (Lk 24:19; Jn 7:40). Ransom (1Ti 2:6). Redeemer (Job 19:25; Isa 59:20; 60:16). Resurrection and Life (Jn 11:25). Righteous One (Ac 7:52). Rock (1Co 10:4). Root of David (Rev 22:16). Root of Jesse (Isa 11:10). Ruler (Mt 2:6). Ruler of the creation of God (Rev 3:14). Ruler over Israel (Mic 5:2). Ruler of the kings of the earth (Rev 1:5). Savior (2Pe 2:20; 3:18). Servant (Isa 42:1; 52:13). Shepherd and Overseer of souls (1Pe 2:25). Son of the Blessed One (Mk 14:61). Son of David (Mt 9:27). Son of God (Lk 1:35; Jn 1:49). Son of Man (Jn 5:27; 6:37). Son of the Most High (Lk 1:32). Star (Nu 24:17). Sun of righteousness (Mal 4:2). True God (1Jn 5:20). True Light (Jn 1:9). True Vine (Jn 15:1). Truth (Jn 14:6). Way (Jn 14:6). Wisdom (Pr 8:12). Witness (Isa 55:4). Wonderful (Isa 9:6). Word (Jn 1:1; 1Jn 5:7). Word of God (Rev 19:13). Word of Life (1Jn 1:1).

Of the Church:

Assembly of the saints (Ps 149:1). Body of Christ (Eph 1:22–23; Col 1:24). Bride of Christ (Rev 21:9). Church of the firstborn (Heb 12:23). Church of God (Ac 20:28). Church of the living God (1Ti 3:15). City of the Living God (Heb 12:22). Council of the holy ones (Ps 89:7). Council of the upright (Ps 111:1). Dwelling of God (Eph 2:22). Family in heaven and on earth (Eph 3:15). Flock of Christ (Jn 10:16). Flock of God (Eze 34:15; 1Pe 5:2). God's building (1Co 3:9). God's field (1Co 3:9). God's inheritance (Joel 3:2; 1Pe 5:3). Golden lampstand (Rev 1:20). Holy City (Rev 21:2). House of Christ (Heb 3:6). House of the God of Jacob (Isa 2:3). House(hold) of God (1Ti 3:15; Heb 10:21; Eph 2:19). Inheritance (Ps 28:9; Isa 19:25). Israel of God (Gal 6:16). Lamb's bride (Rev 19:7; 21). Mount Zion (Ps 2:6; Heb 12:22). Mountain of the Lord's house (Isa 2:2). New Jerusalem (Rev 21:2). Pillar and foundation of the truth (1Ti 3:15). Portion of the Lord (Dt 32:9). Princess (Ps 45:13). Sanctuary of God (Ps 114:2). Shoot of God's planting (Isa 60:21). Sought After, the City No Longer Deserted (Isa 62:12). Spiritual house (1Pe 2:5). Temple of God (1Co 3:16–17). Temple of the living God (2Co 6:16). Vineyard (Jer 12:10; Mt 21:41).

Of the Devil:
Abaddon (Rev 9:11). Accuser of our brothers (Rev 12:10). Ancient serpent (Rev 12:9; 20:2). Angel of the Abyss (Rev 9:11). Apollyon (Rev 9:11). Beelzebub (Mt 12:24). Belial (2Co 6:15). Coiling serpent (Isa 27:1). Dominion of darkness (Col 1:13). Dragon (Isa 27:1; Rev 20:2). Enemy (Mt 13:39; 1Pe 5:8). Evil one (Mt 13:19, 38). Evil spirit (1Sa 16:14; Mt 12:43). Father of lies (Jn 8:44). Gliding serpent (Isa 27:1). God of this age (2Co 4:4). Leviathan (Isa 27:1). Liar (Jn 8:44). Lying spirit (1Ki 22:22). Murderer (Jn 8:44). Powers of this dark world (Eph 6:12). Prince of demons (Mt 12:24). Prince of this world (Jn 14:30). Red dragon (Rev 12:3). Ruler of the kingdom of the air (Eph 2:2). Satan (1Ch 21:1; Job 1:6). Serpent (Ge 3:4, 14; 2Co 11:3). Spirit that works in those disobedient (Eph 2:2). Tempter (Mt 4:3; 1Th 3:5).

Of the Holy Spirit:
Breath of the Almighty (Job 33:4). Counselor (Jn 14:16, 26; 15:26). Eternal Spirit (Heb 9:14). God (Ac 5:3–4). Good Spirit (Ne 9:20; Ps 143:10). Holy Spirit (Ps 51:11; Lk 11:13; Eph 1:13; 4:30). Power of the Most High (Lk 1:35). Sevenfold Spirit (Rev 1:4, n.). Spirit, the (Mt 4:1; Jn 3:6; 1Ti 4:1). Spirit of Christ (Ro 8:9; 1Pe 1:11). Spirit of counsel (Isa 11:2). Spirit of the Father (Mt 10:20). Spirit of fear of the Lord (Isa 11:2). Spirit of fire (Isa 4:4). Spirit of glory (1Pe 4:14). Spirit of God (Ge 1:2; 1Co 2:11; Job 33:4). Spirit of grace (Zec 12:10; Heb 10:29). Spirit of holiness (Ro 1:4). Spirit of judgment (Isa 4:4; 28:6). Spirit of knowledge (Isa 11:2). Spirit of life (Ro 8:2; Rev 11:11). Spirit of the Lord (Isa

11:2; Ac 5:9). Spirit of power (Isa 11:2). Spirit of prophecy (Rev 19:10). Spirit of revelation (Eph 1:17). Spirit of his Son (Gal 4:6). Spirit of sonship (Ro 8:15). Spirit of truth (Jn 14:17; 15:26). Spirit of understanding (Isa 11:2). Spirit of wisdom (Isa 11:2; Eph 1:17). Willing Spirit (Ps 51:12).

Of Ministers:
Administers of the grace of God (1Pe 4:10). Ambassadors for Christ (2Co 5:20). Apostles (Lk 6:13; Eph 4:11; Rev 18:20). Apostles of Jesus Christ (Tit 1:1). Deacons (Ac 6:1ff; 1Ti 3:8; Php 1:1). Elders (1Ti 5:17; 1Pe 5:1). Entrusted with God's work (Tit 1:7). Entrusted with the secrets of God (1Co 4:1). Evangelists (Eph 4:11; 2Ti 4:5). Fellow workers with God (2Co 6:1). Fishers of men (Mt 4:19; Mk 1:17). Messengers of the church (Rev 1:20; 2:1, n.). Messengers of the Lord Almighty (Mal 2:7). Ministers of Christ (Ro 15:16; 1Co 4:1). Ministers of the Lord (Joel 2:17). Ministers of the new covenant (2Co 3:6). Ministers in the sanctuary (Eze 45:4). Overseers (Ac 20:28; Php 1:1; 1Ti 3:1; Tit 1:7). Pastors (Jer 3:15; Eph 4:11). Preachers (Ro 10:14; 1Ti 2:7). Representatives of the church (2Co 8:23). Servant of the church (2Co 4:5; Col 1:24–25). Servant of this gospel (Eph 3:7; Col 1:23). Servants of God (2Co 6:4; Tit 1:1; Jas 1:1). Servants of Jesus Christ (Php 1:1; Jude 1). Servants of the Lord (2Ti 2:24). Servants of righteousness (2Co 11:15). Servants of the word (Lk 1:2). Shepherds (Jer 23:4). Soldiers of Christ (Php 2:25; 2Ti 2:3). Stars (Rev 1:20; 2:1). Teachers (Isa 30:20; Eph 4:11). Watchmen (Isa 62:6; Eze 33:7). Witnesses (Ac 1:8; 5:32; 26:16). Workers (Mt 9:38, w Phm 1; 1Th 2:2).

Of Saints:
Believers (Ac 5:14; 1Ti 4:12). Blessed by the Father (Mt 25:34). Blessed by the Lord (Ge 24:31; 26:29). Brothers (Mt 23:8; Ac 12:17). Brothers of Christ (Lk 8:21; Jn 20:17). Called to belong to Jesus Christ (Ro 1:6). Children (Jn 13:33; 1Jn 2:1). Children of Abraham (Gal 3:7). Children of the free woman (Gal 4:31). Children of God

(Jn 1:12; 11:52; Php 2:15; 1Jn 3:1 – 2, 10). Children of the Lord (Dt 14:1). Children of promise (Ro 9:8; Gal 4:28). Children of the resurrection (Lk 20:36). Chosen of God (Col 3:12; Tit 1:1). Chosen instrument (Ac 9:15). Chosen ones (1Ch 16:13). Chosen people (1Pe 2:9). Christians (Ac 11:26; 26:28). Coheirs with Christ (Ro 8:17). Dear brothers (1Co 15:58; Jas 2:5). Dearly loved children (Eph 5:1). Disciples of Christ (Jn 8:31; 15:8). Faithful, the (Ps 12:1). Faithful brothers in Christ (Col 1:2). Faithful in the land, the (Ps 101:6). Fellow citizens with God's people (Eph 2:19). Fellow servants (Rev 6:11). Freedman (1Co 7:22). Friends of Christ (Jn 15:15). Friends of God (2Ch 20:7; Jas 2:23). Glorious ones (Ps 16:3). Godly, the (Ps 4:3; 2Pe 2:9). Guests of the bridegroom (Mt 9:15). Heirs of God (Ro 8:17; Gal 4:7). Heirs of promise (Heb 6:17; Gal 3:29). Heirs together with Israel (Eph 3:6). Heirs with you of the gracious gift of life (1Pe 3:7). Holy brothers (Heb 3:1). Holy nation (Ex 19:6; 1Pe 2:9). Holy people (Dt 26:19; Isa 62:12). Holy priesthood (1Pe 2:5). Inheritors of the kingdom (Jas 2:5). Inheritors of salvation (Heb 1:14). Instrument for noble purposes (2Ti 2:21). Kingdom of priests (Ex 19:6). Kings and priests to serve God (Rev 1:6). Lambs (Isa 40:11; Jn 21:15). Letter from Christ (2Co 3:3). Light of the world (Mt 5:14). Living stones (1Pe 2:5). Loved of God (Ro 1:7). Man of God (1Ti 6:11; 2Ti 3:17). Members of Christ (1Co 6:15; Eph 5:30). Oaks of righteousness (Isa 61:3). Obedient children (1Pe 1:14). Objects of mercy (Ro 9:23). People close to God's heart (Ps 148:14). People of God (Heb 4:9; 1Pe 2:10). People saved by the Lord (Dt 33:29). People of Zion (Ps 149:2; Joel 2:23). Pillars in the temple of God (Rev 3:12). Ransomed of the Lord (Isa 35:10; Isa 51:11). Righteous, the (Hab 2:4). Royal priesthood (1Pe 2:9). Salt of the earth (Mt 5:13). Sheep of Christ (Jn 10:1 – 16; 21:16). Slaves of Christ (1Co 7:22; Eph 6:6). Slaves to Righteousness (Ro 6:18). Sons of the day (1Th 5:5). Sons of the Father (Mt 5:45). Sons of Jacob (Ps 105:6). Sons of the kingdom (Mt 13:38). Sons of light (Lk 16:8; Eph 5:8; 1Th 5:5). Sons of the Living God (Ro 9:26). Sons of the Most High (Lk 6:35). Treasured possession (Ex 19:5; Dt 14:2; Tit 2:14; 1Pe 2:9). Witnesses for God (Isa 44:8).

TITUS [5519] (tī'tŭs, Gr. *Titos*). A convert, friend, and helper of Paul (Tit 1:4), in the NT mentioned only in Paul's letters, especially in 2 Corinthians. He was a Greek, a son of Gentile parents (Gal 2:3). After his conversion he accompanied Paul to Jerusalem, where Paul rejected the demand of the Judaizers that Titus be circumcised. Hence, Titus became a person of significance for the principle of Gentile admission to the church solely on the basis of faith in Christ. During Paul's third missionary journey, Titus was assigned missions to Corinth to solve its vexing problems (1Co 1 – 6; 2Co 2:13; 7:5 – 16) and to encourage material assistance to the needy at Jerusalem (2Co 8). Much later Titus was in Crete, left behind there by Paul to organize its churches (Tit 1:4 – 5). He was requested to meet Paul at Nicopolis (3:12). Titus was consecrated, courageous, resourceful. He knew how to handle the quarrelsome Corinthians, the mendacious Cretans, and the pugnacious Dalmatians (2Ti 4:10).

Paul's love for (2Co 2:13; 7:6 – 7, 13 – 14; 8:23; Tit 1:4); With Paul in Macedonia (2Co 7:5 – 6); Affection of, for the Corinthians (2Co 7:15); Sent to Corinth (2Co 8:6, 16 – 22; 12:17 – 18); Character of (2Co 12:18); Accompanies Paul to Jerusalem (Gal 2:1 – 3, w Ac 15:1 – 29); Left by Paul in Crete (Tit 1:5), to rejoin him in Nicopolis (Tit 3:12); Paul writes to (Tit 1:1 – 4); With Paul in Rome; goes to Dalmatia (2Ti 4:10)

TITUS, LETTER TO *See 1 Timothy for further background.*

BACKGROUND AND PURPOSE OF TITUS.

The reputation of the Cretans was poor. True sanctification was needed (2:11 – 14; 3:10). Gospel workers (such as Zenas and Apollos, whose itinerary included Crete and who probably carried with them Paul's letter) had to receive every assistance. As to Paul himself, having recently met Timothy, and the situation in Crete being critical, it is natural that he wished to have a face-to-face conference with Titus also.

The purpose of Paul's letter to Titus was (1) to stress the need of thorough sanctification; (2) to speed on their way Zenas the law expert and Apollos the evangelist (3:13); and (3) to urge Titus to meet Paul at Nicopolis (3:12).

Outline:

    I. Salutation (1:1 – 4).
    II. Concerning Elders (1:5 – 9).
    III. Concerning False Teachers (1:10 – 16).
    IV. Concerning Various Groups in the Congregations (ch. 2).
    V. Concerning Believers in General (3:1 – 8).
    VI. Concerning Response to Spiritual Error (3:9 – 11).
    VII. Conclusion (3:12 – 15).

TOMB [1074, 1539, 7690, 7700, 3645, 3646, 5439] (Gr. *taphos*). The word *tomb* is used rather loosely. It may mean a chamber, vault, or crypt, either underground or above. It may refer to a pretentious burying place on a special site. It may be a beehive structure where many bodies can be placed. In general, any burying place is a tomb. The Hebrews were not impressed by the tombs of Egypt, thus their burials remained simple, most burying sites being unmarked. Some kings were interred in a vault in Jerusalem (1Ki 2:10; 11:43); just where this burial place was located has not been determined. Some mention their "father's tomb" (2Sa 2:32; Ne 2:3).

Tombs of NT times were either caves or holes dug into stone cliffs. Since only grave clothes are mentioned in connection with tombs, it seems certain that the Jews used neither caskets nor sarcophagi. Tombs carried no inscriptions, no paintings. Embalming, learned in Egypt (Ge 50:2), was soon a lost art (Jn 11:39). A general opening gave access to vaults that opened on ledges to provide support for the stone doors. The door to such a grave weighed from one to three tons (.9 to 2.7 metric tons), hence the miracle of the stone being rolled away from Jesus' tomb (Lk 24:2; Jn 20:1).

TONGUES, CONFUSION OF The Tower of Babel presents an answer to an otherwise insoluble mystery and reveals God's anger against human vanity and disobedience. That there was originally a common language among people becomes more certain as linguistic research progresses. Many theories have arisen to account for the sudden confusion of tongues at Babel. One is that the whole account is a myth, adapted by Moses to account for the varied speeches that he heard. Another attributes the confusion to a slow change in speech caused by an ancient population explosion resulting in widely scattered peoples who, having no written language, soon developed various forms of speech. But for one to whom miracles exist, it is easy to understand the account in Ge 11:1 – 9, for he who designed the media of speech could have, in an instant, made the modifications in speech that caused such confusion.

TONGUES, GIFT OF A spiritual gift mentioned in Mk 16:17; Ac 2:1 – 13; 10:44 – 46; 19:6; 1Co 12, 14. The gift appeared on the day of Pentecost with the outpouring of the Holy Spirit on the assembled believers (Ac 2:1 – 13). The *external* phenomena heralding the Spirit's coming were followed by the *internal* filling of all those gathered together there. The immediate result was that they "began to speak in other tongues." "Began" implies that the phenomenon recorded was now first imparted and that it was afterward repeated (cf. 8:17 – 18; 10:44 – 46; 19:6). The context makes it clear that "other tongues" means languages different from their own, and by implication, previously unknown to the speakers, for the amazement of the crowd, coming from many lands, was caused by the fact that *Galileans* could speak these varied languages. Under the Spirit's control they spoke "as the Spirit enabled"; the utterances were praise to God (2:11; 10:46). The gift was not designed merely to facilitate the preaching of the gospel; the message in 2:14 – 36 was not delivered in more than one language. There is no express NT instance of this gift being used to evangelize others. (At Lystra, Paul and Barnabas preached in Greek, not the native Lycaonian, which they did not understand.) The gift of tongues on Pentecost was a direct witness to God's presence and work in their midst. While the gift came upon all those assembled when the Spirit was poured out (2:4), there is no indication that the three thousand converts at Pentecost received the gift.

It is not stated that the Samaritans received this gift when the Spirit was imparted to them, but the request of Simon to buy the power to bestow the Spirit indicates that some *external* manifestation did result (Ac 8:14 – 19). The Pentecostal phenomenon clearly appeared again when the Holy Spirit was poured out on the Gentiles in the house of Cornelius (10:44 – 46). Here again it served as a miraculous token of the divine approval and acceptance of these Gentile believers (11:15 – 17; 15:7 – 9). The appearing of the phenomenon in connection with the twelve disciples at Ephesus (19:6), who dispensationally stood before Pentecost, marked the full incorporation of this group into the church and authenticated Paul's teaching.

The gift of tongues is mentioned by Paul as one of the spiritual gifts so richly bestowed on the Corinthian believers. Their reaction to this gift drew forth Paul's discussion of the varied gifts. They are enumerated, compared, and evaluated by their usefulness to the church. He lists the gifts twice and places tongues and their interpretation at the very bottom of the scale (1Co 12:8 – 10, 28 – 30), thus rebuking the Corinthians' improper evaluation of this spectacular gift. He emphasized the comparative value of tongues and prophecy by insisting that "five intelligible words" spoken in the church were of more value than "ten thousand words in a tongue" not understood (14:19). Paul felt it necessary to regulate the use of tongues in their assembly; the ideal place for their exercise was in private (14:28). He insisted that not more than two or three speak in tongues, and that they do so in turn, and one should interpret; no one was to speak in tongues if no interpreter was present (14:27 – 28). Speaking in tongues was not prohibited (14:39), but intelligent preaching in understandable words was vastly superior. He further insisted that women were not to speak in their meetings (14:34).

Two views are held as to the exact nature of the Corinthian "tongues." One view holds that they were foreign languages that the speakers were miraculously enabled to speak without having previously learned them. This view is demanded by Ac 2:1 – 13, unless it is maintained that the two phenomena are quite distinct. That they were intelligible utterances is urged from the fact that they could be interpreted and were the vehicle of prayer, praise, and thanksgiving (1Co 14:14 – 17).

Modern commentators, however, generally hold that the Corinthian tongues were not identical with the tongues at Pentecost but were ecstatic outbursts of prayer and praise in which the utterances often became abnormal and incoherent and the connection with the speaker's own conscious intellectual activity was suspended. It is held that the utterances were incomprehensible to the speaker as well as to the audience (14:14) and that the resultant edification was emotional only (14:4). But 14:4 may only mean that the person's understanding was "unfruitful" to others. Its advocates further hold that this view is indicated in the fact that interpretation was likewise a special gift (12:10).

From 14:27 – 28 it is clear that this speaking in tongues was not uncontrollable. It was very different from the religious frenzy that marked some pagan rites in which the worshiper lost control both of reason and the power of will. Any manifestation of tongues that is not under the speaker's control is thereby suspect (14:32).

TORAH [9368; NT *nomos*: 3795] (tō′ra, Heb. *tôrâh*, *direction*, *instruction*, *law*). The common Hebrew word for "law." It is so translated over two hundred times in the OT, even though this is far from being the best translation. The word is used for human instruction such as takes place between caring parents and beloved children (e.g., Pr 4:1 – 2 KJV). In our ears the word *law* carries the overtones of "authoritative imposition"; but while the Torah of the Lord certainly does not lack such authority (Dt 6:1 – 2), it is rather his loving and caring "instruction" of his people.

The division of the Hebrew Scriptures into the Law (*tôrâh*), the Prophets, and the Writings comes from ancient times. The Samaritans have had only the Pentateuch for their Scripture since ancient times. Perhaps that means that only these five books of Moses were in the sacred canon when the Samaritans began their separate worship. The Torah was divided into 154 sections for use in the synagogue services. It was read through, a section at a time, in three years.

> **General References to:**
> *Divine law (Ex 13:9); instruction (Ex 16:4, 28); the law of Moses (1Ki 2:3); the book of the law (Dt 28:61); the entire Jewish Scriptures (Jn 10:34). See Law.*

TRADITION [2976, 4600, 4142, 4161] (Gr. *parado-sis, a giving over*, by word of mouth or in writing). This term does not occur in the Hebrew OT. There are three types of tradition mentioned in the NT. First, the most common use is the kind of tradition handed down by the Jewish fathers or elders that constituted the oral law, regarded by many of the Jews as of equal authority with the revealed law of Moses. Indeed, the Pharisees tended to make these traditions of even greater authority than the Scriptures (Mt 15:2 – 3; Mk 7:3 – 4). The Pharisees were incensed at Christ because he disregarded their traditions and also permitted his disciples to do so. A classic example of their traditions is recorded in the Gospels (Mt 15:2 – 6; Mk 7:1 – 13).

Paul refers to his former zeal for the traditions of his fathers (Gal 1:14). Josephus says that "the Pharisees have delivered to the people a great many observances by succession from their fathers which are not written in the law of Moses" (*Antiq.* 12.10.6).

The second type of tradition is mentioned in Col 2:8. Some scholars hold that this verse refers to Judaistic heresies, but the emphasis seems to be on the *human*, not necessarily Jewish, origin of these teachings.

The third type of tradition is the gospel truths that the apostle Paul taught. He uses the word three times (1Co 11:2 ASV; 2Th 2:15; 3:6 KJV). The meaning of this kind of tradition is "instruction" (NIV "teachings"). Paul had taught the believers in Corinth and Thessalonica the doctrines of the gospel, and he urged them to keep those instructions in mind.

Mt	15:2	"Why do your disciples break the **t**
	15:6	word of God for the sake of your **t**.
Mk	7:13	by your **t** that you have handed
Col	2:8	which depends on human **t**

TRANSFIGURATION [3565]. The name given to that singular event recorded in all the Synoptic Gospels (Mt 17:1 – 8; Mk 9:2 – 8; Lk 9:28 – 36), when Jesus was visibly glorified in the presence of three select disciples. The name is derived from the Latin term used to translate the Greek *metamorphoō*, meaning "to change into another form." The accounts portray the transformation as outwardly visible and consisting in an actual physical change in the body of Jesus: "The appearance of his face changed" (Lk 9:29), "his face shone like the sun" (Mt 17:2), while "his clothes became dazzling white" (Mk 9:3). The glory was not caused by the falling of a heavenly light on him from without but by the flashing forth of the radiant splendor within. He had passed into a higher state of existence, his body assuming properties of the resurrection body.

The experience gave encouragement to Jesus, who was setting his face to the cross. To the shocked disciples, it confirmed the necessity of the cross through the conversation of the heavenly visitors about Christ's coming "departure" (Gr. *exodus*, Lk 9:31) as well as the divine endorsement of Christ's teaching. It inseparably linked the suffering with the glory. It was the crowning with glory of the perfect human life of Jesus, God's stamp of approval on his sinless humanity. The divine approval established his fitness to be our sinbearer on the cross. It was also an entry for Jesus into the glory in which he would reign, thus constituting a typical manifestation of the king coming into his kingdom (Mt 16:28).

TRANSGRESSION [6296, 7321, 7322, 490, 491, 4126, 4183]. Breaking of a law (Pr 17:19; Ro 4:15).

Ps	19:13	innocent of great **t**.
Isa	53:8	for the **t** of my people he was
Mic	1:5	All this is because of Jacob's **t**,
	6:7	Shall I offer my firstborn for my **t**,
	7:18	who pardons sin and forgives the **t**
Ro	4:15	where there is no law there is no **t**.
	11:11	Rather, because of their **t**,

TRANSJORDAN (trăns-jôr'dăn, *beyond [east of] the Jordan*). A large plateau east of Jordan, comprised in the modern Hashemite kingdom of Jordan; in the NT times, Perea and the Decapolis; in OT times, Moab, Ammon, Gilead, and Bashan. Associated with Moses; Joshua; the tribes of Reuben, Gad, and Manasseh; David; Nabateans.

TRAP

Ps	69:22	may it become retribution and a **t**.
Pr	20:25	a **t** for a man to dedicate something
	28:10	will fall into his own **t**,
Isa	8:14	a **t** and a snare.
Mt	22:15	and laid plans to **t** him in his words.
Lk	21:34	close on you unexpectedly like a **t**.
Ro	11:9	their table become a snare and a **t**,
1Ti	3:7	into disgrace and into the devil's **t**.
	6:9	and a **t** and into many foolish
2Ti	2:26	and escape from the **t** of the devil,

TREASURE [238, 1709, 2773, 2890, 4718, 4759, 4837, 6035, 7621, 10133, 1126, 2565]. A thing of highly estimated value.

Money (Ge 42:25, 27 – 28, 35; 43:23, w 43:18, 21 – 22). Valuables of the temple and royal residence (1Ki 14:26; 2Ki 20:13). Cannot save life (Job 20:20).

Jesus forbids the hoarding of (Mt 6:19; 19:21; Lk 12:33). Hidden (Mt 13:44).

Pr	2:4	and search for it as for hidden **t**,
Isa	33:6	of the LORD is the key to this **t**.
Mt	6:21	For where your **t** is, there your
	13:44	of heaven is like **t** hidden in a field.
Lk	12:33	a **t** in heaven that will not be
2Co	4:7	But we have this **t** in jars of clay
1Ti	6:19	In this way they will lay up **t**

TREE OF KNOWLEDGE A special tree in the garden of Eden, set apart by the Lord as an instrument to test the obedience of Adam and Eve (Ge 2:9, 17). It must have been a real tree since the test was real, by real people, with real results. Its fruit probably was not much different from that of other trees from which they ate. The sin in eating its fruit did not lie in the tree but in the disobedience of the persons who ate.

The phrase "to know good and evil" is used in other places: Infants do not know good and evil (Dt 1:39), nor does an old man of failing mind (2Sa 19:35); but a king does know good and evil (1Ki 3:9), as do angels (2Sa 14:17) and God himself (Ge 3:5, 22).

TREE OF LIFE A special tree in the garden of Eden (Ge 2:9; 3:22). This tree appears again in Rev 22:2 as a fruit-bearing tree with leaves. It will have healing in its leaves (22:2). The phrase "tree of life" in Proverbs (3:18; 11:30; 13:12; 15:4) is figurative for an exhilarating experience.

TRESPASS [4183] (Heb. *'ashām*, Gr. *paraptōma*). Used in the KJV of the OT to express the rights of others, whether of God or of another person. In Jewish law acknowledged violation of a person's rights required restoration plus one-fifth of the amount or value of the thing involved and the presentation of a guilt offering (KJV "trespass offering"). Unintentional trespass against God, when the guilty person became aware of it, required a guilt offering to remove guilt. Trespasses against us must be forgiven by us because God has forgiven our sin.

Ro	5:15	But the gift is not like the **t**.

	5:15	died by the **t** of the one man,
	5:17	For if, by the **t** of the one man,
	5:18	result of one **t** was condemnation
	5:20	added so that the **t** might increase.

TRIAL

Ps	37:33	condemned when brought to **t**.
Mk	13:11	you are arrested and brought to **t**,
2Co	8:2	most severe **t**, their overflowing
Jas	1:12	is the man who perseveres under **t**,
1Pe	4:12	at the painful **t** you are suffering,
Rev	3:10	you from the hour of **t** that is going

TRIAL OF JESUS The tumultuous proceedings before the Jewish and Roman authorities resulting in the crucifixion of Jesus. All four gospels record at least part of the twofold trial (Mt 26:57 – 27:31; Mk 14:53 – 15:20; Lk 22:54 – 23:25; Jn 18:12 – 19:16), but because of the brief and selective nature of their narratives, the precise chronological order of events is not always certain. It is clear that both parts of the trial were marked by great irregularities, but the writers of the Gospels never assert that this or that in the trial was illegal, for they wrote not as lawyers but as witnesses.

Following his arrest in Gethsemane, Jesus was at once taken before the Jewish authorities in Jerusalem. John alone tells us that he was first brought before the former high priest Annas, who conducted a preliminary examination by questioning Jesus about his disciples and teaching. With dignity Jesus reminded him of its illegality, only to be basely struck by an attendant (Jn 18:12 – 14, 19 – 23). Meanwhile the Sanhedrin members had assembled in the palace of Caiaphas, the president of the Sanhedrin, for an illegal night session. Annas sent Jesus to them bound (18:24). The attempt to convict Jesus through false witnesses collected and instructed by the Sanhedrin failed because of their contradictory testimony (Mt 26:59 – 61; Mk 14:55 – 59). Before their charges Jesus maintained a dignified silence, even when blustering Caiaphas demanded an answer (Mt 26:62), thus denying the validity of the process. Aware that their case had collapsed, Caiaphas brushed aside the witnesses and put Jesus under oath to tell the court if he was "the Christ, the Son of God" (26:63). The answer, in deliberate self-incrimination, was used to condemn Jesus for blasphemy (26:64 – 66; Mk 14:61 – 64). The session broke up in disorder, with indignities being heaped on Jesus (Mt 26:67 – 68; Mk 14:65; Lk 22:63 – 65). After dawn the Sanhedrin assembled in its council chamber and reenacted their trial by questioning Jesus on his messianic claims and deity (Lk 22:66 – 71). This meeting was held to give a semblance of legality to the condemnation.

Since the Romans had deprived the Sanhedrin of the power of capital punishment, it was necessary to secure a confirmatory death sentence from the Roman governor, who found it expedient to be in Jerusalem during the Passover season. Accordingly, "the whole assembly" (Lk 23:1) in formal procession brought Jesus, bound, to Pilate. When Pilate asked their charges, they indicated that they wanted him simply to sanction their condemnation of Jesus without a full trial (Jn 18:29 – 32). When Pilate insisted on knowing what the charges were, the people presented three (Lk 23:2). The charge of treason alone Pilate deemed worthy of investigation. When Jesus explained to him the nature of his kingdom, Pilate concluded that Jesus was harmless and announced a verdict of acquittal (Jn 18:33 – 38). This verdict should have ended the trial, but it only evoked a torrent of further charges against Jesus by the Jews, charges that Jesus refused to answer, to Pilate's surprise (Mt 27:12 – 14). Having learned that Jesus was a Galilean, Pilate decided to be rid of the unpleasant task by sending him to Herod Antipas, also present for the Passover, on the plea that Jesus belonged to Herod's jurisdiction. When Jesus refused to amuse Herod with a miracle, maintaining complete silence before him, Herod mocked him and returned him to Pilate uncondemned (Lk 23:2 – 12).

With the return of Jesus, Pilate realized that he must handle the trial. Summoning the chief priests "and the people," he reviewed the case to prove the innocence of Jesus but weakly proposed a compromise by offering to scourge Jesus before releasing him (Lk 23:13 – 16). When the multitude requested the customary release of one prisoner (Mk 15:8), Pilate offered them the choice between the notorious Barabbas and Jesus (Mt 27:17). He hoped that the crowd would choose Jesus, thus overruling the chief priests. Before the vote was taken, Pilate received an impressive warning from his wife (27:19 – 21). Meanwhile the Jewish leaders persuaded the people to vote for Barabbas. When asked their choice, the people shouted for Barabbas, demanding that Jesus be crucified (Mt 27:20 – 21; Lk 23:18 – 19). Further remonstrance by Pilate proved useless (Lk 23:20 – 22).

According to John's gospel, as a last resort to avoid crucifying Jesus, Pilate had him scourged, allowed the soldiers to stage a mock coronation, and then brought out the pathetic figure before the people, hoping that the punishment would satisfy them. It only intensified their shouts for his crucifixion (Jn 19:1 – 6). A new charge, that Jesus made himself the Son of God, aroused the superstitious fears of Pilate, causing him to make further futile efforts to release him (19:7 – 12). Using their last weapon, the Jewish leaders threatened to report Pilate to Caesar if he released Jesus (19:12). This threat, because of Pilate's grievous maladministration, broke all further resistance in the vacillating governor. To his last appeal whether he should crucify their king, the Jews gave the blasphemous answer that they had no king but Caesar (19:15). When Pilate sought to absolve himself of the guilt of Christ's death by publicly washing his hands, the people voluntarily accepted the responsibility (Mt 27:24 – 26). Keenly conscious of the gross miscarriage of justice, Pilate yielded by releasing Barabbas and sentencing Jesus to the cross. *See also Jesus the Christ.*

TRIBE [1074, 1201, 1228, 4722, 4751, 4985, 7259, 7470, 8657, 10694, 1559, 5876] (Heb. *matteh, rod, staff, tribe, shēvĕt, rod, scepter, tribe,* Gr. *phylē, tribe*). The tribes of Israel were descended from the

twelve sons of Jacob, with Joseph's sons, Ephraim and Manasseh forming two, while no tribal territory was allotted to Levi (Ge 48:5; Nu 26:5 – 51; Jos 13:7 – 33; 15 – 19). The leaders of the tribes are called by various names: princes, rulers, heads, chiefs (Ex 34:31; Nu 1:16; Ge 36:1ff.). Before the Israelites entered the Promised Land two tribes, Reuben and Gad, and half of Manasseh, chose to settle on the east side of the Jordan (Nu 32:33). During the period of the judges in Israel, the tribes were each one a law to themselves. When David became king over the whole land, the twelve tribes were unified. He appointed a captain over each tribe (1Ch 27:16 – 22). The captivities wiped out tribal distinctions.

Heb	7:13	no one from that **t** has ever served
Rev	5:5	See, the Lion of the **t** of Judah,
	5:9	God from every **t** and language
	11:9	men from every people, **t**,
	14:6	to every nation, **t**, language

TRIBULATION, THE GREAT (Heb. *tsar, narrow,* Gr. *thlipsis, pressure*). The Hebrew word for "tribulation" has a large variety of meanings in the OT, but it usually refers to trouble of a general sort (Ps 13:4). Likewise, the Greek word refers to tribulation of a general sort (Mt 13:21; Jn 16:33). Sometimes this suffering is just the natural part of one's life (Ro 12:12; Jas 1:27), while at other times it is looked on as a definite punishment or chastening from the Lord for misbehavior (Ro 2:9).

The great tribulation is a definite period of suffering sent from God on the earth to accomplish several purposes. According to premillennial eschatology, it precedes the millennial reign of Christ. Postmillennial theology places it at the end of the thousand-year reign of Christ. Amillennial theology places it just before the new heavens and the new earth are brought in. This period of suffering will be unlike any other period in the past or future (Da 12:1; Mt 24:21 KJV; NIV "distress").

TRINITY (*triad, union of three*). There is one eternal God, the Lord, who is holy love. Through his self-revelation, he has disclosed to his people that he is the Father, the Son, and the Holy Spirit. Yet he is not three deities but one Godhead, since all three Persons share the one Deity/Godhead. The biblical teaching of the Trinity is, in a sense, a mystery; and the more we enter into union with God and deepen our understanding of him, the more we recognize how much there is yet to know. The biblical teaching has led to the Christian confession that God is one in three and three in one.

THE UNITY OF GOD.

God is one. The OT condemns polytheism and declares that God is one and is to be worshiped and loved as such. "Hear, O Israel: The LORD our God, the LORD is one. Love the LORD your God with all your heart and with all your soul and with all your strength" (Dt 6:4 – 5). He said through Isaiah, "There is no God apart from me, a righteous God and a Savior; there is none but me" (Isa 45:21). And this conviction of the unity of God is continued in the NT (see Mk 10:18; 12:29; Gal 3:20; 1Co 8:4; 1Ti 2:5).

THE FATHER IS GOD.

God is the Father of Israel (Isa 64:8; Jer 31:9) and of the anointed king of his people (2Sa 7:14; Pss 2:7; 89:27). Jesus lived in communion with his heavenly Father, always doing his will and recognizing him as truly and eternally God (Mt 11:25 – 27; Lk 10:21 – 22; Jn 10:25 – 28; Ro 15:6; 2Co 1:3; 11:31). Before his ascension, Jesus said he was going to his Father (with whom he had a unique relation) and to the Father of the disciples (Jn 20:17). He taught his disciples to pray, "Our Father...," and to live in communion with him.

JESUS OF NAZARETH, THE MESSIAH, IS THE INCARNATE SON OF GOD.

The disciples came to see that Jesus was the long-expected Messiah of Israel (Mt 16:13 – 20; Mk 8:27 – 30). Later they came to see also that to be the Messiah, Jesus must also be God made man

(see Jn 1:1 – 2, 18; 20:28; Ro 9:5; Tit 2:13; Heb 1:8; 2Pe 1:1). Thus doxologies were offered to him as God (Heb 13:20 – 21; 2Pe 3:18; Rev 1:5 – 6; 5:13; 7:10).

THE SPIRIT IS ALSO GOD.

He comes in the name of Jesus Christ, incarnate Son from the Father in heaven. The way in which the apostles, following Jesus, refer to the Holy Spirit shows that they looked on the Spirit as a person. In the Acts, the Spirit inspires Scripture, is lied to, is tempted, bears witness, is resisted, directs, carries someone away, informs, commands, calls, sends, thinks a certain decision is good, forbids, prevents, warns, appoints, and reveals prophetic truth (see Ac 1:16; 5:3, 9, 32; 7:51; 8:29, 39; 10:19; 11:12; 13:2, 4; 15:28; 16:6, 7; 20:23, 28; 28:25). Paul describes the Spirit as bearing witness, speaking, teaching, and acting as guide (Ro 8:14, 16, 26; Gal 4:6; Eph 4:30). In John's gospel Jesus calls himself the *parakletos* (Paraclete), and refers to the Holy Spirit as another *parakletos* (Jn 14:16; 15:26 – 27; 16:13 – 15).

GOD, THE LORD, IS FATHER, SON, AND HOLY SPIRIT.

This confession and understanding may be said to be basic to the faith of the writers of the NT, though they rarely express it in precise terms. But in certain passages the doctrine is articulated (Mt 28:19; 1Co 12:4 – 6; 2Co 13:14; 2Th 2:13 – 14; 1Pe 1:2).

BIBLICAL DOCTRINE AND CHURCH DOGMA.

There is no systematic explanation of the doctrine of God as Trinity in the NT, though the Trinitarian pattern (see Ac 20:28; Tit 3:4 – 6; Heb 10:29; Rev 1:4 – 5) is present. The dogma of the Trinity found in the Nicene Creed may be said to be the systematic presentation of the implications of the Trinitarian suggestions, hints, and patterns of the NT, against the background of the OT. The classic formula is that there is one God and three persons, and that each person shares the one Being or Godhead with the two other persons.

Implied in the OT:

*God speaks of self in the plural (Ge 1:26; 3:22; Isa 6:3, 8). L*ORD*, Servant, and Spirit (Isa 11:2 – 3; 42:1, w Mt 12:48; Isa 48:16). Tri-holiness of God suggests (Isa 6:3; Rev 4:8).*

Implied in the NT:

Father, Son, and Spirit (Mt 28:19; Lk 3:22 with Mt 3:16; Jn 3:34 – 35; 14:16 – 17, 26; 15:26; 16:7, 13 – 15; Ac 1:2, 4 – 5; 2:33; 10:36 – 38; Ro 1:3 – 4; 8:9 – 11, 26 – 27; 1Co 12:3 – 6; 2Co 1:21 – 22; 5:5; 13:14; Gal 4:4, 6; 2Th 2:13 – 14, 16; 1Ti 3:16; Tit 3:4 – 6; Heb 9:14; 1Pe 1:2; 3:18; 1Jn 5:6 – 7). Tri-holiness of God suggests (Isa 6:3; Rev 4:8).

Relationships within the Godhead:

The Father and the Son (Mt 11:27; Lk 9:26; Jn 3:35; 5:19 – 27; 6:27; 10:36; 17:1; Ac 13:33; Heb 1:5; 5:5; 2Pe 1:17; 1Jn 1:3; 2:22 – 24). The Father and the Holy Spirit (Isa 42:1; 48:16; 63:9 – 10; 1Co 2:10 – 11; 6:19). Jesus and the Holy Spirit (Isa 61:1 – 3; Mt 1:18, 20; 12:28; 28:19; Lk 1:35; 4:1, 14, 18; Jn 1:32 – 33; 7:39; 20:22; 1Co 8:6; 2Co 3:17; Php 1:19; Col 2:2). See Angel of the Lord.

TROAS [5590]. A chief city and port of the Roman province of Asia, on the Aegean coast, about ten miles from the ruins of ancient Troy; known as Alexandria Troas (Ac 16:8; 20:5; 2Co 2:12).

TRUE

Dt	18:22	does not take place or come **t**,
Jos	23:15	of the LORD your God has come **t**
1Sa	9:6	and everything he says comes **t**.
1Ki	10:6	and your wisdom is **t**.
2Ch	15:3	was without the **t** God,
Ps	33:4	of the LORD is right and **t**;
	119:160	All your words are **t**;
Pr	8:7	My mouth speaks what is **t**,
	22:21	teaching you **t** and reliable words,
Jer	10:10	But the LORD is the **t** God;
	28:9	only if his prediction comes **t**."
Lk	16:11	who will trust you with **t** riches?

Jn	1:9	The **t** light that gives light
	4:23	when the **t** worshipers will worship
	6:32	Father who gives you the **t** bread
	7:28	on my own, but he who sent me is **t**
	15:1	"I am the **t** vine, and my Father is
	17:3	the only **t** God, and Jesus Christ,
	19:35	testimony, and his testimony is **t**.
	21:24	We know that his testimony is **t**.
Ac	11:23	all to remain **t** to the Lord
	14:22	them to remain **t** to the faith.
	17:11	day to see if what Paul said was **t**.
Ro	3:4	Let God be **t**, and every man a liar.
Php	4:8	whatever is **t**, whatever is noble,
1Jn	2:8	and the **t** light is already shining.
	5:20	He is the **t** God and eternal life.
Rev	19:9	"These are the **t** words of God."
	22:6	These words are trustworthy and **t**.

TRUMPET

Isa	27:13	And in that day a great **t** will sound
Eze	33:5	Since he heard the sound of the **t**
Zec	9:14	Sovereign LORD will sound the **t**;
Mt	24:31	send his angels with a loud **t** call,
1Co	14:8	if the **t** does not sound a clear call,
	15:52	For the **t** will sound, the dead will
1Th	4:16	and with the **t** call of God,
Rev	8:7	The first angel sounded his **t**,

TRUMPETS, FEAST OF When and how observed (Lev 23:24 – 25; Nu 29:1 – 6). Celebrated with joy after the captivity (Ne 8:2, 9 – 12). *See Feasts.*

TRUST

Ex	14:31	put their **t** in him and in Moses his
	19:9	and will always put their **t** in you."
Nu	20:12	"Because you did not **t**
Dt	1:32	you did not **t** in the LORD your
	9:23	You did not **t** him or obey him.
Ps	4:5	and **t** in the LORD.
	13:5	But I **t** in your unfailing love;
	20:7	Some **t** in chariots and some
	20:7	we **t** in the name of the LORD our
	22:4	In you our fathers put their **t**;

	22:9	you made me **t** in you
	37:3	**T** in the LORD and do good;
	37:5	**t** in him and he will do this:
	40:4	who makes the LORD his **t**,
	44:6	I do not **t** in my bow,
	49:6	those who **t** in their wealth
	49:13	of those who **t** in themselves,
	52:8	I **t** in God's unfailing love
	56:4	in God I **t**; I will not be afraid.
	62:8	**T** in him at all times, O people;
	119:42	for I **t** in your word.
	125:1	Those who **t** in the LORD are like
Pr	3:5	**T** in the LORD with all your heart
	21:22	the stronghold in which they **t**.
	22:19	So that your **t** may be in the LORD
Isa	12:2	I will **t** and not be afraid.
	26:4	**T** in the LORD forever,
	42:17	But those who **t** in idols,
Jer	7:4	Do not **t** in deceptive words
	39:18	you **t** in me, declares the LORD.' "
	48:7	Since you **t** in your deeds
	49:4	you **t** in your riches and say,
Mic	7:5	Do not **t** a neighbor;
Na	1:7	He cares for those who **t** in him,
Zep	3:2	She does not **t** in the LORD,
	3:12	who **t** in the name of the LORD.
Lk	16:11	who will **t** you with true riches?
Jn	12:36	Put your **t** in the light
	14:1	**T** in God; **t** also in me.
Ac	14:23	Lord, in whom they had put their **t**.
Ro	15:13	you with all joy and peace as you **t**
1Co	4:2	been given a **t** must prove faithful.
	9:17	discharging the **t** committed
2Co	13:6	I **t** that you will discover that we
Heb	2:13	"I will put my **t** in him."

TRUTH [575, 586, 589, 597, 622, 995, 4027, 7406, 7999, 9214, 10327, 237, 238, 239, 240, 242, 297, 1188, 4048]. The word "truth," *alētheia* in the NT and a variety of words (chiefly *'emeth*) in the OT, always connotes (1) the interrelated consistency of statements and their correspondence with the facts of reality, and (2) the facts themselves. The former may be called propositional truth, and the latter, ontological truth. Truth and faithful(ness) are translated from the same Hebrew and Greek words.

The biblical use of the word has rich suggestive meanings that go beyond the literal connotations. When Moses (Ex 18:21 KJV) refers to "able men, such as fear God, men of truth, hating covetousness," there is suggested integrity of character — a kind of reliability that goes beyond the literal meaning to include those aspects of personal behavior that seem to be implied by the love of truth. The concept of truth is assumed to be derived from the character of God and is the exact opposite of the concept of lying. "It is impossible for God to lie" (Heb 6:18; cf. 2Ti 2:13; Tit 1:2).

Characteristics of:
(Ps 85:10 – 11). Precious (Pr 23:23). Preserves (Pss 46:11; 61:7; 91:4; Pr 20:28). Purifies (Pr 16:6; 1Pe 1:22). Sanctifies (Jn 17:17, 19; 2Th 2:13). Brings freedom (Jn 8:32). Reaches to the clouds (Pss 57:10; 108:4). Endures forever (Pss 100:5; 117:2). Ways of the Lord in (Ps 25:10). The foundation of which Christ is the cornerstone (Eph 2:20). Came by Jesus Christ (Jn 1:17; 8:45; 14:6; 18:37 – 38; Eph 2:20). Revealed to the righteous (Pss 57:3; 86:11). Word of God called the word of (Jn 17:17; Eph 1:13; Col 1:5; 2Ti 2:15; Jas 1:18). Scripture of (Da 10:21). Acceptance of, necessary to salvation (2Th 2:12 – 13; 1Ti 2:4; 2Ti 2:25; 3:7; Heb 10:26). Rejection of, brings condemnation (2Th 2:10 – 12; Tit 1:14). To be taught by parents to children (Isa 38:19). Church is the pillar of (1Ti 3:15). Believers should worship God in (Jn 4:24, w Ps 145:18); serve God in (Jos 24:14; 1Sa 12:24); walk before God in (1Ki 2:4; 2Ki 20:3); keep religious feasts with (1Co 5:8); value as inestimable (Pr 23:23); love (Zec 8:19); rejoice in (1Co 13:6); speak to one another in (Zec 8:16; Eph 4:25); execute judgment with (Zec 8:16); meditate on (Php 4:8); bind about the neck (Pr 3:3); write on the tables of the heart (Pr 3:3). The fruit of the light (Eph 5:9). They

who speak, show righteousness (Pr 12:17); are the delight of God (Pr 12:22); will be established forever (Pr 2:1). The wicked are destitute of truth (Isa 59:14 – 15; Da 9:13; Hos 4:1; 1Ti 6:5). The wicked resist (2Ti 3:8; 4:4); turn away from (2Ti 4:4); speak not (Jer 9:5); plead not for (Isa 59:4); are not valiant for (Jer 9:3); are punished for lack of (Jer 9:5, 9; Hos 4:1, 3). See Wicked.

The Gospel as:

Came by Christ (Jn 1:17). Is in Christ (1Ti 2:7). John bore witness to (Jn 5:33). Is according to godliness (Tit 1:1). Is sanctifying (Jn 17:17, 19). Is purifying (1Pe 1:22). Is part of the Christian armor (Eph 6:14). Revealed abundantly to saints (Jer 33:6). Abides continually with saints (2Jn 2). Should be acknowledged (2Ti 2:25). Should be believed (2Th 2:12 – 13; 1Ti 4:3). Should be obeyed (Ro 2:8; Gal 3:1). Should be loved (2Th 2:10). Should be manifested (2Co 4:2). Should be rightly divided (2Ti 2:15). The church is the pillar and ground of (1Ti 3:15). The devil is devoid of (Jn 8:44).

Of the Gospel:

(2Ti 4:3 – 4; Tit 1:1, 14; 2:1; Jas 1:18, 21, 23, 25; 2:13; 5:19; 1Pe 1:22 – 25; 2:2, 8; 3:1; 5:12; 2Pe 1:12).

Of God:

Is one of his attributes (Dt 32:4; Isa 65:16). Often linked with his mercy (Pss 85:10 – 11; 93:3; 100:5). He keeps, forever (Ps 146:6); abundant (Ex 34:6); inviable (Nu 23:19; Tit 1:2); enduring to all generations (Ps 100:5). Exhibited in his ways (Rev 15:3); works (Pss 33:4; 111:7; Da 4:37); judicial statutes (Ps 19:9); word (Ps 119:160; Jn 17:17); fulfillment of promises in Christ (2Co 1:20); fulfillment of his covenant (Mic 7:20); dealings with saints (Ps 25:10); deliverance of saints (Ps 57:3); punishment of the wicked (Rev 16:7). Is a shield and buckler to saints (Ps 91:4). Believers should confide in (Ps 31:5; Tit 1:2); plead in prayer (Ps 89:49); pray for its manifestation to ourselves (2Ch 6:17); pray for its exhi-

bition to others (2Sa 2:6); make known to others (Isa 38:19); magnify (Pss 71:22; 138:2). Is denied by the devil (Ge 3:4 – 5); the self-righteous (1Jn 1:10); unbelievers (1Jn 5:10).

Attribute:

Of God (Ex 34:6; Dt 32:4; Pss 31:5; 40:10 – 11; 71:22; 86:15; 89:14; 115:1; 117:2; 138:2; 146:6; Isa 25:1; 65:16; Jer 4:2; 5:3). Exhibited in his government (Ps 119:151); in his judgments (Ps 96:13; Ro 2:2); in his word (Jn 17:19); in his works (Ps 111:7 – 8; Da 4:37). Of Christ (Jn 1:14; 14:6). Of the Holy Spirit (Jn 14:17; 16:13; 1Jn 5:7 – 8). Of the righteous (Ps 51:6; Pr 3:3; Jn 3:21; 3Jn 3). Righteous, should be prepared with (Eph 6:14); should know (1Ti 4:3; 1Jn 2:21; 3:19; 4:6); should love (Zec 8:19; 2Th 2:10); should rejoice in (1Co 13:6); should meditate on (Php 4:8).

Ge	42:16	tested to see if you are telling the **t**.
1Ki	17:24	Lord from your mouth is the **t**."
2Ch	18:15	the **t** in the name of the Lord?"
Ps	25:5	guide me in your **t** and teach me,
	26:3	and I walk continually in your **t**.
	40:11	your **t** always protect me.
	43:3	Send forth your light and your **t**,
	119:30	I have chosen the way of **t**;
Pr	16:13	they value a man who speaks the **t**.
	23:23	Buy the **t** and do not sell it;
Isa	45:19	I, the Lord, speak the **t**;
	59:15	**T** is nowhere to be found,
Jer	5:1	who deals honestly and seeks the **t**,
Da	10:21	what is written in the Book of **T**.
Am	5:10	and despise him who tells the **t**.
Zec	8:3	will be called the City of **T**,
	8:19	Therefore love **t** and peace."
Mt	5:18	I tell you the **t**, until heaven
	18:18	"I tell you the **t**, whatever you bind
Mk	3:28	I tell you the **t**, all the sins
	12:14	of God in accordance with the **t**.
Jn	1:14	from the Father, full of grace and **t**.
	1:17	and **t** came through Jesus Christ.
	3:21	But whoever lives by the **t** comes
	4:23	worship the Father in spirit and **t**,

	5:24	"I tell you the **t**, whoever hears my
	8:32	and the **t** will set you free."
	8:44	to the **t**, for there is no **t** in him.
	14:17	with you forever — the Spirit of **t**.
	16:13	comes, he will guide you into all **t**.
	17:17	them by the **t**; your word is **t**.
	18:23	if I spoke the **t**, why did you strike
	18:37	into the world, to testify to the **t**.
	18:38	"What is **t**?" Pilate asked.
Ac	20:30	and distort the **t** in order
	21:24	everybody will know there is no **t**
	28:25	"The Holy Spirit spoke the **t**
Ro	1:18	of men who suppress the **t**
	1:25	They exchanged the **t** of God
	2:2	who do such things is based on **t**.
	2:8	who reject the **t** and follow evil,
	2:20	embodiment of knowledge and **t** —
	9:1	I speak the **t** in Christ — I am not
1Co	5:8	the bread of sincerity and **t**.
	13:6	in evil but rejoices with the **t**.
2Co	4:2	setting forth the **t** plainly we
	11:10	As surely as the **t** of Christ is in me,
	13:8	against the **t**, but only for the **t**.
Gal	2:5	so that the **t** of the gospel might
	5:7	and kept you from obeying the **t**?
Eph	1:13	when you heard the word of **t**,
	4:15	Instead, speaking the **t** in love,
	4:21	him in accordance with the **t** that is
	6:14	with the belt of **t** buckled
Col	1:5	heard about in the word of **t**,
2Th	2:10	because they refused to love the **t**
	2:12	who have not believed the **t**
1Ti	2:4	to come to a knowledge of the **t**.
	3:15	the pillar and foundation of the **t**.
	4:3	who believe and who know the **t**.
	6:5	who have been robbed of the **t**
2Ti	2:15	correctly handles the word of **t**.
	2:18	have wandered away from the **t**.
	3:7	never able to acknowledge the **t**.
	4:4	will turn their ears away from the **t**
Tit	1:14	of those who reject the **t**.
Heb	10:26	received the knowledge of the **t**,
Jas	1:18	birth through the word of **t**,

	3:14	do not boast about it or deny the **t**.
	5:19	of you should wander from the **t**
1Pe	1:22	by obeying the **t** so that you have
2Pe	1:12	established in the **t** you now have.
	2:2	the way of **t** into disrepute.
1Jn	1:6	we lie and do not live by the **t**.
	1:8	deceive ourselves and the **t** is not
	2:4	commands is a liar, and the **t** is not
	2:21	because no lie comes from the **t**.
	3:18	or tongue but with actions and in **t**.
	3:19	we know that we belong to the **t**,
	4:6	is how we recognize the Spirit of **t**
	5:6	testifies, because the Spirit is the **t**.
2Jn	1:4	of your children walking in the **t**,
3Jn	1:3	how you continue to walk in the **t**.
	1:4	my children are walking in the **t**.
	1:8	we may work together for the **t**.

TUNIC [955, 4189, 4230+4496, 4496, 5945]. A shirt-like garment worn in Bible times by men and women under other clothes. Worn by priests (Ex 28:4, 39 – 40). Saul offers his to David (1Sa 17:38 – 39), as does Jonathan (1Sa 18:4).

TURN

Ex	32:12	**T** from your fierce anger; relent
Nu	32:15	If you **t** away from following him,
Dt	5:32	do not **t** aside to the right
	30:10	and **t** to the LORD your God
Jos	1:7	do not **t** from it to the right
1Ki	8:58	May he **t** our hearts to him,
2Ch	7:14	and **t** from their wicked ways,
	30:9	He will not **t** his face from you
Ps	28:1	do not **t** a deaf ear to me.
	34:14	**T** from evil and do good;
	51:13	and sinners will **t** back to you.
	119:36	**T** my heart toward your statutes
Pr	22:6	when he is old he will not **t** from it.
Isa	45:22	"**T** to me and be saved,
Jer	31:13	I will **t** their mourning
Eze	33:9	if you do warn the wicked man to **t**
	33:11	**T**! **T** from your evil ways!
Jnh	3:9	and with compassion **t**

Mal	4:6	He will **t** the hearts of the fathers
Mt	5:39	you on the right cheek, **t**
	10:35	For I have come to **t**
Jn	12:40	nor **t** — and I would heal them."
	16:20	but your grief will **t** to joy.
Ac	3:19	Repent, then, and **t** to God,
	26:18	and **t** them from darkness to light,
1Ti	6:20	**T** away from godless chatter
1Pe	3:11	He must **t** from evil and do good;

TYRE, TYRIANS [7450, 7660, 5601, 5602] (tīr, Heb. *tsôr, a rock*, Gr. *Tyros, rocky place*).

1. Kingdom of; Hiram, king of (1Ki 5:1 – 2; 2Ch 2:3). Sends material to David for his palace (2Ch 2:3). Men and materials sent from, to Solomon, for the building of the temple and palaces (1Ki 5:1 – 11; 9:10 – 11; 2Ch 2:3 – 16).

2. City of, situated on the shore of the Mediterranean. On the northern boundary of Asher (Jos 19:29). Pleasant site of (Hos 9:13). Fortified (Jos 19:29; 2Sa 24:7). Commerce of (1Ki 9:26 – 28; 10:11; Isa 23; Eze 27; 28:1 – 19; Zec 9:2; Ac 21:3). Merchants of (Isa 23:8). Antiquity of (Isa 23:7). Riches of (Isa 23:8; Zec 9:3). Besieged by Nebuchadnezzar (Eze 26:7; 29:18). Jesus goes to the coasts of (Mt 15:21). Heals the daughter of the Syrian Phoenician woman near (Mt 15:21 – 28; Mk 7:24 – 31). Multitudes from, come to hear Jesus and to be healed of their diseases (Mk 3:8; Lk 6:17). Herod's hostility toward (Ac 12:20 – 23). Paul visits (Ac 21:3 – 7). To be judged according to its opportunity and privileges (Mt 11:21 – 22; Lk 10:13 – 14). Prophecies relating to (Pss 45:12; 87:4; Isa 23; Jer 25:22; 27:1 – 11; 47:4; Eze 26 – 28; Joel 3:4 – 8; Am 1:9 – 10; Zec 9:2 – 4).

UNBELIEF [602].

Characteristics of:

Caused by spiritual blindness (Isa 6:9 – 10; Mt 13:13 – 15, 58; Lk 13:34; 19:41 – 42; Jn 12:37, 39 – 40, 47). Hardens the heart (Ps 95:8 – 11; Heb 3:12, 16 – 19; Ac 19:9). Rejects Christ (Isa 53:1 – 3; Mk 6:3, 6; Jn 1:11; 5:38, 40, 44, 46 – 47; 10:25 – 26; 12:38). Displeases God (Ps 78:19 – 22; Heb 11:6). Makes God a liar (1Jn 5:10). Does not nullify God's faithfulness (Ro 3:3 – 4). Allows God to extend his mercy (Ro 11:20, 30 – 32). Characteristic of all humankind (Ro 11:20, 30 – 32; 2Th 3:2). Illustrated (Ro 10:6 – 7, 16; 2Pe 3:4). Parable of (Mk 4:24 – 25; Lk 8:12, 18; 14:16 – 24). At Christ's second coming (Lk 18:8). The spirit of the antichrist (1Jn 2:22 – 23; 4:3). Of others, used as an excuse by Moses (Ex 4:1).

Condemned:

Leads to: defeat (Isa 7:9); destruction (Ro 11:20; 2Th 2:12); reproof (Jn 16:8 – 9); condemnation (Ro 14:23); rejection (1Pe 2:7 – 8); instability (Jas 1:6 – 7). Admonitions against (Ac 13:40 – 41; 2Co 6:14 – 16; Heb 3:12, 16 – 19; 4:1 – 3, 6, 11; 12:25).

Mk	9:24	help me overcome my **u**!"
Ro	4:20	through **u** regarding the promise
	11:20	they were broken off because of **u**,
	11:23	And if they do not persist in **u**,
1Ti	1:13	because I acted in ignorance and **u**.
Heb	3:19	able to enter, because of their **u**.

UNBELIEVER [UNBELIEF]

1Co	7:15	But if the **u** leaves, let him do so.
	10:27	If some **u** invites you to a meal
	14:24	if an **u** or someone who does not
2Co	6:15	have in common with an **u**?
1Ti	5:8	the faith and is worse than an **u**.

UNBELIEVERS [578, 602, 603].

Are spiritually blind (Jn 14:17; 1Co 2:14; 2Pe 3:4 – 7). Are impure (Tit 1:15). Make God a liar (1Jn 5:10). Will not be convinced (Lk 16:31; 22:67; Jn 4:48; 12:37 – 40). God's forbearance toward (Ro 10:16, 21). Shall be destroyed (Jer 5:12 – 14; Mt 10:14 – 15; Lk 12:46; Jn 8:24; 12:48; Ac 13:41; 1Co 1:18; 2Th 2:11 – 12; Jude 5 – 7; Rev 21:8). Tongues, a sign to (1Co 14:22).

Instances of:

Eve (Ge 3:4 – 6); Moses (Nu 11:21 – 23) and Aaron (Nu 20:12); Israelites (Dt 9:23; 2Ki 17:14; Pss 78; 106:7, 24; Isa 58:3; Mal 1:2, 7); Naaman (2Ki 5:12); Samaritan lord (2Ki 7:2); disciples (Mt 17:17; Lk 24:11, 25); Zechariah (Lk 1:20); chief priests (Mt 21:32; Lk 22:67); the Jews (Mt 11:16 – 19; Mk 1:45; 2:6 – 11; 8:11 – 12; 15:29 – 32; Lk 7:31 – 35; Jn 5:38, 40, 43, 46 – 47; Ac 22:18; 28:24); disciples (Mt 17:20; Mk 4:38, 40; 16:14, 16; Lk 24:11, 21, 25 – 26, 36 – 45; Jn 6:36, 60 – 62, 64, 66, 70 – 71; father of a child possessed with a spirit (Mk 9:24); brothers of Christ (Jn 7:5); Thomas (Jn 20:25); Jews of Iconium (Ac 14:2); Thessalonian Jews (Ac 17:5); Jews in Jerusalem (Ro 15:31); Ephesians (Ac 19:9); Saul (1Ti 1:13); people of Jericho (Heb 11:31).

Lk	12:46	and assign him a place with the **u**.
Ro	15:31	rescued from the **u** in Judea
1Co	6:6	another — and this in front of **u**!
	14:22	however, is for believers, not for **u**.
2Co	4:4	this age has blinded the minds of **u**,
	6:14	Do not be yoked together with **u**.

UNBELIEVING [UNBELIEF]

Mt	17:17	"O **u** and perverse generation,"
1Co	7:14	For the **u** husband has been
	7:14	and the **u** wife has been sanctified
Heb	3:12	**u** heart that turns away
Rev	21:8	But the cowardly, the **u**, the vile,

UNCIAL LETTERS A style of handwriting that uses capitals for most letters. Early Greek manuscripts of the NT were written in uncials.

UNCIRCUMCISED [6888, 213+, 598, 2177] (ŭn-sûr′kŭm-sīzd, Heb. ʾārēl, Gr. akrobystia). A word used in both OT and NT in several ways. Literally it refers to one who has not submitted to the Jewish rite of circumcision. Figuratively, it signifies a pagan (Jdg 14:3; Ro 4:9). In a similar sense it is used of the unresponsive heart (Lev 26:41) and the unhearing ear (Jer 6:10 KJV).

Lev	26:41	when their **u** hearts are humbled
1Sa	17:26	Who is this **u** Philistine that he
Jer	9:26	house of Israel is **u** in heart."
Ac	7:51	stiff-necked people, with **u** hearts
Ro	4:11	had by faith while he was still **u**.
1Co	7:18	Was a man **u** when he was called?
Col	3:11	circumcised or **u**, barbarian,

UNCLEAN, UNCLEANNESS [1458, 3237, 3238, 3240, 5614, 7002, 176, 3123, 3124] (Heb. tūm′âh, uncleanness, defilement; niddâh, separation, impurity; ʾerwâh, ʾerwath dāvār, unclean things; tamēʾ, defiled unclean; tāmēʾ, to make or declare unclean; Gr. akatharsia, miasmos, pollution; akathartos, unclean; koinoō, to defile; mianō, to defile; molynō, to make filthy; spiloō, phtheirō, to corrupt). Sin arose very early in the history of humankind and brought about changes in both the physical and spiritual lives of people. It has greatly affected the entire universe, making the terms clean and unclean very common in the thinking of the human race from the earliest times. These words have been factors in determining people's diets, friends, and habits, in fact, their entire deportment. These words took on a new meaning when God began to call the nation of Israel into being. They fall largely into two main divisions: spiritual or moral uncleanness and ceremonial uncleanness.

In the NT one notes the cumbersome systems of defilement, developed by the scribes and Pharisees, which Jesus condemned. Most of the OT regulations passed away with the passing of the Law, and when the matter was discussed at the Jerusalem Council, only four restrictions were placed on the new believers (Ac 15:28 – 29). In the NT era, uncleanness has become moral, not ceremonial.

Ge	7:2	and two of every kind of **u** animal,
Lev	10:10	between the **u** and the clean,
	11:4	it is ceremonially **u** for you.
	17:15	he will be ceremonially **u** till evening.
Isa	6:5	ruined! For I am a man of **u** lips,
	52:11	Touch no **u** thing!
Mt	15:11	mouth does not make him 'u,'
Ac	10:14	never eaten anything impure or **u**."
Ro	14:14	fully convinced that no food is **u**
2Co	6:17	Touch no **u** thing,

UNDERSTAND [UNDERSTOOD]

Ne	8:8	the people could **u** what was being
Job	42:3	Surely I spoke of things I did not **u**,
Ps	14:2	men to see if there are any who **u**,
	119:125	that I may **u** your statutes.
Pr	2:5	then you will **u** the fear
	2:9	Then you will **u** what is right
	30:18	four that I do not **u**:
Ecc	7:25	to **u** the stupidity of wickedness
	11:5	so you cannot **u** the work of God,
Isa	6:10	**u** with their hearts,
Jer	17:9	Who can **u** it?
Hos	14:9	Who is discerning? He will **u** them.
Mt	13:15	**u** with their hearts,
	24:15	Daniel — let the reader **u** —
Lk	24:45	so they could **u** the Scriptures.
Ac	8:30	"Do you **u** what you are reading?"
Ro	7:15	I do not **u** what I do.
	15:21	those who have not heard will **u**."
1Co	2:12	that we may **u** what God has freely
Eph	5:17	but **u** what the Lord's will is.
Heb	11:3	By faith we **u** that the universe was
2Pe	1:20	you must **u** that no prophecy
	3:16	some things that are hard to **u**,

UNDERSTOOD [UNDERSTAND]

Ne	8:12	they now **u** the words that had
Ps	73:17	then I **u** their final destiny.
Isa	40:13	Who has **u** the mind of the LORD,

	40:21	Have you not **u** since the earth was
Jn	1:5	but the darkness has not **u** it.
Ro	1:20	being **u** from what has been made,

UNFAILING

Ex	15:13	"In your **u** love you will lead
1Sa	20:14	But show me **u** kindness like that
2Sa	22:51	he shows **u** kindness
Ps	6:4	save me because of your **u** love.
	13:5	But I trust in your **u** love;
	33:18	those whose hope is in his **u** love,
	33:22	May your **u** love rest upon us,
	48:9	we meditate on your **u** love.
	77:8	Has his **u** love vanished forever?
	85:7	Show us your **u** love, O LORD,
	107:15	thanks to the LORD for his **u** love
Pr	19:22	What a man desires is **u** love;
	20:6	Many a man claims to have **u** love,
Isa	54:10	yet my **u** love for you will not be
La	3:32	so great is his **u** love.
Hos	10:12	reap the fruit of **u** love,

UNFAITHFULNESS [574+4202, 953, 957, 2388, 2393, 2394, 3950, 5085, 5086, 5538, 8745, 4518].

Characteristics of:

Unfaithful in little, unfaithful in much (Lk 16:10). Brings spiritual bankruptcy (Mt 13:12; 25:29). Brings destruction (Jn 15:2). Brings condemnation (Mt 25:41 – 46; Lk 19:12 – 27). God deals with accordingly (Pr 24:11 – 12; Mt 25:8 – 13, 24 – 30, 41 – 46).

Denounced:

In the parables of the vineyard (Isa 5:1 – 7; Mt 21:33 – 43; Mk 12:1 – 9). In the parable of the empty vine (Hos 10:1 – 2). In the parable of the slothful servant (Mt 25:24 – 30; Lk 19:20 – 27).

Illustrated by:

The unfruitful tree (Mt 3:10; Mk 11:13 – 14). The unfruitful branch (Jn 15:2, 4, 6). Blindness (2Pe 1:8 – 9).

| 1Ch | 9:1 | to Babylon because of their **u**. |
| Mt | 5:32 | except for marital **u**, causes her |

| | 19:9 | for marital **u**, and marries another |

UNFRUITFULNESS [182].

Punished (Isa 5:1 – 10; Mt 3:10, w Lk 3:9; Mt 7:19; 13:3 – 7, w Mk 4:3 – 7, 14 – 19 & Lk 8:4 – 14; Mt 21:19 – 20; Mk 11:13; Lk 3:9; 13:6 – 9; Jn 15:2, 4; 15:6).

UNGODLY [2868, 2869, 2870, 2883+4202, 8401, 96, 813, 814, 815].

To be avoided (Ps 1:1). Seem to materially prosper (Ps 73:11). Judged (Pss 1:6; 3:7; 2Pe 3:7). Christ died for (Ro 5:6), therefore God justifies (Ro 4:5). Law made for (1Ti 1:9).

Ro	5:6	powerless, Christ died for the **u**.
1Ti	1:9	the **u** and sinful, the unholy
2Ti	2:16	in it will become more and more **u**.
2Pe	2:6	of what is going to happen to the **u**;
Jude	1:15	and to convict all the **u**

UNIVERSE

1Co	4:9	made a spectacle to the whole **u**,
Eph	4:10	in order to fill the whole **u**.)
Php	2:15	which you shine like stars in the **u**
Heb	1:2	and through whom he made the **u**.
	11:3	understand that the **u** was formed

UNKNOWN GOD (Gr. *agnōstos theos*). These words occur only in Ac 17:23. When Paul came into Athens on his second missionary journey, he found the city "full of idols." While disputing with the Jews in their synagogues and marketplaces, he was asked by the philosophers concerning his faith. On Mars Hill Paul began his message by saying, "I even found an altar with this inscription: TO AN UNKNOWN GOD" (17:23). This was probably a votive altar erected by some worshiper who did not know what god to thank for some benefit he had received. Using this as a starting point, Paul preached the true God to them. Altars erected to unknown gods were common in Athens.

UNKNOWN TONGUE The KJV "unknown" is a translator's insertion (in italics) for the term normally rendered simply "tongue" (1Co 14:2, 4, 13 – 14, 19, 27).

UNLEAVENED [5174, 109] (Heb. *matstsâh*, *sweet*, Gr. *azymos*). A word often found in both Testaments, usually in a literal but sometimes in a figurative sense. When used literally, it refers to bread made without any fermented dough (yeast, leaven) or to the Passover Feast, when only unleavened bread could be used. When used figuratively, it means "unmixed" (1Co 5:7 – 8 KJV; NIV "without yeast").

UNPARDONABLE SIN Not a phrase used in the Bible, but the usual way of referring to blasphemy against the Holy Spirit (Mt 12:31 – 32; Mk 3:28 – 29; Lk 12:10). There is much difference of opinion as to the meaning of this sin, but one of the most popular and likely views is that the sin involves decisively and finally rejecting the testimony of the Holy Spirit regarding the person and work of Jesus Christ.

UNSELFISHNESS

Commanded:

In the royal law (Jas 2:8). In the church (Ro 12:10; 15:1; 1Co 10:24; Gal 6:2; Php 2:3 – 4).

Inspired by:

Love (1Co 13:4 – 5). Jesus' love (2Co 5:14 – 15).

Exemplified by:

Abraham (Ge 13:9; 14:23 – 24); king of Sodom (Ge 14:21); Hittites (Ge 23:6, 11); Judah (Ge 44:33 – 34); Moses (Nu 11:29; 14:12 – 19); Gideon (Jdg 8:22 – 23); Saul (1Sa 11:12 – 13); Jonathan (1Sa 23:17 – 18); David (1Sa 24:17; 2Sa 15:19 – 20; 23:16 – 17; 1Ch 21:17; Ps 69:6); Araunah (2Sa 24:22 – 24); Nehemiah (Ne 5:14 – 18); Jews (Est 9:15); Daniel (Da 5:17); Jonah (Jnh 1:12 – 13); Joseph (Mt 1:19); Jesus (Ro 15:3; 2Co 8:9); disciples (Ac 4:34 – 35); Priscilla and Aquila (Ro 16:3 – 4); Paul (1Co 10:33; Php 1:18; 4:17; 2Th 3:8); Philemon (Phm 13 – 14); Onesiphorus (2Ti 1:16 – 18).

UNSPIRITUAL

Ro	7:14	but I am **u**, sold as a slave to sin.
Col	2:18	and his **u** mind puffs him up
Jas	3:15	down from heaven but is earthly, **u**,

UPPER CHAMBER, UPPER ROOM [6608, 333] (Heb. *ʿălîyâh*, *lofty*, Gr. *anōgeon*, *a room upstairs*, *hyperōon*, *upper*). A room frequently built on the roofs of houses and used in summer because it was cooler than the regular living quarters (Mk 14:15; Lk 22:12; Ac 1:13; 20:8). One of these was the scene of the Lord's Last Supper (Lk 22:12).

UPRIGHT

Dt	32:4	**u** and just is he.
Job	1:1	This man was blameless and **u**;
Ps	7:10	who saves the **u** in heart.
	11:7	**u** men will see his face.
	25:8	Good and **u** is the LORD;
	119:7	I will praise you with an **u** heart
Pr	2:7	He holds victory in store for the **u**,
	3:32	but takes the **u** into his confidence.
	14:2	whose walk is **u** fears the LORD,
	15:8	but the prayer of the **u** pleases him.
	21:29	an **u** man gives thought to his ways.
Isa	26:7	O **u** One, you make the way
Tit	1:8	who is self-controlled, **u**, holy
	2:12	**u** and godly lives in this present

UR OF THE CHALDEANS The early home of Abraham, mentioned in Ge 11:28, 31; 15:7; and in Ne 9:7. Through extensive archaeological excavations, it is now known that this city was located in southern Mesopotamia, about 140 miles (233 km.) SE of the site of old Babylon. The most extensive archaeological work was done by Sir Charles Leonard Woolley between AD 1922 and 1934.

Education was well developed at Ur, for a school was found there with its array of clay tablets. Students learned to read, write, and do varied forms of arithmetic. Further studies have revealed that commerce was well developed and that ships came into Ur from the Persian Gulf, bringing copper ore, ivory, gold, hardwoods, and diorite and alabaster used in statue making.

Much light has been shed on the worship and religious life of Abraham's day. Nanna was the moon god worshiped there. The temple, ziggurat, and other buildings used in connection with the worship of this pagan deity have been found. Evidences of worship in the homes of the day are revealed by idols found in private niches in the home walls.

From this city of idolatry God called Abraham and sent him with a promise to the land of Canaan.

URIAH, URIAS, URIJAH [249, 250, 4043] (ū-rī′a, ū-rī′ăs, ū-rī′ja, Heb. *'ûrîyâh, Jehovah is light*).

1. A Hittite, the husband of Bathsheba (2Sa 11:3). The fact that he had married a Hebrew wife, his Hebrew name, and his loyalty and devotion as a soldier (2Sa 11:11) all indicate that he probably was a worshiper of the Lord. After David had committed adultery with Bathsheba, he recalled Uriah from the battle and sent him to his house, trying in this way to hide his sin. When Uriah refused the comforts of home and wife when his men were on the battlefield, David sent him back to the war with special instructions for Joab to place him in the thick of the fight that he might die. When Uriah was killed, David took Bathsheba for his own wife.

2. A priest during the kingship of Ahaz. He was one of the "reliable witnesses" (Isa 8:2) taken by the king to record the matter concerning Maher-Shalal-Hash-Baz. It also seems highly probable that he was the one who carried out the king's command to build in the temple an Assyrian altar that was to be used for sacrifice (2Ki 16:10 – 16; KJV "Urijah").

3. A priest who aided Ezra in carrying on his ministry (Ne 8:4). He may be the Uriah referred to as the father of Meremoth (Ezr 8:33; Ne 3:4, 21, KJV "Urijah").

4. A prophet, the son of Shemaiah of Kiriath Jearim. He predicted the destruction of Judah (Jer 26:20). When the king, angry at his predictions, sought to put him to death, he fled to Egypt, but he was apprehended by the king and killed (Jer 26:21 – 23, KJV "Urijah").

URIM AND THUMMIM [H242] (ū′rĭm and thŭm′ĭm, Heb. *hā'ûrîm wehatûmmîm, lights and perfections*). Objects not specifically described, perhaps stones, placed in the breastplate of the high priest, which he wore when he went into the presence of the Lord and by which he ascertained the will of God in any important matter affecting the nation (Ex 28:30; Lev 8:8). It is uncertain what they were and what they looked like and how they were used. One theory is that they were used as the lot and cast like dice, the manner of their fall somehow revealing the Lord's will (1Sa 10:19 – 22; 14:37 – 42). Another theory is that they served as a symbol of the high priest's authority to seek counsel of the Lord, God's will being revealed to him through inner illumination.

They are first mentioned in Ex 28:30 with no explanation, showing that Israel was already familiar with them. They seemed to form a necessary part of the equipment of the high priest, for they were passed on from Aaron to Eleazer (Nu 20:28). The last reference to them in Scripture is in Ne 7:65.

USEFUL

Eph	4:28	doing something **u**
2Ti	2:21	**u** to the Master and prepared
	3:16	Scripture is God-breathed and is **u**
Phm	11	now he has become **u** both to you

USURY [5391, 5957, 5968] (Heb. *neshekh, interest; nāshakh, to bite, to lend on interest; nāshâh, to remove; nash', lead astray*; Gr. *tokos, interest on money*). God gave specific instructions to Israel with regard to interest on money loaned. Any money that a Jew loaned to his brother was to be without interest (Ex 22:25; Dt 23:19). Money could, however, be loaned to a stranger with interest (Dt 23:20). The main purpose for lending money among the Israelites was for the relief of the poor, for which, according to law, no interest was to be demanded (Lev 25:35 – 36). During Israel's time in Babylon, many abuses arose regarding the lending of money (Eze 18:8, 17). Because of this, Nehemiah, after the return from exile, took measures to have the practice stopped (Ne 5:10 – 12).

In the NT reasonable rates of interest received for money loaned are never condemned. It was a common practice in the days of our Lord and is referred to in the parable of the talents. The meaning of the English word *usury* has changed in recent centuries. While it once meant simply the charging of interest on money loaned, it has now come to mean excessive interest.

General References to:

Interest, not necessarily unreasonable exaction, but all income from loans. Forbidden (Ex 22:25; Lev 25:35 – 37; Dt 23:19; Ps 15:5; Pr 28:8; Jer 15:10; Eze 18:8, 13, 17; 22:12). Exaction of, rebuked (Ne 5:1 – 13). Authorized, of strangers (Dt 23:20). Exacted by the Jews (Eze 22:12). Just men innocent of the vice of requiring (Eze 18:8).

UZZIAH [6459, 6460, 3852] (ŭzī′a, Heb. *'uzzîyâh, the* LORD *is strength*).

1. Uzziah, also called Azariah, the son of Amaziah. At the age of sixteen he became Judah's tenth king (2Ki 14:21) and ruled fifty-two years. He came to the throne at a difficult time. His father, because of a military failure, had been killed (14:19). Uzziah was the people's choice as his successor (14:21). He undertook, very early in his career, an expedition against his father's enemies and won battles against the Edomites, Philistines, Arabians, and Meunites (2Ki 14:22; 2Ch 26:1 – 7). He strengthened his kingdom (26:2), and the report of his strength spread as far as Egypt (26:8). He made many improvements on his home front (26:9 – 10), and he possessed real ability at organization (26:11 – 15).

In spite of these successes, he strayed far from the Lord at the end of his life. Apparently as long as the prophet Zechariah lived, his influence was great on the king, and "as long as he sought the LORD, God gave him success" (2Ch 26:5). However, when he became strong, pride filled his heart, and one day he went into the temple, determined to burn incense to the Lord, a duty to be performed only by the priest. The chief priest, Azariah, with eighty priests went into the temple to reason with him, but he would not listen. Because of his self-will, God struck him with leprosy, which stayed with him until his death (26:16 – 21).

2. A Levite descended from Kohath (1Ch 6:24).

3. The father of a certain Jonathan in David's time (1Ch 27:25).

4. One of the sons of Harim who put away his foreign wife when admonished by Ezra the priest (Ezr 10:16 – 21).

5. The father of Athaiah who came to Jerusalem after the exile (Ne 11:4).

VAIN

Ps	33:17	A horse is a **v** hope for deliverance;
	73:13	in **v** have I kept my heart pure;
	127:1	its builders labor in **v**.
Isa	65:23	They will not toil in **v**
1Co	15:2	Otherwise, you have believed in **v**.
	15:58	labor in the Lord is not in **v**.
2Co	6:1	not to receive God's grace in **v**.
Gal	2:2	running or had run my race in **v**.

VALUABLE

| Lk | 12:24 | And how much more **v** you are |

VANITY [401, 448+2855, 2039, 4200+8198, 4202, 8198, 8736, 9214, 9332, 1632, 3029, 3031, 3472] (Heb. *hevel, 'āwen, shāw', Gr. kenos, mataiotēs*). Archaic word meaning "temporary" or "meaningless" that occurs almost one hundred times in the KJV, but never in the sense of conceit or undue self-esteem. The word *vanity* is not used in the NIV, but the Hebrew and Greek words are translated "emptiness," "worthlessness," "futility." These words designate things that are vain and useless, such as the fruitlessness of human endeavors, the worthlessness of idolatry, and the futility of wickedness. This thought appears most often (thirty-seven times) in the book of Ecclesiastes.

General References to:

Beauty is fleeting (Ps 39:11; Pr 31:30). Wealth acquired by lies (Pr 21:6). Consequence of the fall (Ro 8:20). Human life (Job 7:16; Ecc 6:12). Youth and vigor (Ecc 11:10). Thoughts (Ps 94:11). Help (Ps 60:11; La 4:17). Worldly wisdom (Ecc 2:15, 21; 1Co 3:20). Pleasure (Ecc 2:1 – 3, 10 – 11). Activity (Pss 39:6; 127:2). Achievement (Ecc 2:11; 4:4). Possessions (Ecc 2:4 – 11). Accumulating wealth (Ecc 2:26; 4:8). Love of wealth (Ecc 5:10; 6:2). Everything (Ecc 1:2). Foolish controversies (1Ti 1:6 – 7; 6:20; 2Ti 2:14, 16; Tit 3:9). Conduct of the ungodly (1Pe 1:18). Religion of hypocrites (Isa 1:13; Jas 1:26). Pagans (Mt 6:7). Faith without works (Jas 2:14). The wicked, especially characterized by (Job 11:11). Fools follow those given to (Pr 12:11); leading to poverty (Pr 28:19). Saints hate the thoughts of (Ps 119:113); pray to be kept from (Ps 119:37; Pr 30:8); avoid (Ps 24:4); avoid those given to (Ps 26:4).

VASHTI [2267] (vǎsh'tī Heb. *washtî, beautiful woman, from the Persian*). Xerxes' queen, whom he divorced because of her refusal to show herself to the king's guests at a feast. Her place was taken by Esther (Est 1:11).

VENGEANCE [1947, 5933, 5934, 5935] (Heb. *nāqam, to grudge*). Any punishment meted out in the sense of retribution. The word occurs in thirty-two OT verses (sixteen of them in Isa and Jer — e.g., Ge 4:15; Dt 32:35, 41, 43; Pss 94:1; 99:8; Jer 50:15, 28; 51:6, 11, 36). In the NT (KJV) the English word translates three Greek words: in two verses *dikē* is translated "vengeance," in both cases in the sense of punishment for wrong done (Ac 28:4; Jude 7); *ekdikēsis* is used in much the same sense (Lk 21:22; Ro 12:19; 2Th 1:8; Heb 10:30); and *orgē* is used of God punishing evil in human beings (Ro 3:5).

VIA DOLOROSA "The Sorrowful Way," the traditional route Jesus traveled on the day of his crucifixion from the judgment seat of Pilate (Mt 27:26, 31; Mk 15:20; Lk 22:25; Jn 19:16) to the place of his crucifixion on Mount Calvary (Mt 27:33; Mk 15:22; Lk 23:33; Jn 19:18). Nothing is surely known of the exact location of Pilate's judgment hall. Jerusalem was destroyed by the Romans under Titus (AD 70), and again at the rebellion of Bar Kokba (AD 135), when it was so thoroughly demolished that the very marks of the ancient streets were obliterated. By tradition the "fourteen stations of the cross" are marked in the modern city and also are denoted by pictures or images in many churches and private homes as helps to devotion. The stations are as follows: (1) Christ is condemned to die in Pilate's hall; (2) he receives the cross; (3) he falls under its weight; (4) he meets his mother; (5) Simon of Cyrene is forced to bear the cross (Mt 27:32; Mk 15:21; Lk 23:26); (6) his face is wiped by Veronica; (7) he falls again; (8) he meets the women of Jerusalem (Lk 23:28 – 31); (9) he falls a third time; (10) he is stripped of his garments (cf. Mt 27:35); (11) he is nailed to the cross (Mt 27:35; Mk 15:24; Lk 23:33; Jn 19:23); (12) he dies (Mt 27:50; Mk 15:37; Lk 23:46; Jn 19:30); (13) his body is taken down (Mt 27:59; Mk 15:46; Lk 23:53; Jn 19:40); (14) his body is laid in the tomb (Mt 27:60; Mk 15:46; Lk 23:53; Jn 19:41 – 42).

VICTORY

2Sa	8:6	gave David **v** wherever he
Ps	44:6	my sword does not bring me **v**;
	60:12	With God we will gain the **v**,
Pr	11:14	but many advisers make **v** sure.
1Co	15:54	"Death has been swallowed up in **v**
	15:57	He gives us the **v** through our Lord
1Jn	5:4	This is the **v** that has overcome

VIRGIN [408+3359+4202, 1435, 1436, 2351+3359 +5435, 6625, 4221].

The OT has two words that the English versions translate "virgin." The word *bethûlâh* is widely supposed to be the Hebrew technical word for an unmarried and therefore virgin girl, while *'almâh* is said to mean a young woman of marriageable age and, if the context requires, married. The evidence of the way the words are used in the OT is, however, as follows. Nine times *'almâh* is found — four singular (Ge 24:43; Ex 2:8; Pr 30:19; Isa 7:14) and five plural (1Ch 15:20; Pss 46 title, 68:25; SS 1:3; 6:8). In the title of Ps 46 and in 1Ch 15, the word occurs in a way no longer understood and can therefore tell us nothing of its meaning.

Proverbs 30:19 is best taken as a reference to the mystery of sexual attraction leading to courtship and marriage, in which case the *'almâh* is a virgin. In Ge 24:43 and Ex 2:8 the girl is unquestionably a virgin and so also in SS 6:8, where there is a contrast with queens and concubines, i.e., married women. The evidence so far, then, is that *'almâh* is a virgin, not a woman of some indefinite sexual state; and it may be worth mentioning here that outside of the Bible, as far as is presently known, the cognates of *'almâh* are never used of a married woman.

Turning now to *bethûlâh*, and leaving aside metaphorical uses (such as references to cities and tribes; e.g., Isa 37:22), there are fourteen occurrences that are noncommittal (e.g., Dt 32:25), grouping girls and young men simply as "young people," without any more implying that the young women are married or unmarried than that the young men are bachelors. There are twenty-one cases where the girls certainly are virgins (e.g., Ex 22:16; Jdg 19:24). All that this means is that *bethûlâh* can mean "virgin" where the context requires it; but there are three cases where it is especially important to know that the girl in question is a virgin, and in these the word *bethûlâh* apparently was not by itself sufficient but needed to be amplified by saying that she had never had sexual intercourse (Ge 24:16; Lev 21:3; Jdg 21:12). If *bethûlâh* were, as is so confidently claimed by many, a technical term for a virgin, why would the amplifying words ever be needed? By comparison, *'almâh* is never qualified or amplified.

Special importance attaches to Ge 24, which is the only passage in which the words occur so as to enable comparison. Concerned to find a bride for Isaac, Abraham's servant first prays about the "girl" who would turn out to be the right one. He uses the term *na'arah* (24:14). In v. 16 Rebekah arrives and, knowing only what his eyes tell him, she is described as female (*na'arah*) of marriageable age (*bethûlâh*) but unmarried (whom no man had known). If *bethûlâh* necessarily meant "unmarried," no definition would be needed. But in v. 43 the servant, recounting all that has happened, simply describes Rebekah as *'almâh*, i.e., using it as a summary word for all he now knows: female, marriageable, and unmarried.

This conclusion has great bearing on the NT use of *parthenos*, especially as it occurs in Mt 1:23, and on the virgin birth of the Lord Jesus Christ.

Dt	22:15	shall bring proof that she was a **v**
Isa	7:14	The **v** will be with child
Mt	1:23	"The **v** will be with child
Lk	1:34	I am a **v**?" The angel answered,
2Co	11: 2	that I might present you as a pure **v**

VIRGIN BIRTH The teaching that Mary, the mother of Jesus was a virgin both when she conceived and when she gave birth to Jesus, the child who was Immanuel ("God with us"). The source of this doctrine is threefold: (1) The account in Mt 1:18 – 25. Here we learn that before Mary and Joseph came together in marriage, "she was found to be with child through the Holy Spirit." Further, an angel of the Lord appeared to Joseph to tell him, "Do not be afraid to take Mary home as your wife, because what is conceived in her is from the Holy Spirit." (2) The account in Lk 1:26 – 38. Here we learn that the angel told Mary that she had found favor with God and that she would "be with child and give birth to a son." When she asked how this could be since she was a pure virgin, she was told, "The Holy Spirit will come upon you and the power of the Most High will overshadow you. So the holy one to be born will be called the Son of God." (3) The prophecy recorded in Isaiah: "Therefore the Lord himself will give you a sign: The virgin will be with child and will give birth to a son, and will call him Immanuel" (Isa 7:14; Mt 1:23).

Although the conception of Jesus was miraculous and unique, his growth within the womb of Mary and his birth were "normal." The writers of Matthew and Luke probably got their information from Joseph and Mary, and they recorded it with reverence and reticence. Within their accounts several theological motifs may be recognized. First, they record the facts in such a manner as to convey the idea that conception by a virgin was the appropriate way for the eternal Son to become a man, "bone of our bone, flesh of our flesh." Second, as the Holy Spirit had "hovered" over the old creation (Ge 1:2), so now the Holy Spirit is present to superintend the origin of a new creation, of which the incarnate Son will be the center.

Third, the virginal conception points to the unique relation of the incarnate Son to the human race he came to save: There is a basic continuity with us in that he shares our flesh and was born in the "normal" way. There is a basic discontinuity in that he was conceived in regard to his manhood in a unique way — as a new creation. So he is the same but different, and thus he is one of us but able to save us, and that is what his name "Jesus" means.

VIRTUE (Heb. *hayil, strength, ability*, often involving moral worth, Gr. *arete*, any excellence of a person or a thing, *dynamis, power, influence*). The phrase "a virtuous woman" found in the KJV (Ru 3:11; Pr 12:4; 31:10) is literally "a woman of worth" (so rendered once by the RSV, where the NIV has "a woman of noble character"). Sometimes the word is used in its Old English sense of "power" (thus the NIV of Mk 5:30; Lk 6:19; 8:46) and "strength" (2Co 12:9; Heb 11:11).

VISION [2600, 2606, 2607, 2608, 2612, 4690, 5260, 5261, 8011, 8015, 10255, 10256, 3965, 3969+3972, 3969, 3970] (Heb. *hāzôn, hizzāyôn, mar'âh*, Gr. *horama, optasia*). It is impossible to draw a sharp line of demarcation between dreams and visions. The Hebrew and Greek words all have to do with seeing. Visions in the Bible were for the most part given to individuals and were not apprehended by their companions. Through them God revealed to the seers truth in pictorial form. They came under various circumstances, in men's waking hours (Da 10:7; Ac 9:7), by day (Ac 10:3) or by night (Ge 46:2). In the OT both "writing" and "nonwriting" prophets were recipients of visions (Isa 1:1; Ob 1; Na 1:1; and 2Sa 7:17; 1Ki 22:17 – 19; 2Ch 9:29). With perhaps one exception (Nu 24:4), they were given only to holy men in the service of God, and those of a revelatory nature were always recognized as coming from God. In the NT Luke especially manifests great interest in visions (Lk 1:22; Ac 9:10; 10:3, 10ff.; 18:9). Biblical visions concerned both immediate situations (Ge 15:1 – 2; Ac 12:7) and more distant ones connected with the development of the kingdom of God, as may be seen in the writings of Isaiah,

Ezekiel, Hosea, Micah, Daniel, and John. In the OT false prophets feigned visions and were denounced by Jeremiah (14:14; 23:16) and Ezekiel (13:7).

VOICE

Dt	30:20	listen to his **v**, and hold fast to him.
1Sa	15:22	as in obeying the **v** of the LORD?
Ps	29:3	The **v** of the LORD is
	66:19	and heard my **v** in prayer.
	95:7	Today, if you hear his **v**,
Pr	8:1	Does not understanding raise her **v**
Isa	40:3	A **v** of one calling:
Mk	1:3	"a **v** of one calling in the desert,
Jn	5:28	are in their graves will hear his **v**
	10:3	and the sheep listen to his **v**.
Ro	10:18	"Their **v** has gone out
Heb	3:7	"Today, if you hear his **v**,
Rev	3:20	If anyone hears my **v** and opens

VOW [5623, 5624, 5883+6886, 7023+7198, 2376] (Heb. *nedher*, Gr. *euchē*). A voluntary promise to God to perform some service or do something pleasing to him in return for some hoped-for benefits (Ge 28:20 – 22; Lev 27:2, 8; Nu 30; Jdg 11:30); or to abstain from certain things (Nu 30:3). In the OT, vows were never regarded as a religious duty (Dt 23:22), but once they were made, they were considered sacred and binding (Dt 23:21 – 23; Jdg 11:35; Ps 66:13; Ecc 5:4). Fathers could veto vows made by their daughters, and husbands could veto their wives' vows; but if a husband did not veto a wife's vow and then caused her to break it, the blame was his, not hers (Nu 30). A vow had to be uttered to be binding (Dt 23:23). Almost anything — people, possessions, oneself — except what was already the Lord's or was an abomination to the Lord (23:18), could be vowed; and all these things could be redeemed with money, their value to be determined by a priest. Houses, lands, and unclean animals that were redeemed had to have a fifth of their value added to make up the redemption money. Jesus referred to vows only once, and that was to condemn the abuse of them

(Mt 15:4 – 6; Mk 7:10 – 13). Paul's vow in Ac 18:18 was probably a temporary Nazirite vow.

General References to:

A part of Israel's worship (Pss 22:25; 61:8; 65:1). Heard by God (Ps 61:5). Obligatory (Nu 30:2; Dt 23:21 – 23; Job 22:27; Pss 50:14; 56:12; 66:13 – 14; 76:11; Ecc 5:4 – 5; Na 1:15). In affliction (Ps 116:14 – 19).

Mosaic Laws Concerning:

Must be voluntary (Lev 22:18 – 25; 23:37 – 38; Nu 15:2 – 16; 29:39). Must be performed (Lev 5:4 – 13; Nu 30:2 – 16). See above, Obligatory. Estimation of the redemption price of things offered in vows, to be made by the priest, according to age and gender of the person making the offering (Lev 27:1 – 13). The redemptive price of the offering of real estate, to be valued by the priest (Lev 27:14 – 15); of a field (Lev 27:16 – 25). Of women (Nu 30:3 – 16). Of Nazirites (Nu 6:1 – 21). Unintentional (Lev 5:4 – 5). Offerings devoted under (Lev 5:6 – 13; 7:16 – 18; 27:1 – 25; Nu 15:2 – 16). Things offered in, must be perfect (Lev 22:18 – 25). Edible things offered in, to be eaten the same day they were offered (Lev 7:16 – 18). Things offered in, to be brought to the tabernacle or temple (Dt 12:6, 11, 17 – 18, 26); belonged to the priests (Nu 18:14). Things forbidden to pay a vow (Dt 23:18). Traditions that invalidate vows (Mk 7:11 – 13).

Rash Vows:

(Pr 20:25; Ecc 5:6). By Jephthah (Jdg 11:29 – 40); by Israelites (Jdg 20:7 – 11).

Instances of:

Of Jacob (Ge 28:20 – 22); of the mother of Micah, in the dedication of silver for the making of an idol (Jdg 17:2 – 3); of Hannah, to consecrate to the Lord the child for which she prayed (1Sa 1:11, w 1:27 – 28); of Elkanah (1Sa 1:21); of Absalom (2Sa 15:7 – 8); of Job, not to entertain thoughts of fornication (Job 31:1); of David (Ps 132:2); of Jephthah, and of the Israelites (see above, Rash Vows); of Ananias and Sapphira, in the dedica-

tion of the proceeds of the sale of their land (Ac 5:1 – 11); of the Jews, to kill Paul (Ac 23:12 – 15).

Nu	6:2	a **v** of separation to the LORD
	30:2	When a man makes a **v**
Jdg	11:30	Jephthah made a **v** to the LORD:

VOWS

Ps	116:14	I will fulfill my **v** to the LORD
Pr	20:25	and only later to consider his **v**.

WADI [5707, 5711] (wa'dĕ *ravine, valley*). A valley that forms the bed of a stream during the winter but dries up in the summer (Ge 26:19).

WAGES [924, 5382, 7189, 7190, 8509, 8510, 1324, 3635, 4072] (Heb. *hennām, maskōreth, pe'ullâh, sā-khar,* Gr. *misthos, opsōnion*). Pay given for labor, generally reckoned by the day, and distinguished from fees paid for professional service or salaries that may be paid by the month or the year. In civilizations where slavery was a regular institution, the servant or slave necessarily received his living, but not much more, except when the master was kind and loving and made the servant practically a member of the family. The earliest mention of wages is in the bargaining between Laban and his nephew Jacob (Ge 29). It is implicit in the narrative that he must also have received his living during those fourteen years; then he labored for another six years, receiving as his wages considerable herds and flocks (Ge 29 – 30). Pharaoh's daughter promised wages to the mother of Moses for acting as his nurse (Ex 2:5 – 9). In the Mosaic law a hired servant must be paid at the end of the day (Lev 19:13; Dt 24:14 – 15), thus implying a hand-to-mouth existence. The same sort of poverty is in the parable of the eleventh-hour laborers (Mt 20:1 – 16), but too much emphasis should not be put on the supposed value of the denarius (*see Money*), for whether "a penny" as in KJV or "a shilling" as in ASV, the fact remains that the laborer, and presumably his family, could live on it. Mercenary soldiers were advised by John the Baptist to be content with their pay (Lk 3:14). The idea of wages is spiritualized in the statement "The wages of sin is death" (Ro 6:23), where it is contrasted with another: "The gift of God is eternal life in Christ Jesus our Lord." Paul speaks of his gifts from churches at Philippi as "wages" (2Co 11:8 KJV; NIV "support"; cf. Php 4:15 – 18). He earned his living with his hands, and he teaches the right of the laborer to his wages (1Ti 5:18).

General References to:

Of Jacob (Ge 29:15 – 30; 30:28 – 34; 31:7, 41). Laborer entitled to (Dt 25:4; Mt 10:10; Lk 10:7; Ro 4:4). Must be just (Col 4:1). Must be paid promptly (Lev 19:13; Dt 24:15). Withholding of, denounced (Jer 22:13; Mal 3:5; Jas 5:4). Wasting of, denounced (Hag 1:6). Contentment with, commanded (Lk 3:14). Parable concerning (Mt 20:1 – 15). Figurative (Ro 6:23).

Mal	3:5	who defraud laborers of their **w**,
Lk	10:7	for the worker deserves his **w**.
Ro	4:4	his **w** are not credited to him
	6:23	For the **w** of sin is death,
1Ti	5:18	and "The worker deserves his **w**."

WAIL [1134, 3536, 3538, 5027, 5631, 7591, 3081] (Heb. *mispēdh, nehî,* Gr. *alalazō, pentheō*). In ancient funeral processions wailing relatives, often accompanied by hired female (sometimes male) mourners and musicians, preceded the body to the grave (Jer 9:17 – 18; Am 5:16; Mt 9:23).

WAIT

Ps	27:14	**W** for the LORD;
Isa	30:18	Blessed are all who **w** for him!
Ac	1:4	**w** for the gift my Father promised,
Ro	8:23	as we **w** eagerly for our adoption
1Th	1:10	and to **w** for his Son from heaven,
Tit	2:13	while we **w** for the blessed hope —

WAITING [741, 2565, 2675, 3498, 3782, 4538, 5893, 6218, 6641, 7595, 7747, 8432, 9068, 587, 1354, 1683, 1910, 2705, 4657, 4659].

Upon God:

As the God of providence (Jer 14:22); as the God of salvation (Ps 25:5); as the giver of all temporal blessings (Pss 104:27 – 28; 145:15 – 16). Is good (Ps 52:9). God calls us to (Zep 3:8). Exhortations and encouragements to (Pss 27:14; 37:7; Hos 12:6).

For: mercy (Ps 123:2); pardon (Ps 39:7 – 8); the consolation of Israel (Lk 2:25); salvation (Ge 49:18; Ps 62:1 – 2); guidance and teaching (Ps 25:5);

protection (Pss 33:20; 59:9 – 10); fulfillment of his word (Hab 2:3); fulfillment of his promises (Ac 1:4); hope of righteousness by faith (Gal 5:5); coming of Christ (1Co 1:7; 1Th 1:10).

Attitudes in: with the soul (Ps 62:1, 5); with earnest desire (Ps 130:6); with patience (Pss 37:7; 40:1); with resignation (La 3:26); with hope in his word (Ps 130:5); with full confidence (Mic 7:7); continually (Hos 12:6); all the day (Ps 25:5); specially in adversity (Ps 59:1 – 9; Isa 8:17); in the way of his judgments (Isa 26:8).

Those Who Wait upon God: wait upon him only (Ps 62:5); are heard (Ps 40:1); are blessed (Isa 30:18; Da 12:12); experience his goodness (La 3:24 – 26); shall not be ashamed (Ps 25:3; Isa 49:23); shall renew their strength (Isa 40:31); shall inherit the earth (Ps 37:9); shall be saved (Pr 20:22; Isa 25:9); shall rejoice in salvation (Isa 25:9); shall receive the glorious things prepared by God for them (Isa 64:4). Saints resolve on (Pss 52:9; 59:9). Saints have expectation from (Ps 62:5). Saints plead in prayer (Ps 25:21; Isa 33:2). The patience of saints often tried in (Ps 69:3). Predicted of the Gentiles (Isa 42:4; 60:9). Illustrated (Ps 123:2; Lk 12:36; Jas 5:7).

Exemplified:

Jacob (Ge 49:18); David (Ps 39:7); Isaiah (Isa 8:17); Micah (Mic 7:7); Joseph (Mk 15:43).

WALK

Lev	26:12	I will **w** among you and be your
Dt	6:7	and when you **w** along the road,
	10:12	to **w** in all his ways, to love him,
Jos	22:5	to **w** in all his ways,
Ps	1:1	who does not **w** in the counsel
	15:2	He whose **w** is blameless
	89:15	who **w** in the light of your presence
	119:45	I will **w** about in freedom,
Pr	4:12	When you **w**, your steps will not be
	6:22	When you **w**, they will guide you;
Isa	2:3	so that we may **w** in his paths."
	2:5	let us **w** in the light of the LORD.
	40:31	they will **w** and not be faint.
	57:2	Those who **w** uprightly

Jer	6:16	ask where the good way is, and **w**
Am	3:3	Do two **w** together
Mic	6:8	and to **w** humbly with your God.
Mk	2:9	'Get up, take your mat and **w**'?
Jn	8:12	Whoever follows me will never **w**
1Jn	1:6	with him yet **w** in the darkness,
	1:7	But if we **w** in the light,
2Jn	1:6	his command is that you **w** in love.

WALKING [886, 2006, 2143, 6015, 6296, 7575, 10207, 1451, 4135, 4344, 4513].

With God:

According to his commands (Dt 5:33; Ps 1; Jer 7:23); in his ways (Dt 28:9; Jos 22:5); in the old paths (Jer 6:16); as taught by him (1Ki 8:36; Isa 2:3; 30:21); uprightly (Pr 2:7); in his statutes and judgments (Eze 37:24); in newness of life (Ro 6:4); not after the flesh, but after the Spirit (Ro 8:1; Gal 5:16); honestly, as in the day (Ro 13:13); by faith, not by sight (2Co 5:7); in love, following Christ (Eph 5:2); worthy of the Lord (Col 1:10); in Christ (Col 2:6); by the gospel rule (Php 3:16); in the light, as God is (1Jn 1:7); in white clothing (Rev 3:4); in the light of heaven (Rev 21:24).

Instances of: *Enoch (Ge 5:24); Noah (Ge 6:9).*

WAR [1741, 2995, 4309, 4878, 7304, 7372, 7930, 8131, 8569, 9558, 4482, 4483, 5129] (Heb. *milhāmâh*, from *laham, to fight,* Gr. *polemos*). Every phase of Israel's life, including their warfare, was bound up with their God. War therefore had religious significance. It was customary for priests to accompany Israel's armies into battle (Dt 20:1 – 4). Campaigns were begun and engagements entered into with sacrificial rites (1Sa 7:8 – 10; 13:9) and after consulting the Lord (Jdg 20:18ff.; 1Sa 14:37; 23:2; 28:6; 30:8). Prophets were sometimes asked for guidance before a campaign (1Ki 22:5; 2Ki 3:11).

The blowing of a trumpet throughout the land announced the call to arms (Jdg 3:27; 1Sa 13:3; 2Sa 15:10), and priests sounded an alarm with trumpets (2Ch 13:12 – 16). Weapons included slings, spears, javelins, bows and arrows, swords, and battering rams. Strategical movements included the ambush (Jos 8:3ff.), the feint (Jdg 20:20ff.), the flank movement (2Sa 5:22ff.), the surprise attack (Jos 11:1 – 2), the raid (1Ch 14:9), the foray (2Sa 3:22), and foraging to secure supplies (23:11). Sometimes when opposing armies were drawn up in battle array, champions from each side fought one another (1Sa 17). Armies engaged in hand-to-hand combat. Victorious armies pillaged the camp of the enemy, robbed the dead (Jdg 8:24 – 26; 1Sa 31:9; 2Ch 20:25), and often killed or mutilated prisoners (Jos 8:23, 29; 10:22 – 27; Jdg 1:6), though prisoners were usually sold into slavery. Booty was divided equally between those who had taken part in the battle and those who had been left behind in camp (Nu 31:27; Jos 22:8; 1Sa 30:24 – 25), but some of the spoils were reserved for the Levites and for the Lord (Nu 31:28, 30).

When a city was besieged, the besiegers built up huge mounds of earth against the walls, and from these mounds battering rams were used against the walls (2Sa 20:15; Eze 4:2). The besieged tried to drive off the enemy by throwing darts and stones and shooting arrows at them from the walls. Captured cities were often completely destroyed, and victory was celebrated with song and dance (Ex 15:1 – 21; Jdg 5:1; 1Sa 18:6).

Some point out that Jesus accepted war as an inevitable part of the present sinful world order (Mt 24:6) but warned that those who take the sword will perish by it (26:52). In the NT letters the Christian is said to be a soldier (2Ti 2:3; 1Pe 2:11). The Apocalypse uses the figure of battle and war to describe the final triumph of Christ over Satan (Rev 16:14 – 16; 17:14; 19:14).

General References to:
Divine approval of (2Sa 22:35). Civil (Jdg 12:1 – 6; 20; 2Sa 2:12 – 31; 3:1; 20; 1Ki 14:30; 16:21; Isa 19:2); forbidden (2Ch 11:4); averted (Jos 22:11 – 34). Enemy harangued by general of opposing side (2Ki 18:19 – 36; 2Ch 13:4 – 12). Extermination (Nu 31:7 – 17; Dt 2:33 – 34; 3:6; 20:13 – 18; Jos 6:21, 24; 8:24 – 25; 10:2 – 40; 11:11 – 23; 1Sa

15:3 – 9; 27:8 – 11). Tumult of (Am 2:2). Slain in, neglected (Isa 14:19; 18:6). Evils of (2Sa 2:26; Pss 46:8; 79:1 – 3; 137:9; Isa 3:5, 25 – 26; 5:29 – 30; 6:11 – 12; 9:5, 19 – 21; 13:15 – 16; 15; 16:9 – 10; 18:6; 19:2 – 16; 32:13 – 14; 33:8 – 9; 34:7 – 15; Jer 4:19 – 31; 5:16 – 17; 6:24 – 26; 7:33 – 34; 8:16 – 17; 9:10 – 21; 10:20; 13:14; 14:18; 15:8 – 9; 19:7 – 9; 25:33; 46:3 – 12; 47:3; 48:28, 33; 51:30 – 58; La 1 – 5; Eze 33:27; 39:17 – 19; Hos 10:14; 13:16; Joel 2:2 – 10; Am 1:13; 6:9 – 10; 8:3; Na 2:10; 3:3, 10; Zec 14:2; Lk 21:20 – 26; Rev 19:17 – 18). To cease (Ps 46:9; Isa 2:4; Mic 4:3). Wars and rumors of (Mt 24:6; Mk 13:7; Lk 21:9).

God and War:
God in (Ex 14:13 – 14; Dt 1:30; 3:21 – 22; 7:17 – 24; 20:1, 4; 31:6 – 8, 23; 32:29 – 30; Jos 1:1, 5 – 7, 9; Jdg 1:2; 6:16; 7:9; 11:29; 1Sa 17:45 – 47; 19:5; 30:7 – 8; 2Sa 5:22 – 24; 22:18; 1Ki 20:28; Pss 18:34; 76:3; Jer 46:15; Am 5:8 – 9; Zec 10:5). God uses, as a judgment (Ex 23:24; Lev 26:17, 31 – 39; Dt 28:25 – 68; 32:30; Jdg 2:14; 2Ki 15:37; 1Ch 5:22, 26; 21:12; 2Ch 12:1 – 12; 15:6; 24:23 – 24; 33:11; 36; Job 19:29; Pss 44:9 – 16; 60:1 – 3; 105:25; Isa 5:1 – 8, 25 – 30; 9:8 – 12; 13:3 – 4, 9; 19:2; 34:2 – 6; 43:28; 45:7; Jer 12:7, 12; 46:15 – 17, 21; 47:6 – 7; 48:10; 49:5; 50:25; Eze 23:22 – 25; Am 3:6; 4:11; Zep 1:7 – 18; Zec 8:10; 14:2). Repugnant to God (1Ch 22:8 – 9; Pss 68:30; 120:6 – 7; Rev 13:10). God sends panic in (Ex 15:14 – 16); threatens defeat in (Dt 32:25; 1Sa 2:10; 2Ch 18:12 – 16; Isa 30:15 – 17; Eze 15:6 – 8; 21:9 – 17); inflicts defeat in (Jos 7:12 – 13; 2Ch 12:5 – 8; 24:23 – 24; Ps 48:4 – 7; Pr 11:14; 20:18). Wisdom required in (Pr 21:22; 24:6; Ecc 9:14 – 18; Lk 14:31 – 32). See Armies; Armor; Army; Watchman.

Spiritual Warfare:
Is not after the flesh (2Co 10:3); is a good warfare (1Ti 1:18 – 19). Called the good fight of faith (1Ti 6:12). Is against the devil (Ge 3:15; 2Co 2:11; Eph 6:12; Jas 4:7; 1Pe 5:8; Rev 12:17); the flesh (Ro 7:23; 1Co 9:25 – 27; 2Co 12:7; Gal 5:17; 1Pe

2:11); enemies (Pss 38:19; 56:2; 59:3); the world (Jn 16:33; 1Jn 5:4 – 5); death (1Co 15:26, w Heb 2:14 – 15). Often arises from the opposition of friends or relatives (Mic 7:6; Mt 10:35 – 36). To be carried on under Christ, as our Captain (Heb 2:10); under the Lord's banner (Ps 60:4); with faith (1Ti 1:18 – 19); with a good conscience (1Ti 1:18 – 19); with steadfastness in the faith (1Co 16:13; 1Pe 5:9, w Heb 10:23); with earnestness (Jude 3); with watchfulness (1Co 16:13; 1Pe 5:8); with sobriety (1Th 5:6; 1Pe 5:8); with endurance of hardship (2Ti 2:3, 10); with self-denial (1Co 9:25 – 27); with confidence in God (Ps 27:1 – 3); with prayer (Ps 35:1 – 3; Eph 6:18); without earthly entanglements (2Ti 2:4). Mere professors do not maintain (Jer 9:3). Saints are all engaged in (Php 1:30); must stand firm in (Eph 6:13 – 14); exhorted to diligence in (1Ti 6:12; Jude 3). Encouraged in (Isa 41:11 – 12; 51:12; Mic 7:8; 1Jn 4:4); helped by God in (Ps 118:13; Isa 41:13 – 14); protected by God in (Ps 140:7); comforted by God in (2Co 7:5 – 6); strengthened by God in (Pss 20:2; 27:14; Isa 41:10); strengthened by Christ in (2Co 12:9; 2Ti 4:17); delivered by Christ in (2Ti 4:18); thank God for victory in (Ro 7:25; 1Co 15:57).
Armor for: Belt of truth (Eph 6:14); breastplate of righteousness (Eph 6:14); readiness from the gospel (Eph 6:15); shield of faith (Eph 6:16); helmet of salvation (Eph 6:17; 1Th 5:8); sword of the Spirit (Eph 6:17). Called armor of God (Eph 6:11); weapons of righteousness (2Co 6:7); armor of light (Ro 13:12); not weapons of the world (2Co 10:4). Mighty through God (2Co 10:4 – 5); the whole is required (Eph 6:13); must be put on (Ro 13:12; Eph 6:11); to be on the right hand and the left (2Co 6:7).
Victory in: from God (1Co 15:57; 2Co 2:14); through Christ (Ro 7:25; 1Co 15:57; 2Co 12:9; Rev 12:11); by faith (Heb 11:33 – 37; 1Jn 5:4 – 5); over the devil (Ro 16:20; 1Jn 2:14); over the flesh (Ro 7:24 – 25; Gal 5:24); over the world (1Jn 5:4 – 5); over all that exalts itself (2Co 10:5); over death and the grave (Isa 25:8; 26:19; Hos 13:14; 1Co

15:54 – 55); triumphant (Ro 8:37; 2Co 10:5). They who overcome in, shall: eat of the hidden manna (Rev 2:17); eat of the Tree of Life (Rev 2:7); be clothed in white garments (Rev 3:5); be pillars in the temple of God (Rev 3:12); sit with Christ on his throne (Rev 3:21); have a white stone and on it a new name written (Rev 2:17); have power over the nations (Rev 2:26); have the name of God written on them by Christ (Rev 3:12); inherit all things (Rev 21:7); be confessed by Christ before God the Father (Rev 3:5); not be hurt by the second death (Rev 2:11); not have their names blotted out of the Book of Life (Rev 3:5).

WASH

Ps	51:7	**w** me, and I will be whiter
Jer	4:14	**w** the evil from your heart
Jn	13:5	and began to **w** his disciples' feet,
Ac	22:16	be baptized and **w** your sins away,
Jas	4:8	**W** your hands, you sinners,
Rev	22:14	Blessed are those who **w** their robes

WASHING (Heb. *rāhats*, *kāvas*, Gr. *niptō*, *louō*, *loutron*). Frequent bathing was necessary in the warm climate of the East. In Egypt, Syria, and Palestine people washed the dust from their feet when they entered a house (Ge 18:4; Jn 13:10). Ceremonial defilement was removed by bathing the body and washing the clothing (Lev 14:8; Nu 19:7 – 8). The priests washed their hands and feet before entering the sanctuary or offering a sacrifice (Ex 30:19 – 21). In the time of Christ, the Jews did much ceremonial washing of hands before eating (Mk 7:3 – 4) and used public baths as the Greeks and Romans did.

Eph	5:26	cleansing her by the **w** with water
1Ti	5:10	showing hospitality, **w** the feet
Tit	3:5	us through the **w** of rebirth

WATCH

Ge	31:49	"May the LORD keep **w**
Ps	90:4	or like a **w** in the night.
	141:3	keep **w** over the door of my lips.
Pr	4:6	love her, and she will **w** over you.

	6:22	when you sleep, they will **w**
Jer	31:10	will **w** over his flock like a shepherd
Mic	7:7	I **w** in hope for the LORD,
Mt	24:42	"Therefore keep **w**, because you do
	26:41	**W** and pray so that you will not fall
Mk	13:35	"Therefore keep **w** because you do
Lk	2:8	keeping **w** over their flocks at night
1Ti	4:16	**W** your life and doctrine closely.
Heb	13:17	They keep **w** over you

WATCHES OF THE NIGHT The divisions into which the twelve hours of the night were divided. The Jews had a threefold division (Jdg 7:19), while the Romans had four watches (Mk 6:48).

WATCHMAN [5915, 7595, 9068, 2601]. A sentinel.

On the walls of cities (SS 3:3; 5:7); of Jerusalem (2Sa 13:34; 18:24 – 25; Ne 4:9; 7:3; Isa 52:8; 62:6); of Babylon (Jer 51:12). On towers (2Ki 9:17; 2Ch 20:24; Isa 21:5 – 12; Jer 31:6). At the gates of the temple (2Ki 11:6 – 7). Alarm of, given by trumpets (Eze 33:3 – 6). Unfaithfulness in the discharge of duty of, punished by death (Eze 33:6; Mt 28:14; Ac 12:19).

WATER (Heb. *mayim*, Gr. *hydōr*). Because of its scarcity in Palestine, water is much appreciated there. For its people, absence of water was very serious (1Ki 17:1ff.; Jer 14:3; Joel 1:20), and rain was a sign of God's favor. The rivers of Palestine are mostly small and have little if any water in summer. Consequently, in Bible times the country depended on rain as its source of water. This supplied springs and fountains. Cisterns were a necessity for the storing of water, but if water was stored too long, it became brackish and filthy and a menace to health. In the summer there was no rain, so vegetation was dependent on the heavy dews. Irrigation was carried on where there was sufficient water. When water was scarce, as during a time of siege, it had to be rationed. Drinking water, carried in goatskins, was often sold in the streets. Wells and pools, although comparatively scarce, are often mentioned in the Bible (Ge 21:19; 24:11; Jn 4:6; 9:7). Water was used not only for refreshment, but for ceremonial washings before meals and in the Jewish temple ceremony (Lev 11:32; 16:4; Nu 19:7). The Bible uses it as a symbol of the cleansing of the soul from sin (Eze 16:4, 9; 36:25; Jn 3:5; Eph 5:26; Heb 10:22; 1Jn 5:6, 8).

Ex	7:20	all the **w** was changed into blood.
	17:1	but there was no **w** for the people
Nu	20:2	there was no **w** for the community,
Ps	1:3	like a tree planted by streams of **w**,
	42:1	As the deer pants for streams of **w**,
Pr	25:21	if he is thirsty, give him **w** to drink.
Isa	12:3	With joy you will draw **w**
	32:2	like streams of **w** in the desert
	49:10	and lead them beside springs of **w**.
Jer	2:13	broken cisterns that cannot hold **w**.
	31:9	I will lead them beside streams of **w**
Zec	14:8	On that day living **w** will flow out
Mt	14:29	walked on the **w** and came toward Jesus.
Mk	9:41	anyone who gives you a cup of **w**
Jn	3:5	unless he is born of **w** and the Spirit.
	4:10	he would have given you living **w**."
	7:38	streams of living **w** will flow
Eph	5:26	washing with **w** through the word,
Heb	10:22	our bodies washed with pure **w**.
1Pe	3:21	this **w** symbolizes baptism that now
2Pe	2:17	These men are springs without **w**
1Jn	5:6	This is the one who came by **w**
	5:6	come by **w** only, but by **w**
	5:8	the Spirit, the **w** and the blood;
Rev	7:17	to springs of living **w**.
	21:6	cost from the spring of the **w** of life.

WATER OF BITTERNESS Water mingled with dust which a woman suspected of unfaithfulness was expected to drink to prove her innocence (Nu 5:12 – 31).

WAY There are about twenty-five Hebrew and Greek words translated "way" in the Bible. It is often used metaphorically to describe the conduct or manner of life, whether of God or of man (Dt 5:33; Ps 1:6; Pr 16:17). In the NT God's plan of salvation is called "the way of the Lord" (Mt 3:3). The term is also used to mean Christianity or Judaism (Ac 9:2; 19:9; 22:4).

Ex	13:21	of cloud to guide them on their **w**
	18:20	and show them the **w** to live
Dt	1:33	to show you the **w** you should go.
2Sa	22:31	"As for God, his **w** is perfect;
1Ki	8:23	wholeheartedly in your **w**.
	8:36	Teach them the right **w** to live,
Ps	1:1	or stand in the **w** of sinners
	32:8	teach you in the **w** you should go;
	37:5	Commit your **w** to the Lord;
	86:11	Teach me your **w**, O Lord,
	119:9	can a young man keep his **w** pure?
	139:24	See if there is any offensive **w** in me
Pr	4:11	I guide you in the **w** of wisdom
	12:15	The **w** of a fool seems right to him,
	14:12	There is a **w** that seems right
	22:6	Train a child in the **w** he should go,
Isa	35:8	it will be called the **W** of Holiness.
	53:6	each of us has turned to his own **w**;
	55:7	Let the wicked forsake his **w**
Mal	3:1	who will prepare the **w** before me.
Mt	3:3	'Prepare the **w** for the Lord,
Lk	7:27	who will prepare your **w** before you
Jn	14:6	"I am the **w** and the truth
Ac	1:11	in the same **w** you have seen him go
	9:2	any there who belonged to the **W**,
	24:14	of the **W**, which they call a sect.
1Co	10:13	also provide a **w** out so that you can
	12:31	will show you the most excellent **w**.
	14:1	Follow the **w** of love and eagerly
Col	1:10	and may please him in every **w**:
Heb	4:15	who has been tempted in every **w**,
	9:8	was showing by this that the **w**
	10:20	and living **w** opened for us
	13:18	desire to live honorably in every **w**.

WEAK

Ps	41:1	is he who has regard for the **w**;
	72:13	He will take pity on the **w**
	82:3	Defend the cause of the **w**

Mt	26:41	spirit is willing, but the body is **w**."
Ac	20:35	of hard work we must help the **w**,
Ro	14:1	Accept him whose faith is **w**,
	15:1	to bear with the failings of the **w**
1Co	1:27	God chose the **w** things
	8:9	become a stumbling block to the **w**.
	9:22	To the **w** I became **w**, to win the **w**.
	11:30	That is why many among you are **w**
2Co	12:10	For when I am **w**, then I am strong.
1Th	5:14	help the **w**, be patient
Heb	12:12	your feeble arms and **w** knees.

WEALTH [226, 1524, 1540, 2104, 2162, 2657, 3856, 3860, 3877, 3883, 3946, 6938, 6947, 6948, 8214, 3228, 3440, 4355, 4454, 4456, 4458] (Heb. *hôn, hayil, nekhāsîm*, Gr. *euporia*). Abundance of possessions whether material, social, or spiritual. In the nomadic civilization of the early Hebrews, wealth consisted largely of flocks and herds, silver and gold, brass, iron, and clothing (Jos 22:8). In the days of Job, his sons had houses, but their wealth consisted largely of camels, donkeys, flocks, and herds, and "a large number of servants" (Job 1:3). Wealth can come from sinful endeavors (Ac 19:25). From the beginning of Israel, God taught his people that he was the giver of their wealth (Dt 8:18): "For it is he who gives you the ability to produce wealth." He taught them to be liberal: "One man gives freely, yet gains even more; another withholds unduly, but comes to poverty" (Pr 11:24). NT teaching goes even further: "Nobody should seek his own good, but the good of others" (1Co 10:24). Some OT passages give the impression that wealth always went with godliness (Ps 112:3) and that poverty was for the wicked (Pr 13:18), but this outlook can be debated.

Dt	8:18	gives you the ability to produce **w**,
Pr	3:9	Honor the Lord with your **w**,
	10:4	but diligent hands bring **w**.
	11:4	**W** is worthless in the day of wrath,
	13:7	to be poor, yet has great **w**.
Ecc	5:10	whoever loves **w** is never satisfied
	5:13	**w** hoarded to the harm of its owner,
Mt	13:22	and the deceitfulness of **w** choke it,

Mk	10:22	away sad, because he had great **w**.
	12:44	They all gave out of their **w**; but she
Lk	15:13	and there squandered his **w**
1Ti	6:17	nor to put their hope in **w**,
Jas	5:2	Your **w** has rotted, and moths have
	5:3	You have hoarded **w**

WEARY

Isa	40:28	He will not grow tired or **w**,
	40:31	they will run and not grow **w**,
	50:4	know the word that sustains the **w**.
Mt	11:28	all you who are **w** and burdened,
Gal	6:9	Let us not become **w** in doing good,
Heb	12:3	so that you will not grow **w**
Rev	2:3	my name, and have not grown **w**.

WEDDING [2146, 3164, 3353, 8005, 8287, 8933, 1141] (Gr. *gamos*). An event regarded in Scripture as the ceremony by which a man and a woman were joined together as husband and wife and legally entitled to form a separate family unit. The betrothal was a significant, binding, legal commitment for the forthcoming marriage (Dt 20:7), a commitment that could be broken only by death or divorce. At the time of the betrothal, gifts of jewelry (which were often made of gold set with semiprecious stones) would be presented to the girl and sometimes to her mother, and, depending on the society, the bride price, dowry, or contract would also be exchanged. After the invention of coinage, it became increasingly common for gold coins to form part of the betrothal gifts. During the period of the betrothal, which normally lasted for one year, the girl was already deemed to belong to her future husband, and the punishment for any man who violated her sexually was death by stoning.

WEEKS, FEAST OF [8651]. Pentecost, celebrated fifty days after the sheaf waving on the sixteenth of Nisan (Ex 34:18 – 26).

WHITE

| Isa | 1:18 | they shall be as **w** as snow; |

Da	7:9	His clothing was as **w** as snow;
Mt	28:3	and his clothes were **w** as snow.
Rev	1:14	hair were **w** like wool, as **w** as snow,
	3:4	dressed in **w**, for they are worthy.
	6:2	and there before me was a **w** horse!
	7:13	"These in **w** robes — who are they,
	19:11	and there before me was a **w** horse,
	20:11	Then I saw a great **w** throne

WHITEWASH [3212, 3225, 9521, 3154]. Used to "repair" a flimsy wall (Eze 13:10 – 16). Whitewashed tomb or wall, a picture of hypocrisy (Mt 23:27 – 28; Ac 23:3).

WHOLE

Ge	11:1	Now the **w** world had one language
Ex	19:5	Although the **w** earth is mine,
Lev	16:17	and the **w** community of Israel.
Nu	14:21	of the LORD fills the **w** earth,
	32:13	until the **w** generation
1Sa	1:28	For his **w** life he will be given
2Ki	21:8	and will keep the **w** Law that my
Ps	72:19	may the **w** earth be filled
Pr	4:22	and health to a man's **w** body.
	8:31	rejoicing in his **w** world
Ecc	12:13	for this is the **w** duty of man.
Isa	6:3	the **w** earth is full of his glory."
	14:26	plan determined for the **w** world;
Eze	37:11	these bones are the **w** house
Zep	1:18	the **w** world will be consumed,
Zec	14:9	will be king over the **w** earth.
Mal	3:10	the **w** tithe into the storehouse,
Mt	5:29	than for your **w** body to be thrown
	6:22	your **w** body will be full of light.
	16:26	for a man if he gains the **w** world,
	24:14	will be preached in the **w** world
Lk	21:35	live on the face of the **w** earth.
Jn	12:19	Look how the **w** world has gone
	13:10	to wash his feet; his **w** body is clean
	21:25	the **w** world would not have room
Ac	20:27	proclaim to you the **w** will of God.
Ro	1:9	whom I serve with my **w** heart

	8:22	know that the **w** creation has been
1Co	12:17	If the **w** body were an ear,
Gal	5:3	obligated to obey the **w** law.
Eph	4:10	in order to fill the **w** universe.)
	4:13	attaining to the **w** measure
1Th	5:23	May your **w** spirit, soul
Jas	2:10	For whoever keeps the **w** law
1Jn	2:2	but also for the sins of the **w** world.
Rev	3:10	going to come upon the **w** world

WHOLEHEARTED

2Ki	20:3	you faithfully and with **w** devotion
1Ch	28:9	and serve him with **w** devotion
Isa	38:3	you faithfully and with **w** devotion

WICKED, WICKEDNESS [1175, 2365, 4659, 6405, 6406, 6411, 8273, 8278, 8288, 8317, 8399, 8400, 8401, 8402, 94, 96, 490, 2805, 4505] (Heb. *ra, rasha,* Gr. *ponēros, ponēria*). The KJV often uses these words, but later translations prefer "evil," especially in the NT. The idea is that of a person or thing that is bad, worthless, depraved, and corrupt, and especially of a person or thing that opposes God, his will, his Messiah, and his gospel. It can describe a whole people or an individual or the state in which they are (as seen by God).

General References to:

God is angry with (Pss 5:5 – 6; 7:11; Ro 9:13; 1Co 10:5). Spirit of God withdrawn from (Ge 6:3; Hos 4:17 – 19; Ro 1:24, 26, 28). Hate the righteous (Mt 5:11 – 12; Lk 6:22 – 23). Worship of, offensive to God (Ps 50:16 – 17; Isa 1:10 – 15). God's mercy to (Job 33:14 – 30); love for (Dt 5:29; 32:29; Mt 18:11 – 14; Jn 3:16 – 17; Ro 5:8; 1Jn 3:16; 4:9 – 10). Gospel invitation to, illustrated by the parables of the householder (Mt 20:1 – 16), and marriage supper (Mt 22:1 – 14). Prosperity of (Job 5:3 – 5; 12:6; 15:21 – 23, 27, 29; 20:5, 22; 21:7 – 13; Pss 37:1, 35 – 36; 49:10 – 15; 73:3 – 22; 92:6 – 7; Ecc 8:12 – 13; Jer 12:1 – 2; Hab 1:3 – 4, 13 – 17; Mal 3:15). Hate reproof (1Ki 22:8; 2Ch 18:7). Dread God (Job 18:11). Temporal pun-ishment of (Job 15:20 – 35; 18:5 – 21; 20:5 – 29; 21:7 – 33; 24:2 – 24; 27:13 – 23; Jer 5:25; Eze 11:10; 12:19 – 20; Zec 14:17 – 19). False hope to (Job 8:13 – 18). Warned (Jer 7:13 – 15, 23 – 25; 25:4 – 6; 26:2 – 7, 12 – 13; 29:17 – 19; Eze 33:8; Da 4:4 – 27; 5:4 – 29; Zep 2:1 – 2; Lk 3:7 – 9; 1Co 10:11; Jude 4 – 7; Rev 3:1 – 3, 16 – 19). Terrors of, at the judgment (Rev 1:7). Death of (Pss 49:14; 73:4).

Compared with:

Ashes under the feet (Mal 4:3); bad fish (Mt 13:48); bad trees (Lk 6:43); beasts (Ps 49:12; 2Pe 2:12); the blind (Zep 1:17; Mt 15:14); bronze and iron (Jer 6:28; Eze 22:18); briers and thorns (Isa 55:13; Eze 2:6); bulls of Bashan (Ps 22:12); burning thorns (Ps 118:12); bushes in the waste-lands (Jer 17:6); chaff (Job 21:18; Ps 1:4; Mt 3:12); clouds without rain (Jude 12); corpses trampled underfoot (Isa 14:19); deaf cobras (Ps 58:4); dogs (Pr 26:11; Mt 7:6; 2Pe 2:22); dross (Ps 119:119; Eze 22:18 – 19); early dew that passes away (Hos 13:3); earthenware coated with glaze (Pr 26:23); fading leaves (Isa 1:30); fiery furnace (Ps 21:9; Hos 7:4); fools building on sand (Mt 7:26); fuel for the fire (Isa 9:19); garden without water (Isa 1:30); goats (Mt 25:32); grass that withers (2Ki 19:26; Pss 37:2; 92:7); green plants that die away (Ps 37:2); horses charging into battle (Jer 8:6); idols (Ps 115:8); lions hungry for prey (Ps 17:12); melting wax (Ps 68:2); morning mist (Hos 13:3); moth-eaten garments (Isa 50:9; 51:8); pigs (Mt 7:6); poor figs (Jer 24:8); rejected branches (Isa 14:19); rejected silver (Jer 6:30); rocky places (Mt 13:5); scorpions (Eze 2:6); serpents (Ps 58:4; Mt 23:33); smoke through a window (Hos 13:3); sows (2Pe 2:22); springs without water (2Pe 2:17); storms sweeping by (Pr 10:25); straw before the wind (Job 21:18); stubble (Mal 4:1); tossing sea (Isa 57:20); tumbleweeds (Ps 83:13); visions of the night (Job 20:8); wandering stars (Jude 13); wayward children (Mt 11:16); weeds (Mt 13:38); whitewashed tombs (Mt 23:27); wild donkey's colts (Job 11:12); wild waves of the sea (Jude 13). See Reprobate; Seekers; Sin, Confession of.

Contrasted with the Righteous:

(Pss 1:1–6; 11:5; 17:14–15; 32:10; 37:17–22, 37–38; 73:1–28; 75:10; 91:7–8; 107:33–38; 125:5; Pr 2:21–22; 3:32–33; 4:16–19; 10:3, 6, 9, 11, 16, 20–21, 23–25, 28–32; 11:3, 5–6, 8–11, 18–21, 23, 31; 12:2–3, 5–7, 10, 12–13, 21, 26; 13:5–6, 9, 17, 21–22, 25; 14:2, 11, 19, 22, 32; 15:6, 8–9, 28–29; 21:15, 18, 26, 29; 22:5, 8–9; 24:16; 28:1, 4–5, 13–14, 18; 29:2, 6–7, 27; Isa 32:1–8; 65:13–14; Mal 3:18; Ro 2:7–10; Eph 2:12–14; Php 2:15; 1Th 5:5–8; Tit 1:15; 1Pe 4:17–18; 1Jn 1:6–7; 3:3–17). Present and future state of the wicked and righteous contrasted (Job 8; Ps 49). See below.

Described as:

(Job 8:13–17; 15:16, 20–35; Pss 10:4–11; 36:1–4; 73:4–12; Isa 59:2–8; Jer 2:22–25); abomination (Pr 13:9; 15:9; Hos 9:10); alienated (Col 1:21); beasts (Ps 49:20); dogs (Ps 59:6; 2Pe 2:22; Rev 22:15); horse rushing into battle (Jer 8:6); blind (Eze 12:2); carnal (Ro 8:5, 7–8; 9:8); children of the devil (Jn 8:44; Ac 13:10; 1Jn 3:10); perverse (Jer 9:6; Ro 1:21; 2:4–5; Php 2:15); despising God (Job 21:14; Ro 11:28); contentious (Ro 2:8); corrupt (Pss 53:1; 73:8; Isa 59:3; Jer 2:22; Eze 16:47; 20:16; Mic 7:2–4; Tit 1:15); loving darkness (Jn 3:19–20); dead in sin (Eph 2:1–3; 1Jn 3:14); delighting in lies (Ps 62:4), delighting in perversity (Pr 2:13–19); defiled (Tit 1:15–16); depraved (Isa 1:4–6; Jer 17:9; 30:12–15; Ro 1:20–32; 3:10–18; 1Ti 1:9–10; 2Ti 3:2–9, 13; Tit 3:2; 2Pe 2:10, 12–19; Jude 12–13); destitute of faithfulness (Ps 5:9); destitute of the love of God (Jn 5:42); devilish (1Jn 3:8); devisers of evil (Pss 52:1–4; 64:3–6; Pr 4:16; 6:12–15; 10:23; Isa 32:6–7; Jer 4:22); enemies (Ro 5:10; Col 1:21); filthy (Ezr 9:11); full of bitterness (Ac 8:23); uncircumcised (Isa 52:1; Jer 6:10; Eze 28:10; 31:18; 32:19–32); uncircumcised of heart (Lev 26:41; Eze 44:7; Ac 7:51), uncircumcised of lips (Ex 6:12); disobedient (Jer 11:8; Tit 1:16); alienated from God (Col 1:21); full of bitterness and venom (Dt 32:32–33; Ps 58:3–5); grievous sinners (Ge 13:13; 18:20; Job 22:5; Isa

1:4–6); being in moral darkness (Mt 4:16; 6:23; Lk 1:79; Eph 4:17–18); not knowing the way of the Lord (Jer 5:4); lewd (Jer 11:15); lost (Lk 19:10); loving wickedness (Ps 7:14; Jer 14:10; Hos 4:8; Mic 3:2); malicious toward the righteous (Pss 37:12; 94:3–8; 140:9); mocking sin (Pr 14:9); obdurate (Ps 10:4, 11; Pr 1:29–30; Isa 26:10–11; Eze 3:7); outsiders (Mk 4:11); past feeling (Eph 4:19); progressing in wickedness (Isa 30:1, 10–11; Jer 9:3; 2Ti 3:13); rebellious (Dt 9:24); sensual (Php 3:19; Jude 19); servants of sin (Jn 8:34); shameful (Eph 5:11–12); shameless (Jer 6:15; 8:12; Zep 3:5); unscrupulous (Job 24:2–24; Ps 10:4–10; Isa 5:18–23; Jer 5:26–28; 9:2–6); sold to work iniquity (1Ki 21:20); stiff-necked (Dt 9:13; Ac 7:51); under condemnation (Jn 3:18–19); unclean (Ezr 9:11; Job 14:4; Hag 2:14); ungodly (Ro 5:6); without strength (Ro 5:6); vomit (Lev 18:25); wretched, miserable, poor, blind, naked (Rev 3:17–18); hating: correction (Pr 15:10; Am 5:10), instruction (Ps 50:17; Pr 1:29–30), the light (Jn 3:20).

Happiness of:

Sensual (Isa 22:13; 56:12). Limited to this life (Lk 16:25). Ends suddenly (Job 21:12–13; Lk 12:19–20).

Prayers of:

Abominable to God (Pr 15:8, 29; 21:27; 28:9). Not answered (Dt 1:45; 1Sa 28:6; 2Sa 22:42; Job 27:9; 35:12–13; Pss 18:41; 66:18; Pr 1:24–28; 21:13, 27; Isa 1:15; 59:2; Jer 11:11; 14:12; 18:17; La 3:8, 44; Eze 8:18; 20:3, 31; Hos 5:6; Mic 3:4; Zec 7:13; Mal 1:9; 2:11–13; Jn 9:31; Jas 1:6–7; 4:3; 1Pe 3:7). On behalf of, not answered (Dt 3:26; Jer 15:11).

Prosperity of:

(Job 12:6; 21:7–13; Ps 73:3–12; Jer 12:1–2; Mal 3:15). Brief (Job 5:3–5; 15:21, 23, 27, 29; 20:5, 22–23; 21:17–18; 24:24; Pss 37:35–36; 49:10–14; 73:18–19; 92:7; Ecc 8:12–13).

Punishment of:

(Ge 4:7; Ex 20:5; 34:7; Nu 32:23; 1Sa 3:11–14; 2Sa 3:39; 7:14; 22:27–28; 23:6–7; 1Ki 21:20–21;

Job 8:20, 22; 11:20; 18:5 – 21; 19:29; 21:7 – 33; 27:13 – 23; 36:12, 17; Pss 3:7; 5:5; 18:14, 26 – 27; 36:12; 37:1 – 2, 9 – 10, 17, 20, 22, 34 – 38; 64:7 – 8; 73:18 – 20, 27; 91:8; 97:3; 107:17, 33 – 34; 119:21, 118 – 119, 155; 129:4; 146:9; 147:6; Pr 3:33; 10:3, 6 – 8, 14, 24 – 25, 27 – 31; 11:3, 5 – 8, 19, 21, 23, 31; 13:2, 5 – 6, 9, 21, 25; 14:12, 19, 32; 16:4 – 5; 22:5, 23; Ecc 8:12 – 13; Isa 3:11; 26:21; Jer 21:14; 36:31; La 3:39; Eze 3:18 – 20; 18:1 – 32; 33:7 – 20; Hos 14:9; Am 3:2; Mic 2:3; 6:13; Mt 15:13; Ro 1:18; 2:5, 8 – 9; Col 3:25; 1Th 1:10; 1Pe 3:12; 2Pe 2:3 – 9, 12 – 17; Jude 5 – 7; Rev 14:10 – 11).

By: Chastisements (Ps 89:32; 1Co 5:5; 1Ti 1:20). Judgments (Ex 32:35; Lev 26:14 – 39; Dt 11:26 – 28; 28:15 – 68; 30:15, 18 – 19; Job 20:5 – 29; Pss 11:6; 21:9 – 10; 39:11; 75:8; 78:49 – 51; Isa 5:11 – 14, 24; 9:18; 10:3; 13:9, 11, 14 – 22; 24:17 – 18; 28:18 – 22; 65:12 – 15; Jer 5:25; 8:12 – 14, 20 – 22; 14:10, 12; 25:31; 44:2 – 14, 23 – 29; 49:10; La 3:39; 4:22; 5:16 – 17; Eze 5:4, 8 – 17; 9:5 – 7, 10; 20:8; 22:14, 20 – 21, 31; 24:13 – 14; Hos 2:9 – 13; 5:4 – 6, 9; 9:7, 9, 15; Joel 2:1 – 2; 3:13 – 16; Am 5:18 – 20; Lk 12:46; 1Co 10:5 – 11; 1Ti 5:24; Heb 10:26 – 31; 1Pe 4:17 – 18). Sorrow (Ge 3:16 – 19; Job 15:20 – 24; Ps 32:10; Ecc 2:26; Isa 50:11). Trouble (Isa 48:22; 57:20 – 21). Being rejected of the Lord (1Ch 28:9; 2Ch 15:2; Mt 7:23; 10:33; Mk 8:38; Lk 9:26; 13:27 – 28; Jn 8:21; 2Ti 2:12 – 13; Heb 6:8). Being excluded from the kingdom of heaven (1Co 6:9 – 10; Gal 5:19 – 21; Eph 5:5; Rev 21:27; 22:19). Being blotted from God's book (Ex 32:33). Destruction (Ge 6:3, 7, 12 – 13; Nu 15:31; Dt 7:9 – 10; 1Sa 12:25; 1Ch 10:13 – 14; Job 4:8 – 9; 31:3; Pss 2:9; 7:11 – 13; 9:5, 17; 34:16, 21; 52:5; 55:19, 23; 92:7, 9; 94:13, 23; 101:8; 104:35; 106:18, 43; 145:20; Pr 2:22; 12:7; 21:12, 15 – 16; 24:20; Isa 11:4; 13:8; 64:5 – 7; Jer 13:14, 16, 22; Eze 25:7; Hos 7:12 – 13; Am 8:14; Na 1:2, 8 – 10; Zep 1:12 – 18; Zec 5:2 – 4; Mal 4:1; Mt 3:10, 12, w Lk 3:17; Mt 7:13, 19; 10:28, w Lk 12:4 – 5; Mt 21:41, 44, w Mk 12:1 – 9 & Lk 20:16, 18; Mt 24:50 – 51; Lk 9:24 – 25, w Mt 16:26 & Mk 8:36; Lk 19:27; Jn 5:29; Ac 3:23; Ro 2:12; 9:22; 1Co 3:17; Php 3:19; 1Th 5:3; 2Th

2:8 – 10). Sudden destruction (Pr 6:15; 24:22; 28:18; 29:1). Everlasting destruction (2Th 1:9). Everlasting contempt (Da 12:2). Everlasting fire (Isa 28:18 – 22; Mt 18:8 – 9; 25:41; Mk 9:43; Rev 20:15; 21:8). Death (Ge 2:17; Ps 1:4 – 6; Pr 16:25; 19:16; Hos 13:1, 3; Am 9:1 – 5, 10; Ro 5:12, 21; 6:16, 21; 8:2, 6, 13; 1Co 15:21 – 22; 2Co 7:10; Gal 6:8; 1Jn 3:14 – 15; Jas 1:15; 5:20; Rev 2:22 – 23). The second death (Rev 21:8). Condemnation to hell (Mt 23:33; Mk 16:16; Jn 3:15 – 16, 18, 36). Being cast into outer darkness (Mt 8:12; 22:13; 25:30). The last judgments (Rev 6:15 – 17; 9:4 – 6, 15, 18; 11:18; 16:2 – 21; 18:5; 19:15, 17 – 21; 20:10, 15; 21:8, 27; 22:19). Everlasting (Mt 25:46; Rev 14:10 – 11; 20:10). Degrees in (Mt 10:15; 11:22, 24; Mk 12:40). No escape from (Job 34:22; 1Th 5:3; Heb 2:3). God has no pleasure in the death of (Eze 18:23; 33:11).

Illustrated in Parables: the weeds (Mt 13:24 – 30, 38 – 42, 49 – 50); the talents (Mt 25:14 – 30); the barren fig tree (Lk 13:6 – 9); the man who built his house on the sand (Mt 7:26 – 27; Lk 6:49); Lazarus and the rich man (Lk 16:22 – 28).

Woes against the Wicked:

(Isa 5:8, 11, 18 – 23; Mt 26:24; Mk 14:21; Lk 11:52; 17:1 – 2; 22:22; Jude 11).

Warned:

(Jer 7:13 – 15, 23 – 25; 25:4 – 6; 26:2 – 7, 12 – 13; 29:17 – 19; Eze 33:8; Da 4:4 – 27; 5:4 – 29; Zep 2:1 – 2; Lk 3:7 – 9; 1Co 10:11; Rev 3:1 – 3, 16 – 19).

Ge	13:13	Now the men of Sodom were **w**
Ex	23:1	Do not help a **w** man
Nu	14:35	things to this whole **w** community,
Dt	15:9	not to harbor this **w** thought:
1Sa	2:12	Eli's sons were **w** men; they had no
2Sa	13:12	in Israel! Don't do this **w** thing.
2Ki	17:11	They did **w** things that provoked
2Ch	7:14	and turn from their **w** ways,
Ps	1:1	walk in the counsel of the **w**
	1:5	Therefore the **w** will not stand

	12:8	The **w** freely strut about
	26:5	and refuse to sit with the **w**.
	36:1	concerning the sinfulness of the **w**:
	37:13	but the Lord laughs at the **w**,
	50:16	But to the **w**, God says:
	58:3	Even from birth the **w** go astray;
	73:3	when I saw the prosperity of the **w**.
	119:155	Salvation is far from the **w**,
	141:10	Let the **w** fall into their own nets,
	146:9	but he frustrates the ways of the **w**.
Pr	2:12	you from the ways of **w** men,
	4:14	Do not set foot on the path of the **w**
	6:18	a heart that devises **w** schemes,
	9:7	whoever rebukes a **w** man incurs
	10:28	the hopes of the **w** come to nothing
	11:5	**w** are brought down by their own
	12:10	the kindest acts of the **w** are cruel.
	21:10	The **w** man craves evil;
	21:29	A **w** man puts up a bold front,
	29:16	When the **w** thrive, so does sin,
	29:27	the **w** detest the upright.
Isa	11:4	breath of his lips he will slay the **w**.
	26:10	Though grace is shown to the **w**,
	53:9	He was assigned a grave with the **w**
	55:7	Let the **w** forsake his way
Jer	35:15	of you must turn from your **w** ways
Eze	3:18	that **w** man will die for his sin,
	33:14	to the **w** man, 'You will surely die,'
	33:19	And if a **w** man turns away
Da	12:10	but the **w** will continue to be **w**.
Mt	12:39	**w** and adulterous generation asks
	12:45	with it seven other spirits more **w**
Lk	6:35	he is kind to the ungrateful and **w**.
Ac	2:23	and you, with the help of **w** men,
Ro	4:5	but trusts God who justifies the **w**,
1Co	5:13	"Expel the **w** man from among you
	6:9	not know that the **w** will not inherit
Rev	2:2	that you cannot tolerate **w** men,

WIDOW [530, 531, 851+4637, 851, 3304, 1222, 5939] (Heb. *'almānâh*, Gr. *chēra*). Widows in the OT are regarded as being under God's special care (Pss 68:5; 146:9; Pr 15:25). From early times they wore a dis-tinctive garb. The Hebrews were commanded to treat them with special consideration and were punished if they did otherwise (Ex 22:22; Dt 14:29; Isa 1:17; Jer 7:6). The church looked after poor widows in apostolic times (Ac 6:1; Jas 1:27). Paul gives instructions to Timothy about the care of widows by the church (1Ti 5:4); but only those were taken care of who were at least sixty years of age, had been married only once, and had a reputation for good works (5:9–10). In the second and third centuries there was an order of widows in the church. Its members looked after the women of the congregation. This order was abolished by the Synod of Laodicea, AD 364.

Mosaic Laws Concerning:
High priest forbidden to marry (Lev 21:14). Supported by father, when daughter of priest (Lev 22:13). Vows of, binding (Nu 30:9). Entitled to glean in the orchards and harvest fields (Dt 24:19–21). Levirate marriage of (Dt 25:5–10). Care of commanded (Dt 14:28–29; 16:11, 14; Isa 1:17; Jer 7:6–7).

In the Church:
Remarriage of, authorized (Ro 7:3; 1Co 7:39; 1Ti 5:14). Remarriage of, discouraged (1Co 7:8–9). Qualifications for widows in 1Ti 5:3–16 may indicate a church office.

Kindness to:
Exemplified: by Job (Job 29:13; 31:16, 22); by God, the friend of (Dt 10:18; Pss 68:5; 146:9; Pr 15:25; Jer 49:11). Care of, in the church (Ac 6:1; 1Ti 5:3–6, 9–12, 16; Jas 1:27).

Oppression of:
(Job 22:9; 24:3, 21; Ps 94:6; Isa 1:23; Eze 22:7; Mk 12:40; Lk 20:47); forbidden (Ex 22:22–24; Dt 24:17; 27:19; Isa 10:2; Jer 22:3; Zec 7:10; Mal 3:5).

Instances of:
Naomi (Ru 1:3); Ruth (Ru 1–4); widow of Zarephath, who sustained Elijah during a famine (1Ki 17); the woman whose sons Elisha saved from being sold for debt (2Ki 4:1–7); Anna (Lk 2:36–37); the woman who gave two mites in the

temple (Mk 12:41 – 44; Lk 21:2); widow of Nain, whose only son Jesus raised from the dead (Lk 7:11 – 15).

Ex	22:22	"Do not take advantage of a **w**
Dt	10:18	cause of the fatherless and the **w**,
Ps	146:9	sustains the fatherless and the **w**,
Isa	1:17	plead the case of the **w**.
Lk	21:2	saw a poor **w** put in two very small
1Ti	5:4	But if a **w** has children

WIFE [851+, 3304, 7675, 1222+, 3836].

Described:

Called a helper (Ge 2:18, 20); desire of the eyes (Eze 24:10). Compared to a fruitful vine (Ps 128:3). Beloved, by Isaac (Ge 24:67); by Jacob (Ge 29:30). Hated (Ge 29:31 – 33). Contentious (Pr 19:13; 21:9, 19; 25:24). Instances of: Zipporah (Ex 4:25), Peninnah (1Sa 1:6 – 7). Loyal, Jacob's (Ge 31:14 – 16). Unfaithful (Nu 5:12 – 31). Instances of: Potiphar's (Ge 39:7); Bathsheba (2Sa 11:2 – 5). Prudent (Pr 19:14). Tactful: Abigail (1Sa 25:3, 14 – 34); Esther (Est 5:5 – 8; 7:1 – 4). Virtuous (Pr 12:4; 31:10 – 12). Incorruptible or strong-willed: Vashti (Est 1:10 – 12). Wise (Pr 14:1).

Marrying of:

Commended (Pr 18:22; 1Co 7:2; 1Ti 5:14). Bought (Ge 29:18 – 30; 31:41; Ex 21:7 – 11; Ru 4:10). Obtained by kidnapping (Jdg 21:21). Procured (Ge 24; 34:4 – 10; 38:6).

Duty:

Husband to wife (1Co 7:2 – 5, 27; Eph 5:25, 28, 31, 33; Col 3:19; 1Pe 3:7). Wife to husband: to be obedient (1Co 14:34 – 35; Eph 5:22, 24; Col 3:18; Tit 2:5; 1Pe 3:1, 6); to be affectionate (Tit 2:4); to be faithful (Tit 3:11). Relation of, to the husband (Ge 2:18, 23 – 24; 1Co 7:2 – 5, 10 – 11, 13, 39; 11:3, 8 – 9, 11 – 12). Domestic duties of (Ge 18:6; Pr 31:13 – 27). Vows of (Nu 30:6 – 16). See Vow.

Instances of Evil Influence of:

Eve (Ge 3:6, 12); Solomon's wives (1Ki 11:1 – 8; Ne 13:26); Jezebel (1Ki 21:25; 2Ki 9:30 – 37);

Haman's (Est 5:14); Herodias (Mt 14:3, 6 – 11; Mk 6:17, 24 – 28).

Ge	2:24	and mother and be united to his **w**,
Ex	20:17	shall not covet your neighbor's **w**,
Lev	20:10	adultery with another man's **w** —
Dt	24:5	happiness to the **w** he has married.
Ru	4:13	took Ruth and she became his **w**.
Pr	5:18	in the **w** of your youth.
	12:4	**w** of noble character is her
	18:22	He who finds a **w** finds what is
	19:13	quarrelsome **w** is like a constant
	31:10	**w** of noble character who can find?
Hos	1:2	take to yourself an adulterous **w**
Mal	2:14	the witness between you and the **w**
Mt	1:20	to take Mary home as your **w**,
	19:3	for a man to divorce his **w** for any
Lk	18:29	or **w** or brothers or parents
1Co	7:2	each man should have his own **w**,
	7:33	how he can please his **w** —
Eph	5:23	the husband is the head of the **w**
	5:33	must love his **w** as he loves himself,
1Ti	3:2	husband of but one **w**, temperate,
Rev	21:9	I will show you the bride, the **w**

WILL [2911, 2914, 4213, 8356, 10668, 1087, 1088, 1089, 2525, 2526, 2527].

Mental Faculty:

Freedom of, recognized by God (Ge 4:6 – 10; Dt 5:29; 1Ki 20:42; Isa 1:18 – 20; 43:26; Jer 36:3, 7; Jn 7:17). See Blessings, Spiritual, Contingent upon Obedience.

Of God:

Defined: God's purpose (2Ti 1:9, w Eph 1:9); God's plan (1Co 12:11; 2Co 1:15; Jas 3:4); God's will (Ac 27:12; Eph 1:11). The supreme rule of duty (Mt 6:10; 12:50, w Mk 3:35; Mt 26:39, 42; Mk 14:36; Lk 22:42; Jn 4:34; 5:30; 6:38 – 40; Ro 12:2; Eph 5:17). Plans of the righteous subject to (Ac 18:21; Ro 1:10; 15:32; 1Co 4:19; 16:7; Heb 6:3; Jas 4:15). Lord's Prayer concerns (Mt 6:10; Lk 11:2).

Reasons for Wanting to Know: *love for God (Jn 14:15, 21, 23 – 24); desire to please God (1Jn 3:22); blessings in this life (1Pe 3:10 – 12); rewards in the future life (1Co 3:10 – 15; 2Ti 4:8; Heb 10:35); to avoid discipline (1Co 3:16 – 17; 11:31 – 32; 1Pe 4:17); good example to other believers (1Co 4:16; 1Th 1:7; 2Th 3:9; Heb 13:7); will not be ashamed at the second coming (1Jn 2:28); to glorify God (1Co 10:31; Col 3:17, 23; Heb 12:10; 2Pe 1:4); obligation to know (Eph 5:15 – 17).*

How God Reveals: *through his Word (Ps 119:105; 2Ti 3:16 – 17); through control of thoughts, indirectly (2Co 7:8 – 11; 12:7; 1Pe 1:6 – 7; 4:12 – 13; Jas 1:2 – 4), directly (Pr 16:1, 9; 21:1; Eph 2:13); through Satan (Job 1:12; 2:6); through the control of circumstances (Pr 16:9; 20:24; Ac 2:23; 4:28; Eph 1:11); until revelation is complete, through dreams (Ge 20:3, 6; 31:11, 24; 1Ki 3:5; Mt 2:12 – 13) and visions (Ge 15:1; Zec 1:7 – 8; Ac 10:10 – 11). Prerequisites for discerning: spiritual maturity (Isa 55:8 – 9; 1Co 2:7; Eph 4:14; Col 1:9; 1Ti 3:6; Heb 5:13 – 14; 13:21); teaching ministry of the Holy Spirit (Jn 16:13 – 14; 1Co 2:12 – 14; 1Jn 2:27); application in testings (Php 3:15; Heb 5:14; 12:7, 11; Jas 1:2 – 5); yieldedness or self-denial (Ro 6:13, 19; 12:1; 1Pe 2:9; Rev 1:6); discipleship (Mt 16:24; Mk 8:34; Lk 9:23); desire to know God's will (Jn 7:17), to do it (Mk 4:24 – 25; Ac 10:22, 35, 44, 47; 1Jn 2:11); willingness to obey daily (Mt 16:24; Mk 8:34; Lk 9:23; Ro 6:16; Php 2:13; 2Pe 2:19); faith (Ps 37:5; Pr 3:5 – 6; Ro 14:23; 2Co 5:7; Php 2:13; Heb 11:17, 27); patience (Ps 37:7; Jas 1:5 – 6); common sense (Tit 2:12); peace of God (Col 3:15); a clear conscience (Ro 14:23).*

Ps	40:8	I desire to do your **w**, O my God;
	143:10	Teach me to do your **w**,
Isa	53:10	Yet it was the Lord's **w**
Mt	6:10	your **w** be done
	7:21	who does the **w** of my Father
	10:29	apart from the **w** of your Father.
	26:39	Yet not as I **w**, but as you **w**."
	26:42	I drink it, may your **w** be done."
Jn	6:38	but to do the **w** of him who sent me.
	7:17	If anyone chooses to do God's **w**,
Ac	20:27	to you the whole **w** of God.
Ro	12:2	and approve what God's **w** is—
1Co	7:37	but has control over his own **w**,
Eph	5:17	understand what the Lord's **w** is.
Php	2:13	for it is God who works in you to **w**
1Th	4:3	God's **w** that you should be sanctified:
	5:18	for this is God's **w** for you
2Ti	2:26	has taken them captive to do his **w**.
Heb	2:4	distributed according to his **w**.
	10:7	I have come to do your **w**, O God
	13:21	everything good for doing his **w**,
Jas	4:15	"If it is the Lord's **w**,
1Pe	3:17	It is better, if it is God's **w**,
	4:2	but rather for the **w** of God.
2Pe	1:21	never had its origin in the **w**
1Jn	5:14	we ask anything according to his **w**,
Rev	4:11	and by your **w** they were created

WINE [1074+8042, 2810, 3516, 3676, 4641, 4932, 6011, 6747, 9069, 9197, 9408, 10271, 1183, 3885, 3954].

General References to:

Made from grapes (Ge 49:11; Jer 40:10, 12); from pomegranates (SS 8:2). Kept in wineskins (Jos 9:4, 13; Job 32:19; Jer 13:12; Mt 9:17; Lk 5:37 – 38); in jars (Jer 48:12); in vats (1Ch 27:27); in buildings (2Ch 32:28). Commerce in (Rev 18:13). Banquets of (Est 5:6). Plentiful in Canaan (Dt 33:28; 2Ki 18:32). Fermented (Lev 10:9; Nu 6:3; Dt 14:26; 29:6). New wine, a staple (Hos 2:8, 22; 7:14; Joel 2:24; Hag 1:11; Mk 2:22; Lk 5:37 – 39). Aged wine, a delicacy (Isa 25:6; Jer 48:11). Old wine (Lk 5:39).

Positive Use of:

Offered with sacrifices (Ex 29:40; Lev 23:13; Nu 15:5, 10; 18:12; 28:7, 14; Dt 14:23; Ne 10:39). For enjoyment (Pss 4:7; 104:15; Pr 31:6 – 7; Ecc 2:3; Isa 25:6; Zec 9:17; 10:7). Recommended by Paul to Timothy (1Ti 5:23). Given by Melchizedek to Abraham (Ge 14:18). Used at meals (Mt 26:27 – 29; Mk 14:23). Made by Jesus at the marriage feast in Cana (Jn 2:9 – 10). Used in the Lord's

Supper (*Mt 26:27 – 29; Lk 22:17 – 20*). *Given to Jesus at the crucifixion, possibly as a painkiller (Mt 27:48; Mk 15:23; Lk 23:36; Jn 19:29).*

Negative Use of:

Drunkenness condemned (Pr 20:1; Isa 5:11, 22; 24:9; 28:1, 3, 7; 56:12; Jer 23:9; Hos 4:11; Joel 1:5; Am 6:6; Hab 2:5; Eph 5:18; 1Ti 3:8; Tit 2:3). Addiction and craving condemned (Pr 21:17; 23:29 – 32; Joel 1:5). Children sold for (Joel 3:3). **Instances of drunkenness:** *Noah (Ge 9:21); Lot (Ge 19:32); Joseph and his brothers (Ge 43:34); Nabal (1Sa 25:36); Amnon (2Sa 13:28 – 29); Xerxes (Est 1:10); kings of Israel (Hos 7:5). Falsely charged against Jesus (Mt 11:19; Lk 7:34) and the disciples (Ac 2:13).*

Abstinence from:

Required: of Levites while on duty (Lev 10:9; Eze 44:21); of Nazirites during their vow (Nu 6:3); of Samson's mother during her pregnancy (Jdg 13:4 – 5). See Nazirite(s). Required of kings and rulers (Pr 31:4 – 5); of John the Baptist (Lk 1:15). **Chosen:** *by Daniel to avoid defilement (Da 1:8 – 20), in mourning (Da 10:3); by the Recabites to honor a vow (Jer 35:6, 8, 14, 16); with bread, denied to the Israelites in the desert (Dt 29:6). Temperance allowed the guests at Xerxes' banquet (Est 1:8). For the sake of the weaker brother (Ro 14:21). Possibly, by Timothy (1Ti 5:23).*

Figurative:

Of the divine judgments (Pss 60:3; 75:8; Jer 51:7; Rev 14:10; 16:19); of the joy of wisdom (Pr 9:2, 5); of the joys of religion (Isa 25:6; 55:1; Joel 2:19); of abominations (Rev 14:9; 17:2; 18:3).

Symbolic:

Of the blood of Jesus (Mt 26:28; Mk 14:23 – 24; Lk 22:20; Jn 6:53 – 56).

Ps	104:15	**w** that gladdens the heart of man,
Pr	20:1	**W** is a mocker and beer a brawler;
	23:31	Do not gaze at **w** when it is red,
	31:6	**w** to those who are in anguish;
SS	1:2	your love is more delightful than **w**.
Isa	28:7	And these also stagger from **w**
Mt	9:17	Neither do men pour new **w**
Lk	23:36	They offered him **w** vinegar
Jn	2:3	When the **w** was gone, Jesus' mother
Ro	14:21	not to eat meat or drink **w**
Eph	5:18	on **w**, which leads to debauchery.
1Ti	5:23	a little **w** because of your stomach
Rev	16:19	with the **w** of the fury of his wrath.

WINNOWING FORK (Heb. *mizreh*). A fork with two or more prongs used to throw grain into the air after it had been threshed, so that the chaff might be blown away. The work was done toward evening and at night when a wind came in from the sea and carried away the light chaff. Sometimes a shovel was used for the same purpose. A winnowing fork is referred to in Jer 15:7; Mt 3:12; Lk 3:17.

WISDOM [1069, 2681, 2682, 2683, 2684, 4213, 4220, 8505, 8507, 9312, 9370, 10265, 10266, 10539, 5053, 5054, 5055, 5317, 5860, 5861]. The most common OT words for wisdom are Hebrew *hākham* and related forms and Greek *sophia*. In God wisdom is the infinite, perfect comprehension of all that is or might be (Ro 11:33 – 36). God is the source of wisdom as of power, and wisdom is given to people through the fear of the Lord (Job 28:28; Ps 111:10). In man wisdom is an eminently practical attribute, including technical skill (Ex 28:3; RSV "an able mind"), military prowess (Isa 10:13), and shrewdness for questionable ends (1Ki 2:6). Wisdom is shown in getting desired ends by effective means. People of the world are often wiser in their generation than the children of light (Lk 16:8). The wisdom of Solomon was far-ranging in statesmanship (1Ki 10:23 – 24); in understanding of human nature (3:16 – 25); and in natural history, literature, and popular proverbs (4:29 – 34). Wisdom is personified (Pr 8) in terms related to the concept of the Word in Jn 1:1 – 18, and became one of the names of God the Father and the Son, the Holy Spirit being the Spirit of Wisdom.

Wisdom Literature in the OT consists of Proverbs, Ecclesiastes, and Job, with Pss 19, 37, 104, 107, 147, 148, and short passages in other books; and in the OT Apocrypha, Ecclesiasticus, and Wisdom of Solomon. Hebrew wisdom was not all religious; it dealt, as in Proverbs, with everyday conduct in business, family and social relations, and basic morality. The sayings of Jesus, largely proverbial and parabolical, are the crown of biblical wisdom. Paul calls Jesus "the wisdom of God" (1Co 1:24, 30) and says that in him all the treasures of wisdom are hidden (Col 2:3). When Paul compares the wisdom of people with the wisdom of God (1Co 2), he is thinking of the former as that of Greek philosophers rather than OT biblical wisdom. James's letter is wisdom literature at its best, a clear mirror of the teaching of Jesus.

Spiritual:

(Dt 32:29; Job 5:27; 8:8, 10; 12:2 – 3, 7 – 13, 16 – 17, 22). The fear of the Lord is the beginning of (Ps 111:10; Pr 1:7; 9:10; Isa 33:6). Is revealed to the obedient (Ps 107:43; Pr 28:5, 7; 29:3; Ecc 8:5; Da 12:3 – 4, 10; Hos 6:3, 6; 14:9; Mt 6:22 – 23; Lk 11:34 – 36; Jn 7:17; 10:4, 14; 1Co 2:6 – 10; 8:3; 1Jn 4:6). Exemplified (Pss 9:10; 76:1; Pr 1:5; 11:12; Mt 7:24 – 25; 25:1 – 13; Mk 12:32 – 34; Ac 6:10; Ro 15:14; 1Co 13:11; Php 3:7 – 8, 10; 1Th 5:4 – 5; Jas 3:13).

Commended: *(Pr 3:13 – 26; 24:3 – 7; Ecc 7:11 – 12, 19; 10:1, 12). Is above value (Job 28:12 – 19; Pr 3:13 – 15; 16:16). Exhortations to attain to (Pr 2:1 – 20; 4:4 – 13, 18 – 20; 22:17 – 21; 23:12, 19, 23; 24:13 – 14; Ro 16:19; 1Co 8:3; 14:20; 2Co 8:7; Eph 5:15 – 17; Col 3:10, 16; 2Pe 3:18). Parable of (Mt 25:1 – 13). Personified (Pr 1:20 – 33; 8; 9:1 – 18). See Knowledge.*

From God: *(Ex 4:12; 8:4, 10; Dt 4:5 – 6, 35 – 36; 29:4; 1Ch 22:12; Ne 9:20; Job 4:3; 11:5 – 6; 22:21 – 22; 28:20 – 28; 32:7 – 8; 33:16; 35:10 – 11; 36:22; 38:36 – 37; Pss 16:7; 19:1 – 2; 25:8 – 9, 12, 14; 32:8; 36:9; 51:6; 71:17; 94:12; 112:4; 119:130; Pr 1:23; 2:6 – 7; 3:5 – 6; Ecc 2:26; Isa 2:3; 11:1 – 3; 30:21; 42:6 – 7, 16; 48:17; 54:13; Jer 9:23 – 24; 24:7; Da 1:17; 2:21 – 23; 11:32 – 33; Mt 11:25 – 27;*

13:11; 16:16 – 17; Lk 1:76 – 79; 12:11 – 12; 21:15; 24:32, 45; Jn 1:1, 4 – 5, 7 – 9, 17; 6:45; 8:12, 31 – 32; 9:5, 39; 12:46; 14:7; 16:13 – 14; 17:3, 6 – 8, 25 – 26; 18:37; Ro 1:19 – 20; 1Co 1:30; 2:9, 11 – 14; 12:8; 2Co 3:15; 4:6; Gal 4:9; Eph 4:11 – 13; Php 3:15; Col 1:26 – 28; 1Ti 2:4; 2Ti 1:7; 3:15; Jas 3:17; 2Pe 1:2 – 5, 8, 12; 3:18; 1Jn 2:20, 27; 5:20). See God, Wisdom of.

Exemplified: *of Joseph (Ge 41:16, 25 – 39; Ac 7:10); of Moses (Ac 7:22); of Bezalel (Ex 31:3 – 5; 35:31 – 35; 36:1); of Oholiab (Ex 31:6; 35:34 – 35; 36:1); of other skilled artisans (Ex 36:2); of women (Ex 35:26); of Hiram (1Ki 7:14; 2Ch 2:14); of Solomon (1Ki 3:12, 16 – 28; 4:29 – 34; 5:12; 10:24); of Ethan, Heman, Calcol, and Darda (1Ki 4:31); of the princes of Issachar (1Ch 12:32); of Ezra (Ezr 7:25); of Daniel (Da 1:17; 5:14); of Paul (2Pe 3:15); of the magi (Mt 2:1 – 12).*

Prayer for: *(Nu 27:21; Jdg 20:18, 23, 26 – 28; 1Ki 3:7, 9; 8:36; 2Ch 1:10; Job 34:32; Pss 5:8; 25:4 – 5; 27:11; 31:3; 39:4; 43:3; 86:11; 90:12; 119:12, 18 – 19, 26 – 27, 33 – 34, 66, 68, 73, 80, 124 – 125, 135, 144, 169, 171; 139:24; Eph 1:16 – 19; 3:14 – 19; 6:18 – 20; Php 1:9; Col 1:9 – 10; 2:1 – 3; 4:2 – 4; 2Ti 2:7; Jas 1:5). To be possessed in humility (Jer 9:23 – 24; Jas 3:13). Solomon's prayer for. See Solomon. Promised (Jn 8:22). Opportunity to obtain, forfeited (Pr 1:24 – 31). Shall become universal.*

Worldly:

Condemned: *(Job 4:18 – 21; 5:13; 11:2, 12; 37:24). Desired by Eve (Ge 3:6 – 7). Misleading (Pr 21:30; Isa 47:10; 1Co 8:1 – 2). Ending in death (Pr 16:25). Folly of (Ecc 2:1 – 26; 7:11 – 13, 16 – 25; 8:1, 16 – 17; Jer 8:7 – 9; 49:7; Mt 6:23; Ro 1:21 – 23). Increases sorrow (Ecc 1:18; Isa 47:10 – 11). Denounced (2Co 1:12). Woe pronounced against (Isa 5:21). Shall perish (Isa 29:14 – 16). Illustration of (Mt 7:24 – 27; Lk 16:8). Admonitions against (Pr 3:7; Col 2:8; 1Ti 6:20 – 21). Admonitions against glorying in (Jer 9:23 – 24). Heavenly things not discerned by (Mt*

11:25; Lk 10:21). Gospel not to be preached with (1Co 1:17 – 26; 2:1 – 14). To be renounced in order to attain spiritual wisdom (1Co 3:18 – 20).
Commended: *Council of others commanded (Pr 15:22; 20:18; 24:3 – 7). Wise application of, profitable (Ecc 10:10; Isa 28:24 – 29).*

Ge	3:6	and also desirable for gaining **w**,
1Ki	4:29	God gave Solomon **w** and very
2Ch	1:10	Give me **w** and knowledge,
Ps	51:6	you teach me **w** in the inmost place
	111:10	of the LORD is the beginning of **w**;
Pr	2:6	For the LORD gives **w**,
	3:13	Blessed is the man who finds **w**,
	4:7	**W** is supreme; therefore get
	8:11	for **w** is more precious than rubies,
	11:2	but with humility comes **w**.
	23:23	get **w**, discipline and understanding
	29:3	A man who loves **w** brings joy
	29:15	The rod of correction imparts **w**,
Jer	10:12	he founded the world by his **w**
Mic	6:9	and to fear your name is **w**—
Lk	2:52	And Jesus grew in **w** and stature,
Ac	6:3	known to be full of the Spirit and **w**.
Ro	11:33	the depth of the riches of the **w**
1Co	1:17	not with words of human **w**,
	1:30	who has become for us **w** from God
	12:8	through the Spirit the message of **w**
Eph	1:17	may give you the Spirit of **w**
Col	2:3	are hidden all the treasures of **w**
	2:23	indeed have an appearance of **w**,
Jas	1:5	of you lacks **w**, he should ask God,
	3:13	in the humility that comes from **w**.
Rev	5:12	and wealth and **w** and strength

WISE

1Ki	3:12	give you a **w** and discerning heart,
Ps	19:7	making **w** the simple.
Pr	3:7	Do not be **w** in your own eyes;
	9:8	rebuke a **w** man and he will love
	10:1	A **w** son brings joy to his father,
	13:1	A **w** son heeds his father's
	13:20	He who walks with the **w** grows **w**,

	16:23	A **w** man's heart guides his mouth,
	17:28	Even a fool is thought **w**
Ecc	9:17	The quiet words of the **w** are more
Da	2:21	He gives wisdom to the **w**
	12:3	Those who are **w** will shine like
Mt	11:25	hidden these things from the **w**
1Co	1:19	I will destroy the wisdom of the **w**;
Eph	5:15	but as **w**, making the most
2Ti	3:15	able to make you **w** for salvation
Jas	3:13	Who is **w** and understanding

WISE MEN

1. Men of understanding and skill in ordinary affairs (Pr 1:5; Job 15:2; Ps 49:10), came to be recognized as a distinct class, listed with priests and prophets (Jer 18:18), and also found outside Israel (Ge 41:8; Ex 7:11; Da 2:12 – 5:15).

2. The magi (Mt 2:1 – 12), astrologers who came from the East. Their number and names are not given in Scripture.

WITCH, WITCHCRAFT [4175, 4176, 5758]. A title commonly linked with those in league with evil spirits and their practices. Hebrew *kāshaph*, "to practice sorcery" is sometimes so translated in NIV, ASV, often in RSV (Ex 22:18; Dt 18:10; 2Ki 9:22; 2Ch 33:6; Mic 5:12; Na 3:4). Hebrew *qesem*, "divination," is once translated "witchcraft" (1Sa 15:23, KJV, ASV), otherwise "divination." Greek *pharmakeia* (Gal 5:20 ASV; RSV "sorcery") means the use of drugs, charms, or magic words. In Ac 8:9, 11 KJV, "bewitch" is a translation of the Greek *existēmi* (NIV "amazed"). In Gal 3:1 the Greek *baskainō*, "to use the evil eye on one," is rendered "bewitched." The famous witch of Endor (1Sa 28:7 – 25) is not so called in the Bible, but is referred to as a woman who had a "familiar spirit" (KJV, ASV) or who was a "medium" (RSV, NIV). All practices of witchcraft are strictly condemned (Ex 22:18; Dt 18:9 – 14; 1Sa 28:3, 9; 2Ki 23:24; Isa 8:19; Ac 19:18 – 19).

WITNESS [1068+9048, 6332, 6338, 6386, 7032, 3455, 3456, 3457, 3459, 5210, 6019, 6020] (Lev 5:1; Pr 18:17).

Qualified by oath (Ex 22:11; Nu 5:19, 21; 1Ki 8:31 – 32); by laying hands on the accused (Lev 24:14). Two necessary to establish a fact (Nu 35:30; Dt 17:6; 19:15; Mt 18:16; Jn 8:17; 2Co 13:1; 1Ti 5:19; Heb 10:28). Required: to cast the first stone in executing sentence (Dt 13:9; 17:5 – 7; Ac 7:58); to the transfer of land (Ge 21:25 – 30; 23:11, 16 – 18; Ru 4:1 – 9; Jer 32:9 – 12, 25, 44); to marriage (Ru 4:10 – 11; Isa 8:2 – 3). Incorruptible (Ps 15:4). Corrupted by money (Mt 28:11 – 15; Ac 6:11, 13). Figurative of instruction in righteousness (Rev 11:3).

WOMAN [851, 1426, 1435, 3251, 5922, 9148, 1222, 4087] (Heb. *'ishshâh*, Gr. *gynē*). The general account of creation implies the full humanity of Eve (Ge 1:26 – 27), and the special account of her creation (2:18 – 24) emphasizes her superiority over all lower animals, Adam's need of her as helper, her intimate relationship to him as a part of his inmost being, and the nature of marriage as a "one flesh" relationship. Though many OT women do not stand out, three patriarchal wives (Sarah, Rebekah, and Rachel) played significant roles, as did also Moses' sister Miriam (Ex 2:1 – 9; 15:21; Nu 12). In the period of the judges, Deborah exercised unusual leadership (Jdg 4 – 5), and the Moabitess Ruth became a chaste blessing to Israel. Hannah (1Sa 1:1 – 2:11) illustrates both the despair of a childless woman and the grace of godly motherhood. The advice of Lemuel's mother to her son (Pr 31) pictures an ideal, industrious wife in a prosperous family. Queens, good and bad, and evil women of other classes of society are frankly portrayed in the Bible. The ancient world was a man's world: such prominence as women attained was achieved by force of character — sometimes, as in the case of Esther, aided by circumstances not of her seeking.

The teaching of Jesus stressed the original nature of marriage and of a man's obligation of purity in his thoughts and actions toward women (Mt 5:27 – 32). Jesus' example in healing (9:18 – 26) and in social intercourse (Lk 10:38 – 42) reinforced his words. The Gospels are full of evidence of Jesus' understanding and appreciation of women, thus setting a pattern for normal Christian living. Paul (1Co 11:2 – 16;

14:34 – 35) urges subordination for Christian women, but he exalts the believing wife as a type of the church, the bride of Christ (Eph 5:21 – 33). He sets high standards for the wives of church officers and for women in official positions (1Ti 3:11; Tit 2:3 – 5). Likewise, 1Pe 3:1 – 6 urges a subordinate but noble role for married women. To evaluate Bible teaching with regard to women, it is necessary to consider carefully all the pertinent material and to hold firmly to the normative and authoritative character of the words, deeds, and attitude of Jesus Christ.

General References to:

Creation of (Ge 1:27; 2:21 – 22). Named (Ge 2:23). Fall of and curse upon (Ge 3:1 – 16; 2Co 11:3; 1Ti 2:14). Promise to (Ge 3:15). Took part in ancient worship (Ex 15:20 – 21; 38:8; 1Sa 2:22); in choir (1Ch 25:5 – 6; Ezr 2:65; Ne 7:67). Served at the entrance to the Tent of Meeting (Ex 38:8; 1Sa 2:22). Consecrated jewels to tabernacle (Ex 35:22); mirrors (Ex 38:8). Required to attend the reading of the law (Dt 31:12; Jos 8:35). Ministered in the tabernacle (Ex 38:8; 1Sa 2:22). Religious privileges of, among early Christians (Ac 1:14; 12:12 – 13; 1Co 11:5; 14:34; 1Ti 2:11). Purifications of, after menstruation (Lev 15:19 – 33; 2Sa 11:4); childbirth (Lev 12; Lk 2:22). Difference in ceremonies made between male and female children (Lev 12). Vows of (Nu 30:3 – 16). Had their own tents (Ge 24:67; 31:33). Domestic duties of (Ge 18:6; Pr 31:15 – 19; Mt 24:41). Cooked (Ge 18:6). Spun (Ex 35:25 – 26; 1Sa 2:19; Pr 31:19 – 24). Embroidered (Pr 31:22). Made garments (1Sa 2:19; Ac 9:39). Gleaned (Ru 2:7 – 8, 15 – 23). Kept vineyards (SS 1:6). Tended flocks and herds (Ge 24:11, 13 – 14, 19 – 20; 29:9; Ex 2:16). Worked in fields (Isa 27:11; Eze 26:6, 8). Doorkeeper (Mt 26:69; Jn 18:16 – 17; Ac 12:13 – 14). Did not serve in army (Isa 19:16; Jer 50:37; 51:30; Na 3:13). Veiled face (Ge 24:65). Forbidden to wear men's clothing (Dt 22:5). Ornaments of (Isa 3:16 – 23; Jer 3:32). Wore hair long (1Co 11:5 – 15). Commended for modesty in dress

(1Ti 2:9 – 10; 1Pe 3:3 – 6). Compassionate to her children (Isa 49:15); rejoices with dancing (Jdg 11:34; 21:21; Jer 31:13); courteous to strangers (Ge 24:17 – 20); wise (1Sa 25:3; 2Sa 20:16 – 22); weaker partner but coheir (1Pe 3:7). Property rights of: in inheritance (Nu 27:1 – 11; 36; Jos 17:3 – 6; Job 42:15); to sell real estate (Ru 4:3 – 9). First to sin (Ge 3:6). Remained longest at the cross (Mt 27:55 – 56; Mk 15:40 – 41). First at the tomb (Mk 15:46 – 47; 16:1 – 6; Lk 23:27 – 28, 49, 55 – 56; 24:1 – 10). First to whom the risen Lord appeared (Mk 16:9; Jn 20:14 – 18). Converted by preaching of Paul (Ac 16:14 – 15; 17:4, 12, 34). Virtuous, held in high esteem (Ru 3:11; Pr 11:16, 22; 12:4; 14:1; 31:10 – 30). See below, Good. Zealous in promoting superstition and idolatry (Jer 7:18; Eze 13:17, 23). Active in instigating iniquity (Nu 31:15 – 16; 1Ki 21:25; Ne 13:26). Guilty of lesbianism (Ro 1:26). See below, Wicked. Could not marry without consent of parents, father (Ge 24:3 – 4; 34:6; Ex 22:17; Jos 3:16 – 17; 1Sa 17:25; 18:17 – 27). Not to be given in marriage considered a calamity (Jdg 11:37; Ps 78:63; Isa 4:1). When charged with infidelity, guilt or innocence determined by trial (Nu 5:12 – 31). Sold for husband's debts (Mt 18:25). Taken captive (Nu 31:9, 15, 17 – 18, 35; La 1:18; Eze 30:17 – 18). Punishment to be inflicted on men for seducing, when betrothed (Dt 22:23 – 27). Punishment for seducing, when not betrothed (Ex 22:16 – 17; Dt 22:28 – 29). Protected during menstruation (Lev 18:19; 20:18). Treated with cruelty in war (Dt 32:25; La 2:21; 5:11).

In Leadership:

Rulers of nations: Deborah, judge and prophetess (Jdg 4:4); Athaliah, queen of Judah (2Ki 11:1 – 16; 2Ch 22:2 – 3, 10 – 12; 23:1 – 15); Jezebel, queen of Israel (1Ki 16:31); as rulers in Israel (Isa 3:12); queen of Sheba (1Ki 10:1 – 13; 2Ch 9:1 – 9, 12); Esther, queen of Persia (Est 2:17); Candace, queen of Ethiopia (Ac 8:27).

Patriots: *Miriam (Ex 15:20); Deborah (Jdg 4:4 – 16; 5); women of Israel (1Sa 18:6), women of Thebez (Jdg 9:50); women of Abel (2Sa 20:16 – 22); Esther (Est 4:4 – 17; 5:1 – 8; 7:1 – 6; 8:1 – 8), Philistine women (2Sa 1:20). Aid in defensive operations (Jdg 9:53).*

Influential in public affairs: *wise woman from Tekoa (2Sa 14:1 – 21); Bathsheba (1Ki 1:15 – 21); Jezebel (1Ki 21:7 – 15, 25); Athaliah (2Ki 11:1, 3; 2Ch 21:6; 22:3); Huldah (2Ki 22:14 – 20; 2Ch 34:22 – 28); the queen of Babylon (Da 5:9 – 13); Pilate's wife (Mt 27:19). In business (1Ch 7:24; Pr 31:14 – 18, 24).*

Poets: Miriam (Ex 15:21); Deborah (Jdg 5); Hannah (1Sa 2:1 – 10); Elizabeth (Lk 1:42 – 45); Mary (Lk 1:46 – 55).

Prophets: *Miriam (Ex 15:20 – 21; Mic 6:4); Deborah (Jdg 4:4 – 5); Huldah (2Ki 22:14 – 20; 2Ch 34:22 – 28); Anna (Lk 2:36 – 38); Philip's daughters (Ac 21:9).*

False prophets and mediums: *medium at Endor (1Sa 28:7 – 25); false prophets (Eze 13:17 – 23); Noadiah the prophetess (Ne 6:14).*

In the church: *present at the selection of Matthias (Ac 1:13 – 26); present at Pentecost (Ac 2:1 – 18); churches met in women's homes (Ac 12:12; 16:40; Ro 16:3 – 5; 1Co 1:11; 16:19; Col 4:15; 2Jn); teachers (Ac 18:26; Tit 2:3 – 5); deaconesses or wives of deacons (Ro 16:1 – 2; 1Ti 3:11); if Junias was a woman, apostles (Ro 16:7). Widow may have been a church office (1Ti 5:1 – 16).*

Social Status of:

In Persia (Est 1:10 – 22; Da 5:1 – 12). In Roman Empire (Ac 24:24; 25:13, 23; 26:30). Paul's precepts concerning women in the church (Gal 3:28; 1Co 11:5 – 15; 14:34 – 35; Eph 5:22 – 24; Col 3:18; 1Ti 2:9 – 12; 3:11; 5:1 – 16; Tit 2:3 – 5). See Widow; Wife. See also Parents.

Good:

Good wife, from the Lord (Pr 12:4; 18:22; 19:13 – 14; 31:10 – 31; 1Ti 2:9 – 10; 3:11; 5:3 – 16; Tit 2:3 – 5). Virtuous (Ru 3:11; Pr 11:16, 22; 12:4; 14:1). Affectionate (2Sa 1:26), to offspring (Isa 49:15). Illustrated by five wise virgins (Mt 25:1 – 10).

Instances of: *Deborah, a judge, prophetess, and military leader (Jdg 4:5); mother of Samson (Jdg 13:23); Naomi (Ru 1:2; 3:1; 4:14 – 17); Ruth (Ru 1:4, 14 – 22; 2:1 – 4); Hannah, the mother of Samuel (1Sa 1:9 – 18, 24 – 28); widow of Zarephath, who fed Elijah during the famine (1Ki 17:8 – 24); the Shunammite, who gave hospitality to Elisha (2Ki 4:8 – 38); Vashti (Est 1:11 – 12); Esther (Est 4:15 – 17; 5:1 – 8; 7:1 – 6; 8:1 – 8); Mary (Lk 1:26 – 38); Elizabeth (Lk 1:6, 41 – 45); Anna (Lk 2:37); the widow who cast her mite into the treasury (Mk 12:41 – 44; Lk 21:2 – 4); Mary and Martha (Mk 14:3 – 9; Lk 10:42; Jn 11:5); Mary Magdalene (Mk 16:1; Lk 8:2; Jn 20:1 – 2, 11 – 16); Pilate's wife (Mt 27:19); Dorcas (Ac 9:36); Lydia (Ac 19:14); Priscilla (Ac 18:26); Phoebe (Ro 16:1 – 2); Julia (Ro 16:15); Mary (Ro 16:6); Lois and Eunice (2Ti 1:5); Philippians (Php 4:3); the chosen lady (2Jn).*

Wicked:

(2Ki 9:30 – 37; 23:7; Jer 44:15 – 19, 25; Eze 8:14; Ro 1:26). Zeal of, in licentious practices of idolatry (2Ki 23:7; Hos 4:13 – 14); in promoting superstition and idolatry (Jer 7:18; Eze 13:17, 23). Careless (Isa 32:9 – 11). Contentious (Pr 27:15 – 16). Fond of self-indulgence (Isa 32:9 – 11); of ornaments (Jer 2:32). Guilty of lesbianism (Ro 1:26). Subtle and deceitful (Pr 6:24 – 29, 32 – 35; 7:6 – 27; Ecc 7:26). Weak-willed (2Ti 3:6). Active in instigating iniquity (Nu 31:15 – 16; 1Ki 21:25; Ne 13:26). Idolatrous (Nu 31:15 – 16; 2Ki 23:7; Ne 13:26; Jer 7:18). Gossips (1Ti 5:11 – 13). Haughty and vain (Isa 3:16). Odious (Pr 30:23). Guileful and licentious (Pr 2:16 – 19; 5:3 – 20; 6:24 – 29, 32 – 35; Ecc 7:26; Eze 16:32; Ro 1:26). Commits forgery (1Ki 21:8). Subtle and deceitful (Pr 6:24 – 29, 32 – 35; 7:6 – 27; Ecc 7:26). Illustrated by the five foolish virgins (Mt 25:1 – 12).

Instances of: *Eve, in yielding to temptation and seducing her husband (Ge 3:6; 1Ti 2:14); Sarah, in her jealousy and malice toward Hagar (Ge 21:9 – 21); Lot's wife, in her rebellion against her situation, and against the destruction of Sodom (Ge 19:26; Lk 17:32); the daughters of Lot, in their incestuous lust (Ge 19:31 – 38); Rebekah, in her partiality for Jacob and her actions to secure for him Isaac's blessing (Ge 27:11 – 17); Rachel, in her jealousy of Leah (Ge 30:1), in stealing images (Ge 31:19, 34); Leah in her imitation of Rachel in the matter of children (Ge 30:9 – 18); Tamar, in her adultery (Ge 38:14 – 24); Potiphar's wife, in her lust and slander against Joseph (Ge 39:7 – 20); Miriam, in her sedition with Aaron against Moses (Nu 12); Rahab, in her harlotry (Jos 2:1); Delilah, in her conspiracy against Samson (Jdg 16:4 – 20); Peninnah, the wife of Elkanah, in her jealous taunting of Hannah (1Sa 1:4 – 8); the Midianite woman in the camp of Israel, taken in adultery (Nu 25:6 – 8); Michal, in her derision of David's religious zeal (2Sa 6:16, 20 – 23); Bathsheba, in her adultery and in becoming the wife of her husband's murderer (2Sa 11:4 – 5, 27; 12:9 – 10); Solomon's wives, in their idolatrous and wicked influence over Solomon (1Ki 11:1 – 11; Ne 13:26); Jezebel, in her persecution and destruction of the prophets of the Lord (1Ki 18:4, 13), in her persecution of Elijah (1Ki 19:2), in her conspiracy against Naboth to despoil him of his vineyard (1Ki 21:1 – 16), in her evil influence over Ahab (1Ki 21:17 – 27, & 2Ki 9:30 – 37); the cannibal mothers of Samaria (2Ki 6:28 – 29); Athaliah, in destroying the royal household and usurping the throne (2Ki 11:1 – 16; 2Ch 22:10, 12; 23:12 – 15); Noadiah, a false prophetess, in troubling the Jews when they were restoring Jerusalem (Ne 6:14); Haman's wife, in counseling him to hang Mordecai (Est 5:14; 6:13); Job's wife, in counseling him to curse God (Job 2:9; 19:17); the idolatrous wife of Hosea (Hos 1:2 – 3; 3:1); Herodias, in her incestuous marriage with Herod (Mt 14:3 – 4; Mk 6:17 – 19; Lk 3:19) and causing the death of John the Baptist (Mt 14:6 – 11; Mk 6:24 – 28); the daughter of Herodias, in her complicity with her mother in causing the death of John the Baptist (Mt 14:8;*

> *Mk 6:18 – 28); Sapphira, in her blasphemous falsehood (Ac 5:2 – 10).*

Ge	2:22	God made a **w** from
	2:23	she shall be called '**w**,'
	3:6	**w** saw that the fruit
	3:12	The **w** you put here with
	3:15	between you and the **w**,
	3:16	To the **w** he said,
Ex	21:10	If he marries another **w**
Lev	12:2	**w** who becomes pregnant
	15:19	**w** has her regular flow
	15:25	a **w** has a discharge
	18:17	sexual relations with both a **w**
	20:13	as one lies with a **w**,
Nu	5:29	when a **w** goes astray
	30:3	young **w** still living in
	30:9	by a widow or divorced **w**
	30:10	**w** living with her husband
Dt	20:7	become pledged to a **w**
	22:5	**w** must not wear men's
	22:13	married this **w** but when
Ru	3:11	a **w** of noble character
1Sa	1:15	a **w** who is deeply troubled
	25:3	intelligent and beautiful **w**,
2Sa	11:2	he saw a **w** bathing
1Ki	3:18	this **w** also had a baby.
Pr	11:16	A kindhearted **w** gains respect,
	11:22	a beautiful **w** who shows no
	14:1	a wise **w** builds her house,
	30:23	unloved **w** who is married,
	31:30	a **w** who fears the LORD
Mt	5:28	looks at a **w** lustfully
	15:28	**W** you have great faith!
Mk	5:25	a **w** was there who had
	7:25	a **w** whose little daughter
Lk	7:39	what kind of a **w** she is
	10:38	a **w** named Martha opened
	13:12	"**W**, you are set free
	15:8	suppose a **w** has ten silver
Jn	2:4	**w**, why do you involve
	4:7	a Samaritan **w** came
	8:3	a **w** caught in adultery.
	19:26	**w**, here is your son,"

Ac	9:40	Turning toward the dead **w**,
	16:14	was a **w** named Lydia,
Ro	7:2	a married **w** is bound to
1Co	7:2	each **w** her own husband
	7:15	a believing man or **w** is
	7:34	an unmarried **w** or virgin
	7:39	**w** is bound to her husband
	11:3	the head of the **w** is man,
	11:7	the **w** is the glory of man
	11:13	a **w** to pray to God with
Gal	4:4	his Son, born of a **w**,
	4:31	not children of the slave **w**,
1Ti	2:11	A **w** should learn in
	5:16	any **w** who is a believer
Rev	2:20	You tolerate that **w** Jezebel,
	12:1	a **w** clothed with the sun
	12:13	he pursued the **w** who had
	17:3	a **w** sitting on a scarlet

WOMEN

Mt	11:11	among those born of **w**,
	28:5	The angel said to the **w**,
Mk	15:41	Many other **w** who had come
Lk	1:42	Blessed are you among **w**,
	8:2	also some **w** who had been
	23:27	**w** who mourned and wailed
	24:11	they did not believe the **w**,
Ac	1:14	along with the **w** and Mary
	16:13	speak to the **w** who had
	17:4	not a few prominent **w**.
Ro	1:26	**w** exchanged natural relations
1Co	14:34	**w** should remain silent in
Php	4:3	help these **w** who have
1Ti	2:9	want **w** to dress modestly
	5:2	older **w** as mothers,
Tit	2:3	teach the older **w** to be
	2:4	train the younger **w** to love
Heb	11:35	**W** received back their dead
1Pe	3:5	the holy **w** of the past

WONDERS

Ex	3:20	with all the **w** that I will perform
Dt	10:21	and awesome **w** you saw

Job	37:14	stop and consider God's **w**.
Ps	9:1	I will tell of all your **w**.
	89:5	The heavens praise your **w**,
	119:27	then I will meditate on your **w**.
Joel	2:30	I will show **w** in the heavens
Ac	2:11	we hear them declaring the **w**
	5:12	many miraculous signs and **w**
2Co	12:12	that mark an apostle — signs, **w**
2Th	2:9	and **w**, and in every sort
Heb	2:4	also testified to it by signs, **w**

WORD (Heb. *dābhār*, Gr. *logos*). The Bible contains much that is literally the word *of*, and *from*, the Lord — and so it is called "the Word of the Lord." That expression occurs hundreds of times in the OT and usually denotes the prophetic word (word from God through the mouth of the prophet); however, it also can refer to the law of God (Ps 147:19ff.) and to the creative activity of God, who speaks and causes to be (Ge 1; Ps 33:6 – 9). In the case of the prophet, it is never that the prophet chooses to speak a word, but rather that the word from God takes the prophet into its service so that he becomes a mouthpiece for God (Isa 6; Jer 1:4 – 10; Eze 1). And, once uttered, God's word does not return to him empty but accomplishes what he purposes (Isa 55:11). Thus the word of God is the fundamental aspect of God's self-revelation, for by his word he makes known who he is, what he is like, and what his will is for the world.

In the NT the "word of the Lord" or "word of God" (Ac 4:29; 6:2; 1Th 1:8) is primarily good news from God (Ac 15:7). It is the word concerning Jesus Christ and God's kingdom in and through him (16:31 – 32; 17:13); and it is also the word of the cross (1Co 1:18), of reconciliation (2Co 5:19), of eternal life (Php 2:16), and of salvation (Ac 13:26). Christians are told to abide in this word (Jn 8:31), to keep it (8:51; 14:23), and serve it (Ac 6:4).

Jesus himself did not speak like an OT prophet. He said, "I say unto you," not "The Lord says to you" (see Mt 5 – 7). The words of Jesus are the words of the heavenly Father, and so to receive and accept them is to receive eternal salvation (Jn 5:24; 8:51; 12:48; 14:24). But not only is the word spoken by Jesus truly the word from heaven — he himself is the true Word who has come to earth from heaven (1:1 – 14). As the Word (Logos) he is the preexistent Word (Son) who exists eternally and so existed before he became the incarnate Word, when he was rejected by the world he had made. But as incarnate Word, truly sharing our human nature and flesh, he achieved the redemption of the world through his life, death, and resurrection.

The reason why John chose to call the eternal Son by the title *Logos* has caused much research. It is generally assumed that there is a Greek background (*logos* was a prominent concept in metaphysical philosophy) and a Hebrew background (for the word of God is virtually personified in parts of the OT — e.g., Pr 8). Thus this title of Jesus appealed to both Jew and Greek.

Nu	30:2	he must not break his **w**
Dt	8:3	but on every **w** that comes
2Sa	22:31	the **w** of the LORD is flawless.
Ps	119:9	By living according to your **w**.
	119:11	I have hidden your **w** in my heart
	119:105	Your **w** is a lamp to my feet
Pr	12:25	but a kind **w** cheers him up.
	15:1	but a harsh **w** stirs up anger.
	25:11	A **w** aptly spoken
Isa	55:11	so is my **w** that goes out
Jer	23:29	"Is not my **w** like fire," declares
Mt	4:4	but on every **w** that comes
	12:36	for every careless **w** they have
	15:6	Thus you nullify the **w** of God
Mk	4:14	parable? The farmer sows the **w**.
Jn	1:1	was the **W**, and the **W** was
	1:14	The **W** became flesh and made his
	17:17	them by the truth; your **w** is truth.
Ac	6:4	and the ministry of the **w**."
2Co	2:17	we do not peddle the **w** of God
	4:2	nor do we distort the **w** of God.
Eph	6:17	of the Spirit, which is the **w** of God.

Php	2:16	as you hold out the **w** of life —
Col	3:16	Let the **w** of Christ dwell
2Ti	2:15	and who correctly handles the **w**
Heb	4:12	For the **w** of God is living
Jas	1:22	Do not merely listen to the **w**,
2Pe	1:19	And we have the **w** of the prophets

WORD OF GOD

Written Word; the Bible:

Called: book (Ps 40:7; Rev 22:19); book of the Lord (Isa 34:16); book of the law (Ne 8:3; Gal 3:10); holy Scriptures (Ro 1:2; 2Ti 3:15); law of the Lord (Ps 1:2; Isa 30:9); oracles (Zec 9:1; 12:1; Mal 1:1); Scriptures (1Co 15:3); Scriptures of truth (Da 10:21); sword of the Spirit (Eph 6:17); the Word (Jas 1:21 – 23; 1Pe 2:2); Word of God (Lk 11:28; Heb 4:12); good word of God (Heb 6:5); word of Christ (Col 3:16); word of life (Php 2:16); word of truth (Pr 22:21; Eph 1:13; 2Ti 2:15; Jas 1:18).

Compared to: *a lamp (Ps 119:105; Pr 6:23); fire (Jer 23:29); seed (Mt 13:38, 18 – 23, 37 – 38; Mk 4:3 – 20, 26 – 32; Lk 8:5 – 15); two-edged sword (Heb 4:12).*

To Be: *publicly read (Ex 24:7; Dt 31:11 – 13; Jos 8:33 – 35; 2Ki 23:2; 2Ch 17:7 – 9; Ne 8:1 – 8, 13, 18; Isa 2:3; Jer 36:6; Ac 13:15, 27; Col 4:16; 1Th 5:27). Instruction of, to be desired (Ps 119:18 – 19). The people stood and responded, saying, "Amen" (Ex 24:7; Dt 27:12 – 26; Ne 8:5 – 6). Publicly expounded (Ne 8:8); by Jesus (Lk 4:16 – 27; 24:27, 45; Jn 2:22); by the apostles (Ac 2:16 – 47; 8:32, 35; 17:2; 28:23). Searched (Ac 17:11). Searching of, commanded (Isa 34:16; Jn 5:39; 7:52). To be studied (2Ti 2:15; 1Pe 2:2 – 3). Various portions to be compared (2Pe 2:20). Studied by rulers (Dt 17:18 – 19; Jos 1:8). Taught to children (Dt 6:7; 11:19; 21:12 – 13; Ps 78:5). Obeyed (Dt 4:5 – 6; 29:29; Ps 78:1, 7; Isa 34:16; Eze 44:5; Hab 2:2; Mt 7:24 – 25; Lk 6:47 – 48; 11:28; Ro 16:26; 1Co 11:2; 1Th 4:1 – 2; 2Th 2:14 – 15; Heb 2:1 – 3; Jas 1:25; 2Pe 3:1 – 2; Jude 3, 17; Rev 1:3). Believed*

(Mk 1:15; 1Jn 5:11, 13). Longed for (Ps 119:20, 131; Am 8:11 – 13). Walked after (Ps 119:30). In the heart (Dt 30:11 – 14; Job 22:22; Pss 37:31; 40:8; 119:11; Pr 6:20 – 21; Isa 51:7; Eze 3:10; Ro 10:6 – 8). Meditated upon (Jos 1:8; Pss 1:2; 119:15, 23, 48, 78, 97, 99, 148). Worn on the hand and forehead (Ex 13:9; Dt 6:8; 11:18). Written on door frames (Dt 6:9; 11:20). In public places (Dt 27:2 – 3, 8; Jos 8:32). Placed inside of ark of the covenant (Ex 40:20); beside ark (Dt 31:26). Taught in the Psalms (Dt 31:19, 21; Ps 119:54). Used for teaching and admonishing one another (1Co 10:11; Col 3:16). Instruction (2Ti 3:16 – 17).

Not to Be: *added to nor taken from (Dt 4:2; 12:32; Pr 30:6; Rev 22:18 – 19); handled deceitfully (2Co 4:2); broken (Jn 10:35).*

Nature of: *Comforting (Ps 119:28, 50, 52, 76, 83, 92). Delight of the righteous (Job 23:12; Pss 1:2; 119:16, 24, 35, 77, 103, 143, 162, 174). Desired more than gold (Ps 119:72, 127). Edifying (Ps 119:98, 99, 104, 130; Ac 20:32; Ro 4:23 – 24; 15:4; 1Ti 4:6; 1Jn 2:7 – 8, 12, 14, 21). Effective (Isa 55:11). Enduring forever (Ps 119:89, 138, 152; Isa 40:8; Mk 13:31; Lk 16:17; 1Pe 1:23 – 25). Full of hope (Ps 119:81; Col 1:5). Full of joy (Jer 15:16; 1Jn 1:4). Inspired (Ex 19:7; 20:1; 24:3 – 4, 12; 31:18; 32:16; 34:27, 32; Lev 26:46; Dt 4:5, 10, 14; 2Ki 17:13; 2Ch 33:18; Pss 99:7; 147:19; Isa 34:16; 59:21; Jer 30:2; 36:1 – 2, 27 – 28, 32, 59 – 64; Eze 11:25; Da 10:21; Hos 8:12; Zec 7:12; Ac 1:16; 28:25; Ro 3:1 – 2; 1Co 2:12 – 13; 14:37; Eph 6:17; 1Th 2:13; 2Ti 3:16 – 17; Heb 1:1 – 2; 3:7 – 8; 4:12; 2Pe 1:21; 3:2, 15; Rev 1:1 – 2, 11, 17 – 19; 2:7; 22:6 – 8). Life giving (Ps 119:25, 93; Jas 1:18; 1Pe 1:23). Living (Heb 4:12). Loved (Ps 119:47 – 48, 70, 97, 111, 113, 119, 159, 163, 167). Part of the Christian armor (Eph 6:17). Perfect (Ps 19:7; Jas 1:24). Powerful (Lk 1:37; Heb 4:12). Praiseworthy (Ps 56:4). Pure (Pss 12:6; 19:8; 119:140; Pr 30:5). Restraining (Pss 17:4; 119:11). Revered (Pss 119:161; 138:2). Sanctifying (Jn 15:3; 17:17, 19; Eph 5:26; 1Ti 4:5). Spirit* *and life (Jn 6:63). Spiritual food, bread (Dt 8:3; Mt 4:4). Standard of righteous (Ps 119:138, 144, 172; Isa 8:20). Trustworthy (Pss 19:7, 9; 33:4, 6; 93:5; 111:7 – 8; 119:86). Truth (Ps 119:142, 151, 160; 1Th 2:13; Jas 1:18). Wonderful (Ps 119:129). Bears the test of criticism and experience (2Sa 22:31; Ps 18:30). Cleanses life of youth (Ps 119:9). Convicts of sin (2Ki 22:9 – 13; 2Ch 17:7 – 10; 34:14 – 33). Gives peace (Ps 119:165). Inspires faith (Ro 10:17; Heb 11:3). Makes free (Ps 119:45; Jn 8:32). Makes wise (Ps 119:99; 2Ti 3:15). Rejoices the heart (Ps 119:111; Jer 15:16). Spirit of, gives life (2Co 3:6). Standard of judgment, the world to be judged by (Jn 12:48; Ro 2:16). Works salvation (1Th 2:13; 1Pe 1:23). Fulfilled by Jesus (Mt 5:17; Lk 24:27; Jn 19:24). Testifies of Jesus (Jn 5:39; 20:31; Ac 10:43; 18:28; 1Co 15:3; Heb 10:7). See Jesus the Christ, Prophecies Concerning.*

Ignorance of: *(Mt 22:29; Mk 12:24). Disbelief in (Lk 16:31; 24:25; Jn 5:46 – 47; 8:37; 2Ti 4:3 – 4; 1Pe 2:8; 2Pe 3:15 – 16). Rejected by the wicked (Ps 50:16 – 17; Pr 1:29; 13:13; Isa 5:24; 28:9 – 14; 30:9 – 11; 53:1; Jer 6:10; 8:9; Hos 8:12; Am 2:12; Mic 2:6; Mk 7:9, 13; Lk 16:31; 24:25; Jn 3:20; 5:46 – 47; 8:37, 45; Ac 13:46; 1Co 1:18, 22 – 23; 2Ti 4:3 – 4; 1Pe 2:8; 2Pe 3:15 – 16; Rev 22:19). See Commandment.*

Jesus, the Living Word:

(Jn 1:1, 14; 1Jn 5:7; Rev 19:13). See Jesus the Christ, Names of; Titles and Names.

WORK

Ge	2:2	day he rested from all his **w**.
Ex	23:12	"Six days do your **w**,
Nu	8:11	ready to do the **w** of the LORD.
Dt	5:14	On it you shall not do any **w**,
Ps	19:1	the skies proclaim the **w**
Ecc	5:19	his lot and be happy in his **w** —
Jer	48:10	lax in doing the LORD's **w**!
Jn	6:27	Do not **w** for food that spoils,
	9:4	we must do the **w** of him who sent
Ac	13:2	for the **w** to which I have called

1Co	3:13	test the quality of each man's **w**.
	4:12	We **w** hard with our own hands.
Eph	4:16	up in love, as each part does its **w**.
Php	1:6	that he who began a good **w**
	2:12	continue to **w** out your salvation
Col	3:23	Whatever you do, **w** at it
1Th	4:11	and to **w** with your hands,
	5:12	to respect those who **w** hard
2Th	3:10	If a man will not **w**, he shall not eat
2Ti	3:17	equipped for every good **w**.
Heb	6:10	he will not forget your **w**
2Jn	1:11	him shares in his wicked **w**.
3Jn	1:8	men so that we may **w** together

WORKS (Heb. *ma'aseh*, work, deed, *pa'al*, a work, Gr. *ergon*, work, *erga*, works). Used of deeds done by God out of holy love, and by human beings as God's creatures. In the OT the work/works of God (often in the singular, reflecting that the total activity of the Lord is seen as a unity, one work) refer to his creating and preserving the cosmos (Ge 2:2; Ps 8:3), and his deeds of salvation and judgment on behalf of Israel (Ps 28:5; Isa 5:12, 19). God's work is "awesome" (Ps 66:3), "great" (92:5), "wonderful" (139:14), and done in "faithfulness" (33:4). The godly meditate on God's work and works (77:12; 143:5) and praise him for them (72:18; 105:1 – 2). In the NT God is presented as working in and through the Messiah both in creation (Jn 1:1 – 3) and in redemption (9:3 – 4). By his works Jesus reveals his true identity and from whom he comes (Mt 9:2 – 5; Jn 5:36; 10:37 – 38).

Being made in God's image, human beings perform works as they live in God's world in relationship with other human beings. What deeds they perform cannot be isolated from the state of their hearts and their motivation (Ps 28:3 – 4). Works done out of evil motivation are "acts of the sinful nature" (Gal 5:19). Works done in order to earn the favorable judgment of God at the end of life — seeking justification by works — are not acceptable for this end (Ro 3:20; Gal 2:16; 2Ti 1:9). True works, in which God delights, are those that arise from an inward gratitude to God for his goodness and salvation. These spring from faith, the faith that holds to Christ as Savior and Lord (Eph 2:10; Col 1:10). While Paul emphasized the need for faith leading to faithfulness to God in good deeds, James (facing a different situation) emphasized that genuine good works are the evidence of true faith (Jas 2:14ff.).

Ps	145:6	of the power of your awesome **w**,
Pr	31:31	let her **w** bring her praise
Ro	4:2	in fact, Abraham was justified by **w**
	8:28	in all things God **w** for the good
Eph	2:9	not by **w**, so that no one can boast.
	4:12	to prepare God's people for **w**

WORKS, GOOD [1911, 2006, 5126, 6268, 6913, 7188, 7189, 1919, 2240, 2435].

General References to:
(2Co 9:8; Eph 2:10; Php 2:13; Col 1:10; 1Th 1:3, 7 – 8; 2Th 2:17, 21; Jas 1:22 – 27; 3:17 – 18). Under the law (Lev 18:5; Eze 20:11, 13, 20; Lk 10:28; Ro 10:5; Gal 3:12). In humanitarian service (Eze 18:7 – 8; Mt 10:42; 25:35 – 46; Jas 1:27). Hypocritical (Mt 6:1 – 4). Jesus an example of (Jn 10:32; Ac 10:38). Ministers should be patterns of (Tit 2:7). Ministers should exhort to (1Ti 6:17 – 18; Tit 3:1, 8, 14). Holy women should manifest (1Ti 2:10; 5:10). Manifest faith (Ps 37:3; Mt 19:16 – 21; Ro 2:13; Gal 6:4; Jas 2:14 – 26). Scriptures given for (Tit 2:14). God is glorified by (Mt 25:34 – 46; Jn 15:2 – 8, 14; 1Co 3:6 – 9; Php 1:11; Heb 13:21). Designed to lead others to glorify God (Mt 5:16; 1Pe 2:12). A blessing attends (Jas 1:25). God remembers (Dt 6:25; 24:13; Ps 106:30 – 31; Jer 22:15 – 16; Eze 18:5 – 9; Mt 6:1 – 4; 18:5; 25:34 – 36; Jn 15:2 – 8, 14; Ac 10:14, 38; Heb 6:9 – 10; Rev 14:13; 22:14). Of the righteous, are manifest (1Ti 5:25). God remembers (Ne 13:14; Heb 6:9 – 10). Shall be brought into judgment (Ecc 12:14, w 2Co 5:10). In the judgment, will be an evidence of faith (Mt 25:34 – 40, w Jas 2:14 – 20). Parables relating to: the talents and pounds (Mt 25:14 – 29; Lk 19:12 – 27); the labor-

ers in the vineyard (Mt 20:11 – 15); the two sons (Mt 21:28 – 31); the barren fig tree (Lk 13:6 – 9).

Commanded:
(Ps 37:3; Mt 3:8; Jn 14:2 – 8, 14). To ministers (Tit 2:7); women professing godliness (1Ti 2:10); widows (1Ti 5:10). To Christians (Mt 5:16; Col 3:13; Tit 3:1 – 2, 8, 14; Heb 10:24; Jas 1:22 – 27; 3:13; 1Pe 2:12). To the rich (1Ti 6:18). To be done without a show (Mt 6:1 – 4). Following the example of the faithful (Heb 10 – 14). Zeal in (Tit 2:14).

Insufficient for Salvation:
(Pss 49:7 – 8; 127:1 – 2; Ecc 1:14; Isa 13:14; 57:12; 64:6; Eze 7:19; 33:12 – 19; Da 9:18; Mt 5:20; Lk 17:7 – 10; 18:9 – 14; Ac 13:39; Ro 3:20 – 21; 4:1 – 25; 8:3; 9:16, 31 – 32; 11:6; 1Co 13:1 – 3; Gal 2:16, 21; 3:10 – 12, 21; 4:9 – 11; 5:2, 4, 6, 18; 6:15; Eph 2:8 – 9; Php 3:3 – 9; Col 2:20 – 23; 2Ti 1:9; Tit 3:4 – 5; Heb 4:3 – 10; 6:1 – 2; 9:1 – 14; Jas 2:10 – 11).

WORLD [824, 2535, 2698, 9315, 10075, 172, 1178, 3179, 3180, 3232, 3876, 4246, 4920, 4922]. The most common Hebrew word for "world" is *tēvēl*, "the habitable earth," the earth as made for man, often parallel and synonymous with "earth." The Hebrew words for "world" refer either to the earth itself, or as formed for and inhabited by man. Greek cosmology must be reckoned with in the use of such terms as *aiōn* and *kosmos* in the LXX and in the NT. The former term denotes the temporal or durative aspect of that which exists; *kosmos* includes angels, spiritual principalities and powers, men, beasts, earth, heavenly bodies, and Hades. In the NT *kosmos* commonly refers to man and his affairs, especially in an evil sense, over against the new life in Christ, the kingdom of God, the body of Christ, the church. As God is in the world but not of it, so are we: God's mode of being penetrates without mixture the world's mode of being, just as iron is penetrated by magnetism or copper by electricity (cf. Jn 17:14 – 18).

Ps	9:8	He will judge the **w**
	50:12	for the **w** is mine, and all that is in it
	96:13	He will judge the **w**

Pr	8:23	before the **w** began.
Isa	13:11	I will punish the **w** for its evil,
Zep	1:18	the whole **w** will be consumed,
Mt	5:14	"You are the light of the **w**.
	16:26	for a man if he gains the whole **w**,
Mk	16:15	into all the **w** and preach the good
Jn	1:29	who takes away the sin of the **w**!
	3:16	so loved the **w** that he gave his one
	8:12	he said, "I am the light of the **w**.
	15:19	As it is, you do not belong to the **w**,
	16:33	In this **w** you will have trouble.
	17:5	had with you before the **w** began.
	18:36	"My kingdom is not of this **w**.
Ac	17:24	"The God who made the **w**
Ro	10:18	their words to the ends of the **w**."
1Co	1:27	things of the **w** to shame the strong.
	3:19	the wisdom of this **w** is foolishness
	6:2	that the saints will judge the **w**?
2Co	5:19	that God was reconciling the **w**
	10:3	For though we live in the **w**,
1Ti	6:7	For we brought nothing into the **w**,
Heb	11:38	the **w** was not worthy of them.
Jas	2:5	poor in the eyes of the **w** to be rich
	4:4	with the **w** is hatred toward God?
1Pe	1:20	before the creation of the **w**,
1Jn	2:2	but also for the sins of the whole **w**.
	2:15	not love the **w** or anything in the **w**.
	5:4	born of God overcomes the **w**.
Rev	13:8	slain from the creation of the **w**.

WORLDLINESS [94, 96, 3176, 3180+ 3836, 4920, 4921, 4922].

Described:
(Ecc 1:8; 8:15; Isa 56:12; Jn 15:19; Tit 3:3; 2Pe 2:12 – 15, 18 – 19). Proverbial theme (Isa 22:13; Lk 12:19; 1Co 15:32). Tends to poverty (Pr 21:17; Hag 1:6). Fatal to spirituality (Gal 6:8; Php 3:19; 1Ti 5:6). Chokes the Word (Mt 13:22; Mk 4:19; Lk 8:14). Leads to: the rejection of the gospel (Mt 22:2 – 6; Lk 14:17 – 24); the rejection of Christ (Jn 5:44; 12:43). Moral insensibility (Isa 22:13; 32:9 – 11; 47:7 – 9). Death (Pr 14:12 – 13). Pros-

perity of, is short-lived (Job 20:4 – 29; 21:11 – 15; Ps 49:16 – 18; Isa 24:7 – 11; 28:4). Prayer regarding (Ps 73:2 – 22). Parables of (Lk 16:1 – 13, 19 – 25). Vanity of (Ecc 2:1 – 12; 6:11 – 12).

Admonitions against:
(Pr 23:20 – 21; 27:1, 7; Ecc 7:2 – 4; 11:9 – 10; Hos 9:1, 11, 13; Am 6:3 – 7; 8:10; Mic 2:10; 6:14, 19, 24; Mt 6:25 – 34; 16:26; 24:28; Mk 8:36 – 37; Lk 17:26 – 29, 33; 21:34; Jn 12:25; Ro 12:2; 1Co 7:29 – 31; 10:6; Col 3:2, 5; 2Ti 2:4, 22; 3:2 – 9; Tit 2:12; Jas 2:1 – 4; 4:4, 9; 5:5; 1Pe 1:14, 24; 2:11; 4:1 – 4; 1Jn 2:15 – 17). Denounced (Isa 5:11 – 12; 47:8 – 9; Jude 11 – 13, 16, 19). Moses' choice against (Heb 11:24 – 26).

Instances of:
Antediluvians (Mt 24:38 – 39; Lk 17:26 – 27); Sodomites (Lk 17:28 – 29); Esau (Ge 25:31 – 34; Heb 12:16); Jacob (Ge 25:31 – 34; 27:36; 30:37 – 43); Judah (Ge 37:26 – 27); Israelites (1Sa 8:19 – 20); Balaam (2Pe 2:15; Jude 11, w Nu 22; 23; 24); Eli's sons (1Sa 2:12 – 17); Gehazi (2Ki 5:20 – 27); Herod (Mt 14:6 – 7); the disciples (Mt 18:1 – 4; Mk 9:34; Lk 9:46 – 48); the rich fool (Lk 12:16 – 21); Dives (Lk 16:19 – 25); the worldly steward (Lk 16:1 – 13); Cretans (Tit 1:12).

WORLDLY [WORLD]

1Co	3:1	address you as spiritual but as **w** —
Tit	2:12	to ungodliness and **w** passions,

WORLDLY PLEASURE (Job 20:12; Ecc 7:4; Isa 22:13; 2Ti 3:4; Tit 3:3).

Rejected by Moses (Heb 11:25). To be rejected by the righteous (1Pe 4:3 – 4). Brings poverty (Pr 21:17). Chokes righteousness (Lk 8:14). Leads to suffering (Isa 47:8 – 9; 2Pe 3:13); spiritual death (1Ti 5:6). Denounced (Isa 5:11 – 12; Jas 5:5). Folly of (Ecc 1:17; 2:1 – 13). See Worldliness.

WORLDLY WISDOM Desired by Eve (Ge 3:6 – 7). Misleading (Isa 47:10). Increases sorrow (Ecc 1:18). Shall perish (Isa 29:14). Heavenly things not discerned by (Mt 11:25; Lk 10:21). Gospel not to be preached with (1Co 1:17 – 26; 2:1 – 14). To be renounced in order to attain spiritual wisdom (1Co 3:18 – 20). Admonitions against (Col 2:8; 1Ti 6:20 – 21). Admonitions against glorying in (Jer 9:23 – 24). *See Wisdom.*

WORM [6182, 8231, 9357, 1905, 5037, 5038].

Low form of life (Ex 16:24; Isa 51:8; Ac 12:23), used metaphorically of humankind's insignificance (Job 25:6; Isa 41:14).

WORSHIP [1251, 2556, 3707, 3710, 6268, 6913, 7537, 10504, 10586, 3301, 3302, 4686, 4934, 4936] (Heb. *shāhâh, bow down, prostrate,* Gr. *proskyneō, to prostrate, do obeisance to*). The honor, reverence, and homage paid to superior beings or powers, whether men, angels, or God. The English word means "worthship" and denotes the worthiness of the individual receiving the special honor due to his or her worth. While the word is used of humans, it is especially used of the divine honors paid to a deity, whether of the heathen religions or the true and living God.

When given to God, worship involves an acknowledgment of divine perfections. It may express itself in the form of direct address, as in adoration or thanksgiving, or in service to God; it may be private, or it may be public, involving a cultus. Worship presupposes that God is, that he can be known by humans, and that his perfections set him far above humans.

The Bible records that public worship has always existed. In patriarchal times there was both the privacy of prayer (e.g., Ge 18) and the public act of setting up an altar (e.g., 12:7). From the patriarchs onward, we can divide the Bible into four periods. First, while Moses established the basis of the public worship of Israel and gave it its focal point in the tabernacle, we know little about the actual performance of worship. As 1Sa 1:1, for example, shows, the tabernacle remained the center for the pilgrimage festivals with their round of sacrifices; at the same time it shows the wealth and depth of private devotion that they represented. In the second period, worship became highly organized in

the temple ritual, which had its origin in the tabernacle set up in the wilderness. It was led by priests assisted by the Levites, and it included a complex ritual and system of sacrifices. The third stage was that of the synagogue, which developed among those who remained in exile. This greatly differed from worship in the temple. Whereas the latter was centralized in Jerusalem, the former was found wherever there were Jews. In the synagogues, however, the emphasis was more on instruction than on worship, although the latter was not neglected. The fourth stage was that of the early Christian churches. Jewish Christians continued, as long as they were permitted, to worship in the temple and in the synagogue, though for them the whole ceremonial and sacrificial system ended with the death and resurrection of Jesus. Public Christian worship developed along the lines of the synagogue. It appears that from the first, Christians met in homes for private brotherhood meetings, and the time was the Lord's Day (Jn 20:19, 26; Ac 20:7; 1Co 16:2). Christian public worship consisted of preaching (Ac 20:7; 1Co 14:9), reading of Scripture (Col 4:16; Jas 1:22), prayer (1Co 14:14 – 16), singing (Eph 5:19; Col 3:16), baptism and the Lord's Supper (Ac 2:41; 1Co 11:18 – 34), almsgiving (1Co 16:1 – 2), and sometimes prophesying and tongues.

General References to:
To be rendered to God only (Ex 20:3; Dt 5:7; 6:13; Mt 4:10; Lk 4:8; Ac 10:26; 14:15; Col 2:18; Rev 19:10; 22:8). Not needed by God (Ac 17:24 – 25). Divine presence in (Ex 29:42 – 43; 40:34 – 35; Lev 19:30; Nu 17:4; 1Ki 8:3 – 11; 2Ch 5:13 – 14; Pss 77:13; 84:4; Isa 56:7; Mt 18:20; Ac 2:1 – 4; Heb 10:25). Origin of (Ge 4:26). Of Jesus. See Jesus the Christ, Worship of. Acceptable to God (Ge 4:4; 8:21). Of the wicked, rejected (Ge 4:5, 7). See Prayer, of the Wicked. "Iniquity of the holy things" (Ex 28:38). Sanctuary instituted for (Ex 25:8, 22; 29:43; 40:34 – 35; Nu 17:4). Attitudes in: bowing (Ex 34:8; 2Ch 20:18); lying prostrate (Ge 17:3; Mk 3:11). Prayer in. See Prayer. Benedictions pronounced. See Benedictions. With music (2Ch

5:13 – 14; Ezr 3:10 – 11; Pss 100:1 – 2; 126:1 – 3; Isa 30:29; 38:20). *Rendering praise* (Pss 22:22; 138:2; 149:1). *Thanksgiving* (Pss 35:18; 100:4; 116:17). *In spirit and in truth* (Jn 4:23 – 24; 1Co 14:15; Php 3:3). *Renews strength* (Isa 40:31). *Loved by God's people* (Pss 27:4; 84:1 – 4, 10; Zec 8:21). *Reward of* (Pss 65:4; 92:13 – 14; 122:1). *Preparation for* (Ex 19:10 – 13, 21 – 24; 20:24 – 25; 30:19, 21; Lev 10:3; Ps 26:6; Isa 56:6 – 7; Zep 3:18; Mal 3:3 – 4). *Requirements of* (Pss 24:3 – 6; 51:18 – 19). *Proprieties in* (Ecc 5:1 – 2; 1Co 11:13, 20 – 22; 14:2 – 19). *Reverence in* (Ex 3:5; 19:10 – 12, 21 – 24; 24:1 – 2; Ecc 5:1; Hab 2:20). *Private* (Mt 6:6; 14:23; Lk 6:12). *At night* (Isa 30:29; Ac 16:25). *Jesus prays at night* (Lk 6:12). *In the temple* (Jer 26:2; Lk 18:10; 24:53; Ac 3:1). *In the heavenly temple* (Rev 11:1). *In private homes* (Ac 1:13 – 14; 5:42; 12:12; 20:7 – 9; Ro 16:5; 1Co 16:19; Col 4:15; Phm 2). *Anywhere* (Jn 4:21 – 24). *To become universal* (Isa 45:23; Ro 14:11; Php 2:10). *Of hypocrites, despised by God* (Isa 1:11 – 15; 29:13 – 16; Hos 6:6; Am 5:21 – 24). *Of the wicked, rejected* (Ge 4:5, 7). *Of angels, forbidden* (Rev 19:10; 22:8 – 9).

Commanded:

(Ge 35:1; Ex 15:1; 23:17 – 18; 34:23; Dt 12:5 – 7, 11 – 12; 16:6 – 8; 31:11 – 13; 33:19; 2Ki 17:36; 1Ch 16:29; Ne 10:39; Pss 29:2; 45:11; 76:11; 96:8 – 9; 97:7; 99:5; Isa 12:5 – 6; 49:13; 52:9; Jer 31:11 – 12; Joel 1:14 – 15; 2:15 – 17; Na 1:15; Hag 1:8; Zec 14:16 – 18; Mt 8:4; Mk 1:44; Lk 4:8; 5:14; 1Ti 2:8; Heb 10:25; 12:28; Rev 14:7; 19:10). *Summons to* (Ps 95:6; Isa 2:3; Mic 4:2).

National:

(Rev 15:4). *The whole nation required to assemble for, including men, women, children, servants, and strangers* (Dt 16:11; 31:11 – 13), *in Mount Gerizim and Mount Ebal* (Jos 8:32 – 35). *The word of God read in public assemblies* (Ex 24:7; Dt 27:12 – 26; 31:11 – 13; Jos 8:33 – 35; 2Ki 23:1 – 3; Ne 8:1 – 8, 13 – 18; Mt 21:23; Lk 4:16 – 17). *See* Affliction, Prayer under; Blasphemy; Child, Children; Church, the Body of

Believers; Consecration; Dedication; Idolatry; Levites; Minister; Music; Offerings; Praise; Prayer; Preaching; Priest; Psalms; Religion; Sacrilege; Servant; Tabernacle; Temple; Thanksgiving; Women; Word of God.

Instances of:

Israel (Ex 15:1 – 2; Ps 107:6 – 8, 32); *Moses* (Ex 34:8); *Solomon* (2Ch 7:1); *priests and Levites* (2Ch 30:27); *psalmists* (Pss 5:7; 42:4; 48:9; 55:14; 63:1 – 2; 66:4, 13 – 14; 89:7; 93:5; 103:1 – 4; 116:12 – 14, 17; 119:108; 132:7, 13 – 14); *Isaiah* (Isa 49:13; 52:9).

Jos	22:27	that we will **w** the LORD
1Ch	16:29	**w** the LORD in the splendor
Ps	95:6	Come, let us bow down in **w**,
	100:2	**w** the LORD with gladness;
Zec	14:17	up to Jerusalem to **w** the King,
Mt	2:2	and have come to **w** him."
	4:9	"if you will bow down and **w** me."
Jn	4:24	and his worshipers must **w** in spirit
Ro	12:1	to God — this is your spiritual act of **w**.
Heb	10:1	perfect those who draw near to **w**.

WORTH

Job	28:13	Man does not comprehend its **w**;
Pr	31:10	She is **w** far more than rubies.
Mt	10:31	are **w** more than many sparrows.
Ro	8:18	sufferings are not **w** comparing
1Pe	1:7	of greater **w** than gold,
	3:4	which is of great **w** in God's sight.

WRATH [399, 678, 2404, 2405, 2408, 2779, 3019, 5757, 6301, 6552, 7288, 7911, 7912, 8075, 10634, 2596, 3973]. The translation of many Hebrew and Greek words, ranging widely in tone, intensity, and effect (Ge 27:25; 2Ch 26:19; Est 1:12; Ps 85:4; Mt 2:16). The first display of human wrath recorded in the Bible (Ge 4:5 – 6) is followed by numerous accounts of disaster wrought by man's wrath, which never works the righteousness of God (Jas 1:20) and is never more than tolerated (Eph 4:26; Ps 37:8; Ro 12:19). The wrath of a just, pure, and holy God is dreadful to evildoers (Nu 11:1 – 10; Heb 10:26 – 31), yet God is slow to anger, eager to forgive (Ps 103:8 – 9), and so should we be (Eph 4:31 – 32). Less often mentioned in the NT than in the OT, the wrath of God is no less terrible, is revealed most dramatically in the wrath of the Lamb (Jn 1:29; Rev 6:16) and abides on "whoever rejects the Son" (Jn 3:36).

2Ch	36:16	scoffed at his prophets until the **w**
Ps	76:10	Surely your **w** against men brings
Pr	15:1	A gentle answer turns away **w**,
Isa	13:13	at the **w** of the Lord Almighty,
Eze	5:13	my **w** against them will subside,
	20:8	So I said I would pour out my **w**
Am	1:3	I will not turn back [my **w**].
Na	1:2	maintains his **w** against his enemies
Zep	1:15	That day will be a day of **w**,
Jn	3:36	for God's **w** remains on him."
Ro	1:18	The **w** of God is being revealed
	2:5	you are storing up **w**
	5:9	saved from God's **w** through him!
	9:22	choosing to show his **w**
1Th	5:9	God did not appoint us to suffer **w**
Rev	6:16	and from the **w** of the Lamb!
	19:15	the fury of the **w** of God Almighty.

WRITTEN [WRITE]

Dt	28:58	which are **w** in this book,
Jos	1:8	careful to do everything **w** in it.

	23:6	to obey all that is **w** in the Book
Ps	40:7	it is **w** about me in the scroll.
Da	12:1	everyone whose name is found **w**
Lk	10:20	but rejoice that your names are **w**
	24:44	must be fulfilled that is **w** about me
Jn	20:31	these are **w** that you may believe
	21:25	for the books that would be **w**.
Ro	2:15	of the law are **w** on their hearts,
2Co	3:3	**w** not with ink but with the Spirit
Col	2:14	having canceled the **w** code,
Heb	10:7	it is **w** about me in the scroll —
	12:23	whose names are **w** in heaven.
Rev	21:27	but only those whose names are **w**

WRONG [WRONGDOING]

Ex	23:2	Do not follow the crowd in doing **w**
Nu	5:7	must make full restitution for his **w**,
Dt	32:4	A faithful God who does no **w**,
Job	34:12	unthinkable that God would do **w**,
Ps	5:5	you hate all who do **w**.
Gal	2:11	to his face, because he was clearly in the **w**.
1Th	5:15	that nobody pays back **w** for **w**,

WRONGDOING [WRONG]

Job	1:22	sin by charging God with **w**.
1Jn	5:17	All **w** is sin, and there is sin that

XERXES [347] (zŭrk′sēz, Gr. form of Heb. ʾăhash-wērôsh, Persian *Khshayarsha*).

1. The father of Darius the Mede, mentioned in Da 9:1.

2. King of Persia, mentioned in the book of Esther. There seems to be little doubt that he is the well-known historical Xerxes, who reigned from 486 to 465 BC. The main support for this identi-fication is to be found in the linguistic equivalence of the names of the KJV "Ahasuerus" and the NIV "Xerxes." In addition, a close similarity has been noted between the character of the historical Xerxes and the character of the king of the Persians por-trayed in the book of Esther. There are also his-torical correlations. The feast that was held in the third year of the reign of Xerxes at Susa (Est 1:3) corresponds to an assembly held by Xerxes in his third year in preparation for the invasion of Greece. Herodotus states that Xerxes, following his defeat at Salamis and Plataea, consoled himself in his sev-enth year with the pleasures of the harem (Herodo-tus, 9.108). This parallels the biblical account that relates that Ahasuerus replaced Vashti by marrying Esther in his seventh year (Est 2:16) after gather-ing all the fair young virgins to Susa. The Xerxes of Ezr 4:6, to whom were written accusations against the Jews of Jerusalem, is in all probability this same Xerxes, though sometimes identified with Camby-ses, son of Cyrus.

YAHWEH [3363, 3378] (*He who is [I am]* or *He who causes to be*). The Hebrew personal name for God, Yahweh, is translated in the NIV as "Lord." God revealed his name as "I AM WHO I AM," his eternal covenant name implying self-existence and saving presence (Ex 3:14 – 17). YHWH is often called the "tetragrammaton," referring to the "four letters" or consonants of Yahweh. *See God, Names of: Yahweh; Jehovah.*

YHWH This is not in reality a word but is known as the "tetragrammaton," the four consonants standing for the ancient Hebrew name for God commonly referred to as "Jehovah" or "Yahweh." The original Hebrew text was not vocalized. YHWH was considered too sacred to pronounce, so *'adonai* ("my Lord") was substituted in reading. When eventually a vowel system was invented, since the Hebrews had forgotten how to pronounce YHWH, they substituted the vowels for *'adonai,* making "Jehovah," a form first attested at the beginning of the twelfth century AD. *See God, Names of, Yahweh; Yahweh.*

YOKE [3998, 4573, 4574, 4593, 6026, 6296, 6585, 7537, 7538, 2282, 2414, 2433] (Heb. *môtâh, an oxbow,* '*ôl,* *a yoke, tsemedh, yoke of oxen, an acre,* i.e., as much land as a yoke of oxen could plow in a day, Gr. *zeugos, a team,* and *zygos, yoke*). In the literal sense, a bar of wood so constructed as to unite two animals, usually oxen, enabling them to work in the fields. Drawing loads and pulling implements used in farming, such as the plow, were two chief functions the yoke made possible. Archaeological studies have shown that the yoke was variously constructed in different periods of history. It was commonly used all over the ancient world. Also used figuratively in the sense of servitude (Jer 27 – 28) and "the law of God."

1Ki	12:4	and the heavy **y** he put on us,
Mt	11:29	Take my **y** upon you and learn
Gal	5:1	be burdened again by a **y**

YOKED [YOKE]

| 2Co | 6:14 | Do not be **y** together |

YOKEFELLOW [5187] (Gr. *syzygos, yoked together*). A common word among Greek writers referring to those united by close bonds, as in marriage, labor, etc. It is found only once in the NT (Php 4:3), and the meaning here is not clear. Some feel that Paul refers here to a fellow worker; others think the word is a proper noun, Syzygos.

ZACCHAEUS [2405] (zăkē´ŭs, Gr. *Zakchaios*, from Heb. *zakkay, pure*). A publican, referred to only in Luke. He resided at Jericho and is described as a "chief" tax collector. When Jesus was passing through Jericho on one occasion, Zacchaeus wished very much to see him. Being short, he climbed a tree by the side of the path. He must have been quite surprised, therefore, when Jesus paused in his journey beneath this very tree and, looking up, urged Zacchaeus to come down, for he had decided to stay at his house (Lk 19:6). Zacchaeus hurried down gladly and invited Jesus to his home. From that day on his life was changed (19:8).

ZAREPHATH [7673, 4919] (zăr´ĕfăth, Heb. *tsārephath, refinement*). An OT town remembered chiefly because Elijah resided there during the latter half of the famine caused by the drought (1Ki 17:9ff.). Its Greek equivalent "Sarepta" is mentioned in the KJV of Lk 4:26, where it is described as being in the land of Sidon. Here God miraculously sustained the prophet through the help of a widow. Ruins of the ancient town survive south of the modern village of Sarafand, about eight miles (thirteen km.) south of Sidon, fourteen miles (twenty-three km.) north of Tyre.

ZEAL [3013, 5883, 7861, 7863, 2419, 2420, 2421, 5080, 5082] (*zeal, jealousy*).

General References to:
Without love, unprofitable (1Co 13:3). Without knowledge (Nu 11:27 – 28; Jdg 11:30 – 31, 34 – 35; Ecc 7:16; Mt 8:19 – 20; Lk 9:57 – 58; Jn 16:2; Ac 21:20; Ro 10:2 – 3; Gal 1:13 – 14). Wisdom of (Pr 11:30). Required (Isa 62:6 – 7; Mt 5:13 – 16; Mk 4:21 – 22; Lk 8:16 – 17; Ac 10:42; 1Co 15:58; Tit 2:14; 3:1). Commanded (Jos 24:15 – 16; Ezr 7:23; Pss 60:4; 96:2; Ecc 9:10; Isa 60:1; Hag 2:4; Ro 12:11; 1Co 7:29 – 35; Gal 6:9; Eph 5:15 – 16; 6:10 – 20; Php 1:27 – 28; Col 4:5; 2Th 3:13; Heb 12:1 – 2; 13:13 – 15; 1Pe 2:2; 2Pe 1:10 – 11; 3:14;

Jude 3, 22 – 23; Rev 3:19). Expected (Hab 2:2; Zec 14:20 – 21; 2Co 4:8 – 10, 13, 16 – 18; Gal 4:18; Php 2:15). Rewards of (Da 12:3; Mt 25:21, 23; Lk 19:17 – 19; Jas 5:20).

Exemplified by:
Moses (Ex 2:12; 11:8; 32:19 – 20, 31 – 32; Nu 10:29; 11:29; Dt 9:18 – 19); Phinehas (Nu 25:7 – 13; Ps 106:30); Joshua (Nu 11:27 – 29; Jos 7:6; 24:14 – 16); Gideon (Jdg 6:11 – 32); Jephthah (Jdg 11:30 – 31, 34 – 39); Samuel (1Sa 12:23; 15:11, 35; 16:1); David (1Sa 17:26; 2Sa 6; 7:2; 8:11 – 12; 24:24; 1Ch 29:17; Pss 40:8 – 10; 42:1 – 2; 51:13; 69:7 – 9; 71:17 – 18); Solomon (1Ki 8:31 – 53; 2Ch 6:22 – 42); Elijah (1Ki 19:10); Obadiah (1Ki 18:3 – 4); Micaiah (1Ki 22:14); Jehu (2Ki 9:10); Jehoiada (2Ki 11:4 – 17; 2Ch 23:1 – 17); Asa (1Ki 15:11 – 15; 2Ch 14:1 – 5, 15); Israelites (2Ch 15:15; Eze 9:4); Jehoshaphat (2Ch 17:3 – 10, 19); Isaiah (Isa 6:8; 62:1); Hezekiah (Isa 37:1); Josiah (2Ki 22:11 – 13; 2Ch 34:3 – 7, 29 – 33); priests (Eze 44:15); Ezra (Ezr 7:10; 9:10; Ne 8:1 – 6, 13, 18); Nehemiah (Ne 4; 5; 13:7 – 9, 15 – 28); Job (Job 16:19); psalmist (Pss 119:53; 126; 136; 139; 158); Jeremiah (Jer 9:1 – 3; 13:17; 18:20; 20:9; 25:3 – 4; 26:12 – 15); three Hebrews (Da 3:17 – 18); Habakkuk (Hab 1:2 – 4); OT faithful (Heb 11); Jesus (Mt 23:27; Lk 19:41; Jn 4:34 – 35; 9:4); Anna (Lk 2:38); Andrew and Philip (Jn 1:41 – 46); apostles (Mk 16:20; Ac 4:31, 33; 5:21, 25, 29 – 32, 41 – 42; 8:4, 25, 30, 35, 40; 11:19 – 20, 24, 26); Two blind men proclaiming the miracle of healing, contrary to the injunction of Jesus (Mt 9:30 – 31); restored leper (Mk 1:44 – 45); man delivered of demons (Mk 5:19 – 20); Peter (Mt 16:22; Mk 14:29 – 31; Lk 22:33; Ac 2:14 – 40; 3:12 – 26; 4:2, 8 – 12, 18 – 20; 5:29 – 32; 2Pe 1:12 – 15); Samaritan woman (Jn 4:28 – 30, 39); Paul and Barnabas (Ac 14:14 – 15); Timothy (Php 2:22); Phoebe (Ro 16:1 – 2); Epaphroditus (Php 2:26, 30); Corinthians (1Co 14:12; 2Co 7:11; 9:2); Thessalonians (1Th 1:2 – 8); Ephesians (Rev 2:2 – 3, 6); Christian Jews (Heb 10:34); John (Ac 4:8 – 13, 18 – 20; 3Jn 4; Rev 5:4).

Paul: *For the evangelization of the Jews (Ro 9:1 – 3; 10:1; 11:14). In his ministry (Ac 9:21 – 29; 14:1 – 28; 15:25 – 26; 17:16 – 17, 22 – 31; 19:8 – 10; 20:18 – 24, 26 – 27, 31, 33 – 34; 21:13; 24:14 – 25; 26:1 – 29; 28:23, 30 – 31; Ro 1:1, 8 – 9, 14 – 32; 1Co 4:1 – 21; 9:12 – 27; 2Co 1:12, 17 – 19; 5:9, 11, 13 – 14, 20; 6:3 – 11; 11:16 – 33; 12:10 – 21; Gal 1:15 – 16; 2:2; 4:19; Eph 6:20; Php 1:18, 20, 24 – 25, 27; 2:16 – 17; 3:4 – 16; Col 1:28 – 29; 2:1, 5; 1Th 1:5 – 6; 2:2 – 11; 2Th 3:7 – 9; 2Ti 1:3, 7, 11 – 13). In his piety (1Co 4:12; 10:33; 15:31; 2Co 4:8 – 18; 11:22 – 33; 12:10; Php 3:4 – 16; 4:11 – 12, 17; 2Ti 3:10 – 11). In providing self-support (Ac 20:33 – 34; 1Co 4:12; 2Co 11:7 – 12; 2Th 3:7 – 9). In suffering for Christ (Ac 21:13; 2Co 6:4 – 5, 8 – 10; 11:22 – 33; 12:10, 14 – 15, 21; 2Ti 2:9 – 10; 3:10 – 11).*

In Punishing the Wicked:
 Moses and Levites (Ex 32:20, 26 – 29); Phinehas (Nu 25:11 – 13; Ps 106:30 – 31); Israelites (Jos 22:11 – 20; Jdg 20); Samuel (1Sa 15:33); David (2Sa 1:14; 4:9 – 12); Elijah (1Ki 18:40); Jehu (2Ki 10:15 – 28); Jehoiada (2Ki 11:18); Josiah (2Ki 23:20).

Ps	69:9	for **z** for your house consumes me,
Pr	19:2	to have **z** without knowledge,
Isa	59:17	and wrapped himself in **z**
Jn	2:17	"**Z** for your house will consume me
Ro	10:2	their **z** is not based on knowledge.
	12:11	Never be lacking in **z**,

ZEALOT [2421, 2831] (zĕl'ŭt, Gr. zēlōtēs, *zealous one*). A member of a Jewish patriotic party started in the time of Quirinius to resist Roman aggression. According to Josephus (*War* 4.3.9; 5.1; 7.8.1), the Zealots resorted to violence and assassination in their hatred of the Romans, their fanatical violence eventually provoking the Roman war. Simon the Zealot was distinguished from Simon Peter by this epithet (Lk 6:15; Ac 1:13).

ZEALOT, SIMON THE [2421, 2831]. An apostle (Mt 10:4; Mk 3:18; Lk 6:15; Ac 1:13) known either for

religious zeal or for membership in the party of the Zealots. *See Simon, 2; Zealot.*

ZEALOUS [ZEAL]

Nu	25:13	he was **z** for the honor of his God
Pr	23:17	always be **z** for the fear
Eze	39:25	and I will be **z** for my holy name.
Gal	4:18	fine to be **z**, provided the purpose is

ZEBEDEE [2411] (zĕb'ĕdĕ Gr. *Zebedaios*, meaning uncertain, possibly *Yahweh bestows*). A fisherman on the Sea of Galilee (Mk 1:20) and the father of James and John (Mt 4:21; Mk 1:19). He was the husband of Salome and in all probability lived in the vicinity of Bethsaida (Mt 27:56; Mk 15:40). Because of Mark's reference to his hired servants, one would judge that he was a man of means and influence (Mk 1:20). Our only glimpse of him in the Bible is with his sons in their boat mending their nets (Mt 4:21 – 22; Mk 1:19 – 20).

ZEBULUN [1201+2282, 2282, 2283, 2404] (zĕb'ū-lŭn, Heb. *zevûlûn, habitation*).

1. Jacob's tenth son, the sixth and last son of Leah (Ge 30:19 – 20). Three sons were born to him in the land of his birth (46:14). Aside from this, little is recorded in the Scriptures of his personal history.

2. One of the twelve tribes of Israel springing from Zebulun. When God asked Moses to number the able-bodied men at Sinai, the tribe of Zebulun had 57,400 (Nu 1:31). The place assigned to this tribe at this period was on the east side of the tabernacle with the standard of Judah (2:7). While the exact boundaries of Zebulun's territory are unknown, its portion lay between the Sea of Galilee and the Mediterranean. This area included many points at which Christ later carried on his ministry, and Matthew records that he thus fulfilled the ancient prophecy of Isaiah (Isa 9:1 – 2; Mt 4:12 – 16).

3. A city located in the tribe of Asher between Beth Dagon and the Valley of Iphtah El (Jos 19:27).

ZECHARIAH [2357, 2358, 10230, 2408] (zĕk'a-rī'a, Heb. *zekharyāhû, Jehovah remembers*).

1. The fourteenth king of Israel, son of Jeroboam II. In fulfillment of 2Ki 10:30 he was the last of the house of Jehu. After reigning six months, he was killed by Shallum, his successor (2Ki 15:8 – 10).

2. A Reubenite chief (1Ch 5:7).

3. A Korahite, son of Meshelemiah. He is described as "the gatekeeper at the entrance to the Tent of Meeting" (1Ch 9:21) and a "a wise counselor" (26:2, 14).

4. A Benjamite, son of Jehiel. He was a brother of Kish (1Ch 9:37).

5. A Levitical doorkeeper in the time of David (1Ch 15:17 – 18) appointed to play the lyre (15:20; 16:5).

6. One of the Davidic priests who was used as a trumpeter to help in bringing the ark from the house of Obed-Edom back to Jerusalem (1Ch 15:24).

7. A Levite from Uzziel. He was a son of Isshiah (1Ch 24:25).

8. A Merarite in David's day, son of Hosah (1Ch 26:11).

9. A Manassite in the time of David. He was the chief of his tribe and the father of Iddo (1Ch 27:21).

10. One of the princes whom Jehoshaphat sent to teach in the cities of Judah (2Ch 17:7).

11. The father of the prophet Jahaziel and son of Benaiah (2Ch 20:14).

12. Jehoshaphat's third son, killed by his brother Jehoram (2Ch 21:2 – 4).

13. A son of Jehoiada, the high priest who lived in the days of King Joash of Judah. Acting in some official capacity, he sought to check the rising tide of idolatry. A conspiracy was formed against him, and on the king's orders he was stoned (2Ch 24:20 – 22).

14. A prophet whose good influence on King Uzziah was outstanding (2Ch 26:5).

15. The father of Abijah. Perhaps "Abijah" should be "Abi," thus making him Hezekiah's grandfather through Abi, Hezekiah's mother (2Ch 29:1).

16. A Levite, the son of Asaph, who in King Hezekiah's day assisted in the purification of the temple (2Ch 29:13).

17. A Kohathite from among the Levites. He was one of the overseers who faithfully assisted in the repair of the temple in the days of King Josiah (2Ch 34:12).

18. One of the temple administrators in the time of King Josiah (2Ch 35:8).

19. One "of the descendants of Parosh" who with 150 men returned to Jerusalem with Ezra (Ezr 8:3).

20. The son of Bebai who returned with Ezra (Ezr 8:11).

21. One of those who stood by Ezra as he read the law to the people (Ne 8:4); a chief whom Ezra had summoned at the canal that flows toward Ahava and with whom he entered into counsel (Ezr 8:15 – 16).

22. A son of Elam who at Ezra's suggestion divorced his Gentile wife (Ezr 10:26).

23. A man from the tribe of Judah. He was a son of Amariah and lived in Jerusalem (Ne 11:4).

24. A descendant of Shelah who lived at Jerusalem (Ne 11:5).

25. The son of Pashhur, who with others aided in the work at Jerusalem after the captivity (Ne 11:12).

26. A son of Iddo. He was one of the priests in the days of Joiakim (Ne 12:16). This man may possibly be identical with the author of the book of Zechariah mentioned in both Ezr 5:1 and 6:14.

27. A priest, the son of Jonathan. He was one of the trumpeters at the dedication of the wall of Jerusalem under the leadership of Ezra and Nehemiah (Ne 12:35, 41).

28. The son of Jeberekiah, contemporary of Isaiah. He was a "reliable witness" to Isaiah's writing (Isa 8:1 – 2).

29. The next to the last of the twelve minor prophets. He came from a line of priests, being the son of Berekiah and the grandson of Iddo (Zec 1:1). He was a prophet as well as a priest (1:7). He returned from the Babylonian captivity to Jerusalem under the leadership of Zerubbabel. It was during the eighth month of the second year of the Persian king Darius that he began his prophetic ministry (1:1). He was contemporary with Haggai, beginning his ministry just two months after the latter prophet.

30. The father of John the Baptist (Lk 1:5). He was a priest of the division of Abijah and was childless in his old age. Both he and his wife were righteous. One day while Zechariah was performing his services in the temple, an angel appeared and reported to him that he was to have a son, whom he was to name John. Because of doubt, he was stricken mute until his son was named, at which time his speech was restored (1:67 – 69).

31. The son of Berakiah, mentioned in Mt 23:35 and Lk 11:51 by Christ as having been murdered between the altar and the temple. His true identity has not been fully determined.

ZECHARIAH, BOOK OF

HISTORICAL BACKGROUND.

Zechariah was the grandson of Iddo, the head of one of the priestly families that returned from the exile (Ne 12:4, 16). Twenty years after the return, the temple still lay a blackened ruin, and the discouraged people did not see how it could be restored. At this critical moment God raised up the prophets Haggai and Zechariah to encourage the Jews to rebuild the temple. The prophecies of the two men were delivered almost at the same time. Haggai appeared first, in August 520 BC, and within a month after his appeal was made, the foundation of the temple was laid. Soon after, Zechariah uttered his first prophecy (Zec 1:1 – 6). Haggai finished his recorded prophecies the same year. The following year Zechariah gave a message consisting of eight symbolic visions and an appendix (1:7 – 6:15). Two years later he gave a third message in answer to an inquiry by the men of Bethel regarding the observance of a fast. The two prophecies found in chs. 9 – 14 are not dated and were probably given at a much later time.

CONTENTS.

Zechariah 1 – 8 contains messages delivered on three separate occasions: 1:1 – 6 is a general introduction, while 1:7 – 6:15 is a series of eight symbolic night visions, followed by a coronation scene. These visions were intended to encourage the Israelites to complete the temple.

Chapters 7 – 8 were spoken two years later than the series of visions described above and represent Zechariah's answer to the questions put to him by certain visitors as to whether the fasts observed in memory of the destruction of Jerusalem should still be kept. The reply is no; for God demands not fasts, but observance of moral laws. God has come to dwell with his people, and even the heathen will desire to worship God in Jerusalem.

Zechariah 9 – 14 is made up of two distinct prophecies, without dates. Chapters 9 – 11 describe how God will visit the nations in judgment and his people in mercy. The Prince of Peace will come and confound the evil shepherds, but he will be rejected by the flock; consequently, they will again experience suffering. Chapters 12 – 14 are a prophecy describing the victories of the new age and the coming day of the Lord. Three apocalyptic pictures are presented: (1) Jerusalem will be saved from a siege by its enemies by the intervention of the Lord. (2) A remnant of Israel will be saved. (3) The nations will come to Jerusalem to share in the joyous Feast of Tabernacles, and all will enjoy the blessings of God's kingdom.

ZEDEKIAH [7408, 7409] (zĕd'ĕkī'a, Heb. *tsidhqîyahû, the LORD is righteous*).

1. The son of Kenaanah, the leader and voice for the four hundred prophets whom Ahab consulted to learn the outcome of his proposed expedition against Ramoth Gilead. In reply to Ahab's question, Zedekiah said that Ahab would be successful in winning a victory over the Syrians. Apparently these were all false prophets, judging from the question raised by Jehoshaphat: "Is there not a prophet of the LORD here whom we can inquire of?" (1Ki 22:7). When the true prophet was finally called and asked about the outcome of this planned battle, he revealed the truth and was consequently struck by Zedekiah (1Ki 22:19 – 24; 2Ch 18:10).

2. The last king of Judah, son of Josiah and Hamutal (2Ki 24:18). Because of the wickedness of Judah, God finally brought on the predicted tBabylonian captivity. Nebuchadnezzar came to Jerusalem, took Judah's king Jehoiachin to Babylon, and made Mattaniah, whose name he changed to Zedekiah, king in his place. Having taken away the men of influence from Judah, he felt the remaining Jews would be easily subdued (Eze 17:11 – 14). Zedekiah, however, rebelled against the king of Babylon, and as a result he was taken by Nebuchadnezzar and bound. His sons were killed before his eyes, and his own eyes were put out. He was then taken to Babylon, where he died (2Ki 24 – 25). Because of his evil he was permitted only eleven years of reign, many details of which are given in Jer 34 – 37.

3. The son of Jehoiachin (1Ch 3:16).

4. The son of Maaseiah. He was a false prophet who carried on his ruinous work among those who had been deported to Babylon. He was singled out by Jeremiah and publicly denounced for having prophesied lies. His death by being "burned in the fire" was foretold by Jeremiah as a warning to other false prophets (Jer 29:21 – 23).

5. The son of Hananiah. He was a prince of Israel in the reign of Jehoiakim (Jer 36:12).

6. A high official who sealed the renewed covenant (Ne 10:1).

ZEPHANIAH [7622, 7623] (zĕf′a-nī′a, Heb. *tsephanyâh*, *hidden of the* Lord).

1. An ancestor of the prophet Samuel (1Ch 6:36).

2. The author of the book of Zephaniah. He was very probably related to the kings of Judah as follows (Zep 1:1): Amariah and King Manasseh were brothers, Gedaliah and King Amon were cousins, Cushi and King Josiah were second cousins, and Zephaniah was third cousin of the three kings Jehoahaz, Jehoiakim, and Zechariah, thus putting the prophet into familiar relationship with the court, to which his message seems to be specially directed (e.g., 1:8). His principal work seems to have been early in Josiah's reign, like that of his contemporaries Nahum and Habakkuk, and before the greater prophecies of his other contemporary, Jeremiah.

3. A priest, son of Masseiah, whom Zedekiah sent to inquire of Jeremiah (2Ki 25:18 – 21; Jer 21:1). The Babylonian captain of the guard took him to Riblah where Nebuchadnezzar had him executed.

4. The father of a Josiah in the days of Darius to whom God sent the prophet Zechariah with a message of comfort and encouragement (Zec 6:9 – 15).

ZEPHANIAH, BOOK OF Dated in the reign of Josiah (Zep 1:1), this book was probably written early in his reign, before the religious reformation that began around the period from 640 to 622 BC. Thus the period from 640 to 622 is the likely time for the giving of the prophecy.

The book is concerned throughout with the day of the Lord. This prophetic concept refers to any intervention of God in history. The ultimate expression of the day of the Lord will occur in the end times.

In Zep 1:2 – 6 the day of the Lord is seen in its effects on Judah and Jerusalem. It comes as a punishment for the idolatry of the people (1:4 – 6). In 1:7 – 13 the prophet pictures the people as though they were coming to a communal sacrifice, but when they arrive, they are suddenly subject to the devastating punishment of God (1:8 – 9). The punishment is for social crimes as well as for idolatry.

The eschatological day of the Lord is described in Zep 1:14 – 18. In ch. 2 the prophet appeals to the humble to return to God, for the day of the Lord will involve universal destruction. The third chapter continues in the same vein, but there the prophet includes a message of hope that is centered in a remnant of God's people, who will be kept secure throughout the turmoil predicted by the prophet (3:12 – 18).

Outline:

III. God's Judgment on the Nations (2:1 – 3:8).
IV. Redemption of the Remnant (3:9 – 20).

ZERUBBABEL [2428, 10239, 2431] (zĕ-rŭb′a-bĕl, Heb. *zerubbāvel*, *shoot of Babylon*). The son of Shealtiel and the grandson of King Jehoiachin (Ezr 3:2; Hag 1:1; Mt 1:13). In 1Ch 3:19 he is declared to be the son of Pedaiah, Shealtiel's brother. The explanation for this apparent discrepancy is very likely that Shealtiel died without issue; and either his nephew was his legal heir and was therefore called his son (Ex 2:10), or Pedaiah married his brother's widow and thus Zerubbabel became Shealtiel's son by Levirate law (Dt 25:5 – 10). He was heir to the throne of Judah (1Ch 3:17 – 19) and is listed in the genealogy of our Lord (Mt 1:13; Lk 3:27).

When Cyrus allowed the Jews to return to their own land, he appointed Zerubbabel governor of the colony (Ezr 1:8, 11; 5:14). Joshua the high priest was the religious leader. When they reached Jerusalem, they first set up the altar of burnt offering, then proceeded to lay the foundation of the new temple. Soon, however, opposition arose. The adversaries of the Jews made an apparently friendly offer of assistance (Ezr 4), but Zerubbabel and the other leaders rebuffed them; therefore they wrote to the king and succeeded in stopping the work during the reigns of Cambyses (the Ahasuerus [KJV] or Xerxes [NIV] of Ezr 4:6) and the pseudo-Smerdis (the Artaxerxes of Ezr 4:7ff.). In 520 BC the work was resumed and was completed four years later. A great celebration was held at the dedication of the new temple (6:16 – 22), and as far as the record tells, the work of Zerubbabel was complete. It is not known when he died.

Directs rebuilding of altar and temple after his return from captivity in Babylon (Ezr 3:2 – 8; 4:2 – 3; 5:2; Hag 1:12 – 14); Leads freed Jews back from Babylon (Ezr 2; Ne 12); Appoints Levites to inaugurate rebuilding of temple (Ezr 3:2 – 8); Prophecies relating to (Hag 2:2; Zec 4:6 – 10); In genealogy of Joseph (Mt 1:12; Lk 3:27); Possibly the same as Sheshbazzar (Ezr 1:8, 11; 5:14, 16)

ZEUS [2416] (zūs, Gr. *Zeus*, *shine*, *bright*). Chief of Greek gods, corresponding to the Roman god Jupiter (Ac 14:12 – 13).

ZILPAH [2364] (zĭl′pa, Heb. *zilpâh*, *short-nosed person* KB). Handmaid of Leah, given to her by her father Laban. Later through Jacob she became the mother of Gad and Asher (Ge 29:24; 30:9 – 13).

ZION [7482, 4994] (zī′ŭn, Heb. *tsîyôn*, Gr. *Siōn*, meaning uncertain, probably *citadel*). One of the hills on which Jerusalem stood. It is first mentioned in the OT as a Jebusite fortress (2Sa 5:6 – 9). David captured it and called it the city of David. At this time the citadel probably stood on the long ridge running south of the temple, although not all scholars are agreed on this point. This location is near the only known spring; it is suitable for defense; its size is about that of other fortified towns. Archaeological remains show that it was inhabited long before David's time, and certain Bible references (1Ki 8:1; 2Ch 5:2; 32:30; 33:14) indicate that this was the original Zion. David brought the ark to Zion, and the hill henceforth became sacred (2Sa 6:10 – 12). When Solomon later moved the ark to the temple on nearby Mount Moriah, the name Zion was extended to take in the temple (Isa 8:18; 18:7; 24:23; Joel 3:17; Mic 4:7). Zion came to stand for the whole of Jerusalem (2Ki 19:21; Pss 48; 69:35; 133:3; Isa 1:8). The name is frequently used figuratively for the Jewish church and polity (Pss 126:1; 129:5; Isa 33:14; 34:8; 49:14; 52:8) and for heaven (Heb 12:22; cf. Rev 14:1).

General References to:
Taken from Jebusites by David (2Sa 5:6 – 9; 1Ch 11:5 – 7). Called thereafter "the city of David" (2Sa 5:7, 9; 6:12, 16; 1Ki 8:1; 1Ch 11:5, 7; 15:1, 29; 2Ch 5:2). Ark of the covenant placed in (2Sa 6:12, 16; 1Ki 8:1; 1Ch 15:1, 29; 2Ch 5:2). Removed from, to Solomon's temple on Mount Moriah (1Ki 8:1; 2Ch 5:2, w 2Ch 3:1). Collectively, the place, forms, and assemblies of Israelite worship (2Ki 19:21, 31; Pss 9:11;

48:2, 11 – 12; 74:2; 132:13; 137:1; Isa 35:10; 40:9; 49:14; 51:16; 52:1 – 2, 7 – 8; 60:14; 62:1, 11; Jer 31:6; 50:5; La 1:4; Joel 2:1, 15; Mt 21:5; Jn 12:15; Ro 9:33; 11:26; 1Pe 2:6). Name of, applied to Jerusalem (Pss 87:2, 5; 149:2; SS 3:11; Isa 33:14, 20; Jer 9:19; 30:17; Zec 9:13). Called "the city of God" (Ps 87:2 – 3; Isa 60:14). Restoration of, promised (Isa 51:3, 11, 16; 52:1 – 2, 7 – 8; 59:20; 60:14; Ob 17, 21; Zep 3:14, 16; Zec 1:14, 17; 2:7, 10; 8:2 – 3; 9:9, 13). Name of, applied to the city of the redeemed (Heb 12:22; Rev 14:1).

2Sa	5:7	David captured the fortress of **Z**,
Ps	2:6	King on **Z**, my holy hill."
	9:11	to the LORD, enthroned in **Z**;
	102:13	and have compassion on **Z**,
Isa	2:3	The law will go out from **Z**,
	28:16	"See, I lay a stone in **Z**,
Jer	50:5	They will ask the way to **Z**

Joel	3:21	The LORD dwells in **Z**!
Zec	9:9	Rejoice greatly, O Daughter of **Z**!
Ro	9:33	I lay in **Z** a stone that causes men
	11:26	"The deliverer will come from **Z**;
Heb	12:22	But you have come to Mount **Z**,
Rev	14:1	standing on Mount **Z**,

ZIPPORAH [7631] (zĭpō′ra, Heb. *tsippōrâh, bird*, fem. of *Zippor*). Daughter of Jethro or Reuel, the priest of Midian, who became the first wife of Moses (Ex 2:21). She was the mother of Gershom and Eliezer (18:1 – 6). Apparently Moses sent her back to her father during the unsettled and turbulent times connected with the exodus, though she had at least started to Egypt with him (cf. 4:20; 18:2).

ZOPHAR [7436] (zō′fêr, Heb. *tsōphar*, possibly *peep, twitter [as a bird]* KB). One of Job's friends who came to comfort him in his affliction (Job 2:11).

Halley's Bible Handbook with the New International Version—Deluxe Edition

Henry H. Halley

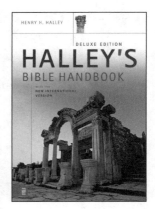

Clear. Simple. Easy to read. Now in full color for its twenty-fifth edition, this world-renowned Bible handbook is treasured by generations of Bible readers for its clarity, insight, and usefulness. *Halley's Bible Handbook* makes the Bible's wisdom and message accessible. You will develop an appreciation for the cultural, religious, and geographic settings in which the story of the Bible unfolds. You will see how its different themes fit together in a remarkable way. And you will see the heart of God and the person of Jesus Christ revealed from Genesis to Revelation.

Written for both mind and heart, this expanded edition of *Halley's Bible Handbook* retains Dr. Halley's highly personal style. It features brilliant maps, photographs, and illustrations; contemporary four-color design; Bible references in the easy-to-read, bestselling New International Version; practical Bible reading programs; helpful tips for Bible study; fascinating archaeological information; easy-to-understand sections on how we got the Bible and on church history; and helpful indexes.

Hardcover, Printed: 0-310-25994-0

Mounce's Complete Expository Dictionary of Old and New Testament Words

William D. Mounce

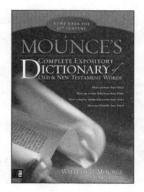

For years, *Vine's Expository Dictionary* has been the standard word study tool for pastors and laypeople, selling millions of copies. But sixty-plus years of scholarship have shed extensive new light on the use of biblical Greek and Hebrew, creating the need for a new, more accurate, more thorough dictionary of Bible words. William Mounce, whose Greek grammar has been used by more than 100,000 college and seminary students, is the editor of this new dictionary, which will become the layperson's gold standard for biblical word studies.

Mounce's is ideal for the reader with limited or no knowledge of Greek or Hebrew who wants greater insight into the meanings of biblical words to enhance Bible study. It is also the perfect reference for busy pastors needing to quickly get at the heart of a word's meaning without wading through more technical studies.

What makes Mounce's superior to Vine's?

- It has the most accurate, in-depth definitions based on the best of modern evangelical scholarship
- Both Greek and Hebrew words are found under each English entry, whereas Vine's separates them
- It employs both Strong's and G/K numbering systems, whereas Vine's only uses Strong's
- Mounce's accuracy is endorsed by leading scholars

Hardcover, Jacketed: 978-0-310-24878-1

In the Steps of Jesus

An Illustrated Guide to the Places of the Holy Land

Peter Walker

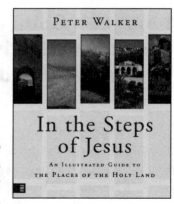

In the Steps of Jesus presents a visually stimulating tour of the places Jesus visited and ministered in during his time on earth as recorded in the Gospels. Each location is addressed separately and includes such cities as Capernaum, Nazareth, and Jerusalem. Full-color photos bring to life the ancient world of the Bible few will ever be able to visit in person. With every page, the reader will gain greater insight into the history, geography, and unique features of these historic places.

A must-have reference book for those interested in the study of the New Testament and the life of Christ.

Hardcover, Printed: 0-310-27647-0

1001 Quotations That Connect

Timeless Wisdom for Preaching, Teaching, and Writing

Craig Brian Larson and Brian Lowery, General Editors

Many times people wrack their brains for succinct, "preachable" quotations to drop into sermons or teaching materials. Now they can relax! *1001 Quotations That Connect* features inspiring observations from a wide spectrum of influential people of the past two millennia, culled from the collection of Christianity Today International. This volume—which contains the reflections of church fathers, missionaries, poets, and celebrities—is a gold mine for preachers, teachers, and writers.

The sayings are arranged under eight descriptive categories, including Ancient Words from Fathers and Founders, Rattling Words from Prophets and Activists, and Keen Words from Writers and Preachers. They are helpfully listed by source, then according to key topics and Scripture references, making retrieval of just the right quote a snap. What's more, a CD-ROM from which text files of all the quotations can easily be pasted into word processing documents comes with the book.

Whether you are driving home the point of a sermon or simply want a quote book for reflective reading, this unparalleled collection is a must-have resource!

Softcover: 978-0-310-28036-1